COLLABORATION AND THE KNOWLEDGE ECONOMY: ISSUES, APPLICATIONS, CASE STUDIES

Information and Communication Technologies and the Knowledge Economy

Volume 5

An associated publication by IOS Press:

ISSN 1574-1230

Collaboration and the Knowledge Economy: Issues, Applications, Case Studies

Part 2

Edited by

Paul Cunningham

and

Miriam Cunningham

IIMC International Information Management Corporation Ltd, Dublin, Ireland

IOS
Press

Amsterdam • Berlin • Oxford • Tokyo • Washington, DC

ISBN 978-1-58603-924-0
Library of Congress Control Number: 2008936390

Publisher
IOS Press
Nieuwe Hemweg 6B
1013 BG Amsterdam
Netherlands
fax: +31 20 687 0019
e-mail: order@iospress.nl

Distributor in the UK and Ireland
Gazelle Books Services Ltd.
White Cross Mills
Hightown
Lancaster LA1 4XS
United Kingdom
fax: +44 1524 63232
e-mail: sales@gazellebooks.co.uk

Distributor in the USA and Canada
IOS Press, Inc.
4502 Rachael Manor Drive
Fairfax, VA 22032
USA
fax: +1 703 323 3668
e-mail: iosbooks@iospress.com

Collaboration and the Knowledge Economy: Issues, Applications, Case Studies
P. Cunningham and M. Cunningham (Eds.)
IOS Press, 2008

Preface

In today's world, even with all the progress and ongoing investment in research there has been made in recent times, there continues to be disparities between the level of take up of Information and Communication Technologies (ICT) as well as the types and complexity of ICT solutions being deployed in different environments.

However, it is important not to underestimate the enormous impact that ICT continues to have in providing opportunities to achieve economic growth and prosperity by leapfrogging previous generations of technology and transforming inefficient work processes. Nowhere is such a transformational effect more noticeable than in the use of mobile and collaborative technologies to enable new ways of working.

Collaboration is critical to building the Knowledge Economy, and considerable work is being carried out not just in industry but also in government and academic research circles to address the often difficult technical, social and legal challenges that cross-organisational collaboration demands in modern society and a post industrial age. Usability, interoperability and secure identity management are no longer simply research challenges – they define what consumers expect in today's fast-moving collaborative world. One of the most difficult challenges of commercialisation today is identifying aspects of solutions that are universal in appeal, while addressing local, national or regional differences that can make or break the successful launch of ICT based or ICT enabled products and services.

This book brings together a comprehensive collection of over 200 contributions on commercial, government or societal exploitation of the Internet and ICT, representing cutting edge research, innovation and good practice from five continents. The strong emphasis on cross border collaboration and adaptation of innovative research results around the world augurs well for the continued development of the European Research Area.

Reflecting the breadth and depth of the ICT related research undertaken by the contributors, the contents are broken down into eleven broad thematic areas. These are: e-Health; e-Government and e-Democracy; Collaborative Working Environments; ICT for Networked Enterprise & RFID; Networked, Smart and Virtual Organisations; SME Issues; Mobility – Issues, Applications & Technologies; Digital Libraries and Cultural Heritage; Intelligent Content and Semantics; Technology Enhanced Learning and ICT Skills; and Security and Identity Management. Papers within each thematic area are in turn grouped under the subheadings of Issues, Applications and Case Studies, reflecting their primary focus.

We would like to acknowledge the valuable contribution of the advisory committee who provided authors with actionable feedback in finalising their papers for publication, and the ongoing encouragement and support of the European Commission.

Paul Cunningham
Miriam Cunningham

Advisory Committee

Ulf Blomqvist, VINNOVA, Sweden
Pete Bramhall, Hewlett Packard Laboratories, United Kingdom
Dr. Jonathan Cave, RAND Europe, United Kingdom
Prof. Stephen Curwell, University of Salford, United Kingdom
Kim Davis, Research Council of Norway, Norway
Prof. Asuman Dogac, Middle East Technical University, Turkey
Prof. Dan Harnesk, Lulea University of Technology, Sweden
Dr. Nenad Ivezic, National Institute of Standards and Technology, United States
Prof. Bernhard Katzy, CeTIM, Netherlands
Gareth MacNaughton, Lane & Hapiak Consulting, United Kingdom
Prof. Ann Macintosh, University of Leeds, United Kingdom
Jesse B.T. Marsh, Atelier Studio Associato, Italy
Mícheál Ó Foghlú, TSSG, WIT, Ireland
Prof. Gregoris Mentzas, National Technical University of Athens, Greece
Alvaro Oliveira, Alfamicro Lda., Portugal
Dr. Stephan Raimer, College of Cooperative Education Schleswig-Holstein, Germany
Prof. Tomás Robles, Universidad Politecnica de Madrid, Spain
Jonathan Sage, IBM Business Consulting Services, United Kingdom
Hans Schaffers, Helsinki School of Economics & ESoCE Net, Netherlands
Dr. Krassimira Paskaleva-Shapira, Karslruhe Research Center, Germany and
　　　Manchester Business School, United Kingdom
Peter Stanbridge, Korora Limited, United Kingdom
Richard Stevens, European Genetics Foundation, Italy
Dr. Volker Stich, FIR at RWTH Aachen University, Germany
Prof. Roger Wallis, Royal Institute of Technology, Sweden
Peter Weiss, AIFB, University of Karlsruhe, Germany
Stefan Wesner, HLRS, Germany
Prof. Jim Yip, University of Huddersfield, UK

Contents

Part 1

Section 2.2. Applications

Section 2.3. Case Studies

Section 3. Collaborative Working Environments

Section 3.1. Issues

Section 3.2. Applications

Section 3.3. Case Studies

Part 2

Section 6. SME Issues

Section 6.1. Issues

Section 6.2. Case Studies

Section 4

ICT for Networked Enterprise & RFID

Section 4.1

Issues

The Internet of Services:
Vision, Scope and Issues

Man-Sze LI[1], Servane CRAVE[2], Jörg P. MÜLLER[3], Steven WILLMOTT[4]

[1]IC Focus, 42 Clifton Road, London, N8 8JA, United Kingdom
Tel: +44 20 8347 7355, Fax: +44 79 6735 9461, Email: msli@icfocus.co.uk
[2]France Telecom Orange Labs, 905 rue Einstein, 06921 Sophia Antipolis cedex, France
Tel: + 33 4 92 94 53 09, Email: servane.crave@orange-ftgroup.com
[3]Clausthal University of Technology, Julius-Albert-Str. 4, 38678, Clausthal-Z., Germany
Tel: +49 5323 727140, Fax: +49 5323 727149, Email: joerg.mueller@tu-clausthal.de
[4]3Scale networks S.L., C/ Llacuna 162, 08018, Barcelona, Spain
Tel: +34 687 021 389, Email: steve@3scale.com

Abstract: The Future Internet and especially the Internet of Services have recently become buzzwords in the European ICT research community. Although the different stakeholders have generally been identified, the research on the Internet of Services is presently at a preliminary stage, fragmented and largely carried out in relative isolation of related areas. The aim of this paper is to support and encourage the development of the Internet of Services by providing an overview of current developments, analyses and insight. It is a contribution towards a holistic vision that encompasses all relevant stakeholders, initiatives and their interests.

Keywords: Services, Service-oriented technologies and paradigms, Future Internet, Internet of Services, Web technologies, Value proposition

1. Introduction

Over the past few years, we have seen a considerable acceleration in the importance of the Internet in our professional and personal lives. This acceleration has been fuelled by both its growth as an infrastructure and its diversity of use as an information delivery channel. The emergence of numerous new paradigms including Peer-to-Peer networks, Software as a Service (or more generally, "X as a Service" - XaaS), highly interactive social networking applications, and an explosion of the number of multimedia content providers add to continuous debates on how the Future Internet infrastructure may develop. In Europe and other parts of the world, the Future Internet is becoming a strategic focus of research. One of the newest and arguably most promising fields of research is the "Internet of Services" (IoS). This is the subject of the present paper, in which we argue that the IoS potentially constitutes a fundamental shift in terms of: (1) the Internet's technical structure; (2) the way in which the Internet will operate and serve its users; and (3) the business models for the provisioning of services, especially service infrastructures.

2. Objectives and Methodology

This paper aims to provide an overview of current developments linked to the concept of the IoS; it will identify and analyse the main issues at stake, and provide preliminary conclusions. It is intended to contribute to a shared understanding and vision of the role of services in the Future Internet. The paper provides the context to help answering major questions such as: What constitute(s) the layer(s) of the IoS? How will the IoS layer(s) relate to the overall Future Internet architecture and how will the different layers be inter-related? How to ensure that the IoS will provide benefits to all stakeholders and have a positive social/societal impact? What are the optimal means to foster sustainable investment in the IoS? What if the research efforts fail? Would the IoS happen anyway?

Throughout the following, we use the term service to denote a software-based component that is delivered via public networks - notably the Internet (as opposed to the more generic sense of service as an economic activity, with a lesser focus on the capability of ICT[i]). We focus on services that are accessed purely electronically, involve interactions between the software systems of the provider and consumer (not excluding interfaces accessible by humans), and are consistent with the notion of services as defined by W3C and others [1]. In particular, we focus on those services that relate directly to the infrastructure of the IoS, as opposed to services offered on top of the infrastructure. We believe the former class of services are of most interest for laying the foundation of the IoS. In contrast, the latter class are more specific to end user needs, more likely to be dependent on the market strategy of a particular provider, and generally more ephemeral.

An underlying perspective of the paper is that the IoS is not just about technology, but also about usage, community building, deployment, business models and public policy – all of which need to be duly considered in bringing the IoS to life. We see four main dimensions to be considered for the IoS: Research and Technology, Business, Individuals and Communities, and Policy and Governance. These four dimensions are inter-related, and development in one impacts on others. However, they are currently being addressed in relative isolation. Therefore, this paper seeks to address these inter-related aspects in a holistic, integrated manner. It attempts to structure what currently is a fragmented landscape into cogent descriptions and arguments, towards a shared understanding of what are the key issues and what may be at stake. The paper addresses the following questions:

- What are the main initiatives, trends, drivers and issues for the IoS?
- What is the value proposition for the IoS and how does this relate to existing and emerging business models of multiple groups of stakeholders?
- What are the preliminary conclusions that can be drawn from the myriad of activities?

Answering these questions is a considerable challenge and so is describing the "big picture" of the IoS. This implies a multi-disciplinary approach which encompasses the sciences of Information and Communication Technologies, Management/Organisational and Services Sciences, Economic and Social Sciences, and potentially others. That approach should ultimately lead to the definition of a common vision for the IoS, which our analysis suggests is currently lacking.

3.   Development and Perspectives towards an IoS Vision

3.1   Scope, Synergies and Complementarities Regarding Future Internet Research

Future Internet research is at the heart of many large initiatives worldwide. The current wave of activities started in 2005 with the US National Science Foundation (NSF)'s announcement of the GENI experimental facility (Global Environment for Network Innovations). GENI originated from the observation that the current Internet infrastructure presents too many limitations which seriously hinder future developments such as mobility, dynamicity, 3D and quality features. The initiative focuses on a US continental-scale, programmable, heterogeneous, networked system driving a "clean-slate" infrastructure and enabling "real experiments with real applications and users". More recently, the Future Internet Design (FIND) initiative, also under the umbrella of the NSF, has started to fund projects and adopts a multi-disciplinary approach for reaching its objectives. There are other national initiatives, such as the AKARI Project and the New Network Architecture Forum in Japan and the Future Internet Forum in Korea. In Europe, of note is the German national "lighthouse project" THESEUS which has the strategic goal to develop products, business models and markets, for enabling consumers and enterprises to access services, contents and knowledge anytime from anywhere. THESEUS seeks to contribute to the creation of a new Internet-based knowledge infrastructure. Already in the late nineties, the French "Réseaux de recherche et d'innovation technologiques" (RNRT) launched working groups on the future of the Internet, with a specific call in 2007 to address major issues under the topic "Rupture". While the scope of these national initiatives varies, there is clearly synergy between them. NSF encourages researchers outside the US to participate in GENI and FIND. In an effort to coordinate Future Internet R&D among countries in Asia and other continents, the Asia Future Internet Forum (AsiaFI) was founded in 2007.

The European Union has accelerated the pace of its actions regarding the Future Internet since 2006, following consultations and publication of "The Future Networked Society" by the EIFFEL Think Tank [2], a voluntary initiative created under the auspices of the European Commission. Under the EU's research programme, some 70 projects of FP6 and FP7 now fall under the Future Internet umbrella [3]. These projects, together with the relevant European Technology Platforms (ETPs), have signed up to The Bled Declaration to further actions on the Future Internet through a European Future Internet Assembly (FIA) [4]. The five ETPs active in the ICT domain (eMobility, EPoSS, ISI, NEM and NESSI) are developing a common vision and exploring joint work. Various FP7 Support Actions are stepping up their community building activities. The EIFFEL Support Action, for example, is creating a pan-European community of scientific/technical experts. All these initiatives present manifold different features in their approach. Coordination at the European level (via, for example, the FIA) would be a challenge.

From the research work available so far, a core debate of the Future Internet is evident, with two major schools of thought for designing the Future Internet. The first is based on a clean-slate approach with radical and disruptive innovation, promoted notably by GENI/FIND[ii] and investigated in FP7 projects such as 4WARD and Trilogy. The second is based on an evolutionary approach, i.e. building the Future Internet on top of the current Internet through incremental enhancements, which has been linked, for example, to the FP7 Future Internet Research and Experimentation (FIRE) experimental facility[iii]. The EIFFEL Support Action strongly recommends a smart combination of these two approaches to design the Future Internet. To complete this context overview, it is of interest to mention the Future Internet "dimensions" as envisioned by the European Commission: the Network of the Future, Internet of Services, Internet of Things, 3D Media Internet, Trust and Security, and Experimental Facilities. Development of the IoS therefore is intrinsic to achieving the full vision of the Future Internet. All these developments underline the need to define a common, holistic view of the IoS.

3.2 Trends and Developments

Recent visions of next generation technologies from a wide variety of viewpoints include connectivity layers and Next Generation Networks (NGN) [5], Grid Computing and Grid Services [6], Semantic Web [7], Service Web [8], Service Wave [9], BPM/ebXML and other application developments enabled by "Web 2.0" technologies. These visions all share a common core view: that the notion of services will play a key role in new architectures and deployment. The trends seen in each of these areas collectively point to: increased automation of software processes (encapsulation of functionality), increased modularity and interoperability (open interfaces and seamless machine-to-machine interaction) and increased flexibility/agility (dynamic software configuration and service composition). These trends are evident in the current state-of-play. For example:

- The complex web of emerging news sharing systems based on RSS syndicated news streams, feed processors and readers – which can be seen as a simple service-based system. News sources increasingly syndicate their content via continuously updated

XML based "feeds" which contain snapshots of new content. Other systems such as feed-burners and feed-readers process this output in order to extract and forward items relevant to specific topics and integrate them for users. Yet other services aggregate posts emerging on the same topic in meta-feeds and so forth. In this case existing Internet and Web protocols provide the service infrastructure.

- Large-scale scientific grid deployments such as EGEE already contain hundreds of services, providing a variety of different types of high capacity computing power, data storage and processing. Highly specialised infrastructure systems support high capacity data transfer, caching, monitoring and other features with value-added systems such as workflow tools. Lastly, domain specific data sources and processing services are available for experiments in areas such as e-Science and e-Health.

- Intra-company focused deployments of current SOA technologies that rely on deployed service infrastructures based on standards such as XML, SOAP, WSDL, UDDI and WS-Security for basic interoperation and BPEL, BPML, WS-CDL, XPDL and others for workflow and coordination. These are often combined with vendor specific add on tools from large organisations such as SAP, ORACLE, Microsoft and others. Businesses are able to progressively expose more and more internal functionality between units and departments for quick re-use.

- The rapid adoption of infrastructure services provided by companies such as Amazon, Google and others, with total traffic by volume to Amazon's S3 and EC2 Web Services even eclipsing global traffic to all other Amazon web properties by Q4, 2007.

- Rapidly emerging new services such as Twitter – which provides a rapid-fire personal micro-bloging service broadcasting short messages; generating well over 50% of their traffic not from their central website, but via a multitude of third party plugins connected to programmatic APIs.

Such developments point to a vision of the Future Internet comprising not just billions of users (compared to the 1.3 billion of users today or 20% of world population; source: Eurescom), but also billions of services, applications and devices; over a multitude of converged networks that are fixed, mobile, hybrid and virtualised; enabling potentially limitless sharing and exchanging of collaborative, user-generated contents both 2D and 3D; and all within trusted as well as trustworthy environments. A fundamental challenge in the current state-of-the-art is to tackle "cross domain" issues in a paradigm of convergence towards a "multi-faceted" Future Internet [10]. For example, in preparation for the Future Internet Assembly, the "Post-Bled" services and software working group has initiated the following cross domain topics: Management & governance; Architectures & infrastructures; Trust at scale and high granularity; and Lifecycle management for Future Internet applications [11]. The IoS should pursue the achievement of a "Continuity of services", encompassing "perfect interactivity" for service consumers (i.e. permanent, transparent, seamless and trustworthy services) and new approaches to service management for service providers (i.e. a move from the complexity of the central control principle to the simplicity of keeping the consistency of each service) [12].

Various players in the telecom industry, on the other hand, have concluded that the current Internet has too many limitations which prevent the convergence of networks and services and the deployment of converged services for delivering "the unified experience" centred on the customer. Specifically, "in order to succeed the FMC (Fixed-Mobile Convergence) must be translated into a new service layer concept and not a new technology" and "future services will be highly individualised, and demand strict quality parameters in terms of latency, jitter and bandwidth" [13]. Orange/France Telecom, for example, has described Future Internet services as those that "focus on user-centric service delivery, with a tight coupling of IMS (IP Multimedia Subsystem) and the Web" [14].

3.3   Towards a Vision for the IoS: Issues for Consideration

At the present juncture of developments as described above, it would be impossible to lay down definitive requirements for the IoS. What seems clear is that the IoS is highly likely to be a fusion of ideas, technologies, practices, and communities. The software industry and the telecom industry are obvious stakeholders, but there are others such as their existing customers, Web 2.0 companies and communities, whose interest should not and cannot be ignored. The convergence of technologies emphasises the need to provide varieties of differentiating services. Our survey of the state of play suggests that there are likely to be one or more service "layers" in the overall architecture of the Future Internet, though the composition of the layer(s) is presently unclear, as is the intersection or intertwining of the network and service layer(s). "User centricity" is another key aspect (see, for example [15]), but what this entails is not sufficiently precise yet. Some of the research orientations to date point to a distinction between the service infrastructure of the IoS and the innovative, value-added services that such an infrastructure supports and enables[iv]. However, there is currently no common view on the definition of "infrastructure" in the context of Future Internet services, let alone what this infrastructure may comprise. Research on these issues is likely to be pursued by different groups of researchers in the coming years. On the other hand, while new technical models, mechanisms and techniques will undoubtedly be developed, will such solutions be able to accommodate billions of users, services and devices? What if the research community fails to produce radically new infrastructures, architectures and platforms? Would the IoS happen anyway? Is there anything that needs to be done to ensure a level playing field for all stakeholders? What are the bottlenecks for and who are the gatekeepers of service development?

We believe that the IoS must first and foremost *have a positive impact on the capabilities of users; be they individuals, organisations, "things" (as in the Internet of Things), or other software-based services.* It must ultimately result in benefits to people in their different roles in society. This has several major implications in respect of the role of the IoS, the paradigm of the IoS, the openness of the IoS and the positioning of the IoS in the Future Internet, as follows:

- The IoS is an *enabler* both for service provision and service consumption, as well as interaction between provision and consumption including "pro-sumption". The technologies and services that comprise the IoS are means to serve the needs of users; they are not ends.
- At the service infrastructure level, the paradigm of the IoS must be any-to-any. The services at this level must be commonly shared, transparently discoverable, and capable of living in an open and dynamic environment. Accordingly, they must have properties that comply with those characteristics and consistent levels of performance that can be guaranteed to the user.
- The IoS infrastructure itself must be open, in the sense that: (1) it is not locked into any technology paradigm or service platform; (2) it is not owned or controlled by any entity; (3) its development and growth is based on participatory input, as opposed to being channelled through makers of the infrastructure; and (4) it has no bias towards business models or service ecosystems, existing or emerging.
- The IoS infrastructure is part of the Future Internet. It should enable and allow for seamlessness of information, applications, services, networks, provisioning and usage to the edge of the network. The IoS should not make a priori assumptions about function placement which restrict business model experimentations by providers or users.
- Just like the current Internet, the serendipitous and disruptive innovation predicted in a variety of Future Internet visions will not be borne out of chaos, but instead rest on a

combination of emerging common and standard infrastructures and the opportunity of creativity this enables.

The above general consideration of requirements strongly indicates that a holistic, multi-disciplinary approach to the IoS is needed. This is also supported by the examples given for the state of play in Section 3.2, which are notable for their variety. Nevertheless, common themes do emerge, including:

- A shift from today's human-readable systems towards facilitating increased machine-to-machine interaction between systems – both in terms of providing new programmatic interfaces to information and functionality and in terms of taking a more structured approach to defining the semantics for machine-to-machine interactions.
- A shift from design time to run-time/late binding of service, from static to dynamic service composition, and from interoperability by design to interoperation by discovery, reuse and on-the-fly assembly.
- A shift towards increased distribution of applications and encapsulation of information as well as functionality; shifting from "download and install" of software applications to "remote pay-per-use" access models and from moving large collections of data around to "always-on remote queries" of information. This change enables three things: the creation of new classes of distributed applications, the creation of new delivery models for functionality and data, and the emergence of new business and revenue models.
- A shift from closed and tightly controlled intra-organisational distributed applications to massively distributed applications functioning in open, public environments.
- A shift from static and standalone content, applications, usage scenarios and systems to dynamic, media-rich content; context-aware, collaborative and intelligent services; ad-hoc value networks and innovation ecosystems; and globally connected and always-on systems of systems.

4.   Internet of Services Value Proposition and Related Challenges

The IoS is becoming a hot topic for research. But research for the sake of research is not enough. The question "Why do we need the IoS infrastructure?" has to be addressed. It is because the answer to that question will help determine the means of realising the IoS. In a world of finite resources and competing strategies, choices will need to be made as regards the means, from architectural design to business alliances. Ultimately, these choices are based on the perception or even conviction of the need. "Doing nothing" about the IoS or "let the market sort it out", for example, are themselves choices.

We believe that the rationale for the IoS lies in the value it offers to its users, actual or potential. In line with our vision, the value of IoS stems from the IoS' positive impact on the capabilities of users. In other words, the demand and supply value creation equation of the IoS must have a positive balance in favour of the demand side. Among others, this is the basis for the user centricity argument of the IoS already noted, and a main ingredient of the global momentum of Web 2.0 companies and related initiatives. User-generated content, user-generated services - and even user-generated service infrastructures - constitute a prominent strand of user centricity, and a source of business-economic friction (see below). "Pro-sumption", where service provision and consumption is blurred, is another.

The full ecosystem of the IoS is vast and still nebulous. Arguably, no definitive chart exists. However, for the purpose of value attribution and accretion, we may identify the users and providers of IoS, on the basis of what could be gleaned from the markets, though not necessarily what might develop in future. This is depicted in Table 1.

Just like the Internet, the IoS should serve equally the individual, business, government and other public environments. It has three main kinds of impact on users' capability: technical, economic and social/societal. *Technical capability* is traditionally the main focus of ICT, where great strides have been made and are continuing in industry and in research (see examples in Section 3). It pertains to all four groups of users (see Table 1).

Table 1: IoS Users and Providers

Users		
• Individuals/communities • Organisations/communities		• Things (as in the "Internet of Things") • Other software-based services
Example providers & their classification[v]		
Utility providers	Aggregators	Integrators
• Specialised software companies • Large companies with specialised service capabilities • Web 2.0 companies • Telcos, ISPs and other current web infrastructure providers • Hardware companies • Focused start-ups	• First generation B2B companies • Industry hubs • Large companies with specialised service capabilities • Web service hosting and management companies • EAI vendors • System integrators • Focused start-ups	• Software vendors • System integrators • Hardware companies • Web 2.0 type (user) communities

Economic capability relates to costs and benefits, usually though not exclusively expressible in monetary terms. It pertains to individuals and organisations as users. Productivity and (economic) growth are key examples. *Social/societal capability* is the most difficult to characterise; it ranges from recent concepts like collective intelligence/wisdom of the crowd to quality of life and eHealth, from eParticipation/eDemocracy to the latest Fifth Freedom of the EU – free movement of knowledge [18]. It pertains to individuals as users and the organisation of users into communities. Unlike the other two capabilities, it is least amenable to direct quantification. In all cases, however, the IoS produces impact on the capability of users through their *use* of the IoS. In this respect, the IoS is no different from other technology paradigms: its use might enable users to reduce efforts/resources; do existing things better; do new things which are judged to be "positive"; and/or reduce risks.

Many attempts are currently being made to characterise services for the Future Internet[vi]. Existing service ecosystems, commercial or otherwise - from Salesforce's AppExchange to Amazon's AWS to Facebook to Dopplr to Google's constellation of labs, codes and online communities are already producing major improvements to users' technical capability as well as economic welfare. Some are "open" in the sense of publishing APIs, widgets and other technical functionality and making them available at low or even nil cost, leading to an explosion of new services from professional developers as well as seasoned "amateurs". Leading actors in the ICT industry and in Web 2.0 are also engaged in initiatives targeting service platform interoperability, inter-network service development and continuity, fusion between the physical world and virtual world and so on[vii]. The impact of technological convergence has been recognised especially in the telecommunication area; efforts are afoot to address seamless service delivery over different types of networks, including fixed, mobile and hybrid, as well as seamless services in Next Generation Networks. All these are important developments and would result in building blocks for the IoS. However, while they contribute to the value proposition of the IoS, they do not by themselves ensure a positive surplus on the demand side in the value creation equation. It is unclear whether or how they would enhance the capability of users - including which specific capability of the user - on a sustainable basis. Importantly, they might create a positive surplus of value for users *within* their own ecosystems. But these benefits are ecosystem dependent; they are lost as soon as users no longer belong to the ecosystem. In other words, the existing service ecosystems do not fully cover, let alone sufficiently address, the range of issues identified for the IoS in Section 3.3.

Given the existing service ecosystems in which major players are aggressively investing[viii], it might be thought that the IoS should be conceived as a global federation of such ecosystems – in other words, the IoS would "happen anyway". However, the technical challenges for service discovery, description, composition, negotiation and orchestration across service ecosystems should not be under-estimated, noting that future ecosystems are likely to mix telecoms, media and web capacities. Nor is not entirely clear how the issues identified in Section 3.3 would play out in this scenario. There is an even larger question mark over the commercial incentive for service ecosystem federation, including that for making services reusable in terms which are commercially attractive to the provider in any given business model[ix]. The competitive positioning of providers (see Table 1) in a nascent "IoS market" with an abundance of novelty fuelled by Web 2.0/X.0, an unclear trajectory of network effect, no sustained records of revenue streams, no clear market structures, and an eclectic population of potential providers spanning multiple industries/domains and those defying traditional classification, add to further uncertainty in the short to medium term. In sum, the business models for providing the IoS are presently at best unclear.

From the perspective of value proposition as described above, what distinguishes the IoS from the many initiatives on the market from Salesforce to Amazon are the specific characteristics of the IoS in creating and delivering usage and producing impact on users' capability. In the previous paragraph, we raised the fundamental question of business models for the IoS infrastructure providers. That, however, is different from the question of business models, which the IoS would enable in order to produce a value surplus for users. In accordance with our analysis in Section 3.3, IoS should not itself be biased towards certain business models of how it is to be used; a potentially unlimited multitude of business models should be supported by the IoS. This raises an important architecture issue of technical interface placement of services, assuming that the architecture be open: where and how should technical interfaces be defined, where economic players can compete (see [20] on the economics of next generation Internet architecture).

That the Internet itself makes no assumptions about and is not biased towards particular business models is a critical factor for the serendipitous and disruptive innovation characterising its success. We believe that the Internet's tradition of being a virtuous circle of network reach (expanding number of users) and new applications (business opportunities) must be preserved and be carried through to the establishment of the IoS. The innovation argument rests on a set of more fundamental notions underpinning usage and impact, namely: *universality of services, accessibility of services and neutrality of services*. Together, they ensure that (1) usage of the IoS is unfettered and unlimited; (2) the pattern of use is in the control of the user; (3) development, growth and impact of use are directly channelled through users, as opposed to providers or makers (also known as the "generative" argument, see [21]). We believe these are the main ingredients for the value proposition of the IoS, and from which the characteristics of the IoS – such as any-to-any, openness, ownership and control – should be derived. Value creation should particularly focus on the edge of the network, where users are located. Benchmarking existing and emerging service ecosystems against these fundamental notions would eventually be a useful or even necessary exercise.

5.   Conclusions and Summary Recommendations

In this paper, we have presented a perspective of the IoS and discussed a number of major issues. Tackling these challenges requires studying and further developing open service architectures and platforms, robust and stable utility-like service infrastructures, context-aware value-added services, methodologies for developing flexible and extensible services and networked applications, methods for experimentation and deployment, as well as (most importantly) models to deepen our understanding of how all these technologies and research activities play together to enable the vision of the Future Internet Economy [22]. These activities need to be developed in a coherent and integrated way. They should also encompass non-technical perspectives in order to guarantee the success of their implementation, i.e. to bridge the future developments regarding the IoS with the activity of the economic actors to ensure that they will foster organisational innovation and as a result develop competitive advantages for the European economy.

While current research on SOA, Web/Enterprise 2.0/X.0, Enterprise Interoperability, Service Web, Grid Services and Semantic Web helps us address important bits of the IoS puzzle, none of these sufficiently addresses the overarching challenge of enabling and improving cooperation between service providers and consumers. Whilst breakthroughs may come in the form of individual projects, there is no obvious means to build up a critical mass of sustainable services and no significant progression towards truly open, universally accessible service infrastructures. The value proposition of the IoS raises fundamental issues about the business model for IoS provisioning. There is, therefore, an urgent need for a unifying perspective for research to position Europe as the leading actor in Future Internet Services. Aggregating all the different perspectives is one necessary step which will help overcome the current obstacles and enable advancement on the IoS challenge.

Acknowledgement: We would like to thank the various colleagues who contributed ideas to this paper. Further information is available at www.e2esu.eu.

References

[1] *Web Services Architecture*, W3C Working Group Note, 11 Feb 2004, http://www.w3.org/TR/ws-arch/
[2] *Future Internet – the Future Networked Society*, a white paper from the EIFFEL Think-Tank, Release 1, December 2006, http://www.fp7-eiffel.eu/docs/EIFFEL-FINAL.pdf
[3] Project listing at http://www.future-internet.eu/activities/fp7-projects.html
[4] *The Bled Declaration: Towards a European Approach to the Future Internet*, 31st March 2008, http://www.future-internet.eu/publications/bled-declaration.html
[5] *Next Generation Networks –General overview of NGN*, ITU-T Recommendation Y.2001 (12/2004)
[6] *The Open Grid Services Architecture*, Version 1.5, 24 July 2006, GFD-I.080, http://www.ogf.org/documents/GFD.80.pdf
[7] *Semantic Web Activity Statement*, W3C, http://www.w3.org/2001/sw/Activity.html
[8] Richard Benjamins et al, *Service Web 3.0*, Vienna, February 20, 2007, http://www.sti-innsbruck.at/fileadmin/documents/technical_report/ServiceWeb3v4h.pdf
[9] *NESSI Strategic Research Agenda*, Vol. 3.FP7-2.exec, NESSI Roadmap, 29 February 2008, http://www.nessi-europe.com/Nessi/Portals/0/Nessi-Repository/SRA/Documents/NESSI_SRA_VOL_3_2009_10.pdf
[10] Issue Papers submitted for the technical discussions at the Bled Future Internet Conference held on 1-2 April 2008, http://forum.future-internet.eu/ (see under Bled Conference Preparation)
[11] Descriptions available at http://services.future-internet.eu/index.php/Main_Page
[12] *The Future Internet: A Services and Software Perspective*, draft to be reviewed by a working group in Bled, 26 February 2008, http://forum.future-internet.eu/viewtopic.php?f=10&t=12
[13] Fabrice Guillemin (ed.), *The future Internet: the operators' vision*, EURESCOM Project Report, P1657, November 2007, http://www.eurescom.eu/Public/projectresults/P1600-series/P1657-D1.asp
[14] B. Cardinael and V. Boutroux, *A possible vision of the Future Internet*, EURESCOM mess@ge, 1/2008
[15] Report of Expert Group on Services for the Future Internet, European Commission, December 2007, ftp://ftp.cordis.europa.eu/pub/fp7/ict/docs/ssai/services-in-future-internet-workshop-report_en.pdf
[16] Man-Sze Li, *A Vision of Next-Generation Software-based Service Provisioning*. In: Expanding the Knowledge Economy: Issues, Applications, Case Studies, P. Cunningham and M. Cunningham (Eds.), IOS Press, 2007, http://www.e2esu.eu/public/Concepts?action=AttachFile&do=get&target=E2ESU_Vision_June_2007.pdf
[17] Report of FP7 ICT Advisory Group (ISTAG) - Working Group on Future Internet Infrastructure, 23 January 2008, ftp://ftp.cordis.europa.eu/pub/ist/docs/future-internet-istag_en.pdf
[18] Council of the European Union, Presidency Conclusions, Brussels, 14th March 2008
[19] See http://www.programmableweb.com/ and http://seekda.com/ (statistics in both are regularly updated)
[20] David Clark et al, *New Arch: Future Generation Internet Architecture*, 6/30/00 – 12/31/03, sponsored by DARPA and ITO, http://www.isi.edu/newarch/iDOCS/final.finalreport.pdf. The economic "tussle" is

further explored in David Clark et al, *Tussle in Cyberspace, Defining Tomorrow's Internet*, SIGCOMM 2002, http://www.sigcomm.org/sigcomm2002/papers/tussle.pdf

[21] Jonathan Zittrain, *The Future of the Internet and How to Stop it*, Yale University Press, 2008
[22] *The Seoul Declaration for the Future of the Internet Economy*, OECD Ministerial Meeting, 17-18 June 2008, http://www.oecd.org/dataoecd/49/28/40839436.pdf

---

[i]   See, for example, the services' definition given by IBM including a description of business services, http://www.research.ibm.com/ssme/services.shtml (as of July 2008).

[ii]   FIND invites the research community to consider what the requirements should be for a global network of 15 years from now, and how we could build such a network if we are not constrained by the current Internet - *if we could design it from scratch*. Some 40 projects are currently involved. See http://www.nets-find.net/.

[iii]   The FIRE experimental facility is intended to support research for the Future Internet at different stages of the R&D cycle based on the design principle of "open coordinated federation of testbeds". See http://cordis.europa.eu/fp7/ict/fire/.

[iv]   A perspective is given in [16], which emphasises the twin notions of utility and end-to-end for the IoS service infrastructure in order to create a level playing field with no technical barriers to market entrants, and to stimulate the wide provisioning of value-added services that are fine tuned to the needs of users, without being locked into particular "ecosystems". Another perspective is offered in [17], which identifies two aspects of the "Future Internet Infrastructure" with the greatest potential for Europe: (1) "Internet of Services – the service infrastructure" and (2) "Internet of Things – the integration of the physical and the digital world". [17] further proposes "a broadened concept of global and open Service Delivery Platform" for the IoS.

[v]   The listing of example providers does not include so-called "prosumers" (end users as providers). It could be argued that prosumers should figure in any classification of providers.

[vi]   Example list on trends and characteristics: Nomadic access becomes the norm; From ad hoc usage to always-on experience; From static information access to dynamic and time-critical services; From free-of-charge access to value-based transactions; Creating trust; Simplification of user interface; Increased M2M interaction [15]. See also the description of IoS in [12].

[vii]   Most recent example as of May 2008: a technology consortium comprising Sprint Nextel, Google, Intel, Comcast, Time Warner and Clearwire to create a US$ 12 billion wireless platform targeting new Internet-based services.

[viii]   Notably Google, Yahoo, Microsoft, Amazon, IBM and Sun; the infrastructures for such ecosystems are now popularly known as "clouds".

[ix]   As evidenced by, for example, the on-going debates of IPR and the relatively small number of publicly available APIs and web services (reported to total respectively 802 and 27563 as of 6 July 2008 [19])

IOS Press, 2008

A New Value Proposition of Interoperability for Enterprises to Advance the Frontiers of the European Knowledge Economy

Man-Sze LI[1], Servane CRAVE[2], Antonio GRILO[3], Roelof VAN DEN BERG[4]

[1]*IC Focus, 42 Clifton Road, London, N8 8JA, UK*
Tel: +44 20 8347 7355, Fax: + 44 7967 359 461, Email: msli@icfocus.co.uk
[2]*France Telecom Orange Labs, 905 rue A.Einstein, 06921 Sophia Antipolis Cedex, France*
Tel: +34 92 94 53 09, Email: servane.crave@orange-ftgroup.com
[3]*Universidade Nova de Lisboa, Campus FCT/UNL, 2829-516 Caparica, Portugal*
Tel: +351 212948542 ext 11233, Email: acbg@fct.unl.pt
[4]*Erasmus Research Institute of Management, P.O. Box 1738, 3000 DR Rotterdam,*
The Netherlands Tel: +31 10 408 2596, Email: RJBerg@rsm.nl

Abstract: Numerous European research projects studied Enterprise Interoperability (EI) in the last decade with a specific emphasis on the development of offerings for SMEs. From our survey of available case studies, it is clear that the main target of these offerings was the search for efficiency with a large focus on supply chain management in the industrial sector. Globalisation, Web 2.0 developments and the rising importance of services for virtually all sectors are new key factors, reinforced by European policies to bring about the Knowledge Economy. This paper argues that the strategic issues of interoperability for enterprises are no longer about basic interconnectivity at the level of technology, or basic information exchange between two entities. Instead, interoperability is now closely coupled with the changing nature of business needs, at the level of the enterprise and the industry, the individual, and the economy. This entails a change in the notion of and approach to interoperability in the enterprise context. The paper presents a new value proposition, an analysis of business models and a discussion of related service offerings.

Keywords: Enterprise Interoperability, value proposition, business models, service infrastructure, Interoperability Service Utility (ISU)

1. Introduction

The online economy and society is anticipated to undergo another wave of transformation and growth over the next decade and beyond. New economic activities will arise with new classes of networked applications and services, new forms of enterprise collaboration, new generations of workers, new business models and new value propositions. It is generally accepted that ICT is an enabler for innovation. What is however less clear, and probably controversial, is the changing nature of innovation and the mechanisms for catalysing innovation. While there is a well established scholarship on innovation and growing research into the wider impact of ICT beyond technological improvements, the relationships between ICT, business models and value proposition *from the perspective of business* is an area that is far less studied. This is notwithstanding the increasing importance being attached to "the business model" for new technology, by the market as well as policy makers and more recently - many researchers. However, there is often an implicit assumption that technology would by itself deliver benefit and value, which is context-neutral or even context-free. This paper challenges that assumption.

Our research shows that the value of ICT for business is dependent upon the level of value a company targets, the type of business model adopted to achieve that value level, the intensity of the company's processes in implementing the business model, and the degree of engagement of the company with its business partners and customers. Specifically, we advance a new notion of Enterprise Interoperability (EI) in a new business context that is characterised by continuous, emergent change; and a pace of change that is likely to accelerate in the coming years under the combined forces of (1) Web 2.0 developments; (2) ICT market trends towards commoditisation and utility; (3) a new generation of Key Enabling Technologies; and (4) globalisation. Those forces impact directly on the kind of business models that are likely to enable companies to be market leaders, to remain competitive or just to survive. This in turn impacts on how ICT as an enabler could support the implementation of the business model in order to generate value in a marketplace. **Interoperability is a strategic issue and an integral part of this new context.** But because the context has changed, the notion of interoperability must evolve accordingly.

In this paper, we submit that interoperability for enterprises is no longer about basic interconnectivity at the technology level, or basic information exchange between two entities, in static contexts of "universal" business models. Instead, interoperability is about ICT infrastructural requirements on the one hand, and serving needs arising from the changing nature of businesses on the other. These new needs relate to those at the enterprise level and community of enterprises, the individual in a myriad of roles, economy and society. Importantly, a value proposition framework of interoperability for enterprises must capture value at the different levels, and value relationships between the levels. Value assessment techniques for interoperability need to pay attention to the potential for value innovation, on the basis of a comprehensive value proposition framework that reflects the changing nature of enterprises and positions the enterprises in a world of change.

The final main issue concerns the role of enterprises in advancing the knowledge economy. That role stems from the contribution of enterprises to the creation of value. Our research suggests that in order for Europe to achieve its Lisbon objectives, it is vital that enterprises take the full advantage of ICT to target value innovation (and not only efficiency).

2.   Objectives

This paper aims to provide a reasoned argument of the relationships between ICT, business models and value proposition from the perspective of business, and assess the requirement for interoperability on the basis of that argument. Specifically, the paper sets out:

- A value proposition framework for EI
- An assessment of different types of business models in relation to the different propositions of value and, related to that, the role of ICT in general and interoperability in particular for enabling the realisation of value
- A new notion of interoperability and the interoperability offerings that are needed for value creation and innovation.

The paper is intended to be a contribution towards ongoing discussions, in research and in industry, on a new perspective of ICT in serving business needs; on how meeting those needs through ICT helps advancing the Knowledge Economy; and on expanding the frontiers of the Knowledge Economy through innovation, particularly value innovation.

3.   Methodology

This paper presents the main findings of the report entitled *Unleashing the potential of the European Knowledge Economy: Value Proposition for Enterprise Interoperability*, published by the European Commission in January 2008 [1]. The technical foundation of that report is based on the *Enterprise Interoperability Research Roadmap*, the latest version of which (Version 5.0) was published by the European Commission in March 2008 [2]. Both documents were developed through an iterative open consultation process coordinated by the European Commission DG Information Society & Media, involving stakeholders of the Enterprise Interoperability Cluster [3] and beyond.

The knowledge presented in this paper is drawn from contributions of the EI community[i], deliverables and submissions from FP6/IST projects belonging to and associated with the EI Cluster, and research associated with the preparation of [1] and [2].

The methodology adopted is based on the outcome of the EI Cluster discussions. Specifically, a distinction is drawn between value propositions for EI, business models for EI, offerings of EI and value analysis of EI. This is reflected in the structure of the present paper. The distinction is itself based on the research framework defined in the *Enterprise Interoperability Research Roadmap Version 4.0*, which positions research challenges in accordance with three inter-linked dimensions: Policy, Business-Economic and Technical [4]. The methodology of the paper adopts the standpoint of the above publications, for closing the gap between the business view and the technical view of interoperability in order for enterprise systems to deliver innovative and sustainable value.

A consequence of the present methodology is a closer coupling between technical research and business research than generally was the case in research projects under previous EU research framework programmes. The need to create a continuous cycle between research and innovation is a key foundation of the i2010 Strategy of the EU [5], most recently highlighted in the EU's high profile "Aho Report", an ex-post evaluation of the ICT theme of FP6 [6]. There is opportunity for the present methodology to be further developed in support of the definition and execution of technical research guided by evolving business needs and complemented by business research.

4.   New Value Propositions, Business Models and Offerings for EI

4.1   A value proposition framework for EI

Value Proposition (VP) is often referenced by scholars and is an important part of a Business Model, but it is extremely difficult to find a commonly accepted definition. For the purpose of this paper, we adopt the definition of Osterwalder et al: "a Value Proposition (*element*) is an overall view of a firm's bundle of products and services that together represent value for a specific customer segment" [7]. A value proposition framework for EI (EIVP) has been developed accordingly in [1]. It is summarised in Figure 1 (see next page).

A key innovation of the above framework is to focus, as a starting point, on the Value Level dimension which measures the utility that interoperability has for enterprises in its strategic positioning and strategy and, as a consequence, how EI deployment is perceived and valued by consumers, citizens, public bodies and other companies. To measure this dimension, it is useful to reference a qualitative description by Kim and Mauborgne: the concept of ***"blue ocean strategy"*** and ***"red ocean strategy"*** [8].

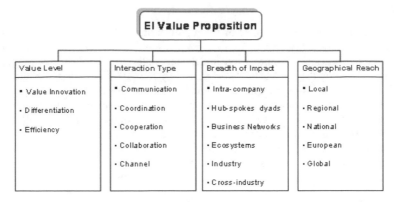

Figure 1: Enterprise Interoperability Value Proposition (EIVP) Framework

Companies competing on blue ocean strategies simultaneously pursue differentiation and low cost. But unlike companies competing on red ocean strategies (see below), their over-riding aim is not to out-perform the competition in the existing industry. Instead, they aim to create new market space or a "blue ocean", **thereby making the competition irrelevant**. They achieve this through *value innovation*, i.e. introducing radical innovations in the products, services, processes, etc., that are genuinely valued by customers. The blue ocean strategies differ from red ocean strategies, where most companies compete, through seeking lower cost, achieved by higher efficiency; or through differentiation, achieved by introducing marginal innovations that are targeted at specific market segments with premium price. Studies demonstrate that blue ocean strategies have a clear impact on companies' revenues and profits, higher than red ocean strategies. **Higher EI value proposition is likely to be achieved when companies are looking to interoperability as a means for developing blue ocean strategies, by creating value innovation for customers**. It should however be noted that interoperability can still be used as an enabler to sustain competitive strategies based on lower costs in order to obtain efficiency gains, or to sustain competitive strategies based on differentiation in order to obtain incremental value-added in products, services and processes. Thus,

Value Level ⎰ Value Innovation ⎱ EI Blue Ocean Strategies
Differentiation
Efficiency ⎰ EI Red Ocean Strategies

Figure 2: Value and Blue/Red Ocean Strategies

Bringing innovation, differentiation and efficiency to customers through EI, as discussed below, may occur in different ways. Importantly, interoperability can relate to that between companies, between companies and consumers/citizens, and between companies and public bodies. Accordingly, while the prime beneficiaries of EI are the customers (enterprises or consumers), citizens in general and public bodies are also beneficiaries. Policy consideration is and must be an intrinsic aspect of EI.

4.2   An Assessment of Different Types of Business models in Relation to Different Value Propositions

Based on the above categorisation of value levels, business models are classified according to the value level they target: Efficiency, Differentiation and Value Innovation. Adapting from the work of Chesbrough (2007) [9], we can distinguish between six main types of business models: *Type 1 Undifferentiated; Type 2 Somewhat differentiated; Type 3 Segmented; Type 4 Externally aware; Type 5 Integrated with the innovation process; and Type 6 Fully open and adaptive.*

Type 5 and 6 are obviously the most promising business model types when aiming at creating value through innovation and differentiation. Type 5 targets efficiency and differentiation in an existing market; it also pays attention to value innovation in new markets. Type 6 not only aims at efficiency and differentiation in an existing market, but is also highly focussed on value innovation in new markets.

The business model analysis yields a key conclusion. The need for EI is progressively greater in support of the business models from Type 1 to Type 6 (see Figure 3). The need increases as the company engages more intensively and openly with its business partners and customers. In other words, *EI as an enabler is directly linked to the openness of the business model, the intensity of the company's innovation process and the degree of engagement of the company with its business partners and customers.* All of these contribute towards increasing the value level that a company may achieve. Importantly, the increase in the value level for the company benefits also its business partners and customers, creating a win-win situation.

Our economic analysis of business models further concludes that investment in EI technologies and infrastructures should focus on:

- Positive feedback: the overall value of the offering as well as the value for the individual participant depends on the number of other participants in the same "network" associated with the offering
- Symmetry of value: all parties involved - including business partners and end-users (who may or may not be paying customers) - gain new value through the relationship
- Innovation: creating or adding value rather than re-distributing value.

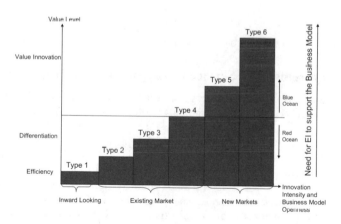

Figure 3: Business Models, Value Level, Innovation and Need for EI (adapted from Chesbrough 2007 [9])

4.3 A New Notion of Interoperability and Interoperability Offerings for Value Creation and Innovation

Successful future enterprise systems will increasingly be aligned with the needs of Type 5 and Type 6 of EI business models as described above. This alignment should be a *full* alignment in the sense that they reflect directly the main characteristics of those business models, namely: **Enterprise systems which are fully open, adaptive and integrated with innovation processes.**

From the four Grand Challenges defined in [4] and updated in [2], four types of EI offerings[ii] can be derived:

- Interoperability Service Utility (ISU): a new **infrastructure** for EI
- Web Technologies for EI: a new generation of **technologies** in support of applying Web 2.0 to the enterprise space ("Enterprise 2.0")
- Knowledge-Oriented Collaboration (KOC): **methods and tools** to support knowledge sharing within a Virtual Organisation to the mutual benefit of partners of the VO
- Science Base: new **scientific foundations** for EI by making use of other scientific disciplines – EI offerings that are rested on and subject to the rigour of science.

By linking the EI offering with the EIVP and EI business models, we can further characterise EI Offerings (Figure 4). Importantly, infrastructures, technologies, methods and tools are valuable in terms of the *overall business impact* they have on the enterprise.

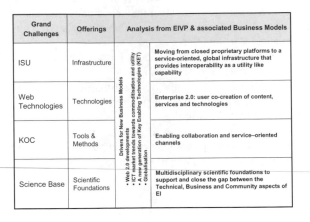

Grand Challenges	Offerings		Analysis from EIVP & associated Business Models
ISU	Infrastructure		Moving from closed proprietary platforms to a service-oriented, global infrastructure that provides interoperability as a utility like capability
Web Technologies	Technologies	Drivers for New Business Models: • Web 2.0 developments towards commoditisation and utility • ICT market trends towards commoditisation and utility • A new generation of Key Enabling Technologies (KET) • Globalisation	Enterprise 2.0: user co-creation of content, services and technologies
KOC	Tools & Methods		Enabling collaboration and service–oriented channels
Science Base	Scientific Foundations		Multidisciplinary scientific foundations to support and close the gap between the Technical, Business and Community aspects of EI

Figure 4: EI Offerings in support of the Grand Challenges of EI Research Roadmap

5.   Key Requirement for Service infrastructure for EI in Future

The foregoing analysis indicates that service infrastructure, such as the ISU, is fundamental to value creation for the EI field as a whole. As noted in [4], *" interoperability is envisioned as a utility-like capability that can be invoked on-the-fly by enterprises in support of their business activities."* The ISU is conceived as a conceptual (i.e. not a functional or technical) "layer" of the Future Internet, atop telecommunications, Internet and the Web. Critically, the ISU is intended to be based on the same principles that secure the openness of the Internet and the Web. It is the **openness of the ISU that drives the value innovation capability of future enterprise systems.** That helps achieve Type 5 and Type 6 EI business models **within an environment of co-existence of different types of business models.** That openness is the key attribute that enables unanticipated change through unfiltered contributions from broad and varied sources. This is in contrast to a closed infrastructure, such as a proprietary IT platform, where growth is channelled through infrastructure maker, regardless of the size and even the "openness" of the ecosystem based on the infrastructure.

The above analysis points to a further distinction between EI offerings: **EI offerings that are open and utility-based** *(utility services),* **and EI offerings that are customised and value-added** *(value added services).* The distinction between these two types can be described as a trade-off between their economic properties (exclusivity and rivalry), as well as the trade-offs between cost and functionality as shown in Figure 5. This further distinction between EI offerings is depicted in Figure 6.

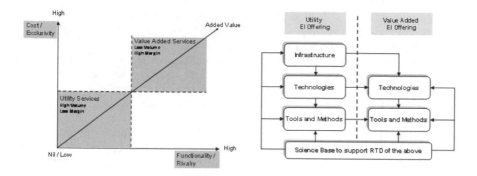

Figure 5: Comparison of Services based on Trade-offs   *Figure 6: Utility and Value Added EI Offerings[iii]*

On this analysis, we can distinguish between *universal* **interoperability** for utility-based EI offering and *conditional* **interoperability** for value-added EI offerings. For universal interoperability, interoperability is needed at two levels:

1. *Between potential providers* **of utility service offerings** – to ensure that connectivity across the services that are required by one or more users can be supported.
2. *Between users and providers of utility service offerings* – to ensure that value added services can be freely added by any user of utility services without fear of losing the investment due to unforeseen changes in the connection, APIs or service conditions.

For conditional interoperability, the degree and level of interoperability needed would be directly derived from the business model of the individual users of value-added services. In other words, specific services may be open under certain circumstances (e.g. for enterprises within an ecosystem) but closed in others (e.g. between competing ecosystems). Value-added services need to be tightly coupled with the business innovation processes of enterprises – they address uniqueness, reflect the proprietary aspects of business assets and operation, and therefore are about exceptions, rather than the business norms and routines of utility services. Importantly, in order to meet the needs of future enterprise systems targeting value innovation, offerings that are traditionally proprietary, i.e. in the value-added category, might usefully be re-categorised as utility offering. Indeed, the history of technology development in general underlines this development: technology that was highly priced and available to a few became, over time, commoditised and affordable to all.

There is already a movement in this direction for some time in the world of IT, such as e-payment in the case of PayPal, identity federation in the case of the Liberty Alliance, location mapping service in the case of Google Maps, and basic data hosting in the case of Amazon's S3. However, while these meet the second level of universal interoperability described above, the first level remains unfulfilled.

Another consequence is that the characteristics of EI offerings at the infrastructure level will drive developments of those at the level above the infrastructure. The kind of EI offerings that could (should?) be available at the infrastructure level is a rich ground of research in terms of technical possibilities, business model configurations (for both providers and customers) and policy enablement.

6.   Business Benefits

Our survey of the state-of-art (see Annex III to [1]) suggests that the business benefits of EI research are generally insufficiently explored. Where they are explored, the predominant focus has been on cost reduction (efficiency) and associated competitive advantage (differentiation). While increasing attention is being paid to innovation including open innovation, processes and mechanisms for innovation are often defined without a clear exposition of value creation, value capture, value assessment and value innovation. We believe that as the four forces for transforming business context (identified in Section 1) intensify in the coming years, competitive advantage will increasingly lie in value innovation, requiring continuous change in business assumptions, culture, (re-) organisation, as well as new and adaptable expertise in products, services and markets.

The corollary is that interoperability in a business context requires re-appraisal. In Section 4.3, we have advanced a notion of EI offerings, which goes beyond the traditional notion of EI solutions. The long-term infrastructure perspective of EI offerings is contrasted with the short-term perspective of EI solutions providing quick fixes and typically dictated by market fashion. We believe that the business benefit of EI lies in the ability of EI to support flexibility and change at the application level, where value could be created and fine-tuned to the specificity of the (individual) businesses as end-users. An open, stable infrastructure is required to make that happen.

In other words, there is a need to differentiate between the general - even universal - benefits of EI at the infrastructure level as a utility and the end-user specific business benefits of EI at the value-added level for value creation and innovation. However, while the thesis has been put forward in research, notably in [1], work on the detailed conceptual and practical (technical) frameworks and business cases is only just beginning in a number of FP7 projects linked to the ISU and its application[iv]. The preliminary research on business models by one of these projects, the COIN Integrated Project, suggests that there is no established literature on applying the notion of utility to interoperability in an enterprise context or regarding business cases or benefits. While there are well known business cases on open innovation[v] and increasingly on the Blue Ocean Strategy[vi], business cases specifically on the value innovation benefits of EI are yet to be developed.

Finally, Future Internet technologies will re-shape interoperability as a capability, leading to the need to reappraise interoperability between enterprises. Future Internet service infrastructures may help lay the utility foundation for EI as described in this paper, leading to new possibilities for value innovation at the application level. The business aspect for such a scenario is described in [13], which concludes that such a development would encourage the emergence of innovative business models and new service providers targeting the traditionally less well-served markets, notably the "Long Tail" of SMEs.

7.   Conclusions

In this paper, we have presented a value proposition framework for EI, an assessment of business model types with reference to that framework, and a new notion of interoperability targeting value innovation, which is dependent on a clear distinction between utility and added value *by leveraging that utility*. In doing so, we have outlined a systemic view of ICT for enterprises and highlighted a number of key research areas. We argued that such work would help reinforce the iterative and virtuous cycle of research and innovation, thus optimising the impact of EI research.

In conclusion, a new approach to interoperability is needed, in order to make interoperability simple, affordable, accessible and reliable, and contribute directly to the sustainability and growth of businesses. Technical research and business research for EI need to be more interlinked and integrated. This paper identifies different types of technical offerings required for future enterprise systems. Equally, it pinpoints the importance of business cases and economic foundations to support the research and development of technical offerings. While the thesis has been made, concrete business cases and clear demonstration of business benefits are currently lacking. In order to advance the frontiers of the European Knowledge Economy, it is vital to lay a new foundation for interoperability – one which focuses on openness, collaboration and innovation as intrinsic aspects of sustainable business models.

References

[1] Li, M-S., Crave S., Grilo A., Van den Berg R. (editors), *Unleashing the Potential of the European Knowledge Economy - Value proposition for Enterprise Interoperability*, 21 January 2008, http://cordis.europa.eu/fp7/ict/enet/ei-isg_en.html

[2] Charalabidis Y., Gionis G., Hermann KM., Martinez C. (editors), *Enterprise Interoperability Research Roadmap, Update (Version 5.0)*, 5 March 2008, http://cordis.europa.eu/fp7/ict/enet/ei-rrrev_en.html

[3] Enterprise Interoperability Cluster coordinated by the European Commission, DG Information Society & Media, Unit D4, http://cordis.europa.eu/fp7/ict/enet/ei_en.html

[4] Li, M-S., Cabral, R., Doumeingts, G. and Popplewell, K. (editors), *Enterprise Interoperability Research Roadmap, Final Version (V4.0)*, 31 July 2006, http://cordis.europa.eu/ist/ict-ent-net/ei-roadmap_en.htm

[5] i2010 - A European Information Society for growth and employment (first announced by EU Commissioner Reding in June 2005), http://ec.europa.eu/information_society/eeurope/i2010/index_en.htm

[6] *Information Society Research and Innovation: Delivering Results with Sustainable Impact* ("Aho Report"), May 2008, http://ec.europa.eu/dgs/information_society/evaluation/data/pdf/fp6_ict_expost/ist-fp6_panel_report.pdf

[7] Osterwalder, A., *The Business Model Ontology: A Proposition in a Design Science Approach*, Doctoral Dissertation, Université de Lausanne, Switzerland, 2004

[8] Kim, W. C and Mauborgne, R., *Blue Ocean Strategy: How to create uncontested market space and make competition irrelevant*, Harvard Business School Press, USA, 2005

[9] Chesbrough, H., *Open Business Models: How to Thrive in the New Innovation Landscape*, Harvard Business School Press, USA, 2007

[10] *103 Ways to success – A portfolio analysis of proposals selected under FP7 ICT Call 1 – Challenge 1 – INFSO.D*, November 2007 (also known as "IPPA Report"; see particularly Section II.3 on Objective 1.3), http://cordis.europa.eu/fp7/ict/programme/publications1/books/ippa2007_en.html

[11] OECD Business Symposium on Open Innovation in Global Networks, Copenhagen, 25-26 February 2008, http://www.oecd.org/document/48/0,3343,en_2649_37417_39858608_1_1_1_37417,00.html

[12] Open Innovation Bibliography, http://www.openinnovation.net/Research/Bibliography.html

[13] Man-Sze Li, *A Vision of Next-Generation Software-based Service Provisioning*. In: Expanding the Knowledge Economy: Issues, Applications, Case Studies, P. Cunningham and M. Cunningham (Eds.), IOS Press, 2007, http://www.e2esu.eu/public/Concepts?action=AttachFile&do=get&target=E2ESU_Vision_June_2007.pdf

---

[i] Who provided inputs to successive draft versions of the report under the public consultation process organised by the European Commission; for full history, see http://cordis.europa.eu/fp7/ict/enet/ei-isg_en.html

[ii] The distinction between EI offerings and the more conventional EI solutions is an important one with reference to particularly publicly financed research. In accordance with [1], provision of EI solutions is a commercial concern and activity. In contrast, provision of EI offerings has a wider perspective of public concern and interest in respect of the changing nature of EI and the long-term research needs of EI.

[iii] Note: A utility offering is open whereas a value-added offering may or may not be open.

[iv] For an analysis of these ISU-related FP7 projects, which currently include COIN, COMMIUS, iSURF and SYNERGY, see [10].

[v] For example, Proctor and Gamble, IBM, Telefonica and Philips. A large number of case studies were presented at the OECD Business Symposium on Open Innovation in Global Networks [11]. See also an extensive bibliography on open innovation [12].

[vi] Announcements to implement Blue Ocean Strategy have recently been made by ING Direct in financial services, HCL in software and KT (Korea Telecom) in telecommunications.

Collaboration and the Knowledge Economy: Issues, Applications, Case Studies
P. Cunningham and M. Cunningham (Eds.)
IOS Press, 2008

How Bytes Meet Coils: ICT and E-business in the Steel Industry

Stefan LILISCHKIS

empirica GmbH, Oxfordstr. 2, 53111 Bonn, Germany
Tel: +49 (0)228 98530-35, Fax: +49 (0)228 98530-12,
Email: stefan.lilischkis@empirica.com

Abstract: This paper presents findings about the use of ICT and e-business in the steel industry as well as related impacts and policy implications. The study was carried out in the framework of the Sectoral e-Business Watch, a service to the European Commission's DG Enterprise and Industry. In the framework of the study, managers from 449 steel firms in the EU and the US were interviewed and ten case studies were conducted. A core finding was that ICT are important along the industry's whole value chain. ICT are used to increase productivity, reduce costs, and improve customer relationships. Almost two thirds of the large steel companies reported that ICT has increased competition. ICT use in steel firms is similar to other manufacturing industries, which may contradict the industry's public image of being old-fashioned. However, current policy activities in the steel industry do not adequately reflect the importance of ICT.

1. Introduction

Of what use is e-business in the steel industry? Why should one study the use of modern technology in an apparently old-fashioned industry? This paper will show that e-business is highly relevant to the steel industry, and that the steel industry does not lag behind other industries in e-business applications. In fact, while the strategic importance of the steel producing industry for Europe has declined during the past decades, steel remains a very important production material.

This paper presents findings about the use of information and communication technology (ICT) as well as e-business applications in the steel industry, including related impacts and policy implications. [1] The study was conducted in the framework of the Sectoral e-Business Watch (SeBW) (http://www.ebusiness-watch.org), a service to the European Commission's Directorate General Enterprise and Industry. Since 2002, the e-Business Watch has been analysing ICT and e-business use in numerous different industries. All results can be downloaded from the project website, in the form of sector reports, annual reports, table reports with survey findings, and datasets in Excel files.

2. Objectives and Industry Background

The objective of this paper is to describe and analyse the state-of-play how steel companies use ICT for managing their business processes – internally and in exchanges with suppliers and customers. It identifies related opportunities and possible barriers for ICT adoption and digital integration, and it assesses the impact of ICT deployment for firms and for the industry as a whole. The analysis leads to implications for possible policy actions. The rationale for conducting the study was enhanced economic policy.

According to the most recent available data from Eurostat, the European steel industry comprised 9,459 enterprises and employed 776,800 people in 2004. The basic metals manufacturing sector to which the steel industry belongs is dominated by large multinational enterprises, with 74% of its EU-27 value added created by enterprises with 250 or more employees. However, the majority of companies in the industry are small or medium-sized [2].

Since 2003 there has been an unprecedented upward cycle in the steel industry, caused by increased demand for steel particularly from China. A further trend is an ongoing process of consolidation of the steel industry, which may lead to further large-scale enterprises. Skills and employment issues are becoming more important since many employees will retire within a few years and hiring new skilled personnel may become difficult. Furthermore, environment issues, energy saving in particular, are becoming more important for the steel industry. In all these contexts, ICT and e-business may play a role.

3. Methodology

The primary data presented here were collected in a representative survey of steel enterprises in seven European Union (EU) Member States and the USA. EU Member States comprised the six largest countries – Germany, France, the United Kingdom, Italy, Spain and Poland as well as Sweden. The survey, referenced as e-Business Survey 2007 in the following, took place in August and September 2007. Decision makers in altogether 449 steel enterprises were interviewed. Interviews were carried out from August to October 2007, using computer-aided telephone interview (CATI) technology. In parallel, a survey with mainly the same questions was conducted in the chemicals and furniture industries.

Another principal part of the study was an econometric analysis of ICT and e-business impacts, based on SeBW survey data and secondary data from the EU KLEMS database. Ten case studies about ICT and e-business use in steel companies were also conducted. The study was guided by an advisory board of five representatives of European steel companies and industry associations as well as of steel experts from the European Commission.

The steel industry as defined for the study purpose covers large parts of division 24 in NACE Rev. 2, "manufacture of basic metals". The steel-related parts of NACE 24 are 24.1 "manufacture of basic iron and steel and of ferro-alloys", 24.2 "manufacture of tubes, pipes, hollow profiles and related fittings, of steel", 24.3 "manufacture of other first processing of iron and steel", 24.51 "casting of iron", and 24.52 "casting of steel".

4. Key Findings

4.1 Infrastructure, Skills, Investment

Steel business can apparently not be done without the internet any longer. Practically all companies in the sector are connected to the internet. However, the share of steel firms that said they have a broadband connection to the internet was 41% (34% weighted by employment) so that there is much scope for improving internet connections. As regards skills, only large companies reported to have experienced difficulties to find ICT practitioners (20%), which reflects their higher demand. As regards budgets, 69% (employment-weighted) said that they would keep the ICT budget at about the same level, and further 30% said they would increase the budget. These figures indicate a continued importance of ICT investment in the steel industry.

4.2 Electronic Procurement

Procurement is fundamentally important in the steel industry, as in most manufacturing industries, because upstream supply chains tend to be complex and fragmented. Firms representing 66% of the EU-7 steel industry's employment were found to procure goods via the internet or other computer-mediated networks – see Figure 1. This is about the same as in the chemicals (70%) and the furniture (64%) industries. The casting sub-sector reported the largest share of firms procuring online (75%). Large firms reported the largest share of online procurers (73%), followed by medium-sized (67%) and small firms (52%). While small firms lag behind, half of them practicing e-procurement can be considered quite a high share. However, in comparison with the US, EU-7 firms lag behind considerably: US steel firms representing 92% of employment reported to procure goods online.

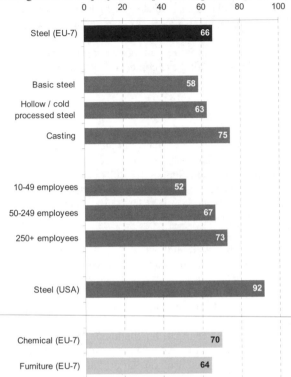

Figure 1: Companies Ordering Goods on the Internet or Via Other Computer-Mediated Networks (2007)
Figures for Sector Totals and Countries are Weighted by Employment ("Firms Representing x% of Employment in the Sector / Country"), Figures for Size-Bands in % of Firms

Electronic sourcing platforms can make procurement processes more efficient and reduce procurement costs. The case of ThyssenKrupp (https://sourcing.thyssenkrupp.info) shows that such platforms may not only be beneficial for the procuring company but also for the suppliers because their tendering procedures can become more streamlined, too. However, steel companies are likely to continue to procure raw materials in long-term offline relationships, due to an oligopolistic market structure in iron ore supply.

4.3 Internal e-Business Systems

Internal e-business systems can significantly enhance workflows and business processes and thus increase productivity and reduce costs in steel enterprises. While large companies may benefit from implementing comprehensive applications such as enterprise resource planning (ERP) systems, small companies may already benefit from simple software and basic ICT. The use of software for managing orders is quite prevalent: Firms representing 76% of the steel sector's employment said they use such software – see Figure 2. 59% reported to have an ERP system. For manufacturing companies, ERP systems are an important "hub" for much of their e-business activities with other companies. B2B data exchanges as well as planning and controlling processes are largely based on functionalities provided by ERP systems. The use of internal systems for document management, supply chain management (both 27%), and customer relationship management (21%) was found to be not so widespread. Internal systems use in the steel industry was found to tend to be smaller than in the chemicals industry but larger than in the furniture industry.

Radio Frequency Identification (RFID) is also not prevalent. Steel firms representing 12% of employment reported to use RFID and 6% said they plan to do so. RFID appears to be a large-firm technology which can be explained by high investment costs. None of the small firms interviewed for the survey reported to use RFID and only 2% said they plan to introduce this technology. RFID use was reported to be much higher in the US: firms representing 26% of the US steel industry employment said they use RFID which is more than twice the EU-7 figure.

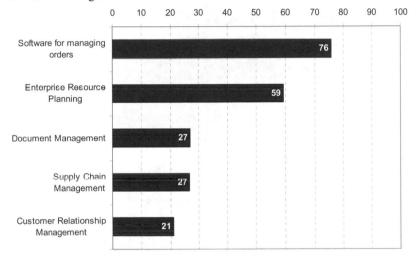

Figure 2: Internal Systems Use in Steel Companies (in %)
Figures are Weighted by Employment ("Firms Representing x% of Employment in the Sector").

Case study evidence from the Śrem iron foundry, Poland, and Farwest Steel, US, indicate considerable productivity benefits from implementing an ERP system. However, the case studies also point to challenges of implementing e-business systems related to ICT acceptance among the workforce. There was a need for changing management practices and offering training.

4.4   Sales-Side e-Business

The steel industry is largely driven by requirements from customers, particularly from the large and powerful automobile industry. Thus the customer interfaces are vitally important. e-Business solutions may enhance communication with customers, including for example product specification, scheduling, and invoicing. Online platforms for data exchange with customers, such as the one at Corus Steel IJmuiden, Netherlands, may improve order processes, reducing orders processing costs and lead times. The case of Baosteel, China, also provides a related example: Workflows were reported to now require on average only 60% of the time spent before introducing digitised operations. However, steel firms representing only 26% of the industry's employment actually sell goods electronically, which is lower than in other industries. Steel products may not be well suited for e-sales due to their specificities.

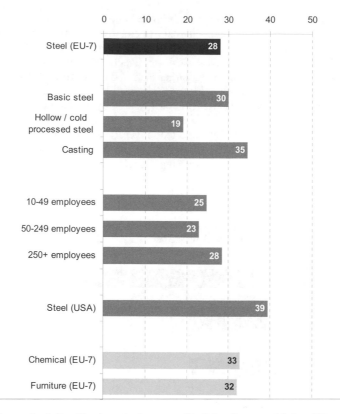

*Figure 3: Companies Selling Goods on the Internet or Via Other Computer-Mediated Networks (2007)
Figures for Sector Totals and Countries are Weighted by Employment ("Firms Representing x% of
Employment in the Sector / Country"), Figures for Size-Bands in % of Firms*

Distribution and logistics of steel products to customers has long been neglected as an important issue in the sector. However, the steel distribution paradigm may now move from a product driven business model to a steel solution model. ICT can contribute to making distribution in the industry more effective. ArcelorMittal Gent, Belgium, provides an example of linking warehouses electronically, enhancing the overview of materials in stock and on transport, thus reducing storage costs and allowing faster invoicing.

4.5 ICT Standardisation May Help to Sophisticate e-Communication

The development of ICT standards in the steel industry may be important for sophisticating e-business communication in the industry and beyond. Eurofer, the European Federation of Iron and Steel Industries, supported the development of the European Steel Industry Exchange Language (ESIDEL) standard. ESIDEL version 1.0 was introduced in 2004; an upgraded version 1.1 was published at the end of 2005. In 2007 the further development of ESIDEL in Europe was stopped. Only 1% of the interviewed EU steel companies reported to use ESIDEL, while even 7% of the US steel firms stated to use it. ESIDEL version 1.1 was however adopted in Australia. At CMC Coil Steels, Australia, the standard was implemented successfully, while opportunities for improvement also emerged.

4.6   Drivers and Barriers of ICT and e-Business Adoption

Companies that stated that they conduct some or none of their business processes as e-businesses were further asked why they do not use e-business more intensively. Two reasons were found to be crucial. The circumstance that "suppliers or customers are not prepared for e-business" appeared to be the most important reason. 64% of the companies agreed to this statement. However, considering the great variety of internal systems, one could argue that many firms blame customers and suppliers while their own efforts are not considerable either. Secondly, size matters: 47% of the steel firms (representing 12% of the industry's employment) said that their company is too small to benefit from e-business.

As regards drivers to use e-business, 22% of the steel firms in the sample reported to have experienced pressure from customers to introduce particular applications. The share of firms reporting such pressure increases by size class; 45% of the large steel firms reported such pressure. Only a tiny share of firms reported pressure from suppliers.

4.7   Overall Differences Between Size Classes, Industries, and Countries

In order to highlight differences between size classes, industries and countries, averages of selected indicators in four domains were calculated: ICT infrastructure, e-procurement, internal systems, e-sales. The following differences were found:

- The steel industry is no laggard – but lacking innovation activity: ICT endowment and e-business use in the European steel industry was found to be broadly in line with other manufacturing industries; on average in between chemicals and furniture which were also included in the survey. This may be in contrast to an image of an old-fashioned industry that may be present in the general public. However, the e-Business Survey 2007 also found that the steel industry is indeed lagging behind other industries in innovative activities. This applies to general product innovation, to process innovation of both general and ICT-related nature, and to organisational innovation.

- SMEs lag behind large firms: In all ICT and e-business domains, small steel firms lag behind medium-sized ones, and medium-sized ones in turn lag behind large firms. The differences between SMEs and large firms are smallest for e-sales indicators and largest for internal systems. The differences for internal systems may reflect SME's limited ability and necessity to invest in comprehensive back-office systems. For e-procurement and ICT infrastructure, the differences are similar.

- EU steel firms lag behind US: EU-7 steel firms lag behind their US counterparts in all domains of ICT and e-business. The differences between the EU and the US were found to be smallest for internal systems and largest for e-procurement indicators. For ICT infrastructure and e-sales indicators, the differences are similar. The data indicate a clear lead of US steel firms over EU-7 steel firms in terms of ICT and e-business. This may potentially contribute to competitive disadvantages of the EU steel industry.

5.   Outlook to Further Possible Developments

In the e-Business Survey 2007, the companies were asked about expected future impacts of ICT on seven selected business functions. The interviewees could state high, medium, low or no impact on the functions. For all business functions, more than 50% of the interviewees stated high or medium impact, indicating that ICT will generally be very important for the steel industry in the future. The highest level of combined high and medium impact was attributed to administration and accounting (86%). A very high share of interviewees (of firms representing 75% of employment) also expected considerable impacts on management and controlling. This confirms the exceptional importance of ICT and e-business for back-office data collection and processing. The second largest impact was expected for logistics (80%) which may indicate that steel companies have switched to attribute crucially high importance on distribution issues. Steel firms representing 72% of the industry's employment expect high or medium future impacts of ICT on production. The values for expected impacts on customer-related functions, namely customer service (66%) and marketing (55%), were relatively low. This indicates that ICT and e-business may continue to play a relatively minor role on the sales side, except logistics. Finally, interviewees from firms representing 58% of the industry's employment expected high or medium future impacts on research and development.

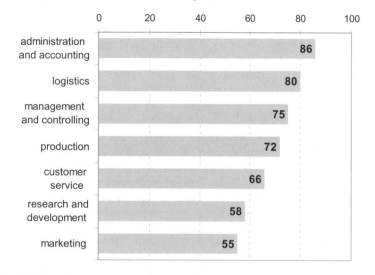

Figure 4: Steel Firms Expecting that ICT Will Have a High or Medium Impact on … in the Future in %
Figures are Weighted by Employment ("Firms Representing x% of Employment in the Sector / Country").

For all business functions, the expected future impacts of ICT were found to be largest for large companies and smallest for small companies. This indicates that SMEs may continue to lag behind large firms in ICT and e-business applications. The levels of expected impact in EU-7 companies were also found to be much higher than in the US. This may be surprising, but it may be explained by the fact that the US steel firms are already far advanced in e-business so that future impacts may be minor. Finally, the levels of expected future ICT impact in the steel industry were found to be higher than in the chemicals and furniture industries. This applies to all indicators except customer service and marketing, further indicating the relatively low importance steel managers attribute to ICT for the sales side.

6.   Conclusions and Policy Implications

Current steel industry policy appears to not adequately reflect the importance of ICT and e-business for the steel industry. Neither the European Commission's mid-term review of industrial policy of July 2007 [3] nor the Communication on competitiveness in the metals industries of February 2008 [4] refer explicitly to ICT, and a steel-industry specific initiative named European Steel Technology Platform (ESTEP) [5] currently does not have a focus on ICT and e-business issues. It may however be important for enhancing the industry's competitiveness to promote competent ICT and e-business use. Several political activities may be suggested:

- Fostering value chains and e-business use: Public organisations may support activities to foster value chain development through ICT in the steel industry. While the European Commission should have a focus on cross-border activities, Member States may promote national or regional activities. In recent years, several EU Member States have launched initiatives to facilitate e-business exchanges within specific industry supply chains. [6] A key objective in most of these initiatives is to enhance SME participation because they are at risk to be eliminated from the supply chain.

- Supporting ICT skills development: The steel industry has the image of a declining industry and may thus face difficulties to attract skilled employees, also in the field of ICT. The steel firms themselves, their industry associations as well as public policy could become more active in this respect. First of all they can promote awareness about and uptake of e-business skills in steel companies. Furthermore they can support e-learning solutions and enhance co-operation activities with universities to support e-skills development.

- Promoting ICT standards: The EC could play a more active role towards standardisation of e-communication processes in the steel industry. The EC could promote the positive Australian experience and the idea of further ESIDEL development among European steel enterprises as well as their customers and suppliers. The EC could also initiate and co-fund European projects to implement this standard. These could focus on SMEs because they tend to be reluctant to adopt standards due to the related investment costs.

- Promoting ICT use for saving energy: ICT and e-business may be used to better protect the natural environment and, in particular, to save energy. Policy makers may promote findings from a related study conducted by the e-Business Watch.

References

[1] European Commission (2008): ICT and e-business impacts in the steel industry. A Sectoral e-Business Watch study by empirica. Final report.
[2] Eurostat (2007): European business. Facts and figures. 2007 edition. Eurostat statistical books. Luxembourg: Office for Official Publications of the European Communities.
[3] European Commission (2007): Mid-term review of industrial policy. A contribution to the EU's Growth and Jobs Strategy. Communication from the Commission to the Council, the European Parliament, the European Economic and Social Committee and the Committee of the Regions, COM(2007)374, SEC(2007)917. Brussels, 4 July 2007.
[4] European Commission (2008): Communication from the Commission to the Council and the European Parliament on the competitiveness of the metals industries. A contribution to the EU's Growth and Jobs Strategy. COM(2008) 108 final. Brussels, 22.2.2008.
Available at: http://ec.europa.eu/enterprise/steel/index_en.htm.
[5] ESTEP, European Steel Technology Platform (2007): 2006 Activity Report. A vision for the future of the Steel sector. March. Available at ftp://ftp.cordis.europa.eu/pub/estep/docs/estep_ar2007.pdf.
[6] European Commission (2007): Sectoral e-Business Policies in Support of SMEs. Innovative approaches, good practices and lessons to be learned. A study by empirica, Databank, IDATE. Version 1.1. November.

Collaboration and the Knowledge Economy: Issues, Applications, Case Studies
P. Cunningham and M. Cunningham (Eds.)
IOS Press, 2008

The Effects of ICT and E-business on EU Trade: a Retail Industry Perspective

Maria WOERNDL
empirica GmbH, Oxfordstr. 2, 53111 Bonn, Germany
Tel: +49 228 985300, Fax: +49 228 9853012, Email: maria.woerndl@empirica.com

Abstract: The retail industry, an important contributor to the European economy, is being affected by changes induced by information and communication technologies (ICT) and e-business. As a result, retailers have come to embrace ICT and e-business to various degrees. This paper aims to illustrate the effects of ICT and e-business on retail firms through adopting a supply chain perspective. The objective is threefold: to explore ICT/e-business effects on e-supply, in-house e-operations and e-sales; to illustrate challenges for e-business adoption; and to identify opportunities for innovation induced by ICT/e-business. In total, 1151 computer-aided telephone interviews (CATI) were conducted with micro, small, medium-sized and large retail enterprises in seven EU countries and the USA. The findings demonstrate that online procurement practice, in-house e-operations and online sales can offer considerable benefits to retailers. Yet, there are also challenges to overcome including the level of readiness for e-business within the retailer's ecosystem. The paper concludes with policy recommendations and areas for further research.

1. Introduction

The retail industry is one of the largest industries in Europe employing more than 15 million people and serving 480 million consumers across the European Community. In 2004, some 3.73 million firms in the EU-27 Member States fell into the retail sector category [1]. The vast majority of the sector's value added was generated by large enterprises and micro enterprises. Overall, EU-25 NACE Division 52 firms generated EUR 1.887 billion of turnover in 2002 with a value added of EUR 351.6 billion [2]. With such strong roots in the European economy, the industry is an important contributor to European productivity and competitiveness. Yet, retail industry performance is heavily dependent on macro-economic developments due to the over-proportional reliance on consumers. In late 2007, the general economic environment for the retail industry has turned less favourable: there is uncertainty about the prospects for economic growth, mainly due to the turmoil in financial markets and rising cost for energy and food. Despite positive developments in real disposable income and favourable labour market conditions, private consumption continues to show signs of weakness in early 2008.

This paper discusses the use of e-business applications and information and communication technologies (ICTs) among European retailers (using data from the US as benchmark). A business process perspective, focusing on three supply chain elements (e-sales, in-house e-operations, and e-supply), is adopted. This perspective provides insight about the role of ICT and e-business in the retail industry and narrows the gap about understanding of entire supply chains: certain 'pockets of research interest' result in a split picture about supply chain management as a whole. There is, for example, a rapidly growing body of knowledge about e-commerce in a business-to-consumer (B2C) context [such as 3, 4] and e-supply in a business-to-business (B2B) context [such as 5] but only few exploit opportunities to study entire supply chains [such as 6].

2.   Objectives

The objectives of this study are threefold. The first objective is to analyse to what extent retailers use ICT and e-business to manage the various elements of their supply chains. For this, the retail supply chain is divided into three elements:

1. the upstream supply chain which enquires about the use of supply chain solutions such as e-procurement and e-storage applications by retail firms
2. the in-house supply chain which looks at e-operations within the retail firms such as distribution and logistics solutions
3. the downstream supply chain which covers all ICT/e-business activities between retail firms and their customers such as selling over the Internet.

The second objective is to explore some of the barriers to e-business adoption in the retail sector. Questions about seven challenges to e-business adoption for retail firms were included in the survey and case firms were also questioned about challenges. The seven challenges included in the questionnaire arc: (a) the company is too small to benefit from e-business activities (b) e-business technologies are too expensive to implement (c) e-business technology is too complicated (d) suppliers or customers are not prepared for e-business (e) firms are concerned about security risks (f) e-business is plagued by important legal problems or complications and (g) it is difficult to find reliable IT providers.

The third objective is to identify opportunities for innovation arising for retail firms from the use of e-business and ICT. In a highly competitive industry such as retailing, firms can gain an advantage over competitors through either using ICT/e-business innovatively or through using ICT and e-business to support product/ service and business process innovations. One of the foci in of this objective is to explore the extent to which innovations in retail firms arc directly related to or enabled by e-business and ICT.

3.   Method

Data about ICT and e-business in the retail industry was collected using a structured questionnaire instrument administered to appropriate company representatives. 1151 telephone interviews with company decision makers (mainly ICT/e-business decision makers, general managers and area managers) were carried out in total. On average, these telephone interviews lasted between twenty and thirty minutes. The survey, which took place between August 2007 and October 2007, covered seven EU countries (France, Germany, Italy, Poland, Spain, Sweden, and the UK) plus the USA. 1026 interviews were done in the EU-7 countries while 125 interviews were conducted with US retail firms. Ten case studies were conducted to further illustrate the findings from the survey.

Retail firms are defined according to the European industry standard classification system (NACE), Rev. 1.1, category 52. All sizes of firms were included in the study and are hereafter structured into micro (fewer than 120 employees), small (between 10 and 49 employees), medium-sized (between 50 and 249 employees) and large firms (more than 2250 employees). Due to the heterogeneous character of the retail sector which covers many different retail formats and firm sizes, three sub-categories are formed: retailers that sell non-food items in store (NACE Rev. 1.1 Class 52.12 and Groups 52.3 to 52.5) and retail sale of food items in store (NACE Class 52.11 and Group 52.2). Retailers in the non-food items in store group accounted for approximately 50% of turnover while the sale of food in store accounted for 44% of total retail turnover in 2002. The remaining NACE groups are summarised as "other retail" in this report: retail sales not in-store (NACE Group 52.6) and repair of personal and household goods (NACE Group 52.7) which accounted for 5% and less than 1% of turnover in 2002 respectively.

4. Findings

The objectives for this study centred on the three elements of the supply chain; challenges to e-business adoption; and innovation driven by e-business and ICT. Findings are discussed in that order.

4.1 Supply Chain Elements: e-Supply, In-House e-Operations and e-Sales

The function of upstream supply chain management (SCM) is to design and manage the processes, information and material flows between retailers and their suppliers. SCM is of utmost importance to retailers as the supply chain can represent between 40% and 70% of a retailer's operating costs, and may comprise half of all company assets [7]. Technology-enabled improvements in SCM promise a high potential not only to cut costs, but also to improve service levels for customers. Therefore, particularly for large retail chains, supply chain management is a highly strategic issue and can be a critical factor for their competitiveness.

In 2007, retailers accounting for 55% of employment in the sector said that they ordered at least some goods from suppliers over the internet or through other computer-mediated networks such as EDI. Their share has increased since 2003 (43%); however, adoption has increased mainly among SMEs, and not significantly among large retailers (Figure 1).

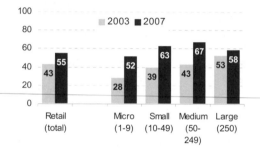

Figure 1: Percentage of Companies Placing Orders for Supplies Online (2003 / 2007)

While the percentage of companies placing orders online is a measure of overall "e-readiness", it does not say a lot about the intensity of e-procurement activity. Hence, retail firms were asked to estimate the share of online orders from suppliers (2007) to total orders. When compared to the number of total purchases from suppliers from 2003 a considerable increase in the intensity of e-procurement since 2003 is evident: the share of those firms for whom e-procurement was a marginal activity has decreased from about 60% in 2003 to 35% in 2007. At the same time, the share of intensive users (procuring more than 25% of goods online) has increased from 17% in 2003 to 40% in 2007.

As retailers do not transform goods, in-house operations supply chain element is concerned with all aspects of organising the in-house processes of receiving, distributing, and selling goods. ICT and e-business applications mainly serve processes inside a company. Interviewees were asked what overall importance e-business has for business processes within the company. They could state "most", "a good deal", "some", or "none". A relative majority of companies representing 47% of the industry's employment said that they conduct some processes by e-business. 22% said "none"; a "good deal" was stated by 20%, and in 11% of firms most processes are conducted electronically.

The most considerable differences between size classes is in the share of firms stating no e-business at all: it is largest in micro firms (35%) and declines with increasing size class. 14% of the large firms said they conduct no e-business at all. On the other hand, the share of firms stating that most of the processes are conducted by e-mail is also the largest in firms with more than 250 employees (15%), while it is similar in micro (7%), small (9%) and medium-sized firms (9%).

While only 16% of retailers use ERP systems, the use of warehouse or depot management systems is widespread among EU-7 retailers: 42% of retailers representing 51% of employment use such systems. The share of firms using warehouse or depot management systems was found to be almost the same in the three sub-sectors. Again the share of firms using such systems was found to increase by size class, with micro firms on a level of 42% and large firms on a level of 65%. In the US (15% of firms, 42% of employment), warehouse or depot management systems are much less prevalent than in the EU-7. The numbers are even lower for ERP with only 6% of US retailers using ERP systems. One e-operations technology that has received considerable amount of interest over the last couple of years is RFID. However, RFID is not very common in the retail industry: retail firms representing 8% of employment reported to use this technology, with usage among micro and small retail firms being scarce.

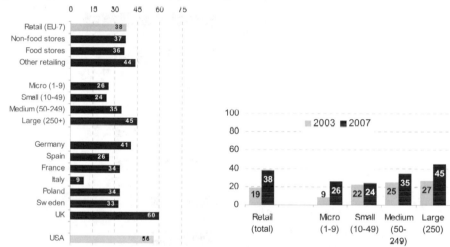

Figure 2: % of Retail Companies Selling Online in 2007

Figure 3: % of Retail Companies Selling Online in 2003 and 2007

The downstream supply chain covers activities and interactions of retail firms with customers. All these activities may take place or may be supported by computerised systems. One of the key changes to the retail industry in recent years is trade via the Internet. Retailers now have the opportunity to sell their products via the Internet to consumers. Retailers representing 38% of the industry's employment stated that they sell goods "through the internet or other computer-mediated networks" (Figure 2). There are no considerable differences between the sub-sectors, but "other retailing" (44%) has a slightly higher share than non-food stores (37%) and food stores (36%). There is a clear distinction between size classes: Almost half of the large retail firms (45%) and 35% of the medium-sized ones sell online, but only 24% of the small retailers and 26% of the micro retailers do so. However, it is notable that micro firms are not far behind their larger counterparts.

The share of companies that sells online doubled from 19% (employment-weighted) in 2003 to 38% in 2007 (Figure 3). There was an apparent increase in all size classes: micro firms made a big jump from 9% of firms to 26%, small retail firms increased their share of online sellers from 22% to 24% and medium-sized ones from 25% to 35%. Large firms made the largest leap in terms of percentage points, from 27% to 45%. This means that while the share of online sellers among large firms was found to be only slightly higher than in SMEs in 2003, the difference was found to be much larger in 2007.

4.2   Challenges to e-Business Adoption

Those companies that stated that they conduct some or none of their business processes as e-businesses were asked why they do not use e-business more intensively. Data indicates that one of the biggest hurdles to e-business adoption for retailers is the business ecosystem: 64% of firms that have not adopted e-business processes report that suppliers and customers are not prepared for e-business. This is the highest overall number of all the seven factors queried, supporting the notion that the business ecosystem can be a major hurdle to e-business adoption. Business ecosystems in the USA seem to be slightly more favourable towards e-business as the overall share in the USA is somewhat lower with 43%. Nevertheless, one could also argue that many firms blame customers and suppliers for not using e-business while their own efforts to introduce e-business are not considerable either.

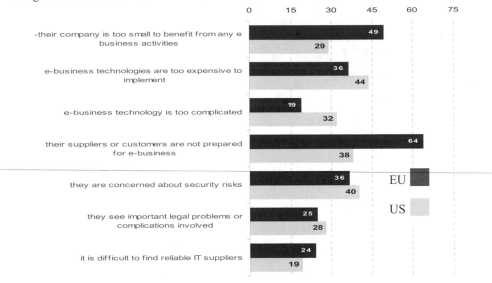

Figure 4: Barriers to e-Business Adoption for Low and Non-Adopters

Firm size also affects e-business adoption: 64% of micro firms and 44% of small firms said their company was too small to benefit from e-business. 47% of micro firms report that ICT was too expensive (average for the retail sector: 36%). These numbers decrease noticeably with firm size from 29% and 30% for small and medium-sized firms respectively to only 20% for firms with over 250 employees. Micro and small firms also consider it to be more difficult to find reliable IT providers than medium-sized and large firms. Security issues in contrast are more relevant for large (40%) and small (39%) firms while only 28% of micro firms and 23% of medium-sized firms report this issue to be a factor affecting the low adoption of e-business. This finding however raises concerns about security awareness among micro and medium-sized firms who might not be fully aware of the exposure to and effects of e-business security issues for their respective companies.

Of the six categories of barriers questioned, the numbers for the US are always lower than for the EU-7 except for 'security issues' where 46% of US retailers face barriers compared to 36% of retailers in the EU-7. This indicates that overall, US retailers seem to face other or even fewer barriers to e-business than EU -7 retailers.

Regarding the three sub-categories, trade in food stores, trade in non-food stores and other retailing, the other retailing group appears to be less affected by the barriers questioned in the survey as fewer low and non-adopters in this group state that the barriers trouble them. No significant differences emerge between the food-in-stores and non-food in stores groups although legal challenges with 30% (28% in food stores), security concerns with 44% (16% in food stores) and difficulties to find reliable IT providers with 28% (20% in food stores) are higher in the non-food stores group.

4.3   Innovation Induced by e-Business and ICT

In order to collect evidence about the role of ICT for innovation, retailers were asked whether they had "launched any new or substantially improved products or services" during the past twelve months, and if they had introduced "new or significantly improved internal processes" in the same period of time. Those firms that had introduced innovations, the so-called 'Innovators' were then asked follow-up questions with the focus being on whether the innovation(s) had been enabled by ICT.

21% of retail enterprises (representing 32% of the sector's employment) said that they had launched new or improved products in 2006/07. Firms representing 70% of employment, i.e. almost two thirds of those that reported product/service innovations, said that their innovations had been directly related to or enabled by ICT (Figure 5). This high share indicates the important role ICT plays for innovative behaviour. With 60% and 67% respectively, micro and large firms are the types of firms benefiting most from ICT enabling innovative behaviour (although the 67% for the large firms is indicative due to a small number of respondents). Overall though, fewer SMEs than large firms have launched new products and services in the 12 months preceding the interview: 44% of large firms, 30% of medium-sized firms, 25% of small firms and 21% of micro firms. Hence product/service innovations are firm-size dependent although there are more opportunities for innovation in larger firms due to them being bigger than smaller ones.

ICT also play a crucial role to support process innovation in the retail industry. Firms representing 45% of the industry's employment said they introduced process innovation in the past twelve months. In firms representing 32% of employment, 36% of the process innovations were ICT-related, and in only 9% the process innovations were not ICT-related. In micro firms again the share of firms innovating with ICT was smaller than in small, medium-sized and large firms. Hence, there appears to be evidence for a relatively higher importance of ICT for business processes innovations in larger companies. Compared the transport and logistics sector, the levels of overall process innovation and of ICT-related process innovation in the retail industry were found to be along the same lines.

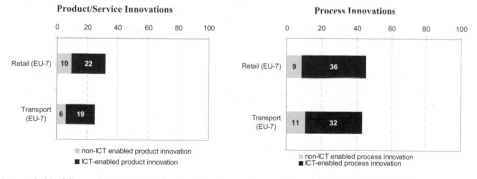

Figure 5: % of Companies Having Introduced Product or Process Innovation (ICT Enabled Versus Non-ICT Enabled, 2007)

5.   Conclusions

5.1   Key Findings

This study finds little indication that the retail industry is doing any better or any worse than other industries studied in terms of e-business. When viewed through the lens of supply chain management, a slight imbalance appears within the industry: retail firms are more active in electronic upstream supply chain and in-house management activities; e-business activities involving customers are not that popular.

Due to the fragmented nature of the sector, firm size differences also become apparent while no significant differences between food and non-food trading in stores emerge. Micro and small retail firms in particular lag behind medium-sized and large firms in almost all indicators of ICT and e-business use. However, micro and small firms have been increasing their ICT adoption in recent years. A previous study on e-business and ICT in the retail sector carried out in 2003 found that the use of e-business in the retail sector was far from being a pervasive reality and below the average adoption rates in other sectors. In 2007 in contrast, ICT and e-business use have become more prevalent in retail firms of all size classes. The 2003 study argued the main opportunities for e-business stem from efficiency and productivity gains and, thus, cost savings. This was found to be still the same for 2007.

For most indicators studied, EU-7 retailers are lagging behind the US: in some cases the differences are large, for example for placing online ads on other companies' website (43% in the US versus 16% in the EU) and for options offered to pay online (higher percentages in the US for all options). Exceptions include the share of firms with Internet access, the average share of employees with internet access, and the use of internal systems for which the levels are similar or even higher in the EU. Surprisingly, the overall importance of e-business stated by the firms is very similar between EU-7 and US retailers. The reason may be that US retailers answered the question about e-business importance with a higher reference level in mind.

5.2   Policy Recommendations

The aforementioned findings call for policy recommendations that consider firm size issues and supply chain management proposals, especially for the downstream supply chain. The following recommendations for policy are considered appropriate:

- Promote electronic supply chain management among SMEs. The share of SMEs placing orders online to suppliers is smaller than in large firms. SMEs therefore could benefit from the increased adoption of e-supply applications and access to e-supply networks through providing opportunities for participation. Similarly, the adoption of e-sales and related downstream supply chain management practices often presents a challenge for retail firms of all sizes because it requires particular management strategies and operations. The retail industry and SMEs in particular could benefit from learning about challenges experienced when adopting e-sales.
- Foster the dissemination of e-business knowledge in the retail industry. Many retail firms may consider ICT as a cost factor rather than an investment in benefits. Improved awareness and knowledge about the effects and sustainability of e-business technologies is therefore deemed an important issue.
- Promoting e-business on a regional level. Since many retailers (with the exception of large multinationals) are usually rooted in the local and regional economy, support to e-business should predominantly take place at the local and regional level. Retailing associations or chambers of commerce could take a leading role in promoting the adoption and extension of e-business practices in retail.

- Promote electronic ordering among European consumers. The low level of e-sales penetration in the EU may be down to a relatively low affinity towards ordering over the internet on the part of the consumer. Retail firms with the support of policy makers should aim to improve trust in online sales through for example better establishing so-called 'trustmarks' for online shops. Another strategy could be to better educate consumers in the use of e-business technologies.

5.3 Further Work Needed

Future research on ICT and e-business in the retail industry could differentiate to a greater extent between micro, small, medium-sized and large firm retailers. The firm size effects identified in this study give good reason for greater attention to issues related to firm size. The heterogeneous structure of the retail industry also calls for further in-depth studies on the different sub-sectors within the NACE classification. Firms in the various sub-sectors engage in quite different retailing activities hence generalisations about the various sub-sectors might be useful for policy makers and retail firms (who could benefit from learning about the experiences of their peers) alike.

References

[1] Eurostat, European business - facts and figures. 2006, Office for Official Publications of the European Communities.
[2] European Commission, European business: facts and figures, European Communities, Editor. 2006, Office for Official Publications of the European Communities: Luxembourg.
[3] To, M.L. and E.W.T. Ngai, Predicting the organisational adoption of B2C e-commerce: an empirical study. Industrial Management & Data Systems, 2006. 106(8): p. 1133-1147.
[4] Lee, B.C.Y., Consumer attitude toward virtual stores and its correlates. Journal of Retailing and Consumer Services, 2007. 14(3): p. 182-191.
[5] Talluri, S., C. Wenming, and R. Narasimhan, An optimization model for phased supplier integration into e-procurement systems. IIE Transactions, 2006. 38(5): p. 389-399.
    Rabinovich, E., Linking e-service quality and markups: The role of imperfect information in the supply chain. Journal of Operations Management, 2007. 25(1): p. 14-41.
[6] Accenture, Retail Supply Chain. Creating and sustaining high performance. 2004.

Collaboration and the Knowledge Economy: Issues, Applications, Case Studies
P. Cunningham and M. Cunningham (Eds.)
IOS Press, 2008

RFID & Wireless Meshed Networks in Europe: *Ticket to Ride*

Ivano Ortis

Global Retail Insights, Viale Monza 14, Milan, Italy

Tel: +39-02-28457344, Fax: +39-02-28457333, Email: iortis@idc.com

Abstract: This paper analyzes the impact of RFID on enterprise productivity and ability to innovate. Payback for RFID implementations typically ranges between 2-3 years, and RFID is expected to become mainstream over the next 5 to 10 years. Over & beyond proven productivity improvements, RFID can enable product and service quality improvement, the optimization of business planning and demand intelligence capabilities, and innovation in the way enterprises can conduct business. This research paper is part of the Sectoral e-Business Watch program.

Keywords: RFID, ROI, Enterprise, Innovation, ICT, Productivity, Retail, Manufacturing, Transportation

1.   Introduction – Why is RFID Relevant to Enterprises?

The development of RFID technology emerges to be one of the most interesting innovations for the improvement of business process efficiency across the manufacturing, transportation & logistics, wholesale distribution and retail trade sectors.

This is due to the fact that RFID systems offer enterprises an advanced way of gathering and processing business data. RFID is becoming a real opportunity to drive business process re-engineering and business models re-thinking through a systematic usage of RFID-collected data in specific-use case scenarios. RFID has been initially implemented in some industries merely as a barcode with an antenna. This proved not to be the right approach to use this technology, even in the early stages of deployment, as demonstrated by pioneering implementations done in the US (the so-called "slap & ship" implementation approach following the RFID mandate issued by WalMart).

Whilst RFID is not a plug-and-play solution, thus requiring painstaking assessments, enterprises no longer focus primarily on the technology in itself, for example aiming to assess if RFID can match specific requirements for read-rate accuracy in rough environmental conditions. Robust business case formulations and long-term sustainability of RFID programs are the two most critical factors to enable the implementation of the technology. Return On Investment (ROI) is the single most important decision criteria to justify financial investments on RFID. In parallel enterprises are concerned about standardization issues, security, privacy, and other factors when evaluating their RFID investment decision.

2.   Objectives

The objective of the paper is to describe how companies in manufacturing, transportation, healthcare and retail industries use RFID for conducting business.

The study informs about the state-of-play how companies use RFID for managing their business processes – internally and in exchanges with suppliers and customers.

1.   Identifies RFID benefits and opportunities

2. Analyze key trends and challenges for the implementation of RFID to enable responsive supply chains, successful Return on Investment (ROI) opportunities and advanced value chain collaboration frameworks
3. Identifies key barriers to RFID adoption
4. Assess impact of RFID on enterprises productivity and innovation
5. Indicate possible implications for policy.

3. Methodology

The Sectoral e-Business Watch (SeBW) approach is based on a well-tuned composition of data collection instruments, including the use of existing sources (e.g. the Eurostat Community Survey on ICT usage in enterprises) as well as primary research (notably the SeBW Survey and case studies). The main sources of information used for this study are:

- SeBW CATI Survey (2007): The SeBW conducted in 2007 a decision-maker survey about RFID activity in sectors covered in this study. 434 interviews were conducted in seven countries. This survey was the main source for analysing the state of play in RFID adoption, process integration, impact on the workforce and ROI expectations.
- Case studies: Ten case studies on RFID adoption in companies from the sectors covered have been conducted specifically for this study. The selection was made with a view to achieve a balanced mix of cases in terms of countries, business activities (sub-sectors), and company size-bands. Cases include best practices, innovative RFID approaches, as well as typical examples of RFID activity (state-of-the-art) in the sector.
- In-depth interviews: In addition to the interviews conducted with firm representatives as part of the case study work, in-depth interviews with company representatives, industry and e-business experts have been conducted.
- Literature analysis: SeBW evaluates literature from various sources, including IDC research, scientific books, journal articles and conference presentations, websites, and newspaper articles.
- For data analysis, descriptive and analytical statistical methods have been used. The study was conducted in consultation with an Advisory Board that was specifically implemented to critically accompany the study from the start.

4. Technology Description

RFID stands for Radio Frequency Identification and it is mostly used for identifying people, objects, transactions or events through a wireless communication connection.

RFID is an automatic identification and data capture method (AIDC), which not only helps to identify, but also to collect data attributes about a certain object or person, including localisation and environmental measurements when integrated with sensor networks. All automatically captured data can then be entered directly into a computer system, avoiding less efficient and more error prone human intervention required to execute operational tasks and business intelligence analysis. The temporarily stored information is then processed to feed other internal IT systems (for example store or factory systems) and external systems alike (for example suppliers portals, business partners and clients information services). Essentially, an RFID system comprises 3 components:

- Multiple RFID tags, also called transponders, a term that comes from the short form of transmitter-responder
- A number of readers or interrogators, also called transceivers,
- The supporting ICT infrastructure (including data communication networks, other hardware such as servers and storage, as well as software components including RFID middleware and information server, front-end RFID-capable applications and back-end systems)

One of the attributes that makes RFID such an innovative feature is that tags can be fit or embedded into almost anything, products, animals or even people, widening possibilities for RFID applications. Companies currently have several options when implementing RFID. They can use static RFID portals, which create a set read field at discrete choke points such as a dock door or sales floor door. Companies may also use mobile devices such as forklift readers or handheld readers. The type of data one wants to capture dictates the choice of technology.

5. Developments

Compared to the estimated RFID adoption rate of 17.7% of enterprises in 2006 and 24.5% in 2007 – resulting from a significant adoption uptake in retail, transportation and logistics - adoption of RFID is expected to grow in the EU-7 at a fast peace over the next 5 years:

- On average, an annual growth of approximately 27% in the number of enterprises adopting RFID is estimated during the period 2007-2009.
- By 2011, approximately 44% of enterprises are estimated to have implemented RFID.
- Potentially, by 2012 half of EU-7 enterprises may have implemented RFID.

In conclusion, a careful assumption is that RFID may become mainstream over the next 5 to 10 years, but research evidence suggests that within the next 5 years RFID adoption will grow significantly.

On an industry level, RFID adoption are mainly driven by transportation, retail and manufacturing, while hospital activities are lagging behind. Supply chain is the premiere area of focus for RFID applications, because automation and real-time detection allow improvements in inbound logistics efficiencies, inventory management accuracy and responsiveness, distribution centre efficiency and loss prevention capabilities. The main applications of RFID are inventory management (70.4% of respondents), labelling single product items (47.2% of respondents), container or pallet tracking, person identification and production tracking. As a result, the principal motivations to implement RFID are:

- Improving product and service safety or authenticity – mainly relevant for manufacturers to overcome counterfeiting and diversion that continue to cause considerable loss and brand reputation damage, but also to improve consumers safety, for example with the introduction of e-pedigree solutions based on RFID in the pharmaceutical industry
- Improving the efficiency of production processes.
- Improving product track-and-trace capabilities, complying with regulations (for example European regulations on consumer products tracking & tracing, Restriction on Hazardous Substances (RoHS) and Waste Electrical and Electronic Equipment (WEEE)), increasing supply chain efficiencies and visibility. Warehouse and logistics productivity improvements emerge as the major supply chain goal in the short-term.
- Improving asset management efficiencies - Due to the faster operational turnarounds and higher process visibility enabled by RFID, there is an opportunity to increase assets' utilisation rates, especially for mobile assets and returnable assets given the current uncertainty over their locations.

Market-driven mandates issued by large retail companies (for example WalMart and the METRO Group) are expected to further stimulate RFID adoption among consumer product goods manufacturers. The ultimate objective being the reduction of out-of-stock situations, and, as a consequence, achieving sales increases by both retailers and suppliers.

Large companies drive adoption of RFID. However, RFID seems relevant also for SMEs with more than 50 employees, with currently a slightly higher percentage of firms in the 250-499 employee size-class (15.4%) that are using, piloting or implementing RFID.

Among the key barriers to RFID adoption, EU-7 enterprises are most concerned about:

- ROI is the major barrier to RFID implementation, for companies of all sizes, but mostly for small companies. ROI concerns are also the result of high technology costs that are indicated by the majority of survey respondents.
- Interoperability concerns represents a key barrier to RFID adoption. Interoperability is a key concern especially for large enterprises.
- Complexity of implementation and IT integration also emerge as a relevant barrier to RFID adoption. In more detail, RFID implementation and IT integration complexity is hampering RFID adoption especially for medium companies with 250-499 employees.
- Privacy – mostly for hospitals - and security concerns – mostly for transportation companies and hospitals - are perceived as key barriers to RFID only by 1 out of 3 organizations.

6. Results

The key finding of the impact analysis, based on empirical evidence, is that the integration of RFID can enable labour and total factor productivity growth as well as innovation in the way enterprises conduct business. Specifically, RFID-enabled innovative activity on products, services and within collaborative value networks, positively affects the likelihood of a firm reporting a turnover increase. As a result, the average payback period for RFID investments is estimated between 2 to 3 years, based on an average lifetime of 10 years for RFID implementations.

Moreover, the increased granularity and real-time business process visibility resulting from RFID will fundamentally improve business intelligence capabilities and support to decision-makers, due to earlier sensing of business issues and potentially more timely and performing reactions to changing market dynamics.

No significant workforce reductions can be expected from RFID, but some workforce reductions will result. In turn, workforce reductions in RFID-enabled departments are often compensated by a reallocation of the workforce to other business functions, for example quality management. Although it is difficult to assess whether an increasing use of RFID creates or destroys jobs, it may be deduced from empirical evidence that high and medium-skilled labour is required to maximize the impact of RFID implementations on productivity, both demand-side (e.g. within end-user organizations) and output-side (e.g. within technology vendor organizations).

However, it is important to remark the following:

- Actual productivity improvements that are obtainable by enterprises depend upon a number of variables that are specific to the actual use case scenario. A phased implementation approach seems the most viable solution to enable quick ROI opportunities (e.g. between 12 to 36 months) while ensuring the long-term strategic goals picture.
- The major cost component of the total value of an RFID project seems to be the cost of project implementation, system integration and business process re-engineering. Cost of RFID tags and reader is the second major component of the total investment, and software costs come third.
- RFID-enabled innovations are correlated with company size - As opposed to large-scale enterprise implementation scenarios, RFID applications by SMEs tend to focus on enabling productivity improvements that have a positive business impact in the short-term.

RFID has some skill-bias towards high- and medium-skilled labour. However, in some areas, the implementation of the technology does not change the labour process significantly (for example warehouse order picking).

7. Business Benefits

Figure 1 presents survey results on the benefits of RFID, reported by companies that are using or planning to use RFID. Over 80% of respondents indicated inventory management enhancements and improved product and service quality as the key benefits of RFID. Survey results also confirm that optimized control and efficiency of inbound logistics, improved efficiency of production and loss prevention gains can result from the integration of RFID, in line with case studies findings.

Figure 1 RFID Benefits for Enterprises (Percentage of Respondents)

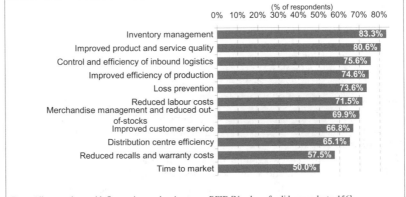

Q. What are the key benefits of RFID for your company?[Source: e-Business Survey 2007]

Base: All respondents with firms using or planning to use RFID [Number of valid respondents: 156]

Each industry has different primary targets, but positive and quantitative results are evident across all industries included in the scope of this study.

RFID integration enables labour and total factor productivity gains due to increase in business process efficiency – Although there is not an instantaneous impact of ICT-capital investments on productivity growth, due to the fact that delays are associated with the introduction of new technologies and organisational changes, because RFID is new in many processes it is easier to achieve efficiency improvements in a relatively short time compared to other ICT investment, for example the implementation of a new ERP system. RFID investments enable labour productivity improvements by eliminating manually assisted processes. In addition, because more accurate information is available, higher process transparency and improved business decisions can be made. As a result total factor productivity can be increased as well thorough improved enterprise assets utilization, improved process efficiencies and reductions of fixed capital. As demonstrated by the following collection of quantitative measures of productivity improvements resulting from RFID implementations, RFID investments have a positive impact on total factor productivity – a measure of the efficiency of input utilization:

- 12% to 17% overall improvements in supply chain process efficiencies
- 17% productivity increase in airline baggage handling
- Up to 83% reductions in shipping errors
- Up to 90% reductions of Full Time Equivalents (FTE) assigned to inventory tracking activities.
- 20% to 25% improvement in production cycle times through greater visibility and control of manufacturing lines process efficiencies
- Up to 20% improvement in WIP (Work In Process)
- 15 to 20 seconds per pallet can be saved by consumer products manufacturers in order picking

- Electronic dispatch note can lead to cost savings of up to €2.84 for each dispatch note
- Loss/theft shrinkage between 11% to 18%
- Up to 30% reductions in inventory levels and 13% reductions of inaccurate understated perpetual inventory
- Qualitative benefits include improved assets utilisation rates, full real-time visibility along the value chain, complete automation of workflow-intensive operational processes, faster invoice matching procedures when fully integrated with ERP and EDI systems, and reduced spoilage of perishable goods.

One of the most promising innovations resulting from the integration of RFID is the opportunity to improve product and service quality. Among the key consequences that enterprises may expect are increasing top-line performance, improved brand recognition and customer loyalty, improved consumers, passengers and patients safety. As a result it may be inferred that RFID-enabled innovative activity positively affects the likelihood of a firm reporting a turnover increase. Quantitative measures of product and service improvements following RFID implementations include:

- In retail, 10% to 60% reductions in out-of-stock situations
- In hospitals activities, up to 100% reductions in transfusion errors
- In logistics, 90% improvement in reliability of delivery time windows

RFID can drive new value creation through the enablement of innovative business models. The opportunity to decrease time to market when introducing new products or services and the ability to improve customer service are important competitive advantages that may result from RFID implementations, as indicated by over 50% of survey respondents. Item-level RFID applications seem mostly relevant and doable for medium and large organizations. Item tagging may also enable new customer-facing strategies and the development of innovative value added services (for example smart-dressing room in fashion retailing and drugs misuse prevention in healthcare) that may result in sales growth. In addition, the increased granularity and real-time business process visibility resulting from RFID will fundamentally improve business intelligence capabilities and support to decision-makers, due to earlier sensing of business issues and potentially more timely and accurate reactions to changing market dynamics.

8. Conclusions

The reality of RFID adoption is expected to ramp up by 2008, and an average annual growth of approximately 27% is estimated during the period 2007-2009 in the number of EU-7 enterprises adopting RFID. Survey findings indicate that by 2012, potentially half of EU-7 enterprises may implement RFID. A more conservative assumption is that RFID will become mainstream in the EU-7 over the next 5 to 10 years.

Empirical evidence suggests that the average payback period for most RFID investments is between 2 to 3 years, due to the achievement of labour and total factor productivity growth as well as innovation in the way enterprises can conduct business.

RFID is not the sole technology choice available to enterprises; for example, reductions in retail out-of-stocks can be achieved using RFID but also with the implementation of advanced demand forecasting tools, automated ordering applications and collaborative replenishment systems. Therefore, enterprises are recommended to assess RFID ROI following the guideline provided in the study, whilst assessing the impact of selected technology options on the specific use case and their eventual synergies. The development of multigenerational RFID programs to accommodate new technologies when they become available is highly advisable.

In addition, enterprises shall consider taking appropriate measures to mitigate risks and pre-emptively address fears that may be raised by employees or consumers; the organisation of a process performance improvement office specifically around data acquisition platforms and business intelligence for the organisation is highly recommended.

Supply chain performance improvement is expected to remain a premiere area of focus for future RFID applications, in line with empirical evidence from the large majority of EU-7 enterprises indicating inventory management and container, pallet, case and returnable assets tracking as the key application areas of RFID. However, the following dynamics are expected to take place:

- The focus of RFID implementations is expected to move gradually from operational execution activities to the optimization of business planning and intelligence capabilities.
- Extending supply chain visibility and performance objectives to the edges, in other words beyond the "4-walls" of an enterprise, will be instrumental to maximise RFID ROI. Therefore, the recommendation is to move gradually from a closed-loop implementation scenario to include the extended boundaries.
- The combination of RFID with sensor network technologies and real-time locating systems (RTLS) is expected to remain a major goal for enterprises across industries.
- Going forward in the next three to five years, a significant trend towards using RFID to enable promotion effectiveness and real consumer value is expected in the retail and consumer product goods industries.
- Person identification also emerges from empirical evidence as a key application area of RFID for both large enterprises and SMEs.
- Improving product and service safety or authenticity is a key business reason driving RFID adoption. Therefore, RFID-based product pedigree applications of RFID seem particularly relevant in the pharmaceutical industry and in high-value goods manufacturing.

The long term scenario, by when RFID will become mainstream, may eventually lead to a situation where any wireless-capable device will benefit from autonomous and unstructured communications capabilities based on meshed communications networks, RFID, digital sensors and other wireless technologies.

Other potential future developments of RFID include:

- Self-service (mobile) automated stores
- Contact-less payments
- Incorporation of RFID directly into products' packaging

Suggested political activities to the European Commission, national and regional governments as well as European and national industry associations include:

- Supporting RFID skills development
- Promoting long-term (e.g. > 10 years) regulatory framework for radio standards
- Overcoming environmental issues arising from mainstream adoption of RFID
- R&D focus on wireless, meshed-network communications protocols

References

[1] Lehtonen, M., Michahelles, F., and Fleisch, E., Trust and Security in RFID-based Product Authentication Systems. IEEE Systems Journal, Special Issue on RFID Technology: Opportunities and Challenges, First Quarter of 2008.
[2] BRIDGE - Building Radio Frequency IDentification for the Global Environment - http://www.bridge-project.eu
[3] Hardgrave, B., Waller, M. and Miller, R., 2006, "RFID's Impact on Out of Stocks: A Sales Velocity Analysis," White Paper, Information Technology Research Institute, Sam M. Walton College of Business, University of Arkansas. Available at: http://itrc.uark.edu/research/display.asp?article=ITRI-WP068-0606
[4] Pharma Traceability Pilot - The Drug Pedigree Requirements Analysis. Deliverable D6.2 of BRIDGE Project, July 2007.

Collaboration and the Knowledge Economy: Issues, Applications, Case Studies
P. Cunningham and M. Cunningham (Eds.)
IOS Press, 2008

A Business-Driven SLA Management Approach Using Policies

Magdalini KARDARA, Dimosthenis KYRIAZIS, Kleopatra KONSTANTELI, Theodora
VARVARIGOU
Dept.of Electrical and Computer Engineering, National Technical University of Athens,
9, Heroon Polytechniou Str, 15773 Athens, Greece
Tel: +30 210 7722558, Fax: + 30 210 7722569,
Email:{mkardara, dkyr, kkonst, dora}@telecom.ntua.gr

Abstract: A new way of service provision, delivering benefits to the end-users is
enabled through the Grid technology. Nevertheless, the business orientation of Grids
is not yet a reality and its final success will primarily depend on its real adopters, the
end-users. In the cases of provision and support of business application services,
what is of major importance is to fulfil the customer's expectations as posed in the
Service Level Agreements. In this context, we present a business-driven SLA
management approach that differentiates the customers and based on that handles
SLA violations on a per-customer basis and proposes loyalties rewards following
specific Policies. Furthermore, we provide implementation details of the
aforementioned approach and describe how it can be adopted in any Grid
environment that seeks to bring customer-specific knowledge during the SLA
management process.

1. Introduction

A Service Level Agreement (SLA) is a contract between the consumer and the provider of a
service that sets out the terms and conditions the two parties have agreed upon and
optionally specifies how the usage of the service is priced. The introduction of SLA
contracts in Grid environments has generated great interest in the Grid community as a
mechanism that Service Providers (SP) may use to offer strong Quality of Service (QoS)
guarantees to potential Grid customers [1]. Since customers will be reluctant to pay for Grid
services without QoS guarantees, which are usually established during the SLA negotiation
phase [2], [3]; SLAs are generally considered to be one of the most vital factors for
commercial Grid applications.

This paper addresses the issue of introducing policies in a Grid system as a solution to
existing requirements in the field of SLA Management. An innovative mechanism will be
demonstrated which uses policies as a means to differentiate among customers and reward
loyalties. Although this has been a well-known and widespread business practice, yielding
very good results to various companies, especially in the field of telecommunications, for
many years now, no work has been done in the area of Grid computing in this direction.
Taking into consideration that SLAs are considered to be prerequisites for the adoption of
Grids in business environments [4], the combination of them with the aforementioned
policy scheme could greatly assist the commercial exploitation of Grid applications and
thus constitute an important step towards a more business oriented Grid.

There are various approaches in the field of SLA management in Grid environments. In
many cases, SLAs are modelled according to business objectives of both customers and
service providers [5]. Following that, authors in [6] propose an SLA management scheme
based upon business objectives, expressed as utility functions, while literature [7] focuses

on SLA management and resource modelling. Other approaches dealing with SLA management by providing QoS guarantees at the same time are presented in [8], [9]. The innovation of the proposed approach lies on the fact that policies are not only used in cases of SLA violations to meet the customer's QoS requirements but also to reward loyalties.

The remainder of the paper is structured as follows. Section 2 presents the objectives of our work while in Section 3 the concept of using policies to differentiate customers and reward loyalties is discussed. Section 4 focuses on the technologies and specifications of the proposed approach, for which implementation details are included in Section 5. The added value and business benefits of the presented concept are described in Section 6. Finally, Section 7 concludes with a discussion on future research and potentials for the current study.

2. Objectives

This section outlines the requirements that are not covered by existing Grid middleware systems and which this paper aims to address. Currently, most Grid systems have a mechanism for monitoring service usage and evaluating conformance to SLA terms. However, the decision making process for selecting the appropriate corrective actions so as to re-establish conformance to the contractual terms of SLAs after a violation has not been properly addressed. In more detail, most existing systems have a standard way of treating all types of violations, namely either dispatching notifications to external components or killing a sufficient number of jobs submitted by the consumer to enforce constraints. In any case, there is no provision of handling violations on a per-customer basis.

Similarly, several Grid middleware systems such as GRASP [10] and GRIA [11], [12] (which will be used as the underlining infrastructure for our approach) have established an SLA–based accounting mechanism and charge users by aligning usage with the billing rules stated in the SLA. However, none of those systems addresses the issue of rewarding customers with heavy usage during the last billing period by granting them special benefits such as discounts.

In this context, the work presented in this paper addresses the two aforementioned issues by introducing a policy-driven SLA management system. The main concept behind it is that the decisions on how to handle a potential breach in an SLA constraint or what promotions should be available to each customer should be made by the provider based on the type of contract the customer has established with the SP and on their usage of the services over the past billing period. In essence, the role of policies in the presented system is to map violations and possible usage cases to the actions that should be triggered according to the customer's contract. Unlike SLAs, policies can change frequently and are ideal for implementing seasonal offers and promotions. The procedure of changing policies is transparent to the customers, and it is up to the provider to inform them for any seasonal offers or discounts. It should be noted that the policies do not override SLA contracts and that SLA terms and conditions will apply regardless of what policy may be currently implemented by the provider.

3. Methodology

The proposed approach is based on a mechanism developed within the GRIA framework. The latter uses SLA templates, which are published to the customers as a means to propose them an SLA contract. SLA templates may be tailored to individual customers or groups of them, which results in a categorisation among customers. According to the desirable level of QoS and the price they are willing to pay, customers select one of the templates available to them. After an SLA template has been signed by the customer, it becomes active and remains so until it reaches its expiration date.

The aforementioned categorisation of customers according to the type of SLA template they have signed has also been used for applying policies. More specifically, an SLA template is associated with a policy in a many-to-one relationship, i.e. an SLA template is mapped to only one policy whereas a policy can be associated with many SLA templates. The SP, who is responsible for this mapping, can thus opt to have the same policy for all customers or differentiate among customers according to their SLA type. Moreover, the policy associated with each SLA template, and thus with each SLA, can change during its lifetime, offering more flexibility to SPs.

In order to charge customers for usage as well as to ensure conformance to the SLA terms, GRIA includes a monitoring and evaluation mechanism, the "SLA Service", which polls the monitored services for usage reports, and uses them to detect violations and to calculate the customer's bill at the end of the billing period. In case of violation of an SLA constraint, a sufficient number of activities (referring to job executions) are killed in an effort to bring the associated metric back to a legitimate value.

First of all, in our approach, each time a violation in an SLA contract is detected, the policy associated with the corresponding SLA Template is retrieved. Depending on the constraint that has been breached and the value of the specific metric, the appropriate corrective action and not only a "kill" action, is decided upon and executed.

A second innovation of our approach lies on the fact that policies are used when calculating the total bill, in order to decide whether, based on the reported usage and number of past violations, the user should be granted a discount or a special promotion. In the case of discount, the amount is subtracted from the total bill, whereas in the case of a promotion, an action implementing the promotion is executed.

4. Technology Description

As already mentioned, the proposed mechanism was developed in the GRIA framework following the specifications under the Web Services Resource Framework (WSRF) [13]. The resulting components were deployed as integral parts of the existing GRIA SLA service. Thus, the XML Schema designed for describing the SLA templates and SLA contracts in GRIA has been adopted.

The Policies are stored as GRIA resources in a repository, while the open source object / relational persistence and query service Hibernate [14] has been used in order to access the repository.

5. Developments

The paper now provides implementation details of the proposed approach, which is compliant to the Open Grid Services Architecture (OGSA). Several changes had to be introduced to the GRIA platform in order to implement the advance SLA management schema that performs a set of actions (while it used to perform only the "kill" action) and to facilitate the proposed policy mechanism in order to handle SLA violations on a per-customer basis and proposes loyalties rewards following specific policies. These changes are described in detail in the paragraphs that follow.

In GRIA, all SLA related functionality is managed by the SLA Service. The main modules of the SLA Service that are involved in billing and detecting violations are the *UsageMonitor*, the *SLA* and the *ConstraintManager*. The *UsageMonitor* polls active services in order to retrieve usage reports, invokes the SLA module in order to perform billing and subsequently invokes the *ConstraintManager* in order to detect violations and decide on the appropriate corrective action. The role of the *ConstraintManager* is to find all SLAs with a breached constraint and decide on what actions need to be taken in order to bring the metric rate down. The necessary actions are then returned to the *UsageMonitor* as a list of *ManagementAction* objects which the *UsageMonitor* is then responsible for executing. The only implementation of the *ManagementAction* interface currently supported by GRIA is the *KillActivityAction* class.

To extend the aforementioned functionality of the GRIA SLA Management system and to implement a policy based one, we have replaced the ConstraintManager with another module, namely the *PolicyManager*. The *UsageMonitor* handles monitoring results to the *PolicyManager* and the latter is responsible for both billing and determining the actions to be taken to handle violations. The functionality of the *PolicyManager* and its interactions with the other components is described in detail in Section 5.1. In order to differentiate between corrective actions and promotions, two sub-interfaces of the *ManagementAction* interface have been developed, i.e. the *CorrectiveAction* and *PromotionAction* respectively. The module structure used to represent management actions is outlined in Section 5.2. Further developments include the modules and database configuration documents required in order to store policies as GRIA resources using hibernate.

5.1   The PolicyManager Component and Interactions with Other Components

The main component responsible for enforcing policies is the *PolicyManager*, which is invoked periodically by the *UsageMonitor* component to detect violations and decide on the corrective action to be taken. As it has been stated before, the *UsageMonitor* is responsible for polling active services for monitoring reports. Once invoked, the *PolicyManager* detects violations by comparing their related reports with SLA terms and subsequently checks the corresponding policy file in order to map the violation to an action. A list of actions is then returned to the *UsageMonitor*, which is responsible for executing them.

At the end of the billing period, the *PolicyManager* uses existing GRIA functionality to calculate the total bill and subsequently parses the policy XML file to find out if reported usage is associated with a discount or a special promotion. For a discount, the amount is subtracted from the total bill. For a promotion, an action implementing the promotion is added to the list of actions returned from *PolicyManager* to the *UsageMonitor*.

The following figure (Figure 1) depicts the sequence of actions and interactions among the components as has been described above.

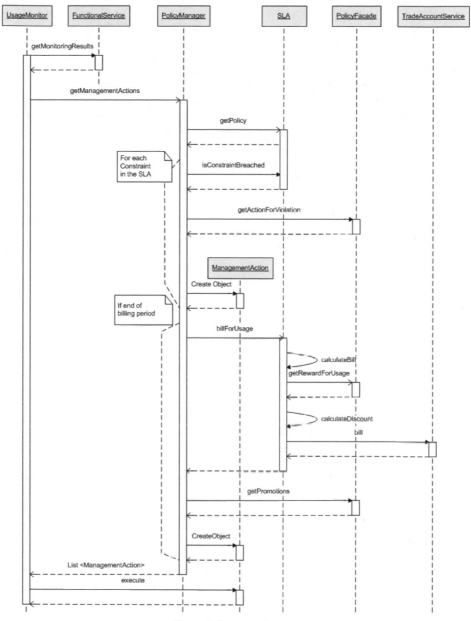

Figure 1: Sequence Diagram

5.2 Corrective Actions and Special Promotions

Corrective actions and special promotions are represented as implementations of the *CorrectiveAction* and *PromotionAction* interfaces which extend the GRIA *ManagementAction* interface. Apart from the *KillActivityAction* already supported by GRIA two (2) more management actions have been developed, namely the *NotifyAction* and the *SuspendActivityAction*. These management actions - classes are implementations of the *CorrectiveAction* interface and handle violations by notifying the owner of the activity and suspending the activity that causes a violation respectively. The *AllowMoreUsageAction* is a sub-interface of the *PromotionAction* interface used for rewarding the customer for their usage by granting them more usage of a specific metric covered by the SLA contract. Several implementations of this interface have been made for different types of metrics (e.g. for the CPU metric, the *AllowMoreCPUAction* was implemented). The structure of the modules described in this section is depicted in Figure 2.

It should be noted here that the aforementioned management actions are only indicative of the mechanism's full potential as in the future a large set of management actions can be integrated into the system with little effort and without modifying any existing components.

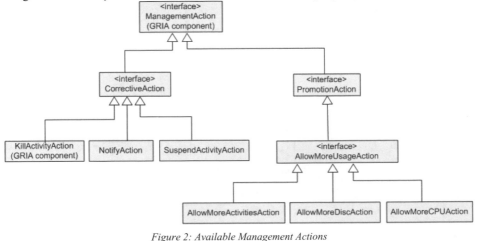

Figure 2: Available Management Actions

5.3   Policy Files

As has been mentioned before, the policies are uploaded by the SP in XML files which are parsed and their data stored in the underlying system as GRIA resources persisted by hibernate. The XML Schema for the policy files defines two (2) major elements: the first for mapping violations to corrective actions and the second for associating usage to promotions or discounts. The former is parsed whenever a violation is detected and the latter at the end of each billing period.

6.   Business Benefits

The mechanism presented in this paper increases the business potential of Grid computing by introducing business practices that have long been utilised and proven to be successful in other domains. As an exemplar scenario for displaying the business benefits of such an approach we will examine how using the proposed mechanism will prove beneficial for an SP, e.g. a telecom provider and their customers.

Firstly, customers would profit from the promotions granted to them as a reward for their loyalty. As a promotion the customer may receive a discount or be granted increased usage of the SP's resources at a future billing period. Furthermore, in cases of violations not only a specific action is performed as until now. Whenever a violation occurs, it is handled more leniently by allowing a set of corrective actions to be applied.

On the other hand, the benefit of this approach for the SPs lies on the fact, that the latter is expected to attract a larger number of customers and at the same time encourage greater usage from existing customers.

7. Conclusions

In this paper, we presented an innovative Service Level Agreement evaluation and accounting mechanism based on the concept of policies. Policies offer a flexible way of tailoring discounts and promotions for particular customers according to their recorded usage and the type of contract they have with the provider. Such a business-driven approach raises the business strength of the usage of SLAs, transforming them into a powerful tool towards the commercial exploitation of Grid to its full potential.

References

[1] R. J. Al-Ali, K. Amin, G. von Laszewski, O. F. Rana, D. W. Walker, M. Hategan, N. J. Zaluzec: "Analysis and Provision of QoS for Distributed Grid Applications", Journal of Grid Computing, pp. 163-182, 2004

[2] P. Hasselmeyer, B. Koller, I. Kotsiopoulos, D. Kuo, M. Parkin, "Negotiating SLAs with Dynamic Pricing Policies", Service Oriented Computing: a look at the Inside (SOC@Inside'07), 2007.

[3] P. Hasselmeyer, H. Mersch, B. Koller, H.-N. Quyen, L. Schubert, P. Wieder, "Implementing an SLA Negotiation Framework", Exploiting the Knowledge Economy: Issues, Applications, Case Studies, eChallenges 2007, Hague, Netherlands, 2007.

[4] P. Masche, B. Mitchell, P. Mckee, "The Increasing Role of Service Level Agreements in B2B Systems", Proceedings of the 2nd international conference on web information systems and technologies, Setubal, Portugal, 2006

[5] B. Mitchell and P. McKee, "SLAs A Key Commercial Tool", Exploiting the Knowledge Economy - Issues, Applications, Case Studies, eChallenges 2006.

[6] Buco, M. J. Chang, R. N. Luan, L. Z. Ward, C. Wolf, J. L. Yu, P. S., Utility computing SLA management based upon business objectives, IBM Systems Journal, 2004,

[7] A. L. M. Ching, Dr L. Sacks and P. McKee, "SLA Management and Resource Modelling for Grid Computing", Whitepaper, UCL, 2003

[8] H. Chen, H. Jin, F. Mao, H. Wu, "Q-GSM: QoS Oriented Grid Service Management", Web Technologies Research and Development - APWeb 2005, Lecture Notes in Computer Science, 2005

[9] Padgett, J., K. Djemame, and P. Dew, "Grid-based SLA Management", Lecture Notes in Computer Science, pp. 1282-1291, 2005

[10] GRASP Grid Based Application Service Provision, http://eu-grasp.net/

[11] GRIA, Grid Resources for Industrial Applications, www.gria.org

[12] M. Surridge, S. Taylor, D. De Roure, and E. Zaluska, "Experiences with GRIA-Industrial Applications on a Web Services Grid", in Proceedings of the First International Conference on e-Science and Grid Computing, pp. 98-105. IEEE Press, 2005

[13] WSRF, The Web Services Resource Framework (WSRF) v1.2, http://www.oasis-open.org/committees/download.php/17833/wsrf-1.2-os.zip

[14] Hibernate - Relational Persistence for Java and .NET http://www.hibernate.org/

[15] The Open Grid Services Architecture, Version 1.5, http://www.ggf.org/documents/GFD.80.pdf

Collaboration and the Knowledge Economy: Issues, Applications, Case Studies
P. Cunningham and M. Cunningham (Eds.)
IOS Press, 2008

An SLA Framework for the GT4 Grid Middleware

Igor ROSENBERG[1], René HEEK[2], Ana JUAN[1]
[1]*Atos Origin, Avenida Diagonal, 200, Barcelona 08016, Spain*
Email:igor.rosenberg@atosorigin.com, ana.juanf@atosorigin.com
[2]*HLRS, Nobelstraße 19, Stuttgart, 70550, Germany*
Tel: +49 711 68560442, Fax: + 49 711 65832, Email: heek@hlrs.de

Abstract: Service Level Agreements are probably the most important documents in every business-aware framework –at least they should be. Every distributed piece of software faces the problem to assure a decent Quality of Service – no matter, if these agreements are legally binding contracts or not. Even though many Grid research or production projects accept the importance of SLAs and even though a specification for describing agreements and related services for SOA is emerging, most do not provide implementation supporting the negotiation and handling of SLAs. Unless the full integration of the complete lifecycle of SLAs is reached, fundamental business requirements cannot be fulfilled and critical barriers of Grid adoption cannot be overcome. Besides, it has to be considered that SLAs are of vital importance for new Grid business models, such as Utility Computing, SaaS or RaaS, due to the requirement for observing a certain QoS when providing a service. Within the BEinGRID project, confronted with this situation, we decided to produce an initial implementation of a comprehensive SLA Framework based on the Globus Toolkit.

Keywords: Service Level Agreement, Globus Toolkit, framework

1. Introduction - The BEinGRID Approach

BEinGRID – Business Experiments in Grid - is an ICT FP6 project of initially 75 partner organisations. The main objective of BEinGRID is to foster the adoption of Grid technologies for businesses and thereby crossing the chasm between the early market dominated by few visionary customers and the mainstream market dominated by a large number of pragmatic customers.

The BEinGRID project originally released 18 so called Grid Business experiments (BEs). Based on a clear business case, each BE developed a prototypic implementation for their specific requirements. The number of BEs was extended to 25 during Spring 2008. The extraordinarily high number of real business scenarios was the basis for a comprehensive field gap analysis, based on real needs expressed by potential users.

The BEs as a whole were analysed within technical cross-activities called clusters. The clusters focussed on a single specific aspect of Grid technologies. Members of the SLA cluster in cooperation with members of the architectures and interoperability cluster have developed the results presented in this article (see section 2).

In section 3, the architecture of BEinGRID SLA Framework for GT4 is presented and discussed. The BEinGRID SLA Management Framework is compared to the TrustCoM, Akogrimo, and AssessGrid SLA frameworks in section 4. Business benefits for the adoption of the BEinGRID SLA Framework are described in section 5. Conclusions, lessons learnt and future work can be found in section 6.

2. SLA Common Technical Requirements, Common Capabilities, Design Patterns and Components – The BEinGRID SLA Approach

Always based on the analysis of the BEs, the approach of BEinGrid was to first extract requirements, define corresponding functionalities, then generic architectures, and finally propose components.

2.1 SLA Common Technical Requirements

The SLA cluster of BEinGRID, specialised in the SLA field, identified common technical requirements, based on the analysis of specific challenges presented by the BEs. These common requirements capture the essence of several challenges mentioned by one or more BEs. The final list of requirements (see [1]) for the SLA cluster in order of appearance in the SLA life cycle is:

a) SLA Template Specification: For a resource provider, a clear step-by-step procedure describing how to write an SLA template to provide with correct (and possible legal) service description

b) Publication and Discovery: Publish the provider offer, the customer QoS needs, and browse/ compare offers in a federated marketplace

c) Negotiation: Bargain-like transaction to agree SLA conditions between the customer and the provider.

d) Optimization of Resource Selection: Optimal resource management on the provider side (selection of the most suitable host) improving the current scheduler solutions.

e) Monitoring: Provide measures of the ongoing process, i.e. system values related to the SLA for internal and external usage

f) Evaluation: Comparing all the terms of the signed SLA with the metrics provided by the monitoring, in order to internally prevent upcoming violations and to externally discover potential violations

g) Re-negotiation: Changing the terms of an already accepted (enforced) SLA

h) Accounting: Charging the consumer for the use of services contracted by signing SLAs

The common technical SLA requirements, which correspond to needs during given periods of the SLA life-cycle, have been prioritised based on their business drivers and technical relevance (see more detail on the classification and the prioritisation of requirements in [1]). All requirements are equally important, but the classification is based on 18 real-world scenarios presented by the BEs.

2.2 SLA Common Capabilities, Design and Implementation Patterns

The SLA requirements have been conflated into Common Capabilities (CCs), which represent a given SLA functionality. A CC is a description of a specific functionality. It represents a single or a group of technical requirements. We decided to merge the Negotiation and the Re-negotiation requirements, and the Monitoring and Evaluation.

Then CCs were refined into Design Patterns (DPs). The DPs are architecture-level documents, which describe a possible implementation of a CC. Only for the most relevant common capabilities have design patterns been produced. The SLA Template Specification is standalone in the sense that it does not require a component being developed. On the other hand, the Publication & Discovery common capability has not lead to the development of a component, even though a solution needs to be proposed - a discussion of a solution is drafted in 3.2.

BEinGrid produced software components by implementing the DPs. The components already developed or under way are:

a) SLA Negotiation for GT4

b) SLA Optimisation of Resource Selection for GRASP, and for GT4

c) SLA Monitoring and Evaluation for GRASP, and for GT4
d) SLA Accounting for GRIA and GT4

Within these, the four GT4 components form the basis for our SLA Framework.

3. Architecture of an SLA framework for GT4

3.1 Preface

The decision to develop an SLA Framework based on the available components for the GT4 Middleware was driven by the high interest expressed by BEs in an integrated and interoperable solution. Nine out of the eighteen business experiments in the first wave are using the Globus Toolkit to build their Grid infrastructure. While writing up the different Implementation Patterns, it became evident that the GT4 middleware lacked of a general mechanism to handle SLAs, unlike other solutions like GRASP [19] or GRIA [16], which come ready with an SLA framework. Based on this strong assumption, we decided to propose a comprehensive framework, which would include the complete lifecycle of an SLA. This framework is meant to be available for direct use in conjunction with the GT4 middleware to provide sufficient SLA functionality for most cases.

3.2 Architectural Overview

The main components and their interaction are shown in Figure 1. Solid boxes and arrows indicate components and interactions or core components of the framework. Dotted boxes and arrows indicate domain-specific components or interaction, which cannot be provided by such a framework in general.

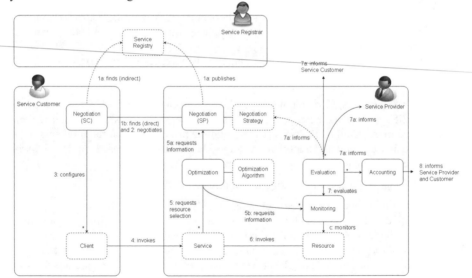

Figure 1 – Architectural Overview of the SLA Management Framework for GT4

The first need, which arises, is the capacity for customer (SC) and provider (SP) to discover each other. In a simple case, direct discovery, the user knows a set of providers, and queries the already known negotiation services for their templates. A more interesting approach is to consider the indirect discovery: a Discovery and Publication component should permit searching for required services, and advertising them. A marketplace or repository system can be envisaged, including advanced search, which should fuzzily match the service providers that offer corresponding services. A big technical issue comes from the fact that since the offer can be very broad-ranged (Grid being about any type of resources, not only computing power), categorizing the offers is problematic [2]. The client interface presents the same problem, as this interface should be generic enough to allow new service integration dynamically, while enabling intuitive search for the user. Related work in this area is covered in the AssessGrid [3], NextGRID [4] and Akogrimo [5] projects (see section 4). A good comparison on various types of service discovery concepts is discussed here [6].

The Negotiation component implements most of the interfaces suggested by the WS-Agreement [7] specification. Only some XML terms of the SLAs documents in WS-Agreement have been removed due to the incompatibility of these terms with Axis 1. The component supports the synchronous as well as the asynchronous negotiation of agreements and therefore provides a high-level of interoperability within the framework and for external clients. An easy plug-in mechanism for domain-specific negotiation strategies allows service providers to adapt the component to their requirements, e.g. respect the information provided by the evaluation component. The same plug-in mechanism for integrating domain-specific implementations of SLA template and SLA repositories is used. Implementations of file-based repositories are available. Related work was taken out by the AssessGrid project [8] and the implementations have been peer reviewed by members of each project.

The Resource Optimization component uses the agreed SLA and the Grid resources information to select the most appropriated resource where to run the job. The optimization algorithm can be customized to adapt to a particular application domain, or provider business rules.

The Monitoring and Evaluation component is in charge of controlling the execution of an SLA. Each resource is monitored, and its metrics are sent to a centralizing point. The information is then archived in a database (to keep records against litigations, but also for accounting). In parallel, the guarantees of the SLA are evaluated against these metrics. Violations and threats (when metrics break a warning threshold) are sent as notifications, for example to the service consumer and the service provider. Different notifications will correspond to different levels of implication in the provider's Grid infrastructure. The component has a set of evaluation rules, which define what functions to apply to discover violations and threats. The proposed implementation relies on the Ganglia [17][18] framework to monitor resources, and offers a bridge to store the metrics in a database. It also offers the notifications as WS-Notifications, with different topics corresponding to different confidence levels.

The SLA Accounting component retrieves from a database the metrics corresponding to the monitoring of the services used. This component then prepares a draft of a billing sheet, based on the price and penalties exposed in the SLA. The official financial department of the provider company must produce the real bill.

3.3   Component Interactions

Customers can discover SLA templates either indirectly (step 1a of Figure 1) or directly (step 1b). With respect to the existing BEs, we are currently focussing on realising the direct discovery approach. Customers can find templates by querying already known negotiation services for templates directly. In principle, customers could discover templates indirectly by querying a registry either for endpoint references to negotiation services or for SLA templates, depending on the type of registry.

After discovering potentially several SLA templates, a customer will select one of them and start to negotiate (step 2) the final SLA with the service provider. WS-Agreement supports an asynchronous negotiation mode, in which the provider will inform customers if he accepts or rejects an SLA offer. In order to support domain-specific negotiation strategies, the negotiation component implements a simple plug-in mechanism for different strategies (e.g. interacting with the service provider). We foresee automatic negotiation strategies, which make use of monitoring and evaluation data (step 7a). In this case, the implementations of these strategies must register for notification by using the WS-Notification interface exposed by the negotiation and monitoring component.

After a successful negotiation of an SLA, two actions happen simultaneously. The negotiation component of the service provider configures the SLA Monitoring and Evaluation component. On the customer's side, the negotiation component must configure the client stub appropriately, allowing the service provider to identify the SLAs for subsequent service invocation (step 4). This can by realised by using an endpoint references containing an SLA identifier.

During a clients service invocation (e.g. a job submission), the optimisation component will make an optimal selection of resources for the service provider based on the negotiated SLA (step 5). When choosing a resource, this component will request information about the SLA for this specific service invocation by using the SLA identifier to query the negotiation component (step 5a). In addition, the optimal resource selection will be based on the current resource states. The optimization component can query the monitoring and evaluation component for further information about available resources (step 5b). The optimization component will send back a list of available and optimal resources to the service, which selects one of them and connects to this resource (step 6).

The resources, continuously monitored (step c) by the monitoring component, produce metrics stored in a database. The evaluation component evaluates this data with respect to an SLA and informs interested entities about relevant events (e.g. an SLA violation). The database also serves the accounting component, which upon receiving notification from the evaluation, starts operating on these historical data sets, before informing the financial department with a pre-bill.

4. Comparisons to other SLAM Frameworks

Comparing our proposal of an SLA framework for GT4 to other results, it becomes evident that it is a very lightweight implementation. This reflects the inversed history of origins of this framework. A comparison of the frameworks studied is presented in Table 1.

The decision for implementing an SLA framework in other projects was made at the very beginning in most cases, sometimes even before the project starts (e.g. during the formulation of the proposal). The BEinGRID approach made it possible to refer to the actual needs of BE and develop firstly components to support them technically in achieving their business requirements by developing common components.

The proposed SLA Framework for GT4 shows similarities with the TrustCoM Contract Management Framework [9]. In terms of components, one could find similar components in the SLA Management of TrustCoM (e.g. the negotiator) in most cases. However, they main difference between the framework described here and the TrustCoM framework is the scope of application. A main objective of TrustCoM was to establish trust between partners in a virtual organisation. Therefore, some SLA components of TrustCoM can be rated as redundant or less important for simpler use cases where a virtual organisation is not established explicitly (e.g. the Notary component and related components, like the SLA Repository). On the other hand, some components, which are represented in the BEinGRID framework, are of higher if not highest importance for business-oriented pilot projects. One example for such a component is the SLA accounting module. Considering the scope of BEinGRID, this seems not to be very surprising: the main objective of each experiment is (potentially) making money. Another point worth mentioning in comparison to TrustCoM is that a majority of BEs have chosen GT4 as middleware, so there is a need for a framework, easily integrated with GT4. The TrustCoM implementations for the SLA management are based on .NET and the Windows Communication Foundation (WCF).

Another compared framework has been the Akogrimo SLA subsystem [5]. It is split into layers, SLA High level services, in charge of the SLA Negotiation phase, and the SLA Enforcement layer, in charge of controlling the execution of a service. In the Akogrimo SLA subsystem, the negotiation interaction protocol follows the WS-Agreement specification adding a final interaction with the Execution Manager to select the most suitable service, in terms of QoS parameters. This latter interaction offers the same functionality as the Optimization component in the BEinGRID framework. Akogrimo uses business high-level terms related to a specific application domain to establish the SLA between service provider and service consumer. The Akogrimo Translator Component makes the translation between the business terms and QoS parameters (CPU usage, memory usage, bandwidth ...). At runtime, the Akogrimo SLA Enforcement layer collects QoS parameters about the execution of the services. These measures are sent to the SLA Decisor module that evaluates them with the thresholds defined in the contract and the system policies, to take the appropriate corrective actions. The interactions that occur at run-time are similar in the BEinGRID framework and the Akogrimo SLA subsystem. The BEinGRID negotiation component allows an easy plug-in of domain-specific negotiation strategies respecting the information provided by the Evaluation component. The Akogrimo SLA subsystem does not provide an Accounting component.

Comparison of SLA capabilities		BEinGRID GTv4 Framework	TrustCoM Contract Management Framework	Akogrimo SLA Subsystem	Assesgrid SLA Architecture
BEinGRID identified SLA capabilities	SLA Template specification	✗	✗	✗	✗
	Publication and Discovery	✗	✓	✓	✗
	Negotiation	✓	✓	✓	✓
	Optimization of Resource Selection	✓	✗	✓	✓
	Monitoring	✓	✓	✓	✓
	Evaluation	✓	✓	✓	✓
	Re-negotiation	✗	✓	✗	✗
	Accounting	✓	✓	✗	✗
Implementation Technology		GTv4	.Net, WCF	.NET, GTv4	GTv4

Table 1: Comparison of capabilities of different SLA frameworks

AssessGrid [3] includes risk management mechanisms to the SLA management in order to move beyond the best-effort approach in the service provision. It considers that negotiating SLAs is a business risk for both the Service provider and the Service Consumer. The AssessGrid architecture considers three roles; the service provider, the broker and the customer. It considers that an SLA must exists between all parties. The life-cycle of the SLA exposed in AssessGrid is the classical vision also followed in the BEinGRID framework. The SLA negotiation follows the WS-Agreement protocol with the restriction that the initiating party is always the customer. The negotiation includes an interaction with the Consultant service to estimate the risk of SLA failure (PoF). The SLA template is based on the standard WS-Agreement structure describing the service terms using the JSDL HPC profile [11]. As in the BEinGRID SLA framework, the AssessGrid architecture does not provide a mechanism to Publish and Discover SLAs. The functionality of selecting the most appropriated resource in which to run a job, provided by the Optimization component in BEinGRID framework, in AssessGrid is performed by Scheduler component that also takes into account potential risk. AssessGrid uses Nagios daemons in the Monitoring services to monitor the Grid resources while BEinGRID uses Ganglia with the same intention.

5. Business Benefits

While research and academic institutions are interested in Grids that provide access to a higher computing performance to satisfy peak demands and support to face collaborative projects, enterprises understand grid computing as a way to address the changing service needs in an organization. Terms such as On-demand and Utility Computing are related to the Enterprise view of Grid [12]. Utility-computing is defined as the capacity to provide computing power as it happens at the moment with other facilities such as water or power, billing it in a pay-per-use model. On-demand computing relates to the ability of acquiring additional resources to meet changing requirements. In both terms, there is a clear separation between the Service provider and consumer and the ability to negotiate a desired quality of service for a determined period. Grid technology, by empathising the requirement of solid SLA management system, is an enabler of this IT provisioning methods.

Grid infrastructures aim to attract and enable new businesses and radically change the relationships between a customer and its supply chain, offering a flexible platform for a global collaboration. Grids can improve industry competitivity by better utilizing heterogeneous resources virtualized as services. Even more, innovative grid-enabled applications can be offered in a SaaS (Software as a Service) manner to new customers creating new business models. However, in all these new business models the Grid is capable to offer are sustained by the ability to establish, negotiate, monitor and evaluate a service level agreement taking part between the service consumer and the service provider.

Recently the convergence and interaction of Grid, SOA and Virtualization as well as Cloud Computing [13] techniques have been largely discussed. All these business models, SaaS, On-demand, Utility and Cloud computing, share the same requirement to be wide adopted in enterprise environments, the need of the establishment of SLAs [14][15] to assure that the business applications meet the required performance benchmarks.

6. Conclusions, lessons learnt and future work

In this paper, we started by presenting the BEinGrid requirement analysis performed on real scenarios (BEs). This provided generic technical requirements (needs expressed in a given scenario), common capabilities (a functionality which answers this technical need), design patterns (the middleware-agnostic architecture needed to provide this functionality), and components (middleware-specific implementations). Based on the gap-analysis, we could justify our proposition of an architecture of a framework for SLAs on the GT4 middleware. This framework is an integrated answer to the needs stressed by the BEs. It is based on components: negotiation, optimization, evaluation & monitoring, and accounting, of which functionalities and interactions were shown. We also highlighted interoperability issues that came up with the component-based approach. This architecture covers the whole lifecycle of an SLA, minus the initial discovery & publication phase. We also compared to other FP7 projects frameworks, namely TrustCoM, Akogrimo, and AssessGrid, highlighting the weaknesses and strong points of each.

The work presented is a software architecture, which was missing in the GT4 middleware. It was discovered that a comprehensive framework, including details for all steps of the life-cycle of an SLA, is not currently required. The basic building blocks are sufficient, as the market is not mature enough to accept open competition and assessment. So a simple implementation based on the core functionalities is proposed to help grid adoption; it will benefit all parties by including SLAs in their business cycle.

Our next step will be to complete our first simple implementation of the proposed architecture, and validate it in real business situations. We are also planning to stress the interoperability problems raised by different middleware stacks, and their solutions (namely, offering interfaces with GRASP and GRIA). We will also re-use existing BEinGrid business analysis to specify in detail the market opportunities of our solution. All this will be done in collaboration with the second wave of BEs, which have the purpose of validating the implementation results of BEinGrid.

References

[1] Design patterns for SOA and Grid. T. Dimitrakos et al., BEinGRID AC1 Meta-Deliverable, 2007
[2] Interoperability and Reuse with WS-Agreement. A. Andrieux, K. Czajkowski, 2004, http://www-unix.mcs.anl.gov/~keahey/Meetings/GRAAP/karl.pdf
[3] Introducing Risk Management into the Grid, Djemame, K.; Gourlay, I.; Padgett, J.; Birkenheuer, G.; Hovestadt, M.; Odej Kao; Voss, K. e-Science and Grid Computing, 2006. e-Science apos;06. Second IEEE International Conference on Volume , Issue , Dec. 2006 Page(s):28 - 28
[4] Towards Autonomous Brokered SLA Negotiation. P. Hasselmeyer, C. Qu, L. Schubert, B. Koller, P. Wieder, Exploiting the Knowledge Economy - Issues, Applications, Case Studies. Volume 3, October 2006
[5] An Enhanced Strategy for SLA Management in the Business Context of New Mobile Dynamic VO, D'Andria, F., Martrat, J., Laria, G., Ritrovato, P., Wesner, S., In Exploiting the Knowledge Economy: Issues, Applications, Case Studies, Paul Cunningham and Miriam Cunningham (Eds), IOS Press, Amsterdam, 2006
[6] On Service Discovery Process Types. P. Hasselmeyer, 3rd International Conference On Service Oriented Computing (ICSOC '05), Amsterdam, The Netherlands, December 2005. Springer-Verlag, LNCS 3826, ISBN 3-540-30817-2, pp. 144-157, December 2005
[7] Web Services Agreement Specification (WS-Agreement). A. Andrieux et al., Specification from the Open Grid Forum (OGF), 2007
[8] Implementing WS-Agreement in a Globus Toolkit 4.0 Environment. D. Battré, O. Kao, K. Voss Usage of Service Level Agreements in Grids Workshop in conjunction with The 8th IEEE International Conference on Grid Computing (Grid 2007), September 2007
[9] TrustCoM Framework V4, M. Wilson, A. Arenas, L. Schubert, Deliverable of the TrustCoM EU FP6 project, 2006, http://213.27.211.106/trustcom/wp-content/uploads/2007/08/d9 trustco.pdf
[10] A Comparison of SLA Use in Six of the European Commissions FP6 Projects, CoreGRID Technical Report Number TR 0129, M. Parkin, R. M. Badia, J. Martrat, http://www.coregrid.net/mambo/images/stories/TechnicalReports/tr-0129.pdf
[11] JSDL HPC Profile Application Extension, Version 1.0. M. Humphrey, C. Smith, M. Theimer, and G. Wasson., V1.0.
[12] The Different Faces of IT as a Service, I. Foster, http://www.ogf.org/documents/Diff_Faces_foster.pdf
[13] Cloud Computing, Greg Boss, http://www.ibm.com/developerworks/websphere/zones/hipods/
[14] SLAs A Key Commercial Tool. B. Mitchell, P. Mckee, Innovation and the Knowledge Economy: Issues, Applications, Case Studies, 2005
[15] The increasing role of SLAs in B2B. P. Masche, B. Mitchell, P. Mckee, Proceedings of the 2nd international conference on web information systems and technologies, Setubal, Portugal, April 2006
[16] GRIA Website, http://www.gria.org/
[17] Ganglia Website, http://ganglia.info
[18] The ganglia distributed monitoring system: design, implementation, and experience. M. L. Massie, B. N. Chun, D. E. Culler, Parallel Computing 30 (2004) 817–840
[19] The GRASP project http://www.eu-grasp.net

Collaboration and the Knowledge Economy: Issues, Applications, Case Studies
P. Cunningham and M. Cunningham (Eds.)
IOS Press, 2008

Asymmetric Information Issues and Solutions for the Broker Executing SLA-Based Workflows

Dang Minh QUAN[1], Jörn ALTMANN[2]

School of Information Technology, International University in Germany, 76646 Bruchsal, Germany
[1] *Tel: +49(0)7251700231, Fax: +49(0)7251700250, Email:* quandm@upb.de,
[2] *Tel: +49(0)7251700130, Fax: +49(0)7251700250, Email:* jorn.altmann@acm.org

Abstract: In the business Grid environment, the user should ask the broker to execute the workflow for him and then pays the broker for the workflow execution service. As the sub-jobs of the workflow must be distributed over many Grid resource providers to ensure the QoS, the broker knows about all aspects of all service providers while it is difficult for user to have this information. Thus, there is an asymmetric information situation. The asymmetric information may bring a negative effect to the broker. This paper will analyze the asymmetric information issues and propose possible solutions to solve the problem.

Keywords: Grid-based workflow, Service Level Agreement, asymmetric information.

1. Introduction

In the Grid Computing environment, many users need the results of their calculations within a specified period of time. Examples of those users are meteorologists running weather forecasting workflows, and automobile producer running dynamic fluid simulation workflows [13]. Those users are willing to pay for having their work completed on time. However, this requirement must be agreed on by both the users and the Grid provider before the application is executed. This agreement is called the Service Level Agreement (SLA) [14]. In general, SLAs are defined as an explicit statement of expectations and obligations in a business relationship between service providers and customers. SLAs specify the a-priori negotiated resource requirements, the quality of service (QoS), and costs. The application of such an SLA represents a legally binding contract. This is a mandatory prerequisite for the Next Generation Grids.

In order to finish the workflow on time, sub-jobs of the workflow must be distributed to Grid resources. Assigning sub-jobs of the workflow to resources requires the consideration of many constraints such as workflow integrity, on-time conditions, and optimal conditions. To free users from those tedious tasks, it is necessary to have an SLA workflow broker performing the co-operating task of many entities in the Grid. Thus, the business relationship of the SLA workflow broker with the users and the Grid service providers will determine the working mechanism of the broker.

We proposed a business model for the system as depicted in Figure 1 [1,11]. There are three main types of entities: end-user, SLA workflow broker and service provider.

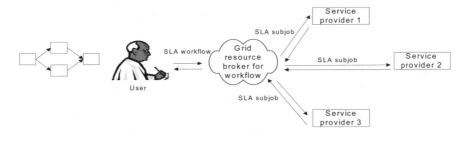

Figure 1: Stakeholders and Their Business Relationship

- The end-user wants to run a workflow within a specific period of time. The user asks the broker to execute the workflow for him and pays the broker for the workflow execution service. It is not necessary for the user to know in detail how much he has to pay to each service provider. He only needs to know the total amount, which depends on the urgency of the workflow and the budget of the user. If there is an SLA violation for example if the runtime deadline has not been met the user will ask the broker for compensation. This compensation is clearly defined in the Service Level Objectives (SLOs) of the SLA.
- The SLA workflow broker represents the user as specified in the SLA with the user and controls the workflow execution. This includes the mapping of sub-jobs to resources, signing SLAs with the services providers, monitoring, and error recovery. When the workflow execution has finished, it settles the accounts. It pays the service providers and charges the end-user. The profit of the broker is the difference. The value-added that the broker provides is the handling of all the tasks for the end-user.
- The service providers execute the sub-jobs of the workflow. In our business model, we assume that each service provider fixes the price for its resources at the time of the SLA negotiation. As the resources of an HPCC usually have the same configuration and quality, each service provider has a fixed policy for compensation in the event its resources fail. For example, such a policy could be that $n\%$ of the cost will be compensated if the sub-job is delayed by one time slot.

From the business model, we can see that the broker has more information about the Grid than the user because he knows about all aspects of all service providers such as resource configurations, pricing scheme, and past performance. It is difficult for the user to know all this information. This situation leads to the asymmetric information issues as the user does not believe the proposed solutions from the broker.

This paper will analyze the effect of the asymmetric information issues and propose possible solutions. In particular, the contribution of the paper includes:

- The description of the asymmetric information about the Grid state and the quality of the mapping solutions.
- The appropriate information which should be revealed during the SLA negotiation to solve the asymmetric information issues.

The paper is organized as follows. Section 2 describes the related works, while Section 3 and 4 analyze the bargaining game and the fuzzy logic, respectively. Section 5 presents the validation, and Section 6 concludes with a short summary.

2. Related Works

The literature records many efforts supporting QoS for workflow. AgFlow is a middleware platform that enables quality-driven composition of Web services [17]. QoS-aware Grid Workflow is a project which aims at extending the basic QoS support to Grid workflow applications [2]. The work in [16] focuses on mapping the sweep task workflow to Grid resources with deadline and budget constraints. However, none of them defines a business model for the system. Recently, there have been many Grid projects working on the SLA issue [12,15]. Most of them focus on single job and thus consider only the direct relation between user and service provider. The business role of the broker in such systems has not been fully evaluated. Thus, the derived problems such as the asymmetric information issue have not been considered in any of the above-mentioned works.

The structure and content of the SLA used in the Grid environment are described in many previous works. According to [3-9], the content of an SLA varies depending on the service offered and incorporates the elements and attributes required for the particular negotiation. In general, it includes:

- An end-point description of the contractors (e.g., information on customer/provider location and facilities)
- Contractual statements (e.g., start date, duration of the agreement, charging clauses, fines)
- Service Level Specification (SLS)s, i.e. the technical QoS description and the associated metrics.

However, all of them do not describe how to set the appropriate value to each parameter in the SLA. In particular, with the case of running SLA-aware workflow, the question of how to give suitable information to solve the asymmetric situations has not been considered.

3. Asymmetric Information Issues

In the contractual context between the user and broker, asymmetric information could bring negative effects as illustrated in the following scenarios.

3.1 Asymmetric about the Grid State

We assume that the price of provider is fixed at the point of doing mapping. This assumption is suitable as many present resource providers such as Sun and Amazon use this model. The cost of running a workflow depends mainly on the cost of the mapping solutions and then cost of a workflow mapping solution depends on the Grid state. When the Grid is free, there are many free resources and the broker could have a large opportunity to assign many sub-jobs of the workflow to inexpensive providers. Moreover, if the resources in each provider are free, there is a strong possibility to exist a solution that dependent sub-jobs of the workflow are executed on the same RMS. Thus, the cost of data transfer among those sub-jobs is neglected. This leads to a low cost mapping solution. In contrast, when the Grid is busy, there are few free resources and the broker may have to assign many sub-jobs of the workflow to more expensive providers. The busy state of the Grid also leads to the strong possibility that sub-jobs of the workflow will have to be executed in different RMSs. In this case, the cost of data transfer could become a significant part of the total workflow running cost, thereby leading to a higher cost.

The user does not know beforehand whether the Grid is free or busy. Therefore, the user's best guess for a mapping solution is that the mapping is done in the average state of the Grid and the user is thus willing to pay a cost correlated to the average. Thus, when the state of the Grid is busy, the higher cost of the mapping solution may irritate and antagonize the user.

3.2 Asymmetric About the Quality of Mapping Solution

The deadline of the workflow has different meanings for different people. The importance of a deadline depends on the urgency of the workflow. For example, the result of the weather forecasting workflow is very important, especially in storm prediction contexts.

Lateness of the weather forecasting workflow in this case may lead to the death of many people. Thus, the urgency is very high. In contrast, the minimal lateness of a dynamic fluid workflow in a scientific research project does not have great effect on the progress of the project. In this case, the urgency is very low.

Under different urgency levels, the user requires different levels of ensuring the deadline. This requirement equates to running the workflow with different risk levels with the risk being defined here as the inability of finishing the workflow on time. Among many factors affecting the risk level of a workflow mapping solution, the failure probability is the most important. The failure probability includes both small-scale and large-scale failures. The small-scale system failure is mainly caused by the breakdown of computing nodes. Large-scale system failures could affect the entire computing system of the provider. Those failures can be large hardware failures, network connection failures and security holes.

Under the workflow with high urgency level, sub-jobs of the workflow should be assigned to RMSs having low failure probability. Under the low urgency workflow level, the demand of mapping sub-jobs to high reliability is not so high. In general, the price of the RMS having the higher reliability level is higher than the price of the RMS having lower reliability level. Thus, the cost of running a high urgency workflow could be higher than the cost of running the lower one.

However, the user does not know beforehand about the failure probability of the RMSs and how to evaluate the risk of the mapping solution. If the user requires a high level of ensuring the deadline and is asked to pay a high price, the user may suspect that the broker has found an unreliable mapping solution to achieve a higher revenue.

In both described scenarios, if the broker does not have suitable ways to resolve the asymmetric information problem, the broker may lose customers. Unlike the scientific Grid where the support is mainly from governments or foundations, the existence of the business Grid depends on the users. The business users always have two choices. They can build the computer system themselves or use the Grid services. If the broker and providers cannot persuade the users to use the Grid service, the end users will build their own computer system and Grid providers will disappear. By using symmetric information policy, the broker and providers make reliable and trustworthy sense for end users while using the Grid. Thus, it contributes to encouraging end users to use the offered service.

4.   Possible Solutions

To solve the asymmetric information issue, the broker should have some ways of revealing the relevant information. Here, we present some such approaches.

4.1   Pricing and Guarantee as the Signal

From the obligation description between user and broker, we refer to the monetary penalty. If the broker cannot finish the workflow execution at the due time, he will be fined. There is a question that what the suitable fining rate is. In this part, we present a way to answer the question.

The user and broker form a contract to execute the Grid-based workflow. The workflow can be finished on time or be late. If the workflow finishes on time, its monetary value to the user is $b1$. If the workflow is late, its monetary value to the user is $b2$. Assume that the late probability of the workflow mapping solution is q. We can also assume that the broker is risk-neutral and the user is risk-averse. The broker proposes a contract that the cost to execute the workflow is p and a guarantee g. If the workflow is late, the broker has to pay the user g. The utility of the buyer is $u(b1-p)$ if the workflow is not late and $u(b2-p+g)$ if it is. As the user is risk-averse, $u'' < 0$. The user will accept the contract when his expected utility is greater or equal to $u(0)=0$. The utility of the broker is presented in Formula 1.

$$B(p,g) = (1-q)*p + q*(p-g) \tag{1}$$

The utility of the user is presented in Formula 2.

$$U = q*u(b2 - p + g) + (1-q)*u(b1 - p) \tag{2}$$

The optimal contract must satisfy following conditions:

Max $\{B(p,g)\}$

S.t $U \geq u(0)$

Using Lagrange multipliers, we have following results:

$$g = b1 - b2 \tag{3}$$

$$p = b1 - u^{-1}(u(0)) = b1 \tag{4}$$

$$\frac{g}{p} = 1 - \frac{b2}{b1} \tag{5}$$

It is possible to say that with low urgency level, the difference in monetary terms between late and on time result is not so large. For example, if a dynamic fluid workflow in a scientific research project is late one or two hours, it has little effect on the progress of the whole project. This means that the $\frac{b2}{b1}$ value is high. Thus, from Formula 5, the $\frac{g}{p}$ value would be low. In contrast, under a high urgency level, for example with the weather forecasting workflow, if the result is late by 1 hour, many ships may not be able to return the harbour to avoid the storm. Thus, the difference in monetary terms is great. This means that the $\frac{b2}{b1}$ value is low and the $\frac{g}{p}$ value is high. From Formula 5 and the analyzed aspect of price and guarantee, we apply to our case as follows.

- The broker provides a menu of contract. Each contract contains the urgency level and the appropriate guarantee. The guarantee is computed in percent of the total cost and the guarantee is higher when the urgency level is higher.
- The user chooses a contract from the menu. Based on this requirement, the broker will do the mapping solution and negotiate the SLA.

The higher guarantee rate with higher price will persuade the user to believe in the quality of the service provided by the broker.

4.2   Signalling During the SLA Negotiation

From the business mode, there are three different types of sub-SLA negotiation using three different kinds of SLA text. User - Broker negotiation focuses on definition of the submitted SLA. Broker – Provider negotiation considers the workflow sub-jobs and uses the analyses of the sub-job SLAs. Provider - Provider negotiation deals with data transfer between sub-jobs (and also between providers) so the SLA part for data transfer is used.

Although there are three types of SLA negotiations, the negotiation procedure remains the same; only service attributes differ. Figure 2 describes this basic procedure in a client - server model. In the first step, the client creates a template SLA with some preliminary service attributes and sends those to the server. The server parses the text and checks the client requirements. In case of conflicts, a new SLA version is compiled and returned.

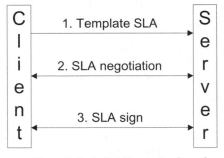

Figure 2: Basic SLA Negotiation Procedure

Here, we focus on the negotiation process between user and broker. When receiving an SLA from a customer, the broker parses it to get all information about the general SLA, sub-jobs, SLO, data transmission, the dependency among sub-jobs and the structure of the workflow. From the information of the sub-jobs and the structure of workflow, the broker does mapping to determine the appropriate provider and the time period to run each sub-job. During the negotiation process, the broker could provide the user the following information to avoid the asymmetric information issue.

• The number of feasible solutions in the reference set created by H-Map algorithm [10].
• Mapping information. The mapping information include the start, stop time of the workflow and the RMS for each sub-job. Depending on the state of the Grid, a mapping module can find a feasible solution in the expected time period or not. If not, it will find the earliest solution and ask for the consumer's approval.
This information contains many signals for the user.
• Firstly, the number of feasible solutions in the reference set created by H-Map algorithm can tell about the Grid state. The H-Map algorithm created a reference set that it distributed over the search space. If the number of feasible solutions is low, this means the Grid is busy and vice versa.
• The second is the start, stop time of the workflow. If this is not within the user's preferred period, it means that the Grid is very busy and the user should prepare for a higher execution cost.
• The third is the RMS for the sub-jobs of the workflow. By providing this information, the broker signals the user about the cost of the mapping solution. With this information, the user can make queries himself in order to know the price from each provider. From this, he can evaluate the cost of the mapping solution.
It is noted that the broker should not provide detail information about start, stop time of the sub-jobs or data transfer. This is because this information does not signal the user about the mapping solution. It may help user bypass the broker to work directly with providers.

5.   Conclusion

This paper has presented the asymmetric information issues between the user and the broker. In particular, the user has less information about the cost of executing the workflow and the quality of mapping solutions than the broker. Thus, the user may suspect that the broker derives a benefit from this information. To avoid these negative effects, the broker should have suitable guarantee policy and reveal suitable signal information in the SLA negotiation phase.

References

[1] J. Altmann, M. Ion, A. A. B. Mohammed, Taxonomy of Grid business models, in Proceedings of the 4th International Workshop on Grid Economics and Business Models, Rennes, France, August 28, 2007, pp. 29-43.

[2] I. Brandic, S. Benkner, G. Engelbrecht, and R. Schmidt, QoS Support for Time-Critical Grid Workflow Applications, in Proceedings of the 1st e-Science 2005, Melbourne, Australia, Dec. 5 - 8, 2005, pp. 108-115.

[3] H. Chen, H. Jin, F. Mao, H. Wu, Q-GSM: A QoS Oriented Grid Service Management Framework, in Proceedings of the 7th Asia-Pacific Web Conference

[4] IBM Corporation, WSLA Language Specification, Version 1.0, 2003.

[5] Open Grid Forum, Web Services Agreement Negotiation Specification (WS-AgreementNegotiation), https://forge.gridforum.org/projects/graap-wg.

[6] Open Grid Forum, Web Services Agreement Specification, http://www.ogf.org/documents/GFD.107.pdf, 2007.

[7] J. Padgett, K. Djemame and P. Dew, Grid Service Level Agreements Combining Resource Reservation and Predictive Run-time Adaptation, in Proceedings of the UK e-Science All Hands Meeting 2005, Nottingham UK, September 19th - 22nd, 2005, pp. 298-305.

[8] D.M. Quan, O. Kao, SLA negotiation protocol for Grid-based workflows, Proceedings of the International Conference on HighPerformance Computing and Communications (HPPC-05), Sorento Italia, 23-25th September, pp.505-510, 2005.

[9] D.M. Quan, O. Kao, On Architecture for an SLA-aware Job Flows inGrid Environments, Journal of Interconnection Networks, World scientific computing, pp. 245 - 264, 2005.

[10] D.M. Quan, Mapping heavy communication workflows onto grid resources within SLA context, in Proceedings of the 2nd International Conference of High Performance Computing and Communication (HPCC06), Munich, Germany, Sep. 12-14, 2006, pp. 727-736.

[11] D.M. Quan, J. Altmann, Business Model and the Policy of Mapping Light Communication Grid-Based Workflow Within the SLA Context, in Proceedings of the 3rd International Conference of High Performance Computing and Communication (HPCC07), Houston, USA, Sept. 26-28, 2007, pp. 285-295.

[12] M. Hovestadt, Scheduling in HPC Resource Management Systems: Queuing vs. Planning, in Proceedings of the 9th Workshop on JSSPP at GGF8, Washington, USA, Jun. 24, 2003, pp. 1-20.

[13] R. Lovas, G. Dózsa, P. Kacsuk, N. Podhorszki, D. Drótos, Workflow Support for Complex Grid Applications: Integrated and Portal Solutions, in Proceedings of the 2nd European Across Grids Conference, Nicosia, Cyprus, Jan. 28-30, 2004, pp. 129-138.

[14] A. Sahai, V. Machiraju, M. Sayal, L. J. Jin, F. Casati: Automated sla monitoring for web services, in Proceedings of the 13th IFIP/IEEE International Workshop on Distributed Systems, Operations and Management (DSOM) 2002, Montreal, Canada, 2002, pp. 292-300.

[15] M. Surridge, S. Taylor, D. De Roure, and E. Zaluska, Experiences with GRIA, in Proceedings of the 1st e-Science 2005, Melbourne, Australia, Dec. 5 - 8, 2005, pp. 98-105.

[16] J. Yu, and R. Buyya, Scheduling Scientific Workflow Applications with Deadline and Budget Constraints using Genetic Algorithms, Scientific Programming Journal, Volume 14 (3-4), pp. 217-230, 2006.

[17] L. Zeng, B. Benatallah, A. Ngu, M. Dumas, J. Kalagnanam, and H. Chang, QoS-Aware Middleware for Web Services Composition, IEEE Transactions on Software Engineering, Volume 30 (5), pp. 311-327, 2004.

Section 4.2

Applications

Collaboration and the Knowledge Economy: Issues, Applications, Case Studies
P. Cunningham and M. Cunningham (Eds.)
IOS Press, 2008

Dynamic Data Mediation in Enterprise Application Integration

Thanassis BOURAS, Panagiotis GOUVAS, Gregoris MENTZAS
*Institute of Communication and Computer Systems, National Technical University of Athens, 9, Iroon Polytechniou str., Zografou Campus, Zografou, Athens 15780, Greece.
Tel: +30 210 7723895; Fax: +30 210 7723550;
Email: {bouras, pgouvas, gmentzas}@mail.ntua.gr*

Abstract: If we try to increase the level of automation in Business-to-Business Enterprise Application Integration (EAI) scenarios, we confront challenges related to the resolution of data and message heterogeneities – that traditional, syntactic EAI technologies are weak to solve, as they miss the documentation of the semantics related to the interfaces and the data structures of the participating services. In this paper, we propose a semantically-enriched approach for dynamic data mediation in EAI scenarios, based on Ontologies, Semantic Web and Semantic Web Services Technologies. The proposed approach focuses on the resolution of message level heterogeneities between collaborative enterprise services exposed from the participating business systems, facilitating automatic, dynamic data mediation during execution time by providing formal transformations of the input and output messages (of the participating Web Services) to a common reference model, i.e. the Enterprise Interoperability Ontology. Moreover, we present a tool that has been designed and developed to support the user to provide business data-related semantic annotations and XSLT transformations if the input and output message parts of given Web Services exposed from business applications, realizing parts of their functionality. Finally, we demonstrate the utilization of the proposed approach and toll in a real-world EAI scenario, i.e. the Stock Replenishment process, across a franchisor-franchisees collaborative value network.

Keywords: Semantic Web, Ontologies, OWL, Data Semantics, Data Mediation, XSLT Transformations, Semantic Web Services, SAWSDL, Enterprise Application Integration.

1. Introduction

In the mid-1990s, a new term called enterprise application integration (EAI) was established, which introduced several methods and software components for efficiently integrating software in an enterprise. Since then available enterprise application integration solutions address integration problems in the following (indicative) ways [1]: by graphically supporting the mapping of systems' interfaces to each other (e.g. SAP NetWeaver Exchange Infrastructure); by reducing complexity using intermediate data-exchange languages (e.g. Extensible Markup Language - XML) or by reducing the number of connection adapters needed through the introduction of hubs (e.g. Enterprise Service Bus). These efforts entail significant costs and - typically due to the "lack of automated support in defining integration, it takes a long time for a human engineer to define semantically correct integration" [2].

The problem that still exists, which the traditional, syntactic EAI technologies are weak to solve, refers to the formalization and the documentation of the semantics related to the interfaces and the data structures of the deployed Web Services. This lack of formal semantics of applications and services to be integrated makes it difficult for software engineers and developers to interconnect heterogeneous applications and thus creates obstacles in the automating EAI activities [3].

There is no doubt that these needs impose the use and interpretation of semantics in EAI and that semantically enriched approaches will hopefully mitigate these problems.

In this paper, we present a semantically-enriched approach for dynamic data mediation in Enterprise Application Integration scenarios, based on Ontologies, Semantic Web and Semantic Web Services Technologies. Our approach, which is presented in the next section, focuses on the resolution of message level heterogeneities between collaborative enterprise services exposed from the participating business systems, facilitating automatic, dynamic data mediation during execution time by providing formal transformations of the input and output messages (of the participating Web Services) to a common reference model, i.e. an enterprise data ontology. In addition, the next section provides an overview of the enterprise data ontology that we have developed and utilized as part of a multi- layered and –faceted interoperability ontology, called Enterprise Interoperability Ontology, which provides a shared, common understanding of data, services and processes within enterprise application integration scenarios.

In Section 4 we present SEAP, the Semantic Annotation and Profiling tool that we designed and developed in order to support the user to provide business data related semantic annotations to specific web services exposed from enterprise applications. The SEAP tool enables the user to graphically define the required transformations of the output and input messages between web services with regard to the respective data entities (used for the annotation of these message parts) of a common ontological model. These transformations are further utilized to enable dynamic data mediation among several interconnected enterprise services, during the execution of a business process which contains these services.

Finally, we provide (in Section 5) an indicative business scenario demonstrating how our proposed approach and tool contributes to the resolution of data heterogeneities among different business, while, in Section 6, we summarize the conclusions and the future work of the research efforts presented.

2. Semantically-Enriched Data Mediation

As already stated the proposed data integration approach facilitates automatic, dynamic data mediation during execution time by providing formal transformations of the input and output messages (of the participating Enterprise Services) to a common reference model (an enterprise interoperability ontology that we developed in OWL, the Web Ontology Language).

More specifically, automatic, dynamic data mediation is enabled by providing a-priori mappings and transformations for all enterprise services inputs. Message parts (of the services' native Web Services) are also output to a common-reference conceptual, ontological model, i.e. the data-intensive enterprise interoperability ontology.

Mappings are created between the enterprise services message elements and ontology concepts, utilizing the schemaMapping attribute to semantically annotate and associate the input and output message elements of the involved enterprise services, towards the creation of the so-called Semantic Profiles of these services, respecting the SAWSDL specification for the deployment of Semantic Web Services [4].

In the literature [5], two types of mappings between enterprise services message elements and semantics have been identified: a) mappings from the Web Service message element to the ontology concept, also called the "up-cast" and/or "up-level", and b) transformations from the ontology concept to the message element, called the "down-cast" and/or "down-level".

Once these transformations are defined, two enterprise services can interoperate by reusing these mappings. Both the mappings and the message transformation occur at the instance level between the WSDL (XML) and the OWL individual.

2.1   Extending Native Web Services Interfaces with Data Semantics

As already mentioned above, the main idea behind the proposed dynamic data mediation approach is that the native descriptions (i.e. WSDL interfaces) of the standard Web Services of the involved service-oriented business applications is extended with data/information semantics. This extension process is called semantic annotation/profiling and the resulting description is the respective SAWSDL-compatible Semantic Profile.

It is obvious that, in order to solve real integration use-cases, the composed processes must also be able to execute/run. Consequently a special start event must trigger the run-time engine to create a process instance. The process instance works with real data which means that it communicates with real Web Services of SOA-enabled business applications. As a result, the process instance includes an invocation of one Web Service with given input data, stores the reply of this Web Service, invokes another Web Service with the stored data, and evaluates logical expressions to decide which execution branch to follow according to stored data, etc.

Because the process instances communicate to the outside world by using the semantic concepts of the common ontological reference model, the standard Web Services of the service-oriented applications can't understand them directly. To solve this, the standard Web Services are encapsulated (through the semantic annotation/profiling process) into semantically-annotated Web Services, which are directly invokable by a given process instance. These services will be referred as "mediated services".

In the next section we introduce a typical semantic annotation/profiling scenario.

2.2   Walkthrough of Enterprise Services Profiling

We assume that Web Services of the service oriented business applications – called native Web services – are described by a WSDL file. This WSDL description contains the data structure (or a reference to it) of the requested input and the provided output data of operations the service provides. This structure is in the format of an XML schema definition (XSD) and is called native data structure. During the annotation process, the standard WSDL description will be extended with semantics as described below.

The exact connection between the native data structure and the used ontological concepts has to be defined first. The concepts of the data-intensive interoperability ontology (i.e. the common reference model), which are the closest to native data, are identified and referenced from the extended description of the native Web Service. This results in a semantic description which is constructed by the guidelines of the SAWSDL recommendation, i.e. creation and utilization of a "*modelReference*" annotation mechanism pointing to a data ontological concept, for every *wsdl:part* of the involved Web Services.

Although one can find concepts that are very close to the native data in meaning, the syntactical differences between the concepts have to be bridged by creating and applying XSLT transformations.

The XSLT transformations are also used to handle data mismatch problems. Data mismatch problems may be caused from differences between native data structures and the selected concepts of the enterprise data ontology. This can be due to the usage of different units (e.g. when a native service uses US units whereas the Ontology concepts use metric units), different currencies, different format for the same data (for example the address, or the date is formatted in many different ways in CRP and ERP systems due to the differences between national traditions).

The created XSLT transformation code is stored at a common repository. After the transformations are present, the reference to them is added to the semantic description, i.e. the Semantic Profile, of the service.

3.   Overview of the Enterprise Interoperability Ontology

Our approach for dynamic data mediation is based on the definition of formal transformations of the input and output messages of the involved Web Services to a common reference model. For this purpose, we are utilizing the Data Facet of the Enterprise Interoperability Ontology (ENIO) that we have designed and developed [6].

The Enterprise Interoperability Ontology represents an explicit specification of the conceptualization of the EAI domain, and structures and formalizes the procedural and operative knowledge needed to describe and resolve the given EAI problem, providing a formal and explicit definition of the data, services and processes that exist within an application integration problem.

Regarding the design principles for constructing ENIO, we have chosen to introduce the model of an upper ontology, which covers generic and domain-independent concepts, with several, domain-related extensions that we call facets. We have developed a three-faceted structure for ENIO: data facet; functional facet and process facet. As the Data Facet of ENIO aims to formally capture the semantics of messages exchanged among collaborative enterprise applications that expose their functionality as web services, it fits perfectly within the scope of the proposed semantically-enriched data mediation approach.

As we do not intend to re-invent the wheel, we based the ENIO Data facet on the Core Components Technical Specification (CCTS). CCTS is the current ISO 15000-5 Technical Specification and supported and used by more than 50 projects and initiatives (including UBL, RosettaNet, CIDX, SWIFT, OAG, etc). The meta-model of the ENIO Data Facet ontologises the meta-modeling elements of CCTS, i.e. Core Components (CC), Data Types (DT), Aggregated CC (ACC), Basic CC (BCC) and Association CC (ASCC).

To populate the Data Facet, we have utilized as knowledge sources the following standards and vocabularies: the OASIS ebXML Core Components Dictionary, RosettaNet Business Dictionary, OAGIS specification, and OASIS Universal Business Language.

Finally, as our goal is to provide a generalized reference ontology for a semantically-enriched data mediation within EAI scenarios, a fine-grained axiomatisation is not needed. A semi-formal ontology providing a common vocabulary with a formal taxonomy, but without detailed logical axioms is enough for our purposes. We therefore chose a common denominator of ontology features which are present in all current ontological formalisms, including but not limited to RDFS, OWL, and WSML.

The features we use are the following: concepts with formal sub-concept relation, instances with formal instantiates relation, and binary properties with single concept domain and range constraints. We have chosen OWL-DL as our implementation language because it is an already available W3C recommendation and has good tool support.

Moreover, other ontology formalisms (including WSML) provide conversion utilities from and to OWL-DL. In the future, we expect that ENIO can be (semi-) automatically translated into various other formats, if needed by the target application domain.

4.   Semantic Annotation and Profiling of Enterprise Services

We developed SEAP (a Semantic Annotation and Profiling tool) which allows the selection and visualization of the native Web Services interfaces and the data-intensive enterprise interoperability ontology and facilitates the user to annotate (through a drag and drop utility) the input and output message parts of the selected Web Service interface with business data entities of the already mentioned enterprise interoperability ontology.

As shown in Figure 1, the graphical user interface of SEAP comprises of five main areas. In the left side, we have the *Native Services Area* that is responsible for the visualization of the selected, native Web Services that are exposed from the existing business system of an enterprise. In the middle, we have the *Ontology Browser area* that is responsible for visualizing all the tree facets of ENIO, i.e. the Functional, the Data and the Behavioral one, as well as, the *Ontology filtering area*, which sorts out the visualized ontological concepts, based on given keywords. Finally, in the right-hand side, the *Adaptation Layer Services* area visualizes the mediated services that comprise the respective collaborative business process, and the *Adaptation Layer Concepts* area, which contains the ontological concepts that annotate inputs and outputs of the services involved in the respective collaborative business process.

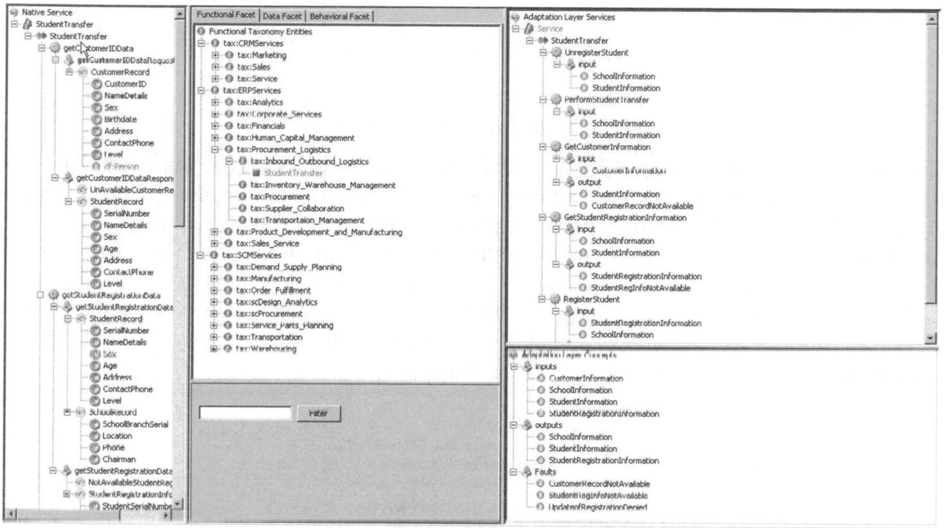

Figure 1: Interface of SEAP (SEmantic Annotation and Profiling Tool)

The user is allowed to drag and drop ontological concepts of the ENIO Data Facet visualized in the Ontology Browser Area, annotating the input and output message elements of the native WSDL interface visualized in the Native Services Area. In parallel, the adaptation layer services and concepts are automatically created. Once the annotation procedure is completed, the user is guided to provide and graphically define the respective XSLT transformations from (for input messages) and to (for output messages) the Enterprise Interoperability Ontology. The up- and down-casting transformations are stored along with data semantics annotations to the SAWSDL-compatible semantic profile of the selected service. These semantic extensions (i.e. data annotations and XSLT transformations) are also used during the execution of generated collaborative business process models that interconnect and orchestrate already annotated enterprise services.

5. Demonstration with a Business Case

Our demonstrator is based on a typical franchisor-franchisees value-added network which includes a complex IT infrastructure in the franchisor headquarters comprising of several centralized, corporate systems, i.e. ERP, CRM and WMS, which are required for the coordination of the retail activity, reimbursements, logistics and the pricing policy of the chain of retail stores. On the other hand, the Point-of-Sales (PoS) retail stores are equipped with an ERP-like Retail System that allows the collaboration with the franchisor and facilitates the business activities of the value network.

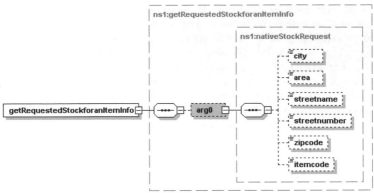

Figure 2: "Address" Object Native XSD

In this enterprise context, we have identified several Collaborative Business Processes (CBPs) that compose and invoke (complex) services exposed from heterogeneous business systems. We have selected the "Stock Replenishment" CBP, in order to demonstrate the usage and applicability of the proposed approach in facilitating dynamic data mediation in complex enterprise application integration. The daily store replenishment cycle constitutes a typical case of process integration scenarios. This replenishment procedure imposes that every day the franchisees have to replenish their stocks by ordering new items from the franchisor that has to invoice and deliver the items requested.

Figure 3: "Address" Object Native XSD

The replenishment procedure involves and triggers, in all way, processes of most of the systems comprising the franchising network infrastructure. We are going to demonstrate the proposed approach and tool through the exchange of the "Address" data object (Figure 2) among the participating services of the involved business systems.

Utilizing the Semantic Annotation and Profiling (SEAP) tool, the user (after having selected and visualized both the native WSDL of the participating Web Service, containing the "Address" object, and the data facet of the Enterprise Interoperability Ontology) annotates the respective message part with the "*DataFacetv3:Address*" term existing in the Enterprise Interoperability Ontology (Figure 3).

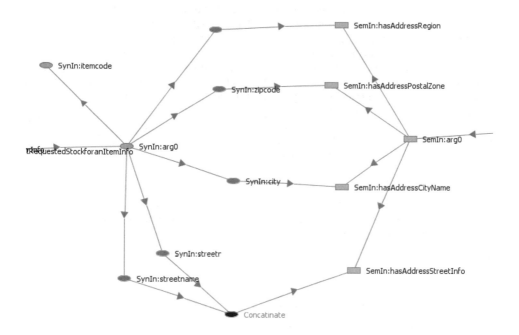

Figure 4: "Address" Object Data XSLT Transformation

Once, the data-related semantic annotation of the "Address" object message part is completed, the user interacts with the "XSLT Transformation Editor" of the "Enterprise Services Semantic Profiling" tool so as to graphically define all the required mappings and transformations from the structure of the native "Address" data object to the respective ontological term (Figure 4).

```
<xsd:choice>
    <xsd:olomont name="stockInformation" type="tns:Item" minOccurs="0" sawsdl:liftingSchemaMapping="
http://lifting.xsl" sawsdl:modelReference="http://www.imu.iccs.gr/fusion/DataFacetv3.owl#Item
http://www.imu.iccs.gr/fusion/State.owl#QuantityReserved"/>
    </xsd:choice>
</xsd:complexType>
<xsd:complexType name="Address">
    <xsd:sequence>
        <xsd:element name="hasAddressCityName" type="xsd:string"/>
        <xsd:element name="hasAddressRegion" type="xsd:string"/>
        <xsd:element name="hasAddressPostalZone" type="xsd:string"/>
        <xsd:element name="hasAddressStreetInfo" type="xsd:string"/>
    </xsd:sequence>
```

Figure 5: "Address" XSLT Transformation

The developed XSLT transformations are stored along with the data semantics annotations to the SAWSDL-compatible semantic profile of the selected service (Figure 5). These XSLT transformations are further utilized during the execution of generated collaborative business process models that interconnect and orchestrate already annotated enterprise services.

6.   Conclusions

In this paper we proposed a semantically-enriched approach for dynamic data mediation among interconnected Web Services in the framework of Collaborative Business Processes.

Moreover, we presented a Semantic Annotation and Profiling (SEAP) tool developed to support the end-user to semantically annotate (with data semantics) the Web Services interfaces of the exposed enterprise services and to graphically define the required up- and down- casting XSLT transformations.

In addition, we presented the applicability of the proposed approach in a realistic B2B integration scenario within a franchisor-franchisees collaborative value network, comprising complex, heterogeneous systemic infrastructure. In the frame of this scenario, we have demonstrated the dynamic resolution of data heterogeneities at execution time.

In the future, we intend to generate and add a transformation repository, containing all the supported transformation types, which can be selected and reused during a service's semantic annotation and profiling process.

Acknowledgement

Work presented in this paper has been partially funded by the European Commission in the project FUSION (Business Process Fusion based on Semantically-enabled Service-Oriented Business Applications) IST 027385.

References

[1] Friesen, A., A. Alazeib, A. Balogh, M. Bauer, A. Bouras, P. Gouvas, G. Mentzas, A. Pace (2007) "Towards semantically-assisted design of collaborative business processes in EAI scenarios", 5th International Conference on Industrial Informatics, INDIN 2007, sponsored by the Industrial Electronics Society of the IEEE, July 23-27 Vienna, Austria.
[2] Bussler, C. (2003) "The Role of Semantic Web Technology in Enterprise Application Integration", In IEE Data Engineering Bulletin 26, 2003, No. 4, pp. 62 – 68.
[3] Haller, A., Gomez, J., & Bussler, C. (2005). Exposing Semantic Web Service principles in SOA to solve EAI scenarios. in Workshop on Web Service Semantics, in WWW2005.
[4] Farrell J. and Lausen H. (eds) Semantic Annotations for WSDL and XML Schema. W3C Candidate Recommendation, January 2007. Available at: http://www.w3.org/TR/sawsdl
[5] Nagarajan, M., Verma, K., Sheth, A., Miller, J., & Lathem, J. (2006). Semantic Interoperability of Web Services - Challenges and Experiences. 2006 IEEE International Conference on Web Services (ICWS 2006).
[6] Bouras, A., Gouvas, P., & Mentzas, G. (2007). ENIO: An Enterprise Application Integration Ontology. In the Proceedings of the 1st International Workshop on Semantic Web Architectures for Enterprises (SWAE), DEXA'07, 3-7 September, 2007, Regensburg, Germany.

Collaboration and the Knowledge Economy: Issues, Applications, Case Studies
P. Cunningham and M. Cunningham (Eds.)
IOS Press, 2008

Semantic-based Integration of Innovative Networking Services and Existing Systems

Flavio BONFATTI[1], Paola Daniela MONARI[2]

[1]University of Modena & Reggio Emilia, via Vignolese 905, Modena, 41100, Italy
Tel: +39 059 2056138, Fax: + 39 059 056129, Email: flavio.bonfatti@unimore.it
[2]SATA srl, via Notari 103, Modena, 41100, Italy
Tel: +39 059 341160, Fax: + 39 059 343299, Email: p.monari@satanet.it

Abstract: The degree of ICT adoption at small and micro companies is still unsatisfactory in most of the EU25 countries and the main barriers to ICT uptake are the lack of basic collaboration services available at reasonable conditions and the need for SMEs to change their current ICT tools. The paper shows how the SEAMLESS services, developed by the homologous FP6 IST project, put every SME in condition to exchange business documents with any other user SME, by overcoming format, language and meaning differences, and enable the user companies to cope with different eInvoicing infrastructures and marketplaces. The SEAMLESS approach addresses very important scenarios such as integration with ERP and SCM systems, with third-party applications providing added-value services to all the network users, with other sectoral, national and international business channels. A number of experiments support a preliminary evaluation of the business benefits generated by this easy, fast and cheap semantic-based integration approach.

Keywords: SME, collaboration, networking, ICT services, semantic integration

1. Introduction

A number of studies have been carried out at the European [1], national and regional level in the last years on the degree of ICT adoption at small and micro companies, and all of them show an unsatisfactory situation in most of the EU25 countries, especially in Central, South-East and South Europe.

This is despite the increasing number of companies with Internet access due to increasing broad-band coverage. As confirmed in the recent European Interoperability Roadmaps [2, 3], two main barriers to ICT uptake are lack of basic collaboration services available at reasonable conditions and need for SMEs to change their current ICT tools.

The SEAMLESS European project (IST-FP6-026476) intends to overcome both problems, by creating a semantic-based service-oriented infrastructure for partner search, negotiation and collaboration, as well as providing software components to make different legacy systems interoperate [4, 5]. The ultimate aim is pushing SMEs to play an active role into the Single European Electronic Market [6, 7].

Every SME using the SEAMLESS service is put in condition to exchange business documents with any other user SME.

At the same time, the SEAMLESS service enables the user companies to cope with different eInvoicing infrastructures and marketplaces.

The paper is aimed at showing the integration models the SEAMLESS infrastructure is offering. Section 1 presents the specific project objectives to introduce with minimal effort and cost increasing levels of interoperability. Section 2 presents the main scenarios of integration between the SEAMLESS platform and the enterprise management systems of the user companies. Section 3 introduces the semantic-based SEAMLESS approach to query and business document translation. Section 4 proposes an overview of the SEAMLESS technological infrastructure and outlines the process of transferring information from SEAMLESS repositories to proprietary information system. Section 5 presents the three possible integration modes. Section 6 recalls the six main integrations implemented so far. Section 7 gives a preliminary evaluation of the business benefits in a cross-border eInvoicing scenario.

2.   Objectives

The use cases supported by the SEAMLESS basic infrastructure are those enabling a small and micro company to enter the electronic market, e.g. (a) gaining visibility in the network, using a proper eService to describe its own profile and present its offer and demand of products and services, (b) extending the number of partners (suppliers, customers), using a proper eService to define the search filter and send it for execution across the network, (c) exploring the collaboration potential of a found potential partner, using a proper eService to start a negotiation process with the exchange of data and quotations, and (d) starting a collaboration with the new partner, using a proper eService to exchange business documents such as order, order status, dispatch advise and invoice.

Special feature of the SEAMLESS infrastructure is that whenever sending (receiving) a query or a document the company keeps working with its usual concepts and language independently of the concepts and language of the receiver (sender).

The integration of the SEAMLESS platform with the enterprise management systems of the user companies includes the following main scenarios:

- *Integration with ERP systems*: establishing a bi-directional data flow where SEAMLESS helps finding new partners and negotiating with them, ERP supports the traditional processing of customer orders and planning internal and external activities, and SEAMLESS helps again in translating, dispatching and tracking the business documents.
- *Integration with SCM systems*: SEAMLESS offers partner search and negotiation functions, the SCM system in turn prepare the business documents to exchange, and SEAMLESS converts and dispatches those documents.
- *Integration of third-party applications into the SEAMLESS platform* to extend its company profiling, partner search, negotiation and collaboration functions.
- *Interoperability with other business channels*. The SEAMLESS platform supports the user companies in generating business documents of different types in electronic form. This is a fundamental condition to help small companies approaching business channels from which they are normally excluded because of their limited resources.

3.   Methodology

Communication and collaboration within the SEAMLESS environment is based on the existence of, and relations between, one global ontology, several regional/sectoral common ontologies, and a number of local (individual) ontologies. This approach is in line with [8] and its implementation in [9] and allows every single company to keep using its own language and data organisation: mapping them (just once) into the mediator knowledge (which in turn maps onto one or more global ontologies) is enough to ensure automatic translation with all the other SEAMLESS ontologies.

- *Global ontology (GLOB)*. Its concepts are reported and described in English intended as *lingua franca*. It is set up and managed by organisations expert in ontology and knowledge management (typically specialised in one sector, Textile and Building & Construction in SEAMLESS), which assures its maintenance and the free access to its contents through proper web services. The SEAMLESS environment must include at least one GLOB, but different organisations can propose partially overlapping GLOBs. In order to achieve a full interoperability condition, every GLOB manager should map the concepts of its GLOB (data model, taxonomies, vocabulary) onto the homologous ones in the other GLOBs.
- *Common ontology (COMM)*. It includes the concepts considered useful to the single SEAMLESS node. It is expected that the COMMs are set up and managed by mediators,

then their concepts are reported and described in the language of the specific region and its can be sectoral. Every COMM is derived from one GLOB so as to establish a relation between its regional/sectoral terms and those of the global ontology. Whenever an addition in introduced in a GLOB it is automatically communicated to all its mapped COMMs.

• *Local ontology (LOC).* It represents the concepts used by the single company when sharing or exchanging information with other companies. For instance, if a company is provided with a legacy system some (not all) of the concepts of its data model are communicated to partners during the negotiation and collaboration phases. In order to establish a relation with other companies, the LOC of each company must be annotated onto the COMM(s) of its mediator(s).

According to such three-level hierarchy, in the worst case a document (or a query) undergoes a five-step translation process. Figure 1 (where DM stands for Data Model, LG for Language and TX for Taxonomy) shows a possible practical example of this worst case, when, within the SEAMLESS network, sender and receiver play the role of LOC belonging to different COMM and different GLOB. This happens when, for instance, a German company of the Building & Construction sector sends a Request for Quotation to an Italian company of the Textile sector.

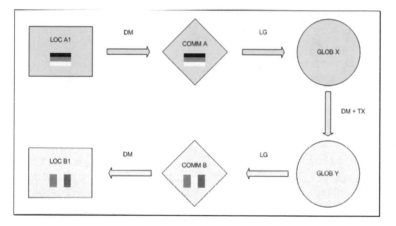

Figure 1 – The SEAMLESS Translation Approach

• *LOC A1 -> COMM A.* LOC A1 manages information according to his legacy schema in German language. Since COMM A needs the information based on the SEAMLESS data model, the LOC is in charge of converting legacy data to the SEAMLESS schema by means of proper mapping files.

• *COMM A -> GLOB X.* COMM A translates the document in English language (franca language for all the GLOB ontologies):

• *GLOB X -> GLOB Y.* GLOB X converts the incoming business document according to the mapping required for GLOB Y ontology. The resulting document is the same order but in adopting the GLOB Y data model and taxonomy terms.

• *GLOB Y -> COMM B.* COMM B translates the document in Italian language in order to be dispatched among the subscribed LOCs.

• COMM B -> LOC B1. LOC B1 needs to insert the received order into his legacy system. Then, he converts the order according to the proper mapping instance.

4. Technology Description

An overview on the overall SEAMLESS architecture is represented in Figure 2. The *Ontology Management Applications* block represents the applications by which the ontology managers edit and maintain their relevant ontologies. The three expected profiles, i.e. GLOB Manager, COMM Manager and LOCL Manager, should access a specific application tailored according to the specific functional requirements.

The *SEAMLESS User Applications* area defines those applications whose role is to ensure the possibilities of SEAMLESS to cover the entire business functionality. SEAMLESS registered users, namely companies, are intended to access all the provided applications. Additionally, a subset of these functions is intended to be available to casual, i.e. not registered, users as well.

The glue of the entire application is the *Services* block. According to a Service-Oriented Architecture (SOA) approach, specific Web Services are required for providing the needed semantic infrastructure for information exchange as well as the information distribution, persistency, accessibility, security and transport.

Third-party User Applications has been introduced for representing those applications, developed outside the SEAMLESS project, that can be integrated with the SEAMLESS applications in order to enrich the offer of business functionalities. Regardless the implementation details of these applications, they are supposed to access the SEAMLESS services in order to share information with the SEAMLESS applications.

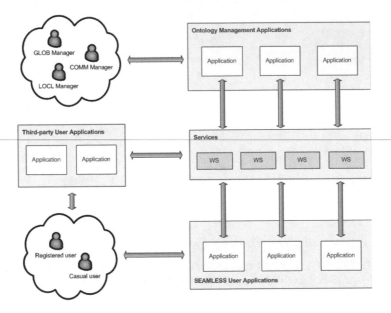

Figure 2 – Overview of the SEAMLESS Architecture

Going deeper in the collaboration aspects, companies interact with each other by exchanging business documents for completing an active transaction (e.g. order, invoice, dispatch advice documents). The SEAMLESS infrastructure supports the whole process of generating a business document by the sender company, translated and dispatching it to the receiver company (see [10] for further details).

Another point of view of the collaboration scenario is the possibility of integrating the business document managed by the SEAMLESS components with the companies' proprietary information systems. Figure 3 outlines the possibility of transferring information from SEAMLESS repositories to proprietary information system (the opposite operation is anyway to be considered feasible as well).

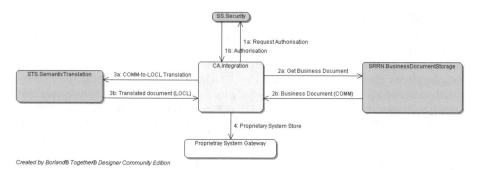

Figure 3 – Integration

1. Company credentials, e.g. username and password, are validated by the Security function. If valid, a session token is returned in order to grant the access to all other services.

2. Documents to be imported in the proprietary system are retrieved by invoking the Business Document Storage function.

3. The document are translated from COMM format to LOCL format by a regular call to the Semantic Translation function. The translated documents are ready to be imported.

4. The Proprietary System Gateway represents a specific module that each company provides to allow the SEAMLESS Integration module to write information in the proprietary system.

5. Developments

Integration is a quite generic concept that can be implemented in different ways. Depending on the required synchronisation and automation degrees there are three main modes of making two applications exchange data with each other:

- *Asynchronous and manual*. The simplest solution enables the user of the exporting application to generate the file and upload it on a permanent storage. After that, the user of the importing application is put in the condition to download the file and acquire its electronic contents. The mode is asynchronous since the two operations are executed in different and independent times, it is manual since the two operators are responsible for launching, respectively, the export and import operations.

- *Asynchronous and automatic*. This mode is similar to the previous case but the export and import operations are executed automatically by the respective applications. For the exporting application this could occur whenever a new datum or document that must be transferred to the other application becomes available, or at certain points in time e.g. twice a day at noon and midnight. In turn, for the importing operation this could occur through a polling function detecting the presence of a new file or on a time basis e.g. twice a day at a quarter past noon and past midnight.

- *Synchronous and automatic*. This is the mode where the two applications can directly communicate with each other e.g. by mutually invoking specific web services. In particular, the exporting application could invoke a function of the importing application to transfer the intended file and trigger the import operation.

The first (and partially the second) of these modes is suited in those cases when it is preferable to keep SEAMLESS and the external application independent of each other and there are no reasons to invest in adapting them.

On the contrary, the third mode should be chosen when it is important for the SEAMLESS platform to assure a high integration degree of the external application to achieve good performances or a seamless swap between the two environments.

6.   Results

Some of the above identified integration scenarios have been practically realized and experimented with the twofold objective to make them behave as proof of concept (living example) and to provide users with advanced solutions since the SEAMLESS platform prototypal phase. The cases that have been studied within the project are [10]:

- *Integration of an open source ERP system (Adempiere).* Adempiere is an Open Source Enterprises Resource Planning system and offers enterprises a complete business suit. It is based on a famous ERP system Compiere. Besides business functionalities to manage internal and external processes of a company, it also offers to import and export business documents in different formats. The decision to integrate Adempiere in SEAMLESS is based on the analysis, in which three different ERP systems were analyzed and after comparing these three, it was decided to use Adempiere.

- *Integration with a B2B portal (Marketline).* The broadly used part of the e-business ICT support is a combination of different e-negotiation services. Marketline offers to its costumers a broad range of services from e-action, e-tendering and supply chain integration. The integration of SEAMLESS with Marketline will expand Marketline usability and diminishing the geographical and cultural barriers, while Marketline can offer in turn those services to SEAMLESS partially free of charge. This is a typical example of asynchronous and manual integration.

- *Integration of a semantic oriented web site Crawler (BIAS).* BIAS is a commercial product from ANTARA, that is being used in different fields, like sectoral web search engines, information aggregator, competitiveness surveillance, etc. In the SEAMLESS integration, BIAS uses the SEAMLESS infrastructure to obtain companies information and mediators ontologies (COMM) in order to be able to extract the company Offer, based on the contents of its website. To achieve this result, the web crawler indexes the company web site pages, and search there the terms of the COMM ontology. Once this is obtained, the matches are exploited in a semantic way in order to find the relationships between the terms found in the site. The result of this inference process is a list of ontology terms that can be grouped to obtain the product families that composes the company Offer.

- *Integration of a Product Configurator (KET-PC).* The integration of KET-PC, a professional Product Configurator made available by KELYAN, is an example of SEAMLESS negotiation function extension and, at the same time, of synchronous and automatic integration mode.

- *Integration of a Transaction Manager (CSF).* The integration of CSF is intended to provide facilities for distributed business transactions management, where the user company can form, plan and perform its business activities via simple, widespread and affordable functionality for business transactions forming and scheduling. In this case it is assumed that the usual business transaction reflects simple business process, i.e. the existing Collaboration Support Functions are applicable for planning and controlling simple business processes. This is an interesting case of asynchronous and manual mode.

- *Cross-border eInvoicing experiment (Austria-Italy-Slovenia).* This last experiment is the demonstration of how some of the main SEAMLESS outcomes could be extracted and applied to solve a hot problem, namely the semantic interoperability of e Invoicing standards. In particular, the translation between the Austrian, Italian and Slovenian data models was tested.

7.   Business Benefits

A preliminary evaluation of the business benefits was made for the cross-border eInvoicing scenario, where companies from Austria, Italy and Slovenia can exchange eInvoices with a minimal effort.

Enabling conditions for the semantic roaming are that the three national reference models are mapped one onto each other, and each company chooses one reference model (typically a standard model adopted in that country) and maps its local model into it.

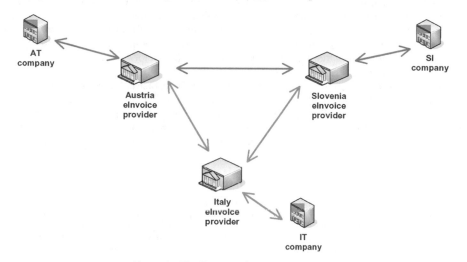

Figure 4 – The Cross-Border eInvoice Experiment

Three bilateral tested cases were created, corresponding to the red arrows in Figure 4: CBI (IT) ⇔ EB21 (AT), CBI (IT) ⇔ SLOG (SI), MS Navision ⇔ CBI (IT), where CBI, EB21 and SLOG are national eInvoicing standards (in Italy, Austria and Slovenia, respectively), and MS Navision is taken as typical example of ERP for SMEs.

The whole experiment took two weeks, including editing of four data models and three bi-directional mapping. More precisely, it takes a couple of days to edit a new standard model (usually very rich and complex, with a wide documentation to understand and interpret). This is the time spent by an ICT engineer fully trained on the use of the SEAMLESS tools and without any previous knowledge of the data model to describe.

For ERP-like data models the time required for editing is less that one day. It depends on the quality of the data model accompanying documentation (filed definitions, relations). It takes about four hours to realises a mapping (80% for the first direction, and 20% for the opposite direction).

The full mapping of all mandatory fields in the output file has been obtained in all the cases. Normally, optional fields like sender codes and comments are excluded. They are just transferred, if there is a correspondence in concepts, or even ignored. The % of concepts and attributes mapped from one data model to the other is the following table:

EB21 (AT) to CBI (IT): 83%	SLOG (SI) to CBI (IT): 78%	CBI (IT) to MS Navision: 75%
CBI (IT) to EB21 (AT): 73%	CBI (IT) to SLOG (SI): 82%	MS Navision to CBI (IT): 68%

Recommendations to data model creators (standardization bodies, ERP producers) suggest to focus on the only fields that are meaningful to the receiver, do not mind if transaction tracking details are lost in the output data structure, avoid as far as possible conditioned field (derived knowledge), provide totals, not only input quantities to computation formulas, replace "text" data with "term" data (meaning pre-defined domains)

The main recommendation to eInvoicing providers is to always associate the original pdf file to the electronic version, to support correct interpretation of minor ambiguities.

8.   Conclusions

The SEAMLESS semantic-based integration services are ready for direct use through the SEAMLESS infrastructure as well as for other integration-oriented third-party applications.

Seven pilot cases, all of them testing a number of business document translations between different sectors and regions, are running and will last also after project completion, i.e. June 2008. The involved micro and small companies act in Building & Construction sector in Poland and Slovenia, in the Textile sector in Italy, Spain, Slovakia and Romania, and in different sectors in Hungary.

Further integration activities are realised with the ICT infrastructures created within the FP6-IST eNVISION, aimed at offering advanced services to SMEs in the Building & Construction sector, and FP6-IST ONE, aimed at providing flexible and powerful negotiation environments according to a model-driven approach. The ENVISION, ONE and SEAMLESS projects belong to the Digital Ecosystem cluster (www.digital-ecosystems.org).

References

[1] www.ebusiness-watch.org, e-Business Watch, European Commission, DG Enterprise.
[2] European Interoperability Research Roadmap (European Commission, DG INFSO, July 2006) ftp.cordis.europa.eu/pub/ist/docs/directorate_d/ebusiness/ei-roadmap-final_en.pdf
[3] Man-Sze Li "Meeting the Grand Challenge of the Enterprise Interoperability Research Roadmap – A business perspective Ecosystems of small companies in the enlarged Europe", eChallenges e2007, The Hague (NL), October 2007.
[4] F. Bonfatti, P.D. Monari "Digital Ecosystems of small companies in the enlarged Europe", eChallenges e2006, Barcelona (SP), October 2006.
[5] F. Bonfatti, P.D. Monari "Putting semantic interoperability between small and micro companies into practice", eChallenges e2007, The Hague (NL), October 2007.
[6] S. Abels, S. Campbell, A. Hahn, "Accessing and managing heterogeneous information in the Single European Electronic Market", e2004, Vienna, October 2004.
[7] The Roadmap to SEEM implementation – www.seemseed.net
[8] D. Beneventano, S. Bergamaschi, F. Guerra, M. Vincini: "Synthesizing an Integrated Ontology", IEEE Internet Computing Magazine, September-October 2003, pp. 42-51.
[9] A. Bokma et al. "Improving busiess information exchange using semantics", eChallenges e2007, The Hague (NL), October 2007.
[10] D4.4.2 Integration of existing systems technical specifications – www.seamless-eu.org

Collaboration and the Knowledge Economy: Issues, Applications, Case Studies
P. Cunningham and M. Cunningham (Eds.)
IOS Press, 2008

Service Oriented Architectural Model for the Development of Disparate Computing Applications

M.R. MAJEDI[1], K.A.OSMAN[2], J. KRASNIEWICZ[3], M. BOYD[1]

[1]*Faculty of Technology, Innovation and Development, Birmingham City University, Millennium Point, Curzon Street, Birmingham B4 7XG, UK*
Tel: +44 121 331 7461, Fax: +44 121 331 5401, Email: matt.majedi@tic.ac.uk
[2]*Corporate Development Centre, Birmingham City University, City North Campus, Perry Barr, Birmingham B42 2SU, UK*
Tel: +44 121 331 6858, Fax: +44 121 331 5256, Email: keith.osman@bcu.ac.uk
[3]*Department of Computing, Birmingham City University, City North Campus, Perry Barr, Birmingham, B42 2SU, UK*
Tel: +44 121 331 5603, Fax: +44 121 331 6281, Email: jan.krasniewicz@bcu.ac.uk

Abstract: This paper introduces a generic Service Oriented architectural model which can be employed for various domains of computing and IT. It explains SOA as a means to overcoming the limitations of traditional software development approaches such as object orientation. For example, limitations such as integrating new hardware devices and software services automatically and seamlessly. Service abstraction and Service grouping are presented as important properties that the SOA model employs to overcome these limitations. The concept of an Abstract Service is proposed as a means by which services with common functionality are organised into service groups. The utility of this model is demonstrated with respect to its successful implementation in three different scenarios. First this model employs to remotely control population of heterogeneous robots through internet. Second, it is evaluated against Enterprise Resource Planning systems to develop enterprise systems. Finally, it is implemented to solve a general integration problem. A service abstraction technique is also introduced for describing groups of services which provide similar functionality.

Keywords: Service Oriented Architecture, Robotic System, Internet-based Control System, Enterprise Applications.

1. Introduction

This paper presents a generic service oriented architectural model which can be employed in the development of disparate IT and ICT applications. The authors have developed this model originally to remotely control an ensemble of robots required to carry out collaborative tasks [1]. The remote control of a single device is not new; this research describes a system in development that is generic and platform independent. The advantages of this system are that it is able to control a population of heterogeneous robots that are required to solve a problem in a dynamic environment.

This research developed a service-oriented architecture (SOA) approach by introducing Service Abstraction and Service Grouping technique to abstract the hardware and software specifics of each device via a robotic abstraction service (RAS) akin to a web-service. This approach allows problem solving, task-allocation and other functionality required to control the population of robot devices to be implemented in a generic way, insulated by the RAS from the hardware specifics of each device.

The key characteristic of this model is that it is generic and provides a robust and adaptive approach to cope with dynamic requirements, technology changes and changes in organization infrastructures. As a result, the authors implemented this model to solve very different problems that share the same requirements.

This paper will demonstrate the efficiency and robustness of this model by employing it to solve three very different problems. First, the model will be employed to remotely control a population of heterogeneous robots through the Internet presented in section 4. Second, the model will be evaluated against an Enterprise Resource Planning System to develop an enterprise system for a case study presented in section 5.1. Finally, the model was employed to solve a general system integration problem presented in section 6.

2.   Overcoming System Evolution and Migration with Service Oriented Architecture

Service Oriented Architecture (SOA) is an architecture that can be adopted in various scenarios [2, 4], developing a common platform for services that are object oriented driven to interconnect between different platform of technologies or applications. Erl [3] emphasis that an ideal SOA presents an ideal vision of a world in which resources are cleanly partitioned and consistently represented.

Software systems need to adapt to new developments in hardware such as in robotic systems where new and more sophisticated robots are being produced. Traditional software development approaches like object orientation can help but there still needs to be some manual intervention in order to make use of new systems.

On the other hand Service Oriented Architecture was introduced as an evolution of Object Orientation (OO) to overcome some of the fundamental limitations of OO regarding system integration and cross platform communication to satisfy today's dynamic industry and develops more robust and adaptive systems.

3.   Service Abstraction and Service Grouping

Some of the most important properties of SOA are loose coupling, abstraction and system integration [3, 4] that are of particular importance for some systems like pervasive applications, heterogeneous multi robot systems and enterprise systems. In a service-based computing environment each component, module or device can be presented as a service. A service can be considered as an agent that provides a distinct process or functionality to clients. As a result, a computing environment can be considered to be a combination of different services that interacts with each other (Figure 1).

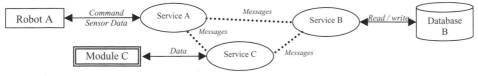

Figure 1: Service-Based Computing Environment

It is advantageous to group together services providing similar functionalities. Grouping together similar services enhances desirable system properties of extensibility, accessibility and loose coupling. Also, in order to identify common functionalities of each group, the authors recommend developing an abstract service for each group. Abstract service defines a list of functions and properties available from each service in the group. Each service would then require presenting an implementation of all these functions. As a result, a computing environment would be partitioned into number of Service Groups (Figure 2).

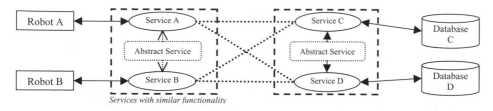

Figure 2: Service Abstraction and Grouping

This model allows different services inside and outside a group to interact with each other via the abstract service. New services can be easily added to a group and become accessible by other services immediately through the abstract service.

4. A Generic SOA Model for Internet-Based Multiple Robot Control

A multi-robot environment can be defined, "as a loosely coupled network of robots that collaborate to solve problems that are beyond the capability or knowledge of an individual robot" [1]. The key to utilising the potential of multi-robot systems is effective coordination and cooperation. To achieve this, the overall control system needs to interact with individual robots irrespective of their hardware dependencies.

Referring to service abstraction and grouping technique, robots can be classified into different groups, for example *worker*, *supervisor* and *observer* groups. By abstracting the services provided by the group, each robot within a group provides a known portfolio of functions to the environment. Thus, each robot provides a "concrete" instance of a particular abstract robotic service within its group. For example, if a particular robot is designated as a worker, it implements the *worker abstract service*, itself inherited from the robotic abstract service (Figure 3).

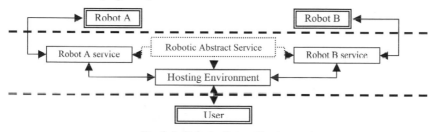

Figure 3: Robotic Abstract Service

Using this model, each robot in the environment can be based on different software and hardware platform with different communication technology.

4.1 Employ SOA for Internet-Based Robotic Control System

In a multiple robotic environment, there needs to be two-way communication between services. A service receives movement command and sends sensors data as an event notification. The traditional Request – Respond architecture of XML web services does not satisfy these requirements, as a result authors implement this model using Decentralized Software Services (DSS) based on Microsoft Robotic Studio. The Microsoft Robotic Studio is an enhanced service oriented tool based on traditional web services with addition of event notification and concurrency that are essential for robotic systems [5].

In order to implement the model, the authors developed a robotic environment containing three Lego NXT Mindstorms robots configured with different capabilities (referred to as Tribot, Grabber and Shooter) and a DRK8080 mobile robot fitted with a number of different sensors and actuators with built-in motor controller and local processor. Lego NXT has Bluetooth connection, whereas DRK8080 is wireless enabled.

Referring service abstraction technique, an abstract service that provides the following functions and events has been developed (this is not a complete list):

- SetDriveSpeed(Left, Right) – set speed of left and right motor
- SetMotorPower(motor, Power) – start a motor with a specified power level (0 – 1)
- SonarDataArrived – notify clients that sonar sensors data has been updated
- IRDataArrived – notify clients that infra red sensor data arrived

Each robot required an implementation of this abstract service. To increase accessibility and extensibility of the services, each has been developed to respond to HTTP, DSSP protocols, and SOAP requests. (DSSP is a SOAP-based protocol used in DSS services)

The hosting environment has been developed as a console application; also two client applications (a desktop and a web application) have been implemented to interact with the services. Both applications are able to control any robot in the environment regardless of underlying technology and also services can send notification messages to the client in real time (Figure 4).

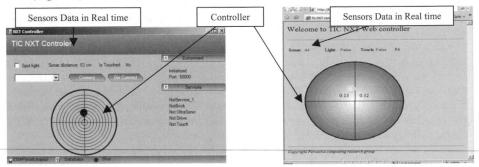

Figure 4: Robot Clients

4.2   Benefits of SOA in Internet-Based Robotic Control System

Using this model it is possible to add new robots to the environment regardless of their platform and specification. A robot can also be a member of more than one group simply by implementing the appropriate abstract service for that group. As a result, a robotic environment based on this model is dynamic: each robot can perform different tasks and new robots can be added to the environment with minimal effort. In principle, an arbitrary number of robots, each with different capabilities, can be controlled within this scheme.

5.   SOA and Enterprise Resource Planning

Enterprise Resource Planning (ERP) systems are seen as a solution to integrate an organization's ICT infrastructure. ERP systems enable communications between different Business Processes (BP), departmental functionalities and ICT systems, from customer enquiries through to providing services and manufacturing products [6, 7]. The key property of an ERP system is a common database that enables different departments to store data in a centralized location and access data in real time. Each component of the system is presented as a module that accesses a common database.

However, implementation of an ERP system can be a cost driven and time consuming process. It requires a deep understanding of business processes and an organization's functionalities. Also, ERP requires changes across the hard - IT and Network resources, and soft – human resources, to form a single integrated solution, abandoning the existing software and systems used in all departments [6, 7]. This is simply no longer acceptable in today's global business market where time and money is the main driver.

On the other hand, Enterprise Application Integration (EAI) is defined as, "the uses of various software models to integrate a set of existing enterprise computer applications" [8]. It was reported that 70% of all EAI projects fail [9] mostly because EAI requires management of the dynamic aspects of the system and also it requires knowledge of many technical aspects. However EAI is focused more on point-to-point integration of enterprise applications and also EAI technologies are still under development [8].

Consequently the authors suggest that the key property of the Enterprise systems should be System integration, unifying the existing software packages used by different departments regardless of their software and hardware platform. Unlike EAI, the authors suggest that an enterprise system should be developed using a single model based on SOA with the aid of service abstraction and grouping.

Any enterprise system contains number of sub systems (Component) like CRM (Customer Relationship Management), Stock control, manufacturing control, *etc*. It is possible to present each of these components as a service to encapsulate functionalities of that particular component. Referring to service abstraction and grouping, it is possible to partition an enterprise system into number of groups like CRM or stock control. In addition each group will be presented with an abstract service (Figure 5).

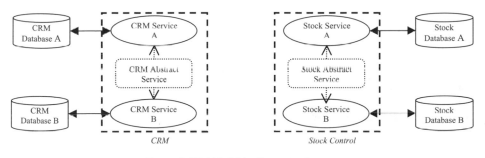

Figure 5: SOA Model for Enterprise Systems

5.1   Implementation of SOA for Enterprise Applications

In order to evaluate the model, the authors decided to implement it for the following case study: Company "A" has number of different systems based on various platforms, namely a CRM application based on SQL server and a Stock control system based on MySQL database. Currently each system is running independently with different front-end causing considerable waste of staff time and effort to keep these two systems synchronized. An ideal solution for this company would be to develop an application that encapsulates both systems without changing the structure of their databases, providing a single coordinator application for users to interact with all systems and databases. It is important to emphasise the fact that this case study is just provided for the purpose of this research, to demonstrate the feasibility of the proposed model, and it is clearly not intended to cover all aspects of enterprise applications. Referring to Figure 5; a CRM abstract service has been introduce which provides the following functionalities:

- GetCustomer(customer number) – get customer data
- GetCustomerOrder(customer number) – get customer orders
  A stock control abstract service providing the following functionalities was developed:
- GetProduct(product id) – get product detail
- GetProductByName(name) – search for a product by name

These abstract services were then implemented for this particular case study using the Windows Communication Foundation (WCF) SOA tool and hosted in a console application developed using C#. Also two client applications (a desktop and a web application) have been developed to interact with these services. Both applications are able to interact with all databases of the system regardless of underlying technology (Figure 6). Based on this model it is possible to integrate another CRM or stock control system into the system simply by implementing the corresponding abstract service. The client applications would then be able to communicate with new service without any change.

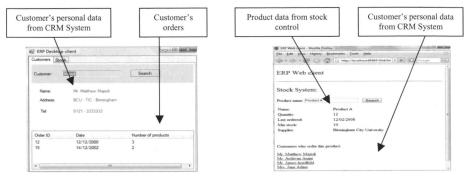

Figure 6: Enterprise Clients

5.2   Benefits of SOA in Enterprise Systems

Using this model, organizations are able to keep their existing systems to form an integrated solution. The proposed model is cost effective in terms of development time and effort; also it meets today's industry in terms of time and money. This model is focused on a single software architectural design whereas an EAI is focused on integration of various models. As a result, this model is more efficient because it does not required knowledge of different technical aspects.

6.   SOA to Solve General System Integration Problems

System integration is a known issue in most companies and organizations, including universities and government bodies. The model introduced in this paper can be implemented for various system integration problems. In order to test this claim, authors proposed the following case study:

Birmingham City University contains number of faculties which all share the same student and course record system centralized in the main campus. However, some faculties like TID have their own local systems such as the Helpdesk software, the Electronic Coursework Management System (ECMS) and Electronic Document Management System (EDMS) all of which have their own local databases. Some of these local systems require accessing centralized data as well as local data in real time. Accessing centralize data has huge implication for data security. Also the centralized database is an Oracle database where as most of the local systems developed using SQL server. Consequently there is a demand for a secure, extendable and interoperable model.

To achieve this goal, the authors proposed a SOA model that includes an abstract service to present centralized student and course record database. A service implementation has been developed that implements the required authentication and authorization and interact with Oracle database (Figure 7).

Figure 7: Data Integration Model for Birmingham City University

The "centralized data abstract service" has been developed which includes the following functionalities:

- GetStudentByStudentNumber (student number) – get a student record
- GetStudentsByDateOfBirth (date of birth) – get list of students with same date of birth.
- GetCourse (faculty, academic period) – get list of active courses in a particular academic year for a particular faculty.

The "centralized data service" has been developed using Windows Communication Foundation (WCF) and hosted using a console application. Also, a client application has been developed that compares course data retrieved from centralized database with local data. This application then categorized the courses according to local system requirements and updates the local database. The client application is also able to validate a student record against centralize database (Figure 8).

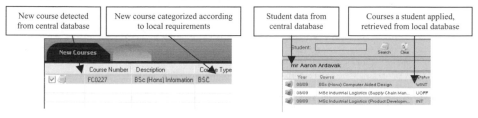

Figure 8: Database Integration

According to this model, the university's corporate ICT can develop number of services as a gateway to the main student and course record system using abstraction and grouping technique. Each faculty will be able to develop their local systems according to their requirements based on these services. Also, the backend databases can be changed later without affecting any of the client applications.

7. Business benefits

Historically, computing systems were developed based on a single platform in an isolated environment without interoperability to other platforms. For example a system developed on a Windows platform could communicate with other systems on the same platform, but there was no easy way to integrate this system with other platforms like UNIX. Today's industry cannot accept this limitation, so computing systems should be developed with interoperability to other platforms and Internet in mind. Service Oriented Architectures have been introduced to tackle these issues and have proven to be a successful and practical methodology. However there needs to be more research and improvement to this architecture to provide more facilities to tackle additional integration problems.

The model presented by this paper intends to extend the conventional SOA approach by introducing Service Abstraction and Service Grouping. Based on this approach, each service-based environment can be partitioned into number of service groups, and the behaviours of each group can be identified using an abstract service. Each service in the environment should be part of at least one group.

Using this model, it is possible to identify behaviour of the entire service-based environment by looking for the abstract services. A single environment could contain thousands of services and hundreds of abstract services, and it is clearly more efficient to examine hundreds of abstract services. Also using this model, new services can be added to the system dynamically, simply by implementing the required abstract services, without requiring other changes.

8.   Conclusion

The authors believe that this paper has demonstrated the feasibility of a generic SOA model to integrate various disparate subsystems such as databases, robots and devices developed under different hardware and software platforms into a single system. Additionally, as a technique inspired by object-orientation, service abstraction has been shown to be an effective means of designating groups of services providing similar functionality.

The authors proposed that a wide variety of enterprise systems can be developed quicker and more efficient by SOA, allowing different departments of a company to use their own local systems. Also SOA can be considered as an ultimate model to overcome most of integration issues facing different companies and organisations. As a result, the authors suggest that SOA could replace the traditional software development methodologies including Object Orientation. However, the authors also conclude that SOA requires further research and improvement to tackle wider integration problems.

References

[1] M.R. Majedi, K.A. Osman, A.J. Wilcox, "A Generic task partitioning framework for internet based control of multiple co-cooperatively working robotic devices", *Proceedings of the second International Conference on pervasive computing and applications*, Birmingham, UK, July. 26-27, 2007, pp. 451-456.
[2] D K Barry (2003), Web services and service-oriented architecture. San Francisco: Morgan Kaufman Publisher.
[3] Thomas Erl. Service-Oriented Architecture (SOA): Concepts, Technology and Design. 2005. Prentice Hall.
[4] Dirk Krafziq. Enterprise SOA: Service oriented architecture best practices. 2004. Prentice Hall.
[5] MSDN (2008). DSS User guide [Website]. Available from:
<http://msdn2.microsoft.com/en-us/library/bb905448.aspx> [Accessed: 12 March 2008]
[6] David L. Olson, "Managerial issues of enterprise resource planning systems". 2003. McGraw-Hill.
[7] Monk, Ellen & Wagner, Bret (2006), Concepts in Enterprise Resource Planning (Second ed.), Boston: Thomson Course Technology, ISBN 0-619-21663-8
[8] Fred A. Cummins, "Enterprise Integration: An Architecture for Enterprise Application and Systems Integration". 2002. Wiley.
[9] Gian Trotta (2003). Integration Best Practices - Dancing around EAI [Website]. Available from:
<http://www.ebizq.net/topics/int_sbp/features/3463.html > [Accessed: 29 April 2008]

CTracker: a Distributed BitTorrent Tracker Based on Chimera

Raúl JIMÉNEZ, Björn KNUTSSON
Kungliga Tekniska högskolan, Isafjordsgatan 39, Stockholm, 164 40, Sweden
Tel: +46 8 790 42 85, Fax: +46 8 751 17 93, Email: rauljc@kth.se; bkn@kth.se

Abstract: There are three major open issues in the BitTorrent peer discovery system, which are not solved by any of the currently deployed solutions. These issues seriously threaten BitTorrent's scalability, especially when considering that mainstream content distributors could start using BitTorrent for distributing content to millions of users simultaneously in the near future.
In this paper these issues are addressed by proposing a topology-aware distributed tracking system as a replacement for both centralized and Kademlia-based trackers.
An experiment measuring most popular open BitTorrent trackers is also presented. It shows that centralized trackers are not topology aware. We conclude that an ideal topology-aware tracker would return peers whose latency to the requester peer is significantly lower than of a centralized tracker.

1. Introduction

The BitTorrent protocol [1] distributes digital content using the resources every participant offers. Every participant is called a peer and a swarm is a set of peers participating in the distribution, i.e., downloading and uploading of a given content.

Nowadays the most popular swarms on the most popular BitTorrent public trackers hold a few tens of thousand peers. BitTorrent usage is continuously increasing and with the participation of legal content distributors we can expect the usage to skyrocket. When content providers start distributing popular TV shows and movies through BitTorrent we should not be surprised to have several millions of peers participating simultaneously in a single swarm.

Big players are already moving towards on-line content distribution by using different peer-to-peer and hybrid systems, for instance, BBC with its successful iPlayer [2]. Furthermore, among others, BBC and the European Broadcaster Union participate in the P2P-Next project [3]. P2P-Next is a Seventh Research Framework Programme project, which aims to become the standard for on-line content distribution using the BitTorrent framework.

The BitTorrent tracker is a key component of the BitTorrent framework. A tracker is set up in order to track the participants within a swarm. Every peer willing to join the swarm contacts the tracker and requests a list of peers participating in the swarm. Then this peer will contact the peers in the list in order to download/upload content from/to them.

Unfortunately, there are three major open issues that threaten the reliability of the tracking system. (1) The tracker is a single point of failure. When a tracker fails the current members of the swarm are not affected but no other peer will be able to join. (2) The tracker faces a scalability issue since it is only able to handle a finite number of peers based on the processing power and bandwidth available. (3) The third issue is locality, and it is more subtle: when you contact the tracker, you will receive a random subset of the available peers. This means that while a local peer may exist, you may only be notified of peers on other continents, resulting in both higher global bandwidth consumption and lower download speed.

The single point of failure issue has been addressed by distributing the tracking tasks among the peers. There are two implementations both based on a DHT (Distributed Hash Table) called Kademlia [4]. Several problems have, however, been found on both of them [5] and there is no visible effort towards fixing them because they are not considered critical but a backup mechanism should the tracker fail.

The scalability issue also affects the distributed trackers because the small set of nodes that are responsible for tracking a specific swarm (8 or 20 nodes in the current implementations) will receive every query. Kademlia partially distributes this responsibility by caching part of the address list on the nearby nodes. This caching feature, however, is not good enough. Although the caching nodes help replying requests, the core nodes must still keep track of every single peer in the swarm.

The locality issue is a consequence of the equality of the peers. From the tracker's point of view there is no discernible difference among peers, therefore it is not able to return a list consisting of the "best" peers, but rather just a random set of peers. In order to improve locality, the tracker could use different heuristics such as geolocation services but that would imply an extra overload. Probably that is the reason why trackers lack this feature.

This paper proposes a system that addresses the three issues described in this section.

2. Objectives

The main objective of this paper is to present a design for a topology-aware scalable distributed tracker based on Chimera, which addresses the issues explained in the introduction. In addition, we will outline some additional benefits of our proposed design.

We also show, through our simple experiment, that there is ample room for improvement. The difference between the ideal tracker and the current centralized tracker implementations is large enough to justify the research on this topic and the replacement of the current tracking system.

3. System Overview

We have undertaken a study of the behavior of the BitTorrent protocol and extensions, and the currently available DHT technologies. Based on the results, we designed and implemented a prototype and compared its behavior with the existing BitTorrent implementations [6].

In this paper a different approach is suggested. Instead of designing, implementing and deploying a completely new protocol we propose to replace just the DHT system in the current BitTorrent framework. We consider that, by being BitTorrent backwards compatible, this DHT replacement can be implemented and deployed more easily, increasing drastically the probability of a large-scale deployment.

Furthermore, we are considering, together with the Tribler research team, to integrate Chimera's key properties into the existing Kademlia-based DHT. If this is possible, the new solution would be fully backwards compatible with Mainline DHT clients. This task, however, is out of the scope of this paper and regarded as future work.

3.1 Distributed Tracker within the BitTorrent Framework

BitTorrent applications using a distributed tracker have two components: (1) a peer which uses the BitTorrent protocol to download/upload data from/to other peers and (2) a node that is a member of the DHT and performs the distributed tracker's tasks.

As stated in the introduction the existing implementations of distributed trackers fail to address the scalability and locality issues. We consider that a topology aware framework offers us the properties needed to address these issues. This framework would allow us to spread small lists of topologically close peers among the nodes; contrary to assigning the task of tracking the whole swarm to a small set of nodes (one node plus a few replicas).

There is a framework called Chimera whose properties fulfill the requirements for such system.

3.2   Chimera's Routing Algorithm

In this subsection a brief description of Chimera's behavior is given. Further information about Chimera is located in the Related Work section.

Chimera [7] is a topology-aware DHT overlay. It routes each message through a number of nodes until it reaches the destination node. Every node in the path processes the message and routes it to another node whose identifier is closer –i.e, more prefix matching bits– to the destination identifier. A node is a destination of a message when there is no node whose identifier is closer in the identifier space –node and destination identifiers might match but that case is very rare.

When routing a message, a node forwards it to the topologically closest node among the candidates. This behavior makes Chimera topology aware, especially during the first hops into the DHT; contrary to the current BitTorrent DHT's behavior, where hops are randomly long all the way to the destination.

Furthermore, intermediate nodes can cache and retrieve results, a key property used by our design, which will be explained in depth later.

3.3   Integrating Chimera as Distributed BitTorrent Tracker

Nodes can send two kind of messages: announce and find_peers. Every message is routed according to a modified version of Chimera's routing algorithm that is explained along this section.

An announce message contains a [IP, port number] pair and its destination is a swarm identifier. This message announces that this peer is participating in a swarm and where it can be contacted by other peers. Every node in the path stores the [peer, swarm] pair and routes the message. There is no reply for this message.

A find_peers message is addressed to a swarm identifier and it is created by a node looking for peers participating in the swarm. Every node in the path checks whether it has information about the swarm. If there is a list of peers for that swarm, that list is sent to the requester. Otherwise the message is forwarded to the next node.

So far the scalability related to the centralized tracker and locality issues have been addressed, allowing intermediate nodes to return small lists of topologically-close peers. This is still not good enough, however, since the destination of a very popular swarm –say 10 million peers– will receive every single announce message and keep track of every peer.

Solving this issue is the main contribution of this paper and it justifies replacing the current DHT used in the BitTorrent framework.

3.4   Scalability Improvement over the Current Distributed Trackers

Chimera's routing algorithm can be modified to forward only a limited number of announce messages. In this way, destination nodes tracking a few tens of peers will keep track of every peer in the swarm but when the swarm reaches 10 millions of peers this node will only track a limited number of peers (the topologically closest peers).

In the modified routing algorithm there are two new parameters m and n where $n \geq m$. The parameter m is the maximum number of announce messages to be forwarded per swarm and n is the maximum number of peers stored in a swarm list. The swarm list is ordered by the distance –network latency– from the node to the peers stored in the list. These parameters can be calculated independently by every node and might be dynamic depending the node's configuration and workload. For instance, a powerful node which wants to store every announcement received might set n to infinite, however, it must be more careful setting m in order to keep the DHT bandwidth overhead low.

Every node in the path of an announce message measures the latency to the new peer and tries to add it to the swarm list. If the list length is already n and the new peer is not closer than any other in the list then the message is dropped. If the list length is between n and m, the new peer will be added to the list, but the message will only be forwarded if the new element is inserted among the m lowest latency peers. Lastly, if the list is shorter than m elements, the message is forwarded following the original Chimera routing algorithm.

One may think that the fact a high latency node (e.g, satellite connections) can be isolated by dropping its announce messages is a design flaw. If this node happens to join a busy swarm and the next node in the Chimera overlay has already a list with n elements, the message will be dropped and there will be no reference to its participation in the whole DHT. Unfortunately for this node, that is exactly what is desired; close nodes are easy to find and the far-away ones are not. This node can, however, always send find_peers messages and discover other peers, therefore there is no risk of total isolation. In a sense, it would have the same effect as a peer behind a NAT or firewall, where the peer can establish connections to others but cannot be contacted by other peers.

3.5   Additional Benefits

Not only will this system improve tracker's scalability, but it can also decrease costs for ISPs. Being able to find topologically close peers, peers can easily discover other peers within the same ISP, thus reducing inter-ISP traffic. Furthermore, ISPs could offer users incentives to decrease inter-ISP traffic even further (e.g., by increasing link speed in connections within the ISP's network and/or setting up an easy to find peer offering cached content).

This is not a minor benefit, since BitTorrent traffic represents an important fraction of the total Internet traffic [8] and some ISPs are trying to control this by caching, throttling or banning BitTorrent traffic, in order to reduce costs and impact on other traffic [9-10].

4. Centralized Tracker Versus Topology-Aware Decentralized Tracker

In this section, the results from a small-scale experiment show how topology (un)aware the most popular BitTorrent centralized trackers are. Then, these results are compared to an ideal topology-aware decentralized tracker.

The BitTorrent specifications [11] do not specify how many peers a tracker should return as a response to a peer's query, nor how these peers should be selected. It is believed that most of the tracker implementations return a list of random peers, i.e., trackers are not topology aware.

In our experiment, the most popular torrent files in Mininova.org were downloaded. Since mininova offers torrent files tracked by different trackers, several tracker implementations are analyzed at once. The results show, however, that there are no discernible differences among different trackers regarding topology awareness.

A total of 79 swarms were analyzed. Every 5 minutes a request was sent to every tracker, obtaining 79 lists of peers. Then, the latency to these peers was measured by using tcptraceroute to every peer in the list. This process was repeated 5 times.

One of the most interesting findings is that most of the peers were not reachable on the port announced to the tracker. The suggested explanations are: peers no longer on-line, NATs, and firewalls; and has been reported by other experiments on BitTorrent [12]. In total, 11578 reachable peers were measured; around 150 peers per swarm (i.e., 30 reachable peers per request on average).

In Figure 1 the average latency to the peers is plotted. For every swarm there are five points and two curves, where five points represent the average latency to the peers in the list returned to each request. One curve represents the average latency to every peer measured within the swarm while the other shows the average latency to the x lowest latency peers in the swarm.

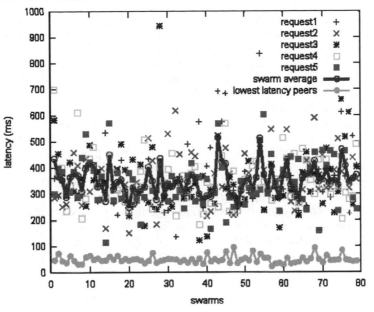

Figure 1: Latency measurements to peers participating in popular BitTorrent swarms

This last curve represents the ideal list of peers that a topology aware tracker should return and it is calculated as follows. The tracker returns 5 lists of torrents as response to our 5 requests. We check the reachability of peers in every list and calculate the average number of reachable peers per request which will be called x. If the tracker were ideally topology-aware it should have returned just the x lowest latency peers whose average is plotted in the figure forming the "lowest latency peers" curve.

The figure shows that the average latency for different requests is as random as we can expect, when assuming that trackers return lists of random peers. It also shows that the difference between the average latency to every peer returned (swarm average) and to the ideal list (lowest latency peers) is between 5 and 10 times. While the former backs our initial assumption, the latter shows a large room for improvement in BitTorrent trackers.

Our measurements so far have confirmed our hypothesis, but we are continuously working to study larger swarms, and we will also start monitoring swarms from multiple vantage points.

5. Related Work

In this section background information about DHT and Chimera is given.

5.1 Distributed Hash Tables

Several structured lookup protocols [13] have been studied in order to choose one that offers the characteristics this system needs. Chord [14] is one of the most well-known DHT. Actually, Kademlia [4] is a Chord derivation used in BitTorrent. Although these protocols provide a distributed lookup system, they do not offer topology awareness.

On the other hand, Tapestry [15] is a structured lookup protocol that provides this characteristic. Moreover, its implementation in C –called Chimera– is flexible enough to be adapted to our needs. In this project, Chimera was chosen as lookup overlay, whose description will be explained next.

5.2   Chimera

As an implementation of Tapestry, Chimera routes messages from one node to a destination's root. In Chimera, each node has a unique identifier. Each node has several routing tables, with references to its nearest neighbors within a level.

A link belongs to a level, depending on the length of the shared prefix of the identifiers of the two nodes involved. For instance, let identifiers in hexadecimal and 4-bit levels, node 6E83 has links of level 4 to nodes whose identifier are 6E8*, level 3 to nodes 6E** and so on. In fact, this is similar to IP routing.

A message from one node to another is routed choosing the highest level link in each step. Since each step routes the message through a greater level, the maximum number of hops is $\log_\beta(N)$, where the identifiers are expressed in base β and N is the length of the identifier. Moreover, since each node routes the messages through its nearest neighbor in that level, the paths are deterministic and topologically aware. At the last hop, the message's and the node's identifiers match, then the message is delivered.

Each object –torrent identifier– has a unique identifier as well. When any node wants to perform an operation over an object (publish, unpublish, lookup, etc.), the message is routed to the block's identifier. Since most likely there will not be a node matching it, the message will reach its destination's root. This is the node whose identifier is the closest to the block's one.

Then, a publish(objectID) is delivered to the objectID's root and this node stores all the references to objectID. In the path, each node which forwards the publish messages also stores the references. A lookup message will be routed in the same manner, however, at any hop it will reach a node which stores a list of references –list of peers participating in the swarm. This node can stop the lookup and return its list of references. This list will be shorter than the root's one and these references were likely published by the closest nodes to the requester.

The main difference between Chimera and Tapestry is that Tapestry reaches the node that actually published an object, while Chimera only routes the messages. Because of the aforementioned property it was possible to use Chimera in this design.

6. Conclusions

In this paper a design of a topology-aware distributed BitTorrent tracker has been presented. This design addresses three key open issues in the current BitTorrent tracker system. We explained how the scalability of the whole system is improved drastically by removing the existence of hot spots in the DHT. This is a desirable property nowadays but it will be absolutely necessary when mainstream content providers offer their content on the BitTorrent framework in the near future.

ISPs will play a key role in P2P content distribution. This design provides mechanisms to reduce inter-ISP traffic, improving user experience (lower lookup latency and increased download speed), without increasing dramatically the ISP's costs.

Our experiment has shown how the most popular open BitTorrent trackers behave and how far their results are from an ideal topology aware system. This backs our initial hypothesis that there is a large room for improvement and encourages us to implement the described system in order to measure its performance.

Future work includes modifying Tribler [16], a BitTorrent-based content distribution framework developed by a research team at Delft University, integrating this design, and comparing performance against the current unmodified version.

Acknowledgment

The research leading to these results has received funding from the Seventh Framework Programme (FP7/2007-2013) under grant agreement n° 21617.

References

[1] B. Cohen. Incentives build robustness in BitTorrent. In Proceedings of the First Workshop on the Economics of Peer-to-Peer Systems, Berkeley, CA, June 2003.

[2] BBC. iPlayer. http://www.bbc.co.uk/iplayer/ (April 2008)

[3] P2P-Next. http://www.p2p-next.org/ (April 2008)

[4] P. Maymounkov and D. Mazieres. Kademlia: A peerto -peer information system based on the xor metric. In Proceedings of IPTPS02, Cambridge, USA, March 2002. http://www.cs.rice.edu/Conferences/IPTPS02/.

[5] Scott A Crosby and Dan S Wallach An Analysis of BitTorrent's Two Kademlia-Based DHTs Technical Report TR-07-04, Department of Computer Science, Rice University, June 2007.

[6] R. Jiménez. Ant: A Distributed Data Storage And Delivery System Aware of the Underlaying Topology. Master Thesis. KTH, Stockholm, Sweden. August 2006.

[7] CURRENT Lab, U. C. Santa Barbara. Chimera Project. http://current.cs.ucsb.edu/projects/chimera/ (April 2008)

[8] A. Parker. The true picture of peer-to-peer filesharing, 2004. http://www.cachelogic.com/. (April 2008)

[9] TorrenFreak. Virgin Media CEO Says Net Neutrality is "A Load of Bollocks". http://torrentfreak.com/virgin-media-ceo-says-net-neutrality-is-a-load-of-bollocks-080413/ (April 2008)

[10] The Register. Californian sues Comcast over BitTorrent throttling. http://www.theregister.co.uk/2007/11/15/comcast_sued_over_bittorrent_blockage/ (April 2008)

[11] Bram Cohen. The BitTorrent Protocol Specification http://www.bittorrent.org/beps/bep_0003.html (April 2008)

[12] J. Pouwelse, P. Garbacki, D. Epema, and H. Sips, "A measurement study of the bittorrent peer-to-peer file-sharing system," Tech. Rep. PDS-2004-007, Delft University of Technology, Apr. 2004.

[13] Frank Dabek, Ben Zhao, Peter Druschel, and Ion Stoica. Towards a common API for structured peer-to-peer overlays. In IPTPS '03, Berkeley, CA, February 2003.

[14] I. Stoica, R. Morris, D. Karger, M. F. Kaashoek, and H. Balakrishnan. Chord: A scalable peer-to-peer lookup service for Internet applications. Technical Report TR-819, MIT, March 2001.

[15] Ben Zhao, John Kubiatowicz, and Anthony Joseph. Tapestry: An infrastructure for fault-tolerant wide-area location and routing. Technical Report UCB/CSD-01-1141, Computer Science Division, U. C. Berkeley, April 2001. 55

[16] J.A. Pouwelse and P. Garbacki and J. Wang and A. Bakker and J. Yang and A. Iosup and D.H.J. Epema and M. Reinders and M. van Steen and H.J. Sips (2008). Tribler: A social-based peer-to-peer system. Concurrency and Computation: Practice and Experience 20:127-138. http://www.tribler.org/

Collaboration and the Knowledge Economy: Issues, Applications, Case Studies
P. Cunningham and M. Cunningham (Eds.)
IOS Press, 2008

iSURF -An Interoperability Service Utility for Collaborative Supply Chain Planning across Multiple Domains: Textile Supply Chain Pilot

Asuman DOGAC[1], Gokce B. LALECI[2], Alper OKCAN[1], Mehmet OLDUZ[2], Michele SESANA[3] and Alessandro CANEPA[4]

[1] *Dept. of Computer Engineering, Middle East Technical University, İnönü Bulvari, Ankara, 06531, Turkey*
Tel: +90 312 2405598, Fax: + 90 312 2101259, Email: asuman@metu.edu.tr
[2]*Software Research, Development and Consultancy Ltd., METU-KOSGEB Tekmer, Ankara, 06531, Turkey*
Tel: +90 312 2102076, Fax: + 90 312 2105572, Email: (gokce,mehmet)@srdc.com.tr
[3] *TXT e-Solutions S.p.A, Via Frigia, 27 - 20126 Milano – Italy*
Tel: +39.0225771804, Fax: +39.0225771828, Email: michele.sesana@txt.it
[4]*Fratelli PIACENZA S.p.A., Regione Cisi, 13814 Pollone - Italy,*
Tel: +390156191237, Email: alessandro.canepa@piacenza1733.it

Abstract: One of the key challenges in supply chain collaboration is to improve the efficiency and effectiveness of the supply chain planning process to handle rapidly changing customer demands. Trading partners usually have different competencies based on their business strategies and investments. They have varying sources of information and also dissimilar views of the marketplace. The distributed intelligence of multiple trading partners needs to be collaboratively exploited in the planning and fulfilment of customer demand in the supply chain so as to enhance supply chain responsiveness.

This paper discusses the technical issues to be addressed for achieving an intelligent collaborative supply chain planning network in which distributed intelligence of multiple trading partners are exploited in the planning and fulfilment of customer demand in the supply chain. This work is supported by the European Commission through ICT- 213031-iSURF project.

1. Introduction

In order to guarantee the survival in today's competitive and demanding digital world of business, the European companies, especially SMEs, should be more agile, self-sustainable and responsive to the changes in the supply chain. Obtaining and maintaining a competitive edge in supply chain is not only the concern of individual SMEs, but should also be jointly addressed by the entire chain. The supply chain partners should collaborate effectively to better align supply and demand forecasts to have a joint strategy for handling exceptions in the way of realizing "the network is the business" vision.

In order to achieve collaborative inter-enterprise planning there is a need for a joint planning process, defining when and how this information should be collected, and which application is responsible for assessing this information in order to create joint supply chain forecasts, replenishment and exception management strategies.

Industry realized this need and has produced "Collaborative Planning, Forecasting, and Replenishment (CPFR)" guidelines. CPFR formalizes the processes between two trading partners used to agree upon a joint plan and forecast, monitor success through replenishment, and recognize and respond to any exceptions [1]. The main idea behind sharing forecast data in the planning phase comes from the fact that trading partners have different competencies based on their strategies and investments. Also, the trading partners have different sources of information and different views of the market. The objective of CPFR is to increase the accuracy of demand forecasts and replenishment plans, which is necessary to lower inventories across the supply chain and attain high service levels of the right products in right locations [2].

CPFR envisions providing significant effects on the supply chain; however the effects will be dramatic only when it is completely integrated with the demand plan of an enterprise, in which the production cycle is synchronized with CPFR order cycle. There are two important challenges in order to facilitate the smooth implementation of CPFR: (I) technical interoperability of the planning and forecasting business documents, (II) costly and labour intensive deployment of CPFR processes within a supply chain consortium.

The key requirement for successful collaboration between partners in a supply chain is the existence of technical infrastructure in accordance with the goals of the collaboration [3]. In order to facilitate CPFR, the trading partners should have the necessary infrastructure to build, share and adjust online forecasts and plans. However, since CPFR does not mandate any messaging standard to be used in the collaboration process, the semantic interoperability of the planning and forecasting business documents exchanged between the companies must be addressed.

In successful CPFR pilot applications, it has been reported that the definition and deployment of CPFR processes within a supply chain consortium is too costly and labour intensive [10]. Although CPFR provides guidelines, no machine processable process templates have been defined. It is necessary to support companies by providing tools in order to build the joint inter-enterprise collaboration process and automate legacy application integration.

In the iSURF project it is aimed to create an open collaborative supply chain planning environment for European SMEs to address these problems.

2. Objectives

The iSURF project aims to develop a collaborative supply chain planning environment based on CPFR guidelines addressing the interoperability challenges of deploying a CPFR process within a supply chain consortium.

The iSURF architecture will be deployed in the premises of Fratelli PIACENZA, a manufacturer of fine woollen fabrics and supplier to many world-leading apparel brand manufacturers, including Boss and INCO/Zegna. In the following sections we introduce the as-is business model of PIACENZA's textile supply chain and describe how we aim to enhance this process through iSURF components enabling collaborative planning.

2.1 AS-IS Business Model of PIACENZA Textile Supply Chain

The PIACENZA textile supply chain is dramatically stressed to optimize highly complex production cycle in a very fragmented sector, where companies with different dimensions, structures, locations and languages must collaborate to manufacture products in a very short production life cycle.

PIACENZA is composed of two different business units: "Fabric division" and "Finished products (knitwear division)". The fabric division receives raw material from the supplier and, after the production phase, sells its products directly to the retailers or to its knitwear division. The latter unit sells the finished products to the retailers at the end of its production phase. In this way each division acts as a customer/supplier of the other and both have highly customized tools for specific production, developed at different times and in different ways and no direct information exchange is possible between them. In this paper we concentrate on the supply chain between PIACENZA Knitwear division and its retailers.

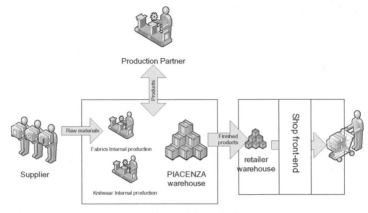

Figure 1 PIACENZA supply chain

The activities performed in this part of the supply chain can be summarized as follows:

- PIACENZA shows a first version of its product to all the retailers
- The retailer sends its order related to the preferred products
- PIACENZA starts its production only when it receives an order
- Finished products are shipped to the customer
- Meanwhile the retailer sells the products
- PIACENZA acts as retailer's warehouse producing the product that can be reordered by customer
- When a new order comes from the retailer, PIACENZA sends the goods available in the warehouse adding a new production activity related to products that are not available in its warehouse
- When the order is accomplished (all the products are available in the PIACENZA warehouse), the goods are shipped

In the current business model, the business documents exchanged between PIACENZA and Retailers are Order, Order confirmation and Transfer documents. Unfortunately, the document formats used by all of the retailers and PIACENZA are not uniform.

Currently one of the biggest problems of this as-is business model for PIACENZA is to forecast the amount of retail sold goods in order to increase the efficiency and efficacy of the item production for the stock service and minimize its final warehouse stock. Retailers today do not share their Point-of-Sale data with PIACENZA; for this reason PIACENZA has to prepare its replenishment plan without any information about the number of sold goods.

This situation generates a lot of problems such as:

- Slow response time to replenishment orders or even infeasibility to respond to the replenishment orders in the stock phase,
- Decreased efficiency of production phase,
- No information about market direction (which products have been sold in-time and which ones are sold only at discount time).

Another important problem in the as-is business model is the different codes used by PIACENZA and the retailers to identify product items. Each kind of product is associated with a product code composed of six fields by PIACENZA. This code is translated into a unique serial number used for internal activities in PIACENZA. The code is applied to the item by a barcode. It is also possible to reconstruct the original coding structure from serial number. Retailers mainly do not use this code; usually they recode it in their proprietary format. For example in the PIACENZA retail point, the product code is composed of three fields that are different from the producer ones and translated into a different serial number. This means that each time a product arrives in the retail point, it has to be recoded manually. The same problem occurs when the retailer is a multibrand retailer. Even in the stock-house owned by PIACENZA there is the recoding problem: the software used in the stock-house has been produced by different companies, and produces different product codes with different purposes and fields.

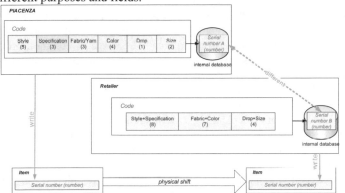

Figure 2: recoding problem between PIACENZA knitwear division and PIACENZA retail

2.2   TO-BE Business Model of PIACENZA Textile Supply Chain

The problems of the as-is business model of PIACENZA can be summarized as follows:

- Product recoding between retailers and PIACENZA
- Inefficient information management through the value chain: Lack of information exchange between PIACENZA and the retailers resulting in unrealistic replenishment plans and entirely order-based production plans
- Document exchanged in Supply chain are in different formats
- Barcodes are slow and do not contains detailed information about product; Manual data entry; No item traceability; No historical data available for items
- Significant time spent in warehouses to calculate inventory levels
- No real planning synchronization between partners; Inaccurate transactions and Long lead times

The available business process of the textile supply chain of PIACENZA is re-engineered based on the functionalities provided by iSURF platform. The enhancements can be summarized as follows:

- The current supply chain visibility gathering architecture based on barcodes and manual information reading will be replaced by an RFID infrastructure: The actual system based on barcodes is not satisfactory: it is slow, requires significant human effort that generates high cost and low precision and does not provide any additional features to the system. The "to be" goal is to set up an RFID based system where each item will be identified by a single identifier in the whole supply-chain. The system will introduce a non-intrusive anti theft system, an auto-shelf utility and an auto inventory/inventory check mechanism. Other benefits can be summarized as:

- Item traceability will be achieved through the RFID based supply chain visibility system. For PIACENZA, it is important to monitor its products: know where they are (warehouse to be shipped, shipped, shop, sold), to know exactly the physical item position (first shelf, on the left part at the middle of the warehouse).
- Item counterfeit control will be achieved by the RFID based supply chain visibility system.
- Item quality control will be handled to identify quality defects and trace these items along the supply chain.

- Master Data Synchronization will be achieved. In order to maintain updated and synchronized information about products, a common reference model will be used based on the available standards. In this way product IDs and master data will be accessible to all partners. PIACENZA will be able to insert/update/delete data into this system, and on the other hand, retailers will be informed about product creation/changes maintaining automatically synchronized data. The usage of common product data will avoid recoding activities between partners, out-of-date information and data mismatches.
- The replenishment efficiency will be increased through a collaborative planning environment that enables the definition and execution of a well defined collaboration process. This collaborative planning environment will make use of the synchronized master data, the real time supply chain visibility data gathered from each member of the supply chain, enable sharing and comparing replenishment plans and forecasts and provide a set of instruments to handle exceptions.
- Document Reconciliation will be achieved in order to address the interoperability problem of the planning documents conforming to different standards that are exchanged in the collaborative planning process.

3. Methodology and Technology Description

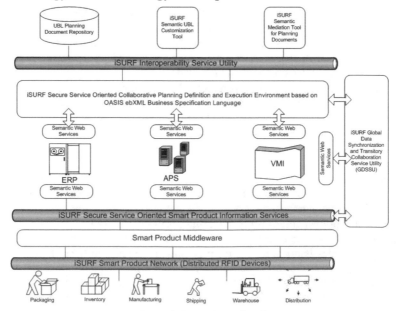

Figure 3 iSURF General Architecture

In this section, we present how to address the problems of PIACENZA as-is business model through iSURF components to enable the to-be business model. The iSURF general architecture is presented in Figure 3. In order to increase the adoption of a collaborative supply chain planning environment, the architecture includes a service oriented supply chain planning process definition and execution architecture. In the iSURF architecture, the interaction with legacy planning applications are achieved through semantically enriched Web services implemented as legacy adapters. The interoperability of business documents exchanged within the scope of this planning process is addressed by iSURF Interoperability Service Utility. Finally, the supply chain visibility data is collected through a smart product architecture implemented based on EPCGlobal [4] guidelines, and master data synchronization is achieved through Global Data Synchronization Service Utility.

The functionalities of these components can be summarized as follows:

- The semantic interoperability of the planning and forecasting business documents exchanged between the companies are achieved through the iSURF Interoperability Service Utility provided. In iSURF Interoperability Service Utility OASIS Universal Business language (UBL) [5] is used as a common denominator. UBL is an OASIS initiative to develop a common vocabulary in exchanging business documents using XML syntax. For this purpose first of all, UBL Planning messages are created using the UN/CEFACT Core Components [6] methodology. The architecture also allows customization of these UBL planning messages to the needs of different industries through a semantic customization process. As a result of this customization process, semantic mediation of planning document instances will be enabled.

- In order to support trading partners to deploy CPFR processes and integrate their internal enterprise planning applications to the joint planning process, the joint collaborative planning process are defined via a graphical interface through predefined CPFR building blocks. These CPFR building blocks are defined in a standard, machine processable business process specification language, namely, OASIS ebXML Business Specification Language, (ebBP) [7]. The companies are enabled to build the joint inter-enterprise collaboration process by grouping these building blocks. Through this platform, it is possible to define the following planning process parameters:
  - What data is needed from the supply chain partners? What data is collaborated on?
  - Which systems provide the data? How the interaction with the underlying legacy systems is achieved?
  - How is the exchanged data translated if they are not directly compatible?
  - Who owns the process for sharing the data and which application will process the data?
  - Is the data publicly shared or is it secured, through which protocols?
  - What frequency is the data communicated?

  The platform produces a service oriented, executable collaborative planning process to be enacted among different supply chain partners.

- iSURF Global Data Synchronization Service Utility ensures the accuracy and reliability of master data used in the supply chain by developing standard based open platform for SMEs. While developing the system the GS1 Global Data Synchronization Network (GDSN) [8] standards are used. GDSN is a network that connects data pools, which are regional sources of manufacturer and retailer data, to the GS1 Global Registry. The GS1 Global Registry lets companies locate the source (manufacturer) or the recipient (retailer) data pools so that data is standardized and synchronized for trading partners on a near real-time basis. The organizations using the GDSN pays fee based on their annual turnover. Since iSURF aims to create a business network addressing the specific needs of SMEs, iSURF project will develop a Global Data Synchronization and

Transitory Collaboration Service Utility (GDSSU) targeting SMEs to share synchronized data on a near real-time basis as presented in Figure 4.

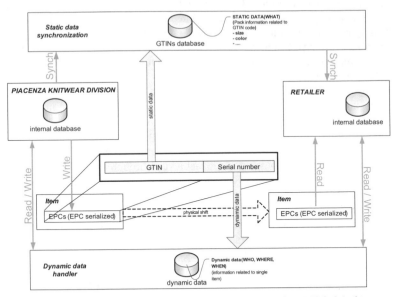

Figure 4 iSURF Global Data synchronization Service Utility and EPCGlobal Architecture

- The iSURF Open Smart Product Infrastructure is capable of filtering and aggregating the acquired smart product data through RFIDs and also correlating them with other business parameters. It is developed based on EPCGlobal Standards. Not all of the data from all of the RFID tags may be interest to the enterprise application. In this respect, the infrastructure eliminates redundant information coming from RFID tags attached to smart products and will provide the filtered data to business applications. When dealing with the processed data, enterprise applications may require dynamic information about the product such as the production or the expiry date. In such a case, iSURF Smart Product Infrastructure will provide required interfaces for gathering necessary data from subscribed party where the product is manufactured.

4. Business Benefits

Voluntary Interindustry Commerce Solutions (VICS) reported that over 300 companies have implemented the process since the publication of CPFR guidelines in 1998. Numerous case studies of CPFR projects report in-stock percentage improvements of from 2-8% for products in stores, accompanied by inventory reductions of 10-40% across the supply chain [9]. Syncra Systems and Industry Directions also conducted a survey of manufacturers, retailers, distributors and logistics providers [2]. According to this survey respondents report:

- An 80% increase in business opportunities for a CPFR partner
- $9M increase in sales
- Simultaneous sales growth and inventory reductions of at least 10%
- Improved availability rates with less inventory

  In parallel with these results, in the textile supply chain planning pilot application of iSURF project we aim to achieve the following business benefits:
- Increase replenishment efficiency and efficacy through collaboration activities

- Improve interoperability among supply chain partners
- Increased product data synchronization
- Reduce human interaction during data gathering
- Quick and synchronized transfer of information between supply chain partners
- Increase the amount of information that can be traced related to product items
- Reduce costs
- Achieve shorter production time during the stock phase
- Allow item traceability

5. Conclusions

The iSURF project develops an intelligent collaborative supply chain planning network that realizes a knowledge-oriented inter-enterprise collaboration environment in which distributed intelligence of multiple trading partners are exploited in the planning and fulfilment of customer demand in the supply chain. The project provides interoperability solutions for achieving the semantic reconciliation of the planning and forecasting business documents exchanged between the companies according to different standards. The developed system will be deployed in textile supply chain to increase efficiency and efficacy of supply chain planning and hence reducing costs. In this paper, we describe how the end user of the iSURF Project, namely PIACENZA, will benefit from the infrastructure.

Acknowledgement

The research leading to these results has received funding from the European Community's Seventh Framework Programme (FP7/2007-2013) under grant agreement n° 213031

References

[1] "Collaborative Planning, Forecasting and Replenishment Version 2.0", Voluntary Interindustry Commerce Standards, Global Commerce Initiative Recommended Guidelines, June 2002.
[2] "The Next Wave of Supply Chain Advantage: Collaborative Planning, Forecasting and Replenishment", Industry Directions Inc. and Syncra Systems, April 2000
[3] "A Guide to CPFR Implementation",
    http://www.ecrnet.org/04-publications/blue_books/pub_2001_a_guide_to_cpfr_implementation.pdf
[4] EPCGlobal, Electronic Product Code Standardization, http://www.epcglobalinc.org/home
[5] OASIS Universal Business Language, www.oasis-open.org/committees/ubl, accessed 04.03.2008.
[6] UN/CEFACT   Core   Components   Technical   Specification,
    http://www.unece.org/cefact/ebxml/CCTS_V2-01_Final.pdf
[7] ebXML Business Process Specification Language, http://www.oasis-open.org/committees/tc_home.
    php?wg_abbrev=ebxml-bp
[8] GS1 Global Data Synchronisation Network (GDSN), http://www.gs1.org/productssolutions/gdsn/
[9] "Collaborative Planning, Forecasting and Replenishment", Voluntary Interindustry Commerce Standards, May 2004.
[10] European CPFR Insights,
    http://www.ecrnet.org/04-publications/blue_books/pub_2002_cpfr_european_insights.pdf

Section 4.3

Case Studies

Evaluation and Testing as Support for a Consistent Architecture Development

Hugo Miguel VIEIRA[1], Fernando Luís FERREIRA[1], John KENNEDY[2],
Ricardo JARDIM-GONCALVES[3]

[1]UNINOVA, Intelligent Robotics Center, Quinta da Torre 2829-516 Monte Caparica, Portugal
Tel: +351212 948337; Fax: +351 212 941253; Email: hmv@uninova.pt, flf@uninova.pt
[2] Intel, Collinstown Industrial Park, Leixlip, Co. Kildare, IRELAND
Tel: +353 1 6068066, Email: john.m.kenedy@intel.com
[3]Faculty of Sciences and Technology, New University of Lisbon,
Campus FCT/UNL, 2829-516 Monte Caparica, Portugal
Tel: +351212 948337; Fax: +351 212 941253; Email: rg@uninova.pt

Abstract: Today, quality needs for software application architectures development are more complex and critical than ever due to the systems complexity, dimension and the interoperability needs to interact with third party applications and infrastructures. This paper defends that system evaluation and testing methods should be based in standard methodologies and processes and that it should be performed through the whole lifecycle of an architecture development. To guarantee the development quality of the architecture, the ISO/IEC CD 2504n of the SQuaRE series of standards will be taken as reference methodology to provides a process description for evaluating the quality of software products and also states the requirements for the components of the architecture. The design, visualization, specification, analysis, development, and report of the test and evaluation procedures that will be applied to the architecture and its components will take as basis the UML testing profile published by OMG. With such an approach, quality assessment establishes a testing methodology trough the lifecycle of the software development that will ensure quality control, reliability and further sustainability on the development of architecture.

1. Introduction

Traditionally, software architecture and design provide the basis for all subsequent system development. The system architecture should meet all requirements prior to the development stage. The implementation of the architecture should be subject to standards and metrics and should be validated at the end to verify aspects such as functional requirements, levels of performance and scalability of the business processes. This confirmed conformity and functionality are the final step of validation for the architecture implementation. Usually, when software components are developed, the main concern of the developers is to have the vision of the global system and to design the architecture towards the goals proposed. Once these are addressed, validation and testing conformance are then introduced, playing a major role at the final stages of the project. However, the problem then arises that the needs for the testing and conformity procedures could conflict with the established architecture. Furthermore, some tests could require the redesign of otherwise complete components. In some cases duplication of work or the development of additional components would be needed in order to cope with the testing requirements. Thus inefficiency is introduced as it implies a return to the initial phases of the design, with the potential for significant recoding.

When working in collaborative environments, establishing a testing methodology at the design phase ensures a more efficient implementation of the test environment. Overcoming those final adjustments that can compromise the initial design of the architecture as testing and evaluation is tackled in parallel with the architecting of the components [1].

Design is an important aspect in software development, because it heavily influences the cost of the implementation and maintenance phases. The design phase only takes 5%-10% of the total effort, but a large part of the total effort goes into improving design decisions/structure [2].

The objective of this paper is to propose an innovative methodology that addresses the evaluation procedures in parallel with the design of the architecture in order to ensure early integration of evaluation components. The methodology is first described, followed by a description of a case study in which it is being applied. Software Architects, Developers and Quality Control Managers are the main targets of the proposed approach in order to minimise code-churn in later stages of projects, thereby reducing the potential for defects and reducing recoding costs.

The methodology is based on the Evaluation reference model ISO/IEC CD 2504n of the SQuaRE [3] series of standards. These describe a process for evaluating the quality of software products and also set the requirements for the components of the architecture. The evaluation process is the basis for determining the software product quality from various perspectives. It can be used for the evaluation of quality in use - determining the effect on relevant quality characteristics for a particular user; external software quality - determining the effect on relevant quality characteristics of the behaviour of a software product within a system; and internal software quality - determining the effect on relevant quality characteristics of the components of a software product. It can also be applied to evaluate the quality of pre-developed software or custom software during the development of the architectural components.

A case study for this methodology is provided by the iSURF[4] project: developing an Interoperability Service Utility for Collaborative Supply Chain Planning. The business case presented in this paper provides a holistic solution enabling collaborative supply chain planning across multiple domains in a non-constraint, flexible and dynamic environment. In particular it will facilitate European SMEs participation in a collaborative supply chain planning process, where evaluation procedures will be applied in the selected domains.

The evaluation and test components are being designed and developed in parallel with the architecture, and using the UML testing profile that defines a language for designing, visualizing, specifying, analyzing, constructing, and documenting the artefacts of test systems[5]. After each phase the evaluation will be compiled from the consolidated feedback of end-users to ensure that their needs for the final product are addressed.

2.   Evaluation Model Proposal

The essential parts of software quality evaluation are the quality model, the method of evaluation, software measurement, and the supporting tools. To develop good software, quality requirements should be specified, the software quality assurance process should be planned, implemented and controlled, and both intermediate products and end products should be evaluated [6].

The performed work adopts the Software Product Quality Evaluation Reference Model that describes the process, activities and tasks performed during the quality evaluation of a software product (see Figure 1). This reference model is defined by the ISO/IEC 25040 standard that contains general requirements for specification and evaluation of software quality. It clarifies the general concepts, providing a process description for evaluating quality of software products, stating the requirements for the application of the evaluation process. This specification is part of the SQuaRE series of standards created by the ISO

(International Organization for Standardization) and the IEC (International Electrotechnical Commission). SQuaRE replaces the current ISO/IEC 9126 series [7] and the 14598 series [8] of standards.

The reference model for software product quality evaluation will detail the activities and tasks required, providing their purpose, outcome and complementary information that can be used to guide a software product quality evaluation.

To evaluate software quality it is first necessary to prepare the evaluation. Then the evaluation requirements must be established, followed by specifying, designing, executing and, finally, reporting the evaluation (see Figure 1).

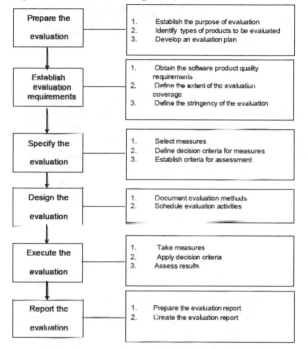

Figure 1: Software Product Quality Evaluation Reference Model

2.1 Prepare the Evaluation

The purpose of the evaluation in our case will be to validate and verify the software to be developed against the collected requirements and perform any further adjustments that may be requested by end users. On top of establishing an evaluation environment for iSURF components, a testing environment will be designed for the proper testing of the entire architecture.

The types of products to be evaluated are the components of the iSURF infrastructure. This evaluation will follow a plan specifying the detailed resources involved, the evaluation methods and criteria to be applied, the evaluation tools, adopted standards and evaluation activities.

2.2 Establish Evaluation Requirements

The establishment of the evaluation requirements will be performed in three steps. Firstly, the software product quality requirements will be obtained using the ISO/IEC 25010 for the quality model and the ISO/IEC 25030 for the software product quality requirements specification. Secondly, the extent of the evaluation will be defined based on criteria such as evaluation budget, target date for the evaluation, purpose of the evaluation and criticality usage of the software product. Finally, the expected evaluation levels will be determined defining the evaluation techniques to be applied and evaluation results to be achieved.

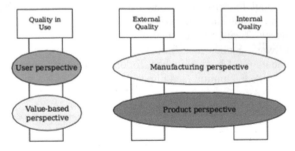

Figure 2: Relationships Between ISO/IEC 25010 and the Perspectives of Quality

Quality requirements like effectiveness, productivity, safety and satisfaction will be defined based on the user perspective of the architecture and quality requirements like functionality, reliability, usability, effectiveness, maintainability and portability considering the manufacturing perspective as defined by the ISO/IEC 25010 (Figure 2). Functional requirements depend on the application domain needs, whilst quality requirements can be identified using the quality model. Some quality requirements should be transformed into functional requirements, such as backup functions for reliability, and usability support. Some other quality requirements should be reflected in design strategies, such as program architecture and modularity.

2.3   Specify the Evaluation

Software product quality evaluation requirements should be allocated to the iSURF architectural components to which they are related in such a way that it is possible to define each appropriate measure and measurement method that can be used to evaluate the specified requirements defined previously. Decision criteria shall be established for the selected measures that can be internal for the evaluation of the component and external for the evaluation of the integrated architecture.

A procedure must be also developed for further summarization, with separate criteria for different quality characteristics and sub characteristics like for instance functionality being a characteristic and suitability, accuracy, interoperability security and compliance its sub characteristics.

2.4   Design the Evaluation

The evaluation methods shall be designed and documented, taking into account the actions to be performed in order to achieve the evaluation results. This will be achieved by using the UML testing profile that extends UML with test-specific concepts like test components, verdicts, and defaults. These concepts are grouped into concepts for test architecture, test data, test behaviour, and time frames.

The description of the evaluation methods shall be completed by the identification of the product components onto which the methods are to be applied. When the evaluation specification is such that expert analysis of the measurements is required in order to interpret the results, the interpretation procedure shall be specified.

2.5   Execute the Evaluation

The evaluation will be executed automatically by using an arbiter that will take the selected measures as input and then apply the decision criteria to validate or not the component under test using a default arbitration algorithm based on functional, conformance testing, which generates Pass, Fail, Unknown or Error as a verdict.

2.6   Report the Evaluation

The evaluation reports will be automatically generated by the testing architecture after the evaluation of each component, ensuring that sufficient information on evaluation results is provided. The evaluation reports format will comply with a common industry format (for instance ISO/IEC 25062).

3.   Case Study on the iSURF Architecture

In order to guarantee survival in today's competitive and demanding digital world of business, European companies, especially SMEs, should be more agile, self-sustainable and responsive to changes in the supply chain. Obtaining and maintaining a competitive edge in the supply chain is not only the concern of individual SMEs, but should be also addressed by the entire chain jointly. The supply chain partners should collaborate effectively so as to better align supply and demand forecasts to have a joint strategy for handling exceptions that will occur along the way of realizing the "the network is the business" vision.

The iSURF project proposes a holistic solution enabling the collaborative supply chain planning across multiple domains in a non-constraint, flexible and dynamic environment, especially to facilitate European SMEs participation in a collaborative supply chain planning process [4]. To achieve this, the project will create a complex architecture composed of four major components that must be tested and evaluated both independently and as a whole. The proposed evaluation methodology will follow the Evaluation reference model ISO/IEC CD 2504n as stated previously.

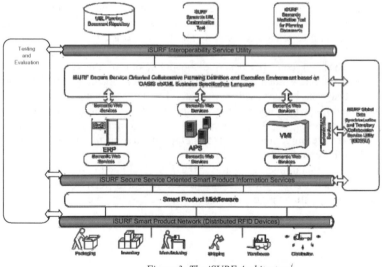

Figure 3: The iSURF Architecture[i]

This paper proposes the establishment of an evaluation and testing process for each of the iSURF software components and for the iSURF integrated architecture by defining the evaluation criteria; designing a testing environment; measuring the test results and performing the overall evaluation. This will validate and verify the developed components and integrated platform against the requirements collected from the end users.

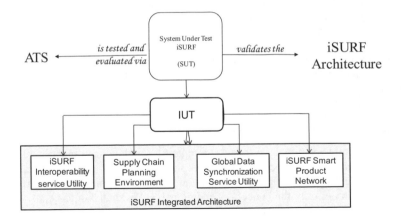

Figure 4: Relationship between Abstract Test Suites and the iSURF Architecture

It is proposed the development Abstract Test Suites (ATS) that will test and evaluate the iSURF architecture via a System Under Test (SUT) that is composed by the implementations of the iSURF components - also known as the Implementations Under Test (IUT). The system under test (SUT) consists of several objects. The SUT is exercised via its public interface operations and signals from the test components. No further information can be obtained from the SUT as it is a black-box.

The first functional test cases for the iSURF software components are being defined based on requirements specified by the end users. The test architecture concepts are related to the organization and realization of the related test cases. These include test contexts, which consist of one or more related test cases. The test cases are potentially realized by test components, and the verdict of a test case is decided by an arbiter.

Similarly, test behaviour concepts describe the behaviour of the test cases that are defined within a test context. Associated with test cases are test objectives, which describe the capabilities the test case is supposed to validate. Test cases consist of behaviour that includes validation actions, which updates the verdict of a test case, and which logs actions that write information to a test log. Behavioural concepts also include the verdicts that are used to define the test case outcomes, as well as default behaviour that is applicable when something other than the specified behaviour is observed.

Figure 5 presents the metamodel diagram for the Test Architecture and Test Behaviour concepts as it is specified by the UML testing profile that will be used from unit level, through integration and system level, up to cross-enterprise system level.

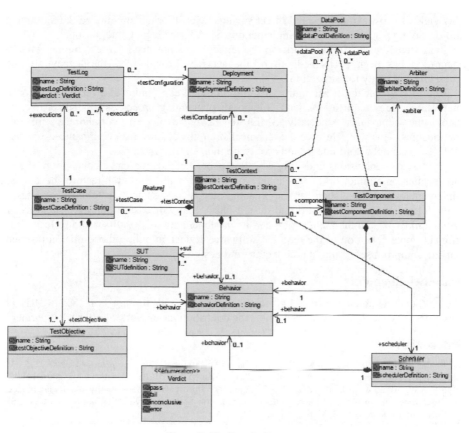

Figure 5: The Test Architecture

4.   Conclusions and Summary

The cost of designing new software in general can be calibrated as the sum of 16% of design cost, 34% of implementation cost, 20% of testing cost and 30 % of maintenance cost [1]. This paper introduces the problems caused by not considering testing and validation in the early phases of architectural definition. It describes a proposed methodology to address this as well as a use case that will be used to demonstrate the methodology.

The chapter "Evaluation model proposal" explains the evaluation model proposal and the steps that must be followed by the methodology to perform the evaluation.

The chapter "Case Study on the iSURF architecture" shows how the proposed methodology can be applied to the evaluation and testing of the architecture that will be developed by the iSurf project, a project funded by the European Commission. The success of this approach shall be measured via appropriate metrics, and an analysis of observed results made available in future publications.

As future plans iSURF aims to tackle the legacy application integration problem by providing a Service Oriented Architecture where the legacy applications will be wrapped as Web services. Following outcomes are expected in enterprises after successful interoperability with legacy applications within the scope of iSURF project.

Reduced Cost: The legacy systems can operate similar to any other application in the architecture, so organizations can build new applications regardless of what's underneath.

This yields to cost avoidances and direct savings. Merill Lynch announced $500,000 to $2 million saving per application by implementing SOA based legacy integration.

Increased Reuse: Service built on the legacy does not need to be rebuilt. After the integration has been performed, all of the services provided by the legacy are fully accessible and ready for utilization.

Reinforcing Technical Strengths: By providing an easy and cost effective solution for integrating legacy applications with collaborative planning processes, iSURF project will enable the companies especially SMEs to easily involve in collaborative planning relationships. This will reinforce the technical strengths of European Companies, especially SMEs who cannot afford integration costs with their limited resources.

By way of conclusions and summary, this paper defends the early conception of a test and evaluation framework, developed in parallel with the architecture design and implementation. With such an approach, quality assessment establishes a testing methodology at the architectural and design phase that will ensure quality, reliability and sustainability of both the architecture and its implementations. Results could reflect a more efficient implementation of the required software product, avoiding those final adjustments that can compromise the initial architecture and design.

Acknowledgements

The authors acknowledge the EC for the support and funding of the iSURF and EuropaINNOVA projects. They recognize the contributions & work of all iSURF partners.

References

[1] Boehm, B., and Basili, V. 'Software Defect Reduction Top 10 Lists', IEEEComputer 34, 1, 2001, 135-137.
[2] Boehm, B., and Basili, V. 'Software Defect Reduction Top 10 Lists', IEEE Computer 34, 1, 2001, 135-137.
[3] Suryn W., Abran A., "ISO/IEC SQuaRE. The 2nd generation of standard for quality of software product". Proceedings of 7th IASTED International Conference on Software Engineering and Applications, SEA 2003, November 3-5, 2003, Marina del Rey, CA, USA
[4] EU project iSURF - An Interoperability Service Utility for Collaborative Supply Chain Planning across Multiple Domains Supported by RFID Devices, Objective ICT-2007-1.3: ICT in support of the networked enterprise
[5] OMG: UML Testing Profile, version 1.0, formal/05-07-07, July 2005
[6] Suryn W., Abran A., Bourque P., Laporte C., "Software Product Quality Practices. Quality Measurement and Evaluation using TL9000 and ISO/IEC 9126". Proceedings of STEP2002, Computer Society Press, 2003.
[7] ISO/IEC. 2001a. ISO/IEC 9126-1: Software Engineering-Software product quality-Part 1 : Quality model. Geneva, Switzerland: International Organization for Standardization.
[8] ISO/IEC. 1999a. ISO/IEC 14598-1: Software product evaluation-Part 1 : General overview. Geneva, Switzerland: International Organization for Standardization.
[9] Trudel S., Lavoie J-M., Paré M-C., Suryn W., "The design of the software quality evaluation method combining CMMI and ISO/IEC 14598: the context of a small company". Proceedings of 12th International Software Quality Management & INSPIRE Conference (BSI) 2004, Canterbury, Kent, UK 5-7 April 2004. Article a obtenu le prix du meilleur article scientifique 2004
[10] Suryn W., Kahlaoui A., Georgiadou E., "Quality engineering process for the Program Design Phase of a generic software life cycle". SQM 2005
[11] Abran A., Khelifi A., Suryn W., Seffah A., "Usability Meanings and Interpretations in ISO Standards". Software Quality Journal. Issue 4, 2003
[12] Côté M-A, Suryn W., Georgiadou E., "Software Quality Model Requirements for Software Quality Engineering", Software Quality Management & INSPIRE Conference (BSI) 2006
[13] Gil B., Suryn W., " The analysis and evaluation of ISO/IEC9126–3 internal quality measures applicability: state-of-the-art 2006" – WHITE PAPER. ICSSEA 2006, Paris, France
E Ramaraj, S. Duraisamy, "Design Phase Testing Model – A Design Assessment", Sri Krishna College of Engineering and Technology

---

[i] This picture was developed by the iSurf consortium and it is reproduced in this paper solely to illustrate the use case demonstration.

Collaboration and the Knowledge Economy: Issues, Applications, Case Studies
P. Cunningham and M. Cunningham (Eds.)
IOS Press, 2008

Inter-enterprise Collaboration Throughout Ontological Orchestration

J. SARRAIPA[1], S. ONOFRE[1], P. MALO[2], R. JARDIM-GONCALVES[2]
[1]UNINOVA – Instituto de Novas Tecnologias
Campus FCT/UNL - Monte da Caparica, 2829-516 Caparica, Portugal
E-mail: jfss@uninova.pt
[2]Faculdade Ciências e Tecnologia da Universidade Nova de Lisboa
Dep. Eng. Electrotécnica - UNINOVA, Campus FCT/UNL
Monte da Caparica, 2829-519 Caparica, Portugal

Abstract: Today, enterprises have information technology that could fulfil their requirements in each operational phase and with external partners, e.g., suppliers. For instance, in industrial environment, many applications are available to support their Product Life Cycle stages. However, organizations typically acquire them, aiming to solve focused needs, without an overall view of the global enterprise's system integration. Researchers have been proposing methodologies and platforms to assist the integration of applications and data. However, implementing new technology in organizations is a complex task, and the advent of continuous technological evolution makes organizations unable to be constantly updated. Thus, the use of appropriate conformance testing and interoperability checking methods is fundamental for the assessment of an accurate seamless inter-enterprise collaborative environment. This paper proposes a methodology to enhance inter-enterprise's interoperability, keeping the same organization's technical and operational environment, improving its methods of work and the usability of the installed technology through ontological harmonization of the enterprises product models in use, assessed by a fitting validation framework.

1. Introduction

Competition keeps increasing and organizations are considering how to improve their position in the market performing strategic partnerships [1]. The formation of cooperation and collaboration alliances between several small organizations is proving, in multiple cases, to be more efficient and competitive by comparison with big companies. This is typically what leads companies to join efforts to survive in very evolutionary and dynamic markets [2]. However, partnerships cause some problems mainly in integrating Product Life Cycle phases, since manufacturers, distributors, designers, retailers, warehouses, often acquire their proprietary solutions which are, typically, not interoperable with another [3].

Due to the large number of worldwide available product catalogues existing in a specific business domain it is very difficult for a customer to find a specific product or a specific class of products from different suppliers. Each enterprise has its own product terminology and classification, thus when it is needed to do business with other enterprises in the same domain, data interoperability problems emerge.

Standardisation in data structures appeared to solve the referred problems. Several initiatives were taken to address this issue, like ISO10303. ISO 10303, also known as STEP, is the standard for the exchange of product model data. STEP Application Protocols have been widely used in industrial environments, to support systems interoperability through the exchange of product data in manufacturing domains. However, this kind of data representation standards did not solve all the problems. Semantics interoperability problems still to be solved. More recently, the development of ontologies, as promising techniques with capabilities to solve semantic issues, has been addressed by important companies and SMEs. Thus, each company is struggling to develop competencies at this ontological level, but inevitably different perspectives will lead to different final results, and achieving different ontologies in the same business domain is the reality. One possible solution is to have a reference ontology for a specific domain where all the domain enterprises should use in their business. Although, to force manufacturers or suppliers to adopt a specific ontology as reference is not an easy task, since each enterprise does not foresee any outcomes by changing their knowledge. Thus, an advantageous solution would be to let them to keep their terminology and classification in use, and adopt a reference ontology. The adopted ontology will be the organization knowledge front-end, enabling inter-enterprises communications sharing the same terminology and semantics. Since this reference ontology will become their front-end, each organizational enterprise should feel motivated to participate in its building process, contributing with their own terminologies, definitions and classification structure.

Nevertheless, interoperability checking applications are required in order to test organization communications conformability. In the next section is presented two methodologies able to guarantee the data exchange conformance level, using a data representation standard with its contents following an agreed common semantics.

2. Methodologies to enhance inter-enterprise's interoperability

The authors propose the use of two existent methodologies to enhance inter-enterprise's interoperability: 1) MENTOR - a methodology for building a reference ontology in a community domain; 2) Interoperability Checking (IC) - a methodology for interoperability checking using conformance testing procedures. Both will facilitate enterprises keep its technical and operational environment, improving its methods of work and the usability of the installed technology through ontological harmonization of the enterprises product models in use, assessed by a fitting validation framework for conformance testing and interoperability checking. The presented work was developed and has been applied in the scope of the Intelligent Manufacturing Systems (IMS) programme[i]; and European EuropaINNOVA INNOVAfun[ii] and ICT ATHENA projects, under real industrial environments.

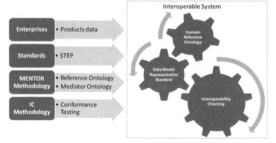

Figure 1: Interoperability drivers

In order to have an enterprise organizational system interoperable, it has to have a domain reference ontology which enhances inter-enterprise's semantics interoperability concerning to the contents of a standardized data representation model. These both components (reference ontology; data representation model) should be complemented with an Interoperability checking methodology able to make the model conformance testing. In the next sub-sections it is presented the MENTOR and the IC methodologies: MENTOR is used by the community to build the reference ontology that produces a mediator ontology to be used as a mapping table between community ontologies; IC methodology is used to perform conformance testing in the representation model.

2.1 The MENTOR methodology

The MENTOR - Methodology for Enterprise Reference Ontology Development is a methodology that helps an organization to adopt or use and to build, a domain reference ontology, after through several main steps as semantic comparisons, basic lexicon establishment, mappings among ontologies and others operations on knowledge base representations. This methodology is composed of two phases: 1) the Lexicon Settlement phase; 2) Reference Ontology Building phase with three steps each.

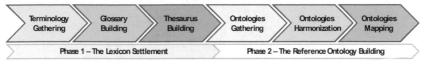

Figure 2: MENTOR Phases and Steps

The Lexicon Settlement phase (Phase 1) represents a domain knowledge acquisition, which comparatively to the human language apprentice phase could be represented in computer science as a semantic organized structure with definitions. The thesaurus can represent such words structure of associated meanings, in order to establish the lexicon of a specific domain.

The Reference Ontology Building phase (Phase 2) is the phase where is built the reference ontology and is established the semantic mappings between the organizational ontologies and the reference one. The first step of this phase is composed by the ontologies gathering in the domain defined. Other type of knowledge representation could be used as input for the harmonization ontologies process together with the thesaurus defined in the previous phase. The harmonization method for building ontologies defined by an adaptation made from Noy [4][5], proposes the development of a single harmonized Ontology's by two cycles where first the structure is discussed until having agreement on it and then the same process for the ontology contents definition. From this process could be found new semantic conflicts, once again, after agreement the resolution could be recorded in the Mediator Ontology (MO) for further mapping establishments. When accomplished all the agreements, the harmonized ontology is finalized together with the mapping tables describing the ontological relationships between the harmonized and each one of the individual ontologies.

Ontology mapping is an activity that attempts to relate the vocabulary of two ontologies that share the same domain of discourse [6]. The process of defining mappings between ontologies is not an easy task and requires a human support. The MENTOR uses the MO as the reference for mediating the mapping establishment and its subsequent "mapping records" reasoning. One example is querying the MO for a correspondence to a reference term in a specific enterprise ontology.

The MO is able to represent ontology semantic operations: the semantic mismatches found in the Glossary Building step; the semantic transformations identified in the harmonization process; the ontologies mapping; and other ontologies operations (e.g. versioning). It was built up as an extension to the Model Traceability Ontology defined by Sarraipa et al [7]. Traceability is ability to chronologically interrelate the uniquely identifiable entities in a way that matters. The mapping relations can be related to a traceability element, in a sense that a specific term defined in the reference ontology has a related one in an organization member ontology, considering ontologies as stages of the desired ontology life-cycle, that is in this case the reference ontology. This makes possible a way to trace ontology elements. The MO structure is represented in Figure 3 using UML class diagrams.

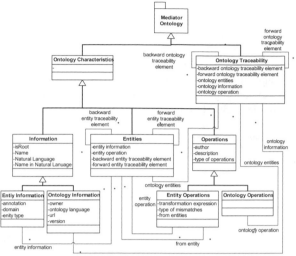

Figure 3 – Mediator Ontology structure

The MO represents two classes: Ontology Characteristics and Ontology Traceability. The Ontology Characteristics class represents: 1) ontology general information related to ontology and ontology entities (Classes: Information; Entity Information; and Ontology Information); 2) ontology operations that an ontology or an ontology entity (e.g. classes; properties; instances) suffered in the various stages of the ontology life cycle (Classes: Entities; Operations; Entity Operations; and Ontology Operations). The Ontology Traceability class represents the information related to the various ontology life-cycle stages.

2.2 Interoperability checking methodology

During latest years, the architecture of the STEP Application Protocols has been revised to promote the reuse of software components, where the testing and quality assurance plays a critical role in the implementation of the STEP software components when applied to different types of manufacturing and e-Business systems.

Interoperability Checking (IC) plays an important role in the company's systems, providing an appropriate mechanism to check if they are able to seamless exchange information between them. The methodology proposed for the presented case is based in the development of an Abstract Test Suite (ATS) that is used to define the set of tests to be used to verify the interoperability between the systems. Figure 4 shows the diagram with the methodology for validation, in this case considering to systems in validation, i.e., "Computer System" and "IC System".

To guarantee the systems interoperability, these steps would be executed to all the cases defined by the ATS [10]. As depicted, the first step consists in reading a XML file provided by the "IC System". Also, the file must be validated with the Conformance Testing (CT), depicted in the system validation section. After the "Computer System" read and "understand" the information in the file, the "Computer System" modifies it with new information and sends it back to the "IC System". Then, the "IC System" analyses the modified file, also improving the CT, and confirms (or not) it is able to understand the modified information that received from the "Computer System".

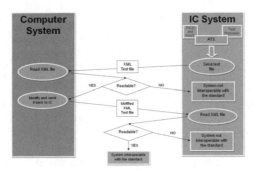

Figure 4 – IC methodology diagram

If the information is correct in the modified file, the IC can notify company that their systems pass the current test. Then the company must pass to the second test, executing the same steps. Doing all the defined test files, IC can ensure the Interoperability of the company's system. This service will be available online, allowing the users to download the test files and check its system. The upload of the modified files will be done by email to the community IC system. After complete the verification of the received file, the community IC system, will notify the user of its interoperability with other complaint systems.

3. Case study

The simple choice of a supplier by a furniture customer, very often brings interoperability problems. Suppliers have defined various nomenclatures for their products and its associated knowledge. Thus, the need to align product data and knowledge emerged as a priority to solve the dilemma. The presented problem was used as a MENTOR use case scenario for validating purposes. The work starts with a reference ontology building related to an organization composed by two furniture suppliers, and then is followed by presenting a MO application for semantic messages translation.

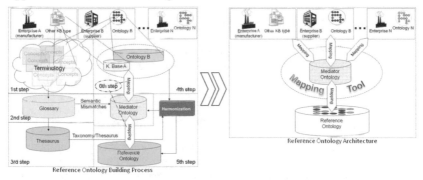

Figure 5 – MENTOR use case scenario

Figure 5 describes the validating scenario, where two enterprises agreed to build a reference ontology to be their knowledge front-end to their clients, though there where the condition to maintain own meaning and nomenclature of products of each other. Although from one side, one of the enterprises has its own product data represented through an ontology, the other still present traditional product catalogues, i.e., regardless the electronic version they merely were digital versions of catalogue pages.

The MENTOR methodology is used to develop this reference ontology. During the reference ontology building phase, it is produced a mediator ontology which records all the semantic operations performed in this process. One of the applications of these semantic operations logs is to use that recorded information for semantic translation. One possible example of such process is when a message with a product request is sent to Enterprise B (the supplier in the figure 5). The mediator ontology is used to get the "semantic translation" of the information present in the message, which uses syntax accordingly to the reference ontology, to the equivalent syntax used in the Enterprise B.

For instance, the request of *"Compact Beds"* with "Light Decorations" is translated to a request of a "Juvenile Bed" that have the "Electric Equipment" attribute as a "Lightning Decoration". Nevertheless these mappings are related only to literal elements (product classes). However, the complexity increases when the mappings are established between property elements, which result in some complex transformations. Back to the same example, the request of a product classified as "Compact Beds" of a "size=3", where "size" is a property in the reference ontology, is "translated" to a "Juvenile Bed" product with a "dimension" which "size" is characterized by a "length" with a value "180" and a "width" with a value *"90"*. Figure 6 depicts an extract of the reference and enterprise B ontologies where the referred mappings are related to.

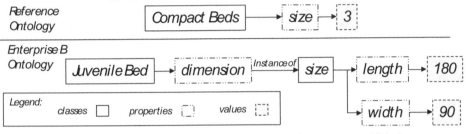

Figure 6 – Extract of two ontologies where mapping relations were established

The transformation resulted from the mapping of this example can be recorded in the mediator ontology as a mathematical expression, that in this specific case is based on the equations presented in the following.

$$F_{R(x)} = size(x) \tag{1}$$
$$F_{E(y,z)} = dimension(size(length(y),width(z))) \tag{2}$$
$$F_{R(x)} = F_{E(y,z)} \tag{3}$$
$$size(x) = dimension(size(length(y),width(z))) \tag{4}$$
$$size(3) = dimension(size(length(180),width(90))) \tag{5}$$
$$y = 120 + 20x \tag{6}$$
$$z = 60 + 10x \tag{7}$$
$$F_{R(x)} = F_{E(y(x),z(x))} \tag{8}$$
$$size(x) = dimension(size(length(120+20x),width(60+10x))) \tag{9}$$

Equation 1 indicates a function that represents the "Compact Beds" property element, which in this case is related to more than one property in Enterprise B representation (equation 2). In order to define the transformation which relates both representations, it is stated an equality between both expressions (equations 3 and 4). After analysing empirically all the existent values that these expressions could take (equation 5 shows one case), it was defined two linear equations which relates them (equations 6 and 7). At the end it was reached an expression that establishes a semantic relation between both representations and establishes the transformation equations related to each variable (equations 8 and 9).

3.1 System validation

To ensure the interoperability between the systems, the first step, must be the application of the Conformance Testing (CT) to its files. Based on the defined methodology for CT, the architecture shown in the Figure 7, is used to validate the exchanged files. The architecture was designed based in web-services, able to receive the files in XML format and checking them against the reference testing model using an Application Engine developed in JAVA, SAX, Schematron and XALAN.

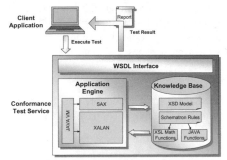

Figure 7 – Architecture for CT system validation [11]

Using the CT the user can check the files against the defined models, ensuring its correct implementation. The CT checks the XML against syntactic and semantic rules and sends back the detected errors enabling its correction.

Following the same example as before, if is defined that an attribute, in the "Compact Beds" entity, named "size" with a value 3 must be related to 90x180 (width, length), and the system detects a relation which have "size=3" with 70x190, the CT with the semantic rules will detect the error reporting it to the user. Also if there is "Compact Bedd" instead "Compact Beds", the CT with syntactic evaluation, will detect and report the error.

With CT executed to its XML files, the next step is the application of the IC. To apply IC, the user will analyze and modify the test files, sent by the IC system, and send it back to evaluation. After check all the files, defined in the ATS for IC, the user receives the confirmation that its system is interoperable. With all the ATS executed (CT ATS and IC ATS), the system validation can ensure that the systems are in conformance with the model defined and is interoperable with others system of this type.

One obvious advantage of this scenario is that this mechanism will enable the computational systems of any enterprise to smoothly communicate with external parties using syntax and semantic present in the reference ontology. This is also the main motivation that enterprises may consider to spend their efforts in contributing for the reference ontology building process.

4. Concluding remarks

The MENTOR methodology enhances inter and intra-organizational knowledge sharing, allowing its actors keeping their own ontologies or knowledge representations by producing a reference ontology in the domain. MENTOR brings together the building and reengineering of ontologies related to mapping competences. After having a reference ontology built, a community should be able to use it as semantic mediator in their business. One example is the use of semantic translators between enterprises exchange data information, which does not share the same semantics. Nevertheless, a validation system is needed to check if the semantics information is recognized by the reference ontology system. The validation methodology presented related to interoperability checking, tests if there are inconsistencies in the information data exchanged between enterprises.

The proposed methodologies and conformance testing services have been applied with good results in a real scenario supervised by the research European ATHENA IP project and European EuropaINNOVA initiative through the INNOVAfun project[iii]. These achievements have been encouraging to the development of further framework functionalities in the future, like the generation of the reports according to a normative schema (e.g., defined in EXPRESS and XML), to enable automatic inference and reasoning on the errors found, and provide automatic correction of the identified errors by an expert system. Interoperability Checking complements the Conformance Testing ensuring that two or more systems can be seamless compliant. For the future, the authors intend to have available a set of web services able to set up knowledge sharing organizations through the web with the conformance testing services.

Acknowledgements

The authors acknowledge the EC for the support and funding of the projects mentioned. Also, they recognize contributions from project partners for the work presented.

References

[1]   The Gallup Organization (2006). Flash Eurobarometer 196 –Survey of the Observatory of European SMEs.
[2]   Camarinha-Matos, L. M.; Afsarmanesh, H. (2008). Concept of Collaboration. In Encyclopedia of Networked and Virtual Organizations, G. Putnik, M. M. Cunha (Ed.s), IGI, ISBN: 978-1-59904-885-7, Jan 2008.
[3]   Jardim-Goncalves, R.; Grilo, A; Steiger-Garcao, A; (2007). Developing interoperability in mass customization information systems, in book Mass Customization Information Systems in Business, ISBN-10: 1599040395, Idea, 2007.
[4]   Noy, Natalya and McGuinness, Deborah, (2002,). Ontology Development 101: A Guide to Creating Your First Ontology'. Stanford Knowledge Systems Laboratory Technical Report KSL-01-05 and Stanford Medical Informatics Technical Report SMI-2001-0880.
[5]   Jardim-Goncalves, R., Sarraipa, J. (2004). Ontology-based framework for advanced networked industrial environments. In: INCOM2004, 11th IFAC Symposium on Information Control Problems in manufacturing. Salvador, Brazil, 2004.
[6]   Jardim-Goncalves, R.; Silva, J. P.M.A.; Steiger-Garcao, A.; Monteiro, A. (2007). Framework for Enhanced Interoperability Through Ontological Harmonization of Enterprise Product Models in book Ontologies: A Handbook of Principles, Concepts and Applications. Integrated Series in Information Systems , Vol. 14-2007, XXIV, 915 p., 245 illus. ISBN: 978-0-387-37019-4.
[7]   Sarraipa, J.; Zouggar, N.; Chen, D; Jardim-Goncalves, R. (2007). Annotation for Enterprise Information Management Traceability. In Proceedings of IDETC/CIE ASME.
[8]   ISO 10303 Standard for Exchange of Product Data (STEP), ISO TC184/SC4, Part31, Conformance testing methodology and framework: General concepts, International Organization for Standardization
[9]   S. Onofre , C. Agostinho, R. Jardim-Gonçalves, and A. Steiger-Garção (2006), "Applying TTCN to enhance B2B Conformance testing frameworks", I-ESA 2007.
[10] Wiles, A.; Relevance of Conformance Testing for Interoperability Testing (2003), ACATS ATS-CONF, 2003.
[11] Jardim-Gonçalves, R., Onofre, S., and Agostinho, C. (2006), "Conformance Testing for XML-based STEP Conceptual Models", ASME 2006 International Design Engineering Technical Conferences & Computers and Information in Engineering Conference, Philadelphia, September, 2006.

---

[i] www.ims.org
[ii] www.funstep.org
[iii] www.funstep.org

Section 5

Networked, Smart and Virtual Organisations

Section 5.1

Issues

Collaboration and the Knowledge Economy: Issues, Applications, Case Studies
P. Cunningham and M. Cunningham (Eds.)
IOS Press, 2008

Fourth Generation Living Labs Quest for Human-Oriented Glocal Society

Bernard CORBINEAU
S3IS, Université Paris-Est, Marne-la-Vallée, 5 Bld Descartes,
Marne-la-Vallée, F77420, CEDEX2, France
Tel: +33164209595, Fax: + 33953859595 Email: Bernard@corbineau.net

Abstract: While mixing a theoretical analysis with practical experiences, this article, emphasizing on rural particularities, tries to define the conditions for creating a Local Living Lab.

1. Introduction

This paper tries to answer some of Jesse Marsh's queries while presenting the Living Labs and Regional Development workshop, which he proposed to eChallenges e-2008.

Theoretically and practically, what are the chances for successful Local Living Labs?[i]

The title of this article refers to a well-documented paper written by Annerstedt and Haselmayer [1] that can be used as a starting block for thinking on a fourth generation of Living Labs, "society-oriented".

This article is on the merge of three major professional concerns (of the author).

The consultant, specialized in the policies and strategies of development within the frame of a Network Society, searches for a clear attitude[ii] on the positioning of the local within the global and vice-versa.

The teacher is looking for the best possible ways to let the students understand the importance of the changes within the Network Society and to help them to define their own tools for a better comprehension of the world.

The researcher is all the time faced to the Network Society comprehension and has to build conceptual and methodological tools which can help the local decision makers to lay down policies which take into account the Network Society environment policies.

The paper, a mix-up of theory and practice, is constantly meshing these triple concerns at defining the conditions for the realization of a Local Living Labs.

2. A More "Society-Oriented" Theoretical Framework

The way the title of this article has been built in regards to the paper of Annerstedt and Haselmayer's [1], gives the tone to the suggested approach:
"Living Labs Europe, Third Generation Living Labs : The Quest for User-Centered Mobile Services"
"Living Labs Glocal - Fourth Generation Living Labs : The Quest for Human-Oriented Society"
"Fourth Generation Living Labs: Quest for Human-Oriented Glocal Society

2.1 Glocal Environment

The prospect is definitely global and insists on the essential and complex link between the closely interlaced dimensions of GLObal and LOCAL. If there can be sometimes a subordinated relation, it is necessary to insist on the fact that neither one nor the other can exist without its other half. The glocal is a social system which determines several dimensions of the Network Society, a geographical one of course and consequently a temporal one. But it also determines a tension, an essential flow. *The flows of interlaced "locals" and their relation to the "global(s)" constitute the glocal.*

2.2   A Human-Oriented Fourth Generation

The paper of Annerstedt and Haselmayer [1] describes the impact of information and communication technologies (ICT) by centering its analysis on the user (user-centered) and not on technology (techno-centered). It seems to us that it is necessary to go further not giving the primacy to the user, who is always technology-centered, but to define another society-oriented[iii] approach. Therefore, it is interesting to analyze the changes of society and to question some of the dimensions[iv] of the Network Society, in regards to the individuals (the inhabitant and not the technology user) or to the collectivity (in this particular case the territory). We could venture speaking of a third approach : after the queen "technology" from the world of "Technocrats", the king "user" from the world of "Consumers", a new "participative" citizen from the "democratic" world (and not the king, as the participative citizen is responsible). It means overtaking the co-design of technology, or of its use, which origins in technology, to search a society co-design, integrating technology as a tool, which origins in a human project.

2.3   A Network Society

The expression "Network Society" is the object of various debates. Let's take it as defined by Castells [6] as a social building in a specific period. The Network Society characteristics differ from the industrial society that it replaces and its features are still under construction. Let's look at it as a new object of study and a new ecosystem. The difficulty of the Network Society considered as an operational concept lies in its historical blur, being at a same time, on one hand a moment of transition between the Middle Age in which we live and, on the other hand, the result of this transition. It can also be seen as... a navigation-light, a mirage, an object of desire, an ideology, a future...

3.   Is the District "La Brie" Excluded from Network Society?

Can anyone think of a Local Living Labs in a low-size rural territory? Let us study this extreme case in order to release an "a minima" model which will then enable to draw results about territories with larger resources. Is a rurally environment without visible resources excluded from the Network Society?

3.1   La Brie, a Case Among Others

*   Location
La Brie belongs to the Seine-et-Marne county which is the most rural and widest county of the Ile-de-France Region (representing 50% of the total surface area) where Paris dominates.

    Hybrid territory, "neither-nor", neither rural nor urban, neither rich nor poor, neither industrial nor service-oriented (among which ICT), neither central nor peripheral, La Brie has difficulty to come together, except for its cheeses which make it famous.

    Paris, close to it, obliterates its chance of survival as a specific entity. Yet 100.000 to 200.000, depending the frontiers definition, inhabitants live there. Some people struggle for its destiny, though obliterating the fact that its destiny will develop within the framework of Network Society.

*   Approaches
Under these circumstances, how can one build a Local Living Lab and which form should it take? Neither the technology-centered analysis nor the users-centered analysis answer the

question. A Local Living Lab can be a development tool only if considering the territory in its domestic, educational, cultural, economic, social, political and … technical dimensions. How to avoid losing the ultimate but still active companies, how to attract new ones, how to develop the countryside for tourism without devitalizing the territory and fighting against an anarchistic urbanization? How one can develop the territory in the Network Society? All these questions are at the core of the future of the Brie.

3.2 Networking of the Actors

Without resources, what to do?   One can rebuild the society by creating new networks, more human than technical ones, integrating the digital networks and the new services they offer or will offer. What the territory can best offer is human resources even if they suffer lack of skill and will. Therefore it needs new means to create new dynamics. It has been the objective of some politicians and citizens who encountered both success and difficulties, but never failure, as a society-oriented experimentation is a success by its own existence! Even if it does not succeed at the very beginning, it creates favorable conditions for future achievements, as long as it has been thought out as a social construction.

A network of small tourism actors has been launched 3 years ago. They have created together their very first products and are now striving for a leveling and an exchange of their skills (Tourisme et Terroir des 2 Morins[v]). Farmers, builders, training centers, territorial collectivities, architects are networking in order to define a new ecology-building cluster. A training organisation has been created and bets on Flexible and Open Distant Training. A popular, open, distant Uuniversity has been launched with ambitious plans but also deep difficulties in finding its rhythm and publics. The project of creating a Regional Nature Park is in process creating a network of 135 villages and small towns. ICTs are not to be found at the core of the projects, neither for the e-training centre nor within the "popular" university, but they are always there. But, much more they are present by they power of networking support to human networks necessary in building a "Network Society" culture. Human beings still are the leavens for developing projects. Politicians are aware of that event if the Network Society dimension is not at the core of their vision. The mayor of one of the most important towns (10.000 inhabitants), vice-president of one of the districts and vice-president of the Region has been initiating a certain number of projects based on real networking and is able to work with good-will people, whatever their political tendencies are. But for lot of them the Network Society is a chimera.

4. To Think a Virtual Local Living Labs

Is a Local Living Labs a relevant instrument in this context? A negative answer seems reasonable. But what does reasonable mean? The acceptance of a destiny tied up to the past or the building of a new future in progress.

Yet, the territory does not have the capacity to build up either an urban Local Living Labs (megapolis type) nor a very large rural region Local Living Labs. Economics, research and even human capacity are lacking. However human resources are the most readily available. They are to be considered as raw material for endogenous development in the frame of sustainable development and as networkers with other territories. The internal and external networking in the territory turns to be the motorization of local development, and the Local Living Labs could become a prime instrument in its binding function and the link between the various actors, their interests and their cultures.

4.1 Which Aggregation of Interests?

Far beyond any political will, "Network Society" culture or any means for implementing it, the most important issue concerns the aggregation of interests, at several levels.

How to outline the aggregation of interests? Should one keep to relatively informal mechanisms or choose more institutional lines, without freezing the aggregation dynamics through networking which is based on the actors' strong autonomy? How to conceive and set up a co-regulation which is thought in a society-oriented perspective for the Network Society, such as the co-design is for the uses and the design of technologies?

How can we apply legitimacy and consequently democratic forms to these new tools of aggregation of interests and to these methods of networking? Which coexistence can be figured out between the new, not yet institutionalized, mechanisms (which may loose its enforcement while becoming institutionalized through traditional criteria) and the current institutions (with tools from the industrial society are not adapted to the Network Society)?

Is the democratic value of innovation the same within techno-centered, user-oriented and society-oriented approaches?

4.2 Frontiers Go-Through as New Aggregators

New intermediaries and gate-keepers are rising up as "frontiers go-through", sorts of network fluidificators and aggregators of interests, at the same time. Nowadays, these new actors, with very different and blurry backgrounds, have a strong impact on the evolution of society whoever they are, either webmasters-organizers of digital resource centers, ICT operation managers of territorial collectivities, "Network Society" or ICT consultants, and, certainly, ... Living Labs by themselves. Their functions are not yet clearly defined. It is the same regarding their legitimacy. Should one still be thinking in terms of gate-keeper in a society which is "frontiers-centered" or at least very hierarchical or should one be thinking in more dynamic terms of "frontiers go-through" in a more open networked Society?

Let us be aware of a great number of boarders to go through: inside versus outside, politicians versus inhabitants, enterprises versus territorial institutions, individuals versus communities and ICT visions versus Network Society visions. The Local Living Labs as frontiers go-through are disclosures and creators... of the rich value of networking.

4.3 Territory and Living Labs with Variable Geometry

The boarders and their territories, whether geographical, professional or institutional, do not superimpose each other. The territories increase with indefinite outlines into a dynamic imbroglio. Particularly in France where the layers of institutional territories have grown fast and do not any longer correspond to the layers of everyday life territories. Generally speaking, everyday life territories have also expanded these past decades under the influence for example of increasing transports and consumption. Expansion is even larger in the Network Society context due to the dematerialization of flows and to the globalization of links.

To understand these new situations it is necessary to think in terms of flexibility of territories and even in terms of territory as a flow. In everyday practice and in the building of representations for the Network Society ideology, the concept of territory with variable geometry is more and more meaningful.

However, is there a territorial node which focuses the capacities and organizes the roles? The relationship between the various levels of territories moves in time and space. There is no standard configuration. New tendencies seem to emerge. Perhaps we can notice lately a possible weakening of the State to the profit of the immediately lower and higher levels. A specialization of the roles seems to be redistributed at least in France and thus according to issues. The local level (NUTS 3, Nomenclature for territorial and statistical units) would be the place for the mutualization of the inhabitants' actions as well as for their training, their sensibilization, their follow-up of ICT uses and their entry in Network Society. The district level (NUTS 2) mutualizes and coordinates the actions of smaller

NUTS but also…. manages intermediate transports among which intermediate numerical infrastructures. It is probably the best nest for clusters. The regional level (NUTS 1), sorts of megapolitan archipelagoes [14] concentrate the R & D resources, lodge the poles of competitiveness, while the States and the EU are tending to become normative levels.

Isn't then the virtual Local Living Labs, which is based on the reality of a potential richness to upcome, a frontier go-through in a world of territories with variable geometry?

4.4   Local Living Labs, Disclosures and Creators of a Territorial Intelligence

What is a territorial intelligence[vi] if it is not the intelligence of living together in a given spacetime. This broad definition of territorial intelligence does not dilute it. Our spacetime changes very quickly. In the Network Society the intelligence of living together results in the co-design of society, its co-regulation, probably its co-administration. However, beyond the democratic dimension, we are facing the dimension[vii] of values production. The virtual Local Living Labs are instruments revealing and operating hidden territorial values (endogenous and interactive), through the actors' mutualization and networking. The territorial intelligence constitutes in Network Society one of the innovation melting pot, underlining its cognitive contents, "a way of interacting that leads to specific competence to innovate" [8, p3].

4.5   Measurements

How to qualify and consequently to measure the Network Society reality of a regional policy or a Living Lab? It is not simply a question of finding out indicators which measure the degree of Network Society with ICT equipment and networks (R&D expenditure, phone and ICT infrastructure, ICT investments and so so…), or in terms of ICT use (eTV watching, number of net-surfers, weight of e-business in total trade, public services on line, etc), but it is a question of refining the measurement of the social and territorial value of practices (capacity to work in network, of co-design, of co-defining the needs and of following-up the development of the methodological and technological tools, etc). The indicators are often poor, even when implemented by an a priori effective institution [10].

However, some territorial public institutions are taking more and more into account society-oriented data in the progress reports of their ICT policies, such as the "Diagnosis of the Information Society in Midi-Pyrenées " [7] which is incremented each year with new prospects and analyzes, especially with sector monographs. "For characterizing the innovative potential of a region, it is necessary to look for qualitative variables and not classical measures scientific and technological production [8].

The experimentation of 2T2M has been the occasion to rethink indicators, even if not put in practice, such as : measurements of confidence, appetite for training, types of leadership and their impacts on confidence, digital literacy, recognition of the proper values of the group, collaborative capacity for an individual or for a group, cognitive potential of the actors, as individuals and as a group [8].

4.6   Which governance for a virtual Living Lab?

In a Network Society context and in the context of social roles for Living Labs, which form of governance is enforced? Governance ruled by each of its members, the Anarchy of nodes? Governance defined by each transaction, the Anarchy of flows? Governance founded on "ruled auto-organization" [5] such as internet and the digital economy, a co-governance (.. of nodes and flows)? Can one make a parallel between an economy "based on the network" where " the delicate control of the exchanges of information applied on the numerical networks federated by Internet makes it possible to found new methods of interactions between the agents" [5] and governorship of the Living Labs where refined creation and exchange of information and knowledge on an intelligent territory would make it possible to found new methods of interactions between the actors of the territory based on new settings in network?

The Living Labs then become a tool, among others, to pilot the territory.

4.7 Does a Briard Local Living Lab exist?

In the light of these developments can one thinks about a Briard Local Living Lab, currently? On first hand, certainly not. No institution and unconscious will, if exists. On the other side, it is possible to draw the first conditions of its creation and even the first scattered achievements which, once put in network, would constitute its own prefiguration. The first actions draw tracks, point out difficulties. The need for institutionalizing is necessary - not to achieve effectiveness because institutionalization is heavy to implement but by need for representation, for visibility, for assertion of oneself with (old-fashioned?) values understandable by all - but also by need for more flexibility in actions, initiatives, ideas in a territorial coherence (with variable geometry!). Making a square of the circle? No, the flows circulate.

To transform the "non-lieu" (the hybrid neither-nor as a nowhere) into virtual territory with a true identity.

5.   Conclusions

Can this too short and too elliptic analysis of the Local Living Labs, positioned in an extreme Briard context, help to read anew the current experiments of the Local Living Labs? Three issues have to be addressed but can already animate the debate of our session.

First, the concepts applied here to a very local territory, the Brie, have to be improved on a larger scope of such territories but also to larger territories even if still local ones.

Frontiers go-through, variable geometry territory, territorial intelligence, actors networking, Network Society and hybrid cultures, all these concepts and practices are transferable and enlightening. The bias of a society-oriented analysis, where the user of technologies is first of all a social being in a social environment, a "co-designer", a Network Society co-author before to be a co-designer of services and technologies, should be probably and generally speaking applied to Local Living Labs and to Living Labs.

The first next job will probably be to focus on the idea of LLL as frontiers go-through, concept that has imposed itself to the analysis and that allowed revisiting the aggregation of interests mechanisms. How LLL and Living Labs in general can be seen and act as a new actor of the aggregation mechanisms by its role of frontiers go-through? The choice of technology, user or society orientated policies of LLL and LL will determine the type of development and so the type de living of the territories.

Secondly, have local territories, especially poor and small ones, the possibility to create LLL that will structure their future? Two conditions seem at least necessary. First, the actors should have the conscientiousness of the challenges that they are facing and the imagination to create new devices, social devices. Secondly, these devices have to fit with the local situation and the global environment. As local means are poor, imagination and will has to be rich. LLL has to rest on human resources and confidence, networking and training in a large assumption.

Such LLL should be conceived as flows, or at least as nodes that capture the necessary wealth of the territory outside and internal flows. For example, LL of bigger areas will feed LLL, but at the demand of the second one. Nevertheless reciprocity must exist, probably not exactly on the same level.

Thirdly, a network of LL, or more generally clusters, including LLL, appears as a new actor by itself. It is breeding the LL and the territories they live in and can structure them for a part. This innovation and innovative networking is of real interest for territories and the LL, each one having its part of work at its level but also in transversal flows.

References

[1] ANNERSTEDT Jan, HASELMAYER Sascha, Living Labs Europe, Third Generation Living Labs : The Quest for User-Centered Mobile Services, paper presented at eChallenge 2006, Barcelona October 2006,
[2] AUGE M., Pour quoi vivons-nous ?, Paris, Fayard, 2003
[3] AUTHIER M., PRADALIER-ROY F., SERRES M., Pays de Connaissances, Editions du Rocher, 1998.
[4] BERTACCHINI Y., QUONIAM L., Information, Réseaux et Projet territorial, 3e Journées de la Proximité, Nouvelles croissances et territoire, Carré des Sciences, Paris, décembre 2001. <http://archivesic.ccsd.cnrs.fr/sic_00000441.html>
[5] BROUSSEAU Éric, Curien Nicolas, Économie d'Internet, économie du numérique, Revue économique, vol. 52, numéro hors série, octobre 2001, p. 7-36. <http://www.cairn.info/revue-economique-2001-7.htm>, p16 et 21
[6] CASTELLS Manuel, The Rise of the Network Society, Blackwell Publishers, Oxford, 1996
[7] Diagnostic de la Société de l'Information en Midi Pyrénées, http://www.ardesi.fr/Le-13-decembre-la-Region-Midi, annuel
[8] HERAUD Jean-Alain, Is there a regional dimension of innovation-oriented knowledge networking ? Fifth Regional Science and Technology Policy Research Symposium (RESTPOR) at Kashikojima (Japan), 5-7 September, 2000.
[9] LEVY P., L'intelligence collective. Pour une anthropologie du cyberspace. La Découverte, 1994
[10] Office fédéral suisse de la statistique, Liste des indicateurs groupés par thème, parmi beaucoup :<http://www.bfs.admin.ch/bfs/portal/fr/index/themen/16/04/key/approche_globale.approach.3 01.ht>
[11] <www.zeknowledge.com >
[12] REIT (Réseau européen d'intelligence territoriale), http://mti.univ-fcomte.fr/reit
[13] RIFKIN, J. L'âge de l'accès. Du capitalisme à l'hypercapitalisme. Ed. La Découverte, 2000.
[14] VELTZ P., Mondialisation, villes et territoires. L'économie d'archipel, Paris, PUF, 1996

---

[i] To simplify the approach, but it will be one of the purposes of the workshop to deepen the definition , a Local Living Lab is defined like a Living Lab with local dimension. "Living Labs Europe opens up the potentials of innovative (mobile) applications and technologies to (mobile) European citizens, companies, researchers and investors for the purpose off pioneering applications for European end-users and markets, enhance attractiveness for visitors, residents, business and to provide a European platform for innovative collaboration and opening markets. " [http://www.livinglabs-europe.com/livinglabs.asp]. We do not treat here the "mobile" dimension.

[ii] or at least the clearest as possible

[iii] A preference for the concept of "centered" when addressing the users and of "oriented" when addressing the society.

[iv] The article focuses on three dimensions of the Network Society that seem particularly important in that analyzing context : ICTs, sustainable development and globalization

[v] www.2t2m.fr

[vi] The expression recovers at least two meanings. The most current, nearer to the marketing than to scientific approach, refers to anglo-saxon expression "Intelligence service". The territorial intelligence "connects (then) the watching practices to the public action for economic and industrial development of a territory" [11]. Territorial Intelligence can have a broader connotation of instrument of sustainable development including territorial management, evaluation, prospective and governance[12]. Another approach Bertacchini, Quoniam [4] refers to collective intelligence , Levy [9] and Michel Authiers [2].

[vii] Another dimension appears essential, object perhaps of future works, that of the esthetics of the Network Society.

Collaboration and the Knowledge Economy: Issues, Applications, Case Studies
P. Cunningham and M. Cunningham (Eds.)
IOS Press, 2008

Living Lab (LL) Business Models for Local Development

Karel CHARVAT, Petr HORAK, Sarka HORAKOVA
WirelessInfo, Cholinska 1048/19, Litovel, 784 01, Czech Republic
Tel: +420604617327, Fax: + 42028197350, Email: charvat@wirelessinfo.cz

Abstract: The paper is focused on analysis of economical processes and management methods inside Living Labs. The study is built on eight year of experience of forming such Living Lab. It tries to compare practical experience from Living Lab building with some theoretical approaches. Current research about LL environment is mainly focused on social and technological aspects of Living Labs, but economical point of view is missing. Also paradigm of openness is in current research not analysed from economical point of view. The objective of analysis is open real economical discussion about LLs.

1. Introduction

Information technologies are in the process of the rapid development. In the whole Europe were established centres with the ability to provide alternative solution of mobile applications and technologies more quickly and effectively. These centres were the base stones for unites called Living Labs (LL). Living Labs respect users´ defined requirements and offer services where users can be involved into research, development and testing and can actively contribute to innovation process of new technologies and their final design. This active connection is a base of modern partnership between research, test centre of LL and end-user [1]. The European Network of Living Labs (ENoLL) was launched by the Finnish EU Presidency on 20 November 2006, as a step towards European Innovation System. In the first wave of ENoLL 19 Living Labs from 15 European countries joined the network: One of them, Czech Living Lab - WIRELESSINFO, was established as the first Living Lab in Czech Republic.

The paper tries to compare experiences from this LL, with analysis of different studies, focused on regional ICT deployment and suggest models for successful building of LL and discusses also advantage and disadvantage of Open Source business model inside and outside of LL

2. Objectives

The objective of this paper is open public discussion focused on sustainable development of LLs. Current research work is focused mainly on social and societal aspect of LL building and there exists no relevant studies answering the basic economical problems of LL sustainability. There exist many social and societal studies about LL, but economical research was not opened. The main objective of this paper is to define until now non answered questions about economical and management issue of living lab and provide some initial opinion. This has to be later study by specialist from economy, management, and probably also legislation. These questions are:

1. What are the economical rules for successful cooperation inside of LL environment?
2. What are key factors influencing successful and sustainable building of Living Lab, what are the advantages and disadvantages of top down and bottom up approach?

3. How to manage ad hoc team?
4. Is Open Source Model of Software Development optimal business model for LL, what are advantages and disadvantages?

This paper is not able to answer deeply above mentioned questions. It can define important objectives for future studies, which have not been discussed by Living Labs communities yet. There are only given some hypothesis, which are formulated on the base of practical experiences.

3. Rules of Benefit

Collaboration inside of LL represents normal economical relation among different subjects. Living labs are usually not chains, but they use more complicated models using both horizontal and vertical collaboration. To manage the potential conflicts among all partners within the LL, a suitable model must be defined and accepted by all partners e can define simple rule of benefit in the case of two cooperating SMEs.

We could expected, that SME 1 has initially profit A and SME 2 has profit B before collaboration. The result of collaboration will be such, partner 1 will lose part of its initial profit (lose is C),, because probably part of its activities will be taken by partner 2- But in the some time, he will also increase its profit as result of collaboration (increasing of profit is D) So it will have final profit

$A - C + D$.

Similar for partner 2 his final profit will be

$B - E + F$

Where E is lose and F is increasing profit from collaboration

The objective for successful collaboration is to define such rules, that the final result has to such that

$D - C > 0$, and $F - E > 0$.

Important question is, how to find good balance of D - C and F - E.
This question is more complicated in collaboration of more organization. Solving such problems could be done by using methods of linear programming.

The problem of currently used methods of LL environment analysis is that the main attention is focused more on qualitative aspects than on quantitative. The qualitative aspects are important, because they differentiate LL from other forms of collaboration. Without solving basic economical problems will be not possible to guarantee long time sustainability of any LL

4. Bottom Up Versus Top Down Model of Living Lab Building

The innovation process inside the LL has three components, which play important role and which are core principle of existence of any living lab. These components could be described by triangle product – project – business.

Product – is the object of business of one or more members inside or outside of the LL and which is developed and innovated during the entire life of LL. Project includes all innovative processes improving products quality and business is a commercialization of product (not necessary only B2B or B2C, but it could be also B2G).

Real innovation process inside of LL has necessary compose from all from these three components. There exist also models, where one component is missing_ For example reduction on business – product: is typical case of selling existing products without any innovation. It tends to lead in long term period to losing competitiveness on the market. Other often case is project – product, which is: often used model in university, which represent research, without real business. The model project – business: is the methods of some organization, where they business strategy is to participate in project without needs of any concrete output), but this models cannot be real business model for LL.

The important aspect of LL business strategy is that, which is from these three components on the top of triangle. We recognized next three models:

1. Project driven LL – is probably most often model, which represent classical top down approach. This model is usually used for building of technological or innovating parks and drivers are usually regions, regional development agency, universities or research organization. The primary goals of building of such LL are usually social, for example increasing employment in region. The big advantage of this approach is existence of political and economical support, which helps in phase of LL building. The potential threat could be lack of interest from the side of SMEs and end users.

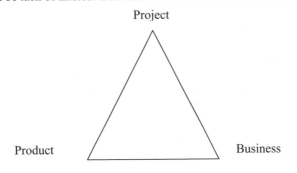

Project

Product   Business

2. Business driven LL- the core principle of this LL is the existence of a large investor (industry, join venture capital, but it could be also government), which needs to solve some concrete economical problem (to developed new product, build regional technical infrastructure, etc.). This investor brings together researchers, SME developers and end-users. Finally he finances the development of this product. As in previous cases, there is big advantage in start phase of LL. Orientation of LL is mainly on economical profit. Threats could be for SMEs that they could become only supplier for this big investor.

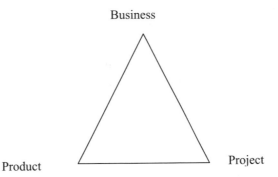

Business

Product   Project

3. Product driven LL is example of bottom up approach to LL building. LL is established mainly by SMEs, to be more competitive on market. The primary objectives of such LL are economical, because activities are driven by local and regional SMEs. This kind of LL has also strong social aspect. Advantage is strong interest of all players, threat could be financial situation. The members have to compete for financial resources on market or compete for research money.

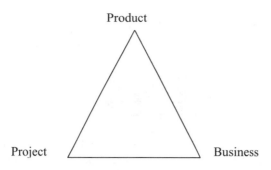

These are only border examples, in reality here could be all scale of other alternatives, which depend on fact how strong are interrelations among single components of triangle. WirelessInfo is an example of the third approach and we believe that it is good strategy for long time development of LL.

Our experiences, in accordance with [3], have shown, that strength of WirelessInfo development projects was their bottom-up approach This was driven by SMEs need rather than centralised intervention. However, the narrow focus of bottom-up projects complicates the extrapolation of sustainable business models or quantitative cost-benefits. While further funding may also be jeopardised, the greater problem may be the difficulty in learning lessons from what is already being done. Living Lab is an innovative approach, but there exist some commonalities with other models, which are used in local and regional development like e-communities of Digital Business Ecosystems. Probably some aspects are more critical for Living Labs, then for other models. Important questions are: "Why exist successful Living Labs in some regions? Why exist they in some regions without direct regional interventions? Why is the LL development so slow in some regions?" Our experience demonstrates that key success factors are presence of so called local or regional champions. This term was introduced by [2] and also other studies focused on this issue [3], demonstrate importance of Local Champions. In local and regional rural context, where WirelessInfo is mainly active, they could be defined as:

1. Local actors who are not interested in technology but take up the role for the greater good of the communities they live in
2. Younger and higher educated people moving to the rural areas, who wanted to have the some level of services as in cities,
3. Local business with clear innovative and knowledge based grooving strategy, which need access and sharing of knowledge

Our experience show, that identification of these Champions is key success factor for successful and sustainable building of Living Lab.

5.   How to Manage Ad Hoc Team

LL is new model of collaboration. What is difference between LL and classical chain model. In chain economy exist simple inter organisational relations.

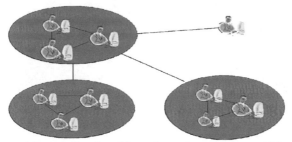

There exist clear hierarchy and model respect hierarchies inside of organisation. If we compare this models with ad hoc cooperation models, which is often used inside of LL, we could see, that there exist two levels of hierarchies, inside of organisation and inside of projects and in principle one person could work on more projects.

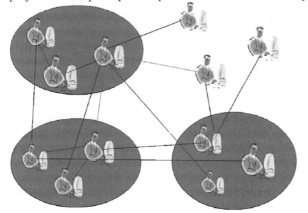

So, there is an important question for management specialists: "How to manage these two hierarchies? How is possible to find the successful models for such kind of collaboration?"

6. Guarantee Open Source Software Development Model Sustainable Development of Living Lab

The current paradigm is that not only development of software, but all knowledge inside of Living Lab has to be built on principle of Open Source. This could of cause speed up innovation inside of Living Lab, but on opposite side, these models doesn't guarantee long time sustainability of Living Lab and cannot be implemented as single unique model. We compare our practical experiences with theoretical results of Humboldt project [4] and we could conclude our experiences into next topics:

There exist real of SME IT developers to use Open Source for building application. As main advantage was mentioned:

a. There can be found the program which suits the end user's needs absolutely
b. The end user can be engaged into the development directly and "leave there his own footprint"
c. Sometimes the program could be very simple and the end user can easily grasp how it works
d. User can just cut off the usable part of the code and starts his own project on this
e. It is possible to use a source code from another project if both licenses allow that

On the opposite side, there is small interest of SME developers to publish their components as Open Source. As main threats are mentioned:

a. According to the open philosophy it is hard to get some fees for the program usage
b. It is necessary to change the business mode. Source of money revenue is not the sales of program, but additional services
c. The user are sometimes quite ungrateful or even rude, so it is hard to deal with them
d. The group can split apart with all the source codes and found the new company, so called „fork". This is mainly caused by personal arguments inside of a team. Or simply rival company can take over the development and introduce better business plan.
e. It can happen, that very important developer can leave the company and the right substitution will not be found. The reason for this (leaving the company) may be also very ridicules.

The above-mentioned points are very important and it is difficult to overcome this opinion. Also our analysis demonstrated that most of useful open source products were in the beginning supported by certain form of public subsidies (direct intervention or development on universities). Our experiences based on eight year of Open Source usage and development from point of view of SMEs could be concluded into next points:

a. For successful opening your products as Open Source on the market you need to have certain, strong market position, which guarantee you, that your profit from opening of your solution will be higher, then your potential loses of part of market
b. It could be very useful to open or your older solution or product, which is not main part of your portfolio. This could bring you big marketing profit
c. It is useful to open as an Open Source such product, which could support selling your other products, for example libraries or solutions, which depend on your commercial products.

Another question is the openness or sharing of knowledge directly inside of Living Lab. Also here is our opinion, that Open Source model cannot be recommended universally From this reason, we introduced new type of a licence (WirelessInfo licence [5]), which combine both approaches and advantages from commercial development and open source developments. Source code is managed by one organisation as for open source, but it is not generally free. The source is open for other organisation (SMEs) after signature of this licence, which guarantee to initial developer certain amount of money after selling applications, which will used this components. The number of payments is usually limited on selling first 10 or 20 licences, after is usage free. New users cannot distribute source code to third persons.

7. Results

WIRELESSINFO is a base stone of the Czech Living Lab (CLL). It is a non-profit consortium, which was established in 2003 on the basis of Living Lab principles. The practical existence of this LL brings new important scientific questions for different specialist. On the base of these questions, paper criticises current research in the area of LL, which is mainly socially and societal oriented. The paper put four questions related to economical and to the management aspects of LL. The results of paper are hypothesis, which has to be analysed by team composed from different specialists.

8. Business Benefits

Authors see business benefit of LL labs as whole, but also business benefit of single members of any member of LL as one from necessary conditions of long time sustainable existence of LL. The social and societal aspects are important, but do not guarantee sustainability. There is a strong need to refocus the current research in the area of Living

Labs and to look for good balance among social, societal and economical aspects of their existence.

9.   Conclusions

This paper introduces four questions, which authors see as important for successful building of living labs. These questions are:

1. What are the economical rules for successful cooperation inside of LL environment? – authors have suggested to define rules of benefits based on comparison of profits and losses of every partner and use theory of game or linear programming for optimization of profit. Further research is needed
2. What are key factors influencing successful and sustainable building of Living Lab? What are advantages and disadvantages of top down and bottom up approach? Authors promote support bottom up approach and support of local champions, which could be core of future LL. This idea is supported by some previous studies, but it is necessary to compare it with other models, when LL situation will be analysed after few years of existence, when there will not be more support for top down formed LL.
3. How to manage ad hoc team – authors don't know the answer
4. Is Open Source Model of Software Development optimal business model for LL, what are advantage and disadvantage authors promote good mix of any kind of licence and eventually to use some combined licence.

References

[1] http://www.wirelessinfo.cz/czechlivinglab/?lang=en&act=living-labs-europe
[2] A-BARD – Analyzing Broadband Access for Rural Development, Coordination Action, Priority SSP-2003-8.1.B.3.5 - Information Society Issues, D7.3 - Final A-BARD Recommendations
[3] Study on Availability of Access to Computer Networks in Rural Areas, Contract No: 30-CE-0099278/00-78, Final Report, Nov-07, Directorate General for Agriculture and Rural Development
[4] Humboldt, A2.4-D1 Software distribution strategies and business models, 2007
[5] www.wirelessinfo.cz WirelessInfo licence

Collaboration and the Knowledge Economy: Issues, Applications, Case Studies
P. Cunningham and M. Cunningham (Eds.)
IOS Press, 2008

An Empirical Classification of Knowledge Sharing Networks in Practice

Robert M. VERBURG, J. H. Erik ANDRIESSEN

Delft University of Technology, Jaffalaan 5, 2628 BX Delft, The Netherlands
Tel: +31 15 278 7234, Fax: +31 15 278 2950, Email: r.m.verburg@tudelft.nl; Erika@tudelft.nl

Abstract: Many knowledge intensive organizations rely on knowledge sharing networks. Such networks, often called 'communities of practice' are found in many organizations but their forms and functions appear to be quite diverse. In this article we determine and discuss a number of basic types of knowledge networks. A literature analysis and a study of 38 networks in large organizations yielded two dimensions of networks, institutionalization and proximity. On the basis of these dimensions four basic types of knowledge networks were discerned: strategic networks, informal networks, question & answer networks, and on line strategic networks. The recognition of this variety of knowledge networks highlights the different ways in which knowledge sharing and creating can be organized and shows that these different forms of organizing require different technological and organizational support

Keywords: Communities of practice; knowledge sharing and transfer; new organizational forms

1. Introduction – Knowledge Processes, Innovation and Networks

Current work environments are characterized by knowledgeable, productive, and flexible employees, who contribute significantly to firm performance through innovation [1]. Communication possibilities have improved high quality collaboration between people across traditional boundaries. The role of learning of both of individuals and groups within these structural organizational realities has become a major challenge for companies. Employee development in a broad sense is crucial for companies in rapidly changing contexts. Increasing expertise within the firm is important for the organization. Also, most employees value opportunities for some form of development at work, increasing the attractiveness of employers able to offer such opportunities.

Learning is equally important on a group level, for example where external collaborations between firms are becoming increasingly important. The concept of knowledge networks has attracted much attention over the years. The concept originates from the realm of knowledge management but as more and more companies are relying on their knowledge base, knowledge networks have become a very visible reality in many organizations. Knowledge intensive organizations are increasingly dependent on transferring and sharing knowledge, experiences and insights among employees. Two ways to deal with this issue are found in organizations, codification and interaction. The first approach leans heavily on knowledge systems and procedures to store and exchange documents. The second approach relies more on interpersonal exchange of knowledge and highlights the role of knowledge intermediaries and knowledge sharing networks. Both approaches can be considered elements in a knowledge-based perspective on firms which highlights the organizational routines and experiences on which individuals draw to perform optimally and use the creative potential of human action [2].

Emergent social networks have been studied by social scientists for a long time. However, organization theorists have only recently recognized their role as vital conduits for knowledge flows [3]. Knowledge sharing networks can be found within and across many organizations nowadays and are often called 'communities of practice'. The forms, functions, and terminology of these knowledge-sharing networks can differ quite dramatically. The problem with networks and interpersonal knowledge sharing is that the transfer of what is learned remains limited to the few people involved. Elsewhere in the network people cannot benefit form this knowledge, since the local knowledge is not 'translated' into new organizational procedures and ways of working. When shared knowledge is accepted by the network, it becomes organizational knowledge, which is than available to be embedded in organizational practices and to be distributed again to individuals or groups. But there has to be a special agency to ensure that the experience becomes embedded in the network [4]. These ideas suggest that knowledge networks may have a double function, that of facilitating the interaction and learning of individual members, and that of bridging the gap between experience-sharing individuals and the network. And indeed some organizations have communities that 'translate' their member's knowledge into overviews of best practices

2. Objectives – the Classification of Knowledge Networks

The purpose of this article is to clarify this conceptual jungle by systematically comparing the various concepts and phenomena that are encountered in this field. We will propose a classification model of knowledge networks, based on the building blocks offered in the literature, and we will identify several basic types of knowledge networks using an empirical analysis of such networks in practice. The existence of identifiable types of knowledge networks has implications for both theory and practice, as unjustifiable theoretical generalizations concerning interaction in or facilitation of knowledge networks may be avoided by specifying different kinds of organizational knowledge networks. Conclusions about how to organize and facilitate knowledge networks have often been too general and a typology of knowledge networks will allow for a better understanding of conditions for success and failure in different contexts.

2.1 In search of knowledge networks

Knowledge networks can be found within one corporation, spanning many business units, but they can also be inter-organizational, comprising members of different companies. For example, such networks could involve researchers working on a similar topic in different research organizations. These networks are clearly different from the more or less co-located groups of colleagues as described by [5,6,7].

Should one then conclude that we are talking about two completely different phenomena? On the one hand, local, informal groups of both experienced and inexperienced traditional workers, and on the other hand often globally distributed groups of expert knowledge professionals? Despite the differences, these groups also have much in common, which justifies bringing them together. Their commonality is to be found in the fact that they are all emergent, autonomous and self-organizing networks, whose primary purpose involves knowledge sharing, knowledge creation, and learning. The traditional local communities of practice have come to be considered as a subset of a general type of learning networks [8, 9,10]. Learning in this sense is an interaction process, where knowledge is socially constructed and situated. Of course, people need to build upon mutual understanding, creatively handling 'cognitive distance' [10] before they can adequately share or jointly develop new knowledge. However, the growth of a common identity and work practice is not necessarily the central function of such communities.

Even within self-organizing groups that are primarily focused on learning, several types can be distinguished either derived from a typology or from differentiating dimensions. Some scholars have distinguished two or three completely different types of knowledge sharing networks, while others have identified dimensions along which knowledge networks can differ (see next section). The objective of this paper is to combine both approaches, in other words to derive basic types from a dimensional analysis of a large set of knowledge networks. We identify dimensions and basic types by analyzing the literature and by assessing the characteristics of a number of knowledge networks. This approach consists of the following steps. The first step is to identify different characteristics of knowledge sharing networks on the basis of .a literature review of major publications on such networks. The list of characteristics of different networks is then used to score a number of different networks. This is done by an expert rating, i.e. we ask a number of scholars who have published research on knowledge sharing networks to score their networks by means of our list of identified characteristics. Before the expert rating a pilot is done in order to test for convergent validity and to eliminate possible ambiguities in the description of the c characteristics. The final step involves the analysis of the expert rating. This includes the extraction of underlying dimensions and the statistical identification of basic network types.

In the next section we will describe the identification of characteristics of knowledge networks from the literature. Then we will provide more details on our methodology of the empirical studies and present the results of our analysis.

2.2   Identifying key characteristics of knowledge sharing networks

The notion of 'knowledge networks' appears to cover a variety of organization related social structures that have a common raison d'être in knowledge sharing. The concept refers to rather loosely coupled networks of employees who cross intra- or inter- organizational boundaries and interact to learn from each other by exchanging information and experiences. According to the literature, however, these social structures may differ in the objectives of their knowledge sharing, in their structure, their composition and distribution, and in the way they interact and communicate. The key characteristics of knowledge networks that were identified by different authors are presented below.

- Purpose: Having a common mission versus only exchanging information, or also: having an organizational orientation, i.e. developing best practices or even innovative solutions, versus an individual orientation, i.e. exchanging information for solving personal problems and learning [11]
- Contract value: degree to which the community has to deliver concrete results [12]
- Formalization: having more or less formal meetings and an appointed coordinator [12]; formally set up by management and clearly visible to management [13]
- Composition: only experts or both experts and newcomers [12].
- Boundary: whether the community is closed or open for new members [12,8], having fixed or shifting relationships and membership [14]
- Reciprocity (connectivity): degree to which members interact mutually and know each other [8,14]
- Identity: Feelings of cohesion, trust and belongingness [14,15]
- Size of the community [8]
- Intra- or inter-organizational [8]
- Geographical dispersion [16,17]
- Mode of interaction: face to face and/or via ICT [16,17]

The list of characteristics presented in table 1 has been used to characterize a set of knowledge networks that have been studied by colleagues in several countries (see below for a description of the method). The relations between the characterizations of the different networks will then be used as the basis for discerning basic dimensions and types of knowledge networks.

3. Methodology - Emprical Analysis of 38 European Networks

For the purpose of this study a total of 38 networks from different countries were rated in terms of the key aspects as presented in table 1. The 38 networks under study were selected on the basis of their descriptions in the current literature. In the past few years, many in depth studies of knowledge networks, both intra-company and inter-company were published and presented at conferences by a variety of authors [17,18,19,20,21]. The authors were approached and asked to apply our scoring method to their networks reported in the literature. All authors agreed to participate, resulting in the sample of 38 networks (eleven from Italy, eleven from Finland, ten from the Netherlands, five from Norway and one from France).

Can this group of knowledge networks be considered as a representative sample? No, they cannot, simply because the population is unknown. This study aims to develop more clarity about the population and about possible sub-populations. The main criterion for selection in the various studies was to find groups of which the primary object was the exchange of knowledge. Another criterion for including cases in this study was variety. In other words, our aim was to collect diverse knowledge networks from different organizations in terms of purpose, size and other characteristics.

4. Results

The 12 variables (characteristics of networks) and 38 knowledge networks were analyzed using a special form of factor analysis. Categorical principal components analysis (CATPCA) was used to accommodate variables of mixed measurement levels. The results are presented in table 1.

Table 1: Results of the Categorical principal components analysis (CATPCA) factor analysis with variable principal normalization.

	Dimension 1	Dimension 2
Organizational. orientation	,796	-,127
Contract value	,750	-,208
Formalization	,685	-,110
Origin	-,331	-,290
Composition	,637	,133
Boundaries	,729	-,300
Reciprocity	-,014	,737
Identity	,422	,347
Size	-,654	-,380
Intra-inter focus	-,256	,678
Mediated interaction	-,283	-,711
Dispersion	-,049	,834

Results show that certain key aspects are highly related, resulting in the identification of two main clusters of characteristics that can be considered as two basic dimensions for differentiating knowledge networks. The identification of clusters does not imply that all aspects in a cluster are basically identical. Characteristics are placed in the same cluster because they tended to be found together in the networks studied.

The first dimension consists of the following five characteristics: organizational orientation, contract value, formalization, boundaries, and composition (Cronbach's α = .76). Knowledge networks that are focused on the development of organizational knowledge also tend to have strong accessibility rules, institutionalized coordination and other formalized rules. At the other pole of the dimension one finds a focus on individual learning and problem solving, on knowledge networks with relatively low formalization that are open for new and even inexperienced members. We labelled this dimension 'institutionalization'.

The second dimension represents four characteristics: reciprocity, focus, dispersion, and mediated interaction. These elements refer to the degree of interaction between members, the inter- or intra-organizational focus of the network, the geographical dispersion of its members, and the degree of mediated versus face-to-face communication (Cronbach's α = .60). We labelled this dimension 'proximity'. The fist component, reciprocity, has clear relations with social network indicators such as density. High on this dimension one finds geographically and organizationally close knowledge networks with high levels of interaction, while knowledge networks low on this dimension are strongly dispersed and do not have high levels of internal interaction.

4.1 Identifying basic types of knowledge sharing networks

The two dimensions are related to important key characteristics of organizational units. Formalization and institutionalization are major control mechanisms for organizational units [22]. It is interesting to note that knowledge networks can strongly differ on these basic mechanisms. The fact that many of the networks are informal in nature is in line with the original theories about communities of practice [5]. However, some knowledge sharing networks are institutionalized to quite a degree, although not to the degree of formalization as in project teams.

The second dimension is also quite central to organizational functioning. Proximity enables groups to interact and communicate frequently, which forms an important condition for groups to develop trust and to cooperate well. This dimension also seems to be related to the distinction between weakly tied and strongly tied networks. Interestingly, this dimension is related to the use of ICT media for communication in the network. A high score on the proximity dimension implies face to face communication as the primary mode of interaction within the network.

It is now possible to see how the 38 knowledge networks are distributed across the two extracted dimensions. Figure 1 consists of a scatter plot with the institutionalization dimension on the x-axis and the proximity dimension on the y-axis. The scores of the networks on the five items of the institutionalization dimension were computed. This dimension has a minimum score of 5 and a maximum score of 15. Scores on the four items of the proximity dimension were computed accordingly leading to a minimum score of 4 and a maximum score of 12. A detailed analysis suggests that the networks cluster in four types as shown in figure 1.

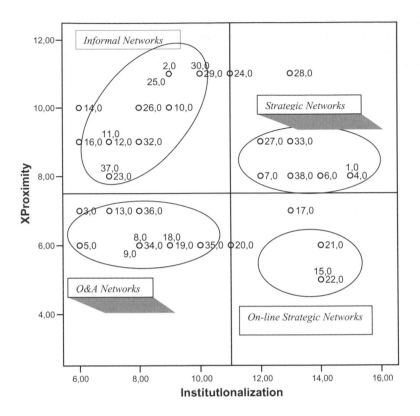

FIGURE 1: A Classification of Knowledge Networks in a two dimensional space

The different types of networks can be described in the following way:

1. Informal Networks: groups of employees with a common area of interest, often closely related to their work (practice), having substantial interaction, a common history and 'culture' involving shared concepts, ideas, stories etc. The main purpose of (people in) these networks is to learn from each other; the transfer of this shared knowledge to the company is of less importance. This type of knowledge networks is generally not very formalized, although some may receive support when they have proven their value. These communities grow spontaneously, are either small or have a small core and a larger circle of peripheral members. According to our studies, a very active coordinator or core group and adequate ICT support are generally required to ensure success of such networks.

2. Question and Answer (Q&A) Networks: knowledge networks with low to intermediate proximity and low levels of institutionalization. These networks consist of employees who exchange, over a company intranet, questions ("Who can help me with ….") and answers concerning the solution of certain practical problems. Although the size of such networks may be quite large (sometimes many hundreds of members), they still display some form of group identity, based on commonality in function and organization. Q&A Networks have limited purposes and seem to thrive without many success conditions, except minimal commitment of those involved as members and good email connections.

3. Strategic Networks: institutionalized groups of experts whose activities are focused on organizational learning. These groups are highly supported with resources and have a strong 'contract value'. In other words, participants are expected, implicitly or

explicitly, to perform for the company, to develop best practices or even innovative solutions. These networks generally consist of a limited number of experts, without a periphery of 'lurkers', since membership is generally not open. The food company network described above is a good example of this type of network. In some cases, these groups may cross the border between knowledge networks (learning oriented groups) and workgroups or task forces (product oriented groups). Like most knowledge networks found in large companies, members of the strategic networks tend to be organizationally and geographically widely distributed. Some of these networks, however, do much interaction in face-to-face meetings. Our studies suggest that strategic networks require intensive preparation, member selection, support, and coordination to be effective.

4. On-line Strategic Networks. A small group of the networks studied here is relatively highly institutionalized yet shows low levels of proximity among its members. These networks have similar institutionalization as the strategic networks described above but low proximity, particularly because of their exclusive communication via electronic means (mainly internet or Intranets). This setting makes interaction, coordination, and cohesion forming within the network quite difficult. Such networks seem to be rare and we have labelled these as 'on-line strategic networks.

5. Business Benefits and Conclusions

There are a great variety of social structures that can be discussed under the heading of knowledge sharing networks. Some try to take the differences into account by distinguishing two or three (sub) types of networks; however, these typologies are not similar and are not usually based on sound theoretical arguments or comparative empirical data. Many new terms have been invented, such as community of interest, community of commitment, interest group, network of practice, knowledge network, knowledge community, internal community, expanded community, formal network and epistemic community. The great variety in terminology has lead to the current situation in which different names are applied to the same phenomenon or that the same label refers to different phenomena.

The recognition of this variety of knowledge network points firstly at the different ways in which knowledge sharing and learning can be organized. Secondly, it has consequences both for technological and organizational support of such networks. The 'availability' of diverse types of networks may promote the realization that before starting knowledge communities, organizations should first consider their objectives and situational constraints. Differences in objectives, desired connectivity and dispersion then have implications for the organizational support that is required. Some networks need extensive top down facilitation, while others are only successful if they grow spontaneously from the bottom up and are left alone by management. As far as technical support is concerned, some communities can thrive well with limited communication tools, others need extensive information services and groupware to function optimally. The identification of the four main types will further enable companies and organizations to make an informed decision about what kind of network will suit their specific purposes.

References

[1]   T.Malone, The Future of Work. Harvard (Mas.):Harvard Business School Press, 2004.
[2]   H. Tsoukas, H, Introduction to the special issue on Knowledge-based Perspectives on Organizations: Situated Knowledge, Novelty, and Communities of Practice. Management Learning 33(4), 2002, pp. 419-426.
[3]   M.M. Appleyard, How does Knowledge Flow? Interfirm Patterns in the Semiconductor Industry. Strategic Management Journal 17, 1996, pp. 137-154.

[4]   C. Argyris & D. Schön, D.A.,Organizational Learning II: Theory, Method, and Practice, Reading (Mass.): Addison-Wesley, 1996

[5]   J. Lave & E. Wenger, Situated Learning. Legitimate Peripheral Participation. Cambridge: University Press, 1991

[6]   J. Brown & P. Duguid, 'Organizational Learning and Communities-of-Practice. Towards a Unified View of Working, Learning, and Innovation'. Organization Science 2(1), 1991, pp. 40-57

[7]   E.Wenger, R. McDermott & W. Snyder, Cultivating Communities of Practice, Harvard (Mas.):Harvard Business School Press, 2002.

[8]   J. Brown & P. Duguid, 'Knowledge and Organization; A Social-practice Perspective'. Organization Science 12(2). 2001, pp. 198-213.

[9]   M.Wasko, S. Faray & R. Teigland, Collective Action and Knowledge Contribution in Electronic Networks of Practice, Journal of the Association for Information Systems (JAIS) 5(11), 2004, pp.12-36

[10]   I. Bogenrieder & B. Noteboom, 'Learning groups: What types are there? A theoretical analysis and an empirical study in a consultancy firm'. Organization Studies 25 (2), 2004, pp.287-313

[11]   P. Gongla & C. Rizzuto, 'Evolving communities of practice: IBM Global Service experience'. IBM Systems Journal, 40(4), 2001, pp.842-862.

[12]   C. Collison , 'Connecting the new organization. How BP Amoco encourages post-merger collaboration'. Knowledge Management Review 7(2), 1999, pp. 12-15.

[13]   J. Botkin, Smart business: how knowledge communities can revolutionize your company. New York: The Free Press, 1999.

[14]   V. Allee, Knowledge Networks and Communities of Practice'. OD Practitioner, 32, 4. Retrieved from http://www.odnetwork.org/odponline/vol32n4/knowledgenets.html, 2000.

[15]   R. McDermott, Learning across Teams: The Role of Communities of Practice in Team Organizations'. Knowledge Management Review, 7(3), 1999, pp. 15-27..

[16]   C. Kimble, P. Hildreth & P.Wright, P, 'Communities of Practice: Going Virtual' in Knowledge Management and Business Model Innovation. Yogesh Malhotra (ed),. Hersey, : Idea Group Publishing, 2000, pp. 220-234

[17]   I. Ruuska & M. Vartiainen, 'Communities and other social structures for knowledge sharing - A case study in an Internet consultancy company' in Communities and Technologies. Marleen Huysman, Etienne Wenger, and Volker Wulf (eds). Dordrecht: Kluwer Academic Publishers, 2003, pp.578-603.

[18]   J. Andriessen, M. Huis in 't Veld & M. Soekıjad, Communities of Practice for Knowledge Sharing' in How to manage experience sharing: From organizational surprises to organizational knowledge J. H. Erik Andriessen and Babette Fahlbruch (eds),. Oxford, UK: Elsevier, 2004, pp. 173-194

[19]   M. Corso & A. Giacobbe, Organizing for continuous innovation: the communities of practice approach'. Paper for CINET Conference, Brighton, UK, 2005

[20]   E. Hustad & R. Teigland, Taking a differentiated view of intra-organizational distributed networks of Practice'. Paper presented at the Communities of Technologies Conference, Milan, Italy, 2005.

[21]   G. Sardone, Supporting Business Community Management through Social Network Analysis. Dissertation. Milan, Italy: Politecnico di Milano, 2006.

[22]   H. Mintzberg, Structure in fives: Designing effective organizations. Englewood Cliffs (NJ): Prentice-Hall, 1983.

Collaboration and the Knowledge Economy: Issues, Applications, Case Studies
P. Cunningham and M. Cunningham (Eds.)
IOS Press, 2008

An Inter-Organizational Configuration Management Database as Key Enabler for Future IT Service Management Processes

Wolfgang HOMMEL[1], Silvia KNITTL[2]

[1]*Leibniz Supercomputing Centre, Boltzmannstr. 1, Garching n. Munich, 85748, Germany*
Tel: +49 089 35831 7821, Fax: + 49 089 35831 7621, Email: hommel@lrz.de
[2]*Technische Universität München, Boltzmannstr. 3, Garching n. Munich, 85748, Germany*
Tel: +49 089 35831 8731, Fax: +49 089 35831 8531, Email: silvia.knittl@mytum.de

Abstract: Outsourcing is the remedy for many enterprises to improve their efficiency. However, to be able to assess the potential of one's own as well as the external providers' services, detailed information about the IT infrastructure and services is needed. In currently predominant IT Service Management Frameworks the so-called Configuration Management process provides an information nexus that is implemented by a database referred to as Configuration Management Database (CMDB). For outsourcing and collaboration scenarios such a CMDB should also provide an information basis for inter-organizational usage. Based on this motivation we first present the concept of an inter-organizational CMDB (ioCMDB). However, several IT Service Management disciplines need to be reconsidered in order to take full advantage of the ioCMDB. Thus, this article also presents the related challenges and the key issues for inter-organizational ITSM process enhancement.

1. Introduction

With technological advances, Information and Communication Technology (ICT) infrastructures become even more complex, while at the same time the demand to operate them cost-efficiently rises. Small and medium, but also an increasing number of large enterprises deem outsourcing or co-sourcing as an appropriate solution to improve the efficiency and maximize their benefits.

But to be able to assess and reassess the potential of their own as well as the external providers' services, detailed information about the IT infrastructure and services in sense of management ratios, such as key performance indicators, is needed. Best practice frameworks for IT Service Management (ITSM), such as the Information Technology Infrastructure Library version 3 (ITILv3) [1][2], and standards, such as ISO-IEC 20000-1 [3], provide guidance for management processes that have proven to work and be efficient.

However, for inter-organizational respectively federated services new requirements emerge, which are not entirely covered by the above mentioned frameworks yet. Basically full control over the services which are in use is assumed traditionally. In inter-organizational service applications this point-to-point nature cannot be taken for granted anymore [4]. Furthermore, there are no standardized mechanisms in place to selectively share management information between various service providers [5]. In the course of adopting ITIL, organizations traditionally adopted merely »the processes« of ITIL. But for inter-organizational services it is necessary that also the IT management »tools« adopt ITIL perspectives [6].

One of the most important ITSM processes is Configuration Management (CM). It provides information about the ICT infrastructure to be able to support all management disciplines like for example Incident Management, Financial Management, and Service Level Management. CM heavily relies on tool support, using the so-called Configuration Management Database (CMDB) as its information nexus, which stores the state of and relationships between Service Assets respectively Configuration Items (CIs). CIs include hardware, software, network components, incident records, policies, and various other information.

We have introduced the concept of an inter-organizational CMDB federation (ioCMDBf), based on the evolving CMDBf standard [7], and discussed its technical architecture concerning access control in previous work [8]. This paper presents the challenges of and proposed solution for inter-organizational ITSM (ioITSM) processes that make efficient use of the ioCMDBf tool support; it can best be described as an extension to well-established best practice frameworks, such as ITILv3.

This paper is structured as follows: In section 2 we describe several real world scenarios, which have in common that the related business services are supplied by the cooperation of multiple organizations. Thus ITSM processes need to cross organizational boundaries. All these cases are lacking from an appropriate tool to support their ioITSM processes. In section 3 we analyze and discuss the resulting disadvantages. Our concept of an ioCMDBf is presented in section 4 as well as the resulting redesign of existing processes by the examples of CM and Incident Management. The benefits of our introduced ioCMDBf are outlined in section 5, and section 6 concludes this article.

2.   Our Inter-organizational Services Scenarios

Our research is motivated by the practical demand for inter-organizational ITSM (ioITSM) in the following real-world business scenarios, which intersect at the Leibniz Supercomputing Centre (LRZ) as a central IT service provider:

*   Scenario 1: As part of the projects IntegraTUM and elecTUM, which are funded by the German Research Foundation (DFG) and the German Federal Ministry of Education and Research (BMBF), multiple IT services for higher education institutions that formerly have been operated locally are being recentralized at the LRZ. The business service is the students' lifecycle with automated access to IT infrastructure like learning management systems or computer labs [9].
*   Scenario 2: The European GÉANT2 project, which is co-funded by the European Commission and Europe's national research and education networks (NRENs), is ensuring high-quality service from one end user to another over multiple interconnected networks (so-called end2end links). End users within GÉANT2 are using such end2end links for transferring data across Europe from one of the endpoints of the 30 participating NRENs to another endpoint within this network [10].
*   Scenario 3: The LRZ is participating in Europe's high performance computing (HPC) infrastructure DEISA, which is partially funded by the European Commission. Its high performance computers are used by researchers from all over Europe as well as Grid partners from other continents [11]. The end users here are performing calculations within a Grid or virtualized HPC infrastructure without requiring direct access to the physical machines.

For each of these projects, the LRZ has to support the project specific ITSM process implementations. All of these projects have the following characteristics in common:

*   The final business service, as it is perceived by the end user, is accomplished not by a single organization but by multiple organizations.
*   For managing the IT services the ITSM has to cross local management domains. However, local management itself is not sufficient for the management of inter-organizational services, thus an inter-organizational ITSM needs to be established.

- There is no appropriate tool support for the respective ITSM processes in place.

The problems resulting from the lack of tool support as they are mitigated by our concept of an ioCMDBf will be described in the next section.

3. Problem Statement and Key Motivation for ioITSM Processes

Inter-organizational services as described in the scenarios above suffer from several drawbacks because an appropriate tool support is missing as of today. By means of the processes of Service Portfolio Management (SPoM), Incident Management, and Financial Management we are demonstrating these challenges in the following.

Within SPoM the service portfolio needs to be managed to improve business value. Without the assistance of an ioCMDBf, it is nearly impossible to quickly gain an overview of which services are offered by whom. This in turn diminishes the capabilities of inter-organizational SPoM, e.g. in order to come to make-or-buy decisions on a profound rationale, such as when almost identical services are offered independently by multiple organizational units. In scenario 1 various IT services are provided by TUM's different organizational units, such as the university's faculties, central administration, and the LRZ as IT service provider (cp. Figure 1). Although the recentralization of email services to the LRZ is already planned within the project IntegraTUM, possible further potential for consolidation might be missed, since there is no information base in place which offers an detailed overview of existing services and their suppliers.

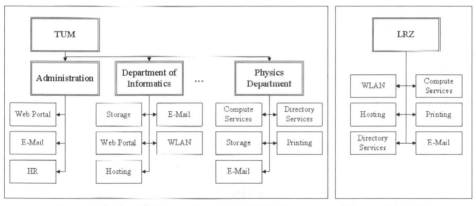

Figure 1: Extract of IT Services Provided by TUM's Organizational Units and the LRZ

Incident Management's goal is to solve interruptions or degradation in service quality as quickly as possible. Without the assistance of an ioCMDBf this process might be rather inefficient, for example if an end-user does not know whom to contact for help during a service incident. The same applies to the service desk agents, e.g. in the case of an email service failure, in order to figure out which of the email servers shown in Figure 1 is the actual root cause.

One of the Financial Management's primary tasks is service accounting. When services are offered by multiple organizations, currently no widely accepted approach is available to support accounting models, such as proposed in [12]. By means of an ioCMDBf, the current state of and the correlation between virtual services, virtual organizations, and real organizations, on which all current Grid models are based, can be derived by a workflow that can be automated to a large degree, which is at present not possible, because there is no ioCMDBf in place yet.

These examples show that on the one hand an appropriate information base like a ioCMDBf is necessary to improve ITSM efficiency like the SPoM's decision processes, the incident resolution times, and laying out a base for automation of accounting mechanism. On the other hand however, the formerly locally operated ITSM processes need to be adapted respectively enhanced for the interactions with the ioCMDBf.

4.   Our Approach for Inter-organizational IT Service Management

Here we describe our concept of an ioCMDBf in section 4.1 and the resulting process enhancements necessary by the introduction of an ioCMDBf in section 4.2.

4.1   Tool Support for Inter-Organizational IT Service Management

Traditionally a CMDBf is used as a logically central information database for the ITSM processes, as depicted for organizations A and B in figure 2. However, for inter-organizationally provided services, the ioCMDBf's logical position shifts to a new ioITSM process layer above the traditional local ITSM layer. This is also the layer that requires the redefinition of ITSM processes, which in turn are adapted to inter-organizational requirements. Therefore, additional roles are required, such as an inter-organizational Change Advisory Board (CAB), and new activities need to be defined, such as the inter-organizational impact analysis based on the properties of CI attributes and relationships across organizational borders.

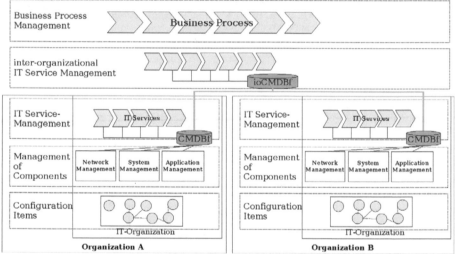

Figure 2: The ioCMDBf is Fully Integrated into the Management Layers

As can be seen from Figure 2, it is essential for the ioCMDBf to have interfaces to each local CMDBf that is deployed within each participating organization. Obviously, data protection aspects are vital because it will often be necessary for external users to have selective access to local data [13]. For this reason we have presented a policy-based access model based on Federated Identity Management (FIM) and Attribute Based Access Control (ABAC) in previous work [8].

4.2   Results of Inter-Organizational Service Management Process Enhancements

A holistic specification of the ioITSM process enhancements would go beyond the scope of this paper. Therefore we will describe the extension and redesign of ITSM processes on the examples of CM and Incident Management in this section.

Following the core ITIL specification [1], the main activities of CM are "management and planning", "configuration identification", "configuration control", "status accounting and reporting", and "verification and audit". For the inter-organizational case, we show the necessary extensions based on the example of "status accounting and reporting". While the former activities of CM are more on a strategic level we chose the operational activities of "status accounting and reporting" to outline the interactions with the ioCMDBf.

The main task of this process activity is to document the state of CIs in all of their life cycles phases. In the case of changing a local service's CI, which has an impact on the inter-organizational service, figure 3 shows the core activities of our redesigned ioITSM process. A local change could be requested within the scope of either a Request for Change (RfC) or a Standard Change, the latter being formally approved by Change Management in advance (also known as pre-authorized change). In GÉANT2 a Standard Change could for example be a customer's request for establishing a new end2end link. In the process of CM this change becomes visibly within the task of "RegisterCI". The local Configuration Manager has to approve this registration and also decide whether any of the inter-organizational services is affected by this change. Such an approval process can be semi-automated if there are appropriate policies and decision rules in place. If an inter-organizational service is affected by this change in the CMDB, the "RegisterCI" activity also has to take place in the ioCMDBf. According to the circumstances, policies need to be defined between CM and ioCMDBf to specify the workflow and consequences, for example, if the registration on either of these sides is missing. This process of status correlation has to be done on the local as well as on the inter-organizational level: In the case of our scenario GÉANT2, this reflects the reality that any local changes could be initiated at each of the 30 involved NRENs.

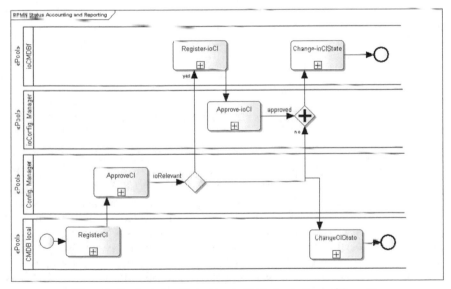

Figure 3: Configuration Management - Status Accounting and Reporting

From the user's perspective, changes and service requests must be submitted to the ioServiceDesk. There the request is approved according to the defined policies within the ioCMDBf, e.g. to figure out whether the user is sufficiently privileged. If this is the case, the corresponding Standard Change procedure is started. In the case of end2end links in the GÉANT2 example, the corresponding local Standard Change procedures are handled via each involved organization's local Service Desk. If the service instance is established successfully, it is necessary that both the local CMDB as well as the ioCMDBf are updated accordingly.

Figure 4 outlines the workflow within the inter-organizational Incident Management process. An Incident Detector reports an incident to the ioServiceDesk. For existing inter-organizational services, it is necessary to introduce this as a new role. It is possible to delegate this role to a local organizational unit, as it has been realized for example in the case of IntegraTUM, where TUM's Service Desk also acts in the role of the ioServiceDesk. Alternatively, a dedicated ioServiceDesk has to be created, as for example in GÉANT2. The activity "DetectIncident" is split into several subprocesses (indicated by the +signs in the diagram), since incidents might be detected either from users or event monitoring systems. These further activities, which are also handled by the ioServiceDesk, are following the Incident Management process description according to ITIL [2] and are not discussed here.

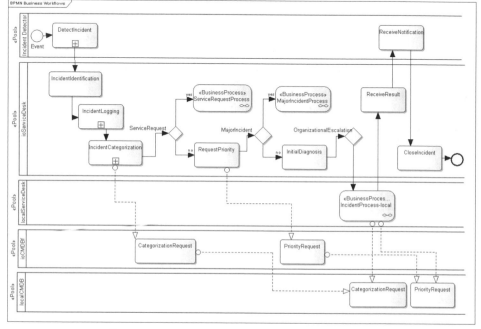

Figure 4 :Inter-Organizational Incident Management Process

The main difference to traditional Incident Management lies in the processing step of "IncidentCategorization", which determines the set of affected services and resources; hence, the ioCMDBf needs to provide the required input for this process, e.g. which of the involved organizational units are responsible for each subservice. A new business process instance needs to be initiated if the process determines that a service request instead of an incident needs to be handled, such as a customer's application for a new end2end link in GÉANT2. In local Incident Management processing, hierarchical as well as functional escalation mechanisms are already present for the exceptional case that the first level support cannot solve an incident. In the ioITSM case, we propose that an additional Organizational Escalation workflow has to be defined: Incident records will be passed on to the appropriate organizational unit, which can handle the request. In figure 4, this is depicted by each organization's local service desk; however, in existing implementations such as GÉANT2, it will be the support contact for any of the 30 NRENs. The ioCMDBf is required to support these processes in order to categorize the incidents correctly and link them to the affected services. Furthermore, the ioCMDBf needs to be connected to each local CMDB in order to synchronize the data; for example, if a subservice's CI reports downtime due to a scheduled maintenance task, incident reports by inter-organizational service monitoring can safely be ignored regarding escalation mechanisms, and the users can be informed accordingly.

5. Business Benefits

The ioCMDBf supports the management of inter-organizational IT services in the same way local CMDBs support the intra-organizational ITSM processes. Both the service providers and the users benefit from it as discussed in this section.

By retrieving Incident Management information for categorization purposes from the ioCMDBf, any subsequent organizational escalation will be much more efficient. Similarly, it will be avoided that trouble tickets are forwarded to the wrong organizational unit. Therefore, incidents will be solved faster, thus increasing the service's availability and the overall customer satisfaction. The introduction of an ioServiceDesk as a new ITSM role offers a single point of contact for inter-organizational services and simplifies the communication between the involved organizations, because the ioServiceDesk coordinates the necessary work tasks. In GÉANT2, this easily scales to all involved organizations of the 30 participating NRENs.

The Change Management can plan the handling of changes much easier, because an inter-organizational Change Advisory Board will coordinate maintenance time slots, and thus the impact of local changes to inter-organizational services can be anticipated reliably and efficiently. As an example, in the IntegraTUM scenario, changes to the central Identity Management System, which is operated at LRZ, must not be made during the online-application phase for study courses, as the TUM's business processes might severely suffer from any service failures. Such service dependencies can be derived from the ioCMDBf, which provides the required input for CM, resulting in a win-win situation for TUM, LRZ, and the customer.

Regarding Financial Management, the ioCMDBf gives an overview of which CIs are used by which services and which customers, and thus is the base for accounting and billing. In the Grid environment, it supports the assignment of virtual to real services and resources, and thus helps to develop a fair sharing of costs and expenses depending on the actual service usage.

The ioCMDBf also provides vital input for the design of Service Level Agreements and the optimized arrangement of service portfolios; while respecting the related business aspects, a detailed model of the infrastructure is provided in a way that SLAs can be adapted to changing customer requirements as discussed in [14].

6. Conclusions

More and more inter-organizational business cases require inter-organizational IT services and consequently a whole new class of ITSM processes. However, as we have shown, ioITSM is currently not adequately tool-supported. To leverage existing infrastructures and to extend existing, well-working best practice frameworks, we have introduced the concept of an inter-organizational Configuration Management Database (ioCMDBf).

This paper presented several of the challenges related to ioITSM and discussed inter-organizational variants of Configuration Management and Incident Management. With the help of three different real world scenarios we have shown that regarding the management of inter-organizational services also the ITSM processes need to be extended, i.e. that new roles like the ioServiceDesk and the ioConfiguration Manager have to be introduced; they cover relationships and activities between local and inter-organizational processes. Furthermore, the activities between the concerned parties have to be adapted.

Our research team is spread over various organizations (see http://www.mnm-team.org/) and taking part in the above described scenarios within Grid, network, and outsourcing projects. Thus one of our current research focal points is inter-organizational ITSM, including both the process design and the technical architectures. Our future work concentrates on the further definition and refinement of the inter-organizational ITSM processes as well as the Configuration Management process specification with the design of the ioCMDBf's interaction model. We also plan to apply our approach to non-public use cases in telecommunication industry.

Acknowledgments

The authors wish to thank the members of the Munich Network Management (MNM) Team for helpful discussions and valuable comments on previous versions of this paper. The MNM-Team, directed by Prof. Dr. Heinz-Gerd Hegering, is a group of researchers of the University of Munich, the Munich University of Technology, the University of the Federal Armed Forces Munich, and the Leibniz Supercomputing Centre of the Bavarian Academy of Sciences. The team's web-server is located at http://www.mnm-team.org/.

The authors also thank the members of the IntegraTUM project team for fruitful discussions and constant encouragement. IntegraTUM is headed by the vice president and CIO of TUM, Prof. Dr. Arndt Bode (see http://portal.mytum.de/iuk/cio/).

References

[1]   Lacy, Shirley and Macfarlane, Ivor. Service Transition, ITIL, Version 3. OGC, Office of Government Commerce. London TSO, The Stationery Office, 2007
[2]   Cannon, David and Wheeldon, David. Service operation, ITIL, Version 3. OGC, Office of Government Commerce. London TSO, The Stationery Office, 2007
[3]   ISO 20000. Available online at http://www.iso.org/iso/catalogue_detail?csnumber=41332
[4]   Candadai, Arun and McKenney, Robert. Federated Service Management - A federated approach to managing highly distributed web services. Feb. 18, 2006. Available online at http://soa.syscon.com/read/183919.htm
[5]   Bhoj, Preeti; Caswell, Deborah; Chutani, Sailesh; Gopal, Gita; Kosarchyn, Marta. Management of New Federated Services. Management of New Federated Services. Integrated Network Management 1997: 327-34
[6]   Leire Bastida, Alayn Cortazar, Pedro Gutiérrez. Ensuring QoS in a European Service Oriented Economy. How can ITIL contribute? Published in: Innovation and the Knowledge Economy: Issues, Applications, Case Studies, Paul Cunningham and Miriam Cunningham (Eds), 2005 IOS Press Amsterdam.
[7]   Forest Carlisle, Klaus Wurster, and et. al. CMDB Federation (CMDBf) - Committee Draft. Technical report, BMC Software, CA, Fujitsu, Hewlett-Packard, IBM, Microsoft, January 2008. http://cmdbf.org/.
[8]   Hommel, W. and Knittl, S. An Access Control Solution For The Inter-Organizational Use Of ITIL Federated Configuration Management Databases. In Proceedings of the 2008 Workshop of HP Software University Association (HP–SUA), Infonomics–Consulting, Marrakech, Morocco, June 2008.
[9]   IntegraTUM. http://portal.mytum.de/iuk/integratum/index_html/document_view?. May 2008.
[10] Hamm, M. K., Yampolskiy, M., Management of Multidomain End–to–End Links. A Federated Approach for the Pan–European Research Network Géant 2, In Moving from Bits to Business Value: Proceedings of the 2007 Integrated Management Symposium, 189–198, IFIP/IEEE, Munich, Germany, May 2007.
[11] DEISA. http://www.deisa.eu/. May 2008.
[12] Göhner, M., et al. An Accounting Model for Dynamic Virtual Organizations. Seventh IEEE International Symposium on Cluster Computing and the Grid (CCGrid 2007), Rio de Janeiro, Brazil, May 2007 .
[13] Ronni J. Colville. CMDB or configuration database: Know the difference, March 2006. Gartner RAS Core Research Note G00137125.
[14] Marques, F.T.; Moura, J.A.B.; Sauvé, J.; Service Level Agreement Design and Service Provisioning for Outsourced Services; In: Proceedings of the 5th Latin American Network Operations and Management Symposium, LANOMS 2007, Petropolis, Brazil, 2007, pp. 106-113.

Collaboration and the Knowledge Economy: Issues, Applications, Case Studies
P. Cunningham and M. Cunningham (Eds.)
IOS Press, 2008

Mastering Demand and Supply Uncertainty with Configurator Software

Cor VERDOUW, Tim VERWAART

LEI Wageningen UR, Postbus 29703, 2502 LS den Haag, The Netherlands
Tel: +31703358330, Fax: +3170 3615624, Email: cor.verdouw@wur.nl

Abstract: This paper evaluates the role of configurator software in agile supply chains that are characterized by a relatively high degree of uncertainty both in the market and in production processes. Product configuration software is successfully used to manage demand uncertainty. The objective of this research is to assess the feasibility of configuration software to manage also supply uncertainty and to identify development strategies and challenges. The paper builds on a typology of supply chain strategies as a frame of reference. A firm's information systems should match the type of supply chain it operates in. By means of a case-study in a young-plant-growing firm it is concluded that current configurator software does not sufficiently support the flexibility at the supply side required in agile supply chains. Main challenges are better integration with flexible back-office systems, and functionality to support process configuration in addition to product configuration.

1. Introduction

Firms in Flowers & Food industry have to cope with great uncertainty in their production planning because of dependency on the growth of living materials. They may reduce uncertainty by improving process control, but remain vulnerable to weather conditions, pests and other incontrollable factors. Moreover, this type of firm may face a high degree of demand uncertainty among others because of weather-dependent sales and changing consumer preferences, especially if it is upstream in the supply chain. Small firms in this sector can cope with the high degree of both demand and supply uncertainty by improvisation. However, growing firms cannot rely on improvisation by some experienced staff members and have to structure their information processing. Traditional Enterprise Resource Planning (ERP) systems are insufficient to manage high uncertainty both at demand and supply side (see among others [1, 2]).

Product configurator software has proven to be a powerful tool to manage demand uncertainty in other industries [3, 4]. Such software supports configuration of products and preparation of offers and contracts in assemble-to-order and make-to-order environments. It is feasible for mass customization of standardized products [5, 6]. The reason for starting this research was the idea that application of configurator software might provide the required flexibility in Flowers & Food industry.

The present paper describes results of a case-study that was carried out in a rapidly growing 350 staff young-plant-growing firm with production locations in The Netherlands, Brazil, Kenya, Zimbabwe, and Israel. The firm is specialized in some particular species and varieties of young plants, for worldwide delivery. The production process is characterized by long lead times and high uncertainty. Logistics are complex due to the global distribution of production locations. The firm's unique selling point is flexibility in meeting customer demands with respect to product specifications and delivery schedules. Up to now it relied heavily on improvisation by experienced employees to manage the uncertain production processes in relation to the high demand variability. However, the rapid growth urges the firm to redesign its business processes. Implementation of ERP software and sales configurator software are considered as options to master uncertainty.

2. Objective

The objective of this paper is to assess the feasibility of configurator software for managing high uncertainty of both supply and demand, and to identify development strategies and challenges for, on the one hand, companies operating in agile supply chains and, on the other hand, suppliers of configurator software that want to add value for firms operating in agile supply chains. Therefore it aims to provide conceptual insight in the way configurators can enhance agility, and to assess the applicability of current configurators.

The paper first develops a theoretical framework to analyze the fit of configuration software to different types of supply chains, and describes the roles that product and process configurators could play in agile supply chains. Subsequently it presents the results of a case study, involving a firm operating in an agile supply chain, and a configuration software supplier. The results include strategic development alternatives for firms in agile supply chains. The paper is concluded by challenges to suppliers of product configuration software to enhance its value for agile supply chains.

3. Methodology

There is no best supply chain design. Fisher [7] introduced the idea that supply chain design should match the degree of demand uncertainty. Fisher discriminates between functional and innovative products. For functional products, having low demand uncertainty, efficient or lean supply chains perform best. For innovative products, that have a high degree of demand uncertainty, flexible or agile chains are a better match. Lee [8] extends Fisher's analysis by adding the dimension of supply uncertainty. Lee distinguishes between stable and evolving supply processes. Stable processes are characterized by controllable production, mature technology and settled industry. In evolving supply processes production and technology are under development and more or less unpredictable. Table 1 summarizes Lee's characterization of the demand and supply dimensions.

Table 1: Characteristics of the Dimensions of Demand and Supply According to Lee [8]

Demand Characteristics		Supply Characteristics	
Functional	*Innovative*	*Stable*	*Evolving*
Low demand uncertainties	High demand uncertainties	Less breakdowns	Vulnerable to breakdowns
More predictable demand	Difficult to forecast	Stable and higher yields	Variable and lower yields
Stable demand	Variable demand	Less quality problems	Potential quality problems
Long product life	Short selling season	More supply sources	Limited supply sources
Low inventory cost	High inventory cost	Reliable suppliers	Unreliable suppliers
Low profit margins	High profit margins	Less process changes	More process changes
Low product variety	High product variety	Less capacity constraints	Potential capacity constrained
Higher volume per SKU	Low volumes per SKU	Easier to changeover	Difficult to changeover
Low stockout cost	High stockout cost	Flexible	Inflexible
Low obsolescence	High obsolescence	Dependable lead time	Variable lead time

The analysis presented in this paper is based on Lee's framework [8] which matches four types of supply chains with characteristics of supply and demand (Figure 1):
- Efficient supply chains focus on cost reduction and match with low supply uncertainty - i.e. a controllable production process - and low demand uncertainty.

- Risk-hedging supply chains focus on pooling resources to reduce supply uncertainty; this type of chain matches with high supply uncertainty and low demand uncertainty.
- Responsive supply chains focus on flexibility through make-to-order process and mass customization; they match with low supply uncertainty and high demand uncertainty.
- Agile supply chains combine risk-hedging and responsive strategies, aiming to cope with both high supply uncertainty and high demand uncertainty.

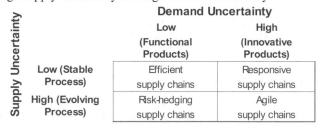

		Demand Uncertainty	
		Low (Functional Products)	High (Innovative Products)
Supply Uncertainty	Low (Stable Process)	Efficient supply chains	Responsive supply chains
	High (Evolving Process)	Risk-hedging supply chains	Agile supply chains

Figure 1: Supply Chain Strategies and Demand and Supply Characteristics [8]

Before selecting a supply chain strategy, a firm should determine if reduction of uncertainty is possible and desirable. Reduction of supply uncertainty might, for instance, be realized by improved production control, cooperation with suppliers of technology. Reduction of especially demand uncertainty - for instance by product standardization and reducing the number of available product options - might decrease added value for customers.

A firm's information systems should match the type of supply chain it operates in. For further analysis we distinguish between front-office systems (coping with the demand side) and back-office systems (coping with the supply side). Front-office systems include order management, contract management, sales configurator, demand forecasting, and customer relations management systems. Back-office systems include resource planning and scheduling, stock management, purchasing, and supplier relations management systems.

The type of supply chain determines the required flexibility of front- and back-office systems.

- Efficient supply chains require stable, straight-forward planning systems for both front-office and back-office. The systems must be well-integrated to reduce waste of resources. Back-office systems support large volume production of standardized products based on long-run forecasts. Front-office systems support efficient order processing, long-run contracts and demand forecasts. Traditional ERP systems cover the demands of efficient supply chains.
- Risk-hedging supply chains require the same type of stable front-office systems as efficient supply chains do. However, they require flexible back-office systems, integrated with production control systems and supplier's systems. Disturbance of production or supply of materials should rapidly be observed and lead to re-planning and rescheduling. The rigid planning and scheduling systems of traditional ERP systems may cause problems in this type of supply chain.
- Responsive supply chains place high demands on the ability to combine fluctuations in demand and available supplies with respect to product specifications and lead times. The most common approach to organize responsiveness is mass customization in an assemble-to-order (ATO) production environment [9, 10]. This type of supply chain quickly responses to demand variability by efficient assembling of order-specific products from standard components. It requires stable back-office systems for efficient production of standardized components and rapid assembly. Traditional ERP systems can meet this demand. However, front-office systems require a flexibility usually not

offered by traditional ERP systems. A responsive supply chain may require a more sophisticated sales configurator.

- Agile supply chains require flexibility in both front-office and back-office systems. They demand flexible ERP in the back-office and sophisticated configurator and customer communications systems in the front-office. Tight integration is required between front-office and back-office and with systems of both suppliers and customers.

The framework described in this section, served as the basis for a theory-building single case-study [11, 12]. The case-study firm was selected on the basis of theoretical and practical criteria, particularly: expressed need for agile information systems, typical representative of Flowers & Food industry, and willingness to cooperate.

4.   The Role of Configuration Software in Agile Supply Chains

Product configuration software is a tool that guides users interactively through specification of customer-specific products [3, 4, 13] . The customer may specify some configuration of predefined components, and may sometimes specify some features like number, colour, capacity, or size of components and their relative position. Product configurators have been around for some 30 years. A well-known early successful application of artificial intelligence was R1, a product configurator for VAX computers [14].

Currently, product configurators play an important role in responsive supply chains. In interaction with the user, the software generates consistent and complete specifications of customized products, taking into account both the customer's requirements (i.e. functional specifications, delivery times and places, technical specifications, quality requirements) and the feasibility of production and delivery. Along with the product specification, current configurators can produce commercial offers and draft contracts, and schedules and contracts for support and maintenance of the product. The software can be designed for use either by a sales representative of the supplier, or by a customer, e.g. through the internet. In both cases the configuration process results in an order specification that can directly be entered into the suppliers production planning and scheduling systems.

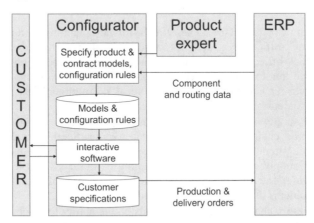

Figure 2: Product Configuration in a Responsive Environment

Current configurators specify the product, not the production process. This makes them excellently fit for demand management in *responsive supply chains*. Figure 2 depicts the data flow for this case. Product experts can enter configuration rules into the configurator's repository. Product data (bill-of-materials, part numbers, prices) and process data (routing, lead times, production cost) can be copied from ERP master data, to ensure that production orders will be in terms that can be interpreted by the ERP system. After configuration, either directly by the customer or through a sales representative, orders can automatically be forwarded to the ERP system.

Through the application of product configurators, suppliers can realize great flexibility in their front-office systems. However, agile supply chains that require process flexibility because of supply uncertainty, would better be served if configurators could offer process configuration in addition to product specification. Agile supply chains require flexibility in their back-office systems as well as in their front-office systems. Unforeseen events may compel them to repeatedly reschedule their production and purchasing. Changes in production and delivery schedules may require frequent feedback to customers, and change of previously entered orders after communication with customers. Figure 3 depicts the architecture required in this case.

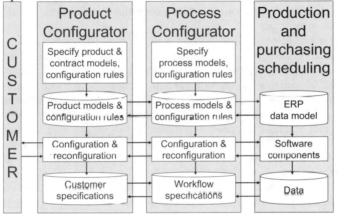

Figure 3: Architecture to Enhance Agility for Coping with Demand and Supply Uncertainty with Configurators

Additional to the architecture for responsive supply chains (figure 2), in agile supply chains unexpected supply events could lead to reconfiguration of the workflow. For instance, components that were originally planned to be produced can be re-planned to be purchased, or suppliers of components can be replaced by others with other delivery processes, or components can be replaced by components that are produced for other orders. If workflow reconfiguration would not satisfy the agreed order specifications, product reconfiguration might be necessary, for instance, by replacing components with other components, or changing delivery dates. This intensive interaction between front-office and back-office and with suppliers and customers, requires process configuration functionality that specifies order-specific workflows, including changes after order conclusion. As such, the process configurator functions as a flexible bridge between the front and back office systems. This requires a solid and flexible integration infrastructure. A service-oriented approach to software configuration might be promising to realize this.

However, dynamic configuration of web services is in it's infancy and has been identified as a research challenge [15]. Once web service composition is a realistic option to implement flexible business processes in the back-office, it still has to be integrated with product configuration software.

To summarize the analysis, it is found that current configurators do not support the combination of order-specific product and process composition. Thus, it can be concluded that agile supply chains are not supported sufficiently by available product configurators.

5.   Case-Study Results

The selected young-plant-growing firm was investigated by semi-structured open interviews with managers and employees (9 interviews with a total of 14 persons) and additional desk research. The results were analyzed by application of the framework. Finally the analysis was tested in 2 workshops   about specific software solutions, respectively ERP and configuration software. Employees of the case-study firm and consultants participated in the workshops.

The interviews indicated that the most urgent bottlenecks in the young-plant firm were:

- Knowledge of production processes and options to reconfigure these processes is only implicitly available in the minds of some experienced staff members. This problem can be managed at the firm's current scale of the firm, but it inhibits further growth.
- Information systems are patchy (island automation) and require a lot of manual data re-entering. Information inconsistency leads to larger safety buffers then strictly required, and many redundant data checks and duplicate registrations are performed.
- Mid-term planning is not coordinated with operational data, due to a lack of integration of information systems.

The company is a niche player that specializes in a few "hard" species of young plants. It is the world market leader in two of these species and has a good position in some other species. The firm considers rapid and customized delivery to be its unique selling point. Combined with the dependence on planning staff's improvisation talents, this sets limits to further growth. Currently, the firm has to deal with high demand uncertainty and high supply uncertainty. Customers have specific demands and demand forecasts are unreliable. Worldwide, great fluctuation occurs with respect to quantity and attributes like color. Supply is hard to plan and hard to adjust, because plants are a living product. Some species have a lead-time of 1.5 year. Moreover, processes are insufficiently controlled and information supply is weak.

Supply chain developing strategies of the young-plant firm should aim at reduction or better management of uncertainty in supply and demand:

- Reduction strategies aim to reduce differentiation by standardization and to eliminate the sources of disruptions.
  - Some possibilities of the case-study firm for reduction of demand uncertainty are product standardization, exchange production planning with customers, or stimulate long-term contracts.
  - Some possibilities for reduction of supply uncertainty are reduction of the influence of nature, by more advanced climate and pest control systems, and standardization of production, e.g., by fixed batch volumes, standard trays, or fixed delivery schedules.
- Strategies for uncertainty management leave differentiation and unpredictability as is, but aim to manage it by better organization, horizontal and vertical cooperation, more advanced tools and better utilization of information.
  - Some possibilities of the case-study firm for better management of demand uncertainty are implementation of mass customization systems, application of product configurators, and information exchange with customers to improve forecasting.
  - Supply uncertainty could be managed by continuous re-planning, decreasing of disruptions' impact by intelligent greenhouse systems and stock management, and by maintaining close relationships with suppliers and service providers.

Based on these strategies, the firm's strategic options are positioned in figure 4. They are:

A. Develop towards responsive supply chains: reduce supply uncertainty and improve demand uncertainty management.
B. Develop towards risk-hedging supply chains: reduce demand uncertainty and improve supply uncertainty management.
C. Develop towards efficient supply chains: reduce both supply and demand uncertainty.
D. Improve the current position in agile supply chains: improve uncertainty management of both demand and supply.

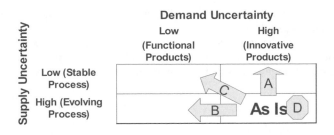

Figure 4: Position and Development Strategies for Case-Study Firm

The choice between uncertainty reduction and uncertainty management strategies is determined by the company-inherent characteristics that determine the reduction possibility and the value the firm wants to add in the market. Especially with respect to demand uncertainty, reduction strategies could reduce the value.

The case-study firm's first priority is to handle supply uncertainty in the back-office: reduce (in options A/C) or manage (in B/D). The choice for reduction would imply the adoption of a traditional ERP system. The choice for supply uncertainty management would require more dynamic production management than a traditional ERP-system can offer.

Application of an existing configuration tool was assessed to be appropriate if the company would decide to develop towards a responsive supply chain (alternative A). If the firm would select a supply uncertainty reduction strategy (A or C), the functionality included in the traditional ERP-software will probably be sufficient, because supply uncertainty is low. This in contrary to alternative B and D which requires flexible back-office systems. Integration of ERP systems and extended configuration software (including process configuration as described in section 4) would fit than.

6. Conclusion and Future Challenges

The research question was how configurator software could contribute to improve information management in the Flowers & Food sector. To answer this question a framework of analysis was developed, based on Lee's supply chain typology. Lee [8] distinguishes four types of supply chains, based on uncertainty of supply and demand. The feasibility of configurator software was evaluated in a young-plant-growing firm, operating in an agile supply chain, i.e. a supply chain with high uncertainty in both demand and supply. Although the case study was performed in the Flowers & Food sector, conclusions may be applicable to agile supply chains in other sectors.

Configuration software can be applied in two ways. First, application of product configuration is relevant for firms that operate in supply chains with high demand uncertainty. If order complexity and product complexity are low, the product configuration functionality built-in in ERP software might be sufficient. Otherwise a specialized product configurator might be required. Second, application of process configuration is relevant for firms that operate in supply chains with high supply uncertainty. The main issue is to integrate the process configuration software with back-office systems, either through inclusion in the ERP-software, or in a service-oriented architecture.

A general conclusion for firms in agile supply chains is that software for both product and process configuration would be valuable. In addition, these firms require intensive interaction, firstly between front-office and back-office, because order fulfillment is not certain to develop according to plan, and secondly with suppliers and customers, because order details and delivery schedules may have to be renegotiated. However, the traditional domain of product configuration software is in responsive supply chains, i.e. high demand uncertainty with reliable and stable supply. Current configurator software does not offer the flexible process configuration and back-office-front-office-customer communication required for agile supply chains.

The conclusion for the case study firm was that configuration software was not feasible in the permanent re-planning of order fulfillment taking place, and investments should be directed to reducing supply uncertainty and managing it with other means than configurator software.

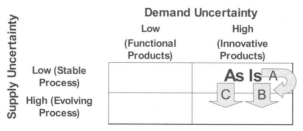

Figure 5: Position and Development Strategies for Configurator Software Suppliers

Figure 5 depicts the main challenges to suppliers of product configuration software to enhance its value for agile supply chains, i.e. to master demand and supply uncertainty:

A. Improve current position in responsive supply chains, e.g. by adding CRM functionality or workflow enactment of multiple partial configurations of one specific contract;

B. Extend product configuration software to agile supply chain by adding functionality for intensive interaction with back office systems, also after contract conclusion.

C. Develop configuration software for managing supply uncertainty by process configuration in agile supply chains.

References

[1] Akkermans, H.A., et al., The impact of ERP on supply chain management: Exploratory findings from a European Delphi study. *European Journal of Operational Research*, 2003. 146(2): p. 284.

[2] Zhao, Y. and Y.S. Fan, Implementation approach of ERP with mass customization. *International Journal of Computer Integrated Manufacturing*, 2007. 20(2-3): p. 160-168.

[3] Piller, F.T., Mass customization: Reflections on the state of the concept. *International Journal Of Flexible Manufacturing Systems*, 2004. 16(4): p. 313-334.

[4] Steger-Jensen, K. and C. Svensson, Issues of mass customisation and supporting IT-solutions. *Computers in Industry*, 2004. 54(1): p. 83-103.

[5] Pine, B.J., B. Victor, and A.C. Boynton, Making Mass Customization Work. *Harvard Business Review*, 1993. 71(5): p. 108-119.

[6] Davis, S., From future perfect: Mass customizing. *Planning Review*, 1989. 17(2): p. 16-21.

[7] Fisher, M. L., What is the right supply chain for your product? *Harvard Business Review* 75(2), 1997, p. 105-116.

[8] Lee, H.L. Aligning Supply Chain Strategies with Product Uncertainties. *California Management Review* 44, 2002, pp. 105-119.

[9] Blecker, T. and G.Friedrich, *Mass Customization: Challenges and Solutions*. New York, Springer, 2006.

[10] Wortmann, J.C., D.R. Muntslag, and P.J.M. Timmermans, *Customer-driven manufacturing*. London, Chapman & Hall, 1997.

[11] Eisenhardt, K.M., Building Theories from Case-Study Research. *Academy of Management Review*, 1989. 14(4): p. 532-550.

[12] Yin, R.K., *Case Study Research: Design and Methods. Third Edition*. 2002: Sage Publications, Inc.

[13] Forza, C. and F. Salvador, Product configuration and inter-firm co-ordination: an innovative solution from a small manufacturing enterprise. *Computers In Industry*, 2002. 49(1): p. 37-46.

[14] McDermott, J., R1: The Formative Years. *AI Magazine* 2(2), 1981, pp. 21-29.

[15] Papazoglou, M.P., P. Traverso, S. Dustdar, and F. Leymann, Service-Oriented Computing: State of the Art and Research Challenges. *IEEE Computer*, November 2007, pp. 64-71.

Collaboration and the Knowledge Economy: Issues, Applications, Case Studies
P. Cunningham and M. Cunningham (Eds.)
IOS Press, 2008

Efficient Trust Aware Resource Allocation in Distributed Computing Environments

Malamati LOUTA[1], Angelos MICHALAS[2], Ioannis ANAGNOSTOPOULOS[3]

[1]Harokopio University of Athens, Department of Informatics and Telematics,
70 El. Venizelou Str., Athens, 17671, Greece
Tel: +302109549100, Fax: + 302109577050, Email: louta@telecom.ntua.gr
[2]Technological Educational Institute of Western Macedonia, Department of Informatics
and Computer Technology, P.O.Box 30, Kastoria, 52100, Greece
Tel: +302467087260, Fax: +302467087063, Email: amichalas@kastoria.teikoz.gr
[3]University of Aegean, Department of Information and Communication Systems
Engineering, Karlovassi, Samos Island, 83200, Greece
Tel: +302273082220, Fax: +302273082008, Email: janag@aegean.gr

Abstract: Dynamic distributed computing environments are composed by various entities, which, seeking for the maximization of their welfare while achieving their own goals and aims, may act selfishly, thus, leading to a significant deterioration of system's performance. In general, system entities may be classified into two main categories, the Resource Requestors (RRs) wishing to use and/or exploit resources offered by the other system entities and the Resource Providers (RPs) that offer the resources requested. In this study, a reputation mechanism is proposed which helps estimating RPs trustworthiness, taking into account their past performance in consistently satisfying RRs' expectations. The trust management framework is distributed, considers both first-hand information (acquired from the RR's direct past experiences with the RPs) and second-hand information (disseminated from other RRs), while it exhibits a robust behaviour against inaccurate reputation ratings. The designed mechanisms have been empirically evaluated, exhibiting improved performance with respect to random RP selection.

1. Introduction

The roles of system entities in dynamic distributed computing environments may be classified into two main categories that, in principle, are in conflict. These two categories are: the entities that wish to use and/or exploit resources offered by other system entities (Resource Requestors - RRs) and the entities that offer the resources requested (Resource Providers - RPs). The aim of this paper is to propose enhancements to the sophistication of the functionality that can be offered by distributed computing environments. Resource Requestors should be provided with mechanisms that enable them to find the most appropriate Resource Providers, i.e., those offering the resources required at an acceptable quality level at a certain time period in a cost efficient manner, while exhibiting a reliable behavior. Such mechanisms may entail a wide variety of negotiation mechanisms in order to establish the 'best' possible service level agreement terms (SLAs) and conditions with respect to resource access and provision [1], in conjunction with trust mechanisms [2] in order to build the necessary trust relationships among the system entities.

Traditional models aiming to avoid strategic misbehaviour are based on authentication of identities and authorization schemes by exchanging digital, cryptographically signed certificates/credentials in order for the involved parties to establish a trust relationship [3], [4] or involve Trusted Third Parties (TTPs) or intermediaries [5] that monitor every transaction. In case RPs do not abide by the agreed SLA terms and conditions, penalties are imposed, so as to reimburse RRs that incur the loss. In parallel, *Reputation Mechanisms* may be employed to provide a "softer" security layer, considered to be sufficient for many multi-agent applications [6], emerging in complex, heterogeneous and highly variable environments. Reputation mechanisms establish trust by exploiting learning from experience concepts [7] in order to obtain a reliability value of system participants in the form of rating based on other entities' view/opinion. Current reputation system implementations in the context of e-commerce systems consider feedback given by Buyers in the form of ratings in order to capture information on Seller's past behavior, while the reputation value is computed as the sum (or the mean) of those ratings either incorporating all ratings or considering only a period of time (e.g., six months) [8]. In general, a reputation system is considered to sustain rational cooperation and serve as an incentive for good behaviour because good players are rewarded by the society, whereas bad players are penalized.

In the context of this study, our focus is laid on the evaluation of the reliability of RPs. To this respect, a collaborative reputation mechanism is proposed, which takes into account the RPs' past performance in consistently satisfying RRs' expectations. To be more specific, the reputation mechanism rates the RPs with respect to whether they honoured or not the agreements established with the RRs, thus introducing the concept of trust among the involved parties.

The rest of the paper is structured as follows. Section 2 presents the software architecture that supports the proposed trust management framework, while the software elements required are identified. Section 3 discusses on the fundamental concepts and methodology followed for the proposed collaborative reputation mechanism, aiming to offer an efficient way of building the necessary level of trust in the distributed computing environments. Section 4 provides a set of indicative results of the efficiency of the proposed trust management framework. Section 5, provides a brief overview of the related research literature and subsequently highlights the contribution of this study. Finally, in Section 6, conclusions are drawn and directions for future plans are given.

2.   Software Architecture & Technology Adopted

In accordance with the service oriented architectures concept [9],[10],[11] and exploiting advanced software paradigms (e.g., distributed object computing [12] and intelligent mobile agents [13],[14]), the service logic is realised by a set of autonomous co-operating components, which interact through middleware functionality that runs over Distributed Processing Environments (e.g., CORBA, Parlay). Intelligent Mobile Agent Technology (MAT) has been considered as a paradigm that can help service designers to handle the potential increased functionality involved in service creation and deployment. According to a simple definition, intelligent mobile agents are software components incorporating intelligent functionality that can at a certain point in time migrate to perform a specific task.

This study is based upon the notion of interacting intelligent agents which participate in activities on behalf of their owners, while exhibiting properties such as autonomy, reactiveness, proactiveness, social ability and adaptivity in order to achieve particular objectives and accomplish their goals [15]. Thus, Resource Requestor Agent (RRA) is introduced and assigned with the role of capturing the RR preferences, requirements and constraints regarding the requested resource, delivering them in a suitable form to the appropriate RP entity, acquiring and evaluating the corresponding RPs' offers, and ultimately, selecting the most appropriate RP on the basis of the quality of its offer and its reputation rating. Resource Provider Agents (RPAs) are the entities acting on behalf of the RPs. Their role would be to collect the RR preferences, requirements and constraints and to make a corresponding offer, taking also into account certain environmental criteria. RRAs and RPAs are both considered to be rational and self-interested, while aiming to maximize their owners' profit.

3. Fundamental Considerations & Methodology Followed

In the following subsections, the authors discuss on the basic concepts and assumptions, taken into account in the overall trust aware resource allocation framework designed.

3.1 RPs' Overall Reputation Rating Estimation

The proposed reputation mechanism for the reliability related factor estimation is collaborative in the sense that it considers both first-hand information (acquired from the RRA's past experiences with the RPAs) and second-hand information (disseminated from other RRAs). To be more specific, each RRA keeps a record of the reputation ratings of the RPAs it has negotiated with and been served by in the past. This rating based on the direct experiences of the evaluator RRA with the target RPA forms the first factor contributing to the overall RPA reputation and is formed on the basis of learning from experience techniques (e.g., reinforcement learning [7]). In the context of this study, a basic assumption is that the reputation ratings lie within the [0,1] range, where a value close to 0 indicates a misbehaving RP. Concerning the RPAs' reputation ratings based on feedback given by other RRA on their experiences in the system (the second factor contributing to the overall RPA reputation based on witness information), a centralized approach may be adopted (e.g., a system component could maintain and update a collective record of the RPAs' reputation ratings formed after taking into account each RRA view on the RPAs' performance [2]). This approach on one hand has significant computational, communicational, time and storage advantages, but on the other hand it may suffer from the classical disadvantages of all centralized methodologies (e.g., introduction of performance bottlenecks and single point of failure in the system).

In the context of this study, we adopt a decentralized approach with respect to witness based information concerning RPAs' reputation ratings. Specifically, a basic assumption is that each RRA is willing to share their experiences and provide whenever asked for the reputation ratings of the RPAs formed on the basis of their past direct interactions. Thus, the problem is reduced in finding proper witnesses, i.e., obtaining a reference of the RRAs that have previously been served by the RPAs under evaluation. In the current version of this paper, we assume that a Resource Provider Reputation Broker component (RPRB) maintains a list of the RPAs providing a specific service / resource as well as a list of RRAs that have previously interacted with a specific RPA.

At this point some clarifications with respect to the proposed model should be made. First, the reliability of RPAs is treated as a behavioural aspect, independent of the resources provided. Thus, the witnesses list may be composed by RRAs which have had direct interactions with the specific RPA in the past, without considering the resource consumed. Second, RPAs have a solid interest in informing RPRB with respect to resources they currently offer, while the RRAs are authorized to access and obtain witness references only in case they send feedback concerning the preferred partner for their past interactions in the system. This policy based approach provides a solution to the inherent incentive based problem of reputation mechanisms in order for the RPRB to keep accurate and up to date information.

3.2 Obtaining Accurate Feedback from Witnesses

True feedback cannot be automatically assumed. Second-hand information can be spurious (e.g., parties may choose to misreport their experience due to jealousy or in order to discredit trustworthy Providers). In general, a mechanism for eliciting true feedback in the absence of TTPs is necessitated. According to the simplest possible approach that may be adopted in order to account for possible inaccuracies to the information provided by the witnesses RRAs (both intentional and unintentional), the evaluator RRA can mostly rely on its own experiences rather on the target RPA's reputation ratings provided after contacting the RRAs. To this respect, RPA's reputation ratings provided by the witness RRAs may be attributed with a relatively low significance factor.

In the context of this study, we consider that each RRA is associated with a weighting factor dynamically updated, which reflects whether the RRA provides feedback with respect to its experiences with the RPAs truthfully and in an accurate manner. In essence, this weighting factor is a measure of the credibility of the witness information. To be more specific, in order to handle intentional inaccurate information, an honesty probability is attributed to each RRA, i.e., a measure of the likelihood that a RRA gives feedback compliant to the real picture concerning service provisioning. Second-hand information obtained from trustworthy RRAs (associated with a high honesty probability), are given a higher significance factor, whereas reports (positive or negative) coming from untrustworthy sources have a small impact on the formation of the RPAs' reputation ratings. Concerning the provision of inaccurate information unintentionally, the authors take into account the number of transactions a witness RRA has performed with the target RPA and the sum of the respective transaction values. Specifically, it is quite safe to assume that RRAs that have been involved with the target RPA only for a few times will not have formed an accurate picture regarding its behaviour. Additionally, if the reputation rating is formed on the basis of low-valued transactions, there is a possibility that it does not reflect the real picture (e.g., an RPA may strategically exhibit good behaviour in case its potential profits in a context of a transaction are low and cheat when the expected earnings are high). Furthermore, time effect has been considered and incorporated in our mechanism in order to model the fact that more recent events should weigh more in the target RP's overall reputation evaluation.

3.3   Decision on the Most Appropriate RP Concerning the Resource Provisioning

Assuming the presence of M RPAs negotiating with a RRA for the terms and conditions of an SLA concerning the provisioning of a resource, the RRA can decide on the most appropriate RPA based on the evaluation of the RPA's offer quality combined with an estimation of the RPA's expected behaviour. In our approach this estimation constitutes the reliability related factor, which is introduced in order to reflect whether the RP finally provides to the RR the resource that corresponds to the established SLA terms or not. The RPA's reliability is reduced whenever the RP does not honour the agreement contract terms reached via the negotiation process. The RPAs' offer quality evaluation factor is based on the fact that there may in general be different levels of satisfaction with respect to the various RPAs' offers. In this respect, there may be RPAs that, in principle, do not satisfy the RRA with their offer.

The evaluator RRA uses the reputation mechanism to decide on the most appropriate RPA, especially in cases where the RRA doubts the accuracy of the information provided by the RPA. A learning period is required in order for the RRAs to obtain fundamental information for the RPAs. During the learning period and in case reputation specific information is not available to the RRA (both through its own experiences and through the witnesses) or it highly possible to be outdated, the reliability related factor is not considered for the RPA selection. Thus, the RP's will be selected only on the basis of the quality of their offers. At this point it should be noted that the reputation mechanism comes at the cost of keeping reputation related information at each RRA and updating it after resource consumption has taken place. Finally, it should be mentioned that the reliability rating value of the RPAs requires in some cases (e.g., when consumption of network or computational resources are entailed in the service provisioning process) a mechanism for evaluating whether the service quality was compliant with the picture promised during the negotiation phase.

3.4 Updating Outdated RPAs' Reputation Related Information

Considering that the RRAs have initially acquired the fundamental reliability related information for the RPAs (that is after the learning period), only the reputation rating of the "best" RPA (i.e., the one selected on the basis of the quality of the offers proposed to the RRA and the RPAs' reliability related values) will be updated, after the user finally accesses the resource. Thus, the system can only verify the behaviour of the "most" appropriate RPA and has no means to identify potential changes to other RPAs' behaviour with respect to their compliance to the established SLA terms and conditions. Furthermore, initial RPAs' reliability rating values are taken equal to 0.1. A quite low reputation rating value has been assumed (that is all RPAs initially are considered to be dishonest entities) in order to avoid the bad consequences of changing identities so as to wipe out possible misbehaviour in the past). Therefore, assuming that the "good" RPAs do not alter their policies (either on the basis of their performance or on the basis of their reliability), the misbehaving RPAs have to improve on their potential performance so as to overcome the barrier raised by their low reputation rating.

In order to take into account new RPAs that enter the system and/or not to exclude RPAs that initially did not honour the terms and conditions of the contracts established, thus being attributed with a small reliability related value after the learning period, and give them a chance to re-enter to the system and improve their reputation rating in case they abide by the SLA terms and conditions, the simplest possible approach that could be adopted is to base the RRAs' decision concerning the most appropriate RPA (after a specific time period, or after the completion of a specific number of transactions) on the RPAs' performance and omit the RPAs' reputation rating values until possible outdated information the system possesses is updated. In the context of this study, the authors consider the reduction of the RPs' reliability related values to the pre-specified minimum (i.e., 0.1) in case a predetermined number of transactions have been completed in the system, whenupon the RPRB component sends a warning message to all RRAs registered in its database. At this point it should be noted that the predetermined number of transactions is considered to assume a quite big value in order not to constitute a disincentive for honest behavior.

4. Results

This section provides some indicative results on the behaviour of the Resource Provider trust aware selection mechanisms that are proposed in this paper. We hereafter assume the existence of an area that falls into the domain of $P = \{P_1, P_2, ...P_M\}$ candidate Resource Providers (that is a specific request may be handled by any of the candidate RPs belonging to the set P). Regarding the different Resource Requestors that access the area, it is assumed that N classes exist. RR classes are interested for the same resource, differentiated however with respect to the quality/quantity level required. Without loss of generality, all RPs are assumed to offer the required quantity/quality levels. Hereafter, it is assumed that $N = 10$ and $M = 10$.

The proposed framework was empirically evaluated by simulating the interactions among RRAs and RPAs. At this point, a basic assumption is that the RPAs propose exactly the same offer to the evaluator RRAs (exactly the same terms and conditions for the potential SLA). In the light of the assumption made, the Resource Provider selection is reduced to choosing the one with the highest reputation value. This way, the acquisition of an initial set of indicative results that show the behaviour of our proposed trust aware framework is enabled.

In order to evaluate the RPs' reliability, each RP has been associated with an honesty probability, i.e., a measure of the likelihood that the RP delivers the service compliant with the agreement established. This probability has been set to the following values: 0.9 for RPAs P_1 and P_5, 0.8 for P_4, 0.7 for P_7 and P_8, 0.6 for P_3 and P_6, 0.4 for P_2 and P_9, and 0.3 for P_{10}. In essence, with probability *0.9* RPA P_5 complies with its promises concerning resource provisioning during simulation runtime, whereas P_{10} maintains its promises with probability *0.3*. A mixture of extreme and moderate values has been chosen in order to test the schemes under diverse conditions.

Figure 1 depicts the formation of the reputation ratings of RP P_6 for five different RRAs, based on their direct experiences. As it may be observed, 20 transactions are required in order to obtain an accurate picture concerning the RP's reputation rating. The reputation rating variations around 0.6 (the honesty probability assigned to RP P_6) illustrated in Figure 1 may be attributed to the fact that the rating estimations are affected by RP's past behaviour concerning resource provisioning, which in our experiments is determined by a random variable.

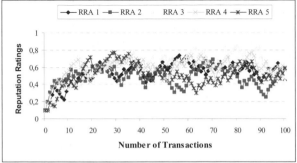

Figure 1: RP's P_6 Reputation Rating Formation for Five Different RRAs
on the Basis of Their Direct Experiences in the System.

Figure 2 illustrates the reputation ratings of each RP, as estimated after 1000 transactions have been conducted (with each RP) in the system. In the context of the experiments conducted, all RR classes are considered to be witnesses and their vast majority is assumed to behave in an honest manner. As may be observed from Figure 2, the most appropriate RP is P_5 (ranked first), followed by RP P_1 (ranked second), followed by RP P_4 (ranked third), followed by P_7, P_8, P_3, P_6, P_2, while the RP P_9 occupies the 9th ranking position and P_{10} the 10th ranking position.

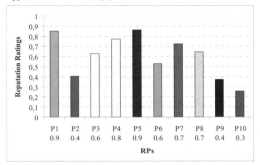

Figure 2: Reputation Ratings for All RPs Serving Resource Requests
Originating from the RR Classes Considered in the System

Finally, comparing the effectiveness of our RP selection mechanism on the basis of the reliability ratings of the RPs with respect to the random RP selection scheme (i.e., the RP for resource provisioning is selected randomly), we may note that in general our designed framework exhibits increased RR satisfaction, which on average is 30%, due to the fact that in our mechanism RPs honouring in the past the agreements established with the RRs are selected for resource provisioning in the future.

5. Related Research Overview

The focus and contribution of this study is laid on the design of a trust management framework, assessing RPs' reliability in an accurate and time – efficient manner by means of a decentralized, collaborative reputation mechanism, forming RPs reputation ratings, which reflect whether RPs provide to the RRs the resource that corresponds to the established contract terms or not. The proposed reputation management mechanism considers both direct RRs experiences with RPs and witnesses information disseminated from other RRs on the basis of their past experiences with the RPs under evaluation, while being resilient to inaccurate information intentionally and/or unintentionally provided.

The work of this paper is related to pertinent previous work in the literature, since trust establishment and management is a topic that attracts attention of the researchers [16], [17]. Most reputation based systems in related research literature aim to enable entities to make decisions on which parties to negotiate/cooperate with or exclude, after they have been informed about the reputation ratings of the parties of interest. The authors in this study do not directly exclude / isolate the RPs that are deemed misbehaving, but instead base the RRs' decision on the most appropriate RP on a weighted combination of the evaluation of the quality of the RPs' offer (potential SLA's terms and conditions) and of their reputation rating (reliability related factor).

Various systems for trust establishment have been presented (e.g., [18], [19]), a number of which utilize the opinion / view other system participants have on the entities under evaluation. However, a number of them do not clearly describe how the evaluator entities find in the system feedback sources used for the overall evaluation of the target entities. Additionally, our mechanism in order to elicit true feedback considers intentional as well as unintentional inaccurate information provisioning, taking into account, in addition to witness trustworthiness, the number of transactions a witness RR has performed with the target RP and the sum of the respective transactional values. Finally, in our framework, time effect has been taken into account and more recent events weigh more in the evaluation of the overall reputation rating of the target entity, while untrustworthy RPs are given a chance to re-enter the system and improve their reputation rating in case they abide by the established SLA terms and conditions.

6. Conclusions

The scope of our paper is to enhance the functionality that may be offered by distributed computing environments. Under the assumption that a number of Resource Providers (RPs) may handle and serve the Resource Requestors (RRs) requests with the same SLA terms and conditions, the RRs may decide on the most appropriate RP for the resource requested on the basis of their reputation rating. The reputation mechanism adopted is distributed, considers both first-hand and second-hand information, while it takes into account potential dissemination of inaccurate reputation ratings. The reputation framework designed has been empirically evaluated by simulating interactions among self-interested RPAs and RRAs and has performed well. Our obtained results indicate that the proposed RP selection scheme exhibits increased RR satisfaction with respect to random RP selection, which is on average 30%, in case honest feedback provision is assumed for the vast majority of the witnesses.

Future plans involve our frameworks' extensive empirical evaluation incorporating various degrees of witnesses' misbehaviour and against existent reputation models and trust frameworks. Furthermore, the authors consider moving the burden of obtaining trust information from the evaluator RRA to the RPAs being evaluated.

References

[1]   N. Jennings, P. Faratin, A. Lomuscio, S. Parsons, C. Sierra and M. Wooldridge, "Automated Negotiation: Prospects, Methods, and Challenges", International Journal of Group Decision and Negotiation, vol. 10, no. 2, pp. 199-215, 2001.
[2]   M. Louta, I. Roussaki, and L. Pechlivanos, "Reputation Based Intelligent Agent Negotiation Frameworks in the E-Marketplace," in 2006 Proc. International Conference on E-Business, Setubal, Portugal, pp. 5-12.
[3]   J. Callas, L. Donnerhacke, H. Finney, D. Shaw, R. Thayer. (2007). OpenPGP Message Format (RFC 4880, IETF). Available: http://www.ietf.org/rfc/rfc4880.txt.
[4]   D. Cooper, S. Santesson, S. Farell, S. Boeyen, R. Housley, W. Polo. (2007). Internet X.509 Public Key Infrastructure Certificate and Certificate Revocation List (CRL) Profile (Internet Draft, IETF). Available: http://www.ietf.org/internet-drafts/draft-ietf-pkix-rfc3280bis-09.txt.
[5]   Y. Atif, "Building Trust in E-Commerce," IEEE Internet Computing Magazine, vol. 6, no. 1, pp. 18-24, 2002.
[6]   G. Zacharia and P. Maes, "Trust management through reputation mechanism," Applied Artificial Intelligence Journal, vol. 14, no. 9, pp. 881-908, 2000.
[7]   R.S. Sutton, A.G. Barto, "Reinforcement learning: An introduction (Adaptive computation and machine learning)", MIT Press, March 1998.
[8]   eBay http://www.ebay.com
[9]   The Parlay Group http://www.parlay.org/
[10]   OSGi (1999) Open Service Gateway Initiative, http://www.osgi.org
[11]   B. Benatallah, Q. Sheng, and M. Dumas "The Self-Serve Environment for Web Services Composistion", IEEE Internet Computing, vol. 7, no.1, pp.40-48, 2003.
[12]   S. Vinoski "CORBA: Integrating diverse applications within distributed heterogeneous environments", IEEE Communications Magazine, vol. 35, no. 2, pp. 46-55, 1997.
[13]   P. Morreale "Agents on the move", IEEE Spectrum, vol. 35, no. 4, pp. 34-41, 1998.
[14]   N. Jennings, K. Sycara, and M. Wooldridge "A Roadmap of Agent Research and Development", Autonomous Agents and Multi-Agent Systems, vol. 1, no. 1, pp. 7-38, 1998.
[15]   M. He, N. Jennings, and H. Leung, "On agent-mediated electronic commerce," IEEE Transactions on Knowledge and Data Engineering, vol. 15, no. 4, pp. 985-1003, 2003.
[16]   J. Sabater and C. Sierra, "Review on Computation Trust and Reputation Models", Artificial Intelligence Review, vol. 24, no. 1, pp. 33-60, 2005.
[17]   H. Li and M. Singhal, "Trust Management in Distributed Systems", IEEE Computer, vol. 40, no. 2, pp. 45-53, 2007.
[18]   L. Xiong and L. Liu, "Reputation and Trust", Advances in Security and Payment Methods for Mobile Commerce, Idea Group Inc, 2005, pp. 19-35.
[19]   G. Zacharia, A. Moukas, and P. Maes, "Collaborative Reputation Mechanisms in Electronic Marketplaces," in Proc. of the 32nd Hawaii International Conference on System Sciences, Los Alamitos, CA, USA, 1999, pp 1-7.

Collaboration and the Knowledge Economy: Issues, Applications, Case Studies
P. Cunningham and M. Cunningham (Eds.)
IOS Press, 2008

BPM4SOA Business Process Models for Semantic Service-Oriented Infrastructures

Dimitris KARAGIANNIS[1], Wilfrid UTZ[2], Robert WOITSCH[2], Hannes EICHNER[2]

[1]*University of Vienna, Department of Business and Knowledge Engineering,*
Brünnerstaße 72, Vienna, 1210, Austria
Tel: +43-1-427738481, Fax: +43-1-427738484 , Email: dk@dke.univie.ac.at
[2]*BOC Asset Management GmbH, Bäckerstraße 5, Vienna, 1010, Austria*
Tel: +43-1-5120534, Fax: +43-1-5120534-5,
Email: {Wilfrid.Utz, Robert.Woitsch, Hannes.Eichner}@boc-eu.com

Abstract: The paper introduces a modelling framework that was developed in the BREIN project to integrate all project related modelling efforts. Based on the project requirements and a state of the art analysis the BREIN related modelling challenges were identified on three levels: syntactical, semantical and contextual. As there are different tools, formats and languages available for the different modelling areas, the key challenge is the integration of the related modelling languages. The paper shows how these challenges are addressed and discusses how business process models can be used for semantic service oriented infrastructures. The implemented modelling framework considers existing standards and establishes a formal integration and transformation among them by realizing a semantic integration service including the syntactical, semantical and contextual level.

Keywords: Business Process Management, Ontology, Service Oriented Architecture

1. Introduction

The following position paper discusses a modelling framework for semantic service-oriented infrastructures that is developed in the IST project BREIN [1], co-funded by the European Commission under the Sixth Framework Programme (2002-2006).

The aim of BREIN is to develop an intelligent grid infrastructure to significantly reduce the complexity of current business-to-business collaborations with a specific focus on SMEs. BREIN will demonstrate its capabilities with two scenarios, the Virtual Engineering scenario and the Airport scenario. Both scenarios involve complex relations between service-providers that need to interact with each other in order to deliver specific services to the customer. The aim of BREIN is to transfer these business collaborations onto grid technology. This means taking the existing business and its services and changing the underlying technology by transferring it to grid technology. In order to succeed in doing this transfer business processes have been selected to perform an analysis of the virtualisation within grid technology. To transfer the business knowledge, ontologies were generated from these business processes as a base of common understanding.

An observation made during the analysis is that business processes are commodity today. Business processes exist in every business field and they need consideration in the related IT-systems. The creation of software is more and more related to the configuration of systems and services using a model-based approach rather than actually implementing it. This paper presents the approach taken to realize the BREIN Modelling Framework covering the observations mentioned above, identifies related challenges and discusses how they are addressed.

The paper at hand is structured as follows: chapter 2 introduces in more detail the objectives of this paper by stating the requirements for the modelling framework and identifying the related challenges. In the third chapter the methodology is presented and chapter 4 presents a case study on the ontology generation approach. Chapter 5 discusses the benefits obtained while chapter 6 provides insight in upcoming research challenges of this approach and gives an outlook on further activities.

2. Integration Objectives and Challenges

As already introduced, business processes are omni-present in business and modelling is continuously gaining importance for the development and the configuration of software systems. A series of national and EU funded projects (e.g. BIG (AUT) [2], FinGrid (GER) [3], BREIN (EU) [1], BEinGRID (EU) [4]) reflect that business aspects need consideration in service-oriented architectures (SOA) and infrastructures (SOI). Within BREIN business related models as well as various technical models have been analysed and discussed aiming to integrate these models into a common modelling framework.

The objective of the BREIN Modelling Framework [5] is to bridge the gap between the demands of the business-oriented end user and the technology-oriented developer. Business experts and developers have the possibility to use the modelling language applicable for specific tasks, which are then integrated by providing a multi-modelling language framework. The semi-formal domain models are transformed into formal and executable ontologies and workflows.

Various modelling services are offered through the BREIN Modelling Framework to support application scenarios such as process-oriented requirements analysis of applications, the specification of the software architecture and the externalisation of expert know-how (knowledge management aspects). In general, the modelling framework separates two levels of abstraction, the business modelling level and the IT modelling level. In addition to these two levels, a "Best Practise Roadmap" deals with knowledge management aspects [6]. The roadmap provides new or external developers that do not belong to the core project team with a model-driven guidance system for system development and extension. Various knowledge services are made available to the developers for collaborative development tasks.

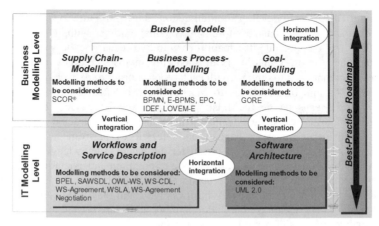

Figure 1: The BREIN Modelling Framework

Considering the BREIN scenarios that are characterized through complex supply chains and inter-organisational collaboration that should be automated, the requirements for the modelling methods used in the business modelling layer and the IT modelling layer, have been derived. As a result the BREIN Modelling Framework has to deal with several modelling languages that have different focus (e.g. business or technical level) and has to consider several languages within one modelling domain. Based on the requirement of the scenarios, the business modelling layer has been instantiated with (see Figure 1):

- Supply chains to model the inter-organisational perspective (SCOR [7]),
- Business processes to represent the intra-organisational view (e.g. BPMN [8], E-BPMS [9], EPC [10]) and
- Goal models to steer the business collaborations (approaches based on GORE (Goal Oriented Requirements Engineering [11])).

The IT modelling layer is split into two building blocks:

- Workflow and Service Description for the discovery and the execution of services and workflows [12] (BPEL [13] and OWL-WS [14]) and
- Software Architecture to document the platform and for the technical specification of services (UML™ [15]).

The integration of all these modelling languages involves several challenges that may be classified according to their level: (1) syntactical, (2) semantical and (3) contextual:

The **syntactical level** concerns models and their representation. The problem here is that modelling languages differ on a syntactical level which means that they are stored in different formats and there is no unified way to access them. Models may be stored as files or in repositories (such as relational or XML databases), and their format may not follow any standard representation. Proprietary formats and different data sources lead to many problems as they require the development of new interfaces for every representation and make the use of models complex.

The **semantical level** deals with modelling languages and raises the question how different modelling languages may be integrated with each other. The integration of two modelling languages usually results in a semantic gap, and the key question is how this gap may be bridged. In particular there are substantial difficulties when it comes to bridge the gap between the business and the IT-view referred to as the "Business-IT Gap". One approach is to use business processes to derive requirements for IT services that will in return automate them. In this case the method used to model the business view has to be integrated with the one representing the technical world (e.g. a business process modelling language for the business view and UML [15] for the modelling of software artefacts).

The third challenge is the **contextual level**, which is concerned with the translation of knowledge from one domain into another domain and the fact that different stakeholders use the same term in different contexts. For instance a business expert might interpret the term *"business process"* referring to a concrete business process in a company e.g. transporting the passengers from the gate to the aircraft at the airport. A technician might understand it as a sequence of web service invocations. The problem is that domain experts have the business expertise but rarely the IT-competence. On the other hand software developers cannot define the business requirements. A common understanding of the domain between all stakeholders is essential and the communication between business people and technician for a successful system implementation.

After setting out the requirements for the modelling framework and the related challenges, the next chapter explains how the framework is realized and how the challenges are addressed. The most challenging objective is the contextual level, which will be explained in more detail.

3.   Conceptual Basis of the BREIN Modelling Framework

As already mentioned in BREIN a modelling framework for all project related modelling tasks was defined. Based on the requirements that BREIN and its scenarios impose on modelling, the definition of the modelling framework started by identifying major technologies involved. The modelling approaches of ATHENA [16], EMI (Enterprise Model Integration) [17], MDD/MDA (Model Driven Design/Model Driven Architecture) [18] and concepts of SOA (Service Oriented Architectures) [19] were analysed.

ATHENA has developed a viewpoint-based integration approach to model interoperability which shows the existence of multiple viewpoints comprising the viewpoints of business analysts, product developers, system architects, and software developers. It becomes evident that these viewpoints share some common objects or concepts that need to be integrated in order to sustain modelling integrity. A quite similar attempt of defining a generic modelling framework is the Enterprise Model Integration (EMI) approach. EMI stands for the integration of the different modelling methods used on the design graph. On the one hand, the design graph includes semi-formal business oriented models, which try to explain the business domain independent of the technology to be used. On the other hand, the design graph includes platform independent technical models which, in the case of processes, can be considered as the basis for process execution.

Considering the observations made in the analysis, the following separations of layers with their respective models, which are also defined in the MDD/MDA approach [18] by the OMG, have been derived (see Figure 2):

1. CIM (Computation Independent Model): models capturing the real world business, serving as the requirements.
2. PIM (Platform Independent Model): workflow models on a platform-independent layer that may be derived from the upper layer.
3. PSM (Platform Specific Model): executable models bound to a specific platform, which are a refinement of the PIM layer.

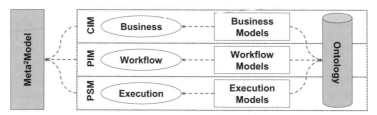

Figure 2: The Concept of the "BREIN Modelling Framework"

3.1   Addressing the BREIN Modelling Challenges

In general shortcomings on a **syntactic level** can be addressed by the use of standards for a specific modelling task. Due to the fact that various modelling languages are made available through the BREIN Modelling Framework a common and generic repository for all models created using different methods is established. BREIN uses a generic model repository that acts as a mediator and allows access to the models through one unified XML format. The functionalities of the generic model repository are exposed through web service interfaces. The framework allows the model interchange with external systems through the implementation of import and export mechanisms with standard formats including EPC, UML/XMI, BPEL and OWL.

On the **semantic level** the BREIN Modelling Framework enables the integration of modelling languages with meta-model integration patterns. The modelling languages are linked using a loose integration pattern. The modelling languages are coupled using a so called transition layer that contains concepts from both methods.   Taking   the   example regarding the "Business-IT Gap" presented before, the language of the business layer (e.g. E-BPMS) and the language of the IT layer (e.g. UML) have been analysed and the common concepts were identified (in the case of E-BPMS and UML, the common concepts are "use-case" related) and may be bridged using the common concept on the transition. There are different types of integration - we consider **vertical and horizontal integration** as well as a **hybrid integration** combining vertical and horizontal approaches:

Vertical integration is a typical top-down or bottom-up approach where different levels of modelling abstraction are integrated. For the top-down-integration the starting point are the elements of the higher level method. Method fragments of the lower layer are selected and integrated based on the requirements from the upper method. Another possibility is the bottom-up integration which is more common in reengineering approaches. To conflate the business modelling layer and the IT modelling layer, vertical integration is needed and, in the case of BREIN that a top down integration approach has been chosen. This means that business goals, strategies and business processes serve as starting points for application development.

Horizontal integration is used for the integration of method fragments on the same layer of modelling abstraction, which means that meta-models on the same level of detail can be integrated. This integration approach is used to integrate the methods within the business modelling layer as well as the methods in the IT modelling layer, respectively.

The modelling challenge on the **contextual level** will be tackled through the integration of meta-models and ontologies to map different modelling languages. A bootstrapping approach [20] where models serve as basis for the creation of ontologies and vice versa has been selected for ontology evolution based upon available content. The main idea is to use business process models for the generation of ontologies, thus also reflecting business aspects. On the other hand a uniform terminology defined as ontology will be used to assist the user when creating models. This issue is treated in chapter 4, presenting two related modelling services that try to overcome the limitations currently existing in this area.

4. BREIN Semantic Modelling Services

From an implementation perspective a service-oriented modelling framework has been established for development and deployment of semantic modelling services supporting the BREIN integration challenges described above. In the following two representative modelling services within this framework have been selected, both dealing with the semantic integration between modelling languages. These services will be described in detail focusing on the Airport Scenario use-case also describing roles involved in using the services.

4.1 Model Mapping Service for Semi-automatic Ontology Generation

The model mapping service allows the semi-automatic generation of an ontology using already existing business process models as a basis. The derived ontology is the basis for refinement and evolution steps and continuous improvements of the system. From the literature of meta-models and their relation to ontologies described in [21], [22] it was reasonable to use business process models, filtering them according to relevant concepts and transforming the relevant ones into formalized ontologies.

As the ontology language (e.g. OWL) and the business process modelling language may be interpreted as meta-models, the meta-modelling reference pattern according to [15] can be applied. For the model integration two dimensions have to be considered, first the direction of integration (vertical, horizontal or hybrid) and second the level of integration (loose, intermediate, and strong). BREIN implements a vertical integration between business process models and ontologies. The integration can be also considered as loose as we consider the business process models and the ontology almost independent.

For the development of the modelling service there are two ontologies that can be applied: an upper ontology on a meta-model layer comprising of a list of concepts for business process modelling as well as derived from the high-level ontology on a model layer comprising of a list of concepts of the scenarios.

The meta-model concepts have been analysed according their usability and the service translates modelling concepts from the business layer to modelling concepts to the ICT layer by applying mapping rules, defined in a language mapping file. As input the modelling constructs of the modelling languages used have been considered and mapped accordingly. For this task the knowledge engineer works in conjunction with the business user to derive and build up a common understanding of the modelling language.

The second approach deals with the transformation of concrete business process models into ontologies. The semi-formal description of business process models using E-BPMS [9] and related business process management languages (e.g. [10]) derived directly from the use-case partner of the Airport scenario and Virtual Engineering scenario (about 100 semi-formal business process models in different iteration for the specific services) were used as the basis to define scenario specific concepts. Again, mapping rules have been established to allow automatic transformation of these models into scenario ontologies.

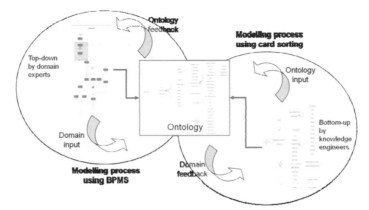

Figure 3: Ontology Generation Approach

In parallel to this top down approach (from the semi-formal models to formalized ontologies), a continuous evaluation and improvement step by knowledge engineers and ontology experts capturing and refining the derived ontologies has been established. The combination of these approaches led to the definition of the ontologies in an iterative way (see Figure 3) leading to a complete domain conceptualisation for the two scenarios.

4.2   Model Assistant Service for Model Consistency Checking

The model assistant service evaluates the derived conceptualisation and makes the formal description usable for the business expert [23]. The ontology is used as input for various checks to be done by the domain user in order to refine and evaluate the models created. The checks/assisting evaluations are available for the user during the modelling tasks performed and makes sure that correct terms are used, suggests synonyms and allows check from a granularity as well as semantic perspective. Apart from this feedback the service also allows to enhance the ontology with new terms or concepts that were not present before. Also other advanced features such as auto-completion or enriched search mechanisms are possible through this integration.

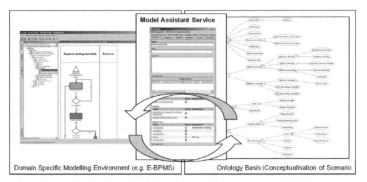

Figure 4: Model Assistant Service for Business Process Modelling

5. BREIN Modelling Framework Business Benefits

Aligning IT with a company's business strategy is critical to its success, and yet, it remains an ongoing challenge. Currently model-based approaches are prominent for this integration. The modelling framework is the first step into this direction providing the integration of different modelling languages to derive IT from business requirements.

The use of business processes to communicate the business needs have been found useful since an early integration of the end user in technical discussions is possible. Business experts can formulate their needs in easy to understand semi-formal models. The first step in modelling was to analyse the scenarios' supply chains to see the interactions between the business actors in the complete end-to-end process. Then business process modelling focused on the intra-organisational perspective.

The modelling activity helped to externalise the dynamic dependencies between participants and processes, increasing the shared understanding of the domain. This semi-formal domain description was the basis to communicate business needs to the systems architects. Based in this common understanding all stakeholders including software developers could take advantage of. An additional aspect is the profit for the knowledge engineer, which is concerned with the ontology building. Through the transformation mechanisms the business processes could be taken as valuable input to complete the rather technology-driven ontology. The integration of the business aspects is a clear enrichment of the system-oriented ontologies.

6. Conclusions

Business processes are commodity today. They exist in every business field and need consideration in the related IT-systems. As there are different tools, formats and languages available a key-challenge is the integration of all these modelling languages into a common and interchangeable framework to ease cooperation and communication efforts.

The presented framework is currently implemented and is used via a prototype by the project consortium and is seen a first step towards the establishment of a common knowledge base in the domain. As the project progresses the BREIN Modelling Framework will evolve including the development of better mappings from business layer towards the ICT layer, more sophisticated modelling services to simplify the handling of ICT models by non-experts and to integrate ontologies into the modelling framework as the underlying model exchange format.

The vision is to evolve the framework to an "IT-socket" that lets business plug-in into IT. Instead of today's IT, which is tightly integrated with the business (i.e. IT is designed for specific business sectors or even applications), in the envisioned future businesses plug into an IT-socket using their business specific plug. To allow this the level of integration has to be lifted from technical to a business level using a model based approach. This is subject to research in a future EU-project.

References

[1]   BREIN project, http://www.gridsforbusiness.eu
[2]   Business In the Grid Infrastructure (BIG) project, http://www.pri.univie.ac.at/workgroups/big/
[3]   Financial Business Grid FinGRID project, http://www.fingrid.de/
[4]   Business Experiments in Grid BEinGRID project, http://www.beingrid.eu/
[5]   Woitsch, R., Eichner H., Hrgovcic V.: Modelling Interoperability: The Modelling Framework of BREIN, In: Interoperability for Enterprises: Software and Applications (I-ESA'08) Workshop Proceedings (2008)
[6]   Woitsch, R., Utz, W.: Roadmap to Akogrimo Convergence: A Sample of Process Oriented Knowledge Management with PROMOTE®, BPOKI'06 at I-KNOW '06, Graz, Austria (2006)
[7]   Supply-Chain Council (Eds.): Supply Chain Operations Reference Model (SCOR®) Version 8.0, http://www.supply-chain.org, (2006)
[8]   OMG: BPMN 1.0, http://www.bpmn.org/
[9]   Bayer, F., Junginger, S., Kühn, H.: A Business Process-oriented Methodology for Developing E-Business Applications. In: Proceedings of the 7th European Concurrent Engineering Conference (ECEC 2000), Society for Computer Simulation (SCS) (2000)
[10] van der Aalst, W.M.P: Formalization and Verification of Event-driven Process Chains, In Computing Science Reports 98/01, Eindhoven University of Technology, Eindhoven, 1998.
[11] Kaiyia, H., Horai, H., Saeki, M.: AGORA: Attributed Goal-Oriented Requirements Analysis Method. In: Proceedings of 10th Anniversary IEEE Joint International Conference on Requirements Engineering. IEEE Computer Society (2002)
[12] Junginger, S., Karagiannis, D.: Entwicklung von Workflow-Anwendungen. In: WISU - Das Wirtschaftsstudium 30, (2001)
[13] IBM: Business Process Execution Language for Web Services, http://www-128.ibm.com/developerworks/library/specification/ws-bpel/
[14] Beco, S., Cantalupo, B., Giammarino, L., Matskanis, N., Surridge, M.: OWL-WS: a workflow ontology for dynamic grid service composition, e-Science and Grid Computing (2005)
[15] Object Management Group (OMG): Unified Modeling Language Superstructure Version 2.0, http://www.omg.org/docs/formal/05-07-04.pdf, (2005)
[16] ATHENA Project, http://www.athena-ip.org/
[17] Kühn, H., Bayer, F., Junginger, S., Karagiannis, D.: Enterprise Model Integration, Proceedings of the 4th International Conference ECWeb (2003)
[18] Object Management Group: MDA Guide Version 1.0.1, http://www.omg.org/docs/omg/03-06-01.pdf
[19] OASIS: OASIS SOA Reference Model, http://www.oasis-open.org/
[20] Karkaletsis, V., Paliouras, G., Spyropoulos, C.: A Bootstrapping Approach to Knowledge Acquisition from Multimedia Content with Ontology Evolution, Adaptive Knowledge Representation & Reasoning, Helsinki, Finland (2005)
[21] Höfferer, P.: Achieving Business Process Model Interoperability using Metamodels and Ontologies. In Österle, Hubert; Schelp, Joachim & Winter, Robert (Eds.): Proceedings of the 15th European Conference on Information Systems (ECIS 2007), St. Gallen, Switzerland, University of St. Gallen (2007)
[22] Woitsch R., Karagiannis D., Fill H.-G., Blazevic V.: Semantic Based Knowledge Flow Systems in European Home Textile: A Process Oriented Approach with PROMOTE. Proceedings of the I-Know (2007)
[23] Leutgeb, A., Eichner, H., Utz, W., Woitsch, R., Fill, H.-G.: Semantic and Adaptive E-Government Processes - A Field Report About Ontology Based Approaches in EU-Projects, In Proceedings of the Eastern European e|Gov Days 2007, Prague, Czech Republic (2007)

Collaboration and the Knowledge Economy: Issues, Applications, Case Studies
P. Cunningham and M. Cunningham (Eds.)
IOS Press, 2008

Environment Friendly E-Environments – Challenges and Perspectives

Syed NAQVI

*Centre d'Excellence en Technologies de l'Information et de la Communication (CETIC),
29/3 Rue des Frères Wright, 6041 Charleroi, Belgium
Tel: +32 71490741, Fax: + 32 71490799, Email: syed.naqvi@cetic.be*

Abstract: This paper presents challenges and perspectives of developing green e-environments. The conception of e-environments that proliferates smart devices engulfing nearly all the activities of our everyday life is facilitating the vision of modern living. However, the negative impact of these scalable technology-rich environments on the global warming is unfortunately nontrivial. It is quasi impossible to opt for the abandonment option as these environments are becoming an inalienable part of our normal lives. This paper illustrates how the energy efficiency can be achieved by using interconnected data and computing resources. A case study of Grid computing is presented to demonstrate the possibility of lowering carbon footprints by using interconnectivity. Moreover, business benefits of these paradigms are also explored as financial aspects are by and large heavier than technological aspects. Based on this work, a number of recommendations for longer term research agenda for greener e-environments are also made in this paper.

1. Introduction

According to a World Bank report on ICT (information and communication technologies) and global economic growth, the pace of digitization is over double the pace of globalisation [1]. This spectacular speed of ICT growth has exorbitant impact on the worldwide carbon dioxide (CO_2) emissions. It is estimated that CO2 emissions of the ICT industry exceeds the carbon output of the entire aviation industry [2]. While the information technology is seemingly taking its toll on the global environment, it is indispensable to identify the ways and means of developing environment-friendly systems and technologies. It is also very important to assure the environment protection throughout the lifecycle of technological products from their fabrication to their disposal. There is a strong need of tackling these challenges in the global perspective as the scope of this problematic cannot be addressed by regional or continental approach. In this context, outsourcing maybe a short-term relief for some nations [3]; but in reality it is like sowing the seeds of disaster for the entire community of global citizens.

ICT like other technologies is contributing to global warming; however, it can be part of a solution. It is already used in technology solutions for monitoring pollution levels, detecting toxic materials, etc. It is also used for raising awareness by providing access to useful information resources. In this paper, we put emphasis on this side of the picture where new ICT solutions can be conceived for the protection of global environment. For example, the next generation networks (NGN) are expected to reduce energy consumption by 40 percent compared to today's public switched telephone network (PSTN) [4]. We have performed a case study of 'Grid Computing' to explore the vision of 'sharing resources implies sharing (lowering) carbon footprints'. We have also analysed the impact of Moore's law on the ecology as the hardware device upgrades generally result in the discarding of old equipments. We have envisioned the post Moore's law era in terms of electronic waste management and in terms of carbon footprints. Business model for Grid computing paradigm is also discussed in this paper.

2. Objectives

The main objective of this work is to provide a pragmatic analysis of the role the information and communication technologies can play for the improvement of global environment in general and of e-environments in particular. Our aim is to present both technical and business interests for the evolution of environment friendly e-environments. The potential challenges and the perspectives of this approach are investigated so that a compelling case can be prepared.

3. Methodology

The methodology used for this work includes a case study of Grid computing.

3.1   Introduction

Grids enable access to, and sharing of geographically distributed heterogeneous resources such as computation, data and information sources, sensors and instruments, for solving large-scale or complex problems. The deployment of Grid infrastructures is now getting momentum after its humble take off from the e-science field over a decade ago. Grid infrastructure is always considered as the best possible solution to accommodate the high volume data produced by contemporary scientific applications [5]. Now Grid computing is emerging as a critical infrastructure for knowledge based economy and is going to be a crucial component of its day-to-day business [6].

Grid computing harnesses the computing and storage capacities of several single computers (also called nodes). The computing jobs are divided over these nodes that enable the simultaneous processing of the various tasks associated with the submitted job. This concurrency not only paves the way for time efficient completion of jobs but also reduces maintenance costs of hardware and software. This scheme also reduces the carbon footprints; e.g. a single computer does not require sophisticated cooling system whereas a dedicated supercomputer does. Grids provide virtual interface to its users so that the underlying complexity of the Grid architecture is taken off from their eyes.

3.2   Case Study

We analysed various aspects of Grid computing paradigm to investigate its potential of providing environment friendly e-environment. The findings of this study are summarized in this section.

3.2.1   Reduction of Heat Generation

Grid paradigm promotes the use of a large number of commodity type servers instead of using a small number of heavy duty symmetric multiprocessing (SMP) servers. The heat generation and carbon footprints of the SMP servers are great challenges faced by the supercomputing centres. The costs associated with their maintenance and cooling is quite high and consequently their impact on the global environment in certainly non-negligible. Small servers and desktop computers generally do not even require air-conditioning for their routine operations. The amount of heat they expel to the environment is not more than the amount of heat released by a couple of humans. They are by and large kept cooled with the natural circulation of the fresh air.

3.2.2   Dispatch of Computing and Storage Jobs to the Energy Efficient Sites

Grid resource broker is a policy driven agent that dispatches the jobs to the appropriate nodes for processing. The definition of 'appropriate node' in this context is driven from the policy of the Grid test bed or from the policy rules of specific virtual organisation (VO) [7]. We can therefore easily envisage the scenario where the Grid/VO policy rules include the clauses that favour the use of environment friendly solutions. For example, priority rule for the selection of a suitable site may depict that "jobs be sent to those sites which employ renewable energy resources". Such policy rule will influence the business model as well because the Grid infrastructure providers' business interests will be associated with the use of renewable energy resources for their establishments.

3.2.3   Facilitate Conception of 'Carbon-Alternative' Applications

The human population is often obliged to participate in 'carbon-generating activities' such as travelling to distant public administration offices; printing voluminous documents for their mass distribution (e.g. yellow pages); commuting to libraries to read the reference books; etc. If we can offer a dependable information technology infrastructure whose utilisation is endorsed by the competent authorities through formal legislation(s) then a big number of carbon-generating activities can be brought to an end. The Grid can realise this paradigm by offering a reliable infrastructure for performing the afore mentioned activities from distance. The legal and social aspects can not be sorted out before the provisioning of some trustworthy Grid test bed, like the reliable internet backbone was made available before embracing the e-business era.

3.2.4   Software Based 'Renewable Applications'

The concept of 'software defined radio (SDR)' [8] is already envisioned and it is seen as future generation of mobile technology. This concept can be extended to cover various other domains where faulty or outdated hardware components are simply thrown away. For example, CDs and DVDs. Grid has the potential of providing efficient distribution of digital contents. If relevant applications are developed that can assure the proprietary rights etc. then a large segment of electronic waste management will be automatically solved like the development of 'media player' has solved the problem of scrapping tape recorders. Grid application developers can envisage the optimal transformation of the current features of the hardware components into their software equivalent for their environment friendly reusability.

3.2.5   Vision for the Post Moore's Law Era

Moore's Law [9], which has been so reliable for so many decades, now seems to be on the verge of losing its relevance [10]. Scientists and engineers have started working on the strategies for the technological solutions that can provide them needful capability of having enhanced capacities for the upgrades of their future endeavours. Grid has the potential of providing a fascinating vision of enhanced computing power in the post Moore's law era due to its capability of harnessing the computing powers of individual computers in a coherent way. Moreover, it's ostensibly environment friendly solutions make it an ideal successor for the Moore's law. Grid is going to transform Moore's "hardware-based evolution" into "software-based evolution" of computing paradigm.

4.   Technology Description

Analytical analysis is used to investigate the impact of various technological factors (both hardware and software) on the global environment. The emerging technology of Grids is targeted for this work as it is indispensable to go along with the new technologies due to their anticipated wide range acceptance in the society. Moreover, it is not realistic to propose an absolute abandonment option for the novel technologies as they are rapidly becoming an integral part of our daily lives. Interpolation and extrapolation of technological evolution especially the Moore's law is carried out so that the impact of this evolution on the electronic waste management can be analysed.

5. Developments

A holistic paradigm to investigate the impact of e-environments on the global environment is developed for this work. A set of recommendations is also prepared for the issues that are not generally fall under the category of mainstream technological concerns, e.g. issues related with other technologies such as material sciences; legal issues such as the legal character of the e-documents; social issues such as the awareness programs; etc.

6. Results

The impact of ubiquitous computing on the global warming is already studied in [11]; however, there is no precedence of the identification of holistic paradigm of the impact of E-environments on the global environments. The follow-up of the work in [11] can be facilitated on the basis of our work, e.g. a comparative analysis of paper versus gadgets that can demonstrate that how much energy costs of producing and printing the paper products (such as road maps, hotel menu, etc.) can be saved by using electronic gadgets; and how the waste management of the aging gadgets be handled in the environment friendly manner. Such a fine grained relationship of paper costs versus electronic waste management costs can provide compelling case for treading towards the technology rich era yet assuring the existence of green environment. This study is necessary for the development of benchmarks to measure the carbon footprints and consequently the evolution of best practises.

We have also analysed the impact of Moore's law on the ecology as the hardware device upgrades generally result in the discarding of old equipments. We have envisioned the post Moore's law era in terms of electronic waste management and in terms of carbon footprints. Moreover, business models for this paradigm are investigated and the benefits are summarized in the section 7 of this paper.

7. Business Benefits

Computational Grid gives a fascinating business prospects as overall data processing costs can be reduced drastically. The reduced processing time on the Grids due to the parallel processing of a job's various components not only lead to the early release of the products into the market but also the overall product price is slashed thanks to quicker and cheaper preparation phase. Although the Grid paradigm still lacks sound security, trust and dependability solutions besides fine-grained billing and accounting models; yet business interests are forcing big companies to invest in this area.

The policy based resource management feature of the Grid can be used to fetch the computing jobs to the sites which are using the renewable energy resources or the sites which produce less $CO2$ than their counterparts. The global sharing of resources has the potential of significantly reduce the use of papers (and consequently printers, cartridges, etc.) as the various stakeholders can use the electronic means to access and process the documents that are otherwise presented to them in paper format.

The Grid paradigm is helpful for telecommuting where people can work from home. Telecommuting is gaining importance today not only for its better impact on the employees' performance but also for the savings associated with this mode of working. According to a survey of the Belgian Wallonia (French-speaking) region, telecommuting is ranked fifth of thirteen solutions to fight against climate change [12].

8. Conclusions and Recommendations

Impact of technology on environment is important with the rise in the global warming. This paper presents the challenges and perspectives of deploying the environment friendly e-environments by using a case study of a contemporary computing paradigm known as Grid computing. The associated concepts such as the scope of hardware evolution to pace overall technological developments and business benefits are analysed. A set of recommendations for long term research agenda is presented here:

- Research on electronic materials and their compositions so that their recycling be made more efficient in such a way that no waste is produced in their lifecycles.
- Coordination is needed with the research developments in other domains. Examples include efficient cooling systems for server/cluster rooms; noise reduction solutions; social engineering methodologies, etc.
- Comprehensive e-Solutions such as E-Government, E-Business that can help curtail the use of papers in the real life administrative and trade situations. Besides technological solutions, legislations are also needed for the equivalence of electronic documents in the legal jurisdictions.
- Possibility of introducing 'environment surcharge' for the IT stakeholders that can be used for planting a tree for every IT unit's fabrication.
- 'Green targets' given by the funding agencies such as ANR in France, IST in Europe, NSF in USA, and DEST in Australia.
- Last but not least is the 'awareness' programs that can persuade people especially young people to play the games in the field rather than playing with the disposable electronic gadgets. For the employees, the concept like 'no email day' [13], etc.

References

[1]   Khuong Minh Vu, 'ICT and Global Economic Growth – Contribution, Impact, and Policy Implications', eDevelopments Services Thematic Group, The World Bank, 16 September 2004
[2]   Bill St. Arnaud's "Green Broadband" website – http://green-broadband.blogspot.com
[3]   Jamie Henn, 'Not In My Country: Outsourcing Pollution', 15 September 2007
      http://itsgettinghotinhere.org/2007/09/15/not-in-my-country-outsourcing-pollution
[4]   Lawrence Harte, Robert Flood, 'Introduction to Public Switched Telephone Networks (PSTN)', ALTHOS Publisher, 2nd edition (May 2005), ISBN: 978-0974278766
[5]   Walter Stewart's article in The Grid Today Magazine, 21 March 2005
[6]   Syed Naqvi, Philippe Massonet, Alvaro Arenas, 'Security Requirements Model for Grid Data Management Systems', Lecture Notes in Computer Science (LNCS 4347), 2006, pp 30-41, ISBN 978-3540690832
[7]   Foster I., Kesselman C., Tuecke S., The Anatomy of the Grid: Enabling Scalable Virtual Organizations, International Journal of Supercomputer Applications, volume 15, issue 3, 2001.
[8]   Walter H.W. Tuttlebee, 'Software Defined Radio: Enabling Technologies', Wiley Publishers, May 2002, ISBN: 978-0470843185
[9]   Gordon E. Moore, Cramming more Components onto Integrated Circuits, Electronics Magazine, 38(8), April 9, 1965.
[10] Zhirnov, V.V.; Cavin, R.K., III; Hutchby, J.A.; Bourianoff, G.I., 'Limits to binary logic switch scaling - a gedanken model', Proceedings of the IEEE, Volume 91, Issue 11, Nov 2003, pp 1934 - 1939
[11] Matsumoto M., Hamano J., Tamura T., Iguchi H., Impacts of Ubiquitous Society on the Global Warming Problem in 2010, Proceedings of the International Symposium on Electronics and the Environment, pp 183-188, 2005
[12] Newspaper "Le Soir" report of 7 April 2008 about the joint survey carried out with the RTBF – quoted by the Belgian Teleworking Association on their website – http://www.bta.be
[13] Intel's No Email Day Concept: http://blogs.intel.com/it/2007/10/quiet_time_on_track_no_email_d.php

Collaboration and the Knowledge Economy: Issues, Applications, Case Studies
P. Cunningham and M. Cunningham (Eds.)
IOS Press, 2008

Soft IP and Markets for Technology

Peter LOTZ[1], Alfonso GAMBARDELLA[2], Jonathan SAGE [3]
[1] *Copenhagen Business School, Kilevej 14A, Frederiksberg, 2000, Denmark*
Tel: +45 38152554, Fax: +45 38152540, Email: pl.ino@cbs.dk
[2] *Università Bocconi, Via Sarfatti 25, 20136 Milan, Italy Tel. +39-02-58363712 (or 3504);*
Fax +39-02-58363591; Email: alfonso.gambardella@unibocconi.it
[3]*IBM United Kingdom Ltd, Hursley Park, Winchester, Hampshire SO21 2JN, UK*
Tel: +44 1962 245418, Fax: (+44) 1962 818927, Email: jonathan.sage@uk.ibm.com

Abstract: Behaviour in the way patents are used in the marketplace has changed over the two decades. Intellectual property has become an industry in its own right with specialist R & D companies concentrating on technology development rather than production. Major industry players are also licensing out their technologies to other players. Technology diffusion and innovation arguably benefit through these trends – there is increased trade in knowledge and more liquidity. However there are still serious problems with the current system – speculative use of patenting to create injunctions and extort large settlement sums being one of these. This paper explores the potential of a novel patenting regime, so called Licenses of Right (LoR) or Soft Intellectual Property (Soft IP), in the European context and its likely impact if it were introduced. An advantage of such a system is that it may facilitate Markets for Technology and reduce the limits caused by the fear of being forced out of business through a patent infringement case. At the same time, such a system might encourage a better understanding of the functioning of this institution and increase awareness of the system itself,. An outcome could be a greater use of technology markets. Yet, if such a system is to function properly there are some questions to answer and problems to resolve.

1. Introduction

Behaviour in the way patents are used in the marketplace has changed over the two decades. Intellectual property has become an industry in its own right with specialist R & D companies concentrating on technology development rather than production. Major industry players are also licensing out their technologies to other players. Society benefits from increased technology diffusion and innovation. However there are still serious problems with the system, the filing of patents that can lead to injunctions being threatened to extort large settlement sums from manufacturers and service providers being one of these.

2. Objectives

This paper explores the potential of a neglected aspect of the patenting regime, the so called Licenses of Right (LoR), in the European context. The goal of this paper is to better understand the functioning of a LoR system. A broad advantage of the LoR system is that it may facilitate markets for technology and reduce the limits due to the fear of litigation by innocent infringers. At the same time, the definition of a LoR system might encourage a better understanding of the functioning of this institution in practice. In turn, this may increase awareness of the system itself, and hence encourage a greater use of technology markets. Yet, a proper functioning of an LoR system still presents some open questions. Generally, we suggest a voluntary scheme under which a patent applicant may choose between a traditional patent with full exclusivity and a patent with only "soft IP". The paper will raise and articulate a series of questions related to a Soft IP scheme and make recommendations.

3. Methodology

The paper is based on research conducted in how markets for technology have developed over the last decades. In addition practical experience of the approach to technology patenting, patent licensing and patent pledging by a major industry player is described as a case study. The hypothesis of what would change under a Licenses of Right regime is made.

4. Background

Markets for technology (henceforth MFT) have grown considerably during the past two decades. At the aggregate level, the chart below (Athreye and Cantwell, 2007 [3]) uses IMF data to show that while licensing royalty rates have been rising only slowly between 1950-1985, they have accelerated sharply thereafter. Similarly, according to OECD (2006) data [9], in the G8 countries, from 1980 to 2003, the technology royalty payments and receipts have increased by an average annual factor of 10.7%, reaching $190,000 million in 2003.

S. Athreye, J. Cantwell / Research Policy 36 (2007) 209–226   217

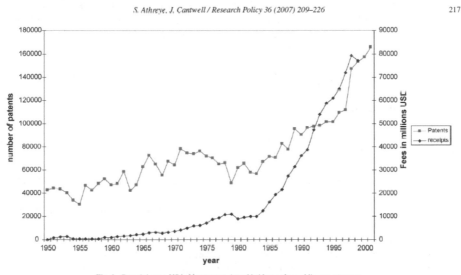

Fig. 2. Growth in non-US held patents and worldwide royalty and license revenues.

Overall, it seems that in the post-war period until the early 1980's, the inventions protected by patents were predominantly used (if used at all) by the patent-holders, whereas from the early 1980's there has been a strong growth in the trade with rights on intellectual property, such as patents.

At the industry level, many high-tech industries – biotechnology, semiconductors, IT, etc. – feature specialist technology suppliers selling their technologies to downstream manufacturers. The division of labor between firms has expanded from manufacturing issues (exemplified by Adam Smith by the making of pins in the early industrial revolution) into the research and development field. This means that new types of firms have appeared, firms that do nothing but produce new knowledge. Prominent examples pertain to the biotech area, where the discovery of gene-splicing in the late 1970's triggered a literal explosion of new non-manufacturing companies (Pisano et al., 1988 [10]). This increasing division of labor may be said to be a natural development following trends in, say, the petrochemical sector, where the immediate port-war period witnessed the emergence of a new type of company, the specialized engineering firm that designed plants and processes (Arora & Gambardella, 1998 [2]).

But the trend not only is based on the creation of new firms. Also larger firms (e.g. IBM) engage in licensing out their technologies more than they used to do in the past. An OECD study (Sheenan et al., 2003 [13]), interviewing 105 large firms in Europe, Japan, and the US, finds that the majority of firms interviewed predict that they will increase their licensing in and out in the 2000s compared to the 1990s.

If the increasing degree of labor in the manufacturing dimensions was a major driving force in the industrial revolution, the MFT promise to enhance the productivity of the entire society in a perfectly similar way. MFT provide several advantages both at the firm and industry level.

Some of the firm-level advantages are:

1) Firms have more strategic options. On the demand side, they can buy or make technology, or both. On the supply side, they can use it internally or sell it, or both.

2) Firms can profit from developing technology even if they do not own the assets to integrate them into products and related markets. This favors in particular firms with limited liquidity or downstream assets, typically start-ups and smaller firms.

3) Established firms produce many technologies that they do not use (e.g. Rivette and Kline, 2000 [12]). Moreover, many of their technologies have multiple uses. MFT enable them to create value from these unexploited assets. This may also encourage companies to think of their large R&D departments as a direct source of economic returns in the market as well.

4) Firms can enjoy liquidity from technology, which is otherwise one of the most illiquid assets. Again, this favors in particular smaller entrepreneurial companies that typically face liquidity constraints.

All of these advantages will provide stronger incentives to develop more technology. Individual firms will expect wider use of their technologies, and henceforth spend more resources on R&D.

This lead to a greater supply of technology that will provide industry-level advantages such as:

1) The greater incentives to invest in technology raise the rate of technological experimentation in the economy.

2) The increased division of "innovative" labor (Arora et al., 2001 [1]), creates greater competition in downstream industries and markets. This is because these firms have an incentive to sell their technology, which in turn diffuses through market trade.

Despite the observed growth and the obvious advantages from an increased specialization in technology development, markets for technology are still faced with problems. The markets are to a very high degree imperfect.

A well-known way of increasing the efficiency of markets is by introducing intermediaries. This is also happening in this area. A series of internet-based technology brokers has emerged over the past few years. Three leading intermediaries worldwide are yet2.com (www.yet2.com), Ocean Tomo (www.oceantomo.com), IP Bewertungs AG (IPB) (www.ipb-ag.com). These companies act as brokers in the increasingly complex markets for knowledge. This vehicle, however, seems not to solve fundamental problems. Lichtenthaler and Ernst (2008) [8] thus reports limited success for these companies.

The main limitation of technology markets is that they are still bound by transaction costs. Razgaitis (2004) [11] notes that out of 100 cases in which a company wants to sell its technology, only in 25 cases a potential partner is found, in only 5-6 cases the parties enter into negotiation, and only 3-4 end up in a licensing transaction. The main reasons for such high attrition rates are the costs of finding a partner, the fear of losing control of relevant intellectual property, the exclusivity or the geographical extension of the deal. In a number of cases the failure may be due to failure of the technology to reach a standard suitable for adoption: the invention may simply be unsuitable for use – or may already have been superseded by better innovation.

Another important (and related) limitation is the increased litigation over IP rights. This may even discourage investments in innovation because firms, especially smaller firms or units, may fear stumbling on some patents and hence incur high litigation costs. The issue has become rather serious and diffused (see eg Bessen and Meurer, 2008 [4]).

In a number of technology areas (such as ICT and biotech) there is concern that patents are increasingly forming "thickets" that effectively are impenetrable, especially for new firms (Bronwyn Hall, Cowan et al., 2007). The increasing patenting has covered large areas with such a complex web of rights that firms may simply give up operating in such areas, or invest in freedom to operate by cross-licensing patents. A recent study (Lichtenthaler, 2007 [7]) concludes that the most important motive for out-licensing is to secure freedom to operate. Generating revenues from licensing seems not to be among the driving forces for licensing. In addition the societal dimension of patenting in pharma, biotech and ITC are attracting increasing attention –Is the balance right between societal interests and commercial objectives?

Thus, while markets for technology are certainly growing, the full potential of this development is far from realized. Trading knowledge requires well-defined property rights, so that efficient contracts can be written. But certain property rights and the enforcements of them on the other hand may hinder the exploitation of technology that is already developed. .

5. Developments in policy considerations

It is in this spirit that the licenses of rights (LoR) scheme now attract renewed attention. It is our conjecture that a sensibly introduced LoR can solve in part these limitations, and they can give new spin to the MFT more generally.

Licences of Rights provisions are well known in several European jurisdictions. More recently, LoR has come on the agenda of the European Union, since an LoR scheme was included in the 2004 proposal by the European Commission for a Community Patent. The recent work on the Community Patent uses the 2004 proposal as its starting point and still includes the LoR provisions although there are concerns that, following the example of the French Patent Office which has recently revoked its LoR provisions, the provisions in the Community Patent regulation may be removed.

This would be very unfortunate. An LoR provision holds promise of mediating some of the transaction cost related obstacles for the expansion of markets for technology. The 2000 Commission proposal included a European Community Patent where the cost of the patent would be prohibitive if translation into all the languages of the European Community were required, and yet those potential infringers in countries not using the language of filing of the patent application will be vulnerable to being an innocent infringer simply because the patent is not in their own language. The Community Patent would not be translated into all the Community languages but would in be in the language of filing with the EPO and it would be automatically endorsed LoR. At the same time, the court system currently proposed for the Community Patent would be perfectly capable of dealing with the Licenses of Right requests in addition to handling normal infringement and validity questions.

6. Soft IP

Soft IP is a new concept that arose in the European Patent Office's Scenario project, which examined the long-term future of the European patent system. Interested stakeholders have since taken the concept forward and are proposing it as a possible component in the European Community Patent. Soft IP is conceived as a system that enables efficient capture and protection of IP, with provision for making licenses available to all interested parties. This is particularly applicable to patents. The Soft IP scenario acknowledges the value of IP in a licensing context, the need for balance between uses of IP in various industries and development models, and the fact that the value of a patent does not always reflect the value of the invention but more the cost of being unable to continue using the invention when an injunction is given.

In particular, the idea behind Soft IP is to encourage the use of LoR in the patent systems. The most immediate and dramatic consequence of LoR is the elimination of the right to seek an injunction to stop an infringer. This is a natural consequence of the LoR: The License of Right in essence changes the exclusive right that a normal patent provides to a remuneration right. Or – in other words – the right comes with a requirement to license, under which the right-holder cannot prevent anyone receiving a license to use the invention. Similar to certain copyrights, the idea is exactly to open the use of the patent to everyone who pays a royalty. Under such a scheme, the patent-holder cannot seek injunction to stop infringers, but it will still be an infringement if a user does not provide notice of the use and pays the royalty.

Instead of the power of injunction, the patent owner would acknowledge that some form of compensation for infringement would be acceptable – the compensation could be monetary with perhaps a cross license being taken into account if appropriate. The fact that a LoR is available greatly assists innocent infringers since they would be assured of obtaining a license, and would not be faced with the prospect of their business being disrupted or closed down. As with the existing LoR systems in the UK, and Germany, if parties cannot agree on terms, terms would be decided by the courts.

The Soft IP approach would be particularly attractive in situations involving the so-called honest concurrent user of the invention. Such people or organizations are "innocent" infringers. Innocent infringers have not engaged in any nefarious or unprincipled behavior but need to use patented inventions. Examples include inventions essential for software interoperability, Internet use and telecommunications projects where interoperability is a must-have, or Open Source projects.

Patent law already recognizes the concept of the "innocent infringer" – one who did not know of the patent or could not reasonably be expected to have known of the patent. The "Soft IP" concept would extend the notion of the innocent infringer.

Introducing Soft IP into the patent systems would facilitate the growth of the markets for technology in two important aspects:

1) It would eliminate the threat of injunctions blocking activities worth much more than the actual values of the invention. Disciplining the so-called patent sharks, this would allow companies a "freedom to operate" subject to royalty payment.

2) It would reduce the transaction costs of negotiating terms of licenses, a serious obstacle for the diffusion of knowledge. This probably would benefit especially small firms and universities.

3) It would partly redress the balance between societal and commercial interests which a patent system should seek to achieve – Soft IP drives a higher degree of collaboration between stakeholders and eliminates "strategic patenting" behavior that is harmful to wide economic interests.

7. Soft IP: benefits, limitations, and open questions

With these obvious benefits in sight, we need a better understand the functioning of a LoR system.

In this respect, a broad advantage of the LoR system is that it may facilitate MFT, and reduce the limits due to the fear of litigation by innocent infringers. At the same time, the definition of a LoR system might encourage a better understanding of the functioning of this institution in practice. In turn, this may increase awareness of the system itself, and hence encourage a greater use of technology markets.

Yet, a proper functioning of an LoR system still presents some open questions. Generally, we suggest a voluntary scheme under which a patent applicant may choose between a traditional patent with full exclusivity and a patent with only "soft IP". However, a specific proposal requires serious consideration. There still is a series of questions related to a Soft IP scheme. Specifically, the relevant questions in this context can be divided in three main areas.

1)   When should a patent applicant decide on whether to opt for Soft IP?

The main question is whether the option of a LoR should be exercised at the time of the patent application rather than grant. This implies that the choice is made when the patent owner does not yet know about the potential uses of the patent. In turn, this reduce the potential opportunistic behavior that the patent owner only chooses to put under LoR less valuable patents (or patents that he has decided to license in any case), while keeping his jewels under the standard regimes. With greater uncertainty, some jewels may turn out to fall onto the LoR scheme, thereby reducing the potential "lemons" problem of this market.

2)   Setting the prices of royalties under Soft IP

Another important question is how the LoR prices should be determined. In addition, one also ought to address the question of how the LoR collection of payments may take place. What can be learned from collecting societies in the copyrights area?

As an example, one can think of some compulsory publication of licensing rates and conditions for patents falling under the LoR regime, so as to increase transparency in transactions and to further encourage the development of the market. It would also avoid discriminating among clients, and the use of licensing as anti-competitive instruments (collusion).

3)   Is Soft IP attractive?

A related set of questions is the following: How big will the LoR incentive be? What extra incentives may be needed to make the system attractive? Should LoR be only voluntary or should it be mandatory for certain patents? Interestingly, this could create a continuum from no LoR to what would basically amount to a Compulsory License (mandatory LoR). To whom should incentives be aimed at, the community at large or the patent owner? What about questions of legal certainty for innocent infringer, viz., should they always get a license in any case?

4)   To what extent is Soft IP really friendly towards SMEs?

Recent practice shows that particularly SMEs are vulnerable in Europe to the threat of infringement. In theory, the Soft IP system means that innocent infringers would not be blocked from pursuing their invention in the case of alleged infringement. Also Soft IP is less costly: it would be cheaper to file LoR endorsed patent and under Soft IP licenses fees could be made easier to collect. Both these hypotheses need further examination.

5)   Is Soft IP compatible with Open Source software licenses?

In theory there is no contradiction between the Soft IP /LoR system and Royalty Free / Open Source licensing regimes. Open Source software is available on a Royalty Free basis, however this does not necessarily mean that it is not protected by patents. Some companies have made pledges not to enforce their patents against open source software. Such companies could endorse their patents under LoR, effectively granting a royalty free license to open source software and granting licenses requiring a royalty payment to proprietary software. However further research needs to be conducted to highlight any possible problems.

A series of other questions relate to enforcement and to the valuation of Soft IP.

LoR schemes exist in several countries. Research into the functioning of these systems might shed light on whether existing LoR systems (e.g. Germany, UK) support the markets for technology. In particular, historical situations (such as the British 1977 Patents Act extension of the patent period) should be examined. Similarly, it could be examined if there is a pattern in the use of the LoR option: Can it be shown that it is taken mostly by firms who plan to license the technology? If so, the current LoR scheme may basically turns out to be a discount to the (few) firms who plan to license their patents.

8. Conclusions

The paper identifies Licenses of Rights as potentially a powerful vehicle for the promotion of markets for technology. It also brings into the equation the importance of achieving a balance between the monopoly rights granted to the patent holder and societal interests. Excluding the right to pursue an injunction means that society benefits from more reasonable services, since the use of injunctive threats arguably adds to costs and supports inappropriate monopoly conditions. However we have raised a series of questions on how to implement such provision in the European context and we also recognize that the various stakeholder interests in a Soft IP system need to be subjected to fuller analysis.

References

[1]   Arora A., Fosfuri A., Gambardella A. 2001. *Markets for Technology: Economics of Innovation and Corporate Strategy*. Cambridge, Mass.: MIT Press.
[2]   Arora A., Gambardella, A. "Chemicals: A U.S. Success Story", …. 1998
[3]   Athreye, S., Cantwell, J., 2007 "Creating Competition? Globalisation and the Emergence of New Technology Producers" Research Policy 36, 209-226.
[4]   Bessen J, Meurer MJ, 2008. *Patent failure*, Princeton and Oxford, Princeton University Press, 2008.
[5]   Cowan, R.,Van der EIJK, W., Elsmore, M., Lissoni, F., Lotz, P., Van Overwalle, G., Schovsbo, J., 2007. "Policy options for the improvement of the European patent system", The European Parliament, IP/A/STOA/FWC/2005-28/SC16.
        http://www.europarl.europa.eu/stoa/publications/studies/stoa16_en.pdf
[6]   Hagedoorn, J. 2002 "Inter-firm R&D Partnership: An Overview of Major Trends and Patterns Since 1960," Research Policy 31, 477-492.
[7]   Lichtenthaler U, 2007. Corporate technology out-licensing: Motives and scope. *World patent Information* 29, 117-121
[8]   Lichtenthaler U, Ernst H, 2008. Innovation intermediaries: Why internet marketplaces for technology have not yet met the expectations, *Creativity and Innovation Management* 17(1).
[9]   OECD 2006. OECD Technology Indicators, Technology Balance of Payment – Payments/Receipts. Paris: OECD.
[10]   Pisano, Gary P., W. Shan, and David Teece. "Joint Ventures and Collaboration in the Biotechnology Industry." In *International Collaborative Ventures in U.S. Manufacturing*, edited by David Mowery. Cambridge, Mass.: Ballinger, 1988.
[11]   Razgaitis S. 2004. US/Canadian Licensing in 2003: Survey Results. *Journal of the Licensing Executive Society* 34 (4): 139–151.
[12]   Rivette, K.G. and Kline, D. (2000) "Discovering New Value of Intellectual Property", *Harvard Business Review*, January-February, 54-66.
[13]   Sheehan, J., Martinez, C. and Guellec, D. 2004. Understanding Business Patenting and Licensing: Results of a Survey. Paris: OECD.

Collaboration and the Knowledge Economy: Issues, Applications, Case Studies
P. Cunningham and M. Cunningham (Eds.)
IOS Press, 2008

Using Semantic Technologies to Improve Negotiation of Service Level Agreements

Ioannis KOTSIOPOULOS[1], Ignacio SOLER JUBERT[2], Axel TENSCHERT[3], Jesus BENEDICTO CIRUJEDA[2], Bastian KOLLER[3]

[1] *The University of Manchester, Kilburn Building, Oxford Road, Manchester, M13 9PL, UK*
Tel: +44 7957 271193, Fax: +44 161 275 6204, Email: ioannis@cs.man.ac.uk
[2] *Atos Origin SAE, Diagonal 200, Barcelona, 08018, Spain*
Tel: +34 93 486 18 18, Fax: +34 93 486 07 66,
Email: {ignacio.solerjubert , jesus.benedicto}@atosorigin.es
[3] *Höchstleistungsrechenzentrum Stuttgart, Universität Stuttgart, Nobelstraße*
Stuttgart, 19,70771, Germany
Tel: +49 711 6856589, Fax: +49 711 68565832, Email: {Tenschert, koller}@hlrs.de

Abstract. The need for automation of the negotiation process between Service Providers and costumers requires flexible protocols that address the issue of Semantic Interoperability. In this work, we present an enhancement of the traditional Service Level Agreement Negotiation Protocols using a lightweight annotation framework borrowed from the SAWSDL specification. We present a complete ontological framework that consists of a set of components that assist the negotiating parties to establish an agreement without having to agree on the same metrics. In order to avoid non-deterministic run times we propose the incorporation of the Monte Carlo algorithm in the negotiation protocol. Finally, we illustrate the applicability and the benefits of our work in a business use case.

1. Introduction

One of the motivations behind the adoption of Service Oriented Architecture (SOA) is the creation of a truly global marketplace where new business opportunities can arise. In this global market Service Providers and costumers need to come to a mutual agreement on the functional and non-functional properties of the service(s) under negotiation. The outcome of the negotiation process is a Service Level Agreement (SLA) and requires that both parties (Service Provider and Service Consumer/costumer) share a common understanding of the terms being used. However, the entities taking part in the negotiation of a Web Service can be coming from different countries or different continents, hence using different vocabularies to describe the terms. Even the definitions of the technical terms might be considerably different even across organisational boundaries. We believe that the use of commonly agreed conceptual models captured in the form of ontologies could greatly improve the interoperability between parties that want to automate the process of service negotiation. In this paper, we will describe an *ontological framework for SLA negotiation*. The remainder of the paper is structured as follows: Section 2 describes the objectives; Section 3 discusses the methodology and how it relates to other research initiatives. Section 4 describes the details of the framework as well as some implementation details and Section 5 analyses the benefits for a business scenario where this framework will be demonstrated. Finally, Section 6 presents conclusions and future work.

2.   Objectives

The objective of the ontological framework is to extend current standardisation efforts on SLA negotiation in a way that the new specification will be backwards compatible and will offer advanced flexibility and performance to users who have deployed the appropriate semantically enabled infrastructure. Overall, the proposed ontological framework aims to provide the means to the user to easily annotate SLA Templates by providing the appropriate contextual information stored in the knowledge base. The knowledge base plays an important role, as it will manage the assembled knowledge such as ontologies, annotations and mappings between different parameters. It will facilitate the translation process during negotiation and will enable the interpretation of semantic annotations of the SLAs. Finally, by incorporating the Monte Carlo algorithm the negotiation process will avoid non-deterministic run times.

3.   Methodology

The methodology for negotiation of Service Level Agreements has been recently the subject of investigations by several research projects. Some early results show that current state of the art in SLA Negotiation lacks flexibility in the protocol and execution. On one side, several European funded projects like NextGRID[1], Akogrimo[2] or TrustCoM[3] have proposed protocols for SLA Negotiation which mainly follow the so-called Discrete Offer Protocol which adopts a "Take it or leave it, terms of SLAs not negotiable" approach. On the other hand, standardisation efforts are still in early stages hindered by competing specifications. In total there is a huge gap in research related to Multiphase Negotiation and Term Adaptation, which implies the necessity for semantic enhancements for SLA Negotiation.

Usually, negotiation protocols are defined on top of existing protocols and standards for the establishment of an agreement between two parties. Two competing standards have been proposed for the establishment of agreements between Service Provider and costumer, namely Web Services Agreement Specification (WS-Agreement)[4] developed with the Grid Resource Allocation Agreement Protocol working group (GRAAP-WG) and the Web Service Level Agreement Language (WSLA)[5] proposed by IBM. WS-Agreement is a Web Service protocol and language for establishing agreements based on Quality of Service parameters. The focus of this specification is to extend current Web Services standards with the appropriate functionality to allow the establishment of an agreement rather than the provisioning of a complete language for the definition of an SLA. WSLA on the other hand provides a framework for monitoring and evaluating Service Level Agreements. The language is defined as an XML schema to be used by both parties in their respective deployments in order to be able to monitor the service. An attempt to merge the two standards initiated by IBM does not seem to have materialised yet. A negotiation protocol based on WS-Agreement has been described in a relatively new specification called WS-AgreementNegotiation [6] which seems to ignore any issues of semantic interoperability caused by the definition of new QoS terms either by the costumer or the Service Provider. Other initiatives include ongoing research from Parkin et al [7] on an abstract definition of SLA Negotiation in combination with an adequate protocol, which is based on contract law principles. To overcome the issues of limitations, Hudert et al [8] proposed a framework augmenting WS-Agreement, and presenting a "meta-protocol" enabling to choose the best fitting protocol (of supported protocols) for negotiation. A more relevant approach to our suggested ontological framework proposed by Oldam et al [9] was based on an extension of WS-Agreement with semantic tags to allow automatic matching between providers and consumers. However, this approach is not generic enough to be considered as an alternative negotiation protocol.

Semi-automated SLA negotiation requires inevitably the involvement of human users who will need to understand the context of the terms being negotiated. In order to assist this task, we propose a Text-Content Analysis (TCA) tool which stores and analyses existing domain ontologies to automatically provide contextual information regarding the SLA terms. The proposed tool enables a more detailed understanding of the text and the content. In order to understand text and content it is necessary to analyze the semantics as well. Information retrieval and text mining techniques can be used for the evaluation of existing domain ontologies stored in the TCA ontology registry. Part of the approach is the creation of a Mapping Syntax between domain ontologies that will allow the negotiation of SLAs mapped to different domain ontologies.

The annotation methodology is based on the lightweight annotation mechanism adopted in SAWSDL[10] which has become the dominant approach in the area of Semantic Web Services. Our main driver behind the adoption of this approach is the need to be able to operate in a mixed environment where some clients will be able to interpret the added semantics while others will just ignore them and graciously fall back to the XML based interpretation of the SLAs. The experience gained from various Semantic Grid projects has led us to the belief that the move towards knowledge based systems will happen gradually, hence in the foreseeable future, Grid middleware will vary in terms of knowledge capabilities.

The terms of the agreement between a Service Provider and a Client is part of a contract signed by both parties. The agreed terms are included in a document called Service Level Agreement while the document containing only the terms of the negotiation is called Service Level Agreement Template (TSLA). Our annotation framework is based on the TrustCoM SLA. We name the annotated version of the TrustCoM TSLA as SATSLA (Semantic Annotated Template Service Level Agreement). This specification will utilize a combination of WS-Agreement and extended WSLA from IBM to enable semantically enhanced negotiation, monitoring and SLA breach detection

Our proposal for an enhanced SLA negotiation tool will extent current state of the art in two ways. Firstly, *interoperability* can be also improved by incorporating automated reasoning based on the semantic annotations that will allow negotiations between parties that use different SLA templates. Secondly, *performance* of the negotiation algorithms can be improved by adding heuristics to avoid local minimums based on the Monte Carlo algorithm [12].

4. Development

In order to clarify how the proposed ontological framework works in practice, we provide an overview of the architecture.

4.1 Architecture

The architecture consists of a set of components that assist the Service Provider and the costumer before or during the negotiation process. The front-end components are:

- The SATSLA GUI provides a friendly way to interact with the SATSLA repository and allows the CRUD operations (Create, Read, Update, Delete) with the SATSLAs stored in the repository.
- The TCA tool manages the ontologies used for the annotation of the SLA documents. The TCA tool is integrated with the SATSLA GUI to present additional contextual information to the user when dealing with an SLA. The bidirectional nature of this tool means that the user can enrich the knowledge base with new facts such as new QoS metrics or mapping between metrics. The possibility to combine new and old metrics

increases the flexibility of the negotiation process and makes it easier for both parties to negotiate without the added burden of translating each others metrics when defining their SLOs.

The back-end components that realise the negotiation processes are:

- A SATSLA Template repository that allows the Service Provider to store all the SATSLA Templates relevant to a specific service as a service can be offered in different ways depending on different circumstances.

- A hierarchy of Ontologies that will be necessary to inform the different aspects of the SLA such as Quality of Service Ontology, Monitoring Ontology, Time Ontology, etc.

The components were developed using different programming languages and platforms, while interoperation was addressed by exposing them as Web Services. However, Web Services do not fulfill yet the promise of interoperation between different platforms, as several incompatibilities still exist. A stable version of the components will be released before in December 2008 while limited demonstrators will be available earlier. The annotation tools will be gradually integrated to the rest of the BREIN platform in order to demonstrate their use within larger business scenarios.

4.2   Semantic Annotation of Templates for Service Level Agreements (SATSLA)

As we mentioned before, our approach is based on the extension of the TrustCoM SLA specification [3] with semantic information using the extensibility points provided by the specification. These extensions are similar to the annotations proposed by Oldham *et al* on their paper "Semantic WS-Agreement Partner Selection" [9] but instead of adding another XML node we adopted the SAWSDL approach. According to this approach, we propose the replacement of the "tag" <OntConcept> that links the SLA term with the ontology with an extension element that carries the semantic information (annotation) following the SAWSDL approach. In the case of TrustCoM SLA, the SLAParameter represents the QoS guarantees (Performance, Response Time, Cost, Availability, etc.) and the Metric represents the metrics used by the Service Provider in relation to a specific QoS.

Currently, the proposed extension with semantic annotations affects the schema of the TrustCoM SLA in the two previous elements, SLAParameter and Metric. Inside the service description element of the WS-Agreement (where the TructCoM is based) we have a service definition based in the WS-Agreement standard and inside this element the SLAParameters which indicate the Service Level Objectives that the Service Provider offer guarantees. Each of these "SLAParameter" is associated directly with one Metric. In Table 1 we present an example that reflects the way the annotations are inserted in the document and the way in which the semantic and non-semantic elements are related.

Adding these sorts of annotations, the schema offered by the service provider is able to contain semantic information, as well as more conventional SLA properties. These annotations will be used during negotiation and monitoring to ensure the service guarantees. These annotations can be in case one party cannot interpret the annotations.

```
<wsla:Operation name="Operation Name" type="OperationDescriptionType">
 <!-- The Total Cost -->
 <SLAParameter name="Total Cost" type="double" unit="Euro"
satsla:modelReference="http://eu-brein.com/ontology/Upper/QoS">
        <Metric>Total Cost Metric</Metric>
 </SLAParameter>
 <!-- Total Cost for Service Usage -->
 <Metric name="total_cost_metric" type="double" unit=""
satsla:modelReference="http://eu-brein.com/ontology/Upper/QoS#PriceMetric">>
        <Source>Provider</Source>
        <Function resultType="double" type="Plus">
                <Operand>
                        <Metric>Usage Time</Metric>
                </Operand>
                <Operand>
                        <Metric>Number of requests</Metric>
                </Operand>
        </Function>
 </Metric>
</Operation>
```

Table 1: Annotated TrustCoM SLA Template

4.3 Ontologies

In order to annotate the SLA, providers and clients can use several ontologies in order to define new QoS parameters. The TCA tool manages the knowledge base that stores and retrieves concepts from the available ontologies in order to allow the user to retrieve the appropriate concept or to find similar concepts in other ontologies. We have defined a hierarchy of ontologies that can be used from both parties of the negotiation. An Upper Business Ontology contains the basic terms related to QoS and its purpose is to the set the basis for the development of other specialised ontologies used in each domain of discourse. For example, the term *performance* in the Upper Business Ontology is abstractly defined as a QoS parameter. However, in the Domain Ontology created for the Virtual Engineering domain investigated in the BREIN project, the term Performance is expanded to other terms such as CPU Speed, Memory, Hard Drive speed, etc. Similarly, the client can import a different ontology or ontologies relevant to the type of service he is offering and use it to annotate her SLA template. Creating and storing mappings between ontologies can lead to the negotiation of services defined using completely different QoS parameters.

4.4 Enhanced Negotiation using Monte Carlo

SLA Negotiation algorithms are hard to develop mainly because they can get stuck on a local minimum. Optimisation is possible but the search for exactly the right answer can lead to indeterminate run time as in the case of the Las Vegas algorithm [11]. The Monte Carlo algorithm can improve the precision of the results the longer it runs and can be stopped whenever a "good enough" solution is found avoiding local minimums.

Let us assume that a SLA has a set of Service Level Objectives (SLO) and there is a Customer that is willing to negotiate within two providers that are offering a set of possible values for a certain SLO. Now, suppose the customer doesn't agree within the values provided by the providers. The customer has two options; on one hand he can decrease his goals, which means that the service that originally is expecting is going to be reduced as well, so indeed he won't achieve his goal. Then the second option is to propose to the Service Providers to alter the original values of the SLOs, keeping in mind their original SLOs but slightly adjusting them to satisfy his needs. By randomising the SLOs over a finite set there is the possibility that the requirements of both parties are met arriving finally to an agreement on the negotiation of the SLA. The Monte Carlo algorithm can be used to iterate over this set of values until it produces a set that satisfies both parties. Let us assume the following parameters of the SLOs defined in TrustCoM specification (see Table 2).

```
<wsag:GuaranteeTerm wsag:Name="SLO_CLOCKSPEED" wsag:Obligated="ServiceProvider">
<wsag:ServiceLevelObjective>
<wsla:Expression>
<wsla:Predicate xsi:type="wsla:Greater">
 <wsla:SLAParameter>ClockSpeed</wsla:SLAParameter>
 <wsla:Value>4</wsla:Value>
   </wsla:Predicate>
   </wsla:Expression>
   </wsag:ServiceLevelObjective>
   </wsag:GuaranteeTerm>
<wsag:GuaranteeTerm wsag:Name="SLO_TOTALCOST" wsag:Obligated="ServiceProvider">
<wsag:ServiceLevelObjective>
<wsla:Expression>
<wsla:Predicate xsi:type="wsla:LessThan">
<wsla:SLAParameter>TotalCost</wsla:SLAParameter>
<wsla:Value>800</wsla:Value>
   </wsla:Predicate>
   </wsla:Expression>
   </wsag:ServiceLevelObjective>
</wsag:GuaranteeTerm>
```

Table 2: SLO definition using the TructCoM SLA specification

Then we provide the following parameters to the Monte Carlo algorithm:
1. For each Service Provider:
    a) W_{spi} Weight or importance that the provider gives to the parameter to provide.
    b) Range: [$Va_{sp(i)}$, $Vb_{sp(i)}$]
    - <wsla:Predicate xsi:type="wsla:Greater"> →Va
    - <wsla:Predicate xsi:type="wsla:LessThan"> →Vb
2. For each customer:
    a) W_{ci} → Weight or importance that the customer gives to be satisfied in the parameter i.
    b) V_{ci} → Desired value for the parameter i.

5.   Business Case

The scenario chosen to demonstrate the applicability of this framework is derived from the need of an engineering company to diversify its offerings by launching a Virtual Engineering platform where small engineering firms can carry out complex engineering simulations without having to buy and configure a complex and expensive infrastructure. In order to facilitate the potential users of this platform coming from all over the globe, we propose the enhancement of the negotiation process using this ontological framework. The parameters (Service Levels Objectives) of the services offered by the engineering company acting as a Service Provider, hosted by the Virtual Engineering platform and consumed by the costumer need to be negotiated. There is clear business mandate addressed by our work that is to make it easier for new clients to participate and consume services within this Virtual Organisation (VO) by improving several aspects such as interoperability, performance and ease of use of the negotiation tools. Improving semantic interoperability during the negotiation phase implies that more costumers will be able to negotiate and possible join the Virtual Organisation. By allowing the users to define their own terms for negotiation and automating large part of the negotiation process we decrease the entrance barrier that deters new clients from joining the VO. The principle behind this framework is to provide additional contextual information to the users during or before the negotiation process, hence giving them the confidence that the result of the negotiation will not contain unwanted terms.

Generalising from this use case, we can infer that companies who want to become key players with a view to establish real and long-term business relationships in the wide market place of the Service Oriented Infrastructure paradigm need to be evaluated and monitored constantly based on well defined QoS metrics. The key factor in the establishment of the parameters to be negotiated and eventually monitored is to know exactly how to define and evaluate them. This process requires the contextual information that will be provided by the proposed ontological framework. A demonstrator with real life data provided by ANSYS UK will be developed in the second half of the BREIN project.

6. Conclusions

Current state of the art in SLA negotiation should be advanced in order to improve the semantic interoperability between negotiating parties. Our work takes a fist step to address some of the challenges but it is by no means complete. We aim to release the complete specification for the annotation of SLAs following the TrustCoM specification along with annotation tools (December 2008). The development of a complete knowledge base containing mappings between several domain ontologies is yet to be addressed. We aim to provide the tools for the community to engage to this process and contribute to the development of this knowledge base. Our business case needs to enriched with real data demonstrating that companies participating in VOs offering business services have vested interests to improve the way service negotiation takes place given that conflict resolution (e.g. the civil court system) can be expensive and time-consuming. Our work aims to meet this need through the use of semantic technologies, which have matured enough to allow us to extend current SLA negotiation frameworks to become more flexible, intelligent and user friendly.

Acknowledgements

This work has been supported by the BREIN project (http://www.gridsforbusiness.eu) and has been partly funded by the European Commission's IST activity of the 6th Framework Programme under contract number 034556. This paper expresses the opinions of the authors and not necessarily those of the European Commission. The European Commission is not liable for any use that may be made of the information contained in this paper.

References

[1] The NextGRID Project, Priority IST-2002-2.3.2.8. Web site, 25 February 2007, http://www.nextgrid.org/.
[2] The Akogrimo Project, Priority IST-2002-2.3.1.18. Web site, 25 February 2007, http://www.mobilegrids.org/.

[3]   TrustCoM, 'A Trust and Contract Management framework enabling secure collaborative business processing in on-demand created, self-managed, scalable, and highly dynamic Virtual Organisations', Web site, 25 February 2007, http://www.eu-trustcom.com

[4]   Grid Resource Allocation Agreement Protocol WG (GRAAP-WG), Web Services Agreement Specification (WS-Agreement),   Version   2005/09,   September   20,   2005, http://www.ggf.org/Public_Comment_Docs/Documents/Oct-2005/WS-AgreementSpecificationDraft050920.pdf

[5]   Web   Service   Level   Agreement   (WSLA)   Language   Specification,   ver.   1.0,   28/01/2003, http://www.research.ibm.com/wsla/WSLASpecV1-20030128.pdf

[6]   Grid Resource Allocation Agreement Protocol WG (GRAAP-WG),Web Services Agreement Negotiation Specification (WS-AgreementNegotiation), ver 1.0, 9/5/08,

[7]   Michael Parkin, Dean Kuo, John Brooke: A Framework & Negotiation Protocol for Service Contracts. In proceedings of the 2006 International Conference on Services Computing (SCC06), Chicago, USA, 18-22 September 2006, pp. 253-256.

[8]   S. Hudert, H. Ludwig, G. Wirtz – A Negotiation Protocol Framework for WS-Agreement, IBM Research Report, October 31, 2006

[9]   Oldham, N., Verma, K., Sheth, A., and Hakimpour, F. 2006. Semantic WS-agreement partner selection. In Proceedings of the 15th International Conference on World Wide Web (Edinburgh, Scotland, May 23 - 26, 2006). WWW '06. ACM Press, New York, NY, 697-706.

[10] Joel Farrell,, Holger Lausen, Semantic Annotations for WSDL and XML Schema, W3C, http://www.w3.org/TR/sawsdl/, Recommendation 28 August 2007

[11] Bernard Bernu1, David M. Ceperley, Path Integral Monte Carlo, Quantum Simulations of Complex Many-Body Systems:From Theory to Algorithms, Lecture Notes,J. Grotendorst, D. Marx, A. Muramatsu (Eds.),John von Neumann Institute for Computing, J¨ ulich,NIC Series, Vol. 10, ISBN 3-00-009057-6, pp. 51-61, 2002.

[12] Algorithms and Theory of Computation Handbook, 15-21, Copyright © 1999 by CRC Press LLC. Appearing in the Dictionary of Computer Science, Engineering and Technology, Copyright © 2000 CRC Press LLC

Collaboration and the Knowledge Economy: Issues, Applications, Case Studies
P. Cunningham and M. Cunningham (Eds.)
IOS Press, 2008

Testing and Evaluation Methods for ICT-based Safety Systems

Micha LESEMANN
Institute for Automotive Engineering (ika) of RWTH Aachen University
Steinbachstr. 7, 52074 Aachen, Germany
Tel: +49 241 80 27535, Fax: + 49 241 80 22417, Email: lesemann@ika.rwth-aachen.de

Abstract: With the massive introduction of active safety systems in modern vehicles, it becomes more and more difficult for the customer to understand the effectiveness of those systems. Objective testing and evaluation methods are necessary to support this and are being developed within the recently started European research project eVALUE. They will also foster the development of new and advanced safety systems for future applications. This paper gives an overview of the systems which will be regarded and a scientific approach for the development of assessment procedures for those systems.

1. Introduction

Modern society strongly depends on mobility, and the need for transport of people and goods is expected to continue to grow. Cleaner, safer and more efficient transport systems are needed. Mobility and especially road transport cause major societal problems: accidents, pollution and congestions. Over 40,000 lives are lost every year due to road accidents in the European Union only, with costs estimated to be about 2% of its GDP [1].

The European Commission and its member states have made major efforts to improve traffic safety, and the results can be seen in a decreasing number of fatalities in many European countries [2]. New ways must be found to further reduce the number of fatalities and injuries. The public awareness of the enormous impact that active safety systems would have on road safety must be raised. It must be easy for the customer to understand the benefits of safety systems based on Information and Communication Technologies (ICT).

The average car buyer cannot assess the performance of active safety systems in vehicles, nor their impact on traffic safety. Today, there are no publicly accepted test methods and no established ways to communicate the test results. The situation is quite different for passive safety systems, where test programs like Euro NCAP have established impact test methods and ways to explain the test results in different levels of detail. While the car buyers may compare star ratings for passive safety between different cars, the professional safety engineer may compare measurement data from the tests.

Going forward to this goal of accident free traffic, evaluation and standardised testing methods for active safety systems are essential. This is the main focus of the European research project "Testing and Evaluation Methods for ICT-based Safety Systems (eVALUE)" which is funded under the 7th Framework Programme of the European Commission. It has a duration of 36 months. The consortium consists of eight partners from four European countries and is led by the Institute for Automotive Engineering (ika) of RWTH Aachen University.

Partners come from both research organisations and industry, including vehicle OEMs. In particular, Centro Ricerche FIAT (Italy) and Volvo Technology Corporation (Sweden) contribute as OEMs while Germany's Ibeo Automobile Sensor is a supplier of laser scanners. SP Technical Research Institute of Sweden and Statens Väg- och

Transportforskningsinstitut (VTI) are research organisations from Sweden with Fundación Robotiker and IDIADA Automotive Technology from Spain being well-know as research and testing suppliers.

2. Objectives

Performance test results presented to the public will help to promote the use of active systems. This has also been underlined by the eSafetyForum working group on Research and Technological Development in their "Recommendations on forthcoming research and development" [3].

By this means, also the research and development of new safety systems is encouraged. The long-term goal is to provide a basis for de-facto standards that will be used by all involved stakeholders. This has already proven to be an effective way in terms of promoting passive safety [4].

In the first phase, the eVALUE project is focusing on safety systems available for today's vehicles. Active systems currently under development or close to market entrance may be included in the project at a later stage. The aim is to identify evaluation and testing methods, especially for primary safety systems, with respect to the user needs, the environment and economic aspects.

An intensive communication with key stakeholders has been started and will accompany the project throughout its duration. The partners are aware of the fact that additional testing methods will not easily be accepted and adopted especially by involved industry. In addition, most manufacturers or suppliers already perform in-house testing of their systems and vehicles. Thus, a harmonisation of those methods is sought wherever possible. Besides industry, other stakeholders like national authorities, customer organisations or standardisation working groups active in this field are also contacted.

However, the project will not perform any activities which lead to a direct standardisation of the methods developed. Furthermore, there will not be any pass or fail criteria defined for the different performance values. The focus will be set on objective and repeatable methods while rating will be up to the users of these methods.

3. Methodology

Today, a number of passive and active safety systems as well as intelligent driver support systems is already in the market. A trend towards more pro-active and increasingly integrated safety systems is apparent. The performance of all these systems is affected substantially by the properties of the vehicle itself. For instance, such vehicle properties include tire characteristics, vehicle dynamics behaviour and friction potential in road/tire contact. Also the control strategy and algorithm quality of the active safety systems can improve the performance towards accident free traffic.

3.1   The Approach in Defining Test Methods

In 2007, the ASTE study [5] has investigated the feasibility of performance testing for active safety systems. It aimed at needed methods and principles for verification and validation of those systems. Therefore, different approaches were considered. The system approach is based on the capabilities of specific systems and mapped to traffic scenarios. Performance of the different systems with similar functions is then assessed.

The scenario approach is directly based on traffic scenarios. The vehicle is tested as a black-box and its overall performance in those scenarios is determined. As a third option, a document-based approach was discussed. This could complement physical testing and might be particularly valuable for HMI testing.

According to the conclusions of the study, vehicle active safety shall be tested following the scenario-based approach. It was further said that performance testing of active safety systems is technically and economically feasible and that a consensus between different stakeholders will be possible. The importance of communicating test results in a very simple way was underlined.

The eVALUE project is a direct follow-up of this study. Most partners are now part of the eVALUE consortium. Together, objective methods will be developed, enabling the estimation of the safety impact the regarded active safety systems have.

Figure 1 gives an overview of a scientific approach for the development of the testing and evaluation methods. Based on accident statistics, relevant scenarios will be derived that represent the majority of accidents in which active safety systems could possibly mitigate the outcome. A vehicle will then be assessed by applying the procedures. Those shall be recognisable also by the end customer as critical situations that can happen at any time. One example could be approaching suddenly congesting traffic or a similar, non-moving obstacle. The benefit of active safety systems (e.g. by automatic braking in this case) will thus be even clearer.

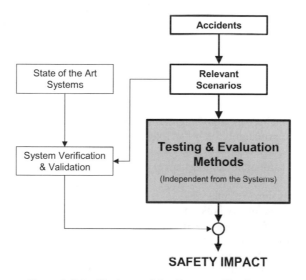

Figure 1: Scientific Approach for Assessment Development

Unlike the assessment of vehicle passive safety, the systems contributing to active safety will be regarded in detail. From verification and validation, e.g. fault rates are be analysed and their influence on the overall safety impact is taken into account. Validation of the systems includes the interaction with the environment/infrastructure and driver actions. For both testing the vehicle as a whole and the systems in detail, relevant scenarios have to be found and/or defined. However, details of this approach are currently under discussion.

3.2 Systems to be Regarded

The road-map of active safety systems with their time horizon is given in Figure 2. They are clustered into four domains. These are the longitudinal domain, the lateral domain, the domain for yaw/stability assistance and an additional domain. Scenarios will be defined for the same domains thus taking into account the interaction of different systems which might come into effect in the same situation.

Figure 2: Clustered Road-map of Active Safety Systems

Out of those domains, the following eight systems have been chosen. This decision is mainly based on the availability on the market with a penetration rate of more than 50,000 vehicles:

- System Cluster 1 (longitudinal assistance)
  1. ACC
  2. Forward Collision Warning
  3. Collision Mitigation, by braking
- System Cluster 2 (lateral assistance)
  4. Blind Spot Detection
  5. Lane Departure Warning
  6. Lane Keeping Assistant
- System Cluster 3 (yaw/stability assistance)
  7. ABS
  8. ESC
- System Cluster 4 (additional assistance)
  - Not defined at this stage

3.3   Challenges and Next Steps

The derivation of relevant scenarios directly from accident statistics has already turned out to be a challenge. No reliable accident databases are available that are capable of delivering a comprehensive analysis of accident circumstances for the whole of Europe. While some European projects like TRACE [6] are currently working on harmonised accident statistics, waiting for those results is not acceptable. The partners will thus define relevant scenarios based on information that is available today. This will include standards for testing of certain systems, results from other projects and the expertise of the involved institutions.

Having defined these scenarios then, the development of the methods themselves will start. The main focus will be on physical testing with a certain support from simulation where this seems appropriate. Verification and validation of the systems will mainly be achieved by lab testing. In general, the most suitable methods and procedures will be taken to reveal the active safety performance in the best way.

4. Conclusions

In the development of automotive active safety systems, no generally accepted standards are available today. Manufacturers of systems, components or vehicles all need to develop their own testing procedures in order to provide both development goals and means to evaluate the system performance. Large R&D efforts are undertaken in parallel by various companies to provide the technological background for development of testing procedures.

Due to this situation of inhomogeneous testing practice throughout the industry, test results acquired in different manufacturer-specific tests cannot be compared by customers and authorities. Furthermore, manufacturers have no means to assess their systems in a generally accepted way.

The outcome of the eVALUE project will be explicit testing procedures/protocols for active safety systems that can found the basis for a de-facto standard whilst and after the duration of this project. In addition, communication with stakeholders that might be involved in a later standardisation process has been established to get a broad picture of currently on-going standardisation efforts towards those systems.

The project started in January 2008 and will continuously generate results. Due to the production deadline, the latest findings cannot be covered by this paper but are available on the project's website under www.evalue-project.eu.

Acknowledgement

The research leading to these results has received funding from the European Community's Seventh Framework Programme (FP7/2007-2013) under grant agreement n° 215607.

This publication solely reflects the author's views. The European Community is not liable for any use that may be made of the information contained herein.

References

[1] Commission of the European Communities, White Paper: European Transport Policy for 2010: Time to Decide. Brussels, 2001
[2] European Transport Safety Council, Transport Safety Performance in the EU – A Statistical Overview. Brussels, 2003
[3] eSafetyForum Working Group RTD, Recommendations on forthcoming R&D in FP7 ICT for Mobility, Brussels, 2007
[4] SARAC II Consortium, Quality Criteria for the Safety Assessment of Cars Based on Real-World Crashes, Paris, 2006
[5] ASTE Consortium, Feasibility Study for the Setting-up of a Performance Testing Programme for ICT-based Safety Systems for Road Transport, Göteborg, 2007
[6] TRACE Consortium, Traffic Accident Causation in Europe, www.trace-project.org

Section 5.2

Applications

Collaboration and the Knowledge Economy: Issues, Applications, Case Studies
P. Cunningham and M. Cunningham (Eds.)
IOS Press, 2008

Supporting Enteprise Networks Set Up Combining ebXML, Semantic Tools and Sectoral Standards

Matteo BUSANELLI, Piero DE SABBATA, Nicola GESSA,
Cristiano NOVELLI, Gianluca D'AGOSTA
ENEA, Via Martiri di Monte Sole 4, Bologna, 40127, Italy
Tel: +390516098671, Fax: +39 051 6098 084, Email: matteo.busanelli@bologna.enea.it,
piero.desabbata@bologna.enea.it, gessa@cs.unibo.it, cristiano.novelli@bologna.enea.it,
gianluca.dagosta@bologna.enea.it

Abstract: The idea that undergoes the proposed paper is to present a collaborative framework, mainly based on the ebXML standard, able to implement the extended Smart Garment Organisation (xSGO*) and Interoperability* concepts in a useful set of tools and reference specifications. We assumed ebXML as a reference for the framework since ebXML represents, at this moment, one of the most important initiatives for the standardisation of collaborative eBusiness processes. The adoption of a standard framework, like ebXML, should reduce the efforts required to set up an electronic collaboration. Nevertheless ebXML lacks, for the moment, of practical implementations in real cases of clusters of enterprises (whilst cases based on Public Administration are known); with the proposed framework we would cover the gap between the ebXML specifications and the needs for a real implementation of the extended Smart Garment Organisation that is focused on a peculiar production chain like the Textile/Clothing sector.

1.   Introduction

The scenario of global commerce relationships requires more and more new mechanisms and tools that, adopting and implementing international standards like ebXML, can ease the establishment and maintenance of new efficient business collaborations.

Starting from our previous experience supporting collaborations between companies, from the Moda-ML[1][2] FP5 project and the TexWeave[3] standardisation initiative of CEN/ISSS and from the concepts of eXtended Smart Garment Organization we create an ebXML-based framework that is composed of a set of resources and a set of tools to address specific problems that need to be solved before starting an industrial collaboration between two or more industrial partners.

The eBusiness Watch report on B2B witnesses the difficulty of the T/C sector [8] in the adoption of ICT in the sector to improve the collaboration between the partners: few installations, regarding only large companies and the relationships with large retail organisations rather than with suppliers and subcontractors.

To overcome these difficulties we adopt a standard-based approach: the main advantage in using the developed tools is the reduction of the efforts required to create a new version of standard documents for enterprise collaboration setup.

This paper describes, in the next section, the ebXML vision for the set-up of an e-business collaboration, how we intend to support such vision and in which steps the developed tools can be helpful. Section 3 will provide a general description of each component that constitutes the framework. Finally, the open issues and the conclusions that could by extracted from this experience will follow.

2.   Setting-Up e-Business Collaboration: How to Support the ebXML Vision

Many efforts have been done to improve enterprise interaction [9]. Our aim was to define a framework that could, on one hand, support the enterprises to face several interoperability issues and, on the other hand, that can rely upon a wide and complete standardisation initiative, also in order to draw up the world of the standards with SME[11]. On this purpose ebXML represents one of the most complete standardisation initiative [10].

The starting point in the ebXML context is the creation of a common understood and of a shared XML document (called ebBP[5]) that describes the whole business process involving different partners, each of which with different roles in the production chain.

ebXML [4] does not specify explicitly the format of the exchanged documents: partners are free to decide what is the format of the documents they want to manage and transfer. But these documents must be explicitly indicated in the ebBP document with some reference information. In some cases the necessity of creation of new documents arises from the specific requests of the partners: in this case the people involved in the ebBP creation or implementation should analyse the requirements of the parties and create the new documents (or adapt the old ones).

It's clear that modelling such type of business collaboration in a complex scenario requires a great experience and a direct communication with the industries. It is also clear that the statement of a standard, or of a public description of a business process, cannot be made directly by one industry that, even if leader in a particular production sector, has not a complete vision of the whole production process.

Our purpose is then mainly to develop enabling tools that can be used both by ICT consultants and internal experts when setting up a business collaboration and that can be easily reused when creating a new collaboration.

The ebXML standard also requires the parties involved in the process to create and manage two different types of document. The first one, called Collaboration Protocol Profile (CPP)[6], defines the data about the party itself (like the role played in the collaboration, the required/expected documents, the communication channels implemented and the transport method available for each channel).

After the creation of the CPP, that is mainly based on the ebBP document, and that is in some sense proprietary of each partner since it describes only the capabilities/requirements of one party, the partners must find a common agreement to implement the collaboration, by the comparison of the different CPPs.

This agreement is written in the Collaboration Protocol Agreement (CPA)[6] and signed by the partners that want to adopt it during the collaboration.

Fig. 1 depicts the "path" to define and establish an ebusiness collaboration, the relationships among all the components of the framework, and interaction between them.

The idea is to start from the definition of an ebBP document. This first step is performed exploiting shared models of business scenarios and data structures. Both the collaborations and the data models can be designed considering the semantic model implemented in a set of OWL ontologies.

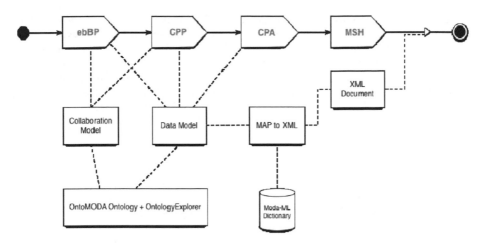

Figure 1: A Graphical Representation of the Interaction Between Different Tools and Resources

3. The Basic Components of the Framework

In the proposed framework, four components have been developed, under the LEAPFROG-IP project [7] to cover the different aspects of the definition of an electronic collaboration:
1. The OntoMODA ontology and the Ontology Explorer, to define data models
2. The CPP Editor and the CPA MatchMaker, to define business processes.
   All these tools, integrated together, support the set up of a business collaboration.

3.1 OntoMODA Ontology and the Ontology Explorer

The OntoMODA ontology and the Ontology Explorer can be used together to build a part of the ebBP document and, eventually, the electronic documents required during the transaction (for example an Order Document that contains all information about the provision of a fabric).

OntoMODA is a multilayered modular domain ontology oriented to the data modelling and e-business data exchange. Its primary purpose is to model a part of the Textile and Clothing sector knowledge through the semantic description of many aspects, like industrial processes and treatments, product description (like fabrics, yarns and fibres) and their characteristics and other information. It also is strictly related with the standardised TexWeave vocabulary for which represents the semantic view.

In fact to support in a helpful manner the data modelling phase, our aim has been to strongly interconnect the semantic model (the ontology) with a practical, formal and standardised set of data structures, as that defined in the TexWeave initiative.

This interconnection is implemented adopting the W3C reccomendation for semantic annotation [12] that allows to add the semantic information to XML Schema documents.

The figure shows the main parts of the architecture that we've implemented:
- OntoMODA, that is mainly composed of two sub-ontologies: Dynamic Ontology (DO), Static Ontology (SO).
- Annotated XML Schemas and Type Libraries: this is a library of XS type and a set of XS document annotated with the concepts defined in OntoMODA.
- ModaML Dictionary: this is a dictionary of business terms upon which it was based the TexWeave standardisation specifications.

The Static Ontology models the Textile/Clothing domain knowledge, defining, for example, concepts like *"fabric"* and specifying all its properties. It is connected with two different types of connections to the Dynamic Ontology that, on the other hands, contains all the semantic descriptions of the representation mechanisms adopted to exchange the information modelled in the Static Ontology. Then, the Dynamic Ontology models the XML components (types, elements and attributes) used as interchange data format in e-business transactions. The Static Ontology itself is modular and therefore composed of several sub-ontologies, each of which addresses different modelling and meta-modelling aspects (i.e. ISO11179 standard, XML Schema meta modelling and real sector knowledge).

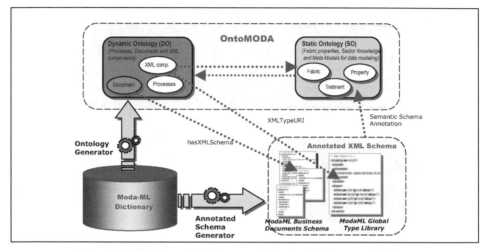

Fig.2 - OntoMODA Overall Architecture with Annotated Schemas and Dictionary

The Dynamic Ontology is generated automatically from the ModaML Dictionary (that can evolve in time - then it is dynamic) and it is split in three sub-ontologies concerning Business Documents (like Order, Invoice, etc...), Business Processes (i.e. Fabric production, Supplying etc...) and the XML Schema Components defined in the real XML Schema files. Here the main connections connect respectively
1. The semantic representations of the business documents with their XML root elements defined in XML Schema and
2. Each semantic representation of the XML components with their real representations in XML Schema files.

As said before the content of OntoMODA is split into its static and dynamic part. The first one mainly describes products, their properties and treatments. It contains a classification of the products and in particular describes the fabrics and their properties. Each fabric property is classified for a particular kind of application. Moreover, a set of relationships has been defined in order to interconnect the classes of the ontology and to model the properties of the instances.

OntoMODA is also a great knowledge source that could be used for documentation purpose. Thanks to the textual description of many concepts it can offer many interesting information useful for who needs to know product definition, industrial treatments, processes and fabric properties.

In order to search and read information through the OWL ontology we developed a web application named Ontology Explorer. The tool lets the user surf the entire OntoMODA, starting from the taxonomy and picking up from it the desired concepts to see more detailed information through apposite panels.

We integrate the ontology with the CPP Editor and the CPA Match Maker to allow an easy and rapid access to the description of the processes defined into OntoMODA. This was done adding simple links that open in a separate window the OE with the ontology loaded on a particular business process.

There are many tools to edit and browse ontology. Protégé [13] is one of the most used one, but there are many others. On the other hand, our aim is to simplify the operation of ontology browsing.

The Ontology Explorer allows the user to navigate, in a simple way, ontologies (it is not strictly related to the OntoMODA ontology and it can show all the online ontologies written in OWL language) and to find concepts and information. Actually all the tools that manage ontologies are really hard to use and to understand: sectorial experts could not be so skilled in computer science or in ontology development to use these tools. Nevertheless, semantic annotation and description ease the comprehension of the information for modelling data and process defining a business collaboration. Then, a relevant problem in developing an ontology for a classical industrial sectors, like the Textile/Garment one, is to create tools to use it easily: the Ontology Explorer is a configurable web tool that is mainly oriented to the Domain Expert rather then to the Ontology Expert or developer.

Usually, domain experts have great knowledge about concepts that concern their expertise area, but their knowledge about ontology implementation is quite absent.

An example of a typical user of the Ontology Explorer (OE) could be a textile expert who consults a sectorial ontology (like OntoMODA) to understand which properties can be used to describe or to characterize a generic fabric.

The Ontology Explorer provides more and better functionalities than other tools dedicated to the same purpose. To enable these functionalities, the Ontology Explorer is designed to be intuitively to use (also for the inexpert user) and many visualization and navigation configuration alternatives are available to the user. It also implements dynamic components that respond to user input, thus enhancing interactivity.

3.2 The CP-NET Tool Set

CP-NET (Collaboration Protocol Networking Enterprises Technology) is a software application set to enable the enterprises, cooperating through a collaborative framework ebXML-based, to establish and to perform Business Collaborations.

To achieve a Business Collaboration it is necessary to provide, for each couple of enterprises, a common base upon which to start doing business. This base is basically a Business Agreement and it is built, following the ebXML standard model, by comparison and by match of two company Business Profiles. ebXML provides a XML standard to describe both Profiles and Agreements: ebXML Collaboration Protocol Profile and Agreement (ebCPPA).

CP-NET provides two web applications to handle the ebXML CPPA specification: the CPP editor and the CPA Match Maker.

The CPP editor allows the enterprises to create and modify their own CPPs (Collaboration Protocol Profile), required to set up the collaboration with other partners and reducing the number of errors, using a simple interface with the aid of a simple inline help. In fact actually the CPPs are created by hand, directly writing the XML, because no tool exists that allows to create it using a human friendly interface. The idea of the CPP editor is to cover this gap, allowing a non XML expert to write a correct CPP.

The CPA MatchMaker wants to simplify the agreement process required to start up the collaboration: it allows to create and to modify, from two CPP Profiles, the Collaboration Protocol Agreements (CPA) for a couple of enterprises. Currently the two CPPs are compared by hand, identifying both the possible problems and the agreements: the problems are solved in a direct contact, using the phone or the fax, by the partners. At the end of the process nowadays one of the partners must write down all the defined agreements in a XML structured document. This document is the final CPA.

This process is very long in time, because the agreement process is, normally, not in real time: when a possible conflict arises during the CPP comparison, the CPA writer must contact the other party and negotiate about the modifications.

The CPA tool simplifies this agreement process reducing the comparison time and highlighting directly the conflicts between the two CPPs. At the end of the agreement process it writes down directly the CPA in the XML format. This reduces the time required by the whole agreement process.

CP-NET framework supports the ebXML Business Process Specifications (ebBP standard), therefore, into the CPP Profiles and into the CPA Agreements the enterprises can describe their characteristics related to one or more Business Processes.

3.3 CP-NET Requirements

The CP-NET tools, CPP-Editor and CPA-MatchMaker, provide:
- A support to upload and store the ebXML CPP and CPA documents, checking and validating them against the proper XML schema;
- A set of Data Access Object to read/write from/to generic DBMS (particularly MySQL and Microsoft Access), remote ebXML ebBP documents, local ebXML CPP and CPA documents;
- Web interfaces, both web applications and web services, that guide users through a logic step sequence to view/change information;
- A software architecture under MVC (Model View Controller) paradigm;

A general vision of the initial objective is showed in the diagram depicted in fig. 3. CP-NET provides an infrastructure to access/edit XML files (particularly ebXML CPP and CPA files) under the MVC (Model View Controller) paradigm. The application is developed in Java language and includes a library set to implement further characteristics not expected by the framework.

To make the application accessible from the web, the tools run on Apache Tomcat Web Server with the support of the Apache Struts framework to develop web applications and Apache Axis to publish web services.

The software architecture is structured in different layers. We can separate them in two main groups:

1) Client/Web
   - Client Layer: users can access to CP-NET tools through a web browser or their own web service client implementation.
   - Web Layer: two ways are provided to access to CP-NET interface, through web applications or web services calls. Both ways are linked with the same Business Delegate layer and the information is arranged in java bean structures.

2) Core Application
- Business Delegate Layer: all the external accesses must go cross this border that is the general interface to CP-NET core application. This layer provides a set of methods that are called from Web Layer. Each method of Business Delegate is called by Servlets of web applications and published as a single web service too;
- Business Logic Layer: this layer contains all the methods to perform the main tasks that characterize CP-NET tools: to receive get/set commands from web layer, to retrieve/insert information from/to XML files and database, to prepare java bean structures, to reply to method calls, to handle errors and exceptions. To access to resources (XML files and database) the business logic use Data Access Business Objects (next layer);
- Data Access Business Object (DAO) Layer: CP-NET tools need to access to two types of resources: XML files (ebXML CPP, CPA and ebBP documents) and database

(MySQL or Microsoft Access). The created DAO classes provide all the methods to get/set information from/to resources.
- X-Lab libraries Layer: the DAO classes of previous layer are specific for CP-NET tools to access to ebXML standards and to CP-NET database. To access to CPP, CPA and ebBP files, the DAO classes extend the XLabDOM class that provides constructors, methods and functionalities for generic XML files. To access to CP-NET database, the DAO classes extend the Xdatabase class that provides constructors, method and functionalities for generic databases. XLabDOM and XDatabase are classes of org.xlab package, developed to reuse and sharing commons procedures into ENEA XML-Laboratory.
- Java libraries Layer: other standard java libraries are included to implement previous layer (for example: Xerces, Xalan, JDOM, ...) to access to resources.

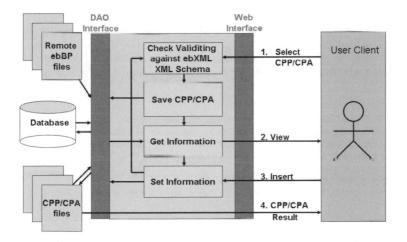

Figure 3: General Vision

4.   Conclusions

The proposed framework has been developed under the LEAPFROG-IP project, in order to define new tools to improve e-business interoperability between the enterprises of the Textile/Clothing sector. The framework will improve the ability of the enterprises to set-up business collaboration, thanks to a complete set of tools that allows the modelling of some relevant aspects related with the definition of a business agreement (from the definition of the data format to exchange information to the definition of the business processes). The benefits of this architecture could be perceived in the next year, when the adoption of ICT tools for data modelling and agreement building will allow the enterprises to formalize the e-business collaborations and then to automize the exchange of business documents. The adoption of the developed framework will also bring to the definition of enterprise profiles that can be used by the enterprises to find and better understand possible collaborations among new and heterogeneous partners. The definition of such profiles represents the premises to populate shared registry of enterprise profiles; CP-NET tools can moreover ease the adoption of standardised documents, like UBL.

One of the next steps in our work will regard the strong integration of such types of tools with applications specific for the exchange of business data (in the ebXML language, a Message Service Handler – MSH), that we are now developing.

The introduction of the semantic vision of the different concepts will ease the usability of the framework itself, allowing a simple access and comprehension also for non ICT skilled users. A learnt lesson during these activities regards the complexity of existing business documents: this complexity makes the adoption of e-business data formats really hard ("customisation" of standard documents is one of the main issues for the enterprises [14]). The testing phase we are now starting includes the exploiting of the ontology to build new, interoperable data format, and the creation of shared business models (ebBP) that will be provided to the enterprise to allow then to design their own profile, following the CPPA specification. These tests will involve both enterprises and domain experts (in the context of the LEAPFROG-IP project) to evaluate the business collaboration design process and to evaluate how to make this operation easy enough for SME.

It is worth to note that our effort does not want to create a brand new interoperability framework, but aim to reinforce and support the adoption of shared standardisation specifications with which it is strongly interconnected. These standards, ebXML and TEXWeave, lack of practical implementations, especially in domains like the Textile/Clothing one, and are consequently not easy to be adopted by the enterprises.

References

[1]   N. Gessa, P. De Sabbata, M. Fraulini, T. Imolesi, G. Cucchiara, M. Marzocchi, F. Vitali, "Moda-ML, an interoperability framework for the textile-clothing sector", IADIS International Conference WWWInternet 2003, p. 61-68, ISBN: 972-98947-1-X , 11/2003, Carvoeiro, Portogallo.
[2]   [Moda-ML]: http://www.Moda-ML.org
[3]   [TEXWeave]: http://www.texweave.org
[4]   [ebXML]: http://www.ebXML.org/
[5]   [ebBP 201]: "ebXML Business Process Specification Schema Technical Specification v2.0.1", July 2005
[6]   [CPPA21]: "Collaboration-Protocol Profile and Agreement Specification Version 2.1", July 2005
[7]   [LEAPFROG IP] (www.leapfrog-eu.org)
[8]   e-Business Watch, sector report n. 01-11, August 2004, electronic Business in the Textile, Clothing and Footwear industries
[9]   B. Medjahed, B. Benatallah, A. Bouguettaya, A. H. H. Ngu, and A. K. Elmagarmid, "Business-to-business interactions: issues and enabling technologies", *VLDB J.*, 12(1):59–85, 2003.
[10] C. Bussler, "B2B Integration, Concepts and Architecture", Springer - Verlag, 2003, ISBN 3-540-43487-9.
[11] K. Jakobs, "Standardisation and SME Users Mutually Exclusive?", Proc. Multi-Conference on Business Information Systems, Cuvillier Verlag, 2004
[12] [SAWSDL] http://www.w3.org/TR/sawsdl/
[13] [Protégé] Protégé home page: http://protege.stanford.edu/
[14] P. De Sabbata, N. Gessa, C. Novelli, A.Frascella, F. Vitali, "B2B: Standardisation or Customistation?", in "Innovation and the Knowledge Economy Issues, Application, Case Studies", e-Challenges 2005 conference, Ljubljiana, October 19-21 2005, pp 1556-1566, Dublin, Ireland, IOS PRESS, ISBN 1-58603-563-0.

Collaboration and the Knowledge Economy: Issues, Applications, Case Studies
P. Cunningham and M. Cunningham (Eds.)
IOS Press, 2008

Process Management Support for Emergency Management Procedures

Thomas Rose[1,2], Gertraud Peinel[1], Emilija Arsenova[2]

[1]*Fraunhofer FIT, Schloss Birlinghoven, 53757 Sankt Augustin, Germany*
Tel: +49 2241 14 2798, Fax: +49 2241 14 2080,
Email:{gertraud.peinel, thomas.rose}@fit.fraunhofer.de, emilija.arsenova@gmail.com
[2]*RWTH Aachen, Ahornstr. 55, 52056 Aachen, Germany*

Abstract: Process management has proven to be instrumental for the engineering and assessment of courses of actions for business operations in many industrial application domains. Processes management means appear therefore as natural vehicle for the definition and analysis of operating procedures also for the emergency management domain. The question arises of what is an appropriate modelling methodology and how tools tailored to the needs of emergency organisations can support this modelling methodology. This paper reports on the experiences gained in the course of modelling specific emergency processes, in our case the cross-organisational treatment of mass casualties. Then, we will introduce the tool platform of project ERMA that has been designed to support such processes.

1. Introduction

Emergency organisations have to prepare for an increasing number of disasters as history shows. Hence, preparation is crucial for the success of the response. Because the size of some incidents might exceed the capabilities of a single organisation, several rescue organizations have to cooperate. Therefore, a corporate planning process is required to prepare for such an event.

Process management appears as natural candidate for such a planning since each planning revolves around activities that have to be conducted and monitored. Starting with early work on process management for software projects [1], process management has been carried to an increasingly growing number of application domains. However, major application domains are confined to manufacturing and production industries that can be characterized by their well-defined processes. Support of knowledge-intensive and complex processes is yet scarce. Although process management has proven its positive impact on organisations' performances in many industrial and commercial applications, customized methodologies are required that are tailored to the terminology and modus operandi of domain experts [2]. In light of this experience, rescue forces also call for a process modelling methodology and tool support that are customized to their objectives for operational planning.

Process management means have not been investigated for fire brigades and rescue forces, besides studies about the use of workflow management for organising information flows [3]. However, our focus is not the automation of processes, but the planning phase for improving the preparation. Communication processes have been studied resulting in multi-agent systems for the support of communication processes [4]. But, the core of their functional reactions, e.g., how to set up a treatment area for injured persons at a larger scale, has not been represented and in particular analysed. Only some standard tactics have been defined for local activities [5]. Yet, fire brigades are embarking upon the development of reference models that can be shared among different organizations.

Therefore, process management methodologies considered as industrial practice appear attractive at first glance. Event-driven process chains (EPC) mimic the nature of rescue processes, since each activity is triggered by an event, which resembles a notification or report in the terminology of fire brigades, and each activity causes by its execution further events. Moreover, fire brigades are used to link each activity with a strategic or tactical goal as essential part of their strategy definition. Hence, EPC appear as natural choice for the capture of know-how on rescue management processes. Even entire rescue plans can be modelled with this kind of modelling method [6]. However, the modelling environment is far too complex to be used by domain experts in the emergency management domain. In particular, assistance amid the guidance of modelling exercises has to be custom-tailored.

In this paper, we first introduce a formal model of an emergency management process that has been formalized in cooperation with a major fire brigade. The topic of this process is the coordination of rescue teams for the treatment of mass casualties, e.g., when 500 to 1200 people are injured. Then we present the electronic risk management architecture of the EC project ERMA, where process modelling support is integrated as a first prototype.

2.   Modelling Mass Casualties Procedures in Cologne

Current practice in the emergency management domain is characterized by the use of paper documents for the representation of process knowledge. Processes are mostly described on a textual basis, as Word documents. They are exchanged among rescue organisations for mutual agreement. Once a communication and discussion process has been successfully concluded, i.e., successful reconciliation of the process, they are used as reference documents. As a result, the process is encoded in an unstructured document consisting of a textual description and images. As such, unstructured documents describe the nature of operations, but the processes described can not be processes in a formal stance with regard to analysis and execution. Graphical notations to the other extreme are easy to use, but do not carry semantic information about the matters modelled, although they provide transparency at first glance compared to the current practice of unstructured documents. With this kind of representation, any formal analysis is also impossible, since the processes cannot be reasoned about. Hence, a formal representation will be beneficial due to its processing facilities. Models can be analyzed as well as views can be defined to focus on specific aspects such as the workload of specific departments.

Several methods have been investigated to represent emergency management processes with different scopes of interest and concern [7], [4], [3], [8]. Our concern is the analysis of quality characteristics of emergency processes, i.e., does one have sufficient resources in place for the processes, does one face a potential overload for specific organisational units in certain periods of relief operations, or do some activities not comply with overall tactical and strategic objectives. In order to check for such kind of properties, the planning process has to result in a formalized process model of the relief procedures that can be analyzed according to this kind of integrity constraints, while each integrity constraint can be formulated in terms of logical conditions. Such a formalization calls for a modelling framework that allows the representation of at least activities and their control flow, resources, organisational units, and goals. Events surface as further natural ingredient of the model, since all operations are triggered by messages or observations.

Therefore, a modelling methodology has to carry these accounts, if one wants to analyse the performance of processes planned. Since our research question has been whether relief organisations can benefit from process management approaches as other application domains do, we surveyed methodologies and tool support in first place. Literature and system evaluation unveil a strong account of control flow coverage. Coverage of complex and ad-hoc organisational and resource aspects is not supported by many systems, as illustrated by workflow-oriented approaches such as WS-BPEL (Web Services Business

Process Execution Language) or YAWL [9] that have automation as prior concern on their agenda. Some commercial workflow management systems have an organisational modelling account, but no elaborated support, such as systems along the lines of the Workflow Management Coalition [10], like Bonapart [11].

Our starting point has been an emergency management process that requires several rescue organisations to cooperate. The process revolves around courses of action to be taken for handling emergency events that involve the medical treatment of mass casualties through supraregional support (ÜMANV – Überregionale Unterstützung beim Massenanfall von Verletzten) [12]. In this context, we particular focus on the planning aspects. The automation of processes is outside of our scope due to the nature of these processes that take place out on the scene.

The need for a balanced representation of control flow-oriented as well as organisational aspects has brought us to the decision to employ extended Event-driven Process Chains (eEPC) [13] as initial modelling methodology for the emergency management domain. Consequently, we selected the ARIS Business Architect [14, 15] as our modelling environment for the modelling exercise with the fire brigade of the city of Cologne. Extended EPC have been "rephrased" in order to comply with the terminology of fire brigades. The concepts and the structure of extended EPC were preserved to a considerable degree by assigning different semantics. However, some modifications were necessary to address requirements of resources or capabilities of measure carriers. Activities were named measures, events were translated into notifications and reports, capabilities and duties of organisational entities and units were explicitly distinguished. In addition, plans were dispatched for classifying activities, e.g., classifying injuries of people according to treatment priority. Information resources of the eEPC were translated into a physical stance, e.g., infra-structure (geographical and traffic management), requirements for a treatment location, instead of using them for the modelling of information logistics.

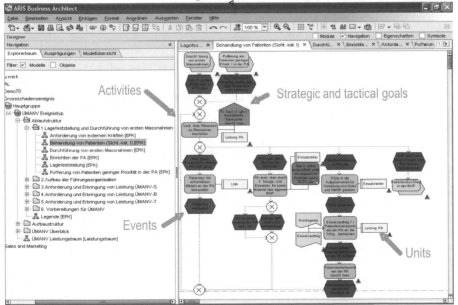

Figure 1: Model of the ÜMANV Presented by the Adopted eEPC

Figure 1 shows a screenshot of the ARIS modelling environment displaying a part of the model for the ÜMANV. It highlights the flow of activities, plans involved for the classification of activities, resources required, and in particular objectives.

The modelling approach based on eEPC has proven beneficial for the fire brigade. First, the domain-specific modelling constructs and views enable emergency organisations to prepare their operational plans as usual. Based on these models, reference models can be established that enable the exchange between regionally different organisations and thus foster consistency of concepts across relief organisations. In addition, best practises can be promoted by encouraging those disaster management organisations to use already assessed operational concepts, to adopt them, and to further adjust them according to the capacities individually. This is especially useful because these organisations are not able to prepare for every possible scenario due to less staff and budget. With regard to modelling economics, single process modules can be extracted from the modelled disaster plan and reused for different scenarios. This possibility for reuse has proven highly useful in particular for coordination phases.

Amid modelling phases, distinctive modelling views are supported. Various process presentations aid in the comprehension of different aspects. For example, the organisational view provides a detailed overview of the organisational structure, the required competencies of each measure carrier as well as their technical resources, while a flow-oriented view focuses on the flow of activities. During reconciliation processes, views further support focusing on those aspects that are only relevant for certain organisational units. Hence, views resemble dynamic summaries.

Once, the model is available, several means for analysis were implemented in terms of reports. As such, reports specify several views on parts of the model, e.g. "show all activities that are carried out by a specific organisational unit". The use of such views allows the fire brigade to immediately analyse their process model with regard to certain criteria, for example whether there is an overload of specific organisational units like the command centre. Actually, certain performance checks delivered directly a benefit for the fire brigade that has not been possible without the formal model. Typical checks include workload on the set of resources and feasibility of services during specific periods. This way, field trials can be significantly enhanced by enforcing a pre-validation of operational concepts, which acquires the required degree of awareness before redundant exercises take place, and in addition saves time and costs.

To summarise, the benefits of the process management approach has been proven and users could directly capitalise on the models due to the provided means for analysis. However, from a usability point of view, the tool chosen as well as other tools evaluated have proven to be too complex for the process planners of the fire brigade. Hence, custom-tailored tool support is required.

3.   ERMA Approach to Risk Management Support

Based on the experiences gained with the fire brigade of Cologne and the tool support evaluated so far, the decision was made to support the modelling of emergency processes with a domain-specific process editor providing its specific structures, terminology, and method. This editor is currently developed in an EU-funded project named ERMA, where it is integrated in a process workbench allowing also manual walkthrough of processes for the demonstration of courses of actions. ERMA (Electronic risk management architecture) [16] strives to support risk management processes in small to medium-sized communities in case of natural or man-made disaster. The supported life cycle of risk episodes ranges from key indicator-based monitoring services, via process-oriented guidance for prevention and relieve, up-to public alerting services that are accompanied by citizen relationship management components to advise the public and gather information from the public. A pivotal element in this life cycle is know-how about processes.

The ERMA emergency management platform comprises:

- Proper risk assessment through a key indicator system: access to monitored sensor data related to various natural and industrial risks existing within their district;
- Process guidance by a process management workbench;
- Information to and from the citizen by enhanced emergency telecommunications systems and a citizen relationship management portal.
- Groupware support by a team collaboration component for integration and connection of different emergency teams enabling information exchange among stakeholders;
- Modular system architecture with SOA interfaces.

The unique features of the ERMA system lies in this combination of modules and their functionalities not available on the current market. In science, individual modules have been tested in the domain of emergency management. Examples include the simulation of events with training purposes [17], the support of information dispatching [18], or collaboration processes [19]. Unfortunately, no commercial system has emerged from these prototypes. This lack of services motivated the birth of ERMA.

The ERMA process workbench serves as core of the system by providing guidance for operation during an event. Main advantage of the ERMA process workbench is the usability of the modelling environment that enables the modelling of processes by crisis management experts themselves.

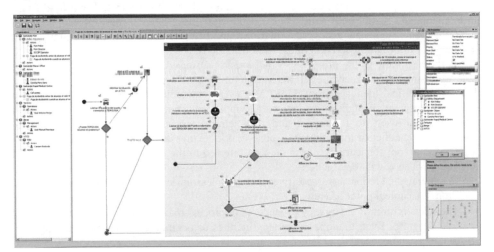

Figure 2: ERMA Process Workbench Editor with a Process from ERMA

The process workbench editor is based on a well-defined data model describing emergency management processes, organisations, and resources. The ERMA user can design processes by using a comfortable lightweight process editor with a typical graphical component for visualising processes as nodes with directed edges as sequences. Main functionalities of the process workbench editor in its current version are:

- Modelling and editing of emergency processes with an intuitive editor;
- Modelling of static and dynamic organisations of the emergency management domain;
- Manual walk-through of process flow (simulation);
- Automatic layout of graphs (hierarchical, incremental hierarchical, organic, orthogonal);
- Easy adaptation to terminology and iconic of the target user group;
- Seamless integration in office environment as well as specific operation centre software by use of SOA.

The user interface of the editor (see Figure 2) deliberately follows common process management tools like ARIS, but is streamlined and simplified. The main window is divided in 3 vertical sections headed by the main menu bar. The left part shows hierarchical trees in (1) the organisational tab: organisations, associated actors and processes, and (2) the process types tab: all processes of the database structured in user-defined classifications. The middle section (3) provides the graph panel showing the process flow of a selected process. Several "open" processes can be displayed in different tabs. The right section presents attributes of nodes or edges selected, and in the right lower corner a graph overview allowing a birds-eye-view of the top process.

Processes consist of activities; processes and activities can be connected by directed edges to show their sequence. In addition, decision nodes can be inserted to allow branching of activity lines. Each activity has several attributes, like name, planned start and end, priority, real start and end, status, actors assigned, and attached files. Activities could be visualised by a standard or user-defined icon. The latter allows an easy and user specific grasp of the purpose of an activity. Figure 2 shows an excerpt of a process modelled for one of the ERMA user, the port authority of Santander in Spain. The modelled scenario describes a chemical toxic cloud due to an accident in a chemical plant in the port area.

4. Lessons Learned in ERMA

The ERMA project has finalised the implementation phase and conducted two field trials, in Romania and Spain, both with success. Both trails have been scenario based, showing how different users can access the platform in different locations, demonstrating the exchange of information and timeliness of notifications.

In the beginning of the project, external experts surmised that rescue staff might not be able to abstract their procedures in such a graph-oriented way in the process workbench. However, the final feedback from the ERMA users and audience in the trials showed, that even the presentation of flows of actions as graph needed some little time to conceive, it stimulated the users to re-arrange and fill their processes with great engagement and convinced the audience immediately. Some visitors expressed spontaneously their interest to use such a tool for learning purposes, and referred to the case of mayors newly elected and inexperienced with emergencies.

In general, the feedback was positive, and some lessons learned can be derived.

From a technical point of view:

- The visualisation of emergency procedures in process management style is intuitive and easy to grasp. Even though, computer-illiterates or beginners need some learning time to understand concepts and interface logic.
- Most communities have very vague emergency plans. Procedures seem to be locked in the head of experienced staff, but are not traceable by electronic or paper means. Determining emergency scenarios and extracting procedures for process models must be accompanied by process modelling and risk experts.
- Authorities often underestimate the spread and usefulness of modern communication channels like mobile phones and Internet during crises situations. But apart from informing people in danger, also citizen feedback and communities' exchange give authorities new means to gather information and also to channel citizen participation [20], [21]. It is also often disregarded, that such communication channels might have their biggest impact before (early warning) and after (recovery) an incident.

From a political point of view:

- Smaller communities tend to delegate responsibilities to superior organisations.
- In many regions several organisations are responsible for different tasks of emergency relief (be it medical support, fire fighting, recovery). These organisations have often

different terminologies, chains of commands, and procedures for emergencies. Not to mention states with a federal structure. Authorities attending the field trials were very pessimistic about common agreements among organisations involved.

- Often, communities concentrate only on direct threats well known and experienced. However, a diversity of risk might surface that is not considered so far. Hence, flexible means are required to adapt to such new kinds of risk once they happen. Knowledge about processes – in particular their strategic objectives – appear as natural ingredient to leverage such changing environments.

5. Conclusions

We have started with the question whether emergency forces can benefit from the employment of process modelling approaches that have proven their potential for various application domains. We experienced that once formal models were in place, fire brigades were immediately in the position to capitalize on our approach due to the means for process analysis. Based on the different views generated from process models, various performance and completeness perspectives were studied. Respective analyses range from the mere evaluation of the sufficient availability of resources, over the adequate distribution of activities across organisational units, up-to a resilient workload for critical operational units. Hence, the question posted at the very beginning has to be answered by *yes*.

Consequently, we started to customize the process modelling tool to their operational and organisational needs. Some of these customisations have already been implemented by the current version of the modelling tool, e.g. adaptation of terminology and constraints on modelling structures. Still, additional adjustments are planned to rectify user acceptance and usability from a domain experts point of view.

Project ERMA has been started to provide an intuitive modelling environment for processes in the emergency management domain. A first prototype has been finalised with positive response from the field trials, first lessons learned are summarised in this paper. ERMA also offers a platform to integrate processes into the overall information flow between emergency management teams and to and from the citizen. Since ERMA uses a SOA approach, it is able to orchestrate services from existing systems. The employment of SOA serves also future business models of ERMA: external information providers can market their services to authorities to be used in case of emergency. Further exploitation steps will include identifying potential end users as customers to summarise requirements and to start with best practice processes. These models can then be shared between communities facing similar risks, and therefore this facilitates the burden of the abstraction task. At the same time, an ERMA user group will be established to support spread of information about the capabilities of such IT-systems in the emergency management domain. This will naturally attract new customers. The planning on this user group is currently in process, news about this and further steps will be published soon.

Acknowledgment

The presented work has been partly supported by research funding from the European Commission within the Community's Sixth Framework Programme (IST project ERMA, IST-2005-034889). The authors would like to acknowledge that this document reflects only the author's views, and that the Community is not liable for any use that may be made of the information contained herein.

References

[1] Curtis, B., Kellner, M.I., and Over, J., *Process modeling*. Communications of the ACM, 1992. **35**(9): p. 75-90.

[2] Sedlmayr, M., Rose, T., Greiser, T., Röhrig, R., Meister, M., and Michel-Backofen, A. *Automating Standard Operating Procedures in Intensive Care*. in *19th Intl. Conference on Advanced Information Systems Engineering (CAiSE'07)*. 2007. Trondheim, Norway.

[3] Mak, H.Y., Mallard, A.P., Bui, T., and Au, G., *Building online crisis management support using workflow systems*. Decision Support Systems, 1999. **25**(3): p. 209-224.

[4] Loper, M. and Presenell, B. *Modelling an emergency operations center with agents*. in *2005 Winter Simulation Conference*. 2005.

[5] Lakenbrink, S., *Kölner Konzepte*, in *BRANDSchutz, German magazine for fire brigades*. 2003. p. 746 - 752

[6] Arsenova, E. *Unterstützung der Prozessmodellierung im Notfallmanagement*. in *Informatiktage 2008*. 2008. B-IT Bonn-Aachen International Center for Information Technology, Bonn: Gesellschaft für Informatik.

[7] Hoogendoorn, M., Jonker, C.M., Popova, V., Sharpanskykh, A., and Xu, L. *Formal Modelling and Comparing of Disaster Plans*. in *Proceedings of the Second International Conference on Information Systems for Crisis Response and Management ISCRAM*. 2005.

[8] Yao, X. and Turoff, M. *Using task structure to improve collaborative scenario creation*. in *4th International ISCRAM Conference*. 2007. Den Haag, Netherlands.

[9] van der Aalst, W.M.P. and ter Hofstede, A.H.M., *YAWL: yet another workflow language*. Information Systems, 2005. **30**(4): p. 245-275.

[10] WfMC. *WFMC.org Homepage*. http://www.wfmc.org/ (5/2008).

[11] Emprise. *BONAPART®   EMPRISE   Process   Management   GmbH*. http://emprise.de/emprise.shtml?id=2757 (5/2008).

[12] Schmidt, J., *Einsatzkonzept MANV Überörtlich. Rheinische Projektgruppe „MANV Überörtlich"*. 2007: Cologne.

[13] Scheer, A.-W. and Thomas, O., *Geschäftsprozessmodellierung mit der ereignisgesteuerten Prozesskette*. Das Wirtschaftsstudium 34 (2005), Nr. 8-9, 2005: p. p. 1069-1078.

[14] Scheer, A.W., *ARIS–From the vision to practical process control*. Business Process Excellence, 2002: p. 1-14.

[15] Scheer, A.W. and Nuettgens, M., *ARIS Architecture and Reference Models for Business Process Management*. Business Process Management: Models, Techniques, and Empirical Studies, ed. W.M.P. van der Aalst, J. Desel, and A. Oberweis. LNCS 1806. 2000, Berlin: Springer. 376-389.

[16] ERMA Consortium. *ERMA Project Homepage*. http://www.erma-project.org.

[17] Pollak, E., Falash, M., Ingraham, L., and Gottesman, V., *Operational analysis framework for emergency operations center preparedness training*. Proceedings of the 36th conference on Winter simulation, 2004: p. 839-848.

[18] Van Someren, M., Netten, N., Evers, V., Cramer, H., De Hoog, R., and Bruinsma, G. *A Trainable Information Distribution System to Support Crisis Management*. in *2nd International ISCRAM Conference*. 2005.

[19] Georgakopoulos, D., *Collaboration Process Management for Advanced Applications*. International Process Technology Workshop, 1999.

[20] Palen, L. and Liu, S.B., *Citizen communications in crisis: anticipating a future of ICT-supported public participation*. Proceedings of the SIGCHI conference on Human factors in computing systems, 2007: p. 727-736.

[21] Careem, M., Silva, C.D., Silva, R.D., Raschid, L., and Weerawarana, S., *Sahana: Overview of a disaster management system*, in *IEEE International Conference on Information and Automation*. 2006.

Business Models on the Web: Application to Most Popular Sites and Related Trends

Roberto GARIGLIANO[2], Luisa MICH[1], Mariangela FRANCH[1],
Pierluigi NOVI INVERARDI[1]

[1] University of Trento, Department of Computer and Management Sciences,
Via Inama 5, 38100 Trento, Italy
Tel: +39 0461 88186 Fax: + 39 0461 88124, Email: {luisa.mich, mariangela.franch,
pierluignoviinveradi}@unitn.it
[2] Soulsim Ltd, (trading as Girland.com), PO Box 377, Durham, DH1 1WU, UK
Tel.: +39 348 4075319, Email: roberto.garigliano@soulsim.co.uk

Abstract: The objectives of this paper are to provide a schema of classification for business on the web – named BM*Web - based on some parameters which are considered to have structural value and to validate it against a significant data set. Interesting results emerge from the statistical analysis, both in terms of original correspondences, and in terms of trend expectations which have then been borne out by actual developments in the online business world. These are particularly evident in the case of community-based businesses.

1. Introduction

Existing categorisations for web-based business models can be organised according to immediately apparent elements, in the sense that these are features that can be observed on the surface of the site by a casual user. However, there is a very large number of such features that could be used as discriminants. Some classifications are based on product or service category, business organisation, type of audience, technology used, etc.

In fact, from an analytical point of view, the best categorisations are those based on a set of pre-defined guidelines or principles. Such principles, in their turn, must be as coherent as possible with respect to some fundamental question (or need, or potential use) one may have. In other words, it is necessary to know first what the purpose of the investigation is, and then use the features most suitable for that purpose. Furthermore, as well as being well-founded in the way just described, these features must have suitable internal properties, i.e. be coherent, be minimal, avoid ad-hocness, etc. Finally, they must be linked via causal connections to observable relevant facts, and must be able to be used for causally inferring new observable phenomena.

In this paper we introduce a new schema, an original multidimensional framework – named BM*Web – that combines issues already present in existing schema describing business models, with innovative aspects. The two main objectives are (a) to provide a schema of classification for business on the web based on some structural parameters and (b) to validate it against a significant data set and to report some business cases that confirm some of the trends and expectations emerged from the project.

The structure of the paper is as following: section 2 introduces related work to establish the context in which the BM*Web framework was defined; section 3 describes our methodology and its application on a large dataset of web sites and reports some results of the ongoing study; section 4 describes the most interesting business cases; finally, section 5 gives some recommendations.

2.   Related Work

Research on web-based BM addresses questions ranging from the definition of business models to the changes due to the inception of the Web and its impact on the economics fundamentals. Focusing on studies related to analysis or classification of BM on the Web, many authors tried to define a taxonomy, among them Timmers [1] and Rappa [2], or even an ontology [3].

Classifications for web-based BMs are founded on a set of criteria of different dimensions and complexity. For example in [2] we have 9 BMs, which are then articulated in 41 different sub-categories, according to the companies' value proposition and the revenues. Other schemas integrate different sets of parameters introducing economics concepts, related to Porter's value chain, e.g., [4].

An interesting comparison among the most relevant contributions is given in [5]. For our goal it is important to cite here those that refer to parameters taken into account by the BM*Web framework.

In particular, the Needs vs. Technology parameter is related to the innovation introduced by the BM and is defined in respect to how the technology satisfies known or unknown users' needs or requirements. One of the first authors that classified BM according to innovation and functional integration was Timmers [6], however, none of the existing schema does explicitly relate the role of technology to the 'satisfaction' of expressed or unexpressed needs of the customer.

To describe a BM, financial aspects are taken into consideration by all authors as they are deeply related to the BM concept. For our approach, we have defined the parameters according to an almost shared set of values; the most critical point was to adopt a level of detail adequate to address the trade-off between being able to identify the different income channels from the client-side and to get useful information.

However, the most largely and deeply investigate aspect is the presence of a web community - most often referred as virtual or online community, that is claimed as relevant for a successful BM in many classification schema; among them [1], [2], [7]. However, the community is usually introduced as one of the elementary web-based BMs, or as a BM in itself and not as one of the parameters necessary to fully define BMs for the Web. Tapscott and Williams [8] identified seven new models of mass collaboration that are completely changing scenarios for large and small companies according to their motto, 'collaborate or perish', towards the creation of the collaboration economy: peer pioneers, ideagoras, prosumers, new alexandrian, platform of participation, global plant floor, wiki workplace. In all these models web technologies are used to change the role of participants – companies and customers - and to support a wide range of online relationships: however, authors do not analytically explain the differences among the identified models. Also, there are not systematic studies about the role of web communities for existing businesses. It is worth naming here the Forum One Communication that started to analyse the community ROI (Return on Investment); according to the last year survey, only 22% of respondents (companies whose BM is based on one or more web communities) had clear ROI Model, but establishing a ROI model was a priority for most of them in the near term [9]. Other statistics gathered by the Forum One Communication support the economics advantages of web communities, e.g. for community users vs. non-community users it stands out that they: (a) remain customers 50% longer; (b) spend 54% more; (c) visit nine times more often; (d) have four times as many page views; while in customer support, live interaction costs 87% more per transaction on average than forums and other web self-service options; and cost per interaction averages $12 via the contact center versus $0.25 via self-service options (http://redplasticmonkey.wordpress.com/2007/05/08/online-community-roi).

3. Methodology

3.1   The BM*Web Framework

Starting from the basic question "What characterises business models on the web?", a linguistic and logical analysis is then carried out, which produces four groups of characterising features: the nature of the market, the novelty of the offer, the type of income and the existence and form of community [10], [11]. The nature of the market is analysed through well-established categories such as B2C and B2B, as well as some which play a special role in online businesses such as C2C and C2B2C. The novelty of the offer is analysed using a scheme based on the existence of perceived needs and solutions. The type of income is classified according to standard criteria, such as 'single payment', 'subscription', 'intermediation', 'advertising', etc. Finally, the community element is analysed in terms of the type of exchange between members and of the level of control over the community. Table 1 reports the version applied in the study described in this paper.

*Table 1. The BM*Web Framework*

PARAMETER	VARIABLE
Market of reference	B2B, B2C, B2(B)2C, C2(B)2C, C2B, C2C
Needs vs. Technology	Copy of business off-line, New answer to existing needs, New answer to unexpressed needs
Income	Subscription, Intermediation, Advertising, Single payment, Other (e.g., donation, tax)
Community	Exchange: information, commercial, complex Employees' control: minimum, light, specific Members' control: minimum, light, specific

The parameters in the table have been refined in a iterative process supported by a web-based application developed to share evaluations given by three analysts, and critical issues were used to identify the parameters and their variables, and to render explicit the application criteria. For example, in the first version of the framework, income categories included a higher number of types and subtypes and have been sorted out and aggregated in different ways until an unambiguous and applicable set was found (e.g., affiliation was included in advertising as it is not easy to clearly identify this form of income using only client-side information).

The first dimension, market of reference, is specified adding to the four traditional acronyms - B2B, B2C, C2B and C2C – two acronyms - B2(B)2C, C2(B)2C – that allow to distinguish those businesses that play an intermediary role for other businesses or customers vs. customers. That happens for example for web sites like Expedia or Lastminute (B2(B)2C); and Ebay and Second Life (C2(B)2C) (for most of the web sites cited in this paper, the URL can be obtained in the following way: www.<name_of_the_company_or_service>.com; also for almost all of them there exist "national" versions that are automatically proposed to the users; otherwise URL is given in the text without "http://"). In some cases the same web site includes different roles – Ebay for example includes also B2(B)2C services: to take into account these cases the analyst can specify both variables, assigning weights according to their relevance for the business.

The second and forth parameters are the most innovative in respect of the existing schema. In particular, for needs vs. technology it is necessary to check if a web site business represents an on-line copy of an off-line business; otherwise, if it represents a new answer to users' needs, we check if these needs were already organized and rendered explicit in some form of the traditional business. In the first category we found newspapers web sites (e.g., New York Times) or encyclopaedia (e.g., Softpedia; while Ebay is an example of a new answer to known users' needs. The last category includes many web communities like Myspace, Secondlife and Youtube, but also web sites offering hosting or communication services to users or developers (e.g., Tripod, Torrentz).

Web communities are analysed at two different levels: exchange among users and control of the interactions. As regard exchanges, users of a web community usually communicate to share information (e.g., Myspace, Youtube); if there is an exchange of real money, the exchange is classified as commercial (e.g., Ebay, PartyPoker); if the web site support complex interactions, members of the community can also exchange virtual objects and assume interacting behaviour, as happen in role playing sites (e.g., Everquest or Geocities).

The interactions among members of a web community can be controlled by employees or by members. In both cases, the BM*Web framework distinguishes three levels of control: minimum, if the only form of control is the presence of recommendations that members have to respect to participate in the community; light, if the web sites check contents by filtering those that are not 'adequate' for the web site; a specific control is based on more strict forms of control and are usually present if there are commercial exchanges among the users. Members' control mechanisms are possible in those web community that distinguish different roles for their member and some of them become 'mentors' or 'expert' thanks to their contributions, as happen for example in the editorial organization of Wikipedia.

3.2   The Study

For the research referred in this paper, the BM*Web framework has been applied to a set of 200 web sites identified extracting from the free list of Global Top 500 web sites given by Alexa (www.alexa.com, 10 June 2006) those in English or with an English version, without pornography or illegal content; for portals a procedure to select the three most relevant sections was applied. The final set was then integrated with a few interesting web sites to be able to validate the framework on all its parameters.

The main results of the study can be summarised as follows:

- Markets of reference are 49% B2C, 31% C2C (always corresponding to web communities) and 10% B2B. The values change significantly for sites with communities (Figure 1).

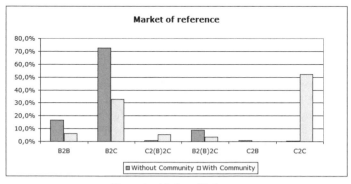

Figure 1 – Market of Reference

- 59% of the web businesses have an active web community; 90% are informative communities; 6% commercial and 4% include complex exchanges. In informative communities, both employees' and member's controls are mainly at the second level (minimum: 63% e 68%, respectively); while for commercial communities, employees' controls are the most important with a 57% of specific controls.

- The most widespread form of income is advertising (46%), then comes subscription (19%) and single payment (18%). But focusing on the web sites with a community, advertising increases from 47% to 52%, confirming the value attributed by analysts to web community (Figure 2).
- The number of income channels is higher for community web sites; also, while for informative communities 48% of the web sites have only one form of income, for commercial and complex communities the percentages change.
- In the general data set, the dominant forms with respect to innovation/needs novelty are the traditional copy-of-business-offline and the totally innovative response to new needs. However, when restricted to the sites with community, the totally innovative response becomes completely dominant.

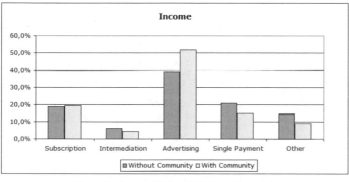

Figure 2 – Income With and Without Community

- Needs vs. technology are distributed in a more uniform way: 36% of the web businesses are a copy of an offline business; 22% answer in a new way to explicit needs and 42% to un-expressed needs. But, again, these percentages change for web sites with and without a community (respectively: 24%, 22%, 54%; 54%, 22%, 24%). (Figure 3).

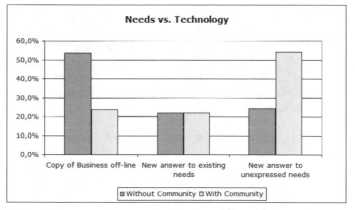

Figure 3 – Needs vs. Technology

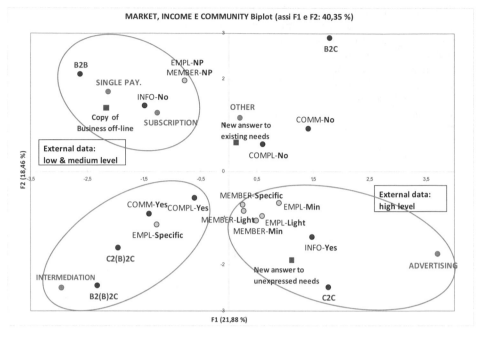

Figure 4 – Three Clusters of Points Related to Successful Business Model

- Figure 4 above shows the results of a multivariate statistical analysis applied to all variables together: it is apparent that two major groupings appear, rapresenting two different successful strategies for business online.

4.   Business Cases Description

Some of the trends and expectations emerged from this analysis have already been supported by recent developments. The list which follows contains the main cases. Some cases are directly based in the European online market; other applies to both European and USA markets; other still are taken from the USA market, but their implications apply to the European frame as well. They all underline the importance of community for successful online business, especially those with highly innovative products/services, and the related move towards forms of income connected to community, as forecast by our schema.
European cases:

- Extension to virtual reality of off-line legal safeguard (successful Habbo prosecution against virtual theft): recently Habbo has launched a successful prosecution for stealing of virtual objects in its virtual world, creating a precedent for the introduction of off-line legal safeguards to the virtual reality worlds (news.bbc.co.uk/1/hi/technology/ 7094764.stm); similarly, there have been attempt in Germany to lauch prosecutions for sexual harassment and rape on Second Life (www.dw-world.de/dw/article/ 0,2144,2481582,00.html).

- Lack of resilience of pure-play online retailers in absence of community barriers (off-line retailers with on-line presence taking more than 50% of online retail market in UK from Oct. 2007): Hitwise data for the online UK market show that pure-play retailers tend to lose their first-mover advantage in absence of a community and are liable to be overtaken by brick-and-mortar competitors adding an online presence to their offline convenience   (www.hitwise.co.uk/press-center/hitwiseHS2004/hotshop.php).   This shows that in absence of community, offline players have an advantage in traditional markets, as predicted by our schema.

- Lack of resilience of dominant players when attacked by new community based ones (more than 50% of email in UK from Oct. 2007 originated from social networks rather than Hotmail, Yahoo, Gmail, etc. according to Hitwise): even free services (such as email) offered by dominant players have lost more than 50% of their traffic to social network, showing that most of the email use is within circles of friends which are best reproduced inside social networks (weblogs.hitwise.com/robin-goad/2007/11/social_networks_overtake_webma.html). This shows that the community factors, in innovative context, is totally dominant with respect to other elements, e.g. market dominance, financial power etc.
- Extension of user investment as a barrier to exit (Girland, Ebay, PartyPoker). This is a predicted trend for sites where the community is the main strategic advantage.
  European/USA cases:
- General increase of integrated advertising (Girland, Second Life, Google, etc.): the general increase in integrated advertising (i.e. advertising which merges seamlessly with the content), and its premium value wrt traditional formats (banners, skyscrapers, overlays etc.) shows the importance of fitting in with the user needs and goals (see e.g., www.kzero.co.uk/blog/?p=783).
- Resilience of established communities based on old technology with respect to those with more advanced technology (e.g. Habbo, Girland v. Second Life): Habbo works on a VR model based on block-world using shockwave; Girland uses a VR 2D+ system (2 Dimensional plus) based on Flash: these systems are still competing, although there are more advanced 3D (three Dimensional) VR such as Second Life; this shows that the user-investment in the site is a formidable barrier to exit, and also that technical complexity may be a barrier to entry for many users.
  USA cases:
- Move of existing businesses towards an internal community (Amazon) or towards acquiring an external one (Google, News Corp): Amazon has modified its business model by adding a marketplace for second-hand items, which is a kind of specialised Ebay community (www.amazonservices.com/promerchant/?ld=AZSOAMakeM); News Corp has acquired Myspace, moving from newspapers and broadcasting to social networks (www.nytimes.com/ 2005/07/18/business/18cnd-newscorp.html), followed by Google acquiring YouTube (www.nytimes.com/2006/10/09/business/09cnd-deal.html?ex=1318046400&en=d3f60bb3f976cfd0&ei=5088&partner=rssnyt&cmc=rss) and more recently launching Lively as an alternative to VR (Virtual Reality) communities such as Second Life (ap.google.com/article/ALeqM5hwfQnhC-NEKfVqcbcWHPE8L2k7dw D91QABG81).
- Move from gaming to community gaming (Sims: thesims2.co.uk/pages.view_frontpage.asp), and extension of community aspects in multi-players gaming (Everquest): The Sims started as single-player program, then it moved to multi-players (www.wired.com/wired/archive/10.11/simcity.html) online and now it has added community elements to it (thesims2.ea.com/community/index.php?pid=Community); Everquest has added external community aspects (e.g. external marketplaces for magic items and characters: forums.station.sony.com/eq/forums/ list.m).
- Move from pure P2P (Peer to Peer) to intermediation (new Napster): originally Napster was a pure P2P; following the adverse trial judgements, it has evolved into a legal tool to sell music online (www.paidcontent.org/entry/419-napster-joins-the-mp3-game-6-million-tracks-all-majors-signed-on).

- Move from single payment to subscription (Ebay): Ebay has recently added premium services for its shop which involve a subscription payment as well as the intermediation fee (pages.ebay.com/storefronts/Subscriptions.html).
- Move of community-based creation models from compilation to search (Wikipedia's move into search engines): the recent announcement of a search engine based on Wikipedia shows that the community-based model of content creation is now strong enough to make it possible a challenge to the most sophisticated statistical engines for search (technology.timesonline.co.uk/tol/news/tech_and_web/article1264117.ece).

5.   Conclusions and Summary Recommendations

The application of the model to the selected sites shows its usefulness against the given criteria: in particular, it is suggested that the model works efficiently, in that it explains various observed phenomena, such as the expansion of communities across most successful sites, the convergence towards some income types (especially intermediation and subscription), the evolution of advertisement towards integrated models (again, particularly suited to communities), and the vulnerability of some dominant business in absence of community. Some of these processes had been forecast by the proposed model and then observed subsequently in the unfolding online business world. The model also produces some unexpected results, in that it discriminates strongly between businesses which appear to be closely related (e.g. on a product type classification), while showing remarkable statistical correlation between apparently highly different businesses. It is also suggested that this shows the useful difference between surface and structural analysis, and furthermore that some action suggestions are not sector-dependent, and as such even more valuable to business leaders.

The main recommendation emerging from the study is that there are different ways for businesses online to be successful, depending on the interplay of the various factors observed: so, it is not important in itself the presence of community or the degree of innovation, but the fact that the set of parameters together be in the appropriate range for the chosen type of online business.

References

[1] Timmers, P.: Business Models for Electronic Markets. Journal on Electronic Markets 8(2): 3-8 (1998).
[2] Rappa, M.: Managing the digital enterprise - Business models on the Web, North Carolina State University. http://digitalenterprise.org (2003).
[3] Osterwalder, A.: The Business Model Ontology - A Proposition and a Design Science Approach, Thesis (2004).
[4] Zeng Q., Huang L., Identifying e-Business Model: A Value Chain-Based Analysis, Journal of Electronic Science and Technology of China, 2(3): 146-150 (2004).
[5] Pateli, A., and Giaglis, G.: A research framework for understanding and analysing e-business models. European Journal of Information Systems 13(4): 302-314 (2004).
[6] Timmers, P.: Electronic Commerce: Strategies and models for business-to-business trading, John Wiley, New Jersey (1999).
[7] Weill, P. and Vitale, M.R.: Place to Space: Migrating to Ebusiness Models. Harward Business School Press (2001).
[8] Tapscott, D., Williams, A.D.: Wikinomics; How Mass Collaboration Changes Everything, Penguin, USA (2006).
[9] Forum One Communication, Online Community ROI: Best Practices Survey, April 2007, http://www.onlinecommunityreport.com/reports/oc_roi2007_final.pdf
[10] Garigliano, R., and eTourism research group: Sintesi degli incontri per la definizione di uno schema per l'analisi dei modelli di business per il Web, eTourism report, DISA, n.20, University of Trento, in Italian (2006).
[11] Mich, L., and Garigliano, R., Novi Inverardi, P.: Business models for the Web: an analysis of success factors, In Baggio R. (Ed.), ICT for Tourism, WCC2008, Milan, 8-10 September 2008.

Business Community Creation Based on Competence Management

Alexey KASHEVNIK[1], Kurt SANDKUHL[2], Nikolay SHILOV[1],
Alexander SMIRNOV[1], Vladimir TARASOV[2]
[1] *St.Petersburg Institute for Informatics and Automation of the RAS,*
39, 14 line, 199178 St.Petersburg, Russia
Tel: +7 812 328 8071, Fax: + +7 812 328 0685, Email: {alexey, nick, smir}@iias.spb.su
[2] *School of Engineering at Jönköping University, P.O. Box 1026, 55111 Jönköping, Sweden*
Tel: +46 36 10 1590, Fax: +46 36 10 17 99, Email: {saku, tavl}@jth.hj.se

Abstract: Business communities are networked organisations with members from different industries aiming at coordinating their activities for production of the final product/service. Forming a network of companies requires "understanding" of the different companies' organisational competences. Competence management can help solving this task. This paper starts with presenting our earlier work in competence management projects aimed at supporting creation of business networks. Three cases are introduced: formation of business relationships with developing countries, competence supply in flexible supply networks, and collaborative product innovation. Based on experiences from these projects, competence management requirements for business community creation are identified and a conceptual framework for supporting the identified requirements is proposed. This framework considers competence management as an essential part of participation in business communities and conceptually integrates organisational and individual competence development. Enterprise models can be employed for supporting competence management and competence development in business community within the framework.

1. Introduction

In many industrial domains, the business environment currently is changing from traditional supply chains within one industry to a more network-centric approach spanning across different industries. This is illustrated by the creation of business communities including members from different industries. A business community can be characterised as an aggregation of resources of independent companies united on the principle of cooperation within the same information environment and capable of coordinating their activities for production of the final product/service. Business communities need to have a clear understanding what the different members can contribute, not only regarding services offered, resource capacity or production capability, but also in terms of organisational competences. Concepts and approaches from competence management can be applied to address this task.

Traditional competence management concepts for large organisations are aiming at the more long-term development and maintenance of organisational competences. For business communities, other approaches are needed, which support flexible short and mid-term competence supply in cooperating groups of smaller companies. Semantic technologies, like ontologies or semantic networks, are expected to support the task of efficient competence supply by providing concepts and solutions for modelling of organizational competence, and by implementing matching mechanisms between required competence and existing partners.

The next section presents our earlier work in competence management relevant for supporting creation of business networks. Three cases are introduced: formation of business relationships with developing countries, competence supply in flexible supply networks, and collaborative product innovation. Based on experiences from these projects, competence management requirements for business community creation are identified in section 3. A frame concept for business community creation is proposed in the last section.

2. Case Studies for Competence-Based Business Community Creation

2.1 Formation of Business Relationships with Developing Countries

Work presented in this section is based on a project for the Swedish International Development Agency aimed at supporting collaboration between enterprises in Sweden and Vietnam. The project considered situations like a company from one country looking for partners in another country in order to open new sales or find manufacturing capacity. Close collaboration of enterprises from different countries often requires overcoming diverse obstacles with regard to differences in products, processes, language, and culture. To facilitate this, companies can be supported by diaspora members having competence in the required industry sector and both cultures.

The applied approach is to model competences of companies and individuals and provide for means to search for needed competence. Figure 1 shows the competence modelling frame concept used in this project [1]. The first part is a meta-model that defines the language for representing competence models. Based on the meta-model, two competence models, for enterprises and individuals, were defined. These competence models were built with the help of an ontology language to represent relevant competences for a given task in a formalized notation. The individual competence model structures and formalizes skills and abilities of a person and includes three major parts: general competence, cultural competence, and occupational competence. The enterprise competence model consists of the industrial and occupational competence parts. The former is subdivided into economic activities, products/services, and specific domain competence.

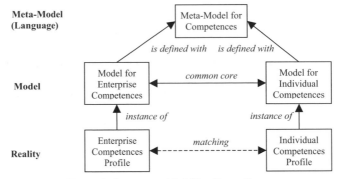

Figure 1: Competence Modelling Frame Concept

The last part of the competence modelling frame concept is competence profiles, which describe particular persons and companies. A competence profile is an instance of the enterprise or individual competence model. A matching mechanism is to be applied on the competence profiles, which are stored in a database, to find instances that match to a given request, like an individual with certain competences required by an enterprise. In this way, a company can find a partner with needed competence as well as get help from a disapora member and learn more about the partner.

2.2   Competence Supply in Flexible Supply Networks

The FP6 project "Intelligent Logistics for Innovative Product Technologies" (ILIPT) is aimed at development of new methods and technologies to facilitate the implementation of "the 5-day car" manufacturing paradigm for the European automotive industry [2]. This is a new paradigm that will approach the building of 'cars to order' in a reduced time scale. ILIPT project will address the conceptual and practical aspects of delivering cars to customers within several days after placing the order [3]. Trying to identify and locate a member that has responsibility and/or competence in a particular part of the supply network can be a laborious, time-consuming process. Developing and maintaining a competence directory of all the relevant parties associated with troubleshooting and solving potential problems can significantly reduce the time. Further, linking this directory to key decision points and frequent problems can further enhance its effectiveness [4].

Depending on the way the competence management system is used, two types of clients can be identified: network members and individuals, who are employees of the network members. The employees are represented with individual competence models. It allows specifying and complementing individual requests with necessary information, and personalizing the knowledge and information flow from the system to the individual. The supply network members are represented with enterprise competence models, which makes it possible to faster and more precisely choose a network member to perform a required operation or to produce/supply required components.

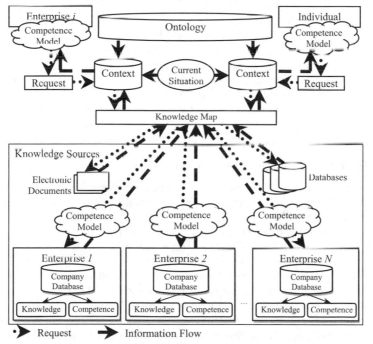

Figure 2: Conceptual Model of Context-Driven Competence Management System

The conceptual model of the context-driven competence management system in flexible supply network is presented in figure 2. Based on requests, ontology of the problem domain, and the current situation, the context is built, which is a description of the individual request and current situation in terms of the ontology. The knowledge map defines references between the ontology and knowledge sources.

2.3   Collaborative Product Innovation

Collaborative product innovation in dispersed groups of engineers creates various kinds of challenges to technology, organization and social environment. Selected examples are knowledge sharing, coordination support or formation of teams. The third case presented in this paper is based on experiences in the FP6 project "Model-Adapted Product and Process Engineering" (MAPPER) [5]. The challenge addressed is how to describe the competences needed for planned collaborative design projects in a way that those individuals best suited for the collaboration can be identified. The selected approach is to model competences of individuals including different competence areas like cultural, professional or occupational competences as part of enterprise models (see also section 4.2).

In order to develop a competence model for collaborative design, which represents all essential and desirable competences needed, we have to understand the nature of collaborative design. Collaborative design can be defined as design task performed in a dispersed group of workers with a joint collaboration objective. This leads to at least three areas, which should be taken into account: (i) the nature of engineering design work itself, (ii) the work of design teams as compared to individuals, and (iii) the effects of distributing design work as compared to co-located design.

We propose to utilize enterprise models to represent required competences. The first part of including enterprise competences is connected to roles. Each role needs certain competences, which can be represented with a specific competence construct being part of the enterprise modelling language. Furthermore, competence sub-items with relations to other competences should be included. As a starting point, the competence classification used in the enterprise under consideration should be applied. The second part of modelling design competences concerns the individuals working in the enterprise. The competence they possess, including a competence measurement has to be represented in the enterprise model as a relation between individual and competence category. The enterprise model developed in the project divided collaborative design competences into three major parts: general competence, competence in certain parts of the design process, and competence in systems and technologies. The main use of the enterprise models was capturing organisational best practices including the competence required for the roles involved.

3.   Competence Management Requirements

Drawing on the experiences from the cases introduced in the previous section, this section identifies and illustrates the requirements for competence management based on the life cycle of business communities.

Business communities experience different phases and situations, which form the "life-cycle" of such a community. The most important phases are community building, formation, integration, operation, discontinuation, and community dissolvement [6]. All the phases show specific requirements to competence development and require support mechanisms for competence management, which is shown in Table 1.

In order to illustrate the above requirements during the different life cycle phases, the case of formation of business relationships with developing countries was selected.

- Community building: during this phase companies need to create their competence profiles and enter them into a database accessible for other companies. Diaspora members should also create competence profiles and enter them into the database.
- Formation: a company, which is willing to find a partner, describes the required competence based on the enterprise competence model and searches the database for potential partners as well as persons who can help to form the business relations.
- Integration: the company selects a partner(s) after examining the competence profiles found in the database.

- Operation: members of the formed community (companies and diaspora members) update their competence profiles in the database to reflect accumulated experience.
- Discontinuation: the same update needed like in the operation phase.
- Community dissolvement: no special requirements for competence management.

Table 1: Characteristics of Business Community Lifecycle Phases and Competence Requirements

Life cycle phase	Description	Typical competence management requirements
Community Building	• Enterprises with joint objectives or interests gather in a community of loosely coupled members • Main purpose is information exchange and communication within the network	• Identification and structuring of competences of community members • Creation of competence models for the members
Formation	• Based on specific requirements for a collaboration, the formation of a project team is started based on the capabilities of the members • Potential partners with respect to the specific requirements have been identified	• Description of competence demand according to the requirements • Search for partner possessing the required competence • Selection of team member based on the search
Integration	• Potential team members have been selected and negotiate the legal and financial conditions for joint project work • A collaboration infrastructure is being implemented for all relevant levels of collaboration • The result is a project network	• Search for new partner possessing the required competence if the negotiation was unsuccessful • Selection of new team member based on the search
Operation	• The collaboration project is carried out within the project network • This is supported by the collaboration infrastructure	• Update of competence models to reflect the relations between partners and changes in members' competences
Discontinuation	• The project network discontinues to exist • Dis-integration at all levels of the collaboration infrastructure and w. r. t. legal and financial issues is carried out	• Update of competence models to reflect the changes in members' competences resulting from the collaboration project
Community dissolvement	• The joint objectives or interests within the community no longer exist • The network is dissolved	

4.   Frame Concept for Business Community Creation

Requirements identified in the previous section and experiences from the industrial cases presented in section 2 form the basis for the conceptual framework for competence management support of business community creation, which will be presented in 4.1. Section 4.2 will illustrate how enterprise models can support implementation of the frame concept.

4.1   Frame Concept

The requirements discussed in section 3 made clear that business community creation requires various organisational competences, some of them specialised for the purpose of the business community under creation, like collaborative design competences in case 2.3, some of them quite general competences, like the ability to quickly select suitable individuals within the organisation who are able to perform a specific business community task. Although organisational competences depend on individual competences, they also include best practices (i.e. competence for performing a process), organisation structures, and resources in the organisation (cf. [7]).

From a competence management viewpoint, there exists a tight interrelation between the business community life cycle, organizational competence development, and individual competence development, which is shown in Figure 3. The involvement in a business community creates different requirements to the competences of an organization (see section 3), which form an input for the organizational competence development life cycle. The needs with respect to organizational development surfacing in a business community can be classified into phase related and lifecycle related needs. Phase related needs concern the execution of tasks in a specific phase of the business community; life cycle related needs address organizational competences for management, monitoring and optimization of the business community. It should be observed that organizational competence development requires a certain lead time, i.e. both phase related and life cycle related development needs should be analyzed and qualification measures should be planned already in the business community creation phase.

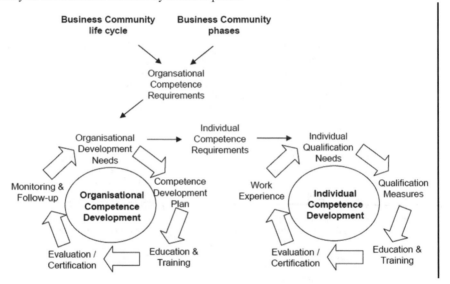

Figure 3: Business Community Life Cycle and Organizational and Individual Competence Development

Business community requirements that cannot be adequately met by the organization show qualification needs on individual and organization level. Organizational and individual competence development cycles both include several stages caused by these qualification needs, like selection or development of qualification measures, education and training, evaluation and certification, resulting in changes organizational/individual competence profiles. Organizational qualification needs might also directly cause qualification needs on individual level, which is indicated by the connection between the two competence development cycles.

4.2   Enterprise Models for Supporting Frame Concept Implementation

Integrating business community lifecycle and competence management results in a number of important elements needed for implementation of IT solutions supporting the framework for competence-based business community creation, including:

- A suitable approach for modelling and representing both organizational and individual competences
- Tools and approaches for populating the competence models
- An appropriate approach for expressing competence demand in the different phases

- Approaches and tools for matching the competence demand with the existing competence profiles for supporting formation phase and integration phase
- A methodology for integrating all above elements including the evolution of competence models.

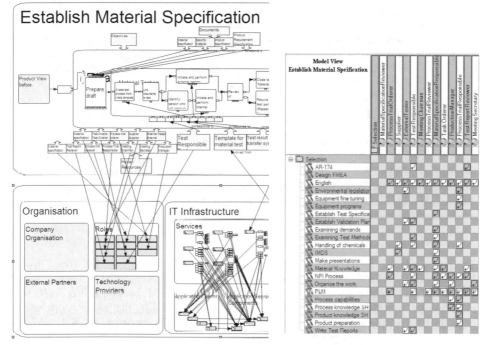

Figure 4a: Visual Enterprise ModelFigure   4b: Competence/Role Matrix

Based on the experiences from the MAPPER project, which was briefly introduced in section 2.3, we propose to use enterprise models[i] for supporting competence management and business community creation. Enterprise models usually capture different aspects of an enterprise including the work processes and activities performed, the organisation structure implemented including roles and actors, the resources used in the processes by roles/actors and the products or services offered by the enterprise. Enterprise models for supporting competence management also have to include the competence required for a specific role and the competences that different actors in the organisation possess.

Figure 4 shows a selected part of an example for such an enterprise model. Figure 4a shows the visual model including the process perspective (illustrated by showing the process for "establish material specification" in the upper half of the figure), the roles involved in the process (shown in the process perspective and in the organisation part, lower part of the picture), the staff available (grey boxes in the lower left part labelled "company organisation and "external partners"), and the IT infrastructure, which is part of the resources used with the processes. Figure 4b shows a matrix created based on the enterprise model listing the different competences as rows, the different roles as columns and the required competences as check marks.

Such an enterprise model describes substantial parts of organisational competences by capturing the processes implemented, the resources available, and the organisational structures in place. At the same time it also includes the individual competences required for the roles and possessed by the actual staff. We consider this kind of model as suitable basis for supporting competence management and business community creation. [9] discusses the use of such models in configuration of flexible supply networks.

5. Conclusions

The main contributions of this paper are to identify competence management requirements for business community creation and to propose a conceptual model for supporting the identified requirements. The main idea in this context consists of (1) considering competence management as an essential part of participation in business communities, (2) conceptually integrating organisational and individual competence development and (3) using the enterprise models for supporting competence management and competence development in business community.

Future work will be of experimental and conceptual nature. From an experimental perspective, the proposed approach has to be implemented and evaluated in controlled environments or real-world cases. This will most likely lead to changes, refinements and improvements of the proposed approach. The conceptual work includes to further elaborate the aspects of expressing competence demands, populating competence models based on existing information sources, and matching approaches for competence demand and models. Approaches from ontology matching seem promising for the latter aspect, as they can be combined and integrated with enterprise models.

Acknowledgements

The paper is based on research carried out as a part of several projects: Integrated Project FP6-IST-NMP 507592-2 "Intelligent Logistics for Innovative Product Technologies", STREP FP6-IST-NMP 016527 "Model-adapted Product and Process Engineering", joint project with Ford Motor Company, project CoReLib supported by the Swedish Institute by grant # 01215-2007, project "Information Logistics for SME" supported by KK-Foundation by grant #2005/0252, and projects funded by grants # 08-07-00264 and # 07-01-00334 of the Russian Foundation for Basic Research, # 14.2.35 of Presidium of RAS, and # 1.9 of the Division of Nanotechnologies and Information Technologies of RAS.

References

[1] Tarassov, V., Sandkuhl, K., & Henoch, B. Using ontologies for representation of individual and enterprise competence models. In P. Bellot, V. Duong, & M. Bui (Eds.), The Fourth IEEE International Conference on Computer Sciences Research, Innovation and Vision for the Future, RIVF 2006. IEEE, 2006, pp. 205–212.
[2] Stone, G., Miemczyk, J., Esser, R. 'Making Build to Order a Reality: The 5-Day Car Initiative', Strengthening Competitiveness through Production Networks. A prospective from European ICT research projects in the field of "Enterprise Networking", 2005, pp. 26--37.
[3] ILIPT: Intelligent Logistics for Innovative Product Technologies (2008), http://www.ilipt.org.
[4] Lesser, E., Butner, K. (2005) 'Knowledge and the Supply Chain', Inside Supply Management, Vol. 16, No. 4, p. 12.
[5] Johnsen, S., Schümmer, T., Haake, J., Pawlak, A., Jørgensen, H., Sandkuhl, K., Stirna, J., Tellioglu, H., Jaccuci, G. (2007) Model-based Adaptive Product and Process Engineering. In: Rabe, M.; Mihók, P. (Eds) New Technologies for the Intelligent Design and Operation of Manufacturing Networks. Fraunhofer IRB Verlag, Stuttgart (Germany), 2007.
[6] Blomqvist E., Levashova T., Öhgren A., Sandkuhl K., Smirnov A.: Formation of Enterprise Networks for Collaborative Engineering. Post-conference proceedings of 3. Intl. Workshop on Collaborative Engineering, Sopron (Hungary), April 2005, ISBN 91-975604-1-3.
[7] Pépiot, G., Cheikhrouhou, N., Furbringer, J., and Glardon, R. 2007. UECML: Unified Enterprise Competence Modelling Language. Comput. Ind. 58, 2 (Feb. 2007), 130-142.
[8] Vernadat, F.B.: Enterprise Modeling and Integration. Chapman & Hall, 1996.
[9] Sandkuhl, K., Smirnov, A., Shilov, N.: "Configuration of Automotive Collaborative Engineering and Flexible Supply Networks". In Cunningham, P. and Cunningham, M. (Eds.): Expanding the Knowledge Economy – Issues, Applications, Case Studies. IOS Press, Amsterdam (NL). ISBN 978-1-58603-801-4.

---

[i] See [8] for an overview to enterprise modeling techniques.

Collaboration and the Knowledge Economy: Issues, Applications, Case Studies   1093
P. Cunningham and M. Cunningham (Eds.)
IOS Press, 2008

Design and Reference Implementation of a Distributed URN Registry: URNreg

Victoriano GIRALT[1], Diego LOPEZ[2], Cándido RODRIGUEZ[3], Milan SOVA[4]

[1]*University of Malaga, Blvd. Louis Pasterur, 33 Ed. SCAI Campus de Teatinos,
Malaga, 29071, Spain
Tel: +34 95 2132366, Email: victoriano@uma.es*
[2]*Red.ES/RedIRIS, Avda. Reina Mercedes s/n Ed. CICA, Sevilla, 41012, Spain
Tel: +34 95 5056621, Email: diego.lopez@rediris.es*
[3]*Red.ES/RedIRIS, Avda. Reina Mercedes s/n Ed. CICA, Sevilla, 41012, Spain
Tel: +34 95 5056613, Email: candido.rodriguez@rediris.es*
[4]*CESNET, Zikova 4, Praha, 160 00, Czech Republic
Fax: +420 2 2432 0269, Email: sova@cesnet.cz*

Abstract: Resource identifiers are critical in our technical environment nowadays. Uniform Resource Names (URNs) are intended to serve as persistent, location-independent resource identifiers and are designed to make it easy to map other name-spaces (that share the properties of URNs) into URN-space. Current instances of URN registries are usually implemented as a set of web pages serving simple enumeration of registered URNs and sometimes their simple descriptions. This paper describes the design and the implementation of URNreg, a novel service which provides a way to get information of a registered URN to both human and non-human users. Also, it supports a distributed delegation model so it is able to get the registry information for delegated namespaces.

1. Introduction

Identity federations are distributed in themselves. Apart from those services enabling the discovery of where to assess user identities, which are not essential and need not be unique, they do not require any central point or authority.

On the other hand, many identity federations, especially in the academic environment, have resorted to URN based values for attributes when it becomes necessary to carry contextual information alongside the value itself.

The use of this type of values is exploding. However, interoperability requires the meaning of the values, at least, to be understood by all the federation participants. Even, in some cases, to be the same for a given attribute, be it at the federation level or some other levels, whether geographical or organizational.

This paper presents the policy and technical mechanism that have been designed to achieve both a distributed control of URNs and the capacity to use such values at an operational level.

The software has been put into production in some projects over the European Research and Academic Network.

2. Basic concepts

Uniform Resource Names (URNs) [1] are intended to serve as persistent, location-independent, resource identifiers. The URN syntax provides a means to encode character data in a form that can be sent in existing protocols, transcribed on most keyboards, etc.

URNs are specially formatted strings with three basic parts:

- The urn: prefix
- The namespace identifier or NID
- The namespace specific string or NSS.

The NSS and the NID are separated by a colon. NSS may be further subdivided into sub-namespaces, possibly managed by different authorities, leading to a hierarchical structure.

Delegations can happen at any point of the hierarchy, and each one should have a corresponding point of publication of assigned values and subsequent delegations. This has been usually done by means of hand maintained web pages, without any service for getting automatic resolution of URNs.

Internet Assigned Numbers Authority (IANA) is the central repository for URN registries [2] containing the highest level of registered and delegated URNs.

3. Service design

The solution proposed in this paper provides a service that can be used for finding registries and it has been designed around registered and delegated URNs.

The protocol of URNreg is based on REST web services [3] with the requirement to provide capabilities for interacting with both human and non-human users. HTML pages are showed to the former group of users whereas XML messages are served to the latter.

The protocol uses basically HTTP requests using GET or POST methods to the URL of a particular URNreg web service. The parameters are being passed the usual way, i. e. as parts of the query string (for the GET method) or within the request body (for POST). Each web service specifies in its definition which parameters it expects to receive and their valid acceptable values.

The defined web services in the specification of the protocol of URNreg are:
- List URNs: request to list URN descriptions or delegation records stored at the particular URNreg server. The service recognizes the following optional parameters:
  o Format: specifies whether the list should be returned in human- or machine-readable format.
  Acceptable values:
    • Human (default) for human readable response (usually HTML)
    • Machine form an XML message
  o Type: specifies which type of records should be listed
  Acceptable values:
    • Description (default) for requesting the description of registered URNs
    • Delegation for requesting the delegation records
- Search for a URN: request for the information about a URN. In case of the namespace of that urn is delegated, it queries the remote registry and returns the obtained information. This service accepts the following parameters:
  o Format: specifies the requested format of the response. The parameter is optional
  Acceptable values:
    • Human (default) for human readable response (usually HTML)
    • Machine form an XML message
  o urn: the requested urn.

Figure 1 describes the scenario after deploying URNreg. An application, with human or non-human interactions, sends a query to the list or search web services. But, in case asks for the information of an URN delegated to another URNreg instance, the service will get that information on behalf of the application. The URNreg front-end is able to perform searches on delegated namespaces. Please note, that the List and Search services behave differently concerning the delegation. While the former just lists the information about delegations the latter actually returns the description even for URNs delegated to other authorities.

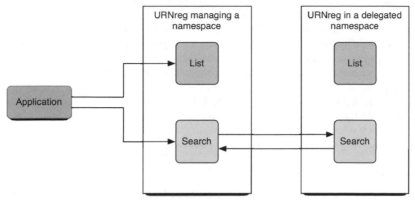

Figure 1: the scenario of URNreg

Each REST request is answered by a REST response, which in case of a machine-readable format is an XML message in a format specific to the particular service. Table 1 provides an example response to the request

http://webserver/urnreg/search/?urn=urn%3Ageant%3Aeduroam&format=machine

```
<?xml version='1.0' encoding='UTF-8' ?>
<Response>
  <urn value="urn:geant:eduroam">
    <descriptions>
      <description value="This is the root URN for eduroam components"/>
    </descriptions>
    <presentations>
      <presentation value="URN raíz para el espacio de nombres de eduroam"
lang="es"/>
    </presentations>
  </urn>
</Response>
```

Table 1: an example of response of URNreg

The data stored when an organization registers an URN is usually quite basic so far, saving only the value of the URN, when it has been registered and who has requested it. URNreg proposes to store more information about the registration of an URN in order to get a full URN resolution service.

The information issued for a registry and for a delegation is different. The registration record consists of the following information:
-   URN value: the registered URN value.
-   Description: description of the URN value.
-   Presentation: human readable representation for the URN value. This attribute allows for multilingual values and its main goal is users can get a well explanation of what the URN is representing.
-   Delegated namespace: in case of URNreg has resolved the delegation of the URN and get its data from the delegated namespace service, it says which web service has been used for.

- Contact person: who has requested the registration of the URN.

On the other hand, the information issued for a delegated URN has the following elements:
- URN value: the delegated URN value.
- Owner: the Internet domain of the institution that owns the URN namespace.
- Register web application: the URL of the web application, or the entry link for a set of HTML pages, used for registering URNs in that delegated namespace.
- Policy document: the URL of the document expressing the policy of that delegated namespace.
- Web services for accessing its URNs: the URL base for the URN web services.
- LDAP URI for accessing its URNs: an optional URI which specified how to get access to an LDAP where URNs are stored.
- Contact person: who has requested the registration of the URN.

4. Reference implementation

A reference implementation has been developed in PHP using the siLeDAP framework [4] for accessing LDAP directories through web services. LDAP has been selected as object store back-end for its performance in search and read operations and for the ease of definition of object classes and attributes. A new schema for storing registered and delegated URNs has been published.

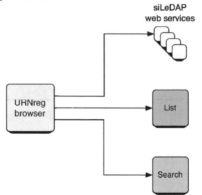

Figure 2: the architecture of the URNreg browser

Also, a PHP user interface has been developed that communicates with the web services to offer a human interface for querying and registering the URNs. This interface allows a user to query all registries from one point following the pointers for machine interface in the delegation objects. The user is also presented with the machine interface links to the web interface of the delegated registries responsible for the namespace. As shown in figure 2, this user interface gets the list of registered and delegated URNs by interacting the web services defined by URNreg.

Using the siLeDAP API, we have developed another set of web services in order to manage the registration of new URNs. Using them, it is possible to register an URN or request a namespace delegation using the URNreg browser.

The human interface is, of course, a web application, that queries the registry that manages the particular namespace. Once a namespace delegation entry is reached, there are two possible paths to follow:
- In order not to confuse the user, the application queries the remote registry and presents the data to the user with the local look and feel. This is probably a less confusing experience for the user, that even allows to present the user with a localized version of

the value, if it is available.
- The application presents the URL of the new registry human interface to the user. Following such link the user will arrive to the registry entry page. This has the risk of landing the user on a page she does not understand, but clearly presents the identity of the namespace owner. This way of operation should follow the standard i18n procedures for selecting the user language and, if it is unavailable either on the request or inside the registry, it must present information in English.

5. Usage

The SChema Harmonisation Committee (SCHAC) schemas [5] mandate the use of URNs as values for certain attributes, allowing for hierarchically assigned encodings, that decouple national- or community-wide variations of otherwise similar values. A clear example of this is schacHomeOrganizationType that describes the sort of institution a certain person is linked to. The simple value "university" has slight but significant differences in meaning in different countries. A URN encoding allow for a consistent spaces of values across national borders and leave each local system the freedom to assign specific, well-defined mapping rules.

The Bologna Process aims to create a European Higher Education Area by 2010, in which students can choose from a wide and transparent range of high quality courses and benefit from smooth recognition procedures. The internal administrative actions made by European universities will use the URNs registered by SCHAC initiative, which is provided by the URNreg of TERENA, since those organizations must work with same definitions around whole Europe.

The root of the namespace for SCHAC attribute values is operated by TERENA, and from the above example it is easy to see that it requires a comprehensive system to manage both common and specific values, including delegations. URNreg combines the ease of user of its Web interface for human administrators, with the possibility of using the Web services from applications using the SCHAC attributes in order to establish correctness and appropriate mappings of their values. The delegation protocol permits applications to query a single point that will appropriately redirect them to the URNreg instance able to satisfy the request.

The URNreg distributed registry is used in the eduGAIN interfederation infrastructure [6] inside the GÉANT2 project. This project uses URNs for providing unique, persistent and well-managed identifiers to the components, either resources or identity repositories, within the participating federations. These identifiers, along with data about when, how, what to and whom for they were assigned, are managed by the eduGAIN Naming Registry.

The values are used in a distributed environment, applying them in all the process required for establishing trust inside the eduGAIN infrastructure. For example, since these URNs serve as identifiers for eduGAIN entities, they are included in their X.509 certificates, as an extension mandated by the eduGAIN certificate profiles. The URN registry provides an invaluable resource for the Certificate Authorities to validate the Certificate Signing Requests, while allowing each participant federation to retain control on the naming schema applied to the components operated inside it. Verifying the meaning, eligibility, and correctness of an attribute value is just one click away.

6. Related work

Both the authors and the working groups on federations in which they participate had no knowledge of any similar work, so we had to develop a totally original system.

Some URN resolution services have developed so far, such as DiVA [7] project, which uses URNs to map electronic resources to URLs and as a primary key of the publications stored in DiVA. But these kinds of service do not provide a generic service.

Also DDDS, an Internet protocol for finding distributed resources using the resource name itself and DNS is being considered for using in URNreg in future releases.

7. Conclusion and future work

The system described in this paper has proved useful for production federations to control the URN explosion and to ease the dissemination of values and their meanings. The system will be deployed during 2008 in many European NREN operators to administer their delegated namespaces from prefixes belonging to projects such as the already mentioned eduGAIN and SCHAC. The Australian Access Federation has also shown interest in the system to manage their URN namespaces.

References

[1] R. Moats, "URN syntax," RFC 2141, IETF, 1997.
[2] "The official IANA registry of URN namespaces," http://www.iana.org/assignments/urn-namespaces.
[3] R. Fielding, "Architectural Styles and the Design of Network-based software Architectures,"
      http://www.ics.uci.edu/~fielding/pubs/dissertation/rest_arch_style.htm.
[4] "The siLeDAP project", https://forja.rediris.es/projects/siledap/
[5] "TF-EMC2 SCHAC project," http://www.terena.nl/activities/tf-emc2/schac.html.
[6] "Deliverable DJ5.2.2,2: GÉANT2 AAI Architecture and Design," GN2-JRA5 deliverable, January 2007.
[7] E. Müller, U. Klosa, P. Hansson, S. Andersson, E. Siira, "Using XML for Long-term Preservation. Experiences from the DiVA Project," Proceedings of the ETD 2003: Next Steps - Electronic Theses and Dissertations Worldwide. The Sixth International Symposium On Electronic Theses and Dissertations, the Humboldt-University in Berlin, Germany, 21 - 24 May 2003.
[8] M. Mealing: Dynamic Delegation Discovery System (DDDS) Part One: The Comprehensive DDDS, RFC 3401, IETF, 2002.

Design and Reference Implementation of a Federated Single Logout

Luis MELÉNDEZ[1], Diego LÓPEZ[2] , Victoriano GIRALT[3], Sergio GÓMEZ[4]
[1]*University of Córdoba, IT Services, Córdoba, 14071, Spain*
Tel: +34 957 211022, Fax: +34 957 218116, Email: luism@uco.es
[2]*RedIRIS, Avda. Reina Mercedes s/n, Sevilla, 41012, Spain*
Tel: +34 95 5056621, Fax: +34 95 5056651, Email: diego.lopez@rediris.es
[3]*University of Málaga, Central Computing Facility, Málaga, 29071, Spain*
Tel: +34 95 2132366, Fax: +34 95 2131492, Email: victoriano@uma.es
[4]*University of Córdoba, IT Services, Córdoba, 14071, Spain*
Tel: +34 957 212132, Fax: +34 957 218116, Email: sergio@uco.es

Abstract: Web Single Sign On (SSO) deployments and Identity Federations, though able to improve user experience and security (no more many passwords to remember, just one place to provide credentials, ...) have also some risks, and maybe the most important of them is associated to situations when the user does not completely close the session when leaving the computer. Both the sessions that are started with applications and the one with the Identity Provider or Authentication Server must be closed to avoid being someone else being able to open applications taking over the user's identity. The Single Log Out (SLO) function is at least as important as the SSO one, but there has been much less effort and research on it. We present one way to implement this functionality that is easy, flexible and compatible with existing AAI and SSO systems.

1. Introduction

When an institution participates in an identity federation [1] its Identity Provider (IdP) normally uses the services of a local WebSSO system (such as CAS [2], PAPI [3], etc.), which in turn will have its own Authentication Server (AS). So, the user may have sessions opened with different Service Providers (SPs) of one or more institutions as well as with other local services. After ending a working session, any user will like to close all of these sessions, as well as the session with the IdP and the AS, so that no other person can use the browser to open new sessions without being required to present any credential.

Given the fact that Single Sign On (SSO) systems automatically provide the authentication information that an application needs in order to grant access, maybe the user ends up not knowing which of the services contacted along a working session have required authentication and which of them have not, so the user is not aware of what applications must be closed. It is usual in corporate environments that many applications share the same look and feel, so the user is not aware of when a 'restricted' zone requiring authentication has been entered, because the SSO system has provided it automatically. We consider this fact a specifically dangerous effect of SSO systems when there is no SLO facility implemented.

An important measure against this danger is to include a clear visual clue indicating the user that the browser is in an authenticated state and should log out before leaving, but this is not always implemented.

The main result of [4] is that when a multiservice environment uses SSO for user authentication, a single logout (SLO) should also be used instead of expecting users to separately log out from each service. We think the same holds true for interinstitutional services such as federations.

We face several problems here:

- How to keep track of the applications opened by the user.
- How to close all of them automatically (or almost).
- How to close every particular session.
- How to close the session with the IdP or AS.

We present an approach to face all of these issues, although the more important and innovative solution lies in the way the sessions opened by the user are tracked and the way to close them. The description provided is concise.

2. Context

There exist several implementations of SLO, but no one is perfect. SAML 2.0 [5] introduces a profile for it, but it will be available only in concrete implementations of its specifications. In this moment there are many deployments of AAI and SSO technologies that lack a SLO facility. Our proposal is aimed to integrate many of these, not only as an interim solution but also as a test bed for some of the concepts and functionality that a SLO system should have.

3. Objectives

We wanted to design a single logout system that could be easily deployed and as little intrusive as possible in pre-existing application or federation code and configurations. We also wanted to explore new ways to expose the closing of open sessions to the user.

That is, the two main concerns for us were that the system should be:

- Simple to implement.
- Applicable to most of the federated identity software in use today.

This is with no doubt an initial step towards a complete solution, since we admit that it has shortcomings that need to be addressed. Anyway it is an already usable option for sites not able to implement another approach or even that prefer the benefits of this one.

4. Description

Our proposal uses two simple Web services that are contacted by the user agent and by other elements of the AAI. Each has, of course, its own URL. This approach splits the complexity and allows for better flexibility, as we will show later.

The first service is the so-called BAR (Browser Activity Registry). Its role is clearly denoted by its name: it associates an opaque identifier with the federated applications the user visits during the working session. It can be contacted by several elements in the AAI, depending on the complexity of the modifications necessary in every element, the pros and cons of every option, etc.

The second service is the SLO, and it is where the user is redirected when log out is requested. It will guide the user through the closing of all the applications that have been opened.

Those services (we have developed reference implementations of both of them) can be deployed in any AAI, since they are independent of any other element. The BAR has not any interface visible to the user, and it is only contacted by other services and by the user agent just to load some element that can set a cookie. The SLO has a user interface, so its appearance can be customized.

4.1   Tracking access to the resources

The sequence of events in a typical Shibboleth [6] deployment can be:
1. The user tries to access a federated application (SP)
2. This redirects the user to the WAYF service to select its local IdP

   The WAYF:
3. Determines that the user has not previously selected an IdP (a cookie is absent, for example)
4. Generates an opaque identifier (token) that may be just a random number.
5. In the user interface where the IdP is selected, it includes an HTML element whose SRC attribute is a URL of the BAR with both that token and the URL of the SP as query parameters.

   Upon receipt of the query generated by the user agent for that element, the BAR:
6. If the browser does not present the cookie called BARtoken, it sets it with the value of the token query parameter. If the cookie is present (subsequent accesses) the token query parameter is ignored.
7. Inserts the URL of the SP in its database, the token and the time stamp.
8. Returns an empty image, an empty script.
9. The WAYF presents the list of IdPs for the user to select the appropriate home institution and does the usual job of this service.

An approximate sequence diagram is:

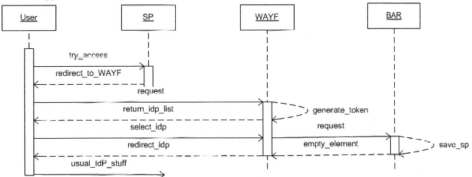

When the user goes to another SP that uses the same WAYF service, the sequence is the same, except that the WAYF service usually does not display again its interface and assumes the same IdP as before (this is indicated by the presence of some cookie). So to force the access to the BAR the WAYF, instead of redirecting immediately to the IdP, returns a simple HTML page that includes a link to an element with SRC attribute pointing to the BAR (like before) and a little javascript that forces the redirection to the IdP as soon as this little page is loaded.

If the user accesses later a different WAYF service or an application that uses an internal WAYF (but has been modified to integrate within the environment we describe in this paper), it generates a BARtoken, but it is not actually used:, When the browser contacts the BAR, sends a previous BARtoken cookie and uses it in its record and not the one that presents the browser in the query parameter.

Since the key to tracking the applications contacted by the user is an opaque identifier, there is no way to link those activities to a person, thus privacy is actively preserved. In the simplest case, such opaque identifier is generated each time by the WAYF, although only the first is used, because the BAR sets its cookie with it.

4.2   The Logout Phase

When an user starts to logout, it is very probable that it is intended to do so from all other applications and from the federation itself, and it is good to let the user decide, but it is not good to provide two links, one for exiting the application and another for exiting all of them.

Our proposal is: the logout link of the applications should be changed so that it redirects to the BAR service (with a URL indicating a Logout), which will redirect to the SLO passing it the value of the BARtoken. This first redirection to the BAR is necessary because the BARtoken cookie was set by it. Another option would be to include the SLO functionality in the BAR service. The SLO service presents the user the choice of closing only this application or all of then opened plus the federation association. The user has also the option to select which applications must be closed. The SLO service asks the BAR for the list of SPs visited (using the BARtoken cookie).

If it is not possible or convenient to change the logout links of the applications, the user can be instructed to contact the SLO service directly, as we will show later.

The approximate sequence diagram:

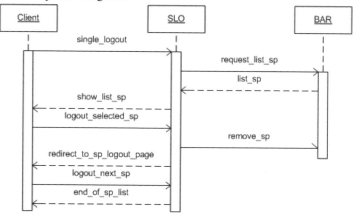

4.3   Sequentially Closing the Sessions

Our proposal for this is simple: not to do it fully automatically. Some applications, like the Moodle e-learning suite for example, asks the user for confirmation after clicking the Logout link. The logout can also be performed using the Logout service of the SP software that protects the application, but this does not allow it to perform the administrative tasks that it should. The logout of a Web application running in a federated environment is a field in which some research has to be done.

So the SLO service presents the user two frames: a bigger one where the closing of the application can be seen and it is possible to interact with it if necessary, for example to confirm the logout. This also serves the purpose of making the user well aware of the closing. Another smaller frame is used for navigation: one button takes the user to the next application to close.

If it is not possible or convenient to change the logout links of the applications, the user can be instructed to contact the SLO service directly, where the applications to close can be selected.

The SLO will contact the BAR to delete the records for the applications the user decides to close, so that a later visit to the same service will show only those that remain open.

For the SLO service to know the target URLs where every application should be contacted to perform the real logout, there are several options. There can be a configuration file, or a SAML 2.0 Metadata file which includes SingleLogoutService element can be used, substitute the /SAML/POST part of the SP with /Logout, etc.

This is also a field of experimentation and improvements.

5. Implementation and deployment

Our initial implementation, just enough for testing the concept, is composed of the following elements:

- Slight modifications to the WAYF service (in our case, a homemade one), no more than 20 lines of PHP code.
- Two simple web applications, the BAR and the SLO. In the very simple initial version, they consist of no more than 60 and 190 lines of PHP code.
- Modification of the logout link of the applications protected by an SP so that they point to the SLO application.

Even in the case of a more elaborated implementation, and without considering other options (see the next section) a basic deployment could simply be done following those same steps. Of course, we will release the source code and detailed instructions as soon as it becomes mature enough.

6. Future Work

In our initial implementation, is the WAYF the one contacting the BAR service, because we considered it was the easiest way to implement the architecture concepts. The connection to the BAR can also be made by the IdP after a successful authentication, but even so the user may be not authorized to access dc application.

The best place could be at the SP, after it has authorized the access. But this can be easy to implement in some cases and very difficult in others. If we cannot adapt all SPs to contact the BAR, we must still let the WAYF service (or equivalent) to do it. If we have an SP adapted to know about the BAR, it should contact the BAR to delete the record placed by the WAYF in the case of an access that is not authorized.

What we have to do then is to further develop these concepts, explore the possible usage scenarios, etc.

7. Conclusions

The system presented here is not perfect, but in some small to medium environments it allows for the relatively easy implementation of a fully functional Single Log Out facility.

Quoting one of the SAML standards: "All that said, it is not intended as a panacea, but simply an alternative to fill another deployment niche"

Talking about the user experience, we propose a way for the user to be visually aware of the closing of every service, and since this process is not totally automatic, she has to click on a button to go through all of them. It can be regarded as uncomfortable, but it is not really so much, and the user is more aware that all gets closed.

We think this is matter that is more subjective than technical, and would like that our proposal promotes some discussion about these usability-related items.

We plan also to do some more research with real users to get feedback about the way they prefer: more automatic or more awareness.

Our system has been implemented and tested in the federated identity infrastructure for the Andalusian Universities, and the user feedback received so far has been positive. As the infrastructure is deployed, we will be able to expose a wider user base to the system and get a better assessment about its usage in the real world.

References

[1]. S. S. Y. Shim, G. Bhalla, V. Pendyala - Federated Identity Management. In: Computer, Vol. 38, No. 12- IEEE Computer Society, December 2005, pp. 120-122

[2] S. Bramhall - Understanding uPortal Security and the Yale Central Authentication Server. 8th JA-SIG Conference,Westminster, Colorado, June 2003

[3] R. Castro-Rojo, D. R. Lopez - The PAPI system: point of access to providers of information. Computer Networks, Volume 37, Issue 6, December 2001, pp 703-710

[4] M.Linden and I.Vilpola, - An Empirical Study on the Usability of Logout in a Single Sign-on System. In: Information Security Practice and Experience. Springer Berlin / Heidelberg, 2005, pp 243-254

[5] Bindings and Profiles for the OASIS Security Assertion Markup Language (SAML). OASIS Standard, September 2003. Available at:
http://www.oasis-open.org/committees/download.php/3405/oasis-sstc-saml-bindings-profiles-1.1.pdf

[6] S. Cantor (editor) - Shibboleth Architecture. Protocols and Profiles.10 September 2005. Available at:
http://shibboleth.internet2.edu/docs/draft-mace-shibboleth-arch-protocols-200509.pdf

Collaboration and the Knowledge Economy: Issues, Applications, Case Studies
P. Cunningham and M. Cunningham (Eds.)
IOS Press, 2008

Co-Design and Web 2.0: Theoretical Foundations and Application

Mikael LIND[1, 2, 3], Olov FORSGREN[1]

[1]*University College of Borås, School of Business and Informatics, S-501 90 Borås, Sweden*
[2]*Jönköping International Business School, P.O Box 1026, S-551 11 Jönköping, Sweden*
[3]*Linköping University, Department of Management and Engineering, S-581 83 Linköping, Sweden*
Tel: +46 705 66 40 97, Fax: +46 46 33 435 40 07, Email: {firstname.lastname}@hb.se

Abstract: Web 2.0 is not just a new buzzword. It represents a new direction of development in the ICT-field strongly related to co-design. The theoretical foundations of co-design as a mean for explaining contemporary practical and theoretical development trends in the ICT-field will be discussed using the e-Me project as an example of a contemporary effort. In this a focus will be put upon both the design process and the resulting artefact as such. By doing this we would manage both to theoretically validate the ongoing trends and also provide inspirational thoughts for how to manage the continual development of the ICT-field in the future. When putting the co-design oriented thinking into application a number of other complimentary trends could be identified. These integrate old classical domains such as private and public, education and work, science and politics, enabling new types of e-services.

Keywords: e-Me, e-empowerment, collaboration, communities, mentality, co-design, web 2.0

1. Introduction

The underlying assumption in this paper is that web 2.0 is not just a new buzzword but represent a direction of development in the ICT-field with both impact and potential. The main idea in this paper is that theoretical explanations may help us to see the potentials of web 2.0 at the same time as they open new views indicating future possibilities. One of the strongest trends in the ICT-field of today is e-empowerment of different kinds of clients, such as citizens and consumers. This means that more emphasis is put upon the possibility for clients to manage and contribute to the information galaxy [2] – both in terms of the use and supply of content as well as services. An often mentioned concept in relation to this trend is Web 2.0. O'Reilley [22], as one of the people who coined term, claim that

"Web 2.0 is the network as platform, spanning all connected devices; Web 2.0 applications are those that make the most of the intrinsic advantages of that platform: delivering software as a continually-updated service that gets better the more people use it, consuming and remixing data from multiple sources, including individual users, while providing their own data and services in a form that allows remixing by others, creating network effects through an "architecture of participation," and going beyond the page metaphor of Web 1.0 to deliver rich user experiences."

Web 2.0 is a concept that put emphasis on participation and co-production of data and services. Some key characteristics of Web 2.0 [22, 23] are especially Rich Internet Applications, User-generated content, Semantic Web, Recommendations, Social Networking, Syndication/mash ups, Open Standards, Software as a service, Personalization, User-generated Services, and Device Independence..

From a theoretical stance these characteristics can to a high degree find explanations within the systems ideas launched by e.g. Churchman [6]. Based on these ideas the notion of co-design was coined by Forsgren [8] (In Swedish: "Samskapande"). His principal idea was that we can design an unlimited number of views on reality. Every view implemented in IT gives new options and benefits for different groups of people. Therefore to optimize the value of these new options the interests of as many as possible of the influenced groups of people should be involved in a co-design of the implemented view. From this angle web 2.0 can be described as a set of models, methods and techniques to bring interest and energy from influenced people into a co-design process. Since the designed perspectives in such process also can be described as knowledge and the implemented views can be regarded as technology the long term development can be described as making influenced people co-producers or co-designers of knowledge and technology.

From a historical perspective we can see a number of different approaches aiming at involvement of users in information systems development in what is called socio/technological approaches [21]. In Scandinavia Langefors [14] with his infological approach was a pioneer for this work. Later Goldkuhl [11] and others have further developed this tradition. All these approaches get theoretical inspiration from philosophical work on how to relate to the fundamental questions of data, information, communication, and knowledge. With our co-design approach we want to take this approach one step further both by considering the philosophical foundation and give examples of such approach have impact on information systems development.

There are today contemporary efforts building on to the idea of web 2.0. One such effort is the e-Me project [2, 3] highly influenced by the necessity of a high degree of stakeholder involvement. The e-Me project is about exploring the concept of an electronic assistant as the next generation of platforms for people-centric e-services. In its start the e-Me project focused students as one category of people. This exploration has been done in conceptual development (refinement of the vision), realization of the e-Me as an artifact, and in a phase of proof of concept involving several future users in the spirit of co-design. The line of action adopted in the e-Me project has been inspired of design science [13]. The users, in their "business" environment, were co-designing a future situation with an electronic assistant supporting them in the management of the lives as students.

2.   Objectives

The objective of this paper is two-folded. First of all some theoretical foundations of co-design as a mean for explaining contemporary practical and theoretical development trends in the ICT-field will be discussed using the e-Me project as an example. In this a focus will be put upon both the design process and as the resulting artefact as such. By doing this we would manage both to theoretically validate the ongoing trends and also provide inspirational thoughts for how to manage the continual development of the ICT-field in the future. Secondly, some claims, founded in the theory of co-design supported by examples from the e-Me project, of future trends going beyond web 2.0 will be discussed.

3.   Methodology

The theoretical sources are both principles of co-design together with what is claimed to be constituents of web 2.0 [5, 22]. Empirical sources are both reports upon contemporary efforts [10, 20] and with experiences from the e-Me project [2, 3, 15]. The e-Me project is to regard as design-oriented action research [16] in which researchers have been collaborating with businesses and organisations as well as end-users in creating new knowledge. Such dynamic interplay between these actors and processes constitutes the core of the co-design knowledge creation process [12]. The result of the work is a new type of infrastructure supporting an ongoing co-design of new citizen centric services.

4.   The Foundations of Co-Design

Co-design is to a high degree inspired by Churchman and his late postmodern writings [7]. The basic fundament can be described as a social constructive pragmatism where it is possible to design an infinite numbers of views of reality. They may differ in their granularity (level of detail), their level of abstraction, and so on. Every such view opens for actions and possibilities in specific directions. People affected by such actions are regarded as stakeholders. A view of a university focusing healthy living opens for possibilities for healthy living students and so on. In that way all views are corresponding to values and interests of different groups of people. As an example a university view showing night life will attract a different group of stakeholders/students compared to the healthy living view. Important is that these groups of people and their values are in a state of continuous change. It is also stated in this theory that quality of information and services is related to stakeholder satisfaction. A university with information about healthy living is of good quality from the point of view of healthiness interested students. This also implies the need for, in this case the university, to decide what type of "ideal" student life they want to support. An effective technique to strengthen the co-design process in this sense is to use short co-design scenarios. In such scenarios we can follow the student in a future ideal episode of importance in the students' life.

To be able to design a good e-Me the students have to reflect and decide what life they want to live as students. When they have an idea about that then they can implement that view into their e-Me mentality. That mentality is part of a general framework where e-me mentalities can be embedded.   In Churchman's terms the co-design of this general framework is the same as to "calibrate" the viewing instrument. This necessity to agree upon some common design for a system has also been put attention on by other scholars [18]. This collective, or individual, process of challenging existing views, designing new views and choosing the best one for re-implementation is called co-design. It has shaped the way we look at knowledge in general and information systems in particular [1, 4, 19].

5.   The Concept of e-Me – Towards an Artefact Enabling Peoples Co-Design of New Services

The e-Me is a (personal) electronic assistant that helps people in organizing their life [2, 3, 15]. So far the e-Me has been explored as a filter and an agent for students. In the student situation this means both in their professional development and in their existence in collaborative environments. This involves, for students, activities such as organizing the course schedule, buying or lending course books, planning public transport, managing study progress, and so on. Today students have to go to a number of places, both physically and virtually, to accomplish that. e-Me will turn that process around. The vision is that the students should not need to go to the information; the information rather comes to the students based on the active profile or e-me mentality set by the student.

Today students, as many other groups of citizens, are offered, indeed required to use, a rapidly increasing number of e-Services. They range from school and course sites to interactions with authorities as well as companies offering student discounts. This forces students to remember a multitude of user IDs, passwords and login procedures. On top of this students are often provided with special email accounts for courses and educations. Many students have four or more different email addresses. Consequently a lot of time is spent on logging on to different mail systems, trying to find passwords and links to various sites. On top of this they also need to organize their life in establishing their identity in collaborative settings. These types of problems are not only restricted to students, but as they are an experienced group of citizens they are the first group of citizens involved.

The e-Me will act both as an agent for individuals and as a filter in the information galaxy. It takes as its starting point the individual and his/her life situation, instead of the organization which is providing services to the individual. An important part of the vision is that the e-Me should evolve over time with input from different stakeholders.

The core of the e-Me consists at the moment of the following components:

- Calendar management, in which the user's calendar can be shared with other e-Me users' calendars.

- Mood management, in which it possible to set and manage in which mood the e-Me user is. Three possible moods have been implemented so far; private, meeting and open. The mood is the individual's desire in its relation to the environment.

- Mail aggregation, in which mail can be popped from different sources and distributed to the user dependent on the mood that is set.

- Contact Management, in which contacts can be grouped into different categories and a status of the contact, can be set in relation to the possible moods.

- Archives, in which files (of different types) can be stored and shared with others.

- Assignment, in which the user manages all tasks assigned to the e-Me. In the pilot version four assignments has been implemented. These are the possibility for e-Me to receive study results, get the schedule into the calendar, receive this weeks lunch menu, as well as matching desires and needs of offers from organizations with students discounts.

- Community, where the stakeholders; users, developers, e-Me project management and service providers can discuss the e-Me, suggest improvements/additional services and share experiences.

In the first pilot study (the phase of proof-of-concept) 120 students became a part of the e-Me project as co-designers [15]. The students co-designed e-Me by writing ideal scenarios. They also tried out the prototype – both in order to identify shortcomings in the application and identify new usage situations, both within and beyond the school setting, when an e-Me would be of assistance. To make this possible a particular (virtual) community space was created as part of e-Me. In this space interaction between different stakeholders, such as the project management, researchers, designers, service providers, programming team, and students as users took place. The goal was to create an on-going and lasting co-design between the various stakeholders in order to create new possible views to be implemented in the concept of an electronic assistant.

During the test period of 3.5 months, the project implemented several refinements. To stimulate continuous interest among the students for being part of the project we used several different mechanisms, such as meetings, workshops, media exposure, continuous updates of the e-Me, and role-plays. The results of the pilot also did show that it was a big range of interests among the students. Some students had very limited ideas of what the e-Me could do to help them while other students had developed ideas on how the e-me could be their bodyguard on the internet. During this process it was clear that the electronic assistant metaphor stimulated ideas about future design options. In the conceptual development it was identified that students, in Sweden and Spain, of today have two important qualities; they are professional and collaborative [2]. This lies well in line with MeWe-generation [17]. This generation is constituted by individualists but no "hardcore" egoists since they put value in friends and collective solutions.

Using the assistant metaphor it would be possible to say that different students could imagine different mentalities of their e-Me assistant. That is also to say that in Forsgren's terms they wanted to implement different views of the reality. In Forsgren [9] this process is described in more detail as co-design where a specific view is co-designed and implemented as solutions in products and services. In the virtual co-design platform they could get inspiration from each other, both in the sense of finding new usage situations and in the sense of helping each other in finding different usage situations when the e-Me would be of value, as well as they could stimulate the development of the general framework.

In that way, a high degree of participation in the co-production of the content, has been an important driver in the design, development, and evaluation of the e-Me artifact as well as in the requirements on the e-Me as an artifact. e-Me, as a personal electronic assistant, should enable users, by its connectivity, to co-produce content and services.

From a Web 2.0 point of view the e-Me pilot as it is now still miss a number of collaborative dimensions to be explored. A deeper investigation, covered in the next section, into the web 2.0 will make that clear.

6.   Contemporary Developments in the ICT-Field

Web 2.0 is to be seen as a reaction against Web 1.0 with static homepages consisting of information meant to be spread to others. Before entering the Web 2.0 world the development towards higher degree of possibilities to interact with organisation-centric web sites became a reality. The 1.0 world has resulted in billions of web sites as part of an increasing information overflow. This has been identified as the electronic service paradox in the sense that there are simply too many sites, services, and communication, but still there are things people cannot do electronically [3]. Key characteristics of Web 2.0 as a collection of trends in Internet development that go beyond the traditional site-html-browser structure are [5, 22]:

- Rich Internet Applications ("Web as Platform"), which is driven from mobility problems created due to locally stored data. These problems have created a need for store data remotely and access the data through applications in different devices.
- User-generated content ("Open Content"), which is driven from the idea that authors generating contents, are of less quality than the co-design of the content from all "readers". The solution is to let users "co-design" the content.
- Semantic Web driven from the problem of that content is categorised using algorithms instead of its semantic meaning. The solution is to let the user categorise or co-design the categorising framework.
- Recommendations driven from the problem of others (than the users) are judging the value of the services. The recommendation is to let users tip each other.
- Social Networking driven from users wanting to find others with similar attributes. The recommendation is to let users to come into contact with each others networks.
- Syndication/mash ups driven from the problem that information is owned by organisations and not distributed to others. The recommendation is let the content become "official" and in that way make it possible for services building on "integration" of information from several sources.
- Open Standards as a consequence of the point before where different systems have problems in interact due to problems of interpretation of different formats. Open standards should be used instead.
- Software as a service ("Light-weight Business Models") driven from the inflexibility resolved in letting users buying licenses for a static product. Other forms, such as subscription, are recommended as an alternative.
- Personalization as a reaction against that systems are not adapted to the desires of the individual. Personal profiles should be stored and continuously adapted based on the behaviour of the user.

- User-generated Services which is a reaction against that most services are built by information providers. The recommendation is to give users a platform for building services for themselves and for others.
- Device Independence, which is driven from the fact that data is only possible to access for certain devices. The recommendation is to develop and use standardised techniques for overcome this problem.

In the table below we put these characteristics in relation to the evolving e-Me artifact as it stands for now.

Table 1: Web 2.0 Characteristics and its Resonance in the e-Me Galaxy

Web 2.0 characteristic	Resonance in the e-Me galaxy
Rich Internet Applications	Data is stored remote and possible to access remotely
User-generated content	The use of archive as a shared area for e-Me users. A more structured approach to this will further explored in coming pilots. The community site, built on share point server, let the users generate content jointly about experiences and desires of e-Me.
Semantic Web	Not implemented yet, but the archive could be developed in this directions. All users have the possibility to include new categories on the community. Some stakeholder groups have the possibility to define higher-level categories.
Recommendations	Some parts of it is implemented through the community by users interacting with each other in recommending services and sharing experiences.
Social Networking	e-Me:s could connect to each other. The scenarios do however not yet show the need for letting the networks of one person's be connected to others (c.f. e.g. LinkedIn).
Syndication/mash ups	A strong design parameter for the design of e-Me has been to stress the question of integration of information aimed for different purposes.
Open Standards	In the next pilot protocols for enabling different services to become part of the e-Me eco system.
Software as a service	In the next pilot the business model for the e-Me galaxy will be further explored.
Personalization	e-Me would let the user make their own settings in regards to e.g. mood, preferred assignments (such as desired offers), calendar, contacts etc.
User-generated Services	Due to that protocols become standardised this will let the user build his/her own services to be deployed in the e-Me galaxy.
Device Independence	e-Me could be accessed from different devices; computer connected to Internet and the mobile phone as the remote control to the e-Me galaxy.

As can be derived from the table there are a number of collaborative potentials in the e-Me for letting people through their use of e-Me's interacting with each other. So far, the community space has this role. This community space does however have a stronger resonance related to the development process. Some initial parts of the e-Me as an artefact have the potential in being developed towards a stronger support in future collaboration.

7.   Implications: What is There to be Seen Next?

In the co-design theory it is stipulated that the overall quality of services will increase if as many as possible of the stakeholders are active involved in co-producing the service. Web 2.0 is mainly a set of techniques making it possible for stakeholders to be involved and to build on results produced by others. In that sense the e-Me pilot, with its community, as it stands now is an example of a web 2.0 artefact.

In the e-Me case both groups of students and individual students are designing their view to be implemented as a mentality in their virtual e-Me assistant. It can be identified that they learn from each other in their discussion about the ideal e-Me. Taking that into account it would be possible to create a library or an arena for exchange of possible e-Me mentalities to download and try out as a learning experience.

Another important discussion and development can be expected in correlation to the e-Me mentality framework. The key question is going to be responsibility and trust. In the university case, should a specific university allow an e-Me framework that makes it possible for students to connect to other competing universities? Who is responsible if a student are designing and using an e-me mentality designed to harm other peoples e-Me? Is that the student or the owner of the e-Me framework? Of course we already have these questions all the way from the birth of the technology itself. The difference is that these earlier "philosophical questions" now become practical concerns.

Related to the question of responsibility is the even bigger question of "world order". A further developed web 2.0 applications as well as a co-design application is challenging the classical borders between public and private in one service as well as it is challenging the classical border between science and politics. One consideration in the same area is whether there should exist a court in the e-Me galaxy governed by the clients (students)

The e-Me service accepts integration of both private financed and public financed services. Maybe new forms of combined financing will be best suited for survival? In a similar way an e-Me mentality designed for selecting the best area to live in will be both scientific in its models but also highly political in its impact. This example also gives a hint to a new future co-design oriented science where the creation of knowledge is regarded as a process of co-design.

Finally we have the co-design communities. They opens for companies to use students as important co-designers of their own services as well as they open for students to be active in real systems development. The border between education and practice is not so easy to see any longer.

8.   Conclusions and Summary Recommendations

Given the foundations of co-design the development towards e-empowerment of clients is a central point. An interesting observation though is whether we have reached far enough. When putting the co-design oriented thinking into application a number of other complimentary trends could be identified. All of them are challenging old classical borders.

The recommendation is obvious: Be open-minded - a fundamental change of old classical beliefs and assumptions are under way. New classification borders are going to be developed in line with the co-design thinking where web 2.0 can be viewed as a first step.

Another important conclusion is the necessity for going beyond the web site as a design metaphor for e-empowering clients. Potentially e-Me as a device-independent platform for e-empowerment distributing user generated e-services in a public-private partnership business model would be an alternative design metaphor. This platform is also a starting enabler for people to exist in a collaborative world without any "real borders" for joint creation of the future. By letting several views of reality be "collided" with each other in co-design processes, by the support of virtual platforms, different desires and roles will evolve. People and organizations acting as clients in this galaxy will individually and jointly form their desires, judgments, and recommendations of what is good and bad. People and organizations acting as service providers in this galaxy will have a chance to contribute with services that the clients actually desire. Due to an increased globalization and development of infrastructure in diverse corners of the world such platforms, as e-Me is an example of, will be an enabler for people to be included in the information galaxy in a preserved way.

References

[1] Ackoff, R. L. (1981). Creating the corporate future. New York: Wiley.
[2] Albinsson L., Forsgren O., Lind M. (2006a). e-Me Stories & Scenarios - The Ideal Electronic Galaxy of the Student, University College of Borås, Sweden
[3] Albinsson, L., Forsgren O., Lind M., Ozan, H. (2006b). Turning the Internet Around – e-Me: The Students ideal e-Service. eChallenges 2006, Barcelona, Spain.
[4] Checkland, P. B. (1988). Soft systems methodology: An overview. J. of Applied Systems Analysis, 15, 27-30.
[5] Christopher L. C. (2007) Understanding Web 2.0, The Seybold Report, Vol 7. (11)
[6] Churchman, C. W. (1968). The Systems Approach. New York: Dell Publishing.
[7] Churchman, C. W. (1979). The systems approach and its enemies. New York, Basic Books
[8] Forsgren O., (1988) Samskapande Datortillämpningar: En systemteoretisk ansats för för lösning av vissa förändringsproblem vid administrativ datoranvändning, (Doctoral thesis), Umeå universitet.
[9] Forsgren O. (1991) Co-constructive computer applications: Core ideas and some compleme§ntary strategies in the development of a humanistic computer science. In: Bazewicz M (ed.) Information systems architecture and technologies - ISAT'91. Politechnika Wroclawska, Wroclaw, pp 45-53.
[10] Forsgren O., Hultén A., Lind M., Salomonson N., Sundström M. (2007) Experiences from setting up an Internet Shopping Collaboratory, eChallenges e-2007, The Hague, The Netherlands
[11] Goldkuhl G. (2006) Collaborative researching - from ISAC to VITS through HUMOR, in Bubenko J et al (eds, 2006) ICT for people. 40 years of academic development in Stockholm, DSV, Stocholm University
[12] Grönlund Å (2000). Managing electronic services: A Public Service Perspective, Springer, London
[13] Hevner A. R., March S. T., Park J., Ram S. (2004) Design Science in Information Systems Research, MIS Quarterly, Vol 28(1), pp. 75-105
[14] Langefors B (1966) Theoretical analysis of information systems, Studentlitteratur, Lund
[15] Lind M., Albinsson L., Forsgren O., Hedman J. (2007) Integrated Development, Use and Learning in a Co-design Setting: Experiences from the Incremental Deployment of e-Me, eChallenges e-2007, The Hague, The Netherlands
[16] Lindgren R., Henfridsson O., Schultze U. (2004) Design Principles for Competence Management Systems: A Synthesis of An Action Research Study, MIS Quarterly, Vol. 28 (3), pp. 435-472
[17] Lindgren M., Lüthi B., Fürth T. (2005) The MeWe Generation – What business and politics must know about the next generation, Fälth & Hässler, Värnamo
[18] Liu K, Sun L and Bennett K (2002) Co-Design of Business and IT Systems. Information Systems Frontiers 4(3), 251-256
[19] Mitroff, I. I., & Mason, R. O. (1981). Creating a dialectical social science. Dordrecht: Reidel.
[20] Mulholland, A., C. Thomas, et al. (2006). Mashup corporations - the end of business as usual. New York, Evolved technologist press
[21] Mumford, E. (1983). Designing human systems, the ETHICS approach. Manchester Business School, Manchester, UK
[22] O'Reilly T. (2005) What Is Web 2.0 - Design Patterns and Business Models for the Next Generation of Software, Available at http://www.oreillynet.com/pub/a/oreilly/tim/news/2005/09/30/what-is-web-20.html
[23] Wikipedia (2008) http://en.wikipedia.org/wiki/Web_2.0

Collaboration and the Knowledge Economy: Issues, Applications, Case Studies
P. Cunningham and M. Cunningham (Eds.)
IOS Press, 2008

Defining Efficient Business Models for Grid-enabled Applications

Katarina STANOEVSKA[1], Davide Maria PARRILLI[2], George THANOS[3]

[1] *Mcm Institute, University St. Gallen, Blumenbergplatz 9, St. Gallen, 9000, Switzerland*
Tel: +41 71 2242793, Fax: + 41 71 2242771, Email: Katarina.Stanoevska@unisg.ch
[2] *Interdisciplinary Centre for Law and ICT, ICRI-K.U.Leuven-IBBT, Sint-Michielsstraat 6,*
Leuven, 3000, Belgium
Tel: +32 16 320787, Fax: + 32 16 325438, Email: davide.parrilli@law.kuleuven.be
[3] *Network Economics and Services Group, Athens University of Business and Economics,*
76 Patission Str. Athens, 11362, Greece
Tel: +30 210 8203693, Fax: +30 210 8203686, Email: gthanos@aueb.gr

Abstract: Driven by the increasing demand, Grid technology is entering the business market in form of utility computing, Grid middleware and Grid-enabled applications. However, the business market is interested in complete Grid solutions. Thus, a successful take up of Grid technology on the business market requires the establishment of Grid value networks. This again can only be achieved by implementation of sound business models for each player providing part of a Grid solution. This paper discusses the business models of providers of Grid-enabled applications.

Keywords: Grid Business Models, Business Grids, Grid-enabled Application

1 Introduction

Newest market research studies report a growing awareness for the potential of Grid technology by industry and increased interest for utility computing and Grid solutions for business application. This trend has been enforced in particular by well-established Internet companies, for example WebEx, Amazon, AOL, who offer their services in form of utility computing [1]. Other players driving utility computing are the telecommunication companies such as T-Systems in Germany. A growing interest for Grid computing can also be observed with Independent Software Vendors (ISV) [1]. This is mostly evident in vertical markets with strong Grid interest for applications that are suitable for Grid (for example data mining).

Driven by the growing interest and demand on the market, Grid technology is entering a new level of maturity and is offered on the business market in three forms [3]: 1) as open source or packaged Grid middleware; 2) as utility computing, that is as hardware and software infrastructure provided according to the Software as a Service (SaaS) paradigm, and 3) in the form of Grid-enabled applications. However, business customers are interested in complete Grid solutions. This means that for a successful take up of Grid technology on the business market the establishment of Grid value networks [15] is required that will be able to provide complete solutions and a critical mass of offerings on all levels of the value network. This again can only be achieved by implementation of sound business models for each player providing part of a Grid solution. While there is a growing body of literature on business models or specific components of them for the utility computing market [3], [15], there is less consideration of business models from the perspective of the providers of Grid applications. This paper provides a contribution in this context and discusses the main aspects of business models of ISV evolving their products from pre-packaged applications towards Grid-enabled application.

The content of the paper is structured as follows: Section 2 provides an overview of state-of-the-art research related to grid-enabled application and the research approach. Section 3 provides an analysis of business models of pilot applications developed as part of the BEinGRID project and their challenges and obstacles driven from those. Section 4 provides a set of guidelines and considerations for the development of business Models for the provision of Grid-Enabled Applications. Finally, Section 5 concludes the paper with a summary and outlook.

2   State-of-the-art and Research Approach

The term "Grid-enabled application" is used in this research paper to denote a software application that has been offered on the market as pre-packaged software and that is being extended in a way that it can run in a distributed manner in a Grid environment. To Grid-enable a pre-packaged software product therefore means that a previously pre-packaged centralized application is enabled or modified to run either on a distributed Grid infrastructure or to be offered as an online service based on the Software as a Service paradigm (SaaS) (see also [4]).

At the first glance the business models of ISVs offering Grid-enabled applications seem similar to the well-known business models of Application Service Providers (ASPs). However, there is a significant difference. The core competence of the ISP is the development of the application itself and not its distribution. On the contrary, the core competence of the ASP is the online provision of applications that are mostly developed by other ISV. Despite of the difference regarding their business models, key learning's from the experiences with the ASP business model can be applied during the development of business models for Grid-enabled applications. Even though ASP was foreseen to be successful, it did not take up on the market and its adoption has been very slow [7]. The main reasons for the failure have been: the inability of early ASPs to produce customized services, the centralized approach for computing, which requires the sending of input and output data and the general lack of trust in the ASP paradigm [6], [7], [9].

At present, the business models for the provision of Grid-enabled applications and ASPs are converging. The convergence of web services and Grid computing technologies is expected to solve current ASP delivery problems [6], [9].

There is a considerable body of literature related to components of business models as well. The definitions range from very broad ones (see for example the definitions proposed by [10] or [11]) to very specific ones (see for example [12] or [13]). While such definitions try to delimit the scope of the meaning of the concept business models, they do not provide insights into components of business models in such a way that it can be used for assessing the activities of a company in more detail. A more concrete definition is the definition of Timmers [14]. According to Timmers, a business model is "...*an architecture for the products, services and information flows, including a description of various business actors and their roles, a description of the potential benefits for the various business actor, and a description of the sources of revenues.*" [14]. Our study of business models for the Grid sector has been performed following this definition i.e. the analysis of all these components and the interactions among them.

To be more precise, for the purpose of our study the business models of technology and application providers were analyzed based on case studies of Grid pilots from the BEinGRID project (www.beingrid.eu – www.gridipedia.eu), an Integrated Project (IP) funded by the European commission under FP6. One of the main objectives of the project is to evaluate the applicability of Grid technology in business through Grid business experiments. In the heart of the project there are 18 business experiments that are piloting Grid technology in various key industrial sectors.

In this paper the business models of the BEinGRID real-life pilots focusing on Grid-enabling applications were analyzed. The findings of the analysis were aggregated to a generic business model for providers of Grid-enabled application. The resulting business model can be applied by providers of Grid-enabled applications as a checklist for developing successful business models.

3 The Business Models for Grid-Enabled Applications in the BEinGRID Project: Challenges and Obstacles

Based on the results of our investigation and cross-analysis of the BEinGRID business experiments, out of the 18 pilots six are aiming towards business models for providing Grid-enabled applications:

- Business experiment (BE) BE16 has developed a Grid-enabled extension of an existing application for ship design and simulation so that it can be offered in cooperation with an infrastructure provider in a SaaS manner.
- BE18 Grid-enabled an existing application for processing of seismic data and plans to offer the service over the Internet in particular to small and medium size enterprises.
- BE07 Grid-enabled an existing application for generation of global aerosol maps using information coming from different satellite sensors.
- BE03 has Grid-enabled an application for 3D rendering and animation.
- BE12 and BE17 are Grid-enabling existing application for supply chain management.

The in-depth analysis of the business models of the above BEs has revealed several advantages and obstacles that need to be considered during the design of the business model. The main advantages are: From the perspective of the ISV the enhancement of an existing application clearly provides a valuable extension of the existing application portfolio. In addition to that, most of the above BEs can achieve a broad competitive advantage, as most of them can leverage a first-mover advantage. In particular for the small ISV (BE12 and BE17) to Grid-enable their application provides a clear competitive advantage and also a needed precondition to stay on the market. To offer the Grid-enabled version of the application also results in an image gain for the companies. For most of the companies the Grid-enabled version of the application is applied to approach a new category of target customers - small and medium size companies.

The main obstacles that need to be overcome are the following: At present all providers of Grid-enabled applications need to establish sound business relationships with utility computing providers, in order to be able to offer a complete solution. This means that the establishment of the whole value chain is necessary. Another major obstacle is the fear of cannibalization effects for the existing centralized application. As the described applications demonstrate, the applications that are being Grid-enabled are those that are needed by the customer companies occasionally. This means that by taking advantage of the SaaS scenario, the customers might try to optimize the usage and pay less than for the licenses for the centralized application. Thus, the existing licensing strategies involving in general a fixed license fee and a variable license fee per user or per CPU needs to be transferred in pay-per-use pricing model that on the one hand meets the expectation of the customers that SaaS should imply lower prices and at the same time enable the ISV to justify the financial risk and sunk costs for development of the application and making it available.

The above findings have been considered for the development of generic business models presented below.

4   Guidelines and Considerations for the Development of Business Models for the provision of Grid-Enabled Applications

Based on the findings from the case studies, general guidelines for the development of the business models were developed. Considering the above obstacles the main emphasis in this paper was on the following components of the business model: design of the product, pricing and legal aspects. The findings are explained in more detail in the sections below.

4.1   Design of the product and licensing

The design of the Grid-enabled application needs to address in particular the cannibalization problem. A careful strategy is necessary, in order to keep existing customers that do not want or cannot use the Grid-enabled application and to meet the requirements of new customers (see also [16]). An important question is: Are different versions for different customer segments and licensing strategies possible and in which form? The problem can be illustrated on the following example:

One ISV offers an application with a given set of functions to the market. A Grid-enabled version of the application is also developed. However, not all of the existing customers have a Grid infrastructure and cannot apply the new functionality. They would like to stay with the centralized version of the application. A small number of the customers already owns a Grid infrastructure and would like to take advantage of the new functionality. These are also the customers that have a high volume of transaction and would also be willing to pay more for the enhanced application. The ISV gets furthermore requests by smaller companies for an occasional use of the application based on the SaaS paradigm. After a certain time a cooperation with a Grid infrastructure provider is agreed upon and the application is also available on a SaaS basis.

The question now is how the different categories of the products should be defined and which licensing and pricing strategy should be defined? A low price for the SaaS application might result in the effect that existing customers of the centralized application - in particular those that use the application occasionally - switch to the SaaS application and save on the licensing costs for the central version of the application. In order to avoid such effects, a carefully designed packaging of the functionality of the different versions of the application together with the licensing and pricing strategy is necessary. The different options regarding versioning of the products are discussed below.

- **Versioning option 1:** Offering the application in the form of pre-packaged software with and without Grid enhancement and without SaaS option (c.f. 2):

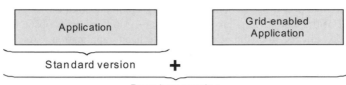

Figure 1: Standard and premium version of a Grid-enabled application sold as commercial product

The versioning example given in Figure 1 enables to keep the existing customer base and the established licensing models for the existing application and provide a premium version for customers that have an own Grid infrastructure. This versioning option provides the opportunity to keep the licensing strategies (for example per user or CPU) and request different prices for the two different versions, to target customers with different needs as well as for additional revenues as the Grid-enabled application, i.e. version can be offered with licenses involving higher prices for it.

- **Versioning option 2:** In case the application is available as a centralized application, Grid-enabled application and SaaS, several different options for versioning and packaging are possible. One possible example is given in figure 2 below.

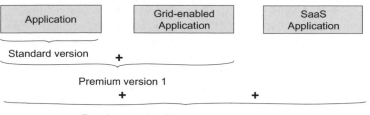

Figure 2: Example of versioning strategies based on three product categories

As in versioning option 1 there might be a standard and a premium version if it is bought by the customer together with the Grid enhancement. The question here is how the SaaS version can be included in a way that it might be suitable to also attract new customers, for example SMEs that cannot afford the premium 1 version, but at the same time not provoke a massive switch from the lucrative licenses for the central pre-packaged application by existing customers. One option is that customers opting for the premium version 1 can add also access to the SaaS version and pay additionally per use, if in addition to their own Grid they use also the SaaS. A similar option might be available for the customers with the standard version of the application. The question is how to differentiate the SaaS version and to prevent cannibalisation of the centralised pre-packaged application. Depending on the target customers, one possibility would be to differentiate the pre-packaged application and the grid enabled application offered as SaaS based on the functionality. For example, if the target customers for the SaaS Grid-enabled application are SMEs than one possibility would be to limit the functionality of the SaaS version or to differentiate a "light" version with respect to the output options or other functionality that are available. For example, an SME that wants the functionality as SaaS might get the output data only in a basic format, while premium customers of the pre-packaged version get it with an option to create different formats. Similar differentiation of the quality of the service can be made also based on other features of the product and service (see also [16]).

How exactly the existing functionality can be packaged in the three product categories and which versions are possible depends on the modularity of the software, the existing customer base, the target customers and the potential for segmentation of the customers depending on their willingness to pay and their specific needs. A good knowledge of the usage patterns of customers as well as their willingness to pay is therefore a clear advantage in determining the right versioning and pricing strategy.

4.2 The Price Strategies of the BEinGRID Business Experiments

The pricing strategy involves two components: the pricing model and the definition of the prices. The major general pricing models for Grid enabled applications are the Pay-per-use pricing models. Thereby, in general the price includes two components: a price per use for the utility computing and a price per use for the Grid-enabled application. A benchmark for pricing the first component of the pricing model might be the published price of SUN of 1$/hour computing resources or the pricing strategy of Amazon: 0.20$ per GB stored or to hire a complete virtual PC for $0.10 per hour. The second pricing component, i.e. the pay-per-use price for the Grid-enabled application includes also the license. Towards the customer this pricing model is either expresses as a single all-in-one price or as a price consisting of two components.

The definition of concrete pricing depends on the specific product. In case where different versions of the product are involved, pricing should not affect the product strategies. For example: BE01 found during the competitive analysis that a license for computational fluid dynamics software can vary from £10'000 to £15'000 per single CPU license and go up to £100'000 for 64 CPUs. In case such an application is Grid-enabled, the question is what the right price might be. Several aspects need to be considered: The typical usage patterns of an average customer, the market prices for similar services and the costs of the provider. For example let's assume that in case of SaaS the same number of CPUs is used. How can the license per CPU be expressed per hour of usage? If a price that is too low is chosen then the ISV does not have interest to provide the application as SaaS as he will lose revenue. In case data about the usage patterns of customers are available the actual average usage per year could be transformed in a price. For example, the provider knows that an average customer is using the application 50% of a person's yearly working time per user. This would mean that the application is used by a typical user for 840 working hours (assuming a yearly total of working hours of 1680). Thus, in order to get the same revenue from the user based on a SaaS version of the application a price of £12 per hour for the application would be required (assuming a basic license of £10'000 for a single CPU) in addition to the pay per use price for the computing infrastructure on which the application runs. In a similar way based on average usage patterns and total number of users a potential price might be calculated.

4.3   Legal Aspects

The analysis of the project's cases shows that in addition to business aspects, major legal issues have to be addressed as well [18].

It is pivotal to address, as starting point, what is, in legal terms, the agreement that encompasses the provision of SaaS. This, of course, depends on the applicable national legal framework but, in general it means to set up an ASP contract. The provision of SaaS implies that there is no physical item delivered to the end user and that, unlike in the contract between a customer and a software house for the writing of a specific computer programme, the software provider keeps the ownership of the application. In case of due diligence, for instance, this element has to be taken into account, as the software can be considered as an asset (and not a liability) of the targeted company only if this undertaking has the ownership of the software.

The service provider will limit as much as possible the rights of the client, which could use the SaaS only during its ordinary course of business, thus he will be liable for breach of contract if, in practice, he sublicenses the supplier's applications. It is pivotal to say that the parties, by virtue of their contractual freedom, would have the possibility to adapt the above clause to their exigencies. As regards the code provided to the client, in a typical SaaS scenario the object of the contract will concern the object code and not the source code.

The contractual freedom of the parties plays a fundamental role also as regards confidentiality obligations. This issue is particularly complex and the experience gained shows that the relative clause should address at least the following issues:

*   Extension of the confidentiality obligations of the supplier and the client as regards, basically and respectively, the data of the customer and the executable code of the software;
*   Duties of the parties;
*   Contractual and Court remedies, taking into account that the latter are heavily influenced by the applicable national legal framework;
*   Exceptions to the rule, i.e. situations in which there are no confidentiality obligations.

We have developed the following template that encompasses the abovementioned elements and that is suitable to be adopted in case of SaaS in a Grid environment: "Customer shall not sell, transfer, publish, disclose, display or otherwise make available any portion of the executable code of the Application to others. Client agrees to secure and protect the Application and the Service in a manner consistent with the maintenance of Supplier's rights therein and to take appropriate action by instruction or agreement with its users to satisfy its obligations hereunder. Client shall use its best efforts to assist Supplier in identifying and preventing any unauthorised access, use, copying or disclosure of the Application or the Service, or any component thereof, or any of the algorithms or logic contained therein. Without limitation of the foregoing, Client shall advise Supplier immediately in the event Client learns or has reason to believe that any person to whom Client has given access to the Service has violated or intends to violate the confidentiality of the executable code of the Application or the proprietary rights of Supplier, and Client will, at Client's expense, cooperate with Supplier in seeking injunctive or other equitable relief in the name of Client and Supplier against any such person.

Client agrees to maintain the confidentiality of the executable code of the Application using at least as great a degree of care as Client uses to maintain the confidentiality of Client's own confidential information (and in no event less than a reasonable degree of care). Client acknowledges that the disclosure of any aspect of the executable code of the Application, including the documentation or any other confidential information referred to herein, or any information which ought to remain confidential, will immediately give rise to continuing irreparable injury to Supplier inadequately compensable in damages at law, and Supplier is entitled to seek and obtain immediate injunctive relief against the breach or threatened breach of any of the foregoing confidentiality undertakings, in addition to any other legal remedies which may be available. In addition, Supplier may immediately terminate this Agreement, including all license rights granted herein, in the event Client breaches any of its confidentiality obligations regarding the Application or the Service.

Furthermore, Supplier agrees that it shall not disclose to any third party or use any information proprietary to Client including information concerning the Client and the users, trade secrets, methods, processes or procedures or any other confidential information of the other party which it learns during the course of its performance of the Service, except for purposes related to Supplier's rendering of the Service to Client under this Agreement or as required by law, regulation, or order of a court or regulatory agency or other authority having jurisdiction there over. In addition, Client may immediately terminate this Agreement in the event Supplier breaches any of its confidentiality obligations set forth herein. Notwithstanding the foregoing, the confidentiality obligations set forth in this Article will not apply to any information which the recipient party can establish to have: (i) become publicly available without breach of this Agreement; (ii) been independently developed by the recipient party outside the scope of this Agreement and without reference to the confidential information received under this Agreement; or (iii) been rightfully obtained by the recipient party from third parties which are not obligated to protect its confidentiality."

5   Conclusions and Further Work

The goal of the paper was the discussion and development of efficient business models for the providers of Grid-enabled applications. Based on five in-depth case studies first major advantages and obstacles for developing business models for Grid-enabled application were identified. Then, general guidelines for the design of the product, the pricing strategy and the legal issues related to provisioning applications in a SaaS manner have been developed. The core consideration has been the avoidance of cannibalization effects of Grid-enabled application offered based on the SaaS paradigm with pre-packaged applications. ISV opting to extend their product portfolio with a Grid-enabled version of their application need to carefully version and price their applications depending on the target customers, existing customers and their needs as well as knowledge about the usage pattern of the applications. Finding the right licensing and pricing model is a major prerequisite for developing successful business models for Grid-enabled application.

Acknowledgement

The research presented in this paper was part of the project BEinGRID (034702), which is supported by the European Commission in the sixth Framework Program.

References

[1]   The 451 Group, Grid computing preview, Section 7.2 (p. 83-89) in Review/Preview 2006-2007, The 451 Group, 2007.
[2]   MomentumSI, Implementing a Successful Service-Oriented Architecture (SOA) Pilot Program, Actional Corporation, 2005.
[3]   Forge, S., Blackmann, C.: Commercial Exploitation of Grid Technologies and Services - Drivers and barriers, Business Models and Impacts of Using Free and Open Source Licensing Schemas. Final Report of the European Study No. 30-CE-065970 /00-56.
[4]   Snjeepan, V.; Matsunaga, A.; Zhu, L.; Lam, H.; Fortes, J.A.B.: A Service-Oriented, Scalable Approach to Grid-Enabling of Legacy Scientific Application. In: Proceedings of the IEEE International Conference on Web Services (ICWS'05), 2005.
[5]   Heart, T; Pliskin, N.: Is e-commerce of IT application services alive and well? Journal of Information Technology Theory and Application, 3(4), pp. 33-41.
[6]   Xu, Huinan; Seltsikas, Ph.; Evolving the ASP Business Model: Web Service Provision in the Grid Era. In: Proceedings of the Second Intzernational Conference on Peer-to-Peer Computing, 2002.
[7]   Desai, B.; Currie, W.: Application Service Providers: A Model in Evolution. In Proceedings of the ICES 2003, Pittsburgg, 2003.
[8]   Stanoevska-Slabeva, K.; Talamanca, C.F; Thanos G; Zsigri C.: Development of a generic value chain for the Grid industry. In: Proceedings of the GeCON'07 Workshop, 2007.
[9]   Mittilä, T.; Lehtinen, K.: Customizing the Application Service Provider Offering. Available online: http://www.ebrc.fi/kuvat/1066.pdf, 2005.
[10]   Rappa, M.: Managing the Digital Enterprise. Available online: http://digitalenterprise.org/index.html, (2005).
[11]   Afuah, A; Tucci, Ch. L.: Internet Business Models and Strategies. McGraw-Hill, New York, 2001.
[12]   Osterwalder A. (2004): The Business Model Ontology. Ph.D. Thesis at the HEC Lausanne.
[13]   Staehli, Patrick, 2002, Geschätsmodelle in der digitalen Ökonomie. Josef Eul Verlag, Lohmar, Köln, 2002.
[14]   Timmers, P (1998): Business Models for Electronic Markets; In: International Journal on Electronic Markets and Business Media, Vo.8 No. 2, 1998. pp. 3-8.
[15]   Hoegg, Roman and Stanoevska-Slabeva, Katarina, 2005, Towards Guidelines for the Design of Mobile Services. In Proceedings of the ECIS 2005 conference, June, 2005.
[16]   Shapiro, C; Varian, Hall, RV.: Information Rules - A Strategic Guide to the Networked Economy. Harvard Business School Press, Boston Massechusets, 1999.
[17]   Tapscott, D.; Ticoll, D.; Lowy, A. Digital Capital - Harnessing the Power of Business Webs. Harvard Business School Press, 2000.
[18]   R. Raysman, P. Brown, Computer Law: Drafting and Negotiating Forms and Agreements, ISBN 9 78158852 024 1. Law Journal Press, New York, 2003.

Collaboration and the Knowledge Economy: Issues, Applications, Case Studies
P. Cunningham and M. Cunningham (Eds.)
IOS Press, 2008

Economically Enhanced Risk-aware Grid SLA Management

Karim DJEMAME[1], James PADGETT[1], Iain GOURLAY[1], Kerstin VOSS[2],
Dominic BATTRE[3], Odej KAO[3]

[1]School of Computing, University of Leeds, Leeds LS2 9JT, UK
Tel: +44 113 3436590, Fax: + 44 113 3435468,
Email: karim@comp.leeds.ac.uk, jamesp@comp.leeds.ac.uk, iain@comp.leeds.ac.uk
[2]Paderborn Center for Parallel Computing, Fürstenallee 11, 33102 Paderborn, Germany
Tel: +49 5251 60-6321, Fax: +49 5251 60-6297, Email: kerstinv@upb.de
[3]Technische Universität Berlin, Department of Telecommunication Systems, Einsteinufer
17, 10587 Berlin, Germany, Tel: +49 30 31424230/21988, Fax: +49 30 31421060
Email: Dominic.Battre@tu-berlin.de, Odej.Kao@tu-berlin.de

Abstract: Grid computing has emerged as a global infrastructure for the next generation of e-Science and commercial applications. This paper reports on recent results on risk-awareness integration in the EU funded project AssessGrid (Advanced Risk Assessment and Management for Trustable Grids) architecture as well as the potential economic issues underlying risk-aware SLA management. Specifically, it will focus on the resource provider, broker and end-user

1. Introduction

Advances in Grid computing research have in recent years resulted in considerable commercial interest in utilising Grid infrastructures to support commercial applications and services. However, significant developments in the areas of risk and dependability are necessary before widespread commercial adoption can become a reality. Specifically, risk management mechanisms need to be incorporated into Grid infrastructures, in order to move beyond the best-effort approach to service provision that current Grid infrastructures follow.

AssessGrid (Advanced Risk Assessment and Management for Trustable Grids) addresses the key issue of risk by developing a framework to support risk assessment and management for all three Grid actors (end-user, broker, and resource provider) [1,2]. To integrate risk awareness and support risk management in all Grid layers, new components are introduced: the provider benefits from access to a consultant service that provides statistical information to support both risk assessment and the identification of infrastructure bottlenecks. The broker makes use of a confidence service that provides a reliability measure of a resource provider's risk assessment, based on historical data. In addition, a workflow assessor supports the broker by providing risk assessments for entire workflows. The end-user interface is realised as a Grid portal that provides the functionality required to support the end-user in using the Grid. The end-user must be able to select whether to negotiate with a provider or with a broker.

On the other hand, AssessGrid is contributing to the establishment of commercial adoption of Grid technology by providing a framework where an end-user can specify a Service Level Agreement (SLA) and choose a provider based on quality and price given, therefore creating a market place and putting the providers in competition with each other.

This paper reports on recent results on risk-awareness integration in the AssessGrid architecture as well as the potential economic issues underlying risk-aware SLA management. Specifically, it will focus on the resource provider, broker and end-user.

2. AssessGrid

AssessGrid focuses on the integration of risk management functionality within Grid middleware. It does this by addressing the concerns of end-users and providers through encouraging greater commercial interest in Grid usage through incorporation of risk assessment mechanisms into Grid infrastructures as well as automated SLA agreement processes utilizing risk information. Incorporation of risk-aware components within the SLA negotiation process as an additional decision support parameter for the end-user is of primary importance. Risk is an ideal decision support parameter within the AssessGrid scenario since it combines both the quantifiable probability of SLA failure with the non-deterministic expected loss, a parameter known only to the beneficiary of the services stated in the SLA. The usage scenarios addressed by the AssessGrid architecture consider 3 principle actors: end-user, broker and provider.

2.1 Resource Provider

The AssessGrid architecture integrates risk-awareness into a Resource Management System (RMS), OpenCCS RMS [3] by extending existing modules (negotiation manager and scheduler) to handle information about Probabilities of SLA Failures (PoFs) and incorporating new components: a risk assessor and a consultant service with associated database. The consultant service uses monitoring information from the historical database in order to generate statistical data required by the risk assessor as input. The risk assessor is responsible for estimating the probability of an SLA failure, for each SLA, in order to determine whether an SLA should be agreed. The probability of an SLA violation is influenced by the availability of spare resources, which can be used in the case of a resource outage, as well as the provider's fault-tolerance capabilities.

OpenCCS makes advance reservations during the SLA negotiation. Resource reservation is used in order to determine the probability of failure of meeting the SLA by considering the resource stability. The RMS functionalities to reduce risk and fulfil the SLA include: 1) checkpointing and migration; 2) dedicated spare resources; 3) pool of spare resources; 4) profit considering scheduling after resource failures, and 5) job outsourcing to another provider.

A provider offers access to resources and services through formal SLA offers specifying the requirements as well as PoF, price, and penalty. Providers need well-balanced infrastructures, so that they can maximise the offerable QoS and minimise the number of SLA violations. Such an approach increases the economic benefit and motivation of end-users to outsource their IT tasks. We report on a number of economic issues that have been identified which affect the provider. These issues can be categorized as belonging to SLA negotiation and post-negotiation phases.

2.2 Broker

After the SLA negotiation has returned an SLA offer, the broker is responsible for performing reliability checks on the PoFs contained in the SLA offers. Without this check, the end-user has no independent view on the provider's assessment, which cannot be assumed to be impartial. SLA offers that are deemed to be unreliable are subjected to an additional risk assessment by the broker using historical data related to the provider making the offer. Where multiple SLA offers are returned by the SLA negotiation process, the broker can rank these according to a price, penalty, PoF matrix depending on the priorities of the end-user.

2.3   End-User

An end-user is a participant from a broad public approaching the Grid in order to perform a specific task that comprises of one or more services. In order to make a request for such services, the end-user must indicate the task and associated requirements formally within an SLA template. The information contained within the template is used to negotiate access for the end-user with providers offering these services, such that the task may be completed. The inclusion of risk information within the SLA negotiation process allows the end-user to make informed, risk-aware decisions on the SLA offers received so that any decision is acceptable and balances cost, time and risk.

The end-user is provided with a number of abstract applications that make use of Grid services deployed within the Grid fabric layer. SLA requests and offers are exchanged between end-user and broker or provider, in order to agree an SLA that grants permission to invoke a Grid service in the fabric layer. Within each layer, the organisation performing the role of each actor must define a policy statement governing the acceptable bounds of negotiation. This restricts end-users and contractors to request or offer SLAs that fall outside of the organization's acceptable limits. For example, in addition to specifying budget constraints, there may be a restriction on a provider's penalty conditions to limit the financial loss incurred because of an SLA violation. Taking these policy limits into consideration, an end-user can negotiate an SLA to run a Grid service by defining requirements as well as the requested QoS in an SLA request. During the definition process the end-user evaluates the importance of the application in terms of its urgency and the consequences of delayed results or failure. A further validation of the policy limits must be made against the SLA offers received from the broker or providers.

Where several SLA offers have been negotiated on behalf of the end user, the broker can return a ranked list - according to price, penalty, and PoF. The challenge for the end-user is to find an SLA offer which offers the best service in terms of price, penalty, and PoF. We report on a mathematical model to help the end-user make the best offer selection based on quality criteria. The end-user defines a ranking of the quality criteria (e.g. PoF is more important than price) in order to measure each of the offers according to its closeness to the criteria.

3. WS-Agreement Extension

The SLA negotiation is based on the WS-Agreement protocol [4], which has been extended in AssessGrid project to allow flexible SLA negotiation schemes between contractors and service providers. Modifications consist in the addition of two operations: *commit()* and *createAgreements()*, with a significant change in the semantics of *createAgreement()* operation. The signature of this operation remains intact. However, the changes in its semantics are important enough to consider that AssessGrid version of WS-Agreement protocol is actually a modification to the WS-Agreement protocol rather than an extension, as the "single round" acceptance model in the original WS-Agreement specification posed an unavoidable limitation to AssessGrid requirements. For more details see [5]. The actual AssessGrid version of the SLA template is based on that defined in the original WS-Agreement specification [4].

4. Economic Issues in Risk-aware SLA Management

The integration of risk-awareness into the Grid provides a number of benefits within an economy framework but also gives rise to numerous research problems. In the following we present an overview of the AssessGrid developments and their impact for continuing research in economic issues.

4.1   Resource Provider

A number of economic issues have been identified which affect the provider. These issues can be categorised as belonging to the pre-runtime (i.e. during SLA negotiation), run-time and post-runtime phases.

In the pre-runtime phase a risk aware negotiation requires that a provider place an advance reservation for the SLA and calculates the PoF. Based on this, a provider determines the price and penalty fee that will be offered to an end-user. In order to increase the chances that a potential end-user accepts an offer, a provider might offer a service with better conditions, i.e. lower price, lower PoF, or higher penalty. A provider's decision whether to agree or reject an SLA depends on the fees and the requested PoF in comparison with the current status of its infrastructure.

For contractors (end-users or brokers), an important provider selection criterion is the price. The SLA template contains pricing information for actions such as data transfer, CPU usage, and storage. Within the AssessGrid model these prices are variable since the price depends on the SLAs PoF value.

The market mechanism will influence the pricing since each provider has only a limited resource set with variable utilisation. Consequently, prices for resource usage will not be fixed but will depend on the economics of supply and demand. Reservations which are well in advance will usually result in a reduced price since there will be access to a greater number of free reservation slots. Equally, immediate resource usage may also result in reduced prices, as providers try to increase their utilisation if demand is low. However, end-users risk resources unavailability if they wait too long before reserving resources.

After an SLA has been agreed by the provider and the end-user, the provider has to ensure during runtime that the SLA will not be violated. Accordingly, the provider's risk management activities are controlled by estimating the penalty payments in the case of an SLA violation. Providers using the AssessGrid developments will be able to initiate precautionary fault tolerance mechanisms in order to prevent SLA violations. The penalty fees, in addition to the PoF (i.e. risk) are the decisive factors in determining which fault tolerance mechanisms are initiated.

In the post-runtime phase the provider has to evaluate the final SLA status to determine whether a penalty fee has to be paid. Even in the case the SLA had been fulfilled the costs for the fulfilment have to be checked since the initiation of a fault tolerance mechanism also consumes resources and therewith results in additional costs. The results of the evaluation process will point out on the one hand whether adjustments in the offer making policies are necessary in order to increase the provider's profit. On the other hand statistics can be generated which show whether initiated fault tolerance mechanisms had been able to prevent an SLA violation.

4.2   Broker

In the following section, we report on 1) how risk assessment is implemented at the broker layer [6], and 2) the workflow scheduling algorithm supported by the broker. Workflow scheduling is one of the key issues in the management of workflow execution and refers to the process of mapping and managing execution of inter-dependent tasks on distributed resources.

4.2.1   Risk Assessment

The Risk Assessor component provides the logic used by the broker's Confidence Service to compute a reliability measure and if necessary a risk assessment. It does this using past SLA data from a historical database. The Risk Assessor uses this data to determine the reliability of the offered PoF value from the provider's SLA. It returns a reliability object which contains the providers name, the number of SLAs on which the reliability is based, a reliability measure and an adjusted PoF. The algorithm for computing the reliability measure is based on a comparison of the total number of observed SLA failures in the historical database with the expected number of failures assuming the provider's PoFs are accurate. This is measured in terms of the number of standard deviations and compared with the expected behaviour of providers that are reliable - in the sense that any systematic errors in their risk assessments are within pre-specified bounds. A key feature of this algorithm is to account for the fact that old SLA data may be less relevant than newer SLA data. A provider's behaviour with regard to risk assessments could change as a consequence of a variety of factors, e.g.

- A provider's infrastructure is updated - this may have an effect on the reliability of subsequent risk assessments.
- A provider's risk assessment methodology or model parameterisation may change.
- A provider's policy may change, for example due to economic considerations. For example, they may decide that they can make more profit if they start to give overoptimistic estimates to end-users/brokers, in order to persuade them to agree offers.

If a provider's behaviour changes (such that a reliable provider becomes unreliable or vice-versa) then a reliability measure that accounts equally for all SLA data could be misleading. Similarly, when a provider is evaluated as unreliable and the broker makes its own PoF estimate, this is unlikely to be accurate when a provider's behaviour has recently changed. In order to address this problem, the reliability measure takes the form of a weighted average. SLAs are split into equally sized categories, according to how recently they were executed. The reliability measure is computed over each category and then weighted, where the category weightings increase linearly, moving forward in time. Hence the most recent category has the largest weight. Simulation results indicate that this approach is superior to both the basic measure (without weights) and a moving average with fixed window size, for providers that change behaviour. If the reliability measure is less than some pre-specified threshold value (chosen according to the level of confidence required that a provider is unreliable) then the broker assumes that the provider's assessment is accurate and its PoF estimate is therefore equal to the provider's. Otherwise, the broker performs its own estimate under the assumption that a single parameter can be used to address systematic errors of the form, $P_{fail} \approx P_{offerred}\,(1+\delta)$ where δ may be positive or negative. Similarly to the reliability measure, the SLAs are split into categories and only SLAs with an offered PoF within $x\%$ of the value in the current SLA offer are considered. If the total number of SLAs considered is less than some threshold value then x is incremented and the process repeated until a sufficiently large sample is found. The value of δ is then computed as a weighted average across the categories and used to estimate the PoF for the SLA offer under consideration.

4.2.2 Workflow Scheduling

The broker can schedule workflows given a correctly formatted SLA request. The workflow scheduling algorithm currently implemented is detailed in the following:

1. Generate a DAG from the end-user's workflow request. Each vertex corresponds to a task in its pending state and edges correspond to dependencies between tasks. The distance of an edge from vertex i to vertex j is the estimated time taken to transit between those states, i.e. the estimated execution time for task i to execute. An end vertex is created and an edge from each exit task to the end vertex, with length(s) corresponding to the execution time of the exit task(s). There is a limiting assumption that the workflows considered will have only one entry and exit task. Scenarios involving multiple entry and exit tasks are the subject of future consideration.

2. Estimate the required workflow execution time, based on the longest path from the entry task to the end vertex. Based on this, the total slack time available is estimated and a slack time ratio is computed to determine the proportion of slack time to be allocated to each task. The amount of slack time allocated to a task is linearly proportional to the task's expected execution time.

3. Compute the maximum acceptable PoF for each task P_{task}, using the approach outlined below and compute the earliest start and latest finish time for each task.

4. Filter providers and send requests for quotes for each task.

5. Once responses are received, compute the reliability and broker's PoF estimate for each quote. Those where the broker's PoF estimate exceeds the task threshold will be rejected.

6.   Check that there is at least one quote for every task. If this is not the case then no workflow mapping can be found. Otherwise,

7.   For each task, choose the best quote according to the cost function. If it is no longer available, move to the next best quote and so on. If no agreements can be secured for a task, roll back and cancel all previously made agreements, i.e., no workflow mapping can be found.

In the simplest algorithm, the PoF threshold is the same for each task and is computed as follows: the maximum acceptable PoF for the workflow is specified by the end-user as P_{max}, or, equivalently, the minimum acceptable probability of success $P_{succ} = 1 - P_{max}$. If all tasks are treated as equivalent in terms of acceptable PoF, then note that if the probability of success for each of the n tasks is $P_{task}(success)$ then the probability of success for the entire workflow is,

$$P_{wf}(success) = (P_{task}(success))^n \qquad (1)$$

The minimum probability of success for each task is then set to $\sqrt[n]{P_{succ}}$, i.e. the PoF for each task must satisfy,

$$P_{fail}^i < (1 - \sqrt[n]{P_{succ}}), \ i = 1 \ldots n$$

An unexplored problem is the economic issue underlying the handling of workflows for the broker. Since the broker is responsible in this case for the SLA fulfilment, it has to react on failures (negotiate with providers for a repeated job execution) in order to prevent paying penalties. Other essential economic issues are the pricing mechanisms for brokers and providers which must take account of the probability of failure in a risk-aware Grid environment.

5. Current Implementation

AssessGrid current software prototype integrates risk-awareness in all three layers of the Grid (end-user, broker and resource provider). The prototype supports direct negotiation between an end-user and a provider, using the broker layer to provide a reliability measure of the provider's risk assessment. In addition, negotiation between an end-user and a provider, using a broker as a mediator is also supported. In this scenario, SLA negotiation between the end-user and multiple providers is performed using the broker Service. This improves the scope of the end-user SLA request and also provides a list of SLA offers ranked by PoF. Also, the broker's functionality is enhanced by allowing it to function as a high-level provider. The broker can now offer its own SLAs combining SLAs from providers into a single SLA, which is useful for workflow mapping.

In this scenario end-users agree SLAs with the broker directly, who in turn agrees SLAs with all providers involved in executing the end-user's tasks or workflow. In the case of single tasks, these may need to be executed redundantly - to achieve a very low PoF (e.g. in cases where a single provider is unable to offer one low enough). For workflow orchestrations the broker is used to map entire workflows to individual SLAs agreed directly with resource providers.

6. Business Benefits

The economic benefit of using a broker within the SLA negotiation process affects all three Grid actors and provides the opportunity for an economy model where SLAs for software services are bought and sold based on differentiated classes of service. The broker's role also creates a competitive market place. In AssessGrid, three business models are identified:

1. *The trusted consulting party model*: a contract is defined through an SLA with the provider and end-user through direct negotiation and the end-user can query the broker's Confidence Service to obtain a reliability measure for an SLA offer.
2. *The intermediate party model*: the end-user submits an SLA request to the broker, which then forwards the request to suitable providers. The broker returns SLA offers to the end-user, ranked by price, penalty, and PoF. The end-user is then free to select and commit to an SLA offer by interacting directly with the corresponding provider.
3. *The virtual provider model*: the end-user agrees an SLA with the broker, which in turn agrees SLAs with all providers involved in executing the end-user's application. The broker can be used to map entire workflows to resources.

7. Conclusion

This paper has reported on recent results on risk-awareness integration in the AssessGrid architecture as well as the potential economic issues underlying risk-aware SLA management.

Resource providers are able to assess an SLA's Probability of Failure (PoF) before committing to it, through risk estimation models. This can be used to identify bottlenecks in their own infrastructure. The ability to assess the risk associated with an SLA request before it commits, enables a resource provider to build a planning based RMS schedule using the computed PoF values.

The problem of evaluating the reliability of the PoF estimates for SLA offers received from providers is also key. A broker that acts on behalf of end-users to find and negotiate for suitable resources benefits from risk management mechanisms.

Further work will focus on further enhancing the software prototype functionality. For example the method used to rank quotes within the broker layer will be improved by considering three criteria, price penalty and PoF, rather than just PoF. Additional effort is needed to address workflow fault tolerance and pricing strategies. Although the current prototype can react to failures in task SLAs belonging to a workflow, the broker needs to determine whether re-submission of the task (in order to ensure completion of the workflow) is appropriate financially. In this case it needs to evaluate whether it is more profitable to pay a penalty fee to the end-user and accept that the SLA has failed. In the latter case it will try to resubmit and retain the rewards set out in the SLA.

References

[1] AssessGrid - Advanced Risk Assessment and Management for Trustable Grids, 2008. http://www.assessgrid.eu

[2] Introducing Risk Management into the Grid. K. Djemame, I. Gourlay, J. Padgett, G. Birkenheuer, M. Hovestadt, K. Voss and O. Kao. In Proceedings of the 2nd IEEE International Conference on e-Science and Grid Computing, Amsterdam, The Netherlands, December 2006

[3] OpenCCS: Computing Center Software, 2008. http://www.openccs.eu

[4] Web Services Agreement Specification (WS-Agreement). A. Andrieux, K. Czajkowski, A. Dan, K. Keahey, H. Ludwig, T. Kakata, J. Pruyne, J. Rofrano, S. Tuecke, M. Xu. OGF Document Series, 2007

[5] AssessGrid Second Software Prototype, Deliverable D3.2 - Broker Scenario – K. Voss, D. Battre, J. Padgett, I. Gourlay, I. Rosenberg, July 2008

[6] I. Gourlay, K. Djemame and J. Padgett. Reliability and Risk in Grid Resource Brokering. In Proceedings of the 2008 IEEE International Conference on Digital Ecosystems and Technologies, Phitsanulok, Thailand, February 2008

Collaboration and the Knowledge Economy: Issues, Applications, Case Studies
P. Cunningham and M. Cunningham (Eds.)
IOS Press, 2008

How Profitable are Intelligent Cars for Society? – Methodology and Results from eIMPACT

Herbert BAUM[1], Torsten GEIßLER[1], Ulrich WESTERKAMP[1], Heiko PETERS[2]

[1]Univ. of Cologne, Inst. for Transport Economics, Universitaetsstr 22, Koeln, 50923, Germany
Tel: +492214702312, Fax: +492214705183, Email: h.baum@uni-koeln.de

[2]Federal Highway Research Institute (BASt), Bruederstr 53, Berg. Gladbach, 51427, Germany
Tel: +49220443419, Fax: +49220443695, Email: heiko.peters@bast.de

Abstract: Intelligent Cars can make road transport safer, cleaner and more efficient. This paper provides – based on the eIMPACT project (FP 6) – a methodology for assessing the socio-economic impacts of Intelligent Vehicle Safety Systems (IVSS). The assessment framework addresses in a comprehensive way the society perspective and stakeholder perspectives on IVSS. In its core the framework relies on cost-benefit analysis which is in the focus of the paper. Results are presented for all twelve systems for which cost-benefit analyses were performed. The benefit-cost results are also tested on sensitivity of results. Overall, it can be concluded that the analysed systems are profitable from the society point of view. The results are mainly driven by the safety benefits. In a temporal perspective, a wider uptake of systems is going to happen in the next decade, which helps to realise the benefits.

1. Introduction

Intelligent Vehicle Safety Systems (IVSS) promise a large potential to reduce the negative societal impacts of road traffic by informing drivers about traffic conditions and assisting them in hazardous situations. As a result, the road transport will be safer, more efficient in terms of time and energy use, and environmental friendly.

Increasing needs for mobility and transport require action to improve road safety, a major concern for European transport policy. Although the development has been distinctly positive in recent years, over 40,000 people still lose their lives on European roads each year, and more than 1.5 million become injured. The costs of those damages amount to 200 billion EUR, representing about 2% of the EU Gross Domestic Product (GDP). In addition, congestion also impairs the European economy by means of time losses and higher fuel consumption. The delay costs are conservatively estimated up to 50 bn EUR per year [1]. Other sources calculate them to roughly another 2% of the EU GDP [2]. Along with this go environmental damages in terms of air pollution and contribution to climate change.

In contrast to the potential, IVSS are not yet widely deployed. The reasons for the slow market take-up involve a lack of user awareness and understanding of the IVSS capabilities, a stakeholder mismatch between beneficiaries and cost bearers because of external effects, network externalities for co-operative systems as well as legal and liability issues. This environment makes the IVSS deployment a complicated case for public-private partnership.

The knowledge about the socio-economic impacts of Intelligent Vehicle Safety Systems is limited so far. Although studies do exist which prove the profitability of particular systems on national or regional level, there is only very limited EU-wide evidence about the socio-economic impacts of intelligent vehicles.

Fundaments for the analysis were laid in the SEiSS study [3] which aimed at exploring the socio-economic impact of IVSS methodologically and demonstrate the workability of the approach by some cost-benefit case studies. A study carried out by COWI made use of the SEiSS framework and covered more than 20 systems [4].

The socio-economic impact assessment within eIMPACT has got two focal points. The first is to develop a broader framework on methodology which integrates the overall society perspective of cost-benefit analysis with economic stakeholder analyses which provide information on individual stakeholders' benefits and costs. The key interest groups within eIMPACT comprise system users, OEMs and suppliers, insurance companies and public authorities. The second focus is to carry out fully-fledged cost-benefit analyses for twelve IVSS and to test the sensitivity of the results. This is made possible by bringing together the latest evidence in system engineering, forecast of safety and traffic data, safety assessment incl. behavioural research, traffic modelling and simulation as well as cost-benefit assessment.

The profitability proof of the systems for the overall society and for key stakeholder groups will actively contribute to a reduction of implementation barriers related to IVSS. With that, guidance for policy measures to facilitate the IVSS market take-up will be provided and the work under the eSafety initiative and the Intelligent Car Initiative of the European Commission is supported [1].

2.   Objectives

The objective of the paper is to describe a comprehensive methodological framework for socio-economic impact assessment and to discuss the results of the cost-benefit analyses for all twelve investigated systems. So clearly, stakeholder analyses have been an important part of the eIMPACT project and the findings are well documented [5]. However, this paper concentrates on the social perspective of CBA. This means, the focus of the analysis is on assessing whether the welfare of the society is improved or not, regardless of the fact who profits and who does not. In order to arrive at this point, the costs of the regarded measure are confronted with this overall economic effect. The benefits are defined in terms of productive resources saved within an economy ("cost-savings approach").

The paper is organised as follows. Chapter 3 gives a brief overview over the methodological framework. It reports about the systems that have been selected for impact assessment throughout eIMPACT. Moreover, the impact channels and the necessary background data for the assessment are explained. Next to methodology, chapter 4 presents the results of the cost-benefit analyses. Furthermore, the main drivers for the results are discussed and the sensitivity of the results is examined. The paper concludes with discussing the conclusions and recommendations, including directions for further research.

3.   Methodological Framework

The goal of the assessment framework is to provide a comprehensive standardised methodology, which enables to perform a socio-economic impact assessment of a set of IVSS in the European Union in pre-selected target years (2010, 2020). Similar to former research, the assessment framework of eIMPACT relies in its core also on cost-benefit analysis. Because of the complex deployment issues, the overall society perspective is complemented by stakeholder analyses for key interest groups [6]. However, as outlined above, the focus of this paper is on the methodology and the results of cost-benefit analysis.

A crucial first step in the overall assessment process is the identification of the most promising vehicle safety technologies for the near- to mid-term future. A workshop in Cologne in March 2006 brought together the relevant expertise inside and outside the consortium. The three-stage selection process (overview over potentially beneficial systems, ranking of the systems according to the criteria "Technical and economic feasibility", "Consumer satisfaction" and "Public concerns", consistency check in order to ensure a balanced choice of systems) ended up in a list of twelve IVSS which formed the basis for the impact assessment throughout the eIMPACT project [7]. The systems comprise (1) Electronic Stability Control (ESC), (2) Full Speed Range ACC (FSR), (3) Emergency Braking (EBR), (4) Pre-Crash Protection of Vulnerable Road Users (PCV), (5) Lane Keeping Support (LKS), (6) Lane Change Assistant (Warning) (LCA), (7) Night Vision Warn (NIW), (8) Driver Drowsiness Monitoring and Warning (DDM), (9) Wireless Local Danger Warning (WLD), (10) eCall (ECA), (11) Intersection Safety (INS) and (12) Speed Alert (SPE).

The assessment on society level relies on information input on impacts, costs and background data (Figure 1). The cost side information comprises the costs of vehicle equipment and infrastructure equipment (where applicable) as well as operating and maintenance costs. The background data set consists of the functional system specification, the forecasted traffic performance (in vehicle kilometres) and safety performance (fatalities and injuries). Moreover, the impact assessment is based on realistic market penetration rates for the reference years 2010 and 2020, reflecting for both years a low scenario representing business-as-usual conditions, and a high scenario which involves focused policy incentives.

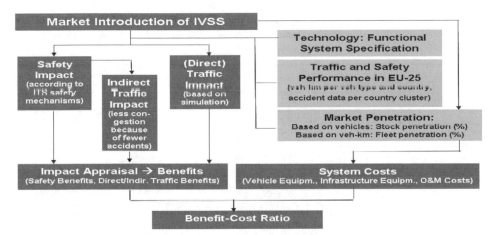

Figure 1: Procedure of the Socio-Economic Impact Assessment

The benefits result from three different impact channels. Most important, at least constitutional for Intelligent Vehicle Safety Systems, is the safety impact channel. It analyses the safety impact of IVSS according to the ITS safety mechanisms [8], including direct effects on accident avoidance and injury mitigation and indirect effects due to behavioural adaptations and exposure. As road safety improvements also release congestion, this add-on effect to the safety impact is also considered. Cost-unit rates for congestion for each of the twelve IVSS are determined. In addition to that, direct traffic impacts are calculated by using micro-simulations such as the ITS modeller [8]. Based on this, effects on travel time, on fuel consumption, on the CO_2 emission, and on the NO_x-equivalent emission can be derived. For each of these categories the corresponding cost-unit rates are applied in order to determine the cost savings. These figures expressed in Euro represent resource savings which can be used elsewhere in the economy to increase the Gross Domestic Product. Thus, this change influences the welfare of the overall society. When the welfare gain is larger than the costs, the system implementation is profitable from the society point of view, indicated by a benefit-cost ratio higher than 1.

4. Results of the Cost-Benefit Analyses

The results of the cost-benefit analyses show that the use of Intelligent Vehicle Safety Systems will contribute actively to the reduction of fatalities and injuries. Hence, IVSS are effective in improving road safety. Moreover, as the benefit-cost ratios prove, they are mostly efficient. In particular, the results can be condensed to the following statements [9].

4.1. All systems contribute actively to the societal goal of improving road safety.

The systems which are considered in eIMPACT are safety systems. Their aim is to reduce the number of accidents and linked to this the number of fatalities and of injuries. As Table 1 illustrates, the safety impact of the IVSS is significant. For instance, Electronic Stability Control in the year 2010 can avoid about 2,000 fatalities (1,914 – 2,240 fatalities, depending on the market penetration secenario). Among the group of the twelve IVSS, Electronic Stability Control, Lane Keeping Support and Speed Alert show the highest absolute numbers in avoiding fatalities and injuries at the estimated penetration rates. The potential of eCall (implying 100% penetration for a fair distribution of infrastructure equipment costs) represents also a significant reduction of fatalities and severe injuries. Overall it becomes clear that improving road safety must include the contributions from all technologies which are analysed here.

Table 1: The number of saved lives and avoided injuries for each IVSS
(The values for eCall and Intersection Safety are only valid for the potential case!)

	Fatalities				Injuries			
	2010		2020		2010		2020	
	low	high	low	high	low	high	low	high
ESC	1,914	2,240	2,577	3,253	32,792	38,265	41,549	52,182
FSR	n.a.	n.a.	49	101	n.a.	n.a.	3,668	9,774
EBR	n.a.	n.a.	72	193	n.a.	n.a.	4,241	10,925
PCV	n.a.	n.a.	14	39	n.a.	n.a.	718	1,918
LCA	2	11	33	86	264	1,189	3,449	8,596
LKS	56	149	197	678	1,420	3,784	5,109	17,296
NIW	2	10	30	73	87	367	1,046	2,542
DDM	4	13	20	94	153	367	682	2,715
ECA	1,955		1,199		severe: 13,691 slight: -15,647		severe: 8,398 slight: -9,598	
INS	n.a.		803		n.a.		63,700	
WLD	n.a.	n.a.	29	66	n.a.	n.a.	989	1,906
SPE	77	119	753	1,076	2,405	3,463	24,643	34,887
Base	33,895		20,791		1,409,415		873,695	

4.2. The improved road safety leads to a significant reduction of accident costs. This means, there are huge safety benefits to be realised.

The reduction of accident costs (= safety benefits) is displayed for the 2020 high scenario in Figure 2. Besides the safety impact in absolute numbers it is also represented to which extent the results accrue to avoided fatalities and avoided injuries. The figures show that Electronic Stability Control, Lane Keeping Support, Speed Alert and eCall lead to the highest safety benefits. The benefits of Electronic Stability Control add up to about 9 Bn EUR. The benefits of Lane Keeping Support, Speed Alert and eCall amount also to more than 1 Bn EUR. In terms of safety benefits distribution, it becomes obvious that for some systems (e.g. Electronic Stability Control, eCall) the majority of safety benefits origins in avoided fatalities whereas other systems (e.g. Full Speed Range ACC, Lane Change Assistance) do merely benefit from avoiding injuries.

Mill. EUR		Fatalities			Injuries		
		0%	20%	40%	60%	80%	100%
ESC	8,831						
FSR	828						
EBR	1,056						
PCV	194						
LCA	723						
LKS	2,276						
NIW	291						
DDM	337						
ECA	2,206						
INS	57						
WLD	237						
SPE	4,118						

Figure 2: Safety Benefits and Distribution for 2020 High Scenario

4.3. The benefits are dominated by the safety benefits. Traffic impacts however represent for all IVSS a considerable add-on to the safety benefits.

The prevention and/or mitigation of accidents reduce congestion caused by accidents. Traffic disturbances are reduced and road transport becomes more efficient. This indirect traffic effect represents a mark-up to the safety benefits of up to 8%. Moreover, at the estimated penetration rates direct effects on the traffic flow can only be expected for the Speed Alert system in the year 2020. The direct traffic benefit represents another 2% mark-up to the safety benefits.

4.4. The safety benefits grow strongly with maturity of systems and policy support.

In the next decade many systems will either enter or penetrate the market. Figure 3 shows the development of the safety benefits in the temporal perspective exemplarily for the Lane Keeping Support system. It becomes clear that the benefits grow strongly in the next decade. Moreover, the achievable benefits in the scenario high (including focused policy incentives) are much higher than in the low scenario for each of the target years.

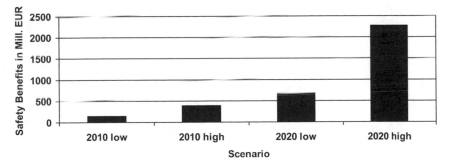

Figure 3: Development of Safety Benefits in Mill. Euro for Lane Keeping Support

4.5. On the basis of benefit-cost ratios, the clear majority of the investigated Intelligent Vehicle Safety Systems is distinctly profitable from the society point of view.

Table 2 provides an overview over the benefit-cost ratios for all scenarios at the estimated penetration rates and share of driven kilometers with the systems. For eCall and Intersection safety – which both require infrastructure investment – the benefit-cost ratio is displayed only for the potential case (equipment of the total vehicle fleet, 100% penetration) for reasons of a fair allocation of infrastructure investment costs.

Table 2: Synopsis of the Benefit-Cost Ratios

Scenario		ESC	FSR	EBR	PCV	LCA	LKS	NIW	DDM	ECA	INS	WLD	SPE
2010	Low	4.4	n.a.	n.a.	n.a.	3.1	2.7	0.8	2.5	2.7	n.a.	n.a.	2.2
	High	4.3	n.a.	n.a.	n.a.	3.7	2.7	0.9	2.9			n.a.	2.0
2020	Low	3.0	1.6	3.6	0.5	2.9	1.9	0.7	1.7	1.9	0.2	1.8	1.9
	High	2.8	1.8	4.1	0.6	2.6	1.9	0.6	2.1			1.6	1.7

n.a. ... not available in this year

Looking at the results for the year 2010, all introduced systems – except Night Vision Warn, which is close to 1 – are fairly above the BC-threshold of 1 which indicates the profitability of a system from the society point of view. Electronic Stability Control and Lane Change Assistant are the two systems which achieve BCR's of more than 3. The result of 4.4 for Electronic Stability Control implies that every spent Euro leads to societal benefit of 4.40 Euro. Four systems are above 2: Lane Keeping Support, Driver Drowsiness Monitoring and Warning, eCall and SpeedAlert. NightVisionWarn is round about 1. The other systems are not available or have no significant market penetration in the year 2010.

In the year 2020 all twelve systems are available on the market. Again, the clear majority of the systems prove their profitability from the society point of view. The best system is Emergency Braking with which has a benefit-cost ratio of above 3. Lane Change Assistant and Electronic Stability Control are in both scenarios close to 3. Six systems have a BCR of between 1.5 and 1.9: eCall, Lane Keeping Support, Driver Drowsiness Monitoring and Warning, Full Speed Range ACC, Wireless Local Danger Warning and SpeedAlert. The remaining systems are – under the estimated conditions – below 1: NightVisionWarn, Pre-Crash Protection of Vulnerable Road Users and Intersection Safety. However, there should not be made any premature conclusions about the profitability of those systems. The result only indicates that from the society point of view they are less efficient than other systems and they are not efficient under the current estimated conditions.

For the less efficient systems the benefit-cost ratio may be significantly higher in the future due to enriched system functionalities or decline of system costs. It is also noteworthy that the results of Table 2 incorporate a considerable safety progress, indicated by the e.g. reduction of fatalities (accident base, see Table 1) from 34,000 (2010) to 21,000 (2020). Sensitivity analyses can provide some indication on the influence of these effects.

4.6.   Results react sensitive to changes of input variables. This holds especially true for the eIMPACT accident trend but also for the estimated safety impact.

Different input variables to the CBA have been tested for their influence on the benefit-cost ratios. Among them, the accident trend reveals the highest sensitivity. When the accident trend between 2010 and 2020 is disregarded, the benefit-cost ratio is changed by more than +1.0. This represents – according to the results classification of the sensitivity analysis – a significant change. The other tested variables (pessimistic / optimistic estimation of the safety impact, based on [4], change of discount rate in CBA from 3% to 8% p.a., change of vehicle lifetime from 12 years to 16 years) change the benefit-cost ratios b more than +/-0.1 which represents a considerable change.

In the following figure the sensitivity of results is exemplarily displayed for the SpeedAlert system under the conditions of 2020 low scenario. The value for the mean BCR (represented by the rectangle) is 1.9. The positive or negative deviations (highest/lowest BCR) represented by the triangle and circle symbol. Generally, the benefit-cost ratios react more sensitive on the tested variables coming from the impact assessment than on those which are core assumptions of the socio-economic assessment.

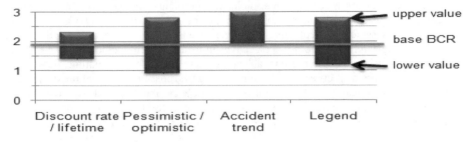

Figure 4: Change of benefit-cost ratios depending on variations of CBA input parameters (Base case: Speed Alert, 2020 low scenario)

5.   Conclusions and Recommendations

The paper presented a methodology to assess the socio-economic impact of Intelligent Vehicle Safety Systems, which is comprehensive and re-usable for future assessment activities. Furthermore, the results of cost-benefit analyses for twelve pre-selected Intelligent Vehicle Safety Systems were discussed.

The results prove that IVSS contribute to improve road safety and that the use of IVSS is profitable from the society point of view. The benefit-cost ratios are distinctly above the threshold of 1. Moreover, the sensitivity analysis reveals that the results react quite sensitive to the accident trend forecast and the estimated safety impact. Overall, it can be concluded that applying IVSS improves the efficiency of road traffic.

Because benefits grow with the maturity of the systems and the level of policy support, measures to enhance the user awareness and understanding of the systems as well as initiatives to support the deployment of the systems [10] can be recommended based on the CBA findings. A deeper discussion of available instruments and the situation in individual EU member states can be found in recent studies [11, 12].

Moreover, the socio-economic impact assessment arrives at some important conclusions, which provide guidance for further research directions:

- In the deployment process of IVSS, bundling strategies will make it possible to realise synergies on the cost side. Within the eIMPACT project, the socio-economic impact of IVSS was assessed assuming that the systems are stand-alone versions. A promising approach for the future is the evaluation of system bundles. System bundles can share components, leading to cost synergies. With that, a stronger decrease of system costs might be possible. When this effect is strong enough, this would also offset the tendency to lower benefit-cost ratios (introduced by the trend reduction of fatalities and injuries) in the long-term. It should also be noted that this analysis has to take into account the path dependency of market introduction. This means, some advanced systems use components from predecessor systems, e.g. Emergency Braking can only be introduced when Electronic Stability Control is on board [13]. Prerequisite for the analysis of system bundles however is the availability of recent in-depth accident data. Foremost it must be clear how systems interact and what this implies for the safety impact (e.g. the bundle impact could represent the sum of impacts from individual systems, it could also be more or less).

- The socio-economic assessment of different deployment strategies represents a promising field for future research. When technologies become mature, the research interest naturally moves from investigating the profitability of a developed system in general to the question of an adequate deployment program. This question is particularly important because IVSS are related to several deployment barriers (involving aspects of market failure such as congruency of beneficiaries and cost bearers, critical mass of systems, hold up problems in the insurance industry, deployment risks and ramping-up effects of the automotive industry). The socio-economic assessment of deployment strategies needs a broader scope than CBA. It has to consider different stakeholder perspectives in its assessment methodology [14]. Multi criteria analysis could represent an appropriate tool for evaluating deployment programs. Assessment criteria could comprise e.g. the cost-efficiency of the deployment strategy, its practicability, the benefit-cost congruency, the financial resources needed for subsidies by the public, the incentives on industrial R&D etc.

- The robustness of CBA results can be improved by considering explicitly the occurrence probability of scenarios. The risk analysis approach in eIMPACT was based on scenarios and on sensitivity analysis. This leads to a wide range of possible BCR. To make the BCR values more robust, it is necessary to determine the probability of occurrence for each scenario. With this information it is possible to get a mean and a variance for the BCR and to get the BCR for the value-at-risk, i.e. the threshold under which BCR will not fall with a certain probability. Monte-Carlo-simulation represents an adequate approach to calculate this distribution of BCR.

References

[1] European Commission, Communication from the Commission to the Council, the European Parliament, the European Economic and Social Committee and the Committee of the Regions, On the Intelligent Car Initiative: "Raising Awareness of ICT for Smarter, Safer and Cleaner Vehicles", Brussels, COM(2006) 59 final, 15.02.2006.

[2] Infras, IWW (2004): External Costs of Transport. Update Study, Zurich / Karlsruhe, October 2004.

[3] Abele, J. et al., Exploratory study on the socio-economic impact of the introduction of Intelligent Safety Systems in Road Vehicles (SEiSS Study), Teltow and Cologne 2005.

[4] Odgaard, Th., et al., Cost-benefit assessment and priorisation of vehicle safety technologies, Final report, January 2006.

[5] Baum, H. et al., Stakeholder Analyses for Intelligent Vehicle Safety Systems, eIMPACT Deliverable D8, June 2008.

[6] Assing, K. et al., Methodological framework and database for socio-economic evaluation of Intelligent Vehicle Safety Systems, eIMPACT Deliverable D3, December 2006.

[7] Vollmer, D., et al., Stand alone and cooperative intelligent vehicle safety systems – inventory and recommendations for in-depth socio-economic impact assessment, eIMPACT Deliverable D2, April 2006.

[8] Wilmink, I. et al., Impact assessment of Intelligent Vehicle Safety Systems, eIMPACT Deliverable D4, April 2008.

[9] Baum, H. et al., Cost-Benefit Analyses for stand-alone and co-operative Intelligent Vehicle Safety Systems, eIMPACT Deliverable D6, June 2008.

[10] European Commission, Proposal for a regulation of the European Parliament and of the Council concerning type-approval requirements for the general safety of motor vehicles, COM (2008) 316 final, Brussels 23.05.2008.

[11] Alkim, T. et al., Policy recommendations to promote selected intelligent vehicle safety systems, eIMPACT Deliverable D7, June 2008.

[12] Zwijnenberg, H. et al., Benchmarking study on activities in promoting and deploying Intelligent Vehicle Safety Systems in the EU, TNO report 2007-D-R0674/B, Delft 2007.

[13] Malone, K. et al., Final Report, integration of results and perspectives for market introduction of IVSS, eIMPACT Deliverable D10, June 2008.

[14] Peters, H., Market failures and the deployment of cooperative vehicle safety systems - a first analytical assessment of potential reasons for the non-diffusion of safety-improving vehicle systems in Europe, Paper presented on the 7th European Congress on Intelligent Transport Systems and Services, Geneva 4-6 June 2008.

Section 5.3

Case Studies

Collaboration and the Knowledge Economy: Issues, Applications, Case Studies
P. Cunningham and M. Cunningham (Eds.)
IOS Press, 2008

Federated Identity Infrastructure for the Andalusian Universities. Deployment of a Multi-technology Federation

Victoriano GIRALT[1], Carmen LOPEZ[2], Diego LOPEZ[3], Luis MELENDEZ[4],
Francisco SANCHEZ[5]

[1]*University of Malaga, Blvd. Louis Pasterur, 33 Ed. SCAI Campus de Teatinos,*
Malaga, 29071, Spain
Tel: +34 95 2132366, Email: victoriano@uma.es
[2]*University of Seville, Spain*
[3]*Red.ES/RedIRIS, Avda. Reina Mercedes s/n Ed. CICA, Sevilla, 41012, Spain*
Tel: +34 95 5056621, Email: diego.lopez@rediris.es
[4]*University of Córdoba, IT Services, Córdoba, 14071, Spain*
[5]*International University of Andalusia, Spain*

Abstract: Identity is a strategic piece in any organization, as it is the key to gain access to services and information. Authentication and authorisation infrastructures (AAI) and, above all, the schemes that allow their integration through federation mechanisms, are a key component of academic institutional ICT. This is specifically relevant for the achievement of the Bologna Process. This paper will present the results of an initiative carried out by several Andalusian universities, focused on producing a standards based multi-technology federated identity infrastructure for the Andalusian Universities. The paper will present the technological options selected, based on open standards and mostly developed by international cooperation. The working group has produced both a document and reference implementations for the main elements of the Federation. The trust model is based upon the Server Certificate Service developed by TERENA. The paper will also present several use cases for the federation.

1. Introduction

The ICT Managers Committee of the Association of Public Universities of Andalusia (AUPA) decided that an Identity Federation for the member Universities would be a desired advancement to allow their students, faculty and personnel access shared resources, following the mobility principles of the Bologna process.

Such decision prompted the creation of a technical working group composed of ICT specialists from some of the participating Universities and the Andalusian regional REN (Research and Educational Network) and chaired by RedIRIS (the Spanish National REN). These experts have produced a test bed operational service and a technical specifications document for the final deployment of the Federation.

The main guiding principle for the works has been a strong commitment to standards and the ability to form a multi-technology federation, provided that the state of maturity of Identity Management technologies and the different level of adoption in the participating institutions, has resulted in several products deployed at various sites.

One of the main deliverables required in the technical specification is the development and deployment of a canonical implementation against which products can be tested before being accepted for use in the Federation.

There are services in the European academic space that allow users that belong to participating institutions to use services provided by institutions other than their own, but they use a single underlying technology.

2. Objectives

The working group set up the following main objectives:

- The federation should serve the needs of any user in the participating institutions, i.e.: students, teachers, researchers, administrative personnel, etc.
- Find a system that will allow the participating institutions to select the technology they prefer for connecting to the federation, based on status of their Identity Management Systems.
- Develop the pieces of software required to fill voids detected in other deployments, specially regarding metadata distribution, trust fabric building and diagnostics.
- Deploy a reference implementation for validation and testing purposes.
- Build a series of common use cases that could be used for deploying services at the institutions joining the federation, with a special focus on those departing from the usual browser-server interactions.
- Use as much open source software as possible.

At first, the work group decided that the federation should be based on Shibboleth 1.3 [1] SAML 2.0 such as the appearance of new versions (Shibboleth 2.0) or totally new software (simpleSAMLphp [3]), have made the group revise that decision and propose the use of full SAML 2.0.

3. Methodology

The project has used collaborative and federated technology from the start. Work has been carried out by technical personnel from the participating institutions.

Each participating institution has installed, at least, one Identity Provider connected to its Identity Management Infrastructure, be it an LDAP directory, a relational database system or any other thing, such that real user identities could be used for the pilot services.

Some of the institutions have also deployed federated services for use by the community.

The new software that was needed to implement some of the new core services, has been developed by members of the working group and made available to the community.

In order to identify needs that should be addressed, the most expert members of the group have pointed out weak points they knew from other federation deployments. Other members of the group have voiced needs and requirements they had in their domains for the federated infrastructure.

Once the requirements and improvements were collected, the working group drafted a document with specifications for the different services.

4. Technology Description

The main characteristic of the federation has been the use of disparate technologies in the participating sites. When the project started, the first three universities already had a Web Single Sign On system in production and diverse IdM system. This a clear difference from other similar deployments in our area, like the Norwegian FEIDE [4] or the Finnish Haka [5] federations, where all the participating institutions use the same technology.

Eduroam [6] is a very successful federated service deployed all over Europe, and beyond. The group engaged with two persons that have been very active in its development and deployment, which has been of great help in identifying issues even before they arose.

This service is different from our federation in that it is based in a common credential transport mechanism: a RADIUS hierarchy. It is similar in that user access the services provided by institutions other than their own with credentials issued and validated by their home institutions, and in allowing the later to decide which credentials and validation mechanisms to use.

The federation uses or is deploying several technical and policy elements.

4.1   Federation Metadata Management

Practice has shown that what conforms a federation is the metadata, so the main design principle for the technical foundations of the Andalusian Federation has been the ease of access to, and the validation of, the services metadata.

Metadata allows IdPs and Sps to build the trust links required for the former to assure that the user data are sent to an authorized receiver, and for the later to be able to authenticate the source of said data. Metadata are the backbone of a federation and should be provided by an entity that all members trust.

Thus the group has produced specifications and reference implementations for:

- Metadata manager with web and web-services interfaces. This is a repository for metadata that can be retrieved both manually, by persons, and automatically, by programs. The retrieved data is properly authenticated using public key cryptography mechanisms. A similar approach has been developed independently, and after our specifications were written, by the authors of SimpleSAMLphp [3]. The metadata manager allows for institution designed persons to update the metadata through a management interface, using X.509 certificates with legal binding value in Spain for identification.
- Metadata based WAYF service. Existing *Where Are You From* service Implementations use local configurations for displaying the available IdPs to the users, thus requiring manual intervention for every addition or removal, which leads, often times, to the existence of just one WAYF per federation. Our approach has been to develop a WAYF service that presents the users with information derived from the federation metadata. This information is securely retrieved from the metadata manager and, thus, easily kept up to date. This also allows for the easy deployment of as many WAYF services as the participating institutions see fit.
- Metadata query facilities. The information model for the metadata conforms to the SAML 2.0 [3] specifications and allows for the participating IdPs to easily obtain all the information needed to configure the services to join the federation. This also allows for a Service Provider wanting to offer its services to the federation to easily obtain the required data with no other intervention.
- Attribute release control. The work group has specified but not yet developed a system for centralized attribute release policy (ARP) management. The ARP system should also allow for locally specified policies at institutional level with web services access to the centralized policies and for user informed consent before sending the data to the SPs. The group has evaluated several existing technologies such as the Australian ShARPE, the works of SWITCH and the controls in SimpleSAMLphp.

4.2   Trust model

TERENA has produced an excellent service, called Server Certificate Service (SCS), for obtaining service and server certificates at a really low cost, it is free for the Universities, the NRENs have absorbed the cost. The procedure for obtaining such certificates is both easy and reasonably secure, which has lead the working group to base the trust model on the use of SCS certificates for the participating entities. Any institution that wants to be part of the federation just needs to designate a representative whose legal personal certificate is sent to the federation operators for access to the metadata manager, obtain an SCS certificate, and upload the information to the service.

- Trust root and trust policy manager. The federation will accept several Certification Authorities (CA) for certificate signing. This trust roots will be distributed off line, outside the federation infrastructure, but there should be mechanisms for obtaining the list of valid root certificates both over normal web queries for persons and over web services for systems. The system will link Internet domains to CA roots, for validation of only certificates pertaining to entities in such domains.
- OCSP. The federation will use the Online Certificate Status Protocol for validating the certificates in the metadata. The service will be offered as an aggregator for those CA that only produce CRLs. This service has not yet been developed.

4.3   Validation service

The federation will provide a service with a minimum of IdP, a SP and a metadata server, with test data, for any one that wants to connect to the federation on either role, to test their set up against a known working mock up, that provides additional logging and analysis mechanisms. Once the service works properly against the validation facility, it can start the process for joining the production federation.

During the design and test phases, this validation has been done against non-production services in some of the participating institutions and, then, against non-critical services.

4.4   Identity Provider for Homeless users

The Federation will include a central Identity Provider for those uses that need to access any service but do not belong to any of the participating Universities. Such a provider will be managed by the Federation operator. This IdP will have a management interface offered as a SP for the federation to be used for those persons with the required privileges. This service is already operational at the Andalusian Scientific Computing Centre (CICA), while the management interface is still in developing stage.

4.5   Attribute exchange model

The federation has selected the eduPerson[7] and SCHAC[8] schemas for attribute exchange, as both are in wide use inside the academic domain.

4.6   Diagnostics tool

The federation participants will offer a federated service for accessing the logs of the services they provide. The group has already developed a Shibboleth log parsing tool that can be queried for specific users or transactions with a federated access control system, so the service operators can easily find the relevant information to support the users. This tool is being expanded to be easily adapted to other log formats.

5. Developments

5.1   Software

The working group has already developed several software pieces to support the requirements of the federation:

- Metadata management tool with metadata query facilities
- Metadata based WAYF service, with extra functionalities (described in other paper in the workshop)
- Log parsing federated tool.

5.2   Documentation

The working group has produced a series of use cases descriptions for the participating institutions to implement. Also, some of this use cases are already in production in some of the participating institutions. Describing each of them in detail here is not possible due to space constraints but they will be publicly available at the federation web site (http://confia.aupa.inf/) once the federation enters full public production.

- Andalusian Virtual Campus. The e-Learning systems of Andalusian Public Universities provide support for the students registered in any of them to take a virtual course in any of the others. This system will be federated both for access control and for exchanging student data using standards that could come out from Bologna process.
- Reciprocal library registration. Federating of the Library Management systems will allow users from any of the participating institutions, physically present at the library of any other one, to get the same level of access to resources, electronic or physical, as in their home organization.
- Federated file swapping repository: Consigna. A tool that has been used as a simple demonstrator for the Federation. The tool allows the exchange of files using a web browser between users of the community and external users. Access to files depends on either client IP address or validated identity of the user against any of the Federation Identity Providers.
- Federated SSH access to systems. The group has developed software for federated and automated provision of accounts for users in need to access Linux based systems over secure shell. The tool allows for either federated retrieval of the users public keys or manual entry.

The group has also produced an animation based on several working services at three different institutions to show how an user identity federation works.

6. Results

The working group has been able to set up a federation with three production IdPs, one preproduction IdP and three more in the works, at the time of writing this paper, using four different technologies. There are also several production or preproduction services put on line.

This has been done in a really short time, which has reassured that a multi-technology federation can be set up with not much effort given the proper level of expertise in the core and with collaborative work for those less proficient.

While we were deploying the test services, some important breakthroughs have occurred, like the release of Shibboleth 2.0 or the appearance of SimpleSAMLphp. This has been of capital importance for the quick set up of some new providers.

Having an easy to deploy, configure and use fedcrated application as the file sharing service has proved a strong driving force for the people doing the deployments as it was a quick a dirty way for testing that their work was successful.

7. Business Benefits

A federation as the one we are setting up will be of capital importance for the Bologna process, in which all the participant universities are involved by law. The framework allows for persons to seamlessly use services provided by several universities simply enrolling in one of them and using the identity this institution provides.

The new concepts and services we have developed for federation administrators and operators eases the configuration and deployment of new services and identity providers, thanks to simple and convenient metadata and trust management.

The experience gained along the project shows the maturity of the federated approach to identity management in institutional environments and its applicability to a great variety of use cases.

Common applications of federated identity so far rely not only on a single technology but also on central elements that control the whole behaviour of the federation. The approach taken by CONFIA demonstrates that an identity federation is essentially characterized by its metadata, and that a collaborative approach to metadata management is possible.

8. Conclusions

The federation framework presented in this paper proposes novel solutions to the problems already detected by practitioners in the evolution of identity federation solution, providing support for a multi-technology environment by means of strong standard commitment and defining a system tightly tied to metadata in what relates to the federation central services. Some specific components for these tasks have been defined and demonstrated and will be deployed soon.

Furthermore, the framework is intended to support services beyond the usual browser-server binomial, and the team is working on use cases related to VoIP and SSH access to computing resources.

Nevertheless, the working group is aware that the results achieved so far are essentially technological, and that there are important policy and business-case challenges ahead the road for the federation and its proposed architecture to be considered a complete success. It is our strong belief that the project technical achievements so far provide a sound basis for supporting a decentralized environment for identity-enabled collaborative application sharing among peer institutions.

References

[1] Internet2(2008). Shibboleth. Located [2.5.2008] on: http://shibboleth.internet2.edu/
[2] SAML 2.0
[3] FEIDE (2008). SimpleSAMLphp. Located [2.5.2008] on: http://rnd.feide.no/simplesamlphp
[4] FEIDE (2008). FEIDE identity federation. Located [2.5.2008] on: http://feide.no/content.ap?thisId=1307
[5] CSC (2008). Haka Identity Federation. Located [2.5.2008] on:
     http://www.csc.fi/english/institutions/haka/index_html
[6] TERENA (2008). Eduroam. Located [2.5.2008] on: http://www.eduroam.org/
[7] EDUCAUSE (2008). eduPerson. Located [2.5.2008] on: http://www.educause.edu/eduperson/
[8] TERENA (2008), SCHAC. Located [2.5.2008] on: http://www.terena.org/activities/tf-emc2/schac.html

Collaboration and the Knowledge Economy: Issues, Applications, Case Studies
P. Cunningham and M. Cunningham (Eds.)
IOS Press, 2008

A Service Oriented Architecture to Support the Federation Lifecycle Management in a Secure B2B Environment

Angelo GAETA[1], Francesco ORCIUOLI[2], Nicola CAPUANO[2],
David BROSSARD[3], Theo DIMITRAKOS[3]
[1]CRMPA, via ponte don Melillo, Fisciano, 84084, Fisciano (SA)
Tel: +39 089 96 43 64, Email: agaeta@crmpa.unisa.it
[2]DIIMA, via ponte don Melillo, Fisciano, 84084, Fisciano (SA)
Email: orciuoli@diima.unisa.it, ncapuano@unisa.it
[3]British Telecommunications plc, Adastral Park, Martlesham Heath, IP5 3RE, UK
Tel: +44 1473 606149, Email: david.brossard@bt.com, theo.dimitrakos@bt.com

Abstract: This paper presents a Service Oriented Architecture to manage the lifecycle of a federation in a secure Business to Business (B2B) environment. The main contribution of the authors to Grid and SOA communities is related to the definition and development of a set of design patterns and software components to support the creation, management and dissolution of a federation of different administrative domains. As case of study we present the application of our components to a concrete business scenario relating to the on-line game application provision, providing also an overview of the main business benefits assessed during the evaluation of the components.

1. Introduction

The paper has the objective of presenting design patterns and software components, based on Grid and Service Oriented Architecture (SOA) technologies, to address the issues related to the federation lifecycle management in a secure B2B environment. In contrast to the current state of the art, that is mainly based of results coming from the eScience community, such as VOMS [4] or GridShib [5], the solutions proposed take into account the needs and requirements of the business communities. This aspect has had a deep impact in the design and implementation of the proposed software components.

While, in fact, most of the eScience solutions propose and implement coarse-grained models to address issues related to membership and management of resources in a Virtual Organization [1] (for instance, allowing the access to a whole resources for job submission) in our case we have requirements that foresees a fine-grained approach (for instance, allowing the access to specific capabilities offered by a Service Provider).

The results presented in this paper are part of the EU FP6 Business Experiments in GRID (BEinGRID) project [6] that is focused around two complementary activities. Firstly, the project is undertaking a series of Business Experiment (BE) pilots designed to implement and deploy Grid solutions in a broad spectrum of business sectors. Secondly, a toolset repository of software components is created to support European businesses that wish to take-up this technology. The work to produce the contents of the repository is divided up into a number of technical Clusters. In BEinGRID project, a Cluster is a thematic activity that focuses on particular technical area relevant for Grid, and produces patterns and generic components by analysing independent requirements and designs provided by each one of the sector-focused pilot projects.

The Clusters defined in the project are: Security, Virtual Organization Management, Service Management (including Service Level Agreements), Data Management and Portals. This paper is concerned with results of the Security and Virtual Organization Management Clusters. For the purpose of this paper, we focus our attention on the issues relating to federation lifecycle management in a secure B2B environment.

The rest of the paper is as follow. In section 2, we briefly recall the methodology adopted to elicit requirements in order to define the patterns and software components, in section 3 we present the software components, and in section 4 we present the case of study. In sections 5 and 6 we discuss main results and business benefits and, eventually, in section 7 we draw our conclusions.

2.   Methodology

The methodology followed to define the components is based on the analysis the BEs. We extract requirements from BEs, identify architectural capabilities and produce design patterns and components. The approach, therefore, is driven from the concrete necessity of the BEs rather than from the theoretical benefits of the Grid technologies.

The BEs selected for analysis cover several vertical markets, including the following: Civil Architecture (BE03 [11]), Retail (BE05 [12]), Leisure & Entertainment (BE09 [13]), Chemistry (BE14 [14]), Finance (BE15 [15]). This diversity further strengthens the value of the results and the commonality of the requirements identified.

It became apparent during the analysis that the business communities are currently more interested in simplifying the management of heterogeneous resources in *a federated business environment* than the dynamicity of the life-cycle of Virtual Organizations. In particular, the BEs analysed present common requirements mainly related to *accessing and managing in a simple and secure way* heterogeneous distributed resources shared among the organisations participating in a collaboration, and issues relating to resource discovery and application/service deployment.

Another key problem that emerges from this analysis is the *dematerialisation* of thc ICT infrastructure underpinning Virtual Organisations: application and ICT resource providers want to reduce or outsource the overhead, also in terms of cost, of managing the distributed Service-Oriented Infrastructure that underpins their Business-to-Business collaborations.

3.   The Software Components

As evidenced in the previous section, common requirements derived from the analysis of the BEs relate to a trend towards either outsourcing or reducing the costs and overhead of managing a shared distributed infrastructure, to simplify access to (and management of) the infrastructure's resources, to support the deployment and distribution of applications on the infrastructure without compromising security or quality-of-service.

This indicates the need for common capabilities and patterns that allow ASPs, ISVs and other providers of business applications to concentrate on the application management and the application service exposure / provisioning to their customers without having to deal with the infrastructure management or administration

In the following subsections we present the main components developed to address the requirements and common capabilities resulted from the BEs analysis. Details on the associated design patterns are presented in [3] and in [7].

3.1   VO Set-Up

This component is required to set up relevant information of a B2B collaboration.

During the VO identification & formation phases, in general, there is the need to perform operations like configuration of the infrastructure, instantiation and orchestration of the application service, assignment and set up of resources and activation of services, notification of the involved members, and manifestation of the new VO.

The high level architecture of this component is presented below:

- *VO Set-up*: this is mainly a façade interacting with the other components.
- *Registries*: these contain new members and service instances of the VO.
- *Federation*: this is in charge to create a federation and to manage the identity of the federation members. This component can be designed according to the Secure Federation Design Patterns [8] and other patterns proposed by the security area of the BEinGRID project such as the Security Token Service one [9] – see below for further details on the STS.

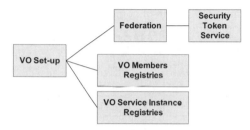

Figure 1: VO Set-Up

The component is useful in several concrete scenarios where there is a low level of dynamicity in the VO (meaning that the other steps of the creation process, such as agreement negotiations and policy definition, may be performed off-line). The federation manager of this component implements and extends the TrustCoM model [16] and is detailed in the next section.

3.2   B2B Federation Management services (FMS) and Security Token Services (STS)

The STS acts as an identity broker for each enterprise, and manages the correlation of identities and security attributes within a security domain with commonly understood credentials across domains. It allows:
1) managing a local participant's perspective of a circle of trust, and
2) adapting local authentication mechanism, token scheme, identity token transformation scheme based on contextual information, secure remote management.

The STS pattern originates research by BT and Microsoft (EMIC) in the TrustCoM project [18].

The key features of this design include:

Context-driven adaptation: A "context selector" inspects issuance, exchange or validation requests for a context element – typically a WS-Federation identifier -   and depending on this selects a configuration from a repository including:
- a business logic explaining how to do the issuance or validation
- a set of security modules implementing info-sets & actions, such as: token format, internal identity profile, inter-organisational claims profile, token signature scheme.

Consequently the observable STS behaviour is different for different federation contexts, and adaptation to a federation context happens at real-time depending on the context of the request.

Contextualisation of token issuance: The same internal resource X – identified by its internal certificate - can be issued different token in content depending on the context of the request. The context of the issuance request is configurable: e.g. Federation identifier, resource to contact, action to be performed, etc. The functionality for issuing or exchanging security tokens (including the token format) is extensible, supporting, for example, custom XML tokens, SAML assertions, and X.509 certificates at the same time.

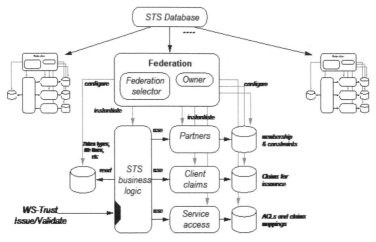

Figure 2: Federation and STS

Manage circle of trust: Each STS holds signed statements identifying the other STSs in a circle of trust and an explicitly defined federation identifier. It also accepts a "local federation context owner" and allows the creation of an association of a global federation identifier with the group of participating STS identities and the identity of the local owner of the federation. The local owner (administrator) manages the local view of the circle of trust underpinning the federation.

The Federation Management Service (FMS) allows managing the full life-cycle of circles of trust, by coordinating a distributed process that establishes trust between the participating STSs. The model allows for STS allows creating asymmetric views of a circle of trust. For example:

- A, B, C participate in the same circle of trust FedID
- A recognizes token issuance authority of A, B and C in FedID
- B recognizes token issuance authority of B and C in FedID
- C recognizes token issuance authority of A and C in FedID

3.3   Policy Enforcement Point

The PEP is an adaptable policy enforcement component that does SOAP level processing on behalf of an application service. In addition, by exposing the application at a given endpoint on the PEP itself, it effectively virtualizes the application. Lastly, the PEP can also handle basic XML threats by providing schema validation, wsdl validation of incoming SOAP messages, XML structure analysis (e.g. XML node depth), etc. For more information on the PEP, please refer to [17] in these proceedings.

3.4   Policy Decision Point

The role of the Policy Decision Point (PDP) is to assist services in their access control. A service can use an associated PDP to determine whether a particular access to the service should be allowed or not. The PDP is policy-based: is based on XACML 3 with some extensions for handling delegation and obligations. For more information on the PDP, please refer to [17] in these proceedings.

4.   The Business Case: Online Game Application

The software components presented are arranged together, adopted and validated in a concrete business experiment of the BEinGRID project, the BE09, whose goal is to develop a Virtual Hosting Environment (VHE) for on-line game provision.

Virtualisation of hosting environments refers to the federation of a set of distributed hosting environments for execution of an application and the possibility to provide a single access point (e.g. a Gateway) to this set of federated hosting environments.

In a typical scenario, a number of host providers offer hosting resources to the Application Providers for deploying and running their applications, which are then "virtualized" with the use of middleware services for managing non-functional aspects of the application, and are transparently exposed to the end user via a single VHE.

With the above in mind, the aim of this business experiment is to improve flexibility, dynamism and performance of the game application exposure and execution. Current gaming platforms, in fact, are very static in nature, with dedicated game servers. As such, the platforms experience extreme peaks and lows in demand, due to the period of the day or week, and ongoing gaming activity. This causes very low utilization of dedicated gaming servers, and therefore high cost of initial investment and maintenance.

The approach taken through the use of VHE is to make available infrastructure services for security, community management and virtualisation that can be used by various service providers, allowing them to link with each other. This is achieved via a generic "business-to-business gateway" component (see Figure 3).

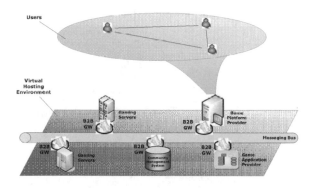

Figure 3: VHE Applied to the Online Gaming Application

In this scenario, the game application provider deploys its gaming application onto two different execution environments (gaming servers), owned by different host providers. The game platform provider, who wants to offer the game to an end user, discovers gaming servers and creates business relationships with them, and also with a separate service provider who offers a system for community management (of gaming clans, tournaments, advanced statistics). Through use of the VHE, these various services are offered transparently to an end user, including the game platform provider's ability to perform the load balancing and server selection based on the defined SLAs

The VHE developed in this business experiment consists of a network of B2B service gateways integrated with common capabilities for B2B trust federation, identity management, access control, SLA management, accounting and monitoring, as well as application service and resource virtualisation. The B2B gateway functionality is complemented by a federated messaging bus and community management services that facilitate the establishment of B2B collaborations (e.g. in the form of Virtual Organisations).

5.   Main Results

The scenario presented above is clearly a B2B collaborative scenario which foresees the federation of several Service and Game providers. In this scenario we have done preliminary validation of the capabilities of the VO set-up and the triplet STS-PDP-PEP.

With respect to the VO Set-up, the purpose of our tests has been to assess the following functionalities required in the VO formation phase: (*i*) Discovery of potential members on the basis of the capabilities they can offer to the VO, (*ii*) Invite potential member to join the VO, (*iii*) Start the secure federation process, and (*iv*) Publish VO members, after their acceptance of the invitation

Our scenario presumes that each potential member of the VO has advertised to the rest of the world its capabilities. This is done, in our scenario, off-line by the Game Provider Administrator. The Game Provider presents a single point of access and a two level hierarchy of registries to publish its business capabilities. One on each hosts of the provider domain there is an Host Instance Registry. One on the provider Gateway, there is a Gateway Instance Registry

The Game Provider has a business relationship with an entity providing a general catalogue and advertises to the rest of the world its capabilities via the catalogue.

The following picture graphically shows the situation.

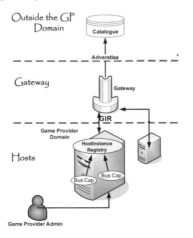

Figure 4: Game Advertising

Apart from the registry management part of the VO set-up component, that involves traditional publish / update operations, our tests have been mainly focused on the secure federation of VO members.

Therefore, a focus from a security perspective was the governance and deployment of security infrastructure services including the PEP, PDP, and STS. The experiment allowed to verify that all three components could be centrally managed and configured in a coherent way. Additionally, there has been significant research into further security components, namely XML security gateways (advanced PEPs), and as a result the experiment has been looking at different vendors' solutions.

From a methodological point of view, we have assessed the added-value of the proposed model for federation of administrative domains with respect to the current state of the art. The proposed model allows, for example, a single administrative domain to federate just a specific capability. This allows a more fine grained approach to resources and services federation more suitable for business applications with respect to the models proposed in the eScience community.

6.   Business Benefits

The validation of the software components in a real business scenario allowed the authors to assess the following business benefits:

Identity and Federation management services: These allow, on the one hand, managing the life-cycle of circles of trust between providers, and therefore the life-cycle management of federation of trust realms, and on the other hand, managing the life-cycled of identities and privileges of users and resources within such federations of trust realms. The obvious benefits of offering these as network-hosted services that can be integrated with application services through the VHE include:

- Facilitating the creation of communities of identity providers that enable identity brokerage and management by supporting open standards such as Liberty Alliance, SAML and WS-Federation, and therefore giving rise to new means of revenue generation.
- Enabling the customer to choose the identity provider that is more appropriate for a specific collaboration instead of being locked into what is incorporated in their SOA platform by some middleware vendor or instead of departing in expensive product integration projects that give them identity provision and federation, at a very high cost, for the specific application at hand.

Flexible, context-aware & adaptive security: the STS-PDP-PEP triplet can be quickly and easily configured to suit the current security situation of exposed services. If new threats are detected such as repetitive failed access attempts, the security infrastructure can reconfigure itself to further prevent such tentative and therefore minimize such risks as denial of service.

7.   Conclusions

While this paper has taken a closer look to a specific experiment, the software components presented can be reused in several common contexts where there is the need to federate different administrative domain and, as evidenced, can be composed in order to address complex issues, such as the creation and management of the VHE previously described.

From a methodological point of view, we have assessed the added-value of the proposed model for federation of administrative domains with respect to the current state of the art. The proposed model allows, for example, a single administrative domain to federate just a specific capability. This allows a more fine grained approach to resources and services federation more suitable for business applications with respect to the models proposed in the eScience community.

From a technological point of view, the main issue encountered has been related to the integration of the software components in the business experiment scenarios. The software components, in fact, have been developed on top of different technologies and different implementations of WS-* specifications.

References

[1]. Foster I., Kesselman C., Tuecke S.: The Anatomy of the Grid: Enabling Scalable Virtual Organizations. International Journal of Supercomputer Applications, 2001, Vol. 15, No. 3, 200-222
[2]. Gamma E., Helm R., Johnson R., Vlissides J.: Design Patterns: Elements of Reusable Object-Oriented Software, Addison-Wesley, 1995 ISBN 0201633612

[3]. A. Gaeta, M. Gaeta, A. Smith, I. Djordjevic, T. Dimitrakos, M. Colombo and S. Miranda "Design patterns for Secure Virtual Organization Management Architecture" proceeding of the First International Workshop on Security, Trust and Privacy in Grid Systems, September 17, Nice, France. Accepted for publication in a Special Issue of Future Generation Computer Systems Elsevier B.V. Journal

[4]. Virtual Organization Membership Service, http://hep-project-grid-scg.web.cern.ch/hep-project-grid-scg/voms.html

[5]. GridShib, http://gridshib.globus.org/

[6]. BEinGRID project website: http://www.beingrid.eu

[7]. Gridipedia Web Site http://www.gridipedia.com

[8]. Secure Federation Design Pattern http://www.gridipedia.com/341.html

[9]. Security Design patterns http://www.gridipedia.com/262.html

[10]. SLA Design patterns http://www.gridipedia.com/204.html

[11]. BEinGRID D3.03.1: BE03 requirements description, BEinGRID Deliverable

[12]. BEinGRID D3.05.1: BE05 requirements description, BEinGRID Deliverable

[13]. BEinGRID D3.09.1: BE09 requirements description, BEinGRID Deliverable

[14]. BEinGRID D3.14.1: BE14 requirements description, BEinGRID Deliverable

[15]. BEinGRID D3.15.1: BE15 requirements description, BEinGRID Deliverable

[16]. TrustCom project: www.eu-trustcom.com/

[17]. Common Capabilities for Trust & Security in Service Oriented Infrastructures

[18]. Christian Geuer-Pollmann. "How to Make a Federation Manageable". In Proc. of "Communications and Multimedia Security" 9th IFIP TC-6 TC-11 International Conference, CMS 2005, Salzburg, Austria, Sept. 19 – 21, 2005.

Collaboration and the Knowledge Economy: Issues, Applications, Case Studies
P. Cunningham and M. Cunningham (Eds.)
IOS Press, 2008

Security Focused Dynamic Virtual Organizations in the Grid based on Contracts

Bartosz KRYZA[1], Lukasz DUTKA[1], Renata SLOTA[2], Jacek KITOWSKI[1,2]
[1]*Academic Computer Centre CYFRONET-AGH, Nawojki 11, Krakow, 30-950, POLAND*
Email: bkryza@agh.edu.pl, dutka@agh.edu.pl
[2]*Institute of Computer Science AGH-UST, Mickiewicza 30, Krakow, POLAND*
Email: rena@agh.edu.pl, kito@agh.edu.pl

Abstract: In the paper our work in the area of supporting dynamic Virtual Organization creation and management with ontologies and contracts is presented. A framework called FiVO (Framework for Intelligent Virtual Organizations) is described, along with its overall application in a Grid setting, its architecture and sample use case.

1. Introduction

Virtual Organizations (VO) are the core concept of Grid computing which allows us to group users and resources into collaboration environments in order to share and use resources such as computing power and services based on proper rules. The main problem faced by Grid administrators and users is the burden of setting up a VO and managing its life-cycle, including inception, deployment, evolution and dissolution. In order to support creation of on-demand dynamic Virtual Organizations we propose a semantic based framework, called FiVO (Framework for Intelligent Virtual Organizations) [1,2]. This framework enables creating a particular VO based on a negotiated semantic contract, which defines the rules of resource sharing as well as SLA parameters that can be used by the monitoring infrastructure to enforce proper Quality of Service within the VO [3]. The framework is aimed at VO administrators and middleware service developers, in order to allow for semi-automatic configuration and deployment of the VO as well as further VO execution.

Current solutions related to contract based management of VO are mostly concerned with simple QoS parameters and SLA. However, we believe that contracts should include much more information, especially that related to the authorization statements which allow to state exact rules of sharing the resources within a VO in case of multiple parties. In order to support that scenario, the contract model must be abstract enough in order to handle various, often highly heterogeneous environments. Our vision is to provide a generic interface and contract model for the purpose of dynamic definition of Virtual Organization by means of contract statements and then properly deploy the VO depending on existing middleware, including security and monitoring components, in particular environment. This issue becomes of particular importance in case of modern large scale integration activities, for instance related to integration of multiple national Grid infrastructures (NGI's), where a need emerges to create Virtual Organizations spanning several infrastructures which often are based on incompatible middleware (e.g. Globus vs. Unicore) and use different models of Virtual Organizations. In that case availability of high level and middleware independent

VO management framework will allow to manage Virtual Organizations while limited the inherent burden on system administrators.

This paper describes a complex approach to addressing VO management issues in Grid environments. It describes the contract ontology we have developed with special focus on its security aspects, which make it possible to define during contract negotiation step of VO inception phase rules under which resources available within a VO can be shared by the participants of the VO and how it is used to configure underlying Grid authorization system used by a particular VO, e.g. PERMIS and VOMS. The framework is being evaluated within the framework of EU-IST project Gredia, on two commercial applications. First one is related to inter-banking solution for automatic credit-scoring of bank users credit requests. The second one is a media application oriented on providing a collaborative environment for nomadic journalists. The paper describes a sample case study based on a bank scenario where bank evaluates on-line requests for their clients, including information from third-party data sources which constitute the Virtual Organization.

2. Related Work

In [4] authors present an SLA negotiation and enforcement tool applicable to business settings based on GRIA middleware and evaluated within the EU-IST SIMDAT project. In the paper they present detailed mathematical model taking into account both resource usage reports as well as various SLA constraints. Authors of [5] present requirements for automating the contract management in a VO. They identify 3 kinds of contracts in a VO: business contract, ICT contract and ASP contract. In the context of the legality of a VO, it could be, in theory at least, registered as a legal entity or not. If it is not its contract is defined by bilateral agreements between the respective partners expressed in the form of contracts. The ICT contract involves the client and the participants of the VO. In [6] attempt was made to formalize a definition of contract-based multi-agent Virtual Organization. The authors define 4 key properties of VOs: Autonomy, Heterogeneity, Dynamism and Structure. They use terminology from agent-based systems, e.g. they refer to the VO itself as an agent. The contract is defined as a set of commitments, goals and agents in some context. The paper introduces a formal definition of a hierarchical VO with a set of agents (which can be VOs themselves), policies, goals and commitments. The VO is then a set of bilateral contracts between agents in a VO, and can be more easily defined in a distributed setting. For example for 3 partners and 2 contracts A<->B and B<->C, A and C don't event need to know about each other. Another example of contract based VO's is presented in [7]. The authors present web-Pilarcos J2EE based agent framework for managing contract based Virtual Organizations. The contract itself is an object (J2EE EntityBean) and can be in several states such as In-negotiation, Terminated etc. The proposed solution is not based on ontologies, and the metadata reasoning is mentioned briefly. The proposed architecture has many different components - which might make it hard for integration with custom systems - should rather provide a more unified interface based on easily adaptable standards. Paper discusses the basic requirements for a VO contract such as modeling of service behaviour, communication services and some non-functional properties such as QoS. It also discusses the operation of VOs, the need for monitoring of security and SLAs for ensuring proper QoS and the evolution of Vos. In [8] the authors propose an architecture of a system which maps Business Level Objectives to SLA and policies. The paper discusses the need to go from abstract SLA concepts understood differently by different parties to low-level configuration concepts - which they refer to Operational Level Agreement. The proposed system aims at supporting configuration of providers systems so that it can guarantee proper BLO and SLA. In [9] authors present a scheme for managing QoS based on SLA contracts with a focus on mobile devices, which functionality is split into two basic phases: discovery and reservation, execution and monitoring. In [10] authors describe the approach to dynamic Virtual Organization of the TrustCOM project, where VO is defined as recursive set of organizations and other Virtual Organizations, which could be created on demand in reaction to a particular business need or market opportunity. The core issue was enabling of trust approach based on requestor experiences control of roles of a participant in a VO.

3. Methodology

The overall aim of the GREDIA is development of a Grid application platform, providing high level support for the implementation of Grid business applications concerned with users mobility. This platform is generic in order to combine both existing and arising Grid middleware, and facilitates the provision of business services, which mainly demand access and sharing of large quantities of distributed annotated numerical and multimedia content. One of the main GREDIA features is its focus on mobile users to exploit Grid technologies in seamless way by enabling mobile access and sharing of distributed content.

The potential results of the platform are being validated through two pilot applications, including media and banking. To handle complexity of allocating heterogeneous resources in the Grid and to make their usage possible with mobile devices, GREDIA strongly focuses on dynamic Virtual Organizations. A significant contribution of GREDIA is to hide the complexity of heterogeneous resources and support dynamic Virtual Organizations of business mobile entities through a special semantic framework.

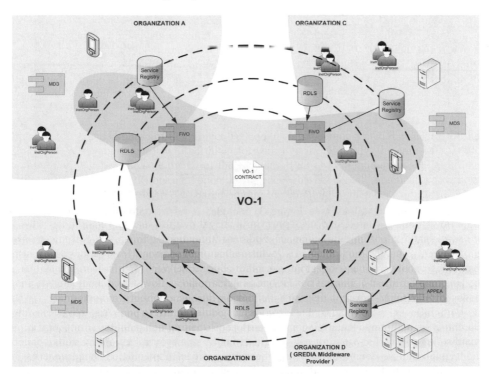

Figure 1. Sample deployment of FiVO in a Grid setting

Figure 1 presents example deployment of the FiVO framework in a distributed GREDIA environment. Four organizations are sharing their resources within the VO-1. FiVO component is deployed logically within each organization and is responsible for storing semantic descriptions of its contents (i.e. resources provided to other organizations). These descriptions can include such aspects of organization as its structure and business logic described in proper ontology as well as hardware, data and service resources available and provide for sharing with other organizations.

The negotiation process is performed in a distributed and iterative manner, where responsible people from each participating organization state their requests and obligations using special Graphical User Interface which allows them to see the changes made by others and either accept or reject them. The user interface is based on Protege ontology editor, thus allowing users to directly have a semantic view over their resources as well as the current state of the contract negotiations (see Figure 2). The contract itself is defined using a special ontology.

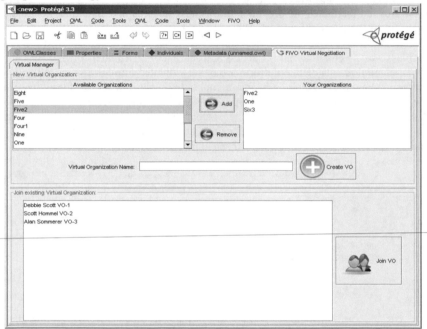

Figure 2. FiVO Graphical User Interface for contract negotiation

The Contract Ontology (see Figure 3) includes a set of ontologies, which allow to specify all issues necessary for the FiVO framework to configure and deploy the Virtual Organization. The main components of this ontology include generic model of Virtual Organization, Security Ontology which allows to defined abstract inter-domain security assertions on resource sharing, a QoS ontology which allows to state the required Quality of Service parameters for accessing resources in the VO and an ontology which describes the contract itself and formalizes the entire negotiation process. In order to reflect the domain specific aspects of the Virtual Organization several domain-level ontologies can be included in the contract ontology for a particular Virtual Organization in order to allow definition of rules for custom resources that will be available in the Virtual Organization.

After the contract between parties is negotiated, our framework configures semi-automatically all dependent Grid middleware such as authorization and monitoring systems in order for the Virtual Organization to be deployed. For instance the configuration of the PERMIS authorization layer is performed by setting up its LDAP certificate registries with proper policies specifying which roles can use which services and under what conditions Additionally the VOMS service is configure with proper attribute certificates specifying which users belong to which roles (see Figure 4).

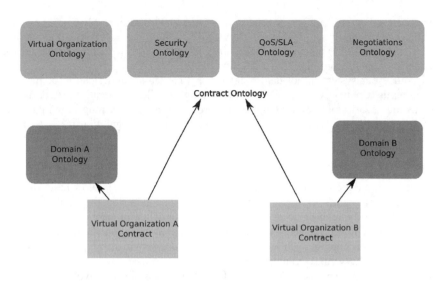

Figure 3. Overview of the contract ontology

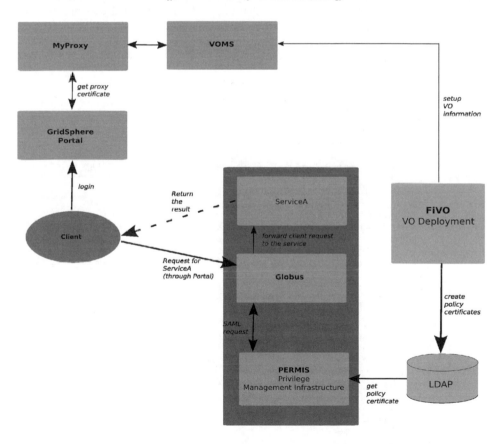

Figure 4. FiVO and authorization infrastructure in a typical Grid setting

The core of our framework is based on a Grid Organizational Memory (GOM) [11] semantic knowledge base, developed previously, which stores information about the contract and performs ontological reasoning in order to infer additional statements necessary to properly configure the middleware.

Of course our system is not dependent on any particular authorization or monitoring solution, as the Contract Ontology is abstract enough to allow generation of configuration in any available Grid middleware component, provided that proper plug-in is implemented in FiVO which can translate the ontology concepts to the configuration rules used by the underlying middleware.

4. Sample Use Case

Our system will be presented here based on a banking use case scenario where users apply for a loan using bank's website. The Virtual Organization for the bank has several requirements mostly relating to security and confidentiality of clients information. The bank's internal credit scoring services require additional information about the client during the loan evaluation process such as client credit history provided by a third-party, which must be a part of the Virtual Organization.

Within the bank itself, several users with various roles can be involved in the credit scoring process and according to their roles only certain operations can be performed on the clients data. Additional issue is assurance that the credit response will be generated in a given time frame, which imposes special requirements on the Quality of Service of the services used in the evaluation process.

Below is a part of the sample contract for this Virtual Organization rendered in Web Ontology Language:

```
<j.0:VirtualOrganization rdf:ID="EasyLoan">
 <j.0:name rdf:datatype="...">
        EasyLoan Application VO</j.0:name>
 <j.0:administeredBy rdf:resource="#Marco"/>
 <j.3:hasContract>
  <j.3:Contract rdf:ID="EasyLoanContract">
   <j.3:hasStatement>
    <j.3:Statement rdf:ID="StCreditCalculation">
     <j.3:hasAtom>
      <j.3:Atom rdf:ID="AtomCreditCalculationService">
       <j.3:hasActor rdf:ID="#Marco"/>
       <j.3:hasResource>
        <j.2:Service rdf:ID="CreditCalculationService">
         <j.0:isOwnedBy rdf:resource="#HappyBank"/>
         <j.0:belongsTo rdf:resource="#EasyLoan"/>
        </j.2:Service>
       </j.3:hasResource>
       <j.3:hasAction>
        <j.3:Action rdf:ID="ProvidesService"/>
       </j.3:hasAction>
       <j.3:hasParameter>
         <j.3:Parameter>
          <j.0:hasQoSAttribute>
          ---- j.5:QoSAttribute - #j.6:TimeToComplete
          </j.0:hasQoSAttribute>
          <j.6:hasValue>
          ---- { "15", #owlTime::unitMinute }
          </j.6:hasValue>
         </j.3:Parameter>
        </j.3:hasParameter>
        <j.3:hasParameter>
         <j.3:Parameter>
          <j.0:hasAuthorizationRestriction>
```

```
     ---- j.5:accessRole
    </j.0:hasAuthorizationRestriction>
    <j.6:hasValue>
     ---- { "#BankClerk" }
    </j.6:hasValue>
    </j.3:Parameter>
   </j.3:hasParameter>
   ---- more parameters ...
   </j.3:Atom>
  </j.3:hasAtom>
  </j.3:Statement>
 </j.3:hasStatement>
 </j.3:Contract>
</j.3:hasContract>
</j.0:VirtualOrganization>
```

This contract is used by FiVO to configure Grid middleware services such as VOMS, PERMIS or MDS in order to actually deploy the Virtual Organization in the Grid environment. This includes generation of for instance PERMIS policies as well as for instance WS-Agreement documents. Further enforcement of the contract statements is performed automatically by these services.

5. Conclusions

In this paper we have presented a framework for supporting dynamic Virtual Organizations inception and management in the Grid setting with a focus on both security of interaction within the VO as well as Quality of Service issues. The framework is currently being evaluated in two pilot applications, and we are still collecting relevant feedback from users that will be taken into account while finalizing the implementation of the system. Major achievements up to date include the definition of the Contract Ontology along with a formal negotiation model and development of the contract negotiation services and Graphical User Interface. The future work includes integration of the framework with most popular Grid middleware security and monitoring components for the purpose of scalable contract enforcement in large heterogeneous Virtual Organizations.

Acknowledgements

The authors want to acknowledge the support of the EU GREDIA Project (IST-FP6-034363) and AGH University of Science and Technology grants 11.11.120.777 and 500-08.

References

[1] Kryza, B., Dutka, L., Slota, R., and Kitowski, J., Supporting Knowledge-based Dynamic Virtual Organizations with Contracts, eChallenges 2007 Conference and Exhibition, The Hague, Netherlands, 24 - 26 October 2007. pp. 937–945. ,

[2] Kryza, B., Dutka, L., Slota, R., and Kitowski, J., Supporting Management of Dynamic Virtual Organizations in the Grid through Contracts, in: M. Bubak, M. Turala, K. Wiatr, Proceedings of Cracow'07 Grid Workshop, Oct 15-17 2007, Cracow, Poland. , ACC Cyfronet AGH, 2008, pp.140-147

[3] M. Zuzek, M. Talik, T. Swierczynski, C. Wisniewski, B. Kryza, L. Dutka, and J. Kitowski, Formal Model for Contract Negotiation in Knowledge-Based Virtual Organizations, in: M. Bubak, G. D. van Albada and J. Dongarra and P. M.A. Sloot (Eds.), Proceedings of Computational Science - ICCS 2008, 8th International Conference Krakow, Poland, June 2008, volume III, LNCS 5103, Springer, 2008, pp. 409-418

[4] Boniface, M., Phillips, S. and Surrige, M., Grid-Based Business Partnerships Using Service Level Agreements. In proc. of Cracow Grid Workshop 2006 (CGW'06), (Eds) Bubak, M., Turala, M., Wiatr, K., ACK-Cyfronet AGH, Krakow 2007, pp. 165–176

[5] M. Shelbourn, T. Hassan and C. Carter, Legal and contractual framework for the VO. In: L.M. Camarinha-Matos, H. Afsarmanesh and M. Ollus, (Eds), Virtual Organizations Systems and Practices. Springer, 2005, pp.167–176.

1160	*B. Kryza et al. / Security Focused Dynamic Virtual Organizations*

[6]	Udupi, Y. B., and Singh, M. P. Contract enactment in virtual organizations: A commitment-based approach. In proc. of AAAI-06. AAAI Press. pp. 722–728
[7]	Metso, J., and Kutvonen, L. Managing virtual organizations with contracts. In Workshop on Contract Architectures and Languages (CoALa2005) (2005). Enschede, The Netherlands, 2005.
[8]	Hasselmeyer, P., Koller, B., Schubert, L., and Wieder, P. Towards SLA-supported resource management. in: M. Gerndt, D. Kranzlmuller (Eds.), Proc. of High Performance Computing and Communications, Second International Conference, HPCC 2006, Munich, Germany, September 2006, LNCS 4208, Springer 2006. pp. 743–752.
[9]	Litke, A., Konstanteli, K., Andronikou, V., Chatzis, S., and Varvarigou, T., Execution Management and SLA Enforcement in Akogrimo. In proc. of Cracow Grid Workshop 2006 (CGW'06). (Eds) Bubak, M., Turala, M., and Wiatr, K. ACK-Cyfronet AGH, Krakow, 2007. pp. 154–164
[10]	T Dimitrakos, G Laria, I Djordjevic, N Romano, F D'Andria, V Trpkovski, et al (6) Towards a Grid Platform Enabling Dynamic Virtual Organisations for Business Applications Proc. Trust Management, Third International Conference (iTrust 2005), Paris, France, 23-26 May 2005, LNCS 3477
[11]	Kryza, B., Slota, R., Majewska, M., Pieczykolan, J., and Kitowski, J., Grid organizational memory: provision of a high-level Grid abstraction layer supported by ontology alignment, The International Journal of FGCS, Grid Computing: Theory, methods & Applications, vol. 23, issue 3, Mar 2007, Elsevier, 2007, pp. 348-358

Collaboration and the Knowledge Economy: Issues, Applications, Case Studies
P. Cunningham and M. Cunningham (Eds.)
IOS Press, 2008

Forecasting Structural and Functional Aspects of Virtual Organisations

Heiko DUIN, Jens ESCHENBÄCHER
BIBA GmbH, Hochschulring 20 , 28359 Bremen, Germany
Tel: +49 421 218-5539, Fax: +49 421 218-5610, Email: esc@biba.uni-bremen.de

Abstract: Planning and management of Virtual Organisations (VOs) depends on accurate prognosis of several organisational aspects. This paper examines how structural and functional aspects of such enterprise networks might be forecasted by using systemic methods. The structural aspects cover the partners and their collaborative interactions while the functional aspects describe the value creation processes accompanied by auxiliary processes. Furthermore, an industrial case study is presented and initial expected results from the application of two selected methods are given. The methods analysed in detail are the cross-impact analysis and the collaborative network analysis method.

1. Introduction

Prognosis and forecasting have been discussed several years [1]. They can be seen as important component of all types of strategic planning [2]. In this respect Wild [3, p. 87] pointed out that decision making on the issue prognosis is indeed the most important information, which will be collected and used in the process of enterprise planning. Regarding the strategic management of companies all aspects of enterprise analysis and environment analysis are subject of prognosis and measurements. Trends in the macro environments such as investments in new ICT solutions [4], changes in competitive situation and evolving changes in resource and competence management of companies do call for new forecasting methods and instruments. A classical systematisation of these methods and instruments differentiates quantitative and qualitative approaches [5], [6], [7]. All these approaches have been developed for the usage in companies. Similar to Weber [8], this paper discusses the forecasting of structural and functional aspects in virtual organisations.

Forecasting business developments have a long tradition [9]. Especially within innovation processes it becomes a key competence to better understand upcoming developments. Boutellier et al show that a systematic planning of R&D and innovation processes can support the competitiveness dramatically. The authors discuss altogether 21 case studies of best-in-class companies dealing with the uncertainties of innovation. [10]. Also MCInerney shows that forecasting can play an enormous benefit to better understand customer requirements as for his case Panasonic [11]. They also state a general trend towards decentralization and cooperation towards virtual organisation can be observed [12]. These aspects can be seen as starting point of our investigations.

This paper addresses the forecast and management of such innovation-oriented VOs. First, based on a systemic view, structural and functional forecasting in VOs is introduced. Here the concept of forecasting structure and functional behaviour of VOs will be discussed. Forecasting can be seen as one very important function for those types of networks. Second, a scenario is presented and will be used to demonstrate the forecasting approach. Thirdly business benefits are presented. The results have been tested in the context of the IST-research project ECOLEAD (www.ecolead.org).

2. Structural and Functional Forecasting of a VO

This chapter provides an overview about the conceptual view of structural and functional aspects of Virtual Organisations.

2.1 Structural and Functional Aspects

Camarinha-Matos and Afsarmanesh have developed a first draft for reference model for collaborative networks, which comprises four dimensions: Structural, componential, functional and behavioural [13]. These dimensions have been created to formalise the issues according to design and coordination of Virtual Organisations. Indeed the structural and functional dimension can be easier coordinated as the other two because informal issues such as componential and behavioural are more difficult to influence. Furthermore, the componential aspects describe the equipment of the network which could easily be adapted to structural and functional needs. The behavioural aspects emerge from a concrete design of structure and function. Consequently, the following focuses on the two most important dimensions:

2.1.1 Structural Dimension

This dimension addresses the structure or composition of the VO constituting elements (its participants and their relationships) as well as the roles performed by those elements including other compositional characteristics of the network nodes such as location, time, etc. The structural perspective is used in many disciplines (e.g. systems and software engineering, economy, politics, cognitive sciences, manufacturing), although with different "wording" and associations.

- Actors/relationships – identifying all the participating actors (nodes) in the network as well as their inter-relationships (edges). Actors can be any kind of organisations (e.g. enterprises) or people. Two (or more) actors can be linked through a number of different types of relationships, e.g. client-supplier, sharing, co-authoring.
- Roles – describing and characterising the roles that can be performed by the actors in the network. A role defines an expected behaviour of an actor in a given context. Examples of roles are: Member, coordinator, broker, planner, etc.

2.1.2 Functional Dimension

The functional dimension addresses the basic operational functions available at the network level consisting of time-sequenced flows of executable operations (processes and procedures) related to the different phases of the VO life cycle.

- Processes – this sub-dimension is concerned with the processes involved in the main line of activities of the network. Processes represent the structured part of operational activities of the network. Examples are distributed business processes in a VO.
- Auxiliary processes – including those processes that are designed to assist the VO in terms of its maintenance and improvement of operations. Examples include performance monitoring, competencies management, etc.
- Methodologies – typically less formalised than processes, represent the body of practices, procedures and rules used by human actors in VO. Often, they are represented as a semi-structured set of steps (informal enumeration of activities) combined with some structured representation of input/output information. An example is the methodology followed by a broker to announce a business opportunity to VO members.

The following chapter provides a system-oriented view on VOs to further narrow the concept of structure and function in Virtual Organisations.

2.2 System Oriented View on Virtual Organisations

A VO can be considered as a system, which is composed of nodes and edges [14]. Then, the dimensions can be characterised in the following way:

- Structural Dimension: Network nodes are represented by system elements and edges describe the relations among the nodes. A number of elements that are connected by relations describe a system. A subgroup of elements and relations can be a sub-system, if all elements and relations also belong to the system. Finally, a system is embedded in a super-system, which creates a framework for the bigger picture. The actors and their relationships are supplemented by roles – both together is characterised by the structural dimension (see Figure 1).

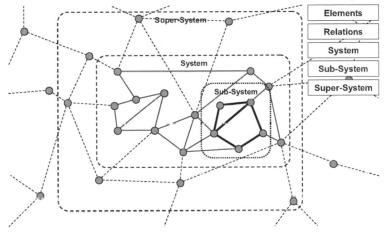

Figure 1: System-Oriented View on Networks like VOs

- Functional Dimension: The functional dimension is described in Figure 3. The VO life cycle is illustrated by the terms VO formation, VO set-up, VO operation and VO dissolution. Indeed, the VO preparation phase is in the focus of the functional dimension, because it is characterised by (distributed) processes and auxiliary processes.

3. Forecasting in Virtual Organisations

3.1 Quantitative and Qualitative Forecasting Approaches

Quantitative forecasting methods deliver on the basis of mathematical and statistical operations results regarding to the intended result. A short overview about the quantitative methods and instruments, including a short characteristic and application fields is shown in several publications [15].

The second group is called qualitative forecasting methods. Those methods have been highlighted in strategic management due to the high uncertainty which continuously increases in companies. They are suited for application in enterprise and network contexts in which either past data is not available or in which data cannot be easily quantified. Simon [16] differentiates quantitative from qualitative forecasting methods with the help of the following characteristics:

- The application is limited on worse structured situations, which are labelled by imperfect information.
- They deliver no guarantee for solutions, but they can be used to reduce the complexity by focusing on a view on most suitable solutions.

- Qualitative methods imply subjective assumptions on individuals or groups.

To summarise, qualitative methods shall be seen as forecasting approaches which are based on a subjective evaluation of the respective prognosis issue.

Both, qualitative and quantitative methods have been developed for the usage in enterprises. As an addition, this paper shows how two approaches can be applied in the dynamic context of smart and virtual organisations. These two methods have been developed towards demonstration of forecasting in VOs.

3.2   Forecasting Approach

The forecasting approach shall improve the planning and management of VOs. One of the main objectives is to reduce the complexity. Figure 2 shows precisely that the approach shall be used to do two things: First, providing information about the structural and functional dimension, and second, to forecast developments of the real world by decomposing it into structural models and further into a rough model. These three layers are presented in Figure 2. By forecasting the "real world" detailed information about structure and processes can be determined.

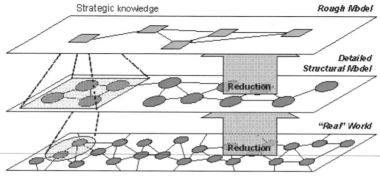

Figure 2: Reduction of Complexity by Modelling

Figure 3 integrates the view of nodes and edges, VO life-cycle and functional and structural dimensions with the ideas of an accurate forecast. Here, the forecast includes not only the estimation about the number of nodes and their edges but also an assumption of the intensity of the collaboration among partners.

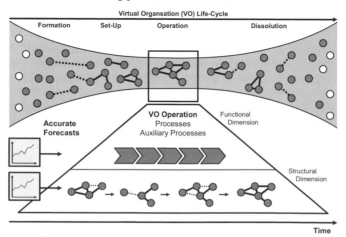

Figure 3: Forecasting Structural and Functional Dimensions

Forecasting of the structural and functional dimensions of the VO should be done using methods based on a systemic approach. As a first attempt, causal cross-impact analysis and network analysis has been chosen for this task.

The next section presents a case study to illustrate the forecasting approach.

4.   Scenario Discussion

In European IST research projects such as TRUSTCOM (www.eu-trustcom.com), ECOLEAD (www.ecolead.org), DBE (www.digital-ecosystem.org) and Intelligrid (intelligrid.info) structure, processes, needs, requirements and IT-Systems for VOs have been analysed. The main focus was constantly on the development and usage of ICT. For some reason the analysis of forecasting methods were only subject in the ECOLEAD project, where the following descriptions are based on.

One of the ECOLEAD cases, the CeBeNetwork scenario, is described in full length in [17]. This case is used for relevant aspects for this paper.

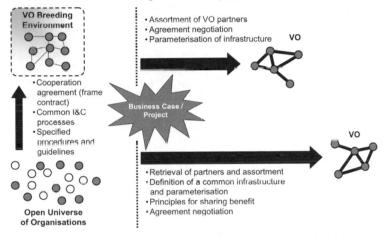

Figure 4: From VBE to the VO in the CeBeNetwork Case (ECOLEAD 2005)

4.1   Collaborative Engineering Scenario

The "CeBeNetwork cooperation group" exists and is proven since November 2002 as an international aerospace subcontractor network of more than 20 partners with over 20 years of experience in aerospace. It provides competitive services for the aviation sector in France, Germany, UK and Spain and additionally in some low-cost countries. It is trying to create new business in automotive and other industries. Figure 4 shows the transformation from the open universe to the CeBeNetwork VBE. Out of this VBE a real VO is created.

4.2   Scenario Specification

Figure 5 shows the ECOLEAD demonstration case scenario. In the cloud a number of new companies (not member of the CeBeNetwork VBE) and new partners (new members of the VBE) are trying to initiate a cooperation. Additionally freelancer's form a Professional virtual community (PVC) which could be freelancers or programming experts are selected which both together create the CeBeNETwork collaborative engineering VO. This dynamic VO is coordinated by CeBeNetwork as VO coordinator that creates the interface to the customer.

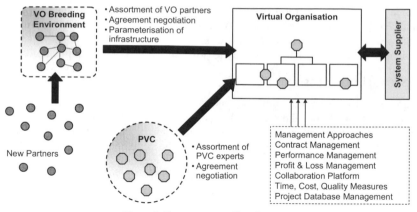

Figure 5: Demonstration Case Scenario

The grey box indicates that all VO functions identified in Figure 5 do play a role in the collaborative engineering case of CeBeNetwork.

4.3　Application of the Forecasting Approach

Baseline of this paper is the conceptual business case of an aeronautical supplier. Actually this supplier is transforming the value chain in a more virtual, smart supply chain. The case has been conducted by using a system analysis point of view (see chapter 2).

The subject of forecasting virtual organisations implies an enormous complexity. This complexity can be structured into three different levels which show a rough model (we call it birds eye view, representing strategic knowledge), detailed model (we call it system model level) and the picture of the real world which includes all the complexity (see Figure 2). Our approach is to use the rough model – the birds eye view – to understand the most important structural elements of the system and to forecast the tendencies within its functional behaviour.

5.　Results

Forecasting methods play a prominent role in enterprise management. They can be used to better understand future trends [18] and developments in order to prepare answers towards the organisation of inter-organizational business processes. The case example has shown that the two presented approaches clearly add value to the prognoses of organizational developments including collaborative networks. Especially virtual organisations need a strong strategic planning to better understand their own structure and behaviour.

5.1　Contributions of Methods

Table 1 gives an overview on the single contributions the two chosen methods provides for the structural and functional dimension.

	Causal Cross-Impact Analysis [20]	Collaboration Network Analysis [19]
Structural Dimension	*Actors relationships*	
	Strategic planning; Assessment of market niche / business opportunity; Competition	Short-term / mid term planning of actors and their relationships; Network structure; Specification of necessary relationships
	Roles	
	Consortium balance; Network size	Roles of VO partners; Value chain structure
Functional Dimension	*Processes*	
	Efficiency and effectiveness; Best competence fit; Process performance	Design of distributed business process by using Porter Value chain model; Stage-Gate-Process; Collaboration intensity
	Auxiliary processes	
	Adequacy of auxiliary processes	Understanding of secondary value chain processes

Table 1: Contributions of Methods to Structural and Functional Dimension

5.2   Expected Business Benefits

Collaborative networks are going to become the major driver for European industry (ECOLEAD 2008, COIN IP 2008). So far the dissemination of such organisational forms are still lacking far behind expectations [22]. The authors claim that one reason is the missing knowledge and understanding about accurate forecast and planning. By using the two approaches the following business benefits can be summarised:

- Better strategic understanding of the potential actors relationships and / or roles with the Virtual Organisation –leads to improvements,
- Better definition of partner roles before starting the operation phase,
- More efficient business process management.

5.3   Feasible results

The application of the Causal Cross-Impact Analysis [20] and the Collaboration Network Analysis at CeBeNetwork shows remarkable results. Regarding the collaboration Network Analysis the following points can be summarised:

- The partners of the Virtual Organisation can a transparent view of the early phase of the innovation process,
- Secondly a structure for collaboration is proposed by the methodology and
- Finally, the CeBeNetwork Case shows the enormous problem to understand the upcoming processes. It happens many times that the future has not been properly understood. This leads to misallocation of resources, late deliveries and so forth. Thanks to the collaboration network analysis these issues can be identified earlier.

The application of the cross impact analysis shows the following results:

- The main strategic developments within innovation processes can be forecasted. Fore CeBeNetwork the careful analysis of the Power 8 program of Airbus indicated dramatic chances within the aeronautical industry.
- The demonstration on alternative scenarios showed CeBeNetwork different alternative routes for the behaviour of the collaboration which provided important support the decision making.

To summarise: The application of the two forecasting methods provided a decision support for the CeBeNetwork cooperation which gained into future business benefits.

6.   Conclusions

The paper has discussed how the cross-impact analysis and the collaborative network analysis can be used to support the forecasting in Virtual Organisations. The methodologies have been conceptually applied in an aeronautical case study. The business benefits clearly show the importance of such approaches in everyday business.

Acknowledgements

The authors thank the partners and the European Commission for support in the context of the COIN project, see more information at http://www.coin-ip.eu/.

References

[1]   Sturm, Flavius, Kemp, Jeroen and Wendel de Joode, Ruben van: Towards Strategic Management in Collaborative Network Structures. In: Collaborative Networked Organisations. Kluwer, 2004, pp. 131-138.
[2]   Mintzberg, Henry: The Rise and Fall of Strategic Planning. 1994.
[3]   Wild, J.: Grundlagen der Unternehmensplanung, 4. Auflagen, Opladen 1982.
[4]   Krauth, Johannes: Simulation for the evaluation of CIM Investments as Part of an Enterprise Strategy. In: EUROSIM '92 Simulation Congress Reprints. 1992. pp. 295-300.
[5]   Götze, K.: Szenario-Technik in der strategischen Unternehmensplanung, 2. Auflage, Wiesbaden 1993.
[6]   Makridakis, S., Wheelwright, SC.: Forecasting methods for management, 5. Auflage, Winchester 1990.
[7]   Bircher, B.: Langfristige Unternehmensplanung, Bern-Stuttgart 1976.
[8]   Weber, D.: Strategische Planung im Unternehmensnetzwerk am Beispiel industrieller Dienstleistungen im Industrieanlagenbau. Shaker Verlag, Aachen 2005.
[9]   Mertens, P.: Prognoserechnung. Physica-Verlag, 5th Edition, Heidelberg 1993.
[10] Boutellier, R., Gassmann, O., Zedtwitz, M.: Managing Global Innovation – Uncovering the Secrets of Future Competitiveness. Third Edition, Springer Verlag, Berlin-Heidelberg 2008.
[11] McInerney, F.: Panasonic the largest corporate restructuring in history. Truman Talley Books St. Martin Press New York 2008.
[12] Gassmann, O., Sutter, P.: Praxiswissen Innovationsmanagement – Von der Idee zum Markterfolg. Hanser Verlag 2008.
[13] Jagdev, Harinder S. and Thoben, Klaus-Dieter: Anatomy of Enterprise Collaborations. In: Production Planning and Control. 12 (2001) 5, pp 437-451.
[14] Camarinha-Matos, L.M., Afsamarnesh, H.: A comprehensive modelling framework for collaborative networked organisations. In: Journal of Intelligent Manufacturing, Springer Science and Business Media, Vol. 18, No. 5, pp. 529-542, (2007).
[15] Welge, M.K.; Al-Laham, A. (2008) Strategisches Management – Grundlagen, Prozess Implementerung, Gabler Verlag Wiesbaden 2008.
[16] Simon, D.: Die Früherkennung von strategischen Diskontinuitäten durch Erfassung von "Weak Signals", Diss. Wien 1985
[17] Eschenbächer, J., Graser, F., Thoben, K.-D., Tiefensee, B.: Management of Dynamic Virtual Organisations: Conclusions from a collaborative engineering case. In: Advanced Manufacturing: An ICT and Systems Perspective. Taylor & Francis Ltd 2007.
[18] Gausemeier, Jürgen, Fink, Alexander and Schlake, Oliver: Scenario Management: An Approach to Develop Future Potentials. In: Technological Forecasting and Social Change. 59 (1998) 2, pp 111-130.
[19] Eschenbächer, J. (2008) Gestaltung von Innovationsprozessen in Virtuellen Organisation durch kooperationsbasierte Netzwerkanalyse, Diss. To be published, 2008.
[20] Duin, H., Schnatmeyer, M., Schumacher, J., Thoben, K.-D. and Zhao, X.: Cross-Impact Analysis of RFID Scenarios for Logistics. In: Logistik Management 2005. Wiesbaden 2005. pp 363-376.

Collaboration and the Knowledge Economy: Issues, Applications, Case Studies
P. Cunningham and M. Cunningham (Eds.)
IOS Press, 2008

eBIZ-TCF: an Initiative to Improve eAdoption in European Textile/Clothing and Footwear Industry

Piero DE SABBATA[1], Mauro SCALIA[2], Martin BAKER[3], Jan SOMERS[4], Milena STEFANOVA[1], Arianna BRUTTI[1], Angelo FRASCELLA[1]

[1]*ENEA, Italy, Tel. +39 0516098111, Email: {firstname.lastname}@bologna.enea.it*
[2]*Euratex, Belgium, Tel. +32-2-285.48.91, Email: mauro.scalia@euratex.org*
[3] *CEC,Belgium, Tel. +44-(0)1458-831131, Email: martin.baker@torisinfo.co.uk*
[4]*GS1, Belgium, Email: JSomers@gs1belu.org*

Abstract: This paper presents an European large scale initiative to foster the adoption of eBusiness (and related technologies and standards) in the Textile/Clothing and Footwear sectors that are characterised by a large presence of SMEs. The project, namely eBiz-TCF (eBusiness for Textile/Clothing and Footwear, www.ebiz-ftc.eu), is funded by DG Enterprise and addressed to "Harmonising eBusiness processes and data exchanges for SMEs in the Textile/Clothing and footwear sectors in the Single Market". The key points of the initiative are a) an eBusiness architecture, based on (as far as it is possible) existing standards, b) a large set of pilots and c) the creation of a wide consensus between the stakeholders. The architecture is based on the adoption of sectorial languages (TexWeave/Moda-ML and EFNET/Shoenet) for the networks of manufacturers, on a use profile of UBL (Universal Business Language) for the relationships with the retail organisations and on common communication architecture (with references to ebXML specifications).

1. Introduction

This paper presents a project that is an European large scale attempt to foster the adoption of eBusiness (eAdoption), and related technologies and standards, at sectorial level in the Textile/Clothing and Footwear (TCF) sectors. These sectors are characterised by a large presence of SMEs and by an average level of adoption of eBusiness and interoperability standards that appears to be lower comparing to similar manufacturing sectors [1][2][3].

The project, namely eBIZ-TCF (eBusiness for Textile/Clothing and Footwear, www.ebiz-ftc.eu), is the answer to a call for tender from the European Commission DG Enterprise and Industry (ENTR/2007/027) called "Harmonising eBusiness processes and data exchanges for SMEs in the Textile/Clothing and Footwear sectors in the Single Market" set out in mid 2007. The duration is about 24 months starting from January 2008 and involves the two concerned sectorial European industrial associations, namely Euratex (European Apparel and Textile Organisation) and CEC (European Confederation of the Footwear Industry) together with ENEA, a public research and technology transfer organisation plus other 40 and more companies across Europe.

The paper presents the approach of the project in order to achieve a wide uptake of eBusiness in sectors which are the core of the fashion industry in Europe.

2. The Challenges and the Objectives

To better understand the goals of the project it is necessary to understand the present challenges of the European fashion industry and the status of the eBusiness adoption.

2.1   The Challenge for the Industry

Innovative e-collaboration combined with other new manufacturing and supply chain paradigms can provide some of the answers to the European companies to strengthen or re-gain global competitiveness.

Success in the fast-moving fashion business is increasingly reaped by companies with lowest response time to changing market and consumers requirements by integrating design, consumer feedback, sourcing and manufacturing, distribution and retailing.

Some traditional retailers and manufacturers try to solve the conflict between long lead times and efficient consumer response (no over-stock, fast re-ordering and delivery) with a vertical integration of the value chain, if possible. And if this is not possible, by e-linking and e-collaboration in the value chain to have the same fast answers to consumer demand. The key for such connectivity is the interoperability of systems based on commonly agreed open standards.

2.2   The Problem Addressed in the Project

A lot of efforts have been done in the field of standardisation for Textile/Clothing and Footwear industry in these years.

Euratex and CEC together with their national member federations, as well as the EU Commission, CEN/ISSS, GS1 and others have been involved in e-business standardisation issues for the fashion industry in recent years. Also pubblic administrations are contributing, like the Department for Technological Innovation - Presidency of the Italian Council of Ministers (DDTA project), to the success of the eBIZ-TCF project.

B2B standard specifications have been developed within the framework of ESOs (European Standardisation Organisations): CEN/ISSS TexSpin [4] and TexWeave [5] for Textile/Clothing (TC), CEN/ISSS FINEC[6] for Footwear and other related to initiatives and projects like eTexML, Visit, Moda-ML [7], EFNET2/3, CecMadeShoe, ShoeNet [8]; all these initiatives, with a wide involvement of industry associations, have prepared a background of analysis and specifications that is (almost) ready to be implemented by the industry. Yet so far an overall harmonisation is lacking and in many cases, the results of these activities have not led to a widespread adoption in the user community.

As a result, the fashion sector remains without globally implemented e-business standards and has not sufficiently succeeded in its efforts to synchronise data and to exchange business documents electronically.

This situation is put in evidence also by the eBusiness Watch reports on ICT uptake for both textiles/clothing and footwear [1][2][3]: IT and e-business uptake is below the average of other sectors in the European Union.

There is a reluctance of many firms and technology providers to implement these specifications (and ICT in general); on the one hand they fear risk of an excessive 'normalisation' of the applications that leads to lose their assets towards the customers; on the other hand they rather wait and see which will be the successful initiative and when the risk on investing on it will be lowered to zero.

As a result the landscape of existing B2B applications is extremely varied, spanning from P2P solutions to a variety of Internet based solutions, all characterised by difficulties in achieving a critical mass of participants and in connecting small companies.

Nevertheless data at European level suggest the existence of an unsatisfied demand for a common standard architecture, for instance according to a survey carried out in the industrial districts of Biella, Italy, (survey made by the local industry trading association) 70% of the fabric producers were asked to electronically supply data to the customers; 70% also received such request by more than one customer and in 100% of the cases each customer required a different data model. A further difficulty was that each customer was asking for few and different documents: one or two out from a wide set of messages (order responses, expected delivery date, despatch advice, defects map, etc), without drawing an holistic design for the future. The result was that the industry did not accepted to invest to satisfy these requests.

2.3 The Project Objectives

Being aware of these issues, both the DG Enterprise & Industry and the industry trade associations Euratex and CEC assumed two objectives.

The first objective was the definition of a reference architecture for eBusiness in Textile/Clothing and Footwear sectors; the target was to tackle the different requisites for both the manufacturer-retail supply chain (downstream part of the architecture) and the manufacturer-supplier network (upstream part of the architecture) with appropriate technological and methodological specifications to cover topics such as data models, communication protocols and product classification.

As main requisite of the architecture, wherever possible, the architecture's specifications had to be based on existing standards; in any case, further standardisation developments have to be realised outside the scope of the project; with the involvement of European Standards Organisations (ESOs) (on this purpose CEN/ISSS is invited to the activities of the project).

The second objective was to achieve consensus between the stakeholders on the architecture and to express this agreement with the ambitious objective to define a Memory of Understanding (MoU) between the stakeholders that could be the basis for a wider diffusion and adoption.

3. Methodology

In general terms, the project does not aim to develop or validate a new technology or a new software but aims to setup an approach to foster eAdoption in two sectors dominated by SMEs through a work of harmonisation that is strongly aware of the standardisation achievements.

Thanks to the large experience gathered with similar initiatives in recent years the project will focus on three key actions:

- Recognition: analysis and evaluation of the existing standards and running experiences and systems.
- Architecture: creation of the reference architecture based on existing standards.
- Pilots: promotion and reporting on meaningful case studies at European scale (involving a large number of actors in many cross-border and cross-sector pilot experiences with the aim to witness the validity of the architecture).

As a first outcome of the project, more than 40 companies have been involved in the pilots, and represent business cases, from Bulgaria, Czech Republic, Croatia, France, Germany, Italy, Netherland, Portugal, Romania, Spain.

They express a wide variety of architectures and actors: some pilots are leaded by final users, others by solution providers with the role of 'facilitators'; the business and the technological scenarios are quite different: some are based on direct P2P message exchange between ERPs (leaded by final users or by ERP providers), others are based on platforms that offer the capability to exchange certified messages (mainly born with the EDI technologies), others on Supply Chain Management service platforms (based on Internet paradigms).

In the project lifetime, beyond a first group of companies that has been selected since the beginning, additional companies will join the project, thanks to a two-stages strategy of the project that foresees a public call for further pilot proposals.

The pilots perform both local and cross-border eBusiness activities that the project supports and monitors in order to obtain meaningful reports that will be the basis to write and diffuse a final Guide to eBusiness in TCF sector at the end of the project.

The key point of the pilots programme is that each pilot is based on the implementation of eBusiness starting from existing IT solutions and with limited adaptations in order to support the standard specifications; thus there will not be a 'unique' solution but a patchwork of collaborating indipendent solutions.

The project supplies pilots with technological assistance, training and specifications, but does not offer a technological solution, a software or a service; the aim is to urge solution and service providers to improve their own offer, without annoying them by delivering yet another rival solution.

According to the mission of the project, the case histories and the technical documentation of the architecture are public and their use is free of charge.

To multiply the impacts, the project also aims to deliver a proposal for the development of any missing standards and, on this purpose, works closely in contact with CEN/ISSS, and organisations like GS1 and others that made the history of the standardisation in both the sectors in these years (like ENEA, INESCOP and others).

4.   Outcomes of the Activities

Within the project, the activities of analysis of the status of art has concerned business to business data exchange in the supply chain (both upstream and downstream), with the inclusion of the mass customisation and B2B Internet based services (like for example, respectively, customised garment provisioning and stock services); the issues related to Internet access, ERP implementation and eCommerce implementation (B2C) were not considered.

4.1   Two Areas

The work of analysis leaded to identify two different challenges related to the different requisites of the different rings of the supply chains of the TCF industry (see also [4]).

A first challenge arises from the highly specialised networks of manufacturing enterprises (upstream area): the producers of final goods rely on complex networks of enterprises (large as well as small) with highly specialised processes; these relationships require a strong integration between the actors and cannot be hampered by rigid or poor models; the keywords are flexibility and completeness. Specific languages (and data models) have to be provided. The collaborations involve a 'reduced' number of actors that know and trust each other with a strong partnership and are extremely '*customised*' to fit the organisation of the partners. In the past we had local networks, now, increasingly, transnational.

A second challenge regards the retail channels for the Textile/Clothing and Footwear final goods (downstream area): based on large organisations as well as small shops, the retail organisations need to achieve a common and efficient connection with the producers; the keywords are efficiency and normalisation. Uniform ways of coding have to be provided. The collaborations involve large numbers of actors that do not know too much each other with an '*anonymous*' partnership that is based only on obligations deriving from purchase contracts and that expire with the goods delivery.

4.2 The Standardisation Path

An aspect that emerged from the analysis is an original path to standardisation in the TCF sectors (see [9]), quite different from the process that usually sees few stakeholders to drive (and, sometimes, fight in) the standardisation processes. In the TCF sector the efforts in the development of the standard specifications were conditioned by the difficulties, for a sector dominated by SMEs, to manage a process of creation of standardised specifications [10][11]; the result has been an original path of standardisation that mixed standardisation initiatives in collaboration with ESOs (mainly CEN) with specific national or European initiatives leaded by 'willing' organisations that attempt to exploit standardisation achievements and to improve them in order to meet the real industry businesses. The result has been a large common background of analysis and a set of outcomes not completely harmonised and only partially recognised as standard specifications.

For example, in the upstream area, the CEN/ISSS TexSpin [4] and the successive CEN/ISSS TexWeave specifications [5] for the TC industry were published but their effective development was supported by a number of initiatives (Moda-ML mainly) and projects that were the laboratory that improved them in order to fit the industry needs. The same, in parallel, happened for the Footwear industry with the CEN/ISSS EFNET [6] specifications that were adopted and improved by the Shoenet community.

Different is the situation in the downstream area where the focus is on company and product identification that are pursued through the adoption of GS1 global coding (GLN and GTN) rather than on sector specific issues. The specifications emerged from different initiatives (CEN/ISSS TexWeave again, CecMadeShoe, for example) demonstrated that the data models and the processes are quite similar between the TCF sectors.

4.3 The Architecture

The architecture that has been established is based on four different types of specifications:
- Business processes (that will be represented using UML notation and ebBP templates[12])
- Data models (document template specifications, based on XML but related to the pre-existing EDI specifications)
- Collaboration and communication protocols
- Product classifications
  The domain of application is based on three sub domains (see figure 1):
- Manufacturing networks of TC industry
- Manufacturing networks of Footwear industry
- Production to retail relationships for TCF industry.
  The production to retail relationship is characterised by:
- Business processes and data models based on XML specifications: common contents, an OASIS UBL [13] profile of use derived from CEN/ISSS TexWeave and CecMadeShoe results
- Interoperability with EDIFACT legacy thanks to an intermediate level of data models.
- Anonymous collaborations (large numbers).

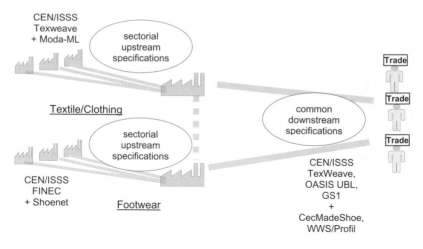

Figure 1. The Domain of the Architecture

The UBL profile of use for the TCF sector will be the first large scale profile of use for UBL in a manufacturing sector in the world (the other larghe scale profile of use of UBL is NES, for the public procurement in North Europe countries). It has the objective to implement:

- Fast and simple connection to hubs and retail organisations
- Use of EAN coding for product and party identification (GTN, GLN)Focus on small & large retail (not huge international) organisations.

The manufacturing networks are characterised by:

- Business processes and data models based on XML specifications specific for business processes: derived from CEN/ISSS TexWeave and Moda-ML for the Textile/Clothing production processes; derived from CEN/ISSS EFNET and Shoenet for the Footwear processes
- Closed collaborations (small numbers; supported at logical level by ebXML CPPA specifications [14]).

It is to note that there is a work to be done to harmonise the different ways to document and represent the specifications that, originally, are quite different and managed by different organisations. The architecture has the objective to:

- Create a favourable environment to setup a collaboration between manufacturers
- Focus on manufacturing industry that has not completely outsorced its production.

The architecture related to collaboration and communication protocols is only partially defined and is characterised by:

- A model of an European TCF logical Network of communication based on three main scenarios: Hub-Hub, Hub-Firm, Firm-Firm (being *hub* is an application connectivity service provider –like EdiCom, eGate, Intesa and others- or an integration service provider –like TXTChain, TextileBusiness,etc-)
- An alternative choice between existing EDIFACT and XML based paradigms
- A strong attention to the issues on security through the network (especially through the hubs of services that must guarantee the identification of the senders)
- Protocols focused on SMTP, while Web Service are foreseen for the future
- ebXML CPPA to model and publish the collaborative reference processes.   The objective is to make each participant able to find a path to interoperate with any other, despite the service and solutions they adopt.

The activities related to product classification are still in progress.

5.   The Benefits

The effective results in terms of eAdoption will be perceived in a period of two/three years after the conclusion of the project, yet some considerations could be done at this stage.

The adopted approach is expected to achieve two relevant objectives:

1. To offer a clear understanding and a roadmap about the reference architecture together with a strong endorsement by the industry associations and the stakeholders;
2. To offer a smooth 'path' for existing solutions to get involved in a seemless space of information exchange and of inter-company collaboration.

From the perspective of business processes, the project will be concluded with a collection of case histories that witness, in different scenarios and to different targets of enterprises, how the exchange of information about the feedback from the market (the sales data) and the activities in the manufacturing networks can improve the efficiency and flexibility of the whole supply chain.

From the perspective of eBusiness implementation, the most evident advantage of this approach for small and medium firms is lowering the threshold to set-up eBusiness with a public reference architecture that includes all that is necessary to participate eBusiness: the investments are based on an European wide common understanding and more solution providers have the skills to support their work.

The players in the field of services for data exchange and supply chain integration: with small investments they can benefit of an architecture that can widen their market and offer them the opportunity to connect small enterprises to their current customers (large retail organisations and large firms).

The same benefits are, in turn, for the large enterprises that encounter less reluctance from their SME partners to invest to get connected: the analysis in the project put in evidence that large enterprises, when reorganising their supply chains, even when they are the driving force of a chain (and of the business), have difficulties to force eBusiness adoption in countries or companies where there is not a common understanding about these methodologies and tools. It is a problem of costs but mainly a problem of organisation and skills that are difficult to create on a single company proprietary basis.

It is worth to observe that even before the launch of the public call for new pilots, a number of organisations, service and solution providers and manufacturing firms have already asked to be involved in the pilot activities, aiming to join the architecture.

In a long term, the TCF sector is expected to gain competitiveness from more sophisticated models of e-collaboration (see for example Leapfrog IP [15] outcomes) and the creation of flexible models and channels of integration between different organisations is a pre-conditions for a wide take-up of tools based on collaborative product design in the fashion industry.

6.   Conclusions

There are some learnt lessons from the project activities at this stage of development:

*   There are two different areas of eBusiness with different priorities: the area of enterprise networking and the area of the relationships with the retail organisations; they require different approaches and technical specifications
*   There is a plurality of actors and scenarios that cannot be forced to one solution or ignored but that can be harmonised;
*   The paradigms from the EDI world and from the Internet eBusiness applications are not mutually exclusive and can complement each other if the focus in on the business processes and in information rather than on technicalities and syntax;

- In sectors dominated by SMEs the creation of standards has its original path that have to be better understood and improved.

This project is the first large scale attempt to foster eAdoption in specific sectors of the European manufacturing industry, it focuses on harmonising existing standards instead of writing 'yet another one'.

The project is build around a sound rational as a starting point and addresses an, existing, key market need. Its large partnership brings together required competences while added value shall be assured by on-the-ground experiences (cross border/sectorial pilots).

The successful cooperation with concerned stakeholders represents a key challenge which is duly pursued for its vital importance to build up consensus. The latter also requires stakeholders openness to achieve the ultimate project goal, namely the durable uptake of results for the benefit of European Textile/Clothing and Footwear companies.

References

[1]   "Special report - e-Business interoperability and standards-A cross sectorial perspective and outlook", e-Business w@tch, September 2005, Brussels
[2]   "Electronic Business in the Textile, Clothing and Footwear Industries", Sector Report: No. 01-II, e-Business w@tch, August 2004, Brussels
[3]   "ICT and e-Business in the Footwear Industry, ICT adoption and e-business activity in 2006", Sector Report: No. 02, e-Business w@tch, 2006, Brussels
[4]   "TexSpin, Guidelines for XML/EDI messages in the Textile/Clothing sector", CWA 14948:2004, CEN/ISSS, March 2004, Bruxelles
[5]   "TexWeave: Scenarios and XML templates for B2B in the Textile Clothing manufacturing and retail", CWA (CEN Workshop Agreement) 15557:2006, CEN/ISSS, 2006, Bruxelles; http://www.TexWeave.org
[6]   "FINEC", CWA 14746:2003, CEN/ISSS, 2003, Bruxelles
[7]   Gessa N., De Sabbata P., Fraulini M., Imolesi T., Cucchiara G., Marzocchi M., Vitali F., "Moda-ML, an interoperability framework for the Textile Clothing sector", IADIS International Conference WWWInternet 2003, p. 61-68, ISBN: 972-98947-1-X , November 2003, Carvoeiro, Portugal.
[8]   Ricardo J. Gonçalves, Müller J.P, Mertins K. and Zelm M., "Enterprise Interoperability II - New Challenges and Approaches", ISBN 978-1-84628-857-9, Springer, October 2007, London
[9]   Gessa N., Cucchiara G., De Sabbata P., Brutti A., "A bottom-up approach to build a B2B sectorial standard: the case of Moda-ML/TexSpin", pp 249-260, in "Interoperability of Enterprise Software Applications", workshops of the INTEROP- ESA International Conference, Geneve 22 February 2005, edited by Hervé Panetto, Hermes Science Publishing, ISBN-1-905209-45-5, 2005, Paris.
[10] Soderstrom E., "Formulating a General Standards Life Cycle", Proceedings of 16th International Conference of Advanced Information Systems Engineering - CaiSE 2004, June 2004, Riga, Latvia.
[11] Jakobs, K., "Standardisation and SME Users; Mutually Exclusive?", Proc. Multi-Conference on Business Information Systems, Cuvillier Verlag, 2004
[12] "ebXML Business Process Specification Schema Technical Specification v2.0.1", July 2005; see also http://www.ebXML.org/
[13] Bosak J., McGrath T., Holman G.K., "Universal Business Language v2.0, Standard", OASIS Open, 12 December 2006; http://docs.oasis-open.org/ubl/os-UBL-2.0/
[14] "Collaboration-Protocol Profile and Agreement Specification Version 2.1", July 2005
[15] Leapfrog Integrated project, FP 7, NMP priority, http://www.leapfrog-eu.org

Section 6

SME Issues

Section 6.1

Issues

Collaboration and the Knowledge Economy: Issues, Applications, Case Studies
P. Cunningham and M. Cunningham (Eds.)
IOS Press, 2008

Empowering SME to Participate in Collaborative Projects

Katrin RESCHWAMM, Andreas WOLF
Fraunhofer Institute for Factory Operation and Automation, Sandtorstrasse 22,
Magdeburg, 39106, Germany
Tel: +49 391 4090 625, Fax: + 49 391 4090 93 901, Email: {firstname.lastname}@iff.fraunhofer.de

Abstract: SMEs make up the majority of companies in Europe and are increasingly instrumental in the development of innovations, yet they continue to face challenges on the road to successful business innovation. Specific efforts have been made to increase the participation of SMEs in collaborative projects funded by national or European programs. While the results are promising, an SME to research gap continues to exist, particularly throughout the innovation process and later during the exploitation phase. The smE-MPOWER approach takes these challenges into account and empowers SMEs to initiate self-defined, long-term international RTD activities of which they have ownership. This paper explains the context in which smE-MPOWER has been implemented and presents the main results of the project, which not only benefit SME but also the coaches interacting with and supporting them. Lessons learned conclude this paper.

Keywords: Cooperation coaching, SME support, collaborative projects, innovation

1. Introduction

1.1 Empowering SME to Participate in Collaborative Projects

SME account for two-thirds of the GDP and two-thirds of the employment and generate half of all new jobs in the European Union [1]. Thus, they are a key structural element of the European economy [2].

Innovation is a key driver of competitiveness. Economic growth and employment in Europe is increasingly dependent on the market launch of innovative products and services and the development of innovative business practices. Sustained innovation raises productivity, adds value and fosters prosperity.

Europe's 23 million SME are playing an increasingly important role in the development of scientific and technological breakthroughs [3]. This is especially true in young, dynamic sectors. Nonetheless, SME face persistent challenges on the road to successful business innovation [4]. These challenges include:

- Bureaucratic hurdles when accessing funding,
- Insufficient access to training and expertise,
- Insufficient access to new markets or international partners and
- Difficulties securing intellectual property rights (IPR) and exploiting research results.

The EU's Seventh Framework Programme endeavors to provide focused support for SME innovation and research activities. Enterprises involved are able to gain experience and knowledge, expand their networks of research and business partners and commercialize their projects by collaborating internationally with complementary organizations.

1.2   The SME to Research Gap

Despite numerous efforts and some evidence of improvement, serious barriers still bar SME from accessing schemes and funds designed to support their innovation and research efforts [5]. The success rate of SME proposals is still surprisingly low [6].

A number of issues explain why SME consistently exhibit a low propensity to take advantage of FP7 and other research opportunities [7].

- SME are little aware of and lack information needed to effectively access and assess the suitability of FP7 schemes.
- The application process takes a long time [8]. Moreover, RTD&I projects can sometimes be counterproductive in a turbulent market [9].
- Human and financial resources are limited, especially in small and micro businesses.
- Joining or assembling a strategic, competitive consortium and clarifying the conditions of related IPR is difficult.
- Managerial expertise to exploit RTD results in a multi-actor scenario is lacking.

2.   Objectives

The smE-MPOWER project (ETI-023401) focused on integrating SME in collaborative projects. A consortium of SME intermediaries and business networks provided SME the support to pursue long-range research interests with appropriate funding by identifying and analyzing the innovative potentials of the SME. Companies with a clear strategy were coached on developing innovation projects around their innovation interests.

The following outlines the support services currently available to SME and addresses remaining gaps. It additionally describes the results of the project as well as the lessons learned, recommendations for improving support for SME and the further approach to continuing smE-MPOWER.

3.   Developments

3.1   Steps Taken

The EC has taken several steps since FP5 to bridge the SME to research gap. In particular, ETI [10] and SSA [11] actions provide SME improved access to scientific and technological information as well as a range of other services intended to facilitate SME participation in framework Programs. The initiatives supporting SME participation have been integrated in the thematic areas of FP7 to eliminate problems of thematic isolation.

FP7 "also includes a number of other incentives for SME participation, such as the increased upper funding rate, and the new CIP Programme [12] offering better conditions and support to SME" [13].

Various European actions and initiatives are aimed at facilitating innovation in European SME, individually addressing the different stages in the process of innovation: Formulation of an idea and the respective concept, management of an innovative project and exploitation of the results. A few these initiatives are presented in more detail below.

3.1.1   Finding and Developing Innovative Ideas

Though innovation is essential to the competitiveness of SME, they often lack the resources needed to initiate innovative projects. The EC is well aware of the need to provide SME assistance identifying needs for innovation and respective funding opportunities. In order to raise awareness and to foster the participation of SME in collaborative projects, many initiatives actively provide support during the first phase initiating projects that correlate with past and current EC objectives to increase the participation of SME in programs and projects.

The Enterprise Europe Network (EEN) combines the former Euro Info Centre (EIC) and Innovation Relay Centre (IRC) networks. In the past, EIC informed, advised, and assisted businesses in EC issues. IRC, on the other hand, focused on supporting innovation and transnational technological cooperation in Europe with a range of specialized business support services. Both EIC and IRC services primarily targeted SME. Launched by the EC in 2008, the Enterprise Europe Network (EEN) combines and builds on the strengths and experiences of both centers. The new integrated network provides a "one-stop shop" to meet all the information needs of European SME and companies, help them develop their innovative potentials and increase awareness of opportunities for EU innovation funding [14]. The network has bundled as well as increased its range of services including assistance to SME to raise their capacity for innovation by participating in collaborative EU projects. Formerly, only IRC in Germany acted as an extended arm of the SME NCP, offering advice on particular funding schemes for SME, now known in FP7 as "Research for the Benefit of SMEs/ SME Associations".

In the former FP6, the Economic and Technological Intelligence (ETI) project scheme was funded to build bridges between SME, researchers, entrepreneurs and investors. Rather than by the SME themselves, mainly intermediary organizations with good access to dissemination channels ran these projects [15]. In FP7, the ETI project scheme has been integrated in the form of Specific Support Actions in the thematic areas to create direct synergies with collaborative projects in future calls. Lessons learned and outcomes of these actions are currently being gathered by the EC and not yet available.

The National Contact Point (NCP) network is the main provider of guidance, practical information and assistance in all aspects of participation in the FP7 in all Member and Associated States. However, since NCP are national structures, the type and level of services they offer varies from country to country. Some NCP are closely tied to projects in FP7, integrating particular partner search facilities that are then offered to clients.

In addition, a number of other services solely provide information (e.g. SME TechWeb sites) or only complete proposal writing (e.g. specialized consulting companies).

3.1.2   Implementing and Managing a Project

The EC provides SME far less support during the implementation phase. Assistance to SME to overcome problems with project management and implementation is thus a weak point in the EC's innovation support strategy.

Although the IPR Helpdesk provides potential and current contractors taking part in EU funded research projects assistance on issues related to IPR, e.g. protection of IPR in preliminary stages and resolution of potential IPR conflicts, this is but one of many issues that emerge during the implementation of collaborative projects [16].

3.1.3   Exploiting Project Results

Little assistance is provided in the last phase too, the exploitation of results. The lack of support for mature innovation projects reflects the European inability to implement and commercialize innovative ideas. If allowed to continue, this gap between having innovative ideas and marketing them will seriously threaten European competitiveness in the long run.

Among others, critical success factors for the market launch of products and services developed in collaborative projects are:

- Professional project management with clear roles for each partner and strict supervision of resources, which is not always the case in EU funded projects
- Allocation of sufficient resources for market assessments and analyses
- Involvement of customers in the development process, e.g. in user groups;
- Clear processes for exploitation rather than just product and service development

- Acquisition and preparation of additional funds for marketing and market launches

These factors need to be already considered during the planning phase of innovative project and measures to address these factors ought to be part of any project plan. Moreover, rather than scientific and technological excellence alone, these factors deserve to be acknowledged when such projects are being evaluated for funding.

3.1.4 The Solution

Improving the access of SME to funding opportunities continues to be a key issue in Framework Programmes. SME need better assistance to transform scientific and technical advances into marketable business innovations. Given the statistically low odds of receiving funding, reducing the burden of self-financing on SME to develop proposals represents another major challenge that has to be addressed on internationally, nationally and regionally. Nonetheless, the next step ought to be to encourage SME to take a long-term and strategic view of the benefits of collaborative research. Professional cooperation coaching to develop innovation projects accordingly provides one suitable approach.

A review of the different initiatives and support services clearly demonstrates that SME need to be empowered to engage long-term in international RTD activities. Experience shows that support only at the outset is insufficient and further assistance is needed, especially during exploitation. Therefore, what is needed is a holistic approach that integrates initiatives or extends particular services throughout the entire innovation cycle.

smE-MPOWER offers a solution focusing on SME and developing their interests in need-demand business innovation. smE-MPOWER coaches work one to one with client SME and share relevant "open knowledge" within the community of coaches.

4. Methodology

4.1 The smE-MPOWER Approach

The smE-MPOWER approach is configured as a standardized system and incorporates the complexity of innovation systems that include various actors such as industry, intermediaries and regional policy makers.

- SMEs are key innovation drivers in the European context but struggle to realize the potential benefits of European Framework Programme Funding because of external and internal barriers. smE-MPOWER addresses these barriers through a highly personalized approach that provides assistance to develop and exploit SME innovation potential.
- Cooperation coaches who guide SMEs into strategic innovation and international partnerships have a complex but poorly defined job profile. Insufficient best practice guidelines and limited support to promote international relations can severely impede their effectiveness. smE-MPOWER provides a common coaching job profile, best practice know-how and access to an international learning community of coaches.

An important side benefit of the smE-MPOWER approach is its stimulation of business cooperation between SME on the one hand and large or multinational enterprises on the other. The global significance and scale of such "open innovation" schemes is expected to grow dramatically in the future. As a highly desired resource in RTD consortia, research organizations and institutions of higher education also profit.

The novelty of the approach is its empowerment of SMEs to initiate self-defined, long-term international RTD activities of which they have ownership. As opposed to other initiatives, smE-MPOWER provides companies assistance to define a strategy and select the most suitable funding opportunity. Exploitation channels and long-term effects resulting from collaboration are taken into account when a project concept is being developed.

5. Results

5.1 The smE-MPOWER SME Mobilizer

Several job profiles critical to the innovation support process were created during the smE-MPOWER project. Two are of central importance. The smE-MPOWER Mobilizer brings SME to a stage of "readiness" to consider engaging in or initiating international RTD projects. Mobilization was identified as a crucial need and a bottleneck to involvement in many European regions. The job's key activities are outlined below. The COROM method designed by CEGOS was applied to also define expertise required for the activities.

Table 1: Key SME Mobilizer Activities

Mission	The smE-MPOWER Mobilizer encourages SME to innovate and raises their awareness of the opportunities that international collaboration and related smE-MPOWER services hold for them. The 7th Framework Programme is a major but not the only opportunity for collaboration. The smE-MPOWER Mobilizer identifies emerging needs of innovative SME and initiates international RTD partnerships that could meet these needs, create synergies and add value to SME.
Key activity 1	Relate to company managers and other employees in face-to-face coaching sessions in a manner that builds trust and is reliable while considering the issues of business strategy, SME challenges and innovation opportunities.
Key activity 2	Analyze potential for business innovation, eligibility for international collaboration and appropriateness of FP7 funding opportunities suggested by the smE-MPOWER Strategic Information Management team.
Key activity 3	Organize multi-company awareness events to raise awareness of the value of international RTD collaboration for business innovation. Also communicate support available through FP7 and smE-MPOWER. Collect, classify and cluster information from attendees and provide them with a roadmap for action.
Key activity 4	Establish SME relationships and raise awareness of business opportunities created by FP7. Follow up on a growing database of interested SME.

5.2 The smE-MPOWER Cooperation Coach

The smE-MPOWER Cooperation Coach is the main job profile in smE-MPOWER and embodies the philosophies of SME orientation, business focus, one on one interaction and open knowledge. Taking over where the Mobilizer leaves off, the coach guides a company through a process of strategic decision-making that culminates in the development of a project concept for internationally collaborative innovation.

Table 2: Key Cooperation Coach Activities

Mission	The smE-MPOWER Cooperation Coach empowers SME and provides them support to successfully participate in (international) RTD project consortia.
Key activity 1	Formalize a common project vision, coherency of goals, expected benefits and contributions of the emerging core consortium (Strategic Interest Group) and design a preliminary project concept in order to assess (EC) funding options and decide how to develop the project proposal.
Key activity 2	Facilitate the project development process by providing support to devise the project structure and project organization, clarification of partners' roles and budgets and strengthen the position of the SME interests in an IPR agreement.
Key activity 3	Identify and recruit complementary project partners for the core consortium (or emerging project consortia) in order to ensure the project consortium possesses all the necessary competencies and resources to achieve a project's objectives.
Key activity 4	Mentor the SME during the contract negotiation phase (documents related to EC contracts and Cooperation Agreement) in order to ensure they will start their project under optimal conditions, especially with regard to collaboration and the exploitation of project results.

This standardized approach is based on several reference processes that have been developed and correlate with the job profiles created. The reference process for the smE-MPOWER Cooperation Coach is one example.

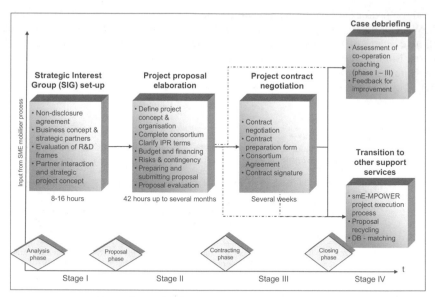

Figure 1: smE-MPOWER Cooperation Coaching Process

Apart from the reference processes and job profiles, an additional asset that was created is the smE-MPOWER community. This is a network of SME coaches who share knowledge and self-developed pragmatic tools based on a common approach to innovation coaching while allowing regional modifications.

6.   Business Benefits

6.1   The smE-MPOWER Message to SME

For an SME to develop a long-term commitment to RTD and innovation it is of paramount importance to focus every effort on the company's priority innovation needs and its potential to innovate. smE-MPOWER empowers SMEs to pursue their self-defined research interests by cooperating internationally. The SME oriented philosophy of smE-MPOWER rests upon the following cornerstones:

- Business innovation: Support is focused on developing a company's capacity to generate value through technological or organizational innovation. Innovation could include a company's products and services, processes, customer relations and methods of distribution. The smE-MPOWER service starts by spreading awareness about the need for and scope of innovation as well as analyzing innovation opportunities in an SME.
- Need-demand driven philosophy: smE-MPOWER provides a "focal SME" support to strategically organize an innovation project and international consortia around its innovation interests. FP7 is a preferred but not the sole framework for action. Every action starts and finishes with the business interest of the SME.
- People-to-people approach: Mobilization and coaching follows an approach geared toward individuals. An smE-MPOWER coach guides a company through a series of customized, small-scale workshops and personally facilitates international partnerships.

This personalized partner search is referral system based on a mutual trust and utilized by the international smE-MPOWER community of regionally established cooperation coaches.

- Open knowledge: When fulfilling their role, smE-MPOWER coaches freely utilize and distribute operational support tools, checklists, templates and decision frames available in the shared knowledge base. An open knowledge license enables all parties to use, modify, share and profit from this open knowledge.

7. Conclusions

7.1 Lessons Learned

European SMEs clearly have innovation needs. They also constitute the foremost breeding ground for new ideas with potential for commercialization. While some SME are aware the FP7 can support their visionary projects, very few believe they can easily access these funding opportunities and rarely pursue them. Empowering SME to strategically think about innovation and their own business innovation is the key to mobilizing them to engage in long-term and self-defined RTD activities. When facing the complexities of international RTD collaboration, SME usually need assistance from professionally equipped and qualified coaches. Such cooperation coaches need to speak the language of SME and therefore build all their support around value creation through business innovation.

While many SME have become reluctant to seek out professional consulting, they tend to be very open to client-centered coaching. Openly sharing knowledge and network resources with a company is a central element of the value provided by a coach. Since coaching to promote cooperation and business innovation only constitutes one element of a complete innovation system, the smE-MPOWER approach should ideally be structurally integrated into existing regional support frameworks. It would then hold potential to empower the regions to achieve the goals of the European knowledge economy.

7.2 Exploiting the smE-MPOWER Approach

Since the EU funded phase of the project has convincingly demonstrated the success of the smE-MPOWER approach, it will be taken forward into the future by the smE-MPOWER community, which is the sole owner of the project's IPR. The community is able to utilize and further develop IPR on an "open knowledge" basis, i.e. all practical know-how generated by the project is freely shared among the community members in a modifiable format.

This community consists of two layers: a growing, distributed, multi-actor network and a lean central support unit. Community members generate value on the regional level by offering services to SME and the regions themselves. The central unit supports the growing circle of regional smE-MPOWER entities that have access to open knowledge generated within the community as well as other services and related training. Structured competence development, training modules and an accreditation system for smE-MPOWER coaches represent a major avenue of future value generation.

Eight of the original ten project consortium members have committed to continue collaboration within this framework. Membership is open to interested parties and subject to an annual membership fee. Business intermediaries with an interest in improving their face-to-face coaching services to SME are the community's target group.

7.3 Recommendations

The EC's intensive incentives and substantial efforts to foster innovation in European SME have led to the emergence of a wide range of SME innovation intermediaries. However, hardly any SME support action has so far developed into a financially independent autonomous organization or initiative. Rather, a complex middle layer of networks and projects between SME and the EC has emerged, which consumes great shares of EC funding while leaving parts of the innovation project stages uncovered. Thus, better coordination between the various actors and a clear separation of tasks would appear to be a desirable and above all beneficial EU policy objective.

References

[1]   European Commission, Directorate-General for Research (2006): SMEs in FP6 – Sharing in Europe's future. Luxembourg, p.5.
[2]   Hübner, D.(2006): SME's: key players in European Regional Policy, speech at: High-level SME stakeholder conference, Brussels, 11 October 2006.
       http://ec.europa.eu/commission_barroso/hubner/speeches/pdf/speech_sme.pdf, checked on 2007-10-09.
[3]   Verheugen, G. (2007): SME – key for delivering more growth and jobs, speech at: High-level SME stakeholder conference, Brussels, 14 September 2007.
       http://ec.europa.eu/enterprise/newsroom/cf/document.cfm?action=display&doc_id=552, checked on 2007-10-09.
[4]   loc. cit.
[5]   A slight increase in participation has been observed during the last years: "For the first two and a half years of the Sixth Framework Programme (FP6), the funding requested by SME for main-listed proposals is estimated at 13.6% against 12.4% for the first year only." in: SME Interservice Task Force (2006): Progress Report 4.
[6]   In FP6 just 22%of SME proposals considered to be of a 'very high standard' received funding, whereas 50% of all projects of a 'very high standard' received funding. Cp. Potocnik, J. (2006): speech at: SME participation in the R&D Framework Programme (FP6), Kortrijk, Belgium, May 2006.
       http://www.waleseic.org.uk/home.php?page_id=184, checked on 2007-10-09.
[7]   European Commission (2005): Europe's SME – contributing and benefiting. in: European Industrial Research, No. 5, p.4-5.
[8]   Morron, M. (2007): The European Union's ICT Program in FP7. Version 1.0, p. 46.
[9]   European Policy Evaluation Consortium (2006): Impact assessment for improving SME specific research schemes and measures to promote SME participation in the Framework Programmes – Final Report, p.30. ftp://ftp.cordis.lu/pub/sme/docs/FPSME_Impact_Final.pdf, checked on 2007-09-28.
[10]   Economic and Technological Intelligence
[11]   Specific Support Actions
[12]   Competitiveness and Innovation Framework Programme
[13]   European Commission (2007): Midterm review of Modern SME policy. p. 4.;
       http://ec.europa.eu/enterprise/entrepreneurship/docs/com_2007_0592_en.pdf. checked on 2007-10-09.
[14]   http://www.enterprise-europe-network.ec.europa.eu/about_network_en.htm
[15]   ftp://ftp.cordis.europa.eu/pub/focus/docs/supplement-sme3_en.pdf. checked on 2008-05-06.
[16]   ftp://ftp.cordis.europa.eu/pub/focus/docs/supplement-sme3_en.pdf. checked on 2008-05-06.

Collaboration and the Knowledge Economy: Issues, Applications, Case Studies
P. Cunningham and M. Cunningham (Eds.)
IOS Press, 2008

Knowledge Circulation in ICT
the Virtue of Practice-oriented Research

Henk DE POOT, Annemiek VAN DER KOLK
Telematica Instituut, Brouwerijstraat 1, Enschede, 7523 XC, Netherlands
Tel: +31 53 4850485, Fax: + 31 53 4850400
Email: Henk.dePoot@telin.nl, Annemiek.vanderKolk@telin.nl

Abstract: Since 2005 the Dutch Ministry of Education has funded regional programmes to stimulate knowledge circulation by Dutch Universities of Applied Science in consortia with small and medium enterprises and communities of professionals from public organizations. In the first 3 years, a striking 45 (34%) of the granted proposals addressed ICT as a main topic on their innovation agenda. Here we investigate the nature of these ICT innovation programmes which rest on a solid basis of multidisciplinary knowledge input from the side of professors and the active participation in knowledge creation from practitioners in the field.

Keywords: ICT, Innovation, SME, Knowledge Circulation, Communities of Practice, Living Labs

1. Regional Attention and Action for Knowledge Circulation

Since 2005 the Dutch Ministry of Education, Culture and Science has funded some 200 "RAAK" regional innovation programmes where Universities of Applied Science (UAS, a.k.a. polytechnic colleges) collaborate in networks with regional partners.

RAAK's goal is to enable practice-oriented research at UASs as well as stimulate the regional network of small and medium enterprises (SMEs) and public institutions in their eco-system. The scheme compares, a.o., to EU's CRAFT, STREPs and Collective Research schemes, the Swiss CTI, the German FH3, the Finnish Tekes and the Romanian ReNITT.

RAAK is an acronym for Regional Attention and Action for Knowledge circulation. Partners in RAAK can be consortia of SMEs as well as professionals from public organizations. The Foundation Innovation Alliance (SIA) manages the RAAK-scheme. SMEs and professionals articulate the research agenda and the collaborative research setting enables a knowledge flow from UASs to practitioners and back [1]. A joint responsibility is essential, as UASs educate the future managers, specialists, and professionals in many SMEs and public institutions. In this paper we look into the large proportion of ICT-related innovation questions that have as yet been articulated.

Some of the topics of the European eCompetences Framework and numerous national ICT research subsidies are prominent in RAAK as well. Yet the scheme fulfils a complementary role to the other innovation grants as our survey among participating SMEs shows. 52,6% of the respondents (N=806) indicated they had not used other innovation grants in the three preceding years. 19,2% used an investigation grant for product development, 8,6% used the Innovation voucher for one-on-one consultancy, 6,7% used EU grants and 8,2% mentioned other grants from regional and national government.

Another aspect of the RAAK subsidy is that the network of participating companies and/or professionals is sufficiently large to bring knowledge circulation about. Depending on the amount of subsidy (typically covering the cost of 1 or more FTEs of research capacity) between 5 and 15 SMEs or some twenty professionals are required upfront. For subsidies amounting to 4 or 5 FTEs the network of SMEs and/or professionals must grow to

40-50 participants. This stimulates partners to address a sufficiently generic innovation agenda. If only one partner signs up for an innovation challenge, that will not be a basis for a joint research programme. The innovation topics are left to the proposers.

2.   ICT Ranks High on Innovation Agenda of SMEs and Professionals

Between 2005 and 2007, 240 RAAK innovation programmes have been proposed of which 149 have been granted. A striking 45 (34%) of these granted proposals include ICT as a main topic on their innovation agenda, even though the RAAK subsidy does not demand that innovations be ICT-based at all. In fact any innovation, whether social, organizational, methodological or technological is equally admissible.

2.1   Why Does ICT Dominate the Innovation Agenda So Strongly?

The prominence of ICT on the innovation agenda might just be that it percolates into all these different domains. As an innovation motor ICT is closely connected to innovation trends: As much as innovation trends are inspired by the possibilities of ICT, ICT developments stem from the societal and economic needs for information and communication. Improved transparency of working, extensive information logistics, tightly coupled activities of business partners or social partners, and intensified communication across a wide range of domains have been identified in innovation agendas since the early 1980s [2, 3]. Notwithstanding this, it often takes decades before visions for business process improvement are implemented. Quite often, ICT is part of these innovation plans.

This raises several questions:

- What ICT innovations are most prominent for SME and professionals?
- Which public and private sectors are most involved in ICT innovation?
- What kind of knowledge circulation is most prominent among different programmes?
- What lessons can be learned from conducting these innovation programmes?

These questions will be addressed in the remainder of this paper.

3.   Methodology Used

The technologies involved, the domain to which programme partners belong, and the methods of knowledge circulation are compared for the different programmes in order to answer these questions. For some of the programmes more information exists, because they have been followed start to end, whereas other programmes are still running at the moment of writing. The results are summarised in Tables 1 through 4, describing and showing the topics (Table 1), the application domains, nr of SMEs, participating professionals, and professors with theoretical and practical skills (Table 2), the innovation goals (Table 3), and ways in which a bidirectional knowledge flow or knowledge circulation is achieved (Table 4).

4.   Comparison of Innovation Programmes

4.1   Prominent ICT Innovations

When ICT innovations of the 45 RAAK Programmes are classified according to technologies proposed, a large part of ICT innovations deal with applying or improving general end-user services for communication (18%), media delivery and gaming (18%).

Next come systems integration solutions applying logistics (18%), sensors (15%), and human interaction in smart solutions such as domotics (7%), location-based services (7%) or solutions targeted to a specific group (4%).

Finally development of software (9%) and hardware (4%) play a role to develop new building bricks and new engineering principles. Table 1 shows examples of the respective topics addressed.

Table 1: Main Topics Addressed in RAAK ICT Innovation Programmes Granted Between 2005 and 2007

Communication (18%)	Media & Gaming (18%)
• distance learning • open cultural collaboration • online training and health log • monitoring based e-care concepts • transparent care solutions • networked healthcare • patient-oriented working • games enticing communication in care	• cross media format development • cross media business network • digital cultural heritage • media literacy • augmented reality (AR) for design & architecture • game and interaction design • artists in media industries
Human Interaction (18%)	Logistics (18%)
• e-business portal for SME • speech therapy portal for professionals • cognitive support for dementia patients • location-based wireless services • location-based tourist services	• logistics and process laboratory • agri-chain logistics information • air cargo/sea freight logistics • business and manufacturing logistics • consented homecare planning
Sensors (15%)	Hardware and Software (13%)
• synthetic insects with embedded sensors • sensing crop growing operations • computer vision-based expertise • computer vision-based microbial analysis • water quality sensing systems	• polymer electronics • embedded Linux • performance management systems • technology-based care concepts • high tech orthopaedics

In Table 1 human centred ICT topics make up 54%, and applied ICT solutions account even for 87%. Even on this limited sample size this teaches us something about the nature of SME-based ICT innovation, being primarily applied and more often than not human centred. Customers still count for SME whereas larger companies and organizations may address markets rather than individuals.

Also the prominence of logistics and sensors into integrated systems is remarkable. In their pioneering phase these technologies were out of reach of SME, but they are rapidly become more affordable and hence a business necessity.

4.2 Prominent Sectors Involved in ICT Innovation

When ICT innovations of the 45 RAAK programmes are classified according to the public and private sectors involved, the inclusion of target groups becomes evident. Table 2 shows the number of innovation programmes for each application domain. A distinction is made between programmes running, and programmes that have finalised. The information about finalised programmes is more complete. As can be seen the consortia grow in size and quality. The proportions of SMEs and professionals as primary target groups (between brackets are the absolute numbers) increase throughout the programmes.

Only among the agriculture and environment programmes, the proportions of SMEs and professionals do not further increase. But these consortia are already large from the start. Two other phenomena in Table 2 deserve attention:

Table 2: Application Domains of RAAK ICT Innovation Programmes Granted Between 2005 and 2007

According to the Application Domains	Programmes		Nr. SMEs		Professionals		Professors
	Run-ning	fina-lised	run-ning	fina-lised	run-ning	fina-lised	Total
Human Centric Domains:	**12**	**8**	**29%** **(40)**	**52%** **(134)**	**57%** **(148)**	**71%** **(93)**	**36**
• Healthcare & Elderly Care	5	5	36% (21)	49% (87)	67% (83)	73% (58)	22
• Culture and Education	6	0	13% (7)	N/A	58% (65)	N/A	8
• Tourism and sports	1	3	44% (12)	60% (47)	0% (0)	67% (35)	6
Technology Centric Domains:	**7**	**18**	**66%** **(51)**	**77%** **(584)**	**36%** **(19)**	**59%** **(164)**	**40**
• Industry	3	10	75% (24)	78% (417)	32% (10)	53% (74)	23
• Business and transport	2	3	44% (8)	81% (128)	0% (0)	67% (39)	7
• Agriculture and environment	2	2	70% (19)	70% (56)	56% (9)	56% (20)	4
• Construction	0	3	N/A	73% (76)	N/A	66% (31)	6

Table 3: Examples of Plans in RAAK ICT Innovation Programmes Across Seven Application Domains

Industry	Care
• coping with chain dependency • mastering computer-aided manufacturing • acceleration through computer vision • joint product development • integrating products in end-to-end systems • innovation through creativity • future product paradigms • pilot cases to test new technologies	• communication platform • from products to systems to services • service prototypes, e.g. for telecare • 21st century hospital • pilots • ICT support for product evaluation • implementation teams
Culture and Education	**Business and transport**
• e-inclusion of students • informal collaboration pilot • access to heritage collections • augmented reality as culture experience • media literacy embedded in curriculum • web-enabled assessment tools	• e-business prototypes • changing rules of business • co-creation • implementation of protocols • value-added ICT utilisation
Tourism and Sports	**Agriculture and environment**
• e-coaching pilot experiment • location-based services • prototype tourist services • integration of hospitality services	• logistic readiness benchmark • GS1 conformance pilot • automated agricultural bookkeeping • sensor-enabled waste water control
	Construction
	• smart home demonstration • domotics system integration • augmented reality for visualisation

1. The proportion of SMEs (compared to other participating organisations) is highest in the technology-centric programmes, whereas the proportion of professionals (compared to other participating individuals in each innovation programme) is highest in human-centric·programmes. Since 2006 this phenomenon was acknowledged by SIA for innovation programmes in general. When social innovation and human factors are heavily involved, professionals from public institutions should become innovation partners like SME entrepreneurs. In some sectors a public institution will invest in innovation, whereas in other sectors (e.g. tourism) private sector investments are key.

2. In the rightmost column the professors (in Dutch: "lectoren") associated with the respective innovation programmes are mentioned. These professors have been appointed at Dutch UASs since 2001 to stimulate multidisciplinary research and improve the collaboration between academia and practitioners [4]. They have a background in science and in the practice of their field of expertise. On average 1,6 professors are involved in the technology-centric innovation programmes, and 1,8 professors are involved in the human-centric innovation programmes. Healthcare and elderly care get most support with 2,2 professors participating on average.

Note that a large proportion of human-centric or end-user applications are found in the domains of healthcare (11%), elderly care (11%), tourism and sports (9%), culture (7%), and education (7%). On the other hand, many technology-centric ICT innovations are just components in larger systems in industry (24%), building & construction (7%), agriculture (7%), business (7%), process industry (4%), transport (4%), and environment (2%).

Together the human-centric domain accounts for 44% of the ICT innovations with a considerable involvement of the public sector, whereas the technology-centric domain seems to be governed by industry and other private sectors. The reason for these separate domains to stand out may be two faces of Baumol and Bowen's theorem [5]. In business, agriculture, and industry, efficiency can always be improved by technology, so this provides a breeding ground for high-tech ICT innovations. In the public sector, high touch is increasingly important. Therefore ICT in should improve rather than replace the human element in numerous services delivered there.

Table 3 shows examples of the respective areas addressed within each innovation domain. The programmes are different in their ambitions.

- The Industry programmes point at strategic questions and hard problems and ICT as an innovation in itself.
- The Business, Transport, and Agriculture programmes emphasize the added value of information logistics.
- The Culture, Education and Tourism programmes seem keenly aware that any service will only work when properly introduced and adopted by the targeted user group.
- The Healthcare programmes are focussed on efficiency through better communication even enabling forms of telecare.
- The construction programmes address new phenomena such as smart homes and augmented reality. To understand their virtues and pitfalls, they need to be explored.

4.3 Comparison of Knowledge Circulation Methods

A mere analysis of innovative ICT technologies and sectors and the ambitions discussed above already hints into what the knowledge circulation in the innovation programmes is about. With knowledge circulation residing in the title of the RAAK scheme, it needs to be properly planned in every innovation programme proposed.

Table 4 shows examples of knowledge circulation methods proposed in the respective programmes. Roughly they fall into five categories, Prototypes, Laboratories, Living Labs, Communication Platforms, and Communities of Practice. In the technology centric programmes, the proposed knowledge circulation techniques, are prototypes (36%), laboratories (36%), and communities of practice (28%).

Table 4: Examples of Forms of Knowledge Circulation Implemented in RAAK ICT Innovation Programmes

Communities of practice:	Living labs
• …for technology-based care concepts • …for speech therapists • …for sea freight logistics • …for sensor technology for water systems • …for manufacturing logistics • …for performance management systems • …for high tech orthopaedics • cross media network • knowledge clusters for transparent care solutions • implementation teams for demand-driven homecare planning • e-business community for e-business consultancy	• laboratory for domotics for handicapped • living laboratory technology based care concepts • laboratory for AR design & architecture • living laboratory location-based wireless services • digital cultural heritage laboratory gaming and design career centre
	Communication platforms:
Prototypes: • educative infrastructure for media literacy • service prototypes for ICT support for dementia patients • 21st century hospital for patient oriented working • integral design principles for domotics for the elderly • development of logistics standard for logistics chain information • value creating concepts for logistics chain information • prototype building for registering growing activities • cross-sectoral innovation by means of computer vision applications	• platform for creative industries for artists in media industries • SportLog open source training log / performance monitor • electronic learning environment distance learning • platform for communication and gaming in care • solutions for healthcare at home / domotics in care • common showcase improving networked healthcare
	Laboratories:
	• polymer electronics laboratory • embedded electronics laboratory • computer vision expertise centre • embedded ICT products laboratory • logistics and process laboratory for testing industry principles

In contrast, the human-centric innovation programmes hinge much stronger on user involvement either as subjects in living labs (40%), or as users of a communication platform (30%), or as peers sharing experiences in a Community of Practice (15%). In the remaining 15% of the programmes a prototype is built to further the discussion on ICT themes in the organization.

So the object being shared in knowledge circulation differs significantly between ICT innovation programmes. In general human-centric ICT innovation programmes tend to involve more non-technical persons, whereas research and development staff are the main target group for the technology-centric ICT innovation. Also there is a difference in emphasis. There is a prototype implicit in every living lab setting, but a prototype does not necessarily involve a user test, let alone a living lab setting. So the technology centric innovations seem to dig deeper whereas the human centric innovations are breadth first.

5. Best Practices and Lessons Learned

As part of the RAAK monitoring activity participants share their best practices and lessons learned throughout the innovation programme. Many of these best practices are generic, in that they could be valid in other innovation programmes where educational institutes and practitioners collaborate. Some of the best practices and lessons learned were specific for ICT innovation however. We summarise them here.

5.1 Best Practices

- Make an explicit separation between the creative and the professional phase (when involving business partners).
- Tower of Babel: realise that disciplines speak different languages.
- Ease of use: Make quick reference guides to relieve users from thick manuals.
- Social pressure: Name and shame list for participants who do not participate.
- Heart of the matter: Involve entrepreneurs in usability laboratories. Make them realise what product or service usability is about.
- Complexity: Use pressure cooker innovation to kick-start the design of ICT services
- Complexity: Take the value chain into account (in domotics, healthcare, agriculture, logistics, business, tourism).
- Joint academic-applied laboratories open to UAS students and SMEs.
- Well-equipped laboratories to attract entrepreneurs, professionals as well as students.
- Use multiple perspectives, e.g. not just healthcare, but also business perspectives.

5.2 Lessons Learned: Threats and Weaknesses

- Divergence through technologies opportunities: Stay on focus.
- Rapid evolution of technology: danger of betting on the wrong horse.
- Confusion of demand-driven problems and problems chosen to train competences.
- Even in high-tech sectors such as installation technology, less than 5% of the workforce is innovation-minded. So a change of mindset must be achieved,

5.3 Lessons Learned: Strengths and Opportunities

- Developments toward digitisation open the hearts and minds for standardisation as well.
- Regional innovation partners can help one another get in touch with new business areas.
- Consider students as new-technology literates.
- Enabling technologies such as augmented reality, location-based services, computer vision, 3D gaming, and logistics all prove to be widely applicable in many areas.

6. Conclusions

6.1 Upfront User Involvement When Necessary

According to IDEO's maxim, failing faster to succeed sooner, upfront user involvement helps to identify system failures [6], but this happens at the expense of limited product development.

Ideally the prototypes for a successful user test are available when a programme starts. The settings that are implicit in public sector programmes encompass more social complexity, which needs to be tested, whereas the settings in private sector programmes allow more technical complexity. Yet, even there, widespread impact is inversely proportional to complexity, and only simple principles run a chance for reasonable adoption.

6.2 Laboratories as a Collaborative Investment

A large part of the ICT-innovation projects encompass setting up laboratories (for technology-centric innovation programmes) and living laboratories (for human-centric innovation programmes) both combined with communities of practice. Obviously the resources for SME and SME-sized public organizations to organise such ICT innovations on their own are only limited and collaboration with UASs, other knowledge institutes, and peers really provides a competitive edge.

6.3 The Virtue of Practice-Oriented Research in ICT-Education

On the one hand the idea to improve both education and practice through collaboration works well, given the many inspiring innovation programmes we have seen so far.

On the other hand, there is something about ICT education that seems to be lacking in general curricula: more often than not the technology comes to life in applications outside the core theoretical or technological domain.

If we want our ICT students to be well-prepared, the lessons learned, and best practices (such as living labs) promoted in the knowledge circulation projects discussed, cannot be left to the mere initiatives of individual teachers and professors in higher education. These aspects of social innovation need to be embedded in the general ICT curricula!

References

[1] van Vliet, Harry; Horvath, Janika. SMEs and innovation in the Netherlands: Spinning the wheel: knowledge circulation in (hydraulic) motion. *Industry and Higher Education*, Volume 18, Number 5, October 2004 , pp. 309-319(11)

[2] Wellborn, Stanley. A world of communications wonders *U.S. News & World Report*, April 1984

[3] Poppel, H. An Overview of Information-Age Trends and Their Impact on Telecom Managers. *Communications News*, June 1, 1985

[4] Leijnse, F. Het Nederlands hoger onderwijs in de komende tien jaar (Dutch Higher Education in the coming ten years), Een essay, *Tijdschift voor Hoger Onderwijs en Management (THEMA)* (4) 2000.

[5] William J. Baumol and William G. Bowen, *Performing Arts - The Economic Dilemma*. New York: The Twentieth Century Fund, 1966.

[6] Bruce Nussbaum. The Power Of Design. *Business Week*. May 17, 2004

Economics-Aware Capacity Planning for Commercial Grids

Marcel RISCH[1], Jörn ALTMANN[1,2], Yannis MAKRYPOULIAS[3], Sergios SOURSOS[3]

[1]*International University in Germany, School of Information Technology,*
Campus 3 Bruchsal, 76646, Germany,
Tel: +49 (0)7251 7000, Fax: + 49 (0)7251 700150, Email: marcel.risch@i-u.de
[2]*TEMEP, School of Engineering, San 56-1, Sillim-Dong,*
Gwanak-Gu, Seoul, 151-742, South-Korea
Tel: +1 510 972 3062, Fax: +1501 641 5384, Email: jorn.altmann@acm.org
[3]*Athens University of Economics and Business, Dept. of Informatics,*
76, Patission str, Athens, 10434, Greece
Tel: +30 210 8203693, Fax: + 30 210 8203693, Email: {makrupoul06, sns}@aueb.gr.

Abstract: Currently, capacity planning is fairly simple, due to the few options that are available. With the advent of Grid markets, this discipline for analyzing resource purchases must be adapted. A commercial Grid provides many different resource types at variable prices, making capacity planning more complicated than it currently is. In this paper, we describe the functionality of an online Grid Capacity Planning Service, which helps companies with little IT expertise to make use of the Grid in a cost-effective manner. The requirements of the capacity planning service are derived in part from a survey carried out among SMEs in the region of the German city of Bruchsal. Using the requirements, we identified all the necessary information from the Grid and we designed and implemented parts of the capacity planning service.

1. Introduction

The main foci of Grid research fall into two categories: In the first category are the research and development projects, which aim at developing Grid architectures. These include Globus [1], GRIA [2], Gridbus [3], glite [4] and NextGRID [5]. In the second category are the business-related projects, which analyze and develop business models for Grid systems. These include, amongst others, AssessGrid [6], Biz2Grid [7] and BeInGrid [8].

However, the commercial Grids, which are slowly developing, do not seem to rely on the principles developed by these projects. Instead, existing commercial Grids have been developed by companies, which have created their own approaches to Grid computing, such as the Amazon.com EC2 [9], the Sun Grid [10], and the Tsunami Technologies Grid [11]. Some of these services have started to become very popular and, thus, prove that the idea of commercial Grid computing is indeed acceptable to resource providers and buyers [12]. This is illustrated in SecondLife Blog [13], which illustrated that for short demand peaks, the Amazon service was cheaper than installing additional in-house bandwidth capacity.

Existing research in commercial Grids has largely failed to consider the economic aspects of Grid computing. It has been tacitly assumed that, by providing the proper technical environment, customers would be convinced of the advantages of Grid technologies. This shortcoming of existing Grid research has been identified by the GridEcon project [14], which started out with the premise that economic considerations complement technical solutions. A number of economic-enhanced support services have been identified which are needed for a commercial Grid to function. These services include various brokers but also a capacity planning service, which helps customers to determine their resource needs.

This paper shows the steps towards the development of a Grid Capacity Planning Service, which will help Grid users to plan their capacity requirements. First, we will define the term 'capacity planning', since capacity planning has lost some of its importance in data center planning and since there are many different definitions for this task. Second, we demonstrate the need for a capacity planning service in a commercial Grid environment through the analysis of the differences between traditional capacity planning and Grid capacity planning as well as through the analysis of a qualitative survey. The survey addressed SMEs from diverse fields such as banking, software development, and car sales. From the survey results, we determined the requirements that SMEs have towards Grid markets and towards capacity planning in particular. Based on these results, the requirements of the capacity planning service are determined and an architecture of a Grid Capacity Planning Service is designed and developed.

The structure of the paper is devised as follows: In Section 2, capacity planning is put into context with other data center tasks. In Section 3, the differences between traditional and Grid capacity planning are explained and, from these differences, the requirements for a Grid capacity planning service as well as the design of the service are derived. The Short-Term Capacity Planning Service is then explained in more detail in Section 4, before the paper is concluded in Section 5.

2.   Capacity Planning Definition

2.1   Capacity Planning Definition

In [15], it has been remarked that the term "capacity planning" is frequently used but rarely defined. To correct this deficiency, we will start by defining the term, using the definition given by IBM in [16]:

> *"Capacity Planning encompasses the process of planning for adequate IT resources required to fulfill current and future resource requirements so that the customer's workload requirements are met and the service provider's costs are recovered."*

This definition allows us to categorize the users of capacity planning into two groups: customers and providers. While some research has been done on the provider's capacity planning problems [17][18], no research has been done, as of yet, on the customer's need for capacity planning in a Grid environment.

According to the definition, the following three tasks are at the heart of the capacity planning process: (1) Monitoring the current resource utilization rate and the application response times; (2) Estimating the future resource requirements of applications; (3) Cost monitoring to ensure that a company does not overspend. Based on these tasks, four courses of action are open to companies: (1) purchasing in-house resources, (2) renting or leasing in-house resources, (3) doing nothing, or (4), in the case of the existence of a commercial Grid, purchasing Grid resources.

2.2   Conceptual Classification of Capacity Planning

The capacity planning process should guarantee that a basic mapping of applications to resources (i.e. resource allocation) is always possible. This implies that resource allocation is a sub-task of the capacity planning process. At the same time, the capacity planning process should ensure that resources have similar load levels, which implies that load balancing is also a subtask of the capacity planning process. Load balancing and resource allocation already have one task in common, namely monitoring.

Economic aspects have always been a part of capacity planning. Since data centers have budget constraints, the IT personnel needs to determine which resource has the best value for the price. These issues are also faced in a commercial Grid, where the IT personnel has to compare different Grid alternatives. As we will outline in the next section, the task of choosing the optimal resource is even more complex because of the usage-based pricing structure of commercial Grids. It forces the data center personnel to predict the resource usage very precisely, in order to achieve low costs for Grid usage.

3. Towards a Grid Capacity Planning Service

3.1 Complexity of Decision Making in Capacity Planning

This section demonstrates why capacity planning is very important in a Grid environment. It also discusses the differences between traditional capacity planning and Grid capacity planning. For this analysis, we assume that a functioning Grid economy exists, that is, prices are determined according to the supply and demand situation. The currently existing Grid computing offers (such as Amazon EC2, Sun and Tsunamic) have fixed prices.

3.1.1 Effort of Capacity Planning

Capacity planning is not popular with companies, since the effort does not bear any relation to the expected benefits, as can be demonstrated with the following example:

We assume that an employee incurs costs of $4500 per month (salary and human resource management) to a company. Thus, one week of work on planning the computing resources costs the company about $1000. This cost must be added to the cost of the computing resources. If this company is a small company, the actual savings through an accurate capacity planning procedure is very low or even non-existent. Consequently, capacity planning is not widely used. This fact could be verified during a qualitative survey of SMEs in the Bruchsal region (Germany): When asked to describe their capacity planning process, companies stated that they used their "gut feeling" to decide which resource to purchase. Other companies simply bought one of the most powerful computing resources available to ensure that it would be able to run future applications, which are expected to require more powerful resources.

In a commercial Grid environment, provider companies have even more capacity planning inputs to consider to determine the best resource allocation. Thus, the capacity planning process becomes even more expensive. This process is further complicated by the fact that Grid users may be willing to sell excess resources on the Grid. In this case, the expected income must be taken into account when calculating the Grid usage costs. This increased complexity will require the data center staff to spend more time on the capacity planning process, which in turn reduces the benefit of capacity planning further.

3.1.2 Resource Diversity

In traditional capacity planning, the IT personnel only has to select new hardware from the resources currently available in the market. Although not standardized, these resources usually have similar features and thus pose few difficulties for professional staff. Therefore, should a resource be added or replaced, the data center staff will be able to find a similar resource that can perform the job adequately well, without having to perform any performance testing. This has also been reported in the survey: Companies stated that new resources are better in every aspect than existing resources, so that all existing applications and future applications (with increased resource requirements) can still be executed.

In a Grid environment, however, the diversity of resources is much greater, since providers may offer any kind of resource (e.g. virtual machines of old computers).

3.1.3   Price Volatility

The current computing resource market is fairly static in that resource prices do not change frequently. Since current resources are usually bought for in-house installation, price variations only occur because of special offers or economies of scale. Therefore, the capacity planning team does not need to rush the capacity planning process to avoid changing prices. Even if the capacity planning team decides to make use of current commercial Grid resources (e.g. Amazon [9], Sun [10], Tsunamic [11]), those prices, although high, remain unchanged [19].

With the advent of commercial Grids, which sell resources at competitive prices, prices will change according to the variation in supply and demand. The capacity planning team has to consider these price fluctuations and has to predict how the prices will develop. Furthermore, with changing prices, the timing of purchases may become a relevant parameter in the capacity planning process: The demand peaks have to be analyzed with respect to the market prices, in order to determine whether the demand peaks coincide with times of high Grid prices.

3.2   Requirements of a Grid Capacity Planning Service

In order to be accepted by Grid users, a Grid Capacity Planning Service (GCPS) should fulfill a number of requirements and provide a set of basic functionality.

The functionality that should be offered by the GCPS is the monitoring service. It monitors Grid and in-house resources. If a performance requirement is no longer met (e.g. an exceeded response time limit or exceeded load level), the GCPS triggers the resource analysis process in order to determine a course of action to satisfy all user demands.

During the resource analysis process, the Grid Capacity Planning Service should take the user's in-house resources into account and should ensure that these are used. Since these resources have been purchased and have been installed, they should be used as much as possible to reduce costs. However, if the user is willing to sell certain resources on the Grid, the GCPS has to take this into account as well. There may be cases in which it is advantageous to sell some of the in-house resources on the Grid.

When the GCPS has determined which courses of action are viable, it should give a ranked list of options to the user, who can then decide which of these options should be executed. This final selection step allows the user to remain in control of his budget and to ensure that tacit requirements are also met.

Furthermore, the GCPS should perform application-resource-mappings. Since the GCPS needs to determine the requirements of applications under different circumstances, the GCPS has to run performance tests for applications on various resource types. At the same time, this procedure will have to be performed in a cost-effective manner. In a commercial Grid environment in which prices fluctuate, the GCPS should perform these actions during times of low resource prices. The results of the performance tests and the thereby derived requirements for each application should be stored locally within the GCPS to ensure that all information is readily available.

Finally, the Grid Capacity Planning Service should perform as many of these actions as possible automatically, i.e. without the help of a human operator. There are two arguments that count against human involvement: the first is that people are slow and error prone and thus the result generated by the GCPS would not be as accurate. The second reason is that experienced and specialized employees are expensive and, thus, would cause higher costs.

3.3   A Grid Capacity Planning Service Model

To fulfill all requirements, we envision a Grid Capacity Planning Service (GCPS), which consists of two distinct parts that work in concert:

- Part 1: Long-Term Capacity Planning Service (LTCPS): This is an online service, which performs the long-term analysis of the user's resource situation. It takes input parameters (e.g. information about in-house resources, application information, and user requirements, and information from the Short-Term Capacity Planning Service) before determining a ranked list of possible courses of action for in-house resource purchases and rentals, and Grid resource purchases and sales.
- Part 2: Short-Term Capacity Planning Service (STCPS): This service suggests to the user the number of machines required to meet his short-term performance or economic goals, over a specific time period. To do so, it uses information on past usage of Grid resources, considers characteristics of the application the user wants to run on the Grid and estimates the application's load that is expected for the requested time period.

These two capacity planning services complement each other, since one addresses the short-term problems while the other addresses the medium- to long-term problems. The two services will be described in more detail in the following two sections.

3.3.1 The Long-Term Capacity Planning Service

Since the LTCPS should plan as far into the future as possible, it requires a lot of information, which can be grouped into three categories:

The first category includes information about user-owned resources, user-owned applications, as well as user requirements. Information about user-owned resources and applications describe which resources are installed in-house and which applications are to be run. The information about user requirements is more complex. For example, many companies have sensitive data, which should not be processed by applications beyond company boundaries. These applications are not permitted to run on the Grid, since this would violate company policy (i.e. a user requirement). Another example for a user requirement is the maximum expenditures for Grid resources, runtime limits, the response time limits, or the fact that the in-house resources must be used to their full extend.

The second category consists of application requirements. These can be divided into minimum and optimal requirements and include items such as hardware requirements and software requirements. The software requirements provide information about additional software that must be available on a machine. The software requirements also include requirements for communication with other software components (e.g. communication with other sub-jobs within a workflow). Furthermore, the application requirements should also include the usage frequency of the application and the average usage duration.

The third category contains information about the Grid market and is collected by the LTCPS. It comprises the current and past prices of Grid resources, the availability of suitable Grid resources, as well as the prices for in-house resources. This last point is still a challenge, since many resource vendors do not use any standard for composing computers that would allow a potential buyer to determine computer prices automatically.

Next, these three sets of information are used to determine a mapping of applications to resources in such a way that all user requirements are met. The result can fall into one of the following categories: in-house resources are sufficient, purchase Grid resources, purchase in-house resources, sell in-house resources on the Grid, or purchase both in-house and Grid resources. The operation of the LTCPS can be seen in Figure 1 below.

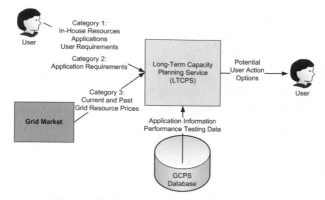

Figure 1: The Long-Term Capacity Planning Service

3.3.2 The Short-Term Capacity Planning Service

The STCPS takes input from the user with respect to the performance and cost-minimization objectives. Then, it proposes the number of machines to be purchased on the Grid, in order to fulfill the user requirements.

We assume that performance objectives are expressed in terms of time delay (i.e. the response time of an application for serving a request). Users (e.g. application providers) find it easy to express their requirements in terms of delays, since the system response time can be experienced by users.

For cost-minimization purposes, further information is required. First, the information about the cost of purchasing a single machine on the Grid market is necessary. Second, it is required that the user provides a cost function, i.e. a function that relates the experienced delay per application request with a monetary value, representing the cost that is incurred to the provider per millisecond of delay per request.

In addition to the information about the objectives of the user, the STCPS needs to have access to monitoring data about the resource load. The monitoring data is needed to make the necessary estimations and predictions of the load (number and type of requests) that the application will face in the future time period for which the plan is required. All these input are summarized in Figure 2 below.

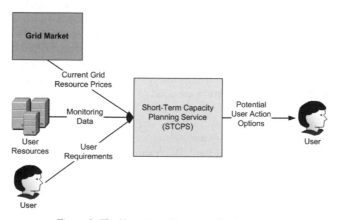

Figure 2: The Short-Term Capacity Planning Service

4. A Closer Look at the Short-Term Capacity Planning Service

Within the GridEcon project [14], we have designed and implemented the Short-Term Capacity Planning Service. In the following sections, we will present the architecture of this system and describe the functionality of the components.

For the STCPS to function, we have to collect monitoring data about every application that runs on the Grid and to be able to categorize applications according to some common characteristics. We assume that every Grid system provides some public interfaces for accessing monitoring data. Using these interfaces, we can obtain all the needed information and store it to a local database, namely the History Component.

After collecting the necessary data, we run a classification algorithm, executed by the Clustering Component. Clustering is necessary for the STCPS, since it allows working with an aggregated set of application-related data. The criterion according to which the application is classified is the execution time of a single request to a virtual machine on the Grid. Our assumption is that applications with similar execution times per request are similar enough to be considered as identical applications. For sake of simplicity, we use clustering with only two classes as an output. This parameter of the system can be changed to allow clustering results with a higher number of classes.

After having aggregated the historical data about the load, we can estimate the load expected for the time period defined by the user. This task is assigned to another module, the Workload Predictor Component. It takes into account the load of the previous hours, along with the load encountered at the same day and time over the past few weeks. Thus, we capture the current trend of the load as well as the behavior that appears periodically.

After the workload prediction is complete, the Decision Support Component has all information necessary to propose to the user the minimum number of virtual machines needed to meet the requirements. To give the user a better recommendation, we have implemented two models: an M/M/k queuing model and a Support Vector Machine model. Both models give answers to the same questions, e.g. how many machines are required such that the application A provides an average service time of Y milliseconds for the next 2 hours? Or, how many machines are required to minimize the provisioning cost, provided that each virtual machine costs x Euros per hour and the cost function is of a certain shape?

All the aforementioned components, along with their internal and external interactions, are depicted in Figure 3.

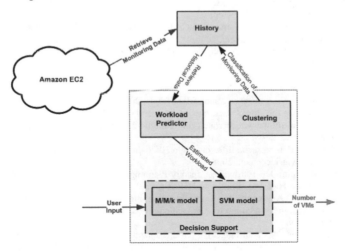

Figure 3: The Architecture of the STCPS

The system is already implemented using the .NET platform and relying on the Amazon EC2 environment. For our tests, we also designed and implemented an application-level monitoring module. The test application that is executed on EC2 is a Web Server with different JSP web pages that emulate the different Web applications. We are currently testing the application and the various approaches used in the design, in order to evaluate the contribution of such a system.

5.   Conclusions

In this paper we have defined the term "capacity planning" and have placed it in a conceptual context for Grid computing. Furthermore, we have shown that capacity planning is rarely used in companies today and that it is more complex in a Grid environment. Due to the complexity, we believe that a Grid Capacity Planning Service (GCPS) is necessary for not only a successful Grid usage but also for making Grid computing widely used.

The GCPS described in this paper has two parts: the Short-Term Capacity Planning Service and the Long-Term Capacity Planning Service. The first is responsible for ensuring that all applications are running as required and will give advice regarding additional resources if they become necessary for a short time period. The latter is responsible for long-term planning of data centers and takes into account the resource requirements of all applications, the available in-house resources, and the user requirements.

Since only an outline of the LTCPS and a basic testing implementation of the STCPS have been developed, several issues still need to be addressed in implementing the GCPS: Firstly, the efficiency of this service needs to be investigated. Since performance testing is expensive, the GCPS needs to perform as little performance testing as possible without ignoring available resource types. Secondly, the GCPS needs to take into account that an application can have different resource requirements depending on how it is used. Finally, the GCPS has to ensure that it performs all capacity planning tasks quickly, even if the user has many courses of action open. This may require storing common resource allocation solutions but, at the same time, avoiding the storing of excessive amounts of data.

References

[1]   The globus alliance, http://www.globus.org/, 2008.
[2]   Gria, http://www.gria.org/, 2008.
[3]   Gridbus, http://www.gridbus.org/, 2008.
[4]   gLite, http://glite.web.cern.ch/glite/, 2008.
[5]   NextGRID: Architecture for Next Generation Grids, http://www.nextgrid.org/, 2008.
[6]   AssessGrid, http://www.assessgrid.eu/, 2008.
[7]   Biz2Grid, http://www.d-grid.de/index.php?id=407&L=1, 2008.
[8]   BeInGrid, http://www.beingrid.eu/, 2008.
[9]   Amazon   Elastic   Compute   Cloud   (Amazon   EC2),   http://www.amazon.com/ gp/browse.html?node=201590011, 2008.
[10] Sun Grid, http://www.sun.com/service/sungrid/index.jsp, 2008.
[11] Tsunamic Technologies Inc., http://www.clusterondemand.com/, 2008.
[12] Techcrunch: http://www.techcrunch.com/2008/04/21/who-are-the-biggest-users-of-amazon-web-services-its-not-startups/, 2008.
[13] SecondLife Blog, http://blog.secondlife.com/2006/10/26/amazon-s3-for-the-win/, 2008.
[14] GridEcon, http://www.gridecon.eu, 2008.
[15] Cortada, J.W.: Managing DP Hardware. Capacity Planning, Cost Justification, Availability and Energy Management. Prentice-Hall, Inc., Englewood Cliffs (1983).
[16] IBM: A Statistical Approach to Capacity Planning for On-Demand Computing Services, http://domino.watson.ibm.com/comm/research.nsf/pages/r.statistics. innovation2.html, 2008.
[17] Siddiqui, M., Villazon, A., Fahringer, T.: Grid Capacity Planning with Negotiation-based Advance Reservation for Optimized QoS. In: Supercomputing, 2006. SC '06. Proceedings of the ACM/IEEE SC 2006 Conference, IEEE, 2006.

[18] Borowsky, E., Golding, R., Jacobson, P., Merchant, A., Schreier, L., Spasojevic, M., and Wilkes, J.: Capacity planning with phased workloads. In: Proceedings of the 1st international Workshop on Software and Performance. WOSP '98, pp. 199-207 ACM, New York, NY, 1998.

[19] Risch, M., Altmann, J.: Cost Analysis of Current Grids and its Implications for Future Grid Markets. In: Proceedings of the Grid Economics and Business Model Workshop. Gecon 2008, pp.13-27. Springer LNCS. Heidelberg, 2008.

Collaboration and the Knowledge Economy: Issues, Applications, Case Studies
P. Cunningham and M. Cunningham (Eds.)
IOS Press, 2008

A Meta-Model for Knowledge Management Approaches

Eckhard AMMANN
Reutlingen University, Alteburgstrasse 150, 72762 Reutlingen, Germany
Tel: +49 7121 2714026, Email: Eckhard.Ammann@Reutlingen-University.de

Abstract: Important known approaches for knowledge management include the classic approach oriented at knowledge assets, the process-oriented approach, the knowledge-intensive business process modeling approach, and the communities of practice. A meta-model for knowledge management is proposed and gives a systematic insight into the variety of models. It lets concrete knowledge management models be derived from it by restriction and instantiation. Full exploitation of the meta-model leads to an integrated approach to knowledge management.Derived knowledge management approaches can be classified and may serve as a decision base for the model of choice in an organisation. Furthermore the meta-model with its generative capability for knowledge management approaches is related to the range of scenarios for 2010 as seen by the European Commission. Keywords: meta-model for knowledge management, model derivation, knowledge management approaches, knowledge-intensive business processes, knowledge conversions.

1. Introduction

A number of approaches for knowledge management has been developed, described and also (partly) implemented ([9], [11], [12]). Important ones are the classic approach focussed on knowledge assets ([11]), the process-oriented approach ([1]), the knowledge-intensive business process modeling approach ([8]), and the communities of practice ([14]). Each approach has its benefits and shortcomings. There are modeling proposals for these approaches, including the high-level 4-entity model by Trier ([13]). Here, from the viewpoint of knowledge, four main entities constitute the building blocks for the models. However, the knowledge itself with its various dimensions is not revealed. In the approach by Gronau ([8]) knowledge is the focus of modeling, but the processing dimension is not represented adaequately. Knowledge management scenarios for the year 2010 are described in the corresponding European Commission report ([5]). Here two dimensions (ontological and epistemological) lead to four scenarios and one further consensus scenario. A different line is followed in the "new knowledge management" approach of the KMCI institut ([6], [7]), where a 3-tier model for knowledge management is proposed, following the critical rationalism paradigm.

A meta-model for knowledge management is proposed in this paper, which supports a systematic insight into the variety of knowledge management approaches and lets concrete models be derived. The description power of the meta-model is provided by six essential entities related to knowledge management and appropriate interrelations between them. It is described as a fully connected graph with self-connecting edges at each node. From this description, concrete models can be gained easily by first restricting to subgraphs and then instantiating the remaining nodes and edges appropriately. In this paper we describe the known knowledge management models by following this derivation procedure.

By taking the full graph as model base, we propose an integrated approach to knowledge management. It is process-oriented and reflects the contributions of different types of knowledge and general conversions between them. Furthermode the human roles as single persons as well as communities of practice in the organisation are subject to modelling. It combines recognized existing approaches of process-oriented and community-oriented knowledge management. The new approach can help to identify patterns in knowledge-intensive business processes.

The derivation of different knowledge management approaches from a common meta-model allows to classify them in a systematic way. Hence a decision base for the model of choice is gained for an organisation having its specific constraints and requirements. Furthermore the meta-model with its generative capability for knowledge management approaches can be related to the scenarios for 2010 as seen by the European Commission.

2. Knowledge Creation, Types and Conversions

The well-known model of dynamic organisational knowledge creation by Nonaka and Takeuchi, the SECI model ([10]), aims at the management of the knowledge creation process.

Two types of knowledge, namely explicit and tacit knowledge, are distinguished. Explicit knowledge can be formulated in a formal and systematic language and is easily transferable and exchangable. Tacit knowledge cannot be formulated and exchanged easily. It is bound to persons, specific in its context and based on personal experiences, intuition, and perception.

The interactions between explicit and tacit knowledge are understood to be responsible to a high degree for knowledge development in an organisation. They can be described as four conversions between the knowledge types: socialisation (tacit-to-tacit), externalisation (tacit-to-explicit), internalisation (explicit-to-tacit), and combination (explicit-to-explicit). Socialisation means exchange of experience and learning-by-doing, externalisation is articulation of tacit knowledge, e.g. by using metaphors, analogies, and models. Internalisation leads to integration of experiences and competences in your own mental model. Finally, combination combines existing explicit knowledge in new forms. The name SECI model stems from taking the first letter of each conversion. The four knowledge conversions interact in a spiral of knowledge creation, which becomes larger in scale as it moves up the ontological dimension from the individuum to groups and the whole organisation.

While the SECI model shows several strengths, its limiting linearity of its knowledge development spiral concept is criticised. This can to a large extent be improved by generalizing the concept of knowledge conversions. The four conversions of the SECI model are now viewed as special atomic conversions, they convert exactly one source knowledge asset into exactly one destination knowledge asset. In addition, general knowledge conversions are modeled converting several source assets (possibly of different types) to several destination assets. For example, a person may extend his tacit knowledge and an explicit knowledge asset in a general conversion, using the tacit knowledge of another person, who is an expert in the relevant topic. Here on the source side of the general conversion we have two tacit and one explicit knowledge assets, while on the destination side one tacit and one explicit knowledge asset arise. In the following we use the term SECI* model to name this generalized model.

3. Meta-Model for Knowledge Management

In general a meta-model abstracts essential entities of a domain of interest and their interrelations. Concrete models can then be derived from it by a process of instantiation of parts or the whole of it. We introduce a meta-model for knowledge management which is based on six general entities (namely Process, Person, Topic, Document, Tacit Knowledge and Explicit Knowledge) and the various interconnections between them. Together they cover the possible relevant parts of knowledge-intensive business activities.

The Process entity represents sequences of activities, the Person entity the human involvement in business activities. The Topic entity aims at themes and topics of relevance. Document represents the information needed, while the two knowledge-related entities Tacit Knowledge and Explicit Knowledge aim at the corresponding knowledge types as described in section 2. Interconnections express relations between the entities and may connect different entities or an entity with itself.

The entities are to understood in a very general way. For example, the Person entity abstracts the whole range of human-related involvements, namely individuals as wells as formal working teams, informal teams, and communities of practice. The interconnections between the two knowledge-related entities Tacit Knowledge and Explicit Knowledge stands for the whole bunch of general or atomic knowledge conversions.

The meta-model is described as a fully connected graph with self-connecting edges at each node as shown in Figure 1. The entities are the nodes of the graph, the interconnections the edges. We use an undirected graph here. In instantiations of this meta-model, the links between concrete entities may be directed.

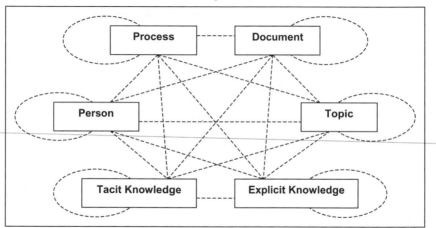

Figure 1: Meta-Model Graph for Knowledge Management

4.   Derivation of Knowledge Management Models

From the meta-model concrete models for knowledge management can be derived. This succeeds by a two-step procedure as follows. First the full meta-model graph is restricted to a subgraph and secondly the remaining entities nodes and edges are instantiated with the relevant objects in the concrete model. The procedure is depicted in Figure 2.

For example, the classic asset-oriented approach to knowledge management ([9], [11]) restricts to a subgraph consisting of the nodes Person, Document, Explicit Knowledge, and Topic and the interconnections between them, but omits the interconnections connecting Person and Explicit Knowledge with themselves. The node Person is only instantiated to a single person. Thus the human interactions and group contributions are not modelled here.

In a similar way, each known model for knowledge management can be derived from this meta-model as described in the next section. Section 6 explains our integrated model, derived from the meta-model by taking the full graph and by then instantiating the nodes and edges.

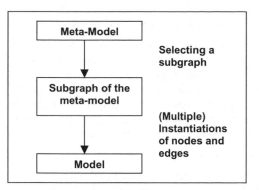

Figure 2: From Meta-Model to Model

5.   Derivation of Known Knowledge Management Models

In this section we shortly describe important existing knowledge management approaches and show their derivation from the meta-model. It will be clear, that each of them uses only a subgraph of the meta-model graph as model base.

5.1   The Asset-Oriented Approach to Knowledge Management

As already mentioned in the previous section, this approach restricts to model subgraph as shown in Figure 3. Historically seen, the first approaches have been of this type.

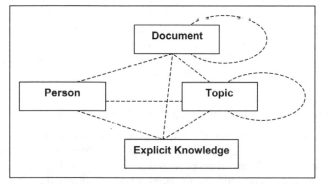

Figure 3: Model Ssubgraph for the Asset-Oriented Approach

In the second step of the model derivation only individuals are instantiated from the *Person* entity, which are not interacting. Therefore human interactions and contributions of group and communities are not modeled at all. Explicit knowledge assets are considered, but no conversions between them. Due to the omission of the *Process* entity in the first derivation step, no processes or activities are considered.

5.2   The Process-Oriented Knowledge Management Approach

In the process-oriented approach ([1]), the Tacit Knowledge and Topic entities with their interconnections are not relevant. Also the self-connecting edge at the Explicit Knowledge and the Person entities are removed. Person is instantiated to individuals, but their interactions with themselves are not considered (only indirectly via explicit knowledge and information, which is instantiated from Document).

5.3   The Knowledge-Intensive Business Process Approach

In the knowledge-intensive business process approach the model base is the full meta-model graph minus the self-connecting edge at the Topic node. As a consequence the relationships and interdependencies of different topics cannot be modeled.

There already exists an approach recognizing the full domain of knowledge types and general conversions as described in section 2 ([8]). The Person entity is instantiated only to individuals and (formal) teams. The Process entity has only weak instantiations, lacking the expressiveness of a business process modeling language as BPMN ([4]).

5.4   Knowledge Communities

Communities of practice have been introduced by Wenger ([14]). They consist of a group of people bound to the organisation as an informal structural unit. Community members volunteer in their membership, they share a concern, a theme, or competence about certain knowledge domains. They care about those domains in the organisation and apply the shared practice in their business processes, e.g. by developing a shared repertoire of resources. While many big companies finally recognize the importance of such communities of practice ([14]), their contribution to the business processes in the enterprise, especially the knowledge-intensive ones, is not formalized. It may be argued, that it is the essence of those communities to be not formally bound to the organisation's hierarchies. Nevertheless, their contributions to the success of the organisation should be taken into account by recognizing their importance for knowledge-intensive business processes. In this paper we focus on the knowledge dimension of those communities and consequently call them knowledge communities. Their possible contribution to business processes will be a substantial part of our new integrated knowledge management approach.

The knowledge community approach omits the Process node with its edges. Besides that, the full remaining subgraph of the meta-model is used. In the second derivation step, the Person entity is instantiated mainly to communities of practice, but may also be instantiated to individuals.

6.   An Integrated Model for Knowledge Management

In Section 5 the derivation of known knowledge management approaches from the meta-model has been described. In each case, a true subgraph of the meta-model graph has been chosen in the first step. What we propose here is an integrated approach for knowledge management. From the perspective of the meta-model it utilizes the whole set of entities and interrelations between them, which exist for knowledge management. The integrated approach covers process orientation, reflects the human role in various forms (as individuals, groups, or knowledge communities) and the two types of knowledge with their mutual general conversions. It is integrated, because its model base is the full graph and consequently a super-graph of other approaches's subgraphs.

The derivation from the meta-model succeeds by first taking the full graph (as shown in Figure 1 in section 3) and then instantiating the nodes and edges with the relevant modeling objects of the model. The Employee entity of the meta-model with its self-connecting edge is instantiated by individuals, teams, communities, and their interactions. Knowledge conversions are instantiated from the edges between the two knowledge entities and the self-connecting edges at the two entities. Information objects instantiate the *Document* entity. The instantiations of the remaining entities are straightforward, instantiated edges model interactions and associations between instantiated entities, for example the transformation from explicit knowledge to information as explained below.

As notation we propose an expressional extension of the Business Process Modeling Notation BPMN ([4]), which we call BPMN-KEC (KEC stands for knowledge, employees, and communities). BPMN is widely used for business process modeling, there exists a whole body of tools to support the visual modeling procedure, to integrate it in service-oriented architectures and to map models to execution environments for appropriate IT-support.

As relation between knowledge and information assets we model transformations from explicit knowledge to information and vice versa, which are performed by either human actors or program components. This is described by an association bound to the transformation. Here information is understood as data in relation with a semantic dimension, but is lacking the pragmatic dimension with the sense of purpose and generative capability of new information, which characterises knowledge. To be able to model very general knowledge conversions as described in section 2, a separate conversion object is included. The list of model symbols in addition to the BPMN symbols include knowledge, information and conversion objects, conversion and transformation objects, association, and the people-related objects person (employee), team and community.

Note that only one object symbol for knowledge is introduced. The distinction between explicit and tacit knowledge is given by the context of the object, be it the conversion leading to it or association with a person object. BPMN-KEC is explained in detail in ([2]).

This model will help to identify several patterns in knowledge-intensive business processes, for example those indicating monopolized knowledge by single persons or the importance of knowledge communities in the enterprise. For example the first pattern may show the necessity to invest in staffing in order to reduce the potential risk of this situation for the organisation. See ([8]) for an extensive taxonomy of patterns.

As an example for the modeling power of the new model and the applicability of the corresponding notation, a business process for product renewal planning is shortly described. A detailed model is given in [3]. The product to be renewed is assumed to be knowledge-intensive and complex. The existing version of it should be possibly renewed. We concentrate on the first of four activities of this process: Propose product idea. The main human actors are the product manager responsible for the product in the company and a knowledge community. The activity relies on two knowledge conversions: Generate Product Idea is a general socialisation conversion, Formulate Product Idea an atomic externalisation conversion. The main origins for Generate Product Idea are on the one side tacit knowledge on new technologies, actual relevant research themes and internal availability in the organisation. This knowledge is not available in a formal teams, but in a informal knowledge community in the organisation. On the other side, knowledge on market trends and the product position of the existing product in the market is available at the product manager. Bringing this together via the knowledge conversion Generate Product Idea will end in a general product idea. This tacit knowledge now will be externalised in the second conversion to end up in a documented product idea.

7. Classification of Knowledge Management Approaches

The derivation of each knowledge management approach from a common meta-model makes it possible to relate the approaches to each other in a systematic way, dependent on the usage of parts or all of the six main entities and interrelations for knowledge management. Figure 4 gives this systematic description. Dependencies between the approaches are shown and the utilisation of the SECI* model is indicated where present.

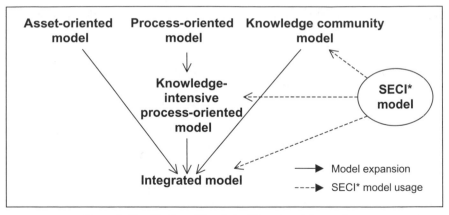

Figure 4: Classification of Knowledge Management Approaches

Note that this classification depends on the first step of the derivation procedure from meta-model to model. This means, that entries in Figure 4 can represent sets of similar approaches each having the same subgraph as model base, but different instantiations in the second step of derivation. For example, model instantiations of "knowledge-intensive process-oriented model" may differ in the extent of generalizing conversions of the original SECI model.

The classification can be used as a decision base for the knowledge management model of choice in an organisation having its specific constraints and requirements. That means, that in a kind of "backward engineering" of the model derivation procedure from the meta-model, an organisation (or a part of it) would first identify the needs and constraints and then choose the model out of the classification given in Figure 4, which at least fits those needs and constraints. For the case of several matching approaches, a simpler model (nearer to the top of Figure 4) would demand less effort for the organisation. The integrated model as introduced in section 6 would work in every case. The chosen model could then be implemented in the organisation.

Furthermore the meta-model with its generative capability for knowledge management approaches can be related to the range of knowledge management trends and scenarios for 2010 as seen and described by the European Commission ([5]). Figure 5 classifies the 5 scenarios along a ontological dimension (designed vs. emergent) and an epistemological dimension (rules vs. heuristics).

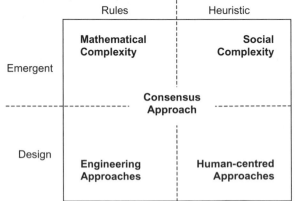

Figure 5: KM Scenarios for the Year 2010 (Taken with Changes from [5])

The three scenarios in the bottom left triangle including the corresponding part of the consensus approach can be fully covered by our meta-model and its generative capability of new approaches. The social complexity approach views knowledge as a flow, not as an asset. Both paradigms (asset and flow) can coexist, despite of the (alleged) paradoxon they produce. Organisational strategies are not deterministic and, seen in longer terms, backward sense making (see [12]). In a narrow sense, this approach is not within the scope of our meta-model. In a wider sense, one could extend the scope of the *Person* entity of our approach with its various instantiations (especially as knowledge communities) together with the instantiations of the two *Knowledge* entities as kind of "germ cell" for a fit to the approach.

8. Conclusion

A meta-model for knowledge management approaches has been presented. By appropriate subgraphing of the full graph of the meta-model and subsequent instantiating the remaining constituents, each existing knowledge management approach can be modeled and classified. Taking the full graph as model graph leads to a new integrated knowledge management approach, which recognizes the contribution of persons, groups and communities as well as the different knowledge types and the conversions between them. The systematic classification of knowledge management approaches can support the decision for the right approach in organisations with their specific constraints and requirements. Relationships of the new integrated approach to the scenarios seen by the European Commission have been discussed. Further work to do includes a refinement of the classification of knowledge management approaches by differentiating models having the same model subgraph of the meta-model graph. This will further improve the usage and benefit of the classification as decision base for an organisation, especially for a small or medium enterprise.

References

[1] Abecker, A., Hinkelmann, K., Maus, H. (2002) *Geschäftsprozessorientiertes Wissensmanagement – Effektive Wissensnutzung bei Planung und Umsetzung von Geschäftsprozessen* (in German), Springer, Berlin.
[2] Ammann, E. (2008a) *BPMN-KEC – An Extension of BPMN for Knowledge-Related Business Process Modeling*, Internal Report 2008, Reutlingen University.
[3] Ammann, E. (2008b) *Enterprise Knowledge Communities and Business Process Modeling*, accepted for the 9th European Conference on Knowledge Management, Southampton, UK, 4-5 Sept. 2008.
[4] BPMN (2006) *Business Process Modeling Notation Specification*, OMG Final Adopted Specification, *http://www.omg.org/docs/dtc/06-02-01.pdf*.
[5] European Commission (2004) *Business Knowledge Management: A study on market prospects, business needs and technological trends*, European Commission, *http://ec.europa.eu/information_society/doc/library/business_knowledge_management.pdf*.
[6] Firestone, J., McElroy M. (2003) *Corporate Epistemology*, EIS Inc., *http://www.kmci.org*.
[7] Firestone, J. (2004) *Introduction to KMCI's Conceptual Frameworks*, EIS Inc., *http://www.kmci.org*
[8] Gronau, N.,Fröming, J. (2006) „KMDL® - Eine semiformale Beschreibungssprache zur Modellierung Modellierung von Wissenskonversionen" (in German), *Wirtschaftsinformatik* Vol. 48, No. 5, pp. 349-360.
[9] Mertens, K., Heisig, P., Vorbeck, J. (2003) *Knowledge Management, Concepts and Best Practice*, Springer, Berlin.
[10] Nonaka, I., Takeuchi, H. (1995) *The Knowledge-Creating Company – How Japanese Companies Foster Creativity and Innovation for Competitive Advantage*, Oxford University Press, London.
[11] Schreiber, G. Akkermans, H., et al. (2000) *Knowledge Engineering and Management – The CommonKADS Methodology*, MIT Press, Cambridge.
[12] Snowden, D. (2002) *Complex Acts of Knowing: Paradox and descriptive Self-Awareness*, Journal of Knowledge Management, Vol.6, No.2, 2002, pp.100-111.
[13] Trier, M. (2007) *Virtual Knowledge Communities*, VDM Verlag Dr.Müller, Saarbrücken, Germany.
[14] Wenger, E., McDermott, R., Snyder, W.M. (2002) *Cultivating Communities of Practice*, Harward Business School Press, Boston.

Section 6.2

Case Studies

Collaboration and the Knowledge Economy: Issues, Applications, Case Studies
P. Cunningham and M. Cunningham (Eds.)
IOS Press, 2008

A Total Cost of Ownership Model
for Global Sourcing

Philipp BREMEN

ETH Zurich, Center for Enterprise Sciences (BWI), Kreuzplatz 5, Zurich, 8032, Switzerland
Tel: +41 44 632 05 29, Fax: +41 44 632 10 40, Email: pbremen@ethz.ch

Abstract: Global sourcing of electrical and mechanical components for
manufacturing industry from offshore suppliers in Asia poses challenges for Western
companies especially for small and medium enterprises. The expected cost savings
can seldom be obtained due to additional transaction and opportunity costs that are
not considered thoroughly. The approach of total cost of ownership facilitates a
holistic analysis of cost objects. This paper presents a method for categorizing
various cost objects of an integral TCO analysis, suggests an approach for
identifying cost objects in enterprises and introduces a model for incorporating
opportunity costs. The integration of monetary costs, transaction costs and
opportunity costs into a holistic total cost of ownership model allows a transparent
evaluation and comparison of several sourcing options.

1. Introduction

Supply chain management has strongly gained in importance during the last decades. While
in the past companies from the manufacturing industry solely needed to satisfy their need
for raw material and commodities, nowadays, they have reduced their vertical range of
manufacture concentrating on core competencies. The increased importance has promoted
the function of supply chain management to a key function even in small and medium
enterprises (SME). Currently, the development of emerging markets forms new
opportunities for global sourcing. Especially China has advanced to one of the most
important supply markets for goods of the manufacturing industry with high volumes and
with a significant share of labour costs. But there are more reasons for companies to spread
their supplier base all over the world. In general, the main reasons for outsourcing are
reducing costs of production factors, gaining access to new sales markets, ensuring
flexibility and delivery, avoiding capacity shortages, taking advantage of foreign tax
systems and subventions, and benefiting from the proximity to customers [1].

Explorative interviews with eight companies in Switzerland showed that global
sourcing activities are characterized by pragmatic practices and that there is a need for
analytic approaches to support decision making. In many cases, the expected cost savings
of global sourcing projects due to lower labour costs are diminished by hidden costs [2].
The theory of transaction costs for search and initiation, negotiation, and control of an inter
company business relation explain additional efforts to a certain extent [3]. Nevertheless,
companies do not have sufficient knowledge about their transaction costs especially when
sourcing from offshore suppliers. A study in Germany recently discovered that 63% of 203
German companies that source from China do not use performance measures to control
their logistics [4].

The analysis of purchasing costs is related to the concept of total cost of ownership
(TCO), a buzz word that was born in the IT industry in the 90s. The concept analyses the
total operation costs of software and hardware. Nowadays, the concept of TCO is
commonly known in purchasing departments as well but seldom applied in an integral way

[5]. The objective of TCO is to understand the true costs of goods and not just the pure purchase price [6]. The core idea behind the accounting concept of TCO is to allocate all costs, additional efforts and opportunity costs of a purchase to the price per unit. For example, the initiation of business with a new supplier, higher efforts in the own company due to larger coordination necessities with offshore suppliers, and – especially when talking about sourcing from low labour cost countries – intensified quality inspection on arrival of purchased goods are normally not considered when calculating the costs of a product.

TCO has been recently discussed in scientific journals as well as rather populist magazines. In scientific literature, the common incentive in the model constructing publications is understanding the firm's true cost, not just price, for a given purchase [7]. Ex-post supplier performance measurement is the motivation stated most often for applying TCO. Related tasks are the strategic make-or-buy decision [8], supplier selection [9] and ex-ante supplier evaluation [10]. The common benefit of the cited scholars is transparency by detailed knowledge of all costs involved in purchasing goods. Cost information might also be used to enhance price negotiations with suppliers [10], to incorporate non-price considerations into the make-or-buy decision [8], and to control the assessment of sourcing risks [11]. Some scholars considered barriers and difficulties when implementing TCO in enterprises [6, 9, 12]. The lack of data sources is the biggest challenge for implementing an integral TCO model. Furthermore, in smaller enterprises cost transparency is often not appreciated because employees do not like their performance to be measured and do not want their efforts be allocated to certain jobs.

The biggest achievement of the publications focussing on model building is developing awareness of additional costs to be incorporated on top of the purchase price by listing cost objectives that should be considered (see [5] for the most complete overview of TCO cost objects). Three different methods of structuring cost objects are discussed. First, most of the authors suggest a structure that is aligned with the functional departments of a company including product-related categories like management, delivery, service, communication, price and quality [6]. Second, objects can be categorized according to the phases of the product life cycle like acquisition, reception, possession, utilization, and elimination [10]. Third, purchase hierarchies can be utilized considering costs objects related to unit, batch, order, or supplier [13].

The most detailed case study of TCO is presented by [14]. The TCO model for a vehicle glass repair and replacement expert operating in the after-sales market consists of 8 aggregated cost categories. Each cost category is quantified by a formula containing simple key performance indicators as variables. The target of the presented TCO model is making volume-allocation decisions in the service industry.

There are two shortcomings in the presented literature. First, the integration of opportunity costs has not been considered thoroughly. Second, the concept of TCO has not been applied to global sourcing yet. What are the opportunity costs of switching to a supplier in a low labour cost country with average lead time of 6 weeks instead of one week from a local supplier? What are the opportunity costs of low quality due to personnel fluctuation at the supplier's? These questions show that low cost is not the only entrepreneurial objective. There are other objectives like quality, delivery and flexibility [15] that have to be considered as well in terms of opportunity costs.

2. Objectives

The objectives of this paper are threefold. First, it presents a method for categorizing various cost objects of an integral TCO analysis. The second objective is an approach for identifying cost objects to be applied in practice. Last, the paper shows the analysis of opportunity costs concerning entrepreneurial objectives that are not related to costs as there are quality, delivery and flexibility. The paper proposes a method for transferring supply chain metrics into surcharges to be added on top of the unit price of purchased goods.

The focus of this research is the evaluation of procurement activities of Swiss companies sourcing offshore from external suppliers in Asia. The considered products are mechanical and electrical components that are finally assembled and sold in Europe. The integration of monetary costs, transaction costs and opportunity costs into a holistic total cost of ownership calculation facilitates a transparent evaluation and comparison of several sourcing options.

3. Methodology

The presented research is embedded in the framework of action research consisting of four main stages: problem definition, state-of-the-art of science, conception and validation [16]. The close interaction of researchers and industry partners ensures the formulation of target-oriented approaches that are applied in industry. Up to eight industry partners were involved in the phases of problem definition, conception and validation.

4. Model Description

4.1 Categorization of Cost Objects

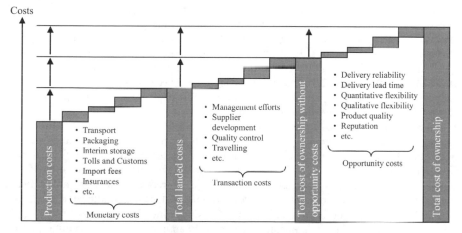

Figure 1: Categorization of TCO Cost Objects

In industry, the use of landed costs for analyzing procured goods is very common as interviews with Swiss companies have shown. Landed costs usually cover the manufacturing costs and monetary costs related to transport logistics like packaging, transport, interim storage, tolls, custom clearance, import fees and insurances (total landed costs). Furthermore, transaction costs related to additional company-internal efforts for globally sourced goods have to be identified and quantified. Travelling costs, communication problems and higher efforts in managing the supply chain are examples of these. Last, entrepreneurial objectives other than costs like quality, delivery and flexibility are incorporated in the concept by opportunity costs. In order to meet the customer's tolerance time, a delivery lead time of 6 weeks from China compared to much shorter lead times when sourcing locally causes opportunity costs, for example, due to increasing inventory requirements (see Figure 1).

4.2 Identification of Cost Objects

The identification of cost objects related to global sourcing projects is a complex problem involving many stakeholders and scarcity of data. The target of the presented method is identifying and quantifying costs of the categories cash flow, working effort and capital employed that exceed the analysis of landed costs, and assigning them to the price per unit of procured goods. Five steps are proposed:

1. Kick-off workshop,
2. Allocation of cost objects,
3. Prioritization,
4. Data collection and
5. Quantification.

The workshop is held with representatives from several departments like procurement, supply chain management, research and development, product management and controlling. After the definition and delimitation of the addressed problem, the team agrees on an exemplary case of an existing supply chain. The method of brainstorming is used to collect a first set of cost objects. In a second step, a reference process model for sourcing is employed to find more detailed objects. The sourcing processes cover strategic and operational elements which are necessary to accomplish global sourcing projects successfully. The process chain starts with the design of the production and procurement strategy. Procurement market research and supplier selection complete the strategic process elements. On the operational side there is design adaptation, production ramp-up, supplier development, operational sourcing, transport logistics, and after sales services. Using this method of categorizing cost objects, a purchasing manager can easily identify the origin of lavish processes. At last, a standard list of potential cost objects is presented (compare [5]) and synchronized with the existent collection.

The collected cost objects are allocated to the stakeholder they belong to. In bilateral sessions with the researcher these owners decide on the relevance and priority of a cost object. Furthermore, the method of quantification is selected as there are simple proportional calculation, activity based costing and the net present value method. The necessary data is defined and collected or estimated if precise figures are not available. Finally, the quantified cost objects are consolidated in a database and allocated to the price per unit of the selected good resulting in the total cost of ownership.

In a case study with three companies the described approach was carried out (see Table 1). The matrix contains the TCO cost objects allocated to the cost categories on the x-axis and to the sourcing processes on the y-axis.

		Cost categories		
		Monetary costs	Transaction costs	Opportunity costs
Sourcing processes	Production and procurement strategy	• Layoffs • Local Sourcing Office • Sourcing Agent / Freelancer	• Strategic planning of supply chain • Implementation of multiple sourcing strategy • Integration into production network • Compliance of ROHS and WEEE	• Higher safety stock due to deficient delivery reliability, quality fluctuation and longer lead times • Inappropriate payment terms • All-time buys • Capital employed for goods in transit • Fix costs for idle inhouse production factors • Reputation loss due to foreign content
	Procurement market research	• Purchase of studies	• Search for potential suppliers • Study of literature	
	Supplier selection	• Contracting and legal fees	• Supplier audits • Adaptation of documents to new language and norms • Analyses of cost structure of supplier	
	Design adaptation	• PDM/PLM System	• Split of order because of IPR-protection • Iterative design adaptation	
	Production ramp-up	• Prototypes with new supplier • External quality control • Materials, tools, and machines • Testing equipment and tools	• Production trial / sample runs • Preparation of work & test instructions • Development of testing tools	
	Supplier development	• Production costs	• Continuous development and coaching of supplier • Supplier performance measurement • Supply management of raw material	
	Operational sourcing	• External quality control • Safety stock	• Language and time difference • Planning and forecasting • Internal quality control • Ordering and monitoring of delivery date • Negotiation of terms	
	Transport logistics	• Customs and taxes • Transport • Quota costs • Interim inventory holding • Insurances	• Know-how about international import and export	
	After sales services	(n.a.)	• Analyses of returns	

Table 1: TCO Cost Objects from a Case Study with Three Companies

4.3   Opportunity Costs

In industry, the achievement of low manufacturing costs is not the only entrepreneurial objective. Quality, delivery and flexibility are other objectives mentioned in literature [15]. The SCOR model proposes five objectives of managing a supply chain, three customer-faced performance attributes – reliability, responsiveness, agility – and two internal-faced ones – costs, assets [17]. The performance of a supply chain concerning these objectives can be measured by specific metrics that facilitate the rating of a supply chain. How can those characteristics of a supply chain be related to the costs per unit? What are additional costs when purchasing goods from an offshore supplier with a delivery reliability of 92% and a delivery lead time of four weeks?

A general model assists companies to incorporate opportunity costs into their decision making methods. The company specific set of entrepreneurial objectives is denoted by $O := \{o_a \mid a = 1,2,...,A\}$. Each objective may be affected by a set of quantifiable drivers or supply chain metrics. The company has to establish a supply chain measurement system defining metrics that are maintained continuously as represented by the set $D_a := \{d_{a,b} \mid b = 1,2,...,B\}$. The drivers cause opportunity costs that are denoted in the set $C_{a,b} := \{c_{a,b,e} \mid e = 1,2,...,E\}$.

Each term of opportunity cost elements $c_{a,b,e}$ is a function of the corresponding driver $d_{a,b}$.

$$c_{a,b,e} = f(d_{a,b})$$

The aggregated opportunity costs for each entrepreneurial objective as surcharge per unit is the sum of all driver-affected costs divided by the number of considered units of sourced goods N.

$$c_{aggr,a} = \frac{\sum_{b=1}^{B}\sum_{e=1}^{E} c_{a,b,e}}{N}$$

A simple spreadsheet can visualize the production costs, total landed cost and total cost of ownership without opportunity costs and total cost of ownership including opportunity costs. This enables the supply chain manager to compare sourcing options.

An example of the general calculation model for opportunity costs stresses the impact of longer lead times in case of sea freight resulting in increased requirements of safety stock. The corresponding entrepreneurial objective $o_1 = delivery$, driver $d_{1,1} = lead\ time$, opportunity cost element $c_{1,1,1} = safety\ stock$ and formula f,

$$c_{1,1,1} = f(d_{1,1}) = s_c \cdot s_f \cdot \sqrt{\frac{d_{1,1}}{1a}} \cdot \sigma_{1a},$$

given that s_c is a proportional factor converting safety stocks into monetary units, s_f is the safety factor and σ_{1a} is the standard deviation of the demand during the statistic period of 1 year (compare [15]). A delivery lead time of 6 weeks compared to a delivery lead time of 1 week results in safety stocks that are 2.45 times higher granting the same service level.

5. Conclusions

The paper presents a model to analyze the total cost of ownership of globally procured goods for manufacturing industries. The integration of monetary costs, transaction costs and opportunity costs into a holistic total cost of ownership model allows a transparent evaluation and comparison of several sourcing options. The model enables decision makers to understand the true costs of a purchase (ex-post) and to draw strategic conclusions for the management of their supply chains (ex-ante).

Supply chain risks have lately been discussed in literature stressing the importance of risk analyses especially in global supply chains [18]. A sudden breakdown of a single source supplier or the loss of a whole shipment can affect a company's supply with significant impact. Results of a supply chain risk analysis are not integrated in the total cost of ownership model.

Further research will be necessary to identify all relevant cost drivers of opportunity costs concerning global sourcing and to derive corresponding formulas that convert cost drivers into opportunity costs.

Acknowledgement

The author would like to thank the Swiss Federal Innovation Promotion Agency CTI for their support through project 8353.1 ESPP-ES (DC-SC-M) and the industry partners.

References

[1] B. Dachs, "Produktionsverlagerungen und Rückverlagerungen im europäischen Vergleich, Mitteilung aus der EMS-Erhebung – Schweiz," *Studie des Frauenhofer Insitut für Systemtechnik und Innovationsforschung (ISI)*, 2006.
[2] R. Bogaschewsky, *China Sourcing Survey 2006*: BearingPoint GmbH and the Chair of Business Administration and Industrial Management at the University of Wuerzburg, 2006.

[3]   R. H. Coase, O. E. Williamson, and S. G. Winter, *The nature of the firm origins, evolution, and development.* New York etc.: Oxford University Press, 1991.

[4]   Y. Fritzsche-Sterr, "Beschaffungslogistik im China-Geschäft. Kosten - Prozesse - Strategien," *Bundesverband Materialwirtschaft, Einkauf und Logistik e. V.,* 2008.

[5]   B. G. P. Ferrin, Richard E. , "Total Cost of Ownership: An Exploratory Study," *The Journal of Supply Chain Management,* vol. 38, p. 18, 2002.

[6]   L. M. Ellram, "A framework for total cost of ownership," *The International Journal of Logistics Management,* vol. 4, pp. 49-60, 1993.

[7]   L. M. Ellram and S. P. Siferd, "Purchasing: The Cornerstone of the Total Cost of Ownership Concept," *Journal of Business Logistics,* vol. 14, pp. 163-184, 1993.

[8]   A. B. Maltz and L. M. Ellram, "Total cost of relationship: an analytical framework for the logistics outsourcing decision," *Journal of Business Logistics,* vol. 18, pp. 45-66, 1997.

[9]   K. S. Bhutta and F. Huq, "Supplier selection problem: a comparison of the total cost of ownership and analytical hierarchy process approaches," *Supply Chain Management: An International Journal,* vol. 7, pp. 126-135, 2002.

[10] Z. Degraeve and F. Roodhooft, "Improving the efficiency of the purchasing process using total cost of ownership information: The case of heating electrodes at Cockerill Sambre SA," *European Journal of Operational Research,* vol. 112, pp. 42-53, 1999.

[11] R. M. Monczka and S. J. Trecha, "Cost-based supplier performance evaluation," *Journal of Purchasing and Materials Management,* vol. 24, pp. 2-7, 1988.

[12] L. M. Ellram, "A taxonomy of total cost of ownership models," *Journal of Business Logistics,* vol. 15, p. 171, 1994.

[13] Z. Degraeve, F. Roodhooft, and B. van Doveren, "The use of total cost of ownership for strategic procurement: a company-wide management information system," *Journal ofthe Operational Research Society,* vol. 56, pp. 51-59, 2005.

[14] K. Hurkens, W. van der Valk, and F. Wynstra, "Total Cost of Ownership in the Services Sector: A Case Study," *Journal of Supply Chain Management,* vol. 42, p. 27, 2006.

[15] P. Schönsleben, *Integrales Logistikmanagement Operations und Supply Chain Management in umfassenden Wertschöpfungsnetzwerken,* 5., bearb. u. erw. Aufl. ed. Berlin: Springer, 2007.

[16] D. J. Greenwood and M. Levin, *Introduction to action research social research for social change.* Thousand Oaks etc.: Sage Publications, 1998.

[17] S. C. Council, "Supply Chain Operations Reference (SCOR) Model. Version 9.0," *Supply Chain Council,* Pittsburgh, PA, 2008.

[18] A. Ziegenbein and P. Schönsleben, *Supply Chain Risiken Identifikation, Bewertung und Steuerung.* Zürich: vdf Hochschulverlag AG an der ETH Zürich, 2007.

Collaboration and the Knowledge Economy: Issues, Applications, Case Studies
P. Cunningham and M. Cunningham (Eds.)
IOS Press, 2008

Importance of ICT for Technology-Based Small Firms' Networking

Vinit PARIDA, Mats WESTERBERG, Håkan YLINENPÄÄ
Entreprenuership, Luleå University of Technology, Luleå, 97187, Sweden
Tel: +46 920 492469, Fax: +46 920 492160, Email: Vinit.Parida@ltu.se,
Mats.Westerberg@ltu.se, Hakan.Ylinenpaa@ltu.se

Abstract: Modern ICT is widely understood as important for enabling more effective communication, collaboration and internal operational efficiency for today's businesses. For small firms with limited in-house resources, and especially for technology-based small firms, ICT is expected to play a vital role. The empirical evidence supporting such an understanding are however rare. This paper elaborates on the extent to which ICT capability is employed by technology-based small firms and investigates the influence of ICT capability on network configuration and networking capability. The results provide some new evidence on how ICT may enable more effective networking in this specific category of small firms, and indicates e.g. that technology-based small firms are high users of ICT for gaining flexibility in working hours, accessing vital information, maintaining collaboration with existing business partners, enable a better handling communication within the firm and providing superior customer service. ICT capability was also found to influence small firms networking configuration. Particularly, there is a clear link between higher ICT use for collaboration and more extensive partnership networking, and a higher ICT use for communication and more extensive customer networking. Furthermore, we also found support for a strong relation between ICT capability and networking capability.

Keywords: Information and communication technology (ICT), networking, small firms, competitiveness and capability

1. Introduction

Small firms are a vital part of our modern economy, as they not only offer employment, but also promote growth and instil innovation. In Sweden, particularly technology-based small firms are considered as potentially high growth orientated firms which mean that studying these firms source for competitiveness should have a great impact on the national economy [1]. Many would argue that these firms are frontrunners or elites in-terms of using information and communication technology (ICT). However, to what extent does technology-based small firms use their ICT capability and what impact it has on their competitiveness still needs to be investigated.

The small firm's ability to network with different actors can be an important source of achieving competitive advantage. Networking enables small firms to get access to different resources, enhance learning, and facilitate innovations [2] [3]. Networking as a concept, can be viewed from several perspectives such as, intensity of ties between different actors, social capital, embeddedness, organization networks, etc. This study focuses on such two important aspects, the network configuration (i.e. the pattern of relationships that between actors) and the networking capability (i.e. ability to develop and utilize inter-organizational relationships). In this first section we briefly discuss these concepts and state the objectives and research questions. The next section presents the methodology used, followed by the results from the empirical study. Finally, business benefits are then discussed, followed by a concluding discussion on the results from this paper.

1.1 Small Firms ICT Capability

ICT for long has been associated with something positive and promising for firms. Particularly, ICT could be a highly valuable tool for small firms, as they have limited access to in-house resources and capabilities. By making low investments small firms can increase their business opportunities such as, have closer relations with customers/partners, lower the cost of production, better information flow, etc. This has driven many governmental initiatives around Europe for promoting the use of ICT [4]. However, the real impact of these initiatives can only be tested and/or understood by observing the current level of ICT use by small firms. In this study we conceptualize ICT capability as closely linked with the strategic use of ICT for business purposes. Thus, the focus lies on utilizing or using ICT, not merely possessing ICT tools.

ICT capability is defined as firms "ability to mobilize and deploy IT-based resources in combination or copresent with other resources and capabilities" [5]. A literature review on small firms ICT capability resulted in identification of thirteen different uses (see Table 1). These different uses will guide us in mapping the extent to which technology-based small firms posses ICT capability and also illustrate the most extensive usages of ICT capability.

Table 1· Thirteen Dimensions of ICT Capability

ICT1 EXISTINGCOL	Maintaining collaboration with existing business partners
ICT2 NEWCOL	Establishing business collaboration with new partners
ICT3 INTCOMM	Handling communication within the firms (e.g. intranet)
ICT4 EXTCOMM	Handling external communication with the firm's stakeholders (e.g. extranet)
ICT5 ACCESSINFO	Accessing information (e.g. market, customers)
ICT6 STRATPLAN	Enable strategic planning
ICT7 COSTSAVE	Enable cost savings
ICT8 GLOBALBUS	Enable global business with partner far away
ICT9 COMPDEV	Enable competence/skills development for employees
ICT10 WORKFLEX	Enable work flexibility (e.g. work outside the office)
ICT11 PRODEVELOP	Enable the product development process
ICT12 SERVQUAL	Enable better customer service quality
ICT13 MARKACTIVTY	Promoting marketing activities

Adapted from [6] [7]

1.2 Network Configuration, Networking Capability and ICT Capability

As suggested before, networking can be a viable source of achieving competitiveness for small firms [2]. Firms can have different network practices or configurations that may involve several actors such as, small firms, large firms, universities or even government bodies [8]. These actors can be customers or partners to the small firm. A possible reason for selecting any particular kind of networking configuration can be due to the expected benefits related with each relation [9]. We define network configuration as "the pattern of relationships that are engendered from the direct and indirect ties between actors" [10]. In Sweden, around 60% of small firms have some kind of organized collaboration with at least one other firm and another 15% have some sort of collaboration with another type of partner [11]. Thus, it seems that small firms, contrary to the understanding of them as individualistic and non-cooperative entities, extensively use and rely on their networking.

However, according to [12], it is not enough to practice networking, it's also essential for firms to be able to successfully and in-practice utilize their networks. This presumes a networking capability, which according to [13] is a firm's ability to develop and utilize inter-organizational relationships to gain access to various resources held by other actors and which includes five components: a) the firm's coordination activities between collaborating firms, b) the firm's relational skills due to their ability of inter-personal exchange, c) its partner knowledge, i.e. possessing organized and structured information about their collaborating firms and competitors, d) the firm's internal communication to attain organizational learning within partnerships, and e) skills in locating and building up new relations with potential partners. A small firm with such capability would be able to strengthen their relations with different actors and gain more benefits from their network, which would lead to increased entrepreneurial behavior and better performance [14].

ICT capability can have strong influence on firms' networking configuration and capability. According to [15], ICT is seen as an important tool for working together and for having constant availability of information and communication with partner firms, which can lead to development of trust, satisfaction and commitment. Further, small firms with ICT capability can find it easier to meet the needs of their clients and offer customized products and services to conform those needs. It can also reduce physical barriers, and firms can focus on establishing most suitable partnerships [16]. Thus, we would like to propose that firms with high ICT capability would not only have ease in creating appropriate network configuration, but also gain more in term of networking capability.

2. Objectives

The overall objectives of this paper is two-fold: first to examine the extent to which ICT capability is possessed by technology-based small firms and second to investigate the influence of ICT capability on network configuration and networking capability.

These objectives can be further divided into four research questions.
1. What level of ICT capability is currently possessed by technology-based small firms?
2. Which dimensions of ICT capability are widely used by technology-based small firms?
3. How does ICT capability influence network configuration for technology-based SMEs?
4. How does ICT capability influence networking capability for technology-based SMEs?

3. Methodology

To achieve the above stated objectives, a survey was conducted involving Swedish technology-based small firms. This study is built on a pre-study that was done in autumn 2006 (see [7]). The pre-study included three in-depth case studies which were used as the baseline for defining criteria for selecting survey firms and for developing the questionnaire. The survey firms targeted were "consultancy-related computer systems or computer software firms" (Swedish industry index code of 72220). From the entire sample of 9,000 active firms, 1,471 firms were selected based on the following criteria: The firm should have less than 50 employees (i.e. small firms according to EU definition) and more than 1 MSEK/0,11 MEUR in sales (to ensure an active firm).

The questionnaires were sent in three waves during May- July 2007. Each questionnaire included three items: (1) a cover letter addressed to the CEO of the firm, explaining the motivation for this study. This letter was also signed by the researchers and personalized for each firm; (2) a business reply envelope; and (3) an eight-page questionnaire. A total of 291 usable replies (21% response rate) were received. Our key measurements were based on well-established scales from literature and the questionnaire was tested before-hand using inputs from small firm managers in similar industries as the targeted. During exploratory and confirmatory factor analysis, we did not observe any unexpected cross loading or irregularity and the alpha value were satisfactory (between 0.67 - 0.88). In order to contrast our two final research questions, regression analysis was conducted using SPSS 15.0. We moreover controlled for environment factors (dynamism, and hostility), firm age and firms size (number of employees).

4.   Results

The analysis shows that technology-based small firms have a high level of ICT capability. However, from the thirteen different uses of ICT capabilities, five were extensively used by small firms, namely, ICT 10 WORKFLEX, ICT 5 ACCESSINFO, ICT 1 EXISTINGCOL, ICT 12 SERVQUAL, and ICT 3 INTCOMM. On the scale of 0 to 6 these usages were all rated above 4.

Table 2: Mean Value of ICT Capabilities Dimensions (A Key to Used Abbreviations is Provided in Table 1).

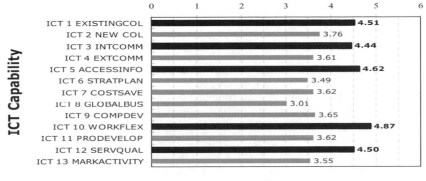

Factor analysis was used to group the different dimensions of ICT capability into more specific groups. Three groups were identified: ICT use for internal purpose, ICT use for communication, and ICT use for collaboration (see Table 3). At the bottom of the table the main characteristics associated to each group is stated. Three dimensions associated with ICT capabilities were removed from these groups as they did not explicitly relate to any particular group shown in italics in table 3 (ICT 8, ICT11, and ICT 12).

Table 3: The Main Groups for ICT Capability

	Internal use of ICT	ICT use for Communcation	ICT use for Collboration
ICT1 EXISTINGCOL			◆
ICT2 NEWCOL			◆
ICT3 INTCOMM		◆	
ICT4 EXTCOMM		◆	
ICT5 ACCESSINFO	◆		
ICT6 STRATPLAN	◆		
ICT7 COSTSAVE	◆		
ICT8 GLOBALBUS			
ICT9 COMPDEV	◆		
ICT10 WORKFLEX		◆	
ICT11 PRODEVELOP			
ICT12 SERVQUAL			
ICT13 MARKACTIVTY			◆
Main Characteristics	Internal use of ICT refers to those firm activities which are closely related with achieving internal efficiency	ICT use for communication refers to better flow of information inside and outside the firm	ICT use for collaboration addresses maintaining and establishing new relationships with different actors

Finally, for investigating the influence of ICT capability on network configuration and networking capability, regression analyses was performed (see Table 4). Two aspects of ICT capability significantly influenced network configuration. Particularly, it is the ICT use for communication that effects networking with customers ($\beta=0.177$, $p<0.05$) and ICT use for collaboration that effects networking with partners ($\beta=0.068$, $p<0.10$).

Table 4: Results from Regression Analysis

Dependent Variable ⟶	Network Configuration			Networking Capability			
	Networking with partners	Networking with customer	Internal communication	Coordination	Relationship skills	Building relations	Partner knowledge
Firm age (log)	-0.050	-0.207	-0.071	-0.258***	-0.027	-0.109	-0.185**
Firm size (log)	0.246***	0.273**	0.264***	0.173***	-0.017	0.239***	0.025
Environmental dynamism	0.049	0.409***	0.143***	0.098	0.108*	0.010	0.029
Environmental hostility	-0.101**	-0.086	-0.026	-0.061	-0.146**	-0.048	-0.097
ICT collaboration	0.068*	-0.014	0.122**	0.187***	0.141***	0.116**	0.191***
ICT internal	-0.013	0.086	0.028	-0.028	0.034	0.104*	0.040
ICT communication	-0.028	0.177**	0.117***	0.088*	0.087*	0.011	0.026
Model Summary							
R square	0.122	0.192	0.217	0.175	0.153	0.143	0.114
R square adjusted	0.098	0.170	0.197	0.153	0.130	0.120	0.090
Std. Error of the estimate	0.714	1.354	0.903	0.937	0.809	0.973	1.000
F-ratio	5.126	8.800	10.795	7.868	6.670	6.220	4.788
Significance	<0.001	<0.001	<0.001	<0.001	<0.001	<0.001	<0.001

p<.10, **p<.05, ***p<.01 Regression coefficients shown are beta coefficients

For the networking capability, all its components are significantly affected by ICT capability. Specifically, the component of relationship skills was strongly influenced from ICT use for collaboration (β=0.141, p<0.01) and marginally from ICT use for communication (β=0.087, p<0.10). Similar result was also received for coordination where ICT used for collaboration (β=0.187, p<0.01) and communication (β=0.088, p<0.10) had a significant influence. However, the internal communication component revealed an opposite relation to ICT capability where ICT use for communication (β=0.117, p<0.01) played a stronger role and ICT use for collaboration (β=0.122, p<0.05) a weaker. Additionally, partner knowledge was influenced by ICT use for collaboration (β=0.191, p<0.01) solely and the component of building relation was influenced from ICT use for collaboration (β=0.116, p<0.05) and internal use of ICT (β=0.104, p<0.10). All the models in the regression analyses have above satisfactory explanation power as the R square are between 0.144 and 0.217. Thus, the results indicate that ICT use for maintaining and establishing closer relations with business partners pays off in terms of developing the firm's network and its networking capability.

5.　Business Benefits

We will now discuss the business benefits emerging from our results using two themes: (1) the level of ICT capability possessed by Swedish technology-based small firms and (2) the influence on ICT capability on network configuration and networking capability.

The level of ICT capability is mapped using the thirteen dimensions given in Table 1. Each dimension was carefully selected based on a literature review and inputs from our preceding case studies. Many studies in past have highlighted the problems faced by small firms in successfully using ICT. However, in the context of technology-based small firms, this does not seem to hold true. Our results clearly show that the small firms currently have a rather high ICT capability. On the scale of 0 to 6, the minimum mean value was 3.01 and the highest 4.87. A possible reason for this high level of ICT capability may be related with the maturity in using technology tools and technological standardizations [6]. Furthermore, technology-based small firms might have a higher level of ICT capability compared to other industries where e.g. their employees can find it easier to effectively use ICT tools for business purposes [7].

Five dimensions of ICT capability have high mean values. Thus, they can be considered as those ICT related activities, which are widely used by technology-based small firms. ICT 10 WORKFLEX refers to ease in work from different locations and also having flexibility with working hours. This dimension has the highest mean value. Thus, it shows that for small firms it is vital that employees can work according to their needs and convenience. And as several employees might work part-time in these small firms ICT enabled work flexibility would hold a special value. The next dimension refers to the use of ICT for accessing information (ICT5 ACCESSINFO). Easy access to information is precious for firms operating in a dynamic environment, and as firms need to be updated on new technologies or innovations that might influence firms' future competitiveness. Wold wide web become an essential enabler for information search/exchange and this role seems to be considerably high for small firms. ICT12 SERVQUAL deals with use of ICT for better customer service. ICT has long been associated as a tool for providing customers with better services in terms of quicker response and closer interactions. Certainly ICT capability would be useful for achieving better service quality as customers' needs can be effectively met e.g. customer relationship management (CRM) systems. The next two dimensions deals with ICT use for maintaining relations with partners (ICT1 EXISTINCOL) and achieving better internal communication (ICT3 INTCOMM). Both these usages hold high significance for small firms and in some ways they compliment each other. With the help of intranet and extranet, small firms can attain effective internal communication, which might make them, operate closely and facilitate closer relation with existing partners [15]. Thus, clearly these dimensions hold the highest ICT valuable for technology-based small firms.

The second theme discusses the influence of ICT capability on network configuration and networking capability. These relationships have several significant links. The network configuration includes two aspects (partnerships and customers integration). Although, these two aspects are closely related, firms usually get involved in each of them due to different motives [9]. Networking in form of partnerships is mainly driven by the need of small firms to find prospective partners and projects. In this scenario, ICT use for collaboration has a positive impact as firms can put emphasis on using ICT tools for establishing and maintaining new inter-firm relationships. Having this closeness can also allow them to be informed about future market trend, new technological developments and more importantly regarding prospective business partners. Similarly, for networking with customers, one purpose can be to develop better products and services, where ICT use for communication has significant influence. And as in this form of networking the relationship already exists ICT use for collaboration does not seem to have any significant impact. However, with the use of CRM solutions, small firms can achieve a higher level of communication and interaction that makes it simpler for firms to understand customers' need and wants. Also, it would be more feasible to integrate the customers' feedback early in the product development phase, which will save costs.

The results from this study indicate that most components of networking capability are either influenced from ICT use for collaboration or/and from ICT use for communication. Specifically, coordination, relationship skills and partner knowledge have stronger relations to ICT use for collaboration. Technological tools such as EDI (electronic data interchange) can provide firms with the possibility to have a constant connection with trading partners, which fosters knowledge sharing and better customer/supplier information exchange [17]. These advantages have positive impact on firms' ability to better coordinate its actions and gather valuable information about customers. Furthermore, ICT can enable firms to offer extra services to their partners such as updated records of transactions, just-in-time deliveries, quick responses on inquiries, etc. Thus, creating an environment of mutual benefit and manifesting better relationship skills. ICT can also facilitate small firm to build goodwill among peers and help them in becoming an attractive partner for business. This will be helpful in building new relations and maintaining existing ones where ICT use for collaboration, and specifically on the component of building new relations, seems viable. ICT use for communication has on the other hand a significant impact on firms' internal communication. This could be the result of reduced structural barriers within firms which makes the communication channels more efficient. The firms' websites can also serve as an important tool for information and communication exchange for different stakeholders.

6. Discussion and Conclusions

To conclude, our results suggest that technology-based small firms are high users of ICT. Most of our sample firms view ICT as a vital part of their business practice. In this study, thirteen different uses of ICT were identified based on theory and practice. However, some of them are more widely used than others. The important ones are aimed at gaining flexibility in working hours, accessing vital information, maintaining collaboration with existing business partners, better handling communication within the firm and providing superior customer service. ICT capability does seem to influence small firms networking configuration. Particularly, there is a clear link between higher ICT use for collaboration and more extensive partnership networking, and a higher ICT use for communication and more extensive customer networking. The regression analysis also shows that ICT capability plays a significant role in enhancing networking capabilities. All components of networking capability are either influenced by ICT use for collaboration or communication. Thus, using technology for maintaining and establishing closer relations with business partners pays off in terms of developing the firm's network and its networking capability.

The theoretical contribution of this study provides further evidence regarding the importance of ICT capability for small firms' competitiveness. Previous studies have empirically linked ICT to performance and innovation [5] [9] [18]. However, the strong influence of ICT capability on networking related aspects has rarely been studied. This study makes a modest attempt to build the gap by empirically relating both these concepts. The main practical contribution of this study is towards providing a compressive picture to the small firms' mangers and policy makers. They can reflect on these results and might find similar or dissimilar scenario with-in their firm or region. The current level of ICT seems to be high at least for technology-based small firms and has large impact on there networking practices. Thus, ICT should be given special value within small firms and not just viewed as an ad-hoc process.

Future research can aim at replicating this study in another setting thus investigating a broader empirical perspective. It may be expected that the results from another industrial setting would be different and these differences can be appealing to investigate further. Another avenue for further research could be to elaborate on the causalities involved. This study has focused upon the influence of ICT on networking. However, this relation can also be the opposite, as many small firms might have adopted ICT due to their reliance networks. All these prospective tracks can be help in further building the research field and provide answers that have been lacking in the current study.

References

[1]   F. Delmar, P. Davidsson, & W. Gartner, Arriving At The High Growth Firm, Journal of Business Venturing, 2003, 18, pp. 189-216.
[2]   W. Powell, K. Koput, & L. Smith-Doerr, Interorganizational Collaboration And The Locus Of Innovation: Networks Of Learning In Biotechnology, Administrative Science Quarterly, 1996, 41, pp. 116-145.
[3]   A. Oliver, Strategic Alliances And The Learning Life-Cycle Of Biotechnology Firms, Organization Studies, 2001, 22, pp. 467-489.
[4]   A. Sourthern, & F. Tilley, Small Firms And Information And Communication Technologies (ICTs): Towards A Typology Of ICTs Usage, New Technology, Work and Employment, 2000, 15, pp. 138-154.
[5]   A. Bharadwaj, A Resource-Based Perspective On Information Technology Capability And Firm Performance: An Empirical Investigation, MIS Quarterly, 2000, 24, pp. 169-196.
[6]   J-A. Johannessen, J. Olaisen, & B. Olsen, Strategic Use Of Information Technology For Increased Innovation And Performance, Information Management & Computer Security, 1999, 7, pp. 5-22.
[7]   V. Parida, & M. Westerberg, ICT Use For Innovation And Competitiveness In Swedish Industrial Service SMEs, The 1st Nordic Innovation Research Conference, Oulu, Finland, 7th – 8th December, 2006.

[8]   L. Pittaway, M. Robertos, K. Munir, D. Denyer, & A. Neely, Networking And Innovation: A Systematic Review Of The Evidence, International Journal of Management Reviews, 2004, 5, pp. 137-168.

[9]   H. Etzkowitz, & L. Leydesdorff, The Dynamics Of Innovation: From National Systems And "Mode A" To A Triple Helix Of University-Industry-Government Relations, Research Policy, 2000, 29, pp. 109-123.

[10]   H. Hoang, & B. Antoncic, Network-Based Research In Entrepreneurship: A Critical Review, Journal of Business Venturing, 2003, 18, pp. 165-187.

[11]   M. Westerberg, & H. Ylinenpää, Cooperation Among Smaller Firms And Its Relation To Competence, Entrepreneurship And Performance, 17th Nordic Conference on Business Studies, Reykjavik, Iceland, 14-16 August, 2003.

[12]   P. Kale, J. Dyer, & H. Singh, Alliance Capability, Stock Market Response, And Long-Term Alliance Success: The Role Of The Alliance Function, Strategic Management Journal, 2002, 23, pp. 747-767.

[13]   A. Walter, M. Auer, & T. Ritter, The Impact Of Networking Capabilities And Entrepreneurial Orientation On University Spin-Off Performance, Journal of Business Venturing, 2006, 21, pp. 541-567.

[14]   M. Westerberg, & J. Wincent, Network Capability And Entrepreneurship: Refinement Of A Scale And Test Of A Framework, AGSE-Babson Regional Entrepreneurship Research, Melbourne, Australia, 5-8 February, 2007.

[15]   M. Ozer, The Role Of The Internet In New Product Performance: A Conceptual Investigation, Industrial Marketing Management, 2004, 33, pp. 355-369.

[16]   M. Nieto, & Z. Fernández, The Role Of Information Technology In Corporate Strategy Of Small And Medium Enterprises, Journal of International Entrepreneurship, 2005, 4, pp. 251-262.

[17]   N. Venkatraman, IT-Enabled Business Transformation. Form Automation to Business Scope Redefinition, Sloan management Review, 1994, 35, pp. 73-88.

[18]   J. Ruiz-Mercader, A. L. Meroño-Cerdan, & R. Sabater-Sánchez, Information Technology and Learning: Their Relationship and Impact on Organisational Performance in Small Businesses, International journal of Information Management, 2006, 1, pp. 16-29.

Collaboration and the Knowledge Economy: Issues, Applications, Case Studies
P. Cunningham and M. Cunningham (Eds.)
IOS Press, 2008

Implementation of an AmI System in a Manufacturing SME

Simrn Kaur GILL[1], Kathryn CORMICAN[2]
CIMRU, Department of Industrial Engineering, College of Engineering and Informatics,
National University of Ireland, Galway, Galway, Ireland
[1]*Tel: + 353 91 493429, Fax: + 353 91 562894, Email: s.gill1@nuigalway.ie*
[2] *Tel: + 353 91 493975, Fax: + 353 91 562894, Email: kathryn.cormican@nuigalway.ie*

Abstract: SME are facing greater challenges due to increased labour cost and reduced cycle times. To adapt to this change more effectively and efficiently they need systems in place that adapt to change easily and seamlessly. This is the case in the customised product and service manufacturing SME sector. Ambient intelligence (AmI) has the ability to help SME to become more flexible to change and build on their already dynamic nature. The ability of the AmI system to adapt and learn in different situations is the key to maintaining the competitiveness in an organisation. This paper seeks to demonstrate the development and implementation of an AmI system in the manufacturing SME environment. It presents an AmI system in industry reference model that highlights the implicit and explicit interaction between the user, process and environment in an AmI system. The reference model is applied to a case study and the benefits arising from implementation are highlighted and discussed.

1. Introduction

Manufacturing is an important part of the economic development in Europe. It has a multiplier effect on the economy as both a generator of employment and wealth [1]. Over recent year it has been in a state of flux due to various factors including reduced cycle times and increased labour costs. Small to medium size manufacturing outlets are especially facing these pressures. Small to medium enterprises (SME) retain their completive advantage by remaining flexible however responding to price competition involves streamlining manufacturing processes and practices. This has a knock-on effect of reducing the flexibility previously mentioned. This creates a dichotomy for many SME's involved in manufacturing, these pressures are causing challenges for SME. They need the ability to adapt to the rapidly changing business environment and to compete in the market place efficiently and effectively [2]. They also need to be more flexible and dynamic in adapting to change in demand from customers [3]. Existing systems in manufacturing are suitable for large scale manufacturing whereby products are standardised and there is a high range of production volume. If SME's are to remain competitive a new type of system is called for, one that can overcome such a dichotomy. Enhanced flexibility while at the same time promoting efficiently and effectiveness of processes requires knowledge from the surrounding environment to become readily available to the decision maker. The new system should have the ability of controlling the environment or ambience. Ambient intelligence is such a solution.

Ambient intelligence (AmI) is a means of integrating electronic technology with information technology creating the ability to adapt and learn in the physical environment that encircles the user [4]. Ambient can be described as the environment that surrounds the user, where the physical environment becomes the users interface with technology [5].

Intelligence is the ability to adapt knowledge to different situations and to be capable of taking advantage of them [6]. Technology moves into the background through the use of embedded technology such as radio frequency identification tags and speech recognition systems which results in a more human orientated interaction between the user and the technology that surrounds them [7, 8]. The use of speech and gestures to communicate with technology creates a more dynamic and flexible surroundings in manufacturing, particularly on the shop floor. It can be said that AmI is an adaptive and flexible technology that caters to the needs and wants of the user by modifying its responses inline with the changing manufacturing environment.

2. Objectives

The proliferation of ambient situations and the approach for identifying and developing such solutions to ensure accurate and effective results currently does not exist. The aim of the paper is to demonstrate the development and implementation of an AmI system in the manufacturing SME environment. This is done to alleviate the problems that are facing SME that manufacture customised products and services. The paper examines the analysis and development of an AmI system in the areas of scheduling and materials management within a SME case study. To accomplish this, an outline of the concept of ambient intelligence is provided. The review of the concept leads to the development of an AmI in industry reference model. The reference model examines the user in the AmI system with regard to their implicit and explicit interaction with the process, environment and the AmI system, which works as both an observer and controller of the manufacturing surroundings. The model outlines the generic requirements of the system in the manufacturing environment. The reference model is discussed further in the paper. The technologies used in developing the AmI system within the case study are examined. A manufacturing SME case study is analysed through the application of the reference model. Problems specific to the SME are identified and overcome using the AmI reference model. The implications of the system developed using the reference model is discussed with regard to the benefits and the issues of implementations.

3. Methodology

A case study was used in this case as there was little understanding of the AmI concept except through definitions. Therefore the case study approach was taken to find out the 'how' as to the application of AmI to a SME manufacturing setting [9]. A case study approach was also chosen as it assumes that the human is the variable in the situation and is in a state of flux and in AmI the user is placed at the centre of the system [4, 9]. The researcher is required to investigate the whole system and look for similarities and find explanations [10]. As part of the case study, the requirements of the company were gathered, and an analysis of the current situation was conducted. The weak points from the analysis were categorised and further analysed. This resulted in the identification of the problems effecting the organisation. The problems that would be covered in the solution were then selected. The solution was developed using the AmI in industry reference model and implemented in the case study. The reference model was validated through the case study and the findings were analysed with regard to the benefits and drawbacks of the solution. [9, 11, 12]

4. Technology Description

Ambient solutions place the human decision maker at the centre of the solution. Hence optimising the role and impact of the decision maker is a key objective of such technologies. AmI can provide greater product efficiency by providing improved visibility over the user, process and environment in manufacturing. This visibility can be utilised to make more informed decisions by all users of the AmI system and in turn improve the time frame in which decisions are made, as well as providing the decision maker with the relevant information that they need to make an informed decision. Through accomplishing this it will empower the human worker to make more effective and efficient decisions. Therefore all aspects of manufacturing will be built around them. This section reviews the concept of ambient intelligence within a manufacturing setting and some of the technologies that can be used to achieve an AmI system.

4.1   What is Ambient Intelligence?

Ambient intelligence is a user centred concept. This means that the user is placed at the centre of the technology embedded environment. In essence the move is away from one computer one user to an environment where many computers interact seamlessly with one user [13]. Gill and Cormican [14] define ambient intelligence "as a people centred technology that is intuitive to the needs and requirements of the human actor. They are non-intrusive systems that are adaptive and responsive to the needs and wants of different individuals." Technology in the AmI environment moves to the background by becoming embedded in everyday objects like cloths and furniture [15-17]. The AmI system works on the principles of evaluated inputs and outputs from the user, process and environment in which the user inhabits.

In developing an AmI system the AmI in industry reference model and the technologies applied in the case study are outlined below.

4.2   Modelling AmI

The model attempts to present a structured approach to understanding AmI in the manufacturing setting. The AmI in industry reference model (see Figure 1) was developed based on the findings of the AmI-4-SME project in conjunction with project partners. The models incorporate the user, process and environment within the manufacturing setting.

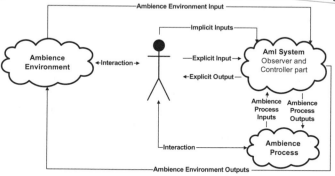

Figure 1: AmI in Industry Reference Model Adapted from Stokic et al[18].

The model identifies the information inputs and outputs of the system; it incorporates the user, process and environment within the information and data retrieval, processing and output. This provides for implicit interaction between the human operator and the AmI system. The AmI system takes a holistic view of the manufacturing system by incorporating the user, process and the environment. This is accomplished through a network of devices that are embedded into the background and can collect information implicitly. The acquisition of information from the shop floor is processed to incorporate context. To communicate the gathered information requires the need for high intelligence in the system. The system needs to provide information in context for it to be of use, to the users of the AmI system. Therefore the AmI system acts as both an observer and controller as the information is provided to it through the network of embedded devices and it has the ability to process the information and take action.

In the case of a machine losing calibration and slowing down production the AmI system can notify a technician of the problem immediately so that there will be less of an impact on the production schedule. The AmI system can also assist the scheduler by providing them with real-time information from the shop floor so that production can be adapted to take account of the machine that requires calibration and testing. Different technologies are used in combination to achieve the AmI system. Some of these are examined in the following section.

4.3   Enabling Technologies

For the AmI system to be achieved requires the advancement of traditional information communication technology (ICT). As such AmI is an advancement of ICT. The technology requirements for achieving an AmI system are "very unobtrusive hardware, seamless mobile or fixed web-based communication infrastructure, dynamic and massively distributed device networks, a natural feeling human interface" and "dependability and security" [4]. In achieving these requirements there needs to be an amalgamation of a number of fundamental developments in the area of ICT which will assist in the development of AmI in the manufacturing sector [4, 19]. These developments are needed to achieve a user centred system that is based on having an omnipresent system that adapts to the users needs and requirements. The three technologies that were used in the developing the AmI system in the case study are outlined below. These include semantic web, radio frequency identification and multimodal services.

The semantic web is the next generation in the development of the web. It is designed to provide meaning to web content. By accomplishing this it allows for more intelligent searches of web content, as well as improved interaction between human and computer. In the manufacturing environment this may lead to an intelligent search of the information stored in the database by the technical staff to assist them on repairing machines on the shop floor in the most efficient manner based on previous repairs and similar machine failures. [20, 21]

Radio frequency identification (RFID) tags are considered to be the next generation of bar-coding. It can be used to track shipments around the world as well as products on the production line. Information related to products can be stored on the tag. This information can be read at different distances depending on the tag. There are two main types of tags, active and passive. Active tags as their name implies are continuously sending information to the reader. They also are more expensive then passive tags, which only respond when, read. [22, 23]

Multi-modal services provide the ability to access and interact with data on a computer through the use of multiple interfaces e.g. both text and speech. This can be accomplished through the use of a keyboard and mouse entry system as well as the speech recognition system (SRS) inputs and outputs. This interaction can also be accomplished through the use of multiple input and output devices e.g. mobile telephone, personal digital assistant (PDA) or computer. In the case of a technician repairing a machine on the shop floor they can access the previous repair history of the machine on their PDA and can through the use of SRS input and also receive information with regard to repairing the machine. [24, 25]

No single technology incorporates the characteristics of the AmI environment. Only when combined seamlessly with other enabling technologies is the concept realised.

5.   Business Case Description

The approach outlined in the previous section is validated in the implementation of a case study. The SME case study manufactures customised fabricated emergency vehicles for the

Irish domestic market. It is located in a remote location in the west of Ireland. The company is managed by owners who all work in the organisation in managerial positions. They employ approximately 28 people. The company not only produces emergency vehicles but also services them as well. The main competitive advantage of the company lies in their flexibility to adapt to customer requirements at any time during the design and production process.

The company used a database system to manage all resource planning and scheduling. The database system was designed in house by a member of the engineering staff. The database system evolved with the ever evolving user requirement of manufacturing operations. This created an environment where only the employees that had been at the company from the beginning of the deployment of the system had a full understanding of the system and used it to its full potential. New members of staff were more hesitant to use the system and information in the database became no longer accurate. Particularly in critical areas of raw materials usage, as work orders were sent to the shop floor and only during production were material deficiencies found. On the shop floor the level of traceability was low. It was not always known how many components were used in the production or if they were assembled in the correct manner. The overall problem lies in the area of knowledge management. Due to this the lead time for products was greater than their competitors.

There were three options available to the SME with regard to possible solution. The first is to buy an off the shelf information management system, the second is to design a new in house AmI system that caters to their specific requirement and can be adapted to deal with future changes. The third option is to combine the first two, use the off the shelf system to manage the resource planning and scheduling, and create an in house AmI system that, is interoperable, can interact with the information management system and make it more adaptive and flexible to the needs of the SME. This would help to ensure that they maintain their competitive advantage of being able to adapt to customer requirements at any time during the design and production processes. In this case study the third option was chosen.

5.1   Decision Information Production Algorithm

The solution was developed in relation to the users, process and technology, and applied to two areas, scheduling and materials management, see Figure 2. Within the new system all users, subassemblies and machines have been tagged with passive RFID tags. RFID readers have been mounted at workstations. The RFID readers send the collected information back to the AmI system.

1. The new process begins by the AmI system having all the scheduling and work instructions finalised with the scheduler. This means that the AmI system is ready to execute the work orders on the shop floor and has ensured that all materials for completing the orders will be available for production as they are required.
2. When the operator arrives in the morning or after completing a work task goes to the LCD monitor to interact with the AmI system. The AmI system recognises the operator from his/her RFID tag and can provide the operator with a new work assignment in relation to their skills level competence in that specific area, log a problem, or adapt the work assignment instructions to the operators specific skill requirements for example it can provide a detailed break down of the task to be performed for a less experienced operator or just the specifics of the task for a more highly skilled operator. Not in all but in some areas of the shop floor the operator can interact with the AmI system through SRS.

3. If the AmI system detects a problem or is notified of one it will inform all relevant personnel. For example a technician can be notified of a machine malfunction or rejects being generated by a specific machine.
4. All the manager and supervisors are contactable and can view and update shop floor operations in real-time, due to the integration of PDA's with SRS into the AmI system network. This allows them to track problems and solution on the shop floor as they happen.
5. Materials usage and availability can also be tracked in real-time. The materials manager can then ensure that there is adequate availability of materials for production on the shop floor so that production is not delayed due to lack of raw materials.

The benefits and issues of the implementation of the AmI system are discussed in the following section.

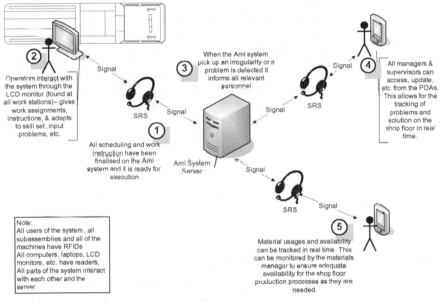

Figure 2: AmI System

6. Business Benefits

The product, which is developed, is a system that enables integration between electronic hardware and software to develop an AmI system. It occurs in three parts:

*   A set of information technology services are provided by the vendors which expands the functionality of the core technologies to allow the system to be integrated in the SME manufacturing environment.
*   Vendors provide for the expansion of existing hardware and middleware. This is accomplished through the development of services that are available for download to provide middleware for integration of legacy systems.
*   Developers are provided for implementation of the ambient system. The ambient consultants will guide the implementation and integration of both the technology vendors and service providers.

For these solutions to be successfully available all three stakeholders must play a role.

In the case study the production schedule was improved by providing real-time updates on production progress information by operators and reducing downtime with improved time and resource management. Materials management benefited from the material in the warehouse being tracked on the shop floor, so keeping accurate records of stocks and its utilisation. The holding cost of stock could be reduced by reducing the lead time as well as improving the accuracy due to traceability of materials and work being conducted on the shop floor. As a result, the manager now has greater visibility over the shop floor, the traceability of raw materials usage in production and utilisation of personnel is improved. The AmI system assists scheduling and materials management in four ways, by collecting real-time information from the shop floor and using it to update the existing schedule, providing decision support to the scheduler, providing shop floor personnel with the information that they require to complete their assigned tasks, and tracking any and all problems that occur on the shop floor and updating the schedule to reflect them. This resulted in lead time reduction from 14 to 8 weeks through improved decision making

In the implementation of the AmI system in the case study, a number of lessons were learned in relation to system development. Issues included privacy with regard to tagging, training of users, creating boundaries between personal and business time and user involvement through the design and development process. Some of the risks with development and implementation of an AmI system are, will the user use the system, accuracy of information and continual maintenance. Financial investment by SME's must be made. However, the solution will depend on the accuracy and availability of the legacy data, also the willingness of users to adopt the solution. The SME solution needs to be one that promotes efficiency, effectiveness, flexibility and can only be delivered through such ambient solutions. AmI is an inspiring concept and with its introduction will change the way that we work and live our lives.

7.   Conclusions

SME are facing greater challenges due to the faster changing business environment. To adapt to this change more effectively and efficiently they need systems in place that adapt to change easily and seamlessly. This is the case in the customise product and service manufacturing SME sector. AmI has the ability to help SME to become more flexible to change and build on their already dynamic nature. The ability of the AmI system to adapt and learn in different situations is the key to maintaining the competitiveness in an organisation. This paper examines the implementation of an ambient intelligence (AmI) system in a manufacturing SME. To achieve this, an AmI in Industry reference model is applied in a SME manufacturing case study. To create an AmI environment, requires the use of a combination of technologies as well as an understanding of the need and requirements of the user, process and environment in which the AmI system is to be implemented. The aim of the paper is to demonstrate the development and implementation of an AmI system in the customise product and service manufacturing SME environment. To achieve this, the case study is analysed with regard to the weak points to be improved through the development of an AmI system. The AmI in industry reference model is used to assist in developing the system as it shows the user, process, environment and AmI system as well as the interaction between these elements. The solution is discussed with regard to business benefits and issues in implementation.

Acknowledgement

This work has been partly funded by the European Commission through IST Project AmI-4-SME: Revolution in Industrial Environment: Ambient Intelligence Technology for Systemic Innovation in Manufacturing SMEs (FP6-2004-IST-NMP-2-17120) and the National University of Ireland, Galway, College of Engineering Postgraduate Fellowship. We also wish to acknowledge our gratitude and appreciation to all AmI-4-SME project partners for their contribution during the development of various ideas and concepts presented in this paper.

References

[1]   MANUFUTURE, A vision for 2020: Assuring the future of manufacturing in Europe, November 2004.

[2]   D. J. Storey, Understanding the Small Business Sector. London, Routledge, 1995.

[3]   D. K. Koska and J. D. Romano, Profile 21 Issues and Implications, Countdown to the Future: The Manufacturing Engineer in the 21st Century, Society of Manufacturing Engineers, Dearborn, Michigan, US Autumn 1988.

[4]   K. Ducatel, M. Bogdanowicz, F. Scapolo, J. Leijten and J.-C. Burgelman, Scenarios for Ambient Intelligence in 2010 (ISTAG 2001 Final Report), ISTAG, IPTS, Seville February 2001.

[5]   P. Morville, Ambient Findability, First ed. Sebastopol, CA, USA, O'Reilly, 2005.

[6]   D. R. Hofstadter, Gödel, Escher, Bach : An Eternal Golden Braid First ed. Harmondsworth, Penguin Books Ltd., 1980.

[7]   M. Weiser, Ubiquitous computing, In: IEEE Computer, Ronald D. Williams ed IEEE, pp. 71-72, 1993.

[8]   M. Weiser, How computers will be used differently in the next twenty years, In: Symposium on Security and Privacy Oakland, CA, USA, pp. 234-235, 1999.

[9]   R. K. Yin, Case Study Research: Design and Methods, Second ed. Vol. 5. Thousand Oaks, Sage Publications, 1994.

[10] J. Gill and P. Johnson, Research methods for managers. London, Sage Publications, 2002.

[11] I. Benbasat, D. K. Goldstein and M. Mead, The Case Research Strategy in Studies of Information Systems MIS Quarterly, Vol. 11, No. 3, pp. 369-386, September 1987.

[12] P. Darke, G. Shanks and M. Broadbent, Successfully completing case study research: combining rigour, relevance and pragmatism, Information Systems Journal, Vol. 8, No. 4, pp. 273-289, 1998.

[13] G. Riva, F. Vatalaro, F. Davide and M. Alcaniz, Ambient Intelligence: the evolution of technology, communication and cognition towards the future of human-computer interaction, IOS Press, 2005.

[14] S. K. Gill and K. Cormican, Ambience Intelligence (AmI) Systems Development, In: Information Technology Entrepreneurship and Innovation, Fang Zhao, Ed. Idea Group, pp 1-22, 2008.

[15] ITEA, The Ambience Project 2003.

[16] J. Horvath, Making friends with Big Brother?, In: Telepolis http://www.heise.de/tp/r4/artikel/12/12112/1.html, 2002.

[17] M. Lindwer, D. Marculescu, T. Basten, R. Zimmermann, R. Marculescu, S. Jung and E. Cantatore, Ambient Intelligence Vision and Achievement: Linking Abstract Ideas to Real-World Concepts, In: Design, Automation and Test in Europe Conference and Exhibition, pp. 10-15, 2003.

[18] D. Stokic, U. Kirchhoff and H. Sundmaeker, Ambient Intelligence in Manufacturing Industry: Control System Point of View. Paper at the In: Control and Applications 2006 conferenceMontreal, Quebec, Canada, , 2006.

[19] ISTAG, Recommendations of the IST Advisory Group for Work programme 2001 and beyond "implementing the vision", ISTAG June 2000

[20] T. Berners-Lee, J. Handler and O. Lassila, The Semantic Web, Scientific American, Vol. 284, No. 5, pp. 28-37, May 2001 2001.

[21] S. Decker, S. Melnik, F. Van Harmelen, D. Fensel, M. Klein, J. Broekstra, M. Erdmann and I. Horrocks, The Semantic Web: The Roles of XML and RDF, IEEE Internet Computing, Vol. 4, No. 5, pp. 63-73, Sept -Oct 2000.

[22] D. Kiritsis, A. Bufardi and P. Xirouchakis, Research issues on product lifecycle management and information tracking using smart embedded systems, Advanced Engineering Informatics, Vol. 17, No. 3-4, pp. 189-202, July - Oct 2003.

[23] B. Potter, RFID: misunderstood or untrustworthy?, Network Security, Vol. 2005, No. 4, pp. 17-18, April 2005.

[24] J. A. Markowitz, Using Speech Recognition. New Jersey, Prentices Hall, 1996.

[25] M. Friedewald and O. Da Costa, Science and Technology Roadmapping: Ambient intelligence in Everyday Life (AmI@Life), JRC-IPTS/ESTO, Seville, Spain June 2003.

Collaboration and the Knowledge Economy: Issues, Applications, Case Studies
P. Cunningham and M. Cunningham (Eds.)
IOS Press, 2008

A Mobile Multi-Supplier Sales Information System for Micro-sized Commercial Agencies

Holger KETT, Jochen KOKEMÜLLER, Oliver HÖß,
Wolf ENGELBACH, Anette WEISBECKER
Fraunhofer IAO, Nobelstraße 12, 70569 Stuttgart, Germany
Tel: +49 711 970-2415, Fax: + 49 711 970-5111,
Email: {Holger.Kett, Jochen.Kokemueller, Oliver.Hoess, Wolf.Engelbach,
Anette.Weisbecker}@iao.fraunhofer.de

Abstract: Micro-sized commercial agencies face a poor electronic and mobile sales support. Most of the sales information systems are built for the usage within larger-sized companies. Problems particularly appear when processes of multiple suppliers have to be integrated into the sales processes of the commercial agencies. The paper addresses the issue of process optimization in form of a mobile multi-supplier sales information system for micro-sized commercial agencies. Two major areas of improvements can be realized: Firstly, by an optimized business process integration of multiple SME suppliers and their sales representatives in micro-sized commercial agencies (internal supplier oriented sales processes), and secondly, by an increased mobility in connection with an optimization of sales processes outside of the office infrastructure (external customer oriented sales processes). The paper examines the common processes in commercial agencies and derives relevant processes as well as the appropriate IT-support in form of use cases. The relevant processes and the use cases depend strongly on certain key parameters of a commercial agency's business relationships with its suppliers. Therefore, the paper introduces a branch independent concept for the sales cockpit with the focus on selected sales scenarios, relevant business processes, and derived use cases depending on selected key parameters. By funding the research project M3V, the German Ministry of Economics and Technology aims to create a secure, mobile, multi-supplier sales information system as a service for micro-sized commercial agencies.

Keywords: sales information system, mobile application, business process integration, software-as-a-service

1. Introduction

In the research project M3V (www.m3v-projekt.de), a survey has been conducted in 2007 among 53 micro-sized commercial agencies in the southern part of Germany. It has shown a poor electronic support of their sales processes [1]. 10 percent of them have no E-Mail support, 20 percent no office software, 45 percent no electronic contact administration or customer relationship management software (CRM), and 70 percent no electronic bookkeeping. The contact between the commercial agencies and their sales representatives is based on phone calls and paper-based document exchange.

The requirements for a new sales information system for those commercial agencies are supposed to be as followed [2]:

- One sales cockpit, if required with the differentiation of back office and mobile cockpit, for the micro-sized commercial agencies instead of many different sales portals of each supplier or no IT support at all,
- Exchange of sales information between the commercial agencies and their suppliers by strongly integrated suppliers' processes and systems into one sales system,

- Mobile access to the sales information to support the processes in which interactions with customers occur,
- Reduced IT-administration in comparison to the initial situation,
- Appropriate business model for offering the sales information system as a service for micro-sized commercial agencies [3].

On one hand, the current CRM-systems which are used by the suppliers are mostly developed for one sales organisation and its sales force which has the disadvantage that the commercial agencies need to work with different sales systems for each of their suppliers [4] and often results in a lack of a mobile sales support in front of the customers.

On the other hand the current CRM-systems which are used by the micro-sized commercial agencies do not support the sales processes across organizations and thus do not feature a strong integration of the suppliers' processes and systems. Therefore, they lack up-to-date as well as mobile sales information.

2. Objectives

The overall objective of the research, which is described in the paper, is the development of a concept for sales information system which supports and automates relevant sales processes of micro-sized commercial agencies. The concept is branch independent.
The three main sub objectives are:

- The identification of relevant processes of micro-sized commercial agencies,
- The examination of optimization potentials in each process with a strong focus on integration and mobility aspects,
- The development of a scenario with various commercial agencies for the sales cockpit which supports branch independently the optimization of their sales processes.

3. Methodology

In order to achieve a branch independent solution, several expert interviews and workshops have been conducted. The experts have been retailers, sales agents and sales representatives for food, clothing, facility management, chemicals, packaging, electronic components and devices. Additionally, in order to improve the suppliers' perspective on the topic, some interviews with suppliers have been done who sell via micro-sized sales organisations. The results have been further examined by a survey among commercial agencies in Southern Germany. The survey is not statistically representative. However, it shows first interesting trends in the research questions examined.

The focus of the research has been the identification of relevant business processes of commercial agencies and their potential for optimization and electronic support. The results of the examination form the basis for the concept development of the sales information system for micro-sized commercial agencies which includes the sales IT-platform, the back office and the mobile sales cockpit. The concept has been evaluated by target users.

The approach and the description of the results are according to the meta model of Business Engineering of Österle [5] which was then further developed to PROMET in order to describe business cases. The meta model consists of three levels, i.e. strategy, process, and system level. Each level provides different elements to describe an IT solution.

4. Initial Situation

For the concrete business case of micro-sized commercial agencies the following elements have been identified to describe the initial situation.

4.1 Strategic Level

The work of sales representatives is based on a legal framework, which defines their rights and duties. However, other aspects also strongly influence their work and thus the IT-support. Table 1 illustrates the main strategic aspects that are relevant for sales representative of micro-sized commercial agencies.

Table 1: Strategic Background of Commercial Agencies

Strategic Aspect	Origin	Right/Duty
Right for representing multiple suppliers	legal	right
Non-competition clause for sales representatives	implicitly legal	duty
Commission claim	legal	right
Comprehensive reporting of the suppliers of all bookings leading to commissions	legal	right
Duty for endeavour and reporting of the sales representatives	legal	duty
Strong strategy of differentiation towards other competitors	business	-
Carefully selected product range	business	-

4.2 Process Level

During the research, 27 processes have been identified which support the sales phases of a commercial agency, i.e. communication and information, consulting, sales, order processing, and after sales and support (see Figure 1).

Commercial agencies take different roles which influence the business processes between them and their suppliers. The main roles are sales agent, sales representative, and retailer (explanation see Table 2). Very often a commercial agency has got different roles with even one supplier. Thus, depending on the role of the agency, the processes need to be combined and supported by the sales cockpit accordingly. The different roles and their influence on the processes are shown in Figure 1. Next to the role there are other key parameters that influence the processes (see tables 4 and 5).

Table 2: Different Roles of Commercial Agencies

Role	Explanation	Type of Contracting
Sales agent	The service of a sales agent is to bring two parties together which are willing to contract.	None
Sales representative	The sales representative is able to contract in the name of the representing supplier.	Representation of supplier also in terms of contracting
Retailer	The retailer contracts in his own name for his organisation.	Power of contracting in his own name

Each of the 27 processes has been examined in terms of frequency, personal effort, weaknesses, future mobile importance and potential for improvement. The examination results can be seen in Figure 1 with the aspects of optimization potential (combines frequency and personal effort of processes), mobile importance, and mobile potential.

When having a closer look to the optimization potential it becomes obvious that the sales cockpit should support the integrative processes between commercial agencies and their suppliers, i.e. providing reports of customer meetings to suppliers, clarification of customer requests with suppliers, matching payments for commissions with suppliers, and matching status of business transactions with suppliers. The (multimedia) introduction of products and the support of the product selection are processes in front of the customers that are also badly supported by current IT-systems.

The processes with a high mobility importance for the commercial agencies are often processes which are conducted in interaction with customers, i.e. providing product information to customers, (multimedia) introduction of products, supporting the product selection, clarification of customer requests with suppliers, checking status of customers' business transactions, administration of contacts, and preparation of a customer meeting (see also [6]). However, processes of the sales phases communication and information, consulting, and order processing show potential for improving mobility. Especially, the product selection process can be supported better.

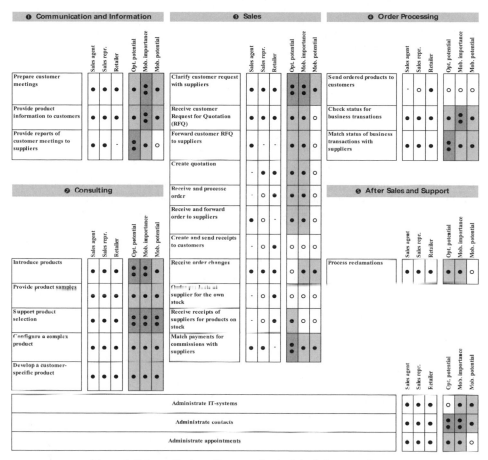

Figure 1: Relevant Business Processes for the Sales Information System

(roles: "-" = process not relevant, "o" = partially relevant process, "●" = relevant process, optimization/mobile potential and mobile importance: "o" = none or low potential/importance, "●" = middle potential/importance, "●●" = high potential/importance)

The sales information system should be able to improve the identified processes. The main weaknesses of the current processes are:

- High manual effort for the sales representatives for maintaining information (integration problem, e.g. orders entered at the suppliers' side),
- Lack of up-to-date information (integration problem, e.g. turn-over which is relevant for the commission of a sales representative, status of transactions),
- Problems of not having the required information at the right place (mobility problem, e.g. product information, information of transactions in front of the customers).

4.3   System Level

Some of the commercial agencies use IT-systems, e.g. ERP and CRM solutions. However, the solutions are characterised by:

- A high usage of single IT-systems without considering a holistic and integrative approach,

- Little IT-knowledge within the commercial agencies despite many of them administrate their IT-systems themselves.

Therefore, the aim of the cockpit and the underlying sales information system is to support the integration of the relevant IT-solutions of the suppliers in order to achieve up-to-date information for each of the sales processes as well as to provide the required information on mobile devices.

5.   Concept of the Sales Information System

From the information gathered in the interviews and workshops with commercial agencies and suppliers, a suitable IT-infrastructure, 27 relevant processes, and the corresponding IT-functionality in form of use cases were derived. Figure 2 provides an overview over the key players, systems, and interfaces of the ideal sales information system which consists of two main parts:

- A sales IT-platform which mainly integrates the systems of suppliers and commercial agencies and assures the provision of up-to-date sales information,

- Back office and mobile sales cockpits which are user interfaces for the commercial agencies to access the stored sales information of the sales information system with mobile and back office IT-devices and -systems.

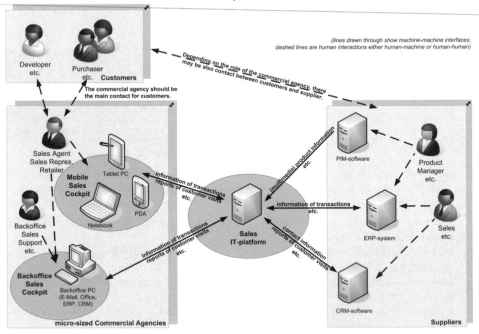

Figure 2: Overview of Key Players, Systems, and Interfaces

The sales information system provides a complete set of functions for supporting most sales processes. Depending on the IT-infrastructure, the specific needs, and requirements of a commercial agency, the set of functions can be adapted. In order to support the work processes of the commercial agencies efficiently, the set of functions contains the use cases shown in Table 3. The use cases are documented by applying the UML notation. With the description of the use cases the main functions of the IT-platform from the viewpoint of commercial agencies are specified [7]. Additional use cases may be required by the suppliers if the integration of the suppliers' backend systems is not realizable. In this case, the platform needs to provide certain functions to replaces the information exchange with the backend systems.

Table 3: Relevant Processes and Use Cases

Processes	Activities in each process which is the basis for deriving the use cases
Prepare customer meeting	Collect relevant information for customer meeting, configure the structure of the information export
Introduce product	Search products, retrieve and present multimedia product information (e.g. videos)
Provide product information to customer	Search products, retrieve product information (e.g. handbooks, datasheets), send product information to customer
Provide product sample	Create and send request for product sample, gather customer's feedback after checking the product sample, retrieve information of a request for product sample
Support the product selection	Search products, retrieve product information, put products into shopping cart, create a request for quotation/order from shopping cart
Configure a complex product (if necessary with the customer)	Configure a complex product, save/administrate a product configuration, create a request for quotation/order from product configuration
Develop a customer-specific product	Create project, handle project correspondence, handle project documents
Clarify customer request with supplier	Handle correspondence for customer requests
Receive customer request for quotations	Receive and enter a customer's request for quotation
Forward customer requests for quotations to supplier	Forward a customer's request for quotation to supplier
Create quotations	Create a quotation, send a quotation to a customer
Receive and process order	Create an order, handle an order, send an order to a supplier
Provide reports of customer meetings to suppliers	Create a report of a customer meeting, handle a report of a customer meeting (e.g. process the open tasks), send report of a customer meeting to a supplier
Create and send receipts to customer	Create a receipt, print a receipt
Receive order changes	Enter order changes, send order changes to a supplier
Send receipts from a supplier to a customer	Print receipt
Match payments for commissions with suppliers	Retrieve amount of payments for commissions
Check status information of business transactions	Retrieve status information of business transactions (list), retrieve detailed information of business transactions
Synchronise electronic documents with a supplier	Administrate electronic documents (i.e. requests for quotations, quotations, orders, order acknowledgements, receipts, reclamations)
Process reclamation	Create a reclamation, check a reclamation, send a reclamation to a supplier
Administrate IT-systems	Administrate employee accounts, configure integration of systems, adjust use cases to commercial agency, import product information, insert product information
Administrate contacts	Administrate contacts, manage leads, administrate correspondence
Administrate appointments	Administrate appointments

As mentioned above the functionality of the sales information system needs to be adapted according to certain prerequisites. For the suppliers' integration the parameters which are shown in need to be clarified.

For example, a sales agent does neither create any quotations nor process any orders. A sales representative without a stock usually does not order products for his stock or send products directly to the customers. This way, the key parameters stock and role have influence on the processes mentioned above.

Table 4: Key Parameters Which May Be Different for Each Supplier

Key Parameters	Characteristics				
Role	Sales Agency	Sales Representative	Retailer		
Types of Products sold	Standard Products	Configurable Products	Individual Products		
Systemintegration	none	ERP	CRM	PIM	...
Stock	yes	no			
direct Customer Contact	yes	no			

Table 5 shows some important key parameters that need to be defined once for the commercial agency. They influence mainly the processes which are done among them and their customers, e.g. the processes are influenced by the possibility of using a mobile device in front of a customer and thus may have real time information, i.e. about stock, delivery time, and status of business transactions.

Key Parameters	Characteristics				
Mobile Devices in front of Customers	yes	no			
Mobile Device	Fullscreen	Smallscreen			
Connectivity of mobile Device	offline	online			
Mobile Output Devices	Screen	Printer	Audio	Fax	...
Systemintegration	none	ERP	CRM	...	

Table 5: Key Parameters Provided Once by the Commercial Agency

The use cases of some selected processes have been implemented in a software prototype based on Java, the Grails framework and .NET for the mobile client [2]. The prototype has been the basis for the concept evaluation by key users.

## 6.	Business Benefits

The evaluation by the key users shows benefits of the sales information system in terms of time/effort reduction, cost savings as well as turnover increase in comparison to the initial situation. The main benefits when looking at reducing time/effort and saving costs are:

- Less manual work in terms of reviewing and filing of paper-based documents, e.g. requests for quotations, orders, and reclamations,
- Mobile fulfilment of documentation activities and thus a reduction in revision of customer meetings and talks,
- A strong concentration on core competencies of commercial agencies, e.g. reduction in IT-administration by applying the Software-as-a-Service approach (SaaS).

The main benefits when evaluating the sales information system in terms of turn-over increase are:

- A high availability of up-to-date sales information and thus a good basis for providing relevant sales information to customers, e.g. information about products and status of transactions,
- A location-independent information provision even in front of customers, e.g. in customer meetings,
- An increase in information transparency due to tracking of transactional information in the sales information system,
- A better information quality as a result of less media breaks when electronically exchanging information.

7. Conclusions and Future Work

A very crucial aspect of the sales information system for micro-sized commercial agencies has been a high adaptability of the sales cockpit to the needs of the sales people so that they get quickly used and accustomed to the application. The adaptation is carried out on the basis of the identified relevant sales processes and their influencing key parameters.

The main benefit of the mobile multi-supplier sales information system is the broad electronic support of the relevant sales processes with a strong focus on the needs of commercial agencies which profit of constantly up-to-date sales information from highly integrated (multiple) suppliers and their systems and a location-independent usage of the application even when interacting with customers. A high adaptability of the IT-platform is needed in order to increase the acceptance by the customers. However, next to the issue of acceptance there are other crucial issues to be solved to run the IT-platform as SaaS successfully, e.g. security, availability, usability, and integration.

The next activities strongly focus on the development of a business model which complements the functional and technical requirements by the business requirements of micro-sized commercial agencies and addresses the above-mentioned issues. Here, the aim is to run the system as a service in an economic way and simultaneously provide an appropriate support to the users which features a high acceptance.

References

[1] Spath, D.; Weisbecker, A.; Kett, H. (Ed.): Mobile Multilieferanten-Vertriebsinformationssysteme für Handelsvertretungen und –vermittlungen - Prozesse, Potenziale und Anforderungen, Fraunhofer IRB, 2008,

[2] Kokemüller, J.; Kett, H.; Höß, O.; Weisbecker, A.: A Mobile Support System for Collaborative Multi-Vendor Sales Processes. Proceedings of the Fourteenth Americas Conference on Information Systems, August 14th-17th, Toronto, ON, Canada: 2008,

[3] Schillewaert, N., Ahearne, M. J., Frambach, R. T., Moenaert, R. K. (2005) The adoption of information technology in the sales force, Industrial Marketing Management, 34, 323-336,

[4] Benz, A.; Ritz, T. & Stender, M.: Marktstudie mobile CRM-Systeme, Fraunhofer IRB, 2003,

[5] Senger, E. & Österle, H.: PROMET - Business Engineering Cases Studies (BECS), 06/2004,

[6] Leek, S., Turnbull, P. W., Naudé, P. (2003) How is information technology affecting business relationships? Results from a UK survey, Industrial Marketing Management, 32, 119-126,.

[7] OMG: OMG Unified Modeling Language (OMG UML), Superstructure, V2.1.2, OMG, 2007, URL: http://www.omg.org/docs/formal/07-11-02.pdf.

Collaboration and the Knowledge Economy: Issues, Applications, Case Studies
P. Cunningham and M. Cunningham (Eds.)
IOS Press, 2008

SME Collaboration: Trick or Treat?

Manon VAN LEEUWEN[1],Teresa MUÑOZ DURAN[1], Kathryn CORMICAN[2]
[1] *FUNDECYT, Manuel Fdez. Mejías sn 2 Planta, Badajoz 06002 Spain*
Tel: +34 924 014 600, Fax: +34 924 001996, Email: manon@fundecyt.es*;*
[2] *National University of Ireland, Galway, Ireland*
Tel: +353 91524411, Email: Kathryn.Cormican@nuigalway.ie

Abstract: Collaboration is a major new source of competitive advantage and an essential regional, and indeed, global management requirement. The collaboration process will ultimately be successful if there is an existence of appropriate systems and structures, open channels of communication, a strong sense of purpose and availability of the necessary resources. Support organizations for SMEs play a vital role in creating the environment in which SMEs can collaborate, focus in this article on support organisations whose main tasks are those of activating and assistance aiming at increasing, encouraging and stimulating innovation, rather than financing or creating it. A concrete example of the interplay of different actions related to training and the customized and personalized support is described.

Keywords: collaboration, innovation, support organisations

1. Introduction

Globalisation has forged a shift from the traditional corporate hierarchy and big business conglomerate to an economy in which both global and regional companies can be equally successful. However, research suggests that they must be part of an integrated network in which core competencies, localisation and customisation are achieved. The networked economy has shifted the focus from wholly owned value chains - encompassing everything from product development, operations, logistics and delivery, - to knowledge and relationships. How then should a business develop and expand in today's knowledge economy? Various authors indicate that network building is a major new source of competitive advantage and an essential regional, and indeed, global management requirement.

Collaboration takes place in a very different business environment and has different requirements than large organisations, therefore approaches and systems for SME collaboration need to be designed specifically for their unique needs and requirements. For example, on the one hand it does not have the potential to dedicate large resources to experimenting within areas of collaborative work and innovation, but on the other hand the flexibility and the responsive nature have a positive impact on collaboration.

The collaboration process will ultimately be successful if there is an existence of appropriate systems and structures, open channels of communication, a strong sense of purpose and availability of the necessary resources. However, it must be noted that without a healthy interpersonal relationship including the existence of motivation, trust, loyalty and honesty between all members of the team then the collaborative process of doomed to fail. It is often the softer issues "people" issues that affects the success of the collaborative work. It is clear that SMEs need these skills to take maximum advantage of the opportunities offered by collaboration and the participation in enterprise networks.

1.1 Collaboration and Innovation

Continuous innovation is key to future survival and growth of businesses operating in increasingly competitive global markets. Innovation has become a necessary component of a successful business strategy among firms of all sizes. In fact, many studies demonstrate that research and development (R&D) and technology-based innovation strategies are strongly associated with superior business performance. Smaller firms may face limited resources for R&D and commercialization and, consequently, incur higher risks. In addition, the innovation process is not solely dependent on R&D, as factors such as human resource strategies and management capabilities of the firm are also key. No longer is the creation and pursuit of new ideas the bastion of large central R&D departments within vertically integrated organizations. Instead, innovations are increasingly brought to the market by networks of firms, selected according to their comparative advantages, and operating in a coordinated manner. The need for collaborative R&D and commercialization is particularly critical for small and medium-sized enterprises (SMEs) hoping to make gains in terms of innovation.

But many SMEs find it difficult to collaborate or network with other organisations. While SMEs are often more flexible and responsive than larger organisations, they frequently lack the skills and resources necessary to collaborate or network. Collaboration takes place in a very different business environment and has different requirements than large organisations, therefore approaches and systems for SME collaboration need to be designed specifically for their unique needs and requirements. For example, on the one hand it does not have the potential to dedicate large resources to experimenting within areas of collaborative work and innovation [1], but on the other hand the flexibility and the responsive nature have a positive impact on collaboration.

2. Barriers to Collaboration and Innovation

2.1 Barriers to Collaboration

We found in our research and interactions with companies that many small organisations find it difficult to collaborate or network with other organisations. While Small to Medium Sized Organizations (SMEs) are lauded to be more flexible and responsive than their larger counterparts, they often lack the skills and resources to collaborate or network. We have found four main obstacles to successful collaboration:

a. Semantics/language: There is a lack of a common language between representatives from different organisations and consequently there can be many different interpretations of the same statement. Therefore, information is often misinterpreted between its creation and incorporation. Furthermore, information is often incorrectly formatted in documents and files and people are unable to communicate effectively. These factors also impede effective information sharing. Therefore, a common and agreed language and format must be finalised from the outset in order to allow the members to understand each other.

b. Motivation: Many people are unclear of the benefits for inter firm collaboration. In other words, they do not know what are the drivers, advantages, rewards and returns of sharing information with others. Unless mutual benefits to collaboration are established and communicated to all parties, people will remain unwilling to participate and reluctant to learn new procedures for information exchange.

c. Trust: SMEs often lack the confidence to share propriety information with other organisations. They often fear that competitors will gain access to proprietary data if they share information such as sales forecasts, or promotional plans with collaborating partners. Nevertheless this kind of real-time sharing of vital operational information is essential if companies want to work together towards a common goal. Establishing trust is potentially the greatest barrier to overcome in collaboration, and it must be established from the outset to allow knowledge sharing.

d. Access: There is a lack of common standard to enable information access and transfer. Therefore SMES often do not know what information to share, where critical information can be found and how to transfer it to others. Software is a key enabler for collaboration and information sharing with the Internet playing a leading role. In the case of SMEs, access to sophisticated IT is often not necessary, however an adequate knowledge of the methods and mechanisms available for communication is important

2.2   Barriers to Innovation

A survey with senior executives in on the key barriers to effective innovation [2], showed some interesting statistics regarding the top factors cited as barriers...

*   Short-term focus/ focus on operations (63%)
*   Lack of time, resources or staff (52%)
*   Lack of systematic innovation process (33%)
*   Leadership expects payoff sooner than is expected (31%)
*   Management incentives not structured to reward innovation (31%)

Innovations usually do not take place in a given, static environment. They are rather a result of a dynamic process in an organisation that involves interplay of several internal and external factors. In this sense there is a clear connection between innovation and collaboration, as the level of collaboration between the different departments or between different companies within the same enterprise group determines to a large extent its innovative capacity. Indeed, just as innovation supports competitivity, networking supports innovation, this is especially true for SMEs, it is evident that innovation would rarely occur in isolation.

3.   Overcoming the Barriers

3.1   The Role of Support Organisations

In today's world, where knowledge is available from a variety of sources, neither companies nor regions can afford to rely exclusively on their own resources for innovation. They need to interact with other people and organisations and draw on other fields of expertise to exploit their full innovation potential. Many regions have discovered that being a host to useful resources such as companies, research institutes and innovation support organisations is not enough – a climate with networking, exchange and trust between the various actors is necessary.

R&D is widely regarded as one of the most important factors in the innovation process; it is therefore imperative to stimulate and encourage more collaborative projects in R&D through partnership schemes linking institutes, universities, and industry. Independent SME support organisations play a vital role in this scheme.

Exhibit 1: Support organisations

According to a wide definition of support organisation such an organisation covers both 1) transfer of substance related information and 2) direct or indirect influence of the intermediary organisations on structures and dynamics of the region – i.e. having a role of a catalyst1. Thus may include centres of technology and/or expertise, development agencies, science parks, business incubators as well as education and research institutions [4]

Here the focus is on support organisations whose main tasks are those of activating and assistance aiming at increasing, encouraging and stimulating innovation, rather than financing or creating it.

Currently literature states that SME owner managers rely heavily on their previous industry experience to develop effective strategies for their businesses. Governments around Europe have not been slow to uptake on the support required for SME's and a number of training and funding schemes have been organised in order to help SME's to remain competitive and become more innovative. Despite the support SMEs have received there are emerging trends within SME's that have characterised their support [3]:

- Firstly there is a lack of networking among support agencies. Referral activity may occur from one agency to another, however often little in terms of partnerships occur.
- Confusion amongst the small business community as to whom from the "support network" to approach for advice and guidance.
- Overlaps and gaps in support provision.
- Clear variations in the quality of business support within and between areas. The level and quality of staffing, the emphasis on training and development of staff and the level of funding vary significantly amongst agencies in the small business policy community.
- Lack of pro-activity in the small business policy community in contacting businesses developing relationships and being able to formulate and deliver services that are required by businesses as opposed to derivatives of national programmes.
- Relatively low level of take-up of small business services. These are shown as up to 10% take up of courses.
- Lack of specific structures and systems for SMEs

Several projects and initiatives have been set up in the region of Extremadura to give an answer to the challenges described and the skills needed by SMEs, and as such allow the SMEs of the region to take maximum innovative advantage of collaboration, both between enterprises, as well as with research institutes and university.

3.2   Training for Collaboration

Training is an effective strategy employed by many organisations in order to increase the skills required for effective collaboration, however there has been low take up rates of the training put on offer. This is because the training is not specifically designed for and targeted at the unique needs of SMEs. The knowledge support organizations have of these specific needs and the day-to-day reality of SMEs, makes them ideal for being a catalyst towards SMEs geared training for innovation, either through their interactions with training and content developers, or by developing training contents themselves. An example of the latter is the MENS project, lead by an SME support organisations, the project provided learning materials for SMEs on enterprise collaboration and pretended to lower the barriers for collaboration by providing SMEs with the knowledge and preparation to upfront these types of collaboration. The research results concerning the analysis of the training needs show a clear tendency towards the "softer" issues, mainly concerning people management, for example related to creating a basis for trust, such as the need for competencies regarding to emotional intelligence; or related to the improvement of the motivation for collaboration, for example by increasing the management skills and communication skill (both of management and the organisational members).

Although this does not mean that the "harder" issues were not mentioned, the related competencies and skills that were considered important and needed for successful collaboration can be classified in three groups: performance (e.g. negotiating skills); structures (e.g. creating the legal structure of the collaboration); and finance (e.g. participating in shared results).

One of the issues that came up during the project in relation to the development of learning and training programmes for SMEs is a paradox concerning the expressed need for e-learning based training solutions and the reality of the uptake of these type of solutions. In fact, the SMEs analysed in the MENS project indicated that they would need "pragmatic training, which is very flexible in time scale, and that is not much need for a tutor or to have direct personal contact". However, the use of e-learning by SMEs still remains at a very low level. The DELID project addresses this issue, and has found out that one of the problems lays in a lack of knowledge concerning learners by those in charge of developing and carrying out e-learning courses. A team of content developers, elearning experts and intermediary organizations joined forces to develop a methodology which describes how e-learning courses can be adapted to better fit SME needs of SMEs in general.

The methodology will allow intermediary and innovation support organizations to better adapt their training for innovation to the real needs and eLearning characteristics of SMEs.

3.3   Innovation Agents

But training is only one side of the coin, making SMEs collaborate and collaborate with the aim of innovation, requires a more broad approach and needs to include customized and personalized support by skilled staff in intermediary organizations.

A good example is the CODICES project, the result of a collaboration agreement between the Spanish Ministry of Education, Science and Technology, the Extremadura Regional Government and FUNDECYT. It puts into practice a series of actions for the promotion of Research, Development and Innovation (RTD+i) within the Extremadura businesses by means of the following activities:

* Promotion and management of projects
* Technological surveillance and technical prospective
* Training and dissemination of RTD actions
* Transference of technology

The main aim is contribute to the technological emergence and excellence research in the enterprises in the region, in order to make them cope with the research and technological development activities, which are normally considered as an option. This action is complemented by a series of activities and actions aimed at improving cooperation between regional knowledge-generating entities (University, research and technology centres) and knowledge-demanding entities (enterprises).

Since the start of CODICES in October 2006, over 40 individual strategic innovation plans have been developed for SMEs in the region, and 7 technology transfer agreements have been signed. Fundecyt as intermediary and support organisation has provided the framework for these agreements and has developed the plans. But the mayor results in terms of collaboration for innovation is the role the organisation has played as intermediary in the setting up of more than 50 projects with regional SMEs.

4.   Conclusions

Continuous innovation is key to future survival and growth of businesses operating in increasingly competitive global markets. Innovation has become a necessary component of a successful business strategy among firms of all sizes.

Innovations are increasingly brought to the market by networks of firms, selected according to their comparative advantages, and operating in a coordinated manner. The need for collaborative R&D and commercialization is particularly critical for small and medium-sized enterprises (SMEs) hoping to make gains in terms of innovation.

But many SMEs find it difficult to collaborate or network with other organisations. While SMEs are often more flexible and responsive than larger organisations, they frequently lack the skills and resources necessary to collaborate or network.

R&D is widely regarded as one of the most important factors in the innovation process; it is therefore imperative to stimulate and encourage more collaborative projects in R&D through partnership schemes linking institutes, universities, and industry. Independent SME support organisations play a vital role in this scheme. The example from MENS, DELID and CODICES show the relevance of these organisations.

The combined interaction of the activities and projects related to training and the customized and personalized support of qualified staff has lead to results.

One of the keys for the success of the strategy is related to the fact that, it combines actions in the field of technology and transfer of knowledge, it does not loose sight of the needs related to the "softer" issues, mainly concerning people management, for example related to creating a basis for trust, such as the need for competencies regarding emotional intelligence; or related to the improvement of the motivation for collaboration, for example by increasing the management skills and communication skill (both of management and the organisational members). The innovation agents in charge of executing the tasks and activities of CODICES, used the training materials developed in MENS to create this environment, and will be taking into account the DELID results to construct eLearning that is well adjusted to the needs of SMEs.

The lessons learned demonstrate that the role of support organisations lays in the creation of a trustworthy environment, which focuses also on the human aspects of collaboration and innovation, are key.

References

[1] www.strategos.com, survey with senior executives in 2004 on the key barriers to effective innovation
[2] F.Bougrain,, B.Haudeville, Innovation, collaboration and SMEs internal research capacities. Research Policy, 2002 31(5): 735-747
[3] Carter, S. and Jones-Evans, D. (2000), "Enterprise and Small Business: Principles, Practice and Policy", Financial Times Prentice Hall.
[4] R. Alajärvi-Kauppi, P. Ervast, Intermediaries' role in Regional Innovation System - a descriptive study in less advantaged regions, http://www.congreszon.fi

Collaboration and the Knowledge Economy: Issues, Applications, Case Studies
P. Cunningham and M. Cunningham (Eds.)
IOS Press, 2008

Building Data Management Components for Business Applications

Craig THOMSON, Kostas KAVOUSSANAKIS, Arthur TREW
EPCC, The University Of Edinburgh, Edinburgh, EH9 3JZ, Scotland
Tel: +44 131 6505030, Fax: +44 131 6505555, Email: c.thomson@epcc.ed.ac.uk
kavousan@epcc.ed.ac.uk, a.trew@epcc.ed.ac.uk

Abstract: With the growing use of information technology-based tools across a broad spectrum of industries, it has become increasingly important to manage data effectively. These tools have also begun to offer the possibility of greater collaboration between organisations. This has led to new requirements to better share and integrate data. The BEinGRID[1] (Business Experiments in Grid) project has been set up to investigate the real requirements of industry as they use Grid software to develop their business. In the context of data management, the goal has been to enhance Grid middleware and bring its capabilities closer to those required by business. This paper describes some of the findings of this investigation and documents work already done to extend the OGSA-DAI middleware to meet the challenges identified in the business experiments.

Keywords: Grid, OGSA-DAI, BEinGRID, Data Management

1. Introduction

Data management is important in a wide variety of business situations. High tech companies are processing increasingly large and complex datasets for diverse tasks like ship design and geological modelling. Companies are also increasing their reliance on electronic storage and processing of information in the day-to-day running of their businesses. Even small organisations will often use electronic order and invoicing software.

The BEinGRID project was set up to explore the technology gap between the current uses of European funded Grid middleware and the businesses that could be using it. The goal is to increase the uptake of Grid software. One of the main ways of achieving this aim is by enhancing existing Grid middleware to make it better suited to the needs of business.

This paper examines business use cases for data management and the requirements that came from them. It then details some of the enhancements undertaken as part of the BEinGRID project to extend the OGSA-DAI[2] middleware. The results of the project will be illustrated by a use case, which describes how the OGSA-DAI middleware and extensions will be deployed in a real business scenario.

2. Objectives

The purpose of this paper is to highlight some of the innovative work done by the BEinGRID project in the area of data management. This involves both component-based extensions to existing Grid middleware as well as descriptions of underlying patterns which would be of use to businesses starting to look at Grid-based enhancements to their current business models. The overall objectives of the data management part of the project are:

- Analyse a number of business pilots to identify the gap between their needs and the capabilities of current Grid middleware
- Develop recommendations on the use of Grid middleware by business

- Extend and Enhance Grid middleware based on real problems

This work will help to make Grid middleware more relevant and accessible to a wider audience of business users. It aims to bridge the gap between the early adopters of Grid technology and the wider market of potential users. The results of the project will provide benefits for companies with data management problems in a broad range of business sectors and allows for greater exploitation of the research results developed within the EU.

3.   Methodology

An initial group of Business Experiments have been analysed from the point of view of data management. The project took the approach of selecting a number of business experiments to form the basis of the requirements capture. Though it was not possible to know at the time of selection how representative these experiments would be of the business landscape, they were chosen to cover a broad range of industrial sectors and areas of interest.

The experiments produced requirements, documentation and designs, which outlined the work they intended to do to achieve their business objectives. These documents were then analysed to extract the requirements that appeared more than once.

These common technical requirements were then refined and patterns were developed to describe useful generic behaviours that could address the requirements. The intention of these patterns was to make them generic enough to be applicable to more than one business sector, but specific enough to relate directly to Grid techniques.

A number of components have been developed to implement these design patterns. The components have been developed to extend the OGSA-DAI middleware. The choice of middleware to extend was based on in house expertise as well as on the analysis of the middleware being used by the business experiments.

Finally a second wave of experiments is being used to validate the utility of the components. The experiments will use the components produced during the project and provide feedback to motivate further development that is continuing in parallel.

4.   Requirements and Use Cases

The first step in producing useful Grid middleware extensions was to identify the important data management requirements and use cases. Eighteen Business Experiments were analysed and they produced a number of requirements. These included:

- Ease of use of middleware
- Allowing middleware to interface with existing software
- The ability to react to changes in a database

One of the experiments which provides a motivation for why a number of these requirements is useful is Business Experiment 24 – GRID2(B2B). This experiment is part of the second wave and aims to develop an extension to existing Business-to-Business (B2B) software.

The Experiment will allow B2B platforms to significantly evolve from the current state-of-the art. Currently data and process synchronisation between the participants of the B2B network requires a human operator, logging in on a portal or generating and processing files that represent supply-chain activities. What is missing is an affordable B2B platform extension to automate this synchronisation. While bigger companies can adopt new software, SMEs can only afford synchronisation if they can retain their original (legacy) infrastructure.

The technical partners of the project are EPCC, CINECA and Joinet. Joinet is the developer of the MaNeM[3] B2B platform which is being used in this experiment. In addition three of Joinet's customers are part of the consortium. Ducati, who make sports motorcycles, and PM and Bentivogli, two of Ducati's suppliers.

MaNeM is used to manage the flow of information between partners in a B2B network. Different legacy software exists to perform supply-chain operations inside each company. The B2B platform provides workflows that manage the interaction between the companies but data exists in parallel in the legacy systems and the same information has to be inputted twice. This is achieved either through the use of a custom script, which is run manually or by data entry by an employee at the company.

The goal of the experiment is to produce a stand alone extension to B2B platforms (not just MaNeM, but potentially others). This extension will allow information changes in one system to automatically update the B2B platform and other legacy systems.

To achieve the goal, a new application is being developed. To succeed it needs to:

- Be flexible
    o The intention is to market the solution to multiple B2B platform vendors
- Interface with existing legacy applications
    o One of the key benefits to the SMEs in B2B networks is that they keep their legacy systems
- React to changes in the legacy system data
    o The information from the legacy system should be automatically propagated to the B2B platform
- Be easy to set up
    o The IT providers of the SMEs involved in a B2B should not have to spend a lot of time deploying the software

These requirements are critical to the success of the experiment and match well with requirements that came from the first phase of business experiments.

For example one first wave experiment was developing an extension to a point of sale application for pizza shops. One of their requirements was that the extension would be easy to install by the technicians who maintained the existing point of sale infrastructure.

In another case there was a requirement to be able to react to updates to data. The particular example here was a travel agent and a tour operator. The travel agent might book a tour with a customer. They would then have to manually enter customer information once for their own records and again to add the customer to the tour operators system. The desire was to have an automatic method of keeping the customer information synchronised.

5.   Design Patterns

After examining the use cases and requirements of the business experiments a number of design patterns were identified. They describe generic architectures, which can be used to solve some of the data management problems that emerged from the analysis of the business experiments.

The first two design patterns implemented as components are the Data Source Publisher and the Primary-Secondary Replicator.

5.1   Data Source Publisher

This pattern describes a mechanism for allowing data to be made available for access at another location. It also provides a layer that can be used to translate to or abstract the data type. The goal is to allow an existing system to be grid enabled so that it can be accessed via other grid middleware components.

The pattern works by adding a component, which communicates with the existing data source. This component provides another interface, which allows the information to be accessed remotely. The intention is that this pattern allows any existing applications to use their existing procedures to access data.

5.2   Primary-Secondary Replicator

This pattern allows a backup of a data source to be prepared and made available if the primary data source fails. This allows a more robust system: if one machine goes down for some reason, the secondary replicas can continue to provide a service.

The underlying idea is identifying a change in one database and reacting to it. This very generic pattern describes an event-based reaction to a change in data. Like the data source publisher, this pattern also allows for an interaction with an existing system. Actions which affect the data source can be monitored and actions taken which communicate with other remote systems.

These design patterns provide further motivation to develop these components. They describe a broader setting to help ensure that the enhancements made to existing middleware through the development of new components are done in a generic way.

6.   Component Development

Once the design patterns had been established the next step was to produce components that provide concrete implementations of the patterns. The first two components have been developed. They provide enhancements to the OGSA-DAI middleware. Another requirement for these components was that they be general purpose and flexible.

The components meet the requirements identified by analyzing the first phase of business experiments and contribute to the solution being developed for the GRID2(B2B) experiment.

6.1   Technology Background

The base on which the components have been developed is the OGSA-DAI middleware. The Open Grid Services Architecture - Data Access and Integration (OGSA-DAI) project, currently funded as part of the Open Middleware Infrastructure Institute UK (OMII-UK), aims to provide the e-Science community with a middleware solution to provide access to and integration of data for applications working across administrative domains. OGSA-DAI offers services that add data access and integration capabilities to the core functionality of service-oriented Grids. Structured data resources, whether these are databases, files, or other types of data, can be made available to Grid applications.

OGSA-DAI provides access to a variety of different database types and allows data to be published via a web service interface. It also contains a variety of activities, which allow data access, transformation and delivery. These activities are also an extension point of the middleware so that it can be customised to meet the particular requirements of a given project.

6.2   Data Source Publisher Component

A key requirement for the uptake of a new technology is the ease of adoption. Many companies whose core business is not information technology are turning to it to help improve their competitiveness and efficiency. One way to help them do this is to make it easy to use the new technology. The goal of the Data Source Publisher is not to extend the existing OGSA-DAI functionality, which already implements the underlying Data Source Publisher design pattern. Instead it automates the deployment procedure. This addresses the ease of use requirement of the GRID2(B2B) experiment and will be used to reduce the complexity of installation.

The Data Source Publisher provides a simple, GUI based installer, which deploys OGSA-DAI and publishes a data source via web services. The real benefit over following the instructions in the user guide is not a technical one. It is much more convenient and requires much less effort on the part of the person installing the middleware if everything they need is bundled together and can be installed in a few simple steps. In order to install OGSA-DAI and deploy it on a computer you will need to download and install correct versions of its pre-requisites as well as database drivers.

By using the Data Source Publisher you reduce these requirements and simplify the process to install OGSA-DAI. You no longer need to use a number of command line tools, everything is handled inside a GUI installer. You have one download which contains the correct versions of all the software required to set up OGSA-DAI. All you have to do is configure the component for your application.

6.3   OGSA-DAI Triggers

The Primary-Secondary replicator pattern was defined in the analysis of business experiments. Replication is already handled natively inside many relational databases. There are limitations however when trying to move information between databases developed by different vendors. The more general idea of replication is reacting to a change in a database and performing an action that affects something else (another database for example). The OGSA-DAI Trigger component seeks to enhance OGSA-DAI by providing a mechanism for an OGSA-DAI workflow to be executed when a database is modified.

By providing a general mechanism for reacting to a change in a database, the OGSA-DAI Trigger component allows all the database access, transformation, and data delivery activities of OGSA-DAI to be used in response to a database change. An OGSA-DAI workflow can be executed automatically whenever a relational database changes.

This component will be used to help interface with different B2B platforms in GRID2(B2B). It provides access to a flexible grid middleware for data management and a mechanism, which allows the B2B extension to react to changes in the legacy system.

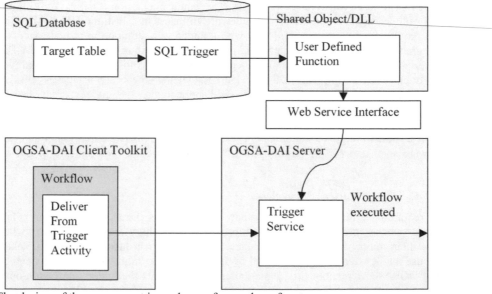

The design of the component is made up of a number of parts:
- An SQL Trigger
- A User Defined Function
- A Web Service Trigger Event Interface
- An OGSA-DAI Service and associated Activities

They provide a mechanism for notifying OGSA-DAI that a database has changed, and allow OGSA-DAI workflows to be stored and executed when the changes occur.

6.3.1 SQL Trigger

The first step in notifying OGSA-DAI that a database event has occurred is to be able to execute an operation whenever the database changes. SQL offers this in the form of triggers. Triggers operate on tables and allow SQL statements to be run when items are added to, updated in or deleted from a table in a database.

In order to minimise the chance of errors and to make it as easy as possible to deploy, the component builds a script that contains the SQL commands required to set up the trigger.

6.3.2 User Defined Function

A conventional SQL Trigger will allow you to run standard SQL commands. No built in command will let us notify OGSA-DAI of the database changes. SQL offers an extension mechanism for its database through user defined functions. This user defined function can then be added to a table and used like the standard set of functions (like SUM() for example). A function has been written to notify a trigger web service that something has changed in the database. It also communicates the values of the changed row. This user defined function is called from the custom trigger.

6.3.3 OGSA-DAI Trigger Web Service

In order to tie in the mechanism with OGSA-DAI we need a target for the trigger information and a place to retrieve it from. In order to do this we need a new Web Service. The UDF can call it directly to notify OGSA-DAI when a table row has changed.

This web service interface also allows standard OGSA-DAI workflows to be submitted by the component user. They are stored along with an identifier for the trigger they should be associated with. When a trigger fires and a notification is sent, any matching workflows are automatically executed.

6.3.4 OGSA-DAI Trigger Activities

The event trigger workflow requires a method of accessing the row information that has been passed into the web service. In order to do this a DeliverFromTrigger activity has been written which presents the row information in an OGSA-DAI format. This activity may form part of the workflow submitted to the web service interface.

7. Results

The outcomes of the initial phase of development are:
- Identification of common requirements from initial Business Experiments
- Description of Design Patterns based on these requirements
- Development of 2 new components to help meet the requirements
- Validation of these components by a new Business Experiment

They provide an analysis of the gaps in existing Grid middleware and their application to a variety of business sectors. They also provide the first steps in closing these gaps and making data management Grid middleware more relevant to business users.

The following key, business-focused requirements have been identified:
- Ease of use
- Integration with legacy systems
- Reacting to changes in an existing database

The Data Source Publisher aims to address ease of use of Grid middleware by simplifying the installation process. The OGSA-DAI Trigger component assists in the integration of existing legacy software with middleware and provides a mechanism to react to changes in an existing database.

The requirements have already been validated by the selection of GRID2(B2B) which is a compelling example of the generality and utility of the components.

8.   Future Work

In addition to the components already produced as part of the experiment, further development is planned. More components will be produced which will further extend the capabilities of the OGSA-DAI middleware.

8.1   Query Translator

The Query Translator helps integrate the databases from different companies together. It does this by allowing the users to produce different views onto the same data. The underlying databases can remain different, but a common schema can be presented on top of the actual database. This allows a company to present a different view of its data to different customers without changing the application they use internally.

This component builds on top of OGSA-DAI. It will allow OGSA-DAI to present an SQL View on to a database that it exposes. This will allow two similar, but not identical, tables to present a common view of their data.

8.2   JDBC Driver Interface to OGSA-DAI

As we have seen, the requirement to interface with existing systems is important. One way of allowing this is to implement an interface, which the legacy application already supports. With the addition of a JDBC driver interface in front of OGSA-DAI it would be possible to very quickly provide data integration to an application, which already supports JDBC with few changes to that application.

The application could continue to use the same interface as before, but could now support integrated data sources through OGSA-DAI.

9.   Business Benefits

A new technology is only of benefit if there is a market for the product, and that product meets the needs of its intended users. In order to better explore the potential benefits of some of the data management components developed as part of BEinGRID, we will again look at the GRID2(B2B) use case.

The GRID2(B2B) experiment will allow the B2B platform provider to enhance its market share by providing a more advanced service. It will allow the manufacturer and suppliers to improve the communication between their organisations. Finally it presents an opportunity to diversify into selling the technology to other B2B providers. It will do this by extensive use of the components developed as part of the BEinGRID project.

The OGSA-DAI trigger component provides functionality that the current B2B software does not provide. It allows for the automatic update of information across organisational boundaries. This allows the B2B provider to give a more advanced service.

The trigger component also increases the speed and frequency with which information is exchanged. It automates the process and minimises the risk of human error. This allows for a more up to date picture of the state of the B2B collaboration. This has benefits in efficiency. In a manufacturing scenario, such as the one in GRID2(B2B) it is important to have up to date delivery information to ensure that the production line is optimally filled.

In order for the B2B platform extensions to be successful, the ICT suppliers as well as the B2B platform developer have to use it. In order to make adoption of the extensions easy, it is essential that the non-Grid software companies can easily deploy and adapt the software. The use of the Data Source Publisher will simplify the installation process.

10. Conclusions

This paper demonstrates the improvements that have been made to Grid-based middleware for data management as part of BEinGRID. It also shows the impact the resulting components can make in a real business scenario. The GRID2(B2B) experiment gives a business-focused use case to highlight the potential benefits of using Grid technology in a business setting. The integration of specific components, Data Source Publisher and OGSA-DAI Trigger, with the OGSA-DAI middleware demonstrates how innovative work can be translated into a real product.

It is intended that the results of BEinGRID be of use to businesses looking at Grid solutions for the first time. To aid knowledge transfer and improve the take-up of Grid Technology, this information will be made available via the Gridipedia website [4].

Acknowledgements

This work is supported by the EU project BEinGRID, sponsored by the European Union under contract number IST-034702.

References

[1] BEinGRID, (2008). BEinGRID project information [online]. Available: http://www.beingrid.eu [accessed 11 July 2008]
[2] OGSA-DAI, (2008) OGSA-DAI information [online]. Available: http://www.ogsadai.org.uk [accessed 11 July 2008]
[3] MaNeM, (2008), MaNeM [online]. Available: http://www.joinetspa.com/supply-chain/prodottosoluzioni.cfm?wid_cat=14&wid_pro=8 [accessed 11 July 2008]
[4] Gridipedia: The European Grid Marketplace, (2008). Gridipedia repository [online]. Available: http://www.gridipedia.eu [accessed 11 July 2008]

Collaboration and the Knowledge Economy: Issues, Applications, Case Studies
P. Cunningham and M. Cunningham (Eds.)
IOS Press, 2008

Support for Client-Server based License Management Schemes in the Grid

Christian SIMMENDINGER[1], Ottmar KRÄMER-FUHRMANN[2],
Yona RAEKOW[2], Hubert HERENGER[3]
[1]*T-Systems SfR, Pfaffenwaldring 38-40, Stuttgart, 70569, Germany*
[2]*Fraunhofer SCAI, Schloss Birlinghoven, Sankt Augustin, 53754, Germany*
[3]*HLRS, Nobelstrasse 19, Stuttgart, 70550, Germany*

Abstract: License Management is currently not supported in any Grid middleware. Since most small and medium enterprises (SME) use commercial applications with associated licensing issues, this lack of support is becoming a major obstacle for the commercial exploitation of these middleware and the corresponding Grid infrastructure. In order to resolve this obstacle, we have designed and implemented a complete grid-friendly License Management architecture, which supports the currently used client-server license schemes. In this paper we discuss the process of eliciting license management related requirements, the subsequently derived common components and their corresponding design patterns as well as details of implementation patterns.

1. Introduction

Over the last few years, Grid technology has evolved from a technology designed largely for the needs of the High Performance Computing (HPC) community towards an open framework supporting the general business domain. In order to foster the adoption of Grid technology in European business and society BEinGRID [1] has gathered the requirements for a commercial Grid environment from a first wave of 18 business experiments. One of the key elements derived from this elicitation of requirements is support for commercial applications from independent software vendors (ISV) in grid environments. In order to meet the requirements of an on-demand computing scenario a pay-per-use License Management scheme needs to be established.

1.1 Background: ISV simulation applications in industry.

Especially small and medium enterprises (SME) from the engineering community stand to profit from pay-per-use HPC Grid scenarios. Very few of these SMEs however maintain their own simulation applications. Instead commercial applications from independent software vendors (ISV) are commonly used with an associated client-server based licensing. For the latter typically FlexNet available from Acresso [2] (formerly Macrovision) is employed, which is the quasi-standard in this area. The authorization of these client-server based license mechanisms relies on an IP-centric scheme - a client within a specific range of IP-adresses is allowed to access the license server.

1.2 Gap Analysis

Due to this IP-centric authorization, arbitrary users of shared (Grid) resources may access an exposed license server, irrespective of whether or not they are authorized to do so. Secure and authorized access to a local or remote license server in grid environments therefore has not been possible so far. The use of commercial ISV applications in grid environments therefore was not possible either. The here presented License Management (LM) architecture resolves this problem. Amongst other features the LM architecture also provides a cost-unit based accounting with the possibility to check validity (e.g. in terms of available funding) of license accounts at job submission time. Neither of these features so far existed. The solution is generic and independent of any grid middleware.

1.3   Business Impact

The lack of a grid solution for client-server based license management readily implies that the vast majority of users from industry has not been able to use their ISV applications in grid environments. The here presented license management architecture thus potentially increases the grid market size in the area of on-demand computing by industry by a large factor.

1.4   The Pay-per-Use model

Prices for licenses for ISV simulation applications in the area of HPC typically exceed the cost of correspondingly required resources (CPU, memory, filespace) by more than two orders of magnitude -- a single license can cost up to 100.000 Euros per year. A pay-per-use model therefore seems to be required in a order to provide a satisfactory on-demand computing scenario with a licensed application from an ISV.

Currently licenses are issued on a yearly basis: Customers buy a fixed number of licenses, with associated features and an included support. The generated revenue for the ISV therefore is predictable and stable. This business model also guarantees that the provided simulation applications are always in line with the requirements of the end-users: There is a close dialog between ISV and end-user.

Contrary to this, in a pay-per use scenario there is no predictable revenue for the ISV – and unless the ISV is also the license service provider (LSP) – the ISVs would loose the direct contact to their end-users. Moreover the currently established business model (yearly licenses) implies a substantial over-provisioning of licenses: End-users need to buy more licenses than they require on a daily basis in order to satisfy their peak requirements. With a pay-per-use scenario this over-provisioning immediately becomes obsolete with a corresponding loss of revenue for the ISVs. On the other hand a pay-per-use model would create a new source of revenue for ISVs, because SME which so far could not afford to purchase licenses can now access the licenses on a pay-per-use basis. Additionally large customers become able to dramatically increase the number of licenses during peak-demand periods.

These contrasting business models make a direct transition towards a pay-per-use license model on a new technology basis rather unrealistic. Instead ISVs will need to constantly evaluate and refine the evolving new business models in a non-interruptive transition on the basis of currently used technology.

From the perspective of the proposed license management architecture this implies that the architecture needs to be able to support a fluent transition from currently used technology towards a grid-friendly pay per use scheme. The here proposed solution provides a solid basis for that transition.

2.   Objectives

The purpose of this paper is to highlight the relevance of license management for the Grid - - where we refer to the introduction -- and to convey the results of the use-case and requirements analysis performed in BEinGRID with respect to license management. From this analysis design patterns and component descriptions for a new license management architecture have been derived. We also describe implementation patterns for the license management components as well as correspondingly developed components.

3.   Methodology

A number of common requirements have been elicited from the initial wave of 18 business experiments in the BEinGRID project. Based upon this analysis design patterns and component descriptions for a client-server based license management scheme have been derived. Implementation patterns are discussed and a reference implementation is presented.

3.1   Requirements

The following license related requirements have been elicited:

1. **Gridification of currently used License Management Systems**: Support for license management was required for four different middlewares: GRIA, GT4, UNICORE and gLite – and all of the four business experiments required support for FlexNet. Since predictably no LSP or ISV is going to support four different middlewares we hence aimed for a generic middleware independent solution, which would support an arbitrary client-server based license scheme including FlexNet. In fact the solution is even usable in a non-Grid LSP context and hence is able to cover the complete spectrum of required scenarios. There are some side-implications with respect to accounting associated with the above requirement: Whereas in the non-Grid scenario the bill already has been paid in advance – and accounting plays a minor role – the pay-per-use model would at least need to support a flexible cost unit based accounting rather than an identity bound accounting: The reason is that usually institutions or research groups own the licenses – not their individual members. Also licenses are typically used in a specific accounting context, namely cost units.

2. **Limited LSP Capability**: The required fluent transition to a pay-per-use model – with respect to the underlying business model – made it likely that at least for a short transitional period (where 'short' can mean: up to a decade) the ISV will also assume the role of the license service provider (LSP) for all its customers: ISVs need to be able to quickly implement and refine the evolving new business models. This immediately implied that scalability of the license service would become an issue. In this transitional period the ISV would have to maintain potentially several thousand simultaneous connections to the FlexNet server. (FlexNet itself is able to handle this amount of connections).

3. **Grid License Models**: The FlexNet scheme (floating licenses from a single – possibly redundant – server) or other Client-Server schemes are limited in their scope and scalability. An extension of such a scheme to a scenario where licenses are offered as standard resources in the Grid therefore seems to be a logical step. This scenario readily implies that licenses have to be scheduled like other resources e.g. networks or CPUs. Licenses are typically an even more precious and expensive resource than compute-power. It therefore is highly important that licenses are not unnecessarily blocked by queued jobs or that jobs, which already have allocated their computing-resources do not get blocked by missing license-keys. Interfaces to e.g. Grid schedulers therefore are needed. An extension of that scenario, where license owners are allowed to re-sell their licenses on a LSP basis should be feasible with respect to technology. This scenario extension would, however, certainly require the cooperation of ISVs. An even bigger step for the ISVs – but maybe a logical one – would be to entirely drop the concept of selling a yearly license and to instead introduce a -- probably token based – system where licenses are accounted and billed on a per job basis.

3.2 Common Capabilities

1. **License Management related Extension of Job Description and Submission**: This Common Capability covers the extension of the job description and its submission with respect to license management. A user needs to provide details about the requested licenses – including authorization – as well as the accounting context. This Common Capability (CC) allows a user to request license resources in a similar manner as currently implemented in Grid middlewares for any other resource (cpu, memory, etc). The resources here can be either own licenses, licenses provided by the service provider or an external LSP.

2. **License Management related Authorization for Job Submission**: This Common Capability covers authorization mechanisms required with respect to License Resource Requests. The sole deviation from current standard authorisation mechanisms is the type of resource, namely whether or not a user is entitled to use a specific license server, specific features of the licensed software or whether limits exist with respect to the number of licenses. In complete analogy possible solutions range from simple locally maintained lists or pin / tan mechanisms up to a full integration into identity management systems like Shibboleth or VOMS with explicit requests to home organizations the of users and/or third party license service providers (LSP) or even requests to License Brokers.

Figure 1:License Management related Authorization

3. **License Management related Scheduler Extension**: This Common Capability covers the extension of a local scheduler. If access to the license servers has been granted, the scheduler needs to schedule the job – according to policies and – possible remote – resources – and to pass the information about the license request details to the resource management system.

4. **License Management related Resource Management Extension:** This Common Capability covers the extension of a local resource management system. In a batch prologue the resource management can dynamically reconfigure the license proxy in order to grant access for a specific userID at the assigned – ideally dedicated – local resources. Correspondingly in a batch epilogue the proxy is reconfigured in order to prohibit non-authorized access. At this point security of access to the license server is transferred from a – e.g. certificate based – authentication/authorization level to the required network level security at which e.g. FlexLM operates. However, this is only required if there is no additional run-time authorization at the license server.

5. **License Proxy:** All external accesses from dedicated local resources are re-routed via to the proxy, which can allow or reject these connections (see License Management related Resource Management Extension) and can re-route this request via a proxy-chain (including run-time authorization) to the remote license server. The proxy and possibly its upstream counterpart both log access time, duration and accounting context.

6. **License Management related Accounting and Billing**: This Common Capability covers the Accounting and Billing of licenses. In order to produce the complete accounting log, information from both the proxy (userID / time-stamp) and the license server (userID / time-stamp, number of licenses, license features) are required. The actual details of billing and accounting not only are depending on middleware, but also

on the underlying business model. Depending on whether licenses are owned by the user, the service provider, an external static LSP or obtained via a Grid broker, the exchange and assembly of the actual accounting and billing information will differ.

7. **Encapsulation of License Server** This Common Capability relates to the integration of existing license servers. It not just addresses a possible encapsulation as a web service but more generally an integration of the license server into the respective Grid middlewares. Remark: In our License Management Architecture Implementation the upstream proxy partly provides this encapsulation. (Run-time authorization)

3.3   License Management Architecture

The License Management Architecture components (LM-Job Description and Submission, , LM-Authorization, LM-Proxy, LM–Monitor, LM-Accounting) are designed to provide a complete License Management for FlexNet (or more generally: client-server license models) based Independent Software Vendor (ISV) applications in Grid environments.

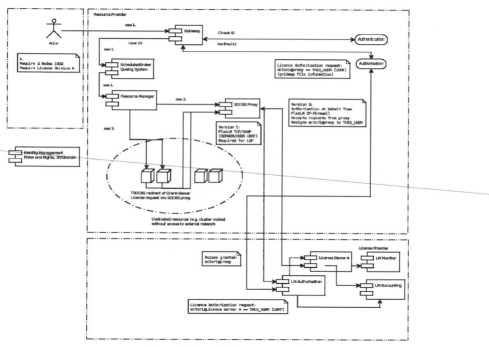

Figure 2:License Management Architecture

Job submission and description are extended with respect to the list of resources (license server) and possibly required authorization credentials. ***License authorization*** then is performed at submit time via a query to a remote service. In a ***first step*** license authorization will be based on a local access list (ACL). Since this latter functionality is frequently required for local usage in a non-Grid context, (e.g. any linux cluster which is shared between different organizations) we will maintain two different versions of license authorization. In a **second step** an optional/alternative run-time authorization (at the remote upstream proxy) via a pin/tan mechanism is implemented. Details of this implementation are presented in Section 4. Usage of licenses is accounted by the ***LM accounting*** module. The ***LM monitor*** monitors the status of available licenses and upon request returns this status to higher-level services like license schedulers/brokers or an SLA monitor.

4. Technology Description

Industrial environments typically rely on commercial applications of ISVs with an associated License Management – usually FlexNet from Acresso [2], which is the de-facto standard in this area. FlexNet has a closed API, is proprietary and based on a simple client-server mechanism. The FlexNet scheme allows 'floating' licenses, which are not bound to a specific host. Rather they are allocated dynamically to arbitrary hosts. Licenses then are checked out at the license server when an application starts and checked in when it ends.

In principle FlexNet therefore is suitable for usage in a Grid environment. There are, however major security and identity issues with respect to the access to the license server in a Grid environment. For example the FlexNet software is able to filter legal and illegal accesses based on the host IP, but is *not* able to grant access on the basis of user/group certificates. This implies that on every Grid site an unauthorized user could check out and use an arbitrary number of licenses once the corresponding license server is exposed.

In order to support this standard (or in general: any client-server license management scheme) we propose to transparently reroute the encrypted socket-based communication between client and server via a SOCKS proxy-chain. The communication from license client then can be transparently forwarded (via a socksified job shell) to a remote upstream proxy and then to the remote license server. The run-time authorization at the upstream proxy is handled via a PIN and associated encrypted one-time passwords. The PIN here represents a license account and can be used to provide the accounting context. License owners (typically institutions) can set up an arbitrary number of these license accounts under a billing account. This mechanism allows institutions or research groups to share access to licenses and to use licenses in a cost unit based accounting context. A self-imposed budget-control for pay-per-use scenarios will be available. The handling of the one-time passwords (generation of tan lists, license accounts and their properties) is implemented as a web service. A design of a portal which enables users to access these web services, conveniently share accounts, automatically extract one-time passwords and submit correspondingly modified jobs is currently in progress.

The local SOCKS proxy (at the service provider site) additionally can be re-configured on a per-job basis by the local resource management systems, thus providing an additional layer of security. The license management architecture is complemented with extended functionalities for job submission and description, license accounting, billing and a License Monitor. Information from FlexNet itself here needs to be synchronized with information from the authorization module in order to provide a complete cost unit based accounting.

5. Developments

5.1 Development

A reference implementation of the license management architecture is currently developed..The implementation of this architecture provides an encapsulation of a standard FlexNet license manager and includes functionalities like authorisation, monitoring and accounting. The technologies that have been used to develop these components are standard Web Services and SOCKS SS5[3] proxies (both local and upstream). The authentication PIN/TAN license scheme is based on OTP Password [4].

5.2 Availability

The "LM-Proxy Standalone" component and the components "LM Job description and Submission for GT4 and Unicore 6" have been released and are available under [5]. The complementing parts of the license management architecture (LM Authorization, LM

Monitor, LM Accounting) will be available by the end of August 2008. All components will be licensed under GPL and will be accessible through [5].

6.   Results

A few selected components of this architecture like the stand-alone proxy and the modified job submission for GT4 and Unicore 6 have been implemented. They have been validated and successfully used by business experiments in BEinGRID. The remaining components of the license management architecture (authorization, monitoring and accounting) will permit secure authorization without the need for out-of-band agreements with potential resource providers. It will allow license providers to map users (or rather: their shared accounts) to the license usage and therefore enable license providers to create the actual bills with a detailed cost-unit based accounting. It will allow end-users to split their license budget in terms of cost-units and to restrict the corresponding usage (Budget control).

7.   Business Benefits

The license management architecture will allow the use of commercial ISV applications in the Grid. The solution is not bound to any specific middleware. Since it also is a non-interruptive solution, which merely complements currently exiting license mechanisms, it will allow the ISVs to extend their business models with respect to pay-per-use in a fluent transition. This eventually established pay-per-use model then in turn will permit all customers who need to use licensed ISV applications to make cost-efficient use of on-demand Grid infrastructures in order to dramatically speed up their design phase and/or quality assurance, to minimize the risks and/or to improve the quality of their products.

A good example for this need to use commercial ISV applications in computing on-demand grid environments are small engineering companies which occasionally need to satisfy peak demands in the area of simulation.

8.   Conclusions

We have succeeded in designing and implementing a novel license management architecture which supports the entire class of client-server based license mechanisms in grid environments. This includes the proprietary FlexNet solution of Acresso[4]. Since this support is a pre-requisite for the use of commercial ISV applications in grid environments, the solution will substantially enlarge the potential grid market size in the area of on-demand computing by industry. The license management architecture also supports the required non-interruptive transition towards a pay-per-use business model for licenses.

The architecture is centered around a dynamically re-configurable SOCKS proxy infrastructure. It is designed to provide excellent scalability. The solution is generic and – with minor modifications (job description and submission) – compatible with all current middlewares. It is also suitable for License Service Provisioning (LSP) in a non-Grid context. Since it provides a very high level of security we think that this solution will play a very significant part in paving the way towards a pay-per-use license model.

References

[1] BEinGRID – Business Experiments in Grid, www.beingrid.eu (as of 08.05.2008)
[2] Acresso Software, www.acresso.com (as of 08.05.2008)
[3] SOCKS SS5, ss5.sourceforge.net (as of 08.05.2008)
[4] PAM_SOTP, www.cavecanen.org/cs/projects/pam_sotp/ (as of 08.05.2008)
[5] LM Architecture, gforge.beingrid.eu (as of 08.05.2008)

Section 7

Mobility – Issues, Applications & Technologies

Section 7.1

Issues

Collaboration and the Knowledge Economy: Issues, Applications, Case Studies   1273
P. Cunningham and M. Cunningham (Eds.)
IOS Press, 2008

Location-Aware Access Control for Mobile Information Systems

Michael DECKER

Institute AIFB, University of Karlsruhe (TH), Englerstraße 11, 76 128 Karlsruhe, Germany
Tel: +49 721 608-0, Fax: + 49 721 608 5998, Email: decker@aifb.uni-karlsruhe.de

Abstract: Location-Aware Access Control (LAAC) means to consider a mobile device's location when making the decision if a request to perform an operation on a particular resource should be granted or not. This is an approach to tackle specific security-related challenges that come along with the employment of mobile information systems but it can also help to support the interaction between user and mobile device in a context-aware sense. For the realization of LAAC two things are essential: the capability to determine a mobile user's location and an appropriate data model to formulate statements about which operations he or she is allowed to perform on which resources at a particular place. Therefore in our paper we first discuss several locating technologies from the perspective of LAAC. Afterwards we introduce a novel location-aware access control model. One special feature of our model is that it supports dynamic location-constraints, i.e. constraints that can only be determined during the runtime of a mobile application.

1. Introduction

Distributed information systems with portable computers like notebooks or PDAs that may have access to stationary backend systems over wireless data communication are called mobile information systems (MIS). Such systems have a great potential for many application scenarios since they can provide computer support almost "anytime, anywhere".

However portable computers are prone to theft and loss which is occasionally brought to the public's awareness by incidences that hit the headlines, e.g. cases like that reported in [15] when notebooks owned by public institutions with sensitive person-related data get lost. Technical measurements against such mishaps are encrypted storage of data (e.g. encrypted hard disks in notebooks), biometric authentication to unlock mobile computers (most notably readers for fingerprints) or triggering deletion of all data stored on a lost device by sending a special command message (so called "kill pill"). In this paper we discuss location-aware access control (LAAC) as another solution to tackle this problem. Access control is concerned with limiting the access to resources that are managed by information systems, e.g. making the decision which operations (e.g. write, read) a user can perform on a particular object stored in a file system or which services he may use (e.g. printing service, querying database) [1]. It is usually based on the consideration of the user's identity as well as individual permissions assigned to the resources under control. LAAC also evaluates the user's current location. So policies like "a nurse is only allowed to access the electronic health record using a PDA while staying in the ward" can be enforced.

But LAAC is also beneficial for reasons beyond security aspects: due to their size mobile computers dispose only over relatively constrained means for user interaction; the display is tiny and of limited quality (contrast, resolution, and colour depth) and data input is cumbersome because there is no full keyboard. One idea to mitigate this is called "context-awareness" [7] and comprehends the evaluation of information about the user's current situation to support his interaction by reducing the number of interaction steps required to perform a particular task. LAAC can be "misused" to hide buttons, options and data sets on the graphical user interface that are not needed at particular locations and thus can help to reduce the data that has to be presented on the display and the navigations steps. Imposing location-aware access restrictions can be motivated by several considerations:

- It may not be plausible to access particular resources outside certain location, e.g. a travelling salesman doesn't need access to a customer record if he stays outside the respective sales district.
- At some places it might be deemed as to dangerous to have access to confidential resources, e.g. at frequented public places, outside a company's premises or in countries where espionage has to be feared.
- Some functions of a MIS may be only useful in the proximity of certain facilities, e.g. remote control of devices installed in rooms like machines, multimedia-equipment or air-condition.
- Staying at particular locations constitutes a form of authentication if physical access to that location is secured, e.g. an area, building or part of a building secured by human guards or doors. In this case LAAC may obviate the need for identity-based authentication and thus providing anonymous access to MIS.

There are already some simple forms of LAAC that can be found in practice: movies on DVD can be protected by the so called region code so discs can be produced that can only be viewed with hardware players manufactured for the European market. There are a few personal navigation devices on the market that are protected by a password which can be only reprogrammed at the place where the initial password was set. Payments with credit cards may be rejected if the payment is attempted at a place where the card holder usually doesn't stay, e.g. shopping in a foreign country or online payment using an internet terminal with an IP-address originating from a foreign country. In some countries there are pay-TV decoders which query the decryption key over a telephone line; the provider will only sent the key if the telephone connection lies in the respective country.

Two things are essential for the realization of advanced forms of LAAC: the possibility to locate a mobile device and an appropriate data model to formulate access restrictions with regard to locations; such data models are called access control models (ACM). In our paper we want to introduce a new location-aware ACM (LAACM) which builds upon the metaphor of different classes of documents. One special feature of our model is the ability to formulate dynamic location-constraints, i.e. location-constraints that can only be determined during the runtime of a process but not in advance at design time. This feature isn't supported by any LAACM we are aware of. We will also discuss several techniques for locating with respect to their suitability for LAAC. Again this aspect is neglected in the pertinent literature.

The remainder of our paper is structured as follows: in section two we first cover the basic models for access control and then discuss the most important LAACMs. Section three is dedicated to locating techniques for LAAC. In section four we introduce an LAACM along with a location-model whereby the focus lies on the possibility to formulate dynamic location constraints. Finally the paper ends with a conclusion given in section five.

2. Models for Access Control

2.1 Basic Models

Access control is the process of determining if a subject's request to perform a particular operation on an information system's resource should be granted or not. Subjects are human users or programs acting on behalf of a user; resources are files, database objects or services. The software component that is responsible for the decision if a request should be allowed or not is termed "reference monitor". There are three basic types of access controls

[1]: discretionary access control (DAC), mandatory access control (MAC) and role-based access control (RBAC). DAC is the approach used by most contemporary operation systems: a resource has an owner who has all rights which he can grant to other subjects; the access decision is made based on the identity of the subject and his rights on that object. For MAC the reference monitor evaluates system-wide rules to make a decision according to labels assigned to subjects as well as objects. These labels might denote several security levels and the rules enforce policies like "a subject with clearance confidential is not allowed to read an object with classification top secret". MAC originally was developed for military systems but meanwhile there are also implementations for civil usage available, e.g. SELinux or AppArmor. RBAC's basic notion is it to have roles that represent job descriptions within organizations, e.g. "manager", "secretary" or "accountant".

These roles are collections of permissions that are assigned to subjects whereas a permission is the right to perform a particular operation on a particular object. It is not allowed to assign permissions directly to a user. The great advantage of RBAC is that it saves a lot of administrative work: if a subject's job within an organization changes (e.g. employee hired or promoted) the administrator just has to adjust the roles assigned to this subject and not to assign all the individual permissions.

2.2 Models for Location-Aware Access Control

In literature several proposals for LAACM can be found; most of them are variants of RBAC. The basic idea to obtain a location-aware RBAC model is to switch off certain RBAC entities if the user stays outside predefined locations. For example in the GEO-RBAC model [5] roles can be disabled depending on the user's location. In the SRBAC-Model [8] the assignment of permissions to a role is active only at defined locations. In LoT-RBAC [16] location-restrictions can be bound to the user-role-assignment, to roles alone and to the role-permission assignment. There are similar LAACMs (e.g. GRBAC, DRBAC, LRBAC) but due to space limitations we can't discuss them here.

Ray and Kumar [13] developed a location-aware model for MAC. In their model security levels are assigned to individual locations. A user is then not allowed to use the MIS if his clearance is below a location's classification and resources can only be accessed at locations that have a classification at least as high as the resource. Leonhardt and Magee [10] propose a location-aware DAC model to formulate policies that express under which conditions a user is allowed to learn about another user's location.

3. Technologies for Location Determination

LAAC relies on the ability to determine a mobile device's location, of course. There are many methods to locate a mobile device, see [9] for an overview. Two generic approaches for locating can be distinguished (see also figure 1): in the case of self-locating the mobile device calculates its position based on signals emitted by a locating network (e.g. satellites, base stations or beacons); in the case of remote-locating the locating networks receives signals from the mobile device and calculates its position. Depending on the deployment scenario it may be necessary that for self-locating the mobile devices forwards its location fix to a stationary backend system; for remote locating the network has to report the location either to the mobile device or to a backend system.

If LAAC is employed not merely to realize interaction support but rather for security reasons we have to assess how prone to manipulations particular locating technologies are. The term "spoofing" with regard to locating is used in literature to describe manipulations performed by the owner of the mobile device as well as by external third-parties. To differentiate we call the former "internal spoofing" (case 2 and 3 in figure 1) and the latter "external spoofing" (case 1 and 4 in figure 1). External spoofing attacks are based on manipulations of the signals for locating exchanged between locating network and mobile device. For GPS (self-locating) an external attack would be to broadcast fake satellite signals that superimpose the genuine signals [16]. In the case of remote-locating external spoofing would mean to fake the signals that are sent by the mobile device to the locating network. However both attacks can be prevented if the respective signals carry a digital signature which is indeed planned for the EU's Galileo system.

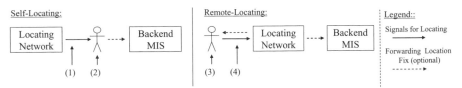

Figure 1: Different Points to Manipulate Location Determination

The case of self-spoofing however is more interesting and is therefore discussed here in more detail: In the case of self-locating the user calculates his own location fix and forwards it to the backend system. He could therefore just "invent" an arbitrary location. One suggesting approach to prevent this attack is that the mobile device has to forward some piece of information that is only visible at the alleged location. This is the basic concept of the CyberLocator system that supplements GPS [6]: here the mobile device forwards also the raw signals received by the GPS satellites. Since the raw signals are influenced by atmospheric effects they cannot be predicted. The backend then compares these signals with signals reported by trusted reference stations not farer away than 2.000 miles. However it is thinkable that the mobile user stays outside the designated location and forwards signals he receives from a colluding party that stays inside the location; this is called "rerouting attack". To prevent rerouting attacks the system demands that the mobile users forwards the signal with a delay of not more than 5 ms since the latency for the rerouting transmission would exceed this time span. Another idea is to broadcast a special location key that can only be received in a particular area [4].

There are other approaches where the locating network sends a special message (including a non-predictable random number) to the mobile device that must be returned within a certain time span, e.g. [14]. This time span is calculated based on estimation of the signals travel time for the distance between mobile device and base station of the locating network. If the mobile device isn't at the location it claims to be its answer won't reach the locating network in time because radio signals cannot travel faster than the speed of light.

There are also proposals for spoof-resistant locating when the reference monitor is operated on the mobile device and no permanent data communication is available. The system for location-aware digital rights management described in [11] is based on satellite navigation and a tamper-proof hardware module as reference monitor. The hardware module hosts a precise clock, an unit for location-determination based on the satellite signals and a decoder to decrypt the content under protection. It is assumed that the satellite signals carry a timestamp and are digitally signed. So the locating unit can determine if navigation signals are manipulated or replayed; it his however necessary to synchronize the clock every couple of hours.

4.   Document-Centric Access Control Model with Dynamic Location-Constraints

4.1   *Core Model*

Our model builds upon the metaphor of virtual documents that are attached to particular places. Each document is an instance of exactly one document class and can be accessed by a user within a defined range. For this paper we think of these documents as files to be edited by some kind of text editor. However the ACM could be easily extended for more general applications where a document instance is a container for different data objects that are processed by several applications. The rationales behind having several document classes is that it allows us to assign different sets of default permissions appropriate for different application scenarios, e.g. class "ordinary note" has the default to allow write operations to users with role "employee" but for class "manager note" only operation "write" is assigned to this role. Further the rules for the dynamic creation of location restrictions will vary greatly depending on the respective application scenario. The user can also configure his device so that only documents of selected classes are displayed.

We depict the model as UML class diagram in figure 2: in the upper part the location model can be found whereas in the lower part the core model is depicted. There are four abstract classes in the model whose names start with "abstract": an abstract class cannot be instantiated but subsumes properties that are shared by several non-abstract classes that inherit from the abstract class.

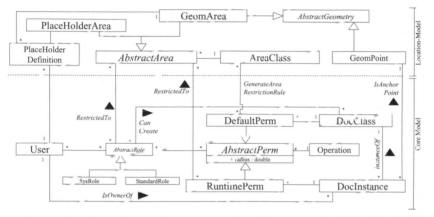

Figure 2: Data Model (Cardinalities for Associations: "*" stands for "0..N", "+" for "1..N")

Following the main idea of RBAC we employ the concept of roles: users can be assigned to roles and roles get assigned to permissions. The permissions assigned to roles are actually abstract permissions. Permissions make a statement about an operation the users of a role are allowed to perform on a document. Operations for the document metaphor are "read", "write", "append", "delete" or "alterPermissions". Class RuntimePerm inherits from AbstractPerm; each instance of this class represents the assignment of one operation to one document instance for one role. Like the name implies these permissions are evaluated to decide if a user is allowed to perform a particular operation on a particular document instance. For example the triple "clerk;customerNote#123;read" allows all users with role "clerk" to perform the operation "read" on document instance "customerNote#123". If a new document instance is created the DefaultPerms are evaluated to find out which initial RuntimePermissions have to be set for the respective DocumentClass. Since the operation "alterPermissions" may allow users to alter the permissions assigned to a document instance it is necessary to have a copy for the permission set for each document instance.

The roles used in the model are either instances of class SysRole or StandardRole since their common super class AbstractRole cannot be instantiated. SysRoles are system roles that cannot be deleted and must be present for each ACM installation; two such roles are "owner" and "admin". StandardRoles however are application-specific roles that must be created for each ACM installation according to the respective scenario and organization.

Using the association "isOwnerOf" we store the owner who created a document instance. The system role "owner" enables to assign special permissions for a document instance's owner. Another association is between AbstractRole and DocClass and named CanCreate. Using this association we can express which roles are allowed to create instances of a particular document class.

4.2   Location Model

At creation of a new document instance the current location of the creating user is assigned as anchor point to the document instance; this anchor point is represented by an instance of class GeomPoint. There is also an attribute called "radius" in class AbstractPerm. If this attribute is set to a non-negative value it says the respective permission can only be used if the user is currently not farther away from the document's anchor point than specified by the radius value. This allows us to have individual location restrictions for each permission and each role. For example a user with role "boss" can read documents of a given class at a distance of 100 meters and write to them at a distance of 10 meters but role "employee" has no write permissions and can only read documents at a distance of up to 5 meters.

Instances of classes AbstractRole and RuntimePerm can be associated with class AbstractArea; if this is the case the respective instance can only be activated while the respective user stays within the denoted area. So we can have a role "nurse" that can only be activated while the users stay within the premises of the hospital. We could also think of other points in the model where a location restriction could get attached to, e.g. to users (i.e. a user is only allowed to access the MIS while staying in a particular area), the canCreate-association (the respective role is only allowed to instantiate that document class in certain areas) or the role-permissions association (a role can only active a permission in certain areas). However due to space limitation we cannot consider this here.

Each AbstractArea stands in association with exactly one AreaClass. An AreaClass is just a symbol to classify AbstractArea-instances into human-understandable categories like "cities", "buildings", "countries" or "regions". AbstractArea has two subclasses: GeomArea and PlaceHolderArea. Instances of GeomArea denote geographic areas; for implementation purposes we assume that these areas are non-empty polygons. The other subclass PlaceHolderArea represents symbolic names of personal areas, i.e. areas that will differ from user to user. Examples are "home town", "office room" or "sales district". To resolve such a PlaceHolderArea to obtain a GeomArea the reference monitor has to resort to the PlaceHolderDefinition which assigns a GeomArea for pairs of "user" and "PlaceHolderArea", e.g. for user Alice the PlaceHolderArea "home town" could point to the GeometricArea "Stockholm".

RuntimePerms can be restricted to AbstractAreas, so the respective role is only authorized to perform that permission in certain areas. If a permission is location restricted the respective DefaultPerm is associated with an instance of AreaClass. At creation time of the respective document class the reference monitor checks for a GeomArea-instance that is an instance of the respective class and contains the current position of the user. If there is such a GeomArea it will be assigned to the newly created RuntimePerm.

A novel feature of our ACM are dynamic location restrictions, i.e. the geometric areas that restrict the respective permission are determined during runtime of the model and don't have to be defined in advance by the administrator like for other LAACMs. There are three different kinds of dynamic location restrictions: (1) restricting permissions according to the anchor point where the document was created and the radius; (2) PlaceHolderAreas are also dynamic location restrictions because to obtain the GeomArea the reference monitor has to know which user is trying to play the respective role; (3) the evaluation of the AreaClass associated with a DefaultPerm to obtain an AbstractArea instance as location restriction for a RuntimePerm instance. To obtain these dynamic location restrictions there are several associations between classes of the core and the location model. This degree of integration between core and location model cannot be found in other LAACMs (if they comprise an explicit location model at all).

4.3 Scenarios

To exemplify the employment of our model we sketch some example applications that use the document metaphor in a natural manner. In all mentioned applications the mobile devices accesses a service on a stationary backend system and the reference monitor resides also on the stationary backend. In literature some descriptions of systems that are based on the metaphor of location-aware documents can be found, e.g. [2] and [12]. However these systems are not based on a general data model or even a LAACM.

Using the "Virtual Graffiti" service a user with role "graffiti-author" can deposit messages at his current location, e.g. "do not visit this pub, the beer is horrible". This message can be read by users with role "graffiti-reader" while staying not further away than 50 meters from the respective anchor point. The message can be altered and deleted by the owner from a distance of up to 1 km; the administrators of the system can do this from any location. If we grant writing permissions also to the "reader"-role we obtain a service where a document can be edited by a community of people; the documents of this service would be some kind of location-aware wiki-pages. If we restrict the "reader"-role to PlaceHolderArea "WikiServiceArea" each user can define individual areas where he would like to use this service. There could also be a document class denoted "personal reminder" whose instances can only be altered, read and deleted by the creating user.

But using this model we can also implement services for mobile workers: service technicians sent to facilities for maintenance work could deposit notes to write down what has to be repaired; they can only alter these notes while staying near the respective facility. For a travelling salesman we could have a service where each document instance represents a customer record. He is only allowed to alter the record (e.g. to enter orders) while staying at the premises of the respective customer. Back office workers however are allowed to alter the record only while staying at the PlaceHolderArea "personal work office", but there is no anchor-point restriction imposed to these permissions.

The next service is an indoor scenario: for a mobile healthcare application a patient's medical record is represented by a document instance. The role nurse is only allowed to view or edit a health record while staying on the hospital's premises, however role "physician" has also the PlaceHolderArea "private residence" as location restriction so physicians can work at home. Abstracting from the document metaphor we could also have distinctive parts of a health record (e.g. section for "vital parameters" and section for "doctor's order" or "diagnosis") which are protected by individual permissions (e.g. "write permission" only for "doctor's order" section). If there is an *AreaClass* "hospital ward" we could also restrict selected permissions (e.g. "append vital data section") to the ward where the patient has his bed.

5. Conclusion

The main contribution of the paper at hand was the description of a location-aware access control model that follows the metaphor of virtual documents. One novel feature of our model are dynamic location constraints, i.e. it is able to express location constraints that can be only determined during runtime of an application. Several application scenarios for consumers as well business users were sketched to demonstrate the versatility of the model.

One notion for further elaboration of the model are security labels that can be assigned to different areas: so a document created at a location classified as "secret" can only be read and edited while staying at a location classified at least as "secret" or above. Further it is worthwhile to devise how to deal with imprecise location determination.

Acknowledgements

This work has been funded by the Federal Ministry of Economics and Technology of Germany (BMWi, Contract No. 01MD06012, Project "MODIFRAME"). The responsibility for the content of this paper lies solely with the author.

References

[1]   M. Benantar, Access Control Systems. Springer, Heidelberg et al., 2006.
[2]   P.J. Brown, The Stick-E Document: A Framework for Creating Context-Aware Application. Electronic Publishing, 8(2 & 3), pp. 259-272, 1995.
[3]   S.M. Chandran & J.B.D. Joshi, LoT-RBAC: A Location and Time-Based RBAC Model. Proceedings of the 6th International Conference on Web Information Systems Engineering (WISE '05), pp. 361-375, 2005.
[4]   Y. Cho, L. Bao & M.T. Goodrich, LAAC: A Location-Aware Access Control Protocol. Third Annunal International Conference on Mobile & Ubiquitous Systems, pp. 1-7, 2006.
[5]   M.L. Damiani & E. Bertino, Data Security in Location-Aware Applications: An Approach   Based   on RBAC. International Journal of Information & Computer Security, 1(1/2), pp. 5-   38, 2007.
[6]   D.E. Denning & P.F. MacDoran, Location-Based Authentication: Grounding Cyberspace for Better Security. Computer Fraud & Security, pp. 12-16, February 1996.
[7]   Dourish, P.: What We Talk About When We Talk About Context. Personal Ubiquitous Computing, 8(1), 2004, 19-30.
[8]   F. Hansen & V. Oleshchuk, SRBAC: A Spatial Role-Based Access Control Model for Mobile Systems. Proceedings of Nordsec '03. pp. 129-141, 2003.
[9]   J. Hightower & G. Borriello, Location Systems for Ubiquitous Computing. IEEE Computer Magazine, 34(8), pp. 57-66, 2001.
[10] U. Leonhardt & J. Magee, Security Considerations for a Distributed Location Service. Journal of Networks and Systems, 6(1), pp. 51-70, 1998.
[11] T. Mundt, Location Dependent Digital Rights Management. Symposium on Computers and Communications (ISCC), pp. 617-622, 2005.
[12] P. Persson et al., GeoNotes: A Location-Based Information System for Public Spaces. Designing Information Spaces: The Social Navigation Approach, Springer, pp. 151-173, 2002.
[13] I. Ray & M. Kumar, Towards a Location-based Mandatory Access Control Model. Computers & Security, 25(1), pp. 36-44, 2006.
[14] N. Sastry, U. Shankar & D. Wagner, Secure Verification of Location Claims, Second Workshop on Wireless Security, ACM, pp. 1-10,   2003.
[15] The Herald: Personnel May Sue MoD Over Stolen Laptop Data (8th February 2008),
      http://www.theherald.co.uk/misc/print.php?artid=2028852
[16] J.S. Warner & R.G. Johnston, GPS-Spoofing Counter Measurements. Los Alamos National Laboratory, Technical Report, 2003.

Section 7.2

Applications

Collaboration and the Knowledge Economy: Issues, Applications, Case Studies
P. Cunningham and M. Cunningham (Eds.)
IOS Press, 2008

Mobile Applications for Public Sector: Balancing Usability and Security

Yuri NATCHETOI[1], Viktor KAUFMAN[2], Konstantin BEZNOSOV[3]

[1]SAP Research, 111 Duke, Montreal, Canada
Tel: +1 613 262 1767, Email: viktor.kaufman@sap.com
[2]SAP Research, Vincenz-Priessnitz-Str. 1, Karlsruhe, Germany
[3]University of British Columbia, 2332 Main Mall, Vancouver, Canada

Abstract: Development of mobile software applications for use in specific domains such as Public Security must conform to stringent security requirements. While mobile devices have many known limitations, assuring complex fine-grained security policies poses an additional challenge to quality mobile services and raises usability concerns. We address these challenges by means of a novel approach to authentication and gradual multi-factor authorization for access to sensitive data. Using our mobile Framework that facilitates low-cost composition of rich applications, we have designed and implemented prototype software that provides secure access to information stored in dedicated online systems, such as Customer Relationship Management, collaboration support, and more for Public Sector workers. Usability of our solution has been confirmed by a first evaluation conducted by a group of volunteers.

1 Introduction

Public Sector organizations are increasingly leveraging mobile devices to support and equip business processes that take place outside. Many government employees work outside of their offices or spend time away from their desks [1]. Public Sector workers such as police officers, social workers, postal workers, employees performing various inspections such as fire, food, buildings, and environmental monitoring need mobile access to information. All these people can benefit from using secure mobile applications, connected to the back-end systems. For example, they could receive assignments and information updates in real time, review contact information before the visit, use maps and routing software in order to find places, and wirelessly submit information to the back-end databases.

In many cases, using a laptop is not appropriate, because of its weight, size, power consumption and WiFi connectivity requirement. Smart phone appears to be a more suitable device, as it is becoming equipped with powerful hardware and software technologies such as J2ME, Bluetooth, GPS, digital cameras, and more – all at a greatly reduced cost and with better infrastructure support. Mobile applications and services continue to be one of the most rapidly evolving areas of technology.

Mobility is especially important for Public Security workers. In order to perform a quality job, police officers, detectives, and forensic investigators would benefit a lot from any-time any-place access to back-end Information Systems.

For this category of workers security is one of the highest priorities. They need advanced capabilities for secure access to very sensitive information. Unfortunately, the high security level is often achieved at the expense of usability and utility. Frequently typing a password is not a convenient task, especially on the tiny keypad. Using multi-modal input capabilities can lead to better usability. At the same time, it can be used for multi-factor authentication and authorization. We propose to combine unique biometric attributes such as user's voice and face image, password, and Bluetooth-connected security token to provide for enhanced security. In the following, we describe our research and a first application that simultaneously enables enhanced security and better usability.

2.   Challenges in Design of Secure Mobile Applications

Mobile applications have, in general, to overcome many obstacles such as limited processing power, unreliable network performance, and limited data storage. Technologies used for desktop applications don't work well on mobile phones. Mobile applications for Public Security introduce additional stringent security requirements.

Designing applications ensuring secure mobile access to online Information Systems poses several challenges:

*   Lack of control over physical location and environment of the user makes usurpation, physical tampering, and shoulder surfing attacks easier.
*   Constrained input and output capabilities limit the choices for authentication and other security-related interactions via the device.
*   Lack of common Operating System and common mobile-application platform implies use of custom or proprietary APIs and tools for secure application development.
*   Relatively slow and intermittent connectivity prevents traditional approaches used to enforce fine-grained access control that relies on authorization verification on each access to the central server.

The state of the practice pervasively relies on password-based authentication and all-or-nothing authorization. A typical example is any application for Blackberry smart phones. It allows the user to use all the application functionality after a successful password-based authentication. For the applications where an extended level of security is required, the BlackBerry® Smart Card Reader connected to the mobile device by means of Bluetooth can be used. It prevents the use of the smart phone without proper signal from the reader. There are some international initiatives dealing with mobile security [2], but they mainly focus on mobile applications that do not require extensive information exchange with a central server. For business applications such information exchange implies the need for additional security measures.

3.   Mobile Support for Public Security Workers

We have designed and implemented a prototype application using a back-end CRM system for support of Investigative Case Management, used by police investigators. The mobile application enables online and offline access to the Incident Reports, Leads, Cases and Contacts database etc.

Figure 1: Example Screenshots of Mobile Investigative Case Management Application

Incident Reports can be immediately assigned to investigators and sent to their mobile devices, together with location-based routing information, historical records relevant to the case (previous similar incidents, personal files of victims, suspects and witnesses, their connections). In the process of investigation, the officer can collaborate with his colleagues using emails, instant messages, voice, video conference, and shared media records [3, 4]. Real-time collaboration among mobile users leverages multi-media features of the phone such as camera and voice recording for documenting user activities. Forensic equipment could be used as well, by means of Bluetooth, to collect and analyze data.

3.1   Enabling Technology

We follow a systematic approach taking into account multiple requirements for the mobile solution, including timely, secure, robust and easy access to the back-end system; transparency between connected, occasionally-connected, and disconnected modes; easy application composition, development, and low total cost of ownership. This requires an innovative approach to Web Services invocation, data exchange and staging, and interfacing with the user, as well as enforcing security policies. The basic technologies that we find appropriate in this case include Service-Oriented Architecture, BPEL, semantic technologies (RDF, OWL), and others.

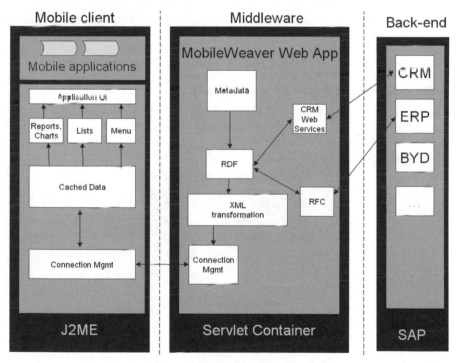

Figure 2: Framework Architecture

Our lightweight mobile service-oriented Framework [5] is designed to facilitate rapid development of rich mobile applications running on Java-enabled devices. In our Framework, the back-end business objects, such as Contact and Activity are being serialized, compressed, encrypted, and transmitted as by-design compact SOAP messages to the client side. The information is stored in the local persistent data store in a compressed and encrypted RDF format. This way, a significantly larger number of business objects as compared to a traditional file system or relational database can be stored. The cached objects are decompressed and decrypted only when requested by an application. Asynchronous remote SOA-based invocation mechanism allows applications to fully function in the disconnected mode, and supports on-demand requests to the server as well as push notifications from the server.

In our solution, neither the business logic nor the user interface forms are hard-coded in the client application. Instead, the client application partially implements interpreters for open industry standards such as SOAP, OWL, RDF, BPEL, XForm and SVG. The application logic and the user interface can be modified or augmented at low cost.

In this paper, we highlight our applied research relevant to Public Security. In particular, we use a novel approach for authentication to handle sensitive data, see Section 4; knowledge of business processes to minimize data transferred to and stored on the mobile device by means of semantic representation of use-case-specific knowledge shared between the client and the server; and flexible composition of business processes by leveraging Web standards [6].

3.2 Deployment Considerations

Our application supporting Public Security workers doesn't require special hardware or network infrastructure. The client application can be deployed on a wide range of mobile phones, supporting J2ME CLDC 1.0, including many mass-market models. It also works with the GPRS and EDGE networks – the advanced networking infrastructure deployed worldwide. Using existing handsets and networks provides for lower costs and faster deployment. Push notifications and compressing wireless traffic additionally reduce communication costs and guarantee almost real-time access to the information.

4.   Fine-Grained Access Policy and Usability

Almost every data piece used by Public Security workers is confidential and requires protection of its integrity. Care must be taken in order to protect the data in the communication channel and on the device in case it is lost or stolen. For most user activities on the device, proper authentication, authorization, and audit are necessary.

Figure 3:Multi-factor authentication.

Multi-media features of the mobile devices provide a unique opportunity to use multi-factor authentication. Our application uses four factors: password authentication, hardware security token connected to the phone by means of Bluetooth, and two biometric factors: voice and face recognition [7]. We provide for voice recordings and photo taking, and plan to call remote services like [8] to perform voice spectrum analysis and similar tasks.

As part of the login procedure, we can use any combination of password typing, voice sample capturing, and image taking. To prevent intruders from using eligible user's photo, randomly selected challenge is supported. For example, application can ask the user to close her left eye. In addition, the application checks if the Bluetooth token is in 10 meters proximity of the device. These four factors, in combinations, enable strong authentication.

Multi-factor authentication takes time and requires significant effort on the part of the user. Given that users often need access to only small pieces of information, which might be not very sensitive, employing all four authentication mechanisms would be redundant, error-prone, and would imply prohibitively high cognitive load of the users.

In order to find the right balance between the security and usability, we use adaptable security policies. All data accessible through the mobile device is being classified using several levels of integrity and confidentiality importance. Depending on the sensitivity level of the information that user attempts to access, different combinations of authentication means can be chosen. For example, in order to grant access to less confidential data, the system only checks that the Bluetooth token is in near proximity. However, if the user accesses more confidential data, voice or face authentication might be requested.

In our approach, we leverage OWL standard and store metadata describing required authorization level along with the business objects accessible through the mobile device. We thus classify all the objects in terms of the required level of identity assurance. We assume that using more authentication factors provides better assurance of the user's identity. If authorization thresholds are defined for both a generic business object and an inherited one, and possibly even its parts, we compute the required authorization level as a maximum of all relevant thresholds.

In order to overcome performance issues related to access validation with high level of access-control granularity and to facilitate offline access control, we "compile" security policies into a Finite-State-Machine graph on the server side. This machine tracks the current security level of the device usage. Authentication actions on the client lead to higher security levels, longer inactivity times reduce this level the same way as absence from a desktop computer leads to computer lock, see also [9]. On the client side, we determine the security state, validate user's permissions and decrypt requested objects accordingly.

For initial login, user only needs the Bluetooth security token, the most convenient and usable factor. It provides basic level of security. Most of the non-confidential information is accessible on this level. However, if user requests access to data with higher security requirements, the application would ask for additional biometric or password-based authentication. The security level is being increased until it is high enough in order to get required data. This relatively simple approach enables reliable security avoiding unnecessary hurdles for the user and without overloading her with security checks.

Finally, all communications between the server and the client are encrypted. In the case of mobile devices, there always exists an additional risk of the device being lost or stolen, so that all data is encrypted as well. A major problem for mobile secure applications is that the asymmetric key encryption scheme works very slowly if the computational power is limited, as is the case for most mobile devices. We chose a compromise solution using asymmetric encryption for most sensitive information and symmetric key encryption for all other data. This approach is also used by the well-known PGP software. The symmetric key is generated once a session and is sent to the client using the asymmetric key.

5.   Outlook and Conclusion

We are further looking into using advanced biometric sensors connected to the phone by Bluetooth etc. and into different algorithms to assure security. While we currently manually define security policies, we hope to take a closer look at a possibility of centralized security policy management. We also hope to perform extensive usability testing. Our first evaluation with a group of few volunteers showed higher level of satisfaction with multi-factor authentication procedure and general secure navigation in our application for Public Security workers in comparison to traditional procedures. In particular, we have given the volunteers a set of ten relatively simple tasks such as finding and viewing certain contact information. Using advanced logger component that records time spent by users during each step, we measured effectiveness (number of tasks performed in a limited time), and satisfaction (perceived level of comfort).

We believe that our innovative approach based on previous works of authors will help to solve many annoying usability problems in the area of enterprise mobile applications. We have implemented a proof of concept solution based on our approach and learned a lesson that secure access to Enterprise information doesn't have to sacrifice application simplicity and usability. Our experiments confirm that we can significantly improve security/usability ratio and should continue working in the direction of flexible security policies for mobile devices.

In conclusion, we proved that it is possible to largely overcome known limitations of mobile devices even in the case of complex additional security requirements in specific domains such as Public Security. To achieve good quality of mobile services we used and improved our mobile Framework based on service-oriented approach and descriptive design approach. Descriptive design and multi-factor authentication turned out to facilitate both usability and secure access management. Furthermore, good quality of service could be achieved by means of limiting the data and services capabilities of a comparable desktop application to those explicitly required in the supported use-cases.

References

[1]   T. Virki, Global cell phone penetration reaches 50 pct, Reuters, 2007. Online.
[2]   GSM Association Mobile Application Security Initiative. Online. Available:
      http://www.gsmworld.com/using/security/mobile_application.shtml .
[3]   Y. Natchetoi, V. Kaufman, L. Hamdi, A. Shapiro, Mobile Web 2.0 Browser for Collaborative Social
      Networking. ECSCW 2007 Workshop. [Online]. Available:
      http://cscwlab1.informatik.unibw-muenchen.de/Main/Ecscw2007Ws .
[4]   ECOSPACE Project. Online. Available: http://www.ip-ecospace.org/ .
[5]   Y. Natchetoi, V. Kaufman, A. Shapiro, Service-Oriented Architecture for Mobile Applications. To be
      published in ICSE companion workshop proceedings, 2008.
[6]   F. Hirsh, J. Kemp, J. Ilkka, Mobile web Services. Wiley, 2006.
[7]   H. Nakasone, B. D. Steven, Forensic automatic speaker recognition. In: ODYSSEY, 2001.
[8]   VoiceVault. Online. Available: http://www.voicevault.com/ca.aspx .
[9]   J. Crampton, W. Leung, K. Beznosov, The secondary and approximate authorization model and its
      application to Bell-LaPadula policies. In: Proceedings of the eleventh ACM symposium on Access
      control models and technologies, SESSION: Access control model, ISBN:1-59593-353-0. ACM, NY,
      USA, 2006.

Collaboration and the Knowledge Economy: Issues, Applications, Case Studies
P. Cunningham and M. Cunningham (Eds.)
IOS Press, 2008

Using Language Technology to Improve Interaction and Provide Skim Reading Abilities to Audio Information Services

Arne JÖNSSON[1], Bjarte BUGGE[2], Mimi AXELSSON[3], Erica BERGENHOLM[3],
Bertil CARLSSON[3], Gro DAHLBOM[3], Robert KREVERS[3], Karin NILSSON[3],
Jonas RYBING[3], Christian SMITH[3]

[1]Santa Anna IT Research Institute AB, 581 83 Linköping, Sweden, E-mail: arnjo@ida.liu.se
[2]Audio To Me AB, Linköping Sweden, E-mail: bjbu@audiotome.se
[3]Linköping University, 581 83 Linköping, Sweden

Abstract: In this paper we present language technology enhancements to audio-based information services (i.e. services where information is presented using spoken language). The enhancements presented in the paper addresses two issues for audio-based services: 1) interaction with the service is rigid and 2) the ability to listen to summaries is limited. Our developments allow for more natural and efficient control of the service and means that facilitates skim reading. Using speech dialogue instead of traditional buttons provides means for more advanced navigation in the audio material. Vector space techniques are used to collect the most relevant sentences in a text and allows for skim reading of varying depth.

1. Introduction

Today most interactions with technical products are realized using variants of visual user interfaces. The same holds for most techniques for information distribution. Many persons, e.g. persons with visual disabilities or dyslexia, or various age related disabilities, have limited access to such information. The need for audio-based information services is significant for these groups. Considering that in a recent survey 98% answer "No" to the question "Did you manage to read what you wanted to read yesterday?" and that more than 90% of today's information is available in text format only, the user group above is extended enormously. For instance, persons listening to PM:s or reports while driving.

The company AudioToMe has developed a large archive of human voice accessible information based on an open Service Oriented Architecture (SOA) enabling various audio based services support for multiple consumer channels/devices, giving consumers access to audio services using standard consumer technologies.

2. Objectives

The objective of this research is to improve interaction of the AudioToMe information services utilizing methods from language technology. Today, users select information to listen to using the keypad on a cell phone or a special device. This provides a robust and easy to use navigation. However, it is not that natural, flexible or efficient.

2.1 Interaction

If an information system instead were controlled through speech interaction, it would be possible to provide flexible and efficient navigation even without visual elements. Speech interaction allows users, not only to skip articles and navigate on subject level but also to search for specific articles using natural language. Natural language dialogue systems are today commercially used for a variety of tasks, and generic dialogue systems are available (e.g. [1,2]) that provide a repository of frameworks and tools in the form of software code that can be shared amongst researchers and that is ready to be used and re-used in industry. To illustrate consider the dialogue excerpt below:

User: Any news about Nokia today?
System: There are stock quotes and an article entitled "Nokia releases new GPS-phone". Which one are you interested in?
User: Read the article
System: <Reads article>
User: Stop. What will the weather be like in Linköping tomorrow?

This short excerpt illustrates how users can navigate a newspaper in a much more natural and efficient way than pressing buttons for moving forward or skipping articles.

2.2   Skim Reading

It should also be possible to efficiently browse information, including skim reading at various levels and present summaries of texts.

Summarizing techniques can already be quite useful when applied to written text, but with such a static, visual media you still have the option of skimming through the area in any direction and at any pace you'd like. Audio, however, is a strictly linear, non-static media where you can only go in one direction while gathering information. Since most of us are able to make out words if they are read to us in normal or a little above normal pace, the shortened material produced by a summariser would be immensely useful to people skimming an audio file

3.   Methodology

Different methods will be used in different sub-projects. Software development is carried out in parallel with the empirical investigations. Thus, agile software development methodology is utilised as it facilitates rapid prototyping and user involvement [3,4].

3.1   Interaction

There are a number of well-explored dialogue phenomena that can be utilised to direct speech interaction, such as clarification request, contextual interpretation, and topic shifts c.f. [3], but these are merely techniques and as such only useful if correctly used. Understanding which features to use in various situations, and how they are realized in language, e.g. various prompts, is therefore of utmost importance for speech controlled interaction to be useful.

To address this, we need to investigate the behaviour of users interacting with a sound-based medium in various situations and consequently we utilise qualitative methods, such as interviews and open prototype evaluations.

3.2   Skim Reading

Skim reading also involves various techniques depending on situation, user and information content. For instance, a politician driving and skim reading a report before a meeting would probably prefer a short summary of the report, whereas a visually impaired person listening to the daily newspaper might prefer keywords reflecting the content of a story. Investigations on user opinions on various techniques for skim reading in different situations are consequently important, combining qualitative and quantitative methods.

4. Technology Description

AudioToMe services include audio mailbox, pod casts, RSS, banking services, landlord information, health care information, and newspapers. The sound files are easy to access and users can create their own profile reflecting the order in which they want to listen to the information, e.g. a newspaper.

4.1 Interaction

Newspaper information is stored in m3u or DAISY (Digital Accessible Information SYstem) files generated every day and contain subject area tags and within each subject area the relevant articles are ordered based on an individual user's normal reading order. The parsed m3u-files provide a basic structure for each user and are used for browsing data.

We will use the Nuance speech recognizer, which is a speaker independent recognizer that allows for full sentence recognition. Interaction can be accomplished using more or less sophisticated commands. Some commands are domain independent, such as READ <x>, where <x> can be the name of a paper, an article, a report etc., NEXT, PAUSE, STOP, BACK etc. Others are domain dependent, e.g. DELETE makes sense in an e-mail system but not when reading the newspaper.

Control in the AudioToMe service system is done using various spoken commands, based on results from the empirical investigations. The commands must be natural to use, but at the same time technically easy to identify. Unfortunately, words that are easy to identify for the speech recognizer need not be the ones that users prefer to use.

4.2 Skim Reading

Skim reading techniques depend on the situation, user, information needs etc. Sometimes whole sentences are preferred, for instance as a summary of a report, but key words, reflecting the content of a text, can also be used as a basis for deciding if an article is interesting to hear.

For skim reading we utilise the DAISY format, which defines how textual information links to corresponding sections in sound files. DAISY also defines a number of standard tags for marking up sections, depending on the source text. For instance, in fiction novels there are tags for chapters, whereas scientific texts have tags down to the level of single sentences. Newspapers are somewhere in between depending on the publisher.

It is, thus, possible to use standard text search techniques to navigate in the information and once selected play the corresponding sound file.

Vector space techniques[5], such as Latent Semantic Analysis[6], and Random Indexing[7], on whole sentences create the set of sentences in a text that best resembles the original content[8]. Using whole sentences means that no speech synthesis is needed, instead sentences are assembled from the original corpus and the sound files are delivered.

Vector space techniques used in a similar way on words provide content information. In such cases pre-processing is used to remove stop words, build term lists (with synonyms), and perform stemming. Finally, speech synthesis is needed to deliver the information.

5. Developments

For skim reading we are using two techniques, PageRank and Random Indexing[9]. Random Indexing is performed using use the Java-toolkit developed by Martin Hassel[10]. Based on Hassel's toolkit we have developed a test bed allowing us to pick out words or sentences from the text and also vary the number of items to present. The program also uses the Snowball-stemmer[11].

Random Indexing is language independent and it is thus possible to produce summaries for many languages. However, stemming and stop word lists are language specific and new such are needed for high quality summaries.

6. Results

This section presents results from experiments on interaction and skim reading.

6.1 Interaction

We have done initial investigations on how people would like to use speech to navigate audio-based newspapers. The pilot tests have been performed on four students from Linköping University in Sweden, three men and one woman. During these tests the experimenter had a computer with a program for audio based newspapers. The newspapers are recorded by the newspaper company and distributed over the Internet or with the radio to the subscribers. The investigations were exploratory. The participants were to pretend that they had access to audio-based newspapers in their daily lives and were instructed to use language freely to control the interaction. We also assigned tasks to the participants like "Read the domestic news" and "Read the second letter in 'Ordet fritt'" (Ordet fritt is the section with letters to the newspaper).

Three of the four participants started immediately by saying the name of the section they wanted to read. The fourth participant said the name of the newspaper and then continued with the name of the section he was interested in. To start reading an article subjects either wanted to say the article name or number of the article in numerical order, the persons that wanted some kind of table of contents read when they entered a section suggested this. Three of the four participants wanted to hear some kind of table of contents. Two of the four participants talked spontaneously about searching with key words. For instance, searching for special words in the text or headlines to find an interesting article.

The difference in expected response from the system varied. One subject wanted to be certain the system had understood his question and preferred paraphrasing like "Do you want to go to domestic news?" One subject preferred if the system started to read articles, or if the command was intended to direct to a section, to read the name of the section.

The study on speech-controlled interaction has provided a corpus that will be used for initial development of the speech-controlled interface.

Further investigations will be carried out to develop the dialogue system and to overcome the problem that it can be hard to make people pretend that they are talking to a computer or in this case something that don't even exist. To handle this, we will use a method similar to[12], where participants will talk to a human that in turn is accessing the current button-based system. These dialogues will be distilled[13] and analysed to provide further knowledge on how persons want to talk to a computer, what kind of commands they want to use and what kind of functions they need.

6.2 Skim Reading

We have also conducted experiments on two types of summaries for skim reading, presenting only words or presenting whole sentences. In the study, 20 students, between 20-30 years old, not visually impaired, listened to sound files of either complete sentences or words. Humans, not synthetic speech, were used to produce the sound files.

The subjects were presented a varying number of sentences, or words, representing the "best" 10, 25, 50 or 70% of the total number of sentences, where "best" is based on the Random Indexing ranking. Stop words were removed when words were presented to the subjects. The order in which sentences, or words, occurred in the original text were preserved when presented to the subjects.

Our results show that subjects prefer whole sentences to words on all four levels (10, 25, 50 or 70% of the sentences or words). 17 out of 20 preferred sentences to words. Note that in the instructions we informed our subjects that 10% should be seen as a way of deciding if an article is worth reading whereas 70% should be seen as a summary of the text. One could assume that on the 10% or 20% level subjects would prefer words to sentences as an indication to whether the article is interesting to listen to or not, but that was not the case.

Thus, our initial experiments conclude that for un-experienced users whole sentences are preferred for skim reading. Further research will include using experienced users of audio-based services.

7. Business Benefits

The core business of Audio To Me is to give consumers access to written information through the use of audio. This includes all aspects from service design and content production to multi channel access and user experience. The research described above is a direct result of field tests and requests from our customers. Adding this to our portfolio will directly enhance the customer value proposition of our services.

Both enhancements, natural dialogue and advanced skim reading, will improve our market position significantly and gives us a strong position to address local, regional and a global market. Our services address a wide range of consumers, from people with defined reading disabilities to the executive enable to find time for reading in a busy schedule.

An example of customer value is how advanced skim reading will help a political active person with dyslexia get an grip of the extensive text material required in all the democratic process.

A segment of special interest is consumers with low technical adoption where audio services can be a new way to give access to media based on RSS, PodCast and blogs etc. We have found the demographic and structurally prerequisites for these type of new audio services positively homogenous within major parts of the European market.

8. Conclusions

We have presented language technology enhancements to support navigating large collections of information material available as audio services.

The research addresses two of the major issues that have been identified in investigations of various uses of audio services. The physical user interface with buttons of various sizes is often a challenge for non-technically skilled users or users with motor dysfunctions. Providing means to use spoken interaction to direct the information services greatly enhances the usability of audio-based services. Furthermore, active persons with reading disabilities face the challenge to orient in and select information from large text masses. Giving such users the possibility to skim read greatly enhances their productivity and hopefully enjoyment using audio-based services.

Currently our results are mainly from investigations on how users would like to use language technology based software in audio-based services. We have not yet integrated the software components for speech-controlled interface or the skim reading techniques to AudioToMe's products.

References

[1] Michael F McTear, Spoken dialogue technology: toward the conversational user interface. Springer Verlag: London, 2004.
[2] J., Hochberg, N., Kambhatla, S., Roukos, A flexible framework for developing mixed-initiative dialog systems. In: *3rd SIGdial Workshop on Discourse and Dialogue*, Philadelphia, Pennsylvania, 2002.

[3]   Pontus Johansson, Lars Degerstedt and Arne Jönsson, Iterative Development of an Information-Providing Dialogue System, *Proceedings of the 7th ERCIM Workshop "User Interfaces for All"* Paris, France, 2002

[4]   Lars Degerstedt and Arne Jönsson, A Method for Iterative Implementation of Dialogue Management, *IJCAI Workshop on Knowledge and Reasoning in Practical Dialogue Systems*, Seattle, 2001.

[5]   Lars Eldén, *Matrix Methods in Data Mining and Pattern Recognition*. Society for Industrial & Applied Mathematics (SIAM), 2007.

[6]   Thomas K. Landauer and Susan T. Dumais, A solution to Plato's problem: The latent semantic analysis theory of the acquisition, induction, and representation of knowledge. *Psychological Review*, 104:211–240, 1997.

[7]   Magnus Sahlgren, An Introduction to Random Indexing. *Methods and Applications of Semantic Indexing Workshop at the 7th International Conference on Terminology and Knowledge Engineering*, 2005

[8]   Martin Hassel, *Resource Lean and Portable Automatic Text Summarization*, PhD Thesis, ISRN-KTH/CSC/A--07/09—SE, KTH, Sweden, 2007.

[9]   Niladri Chatterjee, Shiwali Mohan, Extraction-Based Single-Document Summarization Using Random Indexing, *19th IEEE International Conference on Tools with Artificial Intelligence*, 2007

[10]   http://www.csc.kth.se/~xmartin/java/JavaSDM/

[11]   http://snowball.tartarus.org/

[12]   Pontus Wärnestål Modelling a Dialogue Strategy for Personalized Movie Recommendations. *Proceedings of Beyond Personalization 2005 Workshop (Intelligent User Interfaces 2005)*. San Diego (CA), U.S.A., January 9, 2005. pp. 77-82.

[13]   Arne Jönsson and Nils Dahlbäck, Distilling dialogues - A method using natural dialogue corpora for dialogue systems development *Proceedings of 6th Applied Natural Language Processing Conference,* Seattle, 2000, pp. 44-51.

Section 7.3

Case Studies

Collaboration and the Knowledge Economy: Issues, Applications, Case Studies
P. Cunningham and M. Cunningham (Eds.)
IOS Press, 2008

IMS ARCS - An Industrial Academic Cooperative research program for IMS

Robert MULLINS[1], Ray RICHARDSON[2], Edel MADDEN[1],
Jonathan BRAZIL[1,] Shane DEMPSEY[1]
[1]TSSG, Carriganore Campus, Waterford, Ireland
Tel: +353 51 302964, Fax: + 353 52 302901, Email: rmullins@tssg.org, emadden@tssg.org,
jbrazil@tssg.org, sdempsey@tssg.org
[2]Daysha Consulting, 3 Lincoln Place,Westland Row, Dublin 2, Ireland
Tel: +353 1 287 0104, Fax: + 353 1 287 0104, Email: ray.richardson@dayshaconsulting.com

Abstract: IMS ARCS is an Industrial and Academic cooperative program conducting research in the area of IMS technology with a view to creating a body of intellectual property for the use of the project partners, and serving as a case study on how to develop IMS application software. This paper outlines the objectives of the project, how the research work was planned and executed, and how it intends to transfer knowledge to its industry partners and create a route to allow commercialisation of the research work. The paper also describes how a set of exemplar IMS services and enabler prototypes are being developed to showcase the research work and provide examples of how such services may be developed for commercial purposes. The prototypes will also demonstrate the capabilities of IMS, such as location and presence information, and sophisticated call control. The project employs the OpenIMS testbed from Fraunhofer Fokus, as the basis for the development and execution of the prototypes.

1. Introduction

The IMS ARCS [1] project is an Industry Lead Research Project sponsored by Enterprise Ireland and consists of a partnership of between 25 commercial companies and 4 academic institutions whose objective is to research and develop a number of innovative end user services concepts and service enablers based around, but not limited in the application, to the IP Multimedia Subsystem [2]. This group of companies and academic groups are referred to collectively as the project stakeholders.

The applicability of the various service concepts spans areas such as commerce, health, public transport, personal and child security, education, entertainment and recreation. All such service concepts make use of next generation service capabilities such as mobility, location information, extended presence, multi modal communications, security and anonymisation, mobile wallet functionality and personalisation to provide a high value service and sophisticated user experience.

2. Objectives

This paper proposes to study the various service concepts, their value propositions and business cases, how they might be realised and what their likely societal impacts may be. The paper proceeds to argue the value of such collaborative research projects for both stimulating innovation within the commercial sector and promoting adoption of services by the public.

3.   Methodology Used

The IP Multimedia Subsystem is a collection of 3GPP and ITU standards which propose a technology infrastructure to enable an all IP based Telecommunications Network based around the use of protocols such as SIP [3] and DIAMETER [4]. IMS evolved from an early specification from an industry consortium which sought to create an IP based core networking standard for telecommunications network. It was envisaged that by defining an all IP control layer and adopting IETF track standards such as SIP, network operators could reduce network management overhead, medium to long-term Capital Expenditure and increase Average Revenue Per User (ARPU) through new IP-based services. These services would potentially use capabilities from the telecommunications network control plane and the Internet, hence they've been called Converged Network Services.

The objectives of the project are twofold; the first is to create a body of intellectual property including a number of IMS end user and enabling services, and a set of marketing and business analysis documents evaluating IMS, the various service concepts and the national and international business opportunities that migration to IMS will bring about. The second is to educate the commercial companies about how to develop and deploy IMS applications, including identification of what tools to use, how to use the Open IMS Testbed [5] and the best development processes to follow. This is achieved via the experience gained through bringing a number of the service concepts to realisation.

The key objective of the project is to identify and develop both prototypes to demonstrate a number of end user service concepts, and a number of IMS enablers, or building block type services which can add value on top of the basic IMS infrastructure and be used as reusable components in the creation of end user services.

To achieve this, a top down methodology was employed. It was necessary first to come up with a set of validated end user service concepts, which could be prototyped, followed by a technical analysis which would allow the required and common service building blocks to be identified. The process is shown in Figure 1 below.

To create the set of service concepts, a brainstorming exercise took place. The various stakeholders gathered together to brainstorm the typical lifestyles of various people profiles in the year 2020. Stakeholders divided into groups who were charged with dealing with particular people profiles. From this, the types of services that they might use were imagined and listed. Each group then presented their results, which were then discussed and clarified by the larger gathering. This information was recorded and used as the basic input to a process of analysis that followed.

The first step was to assign each concept that was recorded a unique concept ID. This allowed it to be tracked. The next step was to go through each of the concepts and come up with a one paragraph description of what the service concept was, and eliminate subjectivity in interpretation, as in many cases the output from the brainstorming process was a simple 3 or 4 word description. Having done this, it was recognised that there was a certain degree of duplication in the service concepts that emerged from the various groups, or that certain concepts were very similar and should be merged, so a process of duplicate elimination followed. There were also cases where people had misunderstood what was required and had created technical wish lists or requirements rather than service concepts. These too were eliminated. This left a list of essentially different fleshed out service concepts that were traceable though their ID back to their origin.

The next phase of the project undertook to analyse each of these service concepts under a number of different headings. These were:

- Value Proposition – Why would someone use this service & what alternatives are available
- Business Case – Is there a market for such a service & analysis including charging models
- Technical Feasibility – How feasible is implementing this service – for example would it rely on information that it may not be possible to get.
- Relevance to IMS – is this service relevant to IMS or is it simply an internet type service
- Originality and Patentability – How original is the service concept and what similar services exist. Are there existing patents that might prevent creation of such a service?
- Legal Issues – Data protection, Accessibility
- Deployment issues and Value Chain – What parties are required to deploy this service and how feasible is it. It the service scalable?
- Implementation Effort – How much effort is required to create a service prototype

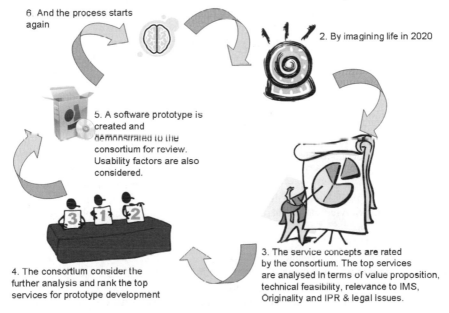

Figure 1: Ten-Month Service Concept Development Cycle

The output of the above analysis process allowed the service concepts to be scored under a number of headings and eventually a list of ranked service concepts were produced. Many of these were eliminated for a number of reasons, while a small number which ranked highly and were deemed technically feasible to prototype were selected. An exercise to identify the IMS enablers required for the project was also executed.

4. Technology Description

The following prototypes were selected for prototyping:

The health monitor consists of a mobile application which gathers vital statistics information through automated sensors, and a data analyzing service that determines what the health data means in the context of the medical history of the service consumer. Automated retrieval of sensor information may use a Bluetooth enabled monitoring device which relays information through the user's mobile phone through to the backend system. The backend system performs a recording function and will also monitor for alarm conditions such as a heart flat line or fibrillation, a diabetic's critical sugar level etc. On detecting such an alarm, a configured response such as notifying emergency services, family members together with location information is triggered.

The LBS home help service provides a virtual golden pages for the user. If for example the user needs a tradesperson (plumber) then the system provides a list of plumbers in the user's direct area. The list will show plumber availability (via presence), cost and can also integrate references (i.e. so that the user can immediately communicate with other people that plumber has worked for). The service would also be applicable to any type of service provided by the golden pages (taxis, electricians, piano fixers etc).

The service provides automated and anonymous call setup between the customer and tradesperson, job management and Identity Verification when the tradesperson arrives at the customer's home.

The Public Transport Adviser integrates the GPS from the user's device with real time public transport information and relays this information to a back end system which then presents the user with all the possible options using public transport from getting from the user's current location to the desired destination. The user wants to take public transport from A to B, so the system calculates the most convenient method to transport, and correct route, for that person. The system can give users voice prompts when they are coming near to a point where they must disembark from the public transport (e.g. as an aid to blind people). The system will also take users preferences into account (cheapest route vs. fastest route,, window seating, 1st class or economy class seating, wheelchair access only, go via a breakfast bar etc). The service will keep the user updated with changes in their journey, due to interruptions such as a broken down bus or by user choice, when perhaps the user decides to interrupt their journey temporarily to grab a coffee or breakfast.

The Gambling Service can build upon existing internet based gambling sites to allow mobile IMS users to:

1. Login to the service
2. Place bets on events on the handheld device
3. View event programs to allow users to study form.
4. Receive notifications about the events; starts, results etc.
5. Offer the user the ability to view or listen to event commentary streamed to their device.
6. Possibly charge bets, credit payoffs against the users IMS provider's account.
7. Notify the user of events that they may be interested in, based on previous betting profile.
8. Inform user of local events (specific to location) on which the service is offering odds.
9. Determine if a user is present at a location based event and offer to place bets on the event.

5.   Example Service Prototype

The LBS Home Help Service was prototyped as a web based application that integrates with various IMS enablers such as location, presence and SIP call control, using these capabilities to allow a user to find a tradesperson within a location and given a radius. By doing a location based search on tradespeople registered with the service, and using presence to determine their availability, the service shows the user a list of those potentially available. It then uses SIP call control to setup a call between the user and the tradesperson while preserving anonymity until the user agrees to place the job. The service then creates a job number and tracks the job until it has been completed.

Figure 2: Screenshots from the LBS Home Help Service

The service is integrated with the OpenIMS Testbed [5] from Fraunhaufer Fokus which supplies the call control functionality, location information and presence through its ParlayX and presence enablers. The service can be deployed on a smartphone with WiFi access capabilities such as the Nokia N95 or Apple iPhone.

IMS ARCS hosted a stand at Mobile World Congress in February 2008 in Barcelona designed to showcase the achievements of the project to date and to highlight the many benefits of IMS technology. The LBS service was demonstrated on this stand and received considerable interest from visitors.

6. Usability Analysis

As part of the service design process, the Interactive Design Centre of the University of Limerick, an IMS ARCS partner, carried out a usability analysis of the fore mentioned prototypes [6]. The initial step in this process was a mock up of the prototypes user interfaces on paper. This was important to ascertain the feasibility and the logistics of implementing a working prototype, while also getting feedback on the user interface design before implementation. In the usability lab, users were given a simplified task analysis for the four IMS applications. These studies were conducted with four different user groups. The heuristic approach involved gaining analysis of the following elements; visibility of system status, match between the system and the real world, user control and freedom, consistency, error prevention, recognition, flexibility, efficiency, aesthetics and navigation.

The data gathered from the usability study was later collated and the results were used to help the development of the services' user interfaces. For LBS, features such as credit card payment capabilities were suggested during the study but not included in the prototype. User's feedback and comments included security issues about using the service and whether the tradesperson quotation was binding or simply an estimate. A second iteration of usability testing based on the prototypes created will provide further feedback.

7. Ongoing Plans for Exploitation of Prototypes

An important objective for the project is to identify and develop opportunities for the commercial exploitation of project deliverables. The project is in fact set up to maximise the potential for commercial exploitation – in particular the project brings together of a broad range of stakeholders with diverse set of expertise and experiences to work on user centric next generation services.

There was a focussed effort at the outset to ensure the industry consortium collectively represented the entire telecommunications value chain – operators, telco ISVs, and Equipment Vendors. The operators (there are three in the consortium) have a specific interest in identifying services which are of interest to their user base and from which they can generate additional ARPU in the face of falling voice revenues. The equipment vendor members are motivated to identify both services and service enablers to demonstrate a return on investment for the IMS platforms they are, in turn, trying to sell to the operators. Finally the 20+ telco ISVs are using their individual domain backgrounds to identify opportunities to extend and combine their existing offerings with project deliverables.

A specific initiative within the project is the commercial exploitation of the Public Transport Advisor service. A preliminary analysis has been conducted on the potential end user take-up and ultimate commercial viability of this service. The focus to date has been on:

- Working with companies in the transport industry to determine what added value can be provided to users beyond what is currently available
- Identifying ISV industry stakeholders with complimentary and enabling product offerings
- Promoting the service amongst the operator stakeholders with a view to setting up user trials within their subscriber bases
The results achieved to date are:
- An opportunity with the Dublin Transport Authority (DTA) has been identified whereby shortest path decision engines could be combined with GPS location services to deliver routing information to mobile users. Additional services are being considered including the use of telemetry data from public transport vehicles to
- Opportunities have been identified for a number of ISV stakeholders to extend the target market for their existing product sets. One particular ISV, a producer of video-based IVR products, has helped define whole new video based use case scenarios for the PTA service. It is expected that these use cases will improve the probability of mass market uptake.
- One of the stakeholder operators has committed to conducting preliminary live user trials of the PTA service based on the results of early usability analysis.

8.   Conclusions and Recommendations

The project aims to take a number of such end user services and bring them to a prototype phase and to the level of usability trials. The prototypes are deployed on the OpenIMS network from Fraunhofer Fokus, an industry standard and open source testbed. The resultant foreground IP created by the project will be available to the project stakeholders for unrestricted exploitation and will be put in the public domain and open sourced 6 months after the end of the project. The project also showcases a development process for IMS services and enablers through combining both internet and telecoms software development paradigms, including the use of various development and testing tools, the use of agile methodology, and incorporating a usability analysis and feedback stage as part of this overall development process.

Projects such as IMS ARCS are a very good way of encouraging research and development activity among companies which often have little or no R&D resources through giving them access to academic research expertise and knowledge, while providing a route to allow commercialisation of existing research work and improving academic industrial cooperation. Simultaneously, academic institutions get access to commercial realism and market requirements, allowing them to tune their research priorities to areas where it is most relevant. Such projects also can have a "stone soup" effect, where the various participants are encouraged to cooperate by contributing some of their background IP and the end result may be far more than the sum of the parts, in which they can all share

Because of the large number of stakeholders in the project, there can sometimes be competing objectives and differences of opinion regarding the direction of the project or where effort should be focused. There can also be a tendency towards "mission drift" where goals can be subtly moved over time. The challenge is met by the academic partners who must sometimes make judgement calls to decide how the project can maximise its value to the overall stakeholder group, and also maintain a clear focus on the project goals while being flexible enough to deliver value to the stakeholders.

References

[1] IMS ARCS Project http://www.ims-arcs.org
[2] IP Multimedia Subsystem http://www.3gpp.org
[3] SIP (Session Initiation Protocol) http://www.ietf.org/rfc/rfc3261.txt
[4] DIAMETER http://www.ietf.org/rfc/rfc3588.txt
[5] http://www.open-ims.org/
[6] IMS Arcs D5.3.1 Usability Analysis Report, Interactive Design Centre, University of Limerick, 2008

Collaboration and the Knowledge Economy: Issues, Applications, Case Studies
P. Cunningham and M. Cunningham (Eds.)
IOS Press, 2008

Emotions, Possession and Willingness to Pay: The Case of iPhone

Jonas HEDMAN, Heidi TSCHERNING
Center for Applied Information and Communication, Copenhagen Business School,
Howitzvej 60, Frederiksberg, 2000, Denmark
Tel: +45 7242 1582 Email: jh.caict@cbs.dk , htj.caict@cbs.dk

Abstract: Emotions are an important factor underlying most human behaviour. The role of emotions is explained by neuroeconomics that is a synthesis of neuropsychology and economics. In this study we test the role of emotions in an exploratory setting, namely the adoption of the iPhone in Demark. To test the role of emotions a research model was developed that includes emotions as independent variables and the intention to buy an iPhone as dependent variable. The hypotheses derived from the research model are tested by regression analysis. The analysis show that positive emotions explain 35 % (R^2 .348) of the variance in people's intention to buy iPhone. Hence, the conclusion suggested in the paper is that emotions should be addressed in research and in the design of mobile artefacts.

1. Introduction

Emotions, such as love, hate, desire, and dislike, are subconscious and have a fundamental impact on human behaviour. However, research into ICT seldom addresses emotions as an factor influencing people when adopting ICT. Instead, very much of the current ICT research implies that human beings behave according to a rational model. This rational view is evident in mainstream models and theories such as Diffusion of Innovations or Technology Acceptance Model. Consequently, underlying mechanisms that shapes our attitudes and beliefs are missed or not addressed, such as our intuitive feelings towards an object. Studies into neuroeconomics have shown the impact of emotions on behaviour and beliefs. It is necessary to investigate the role of emotions in the adoption and diffusion of ICT applications. We explore the role of emotions in peoples intention to buy the iPhone.

1.1 Literature Review: Neuroeconomics

Neuroeconomics is an emerging field that seeks to develop our understanding of human behaviour and in particular the role of emotions and emotional response [1]. The field integrates findings from neuropsychology into social sciences [2]. One of the core findings is that emotional response is an important and underlying mechanism of most human behaviour [1]. The role of emotions has been identified through experiments with people and animals involving neurological techniques (Hansen and Riis Christensen 2007). The role of emotions in human behaviour may be explained by the functioning of the brain, which is addressed next.

According to contemporary neurological and neuropsychological research [1, 3], the brain consists of three basic parts: neo cortex, old cortex, and pre-reptilian part. The neo cortex is the outer part of the brain and the largest. It has several specialized areas for seeing, calculating, reasoning etc and it is here our cognitive processes to a large extent are believed to take place. The old cortex functions as the control system of the brain and is located in the central part of the brain and manages communication between the neo cortex and pre-reptilian brain. The pre-reptilian part is the inner and central part of the brain located in the lower part of the brain and it interacts with the old and neo cortex, where information is processed. It controls basic and elementary processes through three elements. The first is the thalamus where most sensory stimulation passes, such as smells, takes, touches, looks and hearing. The second element is the amygdale which controls our basic responses, such as glandular behaviour (e.g. increase in heart rate) and autonomous responses (e.g. to duck when an object is thrown at you). The third element is the hippocampus, where elementary information is stored, and when interacting with the amygdale it controls emotional responses. The processes controlled by the pre-reptilian part are referred to as emotional responses. They occur before any cognitive process is activated. Every stimulus, from external or internal sources, passes through the thalamus, where an unconscious evaluation of the stimuli occurs. Depending on the stimuli, previous experiences, and the person in question we respond in different ways.

Hansen [4, p. 1432] illustrates brain functionality: "If, for example, an individual in the middle of the road observes a car approaching with fast speed, the perception channelled through the thalamus may, through the amygdale, generate an increased heart rate (autonomous response), sweating in the hands (glandular response) and freezing or running away. All these may occur before any activity in the cortex takes place. Only later, when information has been transmitted here, can the precise nature of the danger be indentified and labelled, and possibly, this may influence the further direction of the response."

Hence, there are several types of brain processes, some are conscious and some are unconscious, activated by affective or cognitive processes. Camerer et al. [2] summarizes different types of brain processes into a two dimensional matrix describing different neural functioning. They distinguish between controlled and automatic processes on one dimension and cognitive and affective processes on the other dimension. Controlled processes are deliberate and sequential when encountering stimuli. In most cases people have a good introspective account of controlled processes. For example, a software developer can recall the development process, such as what problems existed and how they were solved. Automatic processes are parallel and occurs unconscious and are effortless. Parallelism is central. It is the brain's multitasking ability and extremely fast. For example, a person is able to manage numerous of stimulus at the same time, such as seeing, listening, talking, touching, smelling, and tasting. But people have limited introspective account for these processes and are unable to recall why they did something in a certain way.

The other dimension deals with cognitive and affective processes. Affective processes are closely related to motivation and feelings. All affective processes are valence, i.e. they are either positive or negative. They are also labelled as go/no-go questions that elicit behaviour – do or do not. There are two types of affective processes: biological, such as hunger, sex, drug addiction, and social, such as desire to have or to be included. Cognitive processes are brain processes that do not have valance. They answer true and false questions. Hence, cognitive processes cannot lead to action by themselves, only if affective processes are involved. The different brain processes do not exist in a pure form or exist in isolation. According to Camerer et al. [2] all behaviour has to involve affective processes.

In this section we have briefly outlined some of the key ideas of neuroeconomics. The underlying foundation is the new understanding of how the brain functions and the role of emotions and emotional response that underlie all human behaviour. In addition four key brain processes, including controlled, automatic, cognitive and affective, are briefly described. To summarize and integrate the ideas we present the Emotion Cognition Behaviour (ECB) model that relates emotions to behaviour, see figure 1. All behaviour is elicited by some external or internal stimuli. The stimuli are first automatically processed in the pre-reptilian brain leading to either a positive or negative emotion (affective brain processes), which leads to an emotional response. The emotional response may elicit a behavioural response or a cognitive process (controlled or automatic) that may lead to certain behaviour. In the following section we present a research model that incorporates affective (emotions) and cognitive controlled (intention to buy) processes.

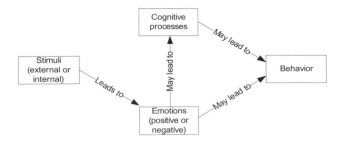

Figure 1: Emotion Cognition and Behaviour Model

1.2   Research Model

Stimuli can be defined as being something that causes a physical response in an organism and stimuli can be either external or internal. External stimuli are stimuli that people sense in their external environment. These can for example be visual stimuli such as images or text. Internal stimuli are peoples' own thoughts on a given product or concept. The external stimulus in this investigation is the questionnaire presented to the respondents. The questionnaire contained a short descriptive text of the iPhones features, a photo of the iPhone, and questions related to our research question. The internal stimuli are the thoughts and possible preferences that people may have formed as a consequence of the continual exposure of the device in different media since its presentation at Macworld Expo in January 2007 and during the process of filling out the questionnaire. This leads to the following hypotheses:

  H1a: Stimuli, external or internal, are related to negative emotions.

  H1b: Stimuli, external or internal, are related to positive emotions.

The emotions elicited by the stimuli leads to emotional responses (behaviour and/or cognitive process. Behaviour (affective and automatic brain processes) elicited directly from emotions is not measured, since it is not relevant for our study. Cognitive processes (thinking about the iPhone and in fact answering the questionnaire) is a response to emotions leading to the following hypothesis:

  H2a: Emotions, positive or negative, elicit emotional response (cognitive processes).

Positive emotions are found to have a great impact on people's choice of consumer products and brand (Hansen and Riis Christensen 2007). Therefore, we hypothesize that positive emotions is a predictor of people's intention to buy iPhone:

  H2b: Emotions, positive, is positively related to people's intention to buy an iPhone.

2.   Objectives

The overall research question is: Can emotions explain the failure or success of information technology? We explore this in the context of the adoption of iPhone in Denmark the purpose is to increase our understanding of how emotions affect people's intention to buy the iPhone. This paper contributes to our understanding of emotions as an underlying mechanism in the adoption and diffusion of mobile services and technology. We acknowledge that emotions and rational behaviour cannot be separated but must be investigated collectively, and believe that it is necessary to rethink the use of existing models to include emotions in order to be able to provide a broader picture of adoption and diffusion of mobile services and technology.

3. Methodology

Given the research question of the paper, to identify the role of emotions in human behaviour, the study conducted is mainly exploratory. One of challenges was to find a behavioural situation, where emotions are likely to be of importance to predict the intention of behaviour. We finally decided to explore our research question in the context of people's intention to acquire the iPhone in Denmark. The reason for this choice was mainly due to the fact that the iPhone was not sold in the Danish market at the time of the data collection. However, it is available through individual parallel import mainly from the UK and the USA. For instance in the beginning of April 2008 there were more than 8.000 iPhone's used in the Danish mobile networks [5]. The iPhone has attracted a lot of attention from customers and competitors, some people find the iPhone so attractive that they go to foreign countries in order to acquire it, and crack it in order to make it work in their home countries. This seemed to be a unique situation for investigating the role of emotions and the intention to acquire a new mobile phone.

3.1 Instrument Development

Affective processes, such as emotions, are difficult to measure directly. But, it is possible to infer the underlying emotions by inquiring about feelings [4, 8]. In psychology there are several instruments available to measure feelings. For example, Ortony and Turner [9] provide a review of different instruments. These measurements are based on verbal expressions and include different feeling words, such as hate, love, joy, distress etc. The instrument used in this study is based on scales from previous empirical studies [6, 7].

The development of the instrument involved three phases: The first phase relates to the development of measurements (feeling words) that measure "emotions". These feeling words came from an initial list of 53 positive and negative feeling words from marketing literature [6] and information systems literature [10, 11]. The initial list was presented and discussed in two workshops with 30 master students. Through these workshops we were able to reduce the number of feeling words to 32.

To test the reliability of the 32 items we developed a questionnaire addressing the impact of "emotions" on potential consumer's "willingness to pay" for an iPhone. The respondents were asked to evaluate the applicability of each of the 32 feeling word to describe their emotions towards the iPhone and its feature. The questionnaire was tested by 39 Ph D students. From the test we selected the five most applicable positive feeling words and the two most applicable negative feeling words. The words were: "excitement", "smart", "doubt", "expectations", "like", "interest", and "uncertainty".

The third phase involved the development of measurements that relates to controlled cognitive processes. The dependent variable or studied behaviour is people's "intention to buy" an iPhone. This was measured by one item "Do you intend to acquire an iPhone". The intention to buy was measured by "positive emotions". The scales were measured using a five-point scale ranging from strongly disagrees to strongly agree.

4. Result

4.1 Population and Sample

Approximately one thousand students enrolled at undergraduate and graduate level at the IT University and the DØK studies (managerial economics and IT) at the Copenhagen Business School were invited to participate in the study. In table 1, we summarise the demographic data of the respondents. Usable responses consist of 158 students including 103 male (66%) and 54 female (34%). The survey was anonymous, and students were asked to respond to all items and in the way consistent with their perceptions and emotions in regard to the iPhone. Respondents were between age 21 and age 57. 103 of the respondents were between 20 and 30 years old which accounts for approximately 65% of the sample. 33 respondents were between 30 and 35 years (21%), 12 were between 35 and 40 years (8%) and 8 respondents were between 40 and 57 years old (5%).

Table 1: Demographic Information of Survey Respondents

Male		Female	
103 (66%)		54 (34%)	
Age 21 – 30	Age 30 - 35	Age 35 – 40	Age 40 - 57
103 (65%)	33 (21%)	33 (21%)	12 (8%)

Table 2, show the respondents experience of Apple products; 82 respondents (52%) stated that they have no or very little experience with MAC computers, 55 (35%) have no or little experience with iTunes and 49 (31%) have no or little experience with iPods. 45 (28%) state that they have much experience with MAC computers, 81 (51%) have much experience with iTunes and 84 (53%) have much experience with iPods.

Table 2: Respondents' Previous Experience with Apple Products

	No or little experience	Much experience
MAC computers	82 = 52%	45 - 28%
ITunes	55 = 35%	81 - 51%
IPods	49 = 31%	84 - 53%

The respondents all have a mobile phone; 72 (45%) have a Nokia phone, 53 (34%) have a Sony Ericsson phone, 6 (4%) have an iPhone and 27 (17%) own a phone of a different brand, such as Samsung, LG, HTC or HP Ipaq. 31 (20%) of these phones are Smartphone's and 127 (80%) of the phones are other phones.

4.2 Analysis

The factor analysis contains three factors (Positive emotions, Negative emotions, and Cognitive processes) explaining 77% of the overall variance. The analysis based on principal component extraction and varimax rotation produced a good factor structure. Kaiser-Meyer-Olkin Measure of Sampling Adequacy gave a result of ,853. The communalities varied between ,571 (Excitement) to ,933 (Cognitive process) indicating that the factors represents the variables well. Nevertheless, the main result of the factor analysis relates to hypothesis 1a, 1b that stimuli elicit to positive and negative emotions, which can be measured by feeling words. This is consistent with studies from marketing [6]. The factor analysis also provides support for the hypothesis 2a that emotions elicit cognitive processes. Another way to illustrate that cognitive processes have been elicited by the stimuli (the survey and its questions) is that 158 persons have participated and spent on average 5 minutes and 47 seconds on the survey.

The second part of our result presentation addresses hypothesis H2b that is based on a linear regression analysis. The dependent variable is intention to buy and the independent are the factor "positive emotions" from the factor analysis. Negative emotion was excluded, since it is not expected to predict intention to buy and the factor cognitive process is an antecedent of cognitive brain processes and not intention to buy. Based on the underlying items of the four factors an index was created for each factor. The indexes were used as independent variables in the regression analysis.

The regression analyses provide acceptable support to the regression models. The squared R reached ,348 and F 80.68 for Positive emotions, thus explaining 35 % of the variance in people's intention to buy iPhone. The results of the study show that cognitive neuroscience is a viable science that can inform information system as suggested. It provides some new insights and illustrates the role of the constructs emotions and emotional response that may force of the revise and rethink some of our models and theories.

5.   Business Benefits

Previous research within other fields has shown that positive emotions have a great impact on people's choice of consumer products and brand [6]. Our study supports this theory and the main benefit of the study is the provision of evidence that positive emotions predict people's intention to buy an iPhone. Benefits of the Emotion Cognition Behavior-model for the various stakeholders are listed below:

- Mobile phone users could experience benefits if businesses use the constructs of the ECB-model and design mobile phones that seek to accommodate the users' emotions towards design and functionality.
- The business community should therefore ensure the incorporation of mobile users' emotions when developing mobile devices. Mobile users have emotions towards the design of the phone and the functionalities supported by the phone. These emotions elicit an emotional response in the form of cognitive processes and these may lead to a certain behavior, such as the acquisition of a particular mobile device. The business community may then benefit even more from their marketing of information and communication technologies that already seems to be approaching peoples' emotions.
- The IS research community could benefit from integrating the discoveries in cognitive neuroscience into IS theories about how the diffusion and adoption of IT supports human processes and should therefore also incorporate emotions in the development of theories and business models. The inclusion of emotions seems to have influence on and predict whether a mobile device, and possibly also information and communication technologies in general, is adopted and thus whether it becomes a failure or success.

The investigation of the failure or success of information and communication technologies as well as the adoption process of technologies feed back to the business community that may use this knowledge in the further development of technologies and marketing, which will in the end benefit the end-users.

6.   Conclusions

This paper has introduced neuroeconomics to the IS community and presented the results of a study that investigates the role of emotions, emotional response and behavior. The purpose was to contribute to the overall question whether emotions can explain the failure or success of information technology. We explored this in the context of iPhone adoption in Denmark and investigated whether emotions influence peoples' intention to buy the iPhone.

After introducing Neuroeconomics, we developed an instrument through three phases to measure feelings and ended up with seven, five positive and two negative, feeling words that may explain the intention to buy an iPhone. 158 respondents participated in the study. Through factor analysis we found that three factors (positive emotions, negative emotions and cognitive processes) explain 77% of the overall variance. We consequently deduce that external and/or internal stimuli are related to positive and negative emotions. Furthermore, the factor analysis shows that positive and/or negative emotions elicit emotional response (cognitive processes). This was further supported by respondents spending on average of 5 minutes and 47 seconds completing the survey. A regression analysis provides evidence that positive emotions are positively related to peoples' intention to buy an iPhone.

Our study therefore shows that cognitive neuroscience is a viable science that can contribute further to information systems research and that constructs such as emotions and emotional response may be incorporated into existing models of diffusion and adoption.

6.1 Future Research

There are numerous opportunities to explore the ECB model and emotions in future information systems research and thereby improve our understanding of different factors influencing the diffusion and adoption of information technology and the design information systems.

The presented research contains certain limitations. These include the technology being studied in a voluntary and not a mandatory context, the role of emotions in regard to the technology is investigated before an adoption can occur at an individual level and the technology itself, which is quite simple as opposed to large complex information systems. These circumstances create an opportunity for IS researcher's to explore the role of emotions in the following settings:

- From voluntary to mandatory context: Our study was conducted in a voluntary context; people's individual intention to buy an iPhone, and therefore the result, referring to the specific feeling words and the impact of positive emotions on intention, cannot necessarily be applied to a mandatory use context. Hence, it could enhance the explanatory power of emotion to study the role of emotions in a mandatory setting. For instance, the role of emotions in sales peoples intention to use CRM system or software developer's intention to comply with procedures in information system development methods. To expand emotions from a voluntary to a mandatory setting requires the inclusion of different feeling words than the seven used in this study, see table 2.
- From before to after diffusion and adoption: The iPhone has not been released in Denmark when this study was conducted and only 4% of respondents own an iPhone, which furthermore demonstrates that diffusion and adoption of the technology has not yet taken place. The current adopters may be categorized as innovators so when the iPhone is released in Denmark it could be of interest to investigate the role of emotions as we go further into the diffusion curve of innovation and the behavior of the iPhone adopters become individual experienced reactions [7].
- From simple to more complex technologies: The intention to buy the iPhone is a simple behavior or at least the decision to buy one does not require a complex decision making process. It would be interesting to study the role of emotions in situations involving adoption decisions of more complex technologies such ERP system. Another situation related to the development of information systems would be the case of software developers solving complex problems, e.g. the design of a new operating system.
- From individual to group or organizational setting: Most existing research within cognitive neuroscience, neuroeconomics, and neuromarketing has been done at the individual level. There are very few attempts to move this research to a group or organizational setting [2]. Thus, there is an opportunity for exploring and exploiting the use of feeling words in both group and organizational settings. For example, are there common emotions towards an object within a workgroup or do common emotions reveal something about the underlying values of an organization. Emotions on technologies introduced in a group or an organizational setting may very well be different from technologies chosen to be used by the individual. The dynamics of a group or an organization are different as well as the benefits of using the technology. It could be relevant to study how emotions influence the implementation of an information system in a change management context. What is the role of employees'

emotions when they respond with resistance against the change? And is this common feeling reinforced in the group as opposed the feeling at the individual level?

These different research settings may help explain the success and failure of information systems and show that positive emotions and cognitive processes towards an information system influence people's intention to make good use of the system and behave as intended and thus make the use of the system a success. Correspondingly negative emotions and cognitive processes towards an information system influence people's resistance against the use of the system and thus cause it to fail.

References

[1] Damasio, A.R., Descartes' error: emotion, reason, and the human brain. 1994, New York: G.P. Putnam. xix, 312 p.

[2] Camerer, C., G. Loewenstein, and D. Prelec, Neuroeconomics: How Neuroscience Can Inform Economics. Journal of Economic Literature, 2005. 43(1): p. 9-64.

[3] LeDoux, J.E., The emotional brain: the mysterious underpinnings of emotional life. [New ed. 1999, London: Phoenix. 384 p.

[4] Hansen, F., Distinguishing between Feelings and Emotions in Understanding Communication Effects. Journal of Business Research, 2005. 58: p. 1426-1436.

[5] Larsen, K.B., 8000 Hackede iPhones florerer frit i Danmark, in Børsen. 2008: Copenhagen.

[6] Hansen and S. Riis Christensen, Emotions, Advertising and Consumer Choice. 2007, Copenhagen: Copenhagen Business School Press. 462 p.

[7] Venkatesh, V., et al., USER ACCEPTANCE OF INFORMATION TECHNOLOGY: TOWARD A UNIFIED VIEW. MIS Quarterly, 2003. 27(3): p. 425-478.

[8] Christensen, S.R., Measuring Consumer Reaction to Sponsoring Partnerships based upon Emotional and Attitudinal Responses. International Journal of Market Research, 2006, 48(1): p. 61-80.

[9] Ortony, A. and T.J. Turner, What's Basic About Basic Emotions? Psychological Review, 1990. 97(3): p. 315-331.

[10] Kalbach, J., I'm Feeling Lucky: The Role of Emotions in Seeking Information on the Web. Journal of the American Society for Information Science & Technology, 2006. 57(6): p. 813-818.

[11] Picard, R.W., Toward Computers that Recognize and Respond to User Emotion. IBM Systems Journal, 2000. 39(3/4): p. 705.

Collaboration and the Knowledge Economy: Issues, Applications, Case Studies
P. Cunningham and M. Cunningham (Eds.)
IOS Press, 2008

Information System for Mobile Devices of the Guàrdia Urbana City Police

Ricard SANJUAN[1], Joan Albert DALMAU[2]

[1]*Municipal Institute of Information Technology, Barcelona City Council,*
Av. Diagonal 220, Barcelona, 08018, Spain
Tel: +34 93 2918252, Fax: + 34 93 2918386, Email: rsanjuan@bcn.cat
[2] *Safety and Mobility, Barcelona City Council, Pl. Carles Pi i Sunyer, 8, Barcelona, 08002,*
Spain   Tel: +34 93 4023368, Fax: + 34 93 4023394, Email: jdalmaub@bcn.cat

Abstract: The Barcelona City Council has focused on the application of the Information Technologies on the government of our city, not only in order to improve the services to the citizens, but also to make City Council internal services more efficient and user-friendly. The case exposed is one of the latest successes that show the benefits of the mobility approach taken in the Guàrdia Urbana City Police. PDA's use with remote access to corporative systems allows improving and speeding up street-level actuations, thanks to a real time access to the corporative information in order to finalize penal actions in-situ. At this point, errors are reduced and exists the possibility to notify and collect the fine at the same moment.

1.   Introduction

As technology moves forward and new products are being offered, its adaptation to work processes is increasingly indispensable. Technological mobility offers have evolved from devices with limited features like agenda and contacts management to great capacity portable offices. Nowadays, the fact that any person can be constantly connected to their organization applications or services entails a good placement and a high competitiveness.

The Guàrdia Urbana City Police agents, who carry out their activities in the street, do an important job for citizens. Furthermore, their activities have a direct impact in the Council internal systems. This is the reason why optimizing their street jobs allows to speed up the Council's internal processes. It also reduces management time and offers the possibility to provide a better service to citizens.

The aim of the action is to improve the efficiency and service level of the Guàrdia Urbana Police using workstations (PDAs) to ease the policemen's activities in the city.

The main reason to carry out this project was to improve the response capacity of the Guàrdia Urbana when finding any incidence on the street. This collective required faster and error free actuations as well as access to more information, such as situation of vehicles, City Council documentation, licenses, sanctions or the land registry. These requirements meant that a more efficient and adaptable treatment circuit was needed.

Thus, the PDAs provide more security to the street-level actuations of the police force and open a portal to communicate with other information systems, such as the Department of Motor Vehicles or other security forces like the Fire Brigade.

2.   Objectives

The main aims of this paper are:

1.   To present the innovative mobility approach proposed in order to improve the Guàrdia Urbana Local Police capacity of response, efficiency and effectiveness.

2. To present a best practices model case description about the implantation of a support system to the mobility platform, common to all users and mobile applications, that gives answer to the universal needs of mobile devices.
3. To show this approach may be transferred to other public administrations to accelerate adoption of new ICT and processes to improve their efficiency and quality of service.

3. Business Case

3.1 Background

The prior system was not mechanized; accusation data was gathered manually by policemen using a fine ticket. The ticket was sent to the Territorial Unit to be classified and reported to a company responsible for mechanized data input. This mechanization included data treatment and depuration to facilitate the work of the different Council collector systems, responsible for denounce procedure and their notification via mail to the offender.

Figure 1: Prior System

3.2 Technological Solution

This system we present changed the whole process, starting with the on-line data input and following with the procedure in the Council systems. Now, the accusation is handled at the same moment that is detected and reported thanks to mobile devices. It is significant to point out the possibility of in-situ notification and the incorporation of new payment possibilities that allow the completion of the procedure at street-level.

The solution used to implement the system is based on the use of the new information technologies in the context of mobile applications. The development on the client side uses the operating system Windows Mobile 2003, including .NET technology, taking benefit of data synchronization with the BackOffice systems allowed by local databases (Oracle Lite). This system is prepared for an on-line operation with or without GSM/GPRS network coverage. Whether being out of range or not, the capacities offered by the synchronization of the PDAs' local databases can be used.

On-line access to the Council systems uses a wireless GSM/GPRS solution that is an extension of the corporate network (LAN) with GSM-LAN. The printers' connection is made via Bluetooth.

In order to compile as much features as possible, the equipment provided to the Guàrdia Urbana agents to support their street-level work consists of:

• PDA terminals fitted with photographic camera, access to the GSM/GPRS network, Bluetooth and Wi-Fi.
• Portable printers fitted with a long-life battery, easy to extract and easy to install in vehicles with Bluetooth connection; digital certificate readers (identification) and magnetic card reader (in order to pay).
• Support material: additional battery, SD cards to load new software versions and download pictures taken.

The complete system consists of a client side installed in the PDA and a server side integrated in the different Council systems. It includes a tax collection system and different enquiry databases that allow the on-line validation. This integration is made using standards such as web services of exchanging XML files.

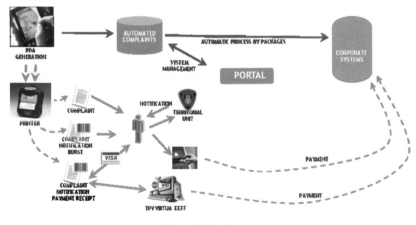

Figure 2: New System

The system is meant to give service to all the Guàrdia Urbana city police working in the street, so it is able to hold around 750 PDAs and 400 printers that will be used by 2500 officers. Nowadays, more than 1500 agents handle 400 PDAs and 200 printers.

4. Methodology

This project started as a partnership between the Guàrdia Urbana and the Municipal Institute of Informatics (IMI). The leading role was held by the Guàrdia Urbana, and the IMI acted as an innovative and technological agent.

Once the project was operative, the Municipal Tax Office (IMH) was included into the leading group to make possible an easier and faster payment of complaints. The automation brought them less data entry work, and generated error reduction and higher income.

During the project implantation, not only manager opinions have been taken into account, but the system users played an important role. Satisfaction surveys have been taken amongst them and have shown a perception of a high quality service meanwhile allowed new evolutions of the system during last year, which includes new features suggested almost entirely by the officers themselves.

Figure 3: Partnership Model

5.   Development

5.1   General Considerations

To understand the different steps of the project we must keep in mind that this is a user-focused project, meaning that it is a tool to improve the working methods of the police officers instead of just an improvement of the inner circuits.

To obtain a better acceptation of the project amongst the Guàrdia Urbana collective, the implantation plan started by presenting a support system to the mobility platform, that was common to all users and mobile applications and gave answer to the usual needs of mobile informatics. In order to create this software, the functional needs of the agents were analyzed when designing the pilot version. The following step was to outline the new improvements included regarding to the ones the operative test formerly had. Then, new functionalities were analyzed with special focus on the officers' most needed tools, like the expansion of the types of sanctions they could mechanize, or the connection with the Council Incidences System (IRIS) and decree violation reports. After that, an integrated mobility solution for municipal agents that work at street-level was created from functional needs detected and analyzed with the Guàrdia Urbana as well as client applications and connectivity systems necessary to its functioning.

Before its final implantation, an operative test was run amongst a reduced group of agents. This test was the key in defining mobility strategies, such as the solution ergonomics or the right mobile devices to be used, according to the Guàrdia Urbana's functional needs. Another step was the impact analysis that a project of this magnitude would have in the daily work of the police officers as they changed their working tool from a notebook to an electronic device.

Finally, the pilot was useful to analyze the different technologies involved (communication, replication and development) as well as the cultural impact the change of tool would have on the officers. Another objective that was achieved was studying the impact of mobile applications on internal circuits and protocols. Volumes, activities and costs were also analyzed with this tool.

Due to needs detected and objective to be achieved, the development was divided into:

- A mobile office, which included a personal agenda, e-mail and alarms.
- Interactive urban guide with access to city infrastructure, visualization systems and location by exact address or crossroad.
- Access to corporate information, incidence's reception and sending or actuation request. Integration with other corporate systems allows remote management.
- On-line reporting of accusations and incidences, attaching photos, that will be managed by a central service locating them territorially.

5.2   Final Planning

The development of the project can be described by these different steps:

1. The project started as a pilot on 2005, with 30 PDAs used by 100 policemen during three months. The PDAs had access to a reduced topology of complaints, and the officers could notify the complaints manually.
2. Next step was the project development, on July 2006, which involved the enlargement to all complaint types. Besides, the fine ticket was replaced by the printing system. During this actuation of the project, a special focus was made on training users and helping them to adopt the system change in order to reduce the cultural impact which can cause reluctance facing change.
3. During 2006 and 2007, the number of PDAs increased to 400, achieving the amount of 1500 users. The final system got integrated with the Council Incidences System (IRIS),

including an access to the web browser, in-situ introduction of the incidences and immediate resolution. A new service offered was to report peddling, with the consequent object confiscation and notification to the offender. This notification could be printed in-situ. Another feature the system included was the option to pay the fine via credit card and get a printed pay receipt. The last new feature was the vehicle information request from the central database.

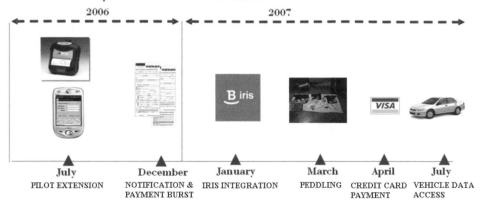

| July | December | January | March | April | July |
| PILOT EXTENSION | NOTIFICATION & PAYMENT BURST | IRIS INTEGRATION | PEDDLING | CREDIT CARD PAYMENT | VEHICLE DATA ACCESS |

Figure 4: Process Development

6. Results

The introduction of PDAs in the Guàrdia Urbana officers' daily life has reduced their amount of work and the errors that were made. Nowadays, about 64% of formal complaints are made via PDA. The 100% is not reached yet because there are not enough handheld devices for all agents. As a measure of comparison, the percentage of formal complaints treated through PDA was of 33% during the pilot project.

The new system was rapidly adopted by the Guàrdia Urbana agents, requiring the acquisition of spare batteries to avoid stopping the working rhythm of a 24 hour day. Exchange and charging areas in the police station (as for patrol radios), have been created.

The new features included in the workstations are really appreciated by the users. On one hand, the officer can access to more information, making his daily job easier; on the other hand, there is a reduction of administrative burden, as shows the fact that around 33% of complaints are notified at the same moment. This percentage is not higher because the officers need to check some information with the offender and they are not always there.

The total investment needed was approximately 2 million euros, including the infrastructure building as well as maintenance cost and GPRS/GSM traffic bills. According to a pessimistic approach, the Return of Investment (ROI) should be achieved in two years. This rapid investment recuperation makes easier to renew the devices more frequently, keeping the handled computers up to date with the latest technology.

7. Business Benefits

The use of PDAs and printers represents a combination of benefits and improvements for the Guàrdia Urbana police:
- Improvement of the capacity of response, efficiency and effectiveness of the activities carried out at street-level by means of the use of mobile technology.
- Access to corporate information and other systems when and where necessary, and therefore the consequent global improvement of the service.

- Immediate introduction of information from the street to the City Council systems so as to speed up data management and to reduce the time of response.
- Introduction of in-situ notification to the offender allowing the legal guarantee of the actions and optimizing the sanctioning process.
  For the City Council, the benefits are:
- Increase in the quality of data entry for future claims.
- Reduction of administrative burden and general administration costs (data entry, sending notifications, executorial procedure, delivery and handling).
- Reduction of time and risk of sanction prescription.
- Better management of denounces and notifications, which means lower cost for the Council, reporting more benefits per fine (33% in-situ notifications).
  The citizen can also recognize some benefits:
- More facilities to pay on the voluntary period, that is, the period comprised between the complaint notification and the start of the legal actions against the offender.
- Citizen's vision of Guàrdia Urbana services changes because of the officers' new tools.
- It means an efficient use of the public expense.

8. Success Key Factors

How to introduce a good change management plan, in order to reduce the impact on the Guàrdia Urbana Police organization, has been the most critical factor of the project.
The key ideas used to this effect are the following:
- It is an "Everybody's Project", for this reason participation at all levels was requested (direction, intermediate commands, agents, logistics responsibles ...).
- Motivation, attitude and implication of the Guàrdia Urbana Police.
- The use of educational and communication channels of the Guàrdia Urbana Police, such as training using didactic tools and participation in periodic meetings, monographs on internal magazines, intranet, etc.
- Progressive deployment by territorial units with in-situ monitoring of the team project.
- Total replacement of the manual fine ticket by the printed one.
- Constant and centralized support for all service shifts including the night ones.

Another key factor has been the previous work done by means of different provisional programs. The group of agents that worked on them played a very important part not just in the application trial but also in the internal promotion, explaining the competitive advantages of the project to the other workmates.

It is remarkable to mention that the user support has been very important. It is a personalized and continuous 24 hour service that was extended during the first two months after the launching in order to guarantee the success of the deployment.

These forces are used to work with rules and commands. This fact facilitates this kind of projects, as long as they are validated by the commands.

9. Transferability

As this is a dynamic and adaptable project, this experience can be useful for other mobile groups inside the Council in different ways.

On the technology side, we have created a model of infrastructure and mobile technology architecture, which can be reused by other collectives and services. The extension of this model as a philosophy can have a great impact on the efficiency of any group that does not work indoor, such as work inspectors or firemen.

This project with the Guàrdia Urbana becomes a model to continue with future deployments of mobile offices. We cannot forget that 66% of the services offered by the Council are developed at street-level.

10. Lessons Learnt

The introduction of eGovernment does not just involve technological improvements; it also means changes in the internal processes and in the organization culture.

The corporate applications mobilization must be aligned with usability aspects and be as user-friendly as possible. In our case, the Council Incidences System has been integrated in the PDAs as a natural evolution of its use. It is also important to adapt the best technological option to the kind of service that will be offered.

Due to a successful change management, we were able to completely renew the working tools of a working group, keeping its productivity and efficiency. Other key factors that made us experience a rapid transition to the daily use of handheld devices were a suitable formation and the Guàrdia Urbana's enthusiasm.

We also learned that the Guàrdia Urbana is more eager for new technologies than we would have imagined. This propels the research into the direction of the technological solutions, expecting a similar welcome in other ambits.

To achieve a profitable solution, the focus must be on an intensive and non-personal use of the technological devices, in order to fit more users in the same device and increase their working rhythm. In a future situation, when a bigger amount of devices and working groups will be implied, a management platform will be needed. As the investment can be recovered in such a short time (ROI), the system can be continuously evolving and it also allows a constant hardware renewal.

11. Conclusions

This project has had a great impact on the organization, which made a qualitative leap forward from manual procedure to PDA use. The incorporation of technology to street-level work implied changes within the organization's daily processes and had a significant impact on people.

Access to corporate information during street operations improves services and minimizes errors. Information is available whenever and wherever necessary and without delay to the City Council in order to be managed.

Thanks to the ITC and the staff's new technical skills, it is possible not only to get efficacy and efficiency improvement, but to strengthen the Guàrdia Urbana's presence on the street reassessing the citizen's point of view.

The constant growth of this project allows us to see future improvements. Renovation to update PDA devices and software to the leading edge technology is already planned within a short time. There will also be an expansion of features which will allow the connection of the Guàrdia Urbana with other forces such as the Traffic Department or the towing service. The new PDAs will be able to connect to Wi-Fi networks as well as GPRS/GSM. They will also be used as a backup communication channel in case the radio fails. Another interesting complement they will include is the possibility to locate the officer via GPS to store the address of the complaint. One extension people will notice is that the new fine tickets will be printed out in three languages: Catalan, Spanish and English.

Due to the great success achieved, we are considering extension to other areas. The municipal services of Urban Planning, Tax Office, Public Highways, Maintenance and Fire Brigade may benefit from what mobility has to offer. The response capacity, efficiency and effectiveness of the municipal services provided at street-level will all be improved.

Collaboration and the Knowledge Economy: Issues, Applications, Case Studies
P. Cunningham and M. Cunningham (Eds.)
IOS Press, 2008

Bringing Wireless Broadband
to Remote Areas

Anna SANGIORGI[1], Paolo DI FRANCESCO[2]
[1]CRES – Centro per la Ricerca Elettronica in Sicilia,
via Regione Siciliana, 49, Monreale, 90046, Italy
Tel: +39 091 6404501, Fax: +39 091 6406200, Email: sangiorgi@cres.it
[2]Teleinform s.p.a., via Regione Siciliana, 49, Monreale, 90046, Italy
Tel: +39 091 6408576, Fax: +39 091 6406200 Email: difrancesco@teleinform.com

Abstract: The term *digital divide* describes how the lack of digital infrastructures divides rural territories from well-served areas; it is still the core of the debate on ICT investments as solutions for socio-economic growth and as a condition for technology transfer and development. Many factors such as cost of infrastructures, low population density and classical business models make up the barriers constituting this problem. In this paper, we describe how an innovative business and social approach – working on the local territory together with local administrations – makes it possible to solve many issues thus giving a new digital life to rural areas. The result is a model suitable for rural regions and NMSs in Europe and the Mediterranean area, where the system proposed – Wikitel WDSL – is just one technical solution but the structured and inclusive approach, oriented to users and local stakeholders, is a guarantee for transferability.

1. Introduction

Access to the information economy in remote areas is notoriously difficult. A gap in technology is a lack of the opportunities offered by information and communication technologies (ICTs), especially when they are unevenly distributed among citizens. The term "digital divide" is an implicit push to bridge this gap, with the most frequent approach focused on technology *tout court*: provide more computers and mobile phones.

The debate on the digital divide also brings up the question of whether large investments in ICT can automatically lead to better living conditions, including those still in a state of poverty, or whether instead this kind of technology needs a developed socio-economic context to have an impact. Here it is not possible to answer, though certainly there is not a strong dependency between opposite positions. The limit of the problem is known and is part of the contradictory process: ICT can have a significant positive impact as an instrument of sustainable development, but without considerable investments it is very difficult to imagine how growth and socio-economic development can be achieved [1]. The need to make information more accessible and provide services via digital means is also well represented at the political and social level. If the Internet is to be the big solution for the problem of marginality, this must be considered in all of its aspects:

- Geographical marginality, which can be solved through digital infrastructures.
- Economical marginality, i.e. how rural areas evolve in terms of their social and economical models.
- Social marginality, which represents the difference in opportunity for interaction between persons in rural or well-served areas.

The most appropriate strategy for local actors is thus a tailored, structured and inclusive approach involving multi-stakeholder partnerships for bridging the digital divide. Only an integrated, multidisciplinary system of players can take the actions required to embed technological convergence (devices, infrastructures, ICT solutions) within the socio-economic environment. Such a model can take due account of the above-mentioned debate – ICT investments before socio-economic development or vice-versa – while keeping in mind the main objective: supporting marginalized areas to lift them out of the gap [2].

In this context, Sicily can be considered as a relevant case study due to the mixture of cultures and economies within which the digital divide occurs. Sicily is the largest region in Italy, with a morphology that varies from the sandy and rocky coasts to the internal mountainous areas (including Etna, the still-active volcano) or the very extensive wheat fields and vineyards. Together with this variety of landscape are the numerous municipalities with different and specific individual situations from the morphological point of view. Many characteristics are shared with rural regions in particular in the southern New Member States (NMSs) and the Mediterranean area: social and economic division, marginality, poor-rich antithesis in terms of areas and individuals.

This opens up the double challenge of offering the same "digital opportunities" other regions have in terms of connectivity:

- To be "always on" for day-to-day activities;
- To gain "proximity status" (with respect to well-served municipalities or areas) independently of geographic, economic and social conditions.

In this situation CRES (Centro per la Ricerca Elettronica in Sicilia), a public-equivalent Sicilian ICT Research Centre in electronics and microelectronics, has defined its challenge as "bringing Wireless Broadband to Remote Areas, especially those ignored by the big Internet Service Providers"

2. Objectives

The aim of this paper is to describe an integrated social approach to addressing the digital divide, using our experience in Sicily as a case study. The initial strategy and actions carried out have the objective of realizing a value added service for the benefit of our region: local municipalities, SMEs and citizens. According to the model of deep co-operation with all the actors potentially affected, together with the technical experience and consequent results, one of the most significant achievements that will be illustrated is the path followed to transform "practice" into a "good practice".

By discussing our concrete experience in the field, we hope to share insights that can be of use to other technology providers and regional development actors working in remote and disadvantaged areas. More than discuss the technological aspects concerning the proposed system (Wikitel [1] WDSL), the objective is to give rural regions, in particular those of New Member States and the Mediterranean basin, a workable and sustainable business model where innovative solutions are adopted not exclusively on the basis of technical features but following rather a process through which the community's needs are expressed and addressed.

3. Methodology

Thanks to the FP6-IST program, CRES has taken part in the ANEMONE [2] project, which realized a "large-scale testbed providing support of mobile users and devices and enhanced services by integrating cutting edge IPv6 mobility and multihoming initiatives together with the majority of current and future wireless access technologies". During the project's lifespan (the project ends in October 2008) CRES decided to take a proactive role in transforming a research experience into a market reality, giving opportunities to local actors to be part of a good "territorial" practice. Teleinform, a very small company controlled by CRES, was transformed into a registered Internet Service Provider and restructured as a commercial company to sell basic and added value products under the unique registered brand Wikitel.

Teleinform's mission thus became to bring wireless broadband to those areas that the large providers consider unprofitable from the standpoint of a traditional cost/benefit business model. The strategy builds on CRES's public role to work "in the field" together with the local municipalities so that connectivity becomes a tool, a service enabler, and not the end goal of the business model. In the end the Wikitel Internet product is seen as a small piece of a more complex puzzle.

This approach has determined the tuning of a fully user-driven model. The specifics of this model vary according to the different characteristics of the rural areas and their marginality, but the same systematic approach is applied in each case:

- Creating synergies between local government and citizens
- Making the right connections with the local environment
- Finding the necessary balance between socio-economical and technical issues and solutions
- D+eploying a multi-disciplinary team with a broad range of competencies, mixing ICT expertise with experience in rural development and technology transfer for SMMEs (Small, Medium and Micro Enterprises).

At this point, the natural but not always obvious step is to find a structured and inclusive solution for areas where traditional market conditions fail. Here, the term "solution" does not indicate a technical one like Wikitel, but must rather capitalise on the experience and results of managing business and rural development together with technicians, local administrators, citizens and micro firms.

The local municipal government is normally selected as the first client to acquire connectivity and/or added value services, who can then spark off a chain reaction progressively involving SMEs and citizens. In the digital divide areas addressed, most municipalities lack an internal system administration service or other IT management facilities. The innovative approach that ensues, compared to the typical strategy of telecom monopolies, consists in a vertical service offer which spans from the pure connectivity and/or LAN infrastructure, to the more complex services (e.g. VPN, Virtual Private Networks) that connect different offices of the Public Administration under the same administrative domain, remotely control firewall and Internet access policies, and so forth.

The total cost of ownership for the municipality is reduced, thanks to the fact that a) some infrastructures can be reused, and b) the overhead due to operational and logistic issues (e.g. the technician is already on site for other tasks) can be dramatically reduced; this last point is of particular importance in the more remote and marginalized areas. This creates an opportunity for CRES/Teleinform to enrich its platform offer with the associated professional services, considering to some degree the entire remote community as part of its customer portfolio. The initial investment with the municipal government can thus be seen in a medium to long-term perspective.

The methodology used to involve local governments has followed two approaches:

1. A "door to door" marketing campaign covering the Sicilian region, contacting the technical office/staff of the Mayors;
2. Participation in a public tender to carry out a connectivity project granted by regional funds for local e-governement (Agenda 2000, POR 2000-2006, measure 6.05 [3]).

In addition to our focus on the municipal governments, there are other "privileged filters" for the local community such as the Areas for Industrial Development, whose aim is to accelerate the growth of local SMEs via special areas; they thus require broadband as part of the infrastructure facilities they offer for businesses.

In any event, initial contacts and the successive partnerships with local governments and agencies are just the starting point of a more systematic approach to involve other actors. Municipalities, more than "official" service points especially in rural or small areas, are considered as the natural hubs that concentrate and deliver "solutions" to those citizens who rise to the role of technology users. This hub function follows from a positive sense of responsibility in local administrators, but although it can suggest a way to the local population, it is unable to make contact with the specific needs of people. The "why is my computer not connecting" or "how can I save money using the Internet" remain *technician to citizen* problems. So in the end, the direct involvement of users, citizens and business owners is the key to the success of technology transfer in digital divide contexts. The approach proposed carries with it a social and economic impact as well, starting from the local municipality or agency and ultimately involving all the actors in the territory in an integrated process of technology upgrading and local development. In fact, the requirement for the multi-disciplinary team mentioned above derives from the need for a comprehensive knowledge of the area concerned, from both the social and technical points of view.

3.1 Business Case Description

In this section we describe our protocol for involving municipalities and then users, within the general approach described above. The concrete examples based on field experiences in five cases offer important insights supporting our conclusions and recommendations.

Following a preliminary contact with the technical staff, a team of experts carries out an on-the-spot inspection and, at the same time, makes a rough technical audit of the potential client's needs in terms of infrastructure and services. The on-spot-inspection is at the core of the whole procedure, to be certain of feasibility. In many cases, for instance, the municipality is organized in several buildings which need to be connected with each other. With this first step, the team has a precise idea of the devices and network apparatus to install and can proceed to make an economical offer which describes how the network will be realized and which services will be delivered. In general, a small municipality suffering from the digital divide asks for:

- Broadband connectivity.
- A private network linking different blocks.
- Connectivity extended to the municipal library, schools (depending on the local municipal government) or other entities directly or indirectly under their administrative domain (e.g. a Pro-loco or tourist information point).
- Replacing existing telephone contracts (PSTN/ISDN) with a better cost/performance solution.

If the offer is considered appropriate to meet the needs, the team installs the required devices and apparatus and the municipality is connected to the Internet. If the contract is assigned by public tender, the team realizes what is described and required in the proposal. In both cases, a main objective is obtained: overcoming the digital divide.

When the last step with the municipality has been concluded, the harmonizing phase between the local government and citizens and SMEs begins. The municipality carefully orchestrates this phase with its technical staff, organizing a public conference to illustrate the adopted technologies and services. The message is clear: if the municipality is "on" the challenge can be taken up by all the others.

At this point, the baton can be handed over to the CRES/Teleinform team, who activates the strategy for citizen and SME involvement. The approach to date has proven very simple but effective, and includes the following steps:

1. CRES/Teleinform contacts a local retailer of personal computers, mobile phones or more in general devices related to ICT technologies;
2. The retailer is offered a percentage for every client who subscribes to the Wikitel system;

3. If the retailer agrees, he/she is informed about the different types of offers/contracts for Wikitel and receives promotional material to inform clients;
4. When a client decides to subscribe, he/she establishes a relationship with CRES /Teleinform for all technical and economic aspects.

During this final phase, CRES/Teleinform audits the client to tailor possible user-driven solutions for specific services. In certain cases, the retailer is involved to install additional equipment.

3.2 Costs and Benefits of the Proposed Model

The business case description addresses the problem of bringing wireless broadband to remote areas. It adopts a general model (container), giving it life with different scenarios (content) that can vary according to specific socio-economic, geographic and technical conditions. In order to transfer the results and adapt them to another context, the following information is required:

*   Characteristics of the area (geography, economy, development policies);
*   Nature of the local stakeholders (local government, technical competitors, SMMEs);
*   Description of services that can potentially promote growth.

In order to evaluate economic sustainability, the following principles are applied:

*   The developers make the investment in the TLC infrastructure, in order to obtain and maintain ownership;
*   The users pay for services and maintenance of the infrastructure, but not for the infrastructure itself.

If this protocol is followed it is possible to identify costs and benefits for both the developer and users. The former bears the cost of the infrastructure but gains the opportunity to theoretically expand business without limits in terms of potential users; it also bears the initial cost for services. The users instead pay for services and system maintenance but are then free from other related problems (choosing the best technical solution, operational problems, etc.) and take advantage of having the infrastructure only "on demand". This reciprocity is undoubtedly a benefit for the whole area: the presence of the TLC infrastructure can increase productivity, generate economic growth, and create jobs and employability, thus improving the quality of life for all.

3.3 Elements to Validate the Proposed Model

The Wikitel system is already on the field, thus representing a commercial "solution". A first indicator to evaluate its success is the number of municipalities and private clients connected, as shown in the table below.

Kind of client	%
Local government	16%
Business	28%
Family	56%
Total	100%

Table 1: Wikitel Installations since 2006

Interestingly, the customers are not migrating due to the fact the product seems to be good enough to contrast the xDSL technology. Most of the customers are not considering the higher price a problem thanks to the customer care service that looks to them superior to the xDSL approach. On the other side it must be noted that the customers that moved to the xDSL are the ones who want to "pay as less as possible" more than considering the overall quality of the product (technical features, customer care, etc.). In all the 3 "oldest territories", i.e. those municipalities where the service has been introduced at the beginning of the commercial launch and the xDSL is now available, the number of customers who have migrated is still under the 10%.

The municipalities seem to be the less sensible to the price gap, because the connectivity is bound together with professional services that make the offer more interesting and complete.

4.   Technology Description

The technological aspect is based on the experience gained during past R&D projects in wireless networks. The process "from idea to product" can be summarized as follows:

- CRES works, often in collaboration with Teleinform, on the prototype of a service, product or device;
- The prototype is then re-engineered by Teleinform and/or CRES to make it cheaper, more robust or simply to make it more attractive to end users;
- Teleinform then defines the commercial strategies and business models for the final product/service.

The Wikitel WikiAir product is based on unlicensed 5Ghz frequencies for both the backbone and access networks. Future technology upgrades (e.g. single or multiple upgrades to licensed frequencies) to provide end users with new services are possible with little effort and in a very short time.

The Wikitel product family is however just the beginning of a medium/long term strategy that includes two main elements – the access medium (e.g. copper, unlicensed/licensed wireless, fibre, etc.) and the set of added value services – where the value is not in either element alone, but in their integration into an attractive and personalized vertical product.

5.   Developments

The proposed model for addressing the digital divide lends itself to transferability in geographical areas and contexts that are completely different from Sicily, due to its ability to adapt to different cultural and social contexts. What should be respected is the operational protocol, as the determining factor of the proposed system.

The choice of such a model, however, depends on a socio-economic analysis of the territory concerned and its reference market. One prerequisite is the existence of conditions of peripherality, rurality and/or low population density, making investment "uneconomical" according to the view of a large Internet Service Provider, but interesting for a connectivity solution such Wikitel. Another positive condition is for example the express wish to have an single supplier for phone and data services.

Every element of technology used is already on the market, thus avoiding any need for special equipment. The cost of these elements is therefore independent of the territory in which the technology will be used. The infrastructure cost will instead depend on the morphology of the territory (harsh conditions), the population density and the required level of service quality. Again, in some cases we have considered all or part of infrastructure costs as a medium/long term investment in order to enlist new customers.

The key determinant of the model's transferability remains the way in which the territorial players have been involved: local government, enterprises, agencies, economic actors and citizens. The better the co-operation, ideally leading to co-design of the services offered, the better the development and success of the system as a whole.

6.   Results

Our experience in applying the proposed model has led, in the first instance, to reaching the primary objective: bringing broadband to remote areas. This occurs not in isolation, but as a function of the broader impacts achieved through important multiplier effects such as increased cooperation between public and private bodies, joining their efforts to transform a territorial challenge into a real and effective participatory process.

One of the central success factors here is gaining the support of the Mayor and his technical staff. Their direct involvement in quickly overcoming the numerous difficulties that arise – e.g. administrative acts concerning permission to install apparatus or environmental impact assessments – is fundamental. The awareness that local government is "on" further stimulates administrators to take on a role in participatory processes towards e-government and e-democracy.

Their support is also crucial for realising the infrastructure in a short time and delivering benefits while enthusiasm is still high. To this end, we take a pragmatic approach towards realising the "last mile", reducing where possible new pylons to the minimum by renting existing ones from other concerns (TV, radio) in exchange for services, in order to shorten the time to full-scale operation.

6.1   Lesson Learned

Through our experience, we have learned that the introduction of broadband in rural areas and the resulting opportunity for all users to be on-line leads to new patterns of consumption for local families, unaccustomed to paying for Internet-based services. This additional cost in the family budget leads to two important considerations for formulating the service offer:

1. A less performing service is preferred if it is more economical; advanced technological elements (e.g. symmetric vs asymmetric, downstream and upstream bandwidth, etc.) are difficult to understand especially for end users more than for technical skilled organizazions (e.g. software companies, public administrations, or local technology resellers).
2. The lack of experience on the part of users should not provide an excuse for un-readiness; enterprises, local administrators and citizens, once they are "on", will immediately ask for additional services, and the provider must be ready to satisfy these requests or its credibility will be irreparably undermined.

7.   Conclusions

The work carried out within the Wikitel project in Sicily demonstrates how a business model that considers the requirements coming from the territory can be sustainable if two key factors are taken into account. First, it is very important to understand and contextualize the local community's needs through interactions with the local Public Administration, SMEs and citizens. Secondly, the ability to customize a complete service offer to meet these specific needs is the key to reaching a fruitful collaboration with local actors.

New research activities in the 7° Framework Programme will speed up the introduction of next generation services and technologies that, according to our experience, will be successful if they take into account not only the technical features, but also business models that are able to scale down from large corporations to small groups of users and from urban scenarios to rural areas.

Despite the awareness that the territories we have worked with have few other options, being cut off from the "big providers" and marginalized by their geographical and socio-economic conditions, we have never fallen to the temptation of identifying a single, top-down model to "solve" the digital divide. Instead we have worked to stimulate, through a participatory, multi-level process (local government - citizens - enterprises), a model of rational experimentation through the co-design of infrastructures and services. The real achievement for the local municipalities and every participant who has joined the initiative, is today constituted by their ownership of what they have chosen and not what the market has imposed on them.

References

[1] For the debate on the digital divide, see among others:"Scegliere con attenzione i driver dello Sviluppo", Linda Lanzillotta (2005 Key4biz.it, in Italian).
[2] World Summit on the Information Society – Outcome Documents – Geneve 2003 – Tunis 2005.
[3] The Wikitel products, http://www.wikitel.it
[4] The FP6 IST ANEMONE home page, http://www.ist-anemone.eu/
[5] www.regione.sicilia.it/bilancio/por/avvisibandi605.htm

Section 8

Digital Libraries and Cultural Heritage

Section 8.1

Applications

Collaboration and the Knowledge Economy: Issues, Applications, Case Studies
P. Cunningham and M. Cunningham (Eds.)
IOS Press, 2008

Encouraging Cultural Exploration: a Dynamic Tour Guide Based on Personalised Contextual Information and Ad-hoc Planning

Benjamin HODGSON[1], Maurizio MEGLIOLA[2], Silvana TOFFOLO[3], Michael ZOELLNER[4], Jonah DEARLOVE[1], Jens KEIL[4]

[1]*British Maritime Technology Ltd, Goodrich House,*
1 Waldegrave Road, Teddington, TW11 8LZ, United Kingdom
Tel: +44 (0)20 8943 5544, Fax: +44 (0)20 8977 9304, Email: enquiries@bmtmail.com
[2]*TXT e-solutions, Via Frigia, 27, Milano, 20126, Italy*
Tel: +39 02 257711, Fax: +39 02 2578994, Email: maurizio.megliola@txt.it
[3]*CSST SpA, Strada Torino 50, Orbassano TORINO, 10043, Italy*
Tel: +39 011 9080701, Fax: +39 011 9080700, Email: silvana.toffolo@csst.it
[4]*Fraunhofer IGD, Fraunhofer Strasse 5, Darmstadt, 64283, Germany*
Tel: +49 6151 155 164, Fax: +49 6151 155 196, Email: michael.zoellner@igd.fraunhofer.de

Abstract: Because of the difficulties in navigating public transport networks and finding out about available activities, cultural tourists tend to follow a pre-planned itinerary and to visit a fairly small set of well known attractions. An analogous situation emerges at the cultural heritage sites themselves: while cultural heritage sites typically have a large amount of archive material, only a small amount of information can be presented, therefore visitors tend not to explore the cultural significance of exhibits in depth. Our solution represents a complete mobile information system for travellers intended to encourage exploration. The system consists of three modules: firstly location-based information intended to enhance the cultural tourists understanding and to suggest exploratory activities based on modelling the users interests; secondly ad-hoc itinerary planning functionality to give the user the confidence to explore and a novel augmented reality system for presenting information in a user friendly way using markerless tracking. This paper covers the research and development aspects of iTACITUS, a sixth framework programme project, reporting on both technical and coordination issues, as well as interaction issues encountered during the project trials.

Keywords: augmented reality, location-based services, wireless.

1. Introduction

Our research work addresses the use of mobile technologies to encourage exploration by the cultural visitor rather than channelling them down a standardised 'tourist trail'. By exploration we mean not only exploring in the geographical sense of visiting places of interest but also exploring intellectually the significance of culturally important features. The problem can be characterised on two scales:

- On a city wide scale, cultural tourists tend to follow a pre-planned itinerary and to visit a fairly small set of well known attractions due to difficulties in navigating public transport networks and finding out about available activities. This has obvious economic implications for smaller attractions and environmental implications due to uncertainty about public transport driving car use. The available information about culturally important landmarks is generally limited to short summaries on physical plaques or guide books. The act of accessing information tends to distract from the overall experience and so the curiosity of the visitor is not captured and engaged.

- At a particular cultural heritage site, visitors are generally not given the full context of the exhibits and features they are looking at. While cultural heritage sites typically have a large amount of archive material only a small amount of information can be presented and so visitors tend not to explore the cultural significance of exhibits in depth. They are also generally presented with a single interpretation or narrative. This problem is particularly acute when the original is damaged. While restoring can allow the visitor to see missing features, the original design is subject to interpretation and physical restoration can in fact damage the original by imposing current preconceptions.

2. Objectives

This paper describes the implementation and early stage trials of a complete mobile information system for cultural visitors. That is the development and trial of a system for:

- Contextual information.
  While several previous studies have looked at provision of contextual information for tourists, these have defined context narrowly in terms of location. Our approach is different in that we added the use of intelligent techniques to profile users and adjust what information present to the user based on a model of their interests and not only on the current geographic location.
- Dynamic ad-hoc itinerary planning.
  Traditional itinerary planning is very much a 'fire and forget' exercise. Previous itinerary planning projects have characterised 'deciding what to do' and 'deciding when to do it and how to get there' as a one shot process. The former is typically done by selecting from a listing the latter by solving the resulting travelling salesman problem. The itinerary is then taken as fixed. Our approach is to view itinerary management as an ongoing interactive process that should allow the visitor to respond to changes and to their own whims.
- Advanced and robust markerless tracking on mobile devices.
  We chose a two-stage approach for development. During the first stage we developed an orientation-only tracking based on optical flow. Only pure camera rotation is estimated, on the assumption that the user remains in one place throughout. This proved the concept, allowing for further iterations to expand upon this method. After that we developed a more flexible texture tracker that enabled orientation and limited translation. Both systems run in real-time frame rates on mobile computers which allows for a wide range of applications both indoors and outdoors.
- User-friendly Augmented Reality (AR) interaction paradigms.
  In this project Augmented Reality is a standard media type next to images, movies and sounds about Cultural Heritage artifacts. In order to provide informative and aesthetic AR applications we have enhanced and implemented three visual and one acoustic communication concepts: Annotated landscapes (Figure 1) filled with pictographic information hotspots in the environment. Superimposed environments (Figure 2) with seamless integrated virtual objects like buildings and paintings. Adapted reality (Figure 3) renders the user's field of view in a visual quality that fits the information's needs. Spatial acoustic AR (Figure 4) transports a place's original ambience via spatial audio clips like conversations and ambient sounds.

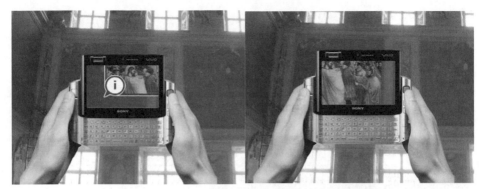

Figure 1: Annotated Landscapes   Figure 2: Superimposed Environments

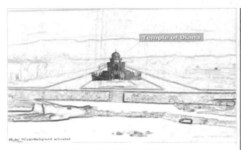

Figure 3: Adapted Reality

Figure 4: Spatial Acoustic AR

3.   Methodology

The methodology we followed during the course of the project was comprised of the following elements:

- Collection of information from cultural heritage site owners and visitors;
- Analysis of state-of-the-art cultural heritage information systems and interaction;
- Lessons learned from previous projects;
- Combinations of different solution approaches for tracking (KTL /randomized trees);
- User trials conducted at Turin and Winchester test sites in terms of usability and the impact of the system on tourist behaviour and learning.

4.   Technology and Developments

From the tourist point of view, our system is composed of the following two complementary applications:

- City Guide: a web platform accessible by any standard browser, merging the features of a tourist assistant and a paper city guide. This application consists of two main collaborative components: the Itinerary Planner and the Progress Module. The latter provides information and services to the Itinerary Planner, partly during the planning phase and especially during the visit.
- Mobile Augmented Reality Viewer (AR Viewer) starts from the City Guide at iTACITUS enhanced sites, providing a number of image/audio/video-advanced contents available.

4.1 Dynamic Ad-hoc Itinerary Planning

The Itinerary Planner allows the user to search for activities and events relating to heritage sites as well as other tourist attractions. These can be selected from various categories and could include visits to cathedrals, art galleries and other cultural sites.

Upon selecting a category, the user will be given a list of possible events that fit in with their itinerary so far. An event can have a specific time window (e.g. a piece of theatre) or more general opening times (e.g. a museum) which would allow the user to select a specific time to add to the itinerary. So, for example, a user has planned to have lunch at a restaurant in Covent Garden (near the opera house), followed by a trip to the Royal Opera House in the evening to see Carmen. So far their itinerary will be:

1300 - 1500	Restaurant
1500 - 1900	Free time
1900 - 2200	Royal Opera House (Carmen).

The user wants to find a suitable event for the free time they have in the afternoon so they consult their Itinerary Planner which contains details on the National Gallery, which has opening times of 9am – 6pm. The Itinerary Planner knows that the user is free from 3pm until 7pm and so checks the travel time between the gallery and the previous and subsequent events. The travel time from the restaurant to the gallery is 15 minutes and the travel time from the gallery to the Opera House is 20 minutes. Therefore the planner suggests a visit to the National Gallery from 3:15pm until 6pm (this is the overlap of the user's free time and the event's time window taking travel times into account). The user wishes to do this so their itinerary is updated to the following:

1300 - 1500	Restaurant
1500 - 1515	Travel to National Gallery
1515 - 1800	National Gallery
1800 - 1840	Free time
1840 - 1900	Travel to Opera House
1900 - 2200	Royal Opera House (Carmen).

In order to achieve this, the Itinerary Planner is connected to a multi-modal routing planner. The route planning incorporates walking as well as using any means of public transport. This route planner runs on a modified version of the A* algorithm with an heuristic to estimate the least time required to reach the destination from any given node. This is written in Java and utilises a MySQL database which contains up-to-date details of all the timetables in the given city. Using this information the router can determine the travel time for each journey on the Itinerary Planner and so only suggest events with sufficient travel time between them.

The Itinerary Planner front end has been designed in Ruby on Rails with a back-end MySQL database. The GUI has been designed for a variety of platforms; in particular it has an iPhone interface as well as a standard Windows interface for use on compact portable PCs (or Ultra Mobile Personal Computer, UMPC) such as the Sony Vaio UX Micro PC.

As well as providing a graphical user interface for the users, the Itinerary Planner also allows Point of Interest (POI) owners to edit details on their POIs. One use of this would be in an art gallery: if there is a special temporary exhibition then this could be entered as a separate event. This is particularly useful in cases where the exhibition does not conform to the standard opening hours of the wider gallery. This approach also allows the POI owner to provide additional information to the user which would otherwise not be available.

4.2　Contextual Information (Progress Module)

The set of applications relating to contextual information is called the Progress Module. It has been implemented as a multi-agent system running on UMPC, following the FIPA conform JADE [1] framework, in order to better handle all its different tasks, and consists of the following agents:

- Location Agent (LA), which provides the GPS coordinates of the user. All the iTACITUS modules rely on this service as the knowledge of the user position represents the main parameter for checking that the visit progress is on time. This is also needed in order to decide when and how provide suitable contextual information and is requested by the AR Viewer
- User Profile Agent (UA), which provides information about the user profile
- Progress Agent (PA), which provides contextual information depending on the user context (i.e. current location, profile, history)
- Gateway Agent (GA), which handles the communication with the external world

The localization exploits a GPS receiver, following the National Marine Electronics Association standard (NMEA 0183) GGA sentences, which contain the basic information about latitude and longitude, as well as a "fix quality" control. The communication with the mobile device has been implemented with the Bluetooth technology. The Location Agent periodically sends the user position to the Progress Agent, which will decide if and what contextual information should be provided.

In this phase of the project, the profiling has been handled by a Personal Rating technique without correlation with the other users i.e. by associating a table (keyword/rating) to each visitor, where "rating" is the probability that the user likes venues/activities about the "keyword" category An initial profile is created when the visitor enters the system for the first time by asking him to fill a short questionnaire about her/his interests in cultural heritage. The following is an example of this:

MUSEUMS	4
ART GALLERIES	4
CASTLES	3
CHURCHES	1
MIDDLE AGE	3

This profile will be constantly updated by refining the "rating" value as the visitor, both explicitly and implicitly, provides feedback about activities and venues; this feedback will be interpreted by the system and accorded different weights. Typical examples include: when the visitor plans or modifies an itinerary (implicit feedback); gives a score after completing an itinerary item (explicit feedback); accepts or refuses contextual information provided by the system (implicit feedback): in the latter case the value of the feedback will be greater if the user accepts information, because the user expressed an interest, whilst in case of refusal the User Profile Agent must take into account that reasons behind a refusal may be different and often not strictly due to thematic interests, so the weight given to this feedback will be lower yet still taken into consideration. Implicit feedback is especially important as by following the user behaviours makes "background"-running systems able to dynamically and transparently update the profile. During the first prototype testing a significant set of profiles will be created in this way in order to provide data for a correlation study (to be carried out in the next phase of the project).

The Progress Agent has the twofold role of providing contextual information and coordinating the other agents. The contextual information is provided or required in the following cases:

- The visitor is approaching a venue not present in her/his planned itinerary but its thematic characteristics are very similar to her/his profile preferences. So, the PM pushes the contextual information
- The visitor explicitly asks for information about what interesting venues are nearby (pull modality)
- The system could also provide other types of information, if available, such as weather and road conditions, that could lead the visitor to re-plan the itinerary

This decision from the PA depends further on two other parameters: the distance covered by the user and the time spent since the last contextual information was provided. When the LA considers both parameters meaningful, it notifies the PA to provide new contextual information Once the PA has received this message it extracts the more profile-relevant information from the appropriate database and informs the Itinerary Planner, which will displays this information to the user (who can accept it or not). The search for contextual information uses a sub-module which returns the XML description of the most relevant information and the relative distance from the user.

The Gateway Agent lets the Itinerary Planner be notified about contextual information availability. The IP alerts the visitor and if her/he is interested, it requests this for them.

4.3   Augmented Reality Applications

The visual Augmented Reality application gives users the ability to explore the digital information about the site in a very intuitive way. Parallel to other media like images, videos and sound it starts out of the City Guide at an iTACITUS enabled site. By holding a mobile computer or tomorrow's mobile phone in front of a point of interest the user immediately gets further information as an Augmented Reality overlay on the screen. This effect is like looking through the mobile computer's display and seeing the real world enhanced with virtual objects or information.

Since a robust markerless tracking system is a requirement for a user-friendly AR application, we chose a two-stage approach. During the first stage we developed an orientation-only tracking based on optical flow; this assured an early implementation of all interaction concepts. After that we developed a more robust texture tracker that enabled orientation and limited translation. Our texture tracker is based on vision and can be decomposed into two distinct phases: the initialization phase, where the object is searched for in the complete image and the tracking phase, where the displacement of the object since the last video frame is computed.

For the initialization phase, we use a method based on keypoint classification: a number of keypoints of the poster are defined, and the possible appearances of these keypoints are learnt in an offline process. The result of the learning stage is a set of classifiers that can be used online to classify an unknown keypoint in the image. Among different classification techniques, we chose the randomized trees classifier for its robustness and speed in the online phase. When a sufficient number of keypoints have been successfully classified, the position of the poster is obtained via a pose estimation algorithm. After a correct position has been found, the system enters the tracking phase, where only the relative displacement of the poster since the last frame is computed. To this end, a number of salient points (the features) are independently tracked in the image, using the KLT tracker [2], which incorporates an affine transformation model and an illumination model for each feature. From the 2D displacement of every feature, a global 3D displacement of the poster can be computed. Adding all the inter-frame displacements to the initial position allows for finding the current position of the poster.

5. Business Benefits

The advantages of our solution are the following:

* The agent model allows a rational subdivision of the tasks amongst many autonomous and collaborative components.
* Contextual information is provided not only depending on the geographical location, but also considering the interests and preferences of the user.
* The Itinerary Planner/Progress Module system allows a dynamic management of the visit itinerary.
* The mobile Augmented Reality Module enables Cultural Heritage sites to provide information interactively on today's UMPC's and tomorrow's mobile phones. But the technique has also other economic impact as IGD already uses it in projects for the industry.
* Tomorrow's mobile phones will benefit from location-based services combined with advanced media like Augmented Reality in all application areas.

6. Conclusions

Two main test sites have been identified in order to evaluate the effectiveness and future potential of a system like iTACITUS in the field: Winchester, Hampshire, UK and Turin, Italy. The Winchester test site is focused on the castle complex, encompassing important cultural sites such as the Great Hall, Westgate and Military Museums, and the Castle Passageways. The other test site is focused on Turin and its surroundings in general and on Venaria for the internal guide.

In conclusion, while the trials are on going, we have started to obtain some technical outcomes, particularly with regard to the Augmented Reality field. AR is finally on the verge of being ready for end users. With more and more powerful mobile computers and better markerless tracking algorithms, the AR experience is becoming better and better.

During the last few years, technology aspects were the main determining criteria of AR applications' success. But as with other digital media, experience and usability will be the next major topic after mastery of technology. The question is how to deal with digital information that blends with real surroundings to make the application as intuitive and easy to pick up as possible and as such increase acceptance of such a young technology.

We are looking today's interfaces in the area of computers, video games and mobile devices. By selecting and evaluating the most successful approaches we are creating a new ideal set of interactions for AR applications. Introducing touch and motion capabilities, for example, could make AR applications an even more intuitive experience. This keeps the learning rate low which is important especially for Cultural Heritage applications.

Our first AR application is designed for the UNESCO World Heritage site Reggia Venaria Reale in Italy. In particular, the partly reconstructed frescos of Sale Diana in the baroque palace and its ruins in the vast gardens are an ideal testing environment. Inside Sale Diana most of the paintings have been restored but there are still some grey areas on the walls. Paintings have not been fully restored because of uncertainties. Thus a grey area is the better choice over an archaeological falsity. There are different approaches of how paintings may have looked; in some cases several approaches are available. Via AR technology we tell the story of Venaria's rooms and its paintings. Grey areas are overlaid with historic drawings of the frescos while looking through the mobile computer's screen. We also provide audio background information about the picture insight by just tapping on it on the screen. Outside in the gardens only the ruins of an impressive temple remain. In order to tell visitors where the temple was located and how the gardens looked in the past we overlay an original historic drawing of the temple right at the spot. Because a black and white drawing would not fit in the colourful gardens we use an adapted reality approach and render the video as a real time sketch (Figure 6).

Figure 6: Temple Diana

Figure 5: Sale Diana

The following points summarize how the consortium views the possible future development of the infrastructure of iTACITUS system:

- Distributed agents: an interesting property of the agents developed in JADE is the possibility to easily migrate between different running environments. A smart distribution of the agents can be obtained by exploiting the LEAP (Lightweight Extensible Agent Platform) libraries implementation of JADE for mobile devices.
- Continuous localization: when next generation mobile devices become available they will probably be more powerful with longer battery life, enabling continuous user localization. The current user direction and the view angle could be exploited in order to further improve the quality of the services. As a matter of fact, the "area of interest", that currently is the circle centred on the user current position, could be refined by about 75%, considering the shifts of the user and keeping into account the direction of origin.
- Profiling: a further profiling phase, called Collaborative Filtering, could utilize the outcomes from the current Personal Rating phase and apply the concepts of similarity to extract more relevant data with a view to improving the current profiling.
- Monitor external data sources such as weather: by using RSS and screen-scraping frameworks, visitors will have further information to modify their itinerary in real-time.
- Markerless Augmented Reality and interaction paradigms are valuable for industry applications in service and construction areas.
- The combined concept of iTACITUS can be transferred to other application areas. Industry Augmented Reality application in the construction and maintenance area will benefit from the agent model and Progress Module for work tasks.

References

[1] F.Bellifemine, G.Caire, D.Greenwood. "Developing Multi-agent Systems with JADE". Wiley Series in Agent Technology. Wiley, 2007.
[2] C. Tomasi and T. Kanade. Detection and tracking of point features. Carnegie Mellon University Technical Report CMU-CS-91-132, Apr.1991.

Collaboration and the Knowledge Economy: Issues, Applications, Case Studies
P. Cunningham and M. Cunningham (Eds.)
IOS Press, 2008

An Integrated ICT Architecture for Intelligent Content Harmonization in European Cultural Heritage Domain

Maurizio MEGLIOLA[1], Krassimira PASKALEVA[2], José AZORIN[3], Daniela CIAFFI[4]

[1]*TXT e-Solutions, Salita S.Barborino 23/R, Genova, 16149, Italy*
Tel: +39 010 4610366, Fax: + 39 010 4610377, Email: maurizio.megliola@txt.it
[2] *Institute for Technology Assessment and Systems Analysis, Forschungzentrum Karlsruhe Gmbh, Hermann-von-Helmholtz-Platz 1, 76344 Eggenstein-Leopoldshafen, Germany, and Herbert Simon Institute, Manchester Business School, University of Manchester, M13 9PL, UK*
Tel: +49 7247 82 6133, Fax: +49 7247 82 4806, Email: Paskaleva@itas.fzk.de
[3] *Institute for Technology Assessment and Systems Analysis, Forschungzentrum Karlsruhe Gmbh, Hermann-von-Helmholtz-Platz 1, 76344 Eggenstein-Leopoldshafen, Germany*
Tel: +49 7247 82 6485, Fax: +49 7247 82 4811, Email: jose.azorin@itas.fzk.de
[4]*Politecnico di Torino, viale Mattioli 39, Turin, 10125, Italy*
Tel: +39 011 5647463, Email: daniela.ciaffi@polito.it

Abstract: Cultural heritage is a wide concept that includes not only monuments, architecture and history (tangibles) but also languages, folklore, traditions, events, music, festivities, customs and life styles (intangibles). The combination between tangible and intangible heritage represents the richness of a specific place therefore the identity of local communities has to be preserved and promoted in order to enhance the benefits for the tourist locality and its customers - visitors, citizens, and businesses, in the general perspective of sustaining multiple cultural identities. The main objective of this research is to develop a novel ICT integrated and participatory system for the cultural heritage destination that can preserve and promote European cultural heritage from its diverse aspects - tangible and intangible - with the objective of experiencing all aspects of the visit and above all, to add value to the cultural heritage itself by the interpretation and valorisation of the cultural goods. The system makes use of Web 2.0 key concepts, such as user-generated content and folksonomies, as a baseline.

1. Introduction

Cultural heritage can be understood as a wide concept that includes not only monuments, architecture and history (tangible goods) but also languages, folklore, traditions, events, music, songs, dance, festivities, customs and life styles (intangible heritage). The combination between tangible and intangible heritage represents the richness of a specific place and have to be preserved and promoted in order to improve the benefits for the destination and its customers – tourist, citizens and businesses, in a general perspective of sustaining multiple cultural identities. In this aspect, a more comprehensive approach needs to be developed in order to appreciate heritage as a source of cultural identity and diversity, while taking into account the existing interaction between the tangible and intangible heritage of the place. Towards this objective, cities and tourism destinations in Europe need intelligent environments that are able to manage, integrate and harmonise their cultural heritage knowledge in order to organize distributed and diverse public information on cultural destinations and sites via existing and new e-services.

The main objective of this research is to develop a novel ICT system for the cultural heritage destination that can preserve and promote European cultural heritage from all its dimensions, with the objective of experiencing all details of the visit and above all, to create new values to the cultural heritage itself by the interpretation of the cultural good.

Against these objectives, the current study is multi-disciplinary in nature aiming to valorise the cultural assets as tourism resources through user-friendly and stakeholder-relevant integrated e-services in urban tourist destinations. For this purpose, a new user-centric, integrated and participatory ICT environment is being developed. It can be understood as a distributed repository of cultural heritage intelligent content and a software architecture enabling content interoperability (service-oriented), content customised access and presentation (agent-oriented) providing integrated e-services to European cultural destinations to support the tourism experience life cycle (pre-visit, during visit and post-visit phases). The work is part of the ongoing EU FP6 Project ISAAC "Integrated e-Services for Advanced Access to Heritage in Cultural Tourist Destinations".

2.   Objectives

This paper has several inter-related objectives.

Firstly, to describe the ICT challenges and innovation aspects of this research from the point of view of data collection and harmonization based on an in depth review of current digitization issues and cultural data interpretation for cultural heritage in tourist destinations' web sites, with a special focus on three case study cities – Amsterdam (The Netherlands), Genoa (Italy) and Leipzig (Germany) [1]. This in depth analysis has identified substantial weaknesses in all e-governance aspects of the destinations' web sites in Europe (relevant to the participation of the users in service development and destination's promotion) and a lack of links between tourism web sites and the main city portals, which has resulted in the short of coordinated action in the cities' promotion among the concerned players. The present study aims to overcome this existing lack in data integration, due to heterogeneity of sources, fragmentation of the information and absence of a unique way to view information, by defining a European reference model to standardise representation, annotation and retrieval of cultural heritage content in cities by using new and emerging semantic harmonisation techniques to support uniform knowledge-based access to distributed information resources and pre-existing heterogeneous databases. In this line, the ICT system resulting from our research collects data from private entities and public administration's resources and harmonizes and integrates them with the publicly available information and databases. This work of harmonization has been based on the definition of a new classification (or taxonomy) [2] that combine a hierarchical classification of general cultural goods categories, from the tangible to intangible, with a particular reference to potential e-services to be integrated in the new platform. The result is an enhanced access in the cultural heritage domain (content interoperability via service-oriented architecture) and content organisation according to the user preferences (customised access and presentation of information via agent technologies). As preferences change over time, in relation to experience, knowledge, perception, awareness and sensitivity, because human being are part of a dynamic community of interest, the proposed taxonomy is designed as a folksonomy, allowing implementation using a "wiki" approach.

Secondly, to describe how our research is based on the Social Web and Web 2.0 approach using the concept of folksonomy. The latter is understood as a dynamic content classification by people who associate terms with content that they generate or consume. Our work attempts to associate this emergent phenomenon of the Social Web with the Semantic Web concept of Ontology (explicit formal specifications of the terms in the domain and relations among them [3]). These two ideas, because of their conceptually different bases (top-down vs. the bottom-up approach), have been highly opposing from the very start. Yet, recent studies highlight that, as the Semantic Web matures and the Social Web grows, there is an increasing value in applying Semantic Web technologies to the data of the Social Web. In this line of emphasis, we create a new ontology defined as folksonomy. This approach allows us to develop a new framework in which the harmonization of the knowledge is based on the ontology viewed as an instrument for sharing information and on a folksonomy, understood as data that is emerging from shared information through tags that introduce distributed human intelligence into the system.

3.   Methodology

Several steps were used for the design and development of the ICT system, which started in 2006 and will be completed in 2009. The system is implemented in three city cases (Amsterdam, Leipzig and Genoa), which were selected because they offer diversity nature and degree of digitalisation of their cultural heritage assets. This, along with other EU relevant practices [2], served to define an ISAAC European reference model to standardize representation, annotation and retrieval of cultural heritage content that can be used not only in Amsterdam, Leipzig and Genoa but in other European cities as well. A five-step methodology has been used as follows:

1.   State-of-the-art analysis of cultural heritage information systems.

In November of 2006, a full assessment of the state-of-the-art, with particular focus on the current multimedia, data representation and harmonisation, and visualisation technology, was carried out. The main aim was to develop the plan for extending and improving the technology within the ISAAC prototype framework to achieve access and management capabilities for the cultural assets from a user perspective view [9].

2.   Review and documentation of lessons learnt from other relevant projects.

In the summer of 2007, fourteen EU projects (AGAMEMNON, BRICKS, CASPAR, CINeSPACE, DELOS, EASAIER, EPOCH, IMAGINATION, MEMORIES, MINERVA PLUS, MOSAICA, MultiMATCH, COLLATE and MICHAEL) were selected and reviewed. This was aimed at using these projects' experiences as a baseline so as to define the ISAAC European reference model. These projects were selected based on their similarities in scope to ISAAC in a sense that they aimed at developing digital and electronic services for tourism and better access to European cultural heritage [2].

3.   Development of the ISAAC concept of folksonomy and principles of Web 2.0.

In parallel with phase 2, an extensive literature review was carried out to provide the basic principles for developing the ISAAC taxonomy. Subsequently, extensive exploration of alternative classification systems and approaches to support the development of metadata for digital content was carried out, including the decentralized social approach named folksonomy. Finally, the latter – a user centred approach (bottom-up approach) - was adopted in parallel to the experts' perception of cultural goods (top-down approach) studied by the ISAAC team [2] and further explained in section five of this paper.

4.   Identification of user requirements.

Between December 2006 and January 2007, seventy-two focus groups workshops were held in the three partner cities (Amsterdam, Leipzig and Genoa) aiming at identifying key user preferences for the development of the system e-services [10]. These activities provided valuable insights in support of the project objectives, the state-of-the-art, and the cities' legacy IT systems and their needs. In this way, our taxonomy has benefited from all actors' views and perceptions in regard to the selected folksonomic approach.

5.   Design, development and testing of the ICT system.

Drawing on the results of the first four phases ISAAC is currently developing the ICT system for the partner cities. The work is divided in three stages: system design, development and pilot testing. In the process, issues of intelligent data harmonization, user requirements and limitations in test cases are being tackled. The effort is coordinated by the project's IT developer, TXT e-Solutions SpA, in close cooperation with the cities' ICT and tourism representatives. Sections four, five and six discuss the major findings from the four first phases of the study and the attributes of the ISAAC ICT system.

4.   Technology and Developments

The ICT system resulting from this research is entirely based on open source software. New Web 2.0 concepts (such as the folksonomy) are used as a basis for dealing with data collection and harmonization issues, encouraging platform independence but also allowing the reduction of development costs for the stakeholders. The instruments related to the social web are regarded as most powerful for translation in technology terms, the concept of interpretation of cultural goods and the perspective domains. Our case study research has shown too that the later emerges as a key driver of future developments in city systems toward the internet technologies, particular with regard to the new instruments allowing the user to be directly involved in city promotion and management (the governance paradigm).

This notion originates from the concept that the user has to be an active actor in the city affairs, not only as a visitor or a static viewer. Instead, the user in our case, tourists, citizens and decision makers has to have the opportunity to enhance the promotion of the cultural goods using the instruments available in the city information system. By surfing the net it is very easy to find official cities' web sites where the cultural goods or the places are presented to the viewer. However, these "conventional" systems have limitations, as far as new roads for cultural promotion are considered within the context of the Web 2.0, and specifically:

- An official site focuses the promotion on "official" cultural goods;
- An official site does not take into consideration "hidden treasures";
- An official site does not take into consideration the intangible aspects of a place;
- Typically the official web site is designed and run by "institutional" actors that for the most part are citizens of the destination.

This last point highlights a very important concept that this study takes forward: citizens even if they love the place where they live, are not as careful to all the destination's aspects as tourists can be. Imagine the place where you live: how many times you discover something unknown in your city just because a friend has come over as a tourist and has discovered something that you have ignored as a citizen?

The essential point is that tourists are more focused on the discovery because when they decide to undertake a cultural tourism experience, their main objective is the discovery of the visited place or attraction. For this reason the latter are the best candidates to discover hidden cultural goods and, most importantly, they are the most adequate users to embrace the immaterial aspects of the place, catching the cultural goods' or the site's soul. We make operational this concept through the so called "interpretation" of the cultural heritage. For this reason the city needs to provide tourists with the right ICT instruments that can help them share their experiences and, in doing so, promote the cultural tangible and intangible aspects of the place and its people.

This is a truly an innovative approach in the domain of cultural heritage that can be viewed as an interactive development of an interpretative strategy. First, it is "interactive" because the user itself is directly involved in the creation of the cultural heritage promotion. And, second, the condition of "interpretative" is given in conformity with the baseline of this strategy, the concept of "interpretation". From a technical point of view, the main way to create a self-promotional strategy is the user-generated content.

In this way, the User-Generated Content (UGC) is considered as either "implicitly generated" or "explicitly generated". Implicit UGC is created by the actions of users as they go about their normal business of viewing pages or selecting search results [4]. This can be used to generate items such as "general most viewed lists" or "you could like also these places", which are based on data generated by people with similar search and browsing patterns. It is important to note that user generated content is not written by random voices from an undifferentiated mass of users. Users are required to create a log-in and content is usually associated with a user name.

Thus, it becomes clear that conventional techniques in the information technology field do not help to catch this objective because they do not allow this interactive interpretative strategy. But, fortunately, there are instruments able to reach the intended results. In this line, the only way to drive the development toward this direction is to focus on the new Web 2.0 concepts and integrated e-services. For instance, social web networks such as "Flickr.com" or "Youtube.com" facilitate greatly the sharing of personal experiences by publishing user-generated content that is based on cultural heritage's real interpretation, accounting for both tangible and intangible aspects.

All of the above mentioned instruments are based on a new and very interesting concept, arisen a few years ago in the content management environment, called folksonomy. While the user generated content allows the collection of new and special content coming from different sources and provides new forms of interpretation for cultural goods, the folksonomy constitutes the cornerstone of the project's objective so long as it harmonizes heterogeneous data. Often cultural objects are described by institutions in language that is highly specialist. Folksonomies allow users to describe contents using their own vernacular language, bridging the "semantic gap" between the institutional language and that language of the user, so facilitating other users find things that interest them.

Of course this way of navigating the cultural goods needs to be moderated, but the system reduces this requirement by setting barriers to entry, such as a login mechanism. This allows users reporting offensive content for review by a moderator and a "reputation" model to help the useful content rise and the non-useful content filter down (tag clouds give prominence to the most popular tags while less popular tags become less visible).

With the folksonomic approach users can get content coming from different resources, official and unofficial, and harmonize them in a unique place, where cultural heritage is interpreted in a better and social-like way. Despite its name, a folksonomy is not taxonomy, because it moves away from the hierarchical approach to an approach more akin to that taken by faceted classification or other flat systems. Folksonomy is not a static classification, but a dynamic organization where the user itself becomes an active actor.

5.   From Taxonomy to Folksonomy

As argued in section one, the ICT system's specific solution is based upon a detailed taxonomy of urban cultural heritage components developed by the ISAAC consortium. A brief conceptualizing framework to the term "taxonomy" is introduced for the purpose:

The word "Taxonomy" (from Greek verb τασσεῖν or tassein = "to classify" and νόμος or nomos = law, science, cf "economy") [...] refers to either a classification of things, or the principles underlying the classification [...]. Taxonomies [...] are frequently hierarchical in structure, commonly displaying parent-child relationships. Simpson's (1961) [5] defines taxonomy as the theoretical study of classification, which includes its bases, principles, procedures and rules. Bailey (1994) [6] also stated that a taxonomy is like a classification, and it can refer to both the process and the end results. He also addressed taxonomies are often hierarchical and evolutionary. The term taxonomy may also be applied to relationship schemes other than hierarchies, such as networked structures. Ravid (2002) [7] defined "Taxonomy is the science of classification according to predetermined system used to provide a conceptual framework for discussion, analysis or information retrieval". A taxonomy might also be a simple organization of objects into groups, clusters or even an alphabetical list (lexicographic order). In current usage within "Knowledge

Management", taxonomies are seen as slightly less broad than onthologies." (Wikipedia). "[…] in digital terms, automated classification of documents in a hierarchy based on information gathered by a metacrawler" (DCMI Glossary [12]).

In the light of ISAAC's integrated ICT system, our taxonomy [2] combines a hierarchical classification of general cultural goods categories, from the tangible to the intangible, with a more user oriented perspective. Attention is paid to the significance that such a taxonomy can enhance access in the cultural heritage domain, with particular reference to the potential new and integrated e-services [11] that are currently being developed for the ISAAC platform.

As a result, the ISAAC architecture classifies both tangible and intangible cultural content according to the ISAAC taxonomy. Hence, content inserted by users will be uploaded onto social networks such as "Youtube" (for videos) and "Flickr" (for pictures) and tagged according to this taxonomy. Additionally, both "Flickr" and "Youtube" provide an API (Application Programming Interface) that enables the system to build contents (photos, video) back into the city website with their own look and feel. In this context, although contents are decentralised from the city website they will have a better exposure since they are accessible from two locations. Moreover, the system also allows the user to insert new tags in order to implement the Web 2.0 concept of folksonomy facilitating a new re-harmonization of the whole content. However, the development of a folksonomy requires a Cultural Heritage's taxonomy as a starting point. The main research activities were first focused on creating an appropriate taxonomy for retrieving cultural heritage assets and, subsequently, on developing the folksonomic approach (see section two).

The next two subsections provide alternative principles and an overview of a hierarchical classification for cultural heritage. This provides an overview of the main cultural heritage characteristics, highlighting the most relevant categories of the users' interests and values associated to cultural heritage, as identified in the field of cultural studies. The development of this taxonomy is strictly linked to the necessity to develop a form of tagging of information, which might help retrieval. Whilst simplifying the articulate nature of cultural goods, it gives the correct information.

5.1   *Alternative Principles for a Classification System in Cultural Heritage Destinations*

There are a number of different alternative principles underlying the development of a classification system. A short overview for cultural heritage destinations should recognize:

a. A hierarchical classification of cultural goods. Examples are:
    − geographical distribution (i.e.: Nation, County, City)
    − authorities in charge of (i.e.: National / Regional / City Tourism Authority)
b. A networked classification of similar cultural goods. Examples are:
    − heritage families (i.e.: Baroque)
    − style life families (i.e.: Slow cities)
c. A plain list of different cultural goods. Examples are:
    − alphabetical list
    − list by amount of yearly number of visitors
    − amount of visitors of the web sites
    − richness in term of cultural goods' availability
d. A short list of basic concepts referred to cultural goods. In contrast to the comprehensive holistic approaches, a different and better operational approach focuses on the selection of a small number of core categories. Examples can be found in Dublin Core Metadata Initiative (DCMI, 2005): the Simple Dublin Core Metadata Element Set (DCMES) consists of 15 metadata elements (Title, Creator, Subject, Description, Publisher, Contributor, Date, Type, Format, Identifier, Source, Language, Relation, Coverage, Rights) [13].

5.2 A Hierarchical Classification of Cultural Heritage

The suggested taxonomy of cultural heritage includes three intermediary levels of hierarchical classification, starting from the most general tangible and intangible CH categories of Goods, Places, Landscapes and Activities, to the most specific elements, supported by examples from the case studies [2].

Firstly, the class of Goods is specified in terms of Monuments, Streets, Buildings, Infrastructure, Popular venues and Settlement. Secondly, the category of Places includes both Public and Private places. Thirdly, the family of (Cultural) Landscapes includes all the followings sub-categories: Agricultural Systems, Environment, Modified Landscapes, Patterns of Settlement and Human Activity, Scene, Urban Landscapes. Fourthly, the last section of the Cultural Heritage hierarchical classification about Activities includes Events for all the three groups of potential users such as Events for Everybody (all stakeholders), Events for Residents and Events for Tourists.

The participants in the ISAAC Focus Groups helped define implementation of the vocabulary. This has confirmed the need to adopt a dynamic system in our IT platform. Overall, the taxonomy list of cultural heritage categories included 257 terms. Following our folksonomic approach, the proposed Cultural Heritage hierarchical classification supports user participation to| implement this initial list. A stakeholder, e.g. manager of a historical café, could be interested to contribute to the third level of the list of private places.

Once the classification criteria has been chosen, the hierarchical approach typical of a taxonomy leaves room for a flat classification created by a group of individuals (folksonomy), typically the resource users, who add natural language tags to online items, such as images, videos, bookmarks and text.

6. The ISAAC Architecture

All instruments described in this paper have been put together to develop an advanced integrated architecture. From a platform perspective, the ISAAC IT platform features the integration of intelligent content, intelligent agents (as the one we developed for the user profiling), information advanced presentation features and new integrated e-services. The ISAAC architecture is designed to incorporate all stages of the cultural tourism experience:
- Pre-visit: during this phase users can plan all details of the cultural experience they are going to live
- Visit: this phase represents the cultural experience itself
- Post-visit: during this phase, users can share their experiences with other people via chat, forums, blog, image and video sharing, etc.

In view of realizing the first step of the interpretative strategy above, this architecture provides a set of advanced services that are integrated in the cities' web sites, allowing users to exploit the ISAAC platform. Thanks to the folksonomy the user generated content is integrated and classified according to the classification. This content is then made available for other users and is presented in an innovative way catching the most complete meaning of a cultural good from its tangible to the intangible aspects. This integrated and participatory architecture and its services present an innovative set of cultural heritage promotional instruments for the benefits of tourists, citizens and the local decision makers in the context of the urban tourist destination.

7. Conclusions

This study attempted to demonstrate that traditional approaches to intelligent content harmonization in the European cultural heritage domain are in need of fundamental revision. It is revealed, through the analysis of existing approaches and case studies, that cultural heritage "consumers" have to be provided with new forms of information tagging that facilitate interactive retrieval processes and, at the same time, support cultural heritage's valorisation, hence preservation and promotion.

Research focused on the ISAAC's specific folksonomy, its main users, and how the later can be further assisted, by the taxonomy, in developing their interests in cultural heritage, when the cultural tourism e-services are organized in relation to timing of the visit and their preferences. The analysis shows that What, Who, How, When, and Why, are five key questions answered by the ISAAC taxonomy:

a. What. The taxonomy provides a systematization of both material and immaterial Cultural Heritage categories (which link directly to the ISAAC Glossary terms) [8];
b. Who. Users may implement the list of activities included in the ISAAC taxonomy of Cultural heritage;
c. How. The Cultural Heritage e-services provided by the ISAAC platform assist users with the opportunity to develop their interests in Cultural Heritage;
d. When. The available Cultural Heritage e-services are organised in relation to the time of the visit (pre, during and post actual visit);
e. Why. Users are motivated to implement ISAAC's Cultural Heritage list as a folksonomy, seen as an asset to participation and e-governance.

Innovation has occurred at the level of data harmonization based on the Web 2.0 approach, and the destination-wide territorial approach to Cultural Heritage promotion and interpretation for both tangible and intangible assets, together with the integration of existing e-services in advanced combinations [11].

The challenge ahead is to merge all the above attributes in an integrated IT system to assist broader access and utilisation of Cultural Heritage in the European destinations. This requires aiming at applications that learn from their users (intelligent agents) through using architecture of participation to build a commanding advantage not just in the software interface but in the richness of the shared data. The test cases for the cities involved in the ISAAC project (Amsterdam, Genoa and Leipzig) are the starting point to prove the system in real environments, currently in progress.

This, in turn, can have important implications on how cities may see their future when using their cultural heritage to promote themselves as centres of culture, heritage and tourism. As the study shows, they need intelligent systems that can increase the access of all users to local riches – tourists, citizens and the decision-makers alike. Moreover, new integrated and user-specific interfaces (folksonomy) are necessary to preserve and promote the diverse but dispersed and heterogeneous cultural heritage contents. Yet, achieving this requires further research not only from a technical point of view but with regard to the users' preferences and cultural heritage interpretation as well as their participation and involvement in the development of integrated ICT systems of European destinations.

References

[1]   N. Mitsche, U. Bauernfeind, P. Lombardi, D. Ciuffi, K. Paskaleva-Shapira, E. Besson (2007). Review of current digitalisation issues and data interpretation. ISAAC Project Research Report D1.1, www.isaac-project.eu

[2]   P. Riganti, W. Strielkowski, J. Wang, K. Paskaleva-Shapira, J. Azorin, P. Lombardi, D. Ciaffi, A. Arezza, E. Wolf, O. Diemer, R. Russo, E. Koomen, L. Fusco Girard, I. Salzano (2007). Defining an EU indexing system to standardise retrieval in the CH domain. ISAAC Project Research Report D1.5, www.isaac-project.eu.

[3]   T. Gruber (2003), "It Is What It Does: The Pragmatics of Ontology", CIDOC Conceptual Reference Model committee, Smithsonian Museum, Washington, D.C.

[4]   T. O'Reilly (2005), What Is Web 2.0, "Design Patterns and Business Models for the Next Generation of Software".

[5]   G.G. Simpson (1961). Principle of Animal Taxonomy. New York: Columbia University Press.

[6]   K.D. Bailey (1994). "Typologies and taxonomies: An introduction to classification techniques", Series: Quantitative Applications in the Social Sciences.102, Sage University Paper.

[7]   Y. Ravid (2002). In "Taxonomy: The Science of Classification - using the library as a metaphor to demystify the process of portal taxonomy development" www.ukoln.ac.uk/web-focus/events/workshops/webmaster- 2004/sessions/milne/taxonomy.ppt.

[8]   ISAAC Task 1.5.1, Part 1 Report, Glossary of Cultural Goods and e-Services from the User Perspective, 27/03/07, Version 0.1.

[9]   A. Arezza, G. Da Bormida (2007). Report on Technology Aspects of Cultural Heritage Access. ISAAC Project Research Report D1.6, www.isaac-project.eu

[10] S. Platt, P. Riganti, W. Strielkowski, J. Wang, A. Chiabai, P. Nijkamp, R. Vreeker, A. Arezza, E. Wolf, O. Diemer, R. Russo (2007). Report on Developing Alternative Platform Scenarios. ISAAC Project Research Report D1.6, www.isaac-project.eu

[11] K. Paskaleva, J. Azorin (2007). Developing integrated e-tourism services for cultural destinations, *International Journal of Services, Technology and Management (IJSTM)*, Special Issue on "Progress in Tourism Service and Sustainable Development", Li, Ch. (ed.), Forthcoming, 2008.

[12] DCMI Glossary, Dublin Core Metadata Initiative, Clement, G., Winn, P. (2005). dublincore.org/documents/usageguide/glossary.shtml.

[13] DCMES, Dublin Core Metadata Element Set, Version 1.1 (2008). dublincore.org/documents/dces/.

Collaboration and the Knowledge Economy: Issues, Applications, Case Studies
P. Cunningham and M. Cunningham (Eds.)
IOS Press, 2008

Designing an Automated Prototype Tool for Preservation Quality Metadata Extraction for Ingest into Digital Repository

Milena DOBREVA[1,2], Yunhyong KIM[3], Seamus ROSS[3]
[1]*Center for Digital Library Research (CDLR), University of Strathclyde,*
Livingstone Tower, 26 Richmond Street, Glasgow, G1 1XH, United Kingdom
Tel: + 44 141 548 4753, Fax: +44 141 548 4523, Email: milena.dobreva@strath.ac.uk
[2]*Institute of Mathematics and informatics, 8 Acad. G. Bonchev St., Sofia, 1113, Bulgaria*
Tel: + 359 2 9792809, Fax: +359 2 9713649, Email: dobreva@math.bas.bg
[3]*Digital Curation Center (DCC) & Humanities Advanced Technology and Information,*
University of Glasgow, 11 University Gardens, Glasgow, G12 8QJ, UK,
Tel: +44 141 330 5512, Fax: F: +44 141 330 3788,
Email: {y.kim/s.ross}@hatii.arts.gla.ac.uk

Abstract: We present a viable framework for the automated extraction of preservation quality metadata, which is adjusted to meet the needs of, ingest to digital repositories. It has three distinctive features: wide coverage, specialisation and emphasis on quality. Wide coverage is achieved through the use of a distributed system of tool repositories, which helps to implement it over a broad range of document object types. Specialisation is maintained through the selection of the most appropriate metadata extraction tool for each case based on the identification of the digital object genre. And quality is sustained by introducing control points at selected stages of the workflow of the system. The integration of these three features as components in the ingest of material into digital repositories is a defining step ahead in the current quest for improved management of digital resources.

1. Introduction

Institutions from different sectors (business, research, education and memory) seek to provide better management and organisation of objects in digital repositories. These repositories differ in aims, size, work procedures and approaches to their users. A study of the digital repositories for research publications carried out by the project DRIVER [1] and published in March 2007, shows that there are about 230 institutes with a digital repository for research output in the countries of the European Union. This report classified the countries in the EU into four groups with respect to the level of activity in establishing digital repositories for research publications: it found that in seven countries out of 27 no digital repositories exist or there is no evidence of existing repositories. Only seven out of 27 countries have well organised digital repositories with country-wide coverage.

As the repository development activities increase it seems paramount for the long term sustainability of these repositories to take a step back and re-examine the question of what methods are most efficient in populating repositories with digital objects that would have preservation quality metadata. It is essential to address the following observations [2]:

- Repositories which are at the beginning of their development need guidance;
- Even well-established repositories rely on manual collection of metadata;

- Manual collection of metadata results in a widely varying level of metadata quality across and within repositories because it is performed by actors with different background, capabilities, experience, expertise, and physical and emotional conditions;
- Manual collection of metadata is labour intensive and expensive.

Automated metadata generation can promote consistent quality across repositories and reduce the cost of collection. It could also lead to efficient means of building collection. The quality of metadata can further be enhanced by using a quality controlled modular approach to automation that employs a distributed management system. The methodological framework which we present here addresses all these issues. Our paper looks into these issues especially in the context of ingest of material into digital repositories, taking into account that sustainable management of digital repositories is dependent on identifying best practices in collecting high quality metadata to be integrated into its architecture from the very beginning, before or at the time of ingest.

2. Objectives

The paper aims to present ongoing research on ingest in repositories with an emphasis on pre-ingest activities featuring automated metadata extraction in a quality controlled environment. Then it suggests a preliminary framework for designing prototype tools for assisting preservation quality metadata extraction for ingest into a digital repository.

An additional objective of this paper is to highlight repository-related issues defined in the DigitalPreservationEurope Research Agenda[1]. It also seeks to raise awareness, amongst the specialists of the community, of future development needs, which would help to achieve excellence in digital repositories technology in the European landscape.

3. Methodology

We investigated previous approaches in extracting descriptive and semantic metadata automatically from digital material, and the tools and related research, which can be, incorporated into a general metadata extraction prototype tool.

The results of our investigations enabled us to define typical ingest workflows for digital repositories and what activities related to the evaluation of the quality of ingested digital objects and metadata should be inherent in the process. Based on our analysis of specific preservation quality metadata requirements and the ingest workflows, the task then examined what kinds of tools might increase both the capacity and quality of document ingest into digital repositories vis-à-vis automated metadata extraction.

We observed that current research and practical work in information extraction targeted at metadata are typically designed for very specific classes of documents (they extract metadata from documents of a specific genre and digital format) and lack generic applicability. The delivery of a generic tool, a 'universal metadata extraction application' capable of extracting metadata from any type of document without prior knowledge of the document type is not a realistic prospect—although it would be welcome. Even a brief consideration of the diversity of file formats, document types and structures, and domains in which information objects (e.g. documents) are created and used indicates the complexity of the problem. This observation has led us to adopt a different approach. We propose an approach that is based on the premise that, if we could determine the genre and technical format of a document, and if we knew what tools could be applied to metadata extraction from documents of the identified genre, we could ensure that the tool which would guarantee the highest recall and precision is selected and applied at the metadata extraction stage.

The genre of the document reflects essential properties relating to physical and conceptual structure of the document, i.e. genre classification clusters documents into groups where each group consists of documents for which named metadata elements are likely to appear in relatively similar locations. We have already investigated the feasibility of automated genre classification including human labelling case studies and have found promising results [6, 7].

4. Technology Description

We propose a practical approach to genre classification which could be used in constructing automated metadata extraction workflow processes and would provide a foundation for the integration of supporting registries of classification and extraction tools with distributed workflow applications.

The model is founded on a consideration of a range of issues inherent in metadata extraction approaches: digital repositories, ingest workflows, automated metadata extraction, genre classification and quality issues. The resulting model proposes a novel approach: pre-ingest of automated metadata extraction based on genre classification of the digital object which allows choosing the most appropriate metadata extraction tool for selected genres. Among the innovative features of this model are that it foresees quality control, and it anticipates that metadata extraction tools will not necessarily be available for all classes of digital objects for which they will be needed and integrates this challenge into the workflow. This guarantees that only digital objects supplied with metadata of the desired quality would be ingested into the digital repository. The workflow provides a general framework for the automated extraction of preservation quality metadata for ingest into digital repositories. Since it follows a service-oriented distributed architecture, various tools within it could be implemented in different organisations and at different times (e.g. in response to specified requirements). To facilitate future implementations we also created a web registry of tools, which could contribute to different metadata extraction subtasks.

5. Developments

In the most popular existing workflows (see for example [3], [4], [5]), the digital objects presented for ingest arrive at the repository either accompanied by their metadata or have their metadata added after ingest. In both scenarios, mechanisms to support metadata quality control are lacking, and this poses risks to the long-term management of the digital objects themselves. Metadata quality has a lasting impact on discovery and retrieval, data and preservation management, and how future users can access the objects. The metadata extraction workflow described here is designed to be a pre-ingest process that includes quality control before the object is submitted to a repository. It is designed to ensure that digital objects ingested into a repository pass a metadata quality threshold; this threshold is defined at repository level.

To improve both quality and state of automation in digital repositories, we introduce automated metadata extraction into our workflow based on the assumption that an intelligent choice of an appropriate metadata extraction tool can be made according to the digital object format, genre and metadata quality requirements. The eventual deployment of a service based on this model depends upon the creation of a public repository of metadata extraction tools as well as the tools themselves.

The input into the workflow is generally a digital object of unidentified genre and format. This is received by the Digital Repository Content Manager, which is a process implemented by a software agent or a human user, or even by a combination of both, at various stages of the task. It initiates and guides the ingest process of digital objects into the repository and includes several transformations and decision-making points. The workflow implements the following core processes:

1. Digital object preparation, including digital object format detection and, if necessary, conversion to PDF.
2. Automated genre classification, involving analysis of the structure of the object and assignment of a genre.
3. Automated metadata extraction, featuring use of a distributed repository of metadata extraction tools for documents of various genres.
4. Quality control. A process where metadata are validated.

The input, output and repositories used in the four core activities are summarised below:

Table 1. *Data flows in the automated metadata extraction workflow activities*

Process	Data input	Data output	Repositories needed
1. *Digital object preparation*	Digital object	Digital object + Digital object in PDF	Repository of PDF converters
2. *Automated Genre Classification*	Digital object + Digital object in PDF	Digital object + Digital object in PDF + Genre	
3. *Automated Metadata Extraction*	Digital object + Digital object in PDF + Genre Format Quality Rights	Digital object + Digital object in PDF + Genre + Metadata **or** Request for a tool (when a metadata extraction tool does not exist)	Repository of automated metadata extraction tools Queue of digital objects of a genre for which a metadata extraction tool is not available
4. *Quality Control*	Quality requirements preset by	Ingest of digital object and metadata **or** repetition of the process.	Digital repository

The idea that we adopted in outlining the general architecture of the workflow was to encapsulate the separate processes described as independent *managers*. The architecture highlighting the managing component on the highest level is presented in Figure 1.

The output of the workflow depends on the outcome of the quality control with respect to the extracted metadata. In general, this outcome would be the document enriched with PDF representation, genre identification and metadata, ready for ingest into the repository. If metadata cannot be generated or do not meet the quality requirements, the process may be repeated. If the reason for the lack of metadata is the lack of availability of an appropriate metadata extraction tool, the digital object will be placed in a queue until the appropriate tool can be acquired (the workflow envisages communication with a public registry of metadata extraction tools).

6. Results

As mentioned above, Figure 1 presents the framework model on the highest level as a combination of processes and data flows. The 3D boxes present the five managers (PDF Conversion, Genre Classification, Metadata Extraction, Quality Control and Metadata Extraction Tools Manager). Decision points are represented by lozenge shapes. The central managing process is handled by the Digital Repository Content Manager (represented by the icon). We have used red dotted arrows to represent its intervention. The regular flow of activities is indicated by black arrows. The digital objects and other data generated by the various processes are presented as blue and green rhombuses. The repositories used at various stages are also represented in Figure 1, as white document stacks with small icons.

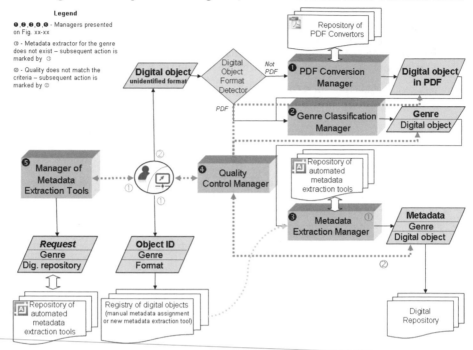

Fig. 1. Ingest framework

The workflow starts with submission of a digital object in an unidentified format for metadata extraction. Operation on the object is initiated by the Digital Repository Content Manager. For the sake of simplicity, we only consider here the situation where one object is processed at a time. Our assumption is that, in the case of multiple objects, the Digital Repository Content Manager will place them in a queue and that they will be processed consecutively.

When a digital object is presented for metadata extraction, the first step is to determine whether it is in PDF format. If it is PDF, then the object is submitted directly to the Genre Classification Manager. Otherwise, it will be submitted to the PDF Conversion Manager for analysis and representation of the object in PDF format. Conversion to PDF is intended to make all documents conform to one format for processing by the Genre Classification Manager, which we have optimised to work with PDF representations. The genre classification method, however, does not rely on PDF conversion, and can be modified to work with other formats in the future. The instance of the object in its original format is also retained and preserved and linked to the process. .

If the object format is not recognised as PDF, the first task of the PDF Conversion Manager is to identify the technical format (e.g. RTF, PS, JPEG) of the object. This is carried out within a Format Recognition Component. Once the format is identified, a tool is located to convert the object to PDF. The format influences the tools that will be needed to convert, render, and/or access the object. If the format is not known or a tool for the particular format is not available or does not exist, the Digital Repository Content Manager will decide how to proceed. A possible scenario might be to publish a public request for the necessary tool.

If a converter exists, it produces a PDF version of the digital object, which is checked for quality and sent to the Genre Classification Manager. When the Genre Classification Manager receives a PDF file, the process starts with an analysis performed by the Compound Object Handler to determine whether this is a simple or compound document. In the case of compound objects, it would create a queue consisting of the object followed by its sub-components. For example, in the case of books, journals or websites it is recommended to extract metadata not only on the higher-level genre but also on the constituent smaller identifiable pieces. For compound objects, the metadata extracted from the components will be integrated to form a composite metadata set at the end of the process. The Genre Classification Manager then proceeds to analyse the genre of the object and each of its components to label them with the genre to which they belong.

Each digital object is processed by a Submission Engine. Its role is to decide which classifiers to apply to a particular digital object. The model incorporates five classifiers: involving visual layout, language model (e.g. N-gram model of words), stylo-metrics (e.g. frequency of definite articles) and semantics of the text (e.g. number of subjective noun phrases), and domain knowledge (e.g. document source or format) [6]. In determining the genre of a digital object, these five classifiers are used discriminatingly, as not all features are necessarily expected to be present in the object, and the feature type most suitable for detecting documents of one genre is not necessarily the best for detecting documents of another genre [7]. Each of the classifiers applied will return a label value. If the classifier had not been used or could not extract any features from the object, it would return a null value, which is also informative in further analysis.

The acquired values are submitted to a Genre Labeller. Its decision-making tool uses an estimated probability distribution of features in relation to classes in a selected training data set to predict the genre class or classes of a document from a predefined schema. If agreement on the genre cannot be achieved, this tool communicates with the Digital Repository Content Manager, which would typically resubmit the object possibly with modifications for a new iteration of the genre-labelling exercise. The output of the tool is the digital object tagged with its genre label. The Quality Manager again takes the lead before the result (an agreed genre label) is submitted to the next component, the Metadata Extraction Manager.

The Metadata Extraction Manager deploys information gathered about the digital object and knowledge of its genre class to select the most appropriate metadata extraction tool from the Repository of Metadata Extraction Tools. Ross, Kim and Dobreva [2] have examined at least eleven research initiatives targeted at metadata extraction for documents belonging to specific genres (e.g. scientific articles or webpages). In selecting the metadata extractor, threshold settings for metadata depth and quality as defined by the Digital Repository Content Manager are taken into account.

A request for tools (from which to select the best available tool) consists of a set of values [g, f, r, q] constructed to represent Genre (g) and Format (f) described above, Quality (q) (described in the next paragraph), and Rights (r), where (r) is intended to convey the Digital Repository Content Manager's preference with respect to product license type (e.g. free or commercial) when selecting tools from the Repository of Metadata Extraction Tools. The Request Dispatcher then selects tools matching the values in the request. The most suitable metadata extractor is selected by submitting the retrieved tools to the Results Optimiser, which chooses the metadata extraction tool that has demonstrated greatest success on earlier occasions. If tools for a particular genre for either the PDF or the format in which the digital object was submitted are not available in the Repository of Metadata Extraction Tools, a check would be carried out to see what formats could be processed. The Metadata Extraction Manager could, as a result, initiate a process to generate a version of the digital object in a format that could be processed by an available metadata extraction tool. After the digital object is submitted to the chosen metadata extractor quality control is applied to the extracted information before ingest. Should an appropriate tool not be available in the Repository of Metadata Extraction Tools the Manager of Metadata Extraction Tools handles the exception. The manager invokes the Request Initiator which starts an external search for an existing tool and if that fails to produce results announces to the community a request for open-source development of such a tool. Second, it adds information about the specific digital object and in which digital repository it is held to a registry of digital objects for which metadata extraction tools are unavailable.

The Quality Control Manager checks the results from the various managers against a predefined and repository-weighted set of quality parameters, including precision and recall, consistency, sufficiency, and trustworthiness: *Quality* threshold value (q). Quality parameters will be of indicative value only if metadata extraction tools have been tested against a transparent benchmark data set before their inclusion in the Repository of Automated Metadata Extraction Tools. This tool is fine-tuned by the Digital Repository Content Manager. It is the basic instrument for assuring the desired quality level. If the quality control leads to a positive result, the object is ingested into the repository or a set of repositories, some which may be distributed. Quality assurance processes would also be implemented for the results of PDF Conversion and Genre Classification Managers. If the quality control finds that the metadata do not pass the defined quality threshold, the digital object returns to the Genre Classification Manager with a request for its genre classification to be re-evaluated. As it would be pointless to return the digital object for genre re-assignment repeatedly after a certain number of failed attempts (although we have not yet identified the optimal number) the object will be sent to the Digital Repository Content Manager for further manual inspection.

There are two scenarios by which a digital object can be removed from the registry. The first depends upon manual extraction of metadata. The second is to return the digital object to the Manager of Metadata Extraction Tools when the necessary metadata extraction tool becomes available.

7. Business Benefits

We have proposed and described a metadata extraction workflow methodology that enables the community to pinpoint domains in which new research is needed and where new tools are required. We have suggested how services could be combined to incorporate automated metadata extraction into the ingest process for digital objects into a digital repository in a distributed environment. This will maximise the effectiveness of applying research results, and enable the exchange of tools developed in different institutions for different parts of the process.

The next step should include further refining the workflow, to elucidate better the processes, completing the survey of available tools and making it extensible by the community via an open-access tools repository, defining protocols and 'application interfaces' to support interoperability at the intersections within the framework, and deploying this conceptual model for practical testing by the community.

The continuation of this research and its implementation will also require additional studies of the user needs for the professionals in digital repository management. While the need of developing such tools is recognised, the diverse ways in which they can be integrated into real-life practices need further research and marketing.

8. Conclusions

The paper presents an approach to automating one particular process – the automated metadata extraction for and prior to the ingest of material into digital repositories. We have suggested a model based on a distributed architecture supported by underlying quality control maximising the potential integration of specialised tools developed across different institutions. The benefits of the implementation of this approach will contribute to several critical components of digital repository management systems:

1. Higher amount of ingested digital objects supplied with preservation quality metadata contributes to sustainability of resources.
2. Improved quality of metadata provides a broader base for the retrieval components and should lead to higher user satisfaction.

Automation, especially in a quality-assured environment, is one of the areas of high demand for research and implementation work in the future years. This paper will help the specialists in digital libraries to understand better the current context of digital repositories and related research needs in realising automated processes. The general principle underlying the approach could be applied also for other repository-related activities.

Acknowledgements

This research has been supported under the DELOS: Network of Excellence on Digital Libraries (G038-507618) project funded under the European Union's Sixth Framework Programme. It also benefited from work being conducted as part of the Digital Curation Centre's (DCC) research programme.

References

[1] Van der Graaf, M.: Inventory study into the present type and level of OAI compliant Digital Repository activities in the EU, White paper, version 0.9, March 2007, http://www.driver-support.eu/documents/DRIVER%20Inventory%20study%202007.pdf

[2] Ross, S., Kim, Y. and Dobreva, M.: Preliminary framework for designing prototype tools for assisting with preservation quality metadata extraction for ingest into digital repository, Pisa, DELOS NoE, December 2007, ISBN 2-912335-39-6.

[3] Reference Model for an Open Archival Information System (OAIS), CCSDS 650.0-B-1 (2002), http://public.ccsds.org/publications/archive/650x0b1.pdf

[4] Bekaert, J. and Van de Sompel, H.: A Standards-based Solution for the Accurate Transfer of Digital Assets, D-Lib Magazine, Vol. 11(6) (2005), http://www.dlib.org/dlib/june05/bekaert/06bekaert.html

[5] Tansley, R., Bass, M., Stuve, D., Branschofsky, M., Chudnov, D., McClellan, G. and Smith, M.: The DSpace Institutional Digital Repository System: Current Functionality, Proceedings of the 3rd ACM/IEEE-CS Joint Conference on Digital Libraries, Houston, Texas, 27-31 May 2003. IEEE Computer Society, Washington, DC, pp. 87-97 (2003), http://ieeexplore.ieee.org/iel5/8569/27127/01204846.pdf

[6] Kim, Y. and Ross, S.: Genre classification in automated ingest and appraisal metadata. In: Gonzalo, J. (ed.): Proceedings of the European Conference on advanced technology and research in Digital Libraries, LNCS, Vol. 4172, pp. 63-74. Springer (2006), http://www.springerlink.com/content/2048x670g9863085/

[7] Kim, Y. and Ross, S.: Examining Variations of Prominent Features in Genre Classification. In Proceedings 41st Hawaiian International Conference on System Sciences, IEEE Computer Society Press, ISSN 1530-1605, (2008), http://ieeexplore.ieee.org/xpls/abs_all.jsp?isnumber=4438696&arnumber=4438835&count=502&index=138

---

[i] DigitalPreservationEurope: DPE Research Roadmap, DPE-D7.2, (2007), http://www.digitalpreservationeurope.eu/publications/reports/dpe_research_roadmap_D72.pdf

Section 8.2

Case Studies

Collaboration and the Knowledge Economy: Issues, Applications, Case Studies
P. Cunningham and M. Cunningham (Eds.)
IOS Press, 2008

Heritage in Digital Times: Yes Please or No Thanks, Not Yet?

Joke BEYL, Gert NULENS

VUB SMIT, Pleinlaan 9, Brussels, B-1050, Belgium

Tel: +32 2 629 16 43, Fax: +32 2 629 17 00

Email: joke.beyl@vub.ac.be, gert.nulens@vub.ac.be

Abstract: Since April 2007, several research teams and heritage organisations in Flanders are involved in a research project that is aimed at developing a demonstrator regarding the online and mobile distribution of digital cultural heritage. This paper intends to outline some of the results that have been achieved within the first year of the project. We focus on the expert survey that was meant to get a notion of the actual needs and of the current level of acceptance for the intended digital heritage applications of this project being on the one hand the creation of a generic metadata model and on the other hand the creation of a personalized, social and location-specific heritage story on a PDA. We can conclude that there is a need for a paradigm shift and for the development of a real vision within the Flemish cultural heritage field. Heritage institutions should reflect carefully upon this challenging landscape of digital media and consider the way in which they can interact with it. This is not to say that they have to interact with it, instead they should think about what is best suited for them to do or not to do.

Keywords: digital heritage, metadata layer, mobile heritage presentation, heritage experts

1. Introduction

Since April 2007, several research teams and heritage organisations in Flanders are involved in a two-year research trajectory called 'Heritage 2.0' in which problems regarding the online and mobile distribution of digital cultural heritage are analysed. This will result in the development of a demonstrator that will be implemented at a specific Flemish heritage site. So while working within the context of a focused case study we go beyond the individual case by researching preconditions and challenges involved. This paper intends to outline some of the results that have been achieved within the first year of the project. With one more year left to go, the main challenge lies in the implementation of these sociological results within the technological developments this project is aimed at.

The Heritage 2.0 project contains two main components. Firstly it intends to develop a generic metadata model for the whole Flemish heritage sector. While this is meant to span the different heritage sectors (movable, immovable, tangible and intangible heritage), the target is not to create a centralised database, but rather to facilitate retrieval and communication among existing heritage databases. Furthermore as well as connecting information originating from different data sources to construct new and rich heritage stories, the project is looking for new ways to distribute these stories. Therefore the second objective of this research project is the creation of a personalised, social and location-specific heritage story that will be presented to the heritage visitor by means of a PDA.

Technological developments have a lot of possibilities to offer. However this does not necessarily mean that these possibilities are desired by the heritage visitor or feasible within the cultural heritage sector. In this paper we focus on the expert survey that was conducted within the context of the research project. The expert survey was meant to get a notion of the actual needs and of the current level of acceptance for digital heritage applications. For that reason we started this research project by trying to answer two fundamental questions. Is the Flemish cultural heritage field ready for using and implementing the expected outcomes of this research project being the metadata layer and the use of a PDA for the presentation of a heritage story? And is there an actual need for this new way of searching and presenting cultural heritage information?

2. Objectives

The innovative aspect of the creation of the proposed metadata layer lies within the fact that it intends to connect different heritage sectors, such as museums, archives and local heritage, that use different ways to describe and to organise their data and that have different opinions concerning the level and the likelihood of opening up their collections. Because of these differences it is not always easy to find out what kind of information is stored where. By facilitating this retrieval process our research project intends to offer an added value to the heritage expert or heritage amateur. There are already some initiatives in Flanders that are aimed at linking heritage content from different heritage institutions. However all of these initiatives are established within a specific heritage sector. For instance the Flemish MOVE [1] project offers a website where the user can search the collections of the 40 member museums of the project by means of a centralised database. Another example is the Flemish ODIS [2] database. This is a centralised database within the archives sector that contains metadata from the 7 partner institutions.

Moreover by implementing the use of a PDA on a specific heritage site in Flanders (i.e. the abbey and herb garden of Herkenrode) for distributing a personalized, social and location-specific heritage story to the visitor we want to reveal the possible bottlenecks this implies. The value lies in the practical approach that is aimed at learning about the needs and wants of the users of the technology. This kind of sociological approach has been used in other heritage related studies [3]. Studying and implementing the use of mobile devices such as a PDA for the presentation of heritage is not new [4]. However the innovative facet of our research lies within our focus on the social characteristics of a heritage visit.

3. Methodology

As was mentioned in the introduction, the first year of this research project was mainly focused on studying the opinions, needs and wants of the users (both the heritage visitor and the heritage expert). In this paper we outline the results of the expert survey.

We conducted a range of focus group conversations with Flemish heritage professionals from different heritage sectors. We asked their opinion concerning the two main components of this research project. Since mobile heritage presentation is still in its infancy in Flanders we decided to extend these focus groups by interviewing several international experts in depth in order to understand how they view the present and future of mobile heritage presentation.

We decided upon this expert survey since they know the heritage field very well and since the project is aimed at them making use of the expected outcomes. So we wanted to find out what would be their level of acceptance as well as to explain why this level is the way it is.

4. Technology Description

The research project tackles two main issues as was mentioned before. However these issues do not necessarily have to be connected. The creation of a metadata layer on top of existing Flemish cultural heritage databases is aimed at facilitating the retrieval of information on a certain heritage topic. We want to smooth the searching process of heritage professionals and heritage amateurs by connecting metadata that is contained in different databases and even more important within different heritage sectors. It would be interesting if a heritage professional that wants to build an exhibition on the impact of the First World War in Flanders for example, is able to easily find out which heritage institutions in Flanders maintain what kind of content concerning this topic.

Since the heritage professional now knows which heritage institutions he needs to contact to get the data he needs, he can start to build a heritage story that is interesting for the visitor. For the raw heritage data is not what a visitor wants. This is something that was mentioned several times during our conversations with heritage experts.

Once the heritage professional has constructed a heritage story he can then choose different means by which to distribute it to the heritage visitor. This can be done by means of a kiosk, a leaflet, a catalogue and an audio guide tour or by means of a PDA.

So taking into account this entire process, the 'Heritage 2.0' research project intends to develop a technological solution to facilitate the retrieval of heritage information, the starting point of the process, and a technological solution to augment the distribution of a heritage story. This however is not the end of the process since there is also a post-visit stage where the visitor might decide to comment or to generate content inspired by the heritage story. Therefore this research project will also take into account the ways in which expert and user generated content can be linked.

5. Developments

We are halfway through the research project and we have now reached the point where the sociological findings have led to recommendations that should be taken into account in the intended technological developments. These being on the one side the creation of a theoretical generic metadata model to connect different databases keeping in mind the specific Flemish heritage context. To cover this context we talked to several Flemish heritage institutions to better understand the way in which they keep and unlock their digital data. We selected these institutions based upon the fact that they maintain different kinds of data (audio, video, photo, text) and use different metadata standards to describe these data. Our technological research partners will use this information as well as the recommendations that followed the expert survey to construct the metadata layer.

At the same time a personalized, social and location-specific heritage story will be developed on a PDA and implemented at the abbey and herb garden of Herkenrode in Flanders. Therefore we work in close collaboration with the organisations responsible for maintaining this heritage site. The results of both the user and the expert study will be taken into consideration when developing the story on the PDA.

To finish the recommendations, the expert survey will be used to reflect upon the possible implementation of Web 2.0 applications within the website that will be dedicated to the Herkenrode site.

6. Results

6.1 An international view on mobile heritage presentation

We asked the opinion of several international experts about the present and future of using mobile devices within the context of a heritage visit. These experts are all doing research within the field of heritage and the use of ICT. Some focus more on the user aspect, others are more into the technological developments this implies.

They all highlight the fact that the use of mobile devices in a heritage context is not always the outcome of a well thought-out and clearly planned process. This means that heritage institutions do not always take into account the possible information overload, the fact that content needs to be adapted to the mobile device and the fact that content needs to be delivered independent from the device, since technology can become obsolete very fast. Furthermore using a PDA for presenting heritage should offer an added value to the visitor and to the institution. If this is not the case, it is not worth investing in. Moreover one has to bear in mind that mobile devices can be very attractive for some visitors, and can be discouraging for others. One of the experts mentioned that a lot of institutions believe that they are capable of creating their own mobile tours while underestimating the fact that this implies a lot of time and knowledge about how to translate the heritage information into a story on a mobile device. In other words, making a traditional exposition or creating a heritage story is not the same as making a multimedia experience. The latter requires a different set of expertise and knowledge. Also it is said that when creating a mobile heritage tour one should always bear in mind that the needs of both heritage staff and heritage visitors have to be taken into account so bottlenecks can be anticipated. Furthermore the experts point out that these new technologies need to be implemented as simple as possible. However, as is said, often institutions just want to get the most out of the numerous possibilities these new technologies have to offer.

To conclude we can say that according to the international experts there is a need for a paradigm shift within the cultural heritage field. Instead of focusing on the collection, heritage institutions should concentrate on the visitor. Secondly, while using technologies such as mobile devices, one should always try to go beyond the technology. Do not let the technology steer the outcome for the visitor, but let the needs of the visitor be a guideline for the usage and implementation of the technology.

6.2   The needs and wants of Flemish heritage professionals

To be able to answer the two fundamental questions of the expert survey we conducted a range of focus group conversations with Flemish heritage professionals from different heritage sectors. The sectors we defined were among others heritage cells whose responsibility it is to promote local heritage, to stimulate collaboration between heritage institutions and so on. We also talked to representatives of museums, of archives and documentation centres, of coordinating bodies, of local heritage and of heritage sites.

To begin with the Flemish heritage professionals see a couple of bottlenecks that could obstruct the creation of the intended metadata layer. They stress the fact that there is a lack of input. In other words there is a lack of a critical mass of digitized and digitally described data. They also mention the fact that different institutions use different systems for organizing their data because they all have their own needs. This makes it difficult to connect these data. Lastly the experts refer to copyright issues. These are not insuperable, but it needs to be made clear, they say, what will be released by means of this metadata layer and what will not be.

They also see some added value related to this communication layer. It would no longer be necessary to consult different heritage institutions to find out whether or not they have some relevant data about a certain topic. Instead the heritage professional would be able to ask just one question and then receive information originating from different sources. Furthermore this layer offers the possibility to discover unknown and unexpected information. Finally by connecting data derived from different institutions it is believed that the opportunity of stimulating collaboration within the broad heritage landscape is created.

Concerning mobile heritage presentation, the second part of this research project, the experts mention some issues that deserve thorough attention. It is important, they say, to guide the visitor, to give him a story but at the same time the visitor should be able to dig deeper into the information he is interested in. This combination is seen to be achievable by offering layered stories. Another issue is user generated content. The experts believe this might be an interesting source of information. But at the same time they argue that this kind of content needs to be filtered. However this requires resources and these are not always available. Furthermore it is noted that a PDA should not be seen as a replacement of other means of heritage presentation. A PDA should only be used when this offers a real added value. The technology is but a means to an end. The experts stress the importance of the content compared to the technology. The story that is delivered by means of the mobile device is the most important but this is also the most time-consuming. However, information needs to be translated into a story that is interesting for the visitor. The visitor wants a precooked story instead of a bunch of information that he needs to tackle him self. So before implementing a PDA in the presentation of heritage this should be given considerable thought. The heritage institution needs to reflect on the longer term.

The experts have some concerns that might hinder the use of mobile devices within a heritage context. They mention the gap between big and small heritage institutions. The latter are at this moment not capable of using mobile technologies for heritage presentation due to a lack of time, knowledge, money, resources and staff to digitally describe data as well as staff to translate these data into a story. The experts point out some other problems. Some doubt the fact that the visitor is ready for using this kind of mobile technology. There is also a danger of overloading the visitor with information or of isolating the visitor from the actual exhibits that surround him. Moreover the experts say that this might cause a problem for heritage institutions since it is not always easy to find enough digital and digitized data to stuff the PDA.

Nonetheless the heritage professionals relate several added values to the use of mobile devices for the delivery of heritage content to the visitor. They emphasize the fact that a PDA offers more possibilities than the classical ways of presenting heritage. It can be used to deliver both sound and vision as well as 3D-reconstructions and it can offer suggestions based upon the interests of the individual visitor. Furthermore it is mentioned that it can be useful in outdoor situations. It also creates the opportunity for heritage institutions to offer serious information in a more pleasant way opening up heritage to a larger and younger audience. There is also an important added value for the heritage institution since it offers the possibility of tracking visitor behaviour and interests. This might be interesting for the development of future exhibitions. Last but not least the experts say that a PDA offers the visitor the possibility to collect and maintain information in an independent way before, during and after the visit because information can be offered by means of different stories and different layers.

To finish the focus group conversations we asked the heritage professionals what they would like to see happen if they possessed unlimited resources. They all emphasized the importance of input. There is a need to digitally describe all data in databases and to connect these data. Because without input there will be no output. Not for the metadata layer and not for the mobile heritage presentation. They say that in essence it should be about making all heritage data available to the visitor in a way that holds an added value for this visitor.

We can say that the Flemish heritage professionals hold a critical stance in relation to our Heritage 2.0 – research project. They acknowledge the fact that both the metadata layer and mobile heritage presentation have benefits for the heritage institutions and their visitors. Nevertheless they mention that a lot of institutions are not ready yet because of a lack of input, knowledge, staff and so on. Furthermore the implementation of these kinds of technological developments needs to be carefully considered in advance. The biggest problem of all however is the fact that a lot of small and local organisations still have a lot of work to do before it is realistic to expect them to follow this path. At the moment they are not willing to invest in something of which they are not sure whether it will be a success. Therefore they will wait and see what happens at the big institutions, it is said.

6.3   What are the real challenges?

Based upon the international interviews and the focus group conversations with Flemish heritage professionals we can conclude that there is a need for a paradigm shift and for the development of a real vision within the cultural heritage field concerning the way they should or could cope with these digital times. Heritage institutions should reflect carefully upon this challenging landscape of digital media and consider the way in which they can interact with it. This is not to say that they have to interact with it, instead they should think about what is best suited for them to do or not to do.

Concerning the experts a lot of institutions are not ready yet to follow this digital path because of the presence of several bottlenecks. Possible solutions we could suggest are the cooperation between large and small heritage organisations to obtain technical support for the latter or the sharing of knowledge about possibilities concerning the use of user generated content as well as the instigation of a follow-up research project focusing on the facilitation of creating a heritage story.

One of the starting points of this research is making the obtained knowledge available for the Flemish heritage sector. That is why we are about to organise a workshop to present some of the results as well as a conference to round off the project in 2009. The goal of this conference will be to frame the project results within the present Flemish and international situation.

7   Business Benefits

The proposed results of the research project offer benefits to the different parties involved. To start with the project creates a benefit for the heritage institutions. The intended metadata layer does not require the heritage institutions to change the way they describe and have described their data. They can however benefit from the opportunity of unlocking their data to a broader audience by means of this layer.

Furthermore this metadata layer holds a benefit for the user that is interested in heritage. We acknowledge the fact that trying to connect databases originating from different heritage sectors is an ambitious goal. However one of the experts we consulted told us that sometimes people assume to fast that this will not work. By creating a theoretical metadata layer we want to show that it is not impossible and that it might be worth the try since this can open up unknown and unexpected information for the user.

Thirdly this project intends to be the first step in a larger trajectory. By running through the entire process of searching heritage content to presenting it by means of a mobile device we want to unveil the possible bottlenecks that might hinder the implementation of the project outcomes on a larger scale.

To finish we want to focus on the collaborative aspect of this research project. On the one hand the project involves the most important coordinating cultural heritage and tourism bodies in Flanders as well as several university research centres and companies that offer solutions within the field of digital and mobile heritage content. On the other hand it was our intention from the start to involve the Flemish cultural heritage field. That is why we conducted the focus group conversations and that is why we will organise the workshop before the end of the project so feedback can be gained. The benefit of this kind of collaboration is the generating of research results that anticipate the specific Flemish context and that are cautious of technological determinism.

8   Conclusions

We return to the two fundamental questions the research project started with. Is the Flemish cultural heritage field ready to use and implement mobile and digital applications? According to the experts it is not, because there is a noticeable lack of digital and digitized data and of knowledge about these technologies. This means that Flemish heritage institutions have a lot of catching up to do. Is there an actual need in the Flemish cultural heritage field for this new way of searching and presenting cultural heritage information? According to the experts there is. However, the expectations they hold are realistic. They emphasize that it is not about using a PDA for the sake of it. There should always be an added value related to it. And even more important, when a heritage institution decides to use a PDA the focus should be on the content and on the context of the visit instead of on the technology. This also implies that the needs of the visitor have to be considered as the starting point of heritage presentation instead of the collection.

So 'Heritage in digital times: yes please or no thanks, not yet?' is a question that cannot be answered in a single manner. For the Flemish heritage field is very diverse. This means that heritage institutions should reflect carefully upon this challenging landscape of digital media and consider the way in which they can interact with it. This is not to say that they have to interact with it, instead they should think about what is best suited for them to do or not to do. This means taking into account possible bottlenecks as well as figuring out suitable solutions. (Table 1)

Table 1: Problems and Solutions

Problem	Solution
A lack of digital data and metadata	Investing in the digitization of data and metadata (for instance by facilitating cooperation between small and large institutions)
A lack of staff to describe and to translate the data	Building and sharing of knowledge about the uses, implementation and management of these technologies (for instance investing in staff that has ICT knowledge)
A lack of knowledge	Enabling of experiments to understand what succeeds and what doesn't
Technology can become obsolete very fast	Investing in the creation of platform-independent digital heritage stories
Not going beyond the technology as well as trying to get the most out of it	Focusing on the needs of visitors and on the mission of the heritage institution to decide upon the most appropriate way for distributing its heritage
Focus limited to the collection	Focus on the visitor

As the research project enters its final year we already point to a possible follow-up whereby research can concentrate on developing a way to support the process of translating the retrieved heritage information into a heritage story.

Acknowledgements

The Heritage 2.0 research project is funded by the Interdisciplinary Institute for Broadband Technology and supported by the Flemish Government. The authors would like to thank the consulted Flemish and international experts for sharing their thoughts and views.

References

[1] MOVE project: www.move.be
[2] ODIS project: www.odis.be
[3] Ename Expertise Centre for Public Archeology and Heritage Presentation. (2004). D.2.1.1: Report on stakeholders needs. In EPOCH WP 2.1, Interim report. Last updated 17-Jan-2007. Consulted 25-April-2008. Available on http://public-repository.epoch-net.org/D2.1.1-Report%20on%20Stakeholder%20Needs.pdf
[4] Lancaster Guide Project (1997); Electronic Guidebook Project (1998); Musepad (2001); Equator (2001); Handscape (2001); Chimer (2001); Archeoguide (2002); Tate Modern UK (2002); Urban Tapestries (2003); City in My Pocket (2004); Archie (2005); San Francisco Museum of Modern Art USA (2006); Übersee Museum Germany (2007)

Collaboration and the Knowledge Economy: Issues, Applications, Case Studies
P. Cunningham and M. Cunningham (Eds.)
IOS Press, 2008

The Construction of a Spatial Data Infrastructure for Cultural Heritage

Nancy OMTZIGT[1], Nils DE REUS[1], Eric KOOMEN[1], Alessandra AREZZA[2]

[1]*SPINlab, Free University, De Boelelaan 1087 Amsterdam, 1081HV, The Netherlands*
Tel: +31(0)5989555, Fax: + 319)020 5989 553, Email: spinlab@ivm.vu.nl
[2]*TXT E-Solutions,Via Frigia 27Milan,20126 Italy*
Tel: +39 02 257711, Fax: +39 02 2578994, Email: info@txtgroup.com

Abstract: This paper describes the setup of a thematic Spatial Data Infrastructure (SDI) for cultural heritage data. Unlocking this data using OGC web services like the Web Feature Service (WFS) and the Web Map Service (WMS) creates a variety of possibilities. It allows to embed interactive maps in touristic web applications and to use the data in management or analyses tools. To implement such a SDI in different European cities, the SDI must be able to adapt to local legislation and customs. Different data sources can be added to the SDI depending on local available data sets. The implementation of the SDI in 3 case study cities illustrates the challenges that this SDI has to face.

1. Introduction

The main objective of the ISAAC project is to valorise the relationship between digital heritage and cultural tourism by developing a novel user-centric ICT environment providing tourism E-services that will meet the needs of both tourists and citizens in European cultural destinations through facilitating a virtual access and stimulating learning experience of European cultural heritage assets before, during and after a real visit. The SDI for the ISAAC project is a re-usable web mapping and spatial data delivery service that, because of its nature, can be used in both touristic e-platforms and for management and research task. Most SDI's are not bounded to thematic data, like the ISAAC SDI is set up for cultural heritage data only.

The next section starts with the objectives of the SDI within the ISAAC project. Section three, the methodology section, describes the three components of a SDI in general. This is background information for section four where the characteristics of these three components in the ISAAC SDI are explained. Section 5 shows the impact of these characteristics for the technical implementation of the SDI, and it is followed by an overview of the results of the implementation so far. This paper ends with conclusions and lessons learned from the implementation of the ISAAC SDI.

2. Objectives

This paper describes the development of a spatial data infrastructure (SDI) that will be a backbone for E-services providing spatial cultural heritage information to tourists, citizens and other users. This SDI is based on the specific requirements of the ISAAC project, but also looks at a wider context of revealing spatial cultural heritage data to researchers, policy makers and the general public. Therefore the ISAAC specific needs are discussed, as well as the conflict of these needs with the general concept of SDI's, and possible solutions for a practical implementation of a sustainable ISAAC SDI.

As mentioned above, the SDI is a backbone for the E-services in the ISAAC platform. These E-services include virtual city tours and tourist satisfaction questionnaires. Three cities implement the ISAAC platform, and these cities differ in important aspects. First, the touristic highlights of these cities are not comparable. And second, the cities are in different countries so aspects like data availability and legislation are not similar. The ISAAC SDI has to take care of these city specific aspects.

3. Methodology

This section introduces the three components of a SDI. Section four will describe the characteristics of these components in the ISAAC SDI.

3.1 The Three Components of a SDI

The components of a SDI are data, technology and organisation. A very important SDI "best practice" regarding data is the concept of distributed databases. This means that data is stored at its original location in its native format. This prevents data duplication and the need for extra procedures regarding data management and updates. Concerning the technology component, the use of OpenGeospatial Consortioum (OGC [1]) standards is applied to make the ISAAC SDI an open infrastructure. These 2 agreements are the fundament of the data, technology and organisation components.

3.2 SDI Technology

The OGC standards for the exchange of spatial data can operate different kind of spatial data requests. First, the Web Map Service (WMS) can deliver rendered maps based on the underlying spatial data. These maps are interactive, and can be queried by the user. The Web Feature Service (WFS) can deliver the spatial data itself. This is useful when the user has his own application to process spatial data, like a Geographic Information System (GIS). WFS can also allow data editing or updating. Data delivery is done using the Geography Markup Language (GML).

The Geography Markup Language (GML) is an OGC creation (filed as ISO 19136) to describe geographical features in general, intended as an open interchange format for geographic transactions on the Internet. Unlike more narrow-purposed vector languages, GML has a grammar allowing for geographic features, coverages, observations, topology, geometry, coordinate reference systems, units of measure, time, and value objects.

Since GML is an upwards compliant sub variant grammar of the general eXtensible Markup Language (XML) it is highly accessible for E-service developers. It is simple to parse, filter and/or transform using generic XML technologies. Besides GML is able to contain, within a single document, all data and metadata about layers, projections, features, attributes and groupings that may be returned by a feature data request. For this all to be wrapped into a single document is ideal for transport of such data over the Internet, where the communication protocols are document based, and the request-response mechanism is limited to returning a single document for each request. In addition, having been an official OGC standard for a number of years has created a third important advantage for the use of GML as an interchange format, which is that its status as official standard has encouraged every major GIS software company to support this format. GML is now a format widely supported as an interchange format by a large array of GIS tools and applications.

One disadvantage of GML is filesize. For large datasets, the filesize can slow down the communication speed between server and client. In most cases where communication speed is of importance, the client will access the WMS service that returns an instant map image and not the WFS service that returns the spatial data itself as GML. Where GML is needed, large datasets are requested and speed is important the use of BXML [2] can be considered.

3.3   SDI Data

All data in the SDI is spatial data, meaning that they have a location on the earth surface. It can be a picture that is taken on a certain spot, or a topographic map with the names of the streets. Spatial data can be stored in different data models. The vector data model describes features as points, lines and polygons, the raster model stores data in a cell based structure like images. Many file formats to store raster or vector data exists. Well known formats include the ESRI shapefile and geo-referenced TIFF's. The data storage format that can be used in a SDI to serve maps to the user depends on the capability of the web mapping application and will not be discussed here.

Meta data is a description of the dataset. It is important to assure a correct use of the data. Items described in the metadata are for example the projection method, the date of data capture and original purpose of the dataset. Metadata should be part of all datasets.

A very important "best practice" regarding data is the concept of distributed databases. This means that data is stored and maintained at its original location so there are no data duplications. Data duplications are the cause of failures concerning for example data versions. Data maintenance remains a responsibility of the data owner, which links this concept to the organisational component.

3.4   SDI Organisation

Since data is preferably kept within the organisation that is responsible for the data collection and maintenance process, a distributed body of data is the natural result of bringing multiple cities into an SDI. Rules and agreements on use of standards for protocols, meta data, the type of services offered etc are necessary to build a coherent and useful SDI [3].

GIS technologies have historically been an expert niche and were more related to the spatial planning office than to mainstream ICT department. There are however trends that suggest that barriers to the establishment of SDI's are decreasing. One of the trends is the incorporation of traditional SDI elements in the common information infrastructure[4] of organisations. As the concept of spatial awareness is spreading through modern organisation thinking, the associated technologies are liberated from their previous niche positions and moving to a level of maturity where the tools to unlock data spatially are available at all points in the organisation. Popularisation of the map as a data presentation medium, brought about by popular and widely used geodata viewers such as NASA's WorldWind and Google's Google Earth and Google Maps products, is driving interest in seeing one's own data in its spatial context. This trend could contribute to the integration of SDI in organisations.

4.   Technology Description

4.1   Description of the ISAAC SDI

At one hand we have the SDI principles, at the other hand the 3 cities with existing ICT infrastructure and fixed internal procedures. The ISAAC SDI has to fit within these existing frameworks, and at the same time remain open, therefore based on accepted standards. The consequences of these considerations have different impact on the implementation of the SDI for each of the case studies. As a consequence, the ISAAC SDI is tailor made for each of the cities. Sometimes the accessibility of data is an issue, sometimes the SDI has to co-exist with existing applications. When lack of data makes a successful implementation of the ISAAC SDI difficult, free data sources like Google Maps or free and open data sources like OpenStreetMap [5] available under de creative commons license [6] can provide a solution. The SDI can also act as a client of other SDI's and deliver spatial data from an other SDI as if it this data was part of the ISAAC SDI. The ISAAC SDI contains two examples of this concept, as can be seen in Table 2.

The ISAAC SDI is being implemented using WMS and WFS services. The implementation shows cases of general application, and city-specific implementations of SDI principles. The software used for the setup of the SDI (UMN MapServer [7] and OpenLayers [8]) was installed on a central location. As more data comes available from the participating cities, the SDI will continue to grow. Tourism E-services will be built upon the SDI backbone by other parties. Since the SDI works with standard formats, communication between SDI and e-services is not complicated to accomplish. Samples of the implementation of the ISAAC SDI are available on www.spinlab.vu.nl/isaac.

4.2 Technology Availability

Since not all cities had a WFS and a WMS service available (see table 1), these services were set up on a central location. For the sustainability of the ISAAC SDI the cities should set up their own SDI node in future.

Table 1: Available Technology

City	WFS/WMS
Leipzig	Not available yet
Amsterdam	WFS & WMS
Genoa	WMS

4.3 Data Availability

For each city, at least 2 datasets are available. Most of them are stored locally, some of them are distributed datasets and served as WMS or WFS layers (see table 2). There is not a compulsory data model, as the WMS and WFS services can handle different data formats.

Data items can be labelled using the ISAAC nomenclature to allow standardised search functions. This labelling is not mandatory for the functioning of the SDI, but useful for services on top of the SDI. The labelling of data items is the task of the data provider, in this case the municipalities.

Table 2: Available Data

Leipzig	Dataset	Storage location
Points of interest	Photo locations	Local, with links to e.g flickr.com
Background	OpenStreetMap	local
Amsterdam	**Dataset**	**Storage location**
Points of interest	Monuments	Local
Background	Topographic map	Local/WFS/WMS
Genoa	**Dataset**	**Storage location**
Points of interest	Points of interest	Local
Background	Topographic map	WMS

4.4 Organisational Issues

Since data is preferably kept within the organisation that is responsible at the source for the data collection and maintenance process, the ISAAC SDI has to deal with multiple organisations One of the challenges of the ISAAC SDI is therefore in the organisational component. The three case study cities have a different cultural and legal background in which they operate. For example where the question of opening data though a map service may be an internal decision for a single department in one city, it could be a complicated matter requiring formal negotiated agreements and higher level management involvement between different departments in another. These differences in organisation have an impact on the current arrangement of the ISAAC SDI.

Cultural and legal aspects can slow down or even hinder the implementation of a SDI in several ways. This can be because of the distribution of tasks and responsibilities within the organisation, or legal directives on for example the use of data. The ISAAC SDI was installed partly on a central location, to avoid organisational issues like time consuming decision making processes. Since the final goal is a sustainable SDI, all nodes on the infrastructure should be independent. Therefore the cities should, in time, implement their own WMS and WFS services.

5.   Implementation

The following sections clarify what services have been combined into demonstrable 'service products' for the three participating cities. It will become appearant from the descriptions that at this stage, many data elements are still hosted by a central ISAAC SDI server at the VU University in Amsterdam. This would in the long term be an undesirable structure, as this server might not be maintained for a sustainable time after the ISAAC project.

5.1 Amsterdam

Although Amsterdam did already have a web map server operational at the start of the ISAAC project, this was not an OGC compliant implementation and as such formed a compatibility problem with the rest of the framework.

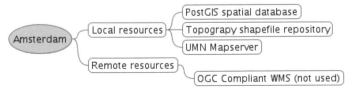

Figure 1 SDI Resources for Amsterdam

However, an alternative WMS implementation (based on UMN Mapserver) was established during the course of the ISAAC project, so that these map layers too are now available through standardized requests. As the ISAAC service demo for Amsterdam was produced at a time when the city's UMN based implementation was not yet in a stable production environment, the service was configured to draw its background layer from shapefiles in a locally mounted filesystem and is currently still in this configuration. The layer of monuments is a large featureset stored in a PostGIS spatial database at the central SDI server. The SDI resources for Amsterdam are graphically represented in figure 1.

5.2 Genua

To make the map service for the city of Genua (see figure 2), a WMS layer provided from the website of civis.comune.genova.it, which would appear to be another UMN mapserver. Unfortunately, metadata to verify this assumption is not present in the service capabilities document. Feature information is based on shapefiles sourced from the city of Genua and hosted from the central SDI server.

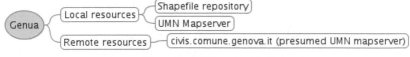

Figure 2: SDI Resources for Genua

There are some remaining issues with matching up the datasets, as the background dataset appears to be in Gauss-Boaga projection, while the overlay features need to be interpreted as lat/lon WGS84 in order to coincide with the correct position for Genua. It is expected that obtaining the appropriate metadata for both datasets will resolve these issues.

5.3 Leipzig

For the city of Leipzig (as illustrated in figure 3) we combine data sourced from five distinct sources, hosted on four distinct services. The background upon which all is drawn is provided by an aerial photograph layer sourced from the Landesvermessungamt Sachsen, and hosted on an OGC compliant Web Mapping Service by this same organisation. This image is then enriched with a layer of road information for additional orientation, sourced from the OpenStreetmap project and hosted on WMS on the central ISAAC SDI server. Feature information in the form of a set of locations associated with images are mapped onto this background. Both the feature lists and one set of images were provided by the city of Leipzig, and are currently hosted centrally. The remainder of linked images is hosted by the online image repositories Flickr and Panoramio, and are sourced from individual members of these communities.

Figure 3: SDI Resources for Leipzig

The services of Landesvermessungamt Sachsen, Flickr, Panoramio and SPINlab do not communicate with or through eachother. The central ISAAC SDI server sends connection information for the other three as part of the website based interface it provides, and it is then the end user software that contacts each of the service providers individually to create the combined service experience.

6. Results

The WMS is a re-usable Web2.0 service that can deliver rendered maps (see figure 4) to the ISAAC platform or any other client: from desktop to palmtop or mobile phone. The potential of displaying maps on mobile devices is one step to the realisation of the literate traveller[9] or could be part of a Location Bases Service (LBS) [10]. Layers can be turned on and off, layers can be queried or contain dynamic links and the user can zoom and pan on the map.

Figure 4: Example of a Rendered Map

Since the WMS is re-usable, it can be applied in different E-services. It can deliver maps to many client types, so means that the SDI can be used by E-services that inform the tourist pro-, on and post-visit, on PC, smartphone or PDA.

The WFS service can also deliver the spatial data behind the map to local or regional administrators that manage the city or region and to scientists that are interested in using the data in their GIS for further analyses. Relevant meta data is delivered on request.

7.   Conclusions

Implementation of the ISAAC SDI so far has proved to be able to solve data accessibility and data availability issues and that the SDI can co-exist with already existing applications in the different organisations. Existing WMS services can be used in the ISAAC SDI for example. This lowers the implementation costs of the SDI for the participating cities.

At this moment, the ISAAC SDI is meant as a backbone of the ICT framework of the ISAAC project, and the cities of Amsterdam, Genoa and Leipzig are case study cities. In future, the use of the ISAAC SDI is not limited to these cities, and also non-urban cultural heritage can be included in this SDI. The purpose of the ISAAC SDI is to be a European framework for the exchange of spatial cultural heritage data, for both tourism, policy making and research. As the ISAAC SDI grows, a SDI catalogue could help to unlock the data sources to a wider public.

The implementation of the SDI for the 3 case studies has proved that the differences in data availability, technological capacities and organisation have impact on the arrangement of the SDI, but not on the functionality of the SDI. Due to the flexibility of the SDI concept it was possible to create a custom made solution for each city. The quality of the data, including the semantics, relevant selections and language issues, remains the responsibility of the individual cities.

The technology has been proven, and suitable data is available. The future challenge is the further implementation of the concept of distributed databases, and to complete the set up of individual nodes in stead of a central location for part of the SDI services.

References

[1]   www.opengeospatial.org

[2] Hong, D. H. Kang, K. Han (2007). "Development of en efficient conversion system for GML documents" in Shi, Y. et al (Eds): ICCS 2007, part II, LNCS 4488, p 511-514.

[3] Nebert, D. (2004) The SDI Cookbook, Developing Spatial Data Infrastructures version2, GSDI

[4] Carrerra, F. and J. Ferreira(2007). The future of spatial data infrastructures: capacity-building for the emergence of municipal SDI's. International Journal of Spatial Data Infrastructures Research, 2: 54-73.

[5] www.openstreetmap.org

[6] www.creativecommons.org

[7] mapserver.gis.umn.edu

[8] www.openlayers.org

[9] Smith, J., W. Mackaness, A. Kealy and I. Williamson (2004). Spatial Data Infrastructure requirements for mobile location based journey planning. Transactions in GIS 8(1): 23-44.

[10] Cartwright, W.E., B. Williams and C. Pettit (2007). Realizing the Literate Traveller. Transactions in GIS 11(1): 9-27.

Collaboration and the Knowledge Economy: Issues, Applications, Case Studies
P. Cunningham and M. Cunningham (Eds.)
IOS Press, 2008

Semantic Multi-language and Multi-ontology Framework for Digital Content Management and Sharing

Stefano BIANCHI[1], Gianni VIANO[1], Christian MASTRODONATO[1],
Gianni VERCELLI[2], Marta GONZALEZ RODRIGUEZ[3]
[1]*Softeco Sismat S.p.A., Via De Marini 1 Torre WTC, Genoa, 16149, Italy*
Tel: +39 010 6026 1, Fax: + 39 010 6026 350,
Email: {stefano.bianchi, gianni.viano, christian.mastrodonato}@softeco.it
[2]*DIST – Università di Genova, Via All'Opera Pia 13, Genoa, 16145, Italy*
Tel: +39 010 3532814, Fax: +39 010 3532154 Email: gianni.vercelli@unige.it
[3]*Robotiker-Tecnalia, Parque Tecnológico Edif 202, Zamudio-Vizcaya, 48170, Spain*
Tel: +34 94 600 22 66, Fax: +34 94 600 22 99, Email: marta@robotiker.es

Abstract: Large amounts of scientific digital contents, potentially available for public sharing and reuse, are nowadays held by scientific and cultural institutions, which institutionally collect, produce and store information valuable for dissemination, work, study and research. Semantic technology offers the possibility to integrate dispersed, heterogeneous yet related resources and to build value-added sharing services (overcoming barriers such as e.g. knowledge domain complexity, different classification, language, data format, localisation) by exploiting semantic annotation and building virtual content aggregation schemas on top of distributed collections. Applications in real cases are anyway often hampered by difficulties related to the proper formalization of complex scientific knowledge (ontology engineering) and the classification of contents (semantic annotation). This paper illustrates the lessons learnt in applying the Semantic Web specifications to support content management and sharing in complex knowledge domains and provides practical examples of application in EC-funded projects.

1. Introduction

Internet and digitisation facilities make large amounts of contents available for public sharing and reuse: this is particularly valid for scientific organizations which institutionally collect, produce and store information valuable for work, study and research in many different contexts.

Nevertheless, complexity of the knowledge domain, lack of unified classification and vocabulary (differences in terminology, syntax and semantics), language, heterogeneous data formats and distributed physical location often hamper access to and use of contents.

By formalizing how raw data relate to real concepts, Semantic Web [1][2] tries to overcome the aforementioned barriers to integrate heterogeneous yet related resources and offer value-added services to audiences living in different countries, speaking different languages, using different vocabularies and having different interests. However, implementations in real life cases are often difficult, as proper knowledge formalization in scientific domains must be ensured to efficiently support content annotation and management functionalities.

This paper describes a semantic framework designed to ease content management and sharing functionalities in complex application domains by means of explicit knowledge formalization. The framework is the result of three EC-funded projects in the eContent, eTen and eContentplus programmes: Worksafe and EuroWorkSafe in the occupational cancer domain [3] and AquaRing which is now aiming at extending and applying the proposed framework to set up a European cross-border digital collection space in aquatic environment by integrating distributed digital collections provided by several European science centres, aquaria and natural history museums [4].

2. Objectives

The framework presented eases aggregation, management, accessibility, sharing and reuse of distributed digital collections by means of semantic content annotation.

On one side, the objective is to allow content providers to structure and annotate digital content collections according to the topics covered by linking contents to domain-specific ontologies (semantic annotation), thus introducing semantics in content management procedures (manual and semi-automatic semantic annotation) and estimating potential benefits (interoperability, reusability etc.).

On the other side, the objective is to open digital collections to the public and exploit expertise-driven classification to develop advanced browsing and searching functionalities as well as resource aggregation services (e.g. virtual exhibitions).

Finally, research in complex knowledge domain also focused on exploiting semantic content annotation to implement a semi-automatic ontology learning mechanism.

3. Methodology

The main steps followed to design, develop, deploy and validate the framework – a validated reference guideline for similar research initiative – can be summarized as follows:
1. Design of a flexible architecture for content space set-up (FTP/HTTP-based);
2. Selection of the most appropriate ontologies for content annotation (considering the realistic cases where domain ontologies do not exist or simply do not cover entirely the knowledge domain, several complementary ontologies must be adopted and merged somehow, or specific extensions are necessary to fill gaps in the domain coverage);
3. Creation of additional knowledge on the basis of content annotation (ontology learning);
4. Development of value-added services to share and re-use the semantically annotated resources (semantic browsing and searching functionalities);
5. Solution opening up to further extensions (additional content providers, knowledge domain extensions, etc.) and to interoperability (e.g. with the European Digital Library initiative).

4. Methodology

State-of-the-art technology and standards were adopted to allow focusing on methodology and development of value-added services rather than on technological innovation.

As for the semantic layer, RDF-based [5] Qualified Dublin Core Metadata Element Set (QDCES) [6] was adopted to formalize content annotation and metadata scheme and Web Ontology Language (OWL) [7] to express the domain ontologies. The first releases of the framework were built on top of Sesame [13] with support for RDF Schema inferencing and querying (RDF-S was used instead of OWL to express ontologies and RQL to query, before SPARQL [14] appeared as a W3C standard). Performance problems and Sesame's limited SPARQL support forced to port the core business logic interacting with the metadata and ontology repository on top of Jena API by HP Labs[TM] [8].

As for the interaction and service layers, state-of-the-art Java-based [9] web technologies (JSP/Servlet, JSF) have been used for information presentation, including AJAX/DHTML to support advanced user interface in content retrieval and navigation.

The framework is based on a simple layered architecture (Figure 1):

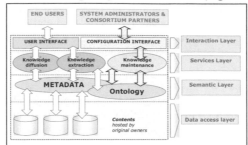

Figure 1: Overall framework architecture

According to the aforementioned technologies, the framework manages all OWL-based domain ontologies through Jena API and stores metadata in QDCES-compliant RDF, supporting multilingual annotation by means of a simple coupling mechanism between metadata instances and physical contents. Contents described by metadata are remotely stored on a distributed virtual content space (data access layer) including several independent HTTP server hosting dedicated file systems easily managed through FTP.

To provide a homogeneous content classification, the semantic layer includes ontologies (which formalize domain knowledge by means of concepts, relations and axioms) and metadata (made up by several standardised complementary descriptive fields which include concepts from domain ontologies). The service layer includes all value added services built on top of the semantic model, wrapped by interfaces included in the interaction layer.

5. Challenges and Development

The following section concentrates on the some of most challenging features of the framework, namely the multi-ontology approach, the ontology learning process and the content management.

5.1   Cultural challenges

The specificity required by domain experts for the coverage of the knowledge model adopted in the application scenarios was one of the biggest cultural challenges issued, as it directly impacted many technical requirements.

As almost all available ontologies were focused on specific issues, the adoption of several complementary ontologies was considered the only practical solution to obtain the expected coverage. This approach directly impacted the way contents could be annotated (e.g. by selecting concepts from different large ontologies) and retrieved (e.g. with acceptable time performances) by knowledge extraction services.

As the framework supports manual semantic annotation, scientific partners defined strict guidelines to ensure similar approaches were followed in analysing contents and selecting the most appropriate descriptive.

In order to relate several complementary ontologies without the overload of additional ontology re-engineering, semi-automatic bottom up solutions were also developed to exploit content annotation as a basis for enriching the available knowledge model, establishing point-to-point relations between the concepts selected for the annotation of a single content on the basis of previously defined general relations between ontologies.

5.2   Technical challenges in ontology management

Two alternative approaches were considered to define a proper domain knowledge model: to develop a single large ontology or to use several disjoint ontologies, each covering a specific portion of the knowledge domain.

The first approach is usually characterized by long development time and management problems, as state-of-the-art semantic technology may encounter serious performance and maintenance problems with large knowledge models. The second approach can not guarantee that meaningful relationships between the different portions of knowledge are neither considered nor established. As reported in literature [10], mixed paths can be followed to find efficient intermediate solutions: to merge all smaller specialised ontologies in an upper ontology or to maintain specialised ontologies separated, adding a "mediator" component to manage relationships and correspondences.

The framework thus applies a mixed scheme enhanced with formal/informal annotation: disjoint specialised ontologies have been used for semantic annotation, whereas hierarchical topic-driven free tagging have been allowed to fill in coverage gaps (e.g. missing concepts).

As a methodological approach, only largely accepted ontologies developed by authoritative institutions [11] were considered (with a particular attention for correctness, multilingualism, use extent, and scientific acceptance). It is worth to notice that the ontology selection process was a demanding task, particularly in terms of *a posteriori* evaluation of coverage and completeness.

The framework links all selected ontologies (up to 7 in the applications considered) by means of an ontology learning technique (Figure 2) that semi-automatically merges concepts and free tags using annotation as information source and exploiting the relationships that are implicitly established when ontologies concepts are used to describe a content.

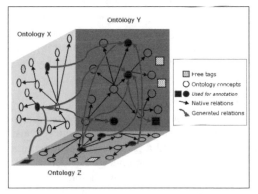

Figure 2: Annotation-based ontology learning (creating relationships between disjoint ontologies)

Provided that several complementary disjoint domain ontologies are adopted (e.g. for the aquatic domain a Biological Species ontology, an Aquatic Environment ontology and an Aquatic Activities ontology) and that high level relations are established between ontologies (e.g. "lives_in"), annotations by domain experts can be used to instantiate relationships between ontology concepts included herein.

The framework is thus able to semi-automatically create a considerable amount of additional knowledge, building a factual relationship network on top of a shared conceptualisation. The result of the ontology learning process can be checked through and corrected by domain experts using an ad hoc ontology editor which provides the following functionalities:

- Translations editing: the translator allows translating some properties of the instances (existing and newly created) as name, synonyms and descriptions to the different languages considered.
- Relationships pruning: as relationships are automatically generated, domain experts can visualise the newly generated ontology and remove those relationships that are not considered scientifically appropriated.
- Hierarchical free tags editing: domain experts can place free tags as instances of the adequate ontology class and create the relationships between these new instances and already existing instances.

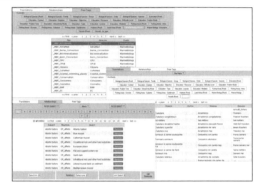

Figure 3: Ontology Editor

Although the functionalities offered by the ontology editor are present in other existing ontology development tools – such as Protégé [15], TopBraid Composer [16], KAON [17] etc. – this editor provides an intuitive and collaborative ontology editing environment to scientists placed in different locations and being specialist on diverse disciplines but not necessarily on ontology engineering. The aforementioned tools do not generally allow collaborative ontology maintenance, whereas OntoStudio [18], which offers collaborative ontology maintenance using the OntoBroker Collaboration server, will support OWL by Autumn 2008.

5.3   Technical challenges in content management

Notwithstanding manual annotation might seem a major drawback in efficiency and performances, in scientific domains this approach is generally considered a mandatory step to guarantee high quality standards and a reviewed content classification, especially when knowledge formalization is strictly based on scientific evidence.

The framework is thus designed to support annotators' work, introducing facilities such as semi-automatic metadata creation (triggered by FTP content transfer) and smart collection management, which allows describing at one go a homogeneous set of resources with the same semantic annotation.

Collections allow content providers to exploit the classification of digital contents as originally available within their premises, provided that the folder structure is based on proper topic-driven aggregation criteria. The proper management of collections is achieved introducing an implicit inheritance of the semantic description which allows annotating only the collection instead of all included contents without any loss of neither information nor meaningfulness, but also allowing to highlight a specific content within a specific collection (when e.g. such content has enough relevance to be found independently of the collection it belongs to under certain circumstances) by simply refining its semantic annotation.

Figure 4: Collection of collections (analogy with structure of folders in plain file systems)

6. Results

The following sections briefly summarize the main technical results (components) included in the framework.

6.1 Semantic knowledge management services

- Metadata Editor: coupled with a FTP client used to transfer contents from local PCs to remote servers included in the Global Content Space, it is designed to formalise content annotation and link metadata to specific ontology concepts, enabling manual annotation of single resources as well as semi-automatic annotation of collections;
- Ontology Learning: it creates a unified ontology on the basis of the ontologies adopted, the semantic content annotations and a set of relationships defined *a priori*.
- Ontology Editor: it allows enriching the unified ontology with concept translation (multilanguage support) and pruning of automatically generated instances and relationships.

6.2 Semantic content sharing services

- Semantic Search Engine: it provides user with domain-related suggestion to improve their search and refines the search algorithms to obtain more meaningful results.

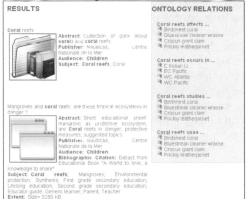

Figure 5: Semantic Search Engine

- Semantic Content Browser: it navigates through the hierarchical ontology providing an immediate feedback on how many contents are available for a specific topic (content browsing) and on how concepts are related (knowledge browsing);
- Semantic Knowledge Map: it provides a tag-cloud visualization on the amount of digital contents available for specific domain ontology concepts;
- Semantic Virtual Exhibition: the homogenous description of contents allows to easily create topic-driven virtual exhibitions, enriching the user experience with explicit associations between multidisciplinary contents.

7. Business benefits

The framework releases delivered within the AquaRing project (first integrated prototype available for preliminary tests in June 2008, stable release scheduled in March 2009) reflects a "roadmap" which aims at a rapid transfer of the product to the market: the framework is flexible, extendable and applicable in different application scenarios where formalized know-how (expressed by a domain ontology) can be used to classify existing digital resources and create additional contextual knowledge by aggregating complementary collections.

Enterprise scenarios where many actors (employees, customers etc.) interchange data and knowledge (product sheet, development guidelines, administrative and corporate data, best practices, quality guidelines, training courses, etc.) represent the best potential business application of the framework. Possible applications addresses e.g. ITC SMEs (to improve the sharing of technical documents usually stored in local pc and poorly classified, as a semantic support for intranets and classical content management systems) and in education departments of scientific institutions (to ease the classification of educational material according to formalized scientific and educational knowledge, thus facilitating the contextual reuse of documents for different targeted purposes).

As a matter of fact, the Semantic Web and in general semantic technologies are still considerably unknown in many domains where content management systems as well as information services might largely benefit from such formalised approaches. As a direct result, simple yet effective knowledge-based solutions are usually positively evaluated by content providers (e.g. scientific institutions) who appreciate the great potential of the methodology. The promising feedback obtained during the evaluation phases allows to say that the framework fulfils the requirements expressed by different categories of stakeholders interested in classifying digital collections according to domain knowledge and in building value-added services. It is also worth noticing that, considering the flexibility of the approach, potential applications range from local intranets (e.g. ontology-driven document management for small companies) to large scale distributed digital content spaces (e.g. in the AquaRing project five European aquaria and natural science museums made their digital collections interoperable and created a homogeneous information system on the aquatic domain based on a common knowledge model including seven complementary ontologies).

Furthermore, the adoption of semantic web standards for metadata and ontology formalization makes the framework and all managed collections interoperable, with evident benefits such as e.g. seamless inclusions of minor content providers and interoperability with the European Digital Library [12].

8. Conclusions

The framework, as a result of the use of semantic technology, is flexible, extendable and applicable to wide and dynamic knowledge domains, allowing seamless integration of distributed resources into a single virtual collection and its exploitation through thematic value-added services (multilingual semantic search, semantic content browser, virtual exhibitions, etc.).

The framework allows the classification and aggregation of contents according to an assessed knowledge model deriving from state-of-the-art ontologies. In all considered cases, value-added services have been designed and extensively tested, providing positive feedback on how semantics can improve the way information is classified, navigated and searched.

The methodology adopted allowed to evaluate also the educational impact of semantic navigation and retrieval functionalities: according to the feedback collected so far (at the time of writing evaluations are still ongoing) semantics is perceived as an innovative approach to efficiently support user's experience by allowing to refine searches and navigations and suggesting alternative domain-related learning paths.

The encouraging results obtained in the application scenarios considered so far suggest that the overall approach can be easily applied in different business cases, offering interesting exploitation possibilities by means of minor contextual adaptation (domain knowledge).

Further work will concentrate mainly on semi-automatic annotation-driven knowledge creation (i.e. ontology learning) and on automatic semantic-driven contents aggregation (i.e. ontology-based content merging) in order to evaluate further potential applications of the methodology defined and to investigate the possibility for exploitation in businesses.

Acknowledgements

The framework described in this paper has been partially funded by the European Commission within the eContent, eTen and eContentplus programmes.

The authors would like to thanks all partners involved in the Worksafe, EuroWorksafe and AquaRing projects for their precious support.

References

[1]   Berners-Lee, Tim, James Hendler and Ora Lassila (May 17, 2001) "The Semantic Web", Scientific American Magazine (http://www.sciam.com/article.cfm?id=the-semantic-web&print=true)
[2]   W3C Semantic Web Activity (www.w3.org/2001/sw/)
[3]   Worksafe / EuroWorksafe Project – European Semantic Portal on Occupational Cancer Risko and Prevention – eContent / cTEN Programme (www.euroworksafe.eu)
[4]   AquaRing Project - Accessible and Qualified Use of Available Digital Resources about Aquatic World In National Gatherings   eContentPlus Programme (www.aquaringweb.eu)
[5]   W3C Semantic Web – Resource Description Framework (RDF) (http://www.w3.org/RDF/)
[6]   Dublin Core Metadata Initiative – Expressing Dublin Core metadata using the Resource Description Framework (RDF) (http://dublincore.org/documents/dc-rdf/)
[7]   W3C Semantic Web – Web Ontology Language (OWL) (http://www.w3.org/2004/OWL/)
[8]   JENA – A Semantic Web Framework for Java (http://jena.sourceforge.net/)
[9]   SUN JavaEE Technology (http://java.sun.com/javaee/technologies/)
[10] "Hacia la definición de ontologías basadas en aspectos" (http://www.dsi.uclm.es/personal/elenanavarro/dsoa/papersCR/CuestaOntologias.pdf)
[11] NeOn Project – Lifecycle Support for Networked Ontologies FP6 IST-2005-027595 (www.neon-project.org)
[12] EDL European Digital Library – Connecting Cultural Heritage (www.europeana.eu)
[13] Sesame – Open source RDF framework with support for RDF Schema inferencing and querying (http://www.openrdf.org/)
[14] SPARQL – Query language for RDF (http://www.w3.org/TR/rdf-sparql-query/)
[15] Protégé – Open source ontology editor (http://protege.stanford.edu/)
[16] TopBraid Composer – Enterprise-class modelling environment (http://www.topquadrant.com/topbraid/composer/)
[17] KAON – Open-source ontology management infrastructure (http://kaon.semanticweb.org/)
[18] OntoStudio – Commercial modeling environment for the creation and maintenance of ontologies (http://www.ontoprise.de/index.php?id=179)
[19] OntoBroker – Commercial Semantic Web-Middleware (http://www.ontoprise.de/index.php?id=180)

Collaboration and the Knowledge Economy: Issues, Applications, Case Studies
P. Cunningham and M. Cunningham (Eds.)
IOS Press, 2008

Meeting Business Challenges – The Move toward a Sharper *"I"* in Intelligent Wells and *e*-Fields

Heidi M. HUSSEIN[1], Yasser EL SHAYAB[1], Amr S. BADAWY[1],
Karim S. ZAKI[2], Ahmed ABOU-SAYED[2]

[1]*Informateks International Inc., 32 El Hussein Street, Dokki, Giza, Egypt*
Tel: +202 37493327, Fax: +202 33386404
Email: {hhussein, yelshayeb, Ashebl}@informateks.com
[2]*Advantek International Corp., 3300 S. Gessner Rd., Suite 257, Houston, Texas 77063, USA*
Tel: +1 713 532 7627, Fax: +1 713 513 5015
Email: {karim, Ahmed}@Advantekinternational.com

Abstract: The major challenge facing the Oil & Gas industry is the nature of field data that exists in large volumes, which might usually be imprecise, chaotic and multi-dimensional. The current paper will discuss recent developments in operations intelligence and knowledge extraction applications to Oil and Gas field data. It will also provide examples of how this technology can optimize productivity of wells, improve performance of injectors and relate major drivers to field responses. A real Field case of operations will be presented.

Keywords: Knowledge Extraction, e- library, Data Mining, Correlation Matrix, Principle Component Analysis, Injection History, Drivers.

1. Introduction

Over the years Data Mining has been used in different industries, and it has proven its efficiency. Data mining was first introduced to deal with massive amount of data that can not be handled by human, and the ultimate goal was to transform this data into knowledge. This extracted knowledge will effectively support and assist decision makers.

Informateks International is an Egyptian data Mining Company working to provide intelligent solutions for the Oil and Gas industry through archiving, analysis and knowledge extraction for oil and gas operations. This Oil and Gas industry is well known to be one of the most technologies attracting due to its size and impact on the world economics.

One special feature of the oil and Gas industry is that E-data collection takes place, without immediate need for data presentation. The low cost of data collection has driven company decision makers to support data storing and sorting as part of Corporate Memory. Company strategists could utilize such sources to extract solutions to current business challenges.

Nevertheless, there is an urging need to augment and complement the human expert with real live models that represent the corporate memory in an adaptable model that continuously self adjusts. This would allow an intelligent knowledge interrogation to take place.

Classical techniques that rely on physics-based methods are not always a practical way to identify and validate suspected relationships between different data attributes. Meanwhile, Data

Mining methods can effectively help identify the rich part of information, and derive hidden relationships inherent in the data. Innovative data mining techniques such as Neural Networks, Evolutionary Algorithms, and Fuzzy Logic is capable of extracting knowledge from attributes in different databases and hence drive performance improvement. The current work will present an example of the exploitation of Data Mining techniques in Oil and Gas applications, along with some proposed innovative directions of future work.

2. Data Mining Cycle

The O&G industry is one of the few industries that are rich in data. Reservoir, field, or well data are needed to perform a successful analysis. Any Data mining project, usually involve the same set of steps or phases, these phases are six sequential phases; which are:

1. **Business Understanding Phase**
   This phase includes the business objective, how data mining can be used, and deciding the success criterion.
2. **Data Understanding Phase**
   This phase includes exploring the data and verifying its quality, identifying outliers.
3. **Data Preparation Phase**
   This phase include a number of tasks; same as data collection, data cleaning, data selection, and data transformation.
4. **Modeling Phase**
   This phase includes selecting the model to be used whether descriptive or predictive one based on the problem understudy.
5. **Evaluation Phase**
   This phase includes assessment of the model built, and interpretation of this model.
6. **Deployment Phase**
   This phase includes how the results will be used, and what is its impact in enhancing this area.

3. Digital Library

One of the crucial steps leading to an effective knowledge extraction / data mining work is the efficiency and the easiness of data storage / handling / extraction. Our model of data storage / handling / extraction is based upon our proper model of Digital Library that is developed and implemented by Informateks®. Such a model has the following characteristics:

1. Web based (for data input and extraction)
2. Secure
3. Easy to use
4. Insure confidentiality of information

Such model is currently used by a consortium of US based Oil companies for data storage where each user from each company have an access to a secured environment that would allow for multiple data input and would insure that the input data are not accessible but to the user. On another front, an interface have been developed in order to give an over view extraction of information from the ensemble of all the data input in the digital library.

Making use of this secured web based digital library will guarantee consistent, high quality data. After data storage, fields of input are mapped into the appropriate fields in different tables that are stored prior to the analysis (All sheets are of the same structure and parameters are of the same units). Another useful option in such digital library is the ability of the user to upload different data formats (data sheets, whether excel or text files. All kind of data are collected in the same database for further analysis).

4. Case Study (Middle East)

4.1 Business Understanding Phase

This case addresses one of the major challenges in the O&G domain which is "relating major drivers to field responses". This particular challenge that is been tackled in this paper describes the situation in which the production wells are no longer satisfying the oil demand. One of the techniques used is the Water Injection technique. It involves converting one of production wells into injector, or drilling new well dedicated for injection. The main objectives of the water injection process are:
-   To push the Oil towards the producer wells
-   To pressurize the reservoir to keep higher production rate

In order to get this process done properly a study of the major impacting factors is highly recommended. The three fields understudy is in the Middle East. The injectivity performance for these fields are quite different, even though they are located near each other (geographically), share many of the same reservoir and fluid properties, and are injecting similar water for the same Enhance Oil Recovery purpose.

4.2 Problem Understanding Phase

The objective of this study was to analyze data from the three fields in order to determine and rank the effects of field variables on the injectivity index. The variables fall into three types:
-   Injection History
-   Water Quality, Physical Properties & Chemical Composition
-   Operational Intervention & Stimulation Events
-   Reservoir/Well Static Properties

4.3 Data Preparation Phase

The data received in different forms hard and soft form. The data mining team at Informateks has combined them into one form. The quality of the data received was low, quadratic curve fitting was used to enhance the data quality. The exploration task involved plotting the raw data to get insights of the kind of data that the analyst will deal with. The aim and sample of the results obtained using the different techniques are shown in a sequential order:

4.3.1 Scatter Plots

The purpose of applying the scatter plot (Figure 1) is to identify over all trend of each variable and if there is any new trends or odd behavior.

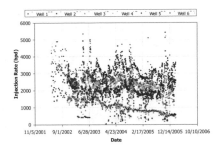

Figure 1: Scatter Plot (Injection Rate vs. Date)

Main Highlights
- Declining injection rate profile for all the wells
- Highest to lowest injection rate rank: 1, 2, 4, 5, 3, 6

4.3.2 Bar Plots

The purpose of applying the bar plot (Figure 2) was to get information about the amount of data available in each field and what variables to include in the analysis.

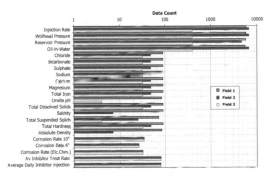

Figure 2: Bar Chart (Data Count vs. All Variables)

Main Highlights
- While there were thousands of data points for injection rate, reservoir pressure, and wellhead pressure, there were two orders of magnitude fewer data points for water properties, and even fewer event data points.
- Field # 1 has the largest amount of water quality data.
- The event data was available for field 2 & 3 only.

5. Data Modeling Phase

5.1 Descriptive Model

5.1.1 Correlation Matrix (Field 1)

It measures the magnitude and direction of the relationship between two variables. Significant correlations are those that exceed the value of the Significance Level, which is inversely proportional to the number of valid samples. It is easier to conclude a correlation is significant when there are more valid data points. Conversely, a correlation must have a higher magnitude to be considered significant when there are fewer valid data points.

Since the data is not of the same amount and also the type of each variable also differ whether static or dynamic, that's why the correlation matrix (Figure 3) was applied three times (Injection rate vs. Injection History variables), (Injection Rate vs. Water Quality Variables), and (Injection Rate vs. Operational Events).

Injection History Variables	
Variable Name	Injection Rate
Well Head Pressure	0.27
Reservoir Pressure	-0.16

Event Variables	
Variable Name	Injection Rate
Tubing Acid Wash	0.06
W/L support	-0.01
Frac support	-0.01
O/U program water injector	-0.04
GC run/well monitoring	-0.11

Static Property Variables	
Variable Name	Injection Rate
Converted	0.49
True Vertical Depth	-0.10
Minimum Horizontal Stress	-0.10
Drilled	-0.49

Water Quality Variables	
Variable Name	Injection Rate
Chloride	0.32
Bicarbonate	0.32
Total Dissolved Solids	0.32
Salinity	0.32
Sodium	0.26
Absolute Density	0.20
Sulphate	0.16
Total Hardness	0.09
Calcium	0.09
Magnesium	-0.19
Oil-in-Water	-0.11
Total Iron	-0.22
Onsite pH	-0.23
Total Suspended Solids	-0.32

Figure 3: Correlation Matrix

Main Highlights
1. Wellhead Pressure – anticipated positive correlation which indicates that there is no plugging occurred.
2. Oil-in-Water has a significantly negative effect on the injection rate.
3. Sodium Chloride (Salinity) had a big positive impact on the injection rate. No indication was given as to the water source and whether mixing of sources occurred.

5.1.2   K means Cluster Analysis

It identifies response behaviors and divides them into different groups. Within each group the behavior is said to be similar. Groups combine data from different wells and periods. The characteristics of each cluster can be extracted from Plot of Mean for Each Cluster (Figure 4).

This method does not produce enough water chemistry data points to interpret key drivers.

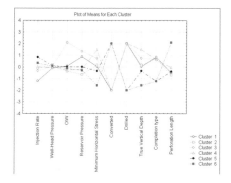

Figure 4: Plot of Means for Each Cluster

Main Highlights
- The cluster analysis has identified 6 behaviors, each of these 6 clusters has different characteristic (- *Cluster 1 & 2 Characteristics*Table 1). For example:

Table 1 - Cluster 1 & 2 Characteristics

Cluster 1 Characteristics	Cluster 2 Characteristics
Low injection rate	Median injection rate
Median wellhead pressure	Median wellhead pressure
High oil-in-water	Low oil-in-water
High reservoir pressure	Low reservoir pressure
Drilled	Drilled
Median Depth	High Depth

5.1.3 Principle Component Analysis

The principle component analysis is a two-step process. First step is to rank the factors (similar variables that are mathematically combined into factors) and then the Eigen value and the percentage of the system information are calculated. This step results in a scree plot (Figure 5). The next step is to choose two factors that contain the most system information and also represents our variable of interest (in this case, injection rate) and project the other variables onto the 2-dimensional plain. The plots show a graphical representation of proportional or inversely proportional correlation. This step results in a projection plot (Figure 6).

5.1.4 Scree Plot

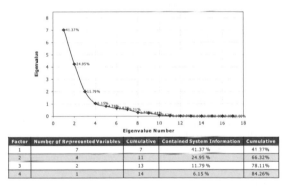

Factor	Number of Represented Variables	Cumulative	Contained System Information	Cumulative
1	7	7	41.37 %	41.37%
2	4	11	24.95 %	66.32%
3	2	13	11.79 %	78.11%
4	1	14	6.15 %	84.26%

Figure 5 - Scree Plot

Main Highlights:
- Factor # 1 & 2 contain of most of system information (66.32%), together they contain 11 variables of the total 18 variables.
- All the variables included in this analysis will be projected on Factor # 1 & 2 so as to identify the correlations between the variables.

5.1.5   Projection Plot

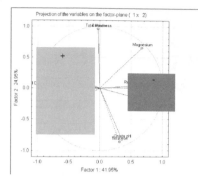

Figure 6: Projection Plot

Main Highlights

- Variables that are directly proportional to the Injection Rate are:
  - Bicarbonate (Positive effect)
  - Sulphate (Positive effect, but not well represented in this plain)
  - Total Dissolved Solids (Positive effect)
  - Salinity (Positive effect) thermal fracturing that would enhance injectivity.
  - Chloride (Positive effect, probably dependant on Salinity)
  - Wellhead Pressure (indicate good performance, as wells undergoing severe plugging exhibit a negative correlation between the injection rate and pressure)
- Variables that are inversely proportional to the Injection Rate are:
  - Reservoir Pressure (negative effect)
  - Total Suspended Solids (negative effect)
  - Oil-in-Water (negative effect)
- Variables that appear to have little to no effect on the Injection Rate are:
  - Magnesium (little effect)
  - Onsite pH (little effect)
  - Total Iron (little effect)
  - Absolute Density
  - Sodium
  - Total Hardness (little effect)
  - Calcium (little effect)

5.2   Predictive Model

5.2.1   Neural Network

These are algorithms that can model the historical behavior of one variable; they can be used to predict the future behavior of that variable, under specific conditions. These models were ranked and the variables on which they relied were listed to identify key drivers (Table 2).

Table 2: Sensitivity Table (Ranking of Variables)

Rank	Model A (R² = 86%)	Model B (R² = 86.2%)	Model C (R² = 86.1%)	Model D (R² = 86.1%)	Model E (R² = 86%)
1	Reservoir Pressure	Reservoir Pressure	Reservoir Pressure	Reservoir Pressure	Reservoir Pressure
2	Oil-in-Water	Oil-in-Water	Oil-in-Water	Oil-in-Water	True Vertical Depth
3	Drill / Complete	W/L support	W/L support	True Vertical Depth	Minimum Horz.Stress
4	W/L support	Frac support	True Vertical Depth	Minimum Horz. Stress	Converted
5	Frac support	True Vertical Depth	Minimum Horz. Stress	Converted	Drilled
6	True Vertical Depth	Minimum Horz. Stress	Converted	Drilled	GC run/well monitoring
7	Minimum Horz. Stress	Drilled	Drilled	GC run/well monitoring	Day Counter
8	Drilled	Converted	GC run/well monitoring	Day Counter	Well-Head Pressure
9	Converted	GC run/well monitoring	Day Counter	Well-Head Pressure	-
10	GC run/well monitoring	Day Counter	Well-Head Pressure	-	-
11	Day Counter	Well-Head Pressure	-	-	-
12	Well-Head Pressure	-	-	-	-

Main Highlights
- It is important to consider the conclusions from the other data mining techniques. Since Oil-in-Water was shown to be an important variable by both the matrix correlation and principle component (radial projection) methods, Model E (which eliminates Oil-in-Water) would not be appropriate to use. Wellhead pressure is not a strong factor in the prediction due to operational restrictions on the injection pressure.

6. Evaluation Phase

The scope of this study was to identify trends and relationships, especially between injection rate and controllable inputs (water quality, operating practices). Below are some of the results obtained from this study:

1. Well 1 and 2 are the best performing injector wells. Cluster analysis high-grades for characteristics that yield the best injection performance. These characteristics include: lower than average reservoir pressure, lower than average minimum horizontal stress, converted wellbore, and deeper than average TVD.

2. The Correlation Matrix technique makes it possible to identify the most significant drivers, regardless of wide dynamic ranges in the variable value, or large differences in the amount of valid data. This method consistently identifies Wellhead Pressure, Reservoir Pressure, and Oil-in-Water as having the most significant influence on Injection Rate.

3. OIW, Total Suspended Solids, and Corrosion each appear to be important drivers in most data mining techniques, but not all techniques in all fields. They may be more important when plugging is more of a problem. OIW will likely form internal filter cake, filter cake formed inside the formation, affecting both the near wellbore pore space and decreasing the relative permeability to water.

4. Several different types of interventions and stimulations were evaluated in the matrix correlation, but few appeared to have significant or even consistent impact. Most interventions exhibited both negative and positive correlations, depending more on the field/location than on the type of intervention.

5. Neural Network (NN) models were generated to match historical injection rates. Successful models were defined as those that produced a high R^2 fit, had the fewest

number of variables as indicators, but still included those variables that were significant drivers from the other data mining techniques.

7.   Deployment Phase

Change in the pressures over the life of the fields is beyond this scope, however, it is recommended to conduct periodic Pressure Falloff Tests and Step Rate Tests to better monitor the system.   This would provide better trend information for the reservoir pressure and minimum horizontal stress, to improve future predictions based on these important variables.

8. Conclusion

The current paper addresses the problem of Data Mining in the Oil and Gas Industry and how the usage of novel techniques of E-Data Collection / digital web based library / Data Mining would need to an enhancement of the performance of the oil field and an enhancement of the ability of future prediction. Part of the work illustrated in this paper have been developed through a grant from the Egyptian Ministry of Communication and Information Technology through its Virtual center of Excellence on "Data Mining and Computer Modeling (DMCM)"

References

[1] Shahab D. Mohaghegh, 2003, Essential Components of an Integrated Data Mining Tool for the Oil & Gas Industry, SPE, West Virginia University
[2] J. F. Hair, R. E. Anderson, R. L. Tatham, W. C. Black, "Multivariate Data Analysis", Fifth Edition, Prentice-Hall International, New Jersey, chapter 3, PP. 87-134.
[3] M. J. Berry, G. S. Linoff, "Data Mining Techniques, Second Edition, Wiley Publishing, U.S.A.
[4] Laura Squier, 2001, what is Data Mining?, SPSS
[5] D. W. Stockburger, "Introductory Statistics: Concepts, Models, And Application", Second Edition, Atomic dog Publishing, 1996, Correlation Chapter.

Collaboration and the Knowledge Economy: Issues, Applications, Case Studies
P. Cunningham and M. Cunningham (Eds.)
IOS Press, 2008

Emerging and Conflicting Business Models for Music Content in the Digital Environment

Anders EDSTRÖM FREJMAN[1], Daniel JOHANSSON[2]

Royal Institute of Technology, Div. Of Media technology and Graphic Arts,
S-100 44 Stockholm, Sweden

[1] *Tel: +46 8 531 81 500, Mobile: + 46 705 89 83 80, Email: frejman@kth.se*
[2] *Tel: +46 70 399 05 00, Email: daniel.johansson@musiclink.se*

Abstract: As music listening is moving from tangible products to digital services, record labels seem to have difficulties in adjusting their business models to the new reality. This study investigates how Swedish record labels have changed their practices and habits when it comes to marketing, promoting as well as selling music. The 360-degree model - more or less used by all majors - where the label owns or partly owns related rights is one clear tendency. A contrary tendency is split risk cooperation found mainly among the independent record companies and their acts. This is one example of the different practises that can be observed in a market where long-time strategies seem to be hard to draw simply because there is not enough knowledge on how the market will evolve, not even on short-term basis.

1. Introduction

Despite the success and booming sales of legal digital downloads (both with and without DRM protection) at iTunes and eMusic, ringtones etcetera, the market for digital music distribution still has a long way to go to cover up for the declining CD-sales observed since all time high sales in 2001 [1].

Plausible explanations for declining sales have been put forward by a number of researchers [2][3][4]. For example the act of listening and purchasing music has faced fierce competition from Internet usage (blogs, Internet-TV, file-sharing), cell-phones, computer games and DVDs. The decreasing diversity in prime time radio-programming (fuelled by big mergers) and the coinciding pattern of concentrating on "low risk" acts by major companies have impoverished the "soundscape" of broadcasted media.

During the latest years a new online ecosystem of companies and stakeholders has emerged with aggregators, distributors, white labels and digital retailers. The value chain for digital distribution of music has somewhat consolidated during the years 2005-2007 and digital sales reached a new global record of 3 billion US$ in 2007. According to most analysing firms and researchers, digital music sales will probably surpass physical sales somewhere around 2011-2013 [5][6].

Therefore, record labels are working hard to try to make use of Internet and mobile networks for marketing and promotion purposes. There are a number of good examples where record labels are active in creating new business models that might have positive effects on future consumption of music. Record labels in the independent sector especially are finding new tools and mechanisms for digital marketing and distribution that is more cost effective and interesting to the consumer.

However these emerging business models sometimes get in conflict with other interests in the music industry. Since the digital landscape is fundamentally different from the physical world, conflicting business models and ideological convictions can be observed throughout the music industry system. Because of these rapid changes, knowledge on how record labels are working in this area is still underdeveloped.

There is a need for new understanding how the record labels themselves are changing their routines and practices and what effects new business models have on their relationship with artists.

2. Objectives

The main objectives of this paper are to

- Understand how new technologies are being used by record companies in promotion and marketing and describe concrete differences and similarities between independent and major record companies.
- Understand the relationship between artists and record companies on all levels. How are investments, risks and revenues divided between artists and record companies? Have the forms for cooperation changed over the last 5-10 years? What are the reasons for starting record companies among well-established artists as well as unsigned and unknown artists/bands?
- Identify the challenges for the players in order to find tools for building sustainable and long-term business models.

3. Methodology

The main data for this paper has been derived from in depth interviews and detailed forms from nine Swedish record companies and distributors. The size varies from 0-40 employees. The companies are Hybris, Songs I Wish I Had Written, Bonnier Amigo, Playground Music, Lights Out, Sound Pollution, Dead Frog Records, Adrian Recordings and Lionheart International. The comprehensive form consisted of four groups of detailed questions regarding (a) the use of aggregators, distributors and retailers, (b) marketing and promotion, (c) the overall development of the company and finally (d) thoughts and visions about the future.

Due to the complex world of digital distribution and the limited time window, the selection of respondents was limited to the Swedish market. Due to the detailed answers from each and one of the respondents, we unfortunately did not have the liberty to reveal any names in relation to specific responses. In addition to the interviews a thorough investigation of the music industry's policies and structure was performed by attending industry conferences as well as interviewing other stakeholders within the industry.

4. Findings

4.1 *Distributors, aggregators, retailers and e-tailers*

The interviews with the respondents confirmed the picture of a slightly complex world of middleman's and varying definitions of the titles above among respondents.

a) Distributor – Historically a distributor is a company that distributes physical goods, e.g. CDs to the sales channels. The sizes of the distributors in terms of turnover vary a lot. All major record companies have always had their own companies for distribution and the gap between these and all others is usually big. Due to the massive workload of finding, recording, producing and promoting acts a distributor can relieve some of the administrative pressure for especially small record companies. For example it is not unusual that smaller record companies use majors as distributors.

b) White Label – A B2B company that has developed a technical platform for sales of digital music. Usually the White Label clears all the rights with the different rights holders and the customer, e.g. a physical store or brand, uses the platform to create a customized online store. 24-7 Entertainment is the largest European White Label. Other examples are Inprodicon and OD2 (owned by Nokia).

c) Aggregator – Typically a company whose main business model is to aggregate digital content from distributors (or directly from record companies). The aggregator provides the content for retailers/e-tailers in other words a distributor of adapted digital content. The border between distributors and aggregators is somewhat fluent but the aggregators main task is to act as a promoter and "push" the digitized music in as many channels as possible. Examples on such Aggregators are The Orchard, Phonofile, CD Baby and IODA Alliance.

d) Retailer/e-tailer – A company selling digital products to consumers. In this context, digital downloads such as digital audio files, music videos or mobile ringtones are being sold. Usually an online shop makes use of a White Label solution, but he largest online music shop, iTunes, is a stand-alone solution.

Figure 1: A common sales chain for digital music.

Record companies can, depending on the product, sell their digital content directly to a consumer. However the most common solution for a record company is to use a distributor (or go directly to an aggregator) in order to minimize the administration and maximize the availability of their products at on-line services. A key issue is namely the huge number of available retailers for music of variable size on different markets, read countries. [7]

Almost all retailers have their own format for metadata, technology for uploading and desired file format. Every song is supposed to appear as different kind of products; ringtone, audio and video. Furthermore, when it comes to downloads for cell phones, the content also needs to be adapted for each model, a process made either by the aggregator or the retailer. On top of that, the major cell phone operators in each country have their own solutions for selling digital content.

The study points out a diverse picture where bigger record companies and distributors try to manage the contacts directly with retailers whereas smaller companies need to use distributors and aggregators. In order to cover the markets in Sweden, Norway, Denmark and Finland with digital downloads via Internet and cell phones, the biggest respondent uses no less than twelve business parties, despite the limited size of the total markets.

The problem is that every middleman of course demands a share in order to cover investment costs [8]. Some respondents claim that e.g. mobile ringtones is a loss in terms of money due to the high billing fees. Video downloads are better, but the earlier mentioned adaption to various cell phone models is costly.

All respondents claim that information they get from digital sales is reliable in most cases. But the level of detail and formats varies a lot, making it sometimes hard to get a compiled image how sales of e.g. a certain single is related to market activities.

One issue addressed by many respondents is the slow handling by some retailers. For example iTunes can take 10 weeks before a tune is available for purchase. It seems like some retailers have different priority lists depending on the customer. A second explanation might be the overall low profitability in this part of the market making it hard to find a balance between staff and pressure for uploads. This type of delays makes it hard for smaller record companies to synchronize sales releases of CDs and downloads.

As even major record labels have started experiment with DRM-free music, the markets acceptance for direct sales through retailers has widened. Some artists have for example started selling mp3s directly to fans. One example is the Swedish retailer Klicktrack who delivers a Do-It-Yourself platform that makes it possible for artists or labels to sell music directly through their own webpage or through a centralized digital store.

Most of the respondents estimate that the time spent on digital sales is 5-15 percent. When asked how much of the sales is digital downloads, the answers was 2-15 percent. Only one respondent replied that they had a digital/physical ratio of 50/50 and 40/60 respectively and that the digital part would soon surpass the physical ditto.

4.2   Marketing and promotion

Most of the respondents still uses "traditional" marketing channels such as TV, radio and ads in printed newspapers, preferably music magazines either directly or indirectly via composite adds by their distributors/retailers. Other respondents (the smallest) question the real effectiveness of using printed media.

Banner ads give better statistic feedback of the overall success for a campaign than printed ditto according to the respondents. A number of other on-line channels also seem to become more important. Since some respondents refer to printed newspapers as something that the younger generation does not read, the interest has turned to the Medias where they think they can meet this audience of growing importance.

Almost all respondents refer above all to MySpace as an important channel of making artists and groups searchable, known and render possibility to listen to their music. The majority of the MySpace sites related to the respondents are maintained and updated by the artists themselves. Sites like YouTube and MySpace are considered as natural channels for promoting videos and recruiting new fans. Official statistics of shows/plays on these and a number of other websites such as Facebook are used to value popularity of artists and releases. In fact some respondents actively plant genuine music files on P2P networks as a part of their marketing strategy and follow the number of downloads. This is the opposite approach of the bigger respondents that share the overall opinion of the majors.

The above-mentioned statistics and, more important, sales and airplay charts are used in contacts with music journalists in order to encourage medial coverage such as interviews or reviews. In the same way, exposure in media is used as arguments in promoting music for both physical and on-line stores. Unfortunately the correlation between observed interest and purchases is not always that good which is frustrating according to some respondents.

So-called street teams are those who talk well and spread the word about a certain group or artist on forums or blogs. It is not unusual that these unofficial on-line street teams are supplied with unique mp3s in order to encourage continued coverage and fuel the traffic to these blogs, forums and communities.

Some respondents stress the importance of building relationships to bloggers, which occasionally also happen to be journalists writing for printed Medias. Search engines for blogs are used daily in order to follow up what is written about a certain act.

When asked how much time that is spent on on-line marketing (both for downloads and physical goods) versus ads in "traditional" medias (print, TV, radio) the answers varied from 5/95 to 50/50. The biggest respondent in terms of employees and turnover had the biggest displacement towards "traditional" medias. But for the second biggest, the division was nearly even. It seems like more niche companies tend to focus on on-line marketing.

It is not expensive (but rather time-consuming) to make music available for digital downloads. In fact, it has never been so inexpensive to produce recordings of high technical quality and make them globally available for digital downloads. At the same time, marketing music with the aim of reaching a broad audience has never been more difficult and expensive.

4.3   The overall development of the companies

The number of signed artists has remained the same or declined according to the respondents and no one reports increasing sales of physical units. Nevertheless physical sales is considered as an important source of income for many years to come.

Digital downloads have remained the same or increased, but not boosted as expected which is a huge disappointment so far. The time-consuming handling of metadata, uploads and contracts is still a limitation and according to some respondents makes digital sales not even profitable. All respondents have adopted new digital platforms but some feel that the major companies have chosen a price model that does not work [9].

The music industry is moving extremely fast and small companies are finding niches, the only way to be profitable as a small player on the market. Short ways between idea and action, flexibility, creativity and focus on digital sales have been the common recipe to adapt to the changing prerequisites. Some respondents are digitalizing their back catalogues in order to make them available for downloads.

When asked about the future of the company, one respondent answered that it is a positive trend that an increasing number of artists want to go independent and thereby take control and make decisions in a world where one need to be flexible. The same respondent believes in developing split-risk-models where both parties get an equal share of a success.

One respondent believes that they will develop from being a pure record company to become a composite music company acting as a publishing house, record company and working with management. This trend is also obvious among majors.

4.4   Visions and thoughts about the future for the music industry

One of the biggest respondents hopes that the majors will be become ever fewer and bigger. Smaller companies will benefit from this development through growing market shares on an overall declining market. The future will namely be more global yet more niche.

A global meta-standard among all rights-holders for distribution of all kind of digital media files is crucial in order to cut administration costs, middlemen and shorten unreasonable lean times. An extension of this would be the dream scenario of a common global database for distribution of digital content. The metadata standard DDEX (Digital Data Exchange) has been developed by the music industry and computer industry. Active members of the consortium are Apple, Microsoft, Real Networks, all the major record labels as well as Ascap, MCPS-PRS and other collecting societies. Apple has already implemented the standard in iTunes but aggregators and other players in the digital ecosystem have not fully embraced the standard [10]. One explanation might be necessary yet expensive adaptions of existing business platforms to the standard.

One of the biggest respondents believe that smaller independents will face a hard time where they will have to choose between bankruptcy or to put their material in the back catalogue of a bigger distributor of digital content. The same respondent think that only a handful of distributors with good local connection can be profitable on a market of the size of Sweden's nine million inhabitants.

Companies with an old back catalogue should be able to receive economical support from the government in order to manage musical cultural heritage as in e.g. Denmark, according to one respondent. One cannot lean on the forces of the market when it comes to maintaining cultural diversity in a global market that is shrinking.

The technological change is considered positive but the biggest respondents are irritated on the slow level of determination showed by politics. The standpoint of politicians and legal authorities against illegal file sharing must be clear. A little bit dejected, one respondent describes Sweden as a world-leader in illegal file sharing activities and that digital downloads therefore are hard to sell.

Perhaps the biggest challenge is to win the upcoming generation. "It is not that young people have stopped buying CDs. They have not even begun." This is a significant quote from one of the respondents. These upcoming consumers have little or no affection to physical music artefacts compared to former generation's CDs and LPs.

It took a long time before digital downloads got widely accepted by majors. Now we are facing the next challenge according to the respondents, namely the lukewarm interest for streaming services by majors. Despite the high level of control and low risk of piracy, majors have not wholehearted embraced services like Pandora and Last.fm.

But in the spring of 2008 some steps have been taken from major labels to license their catalogues to new forms of services [11]. Flat fee, bundled or ad based services like Spotify, Nokia Comes With Music and Qtrax are in advanced stage of planning with the major labels that might lead to a shift in business models during the coming years.

Flat-rate services will be the norm of the future according to many of the respondents. Unlimited file sharing bundled with broadband connections is mentioned as one solution for future income. In the spring of 2008, STIM, the Swedish Performing Rights Society together with some other Swedish music organisations, somewhat unexpectedly, opened the door for cooperation with ISPs concerning monitored but unlimited music downloads for private use [12]. Even though the division model and the technology behind are not clear, this is an interesting step. Completely unthinkable only a few years ago.

A fee of 5 or 10 € on the monthly broadband connection or the TV-license would be an appropriate level for such service according to the respondents in this study. A problem might be the logical somersault: on one hand illegalize file sharing and on the other hand collect fees because of file sharing activities. Nevertheless illegal file sharing is limiting the willingness to invest in new systems and business models in the music industry according to the study.

Another interesting example of Flat-rat services is anywhere.fm where the user uploads his/her music to a web service that can be streamed from any web-browser. Combine this usability with the range of songs in iTunes, add a low monthly fee to get free access to streaming/downloads and make it available through cell phones (where the operator already today uses a flat-rate for data traffic). Majors and indies regardless of size will have the same opportunities and it appeals to the upcoming strictly mobile generation. This is the kind of services that will reshape the landscape of music consumption according to the respondents.

5. Conclusions

An obvious proof for a non-matured digital market observed in these studies is the vast different approaches that the record companies have chosen in order to sell their products. Practices differ as each record label is trying to find their own way of getting revenues from digital distribution. Surprisingly no regular communication seemed to take place between the companies, accept for between two of the smallest companies.

One has to bear in mind that the typical record label entrepreneur often has a history of getting it done "by themselves", not relying on anyone else to run their business. The Swedish music industry has in some senses become institutionalized during the second half of the 20th century leading to groups of companies having more business relations than others [13]. In the light of the latest year's technological development, one could argue that these "islands" are making it harder for new knowledge and business practices to spread within the music industry system, leaving each and everyone of them alone in their struggle.

But the interest for information from diverse channels such as activities on file-sharing networks, social networks, UGC-services and web radio is higher than ever among all players on all levels in the industry. Business models are more and more based on feedback information from online music usage, i.e. the amount of plays on MySpace, YouTube,

Last.fm, iLike, iMeem, MySpace.TV etcetera and record labels are often making decisions based on these sources rather then airplays and record sales.

As a result of these findings a platform that automatically gathers and analyzes usage data from different music services has been developed by Musiclink, the company funding this study. The platform is now being used by all the respondents as well as additional companies in a new research project partly funded by The Swedish Governmental Agency for Innovation Systems. As a further result of this study a spinoff company, named TrendMaze, was started in May 2008. The business model is to be a provider of Business Intelligence focused on online usage of music.

All companies in the study claim that their own activities on file-sharing networks are important, but they refer to different approaches. In fact, some smaller indies actively share their music on file sharing networks and state that this is a vital and effective instrument of their marketing. The tendency among bigger indies is that e.g. spoofing (publishing corrupted files on P2P networks) is an important tool in protecting their assets. In other words, a view similar to major record companies.

The study also shows that the cooperation between record companies and artists in terms of risk-taking, financing of recording and marketing is perhaps the biggest difference compared to earlier years. Because of declining CD-sales the so called 360-degree model has gained large attraction during the latest years where the record labels either owns or share a part of the rights to all relating products, merchandising, tour production, publishing, synchronization (the practice of getting music into movies, TV-shows, commercials), digital distribution etcetera. A second way of cooperating is to share risks, e.g. letting the artist finance or partly finance some part of the production process.

The 360-degree model is probably one reason why some previously signed artists have decided to start their own record companies in order to gain control over rights. For others starting a new record company is the only way to get published.

The straggling approaches draw a diverse picture of a market where long-time strategies seem to be hard to draw simply because there is not enough knowledge on how the market will evolve, not even on short-term basis. This together with mental models and beliefs about how the music business is supposed to work makes it hard for some record labels to adjust to the Internet economy and new consumer behaviour [14]. On the other hand, our study shows that there is a tremendous creativity going on among smaller record labels. New alliances are forming within the industry and some of the respondents are even working together with some of the larger file sharing networks. This is creating somewhat a clash between the larger labels and these new initiatives [15].

In the past national airplays was a vital instrument in establishing a new record on the market and thereby more or less guarantee good record sales. Today not even established record companies can rely solely on airplays. Therefore some of the respondents primarily refer to airplays as sources for royalty income (especially Swedish public service radio with its higher kick-back rate compared to commercial ditto). However the study shows that for some specific genres the commercial radio still is the most important shopping window.

The study has six major conclusions:

- Practices among record labels differs widely when it comes to marketing and promotion online. Majors and somewhat bigger companies emphasize the importance of traditional channels whereas smaller, often very specialized, companies rely on online marketing.
- Approaches to file sharing networks differs depending on how large the record label is. Some of the small labels share their music for free on file sharing networks.
- The relation to the artist has in large changed to the 360-degree model where the label owns or partly owns related rights (major companies) or split-risk solutions (smaller companies).

- Bigger record companies try to cut digital middle hands by working directly with retailers whereas smaller companies need to use aggregators.
- Flat-rate services, e.g. different kind of streaming services or free-music-download through ISPs, was nearly unthinkable only a few years ago. Today collecting societies, record labels and ISPs conduct serious discussions about the future.
- Information from free online music usages is becoming increasingly important to understand the changing wishes of the customers. Business models based on compiling complex information from various on-line sources will find customers on all levels and size of the music industry.

The overall link between these conclusions is declining revenues and a changing market for music that has not yet consolidated.

5.1   The future of the music industry

As the music industry is moving from a product based industry to service based [16] practices, business models are changing drastically. For some record labels digital sales contribute to nearly 50% of the total revenues and the music industry system is no longer homogenous. Telecommunications companies like Ericsson, TeliaSonera, Telenor, France Telecom, 3, Nokia and Samsung are all important parts of the new music ecosystem having an increasing role in the new music distribution system.

During the latest years revenues from performance and private copy levies have increased for every year while revenues from sales of copies have decreased. Between the years 2000 and 2004 revenues increased with 30% for collecting societies in USA, UK and Sweden [14]. At the same time revenues from physical sales decreased with about the same amount. In other words a dramatic shift of sources of income.

It is possible that the music industry is moving from per unit revenues to more flat rate based revenues divided by functions similar to the models collecting societies have used for decades. In such reality there is a large need for getting reliable data on usage of music from music services. TrendMaze is focusing on this area as a result of what has been found in this study.

5.2   Future research

This study has been focused on Swedish record labels. The interviews have revealed that the situation is mainly the same for all record labels in Europe. However, to fully understand the complex landscape for digital music distribution on a European scale further research is needed in countries like United Kingdom, Germany, France and Italy.

References

[1]   IFPI Digital Music Report 2008
[2]   Andersen B., Frenz M. (2007) The Impact of Music Downloads and P2P File-Sharing on the Purchase of Music: A Study for Industry Canada
[3]   Oberholzer F., Strumpf K. (2004) The Effect of File Sharing on Record Sales - An Empirical Analysis
[4]   Adermon A. (2006) Has Illegal Filesharing Caused a Reduction in Record Sales in Sweden?
[5]   Forrester Research (2008) The End of the Music Industry As We Know It
[6]   PricewaterhouseCoopers (2007) Global Entertainment & Media Outlook
[7]   See www.pro-music.org for a complete list of digital music services
[8]   Fridh M. (2006) Internets Influence on the Value Chain within the Music Industry
[9]   Hjelte R. (2006) Does One Price Fit All? A Study of Pricing in the Market for Music Downloads
[10]   www.ddex.net
[11]   Press Release (2008) Last.fm launches largest global free-on-demand music platform
[12]   STIM (2008) How downloading could be made legal
       http://www.stim.se/stim/prod/stimv4eng.nsf/alldocuments/1D66451CBE1B0F81C12573F4002E1CCC
[13]   Arvidsson K. (2007) Skivbolag i Sverige – musikföretagandets 100-åriga institutionalisering
[14]   Wikström P. (2006) Reluctantly Virtual - Modelling Copyright Industry Dynamics
[15]   www.theswedishmodel.org
[16]   Kusek. D, Leonhard.G (2005) The Future of Music: Manifesto for the Digital Music Revolution

Collaboration and the Knowledge Economy: Issues, Applications, Case Studies
P. Cunningham and M. Cunningham (Eds.)
IOS Press, 2008

Tackling the Risk Challenge: DRAMBORA (Digital Repository Audit Method Based on Risk Assessment)

Perla INNOCENTI, Andrew MCHUGH, Seamus ROSS
Humanities Advanced Technology and Information Institute, 11 University Gardens,
Glasgow, G12 8QH, UK
Tel: +44 141 330 {4453, 2675, 5512} Fax: + 44 141 330 3788
Email: {p.innocenti, a.mchugh, s.ross}@hatii.arts.gla.ac.uk

Abstract: The Digital Curation Centre (DCC) in the UK and the EU-funded DigitalPreservationEurope (DPE) project jointly released the Digital Repository Audit Method Based on Risk Assessment (DRAMBORA, http://www.repositoryaudit.eu/) in early 2007, with the goal to provide a practical, evidence-based toolkit for assessing repositories and digital libraries. Subsequent iterative development has let to the refinement of its methodology, and the release of DRAMBORA Interactive, a freely available online tool aimed at streamlining the core risk assessment process. DRAMBORA represents a bottom-up approach that takes risk and risk management as its principle means for determining digital repositories' success and for charting their improvement. The tool's development and ongoing evolution has been informed at all times by practical research. More than twenty international repositories have been subject to assessment using DRAMBORA, enabling the validation of its primary methodology and offering insights into potential shortcomings and the extent of its applicability in a range of diverse preservation contexts. Furthermore, these exercises have enabled initial research into repository profiling, which attempts to identify commonalities within subsets of the repository community in order to inform and facilitate subsequent repository development and evaluation. This paper describes the DRAMBORA methodology, focusing on its benefits and developments, and introduces DRAMBORA Interactive. It goes on to describe the results of some of the most successful pilot assessments. Most notable is the work funded by the DELOS Digital Library project, which sought to identify core characteristics within a range of digital libraries in order to conceive a repository profile that might form the basis for subsequent repository development and evaluation.

Keywords: Digital preservation; digital curation; risk assessment; audits; digital repositories; digital libraries; RBA

1. The landscape of digital repositories assessment criteria

The contemporary domain landscape suggests that information repositories are likely to play a role of considerable importance in the pursuit of digital preservation assurances.

In order to legitimise decentralisation to smaller scale repository environments, it is essential that the community has appropriate mechanisms available to support repository assessment, and determine the competencies of those charged with information stewardship responsibilities. Management, staff, financiers and partners must all be satisfied that their efforts are capable of meeting formal expectations. Similarly, information creators, depositors and consumers naturally hope to obtain similar assurances of the capabilities of the organisations providing maintenance, preservation and dissemination services.

Considerable work has been undertaken to develop preservation audit check-lists, intended to represent the objective benchmarks against which repositories' efforts are judged. The two primary examples, both released in 2007, are:

1. The *Trustworthy Repositories Audit and Certification (TRAC) Criteria and Checklist* [1] describes approximately ninety characteristics that repositories that aspire to a certifiable, trustworthy status must demonstrate they have;

2. The *nestor Catalogue of Criteria for Trusted Digital Repositories* [2] reflects the regional needs of the nestor community. Structured similarly to the TRAC document, this provides examples and perspectives that are more representative of a German operational, legal and economic context.

Both TRAC and nestor are compelling reference materials, and their usefulness in informing the development and retrospective evaluation of repositories is widely acknowledged. However, neither is sufficient in isolation. By their very nature, check-lists like these adopt a top-down assessment philosophy: both examples seeking to define an *objective* consensus of the priorities and responsibilities that should exist within any repository environment. By relying solely on *nestor* or *TRAC*, one implicitly disregards the great variety that is visible across contemporary digital repository platforms. The question persists, is a one-size-fits-all approach to assessment and certification really useful for those within the curation community? Both *TRAC* and *nestor*'s criteria have been painstakingly phrased to ensure their flexibility, and facilitate optimal general applicability. But despite such efforts, it appears evident that within the community there is the need for a more tailored assessment solution that takes into account atypical repository qualities, as either a companion piece, or alternative, to the other existing guidelines.

The *Digital Repository Audit Method Based on Risk Assessment* (DRAMBORA) [3] developed by the Digital Curation Centre and DigitalPreservationEurope is designed to address such shortcomings. Its bottom-up approach enables repositories to relate their benchmarks for success more explicitly to their own aims and contextual environment, enabling an increased granularity of understanding of preservation approaches and challenges. Furthermore, by focusing explicitly on the process of assessment, rather than simply listing desirable repository characteristics, it provides considerably more opportunities for evidence-supported, demonstrable excellence, and consequent repository confidence. A key strength is that DRAMBORA is capable of being used both independently and in association with more objective guidelines.

2. DRAMBORA Opportunities and Outcomes

Digital curation can be characterized as a process of transforming controllable and uncontrollable uncertainties into a framework of manageable risks. The DRAMBORA process focuses on risks, and their classification and evaluation according to individual repositories' activities, assets and contextual constraints. The methodological outcome is a determination of the repository's ability to contain and avoid the risks that threaten its ability to receive, curate and provide access to authentic and contextually, syntactically and semantically understandable digital information.

DRAMBORA acknowledges the heterogeneity that exists within the digital world, refraining from explicitly describing the characteristics that repositories should demonstrate. Instead, parameters for success are aligned with the subjective mandate, objectives and activities of individual repositories. Specific contextual factors and constraints are considered only where they are relevant. This ensures that the results of the audit process are, from the participating repository's perspective, wholly applicable and immediately useful. The process aims to provide repositories with formal understanding of their own mandate and objectives, to provide them with a detailed and manageable breakdown of fundamental challenges, promote communication within the organisation as a whole and facilitate subsequent external audit whether based on TRAC, nestor or any other repository assessment criteria.

2.1 Origins and alignment with international initiatives

In 2006 and early 2007 the Digital Curation Centre (DCC) undertook a series of pilot audits in a diverse range of preservation environments. Various repositories participated, exhibiting a range of different characteristics [4]. As well as providing the participating organisations with an objective and expert insight into the effectiveness of their operation, and determining the robustness and global applicability of those metrics and criteria already conceived [5], the audits were aimed at exploring the optimal means for conducting assessment of repositories. The research set out to develop an increased understanding of how evidence can be practically accumulated, assessed, used and discarded throughout the audit process. A methodology for performing repository audit was quickly established and subjected to considerable subsequent refinement. In March 2007 the process was formalised as the Digital Repository Audit Method Based on Risk Assessment (DRAMBORA), and a first textual version of the toolkit was released.

Important consensus about the breadth of repository characteristics that must be exposed to scrutiny during an assessment process was reached during a meeting of the authors of DRAMBORA, TRAC and nestor in early 2007. Adopting a broad view that echoed the work done by RLG/OCLC in their seminal 2002 "Trusted Digital Repositories – Attributes and Responsibilities", ten general principles of repositories were conceived. The ten principles [6] are varied, encompassing more than simply technological considerations, extending to organisational fitness, legal and regulatory legitimacy, appropriate policy infrastructures, mandate and commitment, and every aspect of object management, including ingest, preservation, documentation and dissemination. For DRAMBORA's purposes, these can be conveniently grouped according to three core criteria classifications, each influenced by contextual factors and exposed to risk, as illustrated in *Figure 1*.

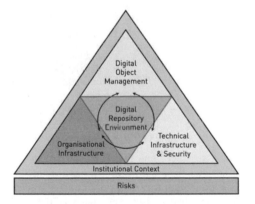

Figure 1: interrelationships within a digital repository environment.
© HATII at the University of Glasgow

2.2 Methodology

DRAMBORA's approach is flexible, and responsive to the structural and contextual variety evident within repositories: its metric for success is directly linked with repositories' own aims. Objective guidance materials such as TRAC, nestor, and even more generic references can be used in combination, informing the process, and prompting analysis of particular issues. Nevertheless, no criteria are objectively deemed to be mandatory.

Evidence and demonstrable success are at the very forefront of the DRAMBORA process. The first phase of assessment reflects this, a process of information accumulation, aggregation and documentation. The repository's strategic purpose, its action plan, and any contextual factors that influence or limit its ability to meet its objectives must each be made explicit. A hierarchical analysis is undertaken; definition of the repository's mandate is the first step of an increasingly focused scrutiny, requiring detailed descriptions of fundamental repository objectives as well as the activities intended to ensure their successful achievement. The outcome of this phase is a comprehensive organisational overview, which immediately leads into the latter phase, concerned with the identification of risk.

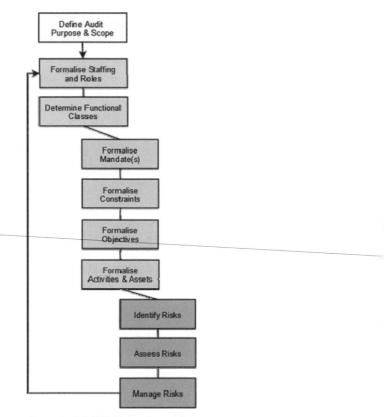

Figure 2: DRAMBORA audit workflow

The risk identification, assessment and management part of the DRAMBORA process is where conclusions are derived from the organisational picture conceived within the first phase. Risk is utilised as a convenient means for comprehending repository success – those repositories most capable of demonstrating the adequacy of their risk management are those that can have, and engender, greater confidence in the adequacy of their efforts. Preservation is after all, at its very heart, a risk management process. The fundamental temporal challenges of preservation are naturally complicated by future uncertainties. Threats relating to any number of social, semantic and technological factors are capable of inhibiting long-term access to digital materials.

3. DRAMBORA Interactive

In early April 2008, in response to usability issues associated with an entirely paper-based approach, a second version of the toolkit was released as DRAMBORA Interactive, a freely available web based tool (Fig. 3,4) [7]. DRAMBORA interactive leads auditors through the individual stages of the assessment process, recording and displaying responses and providing greater structure to facilitate a more comprehensive coverage. The tool provides robust security provisions, supporting multiple repository contributors, but protecting potentially sensitive information from non-authorised access.

The tool's implicit workflow exactly reflects the core DRAMBORA methodology. In addition, characteristics of each registered repository can be described in detailed terms, with technological, organisational and resource related issues made explicit. This facilitates the intelligent comparison of objectives, challenges and risks with those of peer repositories, again, intended to maximize the assessments' breadth of coverage. The tool is equipped with numerous reporting mechanisms to visualize the repository's status, and support the improvement planning process.

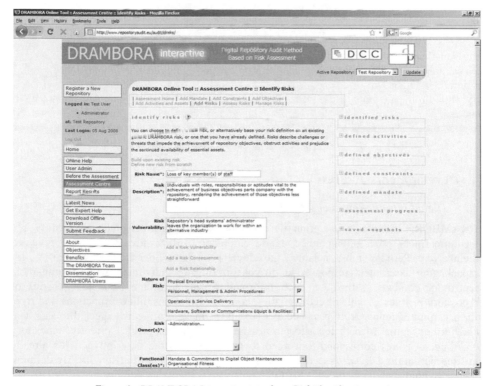

Figure 3: DRAMBORA Interactive interface: Risk identification section

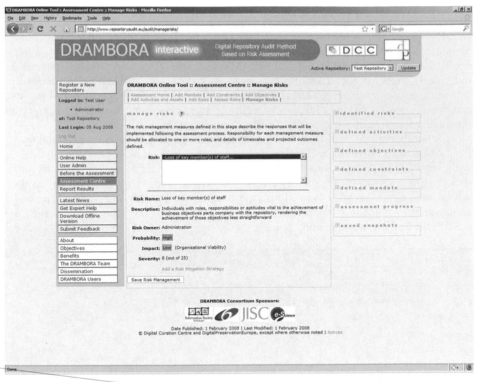

Figure 4: DRAMBORA Interactive interface: Risk management section

4. Developments and results

4.1   Digital Library Repository Profiling: the DELOS audits

DRAMBORA Interactive was primarily developed to inject greater practical usability into
the assessment process, but since its development, further advantages have revealed
themselves. Perhaps most notably, the developers have identified opportunities for
repackaging assessment responses to provoke or inspire individuals within comparable
repository contexts. Ultimately, such information will form the basis for a series of
repository profiles capable of encapsulating core roles, responsibilities, functions and risks
for a variety of repository types. The availability of these profiles is expected to facilitate
and further legitimise both repository assessment and development. Currently, repository
profiling measures correspond (but need to be limited) to the descriptive fields already
utilised within the *DigitalPreservationEurope* project's repository registry [8]. By defining
their own characteristics, the DRAMBORA software is thereafter equipped to offer targeted
suggestions.

Some theoretical work has already indicated the feasibility of these efforts. Within the
context of the DELOS Digital Preservation Cluster four audits of digital library
environments were undertaken, using DRAMBORA [9]. The Michigan-Google Digitization
Project and MBooks at the University of Michigan Library, Gallica at the Bibliothèque
nationale de France, the Digital Library of the National Library of Sweden and CERN's
Document Server exhibit a range of organisational and functional characteristics
representative of most of that which is conceivable within the digital library context. Each
assessment incorporated an onsite visit that took an average of three days, preceded by a

lengthy period of dialogue and information exchange between project facilitators and institutional participants, and considerable desk-based research. The conclusions that followed each would be distilled into a broadly applicable generic template, focusing not on diversity, but the fundamental commonalities that distinguish and characterise digital libraries.

Applying risk analysis based auditing methodology to digital libraries has identified both common strengths and weaknesses in their work. While digital libraries are highly efficient in automating ingest of digitised content, and providing flexible access to their collections, the acquisition of born-digital content poses more difficult requirements that need bespoke solutions and often semi-automatic processing. For metadata and access digital libraries can rely on existing library standards and electronic catalogues that can be linked to simple storage solutions. Relying primarily on standard formats has to some complacency surrounding the digital preservation challenge. This is exaggerated further because digitised collections represent little more than access-facilitating surrogates of their analogue collections, and this is understandable. Each participating institution demonstrated adequate technical infrastructures, and sufficient security to maintain the digital library services.

The areas where the audited digital libraries collectively fail or show weakness relate to:

- lack of policies and procedural manuals and maintenance of the organisation's knowledge-base;
- creation and management of preservation metadata;
- documentation of the systems in use and provision of an audit trail of processing applied to digital objects in library's care;
- maintaining transparency to its stakeholders and involving them in improving the digital library services;
- delegation of responsibility for preservation planning and effective preservation strategy building.

All participating libraries were in the process of expanding and changing their services, which was expected to bring these weaknesses increasingly to the fore. The audited digital libraries can be described as risk-minimal digital repositories, and are certainly aware of their shortcomings. Hence, they were each well placed to earn the status of a trustworthy digital repository. A detailed report [10] on these audits will be publicly available in early autumn 2008.

4.2   Findings from the DELOS audits

The process of assessments yielded almost as many insights about the assessment tool itself as the current state of digital libraries.

4.2.1 Supported self-audits

The most overwhelming response from the audited institutions was that the DRAMBORA audit process yielded numerous benefits, and provided insights that would undoubtedly prompt further investigation and probable response. However, a general response that appeared to be consistent from each of the audited organisations was the value of the process would be lessened if the DELOS facilitators were not present. This is of some concern, given DRAMBORA's role as a self-assessment methodology. If organisations are incapable of exploring their own risks independently then the potential benefits of the process may not be fully exploitable. This reaction may simply be a methodological consequence of the way these audits were undertaken. Generally speaking, facilitators elected to refrain from impressing upon library staff shortcomings that they regarded as self evident, instead preferring to lead them to their own independent realization via the various stages of the DRAMBORA process. In most cases this worked extremely effectively, but although DELOS project members strived to maintain their role as facilitators, and encourage the digital library staff to bear most of the responsibility for analysis and reflection there were inevitably times that, from their experiences of visiting other organisations, they were well positioned to comment on and compare systems to those in place elsewhere. To present these opinions was perhaps an instinctive inevitability, but the result may have been an overdependence on externally arising insights, rather than encouraging the identification, acknowledgment and formalisation of internally perceived challenges. Nevertheless, even before the DELOS audits, this was identified as a potential pitfall of the bottom up approach favoured within DRAMBORA. Fundamental to its success, within its defined self-audit process the parameters for success are associated with the specific aims and mandate of the audited repository. However, there is an implicit vulnerability: self-assessment in isolation can only indicate problems within the bounds of what repositories believe that they should be doing. What happens in cases where organisations are simply oblivious to their shortcomings, or unaware of the available possibilities that they might usefully seize? How can repositories seek to comment on the likelihood or potential impact of unanticipated risks that they are yet to fall foul of? How can they even be confident of identifying a sufficiently comprehensive range of pertinent risks? DRAMBORA Interactive to some extent overcomes these issues. As described above, by requiring users to describe the characteristics of their own repositories the tool presents 'comparable organisations' with insights into the kinds of risks that are faced by their peers, in order to help ensure a more comprehensive coverage. The development of meaningful repository profiles, that reflect contextual realities of the preservation process, is expected to represent the ultimate outcome of this.

4.2.2 Staff participation in the audits

In order to be of real value to the organisation, everyone with any relevant responsibilities or concerns ought to be involved. The audit process is in reality little more than a formalised means of facilitating dialogue and discussion between the stakeholders. In those organisations that did invest time and effort from every functional and organisational unit there were visible benefits, as everything from minor confusions to more long-standing concerns were raised, discussed and generally resolved. Communication on an organisation-wide basis is always acknowledged as vital, but all too often overlooked or underemphasised. The self-audit represents an invaluable opportunity to develop a shared and globally acceptable interpretation and understanding of overall strengths, weakness, opportunities and threats. However, although a wide range of representation is vital to ensure the audit's success, this must be well managed. Representations should be planned to ensure that discussions are logistically feasible and that no more than 4 individuals are involved at any time. As more participants are added beyond that number the discussion will become increasingly difficult to manage, and focus more and more difficult to maintain. Conversational tangents become more common and fundamental audit questions will remain unanswered, or answered only in an incomplete or superficial sense.

4.2.3 Risk scoring

With respect to risk assessment, two priorities for repository staff emerged during the audits. The first was to build a relative array of risks, capable of illustrating where the mildest and most severe challenges within the organisation were evident; the other is to establish how the repository or digital library's maturity compares with that of its peers. The two are far from incompatible, but in order to present useful, globally comparable results the apportioned scores must have some objective significance. Descriptions of the significance of the available scores are presented within DRAMBORA, but these are not immune to further interpretation. It seems likely that self auditors will consider risks as being more or less severe than those already identified and allocate impact and probability scores to reflect their relative status. For this reason, when DRAMBORA is utilised to support a self-assessment process, its results are of most value for internal use. Involving an external (and consistent) facilitator enables these results to have considerably greater objective weight, and may then be the basis for a more global comparison. The benefits of the DELOS process, which enabled a consistent group of individuals to assess four organisations with much in common according to a single methodology, cannot be overstated.

A vital commodity when describing risk is a means to determine, or express risk impact. It appears that the perception of challenge associated with preservation within digital library contexts is quite distinct from that of those dealing with born digital or otherwise unique digital assets. In most cases within the audited institutions, the value of digital content was mainly surrogacy for physical assets. Libraries remain primarily access-focussed and digitised content is considerably more plentiful than born-digital materials. Preservation is naturally prioritised lower since, notwithstanding the significant cost of rescanning large quantities of content, anything that is lost can generally be digitised again. The original DRAMBORA text describes risk impact in terms of only loss of digital object authenticity and understandability. Initial concerns with this limited definition of impact were to some extent met with subsequent reference to the loss of organisations' *ability to ensure* authenticity and understandability of their digital collections. However, the experiences of the DELOS assessments revealed that even this slightly broader definition was too narrow to be either universally usable or applicable. Many of the identified risks could be only loosely related to the digital holdings, rendering any attempt to quantitatively express the extent of potential impact in such terms unfeasible. In addition, adopting an impact scoring system of this kind contrasts markedly with much of the DRAMBORA philosophy, within which organisational priorities are of greatest significance. An objective risk impact scoring system that considers only one manifestation of success or failure is unnecessarily restrictive. Consequently, the risk impact expressions have now been overhauled within DRAMBORA, so that for any risk auditors can select the terms within which impact is realised. The implicit danger in this evolution is well understood; if risks are classified according to multiple impact types it may limit the extent to which they can be compared and prioritised. In order to alleviate such concerns, a weighted model has been favoured, with four 'risk expression' types that can be scored according to a common scale. Irrespective of the specific practical units with which risk impact might be quantified (e.g., in Euros, Gigabytes or a less tangible measure), the impact is described uniformly. The new impact expressions are:

- Reputation and Intangibles
- Organisational Viability
- Service Delivery
- Technology.

These are assumed to be proportionate loss areas, but individual responses can reflect priorities that are adopted by auditing institutions. Impact continues to be measured according to a scale from very low to very high, although the interpretative text that accompanies each has been neutralised to support any of the four risk impact classifications, and permit comparability.

4.2.4 Keeping track of a digital library evolution

A further conclusion highlights the suitability of DRAMBORA within an ever-evolving digital context. The four organisations that participated in this process are all, like the peers they represent, in a state of transition. New services are being developed, expansions are being planned to other areas, new contracts are being signed and new responsibilities embraced as novel legislation emerges. In light of the almost constant development that characterises the repository and digital library community it becomes difficult to say at any particular moment whether a particular organisation merits a trustworthy status. DRAMBORA is equipped to alleviate some of these problems. Its metric is much more focussed on facilitating improvement than on the imposition of transitory judgements. In that respect its iterative workflow has a great deal in common with maturity modelling, which is expected to be integrated in an increasingly formal way within DRAMBORA in subsequent iterations. Concerned with not only validating the effectiveness of existing infrastructures, but also determining the suitability of proposed developments, the process effectively reflects the dynamic characteristics of the repository domain. In general terms, it will be much easier to accredit individual services that the repository is offering, irrespective of their maturity, and then make some conclusions about the organisation as a whole, aimed at its overall development. If the aim of the audit is simply to judge the entire organisation at once, any verdict will have to be accompanied by numerous caveats. This will not really assist those stakeholders concerned about the sustainability or effectiveness of the repository in question, whereas a more general expression of maturity, structured according to available services and measured against mandate and objectives has considerably greater value.

4.3   DRAMBORA and Risk-Benefit Analysis (RBA) for appraisal

DRAMBORA applies RBA at the repository level. It enables repositories to monitor how they are handling the risks associated with preservation through their own repository level management. It is conceivable that much of the process that DRAMBORA encapsulates could be automated for particular kinds of repositories and we intend to investigate this in the future as part of our plan to continue to make DRAMBORA more and more useful to the preservation community. There is plenty of opportunity to develop concepts implicit within RBA to support automation of appraisal at the level of the digital record – using the concept of digital record in its broadest sense. When appraising materials for long-term preservation, risk-benefits analysis offers us proven and developed mechanisms.   It provides a method that can be applied whether at the level of collection, or individual record.   Most importantly it provides a method that is susceptible to automation.   This challenge of automation is one that given the deluge of digital materials that we need to appraise we must embrace.

4.4   Training activities

Six public tutorials (in London, The Hague, Arlington (USA), Manchester, Munich, Stockholm) were held on DRAMBORA 1.0 during 2007. Further DRAMBORA Interactive training courses, targeted for auditors and the general public, will take place in Prague in October 2008 within a joint training initiative organized by DigitalPreservationEurope (DPE), Preservation and Long-term Access through Networked Services (Planets), Cultural, Artistic and Scientific knowledge for Preservation, Access and Retrieval (CASPAR) and Network of expertise in Digital long-term preservation (nestor), to introduce the Principles of Digital Objects Preservation [11]. An additional two training courses organized by DPE and the DCC will take place in the first quarter of 2009 in Europe.

4.5   International audits

Since its release, DRAMBORA is being used by an increasing number of international organizations, ranging from national libraries and archives to universities, and from research and governmental centres to museums. A sample list of organizations can be found at   http://www.repositoryaudit.eu/users/,   and   more   organizations   undertaking   self-assessment with DRAMBORA are periodically being added to the list. Several assessments with DRAMBORA Interactive are currently being conducted by in Europe by the DigitalPreservationEurope partners, while further investigation will be conducted in Japan within a grant provide by the Great Britain Sasakawa Foundation.

4.6   Collaborations

The developers of DRAMBORA have or have had active collaborations with the following international initiatives and projects:

- Trustworthy Repository Audit and Certification (TRAC) Criteria and Checklist Working Group
- Center for Research Libraries (CRL) Certification of Digital Archives Project
- Network of Expertise in Long-term storage of Digital Resources (nestor)
- DELOS Digital Preservation Cluster (WP6)
- International Audit and Certification Birds of a Feather Group
- SHAMAN (Sustaining Heritage Access through Multivalent ArchiviNg)

5. Conclusions

DRAMBORA has now been deployed in a range of evaluative contexts, and the processes of self-assessment and facilitated assessment continue to yield considerable insights into both preservation activities, and the state of preservation assessment. Work associated with DRAMBORA will continue a variety of ways. The DCC and DPE are committed to training a generation of DRAMBORA auditors through a number of planned events taking place in 2008 and 2009. Facilitated audits will continue both interactively and through physical visits, with new organisations registering their repositories and completing self-assessments every week. DRAMBORA Interactive was released in early 2008 and the procedure to submit DRAMBORA as the basis of an ISO standard has been initiated (ISO TC46 /SC 11). DPE and the Digital Curation Centre intend to continue to develop DRAMBORA to support the longer-term management of repositories and ensuring that they are auditable and continue to develop in ways that enable them to consistently improve their levels of service and the longer term sustainability. They will also support its widest possible take-up within the United Kingdom, Europe and broader international contexts.

Acknowledgements

The development of DRAMBORA has been enabled by the European Union through its Framework Six support for DigitalPreservationEurope under the IST Programme (IST-2005-2.5-10) through grant IST-2005-034762. The DigitalCurationCentre (DCC) in the UK was the other key funder of DRAMBORA development.

References

[1]   TRAC was developed by a consortium jointly overseen by the US National Archives and Records Administration and the Research Libraries Group (prior to its absorption within OCLC), and is now maintained by the Center for Research Libraries, http://www.crl.edu/PDF/trac.pdf

[2]   The nestor Catalogue developed in Germany by the Network of expertise in Digital long-term preservation. http://edoc.hu-berlin.de/series/nestor-materialien/8/PDF/8.pdf

[3]   DRAMBORA toolkit, DRAMBORA Interactive and more information on ongoing activities are available at http://www.repositoryaudit.eu/ . See also McHugh, A., Ruusalepp, R., Ross, S., Hofman H.: Digital Repository Audit Method Based on Risk Assessment. Digital Curation Centre (DCC) and DigitalPreservationEurope (DPE), (2007)

[4]   The British Atmospheric Data Centre (BADC); the National Digital Archive of Datasets (NDAD); the National Library of New Zealand's National Digital Heritage Archive (NDHA); the Florida Digital Archive (FDA) at the Florida Centre for Library Automation; and the Beazley Archive (BA) at the University of Oxford were among those that kindly agreed to take part. For a mechanisms to roll out audit and certification services for digital repositories in the United Kingdom, see Ross S., McHugh A.,

The Role of Evidence in Establishing Trust in Repositories, D-Lib Magazine, July/August 2006, Volume 12 Number 7/8, http://www.dlib.org/dlib/july06/ross/07ross.html

[5]   Most notably, at that stage, the RLG/NARA Draft Audit Check-list for Certification of Digital Repositories, which would latterly be published as TRAC.

[6]   Core Requirements for Digital Archives. Center for Research Libraries (CRL), (2007) http://www.crl.edu/content.asp?l1=13&l2=58&l3=162&l4=92

[7]   Available at http://www.repositoryaudit.eu/

[8]   http://www.digitalpreservationeurope.eu/registries/repositories/

[9]   The DELOS report, due to be published imminently at the time of writing describes a range of common objectives, constraints, roles, responsibilities, activities and risks within the University of Michigan Library's MBooks, CERN's Document Server, Gallica at the Bibliothèque Nationale de France and the Swedish National Library's Digital Library.

[10]   S. Ross, A. McHugh, P. Inncoenti, R. Ruusalepp, Investigation of the potential application of the DRAMBORA Toolkit in the context of digital libraries to support the assessment of the repositories aspects of digital libraries, DELOS Noe for HATII at the University of Glasgow, 2008

[11]   http://www.wepreserve.eu/events/prague-2008/

Section 9

Intelligent Content and Semantics

Section 9.1

Issues

Collaboration and the Knowledge Economy: Issues, Applications, Case Studies
P. Cunningham and M. Cunningham (Eds.)
IOS Press, 2008

Multi-level Ontology Mapping for a Cross-culture Collaborative Design

Gianfranco CARRARA, Antonio FIORAVANTI

Dept. Architettura e Urbanistica per l'Ingegneria – Sapienza Università di Roma,
Via Eudossiana 18, Rome, 00184, Italy, Tel: +39 06 44585165, Fax: +39 06 44585186
Email: gianfranco.carrara@uniroma1.it, antonio.fioravanti@uniroma1.it

Abstract: Design process is a very complex activity nowadays due to its cross-disciplinary nature, its delocalization, its new professional figures and its new performing requirements. Computer Supported Collaborative Work (CSCW) together with intelligent content and semantics are up-to-date methodologies to cope with these needs The research work aims at defining new methods, techniques and advanced ICT programs suitable for industries, professionals and technicians who, in various ways and with many specializations, operate in the field of the design and construction of complex building.

In the AEC sector designers (actors) often have difficulties in integrating their own work with others, as a deep collaboration implies working together on the same objects (components), and this can lead to misunderstandings, conflicts, incoherencies.

The purpose of this research has been to enhance, through suitable tools and methodologies together with the exercise of design collaboration, the overall quality of buildings. Such tools and methodologies are founded on correct mapping across ontologies of different cross-culture domains, so it is easier for actors to understand each other, for application programs to interface significant data and for design process to point out contradictory constraints.

The results of this research will be first be applied to provide university students in the schools of architecture and engineering with innovative tools for delocalized design learning enhanced by a cross-disciplinary collaboration.

Keywords: Collaborative Design, Ontologies, Knowledge Bases, Mapping

1. Introduction – Design and Collaboration

The general features of the methodologies and tools reported here have been conceived, developed, implemented, applied and tested on design of Architecture/ Engineering/ Construction (AEC) for the following reasons.

At present, design is a multidisciplinary e interdisciplinary complex activity that covers the entire range of the process leading from the conception to the construction of goods. This complexity has increased in modern times as a result of new needs and new problems, such as environmental sustainability, energy efficiency, new requirements and typology, new materials and products and sectoral regulations, which involve increasing specialization of the various professional figures involved.

The software and methods used today are unable to satisfy present-day needs as they date back to an earlier cultural generation, and are unsuitable for addressing today's challenges involving the global design of goods in their entirety and complexity.

The designers (from now on, actors [1]) actors involved in each phase of the process have to exchange information, knowledge and expertise, thereby fostering mutual understanding. To do this is necessary to have a common dictionary and to collaborate for more agreed goals.

In order to ensure their decisions are approached in such a way as to satisfy the requests/expectations of the various design actors, it is common practice to make use of meetings among actors by means of which relations of close collaboration are established among them.

Many forms of workflow have existed among actors involved in a design process, each of which presents advantages and limitations depending on its specific features and the context. These forms do not depend on the number of collaborating actors, but rather on other decisive features: timing of the actions (the overall time required for the operation and the presence or absence of phases), intersected competences, actor hierarchy, knowledge of the operating context and parallelism of the actions.

Regarding the intersection of competences in teamwork we define the following kinds of design processes.

Coordinate design is an elementary form of workflow where there are no intersections. That allows the design process to be broken down into juxtaposed phases. Information flow is essentially unidirectional and only minimal feedbacks happen; each processing phase begins only after its preceding ones have been completed: a process, a time. This type of interaction works correctly in well defined and steady working environment, which is generally intended to refine the details of the constructive design (Fig. 1).

Cooperative design is a more integrated form of design process where there are little intersections. All the actors strive to attain a common objective by working in a non linear, but pre-defined sequence, where each processing phase can begin even if not all the preceding ones have been carried out: many processes, a time. Just small quantities of information relating to the same entity are generally exchanged.

Collaborative design is the most integrated form of design workflow, in which actors' competences have more intersections, actors can help each other, gain greater insight into how their own work interacts with that of the others and how they can pursue their own objectives more effectively. Each processing phase can begin even if its preceding ones have not been completed, like in Cooperative design, but actors can also act on the same entities (components, concepts) very often exchanging large quantity of information relating to the same entity.

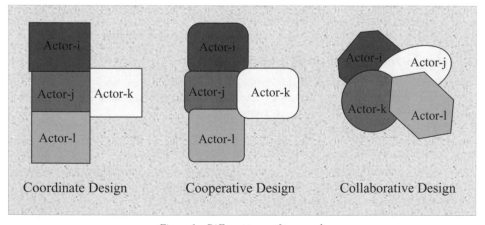

Figure 1 – Different types of teamwork

Collaboration in AEC design activity is suitable for this sector, as any building is a singular, integrated and complex system in a given context with interleaved problems. The global overall solution can be attained only by means of trade-offs among actors so that they can modify their own specialist goals and adapt their own specialist solutions.

The collaboration becomes all the more effective when it takes place at all the hierarchic levels into which a design and construction process is normally subdivided.

Collaboration can thus facilitate the discovery of new design solutions through the proactive contribution of each actor; it allows the various solutions by the different actors to converge towards a single overall solution; it helps the actors reciprocally to modify their own design solutions so that these ones can be more satisfactorily integrated into the overall solution; it allows the reciprocal malfunctions among the solutions proposed by the individual actors to be detected on time; lastly, it encourages the development of creativity through interaction among the different skills [2, 3, 4, 5].

To deal with Collaborative Design problems, software houses have proposed different solutions. In a not so distant past the main problem was to exchange data by means of neutral formats (standards): there were several initiatives such as PHIGS and STEP and so on, that can now be considered to be a small part-of the more general problem that is to find out how to formalize knowledge [6] in all its implications: technical knowledge + expertise + rules of thumbs + context-aware + physical lows, procedures, etc.

2. The State of the Art: BIM and IFC

For the past few decades it appeared that such standards and product models could serve the purpose of collaborative design, they failed as not flexible enough for design process. Moreover it is noticed that in the design process developed by usual application tools (various domain specific applications for analysis, simulation, verification, etc), actors have misunderstandings and lack of data.

In the AEC community several efforts have been devoted to overcome these difficulties in order to integrate competencies in a single application program and to share knowledge. Among the various initiatives, we mention *BIM* and *IFC*.

BIMs (Building Information Modeling) are a product models, recently driven by several CAD system vendors (Autodesk, GraphiSoft, Bentley, Nemetschek, etc.), which can describe the form (e.g., geometric information and its relationships) and attributes (e.g., physical characteristics) of a building throughout its life cycle. BIMs define a building with proprietary formats, their digital models are conceived with a top-down point of view, focus on components and not on the process, are a source of intelligent information about a building. To achieve a better interoperability between disciplines and software applications across the industry and professionals, that has become necessary and urgent, a pragmatic and efficacious basis for information sharing between different BIMs is essential.

For this purpose a second initiative with a different approach has been developed: the Industry Foundation Classes (IFC). It is an open XML standard (OOP) conceived with a bottom-up point of view and non-proprietary data model specifications, proposed by IAI – International Alliance for Interoperability. It is emerging very slowly among industries involved, due to his bottom-up approach. IFC aims at granting software interoperability, at exchanging more significant project data, so that nowadays CAD applications by major software houses, like aforementioned ones, can import and export their proprietary formatted files from/to IFC files. Such specifications represent a data structure supporting a digital project model, useful in sharing structured labelled (more understandable) data across applications, but they are neither intended for design needs nor for mutual understanding among actors, but mainly for (just!) production needs.

Until now exchanging contents among commercial applications has been very difficult. As a matter of fact the translations of proprietary BIMs from their own file formats to the correspondent IFC one, are not equivalent due to the different primary conceptual models of the building.

Even though different specialist actors use the same integrated application tool (e.g. Revit, Triforma, etc.), the entities they consider can have different meanings as belonging to different domains.

BIM has an important role in creating and coordinating components as parts of a building, but actually it does not provide any concept of the building as a "system" (structured set of components with functions aiming at a goal) like architects or engineers have had from centuries. Moreover other difficulties come from the fact that BIM data must co-exist with a number of programs with different task-oriented models, all essential in defining detailed information of a project.

IFC is based on a central model that can be either partially or entirely shared by participants, but must be accepted as a whole, being totally coherent (it is not scalable from this point of view). Although its approach supports different visualizations of the same concept, it is focused on converting and updating the integrated model from multiple sources, at the level of the applications, into a generalized description of the entire building.

As a matter of fact, current interoperability design problems related to commercial application programs are solved within the domain they have been built for, as very often they all have a similar, but particular, point of view: the one of who first modelled the phenomenon, probably some thirty years ago.

Models of a specialist domain allow "data exchange" but not "concepts understanding", so that the research work has been addressed to the specific issues that can enable a higher understanding level among actors.

Therefore the main problem this research has coped with, for improving collaboration in a cross-disciplinary design process, does not concern mere interoperability formats, but the mutual understanding itself of all the different actors over components, concepts and processes, which is still an open one: "the symmetry of ignorance".

3. Methodology

In such a scenario one important task of this research was to develop a methodology for a better mutual understanding by formalizing and managing knowledge in the broadest sense. This allows to integrate the fragmented specialist competences and expertise within an ongoing design project, reducing the "symmetry of ignorance" among the actors. The methodology used consists of analyzing the problem, defining a general model (a framework) of the design process, a common knowledge and a mechanism to interface common with specialist knowledge and to interface knowledge with data.

A fundamental pre-requirement to apply such a methodology and to overcome the above-mentioned mere interoperability format problems is *knowledge understanding*, namely technical knowledge. Technical knowledge concepts can be formalized and structured by means of the technology of *ontologies*, for defining entities; and by means of *explicit semantics* for defining their meanings.

Ontologies provide a valuable support for representing and sharing terminology, concepts and relationships within a given domain, so that an increasing number of communities [6] of experts develop ontologies as an underlying base for their work, including collaboration in design. Actually, beside the use of ontologies manually made explicit by actors, in the growing area of network services, new approaches to composition and orchestration of services are based on ontologies for representing their definitions and semantics, i.e. for disambiguating queries.

At present, most of specialist ontologies are typically not explicit and are inherent in the model of phenomena they are referred to, so that they are hidden in various application tools. i.e. in commercial tools, part of the knowledge is implicit, hidden-coded in application programs and is neither openly available nor understandable to users. It would be needed a reverse engineering…

Explicit semantics (context dependent meaning of knowledge) make entities understandable by humans and tractable by computers.

The only explicit semantics of most specialist application programs have, is at a lower level than IFC as it is linked to datum. Therefore, in many cases, only data can be shared in practice. As a consequence usual application programs that work on data at low semantic level, when applied to the complexity of the architectural product have generated more problems at a higher semantic level than those they had solved at the low one.

Although it was expected that an integrated application program could achieve interoperability among different domains of expertise, at present it is commonly recognized that the fragmentation of the design process increases the "symmetry of ignorance". Moreover it has become clear that a single data model, like integrated application programs, would not be able to serve all the requirements of all the actors and the sheer magnitude of the combined data often exceeds the capability of its management.

To deal with these problems actors have to be aware of entity meanings at the different levels of abstraction they use in a design process, from data level to reasoning level (Fig. 2). An ontology based methodology can also allows the actors to use in a coherent manner different levels of abstraction, or to exploit a conceptual interoperability.

4. Technology Description and Development

The assumption of our research is that actors cannot overcome the "symmetry of ignorance" barrier at data level or at low semantic level by means of usual application programs. Such a goal can only be achieved by means of two basic aspects: 1) matching concepts and mapping ontologies by rules to discover same entities in different domains [7] and 2) using inferential engines and intelligent agents to have an effective support in design.

Regarding the first aspects, at present, for machine interoperability purposes, translation of application programs to/from the common lower ontology level (IFC) is starting to be available to the extent that software houses support new IFC specifications.

The dominant way of using IFC specifications (low-ontology level) today is still a one-direction batch translation of large data sets from an application into the common language and vice versa. Collaboration using IFC specifications exists in the industrial practice, but it is based on "ad-hoc" procedures that are agreed between single specialists at a project level. However, the nature of architectural and building design has proven to be a field of fragmented cross-disciplinary competencies, hard to manage, difficult to formalize in the above-mentioned utopian data-centric approach.

As a matter of fact IFC model servers implemented till now provide limited collaboration support and the existing model servers do not support adequate management of the instance versions (with different meanings) of various specialists.

To solve the aforementioned difficulties it is needed to postulate that each specialist has his own ontology (explicit or that can be explicited) and these ontologies have a partial overlapping meaning: a Common Ontology. Such an ontology can provide a base to capitalise the knowledge and expertise. In facts, matching current problems with past experiences requires to have stored them at the correct level of abstraction.

Moreover Common Ontology can be increased by the use of the semantic power of IFC. This can be done by adding new levels of intelligence: an Upper-Ontology Level (rules) and a Deductive–Reasoning Level [8] above the Ontology one (IFC) (Fig. 2). The first level allows parametric objects and logic/ algorithmic rules - that can adapt themselves to their design contexts - explain constraints, etc. The second level with its deductive capabilities applies inference rules and intelligent agents to the Upper-Ontology Level. This one can be triggered when ontologies at the Lower-Ontology Level match each other and are activated by instantiating a prototype of an ontology within the current context - and transitively, chaining rules as much as possible.

For example one actor may define the use of a room within a building and another actor may be warned when choosing a wrong size for a wall of that room or when a third actor proposes an incompatible material for the surfaces of that room.

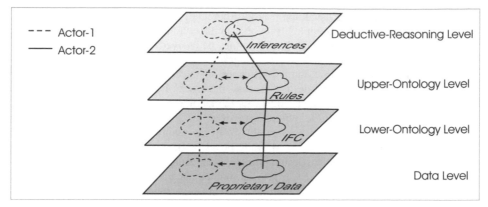

*Figure 2 – Ontologies at Deductive-Reasoning Level map different Actor's ontologies at the Upper Ontology
Level so that inference mechanisms can be applied to rules .*

Concerning the second aspect, the use of inferential engines and intelligent agents, the basic differences of our approach with the present exhaustive and integral approach – consisting in importing and exporting in an agreed and identical format all the information, such as IFC (that anyway is a reference for the semantic matching) – consist of:

- exporting the strictly necessary information among actors;
- leaving to an upper-ontology based tool the task of linking representations of the same entities made by an actor at different levels of abstraction (vertical interfaces);
- making a Reasoning Level for mapping similar entities of different actors at the same upper-ontology level (orthogonal interfaces).

Referring to the first point, in contrast to a centralized database model a distributed ontology model has been developed, based over Personal and Common Design workspaces [9, 10, 11, 12]. Each actor's domain retains its own ontologies in the most appropriate form for his/her needs, while appropriate filters translate ontologies into/from a Common Ontology domain. The discipline-specific "ontology filter" translates the common representations into semantically-specific ones, as needed by their domains of expertise. Conversely, they will translate semantically-specific/domain-specific ontologies into a common ontology representation that can be accessed by means of other domain-specific filters. In turn, at the Low-Semantic Level data structures – representing specialist design instances by means of their own specialist "Data Filter" – are translated into common data structures (i.e. IFC instances) that make up sub-sets of the overall design instance.

To an actor, therefore, an ontology would have semantically specific representation, even though generated by a different actor, thereby facilitating a high level of shared common mutual understanding.

Regarding the second point, the research work has defined an ontology based model that supports actor's design by linking his/her heterogeneous semantics – whose formalization is oriented towards different tasks – with the data of his/her usual application programs, so that the model can point out inconsistency of data, incoherency of constraints, incongruence of goals within the actor's domain.

With respect to the third point, actors ahead of time can acknowledge the implications of their proposed actions, considering other actors' points of view, constraints and goals by means of inference mechanisms at Reasoning Level able to map constraint rules among the ontologies of different domains. The model will also let them achieve better and/or faster their own goals and global goals in decision making and problem solving activities.

The dynamic and semantically-specific representation can allow incoherent/favourable situations (according to different actors) to be highlighted and managed in real time. At the same time it allows actors to make alternatives, reflecting on consequences of their intents more consciously. So the impact of a networked ontology-based collaborative design transforms a hierarchical/linear fragmented process into a distributed and interleaved one, makes actors more aware of overall design problems and allows choices to be more participative and shared.

The integration of the specialist actor's design solutions (instances) translated into sub-sets of the overall design solution (instance) can give rise to inconsistencies and conflicts among instances belonging to ontologies of different domains. These inconsistencies are detected by the inferential mechanisms contained in the Deductive and Reasoning Level It first, points out (if it exists) a common ontology in the Common Ontology by mapping the ontologies of different actors, secondly, checks incoherencies among these ones; thirdly, reports feedback information to actors so that they can provide the necessary action.

The described Collaborative Working Environment has been tested by means of a real use case: a meta-design of a demonstrative Hospital Ward. The implementation is a demonstrative prototype system able to support a highly interactive collaborative design processes among three specialist actors in the field of Architecture, Structural and Mechanical Engineering [13].

Our framework uses a software system for the representation and querying of ontologies, named QuOnto (www.dis.uniroma1.it/~quonto/), developed in the past years at "Sapienza", University of Rome. This system, based on Description Logics, has proven to be computationally very efficient and robust enough to be used in productive environments (with million instances). We used Lisp for Reasoning Level rules, MySQL for the DD and two test bed threads for the development environment. SemanticWorks by Altova for ontologies + Architectural Desktop for graphic objects, or Protégé + SketchUp. See also Carrara e Fioravanti [9, 10].

5. Conclusions

In conclusions, it has been previously shown that all the above-mentioned difficulties can be overcome by means of:
- common and specialist ontologies;
- explicit semantics;
- an upper-ontology level for inference mechanisms;
- a disjoined overall coherence from actor's coherence;
- a storage of knowledge developed along the design process.

Making semantics explicit facilitates the management of design process at many levels. For example, the model can define a quality control level by means of key performance indicators (consistency, coherence, congruence of the design process), or it can manage intellectual property in collaborative design processes according to EU SA 8000 addressed on ethical impact of knowledge sharing.

The impact of the research is very large, as beside the developed use case of the Collaborative Design model in the field of AEC industry, the model has a non-specific structure to be applied to other specialist contents.

Thus conceived, the model confirms the possibility for any actor to work using his own personal methods, algorithms, software and tools to represent the complexity of his own instance of the design problem and to solve any contradictions in his own Personal Design Workspace. An actor has the added advantage that the other actors cannot enter his/her workspace although they are able to trigger yes/no these constraints/opportunities.

From the foregoing it emerges that the model structure is such that any actor defines the data of his own design instance by explicitly attributing them the conceptual ontology they refer to. In turn ontologies are structured by relations and rules in an upper-ontology level.

This evidently differs from what currently takes place in existing CAD systems in which the attribution of the data to concepts is implicit, arbitrary and related to the subjective interpretative capacity of the various actors.

Actually the direct link between ontologies (concepts) and data as well as the translation of both of them into ontologies common to all actors, make it possible to activate a true collaboration, in the broad sense of the term, on the basis of a mutual comprehension and the sharing of the choices.

References

[1] Wix, J.: 1997, ISO 10303 Part 106, BCCM (Building Construction Core Model) /T200 draft (1997).

[2] Gross, M.D., Yi-Luen Do, E., McCall, R., Citrin, W.V., Hamill, P., Warmack, A., Kuczun, K.S.:1998, Collaboration and coordination in architectural design: approaches to computer mediated team work, Automation in Construction, 7(6), 465-473 (1998).

[3] Kvan T.: 2000, Collaborative design: what is it?, Martens, B. (guest ed.), Special Issue eCAADe '97, Automation in Construction, 9(4), 409-415 (2000).

[4] Jeng, T.-S., Eastman, C.M.: 1998, A database architecture for design collaboration, Automation in Construction, 7(6), 475-483 (1998).

[5] Kolarevic, B., Schmitt, G., Hirschberg, U., Kurmann, D., Johnson, B.: 2000, An experiment in design collaboration, Automation in Construction, 9(1), 73-81 (2000).

[6] Ugwu O.O., Anuba C.J. and Thorpe A: 2005, Ontological foundation for agent support in contructability assessment of steel structure – a case study, Automation in Construction, 14(1) 99-114 (2005).

[7] Cheng M.-Y.: 2008, Cross-organization process integration in design-build team, Automation in Construction, 17(2) 151-162 (2008).

[8] Nguyen T.-H, Oloufa A.A. and Nassar K.: 2005, Algorithms for automated deduction of topological information, 14(1), 59-70 (2005).

[9] Fioravanti A., G. Carrara: 2007, Philosophy and structure of a CWE-based Model of Building Design – in P. Cunningham and Miriam Cunningham (eds), eChallenges 2007, ISBN 978-1-905824-05-2, IOS Press The Hague, Amsterdam, 24-26 October 2007, The Netherlands, 2007, CD Rom, pp. 1-12.

[10] Carrara G., Fioravanti A., Nanni U.: 2004, Knowledge Sharing, not MetaKnowledge. How to join a collaborative design Process and safely share one's knowledge, in J. Pohl (ed.) Intelligent Software System for the New Infrastructure. Focus Symposium at InterSymp-2004 Conference Proceedings, Baden-Baden, Germany, 2004, vol. 1, pp. 105-118.

[11] Carrara G, Fioravanti A.: 2001, A Theoretical Model of Shared Distributed Knowledge Bases for Collaborative Architectural Design, in J. Gero e K. Hori eds. Strategic Knowledge and Concept Formation, ISBN/ISSN: 1-86487-114-8. conference Proceeding of the 3° International Workshop 17-18/12/2002, University of Sydney, Australia, 2001, pp. 129-143.

[12] van Leeuwen, J.P., van der Zee, A.: 2005, Distributed object models for collaboration in the construction industry, Automation in Construction, 14(4) 491-499 (2005).

[13] Chen P.-H., Cui L., Wan C., Yang Q., Ting S.K., Tiong R,L.K.: 2004, Implementation of IFC-based web server for collaborative building design between architects and structural engineers, Automation in Construction, 14(1) 115-128 (2004).

Collaboration and the Knowledge Economy: Issues, Applications, Case Studies   1423
P. Cunningham and M. Cunningham (Eds.)
IOS Press, 2008

Ontological Multimedia Information Management System

Hilal TARAKCI[1], Nihan Kesim CICEKLI[2]
[1]MilSOFT Software Technologies, METU, Technopolis, Ankara, 06531, Turkey
Email: hilaltarakci@yahoo.com
[2]Department of Computer Engineering, METU, Ankara, 06531, Turkey
Tel: +90 312 2105582, Fax: + 90 312 2105544, Email: nihan@ceng.metu.edu.tr

Abstract: In order to manage the content of multimedia data, the content must be annotated. Although any user-defined annotation is acceptable, it is better if many systems use the same annotation format. MPEG-7 is a widely accepted standard for multimedia content annotation. In MPEG-7, semantically identical metadata can be represented in multiple ways due to lack of precise semantics in its XML-based syntax. This unfortunately prevents metadata interoperability. To overcome this, MPEG-7 standard is translated into an ontology. In our work, we use an MPEG-7 ontology on top and wrap the given user-defined ontologies with MPEG-7 ontology, thus building MPEG-7 based ontologies automatically. Our proposed system is an ontological multimedia information management framework due to its modular architecture, ease of integrating with user-defined ontologies naturally and automatic harmonization of MPEG-7 ontology and domain-specific ontologies.

Keywords: semantic querying of video content, multimedia content annotation, mpeg-7, mpeg-7 ontology, mpeg-7 based ontology

1. Introduction

Nowadays, using computer technology is the most common way to socialize. People share their special or common multimedia data on youtube, facebook and similar web sites. Besides, everybody has a personal digital library of photos, videos etc. and has experienced the annoyance of looking for a specific video scene inside a huge amount of data without the help of an intelligent multimedia data management system.

Many projects have been developed for the purpose of managing multimedia data with respect to its content. Among these, we can list AceMedia [1], K-Space[2], BilVideo [3], Informedia [4], VideoQ[5]. In this paper, we are concerned with semantic annotation of multimedia data, especially videos. We will summarize the state of the art and then present the difference of our proposed system. In order to manage huge amount of multimedia data, the content must be annotated. The way in which the content is annotated depends on the annotation environment of the multimedia information management system. Although any user-defined annotation is acceptable, it is better if many systems use the same annotation format. In other words, standardizing the metadata of the content is much better than each system using its own defined annotation format. The widely accepted content annotation standard is Multimedia Content Description Standard known as MPEG-7[6]. MPEG-7 is an ISO/IEC standard and developed by MPEG (Moving Picture Experts Group). Furthermore, MPEG-7 uses XML as the language of choice for the textual representation of content description. In MPEG-7, semantically identical metadata can be represented in many different ways due to lack of precise semantics in XML-based syntax. This unfortunately prevents metadata interoperability. In order to overcome the interoperability issues, efforts have been spent to translate MPEG-7 standard into an ontology and to enable its integration with other ontologies through appropriate frameworks, thus enhancing interoperability. There exist four OWL/RDF proposals of MPEG-7. These are Jane Hunter's MPEG-7/ABC ontology [7], Tsinaraki's MPEG-7/Tsinaraki ontology [8], Garcia and Celma's Rhizomik model[9] and Arndt's COMM[10]. In this paper, basics of MPEG-7 ontologies are mentioned and our choice of MPEG-7 ontology is presented. In our work, we use an MPEG-7 ontology on top and wrap the given user-defined ontologies with MPEG-7 ontology, thus building MPEG-7 based ontologies automatically. Prior to wrapping the user-defined ontology, we let the user to select concepts that are going to be used in annotation. On the annotation and querying interface, we let the user to annotate or query the wrapped concepts with their attributes. Our proposed system is an ontological multimedia information management framework due to its modular architecture, ease of integrating with user-defined ontologies naturally and automatic harmonization of MPEG-7 ontology and domain-specific ontologies, which does not include automated or semi-automated annotation but enables integration of any such module. In the paper, these concepts are explained and some user interface screenshots are presented to give a flavour of the usage of the system. The ontological multimedia information framework can be easily used in specific domains naturally. Moreover, the system can easily be modified according to domain-specific requirements due to its modular architecture.

Since our proposed system is based on MPEG-7 ontology, when a mapping between MPEG-7 and another multimedia content description is available, the system can be easily expanded to welcome new annotations. A domain-specific integration of the framework can be easily produced.

The rest of the paper is organized as follows. A brief summary of related projects is given in Section 2, emphasizing the difference between our framework and the existing work. Section 3 reviews MPEG-7 standard and MPEG-7 based ontologies. Our ontological video model is presented in Section 4. Section 5 summarizes the implementation of the proposed multimedia information management system. Section 6 concludes the paper with some comments about future work.

2. Related Work

People want to search and find digital content according to its semantics. In order to achieve this, there should be knowledge about the content. This knowledge comes from the metadata of the content. Metadata can be on different levels of abstraction. On the lowest syntactical level there are basic visual features of content like shape, size, texture, color and movement of a camera or an object in a scene. On a higher level these physical features are interpreted to derive semantic information. This includes taxonomies (e.g. genre), organizational information (e.g. scenes for supporting indexing) and basic descriptions (e.g. identification of objects involved in a scene, roles, etc.). Another type of semantic information is the description of the content as annotations in natural language. As the abstraction level of the metadata increases, the management and querying power of the system increases.

Many projects exist that have been developed on the management of multimedia data with respect to its content [1,2,3,4,5].

AceMedia[1] aims to automate annotation process at all levels and ease content creation, search, access, consumption and re-use.

K-Space [2] focuses on narrowing the semantic gap between content descriptors, which may be computed automatically, and the richness and subjectivity of semantics in high-level human interpretations of audiovisual media.

BilVideo provides an integrated support for queries on spatio-temporal, semantic and low-level features (color, shape, and texture) on video data [3]. BilVideo is an application-independent system. In other words, the system can easily be tailored for the specific

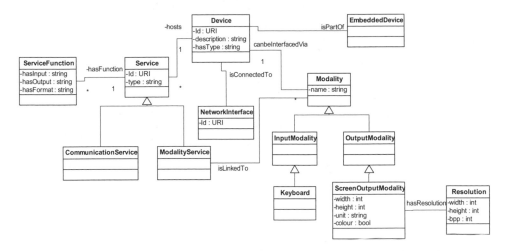

Figure 1: Structure of Domain Ontology

The defined ontology includes the static properties, for instance, the user interface, network interface and other input/output modalities. In addition, the service description concepts are modelled to capture the service behaviour and link the services to the static device modalities. The asserted relationships model the logical relations between the different classes.

The Device class is linked to the Modality, Service and NetworkInterface classes. To model the scenario where a physical device could have independent constituent components, such as a mobile phone with screen, keypad etc., the EmbeddedDevice class inherits all the properties of the Device class and introduces the object property, 'partOf', to identify the link to the parent device. The Modality class is sub-classed into Input and OutputModality, i.e. *InputModality $\subseteq$ Modality* and *OutputModality $\subseteq$ Modality*, with further refinements based on the various types of modalities possible. For instance, the ScreenOutputModality has data type properties specifying its height, width, colour capability and links to the Resolution class for describing the screen resolution in terms of horizontal and vertical resolution in bits per pixel. The Service class has categories for services directly describing devices modalities or those providing other services (e.g. content storage). The ModalityService class thus links to the Modality class. The ServiceFunction is defined in terms of the service input, output and formats to model the service behaviour as a function between input and outputs.

Another ontology that concerns the related domain of service description is the DAML ontology (http://daml.umbc.edu/ontologies/dreggie-ont.owl) which forms part of the DReggie [7] semantic service discovery framework. It describes m-commerce services in terms of their functionality, capability, platform requirements and other attributes. The service component class is the root, with capability and functionality descriptions added as properties. Memory and CPU requirements are considered, though network interfaces are not factored in.

5. Applications

The proposed multimodal ontology forms part of a Personal Assistant Agent (PAA) [8] framework that aims to facilitate context sensitive service provisioning in ubiquitous environments. The technical scenario of the functioning of the framework is presented through a statechart in Figure 2.

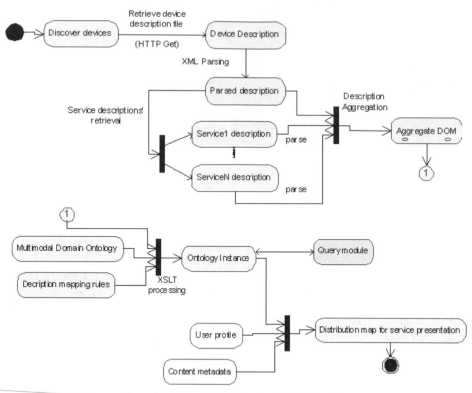

Figure 2: Multimodal Ontology Application StateChart

Multimodal devices in the ambient environment are discovered by a discovery module. In an example use case, the UPnP protocol [9] is used for this step. The descriptions, which consist of device descriptions and hosted software services' descriptions are retrieved by HTTP GET commands. The XML description files are parsed into a DOM (Document Object Model) that converts the XML structure into a tree of nodes in memory and provides interfaces for access and modification. Mapping rules then transform the DOM structure to an OWL ontology instance with reference to the proposed multimodal domain ontology. This is done using XSLT (Extensible Stylesheet Language Transformations). Thus, the ambient environment description based on the developed ontology constitutes the input to a reasoning subsystem that implements a rule based mechanism for matching content metadata and stored user preferences to available device modalities. The output of this reasoning engine shows the best possible modality combination for content presentation to the user.

The ontology formalism also enables semantic querying of the reasoned output. For instance, device capabilities can be queried either by hardware instances (screen availability) or available services (text output), as illustrated by the results shown in [10].

A demonstrator is currently under development for the project [11] of which this work is a part of. This work also fits as an input to adaptation systems [12] developed in this project.

6. Technology Description

The evaluation procedure includes ontology content evaluation as well as a structure-based evaluation that is based on statistics and graph theory. Structural evaluation approximates the ontology structure as a directed acyclic graph, with each node representing a concept and the directed arcs denoting the relationships between them.

The defined metrics analyse the ontology model from different dimensions to provide an evaluation of its structure and alignment to the domain knowledge internal structure. The first defined metric, Property Standard Deviation (PSD), proposed in [13], deals with the distribution of relations amongst the concepts of the ontology. There are two types of properties in ontology: object and datatype property. Since it is the object property that reflects the relations between instances of two classes, it is used to describe the connections in the ontology. Equation (1) depicts the calculation of PSD:

$$PSD = \sqrt{\frac{\sum_{i=1}^{n}(C_i - PE)^2}{n}} \qquad (1)$$

where C_i is the count of the object properties of the ith concept, n is the total number of concepts and PE is the property expectation, given by

$$PE = \frac{\sum_{i=1}^{n} C_i}{n} \qquad (2)$$

Obviously, the higher the PSD, the more uneven the distribution.

The Concept Connectivity (CC) metric gives a measure of the connectivity between the various defined concepts. The ontology can be regarded as an undirected graph $G = \langle V, E \rangle$, with each concept being a vertex in this graph. If a concept has an object property whose value is an instance of another concept, an edge will be drawn between these two concepts. After the whole undirected graph has been created, the number of connectivity branches is calculated.

With the Concept Connectivity metric giving an indication of the width of the ontology, the next two defined metrics consider the height factor. The path-length related metrics, documented in [14], consider only inheritance relationships, such as 'is-a' or 'part-of'. Here, a path is defined as a distinct trace from any given concept to the root. λ_i denotes the longest path length of concept N_i in an ontology of n concepts and is given by

$$\lambda_i = \max(pl_{i,k}), 1 \le k \le p_i \qquad (3)$$

where $pl_{i,k}$ is the set of path lengths for concept N_i.

The max path length of the ontology (Λ) is equal to the longest λ_i; defined by

$$\Lambda = \max(\lambda_i), 1 \le i \le n \qquad (4)$$

$\overline{\Lambda}$, the average path-length metric is calculated using

$$\overline{\Lambda} = \sum_{i=1, j=1}^{n, p_n} pl_{i,j} \Big/ \sum_{i=1}^{n} p_i \qquad (5)$$

These two metrics give an indication of the semantic scope of the ontology by measuring the extension to the most general concept or root.

$\sigma = \Lambda / \overline{\Lambda}$ examines the concept aggregation factor. A σ value of less than 2 means that most concepts surround the root, depicting high concept coherence. A value of more than 2 denotes a loose concept organisation.

7. Results

The evaluation of the domain ontology introduced in this paper has been done both subjectively and with the identified structure-based metrics suite. At a first instance, the defined ontology has been compared with the DReggie ontology, on the basis of domain features captured. This evaluates the ontology content and helps to assess the ontology capability of conveying the given vocabulary's intended meaning. Table 1 shows the results of this subjective evaluation.

Table 1: Subjective evaluation results for multimodal domain ontology

Feature	Multimodal ontology	DReggie ontology
Capability description	√	√
Physical requirements – Service demarcation	√	×
Network interface	√	×
Service formats	√	×
Service cost	×	√
Service properties	√	√
Service inputs and outputs	√	√
Input, output modalities	√	×

The structure-based evaluation focuses on the internal structure of ontology. Table 2 summarises the results of the metrics' (defined in the preceding section) calculation for the two ontologies.

Table 2: Structural evaluation results for multimodal domain ontology

Ontology	PE	PSD	CC	Max path length (Λ)	Avg. path length ($\overline{\Lambda}$)	Concept aggregation (σ)
Multimodal ontology	1.46	0.81	9	3	2.04	1.47
DReggie ontology	1.78	1.42	23	2	1.07	1.87

8. Discussion

As already pointed out in this paper, a multimodal device environment is best described at two different planes: physical hardware description and associated software services interface modelling. To this end, the here discussed ontology models a clear demarcation between these two concepts, while maintaining a comprehensive description of each. It also takes into account the service description requirements outlined in [6]. While the hardware-software decoupling is also apparent in the ontology framework in [4], it suggests separate ontologies for describing devices and services.

This paper, however, proposes that these two concepts should be part of the same ontology. This ensures that the ontology instance populated with real-world data of devices in the ambient environment can be directly input to reasoning subsystems, with all the information being available in one file. Also, this does away with ontology alignment and merging requirements, which would be necessary if the information were to be distributed across different ontologies.

A feature comparison with the complete, publicly available DReggie ontology shows that the here discussed ontology captures the multimodal device domain better. The FIPA standardisation effort for device ontologies is, at a first instance, a frame-based ontology and is aimed at agent communication. From an implementation standpoint of ontology content evaluation, there are important connections between the components used to build the domain ontology (concepts, relations, properties); the knowledge representation used to formalize these components (frames, description logic (DL), first order logic etc.) and the languages used for implementation (with frames, DL in several frames or DL languages). This is so because different KR (knowledge representation) paradigms offer different reasoning mechanisms that can be employed for content evaluation [15]. The proposed ontology is modelled in OWL-DL and thus, implicitly benefits from the DL classifiers to derive concept satisfiability and consistency.

To derive a picture of ontology complexity from its structural organisation, this paper utilises metrics available from current state of the art. These are used to validate the ontology proposed while also comparing it with other published efforts. Moreover, this paper extends the metrics' usability by extending the analysis to interoperability with application logic and domain capture. For instance, this paper analyses how the ontology can perform together with a query application, based on the metric calculations. The related state of the art only theoretically evaluates the ontologies using these metrics [13] or utilises them for ontology evolution tracking [14] and does not relate it to application logic.

From the numbers in table 2, it is apparent that the average relation among concepts is almost similar in both ontologies (PE value comparison). However, our ontology shows the most even distribution of these concepts, as shown from PSD values. The maximum and average path length metrics in unison provide a picture of the ontology depth and by extension, the detail with which concepts are covered. The low value of $\overline{\Lambda}$ (~1) for the DReggie ontology implies that it is essentially a flat structure with most concepts defined very near to the root. Actually, a look at the ontology structure, drawn as a directed acyclic graph, shows that most classes are defined at the same level below the most general concept (owl: Thing) and only 1 concept demonstrates any subsumption relationship. This illustrates that our defined ontology covers the domain in a more detailed manner due to its higher schema depth, while the DReggie ontology depicts general knowledge with a low level of detail. This fact is borne out by the feature evaluation results in table 1. The flat structure of the DReggie ontology is also evident with its large value of CC when compared to its total number of concepts (n); where n=14 for DReggie and n=24 for device ontology. Since both ontologies have σ values less than 2, this means that the concept organization and aggregation is high. A σ value above 2 signifies loose organisation. This also has implication for the intended use of the ontology. Since the low σ value signifies that the concepts tightly surround the root, path traversals can be minimised, i.e. the distance from the most general to the most specific concept is not great. This can help speed up query answering and concept search. Overall, the multimodal domain ontology has a good representation in terms of property and connectivity.

9. Conclusions

The multimodal ontology described in this paper provides a framework for describing devices and services in a formal structure amenable to automated reasoning and effective query procedures. The presented suite of metrics offers an evaluation framework that evaluates ontology models from a plurality of dimensions. An analysis of the identified metrics gives a clear picture of ontology structure and complexity. For instance, the concept aggregation metric can give an indication of output performance when the ontology is plugged into a query mechanism, with higher values translating to longer times to get to any particular concept from the root.

The evaluation figures reveal that the here discussed domain ontology performs well both in terms of property and connectivity properties.

For a more comprehensive evaluation, the other researched device ontologies should be publicly available.

Acknowledgement

The work reported in this paper has formed part of the Ubiquitous Services Core Research Programme of the Virtual Centre of Excellence in Mobile & Personal Communications, Mobile VCE, www.mobilevce.com. This research has been funded by the Industrial Companies who are Members of Mobile VCE, with additional financial support from the UK Government's Technology Strategy Board (previously DTI). Fully detailed technical reports on this research are available to Industrial Members of Mobile VCE.

References

[1]   D. Elenius and M. Ingmarsson, "Ontology-based Service Discovery in P2P Networks," presented at First International Workshop on Peer-to-Peer Knowledge Management (P2PKM), collocated with MobiQuitous 2004, Boston, Massachusetts, 2004.

[2]   A. Gomez-Perez, "Some ideas and examples to evaluate ontologies," in *Proc. 11th Conference on Artificial Intelligence for Applications.* Los Angeles, CA, USA, 1995, pp. 299-305.

[3]   FIPA, "FIPA Device Ontology Specification." Geneva, Switzerland, 2001. [Online]. Available: http://fipa.org.

[4]   A. Bandara, T. Payne, D. d. Roure, and G. Clemo, "An Ontological Framework for Semantic Description of Devices," presented at 3rd International Semantic Web Conference (ISWC), Hiroshima, Japan, 2004.

[5]   N. Kobeissy, M. G. Genet, and D. Zeghlache, "Mapping XML to OWL for seamless information retrieval in context-aware environments," in *Proc. IEEE International Conference on Pervasive Services*, 2007, pp. 361-366.

[6]   O. K. Zein and Y. Kermarrec, "An approach for service description and a flexible way to discover services in distributed systems," in *Proc. International Conference on Information Technology: Coding and Computing (ITCC)*, vol. 1, 2005, pp. 342-347.

[7]   D. Chakraborty, F. Perich, S. Avancha, and A. Joshi, "Dreggie: Semantic Service Discovery for M-commerce Applications," presented at Workshop on Reliable and Secure Applications in Mobile Environment, 20th Symposium on Reliable Distributed Systems, 2001.

[8]   J. Bush, J. Irvine, and J. Dunlop, "Personal Assistant Agent and Content Manager for Ubiquitous Services," presented at International Symposium on Wireless Communication Systems (ISWCS), Valencia, Spain, 2006.

[9]   UPnP Forum, "UPnP™ Device Architecture," December 2003. [Online]. Available: http://www.upnp.org/resources/documents/CleanUPnPDA101-20031202s.pdf.

[10]   S. De and K. Moessner, "Ontology-based Context Inference and Query for Mobile Devices," 19th IEEE International Symposium on Personal, Indoor and Mobile Radio Communications (PIMRC), Cannes, France, September 2008, to be published.

[11]   MVCE, "Ubiquitous Services: Core 4 Research Programme," MobileVCE, [Online]. Available: www.mobilevce.com.

[12]   A. Attou and K. Moessner, "Context-Aware Service Adaptation Management," presented at 18th IEEE International Symposium on Personal, Indoor and Mobile Radio Communications, PIMRC 2007.

[13]   H. Ning and D. Shihan, "Structure-Based Ontology Evaluation," in *Proceedings of the IEEE International Conference on e-Business Engineering* 2006, pp. 132-137.

[14]   Y. Zhe, Z. Dalu, and Y. E. Chuan, "Evaluation Metrics for Ontology Complexity and Evolution Analysis," presented at IEEE International Conference on e-Business Engineering, ICEBE '06, 2006.

[15]   S. Staab, A. Gomez-Perez, W. Daelemana, M. L. Reinberger, and N. F. Noy, "Why evaluate ontology technologies? Because it works!," *Intelligent Systems*, vol. 19, pp. 74-81, 2004.

Section 9.2

Applications

Collaboration and the Knowledge Economy: Issues, Applications, Case Studies
P. Cunningham and M. Cunningham (Eds.)
IOS Press, 2008

Next Generation Modelling: Metamodels As Mediators Between Domain Experts and Ontologies in AsIsKnown

Robert WOITSCH[1], Dimitris KARAGIANNIS[2], Wilfrid UTZ[1]
[1]BOC Asset Management GmbH, Bäckerstraße 5, 1010 Vienna, Austria
Tel: +43-1-5120534, Fax: +43-1-5120534-5,
Email: Robert.Woitsch@boc-eu.com, Wilfrid.Utz@boc-eu.com
[2]University of Vienna, Department of Knowledge Engineering, Brünner Strasse 72, 1210
Vienna, Austria
Tel: +43-1-4277-39581, Fax: +43-1-4277-39584, Email: dk@dke.univie.ac.at

Abstract: This paper presents a Next Generation Modelling approach initially applied in the EU-Project AsIsKnown (FP6-2005-28044) that combines a human-oriented with a document-oriented knowledge modelling approach to define a well-formalised and human-readable knowledge base. Beside traditional ontology management approaches, the meta-modelling approach – applying graphical models – is additionally applied to involve domain experts from different areas when externalising their knowledge. In such a way, graphical meta-models are seen as the mediator between well-formalised ontologies and human-readable graphical meta-models. Through the integration the systems benefit, as the ontology can be partly maintained by domain experts using meta models, and the graphical models get empowered by ontology features such as semantic checks or reasoning.

1. Introduction

Knowledge management is a key for the success of enterprises as according to Lynch [1] 80% of information in enterprises is unstructured and understanding this "hidden" intelligence is the key to improve the interaction with information [2]. The goal of AsIsKnown is creating a common knowledge space for the home textile industry in Europe by enriching knowledge flows between knowledge workers with semantics of the domain and externalise the aforementioned "hidden" knowledge in a well-structure knowledge bases.

The paper focuses on the approach, to use graphical meta models to externalise the "hidden" knowledge out of the head of the domain experts and find mediator mechanism to map this semi-structured knowledge base into an machine interpretable well-structure ontology. In the following the paper distinct between the

- Human-oriented knowledge modelling, which focuses on the externalisation of implicit knowledge from domain experts through the use of graphical meta-models,
- Document-oriented knowledge modelling, which is concerned with formalisation of various input formats to built a well-structured knowledge base using techniques such as Natural Language Processing (NLP) and data/text-mining, and
- Applying meta models as a mediator between these two knowledge bases.

The underlying assumption is that knowledge becomes more important, semantic technology reached a sufficient level of maturity and the collaborative approach summarized in the Web 2.0 phenomenon motivates a collaborative modelling [3], [4].

This paper selected the EC-project AsIsKnown (FP6-2005-28044) [5] to demonstrate the initial step of the Next Generation Modelling in a concrete application scenario. One of the research challenges of AsIsKnown is to support the formalisation of implicit knowledge of domain experts from different areas such as sales representatives, product managers or market trend analyzer and explicit knowledge in form of trend handbooks, system log data, product catalogues and producer databases.

Current techniques of semantic modelling start from a technical point of view, assuming that the knowledge modeller has expertise in formal modelling languages. But in reality domain experts usually do not think in terms of concepts and relations but rather in a language they are familiar with. Therefore the modelling method PROMOTE® (see [6], [7] and [8]) was selected as it provides a graphical modelling language for non-technical end-users to build up a knowledge base. Within the project the human-oriented knowledge base has been implemented by a service called Smart Profiler (SP), whereas the document-oriented knowledge base has been implemented by a service called AsIsKnown Ontology System (AIKOS). Both systems provide a common knowledge base to the other services, which is mediated by a meta-modelling framework. Therefore the Smart Profiler acts as the central repository of meta-data that can be accessed by all AsIsKnown components

In the following section, the paper will briefly present the research challenges of the project and introduce the related work on the problems of end-user driven ontology building and visualisation (section 2). Section 3 deals with the introduction of the graphical meta models by using the PROMOTE® approach. The technical implementation of the approach is dealt with in the subsequent section 4. The paper concludes by providing lessons learned and an outlook on upcoming challenges in the field.

2. The Knowledge Modelling Challenges

2.1 Problem Statement

Semantic Technology has been improved over the last years and has become mature and established in the area known as the Semantic Web. Standards like OWL, a list of free accessible tools like ontology editors and promising features like using inference systems make semantic technology attractive when dealing with knowledge bases. It is therefore well accepted, that there are many applications that can benefit from Semantic Technologies. From an application point of view, however, Semantic Technology comes with two major drawbacks:

1. Although there has been a lot of research in semantic technologies, the tools are more advanced from a technical point of view, requiring experts in order to use them.
2. Finding agreements between domain experts when building and evolving ontologies is difficult and time consuming, as the domain experts do not know how to describe their knowledge and the ontology expert has difficulties to make samples in the domain experts' fields.

In spite of the presence of a number of ontology building methodologies the involvement of the domain expert in the building process is mostly lacking and the visualisation techniques do not consider domain specifics, which hampers the accessibility of ontology modelling by domain experts.

The approach followed within AsIsKnown aims at using domain-specific graphical models as mediator between domain experts and ontologies, based on the assumptions that domain-specific models require less modelling expertise than common ontology specification languages, the models have a formal background as far as they are based on a meta-modelling framework and that meta-models can be transformed into ontology syntax.

Therefore the following goals have been derived:
1. Introduce the concept of meta-model and ontology integration.
2. Provide a modelling environment supporting this approach and enabling collaborative modelling using technologies commonly known as "Web 2.0".

2.2 Research Challenge: Meta-Model and Ontology Integration

One of the conclusions of the WonderWeb market report [9] is that the lack of "visualization" and "multi-modeling paradigm support" is a serious market barrier for semantic technologies.

This conclusion is driving the research challenge of Next Generation Modelling, by involving different roles of knowledge workers using different means of formal knowledge expression. The following two challenges can be identified.

- Multi-modelling paradigm requires research in the field of meta-model mapping, semantic loss and the interpretation of OWL as a meta-model.
- Research is required in the field of graphical representation of domain-specific meta-models – that domain professionals are already familiar with –, as well as concerning these meta-models' relation to the complexity of an ontology.

The goal of the Smart Profiler in AsIsKnown is therefore to represent objects in the language of the domain experts. In the context of AsIsKnown, the sales expert models sales process in a business process notation, the trend analyst models customer profiles in a self-defined notation and the product manager models products and categories in a concept map notation. All three notations are mapped to OWL applying semi-automatic and manual steps.

2.3 Research Challenge: Meta-Model and Ontology Modelling Environment

In traditional ontology development approaches the ontology expert is responsible for the modelling and resolving conflicts. The direct involvement of domain experts in the modelling task enhances this process of ontology development. To enable the direct participation of domain experts the development of a collaborative modelling environment is needed. The technical research challenge of the project is how a system using and extending Web 2.0 technologies can be built. The aim is to use the Web 2.0 principle to enable collaboration, so that domain experts from everywhere can contribute to the ontology building process. The experts can comment on existing models by using a wiki or extend the ontology with new models. The modelling environment also has to consider integrating existing modelling tools ranging from informal, unstructured, text-based to semi-structured and formal ones. The core challenge of the Smart Profiler is hence to apply a Service Oriented approach by providing a range of different modelling services, that use the same meta model core, who acts as a mediator between all modelling services.

2.4 Related Work

The idea to involve domain experts into the building process of an ontology is based on the observation that currently there is a high dependency on few ontology experts and a time and cost-intensive period of ontology generation.

According to Uschold and King [10], Grüninger and Fox [11] as well as Noy and McGuinnes [12] there are top-down, bottom-up or inside-out approaches. The graphical meta-model as an end-user interface extends the top-down approach in providing additional methods for end-user knowledge acquisition. According to the Methontology Methodology described in Fernández, Fómez-Pérez and Juristo [13] the knowledge acquisition phase – using expert interviews – will benefit in providing a graphical representation in the language of the expert. According to Swartout, Ramesh, Knight and Russ [14] describing the SENSUS methodology, the natural language processing will be supported by an end-user driven grouping of concepts via the graphical modelling and additionally providing relations to concepts by applying natural language processing in the textual description of the graphical objects.

In this sense the above-introduced concept is not seen as a complementary approach to ontology building, but as an extension of existing approaches to simplify the knowledge acquisition of end-users.

Current graphical representations of ontologies like OWLViz, Jambalaya, OntoViz, OntoVista, TGViz, Kaon, OL Graphs, RDF Gravity, Vizigator, VisioOWL visualise concepts, instances and relations to support the ontology engineer, but do not support a domain-specific graphical representation.

In this sense the above introduced concept of the Smart Profiler is seen as a new form of a domain specific graphical representation of an ontology using PROMOTE®.

3. Externalising Domain Expert Knowledge

As this paper focuses more on the innovative part in introducing a graphical meta modelling method for ontology generation, the traditional ontology building process applied in AsIsKnown is not explained in this paper. For more information on this and a brief overview on the state of the art in ontology building please refer to [15], [16].

The model based PROMOTE® approach uses graphics to support domain experts in expressing their knowledge. The method has been developed in the EC project PROMOTE (1999-11658) [17] and since then continuously improved in commercial projects [18] and in EU-Projects [19]. PROMOTE® builds on a meta-model as conceptual framework [20]. The meta-modelling approach has already been successfully applied in ADONIS [21] and provides flexibility by allowing customisation. In this sense PROMOTE® is seen as an instance of a meta2-model such as MOF implementing the formal specification of the PROMOTE® meta-model [22]. For a report on the state of the art in meta modelling please refer to the meta model literature survey by Karagiannis [22].

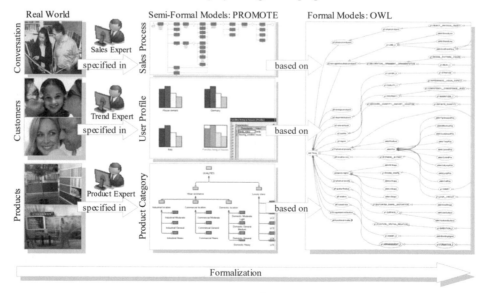

Figure 1: PROMOTE® model stack

Figure 1 depicts how PROMOTE® supports the involvement of domain experts in modelling. According to the identified sub-domains: the sales conversation between customer and sales person can be modelled via process flows and business rules, the customer profile can be modelled via profile models referring to characteristics and preferences, the product categories can be modelled using concept maps. PROMOTE® is used to implement domain specific graphical representations of the ontology to involve domain experts more tightly in the ontology building process. A basis for the model is built by the AsIsKnown ontology that contains the relevant concepts from the home textiles domain. The ontology is used for the validation of the models concerning terminology and semantic and supports correct modelling. Moreover it enhances search and discovery of products by offering inference functionality.

PROMOTE® is a graphical modelling language to model knowledge and therefore has modelling concepts that have a specific meaning e.g. the process sequence can be used to describe the sales process, the profile objects are used to describe user groups and user behaviour and concept maps specify structures (see Figure 1). The provided modelling concepts are defined in the modelling languages. The transformation from PROMOTE® towards OWL is based on transformation rules for the modelling languages. Each modelling concept gets a mapping to the corresponding ontology construct. These mapping rules are manually specified and automatically applied when storing a model. By storing the model, an XML representation of the model is generated and the defined model concepts are parsed. Each identified model concept is then transformed by previously defined mapping rules that map the PROMOTE® XML representation to an OWL representation. Therefore each PROMOTE® model – e.g. a sales process - can be transformed into a valid OWL representation, imported into the ontology base, and manually integrated into the existing ontology. In that case PROMOTE® is an additional source of knowledge that externalises the implicit domain expertise.

Once the sales process is incorporated into the ontology, the ontology can be used to align the modelling of other sales processes, by using checking mechanisms, which control the syntactic and semantic correctness of the model. The next model can therefore be checked against the ontology, to ensure a "common sense ontology" compliant modelling of the graphical models.

In case terms are not properly used, the ontology provides suggestions by following hierarchies, synonyms or by applying searches. The domain expert is involved in the evolution of the ontology, as when unsatisfied suggestions are provided, there is the possibility to insist on new terms. For the communication between the domain expert and the ontology expert, an annotated Wiki has been implemented, which enables a discussion on the terms used in the models. Based on the negotiation between the ontology expert and the domain expert about the graphical models, the Wiki-entries and the meaning of the terms, the transformation rules from PROMOTE® towards the ontology are adapted.

Currently the challenge of the semantic loss is solved by the manual integration process. The support of this manual integration is topic of ongoing research of the project partners.

4. The Project Implementation

From a technical perspective the Smart Profiler deals with the implementation of the Modelling Environment described in section 2.3. The Smart Profiler offers a web-based Knowledge Management System, providing a modelling environment that supports the usage of graphical models as a user interface for ontologies. This allows building and maintenance of ontologies by starting from a domain expert's point of view.

The tools provided by the Smart Profiler support the acquisition and design of knowledge using models, the analysis of knowledge models, their distribution across the organisation, as well as their transformation into different formats including OWL.

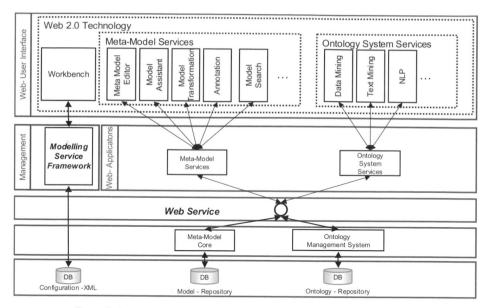

Figure 2: Integration of the Meta Modelling and Ontology Services in AsIsKnown

Figure 2 gives an overview on the implementation of the system. The Smart Profiler consists of a set of services organized in an SOA. In the figure they are referred to as "Meta-Model Services". The other part of the figure shows the AIKOS' part of the AsIsKnown system. The AIKOS' services are refered to as "Ontology System Services" in the figure.

The figure shows the main building blocks of the modelling environment. Starting from the bottom, the persistance layer is presented showing the repositories for ontology- and model data. The ontology repository stores ontologies in OWL format, while the model repository is a relational database for the storage of PROMOTE models. The former is accessible through the Meta-Model Core, while the latter is accessible through an OMS as depicted in the layer above. Both offer a Web-Service interface to their clients.

The layer above contains two types of services. On the left side Meta-Model Services are shown, providing functionality such as meta model editors, model viewer, model search engines, model import/export and transformation services, support for acquisition, analysis or simulation, as well as other services supporting the externalisation, capturing and maintanance of domain experts' knowledge. The ontology system's services support the capturing of knowledge from non-human sources such as documents and provide data mining, text mining, NLP and similar functionality.

At the top the user interface layer is shown, consisting of a web-based workbench integrating the different services.

Model exchange between Smart Profiler and AIKOS: There are two ways of performing this task. The simpler one is on a one to one basis, where graphically modelled ontology models are transformed into OWL syntax.

The more challenging integration step is to exchange semi-formal models, like sale processes or user profiles. For this purpose the Smart Profiler offers a rule based translation mechanism transforming models into ontology concepts as mentioned in the chapter before.

Lexical Translation: The AsIsKnown system supports the translation of input and outputs to the system into different natural languages. This translation is performed using the lexica of the AIKOS, which map lists of natural language terms to the concepts in the domain ontology. The Smart Profiler uses this functionality in order to be able to understand requests, or to provide output in different natural languages. Having this mechanism in place the lexical translation is fully applicable for the product description, product categories and user profiles.

Term Checking: To align the terminology of the domain experts with the ontology each piece of information provided from outside the system needs translation towards the AsIsKnown language. To guarantee the correct translation into the AsIsKnown language, the Smart Profiler checks whether a term is AsIsKnown-compliant or not. The "Model Assistant" checks the correct usage of terms in models and provides reports as well as functionality suggesting terms in case terms are used which are not yet part of the language, including querying of the lexica and browsing in the ontology.

Semantic Checking: The difference between an expert modeller and a beginner in modelling is that the expert knows about modelling guidelines - procedures how to use the available concepts and how to apply the modelling language. In AsIsKnown this knowledge is made explicit in the ontology. A concrete model can be checked against the modelling guidelines on a semantic level. This service uses an inference engine within the ontology to compare models with the modelling guidelines and provides reports and suggestions for error handling. This mechanism helps improving the quality of the knowledge base.

Annotation: In order to enable annotations between the Smart Profiler and the ontology, there is an external annotation repository that stores the references from PROMOTE® models to OWL concepts. Applying the Service Oriented Approach, each of the modelling services can be accessed through a Web-Service interface. In case changes in the annotations occur each Web-Service is informed and is itself responsible for further actions.

Semantic Search: Currently the status of the integration in the project is the usage of discovery within AIKOS. The Smart Profiler offers a search interface to enable the search for modelling constructs, which covers the majority of search requests to the user. In case the concepts of meta-models are insufficient to answer the users request, the request is translated term by term into OWL and passed towards the ontology. An inference engine, searches term by term the ontology (e.g. parent-, children-, sibling-concepts) and sends back the results to the Smart Profiler.

The above-explained mechanisms are seen as the initial implementation of a Next Generation Modelling Framework that needs further investigation and implementation in future EU-projects.

5. Conclusion and Lessons Learned

This paper showed how domain experts from different areas are involved in the creation of a common knowledge base by externalizing and formalizing their knowledge using PROMOTE® and its meta-modelling approach. Through the use of graphical models domain experts directly take the role of knowledge modellers. The AIKOS ontology system allows the management of formalized and thus machine-interpretable models in form of ontologies.

Through the integration of these two knowledge spaces the solution further benefits, as ontology building is user friendly and can be partly maintained by domain experts. The Smart Profiler also benefits from the integration, as the quality of the models is increased by terminology and semantic checks and a translation service is provided. With the help of the ontology also new extensions like semantic search based on annotations are provided.

The use case in AsIsKnown showed that it is beneficiary to use meta-models as mediators between domain experts and ontologies, thus enabling Next Generation Modelling. The goal is that meta-moddels further converges with ontologies leading to a hybrid system based formulates the upcoming research challenges for Next Generation Modelling.

References

[1]   R. Cencion, Intelligent Content in FP7. Intelligent Content and Semantics, Information days, 12-13 December 2007, Luxembourg, ftp://ftp.cordis.europa.eu/pub/ist/docs/kct/intelligentcontent-fp7-ict_en.pdf

[2]   Fraunhofer-Wissensmanagement Community, Semantische Technologien in der betrieblichen An-wendung. www.wissensmanagement-community.de, 2006

[3]   T. O'Reilly, What Is Web 2.0, http://www.oreillynet.com/pub/a/oreilly/tim/news/2005/09/30/

[4]   J. Cardoso, et al, The Semantic Web Vision: Where Are We? In: IEEE Intelligent systems 2007

[5]   AsIsKnown project, http://www.asisknown.org

[6]   R. Woitsch, D. Karagiannis, Process-oriented Knowledge Management Systems based on KM-Services: The PROMOTE® approach. In: Proceedings of the PAKM (Practical Aspects of Knowledge) 2002, Vienna

[7]   R. Woitsch, P. Höfferer, D. Karagiannis, A Meta-Service Framework for Knowledge Management.

[8]   R. Woitsch, D. Karagiannis, H.G. Fill, V. Blazevic, Semantic Based Knowledge Flow System in European Home Textile: A Process Oriented Approach with PROMOTE, IKnow 07

[9]   WonderWeb Project; Deliverable D25; http://wonderweb.man.ac.uk/deliverables/documents/D25.pdf, access: 07.05.2007

[10]   M. Uschold, M. King, Towards a Methodology for Building Ontologies. In: Proceedings of IJCAI95's Workshop on Basic Ontological Issues in Knowledge Sharing, 1995

[11]   M. Grüninger, M. Fox, The Role of Competency Questions in Enterprise Engineering. IFIP WG 5.7 Workshop on Benchmarking. Theory and Practice. Trondheim, Norway.

[12]   N. Noy, D. McGuinness, Ontology Development 101: A Guide to Creating Your First Ontology. Knowledge Systems Laboratory. http://protege.stanford.edu/publications/ontology_development/

[13]   M. Fernández-López, Overview of Methodologies for Building Ontologies. Proceedings of IJCAI99's Workshop on Ontologies and Problem Solving Methods: Lessons Learned and Future Trends, 1999

[14]   W. Swartout, P. Ramesh, K. Knight, T. Russ, Toward Distributed Use of Large-Scale Ontologies. In: Symposium on Ontological Engineering of AAAI. Stanford (California), 1997.

[15]   AsIsKnown project deliverable 9: Ontology Management Systems - http://www.asisknown.org/fileadmin/user_upload/Appendix3_D09_ReportManagementOntologies.pdf

[16]   AsIsKnown project deliverable 10: Software Tool for Engineering Common Sense Ontology - http://www.asisknown.org/fileadmin/user_upload/D10_IPP-BAS.pdf

[17]   D. Karagiannis, R. Telesko, The EU-Project PROMOTE: A Process-Oriented Approach for Knowledge Management. In: PAKM 2000, Third Int. Conf. on Practical Aspects of Knowledge Management, 2000

[18]   K. Mak, Der Einsatz des prozessorientierten Wissensmanagementwerkzeuges PROMOTE® in der Zentraldokumentation der Landesverteidigungsakademie. Landesverteidigungsakademie Wien, 2005

[19]   R. Woitsch, W. Utz, Roadmap to Akogrimo Convergence: A Sample of Process Oriented Knowledge Management with PROMOTE®. BPOKI'06 at I-KNOW '06, Graz, Austria, 2006

[20]   R. Telesko, D. Karagiannis, R. Woitsch, Knowledge management concepts and tools: The PROMOTE project. In: Gronau N., Wissensmanagement - Systeme - Anwendungen - Technologien, Shaker Verlag, Aachen 2001: Proceedings of the 2nd Oldenburger Forum Wissensmanagement, 2001

[21]   S. Junginger, H. Kühn, R. Strobl, D. Karagiannis, Ein Geschäftsprozessmanagement-Werkzeug der nächsten Generation - ADONIS. In: WIRTSCHAFTSINFORMATIK, Vol. 42, Nr. 5, Vieweg-Verlag, 2000

[22]   D. Karagiannis, P. Höfferer: Metamodels in action: An overview. ICSOFT (1) 2006

[23]   D. Karagiannis, H. Kühn, Metamodelling Platforms. In Proceedings of the 3rd International Conference EC-Web 2002 – Dexa 2002, LNCS 2455, Springer-Verlag, Aix-en-Provence, France, 2002

Collaboration and the Knowledge Economy: Issues, Applications, Case Studies
P. Cunningham and M. Cunningham (Eds.)
IOS Press, 2008

STASIS - Creating an Eclipse Based Semantic Mapping Platform

Sven ABELS, Stuart CAMPBELL, Hamzeh Ghazi Ahmad SHEIKHHASAN
TIE Nederland BV, Antareslaan 22-24, 2132 JE Hoofddorp, The Netherlands
Tel: +31-20-658-90 00, Fax: +31-20-658-90 01, Email: sven.abels@tieGlobal.com,
stuart.campbell@tieGlobal.com, hamzeh.sheikhhasan@tieGlobal.com

Abstract: Within this paper the STASIS approach for creating a comprehensive application suite is introduced which allows enterprises to simplify the mapping process between data schemas based on semantics as opposed to syntax. This paper initially introduces the current schema mapping problem and outlines the limitations of existing solutions. The STASIS approach is then presented and contrasted with other semantic projects.

Keywords: Semantic Mapping, Schema Mapping, GMF, EMF, OWL, Eclipse

1. Introduction and Problem Description

In the last decade, a significant number of different e-Business related systems have been developed such as catalogue management tools or online shopping systems. Whenever two or more companies need to collaborate, or even applications within the same company, they invariably need to exchange information electronically and integrate the results in each system. In an ideal scenario, this information exchange and integration is performed in an automatic way allowing business partners to interoperate information seamlessly. However, because of the large number of diverse information systems the data format (syntax) of each exchange (message) usually differs from company to company, or sometimes even within the same company if more than one software product is used. The situation is similar to the Tower of Babel involving many different people that want to work together on a specific task without understanding each other.

This makes it a very challenging to exchange information in an interoperable way. Interoperability in this context means "the ability of two or more systems or components to exchange information and to use the information that has been exchanged" [4]. In those cases, users either have to agree on a common standard or they have to individually map the data format of one business partner to the data format of the other one.

The STASIS project (www.stasis-project.net), funded by the European Commission's FP6 programme [5] is addressing this problem. It provides a set of semantic methods for easing the mapping process between XML, Flatfile, EDI and Database schemas and without relying on any precedence in the ontologies used – "competitive ontologies".

It is addressing a simple key question, which is important for almost all European companies:

"If I have information in my format, and it is integrated into my systems, I want to put minimal effort into mapping this into any format (standardised or not) to do electronic business with another party" [5].

2. Existing Solutions

Mapping processes between schemas today focus on a rather syntactical approach. Tools such as Altova XMLSpy[i] or TIE Integrator[ii] are used to successively map different attributes of two different schemas to each other. Those attributes are in most cases either mapped in a 1:1 relationship or using various connectors such as Methlets (see [7] for explanations and details) for creating complex mappings.

Figure 1 shows an example, mapping the syntactical elements of a source XML Schema file (XSD) to a destination format.

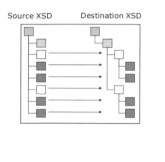

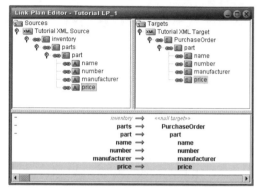

Figure 1: Syntactical Mapping   Figure 2: Link Plan creation with TIE Integrator

This approach has been pretty successful in the past and it allows fast mapping creation if the schema is not too complicated. However, restricting the mapping creation to a syntactical mapping process has some disadvantages. These include:

- The mappings must be performed by a technical person who has schema and syntax knowledge whereas what is wanted is the mapping of business information by business people. Of course comfortable GUIs such as displayed in Figure 2 may ease this task but nevertheless the process is rather technical involving skilled people that know both schemas.
- An in-depth knowledge of both the source and destination schemas is required in advance. New schemas need to be studied in detail before mapping. This is a very expensive step and cannot be avoided
- Mappings are often hard to understand and error-prone because humans normally think in terms of the actual semantics instead of the syntax – e.g. companies usually want to map two addresses instead of mapping Element [ELT4711] to [ELT0815]
- Mappings typically cannot be reused, and must be created from scratch when mapping to a new schema
- Concepts such as inheritance and logical constraints are not supported

3. STASIS Idea and Approach

The STASIS project aims to address many of the problems outlined above and also both introduce the concept of market-drive semantics – "Competitive Semantics" – and to promote a neutral standard mapping format which can be taken advantage of existing transformation tools and technologies.

3.1 Using Semantic Entities

Instead of focussing on syntactical mappings, STASIS concentrates on identifying semantic entities and mapping those semantic pieces. For example, two elements [ELT1] and [ELT2] may be grouped into one logical entity called "Address" which is mapped to a well-defined concept of an Address. After identifying those logical elements and linking the syntactical elements to it, users may concentrate on using those semantic elements for creating their mapping. This allows users to connect elements with identical meanings instead of having to focus on the syntactical elements of two schemas.

3.2   Based on Ontologies

This process is based on ontologies used to define and link semantic entities within a schema. Those ontologies have been defined by the STASIS project team in order to describe semantic elements and their relationship. The link between a semantic element and the syntactical structure of the original schema is expressed in those ontologies. Unlike approaches such as foam [8] and GLUE [2] STASIS does not intend to create an automatic Ontology Mapping, nor does it rely on semantic mapping approaches as analysed in [1]. Instead, it is the goal of STASIS to provide an easy to use GUI, allowing users to identify semantic elements in an easy way. This means that the STASIS project uses ontologies (expressed in the Web Ontology Language OWL) in the background in order to define semantic relationships but users will not notice this nor do they need to know what ontologies are.

3.3   Using STASIS

In order to use STASIS, organisations need to import (or design) their original schema files and identify semantic entries. The overall process involves the following steps:
1. Import of original schema data.
   For example, this can be an XML schema specification (XSD) or a database schema (SQL). The first prototype implementation supports both. Other formats such as EDI are planned for the next versions of the STASIS prototype implementation. All imported data is managed in a neutral format, called SNF (STASIS Neutral Format)
2. Identifying semantic entities
   After importing all data into the neutral format, users need to mark specific elements from their schema file as being semantic entities. For example, two elements [cFirstName] and [cLastName] may be grouped into one logical entity called "Customer Name" as discussed earlier in this section. Each of those semantic entities is called an SSE (STASIS Semantic Entity).
3. Linking to generic concepts (optional)
   Once the semantic entities have been identified, users may decide to link their semantic entities to an overall concept that is provided by STASIS. For example, users may link their semantic entity that they have called "Customer Name" to the global concept "Person Name". Linking own semantic entities to those global concepts allows STASIS to derive some of the mappings automatically. However, their usage is completely optional and may be skipped by the user if preferred.

Figure 3 gives a graphical overview about the process described above.

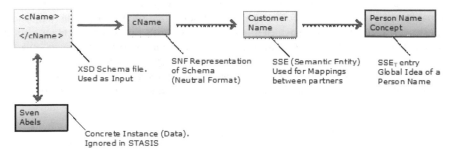

Figure 3: Importing data and preparing it for STASIS

The usage of STASIS is a straightforward process. At first, users have to import schema definitions into the SNF format. Afterwards they need to identify semantic elements and finally they may optionally link those semantic entities to generic concepts.

Once this has been performed, STASIS allows users to map their semantic entities to those of their business partners by simply connecting their Semantic Entities to the Semantic Entries of the business partner as displayed in Figure 4. This allows users to create mappings in a more natural way by considering the meaning of elements rather than their syntactical structure. Some elements might even be connected to a common third party or a chain of them. STASIS automatically detects if such a third party exists. This process will be described within the following section of this paper.

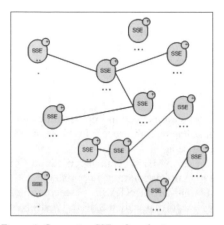

Figure 4: Connecting SSEs of two business partners.

4. Data Distribution and Sharing

All mappings that have been created by STASIS, as well as all semantic entities, are managed in a distributed registry and repository network called the SRRN (see [6]). The SRRN is a cutting-edge Peer-to-Peer network based on WebServices that allows the storage and retrieval of semantic elements in the OWL format. The SRRN has been developed within two European Research projects as described in [6]. It utilises the semantic query language SparQL, [9].

The SRRN is used within the STASIS project in order to allow sharing information among different STASIS users. This gives STASIS another significant advantage over traditional mapping creation tools as STASIS may reuse all mappings. It allows STASIS to make mapping suggestions by reusing mapping information from earlier semantic links. - For example, imagine two companies A and B that would like to map their business schemas in order to exchange information. Let's assume that both have conducted business with company C already in the past. In this situation, STASIS can map the semantic entities of A and B automatically because it knows about their mapping to a common schema from company C. This will become increasingly beneficial as more companies begin to use STASIS and turns into a significant mass of mappings. In addition to this, links of semantic entities to global concepts - as described in the last section – can be used to generate additional links automatically.

5. Technology: From OWL to EMF and Back Again

In order to realize STASIS, the consortium has selected the Eclipse Framework as a base for creating the Graphical User Interface of the mapping editor. Eclipse provides much in-built functionality that may be reused and will therefore reduce the development time in most scenarios.

A definition of what a semantic entity is, and on how a schema is represented in STASIS, is expressed in the STASIS Common Data Model (CDM), which itself is expressed in the ontology format OWL. This logical data model is the base for the graphical editor of STASIS. In order to create this editor, STASIS is reusing two other core concepts of Eclipse: EMF and GMF.

- EMF (Eclipse Modelling Framework, see [3]) is used to create a definition of the CDM model. This is done by describing the CDM model in eCore, which is used by the EMF framework as a base for expressing models (see [3]).
- GMF [3] is a framework that allows creating a graphical editor that is based on EMF.

The overall process is illustrated in Figure 5 and is explained in detail in [10]:

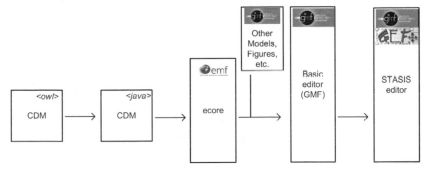

Figure 5: Editor Creation (refer to [10] for details)

As shown in the figure, the overall CDM definition is exported into annotated java classes using the Protégé[iii] EMF export methods. In the next step, the Eclipse functionality is used to derive the model file (eCore) as well as to derive a basic version of the graphical editor (GMF), which is the base for the STASIS schema editor component.

Using OWL parser libraries allows us to continue using OWL based ontologies with the STASIS editor as displayed in Figure 6.

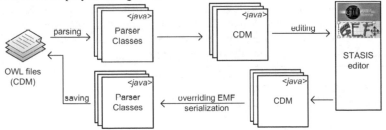

Figure 6: Roundtrip (refer to [10] for details)

6. Prototype Implementation and Results

STASIS has been realized as a prototype already and first results are available allowing the team to start with a formal evaluation process in real world scenarios. Figure 7 shows a screenshot of the first beta version.

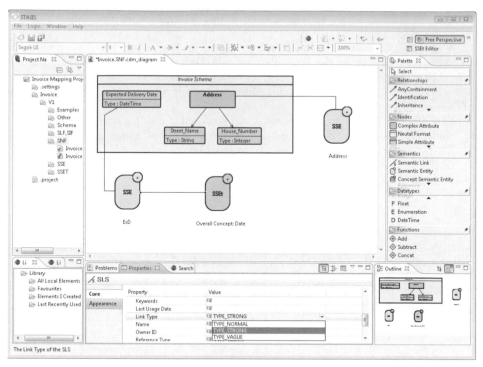

Figure 7: A screenshot of the current prototype

The screenshot shows the main modelling area of STASIS containing a very simple schema on the upper left called "Invoice Schema". This schema contains two elements: (i) a DateTime element called "Expected Delivery Date" and an "Address" which is consisting of two sub-elements called "Street_Name" (String) and "House_Number" (integer). In addition to this, the diagram shows two semantic elements (SSEs) called "Address" and "ExD" and one global concept called "Date".

Users may also use a set of functions to connect elements. For example, Figure 8 shows how the two schema elements "Street_Name" and "House_Number" are connected to an SSE "Address" using a concatenation function. STASIS provides additional dialogs to defile those functions and to define the order to elements.

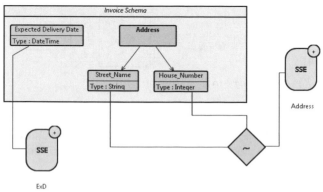

Figure 8: A complex link between schema elements to a semantic element

7. Conclusions and Summary Recommendations

The STASIS project and its implementation is a 'work in progress' and is due to be completed in 2009. In the current state, the main editors have been already implemented as well as most of the modelling functionality. However, there is a still a huge potential for extending STASIS.

Features that will be integrated in the next phase include a query environment allowing users to use simple dialogs for querying the SRRN network for existing elements. In addition to this, STASIS will be able to export mappings into XSLT in the next prototype implementations.

In parallel to the implementation, the STASIS prototype is evaluated in two real-world scenarios from the Automotive and the Furniture domain. The results will be used as an input for the third prototype, which is scheduled for the end of 2008. This will ensure that STASIS is applicable in reality and it will ensure that STASIS is usable by non-experts.

References

[1]   Abels, S.; Haak, L.; Hahn, A.: Identification of Common Methods Used for Ontology Integration Tasks. Proceedings of the first international ACM workshop on Interoperability of Heterogeneous Information Systems, ACM, 2005.
[2]   Doan, A. et al: Ontology matching: A machine learning approach. In Handbook on Ontologies in Information Systems, Springer-Verlag, 2004.
[3]   The Eclipse Project, http://www.eclipse.org, 2008
[4]   Institute of Electrical and Electronics Engineers: IEEE Standard Computer Dictionary: A Compilation of IEEE Standard Computer Glossaries, 1990.
[5]   STASIS project, SofTware for Ambient Semantic Interoperable Services, http://www.stasis-project.net, 2008
[6]   SEAMLESS project, Small Enterprises Accessing the Electronic Market of the Enlarged Europe by a Smart Service Infrastructure, http://www.seamless-eu.org, 2008
[7]   TIE Integrator, An easy-to-use system that can transform and apply business rules to data in any format, passing through enterprise systems around the clock, Product Brochure, http://www.tieglobal.com, 2004
[8]   Ehrig, M., Sure, Y. Ontology Mapping by Axioms. In: Proceedings of the 3rd Conference Professional Knowledge Management. Springer (Heidelberg), 2005.
[9]   SPARQL Query Language for RDF, W3C Recommendation 15 January 2008, http://www.w3.org/TR/rdf-sparql-query/, 2008
[10] Abels, S.; Sheikhhasan, H.; Cranner, P.: Simplifying e-Business Collaboration by providing a Semantic Mapping Platform. In: Proceedings of the 4th International Conference "Interoperability for Enterprise Software and Applications" (I-ESA 2008), Workshop on "Semantic Interoperability: A Practical Approach", Germany, 2008

---

[i] http://www.altova.com
[ii] http://www.tieglobal.com
[iii] http://protege.stanford.edu

Section 9.3

Case Studies

Collaboration and the Knowledge Economy: Issues, Applications, Case Studies
P. Cunningham and M. Cunningham (Eds.)
IOS Press, 2008

E-Business Ontology for European Construction SMEs Collaboration

Sonia BILBAO, Valentín SÁNCHEZ, Iñaki ANGULO
Robotiker-Tecnalia, Parque Tecnológico de Bizkaia, Edificio 202
E-48170 Zamudio Bizkaia, Spain
Tel: +34 94 600 22 66, Fax: +34 94 600 22 99
Email: sbilbao@robotiker.es, vsanchez@robotiker.es, iangulo@robotiker.es

Abstract: This paper provides a description of the e-NVISION ontology, an e-Business ontology for European Construction SMEs Collaboration. The ontology described in this paper covers the construction domain from an e-Business perspective. It does not try to replace existing construction ontologies and should not be considered as the unique ontology for the construction sector. The goal has been to develop a construction e-Business ontology covering the concepts and relations needed to implement four core e-Business scenarios for the construction sector: e-Tendering (participation in calls for tenders), e-Procurement (discovering, evaluating and finally selecting a list of providers of a certain schedule of deliveries), e-Site (coordination at the construction site) and e-Quality (documents management and organising all the information according to the work specification and in compliance with the standards). Research was based on the most relevant currently available national and international knowledge sources, i.e. taxonomies, ontologies and construction models. This ontology re-uses where possible existing classification systems in order to develop a compatible model that may contribute to standards.

Keywords: E-Business, Ontologies, Collaborative environments, Construction SMEs

1. Introduction

One of the main barriers to collaboration is the difficulty to exchange information in a common vocabulary and with the precise meaning intended. This is even more important when exchanging information in electronic format, as is the case of e-Business transactions, or in a domain where great number of actors are involved, as in the construction sector.

In a construction project, different companies and people have to work together: main constructor, subcontractors, designers, investors, material providers, suppliers of machinery, etc. All these actors need to share and reuse knowledge in computational form not only when making business-to-business transactions but also in their internal daily processes.

To this end, it is of great significance to have an e-Business ontology that defines the basic concepts in the construction and e-Business domains and the relations among them.

Regarding e-Business, although many definitions of this term exist, we will use the definition that appears in the European e-Business Report (2006/07 edition). According to this report the term "e-Business" will be used "in the broad sense, relating both to external and to company-internal processes. This includes external communication and transaction functions, but also ICT-supported flows of information within the company, for example, between departments and subsidiaries".

2. Objectives

This paper provides a description of an e-Business ontology for European Construction SMEs Collaboration [1, 2, 3]. This ontology is the result of part of the work developed in the e-NVISION project, "A New Vision for the participation of European SMEs in the future e-Business scenario", a STREP project supported by the European Commission under the 6th Framework Programme in the action line "Strengthening the Integration of the ICT research effort in an Enlarged Europe".

It is not the intention of the authors to consider this e-Business ontology as "THE CONSTRUCTION ONTOLOGY". The goal has been to develop a construction e-Business ontology covering the concepts and relations needed to implement four core e-Business scenarios for the construction sector [4, 5]:

- The e-Tendering scenario tries to enhance SMEs participation in calls for tenders (e.g. as a group of SMEs or as a Virtual Enterprise) on equal footing compared to bigger tenderers, reducing the work needed to analyse paper propositions, in an open and transparent world-wide electronic market, with mechanisms to look for partners internationally, and supported by trust and quality external organizations.
- The e-Site scenario will improve the companies' coordination in the construction time, reporting any change or incident at the construction site in an automatic way to the interested partners so that they can react as soon as possible.
- The e-Procurement scenario looks for potential providers both internally and externally thanks to an effective and rational supplier selection model that allows discovering, evaluating and finally selecting the list of providers of a certain schedule of deliveries.
- The e-Quality system is centred in two main issues: the documents and their management, and organising all the information and data to perform the tasks according to the work specification and in compliance with the standards.

3. Methodology

Ontologies facilitate communication as they provide the terms, their meaning, their relations and constraints that model a certain domain. Due to the fact that ontologies and the related resources are used with different purposes according to their areas of application, it is normal that models that represent the same domain, in this case the construction sector, differ from one and other.

The area of application of the domain varies the perspective of the ontology that determines what aspects of a domain are described. Besides, the extent of the model, i.e. the things at the periphery of the domain that are included or not included, and the granularity of the model, i.e. the level of detail in which a domain is described, also depend on the future use of the ontology. We cannot say that one ontology is better or more appropriate than another for a certain domain without considering its future use.

The opinion supported by the authors of the CEN publication CWA 15142 "European eConstruction Ontology (EeO)" is that a unique ontology for the construction sector will never exist.

Up to now, different construction ontologies have been defined for different purposes. For instance, the bcBuildingDefinitions taxonomy developed by the eConstruct project (www.bcxml.org) was mainly used to support the creation, publication and use of electronic catalogues of construction products - the electronic commerce, to some extent. The e-COGNOS Ontology (www.e-cognos.org) has been developed with one single purpose: support the adoption of Knowledge Management practices in the BC sector. However, there is no single construction ontology that gathers all the concepts that are needed to implement e-Business scenarios in the construction sector.

In accordance to this opinion, the construction e-Business ontology described in this paper does not try to replace existing construction ontologies and should not be considered as the unique ontology for the construction sector. The e-NVISION ontology covers the construction domain from a e-Business perspective. The extent and the granularity of the model have been determined by the detail needed for four core construction e-Business scenarios: e-Tendering, e-Procurement, e-Site and e-Quality.

4. Related national and international knowledge sources

In order to develop the e-Business ontology for European Construction SMEs Collaboration or e-NVISION ontology, research was based on the most relevant currently available national and international knowledge sources, i.e. taxonomies, ontologies and construction models. This ontology reuses where possible existing classification systems in order to develop a compatible model that may contribute to standards.

Firstly, several construction projects and initiatives targeting semantic resources development were analysed. The most relevant for e-NVISION were:

- The e-COGNOS Ontology which supports the adoption of Knowledge Management practices in the BC sector;
- ISO 12006 "Building construction", an international standard for organising the information about construction works. It defines a schema for a taxonomy model.
- The IFC (Industry Foundation Classes) Model which has been developed to enable the exchange and sharing of Building Information Models.

Secondly, the main construction classification systems, taxonomies and vocabularies were looked into: The British Standard 6100 (BS6100), BARBi (Norway), Lexicon (Netherlands), the French Standard Dictionary for Construction (SDC), Uniclass (UK) and OmniClass (North America); the European Common Procurement Vocabulary (CPV) establishes a single classification system for public procurement aimed at standardizing the references used by contracting authorities and entities to describe the subject of procurement contracts.

The main drawback of all these glossaries and classification systems (except for CPV) is that they are focused on the construction terms used in specific countries. Therefore, they are not accepted across Europe.

Finally, research was focused on existing ontologies implemented for other sectors that cover any of the concepts of the e-Business scenarios developed in e-NVISION:

- The Enterprise Ontology (EO) [6] is a collection of terms and definitions relevant to business enterprises, but it needs to be extended to include more detail specific to the construction sector. The e-NVISION ontology has a narrower focus but introduces new concepts such as Virtual Enterprise and groups items not only as products but distinguishes among products, materials, equipment, services and software.
- The Tendering Ontology [7] tries to define the ontological structures needed for a tendering process independent from the sector where it will be used, including the tendering invitation structure (TIS), the sellers' profile structure (SPS) and the buyers' structure. The e-NVISION ontology covers the scope of the tendering ontology with concepts like Tender, Company, Person, Role, etc and allows having groups of SMEs (i.e. Virtual Enterprise) bidding for a tender and not only a company on its own.
- The Scheduling Ontology. Nowadays, SMEs have to use different and incompatible scheduling systems depending on the construction project. The aim is to provide a standardized electronic description of all the scheduling information that will allow interchanging scheduling information among project partners no matter the internal scheduling system they use. Two models have been consulted for the development of the scheduling ontology: Task Ontology for scheduling applications [8] and CMU

Scheduling Ontology [9]. The e-NVISION ontology adds the concept Production Activity Task to define the minimum element/entity of the schedule affected by an unexpected event during construction works. Its hasAsignedActor property is used to store the affected actors (companies or individuals) that have to be notified about the event.

5. Ontology Description

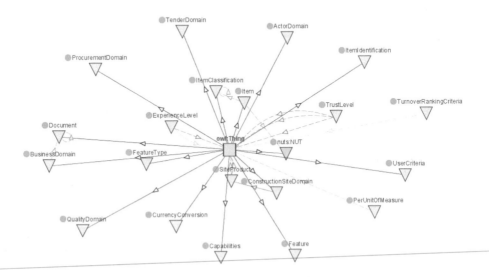

Figure 1: Main concepts of the e-Business ontology for European Construction SMEs Collaboration.

The e-Business ontology for European Construction SMEs Collaboration has been implemented using OWL (Web Ontology Language). The main concepts and relations modelled in this ontology have been grouped by several categories: Actor Domain, Business Domain, Item, Item Classification and User Criteria.

Besides, a domain has been defined to include the specific concepts needed for each of the e-Business scenarios: Tender Domain, Procurement Domain, Construction Site Domain and Quality Domain. This way, the ontology can be easily extended as new e-Business scenarios are considered.

5.1   Actor Domain

The Actor Domain concept groups the classes that contain information related to business actors, i.e., someone or something, outside the business that interacts with the business. This actor can be either a person or a company or a group of enterprises (virtual enterprise).

The Person class represents an employee of a company or independent skilled people (e.g. a company may prefer to use services of an independent designer or advisor on something). Each individual is related to a full name, contact information, certain skills, formal position taken by the person in the company (i.e. manager, administrator, etc.), role (i.e. general designer, subcontractor, supplier, site manager, supervisor, etc.) and responsibilities that the person can have in the company or in the construction works (i.e. responsible for tender analysis, for quality issues, for contracts, for suppliers, etc.).

The Company concept stores among others the trading and registered name of the company, its VAT number, number of employees, contact information, address, the items (product, service or equipment) demanded or offered by the company, its experience and trust information.

The Virtual Enterprise is linked to different companies that can play the role of partner or subcontractor or general contractor. There are different alternatives when an SME participates and bids for a tender. According to these alternatives, the business processes can be divided into four categories:

1. From the point of view of an SME being the General Contractor
2. From the point of view of an SME participating as a partner in the Virtual Enterprise
3. From the point of view of an SME participating as a subcontractor
4. From the point of view of an SME participating in a Virtual Enterprise where there are partners and subcontractors

5.2   Business Domain

Business Domain represents a structured information schema definition used in business transactions. It is equivalent to the Document used in UBL. However, in the e-NVISION ontology the concept Document represents a physical file as this is the term used by the end users of the ontology, that is, the construction sector workers

The main subclasses are: tender, project, request for quotation, quotation, order and schedule of deliveries.

The aim of the tender concept is to provide a standardized description of all the information related with a tender that will enable automatic tender processing of the type of tender, works to be performed, skills required, documentation to be provided, etc. This way, SMEs will reduce time and human resources when analysing tender calls.

The project class represents the proposal presented by a company or virtual enterprise when bidding for a contract in response to a tender call.

The request for quotation is sent by a buyer company to different supplier companies for the purchase of equipment, products, materials or/and machinery. In response, the supplier company sends a quotation to the buyer company. If accepted, the buyer company will send an order to the supplier company.

A schedule of deliveries consists of a list of products, materials, machinery and equipment identified by a standard classification system.

5.3   Item

Item groups the objects: equipment, product, material, service and software. It conceptualizes the possible offerings of a specific company to the external world.

Equipment is any tool, device or machine needed to accomplish a task or activity of the construction works.

By product we mean anything tangible (physical) that can be offered to a market that might satisfy a want or need (Pure Product in Kotler et al., 2006). A product is similar to goods, physical objects that are available in the marketplace.

By service we mean anything intangible (non-physical or non-material) that can be offered to a market that might satisfy a want or need. For example, plumbing, electricity, consultancy, etc.

Material is any simple product used in the process of construction (sand, brick, etc.).

Software represents any software, which is currently used on the site or related to the process of an activity on the site.

5.4   Item Classification

Item Classification groups the different classifications of construction products, materials, services, equipment and machinery. One item classification included in the ontology is CPV (Common Procurement Vocabulary), which establishes a single classification system for public procurement aimed at standardising the references used by contracting authorities and entities to describe the subject of procurement contracts. As CPV is officially used in Europe, it cannot be "not accepted" by the industry because of its application in TED and public tendering and it is related to other standardised (but old-tech) classification of products, buildings, etc.

With regard to construction classification systems, e-NVISION ontology's main advantage is that it is flexible enough to use any classification system. Moreover, it does not restrict the number of classification systems to use.

The Item Classification class can have as many subclasses as existing construction classification systems. This concept has the object property equivalentTo that allows mapping of equivalent items between two classification systems. For example, the item with code 28814000-1 of the Common Procurement Vocabulary classification is described as "concrete" and is equivalent to the item in Uniclass classification with code P22.

In current systems, if Company A registers as able to provide item 28814000-1 of CPV but a tender searches for companies that can provide item P22 of Uniclass classification, then Company A will never be notified of this business opportunity. This obliges SMEs to register and have knowledge of the different construction classification systems. The e-NVISION system does not have this limitation and increases the business opportunities of SMEs as it is flexible enough to use any classification system.

5.5   User Criteria

User Criteria groups the different criteria that a user can define when making decisions in e-Business scenarios, e.g. selecting the most suitable companies or suppliers to work with, analysing quotations, etc.

There are 2 types of criteria: exclusion criteria and ranking criteria. By exclusion criteria we mean all criteria that must be fulfilled in order to provide a valid configuration. Ranking criteria are criteria that can be used to rank the different possible configurations.

5.6   Tender Domain

Tender Domain groups the terms related with the participation in calls for tenders. The two main classes are TenderConfiguratorResult and TenderConfiguratorResultSet.

TenderConfiguratorResult represents each of the results of the tender configurator. It stores a CPV code, a skilled company for this CPV Code, and a ranking position set for this couple (this information is calculated only if a ranking criteria has been entered).

TenderConfiguratorResultSet represents a set of possible configurations of virtual enterprises that can bid for a given tender. The set of results are instances of TenderConfiguratorResult.

5.7   Procurement Domain

Procurement Domain groups the classes related with the e-Procurement scenario. It includes among others:

- Delivery conditions (address where items should/will be delivered, delivery period or time, company responsible for the delivery of items)
- List of items requested by the buyer company in the Request for Quotation with their quantity and description
- Payment conditions (payment deadline, type of payment e.g. bank transfer, cash, checks or credit card, the way of payment e.g. paid after completed fulfillment, paid after every step of fulfillment or part paid in advance rest after delivery of items)
- Price (money amount plus currency e.g. 300 euros)

- Pricing policy (per item e.g. price for 1 brick, per package e.g. price for 1 sack of gypsum, per unit of measure e.g. price for 1 liter of paint, result of negotiation if the price set for the item depends on negotiation.

5.8 Construction Site Domain

Construction Site Domain provides a common category for concepts related to the e-Site scenario. It includes among others:

- Event related classes. The Event concept describes any problem or event happening on a construction site during construction work stage. It can be of 4 kinds: actor event, resource event, task event or a document event. Each event has a time stamp that describes the date and time when the event occurred and it is related with a target which originated the event. At the same time, the events have a status and a level of importance.
- Action ("activity" to be performed by specific actors to solve the problem with its description, identifier, status, date, deadline, companies to notify, etc.)
- environment or the context of the site
- Production activity task represents each of the tasks to be performed in the site. They are defined in the master schedule.

5.9 Quality Domain

Quality Domain provides a common category for concepts related to quality aspects. The two main classes are certificates and quality inspections.

A certificate certifies the quality of a product, a material, an organism or a person. The certificate concept includes information about the type of certificate (CE mark, ISO, etc), its name and identifier, the organization that issued the certificate, the date when it was issued, the date when it expires, etc.

Quality inspections represent the inspections that have to be carried out in certain phases of the construction for the purpose of determining if a work or product is complying with regulations and with the client requirements. This class includes information about the characteristic to control, the frequency and equipment needed to perform the inspection control, the person or company responsible, identifier, date, result of the inspection, etc.

6. Conclusions

It is a fact that the future business scenario will be global, dynamic, open and collaborative. That is why there is the need for exchanging information in a common vocabulary and with the intended precise meaning. Although ontologies have this main motivation, we have come to the conclusion that in order to define a useful ontology, it should be defined specifically for a certain domain and considering its future use.

Up to now, there was no single construction ontology that gathered all the concepts needed to implement e-Business scenarios in the construction sector. For this reason, the e-Business ontology described in this paper fills this gap and provides construction companies with the necessary vocabulary for making business-to-business transactions and for exchanging information in their internal daily processes. The ontology covers the concepts and relations needed to implement four core e-Business scenarios for the construction sector, i.e. e-Tendering, e-Procurement, e-Site and e-Quality, but it can be easily extended as new e-Business scenarios are considered. Besides, it re-uses where possible existing classification systems in order to develop a compatible model that may contribute to standards.

The e-Business ontology will be distributed under an open-source license approved by the Open Source Initiative (OSI: http://opensource.org) in order to facilitate its adoption. Furthermore, the e-NVISION e-Business ontology sustainability approach is based on looking for support and promotion from external organizations, including the European Construction Technological Platform (ECTP), National Construction Platforms of the countries involved in the project and Construction Associations involved in the project. The e-NVISION project has been included among the list of some major recent projects related to the ECTP SRA Implementation Action Plan [10]. The ECTP considers that e-NVISION has synergies especially with Items H6 (Collaboration support) and H8 (ICT enabled business models). Therefore, it is the intention of the project consortium to follow the research line in the framework of the ECTP SRA in order to improve, refine and validate the ontology.

Acknowledgements

e-NVISION project No. IST-028067, "A New Vision for the participation of European SMEs in the future e-Business scenario", a STREP project partially supported by the European Commission under the 6th Framework Programme in the action line "Strengthening the Integration of the ICT research effort in an Enlarged Europe". The consortium is composed by LABEIN, SOFTEC, ASEFAVE, CSTB, BBS-SLAMA, EUROPARAMA, HRONO, KTU, ITERIJA, ASM, K-PSI, ATUTOR, PROCHEM, ZRMK, CCS, NEOSYS (http://www.e-nvision.org).

This paper reflects the authors' view and the Commission is not liable for any use that may be made of the information contained therein.

References

[1]   e-NVISION project, IST-028067, e-Business ontology for European Construction SMEs Collaboration, "http://www.e-nvision.org/ontologies/envision.owl"
[2]   e-NVISION project, IST-028067, D4.1, "e-Business Context Ontologies", February 2008.
[3]   e-NVISION project, IST-028067, D5.1, "Internal Integration Ontologies Definition", February 2008
[4]   S. Bilbao, V. Sánchez, N. Peña, J. A. López, I. Angulo, "The Future e-Business Scenarios of European Construction SMEs", e-Challenges 2007, Expanding the Knowledge Economy: Issues, Applications, Case Studies, Paul Cunningham and Miriam Cunningham (Eds), IOS Press, 2007, ISBN: 1-58603-801-4 (pages 1104-1111)
[5]   I. Angulo, E. García, N.Peña, V. Sánchez, "E-nvisioning the participation of European construction SMEs in a future e-Business scenario", ECPPM-2006, e-Business and e-work in Architecture, Engineering and Construction, Valencia-Spain, September 2006.
[6]   M. Uschold, M. King, S. Moralee, and Y. Zorgios, "The enterprise ontology", The Knowledge Engineering Review, 13 (Special Issue on Putting Ontologies to Use), 1998.
[7]   A. Kayed, R. M. Colomb, "Conceptual Structures for Tendering Ontology", Revised Papers from the PRICAI 2000 Workshop Reader, Four Workshops held at PRICAI 2000 on Advances in Artificial Intelligence, p.135-146, August 28-September 01, 2000.
[8]   D. Rajpathak, E. Motta, and R. Roy, "A Generic Task Ontology for Scheduling Applications", in Proceedings of the International Conference on Artificial Intelligence'2001 (IC-AI'2001), Nevada, Las Vegas, USA, 2001.
[9]   S. F. Smith and M. A. Becker. "An Ontology for Constructing Scheduling Systems", in Working Notes from 1997 AAAI Spring Symposium on Ontological Engineering, Stanford, CA, March 1997.
[10] European Construction Technology Platform (ECTP), "Strategic Research Agenda for the European Construction Sector - Implementation Action Plan", July 20th, 2007

Collaboration and the Knowledge Economy: Issues, Applications, Case Studies
P. Cunningham and M. Cunningham (Eds.)
IOS Press, 2008

Personal Knowledge Management with the Social Semantic Desktop

Niki PAPAILIOU[1], Costas CHRISTIDIS[1], Dimitris APOSTOLOU[2], Gregoris MENTZAS[1],
Rosa GUDJONSDOTTIR[3]

[1]*National Technical University of Athens, Iroon Polytechniou 9 Zografou Athens, 157 80
Greece, Email: nikipa@mail.ntua.gr, gmentzas@mail.ntua.gr*
[2]*University of Piraeus, Karaoli & Dimitriou St. 80 Piraeus Greece 185 34
Email: dapost@unipi.gr*
[2]*KTH – Royal Institute of Technology, Lindstedtsvägen 6, SE-100 44 Stockholm, Sweden
Email: rosag@kth.se*

Abstract: A large number of tools haves recently emerged supporting personal knowledge management. Semantic technologies play an important role in the development of such tools because they allow for advanced organisation, annotation, navigation and search capabilities. In this paper we present SPONGE (Semantic Personal Ontology-based Gadget), a software tool that supports the management of all relevant information in the personal workspace of knowledge workers via cross-media and cross-application linking and browsing of information items based on standard semantic web data structures, together with an intrusive metadata generation support. In SPONGE, we aim to provide a light-weight gadget for easy organisation and access to desktop information plus seamless access to Internet information by means of linking to popular Web search engines or other remote resources.

Keywords: knowledge management

1. Introduction

The discipline of knowledge management addresses four levels of knowledge management: individual, team, organizational and inter-organizational [12]. However, the main focus of research as well as of commercial projects up to now has been the organizational level, which has been analysed from several points of view, mainly the strategic, process, technology and organisational ones [5], [14]. More recently, various attempts have been made to delve into the team and personal levels.

At the personal level, the phrase "personal information management" was first used in the 1980s [9] in the midst of popular excitement over the potential of the personal computer to greatly enhance the human ability to process and manage information. Today, personal information management is meant to support activities such as acquisition, organization, maintenance and retrieval of information captured, used and applied by individuals [18].

A large number of tools has recently emerged supporting personal (e.g. [17], [15], [4]) knowledge management. A knowledge worker is typically using a variety of such tools, often switching between different tools when moving from one assignment to another. This has created the need for novel means to enable users to seamlessly manage more than one personal information management activities. Semantic technologies play an important role in the development of such tools [3], [10].

In this paper we present SPONGE (Semantic Personal Ontology-based Gadget), a software tool that aims to support personal information management. In particular, SPONGE supports users finding, retrieving and annotating desktop resources. The paper is organised as follows: At first we discuss related work and our research motivation. We then present the SPONGE architecture -- SPONGE uses and extends a number of Social Semantic Desktop components developed within the Nepomuk project (see http://nepomuk.semanticdesktop.org). Afterwards, we illustrate the use of SPONGE within a typical scenario of a consulting company. The last section presents our conclusions and areas of further work

2. Related Work and Research Motivation

In recent years the number of ways to keep and manage personal information has increased considerably, in line with the overall increase in the number of devices, technologies, and applications on which knowledge workers rely. The attendant fragmentation of personal information increases the probability of keeping something in the wrong place or form and forgetting that something was ever seen, heard, or read in the first place [11]. Knowledge workers keep information in many different formats, applications, devices and systems. They sometimes keep the same piece of information in several formats to be sure they can get back to it again later and to remind themselves to do so.

Definitions of personal information and knowledge management revolve around a set of core issues: managing and supporting personal knowledge and information so that it is accessible, meaningful and valuable to the individual; maintaining networks, contacts and communities; and exploiting personal capital.

To support individuals better manage their personal knowledge, a wide variety of tools have emerged. Examples of such tools are GNOME-PIM, Gnowsis, Haystack, IRIS Semantic Desktop, KDE, MyLifeBits, etc. Metadata and the application of ontologies in KM tools are important topics affecting the development of personal knowledge management tools. Metadata are used to characterise information; as such they provide means to organize information and make it possible for machines to automatically process and interpret information. Moreover, semantic architectures and the application of ontologies in information systems in the area of KM facilitate the integration of heterogeneous information items within the corporate memory [2], [13]. Nevertheless, ontology-based applications are often associated with high set-up and maintenance costs and with complicated user interfaces that are not suitable for regular users.

Our motivation in this paper is to develop a usable ontology-based personal knowledge management tool that helps typical knowledge workers to overcome some of the above-mentioned problems. We focus on a recent research direction related to the emergence of the Social Semantic Desktop [7], [16]. The Social Semantic Desktop aims to support the management of all relevant information in the personal workspace of knowledge workers via cross-media and cross-application linking and browsing of information items based on standard semantic web data structures, together with un-intrusive metadata generation support. In SPONGE we aim to provide a light-weight gadget for easy organisation and access to desktop information plus seamless access to Internet information by means of linking to popular Web search engines or other remote resources.

3. Research Methodology

3.1. The Application Area and Research Approach

Our work focuses on professional business services (PBS) firms, i.e. firms that provide business services which are based on the application of highly specialized knowledge and expertise such as legal or consulting services [6]. Being knowledge intensive organizations, PBS firms employ professionals that can be characterized as typical examples of knowledge workers. Examples of such firms are law, investment banking, advertising, market research. An   example   of   a   professional   business   services   firm   is   TMI   (see http://www.tmiworld.com/), an international management consultancy. TMI is operating through a network of local partners in 40 countries. It offers solutions through training, consulting, and tools, for individuals, teams and organizations, aiming to transform organisational culture.

In order to understand user needs and requirements, we conducted user research at TMI using ethnographic methods such as contextual observations and interviews. From our study we extracted requirements about typical processes and we created personas [1], [8] as a means to encapsulate user needs. Although personas are fictitious, they are based on the knowledge of real users and therefore identify users' behaviour patterns, motivation, expectations, goals, skills, attitudes and environment. Using these typical processes and personas we developed a number of use cases representing the knowledge creation and sharing work processes within TMI. One of these use cases and persona will later be used to illustrate the developed system functionality. Moreover, based on the elicited requirements we developed a computer-based high-fidelity mock-up, i.e. a partially functioning software prototype that provided typical PKM functionalities and had a User Interface that was similar to the ones of pertinent tools, such as Gnowsis and Haystack (Figure 1).

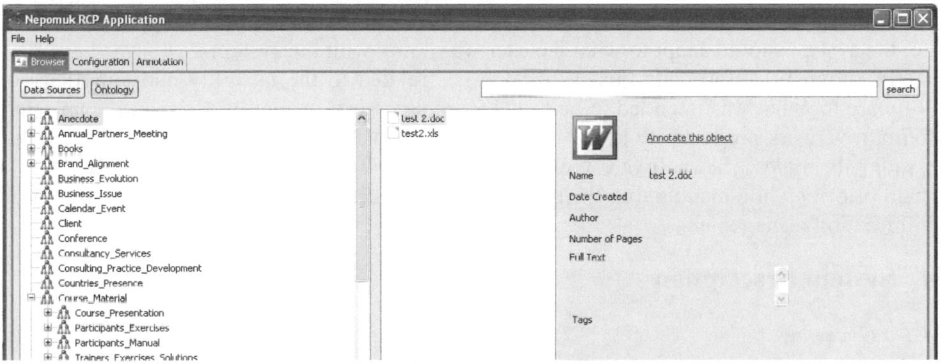

Figure 1: Mock-up used in user research

The high-fidelity mock-up was evaluated by TMI employees in three different office locations; Athens (Greece), Redditch (UK) and Haslev (Denmark). We chose to perform the user research in the informants' work context since it gives an in-depth understanding of their work situation and how the envisaged software fits into their daily work. The evaluation session consisted of a pre-interview, a task phase following pre-defined scripts and a post-interview. The sessions had one moderator and one or more persons observing. The evaluations were videotaped for further analysis. We evaluated the prototype with eleven participants, six men and five women. The medium age of the participants was 42 and it varied from 21 to 64 years old. The informants were both senior and administrative personnel. We had informants working as purchase ledgers, project managers and project support. We also had participants working as trainers, consultants, IT directors, partners and program developers.

3.2. Findings

All informants, when they understood how the mock-up worked, really liked that they were able to search for relevant material from their desktops. They appreciated the fact that they were able to search and collect relevant material, independent of original application and format. User feedback confirmed that the mock-up offered desirable functionalities for supporting management of all relevant information in the personal workspace of knowledge workers. Nevertheless, informants generally felt that the prototype was cumbersome to use because they had to click many times to get to a finished task. Another problem with the prototype was the terminology (both of system labels and ontology terms) because it was not adapted to the target audience. Informants did not understand terms such as 'tag cloud', 'resources', 'wiki', etc. Iinformants also had trouble using the search field of the prototype as it was not easily distinguishable from less important features. Moreover, informants did not understand how to refine the search results as e.g., they did not understand the choice provided to refine search results by selecting classes from the ontology. They also felt that there was too many refine choices.

When informants searched for TMI employees in the mock-up they seemed to be confused as to why they had to search for people in a different way than when they searched for documents. Searching for people should become consistent with searching for documents. There were also issues related to the graphic form and layout of the mock-up as they found the interface to be too grey and with no clear identity. The graphic form is considered vital to the success of the system because the experience during the usage of the system is almost as important as the usability. TMI employees spend a lot of working hours on making their client presentations and other material look attractive and the systems they use should therefore be the same. Informants also commented that there were fields that were empty and not used to execute their scripts. Fields should appear only when needed, i.e. the system should adapt to what the user was doing with the system.

In summary, informants raised many issues related to the usability and simplicity of software tool that was intended to be used by regular users, in a daily basis, and in an effort to improve work productivity in knowledge-intensive tasks. Based on the evaluation results, a radically re-designed software tool was developed, having simplicity and usability as a main priority while maintaining the essential functionalities and benefits of ontology-based information management.

4. System Description

4.1 Overview

SPONGE is a personal information management system that provides advanced search, browse and annotation capabilities based on semantic technologies. SPONGE allows users to search for information resources using free-natural text querying. Resources containing content or metadata that match exactly the query keywords as well as content or metadata that are semantically similar are retrieved. Users are able to search resources either from one specific area/category, such as documents, projects, departments, experts, etc., or from all areas/categories.

Moreover, SPONGE provides users with the ability to browse resources based on semantics. Users are able to navigate through available resources by exploiting relationships between different resources. Different types of resources are shown with different icons. For a selected resource, the system displays resource-specific information, such as metadata, tags, place in the ontology and resource content preview. For example, if a person included in the persons' list of the system is selected, the system provides information, such as his/her profile, his/her documents or other items shared in the system and contact data (email, telephone, address).

Users are able to annotate manually the selected resource. They can add new tags and related items from the ontology while the system automatically restricts the possible options. Metadata are modelled in an ontology that represents the user's conceptualization of his/her domain. This allows a more fine-grained desktop resource classification than the one provided by some operating systems that only allow one file to exist in exactly one folder.

4.2   Technical architecture

SPONGE is a desktop client application that extends the core Social Semantic Desktop services. The Social Semantic Desktop is a software framework comprising a set of interoperable components including:

- The User Context Service component which aims to support the observation of and reasoning about a user's current work context.
- The Task Management component which aims to provide functionalities such as personal task modelling, scheduling, trigger and control, task delegation, task model reuse and retrieval.
- The Personal Information Management Ontology (PIMO) & Metadata Alignment component which aims to host personal ontologies and implement metadata alignment methods.
- The RDF-Store component that is used to store all crawled content and associated metadata in RDF.
- The Distributed Index component that allows users to search across the public spaces of other users' desktops and download the requested document.
- The Local Index component which allows full-text and semantics-based search in the personal desktop.
- The Data Wrapper component which extracts and queries full-text content and metadata from various information systems (file systems, web sites, mail boxes, etc.) and file formats (documents, images, etc.).

The aforementioned components are integrated on a service-oriented architecture and standard communication technologies (Figure 2). The architecture includes a Service Registry, which allows registering, un-registering, and discovery of available services. Moreover, the architecture is based on ontologies to support the use of semantic web technologies.

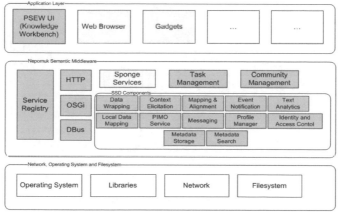

Figure 2: System architecture

PSEW (P2P Semantic Eclipse Workbench) is an effort to integrate the universe of SSD components in a single application with a single user interface. It is built on top of the Eclipse RCP 3.3 and consists of several independent views and editors that allow the user to manage the personal information and its semantic relationships. In this, the usage of Eclipse plug-ins is promoted, thus following the underlying OSGi architecture. The resulting software is an Eclipse Rich Client Platform Application that provides access to available functionalities. In this way PSEW provides a central place to browse, query, view, and edit resources and their metadata.

SPONGE, the focus of this paper, is designed as a combination of a small gadget (a window taking up limited user space) and the user's preferred web browser. The gadget is preferred for user actions where a small part of screen area is required, such as entering a few words, while the web browser is used for presenting more information, for instance the results of a semantic search. The gadget is implemented using Microsoft Visual Studio.NET in an effort to create a simple to install and use application while also keeping a consistent look and feel throughout the user's windows desktop. It can be implemented in other platforms with minimal effort, since the services are provided in a language independent interface. The web pages use open source DOJO JavaScript framework for the presentation of the results and AJAX for asynchronous transfer of data. This interface is integrated using Jetty web server in the PSEW environment, providing functionality to desktop applications through simple xml-rpc.

5. Walkthrough

In order to understand how SPONGE can facilitate a TMI employee to perform his/her daily work we discuss a typical scenario in which the persona of Alistair impersonates a Sales Manager. In a typical situation, Alistair has to prepare a sales meeting for an automotive client. He has to design a solution and write a proposal for the client taking into consideration the clients requirements.

At first, Alistair has to find out TMI experts being able to help him for the sales meeting preparation. Further, Alistair has to find out all proposals and standard products developed by TMI, in order to review the relevant to the case existing TMI offerings. In order to search about TMI experts and relevant existing TMI offerings Alistair enters queries in the SPONGE query interface in free text (free text search). Area A of Figure 3 shows the SPONGE query interface.

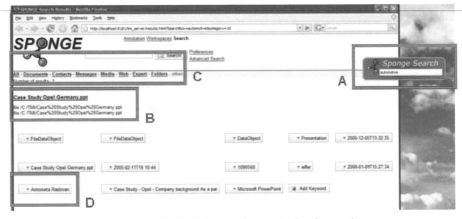

Figure 3: SPONGE Graphical User Interface for search

Results are retrieved in a web page (Area B of Figure 3). Among the retrieved results, Alistair identifies some that seem to be relevant. Alistair is not interested in a particular type of content, so he keeps the 'All' selection on (Area C of Figure 3). In order to clarify if a specific retrieved resource is useful for his work, Alistair selects it. The system provides information about the selected resource (metadata), such as author (Area D of Figure 3).

Metadata have been extracted when the resources were crawled. Metadata are modelled in an ontology that represents the user's conceptualization of his domain. Nevertheless, Alistair may want to alter some metadata or to provide additional ones. Figure 4 realizes the annotation interface.

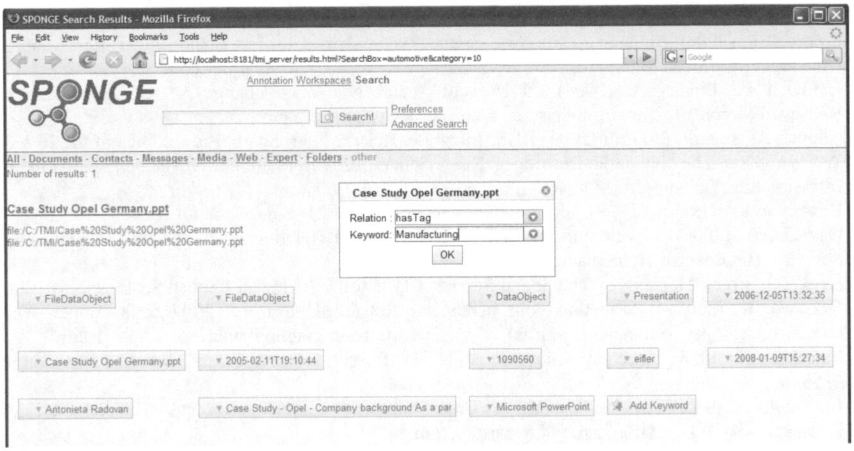

Figure 4: SPONGE Graphical User Interface for annotate

After finding relevant desktop resources, Alistair decides to look for relevant experts. He therefore selects the 'Expert' link in Area C of Figure 3. In addition, he searches for information about the client industrial sector on the Web. Based on the selected information, Alistair is now able to proceed in designing the solution and writing the proposal for his client.

6. Conclusions and Summary Recommendations

The rapid prototyping approach coupled with early user research revealed user needs and issues in an early development phase. Our research revealed a number of important usability issues in ontology-based PKM systems, such as the appropriateness of the terminology used, the degree of integration with desktop activities and the clarity of choices and features offered to the users that exploit the underlying semantic information. To address these issues, a radically re-designed software tool was developed, having simplicity and usability as a main priority while maintaining the essential functionalities and benefits of ontology-based information management. Further evaluation will follow to assess the impact of the improvements on the productivity of the users' daily PKM activities.

Our future plans include extending SPONGE with the ability to access remote desktops in a peer-to-peer topology and with collaborative features which will in turn give users the possibility to create workspaces supporting the accomplishment of their tasks. The idea behind workspaces is to provide a placeholder for storing, organising and sharing resources needed for the accomplishment of personal and collaborative tasks and to organise work-related tasks. This way, users will use SPONGE not only for easy organisation and access to desktop and Internet information but also for seamless access to semantically organised group resources. The planed extensions aim to facilitate wider and easier involvement of knowledge workers in project teams, easier reach to colleagues and experts for advice and information, and persistency of shared knowledge.

Acknowledgement

Research reported in this paper has been partially financed by the European Commission in the Information Society Technologies (IST) project Nepomuk.

References

[1]   Calabria T. (2004) "An introduction to personas and how to create them", Retrieved February 2, 2006 from Step Two Designs PTY LTD Web site:

http://www.steptwo.com.au/papers/kmc_personas/index.html

[2]   Caldwell F. (2006). Managing Philosophies and Risks when Knowledge and information Management Converge. Retrieved March 14, 2006 from Gartner Web site: www.gartner.com

[3]   Caldwell F., Linden A. (2004). "PKN and Social Networks Change Knowledge Management", Retrieved March 10, 2006 from Gartner Web site: www.gartner.com

[4]   Cheyer, A., J. Park, R. Giuli (2006) IRIS: Integrate. Relate. Infer. Share, Proceedings of the ISWC 2005 Workshop on The Semantic Desktop - Next Generation Information Management & Collaboration Infrastructure. Galway, Ireland, November 6, 2005

[5]   Davenport and Prusak (1998). Working Knowledge, Harvard Business School Press.

[6]   Dawson, R. (2000). Developing Knowledge-Based Client Relationships, The Future of Professional Services, Butterworth-Heinemann.

[7]   Decker S., Frank M. (2004). "The Social Semantic Desktop", Technical Report, September 10, 2006

[8]   Goodwin K. (2007). "Perfecting your personas", Retrieved April 16, 2007 from cooper Web site: http://www.cooper.com/insights/journal_of_design/articles/perfecting_your_ personas_1.html

[9]   Lansdale, M. (1988). "The psychology of personal information management", Applied Ergonomics, 19, 1, 55–66.

[10]   Linden A. (2005). "Semantic Web Drives Data Management, Automation and Knowledge Discovery", Retrieved March 14, 2006 from: www.gartner.com

[11]   C. C. Marshall and W. Jones (2006). Keeping Encountered Information, Communications of the ACM, January 2006, 66-67.

[12]   Mentzas, G., Apostolou, D, Abecker, A., Young, R, (2002). Knowledge Asset Management, Springer 2002

[13]   Mika P. (2006). Social Networks and the Semantic Web: The Next Challenge. In Staab S. (2006). Social Networks Applied. IEEE Intelligent Systems, January/February 2006, 80-93.

[14]   Nonaka and Takeuchi (1995). The Knowledge-Creating Company: How Japanese Companies Create the Dynamics of Innovation, Oxford Univ. Press.

[15]   Quan, D., D. Huynh, and D. Karger (2003) Haystack: A Platform for Authoring End User Semantic Web Applications, International Semantic Web Conference, 2003 – Springer.

[16]   Sauermann L., Bernardi A., Dengel A. (2005). "Overview and Outlook on the Semantic Desktop", Procedings of the 1st Workshop on the Semantic Desktop at the ISWC 2005 Conference.

[17]   Sauermann, L. S Schwarz (2004) Introducing the Gnowsis Semantic Desktop, Proceedings of the International Semantic Web Conference, 2004, Springer.

[18]   Teevan J., Jones W., Bederson B. B. (2006). "Personal Information Management", Communications of the ACM, January 2006, 40-43.

Section 10

Technology Enhanced Learning and ICT Skills

Section 10.1

Applications

Collaboration and the Knowledge Economy: Issues, Applications, Case Studies
P. Cunningham and M. Cunningham (Eds.)
IOS Press, 2008

MODA: A Micro Adaptive Intelligent Learning System for Distance Education

Fatma Cemile SERÇE[1], Ferda NUR ALPASLAN[2]

[1]Department of Information Systems Engineering, Atılım University
P.O. Box 06836 , İncek Gölbaşı, Ankara, Turkey, E-mail: cemileserce@gmail.com
[2]Department of Computer Engineering, Middle East Technical University, 06531 Ankara,
Turkey, E-mail: alpaslan@ceng.metu.edu.tr

Abstract: The paper presents a multi-agent module, called MODA, to provide micro-level adaptiveness in learning management systems (LMS). The adaptiveness provides uniquely identifying and monitoring of the learner's learning process according to the learner's profile. The paper covers the pedagogical framework behind the adaptation mechanism, the architecture of MODA and its agents, the protocol providing communication between MODA and LMS, and a sample application of the module to an open source learning management system, OLAT. The study also discusses the possibilities of future interests.

Keywords: Adaptive Learning Systems, Intelligent Learning Management System, Multi-agent Systems, Distance Learning, Learner Profile

1. Introduction

Adaptiveness is a crucial issue in today's online learning environments (OLE). In [1], it is argued that virtual learning environments (VLE) are best at achieving learning effectiveness when they adapt to the needs of individual learners. Learning management systems provide educational services to a wide range of students and they can help students to achieve their learning goals by delivering knowledge in an adaptive or individualized way [1]. In [2], it was argued that as long as the competition on the market of Web-based educational system increases, "being adaptive" or "being intelligent" will become an important factor for winning customers. Web-based adaptive intelligent education systems inherit the advantages of both Intelligent Tutoring Systems (ITS) and adaptive hypermedia systems[2].

Brusilovsky provides some examples of adaptive systems such as InterBook [3], CALAT [4], ACE [5], ELM_ART II [6], ILESA [7], etc. Those systems support different intelligent and adaptive technologies. The author mentions some of technologies including curriculum sequencing, intelligent analysis of student's solutions, interactive problem solving support; adaptive hypermedia technologies such as, adaptive presentation and adaptive navigation support; web-inspired technologies like student model matching, and so on [2].

Pedagogical agents are autonomous agents that support human learning by interacting with students in an intelligent learning environment. They extend and improve upon previous work on intelligent tutoring systems in a number of ways. They adapt their behavior to dynamic state of the learning environment, taking advantage of learning opportunities as they arise. They can support collaborative learning as well as individualized learning, because multiple students and agents can interact in a shared environment. The use of agents in providing adaptiveness has been experienced in some studies such as ADELE [8], PPP Persona [9], etc.

Although these adaptive systems provide important adaptive features, it is not possible to integrate any of them with an existing LMS. Most of them are designed to be used as standalone systems. However, there are lots of LMS used in practice and it might be very effective to plug adaptive features to these already existing and widely used learning management systems.

In this study, a multi-agent intelligent learning system module, named MODA, is proposed. The system is designed to be plugged into any LMS. The aim of MODA is to provide adaptive features to the learning management systems. It provides micro-level adaptation, because, it tracks the learner behavior during the interaction and adapts the content continuously. An LMS, when integrated with MODA, becomes an adaptive learning management system. MODA applies a conceptual framework to be adaptive [10]. This framework bases on the idea that the adaptiveness is the best matching between the learner profile and the course content profile. The framework takes its background from the learning styles and the content types (30 content types including audio, text, exercise, fact, video, etc. are used). In this study, we implemented the learner profile, course profile, matching strategies, and initialization and updating strategies.

MODA's agents were implemented as JADE (Java Agent Development Framework) agents, a middleware that facilitates the development of multi-agent systems. The agent behaviors are defined by learner's actions performed on the LMS, which are explained in the form of scenarios.

In order to have a standalone module for any LMS, we defined a common protocol establishing the communication between LMS and MODA. This protocol includes the structure of the data exchanges among LMS-MODA and the interface to support communication. MODA was integrated into an open source learning management system.

2. Adaptive Technologies and Adaptive Systems

Instructional approaches and techniques that are geared to meet the needs of individually different students are called adaptive instruction technologies [11]. Any type of instruction presented in a one-on-one setting can be considered as individualized instruction, but if it is not flexible enough to meet learner's specific learning needs, it cannot be considered as adaptive.

There are various adaptive technologies or strategies. In [2], these technologies are categorized as: ITS (Intelligent Tutoring Systems) technologies, adaptive hypermedia technologies, and web inspired technologies. InterBook [3] is a tool for delivering adaptive textbooks on the World Wide Web. It uses adaptive annotation technology. CALAT [4] is a web-based intelligent tutoring system (ITS). It employs overlay model and presents the courseware pages so that the student can achieve a learning goal consisting of hierarchical sub-goals. ACE (Adaptive Courseware Environment) [5] is a web-based tutoring framework, which combines methods of knowledge representation, instructional planning, and adaptive media generation to deliver individualized courseware via the web. ELM-ART II [6] is an intelligent interactive textbook to support learning programming in LISP. It supports adaptive navigation as individualized diagnosis and help in problem solving tasks. The system selects the next best step in the curriculum on demand.

There are some adaptive systems that consider cognitive and learning styles, such as iWeaver [12], INSPIRE [13], ARTHUR [14], CS388 [15], and AEC-ES [16]. IWeaver [12] is an interactive web-based adaptive learning environment. iWeaver uses the Dunn and Dunn learning style model. INSPIRE [13] is an adaptive intelligent system developed for personalized instruction in a remote environment. It adapts the lessons according to the learner's knowledge level and learning style, and follows his/her progress. ARTHUR [14] is a web-based system that provides adaptive instruction based on learning styles. It supports adaptive presentation using different teaching strategies. Student learning style is detected and tuned by means of case-based reasoning techniques. CS388 [15] offers a range of learning style tools to students. The learning styles are assessed using the Felder-

Silverman learning style model [17]. AEC-ES [16] categorizes learners as field-dependent and field-independent learners.

The adaptive systems explained above are either intelligent tutoring systems or adaptive hypermedia systems. However, they are not multi-agent. Multi-agent systems can improve the adaptability in online learning settings. As stated in [12], interaction is one (teacher) to many (students) in the traditional classroom environment. Online Learning Environments (OLE), on the other hand, supports one (server) to one (learner) communication. The learner's learning process is very dynamic and there are varieties of different factors affecting the learner's success. It might be effective to provide learners with instructional support assistants having separate responsibilities serving to the same purpose. In this study, we present a multi-agent system to support many (agents) to one (learner) interaction.

Pedagogical agents are autonomous agents that support human learning by interacting with students in the context of Intelligent Learning Environment (ILE). There are some personal agents such as COACH, an intelligent tutor; NOTE-TAKING APPRENTICE; MAXIMS an email-filter; GALOIS an intelligent adviser, etc. However, there are not many pedagogical agents developed so far [18]. ADELE (Agent for Distance Learning Environments)[8] is one of the pedagogical agents that runs on each student's computer and interacts with each student as they work through the Web-based course materials. PPP Persona [9] is an animated pedagogical agent for interactive WWW presentations.

In [19], the authors propose an intelligent agent to guide students throughout the course material in the Internet. They designed an adaptive hypermedia system that functions as a personal assistant to help teachers to generate course curriculum and to help students to navigate through the course material.

Much of the current research in intelligent agents has focused on individual agents. However, in order to be more effective, these agents must work cooperatively with each other as in Multi-Agent Systems (MAS).

3. MODA: A Module for Adaptiveness in LMSs

The aim of MODA is to integrate adaptive behaviour into online learning systems. The main components of the system are as follows:

- Student Modeling
- Adapted Content
- Integration with LMS

3.1 The Pedagogical Architecture

The effectiveness of the adaptation in online learning environments is highly related to the coverage of the adaptation strategy. The better the match between the learner and the instruction is, the higher the adaptation is. In this study, we applied a practical conceptual framework for adaptive systems [10]. The framework takes its background from learning styles and learning standards. The adaptation strategy in the framework is to find the best match between the learner and the instruction set.

The framework defines the learner profile and the course content profile, It also provides the way to find the best match between learner profile and course content profile. The learner profile has the following fields [10]:

- Personality factors: learning style information, IMS LIP (Instructional Management Systems Learner Information Package) fields
- Knowledge factors: identity of the content, identity of the content item (each course concept), type of the content item (one or more of 30 content types), the knowledge

level   of   the   learner   ("UNDERSTOOD","NOTUNDERSTOOD", "MISUNDERSTOOD"), exam results, and last modified date

- Behavioral factors: identity of the actions, identity of the learner, owner of the action (LMS or any other systems), name of the action (search, view lecture notes, login etc.), time to start action, time to end action, description of the action, counts for 30 content types

The course profile is defined by the following information [10]:

- Identification of the course
- Count of each of 30 content types

The 30 content types used in the framework are as follows:

• Activity	• Definition	• Image	• Question
• Advance Organizer	• Diagram	• Innovation	• Sequential content
	• Discussion	• Link	
• Audio	• Example	• Mathematical model	• Suggestion
• Chart	• Exercise		• Syllabus
• Concept	• Experiment	• New concept	• Textual
• Concept Map	• Fact	• Principle	• Theory
• Critique	• Formula	• Problem solving	• Table of contents
• Data		• Procedure	
			• Video

The framework provides a way to classify these content types according to the learning style dimensions. The study also defines a strategy to find the best match between the learner and course profiles. The formulation for finding the best match is as follows [10]:

The learner style values are defined by the vector $x=[x_1, x_2, .., x_8]$, and course content profile values are defined by the vector $y=[y_1, y_2, .., y_8]$, where x_i is the value of the ith dimension of the learner style y_i is the value of the ith dimension of the content profile. The two vectors x and y are normalized as follows:

$$x_{normalized} = [x_1/x_m, x_2/x_m, .., x_8/x_m]$$

$$y_{normalized} = [y_1/y_m, y_2/y_m, .., y_8/y_m]$$

where x_m is the maximum value in the x vector and y_m is the maximum value in the y vector.

The Euclidian distance between these two dimensions is computed as:

$$D(x,y) = ||x-y|| = ((x_{1normalized} - y_{normalized})^2 + ((x_{2normalized} - y_{2normalized})^2 + ... + (x_{8normalized} - y_{8normalized})^2)^{0.5}$$

So, the matching score is found as:

$$S(x, y) = - D(x, y)$$

The $S(x, y)$ gives the matching score between the learner and course content profiles. This score is calculated for each item of the course content profile. The resulting scores are sorted and the course content with the highest score is accepted as the best matched course content regarding the learner profile.

In this study, we implemented the learner profile, course content profile, the classifications of the course content according to the learning styles, and the best matching strategy between the learner-content profiles.

3.2   The Multi-Agent System Architecture

MODA was designed to work with an LMS. We have three main modules: LMS, MODA and LMS-MODA interface module (Figure 1). LMS can be any LMS providing online learning services to learners. MODA is the multi-agent system module. LMS-MODA interface is the communication platform of these two separate modules. We developed a socket-based communication protocol.

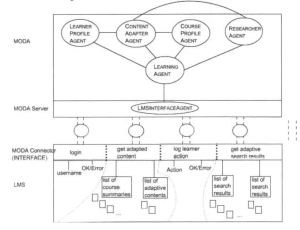

Figure 1 The Architecture of MODA

The system has six learning agents: LEARNINGAGENT, CONTENTADAPTER AGENT, COURSEPROFILEAGENT, LEARNERPROFILEAGENT, RESEARCHER AGENT and AGENTMANAGER. The descriptions and roles of each agent are as follows:

- LMSINTERFACEAGENT is the communication party with the LMS. It behaves as the MODA server.
- LEARNINGAGENT is the central agent, which is responsible for management of the other agents.
- CONTENTADAPTERAGENT is responsible for finding the most appropriate content for the learner using the learner profile. This agent communicates with the PROFILEAGENT, LEARNINGAGENT, and RESEARCHERAGENT.
- COURSEPROFILEAGENT initializes and updates the course profile.
- LEARNERPROFILEAGENT initializes and updates the learner profile.
- RESEARCHERAGENT receives search results, communicates with CONTENTADAPTERAGENT and receives the adapted content.

The agents in MODA were developed as JADE (Java Agent Development Framework) agents.

In the study, it is aimed that any LMS can make use of the adaptive learning module MODA. In order to achieve this modularity, we provide a protocol for communication between LMS and MODA. Any LMS providing necessary information with the required format becomes an adaptive learning management system, when it establishes a communication with MODA. The protocol requires LMS and MODA to read/write the necessary information to TCP sockets. Since the communication occurs in the sockets, we define the data formats exchanged between the systems during either requesting data or responding a request. In the MODA, one of the agents, - LMSINTERFACEAGENT-, serves as a server that receives the requests from the LMS and provides the responses back.

The request and response messages exchanged between LMS and MODA are depicted in Figure 2.

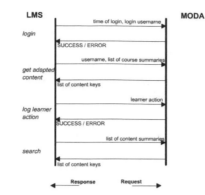

Figure 2 Request and Response Data in Communication Scenarios between LMS and MODA

Communication is performed through data packets. A packet can be either a request or a response packet. The packet structure of request and response are provided in the protocol [10].

4. An Example

MODA has been integrated to an open source learning management system, OLAT. More information on OLAT can be obtained at http://www.olat.org/website/en/html/index.html. Figure 4 shows the welcome page of OLAT integrated with MODA.

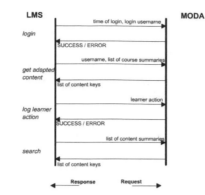

Figure 4 Welcome Page of OLAT with MODA

When the learner clicks "Show Content", OLAT displays all available content resources to the learner. Figure 5 gives the sample screen for the OLAT showing the content after performing adaptation, filtering and sorting through MODA.

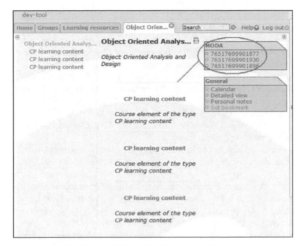

Figure 5 The adaptive content list

5. Conclusion

In this study, we designed and developed an adaptation module, called MODA, for learning management systems. A communication protocol was defined to establish the communication between LMS and MODA. Any LMS obeying the data requirements of the protocol can use MODA to be an adaptive learning system. MODA has been totally implemented using Java programming language. Since the protocol requires communicating through sockets, the development language of LMS becomes unimportant for the integration. This increases the usability of MODA in different LMS without considering the programming language limitations.

MODA is a multi-agent system. It has six agents each having specific roles such as registering agent's services, initializing and updating the learner profile, constructing course profile and performing course content classification, finding out the best match between the learner profile and course profile, and providing communication with LMS.

MODA provides curriculum sequencing and adaptive presentation technologies. It models the learner and the course content using a conceptual framework developed for adaptive systems [10]. It adapts the content according to the best match between the learner profile and the course profile.

The effectiveness of the adaptive strategies and technologies are directly correlated with the number and variety of the learners. This means that the development of MODA is a never-ending process. There will be new adaptive features to be added, or new best matching strategies will be applied as we use it more. It provides a platform to study different research topics.

References

[1] Park, I. & Hannafin, M.J. (1993). Empirically based guidelines for the design of interactive multimedia, *Educational technology Research and Development*, 41(3), Springer, pp.34-43.
[2] Brusilovsky, P. (1999). Adaptive and Intelligent Technologies for Web-basedEducation, *KI - Kunstliche Intelligenz*, Rollinger, Peylo (eds.), 4, pp.19-25.
[3] Brusilovsky, P., Eklund, J. & Schwarz, E. (1998). Web-based education for all: a tool for developing adaptive courseware, *Computer Networks and ISDN Systems,* 30(1), Elsevier, pp.291-300.
[4] Nakabayashi, K., Maruyama, M., Kato, Y., Touhei, H. & Fukuhara, Y. (1997). Architecture of an intelligent tutoring system on the WWW, *Proceedings of the 8th World Conference of the AIED Society*, Kobe, Japan, 18-22 August.

[5]   Specht, M. & Oppermann, R. (1998). ACE - Adaptive Courseware Environment, *The New Review of Hypermedia and Multimedia*, 4, pp. 141-161.

[6]   Weber, G. & Specht, M. (1997). User modeling and adaptive navigation support in WWW-based tutoring systems' *Proceedings of the 6 tn International Conference on User Modeling*, A. Jameson, C. Paris, and C. Tasso, Eds., Berlin Heidelberg: Springer-Verlag, pp. 289-300.

[7]   López, J.M., Millán, E., Pérez-de-la-Cruz, J. L. & Triguero, F. (1998). ILESA: a Web-based Intelligent Learning Environment for the Simplex Algorithm, In: Alvegård, C. (ed.) , *Proceedings of 4th International conference on Computer Aided Learning and Instruction in Science and Engineering(CALISCE'98)*, Göteborg, Sweden, pp. 399-406.

[8]   Johnson, W., Shaw, E., Marshall, A. & Labore, C. (2003). Evolution of user interaction: The case of agent adele, *Intelligent User Interfaces*, pp. 93-100.

[9]   Andr´e, E., M¨uller,J. & Rist,T. (1996). The ppp persona: a multipurpose animated presentation agent, *In Proceedings of the workshop on Advanced visual interfaces(AVI'96)*, ACM, New York, NY, USA, pp. 245–247.

[10]   Serce, F.C. (2007). An adaptive multi-agent system module for learning management systems, doctoral dissertation, Department of Information Systems, Middle East Technical University, Ankara, Turkey.

[11]   Corno, L. & Snow, E. (1986). *Adapting Teaching to Individual Differences among Learners*, Handbook of Research on Teaching, New York: MacMillan Publishers.

[12]   Wolf, C. (2003). iWeaver: towards 'learning style'-based e-learning in computer science education, *In Proceedings of the fifth Australasian conference on Computing Education(ACE'03)*, Darlinghurst, Australia, Australia, 2003, pp. 273–27.

[13]   Grigoriadou, M., Papanikolaou, K., Kornilakis, H. & Magoulas G.(2002). Inspire: an intelligent system for personalized instruction in a remote environment, *Lecture Notes in Computer Science*, 2266, Springer, p. 215.

[14]   Gilbert, C.Y. & Juan, E.H. (1999). Arthur: Adapting instruction to accommodate learning style, *In World Conference on the WWW and Internet Proceedings(WebNet 99)*, Honolulu, Hawaii, October 24-30, p. 7.

[15]   Howard, R.A., Carver, C.A. & Lavelle, E. (1996). Enhancing student learning by incorporating learning styles into adaptive hypermedia, *In Proceedings of World Conference on Educational Multimedia and Hypermedia(ED-MEDIA 1996)*, Boston, USA, pp.118–123.

[16]   Triantafillou, E., Pomportsis, A. & Georgiadou, E. (2002). Aes-cs: Adaptive educational system base on cognitive styles, *Proceedings of AH2002 Workshop, Second International Conference on Adaptive Hypermedia and Adaptive Web-based Systems*, University of Malaga, Spain.

[17]   R. M. Felder and L. K. Silverman. *Learning and teaching styles in engineering education.* Engineering Education, 78(7):674–681, 1998.

[18]   Marzo C. I. Pe˜na, J.L. & Rosa, J.L. (2005). Intelligent Agents to Improve Adaptivity in A0 Web-Based Learning Environment, *Chapter Studies in Fuzziness and Soft Computing, Knowledge-Based Virtual Education*, 178, Springer Berlin / Heidelberg, June, pp. 141–170.

[19]   Ozdemir, B. & Alpaslan, F.N. (2000). An intelligent tutoring system for student guidance in web-based courses, *In Lecture Notes In Computer Science*, 1909, London, UK, Springer-Verlag, pp. 437–448.

Collaboration and the Knowledge Economy: Issues, Applications, Case Studies
P. Cunningham and M. Cunningham (Eds.)
IOS Press, 2008

OKI: The Integration of Technology Enhanced Learning Services

Francesc SANTANACH, Jordi CASAMAJÓ, Magí ALMIRALL, Evaristo DE FRUTOS
Office of Learning Technologies, Universitat Oberta de Catalunya, Av. Tibidabo, 39-43
08035 Barcelona, Spain Tel. +34 93 253 5700, Email: fsantanach@uoc.edu,
jcasamajo@uoc.edu, malmirall@uoc.edu, edefrutos@uoc.edu

Abstract: There is now a whole series of technology enhanced learning platforms available in both the field of free software and in that of proprietary software. Choosing one or another in each circumstance raises many doubts. As a solution, the article shows the use of standards to facilitate the integration of tools and functions with existing platforms.

Keywords: Virtual campus, e-learning, Moodle, Sakai, OKI, OSID, LMS, interoperability, integration.

1. Introduction

The choice of platform has taken up significant efforts in technology enhanced learning projects. Typically, choosing a platform represents a future commitment, as its high installation, configuration and learning costs need to be offset. The type of doubts raised by the choice of platform has evolved as the technology enhanced learning sector has evolved. During the period 1995-2000, the first institutions to work in technology enhanced learning were unsure whether to develop a bespoke platform or buy the licence for a market platform and so when this period came to an end, we found that we had a great number of institutions with platform licences such as Blackboard or WebCT.

Between 2000 and 2005, the question changes, few people envisage bespoke development and the question on everyone's lips is: A market platform or a free software platform? By the end of this period, we see many institutions and companies using platforms such as Moodle or Sakai and developing a large volume of code integrated into these platforms. Given that these are free software platforms, the code is available for modification and with not too much effort high levels of personalisation are achieved. And this is the key to the present question: Should we modify the free software platform or program the personalisation of the platform in a standard layer?

Consequently, many are modifying Moodle[i] or Sakai[ii] and if their new code is not included in the new versions, a significant effort has to be made regarding development in each new version. OKI[iii] is a commitment to providing Moodle and Sakai with a standard layer, a layer that allows connections to academic management, a library and human resources management, without modifying the code of the platforms. In both the university environment[iv] and in the business environment[v], projects concerning the integration of technology enhanced learning services based on OKI have been started.

1.1 Architecture and interoperability based on OKI

An evolution in technology enhanced learning products has been taking place in recent years towards technology enhanced learning frameworks. The majority of products not only offer a certain functionality but allow this to be expanded by the addition of new modules, reprogramming or adapting parts, or accessing a programming API. For example, Moodle offers an entire API for programming new activities or changing certain behaviours. In such a changing and diverse environment as that of technology enhanced learning, the advantages of a framework with regard to a product are evident. So why a specific framework? Why not an abstract and generic e-learning framework? OKI [1][2] is a commitment to providing e-learning services with a standard interoperability layer, a layer that allows connections to many tools and systems like academic management, repositories and others (Fig. 1).

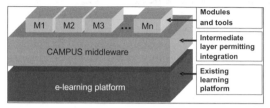

Fig. 1. Architecture by layers.OKI

The Open Knowledge Initiative [1][2], proposes a series of specifications with the aim of fostering the interoperability and adaptability of systems.

1.2   Basic services

Specifications such as OKI OSIDs and IMS Abstract framework [3] define in detail the services that a technology enhanced learning platform should offer. In spite of this, it has been decided to use quite a reduced set of these services. This is because the project focuses on:

- Simplicity.
- Developing in distributed teams.
- Reducing lines of code.
- Keeping the timeline and the investment.

Furthermore, a limited number of services facilitate the integration of external tools. It has been estimated that the average development time needed for tool integration programming through such a set of services is roughly a month.

The criteria to decide the basic services are as follows:

- The minimum set of services
- All of them must be OKI OSIDs.
- Those mandatory for the system to work (authentication and authorization).
- Those enabling the system to be administered and managed as though it were a single product (logging, locale and configuration).

Therefore, the tools developed can communicate with the base platform using a maximum of five services: authentication, authorization, logging, locale (internationalisation) and configuration.

- The authentication service not only allows the user to log into the system but also finds out if the user is logged in. This is a mandatory service in any computer program with user registration.
- The authorization service determines if the user is authorised to act on certain resources and contexts. This is mandatory in any system in which the users play different roles.
- The monitoring service allows program activity data to be stored. It is very useful for finding out what is happening in a system and how it is working.
- The internationalisation service permits the language of a program to be changed and new languages to be added.

- The configuration service allows us to create and change the configuration parameters of a computer application.

These services implement the following OKI OSIDs: all Authentication OSIDs, all Authorization OSIDs, all logging OSIDs, all dictionary OSIDs (used to implement the locale and configuration services), Agent, Id and Group.

1.3   Architecture

The Campus Project started under the assumption that the next step to achieve a real interoperability would rely on adopting a service-oriented model. OASIS [4] defines Service Oriented Architecture (SOA) as a "paradigm for organizing and utilizing distributed capabilities that may be under the control of different ownership domains. It provides a uniform means to offer, discover, interact with and use capabilities to produce desired effects consistent with measurable preconditions and expectations" [5]. In SOA, the system is modelled around a set of modules with a public functionality and responsibility and a set of mechanisms that allow interaction between the services. When these services implement a very clear-cut interface, then it is possible to isolate the interaction mechanisms in a unique layer (see OKI Bus layer further on), facilitating the control of the loose coupling across the systems. If a loose coupling is pursued, the layer can be implemented using web services. This is the case with the Campus Project, in which heterogeneous tools (Java and PHP) interact with some services of an also heterogeneous platform: Moodle (PHP) or Sakai (Java).

The best way to see it is to think of a system of blocks or pieces that fit together (Fig. 2). Each piece is a black box that performs an activity within its limits and invisible to the others [6]. Consequently, each module has its own internal architecture and most appropriate technology to resolve its business logic.

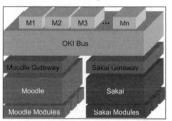

Fig. 2. Architecture by layers.

The modules connect to the system using the base services, which act as a bridge and a link. In turn, the learning platform that wants to use the modules must have an OKI Gateway. An OKI gateway is a piece of software that translates the requests of the base services that use the modules into calls to the platform's API. Each platform has its own. Fig. 2 shows the OKI Moodle gateway (for the Moodle platform) and the OKI Sakai gateway (for the Sakai platform). To integrate a new platform, the corresponding OKI gateway must be used.

One final piece to take into account is the so-called OKIBus. This component is a middle layer that resolves all of the problems relating to the communication between applications. In other words, until now we have described how to make so many base modules speak the same language and be able to understand each other, but what happens if the speakers are far apart and cannot hear each other? And what if there is a lot of noise in the room? The OKIBus layer resolves the equivalent of this type of problem: communication protocols, remote communication, performance optimisation measures, increase in communication quality, etc.

2. The CAMPUS Project

The CAMPUS project [7], promoted by the Secretariat for Telecommunications and the Information Society (STSI) of the Regional Government of Catalonia, grew out of the agreement signed by the majority of Catalan universities to have a virtual campus based on open code and which enables them to offer higher education both online and in a semi face-to-face environment. This initiative came out of the university system open to the world, which aims to become an international benchmark for technology enhanced learning.

This project comes under the Digital University programme fostered by the STSI, the aim of which is to facilitate the transfer and sharing of knowledge using information and communication technologies.

The Universitat Oberta de Catalunya (UOC) is in charge of coordinating and leading the project, which is carried out using the knowledge and experience of each associated university. Each member, therefore, contributes tools and resources to the project, which is organised according to a development community in open code.

Today, the project has over 15 partners who share the development functions of the CAMPUS and the observation and monitoring tasks. The project officially began on 1 April 2006 and delivers its results to the community in 2008.

The aim is to develop a technological infrastructure with free distribution tools to provide online training. The project requirements are: open code and open standards, user-centred design, interoperability between tools and with other systems, scalability of the solution, high concurrence of users and processes, OKI OSIDs [8] specifications as a mechanism of interoperability, which can be executed and integrated into Moodle and Sakai open code e-learning platforms and with a service-based architecture of the solution.

On a functional level, CAMPUS is a solution designed for virtual learning that contemplates the usual functions of an LMS (Learning Management System), but which also offers modules that can be executed and integrated into the model and Sakai platforms (through OKI) and which bring added value to the functionality offered by these platforms. In particular, functionalities are added which are not present in Moodle and Sakai or which are similar tools but with different pedagogical orientations, or which contribute another type of differential value.

2.1 Organisation of the project

Often the organisation and type of relationship established between the constituent agents of a project mark out and determine many of its decisions, risks and results. Therefore, it is important to provide certain data regarding the structure and organisation of the project.

The project members are basically universities and public bodies that play the roles of developer, observer and financer. The project has a budget of around three million euros, financed largely by the Regional Government of Catalonia.

No legal body has been established to represent the project, so each university is legally responsible for maintaining and overseeing the evolution of its tools.

The project management is conducted through a Gforge [9] project development environment; specifically, the La Farga [10] open-code project development and promotion. An environment of this type offers a set of tools that can be used to manage projects. For example, distribution lists, debate forums, wiki, files area and a version control tool, among others.

The project is divided into eleven work packages, each with a set of universities involved. The packages are:
1. User analysis and profile structuring.
2. Model development and interface testing following usability and user-centred design criteria.
3. Central system and security design.

4. Description of subsystems.
5. Central system and security development.
6. Development of subsystems.
7. Usage pilot.
8. Opening up free software to the community.
9. Legal framework and community.
10. Dissemination and opening up of the project.
11. Methodology, quality control and risk management.

2.2   Applications portfolio

CAMPUS offers a portfolio of applications that give added value to the project and which are contributions by the various universities. Some of these tools have already been working successfully in each university and have been brought to the project because of their success and solidity, others offer an added value as they are innovative, others offer specific functions or cover specific pedagogical methodologies; in short, the CAMPUS Project should be seen as a set of applications that fulfil a specific need in the field of technology enhanced learning and which can be integrated on the most common learning platforms.

The following outlines some of the most interesting applications in the portfolio:

- Live e-learning: This is a technology enhanced learning support system based on multicast technology through real-time audio and video broadcast. It permits the broadcasting and recording of multicast sessions of master classes by the lecturers. The lecturer's voice and video and the PC's desktop are broadcast with the application that is currently active.
- Internal messaging: Internal messaging module for the users of a campus.
- External e-mail – Webmail: Webmail manager. It permits the exchange and management of both internal and external mails. It is an integration project of the well-known Zimbra [11] mail management tool. It is not intended that the Internal messaging and External e-mail tools should coexist in the same CAMPUS implementation, rather what is expected is that according to needs, one or the other is used. If external mail is required web mail will be chosen, otherwise internal messaging will be sufficient.
- Results assessment and reporting tool (QTI): System based on the IMS QTI standard to describe the data structure of questions and test results. It allows the creation of questions and exams online, for them to be shared through the QTI specification and for their appearance to be personalised. It is an integration project of the 'Quaderns Virtuals' [12] tool and an extension of the calculation engine to incorporate statistics and advanced graphics on the basis of the QTI Results Reporting data.
- Automatic problem correction: Automatic problem correction is a teaching support virtual environment, which consists of the personalised allocation, correction and assessment of problems for each student. Unlike the QTI application, this tool is designed for problems of complex resolution, such as mathematical problems, programming algorithms or diagramming. It is an integration project of the ACME tool [13].
- 3D Virtual Environments: The most widely known 3D virtual space is Second Life [14] but there are other tools that allow creation and interaction with 3D worlds and which are completely free. The tool developed is integrated in a classroom of a virtual campus and allows users to access a virtual space, using a personalised avatar, where they can view and manipulate 3D objects created by the lecturer. It is an integration project of the OpenSimulator project [15].
- Teaching content monitoring (SCORM): The teaching content management and distribution system in SCORM allows the platform to import, export and display

learning materials that meet the SCORM 2004 specifications. The system enables monitoring data to be stored using an AJAX API and accepts content sequencing strategies.

- Student portfolio: The electronic portfolio is a system that enables the students to submit work to the lecturers to show their progress in the attainment of skills. It is an iterative process where the lecturer comments on the students' work so that the students can improve on it.
- Bookmarks: The aim of these is to provide users with access to key pages on or off the platform on the Internet. As new feature, it offers the capacity of sharing, participating and labelling, which makes it a tool of personalisation and collaboration.
- Wikis, blogs and podcasts: Despite the fact that these tools are now very widespread, that every platform has their own and that their election very often depends on personal preferences, it has been decided to include them as an example of the ease of integration that the CAMPUS offers.
- RSS Mobile/TV: The RSS Mobile/TV is a system that allows information from the campus environment to be received or consulted on various devices, such as hand-held devices (PDA, telephones, etc.) or living-room devices (TV). The system is based on RSS syndication technologies.

3. SUMA Project

The Suma project was created within the eLearning working group [16] of the INES [17] technological platform.

As a result of the experience of the project partners that were part of the INES technological platform e-learning group was the detection of a lack of standardisation in the technology enhanced learning solutions available on the market and which are now being implemented. There are now a great number of both Open Source and proprietary and bespoke platforms.

This situation involves a great deal of individual effort by the companies that implement technology enhanced learning environments to develop the solutions that customers expect in each case. Each project involves significant development technological effort to adapt to the customer's needs and integrate as easily as possible into a business environment.

Consequently, in most cases, the effective incorporation of technology enhanced learning into a company involves a great deal of effort and high costs, which mean that it is not within everyone's reach. Due to this, the major e-learning experiences are found mainly in large companies and in many cases are outside the reach of medium and small companies.

In addition, a significant distance has also been detected between research being carried out in the university environment in both the field of standards and processes and education methodologies in technology enhanced learning. There have been many developments in the theoretical sphere (definitions, models, etc.), but little has been put into practice effectively (beyond reduced pilot trials).

The consortium of companies, technology centres and universities (which participate as subcontracted parties) brings together companies' knowledge on the needs of the technology enhanced learning market with the innovative standards and solutions being developed in the academic field. This situation has enabled an integrating approach to be taken for the construction of a service-oriented platform that unifies new applications and standards currently available in the technology enhanced learning field.

Due to all of this, the Suma Project is also based on the solution proposed by OKI as architecture based on integration standards for e-learning tools, adapting it to the specific needs of the business environment and promoting the transfer of technology between university and business.

There are plans to construct a series of e-learning functions on the services integration layer, which will allow the basic tools of the underlying platform beneath the integration layer to be completed.

These applications will be basically of three types:

- Integration modules with business systems: the aim is to meet the needs in this field based on the experience of implementing technology enhanced learning environments (in both the business and academic sphere) of the companies involved in the project.
- Multimodal access modules: aimed basically at providing access to the platform through Interactive Digital Television (IDTV) and mobile devices as an innovative solution to an access channel to an e-learning platform.
- Intelligent/adaptive learning creation and management environments: to transfer the mature research lines in this field to industry.

This way, the end result will be a complete platform with innovative e-learning functions that facilitate connectivity to pre-existing platforms in both the business and academic field.

The project is presented as a three-year plan (2007-2009) and has secured a subsidy for 2007 from the Ministry of Industry, Tourism and Trade of the PROFIT- ICT Industrial Policy of the 'Avanza Plan'.

4. Conclusions and future work

The CAMPUS project completion date is also a beginning. The commitment is to open all the developments to the community in the form of an open-code project. Therefore, the success of the project will be measured by the use that the community makes of these products and components. A great deal of effort has been invested in ensuring that the developments will be of interest to the educational community and also in providing a sufficiently modular structure that enables everyone to use what strictly interests them.

The structure of the project, with many actors involved, has greatly helped achieve this aim. Each university involved already had experience in virtual teaching and its own learning platform with truly interesting tools. Some universities have a very clear orientation towards free-distribution products, such as Moodle or Sakai, others have their own learning platforms. Achieving a solution design that is compatible with the interests of everyone and which, in addition, is of interest to the educational community in general, has not been easy.

The results of the projects includes the OKIBus and the gateways with a set of technology enhanced learning applications that interoperates with the platform using the OSID standard as one of the first implementation of the OKI OSIDs to build a complete technology enhanced learning solution and that allows the easy integration of new technology enhanced learning platforms (building a new gateway) and any new application that uses OSID.

The innovation of these projects rely on that can guarantee the interoperability of technology enhanced learning platforms and applications using an open standard. To integrate any application to one of the existing technology enhanced learning platforms involves specific development for the platform.

Another important factor is the desire for international projection. To achieve this, from the start we have been committed to open standards and to integrating everything possible and respecting the work lines and objectives of everyone. In this sense, the mechanisms for integration with Moodle and Sakai have been planned and discussed with the managers of these projects. We have worked closely with the MIT OKI working group to transform the project into a benchmark implementation of its specifications and have encouraged the incorporation of education standards in the tools and modules of the project.

The future plans are to develop the use of the project components, to initiate a set of pilot trials to validate developments and to secure more financing to continue working together.

The UOC is committed to basing its Virtual Campus on these components and to follow the architecture and principles set out by the project. The adaptation carried out during 2008 so that UOC's LMS may have OKI OSIDs defined services, is another sample of this concept. The UOC's LMS is a self-made product and has been used as e-learning platform at UOC for more than 10 years. At present, the UOC has over 45000 students, an average level of concurrence over 2500 users connected simultaneously and 6000 maximum users connected simultaneously at peak times like delivery of activities and the beginning of semester. In addition, many of the universities involved are interested in working on evolving tools and integrating them into their organisations.

For its part, the Suma project, which at the time of writing this paper (June 2008) has completed its first year of operation, still has two years to run which will focus on the development of the tools, some necessary and others innovative, to construct a useful platform for the business environment that facilitates the incorporation of technology enhanced learning, with a clear commitment to integration through standards of the multiple applications that currently exist in companies.

References

[1]   Open Knowledge Initiative. http://www.okiproject.org
[2]   Kumar, V., Merriman, J., Thorne, S. . Open Knowledge Initiative Final Report. http://www.okiproject.org/filemgmt/visit.php?lid=44
[3]   IMS Global Learning Consortium. 2003. IMS Abstract Framework: Applications, Services, and Components. Version 1.0. IMS Global Learning Consortium, Inc. http://www.imsglobal.org/af/afv1p0/imsafascv1p0.html
[4]   OASIS. The Organization for the Advancement of Structured Information Standards. http://www.oasis-open.org
[5]   OASIS. 2006. Reference Model for Service Oriented Architecture 1.0. http://docs.oasisopen.org/soa-rm/v1.0/soa-rm.pdf. OASIS.
[6]   The Open Group. 2005. TOGAF Version 8.1 Enterprise Edition. The Open Group. Chapter 32: Building Blocks.]
[7]   Campus Project: http://www.campusproject.org/en/index.php
[8]   Thorne, S., Kahn, J. (2006). O.K.I. Architectural Concepts. Available at http://www.okiproject.org
[9]   Wikipedia. GForge. http://en.wikipedia.org/wiki/GForge
[10] Secretaria de Telecomunicacions i Societat de la Informació (STSI). La Farga. http://www.lafarga.org/
[11] Wikipedia. Zimbra. http://en.wikipedia.org/wiki/Zimbra
[12] Xarxa Telemàtica Educativa de Catalunya (XTEC). Quaderns Virtuals. http://clic.xtec.cat/qv_web/es/index.php
[13] Departamento de Informática y Matemática Aplicada - UDG. Evaluación Continuada y Mejora de la Enseñanza. http://acme.udg.edu/es/
[14] Wikipedia. Second Life. http://en.wikipedia.org/wiki/SecondLife
[15] OpenSimulator: http://opensimulator.org/wiki/Main_Page
[16] eLearning working group of the INES technological platform: http://blogs.uoc.edu/wiki/ines_elearning
[17] INES technological platform: http://www.ines.org.es/

---

[i] www.moodle.org

[ii] www.sakaiproject.org

[iii] www.okiproject.org

[iv] CAMPUS: www.campusproject.org

[v] SUMA: www.ines.org.es/suma/

Virtual Role-Play in the Classroom – Experiences with FearNot!

Sibylle ENZ[1], Carsten ZOLL[1], Natalie VANNINI[2], Scott WATSON[7], Ruth AYLETT[3],
Lynne HALL[4], Ana PAIVA[5], Dieter WOLKE[6], Kerstin DAUTENHAHN[7], Elisabeth
ANDRE[8], Paola RIZZO[9]

[1]Otto-Friedrich Universität Bamberg, Kapuzinerstraße 16, Bamberg, D-96045, Germany
Tel: +49 951 8631965, Fax: +49 951 601511
Email: sibylle.enz@uni-bamberg.de, carsten.zoll@uni-bamberg.de

[2]Julius-Maximilians Universität Würzburg, Sanderring 2, Würzburg, D-97070, Germany
Tel: +49 931 312661, Fax: +49 931 312763
Email: natalie.vannini@psychologie.uni-wuerzburg.de

[3]Heriot Watt University, Riccarton, Edinburgh, EH14 4AS, Scotland
Tel: +44 131 4514189, Fax: +44 131 4513327, Email: ruth@macs.hw.ac.uk

[4]University of Sunderland, Sunderland, SR6 0DD, UK
Tel: +44 191 5153249, Fax: +44 191 515 2781, Email: lynne.hall@sunderland.ac.uk

[5]INESC-ID, Tagus Park, Porto Salvo, 2780-990, Portugal
Tel: +351 214233223, Email: ana.paiva@inesc-id.pt

[6]University of Warwick, Coventry, CV4 7AL, UK
Tel: +44 24 76523537, Fax: +44 24 76524225, Email: D.Wolke@warwick.ac.uk

[7]University of Hertfordshire, College Lane, Hatfield, Herts AL10 9AB, UK
Tel: +44 1707284303, Fax: +44 1707284333,
Email: s.e.j.watson@herts.ac.uk, K.Dautenhahn@herts.ac.uk

[8]Universität Augsburg, Universitätsstraße 2, Augsburg, 86159, Germany
Tel: +49 821 5982340, Fax: +49 821 5985505, Email: andre@informatik.uni-augsburg.de

[9]Interagens s.r.l., Via G. Peroni 444, Rome, 00131, Italy
Tel: +39 3341879778, Email: p.rizzo@interagens.com

Abstract: FearNot! is a novel software application aimed at the age-group of 8-12 year old students with the aim to influence their attitude towards and knowledge about bullying. It is a virtual learning environment for social and emotional learning that allows for individual interaction with synthetic autonomous characters that engage in bullying and ask the learner for help and advice in order to escape victimisation. FearNot! uses an emergent narrative approach that generates stories through the interaction of the learner with the autonomous characters, a highly innovative and believable way to create engaging stories and evoke emotional learning in the user. Whether learning in the virtual environment transfers to real-world attitudes and behaviour about bullying is currently investigated in a comprehensive evaluation study, both in the UK and in Germany.

1. Introduction

The EU funded project eCIRCUS aims at applying educational role-play to social, personal and emotional learning for children and teenagers. This paper focuses on FearNot!, a virtual role-play approach with autonomous agents as social interaction partners in scenarios related to exploring coping strategies for bullying.

In FearNot! children are provided with the opportunity to explore a virtual school environment populated by 3D animated synthetic characters participating in an improvised drama. The children watch the characters engage in bullying episodes and then interact with the victimised characters in order to help them with advice. By empathising with the virtual bullying victim, students become affectively engaged in the role-play and can thus be motivated to become active to stand up against bullying in the real world.

2. Objectives

FearNot!'s novel and highly innovative pedagogical approach to fight bullying in schools builds on the immersive power of virtual role-play. In this paper we will discuss the pedagogical use of virtual role-play, considering the benefits as compared to real-life role-play interventions and the technological challenges.

The domain that we are addressing with FearNot! is bullying: 10-15% of students all over Europe (and in other parts of the world) suffer from being bullied in school [1]. These students are repeatedly victims to behaviours like cruel teasing, social exclusion, physical aggression or thefts and, as a consequence, face long-term effects such as academic regression, social anxiety, somatic and psychiatric symptoms [2]. Our pedagogical goals in eCIRCUS are to enhance children's ability to empathise with the synthetic characters in a virtual bullying scenario and to improve their knowledge about ways of fighting bullying and helping victims. Hence, we will present how FearNot! can be used in primary schools in the UK and Germany and will report some early evaluation results.

3. Methodology

Educational role-play is widely accepted as a powerful instrument to change attitudes and behaviour, by facilitating the ability to take over someone else's perspective (in a holistic sense, integrating thought, feelings, and behaviour) [3]. Through the process of role-taking, students learn how others think and feel in a social situation. With FearNot!, we aim at reconciling the didactical approach of real-world role-play with a more private and less emotionally sensitive (in terms of stigmatisation and further isolation) virtual environment for social and emotional learning. By interacting with the victimised virtual character, we hope to prompt empathic reactions within the child user. Empathy refers to the understanding of the victim's plight as well as experiencing the social and emotional effects of bullying on victims. Apart from the empathic reaction to the victimised character, FearNot! prompts reflection on a variety of coping strategies that the learner can suggest to the character in order to help him or her. If the learner runs out of ideas, the systems will provide further coping strategies through the interaction with the characters. Hence, FearNot! fosters empathic reactions in the child users in order to make them *want* to do something against bullying, and aims at enhancing their knowledge about coping possibilities in order to make them *able* to do something against it.

FearNot! is structured in episodes and interaction sequences. The episodes show bullying incidents between virtual characters in a virtual school, with the learner acting as a spectator. In between the episodes, students engage in a conversation with the victimised character, acting as advisor and friend by suggesting coping strategies. The learner experiences vicariously the situation of the victimised characters including its thoughts and feelings and can influence the storyline in order to help the victim, as the advice given to the victimised character affects its mental state (personality, emotional state, goals etc.) and thus ultimately the victimised character's actions in the next episode.

Role-play can be a powerful instrument to change attitudes and behaviour, if the precondition of immersion is met. In FearNot!, immersion is achieved through character design including the modelling of the agents' minds as well as the narrative structure of the learning experience.

4. Technology Description

As described above, FearNot!'s pedagogical goals are to alter the attitude towards and the knowledge about bullying among primary school students by prompting them to empathise with victims and by providing them with coping strategies to help victims. A core precondition for the child to be able to develop an empathic relationship with the characters is the believability of the characters as well as of their experiences. This believability relates to storylines and drama, which have been continuously evaluated with the target group during the development of FearNot!. But believability also results from the design of the characters, both from their appearances as well as from their reactions and behaviour.

Regarding the issue of appearance, a near-realistic appearance can become a problem for the believability of characters, a paradox, that has been previously named "uncanny valley" [4]; the FearNot! characters and environment are thus cartoon-style, a design decision that has been backed up by the target group's preferences [5].

As far as the issue of reactions and behaviour is concerned, the FearNot! characters are autonomous in the sense that they perceive information from and flexibly react to the virtual environment and other characters as well as the interaction with the learner. To enable agents to do this, each agent has a mind, an emotion-driven architecture named FAtiMA [6] that is based on the cognitive appraisal theory [7] and on findings from research on coping [8]. Characters in FearNot! can perceive all relevant objects, events, and other agents that exist in the virtual environment and appraise them regarding their significance for their emotional state. They then build an internal goal hierarchy and appraise the goals' importance in relation to the current state of the environment. The appraisal processes are influenced by former experiences of the agent and result in an emotional state and action tendencies. Additionally, characters in FearNot! are designed to be more believable than pre-programmed characters (as they have often been used e.g. in many commercial games) since they select their actions autonomously within episodes (see figure 1). Thus, the resulting story has emergent properties, which creates more varied and thus more interesting, and 'life-like' user experiences.

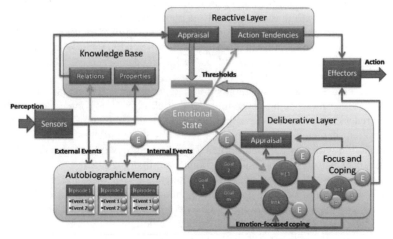

Figure 1: The FAtiMA agent architecture.

Characters are also equipped with an autobiographic memory [9], which gives them the possibility to refer to incidents from past interactions with the child user. In sum, the agent architecture allows for episodes to emerge from interaction between the characters, producing an emergent narrative [10]. In order to engage learners emotionally with the situation of victims of bullying, they are given a certain amount of control over the narrative by interacting with the victimised character, influencing its decisions in the bullying episodes to come. While the development of the narrative is basically driven by actions of the autonomous agents, the combination with the learner's impact on the story results in a highly believable experience for the learner. A narrative facilitator agent controls the characters and locations of an episode and the succession of the episodes to ensure that the learning experience is coherent.

5. Preliminary Results

In this paper, we shall be focusing on those results that relate to the impact of role-play and children's willingness to engage with the characters in FearNot! Earlier results from one-off 20 minutes interactions with FearNot! indicated that in the short term children are not only willing to immerse themselves in the virtual drama, but that they also empathically engage with the characters; they attribute a range of emotions to the characters depending on the events that happen within the respective scenario. Furthermore, the characters are regarded as believable: Hall et al. [5] found that the perceived believability of the conversation with the character is associated with feelings towards the character, i.e. children who felt sorry for the characters rated the conversation as more believable and interesting than children who did not feel sorry, whereas children who felt anger towards the characters rated the conversation as less believable and interesting than children who did not feel angry.

Recent results from Classroom Discussion Forums held as part of the FearNot! evaluation have identified that over a several day time frame, interacting regularly with FearNot!, children become and remain immersed in the world of FearNot! and with the characters who inhabit it. The children do care about and clearly believe in the characters, not only in a single interaction but also over several separated interactions. Achieving this empathic response is a result of immersive role-play for the child.

FearNot! is being currently evaluated with 1180 learners (646 in the UK and 534 in Germany) in terms of whether the software is appropriate for the classroom situation and if it is really able to change victimisation within classrooms. The evaluation study employs a quasi-experimental design with control groups, pre- and post-tests and follow-ups. Initial results from the ongoing evaluation study strongly support the earlier findings reported above. These results regard ratings of the software that were provided as a part of a standardised questionnaire (Character Evaluation Questionnaire, CEQ) and were filled in after the children's third interaction session with FearNot! in three consecutive weeks. Boys rated the episodes featuring male characters; girls rated the "female" episodes.

Analyses of a German subsample of 230 children (age range: 7-10 years; M=8.44; SD=0.56), 122 (or 53%) of them being male, indicate that children enjoy interacting with FearNot!, that they react emotionally to the situation of the victimised character as well as to the bullying behaviour depicted by the perpetrators: 57.1% of the children answered that they had "fun" interacting with FearNot!, additional 23.2% stated they had "rather fun" (on a five-point scale from "fun" to "boring"). Among the male characters (victimised character, bully, assistant to the bully, and two defenders), boys liked the victimised character Jonas best (58.1%) and stated that it would be him they wanted to be friends with (53.0%); when asked who they would want to be if they could choose one of the characters, boys picked Jonas, the victim (37.9%) and Robin, one of the defenders (24.1%). 55.1 % of the boys would vote Lukas, the bully, out, if they could.

For the girls who indicated their preferences among the female characters of another episode with similar roles, 74.0% liked Franziska, the victim, most and 67.0% of them would want to be her friend. They also identified either with Franziska (39.4%) or with Marie, one of the defenders (37.6%) and would vote the bully Jessica out (55.3%). Results are depicted in more detail in table 1.

Table 1: Preferences for and identification with characters in FearNot!

Which character do you like most?		Which character do you like least?		Which character do you like to be friends with?		If you could vote a character out, who would it be?		If you could choose to be one of the characters, which one would you be?		Role
				Boys						
68	**58.1 %**	4	3.4%	62	**53.0%**	23	19.5%	44	**37.9%**	V
8	6.8%	96	81.4%	13	11.1%	65	**55.1%**	13	11.2%	B
16	13.7%	4	3.4%	15	12.8%	11	9.3%	20	17.2%	D
20	17.1%	5	4.3%	23	19.7%	11	9.3%	28	**24.1%**	D
5	4.3%	9	7.6%	4	3.4%	8	6.8%	11	9.5%	BA
				Girls						
80	**74.0%**	1	0.9%	69	**67.0%**	22	21.4%	43	**39.4%**	V
2	1.9%	90	84.1%	4	3.9%	57	**55.3%**	10	9.2%	B
18	16.7%	0	0	20	19.4%	5	4.9%	41	**37.6%**	D
2	1.9%	6	5.6%	3	2.9%	5	4.9%	4	3.7%	BA
1	0.9%	10	9.3%	1	1.0%	8	7.8%	6	5.5%	BA
5	4.6%	0	0	6	5.8%	6	5.8%	5	4.6%	D

V = victimised character; B = bully; D = defender, helps the victim; BA = assistant to the bully

Table 2: Perceived similarity to characters in FearNot!

Which character looks most like you?		Which character looks least like you?		Which character behaves most like you?		Which character behaves least like you?		Which character did you feel sorry for?		Which character did you feel angry with?		Role
						Boys						
23	**22.3%**	38	37.3%	37	**33.6%**	18	15.5%	100	**87.0%**	6	5.3%	V
12	11.7%	20	19.6%	15	13.6%	78	67.2%	8	7.0%	92	**80.7%**	B
6	5.8%	35	34.3%	25	22.7%	7	6.0%	6	5.2%	3	2.6%	D
49	**47.6%**	6	5.9%	28	**25.5%**	6	5.2%	0	0	3	2.6%	D
13	12.6%	3	2.9%	5	4.5%	7	6.0%	1	0.9%	10	8.8%	BA
						Girls						
15	17.2%	32	**32.0%**	52	**53.6%**	10	9.6%	103	**95.4%**	5	4.7%	V
20	23.0%	32	**32.0%**	5	5.2%	75	**72.1%**	2	1.9%	89	**84.0%**	B
28	**32.2%**	9	9.0%	31	**32.0%**	2	1.9%	1	0.9%	1	0.9%	D
2	2.3%	9	9.0%	4	4.1%	6	5.8%	1	0.9%	5	4.7%	BA
8	9.2%	15	15.0%	2	2.1%	10	9.6%	1	0.9%	5	4.7%	BA
14	16.1%	3	3.0%	3	3.1%	1	1.0%	0	0	1	0.9%	D

V = victimised character; B = bully; D = defender, helps the victim; BA = assistant to the bully

Regarding the perceived similarity between the child and the FearNot! characters, the largest group of boys felt similar to Jonas (victim) and Robin (defender), both in terms of appearance as well as in terms of behaviour; accordingly, boys felt sorry for the victimised character (87.0%). 80.7% of the male pupils in the sample also reported to feel angry with the bully. The girls again rated their perceived similarity with and emotional reactions towards the female characters in FearNot!. 95.4% of the girls felt sorry for the victimised character, and 84.0% of them reported feelings of anger with the bully. Concerning perceived similarity in appearance, girls show more variation among the characters, but more than half of them (53.6%) think that the victimised character is most like them in terms of behaviour whereas 72.1% report that the bully is least like them, also in terms of behaviour (for a detailed overview see table 2).

As far as the content and story of FearNot! are concerned, the German subsample deemed it overall interesting and neither too long nor too short (see table 3). They further experienced the interaction with the victimised character as effective and felt they could help a lot to improve the victim's situation (again, see table 3).

Table 3: Ratings on the FearNot! story

Item	Min = 1	Max = 5	M	SD	N
Did you find what the characters talked about…	interesting	boring	1.99	1.16	228
What do you think about the story?	too short	too long	3.03	1.28	227
After talking with [victimised character's name], did you feel that…	they followed your advice	they paid no attention to your advice	2.07	1.17	230
After talking with [victimised character's name], did you feel that…	you helped them a lot	you didn't help them at all	1.72	0.97	229

6. Business Benefits

Regarding the ongoing analysis of the data collected within the comprehensive evaluation of FearNot! outlined above, we hope that the FearNot! application will reduce victimisation and improve knowledge about bullying and about the most effective coping strategies. Assuming that FearNot! is successful in its aims, the e-CIRCUS project team hopes to make it available to the public for educational purposes.

The preliminary evaluation results quoted above indicate that an empathic relationship can be created between a believable graphical character and a human user. This is a significant generic result with possible application well outside this particular system. It can be seen as an important component of any software being used for a persuasive purpose, in which changes in attitude and behaviour rather than only in knowledge are desired. A possible business benefit lies in extending the approach of FearNot! into other domains with adult users, for example in workplace-based courses covering topics such as harassment or gender and race awareness. Health education, in which motivating behaviour change is usually the ultimate objective, is another possible application domain.

There has also been a great deal of interest in FearNot! itself from countries outside of the UK and Germany, in which the more comprehensive evaluation referred to has just taken place. Enquiries have been received from Sweden, Denmark, Italy, the US and the Netherlands amongst others. While the project team does not itself have the resources to implement versions of FearNot! in other countries, there is clearly a demand from educationalists which could produce business benefits to a company that was able to take on this extra development work.

Finally, the FAtiMA agent architecture and the improvising characters that it supports might easily form the basis for much more flexible and versatile graphical characters in computer games, whether console-based and used individually or distributed and used by many hundreds of thousands of users as for example World of Warcraft. Companies that take this type of architecture on board would be able to produce improved products and indeed totally new game genres with a much more engaging narrative content than is currently the case.

7. Conclusions

The main challenge of the approach depicted in this paper is to reconcile the immersiveness and realism of virtual environments as learning spaces. As ongoing and comprehensive evaluation efforts indicate, FearNot! succeeds in engaging children empathically with autonomous characters involved in bullying. Whether this immersion leads to changes in attitudes and behaviour in real bullying incidents is currently investigated in an ongoing evaluation study.

Lessons learned during the development of FearNot! tackle two areas, one relating to the technical equipment in schools, the other relating to the importance of believability of and empathy towards agents:

As far as technical considerations are concerned, the most important aspect is to ensure that the application is running stable on school computers. Due to the fact that software developers usually do not have access to the school computers during software development, they are not aware of the technical limitations attached to these machines. E.g., primary schools tend to purchase lower specification computers because they simply do not need highly powerful machines to meet their basic requirements (e.g. regarding graphic cards, processors, RAM, etc.). Another issue is caused by large variability among the technical equipment, as well as management of administration rights, between different primary schools found both within and between the UK and Germany. This means that educational software for use in primary school classrooms needs to be very flexible and stable in order to run on many different systems. In sum, it is recommended that software developers do not only undertake a thorough survey of the equipment available in the schools they are aiming at, but also to use machines for their development work that are comparable to those available to schools [11]

Another lesson learned regards the engagement of the user in the virtual learning environment. While a nice and appealing appearance of the characters seems not necessary to keep a user's attention [12, 13], believability of the characters seems to be the key consideration when designing a virtual learning environment. Realistic appearance of agents is one approach to believability, which is linked to the danger of the 'uncanny valley' [4]. Autonomy is another way to enhance believability of characters; here, the difficulties lie in the dynamic real-time generation and coordination of verbal and non-verbal expressions and actions, in particular when it comes to emotional expressions. "Even if an agent is able to effectively communicate it's emotions to the user, that agent must also maintain coherence between its emotions and behaviour – an unpredictable character that lacks temporal and/or cross-situational consistency will not be believable" [11].

The believability of the characters and their ability to express emotions is particularly important for applications that aim at facilitating an empathic reaction in the user. This empathic reaction is substantially influenced by the perceived similarity between user and agent [14]. Hence, it seems plausible that different user groups react differently to the FearNot! characters: a small-scale evaluation of FearNot! with children, teachers, and AI experts showed that children responded more positively towards a number of aspects of the software than did teachers or experts, and were also therefore more likely to express empathic reactions [15]. Different users will therefore require different agents in order to empathise with them. It is thus recommended to continuously involve users in the design of characters for virtual learning environments, using a variety of methodologies like design walls, photo-elicitation, mood boards, and focus groups/discussions in different phases of a virtual learning environment's implementation [11].

Acknowledgements

This work was partially supported by European Community (EC) and is currently funded by the eCIRCUS project IST-4-027656-STP. The authors are solely responsible for the content of this publication. It does not represent the opinion of the EC, and the EC is not responsible for any use that might be made of data appearing therein.

References

[1]   Pepler, D. J., & Craig, W. M. (2000). Making a difference in bullying (2000). LaMarsh Research Report # 60. Toronto: York University.

[2]   Wolke, D., Woods, S., Bloomfield, L., & Karstadt, L. (2000). The Association Between Direct and Relational Bullying and Behaviour Problems Among Primary School Children, Journal of Child Psychology and Psychiatry, 41 (8), 989-1002.

[3]   Hungerige, H., & Borg-Laufs, M. (2001). Rollenspiel [Role-Play]. In: M. Borg-Laufs (Ed.), Verhaltenstherapie mit Kindern und Jugendlichen. Tübingen: dgvt-Verlag.

[4]   Mori, M. (2005). On the Uncanny Valley. Proceedings of the Humanoids-2005 workshop: Views of the Uncanny Valley. Dec 5, 2005, Tsukuba, Japan.

[5]   Hall, L., Woods, S., Aylett, R., Newall, L., & Paiva, A. (2005). Achieving empathic engagement through affective interaction with synthetic characters. In: J. Tao, T. Tan, R. W. Picard, (eds.) ACII 2005. LNCS, vol. 3784, pp. 731–731. Heidelberg: Springer.

[6]   Dias, J., & Paiva, A. (2005). Feeling and Reasoning: a Computational Model. In: C. Bento, A. Cardoso, G. Dias (eds.) EPIA 2005. LNCS (LNAI), vol. 3808, pp. 127–140. Heidelberg: Springer.

[7]   Ortony, A., Clore, G., & Collins, A. (1988). The cognitive structure of emotions. Cambridge: University Press.

[8]   Lazarus, R. (1991). Emotion and adaptation. Oxford, NY: University Press.

[9]   Ho, W.C., Dias, J., Figueiredo, R., & Paiva, A. (2007). Agents that remember can tell stories: integrating autobiographic memory into emotional agents. In: AAMAS. Proceedings of Autonomous Agents and Multiagent Systems. New York: ACM Press.

[10]   Aylett, R. S., Louchart, S., Dias, J., Paiva, A., Vala, M., Woods, S., & Hall, L. (2006). Unscripted Narrative for Affectively Driven Characters. IEEE Journal of Graphics and Applications 26(3), 42–52.

[11]   Watson, S., Dautenhahn, K., Ho, W. C, & Dawidowicz, R. (in press). Developing Relationships between Autonomous Agents: Promoting Pro-Social Behaviour through Virtual Learning Environments. In: G. Trajkovski & S. Collins (Eds). Handbook of Agent-Based Societies: Social and Cultural Interactions. IGI Global.

[12]   Woods, S., Hall, L., Sobral, D., Dautenhahn, K., & Wolke, D. (2003) A study into the believability of animated characters in the context of bullying intervention. In: Conference Proceedings IVA 2003, pp. 310-314. Berlin, Germany: Springer.

[13]   Watson, S., Vannini, N., Davis, M., Woods, S., Hall, M., Hall, L., & Dautenhahn, K. (2007). FearNot! an anti-Bullying Intervention: Evaluation of an interactive virtual learning environment. In: Conference Proceedings AISB'07, pp. 446-452.

[14]   Davis, M. H. (1996). Empathy – a social psychological approach. Madison, Wis: Brown & Benchmark Publishers.

[15]   Hall, L., Woods, S., Dautenhahn, K., Sobral, D., Paiva, A., Wolke, D., & Newall, L. (2004). Designing empathic agents: Adults vs Kids. In: Conference Proceedings ITS 2004, pp. 604-613. Berlin, Germany: Springer.

Section 10.2

Case Studies

Collaboration and the Knowledge Economy: Issues, Applications, Case Studies
P. Cunningham and M. Cunningham (Eds.)
IOS Press, 2008

Re-Engineering Assessment and Technology Enhanced Learning: A Blended Approach to Teaching Undergraduate Modules

Dr. Alan HOGARTH[1], Dr. John Biggam[2]

[1]Strategy, Innovation and Enterprise, Glasgow Caledonian University, Glasgow, Scotland,
UK, Tel: +44 141 331 3968 Fax: 44 141 331 3193, Email: A.Hogarth@gcal.ac.uk
[2]People, Management and Leadership, Glasgow Caledonian University, Glasgow,
Scotland, UK; Tel: +44 141 331 3943 Fax: 44 141 331 3193, Email: J.Biggam@gcal.ac.uk

Abstract: The introduction of learning technology is altering the way in which students learn (and tutors teach). With the increasing use of Virtual Learning Environments (VLEs) a more student-centred approach is being encouraged and this in turn leads to a change in the learning and teaching culture from the passive classroom student to one of the active 'independent elearner'. The area of learning, teaching and assessment in education and industry has historically been facilitated by traditional classroom teaching by a teacher in a face-to-face setting. As such, not all institutions, organisations and students are prepared for this change. This paper discusses a blended learning approach, developed by the authors, to teaching undergraduate modules that encourage students to undertake independent learning in a practical and non-threatening manner. This approach is based on the utilisation of aspects of traditional teaching, VLEs and Web 2.0 technologies. The model discussed in this paper is the culmination of a project funded by the Re-Engineering Assessment Project (REAP) and initially involved a questionnaire survey of a group students who were undertaking the traditional module from which a proposal for the 'blended learning' model was posited.

1. Introduction

Traditionally the lecture theatre, seminar room and laboratory, the basis of conventional teaching and learning spaces, have been derived from long-standing teaching and learning models. However, these models are changing. A wider, more diverse student population has created the need for greater flexibility in curriculum design and course delivery, accompanied by innovations in teaching and learning. A more flexible style of teaching and greater independent learning by students is now required to cope with these changes. However, the question is how can independent learning be encouraged, will it be through technology enhanced learning or by one of the older but tried and tested methods such as self-study, videos, computer-based training (CBT), role-plays, groupwork or by teleconferencing or web-based seminars? With all these options to choose from, it can be confusing for many university lecturers and students familiar with the more traditional educational forms. Furthermore, many studies claim that this technology has many advantages over traditional education [8]. However, despite this the use of these technologies by institutions has been at best varied with many tutors and students still coming to terms with Virtual Learning Environments (VLEs) such as Blackboard. Basically the cultural shift to Technology Enhanced Learning has been proving difficult with many lecturing staff and students unwilling to embrace the new approaches [2].

Moreover without proper instruction in the new learning media students are having difficulty becoming 'independent learners' [9]. Fundamentally, most experts agree that more research, experimentation and better tools are needed to approach the maximum potential that this new technology offers, [11] and [8]. How then can all of these techniques become more useful to university staff and students? The answer would appear to be to encourage independent learning by facilitating a 'blended learning' approach. This paper discusses the growing popularity of blended learning and offers a prototype, developed by the authors, utilising this approach to teaching and learning.

2. Objectives

The main objective of the project was to develop a new 'blended learning' model to encourage independent learning. The research was funded by the Re-Engineering Assessment Practices (REAP) project, which was set up by the Scottish Funding Council to encourage changes in teaching and learning through technology. The authors are lecturers of long standing who have worked for several years in the area of developing and using Technology Enhanced Learning. They applied for funding through their institution, Glasgow Caledonian University. Their idea was to consider the adoption of a blended learning approach in order to enhance traditional teaching practices i.e. develop an approach to teaching an undergraduate module using existing some aspects of traditional teaching, Technology Enhanced Learning technology (Blackboard) coupled with Web 2.0 technology. To this end a review of the literature and a student survey were undertaken and a proposal developed [10]. The initial research and idea for a prototype was undertaken in 2006/2007 and the prototype proposed in this paper was developed, based on that research, in the summer of 2007. The next objective is that the findings for this research should hopefully benefit a number of stakeholders including students, staff and also business organisations that employ training schemes as the methods and techniques applied should have a universal benefit. Another objective for any research is to define the terms used in that research. As such it is important to derive a working definition of the main terms in this research, namely 'independent learning' and 'blended learning'. The 'blended learning' model should ultimately alleviate the time, space and geographical location problem of accommodating large numbers of students.

2.1   The Importance of Independent Learning and Blended Learning

The term 'independent learning' is not new, but it does encourage debate on an exact definition of what it is. Discussions on independent learning are awash with synonyms to describe this term. Kesten [12] lists them as, 'autonomous learning, independent study, self-directed learning, student initiated learning, teaching for thinking, learning to learn, self instruction and life-long learning'. Moreover, this proliferation of terms is made worse by the fact that many authors use the same term to mean different things. As Broad [3] says, 'confusion exists due to the number of terms and possible interpretation of those terms'. Furthermore, recent reports highlight the fact that undergraduates, 'struggle to cope with the independent and self directed style of learning expected by higher education tutors' [17]. Given this it can then come as no surprise to discover that students are uncomfortable with independent learning. However the hope of the authors of this paper is that the technology involved in their model will encourage the students to become independent learners. In order that independent learning is successful it will be important that staff and students are competent in VLEs and other learning technologies. Coupled with this they will need new skills in facilitating the relevant instructional methods. There are many views on what blended learning is. However, like so many terms within this field it remains ill defined. For example, Whitelock & Jeffs [16] offer three definitions, 'the integrated combination of traditional learning with web-based online approaches; the combination of media and tools employed in an e-learning environment and the combination of a number of pedagogic approaches, irrespective of learning technology use.' Also, in his support for this approach Masie, cited in Rossett [14] states that, 'We are, as a species, blended learners'. Julian and Boone [12] agree when they argue that, 'The importance of a blended approach to learning is that it ensures the widest possible impact of a learning experience...' The authors of this paper tend to support Valiathan's view of blended learning when he states that, 'Blended learning is also used to describe learning that mixes various event based activities, including face-to-face classrooms, live elearning and self-paced learning'. This view of blended learning is enhanced by three models, skills driven, attitude-driven and competency-driven. However, the problem is that the breadth of interpretations means that almost anything can be seen as blended learning, and consequently this is confusing for academic staff, students and business practitioners. The next section will consider how the utilisation of Web 2.0 technologies for blended learning can encourage independent learning.

2.2   Blended Learning and Web 2.0 Technology

There are a number of areas in Higher Education where, it is argued, that blended learning can help and these include, increasing student numbers, automated assessment, widening participation and improved access to limited resources. However, the most important driver suggested for choosing a blended learning approach is that it will give enhanced benefits to traditional face-to-face teaching and learning and facilitate independent learning. As online tools become more ubiquitous inside and outside the classroom, and the growth of distance learning continues, educational researchers have begun to focus on how best to harness new technologies. As such there are many technologies being researched that can be used to facilitate and stimulate online education including what is referred to as Web 2.0 [5]. This term encompasses a variety of different meanings that include emphasis on user generated content, data and content sharing and collaborative effort together with the use of various kinds of social software such as Second Life, Blogging, WiKis, social book marking, pod casting, vidcasting and (in our case, Compendium software). However technology must not be the driver of blended learning. Technology should never be used simply to substitute face-to-face learning, but must clearly offer an improved educational benefit. Also, coupled with Web 2.0 technology students must involve communication and socialisation and it is here where 'social networking' activity if applied correctly could prove beneficial. The loss of face-to-face presence is, understandably, one of the most contested issues in online learning. Hara and Kling [7] note that, 'Human communication is inherently ambiguous but that these ambiguities are generally resolved adequately in face-to-face contexts'. Garrison et al [6] agree but comment further when they state, 'In face to face interaction communication can be entrusted to habit or instinct...communicators in a virtual environment have to 'think' about their metacommunication'. Therefore a social environment online is necessary. As such, this situation could be improved through the use of social networking tools such as WiKis and web logs. On reviewing the available technologies associated with web 2.0 the authors were impressed by the possibilities for their own model. The next section will discuss the activities that led to the development of the blended learning prototype.

3. Methodology

3.1   The Re-engineering Assessment Practice (REAP) Project

As stated earlier this paper discusses the development of a prototype model funded by the REAP project within Glasgow Caledonian University. The authors' proposal was to convert the existing third year undergraduate module from a traditional face-to-face format into a format based on Technology Enhanced Learning/blended technologies. The existing module format comprises of 12 lectures, 12 seminars, a clinic and a lab and is of 12 weeks duration.

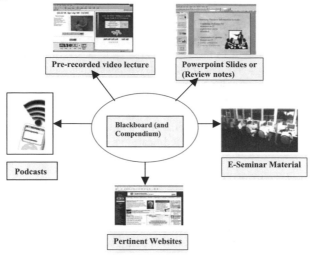

Figure 1: Package for Independent Learning and Teaching (PILAT)

The current assessment is in two parts, group coursework (50%) and a final examination (50%). In general it is envisaged that the changes would encourage independent learning by the students and instigate some degree of online assessment. The model has incorporated 'blended learning' features including face-to-face, Blackboard, Compendium software and social networking technology. The methodology adopted for the original project included a literature search and a survey. This in turn produced a proposal for the development of a blended learning prototype. The methodology for this paper was essentially based on this proposal. The proposal was to convert traditional lectures and seminars to an online format using a combination of the Blackboard VLE, the Open University's 'Compendium' software, Web 2.0 technologies and some element of face-to-face communication. This has now been completed with the production of the prototype, which will be highlighted in this paper. A student survey was previously undertaken where the questionnaire comprised a series of yes/no questions and one opinion based question. Overall the responses were in favour of a 'blended' approach and this led to the proposal (See Figure 1) and a framework on the way forward for the project. The prototype discussed in the paper was based on that proposal.

4. Technology and Developments

When developing the blended learning prototype it was considered from two perspectives; pedagogy and technology. From a pedagogical perspective independent learning and blended learning aspects were incorporated and from a technological perspective how best to encourage the students to access the model were considered. As such a variety of technology platforms were used to build the prototype, however the main vehicles were Compendium software for content management and Blackboard for the group communication element and formative assessment.

Figure 2: eMBIS Lecture on Blackboard

Other Web 2.0 technologies such as Blogging and pod casting are also incorporated in the prototype. Based on the authors' original ideas and enhanced by the student responses to the questionnaire [10] the prototype incorporates many features both in Blackboard (See Figure 2) and by the innovative use of the Compendium software (See Figures 3 – 7 for examples of the content developed). Compendium's advantage is that it allows for the incorporation of all manner of content such as the video lectures, podcasts, Powerpoint slides, seminar material etc., (See figure 6), that the students can access online on a weekly basis (i.e. each teaching week) thus cutting classroom time (and room allocation) and encouraging independent learning. However, access to the tutor will always be available at the weekly clinic to deal with any issues that may arise. The video presentations were recorded with Movie Maker Pro and are of 5-10 minutes duration; podcasts were recorded with Audacity (links to practitioner podcasts are also attached); links to relevant subject websites were included as were PowerPoint slides and seminar material for the lecture topic. E Seminars are facilitated in Blackboard's Virtual Classroom and students' participation will be monitored (contribution rates can be logged in BlackBoard) and this will form part of the module assessment.

Figure 3: Initial Screen Option for eMBIS in Compendium

The weekly face-to-face Clinic will be timetabled for all students for advice and assistance with any aspect of the module and would be held to maintain a personal link with the students.

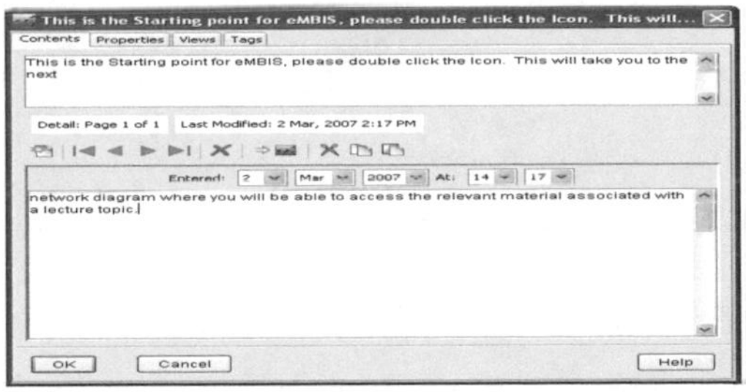

Figure 4: Set up screen for text instructions

Assessment instruments are also catered for in the prototype (See figure 7). Formative assessment using BlackBoard Multiple Choice Questions (MCQ) can be facilitated.

Blogging software is to be used for keeping a diary of issues and developments and web-based presentations will be assessed. The final examination will be held in a traditional format, thus adding to the blended learning ethos. The blended learning prototype is a work in progress and further work will be required. As such the final results will not be known until the prototype goes live at start of the new semester in October 2008 (see Section 5). It does however currently demonstrate how the teaching module will function in this blended learning mode.

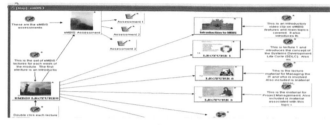

Figure 5: First Screen showing all Lectures and Assessments

The lessons learnt from this research project thus far are that developing such a prototype is very time consuming (the authors worked on the project while still maintaining a full teaching commitment) and although constrained by time and minimal funding the authors have managed to produce a working prototype.

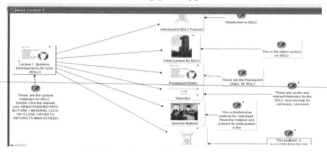

Figure 6: Content of an eMBIS lecture

Essentially the next phase of the project will be to fully convert and set up the full 'content' of the eMBIS module (even completing the prototype was very time consuming) before going live.

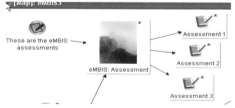

Figure 7: Clicking on the icons will access the assessment task

5. Business Benefits

According to Michael Clouser of eCornell business take up for Technology Enhanced Learning for Continual Professional Development (CPD) is increasing by 25% a year. Coupled with this many business organisations have also adopted blended learning and recognise this as an important component of their overall strategy. For example BUPA have hired Brightwave to train their 2,500 employees. Claire Shell [17], elearning manger at BUPA states that, 'Working with Brightwave... has shaped our use of elearning and blended learning'. County Durham Primary Care Trust [4] have also utilised blended learning to, 'provide a training programme that combines face–to-face and elearning'. Furthermore, blended learning programmes are increasing within business organisations. According to research by Balance Learning and Training Magazine [1],'blended learning is now used by 55% of organisations' and in a further study '81% of organisations surveyed believe blended learning is an effective means of learning'. Given that many business organisations are already familiar with the concept of blended learning, the prototype developed by the authors will not only encourage independent learning amongst university students, but will also provide such business organisations with an easy to use and adaptable approach to teaching and learning. It is expected that the blended learning model will go live in October 2008, when a group of third year undergraduates will be asked to participate. It is envisaged that they will be issued with either a CD or USB flash drive containing the content for the model. These students will then be able to offer their views on the model via questionnaires and interview sessions and the results will be compared with responses from a group of students who did not use the new model. Given that we receive a positive response from the students then the idea initially would be to offer it to other courses and departments via training sessions. The model will hopefully alleviate the issues of increasing student numbers, encourage automated assessment, allow for widening participation and improved access to limited resources.

6. Conclusion

In the literature, in business and in educational institutions it has been recognised that blended learning is being driven by technology and this in turn should encourage independent learning. However, there is some confusion over which technology may be the most suitable to encourage such independent learning. Furthermore some businesses, tutors and students are wary of the change in traditional teaching approaches and as such do not wholly embrace the idea of elearning for all aspects of teaching. However given that blended learning incorporates elements of traditional teaching with those of elearning technology this approach could be the solution to those concerns. To this end the authors have developed a 'blended learning prototype'. Although the model is currently just that, a prototype, the next phase of the project is to test the product with a group of students and evaluate its effectiveness. Depending on the results of this research the blended learning model structure could then be exploited for any module on any course and also be used/adapted in the business environment for training courses. Given our experiences with this project the authors suggest that utilising Web 2.0 technology and Blackboard facilities, with some aspects of traditional teaching, in our blended learning model offers an attractive approach for students and should encourage independent learning. Other avenues to consider include developing an 'eBook' for the eMBIS module content. Further work will also be required to investigate the security and robustness of the final product along with consideration of facilities for disabled and international users.

Acknowledgement

Support for this project was provided by the Scottish Funding Council under the Re-Engineering Assessment Practices (REAP) project, which was initiated to encourage lecturers/tutors in higher education institutions to develop innovative approaches in teaching and learning through technology.

References

[1] Balance Learning and Training (2004). 'Blended Learning in the UK', Survey 2004, Balance Learning and Training Magazine.
[2] Biggam, J. (2004), "Preparing for Elearning in Higher Education: Drivers, Barriers and Pedagogical Issues", PhD thesis, Glasgow Caledonian University.
[3] Broad, J., (2006), "Interpretations of independent learning in further education". Journal of Further and Higher Education, 30, 2, May.
[4] County Durham PCT (2007), "County Durham PCT opts for blended learning" online at: http://www.trainingreference.co.uk/news/b1071008.htm
[5] Franklin, T. and Van Harmelen, M (2007). "Web 2.0 for Content for Learning and Teaching in Higher Education", Report funded by JISC, Franklin Consulting, May 2007.
[6] Garrison, D.R., Anderson, T. and Archer, W. (2001), 'Critical thinking, cognitive presence and computer conferencing in distance education', American Journal of Distance Education, 15, 1, pp7-23.
[7] Hara, N. and Kling, R. (2000), 'Students' frustration with a web based distance education course: a taboo topic in the discourse', First Monday, 4(12), pp1-34.
[8] Higher Education Academy, (2004), Online at: http://www.heacademy.ac.uk/.
[9] Hogarth, A. (2006), "New Conceptual Paradigms for Introducing Groupwork and Group Based Technology in the HE Environment", in Proceedings of eChallenges 2006, Barcelona.
[10] Hogarth and Biggam (2007), "Technology Enhanced Learning in Higher Education: A REAP Case Study", in Proceedings of eChallenges 2007, The Hague, Holland.
[11] Joint Information Systems Committee (JISC), (2002), 'Inform Issue 1: Reviewing our use of technology', Online at: http://www.jisc.ac.uk/index.cfm?name=pub_inform1
[12] Julian, E.H. & Boone, C. (2001).Blended Learning Solutions: Improving the Way Companies Manage Intellectual Capital online at:http://sunned.sun.com/US/images/final_IDC_SES_6_22_01.pdf
[13] Kesten, C. (1987). 'Independent learning: a common essential learning', a study completed for the Saskatchewan Dept of Education: University of Regina.
[14] Rossett, A. (ed.) (2002). The ASTD E-Learning Handbook. New York, McGraw-Hill. http://www.learningcircuits.org/2002/aug2002/valiathan.html
[15] Shell, C. (2007), "Blended Learning supports BUPA project", online at: http://www.trainingreference.co.uk/news/b1070201.htm
[16] Whitelock, D. and Jeffs, A. (2003), Editorial: Journal of Educational Media Special Issue on Blended Learning, Journal of Educational Media, 28(2-3).
[17] Wilde, C., Wright, S., Hayward, G., Johnson, J and Skerrett, R. (2006), Nuffield review of higher education in focus groups preliminary report. Oxford University, Online at: http://www.nuffield14-19review.org.uk/files/news44-2.pdf

Collaboration and the Knowledge Economy: Issues, Applications, Case Studies
P. Cunningham and M. Cunningham (Eds.)
IOS Press, 2008

Model of Impact of Technology-Enhanced Organizational Learning on Business Performance

Tanja ARH[1], Vlado DIMOVSKI[2,] Borka JERMAN BLAŽIČ[1]

[1]*Jožef Stefan Institute, Jamova 39, Ljubljana, 1000, Slovenia*
Tel: +386 1 477 33 36, Fax: +386 1 477 39 95, Email: tanja@e5.ijs.si, borka@e5.ijs.si
[2]*University of Ljubljana, Faculty of Economics, Kardeljeva ploščad 17,*
Ljubljana, 1000, Slovenia
Tel: +386 1 589 25 58, Fax: + 386 589 26 98, Email: vlado.dimovski@ef.lj-uni.si

Abstract: Nowadays, the information-communication technologies and technology-enhanced learning are making access to a wide range of different sources of knowledge. In companies, knowledge is being expressed via employees and their intellectual capital. Mastering of this knowledge is becoming crucial for successful working and presents an important source of competitive advantages in companies. The paper focuses on the presentation of conceptualization of a structural model that had been developed to test the impact of technology-enhanced organizational learning on companies' business performance with more than 50 employees. In accordance with stakeholder theory and balanced scorecard, both financial and non-financial aspects of performance are considered. In this paper, special attention is given to the presentation of definitions of four main construct of research model: technology-enhanced learning, organizational learning, financial and non-financial business performance and their operationalisation. Theoretical and empirical basis for the relationship between the above mentioned constructs are being examined. The paper concludes with the presentation of the hypothesized research model.

Keywords: technology-enhanced learning, organizational learning, business performance, operationalisation, hypothesized research model

1. Introduction

The employees' knowledge significantly contributes to the companies' ability to react to requirements of fast market changes, customer needs and successful business processes. As such, companies need to manage the knowledge of their employees. Maintaining the knowledge means to evaluate the employees' tacit and explicit knowledge as well as provision of the knowledge within the company with suitable tools.

When companies intend to acquire knowledge by educating their employees, suitable methods are based on technology-enhanced learning (TEL). Technology-enhanced learning as a means of knowledge and competences acquisition, has been widely adopted as a promising solution by many companies to offer learning-on-demand opportunities to individual employees in order to reduce training time and cost. Technology-enhanced learning, referring to learning via the Internet, has become a major phenomenon in recent years. Through TEL, workers have access to various online databases, tools and e-services that help them find solutions for work-related problems [13, 14].

To perform effectively, employees and all members of the company need to continuously refresh and enhance their skills and knowledge. As human capital replaces physical capital as the source of competitive advantage, organizational learning (OL) has emerged as a key enabler of success. The study of organizational learning is relevant as it seeks to respond to the challenges that arise in a constantly changing business environment and can help companies to confront to their long-term survival difficulties. Organizational learning thus represents a source of heterogeneity and of potentially sustainable competitive advantages, because of the companies' different capabilities for learning and absorbing knowledge [1, 2].

The analysis of organizational learning has become an increasingly important study area over the recent years. Various works have dealt with the analysis of this construct from different viewpoints. There are studies that focus on this construct using a psychological approach [3, 4], a sociological approach [5, 6], or from the point of view of organizational theory [7, 8, 9]. More recently, learning has been considered, from a strategic perspective, as a source of heterogeneity among organizations, as well as a basis for a possible competitive advantage [10, 11, 16, 17, 18, 19]. Recently it is coupled with the question of organizational business performance. Stakeholder theory addresses organizational performance evaluation from multiple perspectives - shareholders, employees, customers and suppliers of a certain company.

This paper aims at presenting the conceptualisation of a research model for impact and connection assessment of four basic constructs: technology-enhanced learning (TEL), organisational learning (OL), financial (FP) and non-financial (NFP) performance, in accordance with the shareholder theory [12, 25], and balanced scorecard [23]. The paper provides definitions of technology-enhanced learning and technical terms related to it, its scope and the process of organisational learning, as well as a method for business performance assessment. Special attention is afforded to the presentation of the observed correlations between the aforementioned constructs.

The paper is divided in three parts: (1) conceptualisation of a structural sub-model, which entails constructs and relationships among them; (2) operationalisation of constructs (latent variables) with the purpose of developing a measurement sub-model and a measurement instrument, and (3) the presentation of a hypothesized research model, aimed at empirical assessment of impact and correlations among TEL, OL, FP and NFP.

2. Conceptualisation of Structural Sub-model

A complete research model normally consists of two sub-models: measurement and structural. The measurement sub-model shows how each latent variable is operationalised through observations of corresponding indicators. The structural sub-model describes relationships between the latent variables.

Development of a quality model requires first to establish a structural framework, which is usually implemented in two steps: presentation of fundamental constructs and review of potential correlations between them. Consequently, the next sub-sections focus on the presentation of theoretical foundations of the observed constructs, the presentation of hypothesized relationships between the latent variables and the issue of operationalisation of these constructs.

2.1 Technology-Enhanced Leaning

Kirschner and Paas defined technology-enhanced learning as a learning process in which Internet plays the key role in the presentation, support, management and assessment of learning [22]. Rosenberg defines technology-enhanced learning as a learning process in which information technology partially or fully undertakes the role of a mediator between different stakeholders involved in the learning process [34]. We refer to the process of studying and teaching as technology-enhanced learning when it includes information and communication technology, regardless of the mode or the scope of its use [20, 21].

2.2   Organisational Learning

Despite its importance or maybe precisely because of it, organisational learning is defined in numerous ways and approached from different perspectives. The pioneers [26, 8] defined organisational learning as an individual's acquisition of information and knowledge, and development of analytical and communicational skills. Understanding organisational learning as a process, which can take up different levels of development, makes the learning organisational structure an ideal form of organisation, which can only be achieved once the process of organisational learning is fully optimised and the organisation is viewed as a system [8]. Jones emphasizes importance of organizational learning for organizational performance defining it as "a process through which managers try to increase organizational members" capabilities in order to understand better and manage with organization and its environment to accept decisions that increase organizational performance on a continuous basis"[15].

The aforementioned statements regarding the lack of unity of organisational learning definitions are also supported by the findings of [27, 18]. The former states that extensive research carried out in the field of organisational learning has mostly been fragmented, while the latter adds the fragmentation lead to the multitude of definitions, for ex. [28, 29], differing according to the criteria of inclusion, scope and focus [30]. Dimovski provided an overview of previous research and identified four varying perspectives on organizational learning. His model managed to merge informational, interpretational, strategic and behavioural approaches to organizational learning and defined it as a process of information acquisition, information interpretation and resulting behavioural and cognitive changes which should, in turn, have an impact on company's performance [18, 31].

Development of our research model is based on DiBelle and Nevis' model [32] of integrated approach, according to which the organisational learning factors are divided into study guidelines and study promoters, and on the Dimovski approach [18], which combines aforementioned four aspects of organisational learning.

2.3   Companies' performance

Company performance assessments have advanced over the past years, and developed from traditional, exclusively financial criteria, to modern criteria, which include also non-financial indicators. The theory of economics started developing improved models for performance assessment, taking into account all shareholders: employees, customers and supplier's employees and the wider community, also advocated by the Freeman's theory of shareholders [25, 12]. The existing models, based on accounting categories, combine with non-financial data and the assessment of the so called "soft" business areas, which mostly improves the assessment of companies' perspective possibilities [33]. For a good performance of a modern company we need to introduce, along with the financial indicators (FP) also non-financial indicators (NFP). There are several approaches to choosing the non-financial indicators, among the modern performance assessment methods, the best known ones are the Total Quality Management (TQM) model and the Balanced Scorecard model (BSC) [23].

2.4   Relationship among Constructs

Findings based on a rather wide overview and systematisation of literature has shown that we can expect positive impact of ICT and technology-enhanced learning on organisational learning. Robey et al. do warn that technology-enhanced learning and relative ICT may take either the role of a promoter or the role of an inhibitor of organisational learning [35].

Correlation between organisational learning and business success is often a controversial issue when it comes to company's management [36]. Some authors believe better performance is related to organisational learning, though their definitions of business results differ greatly. In relation to this we can mention the capacity of organisational learning to have a positive impact on the financial results [37, 38], on the results related to shareholders [39, 40] and on the business results, such as innovativeness and greater productivity [41]. Mintzberg says the company performance is important feedback, information on effectiveness and efficiency of the learning process [42]. The recent study of Perez, Lopez, Montes Peon and Vazquez Ordas has shown organisational learning has a significant impact on companies' performance [43]. It is also interesting to look at the past findings related to the correlation between financial and non-financial business performance indicators. Empirical literature is still very limited in this field, yet surprisingly enough Chakravarthy's [24] findings indicate there is no correlation between the two.

3. Conceptualisation of Measurement Sub-model

Having understood the hypothesized correlations between the latent variables, the following question is a logical consequence: how should these four constructs be operationalised and measured.

3.1 Development of the research instrument

The questionnaire used has been experiencing constant development and validation for more than 10 years. Dimovski [18] used it on sample of Ohio credit unions in order to measure the organizational learning process as a source of competitive advantage. Škerlavaj [30] upgraded it to include measures of non-financial performance, while he replaced industry-specific measures of financial performance with two measures valid for all companies. For this study the operationalisation of all four construct involved was improved and applied on a sample of Slovenian firms with more than 50 employees in 2007. The reason to include smaller companies is to improve the generalizability of the research findings. The measurement instrument used in this study has 22 items for the technology-enhanced learning construct, 29 items for organizational learning construct, three items for financial and four items for non-financial performance. Pre-testing procedures were conducted in the form of interviews and the studies with managers, focus groups with research and academic colleagues. Table 1 presents constructs, indicators used for construct assessment, number of items summed up to give the value of an indicator and theory or empirical research on the basis of which the measurement items were developed.

Latent Variables (constructs)	Indicators and Number of Items from Questionnaire	Theoretical Grounds, Research, Authors
Technology-Enhanced Learning (TEL)	• Information and Comm. Infrastructure (ICI) – 9 items • Education Technology (ET) – 10 items • Learning Contents (LC) – 3 items	• [22], [20], [34], [41]
Organisational Learning (OL)	• Knowledge Acquisition (KAC) – 9 items • Knowledge Transmission (KTR) – 10 items • Use of Knowledge (UoK) – 10 items	• [18], [32]
Financial Performance (FP)	• Return on Assets (FP1) – 1 item • Return on Equity (FP2) – 1 item • Added value per employee (FP3) – 1 item	
Non-Financial Performance (NFP)	• Employee fluctuation (NFP1) – 1 item • Share of loyal customers (NFP) – 1 item • Number of customer complaints (NFP3) – 1 item • Supplier relations (NFP4) – 1 item	• [12], [23], [25], [45]

Table 1: Specification of constructs

In short, the hypothesized model shall be composed of four constructs and 13 indicators, and will be of recursive nature, meaning that there shall be no cases of two variables appearing simultaneously, i.e. as a cause and a consequence to one another.

4. Research Hypotheses and Model

Once the theoretical frame of the model is devised, illustration of conceptualisation by the means of a flow chart is to be tackled. Flow chart is a graphical representation of interrelations between various elements of a model. Measurement variables belonging to exogenous latent variables are marked with an x, while their measurement deviations are marked with a δ. Endogenous latent variable indicators are marked with a y, and measurement deviations with an ε. Structural equation deviations are ζ, exogenous latent variables are ξ, endogenous constructs are η, and one-way influence of exogenous latent variables on exogenous are γ. To describe relations between latent variables and their indicators (measurement variables) we use λ. Figure 1 below illustrates a conceptualised research model, presenting all basic constructs and hypothesized correlations between them. We aim at proving: (1) that the latent variable of technology-enhanced learning (TEL) has positive impact on organisational learning (OL), (2) financial (FP) and (3) non-financial performance (NFP); (4) that the latent variable of organisational learning (OL) as a process of knowledge creation leads to improved financial results (FP), as well as to (5) improved non-financial results (NFP); (6) that it is impossible to expect significant statistical correlations between financial performance (FP) and non-financial (NFP) performance.

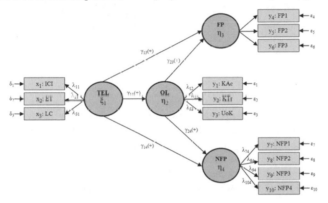

Figure 1: Conceptualised research model

5. Research procedure

Table 2 provides the procedure of analyzing the data. First, item analysis is performed to describe the sample characteristics, to investigate the item means, and to assess item-to-total correlations. Second, exploratory factor analysis is performed to explore whether the items load highly on their intended latent construct, and have low cross-loadings. After the exploratory factor analysis, the reliability of the underlying factors is discussed in terms of Cronbach's alphas. Third, confirmatory analysis (CFA) is performed to ensure that the constructs are valid and reliable; this refers to the measurement part of the model. Consequently, CFAs (without any structural relationships) are performed with LISREL 8.80 to check whether the items meet the criteria for convergent and discriminant validity, as well as construct reliability. In this phase, the presence of multicollinearity is also investigated through regression and correlation analysis. The properties of the four research constructs in the proposed model (Figure 1) and the six hypotheses is tested using a LISREL 8.80 and PRELIS 2.30 package for structural equation analysis and procedures [44]. As estimation method for model evaluation and procedures, the maximum likelihood (ML) method and the two stage testing processes is utilized. Structural Equation Modeling (SEM) is designed to evaluate how well a proposed conceptual model that contains observed indicators and hypothetical constructs explains or fits the collected data. It also provides the ability to measure or specify the structural relationships among sets of unobserved (latent) variables, while describing the amount of unexplained variance. Clearly, the hypothetical model in this study was designed to measure structural relationships among the unobserved constructs that are set up on the basis of relevant theories and prior empirical research and results. Therefore, the SEM procedure is an appropriate solution for testing the proposed structural model and hypotheses for this study. Presentation of research results is planned to take place mid-2008.

Stage	Analysis	Purpose
1.	Item analysis	Investigation of sample characteristics Investigation of item means Investigation of item-to-total correlations
2.	Exploratory factor analysis	Exploration of loadings; removal of items with low loadings and high cross-loadings; Assessment of number of latent factors Assessment of reliability (Cronbach's alpha)
3.	Confirmatory factor analysis	Assessment of convergent validity Assessment of discriminant validity Assessment of construct reliability Assessment of correlations and multicollinearity
4.	Testing the hypothesis	Assessment of structural relationship (H1-H6) Parameter Estimates for Overall Measurement Model Convergent and Discriminant Validity
5.	Presentation of results	Discussion of findings

Table 2: Research procedure

6. Conclusions

The aim of this paper was to present the conceptualisation of a model for assessment of impact of technology-enhanced learning, and the respective information and communication technology on the business performance of Slovene companies with more than 50 employees. We have studied the theoretical and empirical grounds for the correlations between the aforementioned constructs, and in the end presented a hypothesized research model. Empirical analysis of the model shall be presented in the second part of the research.

This study contributes to the technology-enhanced learning and organizational learning base of knowledge in three dimensions: (1) theoretical, (2) methodological, and (3) practical. Technology-enhanced learning contributes to sustainable competitive advantage through its interaction with other resources. Recent literature suggests that organizational learning is a process that plays an important role in enhancing a firm's competitive advantage [37] and which may benefit from the judicious application of technology-enhanced learning. It has also been argued that for firms to be successful they must complement TEL with OL. Within the broader conceptual framework, this study focuses on the relationship between technology-enhanced learning, organizational learning and business performance. As such, the conceptual model offers several research opportunities and provides a solid base for a further empirical testing of hypotheses related to technology-enhanced learning and organizational learning.

References

[1]   Easterby-Smith, M., Crossan, M. and Nicolini, D. Organizational Learning: Debates Past, Present and Future, Journal of Management Studies 37(6), 2000, pp. 783–96.
[2]   Lei, D., Slocum, J. W., & Pitts, R. A. Designing organizations for competitive advantage: The power of unlearning and learning. Organizational Dynamics, 27(3), 1999, pp. 24–38.
[3]   Cyert, R. M., March, J. G. Behavioural Theory of the Firm. Englewood Cliffs: Prentice Hall, 1963.

[4]   Daft, R. L., Weick, K. E. Toward a model of organizations as interpretation systems. The Academy of Management Review, 9(2), 1984, pp. 284–95.

[5]   Nelson, R. R, Winter S. G. An evolutionary theory of economic change. Cambridge: Belknap Press; 1982.

[6]   Levitt, B., March J. G. Organizational learning. Annual Review of Sociology, 14, 1998, pp. 319–340.

[7]   Cangelosi, V. E., Dill W. R. Organizational learning: observations toward a theory. Administrative Science Quarterly, 10, 1965, pp. 175–203.

[8]   Senge, P. M. The fifth discipline: art and practice of the learning organization. New York: Doubleday; 1990.

[9]   Huber, G. P. Organizational Learning: The Contributing Processes and the Literatures. Organization Science, 2(1), 1991, pp. 88–115.

[10]   Grant, R. M. Prospering in dynamically-competitive environments: organizational capability as knowledge integration. Organization Science, 7(4), 1996, pp. 375–387.

[11]   Lei, D., Hitt, M. A., Bettis, R. Dynamic core competencies through meta-learning and strategic context. Journal of Management, 22(4), 1996, pp. 549–69.

[12]   Freeman, E. R. Strategic Management – A Stakeholder Approach, London: Pitman; 1984.

[13]   Zhang, D. Media structuration – Towards an integrated approach to interactive multimedia-based E-Learning. Ph.D. dissertation, The University of Arizona, 2002.

[14]   Zhang, D., & Nunamaker, J. F. Powering e-learning in the new millennium: an overview of e-learning and enabling technology. Information Systems Frontiers, 5(2), 2003, pp. 207–218.

[15]   Jones, G. R. Organizational Theory, 3rd edition. New York: Prentice Hall, 2000.

[16]   Lei, D., Slocum J. W., Pitts R. A. Designing organizations for competitive advantage: the power of unlearning and learning. Organizational dynamics, 1999, pp. 24–38

[17]   Dimovski, V., Škerlavaj, M., Kimman, M., Hernaus, T. Proces organizacijskega učenja v slovenskih, hrvaških in malezijskih podjetjih. Management 1(2), 2007, pp. 101–113.

[18]   Dimovski, V. Organisational learning and competitive advantage. PhD, Cleveland State University, 1994.

[19]   Dimovski, V., Škerlavaj, M. Performance effects of organizational learning in a transitional economy. Problems and Perspectives in Management 3(4), 2005, pp. 56–67

[20]   Henry, P. E-learning technology, content and services, Education + Training, vol. 43(4), MCB University Press, USA, 2001.

[21]   Dinevski, D., Plenković, M. Modern University and e-learning, Media, culture and public relations, Vol 2, 2002, pp. 137–146.

[22]   Kirchner, P. A. & Pass, F. Web enhanced higher education: a Tower of Babel.Computers in human behaviour, 17(4), 2001, pp. 347–53.

[23]   Kaplan, R. S., Norton, D. P. Balanced Scorecard – Measures That Drive Performance, Harvard Business Review, 1-2, 1992, pp. 71–79.

[24]   Chakravarthy, B. S. Measuring Strategic Performance, Strategic Management Journal, 7, 1986, pp. 437–458.

[25]   Freeman, E. R. Politics of Stakeholder Theory: Some Future Directions, Business; Ethics Quarterly, 4, 1994, pp. 409–422.

[26]   Argyris, C. Schön, D. A. Organizational Learning II: Theory, Method and Practice, Reading, MA: Addison-Wesley, 1996.

[27]   Shrivastava, P. A Typology of Organizational Learning Systems, Journal of Management Studies, 20, 1983, pp. 1–28.

[28]   Nonaka, I., Takeuchi, H. A Theory of Organizational Knowledge Creation, International Journal of Technology Management, 11(7/8), 1996, pp. 833–46.

[29]   Wall, B. Measuring the Right Stuff: Identifying and Applying the Right Knowledge, Knowledge Management Review, 1(4), 1998, pp. 20–24.

[30]   Škerlavaj, M. Vpliv informacijsko-komunikacijskih tehnologij in organizacijskega učenja na uspešnost poslovanja: teoretična in empirična analiza, Master thesis, Ljubljana: Ekonomska fakulteta, 2003.

[31]   Dimovski, V., Colnar, T. Organizacijsko učenje, Teorija in praksa, 5(36), 1999, pp. 701–722.

[32]   DiBella, J. A. In Nevis, E.C.: How Organizations Learn – An Integrated Strategy for Building Learning Capability. San Francisco, CA: Jossey-Bass, 1998.

[33]   Bergant, Ž. Sodobni pogledi na ugotavljanje uspešnosti družbe. Slovenska ekonomska revija, 1–2/, Ljubljana, Zveza ekonomistov Slovenije, 1998, pp. 87–101.

[34]   Rosenberg, M. E-Learning, Strategies for Developing Knowledge in the Digital Age,NewYork: McGraw-Hill, 2001.

[35]   Robey, D., M. Boudreau, Rose, G. M. Information Technology and Organizational Learning: a Review and Assessment of Research, Accounting, Management and Information Technologies, 10, 2000, pp. 125–155.

[36]   Inkpen, A., & Crossan, M. M. Believing is seeing: Organizational learning in joint ventures. Journal of Management Studies, 32(5), 1995, pp. 595–618.
[37]   Lei, D., Slocum, J. W., Pitts, R. A. Designing organizations for competitive advantage: the power of unlearning and learning. Organizational dynamics, 1999, pp. 24–38.
[38]   Slater, S. F., & Narver, J. C. Market orientation and the learning organization. Journal of Marketing, 59(3), 1995, pp. 63–74.
[39]   Goh, S., & Richards, G. Benchmarking the learning capability of organizations. European Management Journal, 15(5), 1997, pp. 575–583.
[40]   Ulrich, D., Jick, T., & von Glinow, M. A. High-impact learning: Building and diffusing learning capability. Organizational Dynamics, 22(2), 1993, pp. 52–66.
[41]   Leonard-Barton, D. The factory as a learning laboratory. Sloan Management Review, 34(1), 1992, pp. 23–38.
[42]   Mintzberg, H. Strategy formation: Schools of thought. In J. W. Frederickson (Ed.), Perspectives of strategic management. New York' Harper Business, 1990, pp. 105–235.
[43]   Péréz López, S., Montes Peón, J. M., & Vázquez Ordás, C. Managing knowledge: The link between culture and organizational learning. Journal of Knowledge Management, 8(6), 2004, pp. 93–104.
[44]   Jöreskog, K. G., Sörbrom, D. LISREL 8: Structural Equation Modelling with the SIMPLIS Command Language, London: Lawrence Erlbaum Associates Publishers, 1993.

Collaboration and the Knowledge Economy: Issues, Applications, Case Studies
P. Cunningham and M. Cunningham (Eds.)
IOS Press, 2008

"Whole Language" System for the Technology Enhanced Learning of Handwriting and Reading

Gabor HROTKO

jMind Consulting Ltd, 5-9 Színház u. Budapest, 1014, Hungary
Tel: +36703176050 Fax: +3613768169 Email: Hrotko@t-online.hu

Abstract: Developing the Write&Read technology enhanced learning system we had the following objectives: full autonomy of learning, motivation, personalization. The system allows to learn handwriting and reading autonomously starting from the very beginning up to full acquisition of skills. For motivation the lessons are embedded in an animated series of fairy tales where an active role belongs to the student who is always helping the characters by handwriting and reading in difficult situations. An innovative IT based teaching technology of copying written and spoken words is magnifying learning efficiency. The system is adaptive, the teaching process is tailored to the personal abilities of the student thanks to an automatic switching between exercises with increasing difficulty. In the virtual environment the "whole language approach" is working very naturally to achieve reading comprehension. A special construction of repetition is helping the student to acquire higher-level reading skills.

1. Introduction

The main objective of the Write&Read (WR) project was to build a technology enhanced learning system for the most traditional discipline of education, the teaching of handwriting and reading. In the background of the project there is a patented invention proposing technical and methodological innovations to reform the teaching of literacy on the base of IT solutions such as flash animation, digital voice and image recording, multimedia, automatic speech recognition, automatic handwriting recognition. The result of the implementation is a new teaching technology where the curriculum is embedded in an animated story, the traditional methods of school teaching are improved and integrated using original IT methods. The basic idea was that by copying written and spoken language elements the students will learn the essence of writing and reading. This simple idea evolved into a sophisticated e-learning methodology offering the opportunity for everybody to learn literacy autonomously without the help of teachers, independently of languages, cultural backgrounds and pedagogical infrastructures, economic and social circumstances. The implementation of the system in several languages will open a perspective for the army of illiterates to step into the world of knowledge.

2. State of the art

A rampant activity is going on in the development of computational aids to help children in learning writing and reading. In the last decade a number of lively animated products have been issued to help and stimulate learning, while eliminating its monotony[i].

Start Write is a useful resource for teaching beginners how to write. While it sounds odd to have a computer program, which develops handwriting skills, Start Write lets instructors create customized practice sheets with guidelines which students can trace. It comes with several different sizes and styles of fonts, clip art and a spell checker, as well as all the standard features of a word processor. Instructors can add arrows to show the direction of hand movement, type in dots, dashes or solid letters, and control the shading of the printed text. It will print lines and underlines and is very easy to use, with a simple Point and Click feature. There are template lessons included, and one can create phonics or spelling pages or even letters to a friend, depending on the level of the students. It also lets the user import graphics and pictures, for personalizing the printed page.

There are a large number of computerized aids helping children to learn reading. Probably the most sophisticated experiment was the "Watch-me! Read" program (WMR) developed by IBM[ii]. Using WMR, "…a child can read aloud from an electronic book accompanied by a computerized "pal" who provides assistance throughout the reading session. The "pal" recognizes mistakes and asks students to repeat words they have misread, reading words correctly to them if necessary. … Because teachers often do not have the time to provide every child with individualized reading attention, WMR assists in addressing differences in reading experiences and language backgrounds through an engaging, book-based approach." WMR may be a very useful aid to improve reading after acquiring a certain level of skills and experience.

The objective of the ambitious THRASS system[iii] was to reform the teaching of English writing and reading. Its central module contains 44 phonemes in 120 different written combinations. Choosing one of these combinations the student can hear its proper pronunciation. Inversely, when a phoneme is pronounced the student has to select one of its possible written forms. Reacting to the right choice its pronunciation is repeated and a sample word containing the selected written form is shown. Using the "Writing Module" pronounced sample words are to be typed by the student. In case of wrong typing the correct form is displayed. Finally, in the "Spelling Module" sample words are presented for spelling. The "Teaching Guide", explains how the THRASS multi-sensory resources (audio, magnetic, printed, software and video) are used in the ten-stage phonics program known as THRASS Whole-Picture Keyword Phonics. The program teaches children and adults about the building blocks of English words and the thinking processes, the metacognitive processes or, more formerly, the Phonographic Metacognition involved in reading and writing the five hundred basewords of written English. The guide is divided into eleven main sections, with one section for each of the THRASS 10 stages and a separate Photocopiable Section containing reference and assessment sheets, which if desirable, may be laminated. There was a strong criticism about THRASS[iv], because in spite of the original intention it does not represent an autonomous pedagogical means but remains on the level of a teaching aid.

Several types of electronic storybooks are available for entertaining children and supporting teaching activities[v]. In the animated storybooks, like Mindstorms of Lego, children find themselves in a virtual futuristic world where they face challenging tasks to be solved in interactive working mode and in some cases the course of the story can be controlled by them. Practically the features of THRASS, WMR and electronic storybooks can be observed within the functionalities of the workstations produced by the leaders of the teaching aids market (e.g. Leapfrog, Riverdeep, Pearson). This kind of workstation help children of 5-8 years in learning writing and reading and they represent very useful means to introduce the world of literacy to children in an amusing and informal way.

A common shortfall of the described solutions is that they do not treat the teaching of writing and reading jointly, according the contemporary principles of education. Another common deficiency is that they only cover a certain phase of learning, they do not handle the whole process from the very beginning until the learner fully acquires handwriting and reading skills. A further problem is that the application of computerized teaching solutions requires a significant modification of the curriculum and the appropriate preparation of teachers.

A general problem is that there is no product on the market that can help the students to learn literacy autonomously.

3. Characteristics of the WR system

3.1   General

The student is working on a tablet PC equipped with a display and a pen for handwriting and a headset for reading exercises. An ergonomically suitable arrangement is designed for comfortable writing position. The system can teach students handwriting and reading starting from the very beginning up to the full acquisition of these skills. The use of the system does not require neither the help of a teacher nor the knowledge of computers.

3.2   Motivation

One of the most important elements of the learning technology is the motivating environment built to hide the obligatory character of teaching, to make learning an interesting game. In the school the students are not very much interested in the process and results of learning. Some of them may have positive influence of the parents or the teachers, others may be stimulated by the good guide of eminent students, the competitive spirit in the class. However, all these factors are occasional. Building the WR system it seemed obvious to use the computer not only as a means for teaching but also for the purposes of motivation, the more so, since children are fans of TV and electronic games. In the WR system the writing and reading exercises are embedded in a series of an animated fairy tale. Every scene is embedding a lesson with 4-5 object sentences The story is going on in ABC-land where everything is concerned with letters, writing and reading can make miracle, bring to life the lifeless things, rebuild the ruined houses, cure diseases, feed the hungry and give thirsty to drink. The students are highly motivated because they actively participate in the story helping the characters in problematic situations by writing and reading the object sentences. They feel like a magician seeing that the meaning of written or read sentences is realized and the story takes a positive turn. The constrained nature of teaching disappears, the students are waiting for new adventures where they can help friends, the characters of the story. Thanks to this motivation the students acquire skills of handwriting and reading in an amusing way without any embarrassment.

3.3   Innovative teaching technology

IT allowed us to design and implement a new teaching technology, which transmits the methods of traditional school teaching in very efficient forms. For example functional teaching is working throughout, whole sentences of the story are used in every exercise. To get used to the abstraction of writing letters the students draw schematic pictures of birds, animals and different objects in the first lessons. Most importantly the traditional method of copying is made a central element of the e-learning technology. The copying exercises are technically arranged in the writing area of the display located under the animation. This area reminds 2 lines of the school textbook, in the upper line the object sentences are demonstrated, the students copy them to the lower line. Copying written and spoken samples the students feel are in a close cooperation with the story.

Basic forms of written copying are as follows:
a) Overwriting the letters of the object sentence,
b) Copying the letters of the object sentence,
c) Writing the letters of the object sentence under dictation.

In the last form a machine voice is pronouncing the letter (phoneme) to be written. In our understanding this operation is also a copying action because hearing the sound the student recalls the requested letter and copies it by hart.

d)   Writing words of the object sentence under dictation.

Basic forms of spoken copying are as follows:

a)   Echo like copying of sounds. When the student is overwriting or copying a letter a machine voice is pronouncing its sound and the student is to repeat it.

b)   Echo like copying of syllables. A machine voice is rhythmically pronouncing the syllables of the object word and the student is to copy them in the same rhythm.

c)   Reading the letters of words. When the student is overwriting or copying a letter he/she has to pronounce its sound. In our understanding this operation is also a copying action because when writing a letter the student recalls the proper sound and copies it by hart.

d)   Reading the syllables and words of the object sentence.

The copying phonics exercises teach students the relationships between the letters (graphemes) of written language and the individual sounds (phonemes) of spoken language. They teach students to use these relationships to read and write words.

3.4   Evaluation

An important element of teaching handwriting is the evaluation of letters written by the student. The algorithm measures the quality of the current letter and immediately demonstrates the result by colouring its surface. This gives a new motivation for the student who wants to get only the best colours. The quality check is working also in reading letters, syllables and words. In case of misreading the opportunity to repeat the reading operation is offered to the student before a correction is done by prompting.

3.5   Reading instruction

Technology enhanced learning of reading is based on fine transitions between exercises of increasing difficulty. Initially only spoken copying is taking place. When the student is overwriting the current letter its sound is demonstrated simultaneously and the students is to echo the sound. After numerous repetitions the inseparable connection between letters and sounds becomes fixed. Later the spoken copying goes on with syllables. A machine voice rhythmically pronounces the syllables of the word and the student is to repeat them in the same rhythm watching the written form in the meanwhile. The systematic use of this method helps the student to discover the clue of reading. The result will be cleared in exercises of higher difficulty modes. In the first reading mode the students are reading only letters by themselves. In the next mode the syllables are to be read autonomously and in the most difficult mode the students are reading entire words. In the WR technology enhanced learning system it is natural that the algorithm is checking the correct reading of letters, syllables and words and in case of misreading helps the student by prompting – pronouncing the correct sounds.

3.6.   Personalization

The system is adaptive, the teaching process is automatically tailored to the ability and endeavour of the student because the learning progress is controlled by a feedback mechanism. Students acquire skills gradually, there are 5 levels of writing difficulty and 5 levels of reading difficulty with automatic transitions between them. The program evaluates every sentence written and/or read by the student and sets automatically the proper writing/reading mode for the next sentence according the result of the previous one. When the evaluation discloses progress a more difficult mode will be set, in case of getting a "medium" mark the mode will remain unchanged. When the evaluation algorithm clears that the student had problems in writing or reading in currently finished exercise, it sets a lighter mode for the next exercises. The mode can change from sentence to sentence, up and down and this gives a new motivation to the student to keep on writing and reading in higher-level modes.

The adaptive character of teaching appears also in the tolerance to speech impediments. When the student tries several times to make spoken copies of a specific phoneme and his/her impediment (e.g. lisp) hinders to pronounce it correctly the machine will accept the false pronunciation, according to the level of a built-in predefined tolerance. However the system may help to eliminate speech impediments by giving methodically more exercises on those specific phonemes showing not only the right pronunciation but also the animated pictures of the correctly working vocal organs.

In general, the process reminds teaching by a personal teacher who is sitting with the student, checking the quality of written or read words and sentences and helping when necessary according the progress of the student.

4. The "whole language" approach may work

The technology enhanced learning methodology of WR system described above may develop the basic literacy skills like writing ability, phonological awareness very efficiently. However, it is not easy to develop reading comprehension. If readers can read the words but do not understand what they are reading, they are not really reading. Text comprehension is the reason for reading. The aim of the whole language approach was to construct environments where reading skills evolve in a natural way. According to Kenneth Goodman "Whole language learning builds around whole learners learning whole language in whole situations" [1]. He believed that children should learn reading as they learnt to speak, heuristically, by semantic associations, trials and errors. Presently the method is not used anywhere since school teaching is lacking whole situations and semantic associations.

However, in the WR system this method started to work very naturally thanks to the virtual motivating environment and the IT based teaching methodology. The epic animated scenes with the audible texts are self-explaining. The sentences to read emerge in the plot of the story and they are in intellectual coherence and textual overlap with the previous sentences and with the situation in which they arise for reading. In this environment powerful semantic associations born facilitating the interpretation of written sentences. Understanding the situation the students will fully comprehend the spoken sentences. They learn to read by trials and errors, in case of mistakes the program helps them by prompting the correct sounds or words.

Although the WR technology enhanced learning system has a natural potential to realize the whole language approach, the reading comprehension is developing slowly. There is a long way from the phonological awareness to the reading comprehension. To help the progress we designed and implemented a special construction to build a learning environment richer in semantic associations. For this purpose a traditional pedagogical method, the repetition was introduced to help matching the spoken and written form of sentences. Repetition means that in a lesson the object sentence or its parts appear several times in spoken and written form, in different modifications, e.g. in the following sequence.

1. In a problematic situation of the scene the object sentence is presented in spoken form by one of the characters. It is organically connected with the plot of the scene, with its textual and pictorial context.
2. The object sentence is written by the student under dictation.
3. Finishing the writing exercise the sentence is read aloud by the student (helped by prompting) and its meaning vivifies in the animated story to solve the problematic situation and produce motivating emotions.

4. The lesson is going on with the next situation containing the next object sentence.
5. When the lesson ends its events are summed up by reading of its object sentences.
6. At home the student - using prepared paper worksheets - tells the parents what happened in the scene then writes and reads the object sentences with the help of parents.
7. At the beginning of the next lesson the last lesson is repeated in a narrative form and the reading of its object sentences takes place again.

This arrangement allows the whole language methodology to start working! Recalling the last scene the students remember every aspect of it, especially the problematic situations. They know very well the object sentences, after all they have done several exercises on them. Now, before reading an object sentence a preparation phase helps easier reading. The problem situation connected with the object sentence is demonstrated and retold by the narrator. In his spoken text some expressions are bringing to mind the words of the object sentence in advance. Then the object sentence appears in written form as a target of reading. The students can half read it and half guess its meaning using all the earlier accumulated knowledge of the sentence and the emerging semantic associations. As K. Goodman wrote they predict, select, confirm and correct themselves searching for the meaning. With other words they guess, make hypothesis about the content of the sentence then check the guessed version. In this process of "trial and error" besides image reading deciphering is often used by the students to read some words. The program helps by prompting when misreading takes place.

5. Implementation

In fact the project had a clearly research character. We designed and developed a new method of IT based learning for writing and reading, wrote the curriculum, the scenario of the story and integrated them together. New IT solutions and means have been developed such as the presentation and sequential control of exercises, interaction between the exercises and the animated story, evaluation of writing and reading quality, evaluation of the student's progress and personalisation of teaching. There were also a number of practical means to develop, like prompting in reading, showing the difference between a letter written by the student and its ideal version, the missing roundhand Hungarian font, etc. One of the most difficult things was to compile simple object sentences for writing and reading exercises, which serve at the same time for solving critical situations. Presently, in test applications we observe some practical problems to be corrected, e.g. the optimal time gap between pronunciation of syllables, the optimal distance parameters of the light point leading the pen of the student, etc. The experience of the test applications will be used to develop the final commercial version of the program.

In test applications we use two different hardware solutions for writing: tablet PC and ordinary PC equipped with a digitizing tablet. The use of tablet PC gives better writing results because the work of hand and eyes is not separated in space.

Presently the system is implemented in Hungarian. The methodology allows to implement the system in any languages with modifications requested by the nature of the object language and its teaching traditions.

Problems of dissemination:

In Hungary the official interest to use such a technology enhanced learning tool for teaching is low. For the majority of teachers it will be also difficult to accept the application.

Leading companies producing technology enhanced learning means to help teaching of handwriting and reading are not interested to accommodate a product from an unknown source even if it is more intelligent than their own.

A further problem of spreading is the high price of tablet PC-s providing better results in learning handwriting.

6. Test applications

Test applications have just started in Budapest in K classes of private schools for 6 years old children. After the first 9-10 lessons the results are impressive, children like to learn in the motivating environment and have a quick progress in writing and phonics. They write good quality strokes in requested sequence. After writing and pronouncing a significant number of letters and syllables they are becoming experienced in matching the written and spoken form.

Some children learning in the first class also use the system to improve writing skills and phonological awareness. The whole language approach is helping them to develop reading comprehension.

Predictable areas of early applications:

- Children of the Hungarian minority in the surrounding countries loosing Hungarian literacy (and identity),
- Functional illiterates,
- Handicapped children, children with dyslexia,
- Private schools, individual use.

7. Conclusion

In summary it can be stated that a completely new learning system has been developed allowing students to learn handwriting and reading in an amusing way without the help of teachers or parents. One of innovative features of this automated system is that the teaching process is personalised, tailored to the abilities of the student. Another new achievement is that the virtual motivating environment allowed to apply first the so called "whole language approach" for the development of higher level reading skills.

The whole system consists of 40 lessons what can be passed in 2 months, provided a one-hour per day learning schedule. The experimental use of the system started, the results are very promising according the opinion of teachers and parents. The experimental stage should be expanded to have an overall picture about the applicability and efficiency of the system, its advantages and disadvantages.

The implementation of the system in other languages will allow to acquire literacy in countries where the education system is underdeveloped. The vast number of illiterates in the world (about 900 millions) and even in some developed countries (e.g. 30-40 millions in the USA) gives reasons to set a high priority to the further development and distribution of these type of systems.

Companies are invited to participate in the development of various national versions of the WR system.

References

[1] Goodman, K. (1986). What's whole in whole language. Portsmouth, NH: Heinemann Educational Books.

---

[i] e.g. see www. mrsalphabet.com, Hwww.bbc.co.uk/schools/4_11/literacy.sHhtml
[ii] see www.ibm.com/ibm/ibmgives/grant/education/programs/reinventing/watch.shtml
[iii] see Hwww.thrass.co.ukH
[iv] (see www.rrf.org.uk/
[v] see a survey in Hwww.literacyandtechnology.org/v3n1/Hchenferdigwood.htm

Collaboration and the Knowledge Economy: Issues, Applications, Case Studies
P. Cunningham and M. Cunningham (Eds.)
IOS Press, 2008

Training for Open Source: A Need Not A Luxury

Manon VAN LEEUWEN[1], Guadalupe MORGADO[1], Julia VELKOVA[2]
[1] *FUNDECYT, Manuel Fdez. Mejías sn 2 Planta, Badajoz 06002 Spain*
Tel: +34 924 014 600, Fax: +34 924 001996
Email: manon@fundecyt.es; guadalupe@fundecyt.es
[2] *Internet Society – Bulgari, 31 Ivan Shishman Str., Sofia, 1000, Bulgaria*
Tel: +359-2-9802334, Email: julia@isoc.bg

Abstract: Despite the fact that public sector's interest in open source is intensifying, and there is an increasing demand for skills related to Open Source applications, both from a user as well as from a developer point of view, the uptake in educational and vocational training programmes is not yet mainstream. The TRAIN-OS project presents answers to this challenge by providing access to F/OSS training materials, based upon an analysis of the needs of the trainers and trainees. The paper will present the results from the research and will provide insight into the information, knowledge and training needs from European trainers.

Keywords: Training, Open Source

1. Introduction

Over the last few years, Free and Open Source Software (FOSS) has established itself as a viable alternative to proprietary software in many areas of information and communications technology (ICT) deployment.

A substantial amount of source code has been open since the 1980s. The collaborative model that is one of the central features of the OSS model gained momentum in the late 80s and early 90s. The term "open source software" started to come into general use in 1998. Recently, the development and use of OSS has reached significant proportions globally. The potential benefits and the level of maturity of the OSS model is recognized as a viable alternative, which will in many cases prove to be the preferred approach to software development and deployment. There is now a general acceptance of open source software such as Firefox and even Open Source such as Wikipedia, as viable options

1.1 The definition of F/OSS

In computing, free and open source software, also referred to as OSS, F/OSS, FOSS, or FLOSS (for Free/Libre/Open Source Software) is software which is liberally licensed to grant users the right to study, change, and improve its design through the availability of its source code. This approach has gained both momentum and acceptance as the potential benefits have been increasingly recognised by both individuals and educational players.

'F/OSS' is an inclusive term generally synonymous with both free software and open source software which describes similar development models, but with differing cultures and philosophies. 'Free software' focuses on the philosophical freedoms it gives to users and 'open source' focuses on the perceived strengths of its peer-to-peer development model. However many people relate to both aspects and so 'F/OSS' is a term that can be used without particular bias towards either camp.

Exhibit 1: Definition

A common definition has been developed by the Free Software Foundation Europe, which defines four freedoms regarding free software and is widely used since the 1980's1. These four freedoms are:

1. The freedom to run the programme, for any purpose. Placing restrictions on the use of Free Software, such as time (30 days trial period", "license expires January 1st, 2007"), purpose ("permission granted for research and non-commercial use") or geographic area ("must not be used in country X") makes a programme non-free.

2. The freedom to study how the programme works, and adapt it to your needs. Access to the source code is a precondition for this. Placing legal or practical restrictions on the comprehension or modification of a programme, such as mandatory purchase of special licenses, signing of a Non-Disclosure-Agreement (NDA) or making the preferred human way of comprehending and editing a programme (and its "source code") inaccessible also makes it proprietary.

3. The freedom to make and redistribute copies. If you are not allowed to give a programme to someone else, that makes a programme non-free. Redistributing copies can be done gratis or for a charge, if you choose to do so.

4. The freedom to improve the programme, and release improvements. Access to the source code is a precondition for this. Not everyone is a programmer or a programmer equally good in all fields. This freedom allows those with the necessary skills to share them with those who do not possess them. Such modifications can be made gratis or for a charge. [1]

These freedoms are rights, not obligations, although respecting these freedoms for society may at times oblige the individual. Any person can choose to not make use of them, but may also choose to make use of all of them.

1.2 F/OSS and the need for skilled professionals

The need for professionals competent in differing aspects of F/OSS has increased significantly in the recent years. In other words there is a shortage in skilled workforce in the F/OSS area. This is a result of the success of F/OSS especially in the commercial market in the recent years

An example is the demand for Linux professionals. One of the fastest emerging operating systems in the world, in 2005 Linux was predicted to grow at a rate of 27 percent in next three years. In India, this growth was expected to be almost 80 percent in the country, in the next three to four years. Matching this development is the need for professionals who are well-qualified and experienced to take on different positions in this space, ranging from Linux administrators to principal engineers, browser/Web server developers, senior software engineers for Linux kernel programming, drivers and embedded Linux, etc. [2]

The demand arises not only in technical aspects but also in non-technical aspects (legal issues, business model, organisation, etc.) of F/OSS. In other words such curricula should be developed both as technical programs and as non-technical programs. Educational institutions should develop and implement curricula addressing this specific need. This includes curricula to be developed by institutions in the formal education system, curricula to be developed by professional training organizations, and curricula delivered in settings for life-long learning.

"Most of the people who get any form of computer training get it on proprietary software. That's why they lean on it. That's what they know, what they talk about, what they advocate. There's a need for investing in training for open source software"
James Lunghabo, general manager of the East African Centre for Open Source Software

---

However, despite the clear benefits, which F/OSS can produce, the majority of the educational institutions are still not considering the implementation of F/OSS applications or solutions. One of the main reasons is the lack of knowledge about F/OSS. Even for those educational institutions that do implement F/OSS, it is very common for the delivery of curricula to make use almost exclusively of proprietary software, and F/OSS is rarely mentioned as a topic of study. This is a weakness of the traditional curricula. Lack of basic knowledge on F/OSS is a concern for the graduates of these programs, both from a professional point of view and from a cultural point of view. That means that educational institutions should adopt their curricula to include components to give basic knowledge on F/OSS.

Aside from FOSS desktop applications for general use, there is a lot of Free/Open Source educational software that can be used for teaching specific subjects or courses in schools, colleges and universities, but the development of contents for training on the use of these and other F/OSS is less extended.

This is even true for training materials for the software developers themselves, an example is the situation with respect to secure application design and development. A study conducted by PORT [2] has shown that the majority of the open source developers lack common knowledge on these issues, but there is a lack of good training material that is easily accessible to open source developers.

Another example comes from research conducted by Forrester [3] on the adoption of Linex in US and Canadian businesses. When asked about training, they indicated that training for Linux was more robust, more costly. The investments companies made in training for their IT employees were significantly higher for Linux than Windows, on average, 15% more expensive. When asked why, almost all 14 organizations cited the fact that training materials for Linux were less available than for Windows.

This shows that one of the barriers to the integration of F/OSS contents into the educational and training curricula is the fact that, although many training materials have been developed, they are disperse, and accessing them in an easy way is difficult. Trainers have enormous problems finding the right training materials for a specific learning situation.

TRAIN-OS provides an answer to this need by providing both trainers and teachers with the skills, competences and knowledge needed in order to offer formal and non-formal training within F/OSS field and related issues, to those participants in the learning process.

2. Objectives

Consequently the TRAIN-OS project mission is to ensure that F/OSS priority training needs are met in various educational institutions across the EU. This means maintaining an efficient and effective online repository of F/OSS training material and facilitating the transfer of already existing F/OSS training material to other institutions. Within the context of this mission, the vision for the TRAIN-OS project is to identify F/OSS training requirements and provide an efficient repository of existing F/OSS training material. The following tasks specify the framework by which this vision is being realised:
GOAL 1: Establish a logical, flexible, and responsive OSS training questionnaire to quickly translate field training and education requirements into easily accessible, usable, and effective training materials.
GOAL 2: Implement an efficient, open, and consistent process for categorising OSS training materials and organise them accordingly in an online repository.

The project helps improve the level of quality and innovation regarding the vocational training linked somehow to F/OSS. It will provide trainers and teachers, as well as the institutions and organisations involved in vocational training, with a powerful tool that allows them to access available training material related to F/OSS and choose material that is most relevant to the environment and learning situation. This should improve the training quality that is currently being given in this field. The knowledge base will provide an innovative offer of F/OSS training materials, and in the ICT domain where there is a growing demand for training materials adapted towards every learning situation. TRAIN-OS will respond to these needs by providing trainers and teachers with a powerful tool to facilitate the access and use of F/OSS training material and other related issues. It will also offer relevant support services to improve the quality of training they are giving and ameliorate their own skills and qualifications.

3. Methodology

Research related to obtaining information on educational needs normally combines several of a series of research techniques:

- Documentary investigation, using archives, databases and recent studies that provide information on the organisation in question and on the socio-economic environment in which it deals, and also using the most up-to-date publications and conclusions.
- Questionnaires or standardised forms are relatively inexpensive and above all quantifiable. They can be given to a large number of persons who are able to express themselves without fear.
- In-depth interviews with trainers (key informants) to provide extensive, dense and contextualised information, which will avoid misunderstandings and errors in the interpretation of secondary data, and may reveal causes of and solutions to problems.
- Discussion groups result in a synthesis of different points of views and provide the investigator with many ideas, although there is a risk of group dynamics, which may counteract the validity of data obtained.

The methodology to perform the research in the TRAIN-OS project involves the usage of multiple techniques to collect objective information regarding the educational needs on F/OSS.

The first step has been a documentary investigation in TRAIN-OS, which includes an extensive research on the available educational materials on Free Software and Open Standards. This research is partly done by requesting the inputs of different communities. The goal of such an overview is not only to map the existing educational materials in this area but also to identify those materials that can be integrated in the TRAIN-OS platform. This kind of approach also requires that the training materials are classified in groups and categories. In this way, the classification would allow for a more systematic and clear presentation of the educational materials and will therefore make the selection of materials needed easier, according to the specific needs of the trainee or trainer.

This second research step is requesting the inputs of different target groups via a questionnaire and interview. The goal of such an approach is not only to map the existing educational material in this area but also to identify those materials that can be integrated in the TRAIN-OS platform. Therefore, an evaluation of the quality of these materials will also be performed when possible. Furthermore, an overview of all organisations, communities and platforms that are related with the production of these materials will be prepared. A follow-up interview will permit the identification of which parties can be interested in the TRAIN-OS materials as well as in participating in the uptake of collated materials.

4. Developments

The classification which the TRAIN-OS project decided to use is the following one:
1.1   Introduction to Free Software, Open Standards and OSS.

1.2 Basic and general issues about Free Software, Open Standards and OSS but not centred at any specific application. Basic GNU/Linux Operating System. Note that this area includes multiple applications such as kernels, plain text editors, command shells, the X-Window system, GUI desktops, system configuration tools, developing tools, and many others.

1.3 Office tools, including: formatted text editors and readers, spreadsheets, presentations, E-mail clients, personal information management, project management and others.

1.4 Educational Software. Includes applications that specifically designed for teaching different subjects at different educational levels.

1.5 Enterprise Software Applications, including CMS, CRM, ERP, accounting, groupware and collaboration, mail servers, DB servers and others.

1.6 Multimedia Applications, including image manipulation, audio mixing, video capture, editing and playback applications.

1.7 Others. This category will be used for those applications which do not fit the previous six areas but which are considered interesting for the knowledge base

The categories listed above were defined by the SELF Project. The TRAIN-OS consortium has decided to continue building on this classification structure since it covers the majority of the aspects, which the project aims at. In this way it will be achieved a synergy between these two European projects and their outputs will be complementary to each other. The TRAIN-OS project will add an additional perspective to the training needs related to education on Free and Open Source software by interviewing and performing surveys with companies, higher educational institutions and educators on F/OSS while working within the classifications of the SELF project. On the other hand, the SELF project itself provides a good ground of 2 year work on the topic related to the education on Free Software and Open Standards which would allow the TRAIN-OS project to build upon and create a further basis to respond best to the needs of the trainees.

> **Exhibit 2: SELF project**
>
> SELF is an international project aiming to provide a platform for the collaborative sharing and creation of free educational and training materials on Free Software and Open Standards. The SELF Platform is
> 1. A repository with free educational and training materials on Free Software and Open Standards
> 2. An environment for the collaborative creation of new materials
>
> Inspired by Wikipedia, the SELF Platform provides the materials in different languages and forms. The SELF Platform is also an instrument for evaluation, adaptation, creation and translation of these materials. Most importantly, the SELF Platform is a tool to unite community and professional efforts for public benefit.

Using the basic endpoint of detecting training needs in educational organisation, the following objectives have been sought in the questionnaire:

- To identify know-how, competencies and personal skills of organisations with regards to OSS training.
- To assess educational attitudes towards training related to OSS.
- To analyse the available educational materials on Free Software and Open Standards.
- To analyse the organisations, communities and platforms that are directly or indirectly related with the production of such materials.
- To assess the availability of training offers and material available for inclusion in the TRAIN-OS knowledge platform.

A quantitative technique is used, in the form of a structured questionnaire with mainly closed-ended questions (selection of a series of categories that are assigned in advanced), although some open-ended questions were included in order not to limit information that was contributed. The option of a personal interview is chosen to implement the questionnaire where possible, arranging a prior appointment with each subject.

The interview's main target group are representatives of educational trainers within educational institutions that offer Open Source training, although the business sector and existing developer's communities will not be excluded, as they can provide valuable information. Participants are to be selected according to their involvement in information technology training, preferably open source trainers/teachers.

5. Results

The research and development taking place in the project provides an answer to the main upfront problems when designing and implementing a F/OSS curriculum: there is not a homogeneous and standarized way to describe the training contents; the materials are scattered as there is not just one place to access to the main part of the available materials, and, last but not least, there is no solution to guide trainers through the big amount of available materials, providing knowledge and support to choose the most suitable materials for every learning situation.

Initial results obtained in the test phase of the questionnaires in the region of Extremadura show the enormous interest generated by the training community in the field of Open Source. Trainers and training organisations are showing significant support and willingness to share their F/OSS training materials through the TRAIN-OS knowledge base. The roll out of the questionnaires in the region are being realised with three different type of training institutions and organisations:

1. Training for entrepreneurs and SMEs, recollection the materials related to F/OSS with mainly a business orientation, examples are materials related to business management, or specific enterprise applications, such as ERP and CRM systems.
2. Training materials for non-experienced ICT users, recollection of materials related to digital literacy and the use of desktop applications, such as OpenOffice, Firefox, etc.
3. Training materials for advances ICT users and developers, materials related to programming in Open Source.
4. Train the trainer materials, materials for trainers on how to provide training and learning for F/OSS.

The experience in Extremadura shows that the major demand for materials is to be found in the first two groups, and this is where the most training materials can be found. At the same time there is a clear demand in the region for materials for advanced ICT users and developers, although the demand here is more dispersed, as the amount of themes demanded is significantly larger that for the other groups.

The results obtained with the first set of questionnaires analysed from the different countries provides a similar view, in particular the most demanded ones are the training materials related to:

1. Operating systems,
2. Database systems,
3. Office products,
4. Internet applications and web applications.

Although almost all respondents stated that they would be interested in accessing these type of materials, a subset of these indicated that at the same time they would not be willing to share their materials with others. A paradoxical situation, which can be traced back somehow to the fact that the subset of respondents not willing to share their materials came largely from the private sector and more specifically of organisations whose business is mainly based on providing training.

6. Conclusions

Over the past few years, Free and Open Source Software (FOSS) has established itself as a viable alternative to proprietary software in many areas of information and communications technology (ICT) deployment. There is now a general acceptance of open source software such as Firefox and even Open Source such as Wikipedia, as viable options.

Despite the clear benefits that F/OSS can produce, the majority of the educational institutions are still not considering the implementation of F/OSS applications or solutions. One of the main reasons is the lack of knowledge about F/OSS. Even for those educational institutions that do implement F/OSS, it is very common for the delivery of curricula to make use almost exclusively of proprietary software, and F/OSS is rarely mentioned as a topic of study.

Another one of the barriers to the integration of F/OSS contents into the educational and training curricula is the fact that, although many training materials have been developed, they are disperse, and accessing them in an easy way is difficult. Trainers have enormous problems in finding the right training materials for a specific learning situation.

TRAIN-OS provides an answer to this need by providing both trainers and teachers with the skills, competences and knowledge needed in order to offer formal and non-formal training within F/OSS field and related issues, to those participants in the learning process. A documentary research has been complemented with fieldwork through interviews and questionnaires with trainers and training institutions, and experts on F/OSS. The documentary research has lead to a classification scheme for the training materials to be identified in the fieldwork. Preliminary test results show that the most demanded training materials can be found in the field of business management and for non-experienced ICT users.

The work is ongoing and will lead to the development of a knowledge base, which will describe in a homogeneous way, and using the classification scheme identified in the first phase, all the training materials selected. This knowledge base will provide trainers with a place where they cannot only retrieve F/OSS based training materials, but where they can also upload and thus share the materials they have developed. And although training in FOSS is not normally a part of formal education or training, TRAIN-OS provides support for educational and training institutions, so that they can integrate this service for educational and training institutions in their professional trainings or adult education programmes.

References

[1] This definition has also been used by the EU funded project SELF and was first documented in the GNU's Bulletin, vol. 1, no. 1, published January 1986 1 and used by the SELF project. I will also provide the basis for the TRAIN-OS project. For full definition: http://www.gnu.org/bulletins/bull1.txt
[2] Linux: An emerging career space for creative minds, Punita Jasrotia Phukan. http://www.expressitpeople.com
[3] Training Concepts and Training Plans, report developed by the OPEN-TC project. http://www.opentc.net
[4] Forrester surveyed 140 large companies in North America to find out their open source plans. March 16, 2004, Trends "Open Source Moves Into The Mainstream."

Collaboration and the Knowledge Economy: Issues, Applications, Case Studies
P. Cunningham and M. Cunningham (Eds.)
IOS Press, 2008

Enhanced E-training in the Field of Mechatronics: The Slovenian Case Study

Matija PIPAN, Borka JERMAN BLAZIC
Jozef Stefan Institute, Jamova 39, Ljubljana, 1000, Slovenia
Tel: +386 1 4773863, Fax: +386 1 4773995, Email: matic@e5.ijs.si

Abstract: The main purpose of this paper is to introduce good practices into the areas of vocational training in the field of mechatronics supported with the state-of-the-art ICT, as well as with the established methodological and didactic approaches, all with the view of improving the quality and efficiency of education. The aim and the goals of the new innovative way of training in the field of mechatronics are directly focused on resolving the issue of the current market imbalances of supply and demand of qualified mechatronics staff. This should result in greater recognition and appeal of the profession, and will positively influence on the existing gap on the market.

1. Introduction

The profession of a mechatronic is believed to be a profession of the future, as many EU studies [7,9] have indicated it, placing it among the top three most perspective professions. The mechatronic area offers modern job opportunities, combining three main fields of interest: mechanical engineering, electrical engineering, and information technologies; this is why the mechatronics is considered an interdisciplinary technical field. These professions have just recently been born in the industrially developed states, due to an ever-greater automation of the production processes. Mechatronics is a new way of thinking, a new way of planning products and systems that enable the integration of precision mechanics, electronics, automatic management, and informatics into the basic processes of planning, instead of searching for engineering solutions for every task individually. Mechatronics is therefore an interdisciplinary technical field, founded on the grounds of classical technical science of mechanical engineering, electrical engineering, and computer science. Instead of electromechanically (with bits of electronics) based systems, more and more complex mechatronic systems are entering the market.

In Slovenia and other EU Member States formal training programs in mechatronics are already offered at the level of secondary school, as a programme of higher education and at university level [8]. However, market demand is much greater than supply. For the time being, the market is short of adequately trained staff; for that reason jobs that would call for experts in mechatronics are done, as a rule, by experts in mechanical or electrical engineering, who, due to their narrow orientations and focus on just one area, do not provide the possibility of a comprehensive insight into the installations and processes that require knowledge of mechatronics. Company research has shown that there is a great interest on the side of economy in additional vocational training for the staff, who have already completed their formal studies in mechanical or electrical engineering, to train them for work in the production processes, where mechanical machine installations are controlled by electronic control systems. In this way, the companies could at least partially diminish the currently existing gap on the market, which lacks qualified staff. Companies also voiced a demand for vocational training to be efficient substance-, time-, and cost-wise, and implemented at an independent location, with the purpose of minimizing the effects on the company operations.

2. Objectives

The main purpose of this paper is to introduce good practices into the areas of vocational training in mechatronics supported with the state-of-the-art ICT, as well as with the established methodological and didactic approaches, all with the view of improving the quality and efficiency of education. The purpose and the goals of the project MeRLab (Innovative Remote Laboratory in the E-training of Mechatronics), founded by Leonardo da Vinci Lifelong Learning Programme 2007-2013, are directly focused on resolving the issue of the current market imbalances of supply and demand of qualified staff, trained in the field of mechatronics.

3. Methodology

If we wish to present mechatronic studies in an attractive and innovative way, if we want to facilitate training access to a wide spectrum of potential users, and be at the same time and cost-effective, then implementing e-training is an optimal solution. Therefore the focus of the project is in the preparation of the innovative e-course. E-learning alone, as a teaching method, is not news to the world today, the only thing that can be innovative is the e-learning contents. Besides the preparation of the interactive-multimedia e-materials for the chosen study modules [5], produced in the accordance with the SCORM (Shareable Content Object Reference Model) standard [1] which guarantees their interoperability and enable them to be further used in all e-learning management systems which support this standard, and implementation of a remote laboratory for practical work is another innovative dimension of our project (Figure 1).

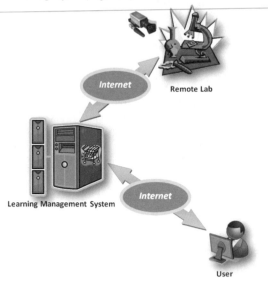

Figure 1: Architecture description

Companies demand more and more practical knowledge and skills from their employees, merely theoretical knowledge is no longer enough. Practical skills can only be developed by working in laboratories. Preparing a practical training course in a classical laboratory is normally very expensive and limited in space, time and number of participants. For this reason, within the E-Learning Distance Interactive Practical Education

(EDIPE) project a product called Remote Laboratory for Practical Lessons was developed, which resolves the above-mentioned problems and limitations [4]. A remote laboratory does not present web-based simulations. It truly makes it possible for students to perform actual experiments in the area of mechanical and electrical engineering, as well as programming, which take place in a physical laboratory. A user accesses the laboratory from a dislocated place using web tools (internet and browser), where (s)he can start to perform an experiment. The remote laboratory enables the user to have a full control over the implementation, measuring and monitoring of the experiment. The greatest advantage of the remote laboratory is that the users can perform their tasks anytime, anywhere, and can do so safely, without a laboratory assistant. The remote laboratory experiments are not only analysis-oriented (measurements and result observation); they can be synthesis-oriented, including also the planning aspect.

4. Case Study

To achieve the objectives of the above described methodology. we needed to accomplish four main concrete goals:

- Needs analysis: determining the actual company needs for mechatronic staff, based on company research, and determining its skill requirements for the employees. According to the needs analysis performed the mechatronic skills are much in demand, and we have noted a strong support from Slovenian employers to develop these types of professions. People with combined work tasks and knowledge in the field of electronics, mechanical engineering, and informatics are needed in automatic production and other processes (eg. for modern purification plants) at three levels of difficulty: as operators, processing installation administrators, and processing technology experts. The first ones – mechatronic operators – manage processing installations, supervise their operation, carry out simple maintenance works and serve them. Processing installation administrators – mechatronics administer the operations of the processing systems, diagnose mistakes, repair processing lines, maintain installations, maintain and archive software and documentation for the maintenance of the processing system. A mechatronic of processing technologies predominantly deals with the line and machine assembly, with production optimisation and adjustments of the processing lines and installations to suit the needs of an individual company. Our e-course is adjusted to serve as an additional vocational training course for the needs of the first two described professional profiles.

- Establishment of an innovative remote laboratory for the practical work in the framework of vocational mechatronics training: adaption of laboratory devices that shall be used by mechatronics e-course participants, translation and transfer of innovative remote laboratory into the Slovenian environment, usability evaluation and adjustment of the user interface for needs of a precisely defined target-user group [2, 3, 6].

- Adaptation of the Learning Management System (LMS): The very nature of technology enhanced learning, implementation dictates the use of modern information technology. For this purpose we shall put to use an already tested, reliable and stable learning environment eCampus®. This LMS system is based on a robust architecture, which facilitates adjustability to specific needs, such as multilayer connectivity with the remote laboratory (at the presentational level, at the data exchange level and user interaction between the two systems, as well as memorisation of past activities according to the identity of an individual user). Given the fact that communication is also an indispensable part of technology enhanced learning, it is supported with multiple options (forum, private message exchange, internal or external mailing list system communication, chat room, blogs, etc.), which offer both the learners and the mentors a wide spectrum of possibilities for communication. The portal will be publicly accessible through a special URL web address. For the purposes of

dissemination we will use the login portal site as an informative web page offering number of articles, news and best practices related to mechatronics.
- Production of multimedia-interactive e-learning contents: based on the company needs analysis we chose relevant mechatronic topics and organised them in modules; using the modern ICT and methods we rearranged them to modern interactive-multimedia e-materials, produced in accordance with the SCORM standard [1].
- Pilot training: with the e-topics prepared and the remote laboratory for practical work implemented, we prepared a 40-hour e-course, which will be entirely conducted via the Internet. We will organise a pilot training of at least 30 course participants, chosen from the main target group who are workers who have already completed formal education in the field of machine or electrical engineering, and are currently employed by SMEs or large enterprises, more precisely working within the production processes, which include mechanical machine devices for electronic control systems. Due to an increased complexity of devices, which require mechatronic know-how, their knowledge in either mechanical or electrical engineering only often proves to be insufficient; resulting as a substantial need for further training of such staff. The pilot training will be performed for the purposes of validation and evaluation of the e-course. Their competences shall be tested at the end of the e-course. The examination will include both theoretical questions and practical tasks. Every course participant who will pass the final exam will receive a training certificate.

5. Expected Business and Education Benefits

In Slovenia, we currently do not have a model and even less an enviable level of cooperation between economy and the systems of education or their institutions, due to some known specific circumstances. Thus, this project should serve as a linking element and an example of how such connections can be improved and cooperation between the two parties enhanced. It shall ensure the establishment of connections between economy and education at the national level and further on EU level, since its main purpose is to meet the demands of economy. The economy, which for the time being is well undernourished with the above mentioned profile of labour force, shall at least partial mitigate the needs. The individuals will acquire an additional professional qualification and upgrade their skills, thus improving their employability potential on the labour market, which fits the spirit of lifelong learning. Through activities such as presentations, dissemination, etc. the project will have a direct impact on the public awareness regarding the new field of mechatronics, regarding the companies' needs of workers with such a profile and regarding the ways and possibilities for education and training in the field of mechatronics. In this way, young people will be encouraged to undergo formal processes of education in this area of expertise, and adults will be encouraged to either participate in the training process as provided by this project or through the system of National Vocational Qualification (NVQ) or in some other way. Potential mechatronic e-course participants, besides the main target group, are also the employed or the unemployed, who have completed their formal education in other fields (eg. textile sciences, chemistry, pharmacy, etc.), but have some experience in managing electronically controlled mechanic machine installation systems. This training will provide such staff with the necessary theoretical and practical knowledge (requalification), which is a necessity for the management of mechatronic installations. Requalification of people with very low and low employment prospects will improve their competitive position on the labour market, and will consequently have an additional impact on diminishing the gap between supply of and demand for qualified mechatronic staff, indicating a high potential for the future use of the results to be achieved by this project.

More direct impact of the project result are mostly for the course participants, because the training will provide them with the necessary new knowledge and skills, which will make them more competent at work and will provide them with better career development opportunities.

Furthermore the project results – e-course – will also be used by the companies, since on the basis of adequately qualified staff they can increase their production efficiency and diminish the number of mistakes, which consequently leads to a higher cost-efficiency and higher profits. The project results may also be used by the institutions of education, who are implementing various professional and vocational training programmes. They will have a possibility of integrating the e-mechatronic course prepared in the framework of this project into their study programmes.

Table 1. Expected Impacts of the project results

	Short term impact	Long term impact
Target group(s)	*Predominantly already educated and trained staff with secondary vocational, specialized or post-secondary education in the field of technical and natural sciences will undergo further training or retraining for the current field of interest – where there is a great demand.*	*Diminishing unemployment levels of those, who might have no employment prospects for the time being. Expand employment possibilities for persons with mechatronical skills.*
Target sector(s)	*Most of all, the employees (or those who intend to become such) in companies with technological processes shall contribute to improved company results and efficiency.*	*Diminishing the gap and lack of staff trained in the field of mechatronics.*
Potential user(s)	*Production and service companies shall increase their efficiency, while it shall facilitate employees' work and increase job satisfaction.*	*It will be easier for the companies to carry out and support undisturbed technological or production process.*
Vocational education training systems & practices	*National Institution for Vocational Education and Training which carry out programmes in the field of mechatronics, they will access new, innovative and, most of all, efficient mechatronics teaching and learning tools.*	*Schools will be able to implement the mechatronics programmes in a more attractive and innovative manner, offering better, more sustainable and, most of all, more innovative know-how to students and future employees.*

6. Conclusions

Given the fact that according to the European Commission's Joint Report on Social Protection and Social Inclusion the number of elderly employees will rise from 41% in 2005 to the foreseen 50% in 2010, and given the fact that mechatronics, or computer technology connecting, foddering and mechanical elements are the third fastest growing sector in Europe [5,7], we have to make sure that the method used in educational process (formal and informal) is effective and reconciliated with the market demands. One step to meet these requirements is also our innovative and efficient teaching method, which is fully technology enhanced learning based, and mechatronic training puts significant emphasis on practical work, the decision to transpose and implement the remote laboratory innovation into this e-course is absolutely necessary. This method offers the possibility for additional vocational training (further training or retraining) of employees and unemployed, who had already completed their formal studies, and whose knowledge has become insufficient due to great technological changes. Since our teaching method provides for time and space independency, it minimizes the company work process disturbances and fulfils the requirements of the companies, as expressed in the research previously carried out.

The added value of the MeRLab project, if compared to the EDIPE project, is that the remote laboratory, which was the end-product of that project, will be upgraded with some additional interactive-multimedia e-contents, connecting them with an established methodological and didactical approach into a modern, attractive and innovative course of mechatronics for a specific user target group. This should result in greater recognition and appeal of the profession and will positively influence the gap between supply and demand of mechatronic staff on the Slovenian as well as on the whole EU market.

References

[1] Bohl O., Schellhase J., Sengler R., Winand U. The Sharable Content Object Reference Model (SCORM)- A Critical Review. Proceedings of the International Conference on Computers in Education, 2002, pp. 950.

[2] Karayel D., Kandara O., Ozkan S. Virtual Laboratory for Machine Education, 3. National Machine Engineering Education Symposium, I. T.Ü., Istanbul, 1997, pp. 16-17.

[3] Shin D., Yoon E. S., Lee K. Y., Lee E. S. A web - based, interactive virtual laboratory system for unit operations and process systems engineering education: issues, design and implementation, Computer and Chemical Engineering, 26, 2002, 319-330.

[4] Uran S., Hercog D., Jezernik K. Remote Control Laboratory with Moodle Booking System. Industrial Electronics, 2007, pp. 2978 – 2983.

[5] Wikander J., Torngren M., Hanson M. The science and education of mechatronics engineering. Robotics & Automation Magazine, IEEE, Volume 8, Issue 2, 2001, pp. 20-26.

[6] Bassily H., Sekhon R., Butts D., Wagner J. A mechatronics educational laboratory – Programmable logic controllers and material handling experiments. Mechatronics, Volume 17, Issue 9, November 2007, pp. 480-488

[7] COMMUNICATION TO THE SPRING EUROPEAN COUNCIL: Working together for growth and jobs A new start for the Lisbon Strategy (Brussels, 02.02.2005 COM (2005) 24)

[8] ManuFuture conference 2006: Implementing the Manu Future strategy (http://ec.europa.eu/research/industrial_technologies/articles/article_3911_en.html).

[9] Cadefopinfo - Vocational Training in Europe 05 (http://www2.trainingvillage.gr/download/Cinfo/Cinfo32005/Cinfo32005EN.pdf)

Collaboration and the Knowledge Economy: Issues, Applications, Case Studies
P. Cunningham and M. Cunningham (Eds.)
IOS Press, 2008

Biometric Identification System in Higher Education Exams: Test in Laboratory Practices

Rosario GIL, Sergio MARTIN, Gabriel DIAZ,
Elio SANCRISTOBAL, Manuel CASTRO, Juan PEIRE
*ETSI Industrial, Electrical and Computer Department, Spanish University for Distance
Education (UNED), C/Juan del Rosal 12, Madrid, 28040, Spain
Tel: +34 91 3987795, Fax: + 34 91 3987785,
Email: {rgil, smartin, gdiaz, elio, mcastro, jpeire}@ieec.uned.es*

Abstract: This paper outlines a way to identify users in a branched institution with a high number of users mainly devoted to secure and evaluation applications. In broad lines it starts from a distance model of education with traditional exams, the scope will be to archive a full distance education equipped with tools to control and assure the identity of every user.

Keywords: Distance Education, Learning Management Systems, Biometric, Lab Test, legal protection.

1. Introduction

The Spanish University of Distance Education is headquartered in Madrid, which coordinates all activities. Its distance model results in it having specific characteristics.

How subjects are taught depends on the characteristics of the subject, i.e. whether it is technical or arts. For technical subjects the structure of activities is as follows:

- Study a subject for oneself
- Ask questions by phone, email, etc.
- Attend physical laboratories
- Evaluation at university

For arts subjects the same structure is followed except there is no laboratory work. This study focuses on subjects taught in the Industrial, Electrical and Computer Department.

2. Objectives

Our main aim is to streamline the entire administrative process associated with a subject in its annual cycle. The administrative load that a teacher may have, results in time being spent on non-teaching related tasks. Our national university handles nearly 200,000 students a year, although this burden is distributed across all faculties and specialties. Since most of them are arts degrees, this high volume causes many management problems.

There are a number of issues that need to be reviewed:

- Quantity of questions that a teacher can manage
- Management of laboratories and devices for the volume of people
- Teachers available to supervise during exams and correction of all exams

The department has developed these three lines of investigation to try to solve or streamline these three key points in the development of a course. This paper provides focuses on the last point, items related to evaluation.

3.   Studying the Environment: Assessment at the Centre

Until very recently each student had a student card received at enrolment and kept for all studies. Along with their ID number, each student had to identify themselves before entering the examination room. Using the student code on the card an exam form was printed with a header on the top describing the characteristics of that exam:

- Personal detail of that student
- Classroom places allocated. All seats were numbered so as to distribute appropriately.
- Restrictions during the exam, namely whether to permit the use of documentation

It thought new applications much faster for access control so they could coexist perfectly with those already implemented. In addition to this new solution raised it intended to go a step further in administrative management. To save on printed documentation, classification of the subjects after an exam and their corresponding distribution to the teacher, could delay the correction of examinations. It raised the examination Web. In this way teachers could have the exams immediately and the degree of dissatisfaction or insistent calls by students asking for their marks would be dramatically diminished.

So it had two objectives:

- Access Control fast and reliable
- Web design exams

The decision taken was to merge these two concepts into one, so that the student entered the classroom and had his own computer. He could identity and carry out his own exam.

4.   Design of Identification Applications

At present there are many technologies used for secure transmission of data over the Internet but it is necessary to know that the person sending the data is not an imposter. Username and Password is inadequate for the rigours of identification now required.

The methods of identification are:

- Something the user knows - password
- Something that the user owns - smart cards
- Something that the user is - quantitative data identifying a person, biometric characteristics

The use of biometric techniques eliminates having to memorize or carry a card because it is something that is always available. The preference of the selection of an identification method was to test the strengths and weaknesses of the available biometric security tools.

Like any technical security in an environment, appear at the same time or almost in parallel ways how to break it or find its weaknesses. Therefore impersonation of people is a fact that this will continue in this technique.

For the characteristics that have such data and information that can shed it becomes necessary to the delimitation of what is seen as biometric data, the treatment being given, as well as legal protection that should have.

As is well known, biometrics is the technique used to measure physical and biological features of the human body. It is worth noting that these biological and physical characteristics are different for each person and that by being able to distinguish certain peculiarities, it is always possible to identify the individual concerned [1].

Biometric data [2] is so named because certain elements distinguish it from other categories of data. Therefore biometric data should be universal, unique and permanent.

Physiological and genetic traits as well as the environment influence the development of a human's personality, with social behaviour acquired through conditioning [3].

Given these influences both hereditary as environmental, biometric data can be obtained on the basis not only in the physical and biological constitution of the individual, but also in specific actions and behaviours taken by that person in achieving their place in society.

According to the class sample is collected, physical-biological or social action, the biometric data may be static or dynamic in nature.

Dynamic biometrics refers to how behavioural aspects relate to the person. Examples include handwritten signature, pressing on keys, analysis of gait and gesture analysis. The problem, is that it is unclear how reliable such biometric data is, as the individual can change how they use a keyboard or how they walk. However, it is possible that with high-tech tools that a person's identity can be reliably confirmed through a combination of variables such as body weight, tilt, force and pressure point.

Static biometric data is based on human anatomy. Physiological aspects are permanent and cannot easily be changed by the individual. Examples include static biometric fingerprints, hand geometry, iris or retina analysis, facial recognition and DNA analysis.

In the use of this new identification technology today, greater priority is given to static biometric data as it margin of error is almost zero.

Static fingerprint biometrics is used to identify persons. Fingerprints are formed by some grooves or ridges on the surface of the phalanx of finger. Their unique position makes it is different and distinctive in each person. The main varieties, which generally have ridges papillary, by their morphology, branching, address and interruptions are commonly known as "minutiae" or points characteristic [4]. These characteristics are different points and are in a different percentage for each person and among the most common are the abrupt, fork, convergence, fragment, cyclet, and point, among others.

In the Table 1 describes different characteristics of some biometric technologies.

Table 1: Comparison of different kinds of Biometrics techniques

Feature	Fingerprint	Geometry of the hand	Retina	Iris	Face	Signature	Voice
Easy to use	High	High	Low	Medium	Medium	High	High
Errors associated	Dryness, dirt, age	Damage in hand, age	Glasses	Poor quality of light	Light, age, glasses, hair	Change the signature	Noise, cold climate
Accuracy	High	High	Very High	Very High	High	High	High
Acceptability of use	Medium	Medium	Medium	Medium	Medium	Very High	High
Security Level	High	Medium	High	Very High	Medium	Medium	Medium
Stability in Long-term	High	Medium	High	High	Medium	Medium	Medium

Figure 1 [5] shows also the percentage of each technique on the market, data collected by International Biometric Group in 2006. Finally another comparison between each technique with the ideal behaviour is shown in Figure 2.

Percentage of Biometric Market in 2006

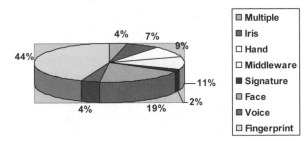

Figure 1: Percentage of Biometric Market in 2006 by International Biometric Group

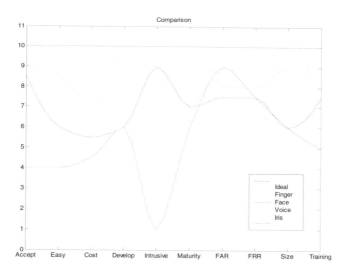

Figure 2: Comparison of Various Biometric Technologies Vs. the Ideal Line One That Would Like to Obtain

Because of its medium-high behaviour to the basic features required in a system, and for its proximity to the line biometric ideal in any environment (Figure 2), fingerprints were selected for integration into our application. The advantages [6] of the fingerprint include:

- Subjects have multiple fingers
- Easy to use, with some training
- Some systems require little space
- Large amounts of existing data to allow background and / or checks watchlist
- You have proven effective in many large scale systems over years of use
- Fingerprints are unique to each finger of each individual and the ridge remains permanent arrangement during one's lifetime
  And their handicaps or weaknesses:
- Public Perceptions
- Privacy concerns of criminal implications
- Health or societal concerns with touching a sensor used by countless individuals
- Collection of high quality nail-to-nail images requires training and skill, but current flat reader technology is very robust
- An individual's age and occupation sensors may cause some difficulty in capturing a complete and accurate fingerprint image

5.   Development in a Controlled Environment

The goal of this test was to create an application that integrates identification and conducting examinations in a learning platform. It was implemented in two phases, the first of which involves registration of personal user details, subjects enrolled and fingerprint. The second phase at exam time, captures a new sample to compare against the database.

Our department (DIEEC Electrical and Computer Engineering Department) of UNED (Spanish University for Distance Education) uses aLF to manage courses. aLF is based on dotLRN and this last one on OpenACS. aLF let us several facilities to develop a course, not just only contents, it can create new forum, surveys and so on. As it is based on OpenACS, it inherited its permissions and associated restrictions. With these permissions we will be able to generate new applications or modify content. However, this does not establish the true identification of the user behind an e-mail account and password. To improve this situation we have developed a new identification package.

The tool used for identification uses the pattern of the fingerprint to verify a person's identity. As it is difficult to manipulate it and is unique for each student, there will be no problems such as lost or exchange as there may be with password or smart cards.

For the first part, a system was designed that enrols a student in subjects related to our department, storing his personal information along with his fingerprint. The development environment was C++ (MFC, Microsoft Foundation Class) and MySQL database. The capture of the fingerprint was carried out through an optical scanner incorporated into a mouse, requiring no prior training and making fingerprint capture easy (Figure 3).

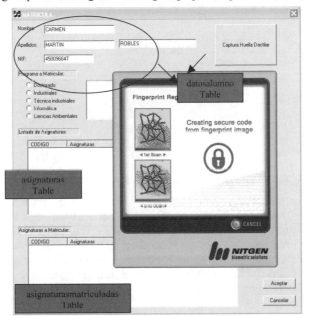

Figure 3: Enrolment Screen

As a result of this first phase, we obtained three tables in MySQL: personal information and biometric student; subjects available in the department and finally permissions allowed students in the form of subjects enrolled (Figure 4). Thus was controlled identification and the proper access that person to do exam.

For the second phase: verification, dotLRN offers the possibility of doing exams. These can be of different kinds, like multiple choices, large explanation, etc. For the pilot of our application we decided to implement in a laboratory practices where students had to write down the results of different experiments. This choice let us have a small-medium number of students and a medium place to perform experiments but it was big enough to get conclusions of our identification module.

We developed a web service, which receives several input data such as username, fingerprint, etc. from an authentication page that is displayed on the student's browser when he is going to access his exam. This input data is compared with the database tables which contain the data stored in the phase of collection of personal information. In the case of this data matches, an xml file is sent containing the exams elements from the assessment database model and the exam will be displayed on the student's browser. Of course this xml file will be able to be managed by the assessment service, if it is needed. In any other case the access to exam will be denied. Also we want to mention the importance of using standards as IMS QTI.

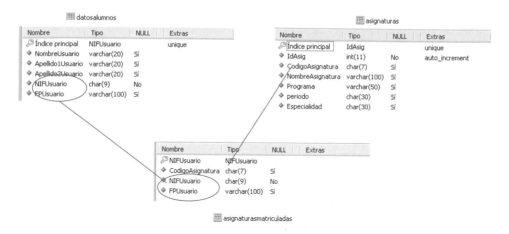

Figure 4: Relationships Between Tables

6.   Business Case Description: Real Environment Tests

Since incorporation and changes in the assessment process at a university can carry risks and errors that previously did not exist, we integrated an early version at the departmental level, doing a first test in a laboratory practice, where it was easier for us to monitor the number of people involved, place and the importance of content to be validated was minor.

At the test time in a laboratory, errors were identified and could be solved in real-time. The common error was the false rejection [7] by no training users or by our own module error. In any case, our implementation return rates from other closest samples.

- Dirty finger, wrong orientation
- Weak template stored

The fingerprint usually remains very stable over time, except for those who perform manual work where the fingerprint can become worn or there is a danger of losing a finger. Errors are focused on the quality of the sensor capturing the traces, and cleaning the sensor.

In this first study we also tested with staff without the permission to access the exam, and such people were rejected. For the first test, the level of participation was high and there was a high acceptability. The errors were more related to the use and understanding of the application than the module itself. The application was tried in "Digital Electronic Lab" over five days. As Distance University it was reserved 3 days for students out of Madrid and 2 days for students from Madrid. 80 students were included, around 16 students a day. In figure 5 shows some data extracted from this first experiment as the false rejection rate (FRR); the false acceptance rate (FAR) [8]; the failure to enroll rate (FTER) [9]; and so on.

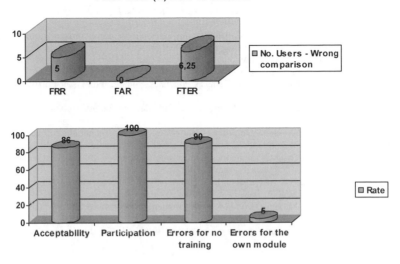

Figure 5: Results from the First Experiments

7.   Conclusions and Summary Recommendations

The first real test in a controllable environment achieved an acceptable rating, both by student and by the person assigned. As a non-intrusive technology there were no comments from the students. Likewise, the false rejection occurred in a minority.

The result to integrate a biometric identification in communities such as aLF or other learning systems can give greater freedom to introduce content or create spaces in adequately controlled way.

After this first test in laboratory, it intends to broaden theoretical courses and exams in classrooms equipped with computers for all students. Likewise remote activities where the support of teachers would be no longer necessary, in such case it would have to cope with the false rejection rates, trying to diminish as much as possible.

It is increasingly common to use biometric data as a mechanism for unambiguous identification of individuals. The definition of what is meant by biometric data is important for the nature of these data and the level and content of such information such data should have greater legal protection. This is the case of facial recognition or the use of DNA.

In a general sense the legal protection of biometric data at the community level is covered at first by the Directive 46/95 on the protection of personal data. It says in principle because, the provisions of this Directive 46/95 is limited in its scope if the use of biometric systems geared to issues related to the security of the Member States of the Union.

We must find the right balance [10] between security and freedom for the sake of respecting the dignity and fundamental rights of everyone.

Acknowledgement

The authors would like to acknowledge the Spanish Science and Education Ministry and the Spanish National Plan I+D+I 2004-2007 the support for this paper as the project TSI2005-08225-C07-03 "MOSAICLearning: Mobile and electronic learning, of open source, based on standards, secure, contextual, personalized and collaborative".

References

[1] Aparicio, J.; Estudio Sobre la Ley Orgánica de Protección de Datos de Carácter Personal, Ed. Aranzadi, Navarra, 2000, pp. 54.

[2] 29th Article European Union Working Group referring to computerized biometric data. Working document about biometrics adopted on August, 1st, 2003, pp. 4.

[3] Garcia-Pablos, A; Manual de Criminología, Ed. Espasa-Calpe, Madrid, 1998, pp. 427.

[4] De Diego Diez, L.A.; La Prueba Dactiloscópica, E. Bosch, Barcelona, 2001, pp. 30. Connected to Anton, F.; Iniciación a la Dactiloscopía y otras Técnicas Policiales, 2nd ed., Ed. Tirant Lo Blanch, Valencia, 1998, pp. 33 and more.

[5] Galvis, C.M.; Introducción a la biometria. Bogotá D.C., February 2007. Accessed in June 2008, http://www.monografias.com/.

[6] Biometrics Frequently Asked Questions. National Science & Technology Council Subcommittee on Biometrics. http://www.biometricscatalog.org/NSTCSubcommittee/. Accessed in July 2006.

[7] Wayman, J.L.; A Generalizad Biometric Identification System Model. Proc. IEEE Asilomar Conference on Signals, Systems, and Computers. November 1997

[8] Uludag, U. and Jain, A.K.; Attacks on Biometric Systems: A Case Study in Fingerprints. Proc. SPIE-EI 2004, pp. 622-633, San Jose, CA, January 18-22, 2004.

[9] Wayman, J., Jain, A., Maltoni, D. and Maio, D.; Biometric Systems: Technology, Design and Performance Evaluation. Ed. Springer, 2005.

[10] Tapia, S.G.; La Protección Jurídica de los Datos Biométricos en la Comunidad Europea. Revista de Derecho Informático. Ed. Alfa-Redi.

Collaboration and the Knowledge Economy: Issues, Applications, Case Studies
P. Cunningham and M. Cunningham (Eds.)
IOS Press, 2008

1557

ORT Argentina Virtual Campus Project

Guillermo LUTZKY

ORT Argentina, Libertador 6796, Buenos Aires, Postcode, Argentina
Tel: +054 11 47896515, Fax: +054 11 47896565, Email: glutzky@ort.edu.ar

Abstract: ORT Argentina currently holds two educational complexes, two technical high schools and two post-secondary junior colleges, with over 7,000 students. ORT Argentina Virtual Campus project has been designed to expose students and teachers to new technologies, especially to collaborative tools usually known as "Web 2.0" applications and services, and also to achieve a richer and stronger interaction between students, teachers, administrators, the Internet as a learning platform and the school community. The aim is to make the processes that take place within the organization, the school and the classroom public, transparent, flat, ubiquitous and adaptable.

The experience achieved higher standards than expected: Web Presence for the organization (almost inexistent before the project) and classrooms production are stronger. Students have paid attention to the observations on spelling, writing style and design, which emphasizes the open nature of the production and its 'permanent beta'.

1. Introduction - ORT Argentina's background

ORT Argentina's academic programmes are intended to cover the educational and training needs of the community, and, by means of a vast range of tracks and careers, to ensure that our students receive first-class training according to their own personal and academic interests.

ORT Argentina has a long and proud tradition. Founded in 1936, and backed by the 125 years of World ORT's rich experience in the field of education and training, it has grown and won recognition in local, national, and international educational circles. We are fully committed to giving our students the highest possible level of education and services.

ORT Argentina currently holds two educational complexes, two technical high-schools with over 4000 students, a post-secondary junior college with 2000 students; a department that develops joint cooperation projects and training programmes with other institutions and enterprises, and around 1000 teachers and support personnel.

2. State of affairs

Information, knowledge, and culture are central to human freedom and human development. How they are produced and exchanged in our society critically affects the way we see the state of the world as it is and might be; who decides these questions; and how we, as societies, come to understand what can and ought to be done.

An educational organization increases and utilizes its intangible assets by creating, sharing, and leveraging knowledge to create economic value and enhance organizational performance. In that sense, one of our main tasks is to incorporate the concrete and practical aspects of Knowledge Management.

Following this scenario, ORT Argentina decided that its structure, its schools and teachers must be more open and flexible, not only to become a sustainable organization, but also to prepare our students to deal with this context of accelerated change and innovation. It is essential for ORT Argentina to be aware of disruptive innovations that appear with increasing frequency into the technological and educational field, and to focus into science, creativity and culture shifts of paradigms.

3. Redefining the organization's focus

3.1 Managing knowledge

To reach a level of excellence and competitive advantage, ORT Argentina aims at redefining knowledge management. We understand culture not as something given, but as an issue in permanent change, which is produced in the social practice.

Besides, we look forward to implementing this strategy in an institution as large as ORT Argentina, which is also -by definition- a very complex organization; in which each student, teacher and family has its own requirements of personalized interaction and attention. Therefore, not only must we intervene in the design of information circulation systems, but we must also "read" the changing social structures of knowledge, and design the strategies that incorporate them to the organization.

3.2 Managing uncertainty

The concept of "emergent" seems to be essential in the near future, which should count on human resources with the necessary flexibility, motivation and interrelation to be able to face such singularities, which will become more frequent.

Management of the unexpected can be applied to almost all the organizations. Edgar Morín observed that "confronting uncertainty" was an important factor for the education of the future. In this sense, managing knowledge is managing chaos: order and systematization are just one part; the other is disorder and creativity. The notion of radical change or technological revolution in the tradition of academic practice is infrequent.

These concepts can also be applied within the classroom, especially when we use ICTs to teach and learn along with our "digital natives". In this sense, it should be pointed out that ORT aims at giving teachers and their students the freedom to develop the solutions and carry out the adequate processes to create communities of practice. Web 2.0 tools are a key instrument to deliver this collaborative and reticular project.

4. Foundation of the project

One of the main factors that determine knowledge worker productivity is that knowledge workers - and we must think of teachers as such - should be treated as an asset. It is extremely important that they are committed to working for the organization. Management has the mission of attracting and retaining the best knowledge workers.

From a strategic viewpoint, the challenge is to help our knowledge workers to contribute to value creation in our organization, and to generate an organizational climate where we do not just acknowledge the importance of this, but we do something about it.

To accomplish the institutional change, we have decided to create a knowledge network in parallel with the formal organizational pyramid, to allow ORT Argentina to reach its full potential. We used every available tool and technology, and looked out for others being developed, to carry out this collaborative and reticular project.

This initiative has been designed to achieve more interaction between students, teachers, administration, and parents, using the Internet as a learning platform, (far beyond the search for information and the use of the e-mail or IM), and to expose our community to new technologies, especially collaborative tools usually known as "Web 2.0" tools.

At the same time, it was important to sense the reaction of the community - other stakeholders, parents and students themselves - towards the responsibility and commitment required to make teaching, learning, socialization and the other processes that take place within the school and within the classroom public, transparent, flat and ubiquitous.

In a first stage, weblogs were chosen to become the technology to deliver the project. It is important to remark that in spite of the fact that weblogs originated within a school subject framework, they were quickly adopted by teachers from other courses, due to their efficiency in communication. Weblogs are reliable, accessible, easy to learn, non-intimidating and incrementally inexpensive. This experience had a great institutional impact, which is reflected on the quantity and quality of the Internet sites and weblogs created (400+ at June 2008).

We are looking for a coordinated emphasis on people, information, process, technology and support – a wide range of factors that together contribute to knowledge work productivity -, and we see a Web 2.0 contributive architecture as a scaffolding to contribute to our vision.

ORT Virtual Campus project looks forward to redesigning knowledge management at schools and into the organization itself. ICTs and Web 2.0 applications are being used as tools for collaborative work and production.

These tools will also provide a friendly, solid scaffolding to turn the school into an organization that manages knowledge. In this framework, it is important to think about the potential of these new media to create learning environments for the transfer of the skills needed to be included in the 21st century society.

Another issue to be considered is that we are living in the economy of attention and nowadays a Web Presence seems mandatory for most of the activities that are going on every day within an educational institution.

5. Goals of the Project

We want to prepare our schools, teachers and students for the Knowledge Society. The use of Web 2.0 applications and of weblogs in particular is an institutional strategy, transversal to the different disciplinary areas. This is oriented towards attaining the following goals:

- To promote the use of these new media among the members of the educational community, i.e. to generate a culture which includes the most experienced users and those who have just started using these tools, with the aim of building a teaching and learning community.
- To promote the construction of knowledge based on students and teachers' collaborative work. The notion of collaboration –central aspect of our project- implies recovering the value of social interaction in the production of knowledge and learning.
- To contribute to the creation of teaching and learning communities based on projects, powered by the blog network of the different areas, disciplines and courses; and to promote the participation of different members of the educational community in the development of the projects.
- To encourage the redesign of didactic strategies on the part of the teachers, and the incorporation of the audiovisual formats and the new mobile devices as teaching and learning tools, to think of how these new ways of representation can help in the understanding and building of knowledge in certain disciplines.

From a pedagogical approach, these additional guidelines were suggested to every teacher and administrator:

- Recast teachers and students as researchers and producers of knowledge. "Teaching to the future demands that we imbue students with a sense of intellectual purpose, instill in them a desire to make a difference, provide them with opportunities to reach a wider audience, furnish them with the tools to break new ground into the future society and do not shield them from innovation and innovative practices."
- Craft assignments that look both forward and backwards. "When we teach only to the future, we abandon our responsibility as the curators of our intellectual and cultural

heritage. Likewise, when we teach only to the past, we forget that our students have already booked tickets in the opposite direction".

6. Initial achievements

During the first few months of this experience, we focused on the creation of a set of blogs oriented towards different goals (see a classification into the universe... below). Now, we are facing a double challenge related to maintaining the production of contents over time and strengthening the networks of collaborative work among the different actors. For that purpose, we have incorporated a series of Web 2.0 tools, on which we will comment here.

To encourage collaborative work and introduce us in the new ways to store, organize and recover information, we have incorporated del.icio.us, a tool of social bookmarking[i], which is gradually integrating –via the most experienced users- to the universe of blogs. This application allows us to share favorites and to start creating a source of shared resources, ordered in terms of categories.

In parallel, there was a need to organize or systematize the set of blogs of the Virtual Campus. Therefore, there is an integration weblog, which aggregates RSS feeds from others Virtual Campus' weblogs that can be found at http://redblogs.ort.edu.ar.

To deepen the interconnection between blogs and to contribute to the creation of potential networks of collaborative work, we have added to most of the blogs an application called Feevy[ii]. Through Feevy we can include within each blog a link to the last posts of other related blogs -either because they are of the same subject or year, etc. The idea is to promote in this way the relationship and exchange between the different disciplines and areas to create a favorable context for the emergence of future projects and learning communities.

At this point, we would like to remark that the teaching and learning communities, based on projects and enabled by these new technologies, have become a fundamental pillar in our project and guide our practice.

7. A classification into the universe of weblogs

The following classification of the blogs that constitute ORT Virtual Campus does not intend to delineate isolated and watertight compartments, but to identify the main points of intersection of the network of blogs, by using the most representative cases as a base of analysis.

7.1 Blogs of a school subject, where teachers and students publish

This type of blogs emphasizes the productions of students, who are co-authors or contributors to the blog, and the interaction among peers and with the teacher by focusing on the activities that are carried out. In the first two cases, for example, the blog was used as a tool to elaborate, develop and publish a survey, by taking advantage of the potential of the blog as a tool.

7.2 Blogs of a school subject, where only teachers publish

At these blogs teachers publish study materials, tasks or other contents in a new audiovisual format.

7.3 Collective blogs: from teachers to teachers

At these blogs teachers are encouraged to experiment and reflect on their own practice in relation to the new technologies (see, for example, this post http://cuadernodelengua.blogspot.com/2007/06/enredados.html published in the blog Cuaderno de Lengua, where a teacher suggests the metaphor of a "trip by train" to analyze her discovery of the blogs). Besides, blogs are a space to share and exchange reading material and activities

7.4 Collective blogs: from teachers to students

These blogs are similar to those of the second category, but they are not restricted to the curricula of a school subject or to the development of classes: they include issues of general interest, different school services and the daily news of the school. The blogs of the Students' Counseling Areas have incorporated a calendar and a diary of the activities. Parents welcomed these blogs and left their comments on them. The weblog of the library, in turn, is characterized by its comments on the last books received, and recommends different articles published on newspapers:

7.5 Students' Blogs

Not only do these blogs register the last version of the students' projects and homework, which is equivalent to the coursework handed in class, but they follow up the elaboration process and, ultimately, the learning process.

7.6 Blogs of School Projects

It is also worth mentioning those projects, which deal with inherent problems of the community or the local context, which demonstrates the social and cultural nature of the construction of knowledge. The most representative example in this sense is the Oral History project, which began in 1993 with the aim of building the "Epistolary, Photographic, and Oral Archive of the migratory experiences of ORT families".

7.7 Oral History and Education[iii]

This blog along with the radio blog called "La Corneta" (i.e. "The Horn") have also incorporated new formats: geolocalization maps to tell stories at the Oral History blog[iv] and podcasts at the radio blog[v]:
La Corneta –radio blog.[vi]

7.8 Institutional Blogs

The blog of the project is included in this category: it is a space to document and reflect on the experience. In addition, we have implemented a "support" blog where we comment on the new tutorials or tools available:
- ORT Virtual Campus[vii]
- Tutorial Blog[viii]

  Other institutional blogs include:
- ORT Entrepreneurship Center[ix]
- News of ORT Argentina[x]
- School's Health Department[xi]

8. Lessons Learnt

In the first place, we would like to highlight the natural way in which students and teachers incorporated these tools to their routine. Even more, enthusiasm and commitment was perceived by the challenging projects they suggested. In general terms, the content achieved a higher standard than the one expected. Students paid attention to the observations on spelling, writing style and design, which emphasizes the open nature of the production and its 'permanent beta' or improvement. Besides, it really caught our attention the fact that there were no complaints about additional workload.

It is also interesting to register, through visit counters, different logics of the adolescents' works, hours at which they produce and publish. Besides, certain "contagion" patterns have emerged: when quality productions are published, there is a need to make contributions following the same high standards.

Weblogs are friendly channels, where teachers publish relevant information for students, correct homework and they even make those corrections 'public' for the rest of the class in the comment's section. Teachers from non-technological subjects have also made use of weblogs, especially Language teachers, who take advantage of them so that students can publish different tasks, such as tales, analysis of literary texts and research.

The institutional areas that have incorporated the project have discovered the potential of this direct channel with the educational community, where they can register the activities they carry out or can generate projects that promote a greater degree of involvement on the part of the different actors of the community. The institution has begun to open new spaces for dialogue and action with the different protagonists of the educational community through the blog. There is a clear reticular and non-pyramidal structure. Spaces for internal communication and production have been generated beyond the traditional formats.

Parents, in turn, have shown their enthusiasm and attention towards these "productive" aspects of the use of ICTs, in contrast with what they perceived as an excessive recreational use of the Internet.

Also, after one full year with the project, we can mention that:
- It is mandatory to create a space of Knowledge Development alive, flexible, active and pertaining to all, to be effective implementing a social framework.
- It is a strong marketing tool for an educational institution, to consider as a single process both action and communication.
- It is a key point to look for the innovator, the teacher on each department who has ideas and enthusiasm, to try new ways to do his job.
- It is very important not to fall into elitism, and asking only the supposedly best teachers to participate. This must be an open opportunity for everybody.
- It is crucial to consider "prosumers" to each one of the members of the community, and to each group.
- It is essential to convince people to work in networks, to create practice communities, (like the English teachers, the students who do charity work, etc).
- And to create at atmosphere which allows experimentation, innovation, and the opportunity to make adjustments.

9. Interim Results and levels of Innovation

To outline at least interim results after only one year, we can mention the jump of productivity of teachers. More activities, more study material, and essentially, more creativity is shown and used into classes and other teaching opportunities.

The project has helped to consolidate the institutional culture, has added value, capitalizing, the production and collective knowledge. Also, the project has allowed management to detect hidden talent, both of teachers and of students, who were otherwise out of sight, because of the departments or classrooms dynamics. Finally, provides scaffolding for different ways to teach, to learn, and to produce knowledge under a school environment.

Some innovations, going much further that what was suggested in the start of the project, (and created by suggestions of teachers and administrators) are:

9.1 Thematic Networks of Weblogs

There are like portals where the user can access all the blogs of a specific category.

- English Language Weblogs Network[xii]
- Spanish Language Weblogs Network[xiii]
- Jewish Ed. Weblogs Network[xiv]

9.2 Networks of Weblogs of Students Graduation Projects

All the students of ORT in his final year must develop a Graduation Project, depending on the track they have chosen. They have academic hours dedicated to the project and a tutor. The weblogs help them to log the advances and challenges that they must solve. And also, as a marketing platform, they show the level of accomplishment of ORT Argentina's Students, and work as an online CV for the students.

- Chemistry Final Projects[xv]
- Electronics Final Projects[xvi]
- ICT Final Projects[xvii]

Some statistics numbers also show the level of production, and the social impact reached by the project:

1. As recorded by Google Analytics, it is significant the growth of visitors to the weblogs, and the retention of viewers.
   May 21 - June 20, 2007: 6,655 Visits   12,270 Pageviews   66.36% New Visits
   May 21 - June 20, 2008: 93,613 Visits   150,608 Pageviews   47.36% New Visits
2. In terms of production, from May 20th to June 20th, 2008, 2060 blog entries were published by teachers (and students in classroom weblogs), plus other additional 320 by students in the Final Project weblogs
3. In terms of visibility, the project appeared, (from November 2007 to June 2008), five times into three of the main newspapers (Clarín, La Nación, La Razón) of Buenos Aires, and two more times into the most visited news site in Argentina (http://www.clarin.com).

10. Final Reflections

In the previous section, we have emphasized students' and teachers' motivation and enthusiasm towards working with these new tools, which they quickly and naturally incorporated, without greater difficulties. Weblogs - especially those where teachers and students publish - have become alternative spaces for socialization, characterized by a flat, informal style that favors communication between administrators, teachers and students. They have also connected the school environment to the student's context (family and friends). This generates a greater sense of ownership, responsibility and belonging, thus facilitating the transfer of the contents learnt between both environments and, in a nutshell, delivers a better service to all the stakeholders involved.

In this sense, it seems that the main changes of the "Knowledge Society" at school affect to a great extent two axis: teacher-student-task on the one hand, and teacher–parent–administrator-educational institution on the other.

We are advancing towards a knowledge management strategy, which takes up not only the explicit but also the non-traditional, tacit knowledge that is incorporated to the routine practices. The starting point of this experience is based on these social networks of knowledge and it aims at incorporating them to the organization. What makes this project more complex, and at the same time, more valuable and fascinating is the need to permanently sense the environment, and recycle the old to develop the new.

The institution, and its management, is fully behind this project. To encourage this pioneering initiative, and in particular the adoption of online communication, ORT Argentina reviewed all of its operating procedures and structures, to ensure that its support was holistic. The cultural change is substantial, especially for a successful academic organization. Without such change, teachers and administrators who have sought to incorporate these new tools to their teaching methods would have been left stranded, and the students would have not received an effective service delivery.

References

[1] CASTELLS, M. (1997). La era de la información: economía, sociedad y cultura. Vol 1: La sociedad red, Alianza Editorial, Madrid.
[2] MORIN, E, (1999). Los siete saberes necesarios para la educación del futuro. UNESCO
[3] BRUNNER, J.J. (2002): Internet y educación. ¿La próxima revolución? Fondo de Cultura Económica, Santiago.
[4] RHEINGOLD H.: (2004) Multitudes inteligentes. La próxima revolución social. Gedisa, Barcelona.
[5] DRUCKER, P. (1993). Post-capitalist society. Nueva York: Butterworth-Heinemann.
[6] NONAKA, I (1995). The knowledge creating company. Oxford : Oxford Press.
[7] SEELY BROWN, J. (1999). Serendip. Learning, working & playing in the Digital Age. http://serendip.brynmawr.edu/sci_edu/seelybrown/
[8] PEÑA, I.; CÓRCOLES, C.; CASADO, C. (2006). El Profesor 2.0: docencia e investigación desde la Red. *UOC Papers.* N. ° 3. http://www.uoc.edu/uocpapers/3/dt/esp/pena_corcoles_casado.pdf
[9] FUMERO, A. y ROCA, G. (2007). Web 2.0: Biblioteca Fundación Orange España
[10] COBO ROMANÍ, C. y PARDO KUKLINSKI, H. (2007). Planeta Web 2.0: FLACSO México
[11] ORTIZ, LUIS FARLEY (2007). Campus Virtual: la educación más allá del LMS. Revista de Universidad y Sociedad del Conocimiento (RUSC). Vol. 4, n.° 1. UOC. http://www.uoc.edu/rusc/4/1/dt/esp/ortiz.pdf
[12] SEELY BROWN, J. and ADLER, R.: (2008). Minds on Fire - Open Education, the Long Tail, and Learning 2.0: Educause Jan/Feb 08

---

[i] http://del.icio.us/campus_virtual
[ii] http://www.feevy.com/
[iii] http://historiaoralort.blogspot.com/
[iv] http://historiaoralort.blogspot.com/2007/07/el-espacio-urbano-otra-representacin.html
[v] http://radioeducativaort.blogspot.com/2007/07/ historia-de-la-msica.html
[vi] http://radioeducativaort.blogspot.com/
[vii] http://campusvirtualort.blogspot.com/
[viii] http://blogsoporte.ort.edu.ar/
[ix] http://ceo-ort.blogspot.com/
[x] http://novedadesort.ort.edu.ar/
[xi] http://deptomedico.blogspot.com/
[xii] http://redblogsingles.blogspot.com/
[xiii] http://redblogslengua.blogspot.com/
[xiv] http://redblogseducacionjudia.blogspot.com/
[xv] http://redblogsquimica.blogspot.com/
[xvi] http://pfelectronica2008.blogspot.com/
[xvii] http://pfinformatica2008.blogspot.com/

Collaboration and the Knowledge Economy: Issues, Applications, Case Studies
P. Cunningham and M. Cunningham (Eds.)
IOS Press, 2008

Bangladesh Virtual Classroom: Technology Enhanced Learning for all – today

Åke GRÖNLUND [1], Yousuf M. ISLAM [2]

[1]Örebro University, Fakultetsgatan 1, Örebro, 701 82, Sweden
Tel: +46 70 5851790, Fax: + 46 19 332546, Email: ake.gronlund@oru.se
[2]Daffodil International University, 102 Shukrabad, Mirpur Road, Dhaka, Bangladesh
Tel: +8801711876909, Email: ymislam@gmail.com

Abstract: We developed low-cost, effective ICT to improve distance education in Bangladesh, using video and SMS to implement innovative pedagogy and to create a large-scale interactive learning environment for students, hitherto not existing. We develop sustainable strategies for ICT use in education including curriculum development, teacher education for interactive learning, and a new business model. Being the first of its kind worldwide, the project will serve as a role model for how to arrange low-cost distance tuition requiring only minimal ICT infrastructure, an example providing valuable experiences transferable to other developing countries. The project addresses technical factors (development of interactive technology) as well as social ones (introducing and sustaining interactivity in education) and the business model for distance tuition (engaging local learning centres, telecommunication management).

1. Introduction

Education is a major factor for development [12, 13,14, 16], yet education in developing countries is a huge challenge [5, 6, 7, 8, 10]. As a complement to traditional education, distance tuition is established in many countries. In Bangladesh, the Bangladesh Open University (BOU) provides distance tuition to some 250 000 students all over Bangladesh since 1992. Students are distributed across vast areas with poor communication facilities. Major problems include low throughput, poor or no communication between teachers and students, traditional inefficient teaching methods, and underdeveloped use of local learning centres. Generally, technology enhanced learning has been promoted as a way to overcome physical distances, availability problems [5, 7], and teacher shortages [15], but most technology enhanced learning projects use web technology which is typically not readily available, neither now nor in the foreseeable future, more so in the rural areas of developing countries. This also deprives the education from adding features of interactivity, which has proven to be a main enabler for student retention, performance and satisfaction [9, 17, 18]. There is hence a need for solutions using existing infrastructure as much as possible.

The Bangladesh Virtual Classroom project (BVC) employs low-cost, effective ICT to improve distance education in Bangladesh, with the prospect of being able to implement both technology and methods in any developing country. Using video and SMS together with a computer server to implement innovative pedagogy we create a learning environment for students, hitherto not existing. The project is a joint effort between Örebro University, Sweden (ÖU) and BOU. We develop sustainable strategies for ICT use in education including curriculum development, teacher education for interactive learning, technical tools for large-scale interactive learning using existing mobile technology infrastructure, and a new business model. Being the first of its kind worldwide, the project will serve as a role model for how to arrange low-cost distance tuition requiring only minimal ICT infrastructure, an example that will provide valuable experiences transferable to other developing countries. The project addresses technical factors (development of interactive technology) as well as social ones (introducing and sustaining interactivity in education) and the business model for distance tuition (engaging local learning centres, telecommunication management).

In terms of technology, the project is feasible and well timed. It is estimated by World Bank that 77 per cent of the world's population is within the reach of mobile phone network and it is estimated that the number of cell phone subscribers worldwide continues to increase at a very rapid rate, with the most significant growth being in developing countries [3]. In Bangladesh GSM technology based mobile phone was introduced in March 1996. Mobile network coverage has today reached about 97 percent of the country's population and 82 percent of the land area [4]. Competition among mobile operators has significantly reduced tariff rates in the past few years and availability of low-cost phone sets attracted subscribers of financially constrained group. Although nearly half of Bangladesh's more than 140 million people still live on less than a dollar a day it has one of Asia's fastest growing cellular markets. Already today Bangladesh has 38.93 million mobile phone subscribers by the end of March 2008 [1]. This means one out of four Bangladeshis have a mobile subscription – on average at least one in every family. The number is forecast to increase to be 44 million by 2009 [4]. Our own estimates suggest that access to mobile phone at the household level is nearing 90 % in the urban area and 70 % in the rural area. We have also done tests with delivering information through mobile phones in Bangladeshi villages that support this picture. Computer access is still miniscule, concentrated to urban areas, and not expected to increase dramatically in the foreseeable future.

Based on these preconditions, the BVC project develops interactive teaching methods and technical tools designed for the infrastructure in developing countries. Many ICT aid programs invest a lot in expensive technology, such as putting computers in schools. This sometimes succeeds, sometimes fails, and the distinguishing factor is whether or not the technology fits into the context in which it is to be utilized and maintained. The BVC project draws on an existing, and very strong, trend in technology use and extends the use of it to becoming a participatory tool in combination with computer based support for teaching and learning activities. The originality lies in non-Internet/broadband dependence, good alignment to technical trends viable also in rural areas of developing countries, and excellent compatibility with social needs by target groups. As there is also no technology investment necessary, the BVC can provide a promising business case in terms of economy as well as time to implementation.

2. Objectives

The aim of this paper is to address the question of how to use existing mobile telephony technical infrastructure to create an interactive learning environments which can reach the majority of the population, be scalable to include many thousand students, and be sustainable from a resource perspective including the business model of institutions providing education.

This question includes challenges relating to pedagogy and teaching methods, technical tools for learning and communication, and institutional arrangements. The paper addresses these challenges by the illustrative case of the BVC. We present technology developed and achievements in pedagogy and course delivery, and we discuss the challenges ahead.

3. Methodology

A research and development endeavour, the project involves both practitioners and researchers. The practitioner side was primarily Sida (Swedish International Development

Cooperation Agency) through its affiliate SPIDER (www.spider-center.org), focusing on ICT4D and acting through a network of Swedish universities. The project was conceived by researchers in Sweden and Bangladesh. Ideas and prototypes were developed and project ideas were conveyed to practitioner organizations in Bangladesh. Finally a partnership was set up with BOU and a local software company in Bangladesh in which roles were clearly distinguished. The research partner (ÖU) does all research involved (including independent software testing), the software company develops the interactive application, BOU supplies teachers, physical facilities, and administrative support. Video recording is done at BOU, by local technicians and with participation of e-learning expertise from the research partner. The research parts of the project are clearly separated from the development work and come in three stages.

1. Preparatory grounding. All prototypes draw on research in several fields; information systems development, human-computer interaction, computer-supported cooperative work, technology enhanced learning, pedagogy, and development.
2. Underway research points are identified which require scientific methods; e.g. usability testing of prototypes, sociological investigations of local communication networks, and technology use patterns.
3. Following real-world implementation are effect studies, including e.g. effects on learning, uptake, and user satisfaction.

4. Technology Description

In the Bangladesh Virtual Classroom project, SMS is used together with TV/video to make lectures interactive. To support course delivery a Mobile Course Management System has been developed.

The mobile application as well as the whole concept have been tested in laboratory-style settings in physical classrooms as well as live on TV at BOU over two years. From this work we have arrived at a technical solution and a working method that works well. During 2008 BOU is running a first large-scale pilot ("English 2", upper secondary level), which involves some 70 000 registered students. Recordings are done in a BOU regional centre in Dhaka, including real students in the studio to give both teachers and viewers the sense of a "real" classroom.

The process change under implementation includes improving teachers' skills on how to teach in an interactive manner and organizing teaching material for interactivity. Curriculums have to be revisited, lectures redesigned, and presentation and interaction practiced. This project develops both interactive technology and interactive teaching methods. The cartoon captures the learning situation we design for at a glance, a student sitting at home or in company with others using TV or video to watch and a mobile phone to communicate with teachers and other students.

Starting with the technology, behind the cartoon view we have built a quite comprehensive SMS-based system involving a number of tools for communication between students and teachers. There are basically three different sets of tools; for learning and communication, for administration, and for teacher support.

4.1   Learning and communication tools

The core of education, of course, has to do with learning, and the basic thrust of our system and our method is to bring the teacher and the students closer to each other, as far as this can be done given the distributed setting. The following tools have been implemented and tested to support and enhance learning.

Self Assessment Quiz: after finishing a chapter, a student can download a quiz based on the chapter. This is done by sending BOU Z <lesson number>. The students can take a quiz whenever they want, as many times as they want. The students are given random questions from a database.

Questions during class: students respond to questions by the teacher during class time by sending BOU Q <selected response>. The response is simply a, b, c or d. The students see a bar graph of the answers sent in. The teacher then discusses the answers and dials a student from among those who have answered wrongly. The conversation is heard by all the viewers.

Participatory Cards: The teacher on video asks a question like, 'In your opinion, how can language learning be made easier?' The students respond by SMS sending keywords after BOU P <opinion>. The opinions are displayed on a monitor as rectangular boxes as they come in. The students are then able to visualize the responses and group the ideas together to come up with collective strategies in response to the question. It has been found that students take ownership of the process and results. This is a workshop technique adapted to students watching a video lesson.

Homework: Not a specific technical function but a task given to students that can be reported using other functions. Homework is coupled to the learning partner idea.

Learning partner: This is also not a technical function but a pedagogical approach. It is well known from distance tuition research and practice that students who have a social network in class are less likely to drop out than those who work alone, hence it is a good idea to group them together so they can share experiences and spur each other. The students have to register as a pair in the language BVC class. They do this by sending an SMS as BOU LP <own ID> <partners ID> <partners mobile number>. When the partner confirms with a similar SMS the pair is registered. Tasks are designed to get the partners works together, e.g., partners have to send in comments on each other's work. Each comment will be recorded in a database. Each comment will be counted as one mark.

Meaning: Students can get the meaning of words given in their text as vocabulary by sending BOU D <word>. This returns the meaning and a sentence with the word. As a future development, students can also get the pronunciation of these words.

Reading: students are encouraged to read and learn by texting BOU R. This returns a short (<160 character) paragraph from a story. In return for key words that express the main idea of the paragraph students get the next paragraph. This way, students can complete stories that are stored in the server.

4.2   Administrative tools

Registration: To participate in electronic course communication students must register. This is done by SMS and checked against BOU course registration files.

Attendance: Students can register for each class. Registration gives access to all the other tools. Students can just watch the TV show, but without registration they cannot take part in activities. This function also gives the teacher a view of who is watching and who is not.

Course information & rules: Practical information about the course is disseminated over SMS, such as performance criteria, available tests, deadlines, etc (e.g. "You have to pass 8 out of 10 classes to pass the course"). These messages are not just one-way information, they also include feedback, such as reminders like "Don't forget to take the quiz, you haven't done that yet".

Results: Results of each student's answers to SMS questions are communicated individually to each student; "Congratulations, you attempted 8 out of 10 Q's, 7 right".

4.3 Teacher support

Many of the above functions are automated so the teacher only does preparatory work, such as preparing or updating the course dictionary, or follow-up analysis such to see how many students took the tests, what the results were, etc. Such statistics, provided by a report generator, give BOU teachers a new view of student activities and results. Previously they had no contact with the students before the final exam after the course is completed by the end of the year.

During class the teacher is busy as the allotted time during a TV show is very limited so s/he needs to be disciplined and informed for the interactive parts. To support a 'live' show our system provides a "dashboard" available during class on the computer. This provides results from SMS questions asked during class and numbers to call. The teacher can see the number of correct and incorrect answers and the telephone number corresponding to who answered what – A, B, C or D. Based on this information s/he can call one of the students, by clicking on one of the telephone numbers, to discuss the answer. For example, if there are many incorrect answers the teacher may want to understand why so many people got it wrong. S/he might then choose to call someone who got it right so as to let that student provide an explanation which may help other students better understand the reasoning.

5. Developments

The mobile application as well as the concepts on how best to run the BVC have been tested in various ways in physical classrooms and live on TV at Bangladesh Open University (BOU) over two years. Starting from the basic idea of interactivity we first developed a prototype for the mobile application as of above and tested it in a setting with two ordinary classrooms. The same teacher served both classes. In one he was physically present, in the other he was visible through TV and interacted through the SMS system. Learning in both classes was compared and found to be the same [2]. This showed that the method of teacher-student interaction through SMS worked. It also showed that the usability of the system was satisfactory.

Next we developed a video designed to be a prototypical BOU TV-sent class, including interactivity between students and teacher. The purpose of this was to demonstrate our idea to BOU in a hands-on way. Traditionally, BOU teachers do not work with students. They produce lectures based on literature and deliver them as speeches on (recorded) TV. Hence, both interaction in general and the specific technical implementation of it had to be clearly demonstrated. The demonstration went well, as we learned from focus groups of teachers and students, and we were able to make an explicit contract with BOU to develop a complete course in this fashion. This course was "English 2", which engages some 70 000 students starting in Spring 2008 and will be completed by the end of the year. 28 interactive lectures have been produced and recorded with live classes. These are shown on TV at a pace of one per week. They are also available on VHS tape/DVD to be viewed at any time at the some 1300 BOU tutorial centers, available across the country.

Technically the SMS applications as well as the TV recordings work well. Students quickly learn to use our course tools, and the mobile phone is already a familiar technology. A challenge of the large-scale test phase was to make teachers learn how to teach in an interactive manner and organize teaching material for interactivity. Curriculums have to be revisited, lectures redesigned, and presentation and interaction practiced. We have done this in the following manner. About a dozen BOU teachers were selected based on personal interest, knowledge and availability. They were given a one-week course on interactive teaching in general and our specific method in particular in December 2007. The purpose was to prepare them for recordings by understanding how the teaching material should be organized so as to be delivered in this interactive manner. In February 2008 two intensive weeks of test recordings took place. By then, teachers had, in cooperation with the project's pedagogical expert, developed scripts for the lessons, and we recorded them with a "live" class present. We could, of course, not produce 28 lectures in two weeks with teachers inexperienced both in interactivity and live teaching, but we wanted to have an intensive session so as to find a smooth way of recording, acquaint as many teachers as possible with the method and the situation, and establish a stable design for the TV shows, meaning one that both fitted our intentions and the teachers' experience and current ambitions. Once this was done we went on with recordings engaging five teachers as the main actors.

Recordings were done with a live class of students, for several purposes. First, teachers needed to have a class present to be able to really learn interactivity. A real class gives real, and immediate, feedback. Second, it gave us a good opportunity to observe students' behavior and to inquire their views on the pedagogy, technology use, and the tools we had developed. Third, as the lectures would be recorded and used for re-plays it would be useful to have the "live feeling" to the show even when it would not be watched in real time.

Beyond this practical approach there is a wider issue about teaching methods in general which this project addresses but which can only be solved gradually and by means of sustained change processes. Interactivity in teaching has since long been found to be a success factor essential for learning. Interactive teaching has developed since the late 1960s in the industrialized world; however, in most developing countries it is a novelty. Interactive teaching puts new demands on teachers, teacher training and education organizers, and full scale implementation will require much effort. Our project has so far mainly addressed these issues by a practical approach so as to get started, but clearly this is only the beginning of a long development. We have opened the door to the benefits of interactive teaching; however addressing the demands for teacher training, change of pedagogical ideals, understanding the importance of enabling students rather than trying to fill them with information is a much more far-reaching endeavor. We are working with BOU to address also these issues; however this effort has a longer-term schedule.

6. Results

This project has, in research-practitioner partnership, developed a complete set of tools for large-scale distance tuition in developing countries including (1) interactive technology with a number of technical tools for learning and course administration, (2) a new pedagogical model designed for interactivity in a developing country context, (3) methods for focused teacher training in interactive e-learning, and (4) curriculum development. We are currently cooperating with BOU to (5) develop and implement a new business model for distance tuition in Bangladesh. We will work to make this model internationally applicable, and we are currently preparing to set up another test site in Ghana.

User acceptance and learning effects have been investigated and found positive. The level of innovation is very high concerning pedagogical methods and distance tuition business model in developing countries. The technical innovation is high concerning adaptation to needs in developing countries, i.e. usefulness, however as it uses existing technical infrastructure there is no imminent need for expansion of this.

7. Business Benefits

The BVC project has developed a model for low-cost interactive technology enhanced learning in developing countries. This is a huge benefit as both technology enhanced learning and distance tuition in general show very poor throughput rates in developing countries and are not aligned with e-learning best practices. Drawing on existing technical infrastructure and existing skills in using technology the tools and methods developed are very feasible. The business model innovation is very high as this is a low-cost scheme with extremely high outreach already as of today. It is both affordable and useful in any developing country. As there is no technical investment necessary, the economy of the approach is promising. Yet to be done is full-scale implementation of the business model. This is beyond this actual project but as the practitioner partner, Bangladesh Open University is the major actor in the country we believe the scene is well set for this challenge.

8. Conclusions

The BVC project has developed a complete set of tools for large-scale distance tuition in developing countries including (1) interactive technology with a number of technical tools for learning and course administration, (2) a new pedagogical model designed for interactivity in a developing country context, replacing repetitious pedagogy with student centred learning, (3) methods for focused teacher training in interactive e-learning, and (4) curriculum development. We are currently cooperating with BOU to (5) develop and implement a new business model for distance tuition in Bangladesh.

There is potentially huge economic and societal significance of this effort. Economic, because it is a low-cost scheme requiring no new technical infrastructure. Societal, because it allows the rural population in developing countries to take a significant step into the "e-society". This said, there are a number of challenges which cannot be met by a single effort but need consistent and sustained change work. These include.

- Technical challenges for education providers: Making the TV shows effective in terms of production efforts and attractive to students. Less of a challenge but still a new task is hosting an SMS server and attached software.
- Organizational challenges: (1) Teacher training: making teachers learn and adopt interactive ways of teaching; (2) Redesigning the basic course model; and (3) Engaging local tutorial centers in new ways
- Cultural challenge: Making "student-centered teaching" the norm, i.e. focusing more on learning and less on teaching. This is a long-term change, which in industrial countries has taken decades. While this process may be faster as examples and methods exist one should not expect educational cultures to change quickly [19, 6, 10, 11].

While these challenges all have to be met by each project it would be beneficial if international aid providers would take care that receiving governments understand the two latter ones. "Development" programs often stop at technical development, and this is often the easiest part; certainly this has been the case in this project. Organisational changes need government support beyond what a single project can achieve alone. Cultural changes cannot be "implemented" they have to be enacted. However, they can be strongly supported by organizational changes providing incentives for innovation.

Further work for our project includes full-scale implementation of the business model, making further tests in other countries, and sustaining the technical tools. The BVC is compatible with increasing use of web technologies, so one strand of further development is to integrate it with existing learning management systems as the feasibility of this emerges.

References

[1] BTRC. (2008). Mobile Phone Subscribers in Bangladesh . Retrieved April 21, 2008, from http://www.btrc.gov.bd/newsandevents/mobile_phone_subscribers/mobile_phone_subscribers_march_2 008.php

[2]   Yousuf M. Islam, Manzur Ashraf, Zillur Rahman, Mawdudur Rahman: Mobile Telephone Technology as a Distance Learning Tool. *ICEIS 2005,* Proceedings of the Seventh International Conference on Enterprise Information Systems, Miami, USA, May 25-28, 2005. ISBN 972-8865-19-8, pp.226-232.

[3]   Kenny C. and Keremane R. The World Bank, Washington, DC 20433, USA. Accessed at http://www.sciencedirect.com/science

[4]   Asian   Development   Bank   press   conference   on   17   May   2007.   Accessed   at http://www.thenews.com.pk/print1.asp?id=56250

[5]   Dhanarajan, G. "Distance Education: promise, performance and potential," Open Learning (16:1) 2001.

[6]   Evans, R. "Explaining low learner participation during interactive television instruction in a developing country context," in: Curriculum Studies, University of Pretoria, Pretoria, 2005, p. 175.

[7]   Grönlund, Å., Andersson, A., and Hedström, K. "NextStep eGovernment in developing countries," Örebro University, Informatics, Örebro, p. 140.

[8] Heeks, R. "Information Systems and Developing Countries: Failure, Success, and Local Improvisations," The Information Society (18:2) 2002, pp 101-112.

[9]   Jiang, M., and Ting, E. "A Study of Factors Influencing Students' Perceived Learning in a Web-Based Course Environment," International Journal of Educational Telecommunications (6:4) 2000, pp 317-338.

[10] Rajesh, M. "A Study of the problems associated with ICT adaptability in Developing Countries in the context of Distance Education," Turkish Online Journal of Distance Education (4:2) 2003.

[11] Sehrt, M. "E-learning in the Developing Countries - Digital Divide into Digital Opportunities," in: *UN Chronicle Online,* UN (ed.), United Nations, 2003.

[12] Soriyan, H.A., Mursu, A.S., Akinde, A.D., and Korpela, M.J. "Information Systems Development in Nigerian Software Companies: Research Methodology and Assessment from the Healthcare Sector's Perspective," The Electronic Journal for Information Systems in Developing Countries (5:4) 2001, pp 1-18.

[13] UNDP "Information and Communication Technology (ICT) for Development," 2005.

[14] UNESCO "United Nations Decade of Education for Sustainable Development," 2005.

[15] UNESCO "Teachers and educational quality: monitoring global needs for 2015" UIS/AP/06-01, UIS, UNESCO Institute for Statistics (UIS), Montreal, Canada, p. 215.

[16] WSIS "World Summit on the Information Society," 2005.

[17] Zhang, D., Zhao, J.L., Zhou, L., and Nunamaker, J.F. "Can E-Learning Replace Classroom Learning?," Association for Computing Machinery. Communications of the ACM (47:5) 2004, pp 75-79.

[18] Zhang, D., Zhou, L., Briggs, R.O., and Nunamaker, J.F. "Instructional video in e-learning: Assessing the impact of interactive video on learning effectiveness," Information & Management (43:1) 2006, pp 15-27.

[19] Eastmond, D. "Realizing the promise of distance education in low technology countries," Educational Technology Research and Development (48:2) 2000, pp 100-111.

Section 11

Security and Identity Management

Section 11.1

Issues

Collaboration and the Knowledge Economy: Issues, Applications, Case Studies
P. Cunningham and M. Cunningham (Eds.)
IOS Press, 2008

Federation of Circles of Trust and Secure Usage of Digital Identity

Alexis DAVOUX[1], Jean-Christophe DEFLINE[2], Ludovic FRANCESCONI[3],
Maryline LAURENT-MAKNAVICIUS[4], Kheira BEKARA[4], Romain GOLA[4],
Jean-Baptiste LEZORAY[5], Vincent ETCHEBARNE[1]

[1]*Orange Labs, R&D, 38-40 Rue du Général Leclerc, Issy les Moulineaux Cedex 9, 92794, France*
Tel: +33 1 45 29 53 86, Email: {adavoux.ext, vincent.etchebarne}@orange-ftgroup.com
[2]*Copilot Partners, 11, rue du chevalier de Saint George, Paris, 75008, France*
Tel: +33 1 42 86 67 26, Fax: +33 1 42 60 19 09, Email: jcdefline@copilotpartners.com
[3] *Groupement des Cartes Bancaires « CB », 31 rue de Berri, Paris, 75008, France*
Tel: +33 1 5389 4068, Fax: +33 1 5389 3500, Email: ludovic-francesconi@cartes-bancaires.com
[4] *TELECOM&Management SudParis, 9 Rue Charles Fourier, Evry, 91011, France*
Tel: +33 1 60 76 44 42 number, Fax: +33 1 60 76 47 11, Email: {firstname.lastname}@it-sudparis.eu
[5]*CEV Group, Zone Neptune 2, Rue Henri Claudel, Saint-Lo, 50000, France*
Tel: +33 2 33 77 65 00 number, Fax: +33 2 33 77 65 01, Email: jean-baptiste.lezoray@cev-sa.com

Abstract: The joint growths of digital services and identity fraud exploiting poor identity management solutions have led to an identity crisis on the Internet. People struggle to keep control over their fragmented digital identities, and user privacy is not correctly enforced. As countermeasures, new digital identity initiatives include several distinct federated identity models, like Liberty Alliance or InfoCard. Based on the results of a French innovative R&D project called FC² (Federation of Circles of Trust), this paper investigates the ways to create a federated identity architecture compatible with the major existing identity technologies while providing a secure and coherent user experience. In the light of a practical use case involving a bike rental service requiring attributes from its users to complete their registration, the card-based identity selector seems to arise as a major client identity component. The first project results highlight the need for clear and simple user information on service providers about identity exchanges. A 'Simplified Sign-On' procedure for users and the need for digitally certified attributes are also exposed. On the business side, possible future models are sketched with their benefits for the different actors of the identity value chain. Eventually, studying the legal issues related to the federated identity model show that the responsibilities of the different actors should carefully be established within a circle of trust.

Keywords: federated identity, circle of trust, digital identity, user experience, FC², security, identity value chain, interoperability, Liberty Alliance, InfoCard, Higgins

1. Introduction

"Jack234", "Jack M.", "Dr Jack Malone"… These are not the signs of some kind of 'digital schizophrenia' but the multiple digital personas used by a same person on the web. And with the always-growing number of online services and the development of dematerialization processes, digital identity usage has become a key subject for the individual (citizen, customer or simple user) and his digital life. As a key requirement for secure electronic transactions and trusted digital exchanges (e-commerce and e-administration are two examples), digital identity management is a ground basis for the modernization of the society.

As security was not an initial goal in the conception of Internet, the users' identity is not widely normalized, and can rely on multiple different supports like certificates, system accounts, local databases linked to applications, directories... Fragmented and incompatible identity management solutions lead to personal and private information spread across service providers and no longer manageable by the end-user. People barely manage to keep trace of their distinct usernames, passwords, personas and personal attributes on the web. Identity fraud is growing fast: as a consequence, users are losing their trust in the e-services. More specifically, regarding personal data and privacy, consumers remain largely concerned about the usage that can be made with their data [1]. To remedy this situation, new identity management solutions have arisen, like an identity credential that could be used by many organizations for multiple functions. However, a majority of consumers remain divided on which organizations they would mostly trust to do so, and how data should be administered. Furthermore, local legislation would forbid a centralized repository for personal data in some countries.

At this time, different initiatives of identity portability already coexist. Among them, the federated identity model allows the use of digital identities over distinct security domains. It gives the users back control over their personal data disseminated amongst organizations. This model supports multiple identity and service providers. Yet it may vary in the way the actual 'identity federation' is done.

2.   Objectives

Based on the previous statements, the following questions arise: how can the various identity management initiatives fit together? Is it possible to provide identity-aware and personalised services while relying on different identity models and respecting the user concerns about their digital identity and privacy?

To answer these questions, this paper proposes a new practical identity federation architecture involving various and multiple identity-aware service providers, aiming to provide a coherent and secure digital experience for the end-user. The adopted model should be interoperable with current major federated identity frameworks (Liberty Alliance [2], InfoCard [3] and Microsoft CardSpace [4] or the Higgins identity framework [5]...). It should also allow the end users to easily access services and securely share their personal data, while considering ergonomics and respect of user privacy as key requirements.

The resulting architecture should meet the user needs in terms of better and simpler identity management. At the same time, it should be considered viable by the actors of the identity value chain like service providers or identity providers. Indeed, it should enhance the development of new identity-based digital services by encouraging the adoption of federated identity management solutions and preventing identity-fraud. Business and legal stakes also have to be carefully considered. This paper analyzes some of them and considers societal issues as well.

3.   Methodology

This paper is built upon the early results from a French R&D innovative project called FC² [6] (Federation of Circles of Trust), started in fall 2007. The main goal of FC² is to develop and validate a comprehensive platform allowing new secure digital online services, based on transparent and federated identity management. The actors of this project are small, medium and large companies from the telecommunications and banking industry, software vendors, universities, research institutes, and the French Home Office. The FC² project plans to deploy a platform demonstrating federated identity management solutions, involving services from three different fields of activities: public/governmental services, banking services and telecommunication services. FC² would like to stay as equitable as possible with regard to the identity technologies used.

This paper proposes to share and explain the first project analyses, with a focus on the relation between the user experience and the technical interoperability between different federated identity models. On one hand, consumers would highly welcome any system that may simplify their life, by allowing them to fulfil almost automatically their personal data (identity, banking card number, etc) in the various daily requests of the digital life. On the other hand, they are frightened by the potential usage being made with those same personal data. For a new identity management to succeed, it's therefore crucial to take into account the users' needs in terms of privacy and at the same time simplicity of use.

Eventually, the functional architecture of one of the main FC² scenario is proposed as a support for this reflexion, which leads to glimpses of a possible technical architecture, based on existing identity-related initiatives. Some innovative ideas and proposals are exposed, based on critical features like authentication and SSO, attributes sharing and payment processes.

4. Technology/Business Case Description

One of the use case studied by the FC² project is a functional and technical use case implicating a French public urban bicycle rental service, directly inspired by the "Vélib'" success story in the city of Paris. This scenario is divided in two steps: a user registration to the bicycle rental service using a dematerialized procedure, and the use of a mobile service providing the journey best journey by bike to the user destination.

The user has to register to the bike rental service and is faced once again with a very tedious web form to fill. But as a regular user of the FC² platform, he has already entered the needed information (i e attributes) into his existing profiles in the different circles: his citizen account, his banking account and his telecommunication operator account. In order to avoid the painful completion of the form by the user, the FC² platform enables the registration website to get these personal attributes stored in various places in order to automatically fill the user form after user approval, even if different identity models and/or technologies are used by the entities involved. As a consequence, the user can easily fill a registration form while enforcing his privacy rights; at the same time, the bike rental service receives user information from trusted sources and offers a nice experience to the user.

Eventually, the user is able to access the mobile cartography website in a convenient but privacy-friendly way. In the use case, he wishes to find the best journey by bike to go visiting his friend. The site should access his geolocation and contact book with the address of his friend to provide an enhanced service. But this attribute sharing step is only allowed according to an access rule predefined by the user or after having explicitly asked 'on-the-fly' for his consent.

The functional description and architecture for this scenario can be seen below for a user called Anne. Each circle of trust, hosting one of Anne's profiles is shown by a different cloud. Arrows between profiles and a service represent the attributes sharing process, while the central circle models Anne's sphere of control on her personal information.

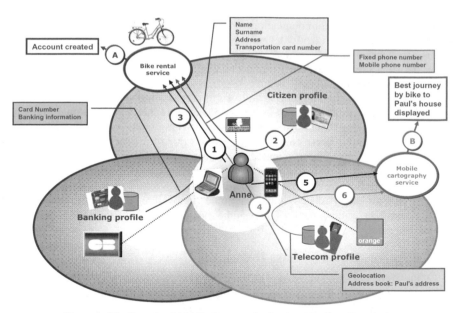

Figure 1: Bike Rental and Mobile Cartography Services Use Case Description

5.   Developments

One of the main challenges with this use case is to achieve technical interoperability, while taking into account the key requirements such as ease of use and respect of user privacy. Indeed, the various services involved in this use case rely on different identity solutions. As a French government directive states for identity-aware citizen services, the 'citizen circle', with local and national identity providers, is based on the Liberty Alliance specifications. In this case, the identity federation is based on links established between the user's identities at the server level. Furthermore, it should also be possible for Anne to share attributes from her smart card, especially her CNIE, the future French electronic identity card. On the contrary, the banking services are more likely to be InfoCard/CardSpace-based. In this model, the identity federation is based entirely around the user, more precisely thanks to his identity selector containing his multiple InfoCards. Eventually, the telecommunication services adopt mixed identity technologies. So let's see what we've learnt from the first story-boards, with a particular focus on the user experience.

First, let's consider a Liberty/SAML-based platform. This solution offers a secure exchange framework, has already been deployed in various projects and is well-tested. However, during the registration process, personal information is gathered from three different circles and involves lots of network exchanges. Multiple redirections in Anne's browser can result in an unpleasant user experience and poor performance (especially on mobile devices). This can be partly avoided with the use of some kind of attributes broker, presenting at once all the personal attributes from the different profiles and waiting for the user consent before disclosure. Anne could also use a rich client installed on her machine. This client might rely on the ID-WSF LUAD (Liberty-enabled User Agent or Devices) or Advanced Client profiles. The main task of this client is to take care of authentication and attributes sharing consent interactions, thus avoiding multiple http redirections. Liberty profiles are natively supported and interactions with a smart card can nicely be integrated within the client. But from a technical point of view, these solutions could be problematic when invoking non-Liberty attributes providers (like the banking ones) or dealing with

InfoCards. Hopefully, on the server side, the Concordia project [7] or other initiatives like [8] have provided interesting material to achieve interoperability between Liberty-based services and InfoCard-based services. Thanks to the design of one of their scenarios, Anne can use one of her InfoCard on the Liberty-compliant bike rental service when needed. As a result, Anne would use redirections when invoking Liberty-based attribute providers, and the InfoCard identity selector to collect other attributes. The main drawback of this solution is the discrepancy in the user experience, which is not consistent within the whole registration process and may confuse Anne in the long run.

But from the user experience point of view, the use of card-based identity selectors remains very appealing. Thus using successively several InfoCard could be an alternative. For the bike rental registration scenario, Anne would select three different cards in three different steps, for citizen, banking and telecommunication information. In this case, this card-based only user experience remains consistent. But an InfoCard identity selector like Microsoft CardSpace cannot natively interact with a Liberty circle of trust. However, an open-source identity selector like the one from Higgins may be more flexible. The Higgins identity selector would work with the 'classical' InfoCard infrastructure and would interact with the Liberty infrastructure thanks to a SAML2/ID-WSF interface, still in development at the time being. Eventually, another additional module in the Higgins identity selector could handle the interactions with Anne's smart card or SIM card.

Thinking a little bit further, although the user experience is coherent, the multiple apparitions of the identity selector, each time showing her the suitable cards may not be so user-friendly and could be confusing. An even more attractive solution could be the use of a card-based identity selector to provide at once all the attributes needed. To achieve this goal, the FC² has considered the use of a "meta-card" FC², dynamically built to respond to the attributes requirements of the registration service. Using this meta-card would spare Anne the trouble of selecting multiple cards one after another in her identity selector by providing a simpler and coherent user experience. During the registration process, Anne clicks on the web page on the link "fill this form with my FC² attributes", invoking her identity selector installed on her machine. Then, she selects her meta-card FC², which collects all the attributes needed. The attributes are gathered automatically from the different attributes providers of the different circles: banking information from her bank, contact information from her telecom operator, address from the citizen circle... Then Anne validates within her identity selector the use of her attributes which are transmitted to the service provider. Indeed, this very idea of a "meta-card" can rely on the Higgins modular client/server identity selector, in current development. It allows the user to dynamically "compose" the identity presented to the service. As a consequence, the FC² project has initiated a collaboration with the Higgins project. Some Higgins components would definitely be helpful to provide a nice card-based user experience. However, for this scenario and others, we have to keep in mind that a full web-based experience should remain feasible and smooth enough for the end user not equipped with an identity selector, even if fewer identity features are available.

6. Results

Based on the first societal studies and story-board results, some recommendations are proposed to leverage the adoption and use of an identity federation system. First, the implementation of a brand / label (like the FC² logo for example) personalizes the supplied services and is perceived by the user as a sign of confidence. This confidence can be enhanced by supplying clear and transparent information about the process of sharing information between the various circles of trust and overall by letting the user be in control of which data he wants to share. It is vital for the various service providers to follow simple and harmonized ergonomic principles for identity-based functionalities, which has been considered as a key requirement in the FC² story-boards. Eventually, implemented security requirements and controls should be adapted to various contexts of use.

The FC² consortium is currently designing the architecture of the interoperability platform, taking into account interoperability constraints and user experience requirements. What kind of identity-related services should be offered by such a platform? Let's have a look at three key features: SSO, attributes sharing and the payment process.

Different identity models offer various kinds of web Single Sign-On. But the FC² project has determined that offering SSO between services belonging to different circles of trust on the web wasn't necessarily one of the most desirable features for users. However, offering "Simplified Sign-On", i.e., facilitating attributes sharing could really be helpful for the user Anne. What really matters is that she can easily share her attributes coming from her various profiles when she needs to register to or use a service, while keeping control on them and authenticating herself the fewer times possible. Furthermore, before the actual disclosure of her attributes, only one common consent interaction step should occur. Whatever user experience is privileged, Anne should remain in control of the disclosure of her personal information.

Indeed, Anne can share her attributes hosted on a distant attribute provider, previously provisioned by herself (her address) or provided by a specific service (her geolocation provided by her mobile operator). In both cases, the attributes can be signed by the attribute provider before being used on the service provider side. If the service and the attribute providers have a trust agreement, the attributes can be associated with a certain confidence level, adding more value for the service provider which receives a "certified" attribute from a "trusted" attribute provider. For example, during the user registration step, the bike rental service may need some mandatory information about the user's address to establish a digital contract. As a part of the dematerialization process, the telecommunication operator can provide, after user approval, a signed customer address as dated information whose origin is certified to the bike rental service. Eventually, Anne can also use a smart card to share some of her attributes stored on it, which are pre-signed by a third party (but not modifiable).

Eventually, the registration process ends with a payment step for the subscription fee. The FC² project has specified an innovative way to combine payment and identity management. 3D-Secure [9] is a secure architecture for online payment. Its main goal is to allow the seller to redirect the buyer to his own bank during a payment process so he could authenticate himself and authorize the current transaction. The innovative idea brought by FC² is to combine this system with InfoCard, so the user could use his identity selector to present a proof of authentication from his own bank and his signed banking attributes (i.e. credit card number) in one step to the seller site, eliminating the need of redirection to the buyer's bank and enhancing the user experience.

7.   Economic and Societal Significance, Business Benefits & Legal Issues

7.1   Economic and Societal Significance

The general objective of the considered identity management service is to further the sound development of the digital economy. In order to deliver high value services on the Internet, service providers (either merchants or administration) will increasingly need to securely identify their customer / user with full certainty.

For the user, the benefits have to be well understood, thus explained carefully. Indeed identity is at the core of the human being, in a sociological way. Behaviours respond to many different factors, and users adapt to the requests by "negotiating" their personal data. In this context, the ergonomics of identity selectors seem well adapted to address the need of reference to a known environment ("my wallet") and transparency (choice and consent).

7.2   Intended Business Benefits

From a business point of view, the FC² platform intends to bring added value to all players of the value chain, with a clear focus on the user experience.

From a user perspective, the platform offers time saving, better ease of use, seamless transaction, increased security, trust and confidentiality, as well as ubiquitous access (on any terminal, even without an installed identity selector).

On the service provider side, the service answers most market needs regardless of the industry. Tangible benefits are provided: productivity gains (decrease of allocated resources mostly), better fraud management and therefore lower costs, increase in quality of service, and better image. On top of this, a significant advantage for e-commerce use cases is the decrease in the rate of abandoned transactions, generating new revenues. Indeed, it is estimated that 46% of e-transactions are abandoned before completion [10] and 31% of customers prefer to shop at stores that don't require them to retype their name, address, and card number [11]. Providing this service, added to better ease of authentication, is likely to translate into better conversion rates. Eventually, by introducing new means of certifying personal data, the FC² platform can provide improved legal security (proof management) to the service provider, in order to tackle fraud and litigation issues.

But the business models adopted by the identity providers and other trusted third parties yet remain to be determined, their success relying partly on volume and recurrence of use. Identity providers should be able to monetize their service if the service provider and/or the consumer consider that the delivered value is worth paying for. However, since wide consumer adoption rate is critical, the main assumption is that service providers will probably bear most of the cost of the service if not all of it. In any case, the service provider should have enough incentive to use the service and will make its decisions on the basis of a cost / benefit analysis, taking into account the acceptable deployment cost of the selected solution, and the estimated return on investment.

7.3   Legal Issues

To cope with identity-related risks such as privacy violation, identity theft and fraud, legal and technical expertise should drive decisions enforcing users' privacy, consumption rights, administrative rights and the overall security of the federated identity architecture.

Within the European perimeter, two EU Directives [12] in the data protection and privacy field are relevant to the activities of most participants of the circles of trust. These directives regulate a number of categories of data and impose specific obligations or restrictions on those who handle this information and allocate compliance responsibilities according to the 'role' that any given participant is performing. In France, the law regarding the protection of the personal data has been amended in August 2004 [13] to comply with the Directives of 1995 and 2000.

Consequently, participants of the circle of trust will need to address the types of data that are being handled, what role they are performing in the CoT in respect of this data and, consequently, what obligations or restrictions this places upon them. The directives are likely to have a direct impact upon the necessary legal and contractual framework for a circle of trust. Indeed, the participants may be required to enter into particular types of agreements between each other. These will be dependent on who is performing which role, what data they are handling and for which purpose, and where that data may be transferred. Addressing the who, what, which and where for a circle of trust is therefore an essential first step in developing the contractual framework.

Nevertheless, the diversity of the legal regimes that apply to the FC² context introduces high complexity in the legal framework definition. Indeed, administrative, commercial, competition and consumption laws are only a subset of the legal relevant codes. Public life and freedom to access information should be considered along with intellectual properties rights and privacy law. For example, proof management and traceability within a circle of trust can be delicate to implement. Eventually, local particularities should be taken into account: there is a special governmental legal regime that applies to data flowing out of France, especially towards USA. Of course, the impact of data protection and privacy laws may differ for the circles of trust and depends on the business sector and the relationship between the participants.

Service providers and identity providers assume the civil and criminal responsibilities in the event of collections of personal data using fraudulent, unfair or illicit means. Those issues are even more emphasized with the multiplicity of actors participating to the service value chain, mainly as identity providers, or service providers. However, the entities collaborating to the circle of trust do not have the same legal responsibilities. Those actors need clarification of their legal duties in relation to customers, and other players. As an early FC^2 outcome, a first recommendation for the legal setup of a circle of trust is to precisely identify actors in the value chain along with their responsibilities according to the role they play and the risks they take.

8. Conclusions

This paper has indeed investigated the ways to build an interoperable identity federation platform providing a coherent user experience related to digital identity across domains on the web. This platform, regardless of the identity technologies used by the different partners, considers user-friendliness, user privacy and user protection against identity fraud as strong common factors. Simple attributes sharing from multiple sources – different circles, different media, and different levels of trust- radically changes registration processes. As we have seen with the bike rental scenario, the use of a card-based identity selector is attractive for a new enhanced user experience. The Higgins project seems to be a promising framework to investigate.

As many other national or European projects prove it, digital identity management becomes the future pillar of digital life. From a societal point of view, the creation of digital trusted and comprehensible space for end users is at stake. For companies or states, mastering identity management technologies is a strategic domain. Eventually, identity-based business should boost the thriving digital economy. A more precise legal framework definition and a strong political will are also necessary requirements.

First results from the FC^2 project are only a glimpse of the expected results fuelling this topic. Next year, the first implementation and interoperability results should be available, which should let us highlight the first lessons learnt and provide more recommendations.

References

[1]   Socio-economical study, FC² project, SP6 official deliverable, April 2008
[2]   Liberty Alliance Project, http://www.projectliberty.org/
[3]   Identity Metasystem , Identity Selector Interoperability Profile V1.0
[4]   Microsoft CardSpace, http://netfx3.com/content/WindowsCardspaceHome.aspx
[5]   Higgins project, http://www.eclipse.org/higgins/
[6]   FC² official website: www.fc2consortium.org
[7]   The Concordia Project: http://projectconcordia.org
[8]   Ivar Jørstad, Do Van Thuan, Tore Jønvik & Do Van Thanh: "Bridging CardSpace and Liberty Alliance with SIM Authentication", ICIN 2007, Bordeaux, France
[9]   3D-Secure, http://partnernetwork.visa.com/pf/3dsec/
[10] Shop.org/Forrester, "State of Online Retailing 2007"
[11] JupiterResearch/PayPal, "Confidence, Convenience, Choice", 2008
[12] Direction on protection of the personal data, 1995 and Directive on electronic commerce, 2000
[13] V. E. Caprioli, Loi du 6 août 2004 : commerce à distance sur Internet et protection des données à *caractère personnel*, Comm. Comm. Elect., Février 2005, n°2, p. 24-28

Collaboration and the Knowledge Economy: Issues, Applications, Case Studies
P. Cunningham and M. Cunningham (Eds.)
IOS Press, 2008

1585

Linkage Control – Integrating the Essence of Privacy Protection into Identity Management Systems

Marit HANSEN

Unabhängiges Landeszentrum für Datenschutz (ULD) Schleswig-Holstein,
Holstenstr. 98, 24103 Kiel, Germany
Tel: +49 431 988 1214, Fax: +49 431 988 1223, Email: marit.hansen@acm.org

Abstract: In the digital world, linkage of data may pose threats to the privacy of individuals. Thus, linkage control by the individuals concerned, based on transparency of the actual and planned data processing, is the main requirement to maintain their private sphere. Today's user-centric identity management systems provide some control for users, but still lack thorough concepts of linkage control. This text introduces the phases of data processing relevant to linkage. After discussing current features of user-centric identity management concepts, an extension towards better and more comprehensive linkage control by individuals is proposed, taking into account information sources from all phases of data processing. Further, economic aspects are briefly sketched. Finally, recommendations for developers and policy makers conclude the text.

1. Introduction

The Eurobarometer survey on data protection from 2008 affirms results from other studies that a majority of EU citizens are concerned about privacy issues [1]. However, people often are not aware of actual or potential risks to their privacy, and even if this is the case, they regularly do not know how to act or react to protect themselves.

Risks to privacy usually stem from abuse of personal data, i.e., data related to individuals [2]. Data controllers often can directly link these data to their owners, namely the individuals concerned. Otherwise different data portions may be linked and accumulated into profiles that give information on the associated individuals. In many cases it is possible to identify individuals from the linked information in the profiles. Different European laws regulate the treatment of personal data. However, it is not enough to rely on European legislation in a globalised world, the more so as laws alone usually are not appropriate safeguards if not implemented in business processes and technologies.

Individuals usually have an intuitive understanding of links and linkabilities, but this understanding does not work well for the digital world with so many potential data controllers and a growing variety of identifiers and attached identity attributes, e.g., as being a citizen of a State, a customer of a company, or a user of an Internet service. User-centric identity management systems (IMS) can support users to better understand privacy risks and to act accordingly.

In the following, it is shown that even today's solutions for *privacy-enhancing* IMS have to be extended by more comprehensive possibilities of linkage controls to truly enable individuals to maintain their private sphere. In sketching this vision, we primarily address developers, vendors, and policy makers. This text is organised as follows: Section 2 introduces the concept of linkage control. Section 3 presents the relevant features in the IMS of the project PRIME – Privacy and Identity Management for Europe. Section 4 elaborates on enhancements of IMS for user-controlled linkage. Section 5 elicits relevant economic aspects. Finally, Section 6 concludes the text and gives recommendations.

2. Important Terms and Concepts

This section introduces basic terms in the field of linkage. A general model for enriching information illustrates important phases and their relation to linkage with various facets. Further it is elaborated why linkage control is the essence of privacy protection.

2.1   Terms

To link entities means to connect those entities or to establish a relationship between them. Usually **linkage** – the act of linking – is done for a specific purpose, and this purpose determines which entities can or will be linked. For example a car can be linked to its owner by checking out the registration number at the authority which stores that information; the IP address can be linked to a computer that has been assigned that number by an Internet Service Provider; transactions of the same eBay user can be linked and compiled into a profile of that user. A typical way of linkage is to relate different portions of data which have the same identifier, but it is also possible to establish links because of other information, e.g., concerning time or location.

Note that an established link does not mean that the linked portions of data belong together. For example two data sets with information on a "John Smith" may be linked even if there are two persons named "John Smith", not knowing each other, totally unrelated except for accidentally having the same name.

Linkability (i.e., the possibility to link) and its negation **unlinkability** are dependent on the attacker's perspective, i.e., the data which are available for him and further knowledge on ways of successfully linking those data [3].

Comparing linkage of data with linkage of chain links, it seems logical that there can be also some **"de-linkage"**, i.e., removing a once established link. This can be achieved by separating data into different databases that cannot be accessed by the same person or by deleting components of a data profile. If separation or deletion is not possible, the validity of the linkage may be challenged by providing contradicting information, e.g., by injecting disinformation. De-linkage often cannot be guaranteed because the linked information may already be memorised by people or copied and further processed by ICT (information and communication technology) systems.

To complete the terms, the uncommonly used word **"de-linkability"** stands for the possibility of de-linkage while **"un-de-linkability"** means the opposite [4].

Linkage control means to know about linkages performed or planned, to influence its conditions (at least in a defined and known scope) and to be able to check afterwards whether the linkage was done properly and as agreed upon. A necessary requirement for linkage control is transparency, i.e., clarity on the terms of data processing. The most effective way of preventing linkage is to prevent **linkability**, i.e., the possibilities of linkages. Related is also **observability control** because if no information is observable, there will be nothing to link. Linkage control can also mean having guarantees that some data portions actually are or will be linked. This may be the case for reputation systems where an individual should not be able to remove unwelcome entries.

2.2   A General Model for Enriching Information Put into the Linkage Context

Digital identities that represent people in the digital world are often linked with information about this very same person, e.g., social contacts or actions performed under that digital identity. In addition, this information can be further specified or extended by linking it with other data sources, e.g., other digital identities of the same person, and utilising scoring models or other sophisticated algorithms which analyse the data.

Figure 1 shows the typical data flow when enriching information for the purpose of generating decisions, as this is done multiple times a day in common data processing systems. Not always the phases are as pronounced as in profiling and scoring systems:

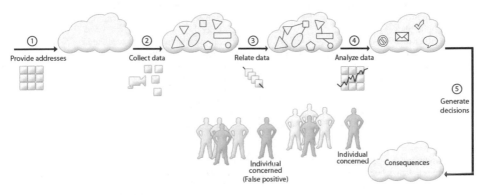

Figure 1: Model of information flow relating to linkage

The successive phases of this model are explained in Table 1, which also discusses the relation of each phase to linkage.

For discussing linkage properties and objectives, it is important to make clearly visible who can access which data and perform which actions on these data. In all identified steps in the model workflow presented in Figure 1, the actors contribute to some aspect of linkage and may have to be cautious to avoid undesired effects. In case of a mistake, it may be hard for individuals concerned to find the error and its cause in this workflow and to achieve that appropriate corrective measures are being taken.

Table 1: Phases in the model of information flow

	Description	Relation to linkage
Provide addresses ❶	In ICT systems, each object has addresses which acts as distinguishing information in a specific scope. Addresses can be names or identifiers which may enable referencing, distinguishing and identifying objects. Often the addresses are assigned according to a defined address schema, e.g., IP addresses or e-mail addresses. Often the addresses contain more information than it is necessary for the purpose of distinguishing.	a) The address may represent an individual, an action of an individual, an object possessed by an individual. b) Information on the assignment of addresses contains the link between the address and what it stands for. c) Even without an assignment table links can be established, e.g., between data sets when addresses occur repeatedly. d) Already the address schema and the assignment process set the context for possible linkages and the interpretation of those links, e.g., whether addresses are unique for single individuals or whether addresses can be taken by other individuals (voluntarily or not, as in the case of identity theft).

Collect data ❷	In addition to the data processing performed on legal grounds or with the user's consent there may be hidden collection of data. There is probably no single entity which can monitor all user actions or data transfers, but there are many which can observe some parts of users' lives or ICT systems. Users are often unaware of data trails they are leaving, e.g., when browsing the Internet or when using mobile phones. Further many people provide personal information to social networks or blogs where they are publicly accessible.	a) All information which is observable can be monitored and collected. b) The data collector is not necessarily related to the party assigning addresses or defining address schemas. c) Once data are disclosed, it usually cannot be guaranteed that they won't be part of some data collection and transfer – either by professional data controllers or by other individuals. d) Also typically temporary data can be stored permanently. e) The information whose personal data are collected may be available in this stage as well. Otherwise information such as identifiers, location, time etc. can be gathered and stored together with the observed data. Then the relation to a person may become clear after linking the data in phase 3.
Relate data ❸	The raw data being collected in the previous phase are linked in this phase. Usually this process of relating data is done for a specific purpose which determines conditions for the linkage, e.g., which data are relevant, when should data be related (e.g., sameness of addresses, similarity of time information etc.). As relating data in a correct way (determined by the purpose of data processing) depends on specified conditions and assumptions, specific linking algorithms can be used.	a) Relating data is linkage on the data set level. b) The related data can be directly linkable to an individual or they can be a pseudonymous profile of an individual with no knowledge of the identity behind. c) The process of relating the data may be conducted by special parties. d) Further the algorithms to be used may be provided by yet other parties which may not be related to the other phases of data processing.
Analyse data ❹	Also the analysis of the compiled profiles and other data portions usually is driven by the given purpose. Different methods can be employed such as scoring functions, expert systems or neural networks, possibly being providers by specific parties. In this phase decisions are prepared.	a) As the data analysis bases on the linked data from the previous phase, the linkage properties are inherited. b) In addition the analysis algorithms may link the data to other information, e.g., facts or assumptions from other sources or rules being applied to the data. c) The process of analysing data may be conducted by special parties. d) Further the algorithms to be used may be provided by yet other parties which may not be related to the other phases of data processing.
Generate decisions ❺	Actual decisions are generated in this phase. They may affect single or multiple individuals. The decisions are not necessarily fair, and sometimes they do not base on accurate data or on correct assumptions when relating or analysing data. In these cases individuals being "false positives" may suffer from consequences of the generated decisions, e.g., if they have to pay more than others for the same service or if they won't get a service at all.	a) The decision maker decides on basis of the information available at that stage, being provided by previous phases. b) This phase links the data processing to real consequences which may affect individuals also in their real lives, not only their digital representations. c) By the decision, the link is (re-)established to the individuals concerned, whether all phases were performed correctly on accurate data or not.

2.3   Linkage Control as Essence of Privacy Protection

There are various definitions for the right to privacy, each of them focusing on specific aspects. Two of the most mentioned concepts are firstly the "right to be let alone" [5] and secondly the right "to control, edit, manage, and delete information about them[selves] and decide when, how, and to what extent that information is communicated to others" [6] or similarly the "right to informational self-determination" stemming from the 1983 ruling of the German Federal Constitutional Court, demanding that each person can at any time ascertain who knows what about him or her. Both definitions are related to linkage control:

For the "right to be let alone", individuals should be able to control (or prevent) the linkage at least in the last stage (phase 5 in Figure 1) when decisions may concern them. For the informational self-determination, in particular earlier phases are relevant, too, because all available data (e.g., disclosed information on the respective individual) is the material for the knowledge acquired by other parties.

Also extended perspectives such as the privacy categories from [7] are based on linkage: The supplementary aspect of group profiling and social sorting describes possibly anonymous profiles which may contain information that can be used to discriminate against specific individuals. Or the link to the individual can be established later, e.g., by additional algorithms, computing power or data. Here all phases from Figure 1 are relevant. Further the need for defining what is public and private [7] again is based on linkage control so that individuals involved in participatory processes can prevent unfavourable consequences.

3. Linkage Control Features in PRIME's Identity Management System

In the digital world, linkage control for users is currently much more difficult due to massive data processing which is mainly opaque for them. Privacy-enhancing identity management systems strive for linkage control by the user. For this reason we list in this section a few interesting functions which support linkage control.

Identity management means managing various partial identities (usually denoted by pseudonyms) of an individual, i.e., administration of identity attributes including the development and choice of the partial identity and pseudonym to be (re-)used in a specific context or role [3]. Identity management systems can be distinguished by the degree of control from individuals respectively organisations when administrating the partial identities. It always depends on the context as well as on the perspectives of the parties involved how much linkage, linkability or unlinkability is desired in a specific situation.

Meanwhile so-called "user-centric identity management systems" [8] dominate the landscape where users are given at least some control on their identity data. Typically users can decide on how much information they are willing to disclose in a specific situation. However, even big systems such as Microsoft's CardSpace by now do not support users in interpreting the privacy policy on the service's side with its linkage-related information.

An enhanced approach is shown in the project "PRIME – Privacy and Identity Management for Europe" [9], as depicted in PRIME's White Paper [10], based on some fundamental work from David Chaum since the early 1980s [11]:

- To achieve better linkage control, the workflows within organisations can be organised in a way that they prevent globally unique identifiers, but instead restrict the identifiers' scope to the necessary domain. In different contexts, different pseudonyms can be used against unwanted context-spanning linkages (cf. the "Identity Protector" [12]).
- Undesired linkage is also prevented by private credentials, i.e., certificates proving identity claims (e.g., "being of age") without revealing information that may identify the individual [11], [13]. Multiple private credentials can be created from a single master certificate that are neither linkable to each other nor to the issuance interaction of the master certificate.
- Individuals are supported in knowing beforehand the conditions of data processing by privacy policies that are both understandable by human beings [14] and machine-readable, i.e., they can be interpreted by the user's system. In addition, the organisation can automatically enforce its privacy policy – and all included statements concerning limitations of linkages – with appropriate tools.
- Such privacy policies can be cryptographically "stuck" to data sets [15], [16]. Thereby these sticky policies can travel together with the data they apply to.

- PRIME integrates multiple transparency functionalities [17] which make users understand better possible linkages and to react accordingly: The main tool is the so-called "Data Track", a logfile of prior transactions which stores a record of what identity information has been disclosed to whom and under which conditions. This logfile enables users to review later what they consented to. It also can warn users against too much data disclosure. Other transparency tools conceptualised in PRIME are the "Security Feed" based on RSS which gives machine-readable information on privacy and security incidents, or the support of individuals to exercise their privacy rights, i.e., managing requests towards the data controller demanding access to their personal data, rectification or erasure as well as giving and withdrawing consent. This kind of tools will be further developed in the FP7 project PrimeLife [18].

4. Extension of IMS to Enable Linkage Control by the User

How can the described features in Section 3 be mapped to the linkage model in Section 2, which illustrates typical data processing phases in the world? Although PRIME's features seem to already cover a lot of what is necessary to enable true linkage control, they cannot give a complete picture, as they mainly address the direct relationship between user and service. An exception is the "Security Feed" which may provide information also from other sources than the service itself. The possible (and on a large scale meanwhile common) data processing by others, be it secret services of other nations or curious peers, is not shown to the user in current IMS. Today, data transfers and integration of other parties are at best roughly described in privacy policies, and information on analysis algorithms actually being applied or assumptions made is usually missing at all.

For an integral whole of linkage control by users, several extensions should be considered that address not only IMS software designers, but also legislators, policy makers, data controllers, standardisation bodies, and data protection authorities:

1. **Transparency on linkability and linkage**
    - Information on possible and actual linkages as well as de-linking options should be available by the individuals concerned. In an abstract way (without mentioning personal data of individual cases) this could be provided in public databases. At least concerning governmental activities this should be legally demanded. Information on quantification of linkability [19] would be helpful.
    - Privacy breaches should be communicated to the individuals concerned.
    - IMS should be able to inform users about possible privacy risks by interpreting the information sources mentioned in the bullet points before.
    - Data controllers should always document the sources of their data and algorithms used as well as the actual recipients (not only categories of recipients as currently demanded by privacy law). They should be able to prove that their data processing is lawful. In case of questions by users or supervisory authorities it should be possible with little effort to review the full audit trail covering all phases of data processing (cf. Figure 1) until decisions are generated.
    - The information obligations should not be limited to clearly and directly personal data, but should also comprise other data suitable to affect individuals.
    - Even if no privacy or security risks occur, individuals should be informed on data processing. This could be implemented, e.g., as an "itemised statement" – similar to telecommunication bills – sent by data controllers to users, stating who has accessed the individual's personal data for which purpose and giving further information.
    - For enabling the IMS to orchestrate the available information on processes and actual and possible linkages, standardised formats and ontologies will be required.

2. Control of linkage

- Data controllers as well as standardisation bodies should take care of observability and linkability issues already when defining address schemas, processes and protocols. In relevant areas privacy impact assessments should be conducted.
- Cross-jurisdiction data processing transferring data out of the area where users can exercise their linkage control and where privacy regulations can be enforced should be avoided. For instance, the European Union should offer their citizens ways to keep their personal data in the EU jurisdiction – also when using mighty search engines, transferring money within the EU or booking inner-European flights.
- Users should be informed on how to check all data processing concerning them and be provided with effective possibilities for correcting occurred errors and for redress. Processes for checking and redress should be handled in an easy way.
- IMS should raise the users' awareness and support them in their linkage control. Good usability as well as high data security and reliability are prerequisites.

5. Economic Aspects of Linkage Control

Today, we are far from offering users linkage control regarding their privacy – neither in the traditional nor in the ICT-enhanced world. The vision of full linkage control bases on manageable ICT systems both at the service's and the user's sides, and it requires a plurality of available information channels which can be interpreted by the user's IMS. On the one hand this calls for new kinds of information providers as well as providers of the supporting infrastructure. These providers have to develop workable business models – supply and demand here is still unknown territory. But linkage control does not only address new services: Starting from existing systems, each business process or ICT system designer should consider supporting linkage control from the outset through the different phases of information flow.

Currently there is no comprehensive analysis of economic aspects regarding linkage control. However, a few specific features are being explored. For instance, transparency of security risks is being discussed for several years – also from the economic point of view [20] – and has gained momentum in the process of reviewing the ePrivacy Directive where data breach notification provisions are being debated. Further, the discussion of business models of privacy-enhancing technologies addresses many linkage control issues [21]. Clearly, the carrot-and-stick approach is promising, i.e., a mixture of firstly economic incentives and secondly sanctions when not adhering to the law or not meeting the required state-of-the-art. This demands a consensus among policy makers on the value of privacy and the consequence of exercising linkage control.

6. Conclusions and Recommendations

Our information society with its data processing is to a great extent based on linkage. Linkage control is one of the most important concepts for self-determination of individuals. In the digital world full of identifiers for digital identities which often can easily be linked, better linkage control by individuals is crucial for maintenance of their private sphere. Control is based on transparency and checkability. This requires that the complex world of today's data processing with manifold actors has to provide all relevant information to check correctness and fairness of decisions.

Privacy-Enhancing Identity Management Systems could act as the users' assistants and guardians if being enhanced to interpret sources with all information relevant to them and supporting them in exercising their control. In a way this would mean to mimic "world knowledge" as linkage aspects cover so many facets of data processing. However, this vision is not totally unrealistic in a world of semantic web, ontologies being standardised and governmental processes in the scope of the EU Services Directive being translated into XML. True linkage control needs information, much more than it is available today. Here a balance between possible trade secrets from data controllers when applying scoring algorithms and the requirement of checkability by supervisory authorities and individuals concerned has to be found. Also a societal consensus on possible limitations of linkage control by individuals should be achieved.

Policy makers as well as system designers should appreciate the value of linkage control and pick up the concept in their respective areas. More work is needed when it comes to linkage-relevant interaction between peers instead of data controllers because the former are typically not subject to privacy regulation.

References

[1] Eurobarometer, Data Protection in the European Union – Citizens' Perceptions. Analytical Report, Flash Eurobarometer No. 225, Survey conducted by the Gallup Organization Hungary upon the request of DG Justice, Freedom and Security, Feb. 2008, http://ec.europa.eu/public_opinion/flash/fl_225_en.pdf.
[2] Article 29 Data Protection Working Party, Opinion 4/2007 on the concept of personal data. 01248/07/EN WP 136, June 20, 2007, http://ec.europa.eu/justice_home/fsj/privacy/docs/wpdocs/2007/wp136_en.pdf.
[3] A. Pfitzmann, M. Hansen, Anonymity, Unlinkability, Undetectability, Unobservability, Pseudonymity, and Identity Management – A Consolidated Proposal for Terminology. Working Paper v0.31, February 15, 2008 (first version from 2000), http://dud.inf.tu-dresden.de/Anon_Terminology.shtml.
[4] M. Hansen, S. Meissner (Eds.), Verkettung digitaler Identitäten. Report commissioned by the German Federal Ministry of Education and Research, October 2007, https://www.datenschutzzentrum.de/projekte/verkettung/2007-uld-tud-verkettung-digitaler-identitaeten-bmbf.pdf, Lulu Inc., Feb. 2008, ISBN 3000234063.
[5] S. Warren, L. Brandeis, The Right to Privacy. In: Harvard Law Review, Vol. 4, 1890, pp. 193-220.
[6] A.F. Westin, Privacy and Freedom. Atheneum, New York, 1967.
[7] D.J. Phillips, Privacy policy and PETs – The influence of policy regimes on the development and social implications of privacy enhancing technologies. In: New Media & Society, Vol. 6, No. 6, SAGE Publications, London, Thousand Oaks, CA and New Delhi, 2004, pp. 691-706.
[8] A. Jøsang, S. Pope, User Centric Identity Management. In: Proceedings of AusCERT Conference 2005, Brisbane, Australia, May 2005.
[9] PRIME – Privacy and Identity Management for Europe, FP6 IST project, https://www.prime-project.eu/.
[10] R. Leenes, J. Schallaböck, M. Hansen (Eds.), PRIME White Paper V3. May 2008, https://www.prime-project.eu/prime_products/whitepaper/.
[11] D. Chaum, Security Without Identification: Transaction Systems to Make Big Brother Obsolete. In: Communications of the ACM, Vol. 28, No. 10, Oct. 1985, pp. 1030-1044.
[12] H. van Rossum, H. Gardeniers, J.J. Borking et al., Privacy-Enhancing Technologies: The Path to Anonymity. Volume I & II, Achtergrondstudies en Verkenningen 5b, Registratiekamer, The Netherlands & Information and Privacy Commissioner/Ontario, Canada, Aug. 1995.
[13] J. Camenisch, A. Lysyanskaya, Efficient non-transferable anonymous multi-show credential system with optional anonymity revocation. Research Report RZ 3295 (# 93341), IBM Research, Nov. 2000.
[14] Article 29 Data Protection Working Party, Opinion on more harmonised information provisions. 11987/0 4/EN WP 100, Nov. 25, 2004, http://ec.europa.eu/justice_home/fsj/privacy/docs/wpdocs/2004/wp100_en.pdf.
[15] G. Karjoth, M. Schunter, M. Waidner, Platform for Enterprise Privacy Practices: Privacy-enabled Management of Customer Data. In: Proceedings of 2nd Workshop on Privacy Enhancing Technologies (PET 2002), LNCS 2482, Springer, pp. 69-84.
[16] M. Casassa Mont, S. Pearson, P. Bramhall, Towards Accountable Management of Identity and Privacy: Sticky Policies and Enforceable Tracing Services. HPL-2003-49, Trusted Systems Laboratory, HP Laboratories Bristol, 2003, http://www.hpl.hp.com/techreports/2003/HPL-2003-49.pdf.
[17] M. Hansen, Marrying Transparency Tools With User-Controlled Identity Management. In: Proceedings of the Third IFIP WG 9.2, 9.6/11.6, 11.7/FIDIS International Summer School, Aug. 2007, IFIP International Federation for Information Processing, Vol. 262, Springer; 2008, pp. 199-220.
[18] PrimeLife – Privacy and Identity Management in Europe for Life, FP7 IST project, http://www.primelife.eu/.
[19] S. Berthold, S. Clauß, Linkability Estimation Between Subjects and Message Contents Using Formal Concepts. In: Proceedings of the 2007 ACM Workshop on Digital Identity Management, 2007, pp. 36-45.
[20] R. Anderson, R. Böhme, R. Clayton, T. Moore, Security Economics and the Internal Market. Report for ENISA, Feb. 2008, http://www.enisa.europa.eu/doc/pdf/report_sec_econ_&_int_mark_20080131.pdf.
[21] P. Ribbers (Ed.), Business Processes and Business Case. PRIME Deliverable, May 2008, https://www.prime-project.eu/prime_products/reports/reqs/pub_del_D2.2.a_ec_WP2.2_v5_Final.pdf.

Collaboration and the Knowledge Economy: Issues, Applications, Case Studies
P. Cunningham and M. Cunningham (Eds.)
IOS Press, 2008

Dynamic Access Control Management for Distributed Biomedical Data Resources

Matthias ASSEL, Onur KALYONCU
High Performance Computer Center of the University Stuttgart,
Intelligent Service Infrastructures, Nobelstr. 19, 70569, Stuttgart, Germany
Tel: +49 711 68562515, Fax: +49 711 68565832, Email: {assel,kalyoncu}@hlrs.de

Abstract: With increasingly dispersed and inhomogeneous resources, sharing knowledge, information or data becomes more and more difficult and manageable for both end-users and providers. To reduce administrative overheads and ease time-consuming management tasks, quite a few solutions for secure data sharing and access have been designed and introduced in several research projects worldwide. In this paper, we focus on the EU-funded research project ViroLab, which tries to build a virtual laboratory that allows health professionals to access distributed data resources in order to perform clinical studies and analyses on the requested data sets. The paper concentrates on the approach and implementation how data sharing in ViroLab is carried out and how these biomedical resources can be easily managed to guarantee the highest level of protection against any abuse. We conclude with an outlook and recommendations on how the system can be enhanced and improved.

1. Introduction

Today, more and more interdisciplinary scientific teams and institutions, which are located at different sites and even in several countries, collaborate together to reach their scientific goals and to facilitate international research activities. Specifically designed collaborative working environments [6] assist scientists during their daily workflows and help them to discuss about their common goals, plan their future tasks, share their knowledge, and evaluate, report and pool their results. These working environments are continuously evolving and becoming more and more complex. A major reason constitutes with the increasing number of inhomogeneous and distributed resources, in particularly data resources and repositories, which could additionally contain sensitive information or private and confidential data sets.

The EU-funded research project ViroLab [1] shall provide researchers and medical doctors a so-called virtual laboratory for infectious diseases. ViroLab develops such a collaborative workspace for different types of end-users like virologists, clinicians, and researchers and enables the interactive sharing of expertise and results while working together on the same data and information sets that are widely dispersed over Europe and currently without cross-national collaboration. The Human Immunodeficiency Virus (HIV) drug resistance problem has become an increasing problem worldwide though it is one medical area where genetic information is widely available and has been collected and used for many years [5]. For these reasons, it was chosen as prototype in the ViroLab project.

In this paper, we describe the approach how access to the distributed and confidential data resources within the ViroLab collaborative working environment is realised and implemented. We explain how existing security concepts like Shibboleth, GSI[i], and XACML[ii] have been combined and linked together in order to build a corresponding environment that ensures the utmost protection for clinical data and provides the users a great flexibility to set up and manage such collaborative working sessions while at the same time reducing administrative overheads. Finally, we also indicate some limitations and peculiarities and provide advice how future systems can be further improved and enhanced.

2.   Motivation and Objectives

Basically, medical experts like doctors or virologists want to use the ViroLab virtual environment for requesting patient information in order to predict any possible drug resistance for their according case. They simply want to retrieve all relevant information without the need of any specific expertise in computer science. The way to gather data must be kept simple and transparent to them but should be as self-explaining as possible

Besides this typical use case, which principally takes place within one organisation or hospital, the virtual laboratory shall also provide possibilities to perform studies on the integrated patient (clinical and genetic) information sets. Those studies usually require lots of data most suitable from several institutions to analyse and observe interesting characteristics of the different virus subtypes and their spread among our society. Since most of the data owners are afraid of sharing all or even single data sets with someone working for ViroLab, the exchange of relevant data shall be handled and controlled by the providers themselves. Hence, the data resource administrators need to be provided with a user-friendly and easy to understand concept, which allows them for dynamically defining and changing access policies in which institutions, departments, or users can be specified to work on their data without browsing and/or accessing their entire repository. In order to reach this difficult endeavour, the ViroLab workspace together with its integrated data resources are developed in close cooperation with clinical partners like hospitals and bioinformatics centres that, in addition to the data and tools, also actively contribute to the overall design of relevant workflows for daily practices being foreseen for integration within the virtual infrastructure. Furthermore, the collaborative and interactive usage of clinical databases beyond the scope of ViroLab shall also be achieved to facilitate future research activities in the field of other infectious diseases.

3.   Related Work

Data management, in particular access control to certain resources, in collaborative and Grid environments respectively has been a subject of study and research for quite a few years. Early solutions, such as those employed in common Grid systems basically relied on replicating data, or prior to performing any calculations, data had to be fetched and staged by a specialised middleware component. The identification of users as well as the access to certain data files has been performed in the traditional way of mapping system users who authenticate themselves via corresponding (Grid) certificates onto local user accounts with specific rights allowing them to access, use and transfer appropriate pieces of data. This was a limiting solution as it took no notice of structured data storage technologies such as databases which additionally require proper user authentication and authorisation.

These constraints gave rise to a number of projects aiming at standardisation and increased flexibility of data management in Grids and collaborative environments, one of the most important of them being OGSA-DAI [7]. This project aimed to develop a toolkit for exploiting different types of data resources onto the Grid through a set of standard Web Service interfaces. Although OGSA-DAI provides the possibility to integrate relational databases smoothly, the authorisation for granting access to such resources still based on the certificate provided and hence, the user's distinguished name which reduces the level of dynamicity and limits administrators to perform fine-grain access control down to the level of single data sets. In order to overcome these restrictions of existing authentication and authorisation concepts, which completely rely on GSI, other projects [8] tried to combine both areas, traditional Grid computing together with decentralised management of user identities to ensure greater flexibilities for both users and resource providers. Unfortunately, these projects do not focus on the dynamic adaption of user rights according to sudden circumstances. However, projects like TrustCoM [9] or BREIN [10] which are dealing with business workflows and collaborations have already applied dynamic policy management but basically for protecting services or applications and without touching the difficult problem of distributed data resources. In ViroLab, we are trying to take and combine results from several previous projects in order to provide the users with the greatest level of flexibility and dynamicity but at the same time guaranteeing the maximum of security and trustworthiness while accessing, sharing and using biomedical data sets.

4. Approach and Methodology

Security issues and policies for collaborative working environments are very different from local ones. The abuse of data not only by third parties but also by so-called trusted organisations must be considered during the design and development of the entire setup. In other words, not all of the integrated resources may be accessible to all of the users known to the system. To protect certain data sources, applications, services, or tools, specific access control policies, which define by whom the shared resources can be accessed and used within the environment, are usually a prerequisite of any virtual collaboration.

In our approach, each partner organisation determines and specifies its own judgment based on the self-defined and self-managed access control policies. According to this judgment the corresponding organisation can make their appropriate authorisation decisions. Thus, in addition to the decentralised control, a fine-grained control of the resources is basically achieved.

To overcome the problems of dynamic and on-demand collaborations, ViroLab makes use of the established security framework Shibboleth [3], which was developed to protect online resources across and within organisational boundaries. Shibboleth provides a federated Web Single Sign-On (SSO), attribute exchange framework and extended privacy functionality, allowing the users and their home site to control the attribute information being released to each service provider. Using Shibboleth-enabled access simplifies the management of identity and access permissions for both identity and service providers.

The access control mechanism that is used within Virolab has some differences from the typical role-based access control. The policy that is created by the resource's owners specifies which minimum set of attributes must be provided in order to gain access to the corresponding resource. In a typical role-based approach within a single organisation a single attribute that defines the users' role could be sufficient to describe a user in a single environment, but for fine-grain access control within multiple organisations supplementary attributes are required which do also reflect the organisation and the organisation type of the user. More attributes are also possible and base on the granularity of entire setup. To make authorisation decisions, the attributes being released by the respective Shibboleth identity provider (IDP) – typically the home organisation of the user (refer to figure 1, step 7) – is evaluated against the attributes specified in the access control policies. Users typically request permissions by being a member of a certain role. Shibboleth eliminates in our attribute-based approach also the need for role assignment policies that define which role can be assigned to which subject like in a role-based approach. In that manner, Shibboleth allows a simple policy management which only concerns about the permission policies. In our approach, permission policies are the single type of policies. The basic security infrastructure components and their interactions are now explained in more detail to clearly depict our approach and its relevance and application within ViroLab .

1. A Doctor logs into the ViroLab Portal (a web-based user frontend). He has to provide his credentials, usually username and password (Authentication);

2. The credentials are now transferred to the local identity management system and verified against the locally stored credentials;
3. In case the user is known to the home organisation's users database, a digital identity token (fingerprint) is created and sent back to the portal;

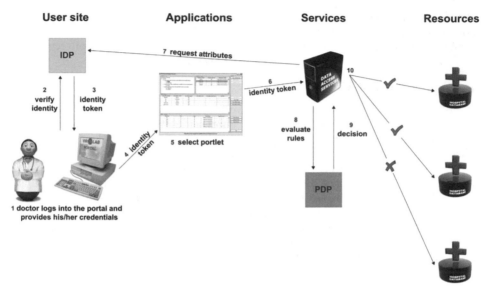

Figure 1: Authentication and Authorisation within ViroLab

4. Once the user is logged in, he can choose between different available applications;
5. He selects the data access application and sends a request to the Data Access Services (DAS) that are responsible for querying distributed databases simultaneously;
6. During that request, the initially created identity token is passed to the DAS that require this token to request the corresponding user attributes;
7. This request is performed by sending the identity token to the user's home organisation (HO) firstly proving whether the user is known and the token is valid. In a second step, the released user attributes like his role, institution or e-mail address are obtained from the local database and returned to the DAS;
8. The final decision whether someone is allowed to access a resource is only known to the PDP (Policy Decision Point). Hence, DAS sends an authorisation request to the PDP;
9. The PDP checks its stored access control policies for the corresponding rules. These rules contain conditions specifying the required set of attributes. If a policy rule matches with the provided attributes, the appropriate resource is cached. Having evaluated each access policy, the PDP returns a list of accessible resources to the DAS;
10. Finally, the DAS take the incoming request and tries to connect to each of the accessible resources and performs the user's query.

5. Technologies and Implementation

In order to meet the specific requirements for exchanging confidential biomedical information within such a virtual environment [2], the solution introduced and developed in ViroLab is built on established Grid technologies – GSI and OGSA-DAI – which provide the core for the own designed services, called Data Access Services (DAS).

These services [4] implement standard user interfaces to support various user groups but they also allow the integration of different data resource types, using the core functionalities of OGSA-DAI, to be smoothly exposed within the entire infrastructure. To guarantee that only persons who are known to the infrastructure can access certain data sets, additional security features, in particular strong access control mechanisms for all integrated data resources, have been defined and applied to protect the sensible information.

The Policy Decision Point (PDP) introduced within ViroLab has been developed during the TrustCoM project [12]. To fulfil certain new requirements related to data resources, it has been slightly modified and extended. The PDP is implemented as a web service and is responsible for controlling any access to a certain resource. The PDP makes its decision based on the access control policies stored in its repository to decide whether the user can access that particular resource and perform queries. It provides quasi dynamic authorisation and user-defined policies which are created and managed by data providers themselves. For the simplicity of the policy management, each data provider writes its own access control policies and a data provider has one access control policy for each of its resources.

The Extensible Access Control Markup Language (XACML) that provides a general policy language as well as an access decision language is used to define these attribute-based access control policies in our approach. XACML is implemented in XML and standardised by the Organisation for the Advancement of Structured Information Standards (OASIS). A XACML policy typically consists of multiple policy rules, and within each policy rule the data providers can describe specific conditions specifying the required attributes a user needs to provide in order to become authorised. In the following figure, this general interpretation is being presented.

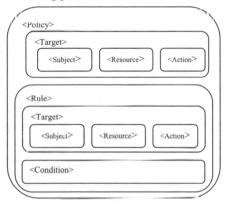

Figure 2: Structure of XACML Policies

In a typical scenario, the PDP initially receives from the DAS a list of available resources and the set of the attributes of the user for whom the access permission is requested. For every available resource, the PDP creates the relevant authorisation requests (see figure 3). The subject field of this request contains the received set of attributes and the resource field corresponds to the one of the available resources (refer to figure 4). In the evaluation process, the PDP matches the subject, resource, and action fields of the request with the target fields of the policies in its repository. In case of a successful match, it evaluates the policy and makes its decision. After the evaluation of the corresponding policies, PDP combines the individual decisions and creates a final authorisation decision being shared with the DAS that provide the users with a list of all accessible resources. The modification and the deletion of corresponding access control policies are also directly provided by the PDP.

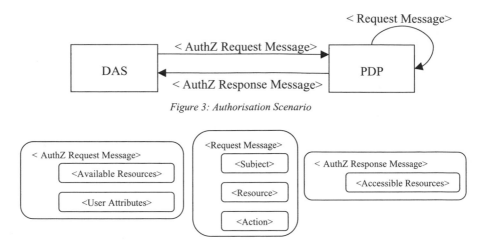

Figure 3: Authorisation Scenario

Figure 4: Structure of the Messages

6.   Preliminary Results

The ViroLab project is in the middle of its implementation phase developing and realising this approach. However, ViroLab already released a first prototype of the virtual laboratory that supports data access and integration of the heterogeneous resources in a limited way. One can deal with these resources as a federated data space, which can be queried by submitting multiple and concurrent requests for gathering any kind of biomedical data sets that still reside in an inhomogeneous state. Basic security features including the encryption of transferred data messages as well as the support for user authorisation based on Shibboleth's authentication and authorisation infrastructure are also in place. Currently, four user sites have been connected to the overall laboratory environment which provides Shibboleth identity provider capabilities to their users. Access control has also been successfully achieved by using the extended version of the TrustCoM PDP and self-defined XACML access control policies following the abovementioned schema. The dynamicity aspect is supported through the creation of a nice and user-friendly graphical interface that enables fast and easy generation, change, and upload of particular policies.

Both virologists and clinicians have successfully applied these activities requesting data within several pre-defined experiments. A detailed description of corresponding experiments and workflows can be found in [11].

7.   Conclusions

XACML provides administrators with a standard access control policy language. Controlling the general access to the resources can be achieved by very simple policies. Highly detailed policies, which are also provided by XACML, can be used in order to support fine-grained access control down to the level of database tables and single data sets. XACML also allows conditional authorisation, policy combination, and conflict resolution. It is a very general extensible language offering lots of flexibility. However, this flexibility and expressiveness can cause complexity and verbosity while creating deeply structured policies. Another limitation of the language is the lack of policy versioning and management in the XACML framework. This must be solved by the administrators themselves.

Using a one standard access control policy language within the entire system has some advantages. The delegated administrators do not have to write their own policies in many different languages but they can reuse their existing codes. Thus, they can create, change and delete the access control policies in a timely manner. There is also no need for an invention of a new and specific policy language.

The role-based approach allows for modeling a single or several complex organisation/s. Instead of considering every single user in the entire system this can save time and money. Distributed administration also reduces the complexity and provides enhanced flexibility.

The solution presented in this paper shows the interaction of Shibboleth with the DAS and a modified version of the TrustCoM PDP. It still resides in a prototyping phase but already achieves the integration of dispersed and heterogeneous biomedical data resources in an easy to manage and secure way. Future work and further usage scenarios including several hospitals and more complex data queries shall validate the usability and effectiveness of XACML for making fine-grained and attribute-based access control that could be applied and used in real clinical workflows.

Acknowledgement

The results presented in this paper are partially funded by the European Commission through the support of the ViroLab Project Grant 027446. The authors want to thank all who contributed to this paper, especially the members of the project consortium.

References

[1] ViroLab – EU IST Project (IST-027446), http://www.virolab.org

[2] M. Assel, B. Krammer, and A. Loehden. Management and Access of Biomedical Data in a Grid Environment. In Proceedings of the 6th Cracow Grid Workshop 2006, pp. 263-270. Cracow, Poland (2006)

[3] M. Assel and A. Kipp. A Secure Infrastructure for Dynamic Collaborative Working Environments. In Proceedings of the 2007 International Conference on Grid Computing and Applications, pp. 212-216. CSREA Press, USA (2007)

[4] M. Assel, B. Krammer, and A. Loehden. Data Access and Virtualization within ViroLab. In Proceedings of the 7th Cracow Grid Workshop 2007, pp. 77-84. Cracow, Poland (2007)

[5] P. Sloot, C. Boucher, M. Bubak, A. Hoekstra, P. Plaszczak, A. Posthumus, D. van de Vijver, S. Wesner and A. Tirado-Ramos. VIROLAB - A Virtual Laboratory for Decision Support in Viral Diseases Treatment. In Proceedings of the 5th Cracow Grid Workshop 2005, Cracow, Poland (2005)

[6] A. Kipp, L. Schubert and M. Assel. Supporting Dynamism and Security in Ad-Hoc Collaborative Working Environments. In Proceedings of the 12th World Multi-Conference on Systemics, Cybernetics and Informatics: WMSCI2008, In Press. Orlando, USA (2008)

[7] M. Antonioletti , M.P. Atkinson , R. Baxter , A. Borley, N.P. Chue Hong, B. Collins, N. Hardman, A. Hume, A. Knox, M. Jackson, A. Krause, S. Laws, J. Magowan, N.W. Paton, D. Pearson, T. Sugden, P. Watson, M. Westhead. The Design and Implementation of Grid Database Services in OGSA-DAI. Concurrency and Computation: Practice and Experience, Volume 17, Issue 2-4, pp. 357-376 (2005)

[8] T. Barton, J. Basney, T. Freeman, T. Scavo, F. Siebenlist, V. Welch, R. Ananthakrishnan, B. Baker, M. Goode, and K. Keahey. Identity Federation and Attribute-based Authorization through the Globus Toolkit, Shibboleth, Grid- Shib, and MyProxy. Proceedings of 5th Annual PKI R\&D Workshop, Gaithersburg, USA (2006)

[9] TrustCoM - EU IST Project (IST-2003-01945), http://www.eu-trustcom.com

[10] BREIN - EU IST Project (IST- 034556), http://www.gridsforbusiness.eu

[11] T. Gubala, B. Balis, M. Malawski, M. Kasztelnik, P. Nowakowski, M. Assel, D. Harezlak, T. Bartynski, J. Kocot, E. Ciepiela, D. Krol, J. Wach, M. Pelczar, W. Funika, and M. Bubak. ViroLab Virtual Laboratory. In Proceedings of the 7th Cracow Grid Workshop 2007, pp. 35-40. Cracow, Poland (2007)

[12] M. Wilson, D. Chadwick, T. Dimitrakos, J. Doser, A. Arenas, P. Giambiagi, D. Golby, C. Geuer-Pollmann, J. Haller, S. Ketil, T. Mahler, L. Martino, X. Parent, S. Ristol, J. Sairamesh, and L. Schubert. The TrustCoM Framework V0.5. In Proceedings 6th IFIP Working Conference on Virtual Enterprises (PRO-VE '05), Valencia, Spain (2005)

---

[i] Grid Security Infrastructure

[ii] eXtensible Access Control Markup Language

Section 11.2

Applications

Collaboration and the Knowledge Economy: Issues, Applications, Case Studies   1603
P. Cunningham and M. Cunningham (Eds.)
IOS Press, 2008

A Meta Model Generator for Implementing Access Control and Security Policies in Distributed Systems Based on Model-Driven Architecture

Mirad ZADIC, Andrea NOWAK
Austrian Research Centers GmbH-ARC, A-2444 Seibersdorf, Austria
Tel: +43 50550-3155, Fax: +43 50550-2813, Email: {firstname.lastname}@acrs.ac.at

Abstract: Specifying security policies, especially access control policies, may be an enormous task for every security administrator. With the current vast and complex IT-infrastructure having sensitive assets, it is preferable to have a tool that simplifies the security policy specification task. Our goal in this work is to present the concept and design of a tool, which should solve the previous problem. To facilitate managing and maintaining security policies we are going to define a specific modeling language for generating tool on the base the features of Meta Modeling Environment. This provides a set of the visualization components and code generation capabilities to build layers of security policies architecture. The policy generator generates the access control policies in the XACML (eXtensible Access Control Mark-up Language) format.

Model-Driven Development (MDD) is a popular approach to creating solutions in a large number of domains. In many cases, however, an organization does not have the resources or time available to develop a graphical modeling environment from scratch using the Eclipse Modeling Framework (EMF), Graphical Editor Framework (GEF), or Graphical Modeling Framework (GMF). A way to reduce complexity of developing a Graphical Modeling and Generating Tool is to examine the Generic Eclipse Modeling System (GEMS), which makes possible rapidly creating such modeling tool from a visual language description or metamodel without any coding in third-generation languages.

Keywords: Model Driven Development, Security policies Architectures, Meta modeling, Domain-specific Modeling Languages, Policy Generator.

1. Introduction

The distributed service architectures without appropriate security guards carry indefinitely risks and for many companies is the security one of the biggest barriers for the realization of linking applications within organizations, across enterprises or across the Internet. If a continuous confidentiality, integrity, non-repudiation and access control is not guaranteed, the use of Web services is in the e-business doomed to failure.

1.1 Fali Recenica

A Web service end-point Security involves a number of aspects, such as: reliable messages, privacy, authorization, trust, authentication and cryptographic security. Each aspect addresses a number of optional features and parameters, which must be coordinated between communicating end-points. Currently, in most companies, the specification policies are manually created and managed by a security administrator as an independent procedure during the deployment stage after the software design and development. Because XACML policies [2] [3] are rich XML-based documents with complex syntax, it is very difficult and time consuming to write error free XML documents by hand, especially for people who do not know the syntax well. This may affect the productivity of the administrator and the quality of the software. Hence, a suitable XACML editor or a tool that can automatically generate XACML policies is needed. Another problem is normally the administrator does not take part directly in the application design process, so he/she may not understand the software structure and details well enough to define policies to fulfil the security requirements.

Many models have been developed to construct and manage the security requirements but our security infrastructure is deployed in a modular way with pre-defined, configurable security components. In this paper we present the a modeling tool and generator which uses the Domain-Specific Modeling Languages (DSMLs), Model-Driven Engineering (MDE), Model-Driven Architectures (MDA), and Model Driven Development (MDD) [6]. The goal in this work is to present the concept and design of a generator, which should support the process of specifying the access control policies. Furthermore, the generator should provide the security administrator with expert knowledge and help him to tackle the well-known problems, which may arise during the security policy specification task.

In Section 1 and 2 we provide some background on the standards and the technologies our work is based and our main research objectives. Our presented Model-Driven-Approach with the metamodel, and there transformations tool for policy specifications are discussed in Section 3 and 4. Section 5 presents a short presentation of results. Section 7 we describe our future work and at least Section 8 gives an overview about related work

2.   Objectives

Systems for model-driven software development can be seen as a new generation of visual programming languages. A system can be modeled at different levels of abstraction or from different perspectives. The syntax of every model is defined by a metamodel that's mean the metamodel defines the syntax of the modeling languages, a model plays the role of the source code, and the generator replaces the compiler.

Using this approach, it is possible to generate automatically large amounts of source code and other artifacts, e.g. deployment descriptors and make files, based on relatively concise models. This improves the productivity of the development process and quality of the resulting systems. It is also a step towards platform independent design of systems.

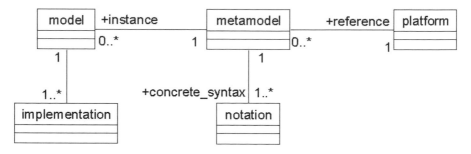

Figure 1: Different Levels of Modeling

The types and relationships have the following meaning: A model represents a software system at an appropriate level of abstraction or from a certain perspective. One or more implementations are generated from a model. A metamodel defines the syntax of a class of models. Every metamodel refers to a particular platform, called its reference platform (reference). A platform is an execution environment for software systems, like the Java platform. The semantics of a metamodel is defined through transformation rules that map every language construct to constructs in the reference platform, Figure 1.

The Generic Eclipse Modeling System (GEMS), a part of the Eclipse Generative Modeling Technologies (GMT) project, helps developers rapidly create a graphical modeling tool from a visual language description (metamodel) without any coding in third-generation languages. GEMS substantially reduces the cost of developing a graphical modeling tool by allowing developers to focus on the key aspects of their tool: the specification of the DSML and the intellectual assets built around the use of the language. The infrastructure to create, edit, and constrain instances of the language is generated automatically by GEMS from the language specification. Moreover, GEMS allows the separation of language development, coding, as well as "look and feel" development, such as changing how modeling elements appear based on domain analyses.

3.   Methodology

3.1   XACML Policies

The policy generator generates the access control policies in XACML (eXtensible Access Control Mark-up Language) format, which is established by OASIS. The XACML standard defines the machine-interpretable and also machine-enforceable security policies [2] [3] [4] [5]. Whenever a principal requests access to a resource, that request is passed to a software component called a Policy Decision Point (PDP). A PDP evaluates the request against the specified access control policies, and permits or denies the request accordingly. Actually the interface of the whole environment to the outside world is Policy Enforcement Point (PEP). It receives the access requests and evaluates them with the help of the other actors and permits or denies the access to the resource. The PEP forms a request based on the requester's attributes, the resource in question, the action, and other information pertaining to the request. The PEP sends then this request to a PDP.

The main goal of policy generator [7] [8] is to derive low-level and enforceable security policies. These policies are deduced from the business process, which acts as the input scenario. In this scenario, the security problems should be already identified, and annotated within the business process. The generator shall generate follows types of XACML components, Figure 2:

<PolicySet> element combines Policies in a PolicySet. It has a target, a policy-combining algorithm-identifier, a set of policies and obligations.

<Policy> element combines rules in a policy. Therefore, a policy consists of a target element, a rule-combining algorithm identifier, a set of rules and obligations. The target element of policy has the same purpose as target element of rule. The rule-combining algorithm determines rule-combining method applied to the rules.

<Rule> element is the most elementary unit of XACML policy. It has the target element, the condition element and the effect element. The target element specifies the environment, on which this rule should apply. The condition element is a Boolean function over subject, resource action and environment attributes. In order to apply the effect of rule on the target, this condition should evaluate to true, otherwise, the rule will return indeterminate. Lastly, the effect element states the decision for this rule: either permit or deny.

<Target> element describes the properties of the environment, on which the Rule, Policy or Policy Set should apply. It contains the subject description, resource description, action performed and environment description.

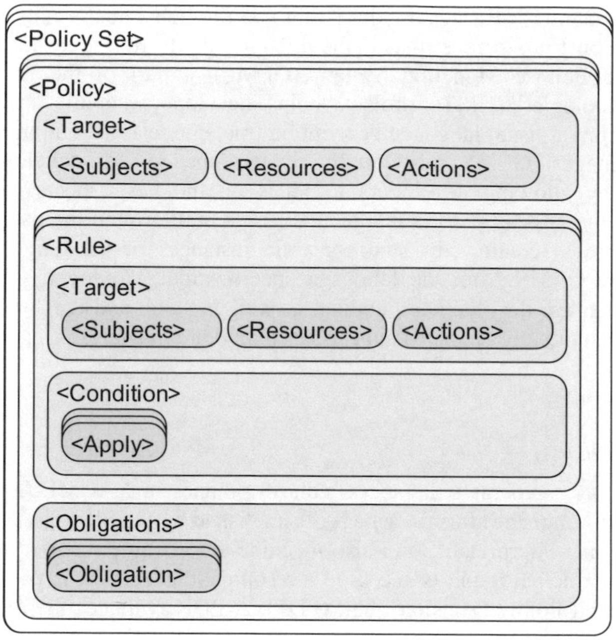

Figure 2: XACML Components

<Condition> element represents a Boolean expression that refines the applicability of the rule beyond the predicates implied by its target.

<Obligations> element of an XACML <Policy> is a directive to the PEP to perform additional processing following the enforcement of an access control decision. It contains one or more <Obligation> elements and typically references elements in the request context. Processing of <Obligations> elements is application-specific.

3.2   Meta Modeling Tool

The Generic Eclipse Modeling System (GEMS) created by the Distributed Object Computing (DOC) Group at the Institute for Software Integrated Systems (ISIS) at Vanderbilt University is an Eclipse-based Meta-configurable Modeling Environment that enables developers to generate Domain-Specific Modeling Language (DSML) tools for customizing software architecture via the following capabilities [9] [10] [11] [12]:

1. A visual interface that supports the creation of do-main-specific modeling languages (DSMLs), i.e., GEMS contains a metamodeling environment that supports the definition of paradigms, which are type systems that describe the roles and relationships in particular domains.

2. The creation of models that are instances of DSML paradigms within the same environment.

3. Customization of such environments so that the elements of the modeling language represent the elements of the domain in a much more intuitive manner than is possible via third-generation programming languages.

4. A flexible type system that allows inheritance and instantiation of elements of modeling languages.

5. An integrated constraint definition and enforcement module that can be used to define rules to be adhered to by elements of the models built using a particular DSML.

6. Facilities to plug-in analysis and synthesis tools that operate on the models.

GEMS provides a mechanism called Model Intelligence Guides (MIGs) to substantially reduce the cost of integrating a constraint solver and reduce the complexity of modeling large and complex domains.

4. Technology Description

4.1 XACML Policies Model Description

This section gives a short overview of our model driven development process for developing a XACML policy specification model. The presented XACML policy model defines end-point policies for Web Services. All model components make a base of challenges that should be generated from the policy generator. XACML components are reflected in the relevant structure of WSDL:

Port → Operation → Message

The established XCAML model has a set of definitions to facilitate combining of end-policies for service-oriented structure.

That means an XACML <PolicySet> element is associated with a concrete Web-service end-point definition. It is usually that its <Target> element has to identify Web-services port and to describe port's parameters. In the case that a policy must be target more finely than a port, as in presented XACML model, the <PolicySet> contains more <Policy> elements. The <Policy> elements define the objectives for each aspect of policy associated with the port. The policy-combining algorithm for <PolicySet> is defined with:

"urn:oasis:names:tc:xacml:1.0:policy-combining-algorithm:deny-overrides".

The content of <PolicySet/Target/Subjects> has only one <Subject> element for service-requestor. The MatchId for the <PolicySet/Target/Subjects/Subject> element is defined with:

"urn:oasis:names:tc:xacml:1.0:function:string-equal"

<AttributeValue> and <SubjectAttributeDesignator> ere defined for a service-requestor.

The content of the <PolicySet/Target/Resources> element is the name attribute of the end-point's port definition. The MatchId for the <PolicySet/Target/Resources> element is defined with:

"urn:oasis:names:tc:xacml:1.0:function:anyURI-equal".

The contents of <PolicySet/Target/Actions> element is defined as <AnyAction/>.

There are two <Policy> elements one for service-requestor and one for service-provider. Therefore each <Policy> element is associated with a single aspect of an end-point policy concept, respectively "sending" and "receiving". The rule-combining algorithm for a <Policy> element is predefined with:

"urn:oasis:names:tc:xacml:1.0:rule-combining-algorithm:permit-overrides".

The <Target> element of a <Policy> element "sending" has to identify the one objective of end-point policy to which to be successfully invoked. The content of <Policy/Target/Actions> element is defined with one <Action> element, which defined invoked object. The MatchId for the <Policy/Target/Actions/Action> is:

"urn:oasis:names:tc:xacml:1.0:function:anyURI-equal"

In <AttributeValue> is defined invoke for an object of Web-service port.

This "sending" <Policy> element has <Rule> element, which define strategy and it is affected as "Permit". In this case, the policy specifies the actions that must be performed, either instead of, or in addition to, actions that may be performed. This facility for action defines the conjunction with policy evaluation in the <Obligations> element. The <Rule> strategy "Permit" is resulted unless PEP understand and discharge all of the <Obligations> elements associated with the applicable policy.

The <Obligations> element is data-processing obligation and annotates defined action operation. The FulfillOn attribute indicates the effect for which this obligation must be fulfilled by the PEP, defined as "Permit". ObligationId (of type URI) is mapped to a specific handler called by the PEP and Obligation parameter values are passed to handler.

<Policy> element "receiving" in presented model carried the <Policy/Target/Subjects> and the <Policy/Target/Resources> elements but they are defined as <AnySubject/> and <AnyResource/>, respectively. In this case should be the contents of the <Policy/Target/Actions> element identify the invocation of Web-service object. The <AttributeValue> and <ActionAttributeDesignator>elements describe the invocation of Web-service object in the <Action> element. The <ActionMatch> element carries MatchId:

"urn:oasis:names:tc:xacml:1.0:function:anyURI-equal".

The <Rule> element contains set of <Apply> elements that define what to do in that invocation. The <Apply> elements are structured as follows:

```
<Apply FunctionId="urn:oasis:names:tc:xacml:1.0:function:string-equal">
    <Apply FunctionId="urn:oasis:names:tc:xacml:1.0:function:string-one-and-only">
        <AttributeSelector RequestContextPath="…" DataType="…"/>
    </Apply>
    <AttributeValue DataType="…"> … </AttributeValue>
</Apply>
```

There are three possible attribute's classes: Unconstrained attributes, Constrained attributes and Authorized attributes. This XACML model preferred a constrained (environmental) attribute, whose value is outside the control of the policy-user. The emergency condition code is an example of an environmental attribute over which a policy-user has no control. In presented model this attribute is used to evaluate any action that the policy-user might take, for instance is mapped to a specific handler.

```
<AttributeSelector RequestContextPath="//Environment/Attribute
                    [...handler...]/AttributeValue/text()" DataType="…"/>
```

There is a subject attribute over handler action in the elements of message. In this case of the environmental attribute a "handler" takes care about signing or encrypting of elements in SOAP messages. The policy-user waits until the predicate involving the result. The <Rule/Target> element is omitted.

4.2   Meta Modeling Environment

The Generic Eclipse Modeling System (GEMS) as part of the Eclipse Generative Modeling Technologies (GMT) project is used for design and implement our generator. GEMS allows domain experts to rapidly create complex graphical modeling tools for Eclipse without writing Graphical User Interface (GUI), EMF, or XML code. GEMS provides extensive support for integrating intelligent mechanisms into a modeling tool to provide visual modeling queues, constraint-compliant batch processing, simulation, and analysis.

The implementation of GEMS reuses the basic Eclipse components such as EMF (Eclipse Modeling Framework) and GEF (Graphical Editing Framework), as well as parts of GMF (Graphical Modeling Framework) runtime. GMF utilizes Eclipse EMF and GEF technologies. EMF is used for model management and GEF for graphical user interface. GMF uses a static-mapping-based approach. It defines a set of meta-models: graphical (presentation), tooling and mapping meta-models. Graphical meta-model defines the graphical element types. Tooling meta-model defines the palette and menus. The mapping meta-model defines the mapping possibilities between the models. In addition, it uses EMF Ecore Model as the domain meta-model.

The main distinguishing feature of GEMS is an appropriately built presentation meta-model. It enables a clear separation of responsibilities between the GEMS presentation engine, which handles all the low-level presentation and layout-related tasks, and transformations, which create and maintain only the domain and the logical structure of presentation. GEMS contains also a universal metamodel-based presentation engine for element property editing, and an advanced project tree engine.

GEMS provides an extensive feature set for rapidly building graphical modeling tools including [13] [14] [15]:

1. A graphical language for metamodel specification that can capture
   o Domain entities
   o Attributes of entities
   o Inheritance relationships
   o Connection and containment relationships between entities
   o Distinct modeling views
   o Graphical information, such as connection styles, colors, and fonts
   o Constraints
2. A code generation framework, which does not require any coding or XML editing, for transforming a GEMS metamodel into a working Draw2D/GEF Eclipse plug-in for editing instances of the language
3. The visual appearance of the generated modeling tool can be customized by creating CSS stylesheets to modify the icons, colors, fonts, connection styles, and other visual attributes of the modeling entities
4. The views available to a modeler can be customized through a mechanism similar to CSS stylesheets
5. The generated graphical modeling plug-ins, created by GEMS, support extensive external customization through extension points for
   o Adding code generators and transformation, such as Open Architecture Ware, Java Emitter Templates, and Atlas Transformation Language
   o Model pre and post processing
   o Model event listeners
   o Triggers for invoking actions (similar to database triggers)
   o Constraint languages
   o Menus
   o Palette customizers
   o Intelligent modeling guides
   o Model serializes
6. GEMS provides built-in support for constraints written in Java, OCL, and Prolog
   o Constraints can also be used as triggers for invoking actions

5.   Developments

This section represents how to generate the XACML Policy Specifications modeling tool based on the metamodel describing syntax of the DSML (GEMS). As a case study, is described the development of a tool, called ARCSecuModel, for specifying and modeling the security policies for access to the Web services. ARCSecuModel allows IT professionals to describe the needed policies component they wish to deploy security requirements of the Web-service and the security goals in the predefined Business processes.

For modeling the presented ARCSecuMetaModel is used GEMS to visually describe a metamodel in Eclipse, to generate the EMF, Draw2D, and GEF code and to implement a modeling tool for the language described by the metamodel. The Meta model is described with follow GEMS objects: Class, Connection, Attribute and Inheritance.

The first entity (class) is the ArcSecuModel, which is represented as the main white canvas containing the Domain and Messages. The ArcSecuModel is the root entity in our metamodel. Domain and Messages entities can be seen on the left and below from ArcSecuModel, respectively. Tree more entity types are present for security goals: IntegrityRequirement, ConfRequirement and NonRepRequirement.

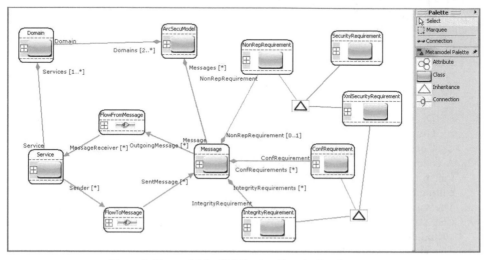

Figure 3: Metamodel for Web-Services Security Requirements

The security goals (IntegrityRequirement, ConfRequirement, NonRepRequirement) are child entities of Message. The Service entity is child entity from Domain. The finishing of ARCSecuMetaModel tool involved also connections between Message and Service. These are defined with FlowFromMessage and FlowToMessage connections that were defined in suitable directions.

Inheritance relationships are created by adding an Inheritance element to the model, and connecting it to the parent type and derived type(s). Derived types inherit any attributes, connections, or containment relationships specified by the parent. The presented ARCSecuMetaModel contains entities with two Inheritance relationships: first Inheritance between IntegrityRequirement (BaseClass), ConfRequirement (BaseClass), XmlSecurityRequirement (DerivedFrom) and the second between NonRepRequirement (BaseClass), XmlSecurityRequirement (BaseClass), SecurityRequirement (DerivedFrom).

The classes IntegrityRequirement and ConfRequirement Attributes inherit the attributes from XmlSecurityRequirement entity (NS1; NS2; NS3; NS4; NS5; NS6; NS7; XPath). Service carries an attribute (string type) named OperationName and Massege carries also an attribute (Boolean type) named IsResponse. Figure 3 shows the complete metamodel ARCSecuMetaModel for our policy generator tool.

After creating a metamodel, GEMS's DSML plug-in generator creates the modeling tool. The code generator first traverses the various entities in the model and generates an Ecore model, which is a set of EMF objects that represent the metamodel or syntax of the visual language. GEMS then invokes the appropriate EMF code generators to produce EMF classes that implement the Ecore definition.

The generated EMF classes are used as the object graph underlying ARCSecuModel. These classes automate key aspects of serialization and de-serialization. By default, GEMS leverages EMF's ability to save EMF models to XMI. Other serializers can be plugged into persist models in a database or use an alternate file format. The EMF object graph also allows GEMS to leverage the libraries available for Eclipse to check Object Constraint Language (OCL) constraints against a model.

The second set of code generated by GEMS, are the classes required to plug the generated EMF code into the GEMS runtime framework. The GEMS runtime provides a layer built on top of GEF (and soon GMF) that provides higher level capabilities, such as applying CSS styles to elements, exposing remote update mechanisms, and providing constraint solver modeling intelligence.

The GEMS runtime provides numerous extension points for adding custom functionality to the generated modeling tool. Extension points are available for adding actions that can be triggered by OCL, Java or role-based object constraint assertions on the model, customization of menus, custom code generators, remoting mechanisms, custom serializers, and many other features.

The third set of code artifacts, generated by GEMS, are the various XML descriptors, build specifications, class path directives, and icons required to integrate the generated tool into Eclipse as a plug-in. When a modeling tool is generated into a Java project, these various artifacts configure the project properly to build the plug-in and make it visible for testing with the runtime workbench. The build artifacts also configure the project so that it can be exported properly as an Eclipse plug-in modeling tool.

One benefit of GEMS is to avoid requiring developers to use third-generation languages to write any graphics code to implement a modeling tool. GEMS allows developers to customize the look and feel of their modeling tools. It supports this capability by allowing developers to change the default icons visible on the palette and in the model, which enables developers to quickly create impressive visualizations matching domain notations.

Swapping icons isn't the only mechanism GEMS provides to customize the look and feel of modeling tools like ARCSecuModel. Developers can use CSS style sheets to change fonts, colors, backgrounds, background images, line styles, and many more features of a GEMS-based modeling tool as shows the Figure 4.

In GEMS CSS styles are applied to elements using traditional CSS selectors. The key difference is that selectors refer to the roles and types specified in the metamodel. Even more complex visual behaviors can be created by leveraging a feature called TAGS in GEMS. TAGS are textual markup that can be added to modeling elements to denote that they have a certain property. The GEMS TAGS facility supports the combination of domain analysis with CSS styles to rapidly develop complex domain-specific visual behaviors, such as changing the icon for a Domain that doesn't have sufficient resources (Services).

Triggers allow constraints to perform a number of actions to guarantee model correctness, such as showing a warning message, vetoing a model change, or adding elements to fix the error. A trigger can also result in a message popping up above the modeling element that has violated the constraint. Much more complex actions can take place as well. For example, a constraint violation can trigger an action that runs policy generating process.

6.   Results

The modeling tool is an Eclipse rich client that is used to visually model the security needs of each communication and generate the XACML policies for each involved domain. Figure 4 shows some instances of a security model that describes the secure communication between domains.

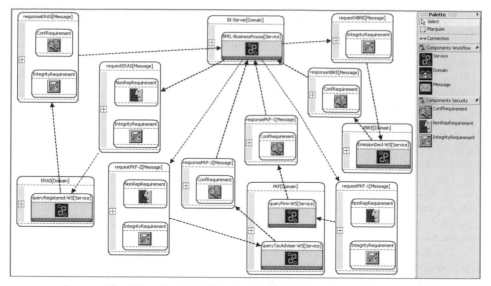

Figure 4: The Eclipse Based Modelling Tool for Web-Services Security Requirements

To model the communication between two domains one first needs to drag two domain model elements from the palette on the right onto the canvas. The bottom panel of the new domain elements is initially colored red. This indicates that some properties have to be set to make the model element valid. The properties can be set in the properties panel at the bottom of the modeling tool. For each domain a name has to be set that denotes its role in the communication. Next one needs to add services to each domain that communicate with each other by dragging services from the palette on each domain. The services need to have a name and an operation name set to be valid. These actually have to correspond to the real names of services. Now the communication needs a message sent between the two nodes. This is done by dragging a message model element on the canvas. The message has to be associated with initiating and receiving services by using the connection tool. Finally the security requirements of communication is configured by dragging security requirements from the palette onto the message. For confidentiality and integrity requirements one has to specify the XPath to the elements on which the requirements shall be enforced and also up to five namespaces. For the non- repudiation requirement no further configuration is needed. The generator can be run by right-clicking on the canvas and selecting ArcSecu Menu->DO IT. For each involved domain the generator creates one folder containing the XACML policies that need to be deployed to the policy folder of each domain.

7.   Conclusions

We presented the Generic Modeling Environment (GME), a configurable modeling and program synthesis tool set, which makes the rapid and cost-effective creation of highly customized, domain-specific system design and analysis environments possible. It is highly applicable for modelling XAMCL policy generator related to security artefact for Web-services. We focus on visually modelling an XACML system to fulfil the XACML profile and automatic generation of the security infrastructure in XACML-formatted documents.

This paper has described the powerful features available for building graphical modeling tools with GEMS. GEMS focuses on allowing developers to create Eclipse-based modeling tools without writing plug-in descriptors, GMF mapping files, GEF code, or EMF code. Furthermore, GEMS provides facilities to support external specification of visualization details so that they can be managed by graphic designers and other individuals not experienced with complex GUI coding. This Meta modelling approach reduces the cost of developing a graphical modeling tool by allowing developers to focus on the key aspects of their tool. The infrastructure to create, edit, and constrain instances of the language is generated automatically and the implementing process makes possible the separation of language development, coding, as well as "look and feel" development.

We introduce the concept of Model Driven Security for a software development process, which allows for the integration of security requirements through system models and supports the generation of security infrastructures and focuses on business logic as well as on inter-organizational workflow management.

8. Future Work

Several improvements and extensions need to be addressed in future work.

Currently our approach focuses on static design models, which are relatively close to the implementation. It is worth considering whether the efficiency of the development process of secure applications can be improved by annotating models at a higher level of abstraction (e.g. analysis) or by annotating dynamic models, e.g. state machines. Moreover, some critical questions concerning the development process are still open, e.g. how are roles and permissions identified? Beyond that, the current prototype does not yet demonstrate the platform independence of our concepts. Future work will focus on modeling security requirements and design information using dynamic models. The development process for secure systems starting with the initial analysis up to the complete secure system design will be investigated. In this context, we will examine the possibility of propagating security requirements between analysis and design models and ways to verify the compatibility of requirements and design information given at different levels.

In future work, we are developing advanced declarative programming, knowledge base, and querying functionality for GEMS, as well as addressing the challenges of maintaining model assets when the underlying meta-model changes.

References

[1] OASIS Standard. XACML profile for Web-services, http://docs.oasis-open.org/committees/documents.php?wg_abbrev=xacml
[2] OASIS Standard. eXtensible Access Control MarkupLanguage (XACML) version 2.0, http://docs.oasis-open.org/xacml/2.0/access_control-xacml-2.0-core-spec-os.pdf, February 2005.
[3] SAML 2.0 profile of XACML. Draft 02, 11 November 2004. - http://docs.oasisopen.org/xacml/access_control-xacml-2.0-saml_profile-spec-cd-02.pdf
[4] Ferraiolo, D. and R. Huhn. Role-Based Access Control. In Proceedings of 15th National Computer Security Conference
[5] Xin Jin, Applying Model Driven Architecture approach to Model Role Based Access Control System, Master Thesis
[6] Object Management Group. MDA Guide Version 1.0.1. [cited 2005 Nov.]; Available from: http://www.omg.org/mda/specs.htm.
[7] Policy Generator, Taufiq Rochaeli, TUD SEC, Ruben Wolf, Fraunhofer-SIT, February 10, 2006.
[8] Simplifying the Development of Product-line Customization Tools via Model Driven Development, Jules White and Douglas Schmidt, Department of Electrical Engineering and Computer Science, Vanderbilt University, Nashville, USA
[9] GEMS EMF Intelligence Tutorial, http://wiki.eclipse.org/GEMS_EMF_Intelligence_Tutorial
[10] GEMS EMF Intelligence Tutorial with Mixed Constraints, http://wiki.eclipse.org/GEMS_EMF_Intelligence_Tutorial_with_Mixed_Constraints
[11] GEMS Metamodeling Tutorial, http://wiki.eclipse.org/GEMS_Metamodeling_Tutorial
[12] The Generic Eclipse Modeling System (GEMS), By Jules White
[13] openArchitectureWare 4.2 Fact Sheet, Markus Völter, voelter@acm.org Date: September 3, 2007
[14] GrTP: Transformation Based Graphical Tool Building Platform, Institute of Mathematics and Computer Science, University of Latvia
[15] Building Tools by Model Transformations in Eclipse, University of Latvia, Audris Kalnins, Oskars Vilitis1, Edgars Celms

Collaboration and the Knowledge Economy: Issues, Applications, Case Studies
P. Cunningham and M. Cunningham (Eds.)
IOS Press, 2008

Enabling True Single Sign-On for Grid Portals

Efstathios KARANASTASIS[1], Piotr GRABOWSKI[2], Vassiliki ANDRONIKOU[1],
Michael RUSSELL[2], Piotr DZIUBECKI[2], Dominik TARNAWCZYK[2],
Dawid SZEJNFELD[2], Tomasz KUCZYNSKI[2], Theodora VARVARIGOU[1], Jarek NABRZYSKI[2]
[1] *National Technical University of Athens, 9 Iroon Polytechniou, Zografou, 15773, Greece*
Tel: +30 210 7722558, Fax: +30 210 7722569, Email: karanastasis@telecom.ntua.gr
[2] *Poznan Supercomputing and Networking Center, Noskowskiego 10, Poznan, 61-704, Poland*
Tel: +48 61 8582174, Fax: + 48 61 8582151, Email: piotrg@man.poznan.pl

Abstract: This paper discusses the security issues arising when incorporating Grid portals in business environments and proposes a viable and robust integrated security solution, which is easy to incorporate into existing platforms, to use and to maintain. The proposed solution enables Single Sign-Up, an innovative concept for automatic user registration in domain specific middleware and remote services, Single Sign-On, and advanced user management. These mechanisms cooperate seamlessly, offering high levels of security, promoting the overall business processes, and thus comprising an important improvement towards the business adoption of the Grid. The design and implementation of the system is based and will be tested on several real life business cases from different sectors.

Keywords: business, Grid, portal, security, registration, authentication, Single Sign-Up, Single Sign-On, user management, toolkit, application, Web

1. Introduction

As "Grid" [1] makes its way to the mainstream, many businesses are looking to see how Grid can enhance their business models to drive growth, improve efficiency and increase production. Here, standards-based approaches to resource management, meta-scheduling, and federation of data and services are considered fundamental reasons to adopt Grid. Another key reason to adopt Grid is to benefit from the plethora of open-source software and tools now available on the market that support the Grid computing paradigm, such as to reduce the overall cost of the IT solution or simply to be inline with current trends in computing. While most open-source Grid platforms offer mechanisms for managing security and trust issues in federated environments, most do not offer practical means for integrating these security mechanisms with Web portals.

Grid portals comprise a collaborative environment which provides a simple and common Web interface to heterogeneous computational Grid resources and services. The offered functionality ranges from the submission and monitoring of computational jobs to the management of remote workspaces, accounting and provision of user and resource related statistics. A Grid portal also simplifies administration and problem solving by offering mechanisms for controlling access and monitoring user actions.

This paper discusses the security issues arising when incorporating Grid portals in business environments. It describes the methodology followed in the framework of the BEinGRID project [3], designing and developing components related to portals security, based on the needs of several real life business cases from different sectors. The components were implemented as enhancements and extensions to the Vine Toolkit [2]. The document describes the design of the proposed solution and the technology choices made. It further presents screenshots of the implementations and discusses their business impact and benefits when using them.

2. Objectives

This paper discusses how the Vine Toolkit, driven by business scenarios examined within the context of the BEinGRID project , aims to fill the Web-to-Grid gap to enable businesses to transparently connect their user communities to their Grid-enabled infrastructures in a secure and easy way. Vine, a Java-based framework that supports a variety of application environments, provides an extensible model for defining how users are granted identities and security tokens for multiple Grid environments, as well as how to introduce that registration process into the Web-site sign-up process. Moreover, it provides a complimentary collection of reusable Web 2.0 [4] interfaces that support user account sign-up and administration and can be adapted to any Java Servlet [5] or Portlet [6] based portal environment.

3. Methodology

The development and evaluation of the Vine Toolkit is based on the technical and business needs of ten different business cases from the aerospace, architectural, financial, environmental engineering, automotive, pharmaceutical, textile, chemistry, IT and geological sectors.

The portal security and user management requirements of these business cases were examined and detailed during the first year of the BEinGRID project. Substantial weight was also given to specific business requirements and the promotion of the overall business processes. Analyses of these requirements led to the design of a general model, which was refined several times in a constant interaction process with the involved businesses. The outcome of this procedure was a set of common components at the portal presentation layer as well at the business-logic layer, which represent viable solutions to address the requested functionality and can be adapted to the various Grid middleware and use cases represented by the business cases that were analysed. Requirements and designs from the OMII Europe project [7] were also included in this effort. The design has been implemented as enhancements and extensions to the Vine Toolkit and verified on a number of small testbeds deployed at the Poznan Supercomputing and Networking Center (PSNC) [8]. One of the main goals comprises the application and evolvement of this work in new business cases within BEinGRID as well as other real-world business problems.

4. Technology

Web portals, whether used internally or as a public offering for products and services, are vital enablers for commerce and production in business today. The most successful Web portals make it easy for users to join and become active members, that is, obtain accounts on the portal, its back-end services and partner sites. Thus, in order for Grid to become truly mainstream, it too needs to support Web-based user registration, the familiar email-verified "sign-up" model we see on many Web-sites today, as well as Web-based "Single Sign-On" and online tools for administering access to resources. Moreover, it must be possible to integrate this support into existing portal platforms.

The Vine Toolkit consists of a core project that defines a base API and programming model upon which sub projects are built. Each sub project addresses a particular problem area. Some, like the Grid Vine, build upon core Vine to define more general concepts and extensible elements. Others, like the Globus Toolkit 4 Vine, are concerned with adding support for particular third party libraries and services. At the time this paper was written, Vine had inherited support for several middleware and standards, including gLite 3 [9], Globus Toolkit 4 [10], JSDL 1.0 [11], OGSA-DAI 2.2 [12], UNICORE 6 [13], Storage Resource Broker [14], and others. Each Vine project conforms to a particular file structure that defines how source code is built as well as how third party libraries and configuration files are packaged and deployed. Users can select the specific Vine projects they require for their applications. Naturally, there are dependencies between certain projects that must also be taken into account.

When Vine is deployed, Vine's build system will deploy and package only those source files that are relevant to the target environment. Source files that are included in the main source tree for each project are deployed to all types of target environments, while source files contained in a project's web source tree are deployed for use only with Web applications. Typically, web source trees include user interfaces developed in one or more Web UI frameworks, such as the Google Web Toolkit [15] or Adobe Flex [16], as well as Java servlets, portlets and any Web services that are intended for use by that project.

Resources are perhaps the most important concept modeled in the Vine Toolkit. Vine defines a resource as anything that can be utilised. A computer, an application, a software library, a person, these are all resources in Vine. In fact, in Vine, resources define the application just as they define Grids. At their most basic level, Grids are collections of resources with policies describing how to use those resources. In order for the different resources to be properly accessible and functional, they must be identified in the resource registry file. Using the Vine Toolkit, one composes applications as collections of resources and services for utilizing those resources. The Vine Toolkit makes it possible to organize resources into a hierarchy of domains to represent one or more virtual organizations (VOs).

The Vine Toolkit is using a standard method of access control that enables a user to only login once and gain access to all resources configured for use with the system, without the need to login separately to each of them (Single Sign-On). It also implements a non-standard method for registering users into the portal system and underlying middleware (Single Sign-Up). Due to non existing standards for this scope, the developers had to implement a novel method supporting this idea. For managing users' credentials, which is required in order to enable Single Sign-On, the MyProxy Credential Management Service [23] is used. The MyProxy client in the Vine Toolkit is using a standard protocol for storing and retrieving X.509 proxy credentials (RFC3820) [24] to and from a server. Vine security is mainly using the authentication and authorisation capabilities of the portlet container and existing MyProxy credential repositories or, in some cases, the component's internal CA and credential repository, thus giving the end user a useful tool that allows using existing middleware and infrastructures. User Management in Vine can be fully integrated with the portal container and the underlying libraries may use different standards for different purposes. For example, Hibernate [25] may be used for database management, or the Java Database Connectivity (JDBC) API [26], an industry standard for database-independent connectivity, may be used.

As mentioned above, the Vine Toolkit was tested on a number of small testbeds deployed at the Poznan Supercomputing and Networking Center (PSNC) running different configurations, including:

- Fury.man.poznan.pl: Fedora 3, Globus Toolkit 4.0.1
- Seagrass.man.poznan.pl: Gentoo, UNICORE 6
- Omiidemo.man.poznan.pl: Gentoo, Globus Toolkit 4.0.4
- Node2.qoscosgrid.man.poznan.pl: Gentoo, OpenDSP
- Desktop / notebook computers running Windows XP, Mac OS, or different versions of Linux.

5.   Developments

In order to support seamless integration with application containers, Vine offers several entry points for introducing security. This section focuses on a wide range of security needs of a typical Web portal application, which are addressed by the Vine Toolkit. However, most of the topics discussed here can apply to other application environments.

The high-level logic of the Vine Toolkit in terms of security related operations is presented in Figure 1. In reality, quite complex business-logic patterns and related components were implemented in order to support this logic.

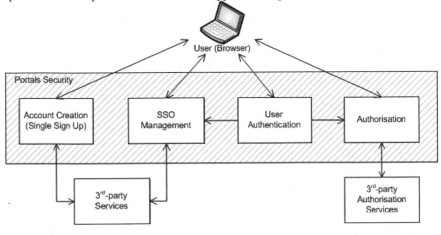

Figure 1: High-Level Architecture of Security in Vine

In brief, Vine offers a number of interfaces covering a Grid portal's security needs, serving at user registration and authentication. It allows automatic creation of user accounts and registration in a number of chosen middleware and services during sign-up or after account approval, simplifying the process of generating credentials and registering them with Grid middleware, or creating accounts on remote systems. It further enables Single Sign-On (SSO), allowing the usage of integrated third party security services in a common way. The mechanism behind this is Security contexts.

Security contexts are Vine services that provide capabilities to other Vine services for handling particular types of security problems, making it easy to add support for third party security libraries and services in a common way. Security contexts include a number of middleware-specific registration and authentication modules. The Grid Vine project provides a General Security Services (GSS) [17] security context for obtaining access to GSS credentials delegated to a Vine application for a particular user. The latest version of Vine incorporates a number of GSS and non-GSS registration and authentication modules supporting, among others, Globus Toolkit 4, UNICORE 6 and VOMS [18] (gLite 3).

Whenever a user accesses resources within a portal, such as a fragment of html or a portlet, or external resources via the portal, such as a file or remote information service, typically some mechanism is required to check whether that user is authorised to access that resource and what level of access they have been granted. Vine does not currently handle authorisation mechanisms explicitly but rather leaves it up to the application programmer to address how authorisation is performed. This is because at times authorisation to portal resources can be performed by the web application server or portal container application to which a Vine application has been deployed. Likewise, authorisation to external resources is often performed by the third party services a Vine application utilises to make those resources available to users.

5.1 User Registration and Single Sign-Up

The moment a portal user first obtains a user account comprises also the appropriate time for the registration of that user with any third party services configured for use with a given

Vine application. Registration with third party services may involve a complex set of procedures and/or human intervention by a portal administrator. The Vine Toolkit provides complete mechanisms for handing user registration, promoting the innovative concept of Single Sign-Up.

An account represents permission by a person to use a Vine application. We call this person a "user" of the application. In order to use a Vine application (i.e. a Vine Grid portal in the context of this paper) a user must first request an account. An account is created when an account request is approved by an account manager module. An account manager is responsible for handling account requests and managing the accounts that result from the approval of account requests. Account manager modules can be configured to automatically accept account requests submitted to them or require manual acceptance.

Account requests have three basic attributes: a unique username, a private password, and a unique and valid email address. An account has an additional attribute, a unique identifier used internally by Vine. Both account request and account may have more attributes depending on the application. As also explained below, an account can have zero or more registrations associated with it. The registrations associated with an account depend on how a Vine application's resource registry is configured and which registration requests have been approved for that account. Once an account request is accepted, an account manager module will process each registration request associated with that account request.

A registration generally represents permission to use one or more third party services configured for use with a Vine application, such as a Grid middleware platform in order to support access to remote computational resources. Their attributes depend on the registration module to which the request is submitted. A registration module is responsible for managing registration requests and the registrations that result by the approval of requests. Registration modules can be configured to automatically accept registration requests submitted to them or require manual acceptance. Registration requests can be submitted to a registration module directly or by an account manager for a given account request. If the registration request has been approved, then a registration is created and managed by the particular registration module.

In case the registration request is part of an account request, then a registration will only be created if the associated account request has been also approved. If a registration's parent account request is denied or fails any time during its processing, then a registration will not be created even if its associated registration request was approved. Instead, that registration request will be rolled back. In the same manner, an account will only be created if all the corresponding registration requests have been approved.

Accounts and registrations have two basic states, active or inactive, permitting or preventing a user from using a Vine application or a service respectively, and their lifetime is configurable. A registration module will notify its parent account manager whenever the status of a registration request changes. Account and registration requests both have a well defined lifecycle, as illustrated in Figure 2.

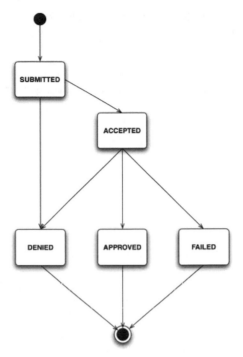

Figure 2: Account Request and Registration Request Lifecycle

5.2   User Authentication and Single Sign-On

When a portal user logs in to a portal, Vine authenticates that user with the third party services configured for use with a given Vine application. Typically, a username and password are supplied at login time. This information can be passed to third party services to which the user has been registered in order to obtain access to resources for as long the user is logged in to the portal. The Vine Toolkit provides authentication modules for handing user authentication issues and enabling single sing-on. Authentication modules, also mentioned above, are Vine services invoked to authenticate a user attempting to create a Vine session. All activity in a Vine application is handled in one or more sessions. Sessions are used to create service contexts.

Authentication to third party services usually results in some credential or security token that is granted to a Vine application to enable Vine to access resources via one or more third party services that accept the given security token. Vine has an extensible mechanism to make these security tokens available to application programmers, as explained above.

5.3   User Management

The User Management in Vine provides the ability for managing accounts of portal users and user-groups and their access to content or resources. This also includes the need for users to manage their own personal information and view information of other users, if authorised. In addition, the portal administrator can manage a user-group and change their access rights to content / resources, resulting in consequent changes to the environment presented to the user and/or the users permissions. This includes changing the list of portlets displayed to a specific user-group, for example a standard user or a first time logged in user, and arranging their layout. As a result of this, the user can only see and navigate the portlets chosen by the administrator. Portlets requiring administrative access rights cannot be presented to a user who does not hold the required privileges.

The high-level logic of the Vine Toolkit in terms of user management related operations is presented in Figure 3. Vine provides the ability to plug into the user account management mechanisms of its container environment, as well as to manage user accounts in standalone applications and services.

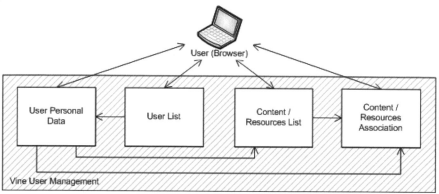

Figure 3: High-Level Architecture of User Management in Vine

In specific, the User Personal Data operation allows users to view and change personal information, like first and last name or email address. The Users List operation, carried out by an account manager in the implementation of Vine, allows users or administrators to view or manage (e.g. add, delete) accounts of portal users. The Content/Resources Association operation covers the need for administrators changing the association between user accounts and Content or Resources. For example, the administrator can choose which components will be available to users and what their portal page will look like, according to their user group. Finally, the Content/Resources List operation serves at presenting the available portal resources users could possibly be assigned.

The reader should keep in mind the individual functionality provided by User Management, as well as the other aforementioned components, is important for achieving high levels of security, and simplicity in usage.

6.   Results

The work committed on the Vine Toolkit was accompanied by a number of sample portlets representing the basic characteristics of the implemented business-logic. The figures below present screenshots of the developed portlets deployed in the GridSphere [19] portlet container.

Before a person can use the Grid portal, he/she will need to get an account on it. A guest user has to navigate to the homepage of the Grid portal and use the Signup portlet to request a new portal account (Figure 4). By following the steps presented, the guest fills in the required fields with his/her details, chooses an account type and submits an account request.

Figure 4: Signup Portlet – New User Account Request

Figure 5: Login Portlet – Login to Domain BEinGRID

When an account request is successfully approved by the administrator, the corresponding account is created and the requester is considered a registered user. Registered users are able to login to the portal by providing their chosen username and password in the Login portlet (Figure 5).

The portal administrator can use the "Requests" tab of the Account Manager portlet (Figure 6) to browse a list of registration requests, undertake the new user's registrations with external middleware or services and finally approve the new user account. In the "Accounts" tab of the Account Manager portlet, the administrator can view and modify existing user accounts.

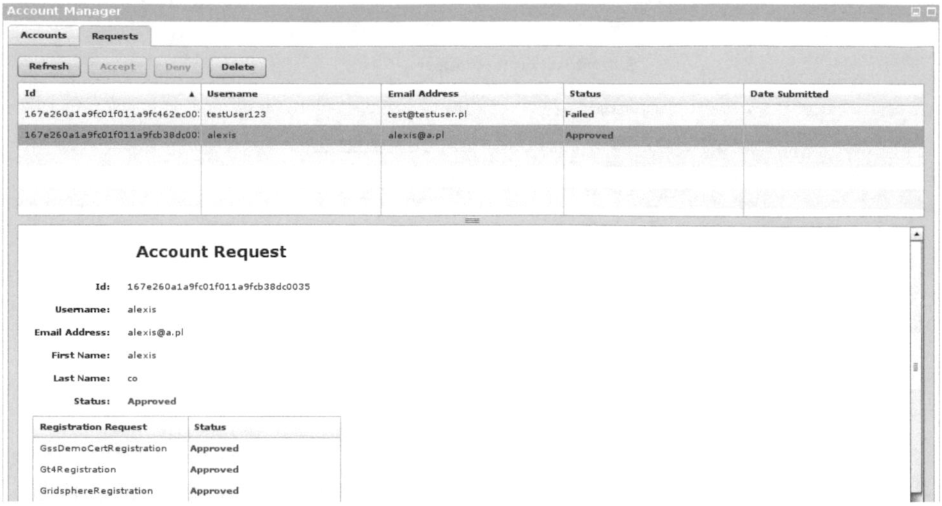

Figure 6: Account Manager Portlet – Account Requests List

In the Credential Manager portlet (Figure 7), a user can view and manage his/her credentials. When viewing a credential, the following details are presented: credential's label, Distinguish Name of the credential owner, status of the credential (active/inactive), remaining lifetime, creation date and date of last retrieval, corresponding MyProxy username for the credential, credential name in MyProxy, and value of lifetime when the credential was retrieved. The user can also check which credential ("Default Credential") was automatically retrieved from MyProxy during the login phase. In the case when no appropriate credential exists and can be loaded, the user can use the "New credential" command to specify a credential to be retrieved from MyProxy to the portal.

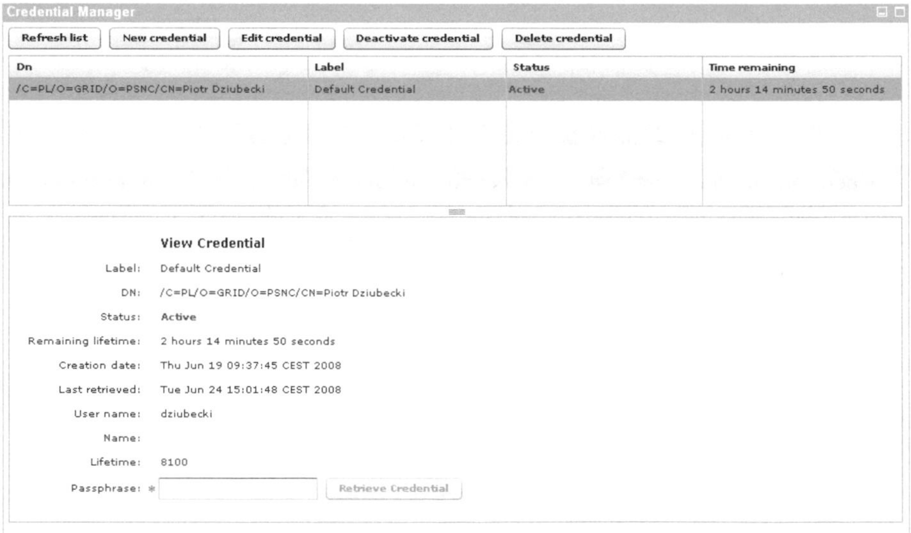

Figure 7: Credential Manager Portlet – View Credential Details

7. Business Benefits

Taking into account current market trends for support of collaborative environments as well as connecting and enabling communication among different businesses, collaboration, connectivity, communication [20] and synchronization of processes comprise decisive factors for business success. A variety of roles with different levels of authorization and varying Quality of Service (QoS) requirements, related among others to security, reliability and performance, must be served by Grid portals.

Grid portals comprise a solution for the rather limited usability of the Grid infrastructure for end users, by offering a user-friendly and much less complicated environment for them to transparently access and manage services and resources aggregated from different, distributed and heterogeneous sources. Moreover, given the customizability potential, based on different end user roles, Grid portals can provide personalized views of information, this way constituting a *significant enhancement* of the Grid business aspect.

Offering Web-based access and management of resources and service capabilities, however, poses strong security requirements. The threats are numerous; an attacker may gain access and manage the resources and the services for running their own jobs on the Grid, obtain information about registered users or retrieve the results of executed jobs, among others. [21] In a business environment, the security requirements become even stronger. Important business data may be exposed, and customers/enterprises may be charged for services they never used or face Denial of Service (DoS), all resulting to possible financial and other important malign problems to their business. An example could be taken from a strongly collaborative environment such as the supply chain, in a case where the system does not allow for customers to submit their orders or for suppliers to view the submitted orders and process them, or when orders and customer information are exposed to the supplier's competitors. The impact of such problems could range from delays in order processing, affecting the speed of the processes in the whole supply chain (distributors, manufacturers and customers) and resulting in a delayed order cycle, to the loss of customers.

Depending on the requirements of the businesses involved, related to data confidentiality, reliability and access control, a "successful" security attack may cause significant costs and have great impact on the reputation of the service providers. Thus, security comprises an important aspect of Grid portals. Data transformation and certificate establishment as well as user authentication, authorization and management work towards this direction. However, depending on the business-related security levels and the scale of the system, the above mentioned processes may be time-consuming and rather complicated for setting up as well as for maintenance. The proposed integration of these security mechanisms with Grid Web portals and the resulting abstraction of the users from the security mechanisms - reducing thus the complexity of the processes and the effort required to perform them - comprise an important improvement towards the business adoption of the Grid. Security and user management can this way be performed in a more cost-effective way and allow for IT staff to focus more on how to plug Grid into their business rather than wonder how to plug Grid into their technology.

Especially in the case of small local businesses that lack the capital to own resources (computational, informational, applications, etc), they can remain profitable and maintain or improve their market share by taking the step to bring Grid into their businesses and accessing resources through a secure portal solution. This way, local economies can remain viable.

By offering automatic creation of user accounts and registration in a number of chosen middleware and services during sign-up or after account approval, the Vine Toolkit enables a simplified process of generating credentials and registering them with Grid middleware, or creating accounts on remote systems through the user-friendly user setup and administration interfaces presented. In fact, our major marketing strategy comprises in demonstrating to Small and Medium-sized Enterprises (SMEs) this simplified process and the success stories produced after its application in real-world businesses within the BEinGRID project.

8.   Conclusions and Future Work

In this paper we demonstrated the Web-based Single Sign-Up and Single Sign-On with the Vine Toolkit, which can be used in several Grid platforms employed by BEinGRID partners or other businesses today. We showed how User Registration, User Authorization and User Management are implemented seamlessly in one package designed to fulfill the real needs of secure and easy Web-access to Grid resources in business environments. The cooperation of the aforementioned mechanisms allows Vine applications to enable a true Single Sign-On capability.

The work in the Vine Toolkit was focused on giving the end user a useful tool that would allow reusing existing middleware and infrastructures. Additional effort was put into building an automated mechanism for user account creation in existing systems and various middleware. Globus Toolkit 4, UNICORE 6 and gLite 3 security is supported, amongst others. Vine was implemented having in mind how to improve business operations and provide business users with an easy to use environment through a Web portal. These characteristics make Vine ideal for use by businesses that wish to "Gridify" their existing infrastructure and processes, in order to remain competitive and exploit the benefits of Grid, as discussed above.

We would further like to point out that the presented software is open source (the Apache License 2.0 applies). Also, although this paper focused on security and user management, additional functionality is packaged in Vine. It supports the submission, monitoring and control of computational jobs in different Grid platforms, as well as the management of file repositories of different types. It thus comprises a fully integrated solution that can be used when building a Web Grid portal.

Although the Vine Toolkit is now in a mature state and available for usage through the Gridipedia [27] Web site, development is still on-going. The users' feedback will lead to the further improvement of some detailed aspects of its functionality, and to fixing any discovered problems. Future work also includes, but is not limited to, testing and evaluating Vine in a new business case within BEinGRID. This business case is mainly concerned with complex computing workflows in Grid enabled enterprise B2B processes, focusing in the aerospace and defense sector and using Web 2.0 technologies. In the context of this work, we also expect to further evolve the functionality provided by all the components of the Vine Toolkit, as well as improve the presentation layer by the adoption of new UI technologies. Furthermore, we aim to the implementation of support for additional middleware and third party services, such as GRIA [22].

References

[1] I. Foster, "What is the Grid? A Three Point Checklist". GRIDToday July 20, 2002.
[2] Russell M., Dziubecki P., Grabowski P., Krysinski M., Kuczynski T., Szjenfeld D., Tarnawczyk D., Wolniewicz G., Nabrzyski J., "The Vine Toolkit: A Java framework for developing Grid applications", Proceedings of the Seventh International Conference on Parallel Processing and Applied Mathematics (PPAM'07), 2007.
[3] BEinGRID Project: http://www.beingrid.eu
[4] Paul Miller, "Web 2.0: Building the New Library", http://www.ariadne.ac.uk/issue45/miller/
[5] Servlet 2.3 API: http://jcp.org/en/jsr/detail?id=53
[6] Java Portlet 1.0 API: http://jcp.org/aboutJava/communityprocess/_nal/jsr168/

[7] OMII-Europe Project: http://www.omii-europe.org

[8] PSNC: http://www.man.poznan.pl/

[9] E. Laure, S. M. Fisher, A. Frohner, C. Grandi, P. Kunszt, A. Krenek, O. Mulmo, F. Pacini, F. Prelz, J. White, M. Barroso, P. Buncic, F. Hemmer, A. Di Meglio, A. Edlund, "Programming the Grid with gLite", Computational Methods In Science And Technology , 2006

[10] I. Foster, "Globus Toolkit Version 4: Software for Service-Oriented Systems", Proceedings of IFIP International Conference on Network and Parallel Computing, 2006.

[11] Job Submission Description Language (JSDL) Specification, Version 1.0: http://www.ogf.org/documents/GFD.56.pdf, Global Grid Forum, Lemont, Illinois, U.S.A., GFD.56, November 2005

[12] Mario Antonioletti, et al., "The design and implementation of Grid database services in OGSA-DAI Concurrency and Computation: Practice and Experience" Volume 17, Issue 2-4

[13] Dietmar W. Erwin, David F. Snelling, "UNICORE: A Grid Computing Environment" Proceedings of Parallel Processing: 7th International Euro-Par Conference Manchester, 2001

[14] Arcot Rajasekar, et al., "Storage Resource Broker-Managing Distributed Data in a Grid Computer", Society of India Journal, Special Issue on SAN, 2003

[15] Google Web Toolkit: http://code.google.com/webtoolkit/

[16] Adobe Flex: http://www.adobe.com/products/ex/

[17] GSS-API: http://www.ietf.org/rfc/rfc2853.txt

[18] R. Alfieri et al., "From gridmap-file to VOMS: managing authorization in a Grid environment", Future Generation computer Systems, Volume 21, Issue 4, April 2005

[19] J Novotny, M Russell, O Wehrens, "GridSphere: a portal framework for building collaborations, Concurrency and Computation", Practice and Experience, Volume 16, Issue 5

[20] Vassiliadis B., Giotopoulos K., Votis K., Sioutas S., Bogonikolos N., Likothanassis S., "Application Service Provision through the Grid: Business models and Architectures", Proceedings of the International Conference on Information Technology: Coding and Computing (ITCC'04), 2004.

[21] Wang, X. D, Yang, X., Allan, R., "Top Ten Questions To Design A Successful Grid Portal", Proceedings of the Second International Conference on Semantics, Knowledge, and Grid (SKG'06), 2006.

[22] Surridge, M. Taylor, S. De Roure, D. Zaluska, E., "Experiences with GRIA Industrial Applications on a Web Services Grid", Proceedings of the First International Conference on e-Science and Grid Computing, 2005

[23] MyProxy Credential Management Service: http://grid.ncsa.uiuc.edu/myproxy/

[24] RFC3820, S. Tuecke, V. Welch, D. Engert, L. Pearlman, and M. Thompson, "Internet X.509 Public Key Infrastructure (PKI) Proxy Certificate Profile," IETF RFC 3820, June 2004 http://www.ietf.org/rfc/rfc3820.txt

[25] Hibernate: http://www.hibernate.org/

[26] Java Database Connectivity (JDBC) API: http://java.sun.com/javase/technologies/database/

[27] Gridipedia: http://www.gridipedia.eu

Collaboration and the Knowledge Economy: Issues, Applications, Case Studies
P. Cunningham and M. Cunningham (Eds.)
IOS Press, 2008

Anonymous, Liberal, and User-Centric Electronic Identity – A New, Systematic Design of eID Infrastructure

Libor NEUMANN
ANECT a.s., Antala Staška 2027/79, Prague 4, 140 00, Czech Republic
Tel: +420 271 100 100, Fax: + 420 271 100 101, Email: Libor.Neumann@anect.com

Abstract: A systematic design of a new eID infrastructure has been carried out and partially verified. The decision to start the design from scratch was based on a critical analysis of the current and known eID infrastructures and tools, their limits, and comparison with current needs and the real world environment. The design is based on ideas of anonymous eID, liberality, and user-centric solution. New ideas improving security and privacy protection together with private data management are used. Also included into the eID design are modern infrastructure features like security management, ICT lifecycle support, and openness to future improvements. The design and verification processes are briefly described together with the results achieved.

1. Introduction

An analysis of current eID architectures [1] shows that none of these fulfils all current needs of eID infrastructure stakeholders (i.e. customers and service providers). The systems were not designed to be used in worldwide public networks with billions of users and millions of service providers. None of the existing eID solutions is a truly up-to-date eID infrastructure supporting seamless and secure personified communication with all the needed features. A new eID design is needed that reflects current reality.

This paper describes an attempt to carry out and verify a new and systematic design of eID infrastructure. As the paper limits do not allow to describe and discuss all interesting and important questions in detail, only a briefly description is given

2. Objectives

The current eID solutions seem to have been built from the bottom up. They are designed to use specific technologies for eID solutions rather than to be based in a systematic top-down design of the eID infrastructure. Solutions for many important systematic issues are frequently missing or insufficiently supported. For instance, they tend to:

- Overestimate or ignore the skills of a regular user,
- Confuse physical identity with the need to distinguish between different remote users of electronic services,
- Use one technology or a single technology principle,
- Underestimate the need for eID infrastructure management,
- Not support the innovation cycle and future technology, and
- Give insufficient attention to protecting private data.

Based on a systematic analysis of existing solutions [1] (where the basic design targets reflecting current needs were formulated), an attempt is ongoing to come up with a new design for an up-to-date eID infrastructure. The design starts from scratch, and it is built from the top down in order to address all the various aspects of the solution. The design recognises and reflects the key stakeholders and their needs. The result is the proposed ALUCID® (Anonymous Liberal and User-Centric electronic IDentity).

3. Design Methodology

The design was carried out in a stepwise manner, starting from scratch, and it included relevant analysis and evaluation at each step.

The first steps were theoretically based. A very critical analysis was made that included scrutinizing the known eID architectures' weaknesses and strengths [1]. The historical environments that had existed during these architectures' designs were quite interesting, too, and these were able to explain many of the weaknesses. An analysis was made also of today's real world needs [1]. Six described common needs were used as design targets and basic evaluation criteria.

Also analysed were the limits that today's real world establishes. That analysis examined two different security domains in the current real world: the global cyberspace, with its billions of interconnected computers having continuously growing power, and the local human environment, characterised by very limited human skills and no possibility for its significant improvement. The existence of two domains with opposing security needs and resources was very important in the theoretical design.

The theoretical analyses yielded the first design principle, which is to using a specific personal device (i.e. a specific computer) to interconnect the security domains and separate the high-power, dynamically changing cyberspace from the conservative human environment. Current technology offers easily portable devices with sufficient computing performance that can be produced in the real word. The specific device has been named the "Personal Electronic Identity Gadget" (PEIG®).

The next design steps were focused more on details. A virtual machine design abstraction was used. The specific instruction set was designed to support basic functionality. The function was verified against the idea of very simplified use by the end-user. The organization of the eID environment was simplified as much as possible. All intermediates and all additional activities were deleted and automated by the virtual machines. Such new principles have been used as anonymous identity, symmetrical authentication, limited validity space of identifiers, and one-time identity. The design includes the dynamics of identifiers and secrets as standard features. Every identity has limited validity time and count and can be automatically changed without loss of the identity link.

Private data management – namely e-government supporting features – was part of the more detailed design. The questions had to be resolved of where the private data can be stored, how this data can be shared, and how to protect end-user privacy. New ideas were combined with such well-known principles as storing personal data only in secured information systems managed by skilled service providers, separating authentication from authorisation [2], "introducing PEIG" to the service provider or "remote heritage of PEIG introduction" supported by one-time identity.

The theoretical design was completed by the first description, whereby the main principles were described and include security management, a basic description of the virtual machine instruction set, and communication between virtual machines for all designed functionalities.

Verification by models and prototypes was the last design step. A global solution with limited technical details was verified by Model 1. The verification resulted in an improved virtual machine instruction set and clarification of interfaces, including interfaces between the standard computer and network environments. Model 2, then, was focused upon security algorithms and security management.

Prototype 1 has been designed to verify interoperability with the real ICT environment. The planned next prototypes will be focused upon solving specific technology issues related to such particular implementations as using specific hardware, communication interfaces, or software environments.

4.   Technology Description

a.   Global Systematic Solution

The basic principle of the designed solution is the transfer of all specific knowledge-demanding activities into the infrastructure. Experience from systematic design of other infrastructures has been used, and especially experience from the internet itself. Well-known, high-quality eID technologies and algorithms have been integrated and modified for the distributed seamless use by millions or even billions of mutually communicating systems.

- The infrastructure topology has been simplified. No intermediate subject, such as a certification authority or identity provider, is included. There are only the electronic service provider and the electronic service user.
- A personification of the eID device is not required. The identical eID devices can be produced without including any user-specific information. The eID devices are interchangeable with regard to their production and sale. The eID device creates an identity automatically by its own use in real life.
- No global identity, no global naming, and no naming authority are used. Identifiers are valid only between the user and service provider. The uniqueness of identifiers is solved automatically by the eID means itself, by the eID infrastructure. The only worldwide coordinated identifiers are those of the service provider. They are based on identifiers that are well-known and widely used on the internet, i.e. URI (DNS).
- No personal information is used in the eID infrastructure. Only pseudorandom numbers with temporary validity are carried over the public networks. No relation exists between the user's eID devices and the information carried over the network.
- The solution is not based on a single eID technology. Rather, it supports several authentication technologies simultaneously and is open for future enhancements.
- Full mesh topology is supported by design.

The systematic design is based on a simple abstraction. The eID infrastructure creates and supports a "secure stable link" between the user-owned eID device (the PEIG, or Personal Electronic Identity Gadget) and the item in the user database at the service provider's site. The link created and managed by the eID infrastructure is not dependent on the real identifiers and credentials used in communication over the network. Only the eID device supporting the link has the information connecting the real identifier and credentials with the link (see Figure 1).

The link is created automatically during the first connection to the service provider. The PEIG performs automatically all the activities needed to manage the user's eID. The user needs not to have any specific skills; the only thing he or she needs is to have the PEIG and to activate it.

The design supports a broad and flexible range of security levels. The length of identifiers and credentials can be changed within a wide range, and authentication levels can be selected together with the authentication method used, the algorithm and its parameters. Security management is supported by the eID infrastructure. The service provider is able to set up a minimal security level for its clients, and clients' PEIGs are able to acknowledge the level automatically if it is supported by PEIG implementation. The security level can range from a very basic level (comparable with RF-ID) to a very high level (comparable with PKI used for electronic signature or electronic citizen cards).

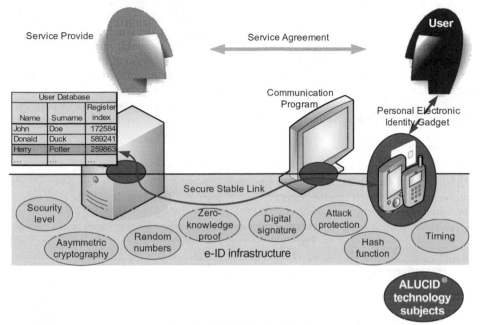

Figure 1: ALUCID Basic Abstraction

The design enables future improvements to the eID infrastructure without synchronisation of the users' and service providers' innovations. It enables changing the technology without severing the secure stable link. The service provider or user can upgrade his or her eID device without losing the link (the personified relation). The link can be transferred or cloned between two PEIGs owned by the same owner without copying of identifiers and credentials. The security level can be changed; the security algorithms used can be changed. New algorithms should be used without the loss of the link in future.

The design includes an integrated protection against network attacks. The protection has especially been improved at the client side of the infrastructure, where lies the weakest part of the current eID solutions. ALUCID uses well-known security systems like firewalls or proxies plus a new idea involving symmetrical authentication.

Open interface is included in the systematic design, as this is a well-proven method of interoperability support [3]. It should support seamless interoperability of different products from different suppliers in one eID infrastructure.

The design enables independent security auditing. The eID products and eID services should be independently verified and the result of verification will be easily accessible and understandable to the users. Together with the selling of empty eID devices without personification, this should simplify the end-user's life and enable selecting the right product on the market without any specific eID training or eID knowledge. Only standard market tools and methods are used.

e-Government specific point of view was described in [4].

b.   eID infrastructure Supplier Point of View

Each supplier can place its own product or service onto the market, and it does not need to produce the entire infrastructure. Suppliers can find their own places position on the market and produce compatible products with specific features for their customers. A supplier can focus on the end-users and produce its own implementations of the PEIG with specific forms and features respecting the interoperability standards and security limits.

A supplier can also focus on the service providers and offer its own implementation of the ALUCID server component that is included or related to a specific ICT environment, such as a specific web server or portal. The supplier can focus on specific applications support, on certain services, or on outsourcing for service providers.

The eID infrastructure supplier should be familiar with all related topics of the eID infrastructure, including interface standards, protocols, security levels, security profiles, supported algorithms and methods, eID creation, updating, access control to identity data, timing, sequencing, and others.

c.   Service Provider Point of View

The service provider's priority is its own service provision. The eID infrastructure can be used in a very simple way from that provider's viewpoint. The service provider buys the product or service from an eID infrastructure supplier and integrates it into its own service implementation.

The eID infrastructure will create and enable security management for the links between the service provider's user database and the users of its service. Identifiers and secrets will be managed automatically by the eID infrastructure with respect of the security parameters set up by the service provider's security manager.

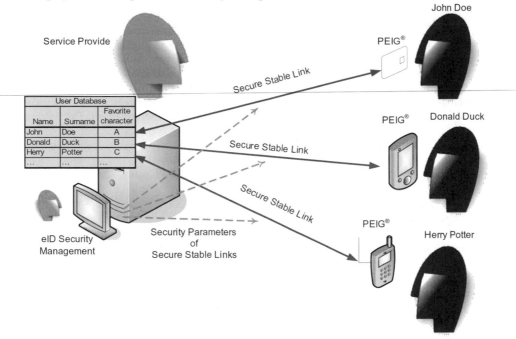

Figure 2: Service Provider Point of View

From a service provider's viewpoint, all its customers are connected through the eID infrastructure directly and independently of other service providers. The service provider is virtually at the centre of all its customers. To the service provider, it looks like virtually no other service provider is connected to the eID infrastructure (see Figure 2).

d. End-User Point of View

The end-user's viewpoint is simple. It is user centric. The user buys one or more PEIGs, as he or she likes. It is his or her free decision. Maybe the form, colour, weight or other parameters are important for him or her. Perhaps the range of security levels supported by the PEIG, the PEIG's activation security, or the certification of the PEIG is important to the user. Then he or she teaches the PEIG to recognise him or her (secure activation of the PEIG), and the PEIG is prepared for use with a variety of service providers.

From the end-user's perspective, he or she is at the centre between all of his or her service providers. The PEIG enables him or her directly to communicate with the personified services. One click suffices to open the service of any of his or her service providers. To the end-user, it looks like virtually no other user is connected to the service providers (see Figure 3). Virtually only his or her personified services are provided by his or her service providers.

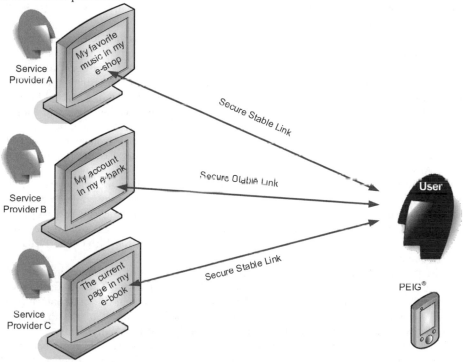

Figure 3: User Point of View

The end-user scenario should be as follows:
1. The user selects a PEIG he or she likes in a shop. It is sold empty. Anybody can buy it.
2. The user teaches his or her PEIG to recognise them when activated. Nobody else knows the activation information. The activation information is not used as any part of the eID.
3. The user connects the first time to the service provider and uses the activated PEIG. The PEIG automatically creates an eID for the user (together with the service provider system's eID means).
4. The user can (but need not) give their personal data to the service provider, and the service provider eID means are able to link this with user eID in a trustworthy manner.

5. The user will be able to open his or her personified service directly if he or she activates his or her PEIG. No login and no authentication process will be seen. It will be done automatically by the PEIG.

6. The same procedure (points 3–5) can be used with any other service provider supporting ALUCID. The number of service providers supported by the PEIG is limited only by the PEIG's internal memory size.

5.   Developments and Results

The ALUCID design has been verified by models and prototypes.

The full range of system functions (e.g. anonymous identity; secure stable link; relation of identity with personal data; fully automatic identity generation; dynamic identity change; sharing of personal data without sharing of eID; one-time identity; data transfers between PEIG, user terminal, and service provider system) was verified in Model 1. The model did not include any real security algorithm. Model 1 was written in Visual Basic for Application [5] in the Microsoft Excel environment.

Model 1 enabled verification of all basic system design ideas and verified the limits of the architecture. The design was then slightly modified with respect of testing.

Security support was implemented in Model 2. The full support of real identities – including random numbers generation, real hash and cryptography algorithms – were used. Model 2 was written in Java [6] using standard Java Cryptography Architecture API [7].

Model 2 enabled verifying security levels, multiple authentication algorithm support, change of security level without loss of identity, use of security profiles, and basic security management. The design was then improved in the area of security management and in the interface description areas as a result of Model 2 development and testing. The first version of the ALUCID interface was then described (using XML/XSD).

Prototype 1 implemented the modified Model 2 in a real web environment. The service provider and the client site were implemented using standard http communication. A standard web browser was used as the user's communication program. The Tomcat [8] was used for implementing the service provider and client sites for ALUCID and for the testing applications. Prototype 1 included the first implementation of the PEIG. The PEIG was implemented in the standard USB flash memory.

The prototype 1 scope has been selected to minimise risks of implementation. The prototype has been implemented as a standard Web Service [9]. The verification was successful. The basic functionality was thereby verified in a real-life environment. The second version of the ALUCID interface was described as a result of the Prototype 1 implementation, and the http communication was slightly modified (simplified).

No significant implementation problem has been met. The objectives described in six eID common needs in [1] were reached at a prototype level. The limited network attack protection and set of e-government support functionality was included in the prototype

New prototypes are being prepared. The implementation of PEIG into mobile (cell) telephone is already prepared. Planned, too, is implementation of the more complex functions like "Identity Link" to support "remote heritage of PEIG introduction" in a real network environment or "Identity Clone" to support migration or copy of the secure stable link between PEIGs of the same user.

6.   Business Benefits

If ALUCID will be successful, it can create an anonymous eID infrastructure where the idea of "A single European information space" [10] can be put into practice. The ordinary user should be able to simply and securely communicate with dozens or even hundreds of his or her personified services. The service providers should be able to manage in a productive and secure way the security of their customers. This could open possibilities for new personified electronic services in many areas. A "virtually private internet" should be created for every end-user. As a consequence, personal data protection could be significantly improved. Personal data could be placed only in secured information systems where the access can be managed. No personal data would be used where no access control could be made, namely in eID systems [4].

7. Conclusions

ALUCID is the outcome of a systematic design of a new eID infrastructure. It aspires to address all existing requirements for an absolute majority of participants in the real environment of today's public networks, and especially the internet.

The solution has been simplified as much as possible to respect real needs and the real skills of the stakeholders.

The design has been verified successfully by the first models and prototype. More advanced testing and verification in pilots is needed to prepare the solution for real-life use.

Many challenges are still ahead, like real standardization of interfaces, deployment strategy, cooperation with market leaders, reaching of critical mass and they should be solved in future. We want to be open and co-operative, we look for partners.

References

[1] Neumann, L. "An Analysis of E-identity Organisational and Technological Solutions within a Single European Information Space", *e-Challenges e-2007*, The Hague, Netherlands, 2007, pp. 1326–1333.

[2] Neumann, L., Sekanina, P. "Distributed Authentication and Authorization in e-Government". *Conference Proceedings, 5th European Conference on E-Government*, University of Antwerp, Belgium, 2005, pp. 597–606.

[3] Neumann, L. "Strategic Options for Pan European E-Government Interoperability", *e-Challenges e-2006*, Barcelona, Spain, 2006, pp. 333–340.

[4] Neumann, L. "Anonymous, Liberal and User-Centric Electronic Identity Supports Citizen Privacy Protection in e-Government". *Conference Proceedings, 8th European Conference on e-Government*, Ecole Polytechnique, Lausanne, Switzerland 10-11 July 2008.

[5] Microsoft, *Visual Basic for Application*, [online], Available: http://msdn2.microsoft.com/cs-cz/isv/bb190538(en-us).aspx [18 April 2008].

[6] Sun   Microsystems,   The   *Java*^{TM} *Tutorials*,   [online],   14   March   2008,   Available: http://java.sun.com/docs/books/tutorial/ [18 April 2008].

[7] Sun Microsystems, *Java*^{TM} *Cryptography Architecture API Specification & Reference*, [online], 25 July 2004, Available: http://java.sun.com/j2se/1.5.0/docs/guide/security/CryptoSpec.html [18 April 2008].

[8] Apache, *Apache Tomcat*, [online], Available: http://tomcat.apache.org/ [18 April 2008].

[9] W3C, *Web Services Architecture*, [online], Available:http://www.w3.org/TR/ws-arch/ [23 Jun 2008].

[10] Commission of the European Communities (2006), *i2010 e-Government Action Plan: Accelerating e-Government in Europe for the Benefits of All*, Communication from the Commission to the Council, the European Parliament, the European Economic and Social Committee and the Committee of Regions, Brussels 25.04.2006, COM(2006) 173 final, pp. 8–9.

Collaboration and the Knowledge Economy: Issues, Applications, Case Studies
P. Cunningham and M. Cunningham (Eds.)
IOS Press, 2008

Common Capabilities for Trust & Security in Service Oriented Infrastructures

David BROSSARD[1], Theo DIMITRAKOS[1], Maurizio COLOMBO[2]

[1]*British Telecommunications plc, Adastral Park, Martlesham Heath, IP5 3RE, UK*
[2]*IIT-CNR, Pisa, Italy*
Contact author. Tel:+44 1473 60614, Email: david.brossard@bt.com

Abstract: Trust and security are of paramount importance to the successful implementation of Service Oriented Infrastructures based on Web Services and Grid technology. Security failures in a networked economy are often the result of exploiting the fuzzy boundaries of independently robust, partial security solutions. In contrast to the current state of the art, that is mainly based of results coming from the efforts of the e-Science community, such as VOMS [4], GSI [14], CAS [14] or GridShib [5], the solutions proposed in this paper are closely related to the needs and requirements of the business world. Following closely the current and future needs of European businesses has been a critical factor in the requirements elicited and the design choices made by the Business Experiments in GRID (BEinGRID) project [1]. The results presented in this paper stem out of Trust & Security activities of the EU FP6 BEinGRID project, and related work contributed by the EU FP7 project GridTrust [4].

1 Introduction

BEinGRID is the largest European research initiative looking into business applications of Service Oriented Infrastructures using SOA Web Services and Grid computing. The BEinGRID initiative has 96 partners including European enterprises of all sizes and is conducting 25 real-world Business Experiments (BE) across most market sectors. Each of these Business Experiments is assessing the relevance of some business solution that takes advantage of Grid computing in a specific market sector.

The BEs are supported by teams of technical consultants and business analysts, with whom they interact closely in order to elicit common requirements; prioritise them in terms of popularity, reusability, innovation potential and business impact; identify common capabilities; and finally validate the reference implementations of these common capabilities on the most relevant Grid and Web Services platforms. BEinGRID is also building a public knowledge repository [2] where case studies, market analyses, technical analyses and software components are going to be provided.

The objective of the paper is to identify the common capabilities of establishing trust and security in service oriented architecture and Grid computing system, so that more applications can be developed based on this platform, more modern services can be provided by service providers and cutting-edge technology can be easily implemented.

The following are some major research challenges identified through the analysis of 25 Business Experiments in several market sectors, conducted by the BEinGRID project:

- *Managing identities and federations in dynamic business collaborations*: How to manage the life-cycle of circles of Trust? How to enhance the structure of a circle of trust? How to coordinate a network of identity brokers in order to support the life-cycle of a Virtual Organisation? How do you contextualise identity issuance, how do you manage virtual identities and claims that are specific vary between virtual communities?

How do you manage revocation of claims in a large-scale distributed system? How do you delegate the authority to issue credentials on one's behalf within given contexts?

- *Security autonomics in large scale, network-centric distributed systems*: How to detect or inform about contextual changes, and how to adapt in response to contextual changes in a large-scale distributed system based on local knowledge? How to interpret and consistently enforce VO-wide policies? How to adapt the way you manage, interpret and security policies in a dynamic environment where resources are shared across multiple, potentially unrelated, administrative domains.

- *Distributed access management in large*-scale decentralised systems: how to manage, reason with and enforce access policies in large-scale, network-centric distributed systems? How to share policy information across administrative domains? How to confirm that obligations are met? How to keep managing the confidentiality of your data and access to your applications once hosted in another's environment?

- *End-to-end security and Governance*: How to achieve end-to-end security of interactions with Grid resources? How to aggregate security services in a Grid? How to securely govern aggregated security services that are distributed over the network?

2 Overview of selected security capabilities

In this section we summarise some of the security capabilities designed and developed by the BEinGRID and other relevant projects such as GridTrust [3] and TrustCoM [4]. These capabilities cover several important functionalities such as offering connectivity to external identity and security attribute providers; supporting the full management life-cycle of federating of trust realms; supporting distributed access control including the delegation of administrative authority in multi-administrative environments; offering real-time monitoring of policy enforcement; supporting real-time policy adaptation in response to events. These security capabilities can be offered as managed security services or as reusable components integrated into a larger security-enabling infrastructure. The following sections offer an overview of these capabilities. For more information please refer to www.gridipedia.eu

2.1 B2B collaboration management

This is a bundle of services that support the full life-cycle of defining, establishing, amending and dissolving collaborations that bring together a circle of trust (federation) of business partners in order to execute some B2B choreography. This capability consists of three distinct services that bundle the functionality as required by the different actors involved in the management of a B2B collaboration infrastructure:

- *Host:* provides common capability inventories, policy registries and notaries. Facilitates sharing the state of the B2B collaboration context.
- *Initiator*: manages the creation of B2B collaboration contexts. It implements a process composing all services required for managing the lifecycle of a B2B collaboration context.
- *Participant*: manages the participation in a B2B collaboration context. It manages the state of the member in each B2B collaboration context and coordinates interactions with the rest of the B2B collaboration management infrastructure.

The lifecycle of the B2B collaboration is divided in four phases:

- *Identification*, which includes the definition of the B2B collaboration and the associated B2B policies and agreements.
- *Formation*, which includes the discovery, invitation and selection of B2B collaboration partners and the initiation of a circle of trust among them.

- *Operation*, which includes initiating the creation of the service instances that are exposed by the B2B collaboration partners, monitoring partner-to-partner interactions and adapting the partner selection or the assignment of resources to the B2B collaboration.
- *Dissolution*, which includes cancelling the B2B collaboration context, the policies and agreements associated with it, and the service instances are destroyed and/or become inaccessible.

Please see [8] in these proceedings for more information on policy-based management of the Virtual Organisation life-cycle. Previous attempts to architect services that capture certain aspects of this functionality include work by BT and SAP Research in the TrustCoM consortium in [4], [9].

2.2   B2B Federation Management services (FMS) and Security Token Services (STS)

The STS acts as an identity broker for each enterprise, and manages the correlation of identities and security attributes within a security domain with commonly understood credentials across domains. It allows:

1) managing a local participant's perspective of a circle of trust, and
2) adapting local authentication mechanism, token scheme, identity token transformation scheme based on contextual information, secure remote management.

The STS pattern originates research by BT and Microsoft (EMIC) in the TrustCoM project [4], [9],[10]. A more elaborate presentation of this capability is also described in [12] and in paper [8] in these proceedings.

2.3   Distributed Access Control (AuthZ Policy Decision Point - PDP)

This capability provides authorisation services that allow the necessary decision making for distributed enforcement of access policies by multiple administrators, ensuring regulatory compliance, accountability and security audits. This is achieved by extending current access control models with (1) validity conditions for each authorisation policy, (2) policy issuance whereby administrators have to digitally sign the policies they produce, and (3) administrative delegation policies that allow a trusted administrator to define who can issue policies about what actions on which subset of the administered resources.

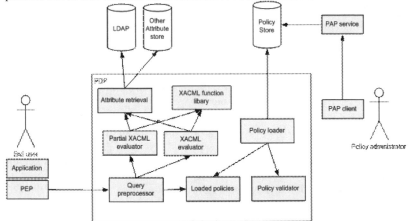

Figure 1: High-level overview of the Policy Decision Point architecture

Key functions include:

- *Policy-based access control*: applicable policies are stored on the system and are analyzed by the PDP. The PDP makes its decision and returns the decision. The policies can all be expressed in standardised access control languages such as XACML 2.0 / 3.0
- *Constrained Administrative Delegation:* the delegation mechanism is used to support decentralized administration of access policies. It allows an authority (delegator) to delegate all or part of its authority to another user (delegate) without any need to involve the central IT-administration. The specific authorization can then be delegated further by the user, in full or constrained to a subset of the original authorization. In this delegation model, the delegation rights are separated from the access rights. These are instead referred to as *administrative control policies* (see the XACML 3.0 draft). These policies can be targeted in the same way as access control policies. Access control and administrative policies work together.
- *Obligation*: when centralizing the security architecture with the XACML model, an obligation is a directive from the PDP to the Policy Enforcement Point (PEP) on what must be carried out before or after an access is granted. If the PEP is unable to comply with the directive, the granted access will not be realized. The augmentation of obligations eliminates the gap between requirements and policy enforcement previously described.
- *Segregation of policy stores*: by means of PDP instantiation and creation of separate stores, it is possible to have instances of the PDP service that each act as a single standalone PDP unaffected by the policies pushed to the other PDP instances. This is particularly important in a virtualized / contextualized environment where different virtual organizations may require their own PDPs.

A more detailed description of this capability is provided in [12]. The design and implementation of capability is based on research by BT, Axiomatics and SICS in the TrustCoM and BEinGRID projects [7], [6], [4], [9].

2.4 Message-based Security Policy Enforcement Engine (PEP)

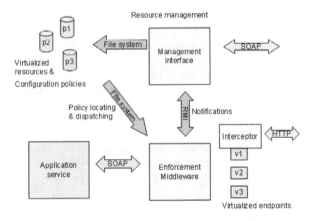

Figure 2: High-level overview of the Policy Enforcement Point architecture

This is a *secure message processing system* that is a fusion of (1) an application service firewall / gateway that protects interactions to XML applications and Web Services, (2) a proxy that intercepts, inspects, authorises and transforms content on outgoing requests to external services, (3) a message bus that enforces content- and context- aware message processing policies and (4) a light-weight core of a service bus that integrates all other SOI security capabilities. The PEP provides message-level security enforcement based on B2B agreement as opposed to the application logic.

The key functions of this capability include:

- *Policy-based message processing:* Processing actions are defined by means of security policy assertions that are executed by message processing engine as well as more complex actions such as remote calls to STS, PDP for token issuance, validation or access control request, etc… The PEP can also perform transformation actions on the content of intercepted or generated messages (including encryption / decryption of elements) as well as content-based routing and message structure or content validation.

- *XML threat protection:* In a more comprehensive variant, the PEP can also handle basic XML threat protection by validation messages against their relevant schemas, checking the format of the request, SOAP operations and their input parameters, and the simple XML threats such as node depth and so on.

- *Context-based security enforcement:* the PEP intercepts a SOAP message, analyzes the SOAP headers (typically the address headers) to locate a suitable enforcement policy which in turn determines which security operations the PEP will enforce.

- *Service contextualization:* the PEP allows exposing an enterprise's internal services externally. This is part of the service virtualization. As a result when incoming messages come in, the PEP not only processes it and applies security, it also routes it to the relevant web service in the back-end.

- *Management:* The PEP management service is based on WSDM (WS-Distributed Management). When a protected application service is virtualized and exposed, a new instance is of a PEP management resource created in order to manage the policies to the protected service. This resource instance can only manage the exposure of the associated protected application service and the corresponding security enforcement policies. This brings a clear separation of concerns regarding the administration of Web service exposures. Furthermore different implementations of PEP can be clustered without affecting the protected service – to – management resource association.

A more detailed presentation of this capability is provided in [12]. See also [15] for an elaboration of an earlier version of this pattern produced within BT's UK research labs.

2.5   Usage Control Service (UCS)

In an environment in which computational services execute unknown applications from different users, the resources must be protected from abuse by the applications through usage monitoring at all levels. At the computational level, such a monitor controls the actions performed by the applications executed on the associated computational service. At service level, it monitors the invocations to services executed on the grid node. At VO level it monitors the invocations to a group of associated services in the VO.

The Usage Control Service (UCS) is a common capability that is typically deployed on the service provider site. It takes as input the VO-level policies, the local resource policies and a user profile and produces the equivalent policy state machines. Based on this input, the UCS service generates policy state machines that are used by the resource-level monitors for policy evaluation.

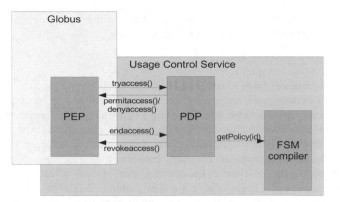

Figure 3: High-level overview of the Usage Control Services deployment architecture

The following components are needed in a UCS implementation:

1. *Policy Enforcement Point (PEP)*: is the component integrated within the middleware platform upon which the UCS is deployed (e.g. the Globus Toolkit). Its main task is the interception of the security relevant actions performed by the execution of the associated security policy; for instance it asks the PDP for a decision and subsequently implements those decisions.

2. *Policy Decision Point (PDP)*: is invoked by the PEP, it evaluates the policy and decides whether the action is allowed. While actions are in progress it interrupts the execution when the right granted to the user has been revoked.

3. *FMS compiler*: takes as input a Global VO policy and a Local policy and produces the appropriate *PDP* policy to be enforced on this Grid Node.

An implementation of this capability is currently being produced by IIT-CNR within the scope of the GridTrust project [3].

2.6   Security Autonomics

<u>*Adaptation Service (ECA)*</u>: implementing novel technology that allows reconfiguring the security services in response to security or QoS events in order to optimise performance and to assure compliance with agreements and enterprise policies. This is achieved by correlating and processing events from managed infrastructure services (e.g. the capabilities above), then applying Event-Condition-Action policies that in turn triggers reconfiguration or other life-cycle management actions on managed infrastructure services under its control. An overview of the pattern for this capability is presented in [12]. It is based on research by BT and Imperial College in TrustCoM [9] and subsequent work [16].

<u>*Security Observer*</u>: implementing an assessment and reporting functionality that observes security changes or violations and generates events that can be in turn be acted upon by other capabilities such as the ones implementing the *Security Autonomics* layer summarised above. The importance of this function stems from the fact that due to the uncertainty and dynamics of Grid infrastructures local security changes may have a global impact (or an impact in certain other localities) but are not necessary observable (or understood) in the localities affected. A publisher-subscriber-based mechanism can be used to disseminate security change events. This can be coupled with a *Complex Event Processing* functionality which will enable the correlation of relevant events in order to achieve a better understanding of their aggregation. Overall the aim of such a system is, on the one hand, to understand the emerging global impact of various local security changes, and on the other hand, to inform those system entities that are interested in such security changes of some type. An initial version of the security observer has been developed by a team at CETIC in

the context of BEinGRID and it is being validated within the scope of BE03 [17], a business experiment on Visualisation and Virtual Reality.

2.7　Virtualisation & life-cycle management

This is a governance layer managing the life-cycle of a secure exposure (aka "virtualisation") of enterprise resources. Service virtualisation is achieved by exposing a service at a given "virtual" endpoint, associating a reference to this endpoint with a profile of a Service Oriented Infrastructure configuration and structure of policy templates for each infrastructure services in the profile. Life-cycle management is achieved by a governance layer that orchestrates the service exposure process, the life-cycle of instances of the infrastructure profile, the life-cycle of the configuration of each infrastructure service in the profile and the life-cycle of each policy for a configuration state of an infrastructure service in the infrastructure profile. Although this component was not part of the initial functionality envisaged for BEinGRID, it arose as a necessary integration and management layer through the contribution of one of the BEinGRID experiments (BE9 – Virtual Hosting Environment for online gaming [13]). Please see [8] in these proceedings for more information on this capability.

3　A Case Study

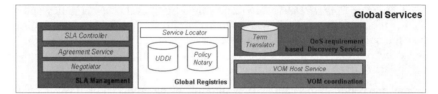

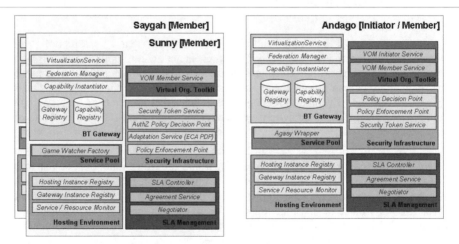

Figure 4: Overview of the VHE infrastructure deployed in [13]

Some of the common capabilities described above have been demonstrated in a Business Experiment of the BEinGRID project [1] within the scope of a Virtual Hosting Environment (VHE) for online gaming [13]. In this scenario a distributed online game application runs over a Virtual Hosting Environment (VHE). The latter is a Service Oriented Infrastructure composed of the following subsystems
(i)　Global services for B2B collaboration management service (VOM),

For each business partner:

(ii) A B2B gateway integrating and governing the following groups of infrastructure services

    (1) VOM participant services

    (2) A Security Infrastructure

    (3) A SLA Management infrastructure

(iii) the hosting environment, and

(iv) a pool of application services, i.e. the online gaming platform, game management services (Game Watcher) and managed game titles.

In a typical scenario, a number of host providers offer hosting resources to the Application Providers for deploying and running their applications, which are then "virtualized" with the use of middleware services for managing non-functional aspects of the application, and are transparently exposed to the end user via a single VHE.

The aim of this business experiment is to improve flexibility, dynamism and performance of the game application exposure and execution. Current gaming platforms, in fact, are very static in nature, with pre-selected dedicated game servers. As such, the platforms experience extreme peaks and lows in demand, due to the period of the day or week, and ongoing gaming activity. This causes very low utilization of dedicated gaming servers, and therefore high cost of initial investment and maintenance.

The approach taken through the use of VHE is to make available infrastructure services for security, community management and virtualisation that can be used by various service providers, allowing them to link with each other. This is achieved via a generic "B2B gateway" component (see Figure 4).

In this scenario, the game application provider deploys its gaming application onto two different execution environments (gaming servers), owned by different host providers. The game platform provider, who wants to offer the game to an end user, discovers gaming servers and creates business relationships with them, and also with a separate service provider who offers a system for community management (of gaming clans, tournaments, advanced statistics). Through use of the VHE, these various services are offered transparently to an end user, including the game platform provider's ability to perform the load balancing and server selection based on the defined SLAs

The VHE developed in this business experiment consists of a network of B2B service gateways integrated with common capabilities for B2B trust federation, identity management, access control, SLA management, accounting and monitoring, as well as application service and resource virtualisation. The B2B gateway functionality is complemented by a federated messaging bus and community management services that facilitate the establishment of B2B collaborations

4   Conclusions and related work

Security is a key challenge because Grid adopters must trust the global infrastructure and this cannot be achieved without proper security by design. This is especially difficult because of intrinsic characteristics of the Grid such as openness, heterogeneity, geographical distribution and dynamicity. Consequently, Grid security has been and is currently being investigated by a number of research groups and projects such as AssessGrid (risk-based approach), GridTrust (design of next-generation security framework), BEinGRID (integrated project involving 25 real-word industrial deployment of Grid Technology), and XtreemOS (Linux-based Operating System to Support Virtual Organizations). Each project is looking at establishing robust security patterns and leveraging existing middleware architecture and software to provide trust, security and privacy. BEinGRID is different from the other related initiatives in that it coordinates a large number of business experiments across various critical market sectors. These drive the elicitation and prioritisation of common requirements, the identification of common capabilities and the validation of reference implementations of these common capabilities on the most relevant Grid and Web Services platforms. The trust and security capabilities presented in this paper have resulted from such a process within the BEinGRID project [11],[12], augmented with selected results from associated targeted research projects such as GridTrust [3]. It is the intention of the authors to make the implementations of the common capabilities described in this paper available through the Gridipedia repository [2].

The trust and security capabilities presented in this paper take the form of a managed (and potentially) network-hosted service that enables an enterprise to achieve the following benefits:

- To virtualize its applications, employee accounts, computing / information resources; this can be achieved by plugging the governance layer into the VO Cluster's application virtualization component
- To govern such virtualised entities, including defining trust relationships enacted by the STS, security and access policies, identity schemes, etc, and to enforce them.
- To adapt the observable behaviour of virtualized entities and the use of infrastructure services in response to contextual changes. Examples include updating the security, privilege provisioning, or access control policy in response to changes of business process activity, changes of membership in a B2B collaboration, etc.
- To securely expose such assets to an open network through the PEP, with the option to apply different security policies in different collaboration contexts while, ensuring process and information separation between services transacting in different collaborations.
- To maintain the management of its participation in B2B collaborations. This includes managing the life-cycle of its participation in B2B collaborations and contributing to the joint management of the B2B collaboration with the other participants.

Through the study, we learnt the following lessons:

Lesson 1 – Security needs to be designed in the Business Experiments: security is a non-functional requirement and as such is often forgotten. So we have to emphasise that security solution and architecture needs to be well-designed and implemented in order to make full use of grid technology.

Lesson 2 – interoperability is essential since several specifications & different implementations are used in the distributed systems communications. For example, some BE has a mixture of Java, .Net, a wide range of web services specifications, and certificates usage. In particular when it comes to web services, because Java and .NET have separate implementations for – say WS-Trust, or WSRF, it was important to thoroughly test and address these issues before final integration stage.

Lesson 3 – Compatibility: the trust and security common capability (PEP-PDP-STS) need to be developed as a modular with a pluggable, extensible architecture to accommodate new security components operating with different standards.

The Best Practices can be summarised as follows from our research:

Best Practice 1 – Use software as a service – the SaaS pattern: Business experiments should pick up the solid security solution from a panel of ready-made components and use them directly in their architecture. In order to do so, security component needs to be developed and easily adopted as a service by an SOA-oriented architecture or a Grid-based architecture.

Best Practice 2 – Make full use of existing security components.

Best Practice 3 – Decouple business logic from security: this avoids poor security patterns, technology lock-ins, incompatibilities, and non-extensible systems. Security should be seen as an add-on layer that can be configured and executed independently of the business logic. With new web service frameworks for instance, such as WSE or WCF, the security configuration has been offloaded to an external layer.

Best Practice 4 – Plan for an extensible architecture: A business experiment's world might grow and new components might be brought in. It is necessary to introduce extensibility by leveraging grid technology to develop pluggable exchangeable components.

Best Practice 5 – Interoperability & impact: When adopting security solutions, business experiments should spend more to consider interoperability issues. Also, as a general rule, the introduction of the additional security layer or components should not downgrade the system performance too much.

Acknowledgments

The paper is the result of work from several FP6 and FP7 European projects including TrustCoM, BEinGRID, and GridTrust. In addition, several components from FP5 European project GRASP were used in the demonstration mentioned in section 3.

References

[1] BEinGRID project site: www.beingrid.eu
[2] Gridiptedia repository site: www.gridipedia.eu
[3] GridTrust project site: www.gridtrust.eu
[4] TrustCoM project site: www.eu-trustcom.com
[5] Seitz L., et al (2007): A Classification of Delegation Schemes for Attribute Authority. In Dimitrakos et al. Formal Aspects in Security and Trust 2006, LNCS, Springer.
[6] J. Alqatawna, E. Rissanen, B. Sadighi. Overriding of Access Control in XACML. POLICY 2007. 87-95
[7] Seitz L., et al (2007): A Classification of Delegation Schemes for Attribute Authority. In Dimitrakos et al. Formal Aspects in Security and Trust 2006, LNCS, Springer.
[8] Angelo Gaeta, F. Orciuoli, N. Capuano, D. Brossard, T. Dimitrakos. A Service Oriented Architecture to support the federation lifecycle management in a secure B2B environment. In proceedings of e2008.
[9] Dimitrakos, Theo. TrustCoM Scientific and Technological Roadmap. Restricted TrustCoM deliverable available upon request. Contact: theo.dimitrakos@bt.com
[10] Christian Geuer-Pollmann. "How to Make a Federation Manageable". In Proc. of "Communications and Multimedia Security" 9th IFIP TC-6 TC-11 International Conference, CMS 2005.
[11] Theo Dimitrakos, et al. "Common Technical Requirements for Grids and Service Oriented Infrastructures". BEinGRID report. Restricted – ontact theo.dimitrakos@bt.com
[12] Dimitrakos, Theo, et al. "Common Capabilities and Design Patterns for Grids and Service Oriented Infrastructures". BEinGRID report. Restricted – please contact theo.dimitrakos@bt.com
[13] BEinGRID Business Experiment 9: http://www.beingrid.eu/index.php?id=be9
[14] GSI: Globus Security Infrastructure. See http://www.globus.org/toolkit/docs/4.0/security/
[15] Andreas Maierhofer, Theodosis Dimitrakos, Leonid Titkov, David Brossard: Extendable and Adaptive Message-Level Security Enforcement Framework. ICNS 2006: 72
[16] K. P. Twidle, E. Lupu: Ponder2 - Policy-Based Self Managed Cells. AIMS 2007: 230
[17] BEinGRID Business Experiment 3: http://www.beingrid.eu/index.php?id=be3

Section 11.3

Case Studies

Collaboration and the Knowledge Economy: Issues, Applications, Case Studies
P. Cunningham and M. Cunningham (Eds.)
IOS Press, 2008

A Secure Environment for Grid-Based Supply Chains

Lorenzo BLASI[1], Alvaro ARENAS[2], Benjamin AZIZ[2], Paolo MORI[3], Umberto ROVATI[1],
Bruno CRISPO[4], Fabio MARTINELLI[3], Philippe MASSONET[5]

[1]Hewlett-Packard Italiana S.r.l., Via G. di Vittorio 9, Cernusco sul Naviglio, 20063, Italy
Tel: +39 02 92121, Email: lorenzo.blasi@hp.com; umberto.rovati@hp.com
[2] e-Science Centre, STFC Rutherford Appleton Laboratory, Didcot, OX11 0QX, UK
Tel: +44 1235 778840, Email: A.E.Arenas@rl.ac.uk, B.Aziz@rl.ac.uk
[3]Istituto Informatica e Telematica CNR, via Moruzzi 1, Pisa, 56124, Italy
Tel: +39 050 3152069, Fax: +39 050 3152593,
Email: paolo.mori@iit.cnr.it, fabio.martinelli@iit.cnr.it
[4]Vrije Universiteit Amsterdam, De Boelelaan 1081a, Amsterdam, 1081HV, The Netherlands
Tel: +31 20 5987829, Fax: + 31 20 5987653, Email: crispo@cs.vu.nl
[5]CETIC, Rue des Frères Wright, 29/3, B-6041 Charleroi, Belgium
Tel: +32 71 490 744, Email: phm@cetic.be

Abstract: This paper introduces a transportation supply chain which exploits Grid services for optimizing both the delivery and cost of each customer order. The proposed case study focuses on an auction-based model to select transporters for given transportation tasks in a generic supply chain. Each transporter uses a Grid based computing service to re-optimize the routes of its vehicles after the addition of each new transportation task. The main objective of this paper is to describe a secure environment for the transportation supply chain by identifying its security issues and developing security components that help to solve these issues. These components are currently under implementation in the EU GridTrust project.

1. Introduction

Logistics is a service that moves its customer's products from one place to another. Big transporter companies may be chosen for their brand, but at the end what makes the difference is the quality and price of the service; thus competition in the transport sector is driven by the two main factors of delivery time and price.

A characteristic of current logistic systems is that only a few big players make use of global optimization techniques. Improving transporters fleets' utilization is an environment-friendly activity because it lowers the number of circulating trucks, but small transporters rarely apply operating-research techniques, as usually they don't have enough customers at the same time.

But how can a small transporter improve its operations to compete with big players? How can a transporter find enough transportation tasks to improve its own fleet utilization? And how can a customer find the best transporter for each given transportation task?

The proposed case study tries to answer the questions above with a solution based on two main ideas. The first is to use an auctioning system that exploits competition between transporters and allows customers to find the best provider for each task. The second idea is to have route computing services, i.e. computational services that provide maps and libraries to execute applications solving the logistic optimization problem, to allow even small (SME) transporters to optimize their routing. Both the auctioning system and the routing computing service will be hosted on Grid resources. This solution raises several security challenges such as selection of services with compatible security policies or continuous control of the execution of unknown applications, among others.

2.   Objectives

The main objective of this paper is to describe a secure inter-enterprise Grid environment for a business case such as a transportation supply chain. The same secure environment can be widely applied to other scenarios as well, be they Grid- or SOA-based.

This paper identifies some security issues of the case study and introduces security components that help solving them, components such as a service for measuring and keeping track of users' trust level or a service providing continuous control to prevent malicious activities. These and other components described below are currently under implementation in the EU GridTrust project [1].

3.   Methodology

The methodology we adopted in GridTrust follows these lines:
- Perform a security analysis of the scenario to define security requirements for the application using the KAOS goal-oriented requirements-engineering methodology [4], as well as to identify use cases and mis-uses cases.
- Identify and develop architecture components that could contribute to meet the main security challenges identified. These components are described in the next section;
- Evaluate how the architecture helps in solving the security challenges of the case study.

Currently GridTrust is in the implementation phase and the evaluation will be carried out in the next year. Our plan is to have a running version of the GridTrust Security Framework components by September 2008.

4.   Technology and Business Case Description

This section describes the Virtual Organisation (VO) model adopted by the GridTrust project, our supply-chain case study, security issues related to the case study, GridTrust architecture, and its application to the case study.

4.1   A Model of Virtual Organisations

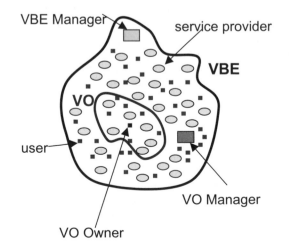

Figure 1: Organisations and Users in a VBE

In order to support rapid formation of VOs, we use the concept of virtual breeding environment (VBE) [3]. A VBE can be defined as an association of organisations adhering to common operating principles and infrastructure with the main objective of participating in potential VOs. We have adopted the view that organisations participating in a VO are selected from a VBE, as illustrated in Figure 1. Such organisations may provide resources/services (ovals), and include users that utilise VO resources (small squares).

4.2   A Grid-Based Supply Chain for Transportation

We have developed a supply chain based on auctions in order to find the best offer for a transportation task. The auctioning system, which runs reverse auctions of type First-Price Sealed-Bid [2], allows producers to propose Requests for Quotation (RfQ) for transportation tasks (such as "move N units of P from A to B"). Each Transporter who wants to make a competitive offer should recalculate its routing with the added transportation task; routing recalculation is performed on Grid resources using the routing computational services. After recalculation each transporter$_i$ can make its offer. Choice of the best offer may be based on price, planned delivery time and transporter's reputation, depending on customer requirements.

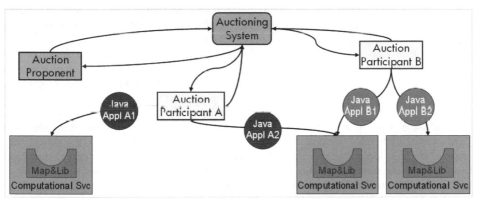

Figure 2 - Full Auctioning Scenario

The components of this business scenario are the following (see Figure 2):
- Auctioning system (a custom Grid service)
- Auction Proponent, it's the Producer application (creates auction, receives result, creates Delivery VO)
- Auction Participant, is the Transporter application (notified of an auction, creates Routing VO, invokes routing calculation, sends an auctioning offer)
- Map&Lib, are Routing support services, (maps, map access library, base routing functionality) made available by the Computational Service provider
- Java Appl, is the Routing application (executed on Computational Service) which may be different for each Auction Participant

The Auction Proponent plays the role of a producer in a supply chain, creating a Delivery VO to manage the whole auctioning and delivering process. Each transporter participating in the auction (i.e. in the Delivery VO) creates its own Routing VO in order to calculate best routes to participate in the auction.

The Grid computational service provider(s) may offer several maps with different levels of accuracy for the underlying distance-time (DT) matrix and libraries implementing different algorithms for solving base routing problems.

In general the transporter already has a certain set of transportation tasks to be performed and already calculated a sequence minimizing the path length for each of its vehicles. Adding the requested transportation task this sequence has to be reoptimized. To perform such a reoptimization, calculating the added cost and thus creating an offer for the new task, the transporter will send to the computational service provider an application exploiting some of the provided maps and libraries.

When either auction time expires or offers are available from all invited bidders, the closing phase starts and the auctioning system selects the winning offer based on the optimization criterion defined at auction creation time.

A future implementation of the system will allow monitoring the whole delivery phase and verifying transporter's compliance with the offered terms of service (considering the offer as a SLA). The reputation index of a transporter is based on a history of its accomplishments; with the current implementation it lowers if the transporter's behaviour is not in line with VO security policies, but using a SLA monitor the reputation can be increased with successful shipments and lowered if the transporter doesn't fully comply with the terms agreed in the SLA.

4.3   Security Issues in a Grid-Based Transportation Supply Chain

The main security issues for the auctioning service are summarized as follows: secure identification of auction participants, secrecy of offers at least until auction closure, data integrity and non-repudiation of both offers and RfQs.

Routing services also raise important security issues, mainly originating from the fact that they execute unknown applications on behalf of potentially unknown or not trusted users. Hence, a security support is required to control that these applications do not perform actions meant to steal valuable data or to gain unauthorized accesses. For example, if a transporter is paying a monthly subscription for using map A, it cannot use map B.

The use of reputation information as one of the parameters for selecting transporters is a fundamental part of the proposed model. Transporters' reputation can be measured with respect to their complying with global and local security policies defined for Grid resources. In the future it will be measured also with respect to the transporters' ability in honouring the agreed SLAs for delivering goods.

4.4   GridTrust Architecture

In this section we describe the main components of the GridTrust Security Framework (GSF) that contribute to meet security challenges identified in the previous section. GSF services are developed at the Grid middleware layer and as Globus has been chosen as reference Grid middleware, they are developed as additional Globus services.

- The **VBE Manager** acts as a service registry, where service providers register their services and other GSF services can retrieve them given abstract service descriptions. Each Virtual Organization (VO) will be created within a specific Virtual Breeding Environment (VBE); a VBE may contain several different VOs.
- The **VO Manager Service (VOM)** coordinates all other security services and is the single point of access for users and service providers participating in the VO. The VO Manager is responsible for handling several functionalities. These include VO creation, populating VOs with services required by VO owners to achieve their goals, updating VO policies, evolving the VO by allowing its member service providers to subcontract part of their services to other service providers and finally, terminating the VO.
- The **Policy and Profile Manager (PPM)** keeps all the knowledge bases needed by GSF services: VBE and VOs users, with security preferences and their trust and

reputation credentials; VOs with their owner and security policies; service providers with their services and security policies regulating access and usage of the services.

- The **Secure Resource Broker (SRB)** is called by VOM with a list of services, needed by the VO Owner to form its VO, and the associated security requirements. It returns the list of providers offering the requested services and also satisfying all the specified security requirements. One of those requirements is the reputation of a service in a VBE.
- The **Trust and Reputation Service (TR)** keeps track of the past and current behavior of VO owners, users and service providers and transforms it into trust and reputation credentials that can be considered by other users, service providers and GSF services when making decisions.
- The **Continuous Usage Control Service (C-UCON)** is an implementation of the UCON policy framework [5], where it is deployed on each service provider and is responsible for the evaluation and runtime enforcement of policies about resource usage in VOs. It also reports feedback to the TR service about users violating these UCON policies.

Each of these services can be invoked only by mean of the API it exports, hiding all the implementation details on how the service is implemented. The framework is flexible so during the project we provide instance implementations for each service, but implementations developed by third parties can easily replace ours. Besides, the framework is modular so it allows the possibility of adding future new security services if needed.

4.5   Applying GridTrust Services in the Transportation Supply Chain

To satisfy the identified security issues a secure Grid environment is needed. When the Producer in the supply chain scenario receives an order from a Customer, it utilizes GSF components to construct a secure Delivery VO whose members are shown in Figure 3.

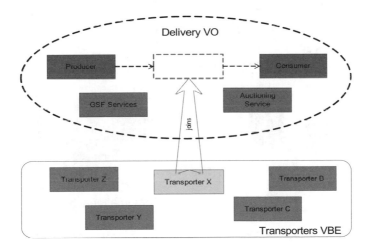

Figure 3: The Delivery VO and its Transporters VBE

This is done over several phases. In the first phase, the producer requests from the VOM service the creation of a Delivery VO. In the next phase, the Producer registers with the PPM service (through the VOM) the list of VO users and their security profiles. Then the Producer requests from the VOM to search for a suitable auctioning service by including the abstract description of the service and of security requirements (e.g.

reputation level). The VOM utilizes the SRB service in its search and once the right candidates are reported back to the Producer, the Producer will inform the VOM of its selection and SRB will negotiate and schedule the selected candidate. The operational phase now commences with the Producer sending to the auctioning service a Request for Quotation (RfQ) for delivering the ordered goods. This triggers each transporter to start a new Route-Calculation VO as shown in Figure 4, which will include Computational Services (CS) needed to compute the route and the bid. The route-calculation services will be derived from a Computational Services VBE. Each transporter chooses the most suitable set of CSs depending on the maps and the libraries offered, and also taking into account the security features, and it will submit its route calculation application to these services. The result returned by the route calculation application executed on the computational services is a new sequence of paths, one for each vehicle, paired with its incremental cost that allows the transporter to define its bid. The winning transporter with the best bid is then reported back to the Producer, which requests from the VOM the addition of that transporter to the delivery VO. The delivery VO is now fully operational.

This flow of events highlights how the GSF components, which build on and complement consolidated Grid security techniques, can satisfy the security issues of the scenario. The SRB service, when receiving from the Producer the security requirements of the auctioning service, is able to select the suitable candidates fulfilling those requirements. Such security requirements may be, for example, that the auctioning service must maintain the integrity of bids and secrecy of offers.

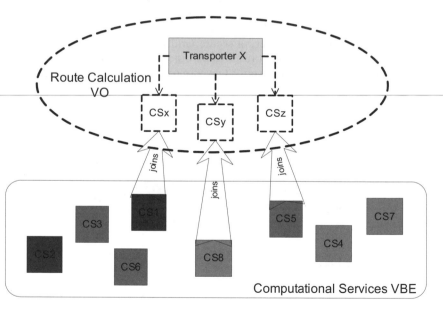

Figure 4: The Route-Calculation VO and its Computational Services VBE

The security of the CSs exploited by the transporters to compute their new paths is addressed by another GSF component, the UCON service. From their point of view, the CSs execute unknown applications on behalf of potentially unknown and untrusted users, and these applications could perform dangerous actions that could harm or damage the services. The UCON service allows to monitor the execution of these applications and to enforce a security policy preventing them from performing dangerous operations. In particular, the policy defines the admitted behaviour of the applications in terms of interactions with the underlying operating system. The CS owner could enforce also policies to regulate the usage of the maps and libraries offered by his service. As an example, the policy could state that the application can, in principle, use any map, but when it accesses one of the maps it cannot access the others anymore. The UCON service can both take into account the user reputation, computed by the TR service, to decide whether to allow a given action of the route calculation application, and can provide feedback to the TR service about the application behaviour to update the user reputation value.

5. Conclusions and Summary Recommendations

We have shown how Grid-based supply chains can be secured by associating them with trust and security management services such as VBE and VO managers, secure-aware resource brokers, reputation services, and usage control services, among others. The solution we have proposed, called the GridTrust Security Framework (GSF), incorporates these services in a manner that is modular, interoperable and security-aware.

Interoperability and Modularity. Since we are re-using an existing Grid infrastructure, which is the Globus middleware, our system components are interoperable with other Globus-based components. This facilitates future development of Globus-based solutions. In fact, the GSF components are modular in that any combination of these can exist in any Globus-based solution.

Security-aware design. The design we propose for the environment of the Grid-based supply chain case study is security-aware in that it tackles current security issues that may arise in any Grid-based system. The security requirements were elicited using a requirements-engineering methodology that has been tailored for Grid systems [4].

There are three main innovations in the GSF. First, in SOAs and Grids have been identified the need for having security into account when selecting services or brokering resources. Our Secure Resource Broker service solves this by having into consideration security information such a policies and reputation values when brokering resources. Second, we are combining in an effective way social-control mechanisms such as reputation and security, by using the Trust and Reputation service to quantify security for both Grid users and resources. Third, the Continuous Usage Control service controls the usage of Grid computational resources by applying fine-grained and history-based access control, and improves state of the art with mutable attributes, obligations and continuous enforcement. Existing authorisation systems in Grid simply check that the remote Grid user has the right to execute an application, considering applications executed on computational resources as atomic entities. Hence, once they authorise the execution of an application, no further controls are executed on the actions performed by this application on the resource. Instead, in GSF authorisation framework, the monitoring is fine grained, because the actions performed by applications on the resource are controlled, and history-based, because to decide whether an action should be allowed all the previous actions performed by the application are taken into account. Moreover, in GSF framework rights are dynamic, because attributes and conditions may vary over time. This means that, while an access is in progress, the factors that authorised it could change and the access right could not hold anymore. Consequently, in our framework, the control of the existence of a right is continuous (i.e. repeatedly performed during the access), to revoke an access that is in progress when the right does not hold anymore.

One lesson we learnt at this stage is that the complexity of Grid-based supply-chain systems (exemplified by our auctioning system and its multiple VOs) has suggested the need for lightweight and dynamic VO models. During the evaluation phase we expect discovering more insights, for example about the role of VBEs or the need for VBE federation, but also about VBE/VO design guidelines and more.

Future work includes further evaluation of the GridTrust services in other scenarios and the addition of new features to the security services such as distributed reputation management and VBE federation. Another important issue is human readability of security policies. Since the security policy enforced by the UCON service can be defined at the VO level, at the computational resource level, or can be a combination of these two, one important issue we are facing is how to express the security policies at VO level in a human readable format and how to translate these policies in an enforceable format.

References

[1] P. Massonet, A.E. Arenas, F. Martinelli, P. Mori, and B. Crispo. *GridTrust – A Usage Control Based Trust and Security Framework for Service-Based Grids*. In E. di Nitto, A.-M. Sassen, P. Traverso, and A. Zwegers, editors, "At your service: Service Engineering in the Information Society Technologies Program". MIT Press, 2008. (To appear).

[2] Carter et al, *Reverse auctions—grounded theory from the buyer and supplier perspective* - http://www.econbiz.de/archiv/myk/whumyk/controlling/auctions_theory_perspective.pdf

[3] L.M. Camarihna-Matos, and H. Afsarmanesh, H. *Elements of a base VE infrastructure*. Journal of Computers in Industry, 51(2):139–163, 2003. (available at http://www.uninova.pt/~cam/ev/CiI.PDF)

[4] van Lamsweerde, *Requirements Engineering in the Year 00: A Research Perspective*, in Proceedings of the 22nd International Conference on Software Engineering, Limerick, Ireland, ACM, pp. 5-19, 2000. (available at http://www.sis.uncc.edu/~seoklee/teaching/Papers/lamsweerde00requirements.pdf)

[5] R. Sandhu and J. Park, *Usage Control: A Vision for Next Generation Access Control*, in Proceedings of the Workshop on Mathematical Methods, Models and Architectures for Computer Networks Security (MMM03), Springer LNCS, 2776, pp. 17--31, 2003. (available at http://www.list.gmu.edu/park/paper/MMM03-UCON-vision.pdf)

Collaboration and the Knowledge Economy: Issues, Applications, Case Studies
P. Cunningham and M. Cunningham (Eds.)
IOS Press, 2008

When Little Brother is Watching You It Is Time to Ask: Who Has the Right to Mediate Personal Data?

John Sören PETTERSSON

Centre for HumanIT, Karlstad University, Karlstad, 651 88, Sweden

Tel: +46 54 700 2553, Fax: + 46 54 700 1446, Email: john_soren.pettersson@kau.se

Abstract: The focus of this presentation is on the commercialisation of various register data exemplified by some cases of mass distribution of personal data in Sweden. Even if many people use such web services, other people find faults with them. The critics want to restrict data dissemination but this is hard when there are data aggregators such as credit-ranking institutes benefiting from mediating personal data. This paper proposes that the mediating could be done by the subject as there is means to let the data be supplemented by proofs of the authentic origin in banks, tax registers, etc., of the data. By this mode of operation, every (computerised) citizen would be informed about the data basis for decisions that concerns them and is thereby in a better position to augment data giving a misleading picture.

1. Introduction

Interests in personal data about neighbours, friends, or famous people seem to be quite wide-spread, to judge from facts revealed during a debate in Sweden last year. When certain web sites started to publish personal data about every citizen these sites attracted a lot of attention. What ordinary gossip columnists writing their chronicles of scandal in colourful magazines cannot provide is this personalised service, which gives civil status and economic reports about exactly the individuals that each reader likes to hear about. So much better then that some web publishers feel the responsibility to offer such services... Well, in fact, it is not good that personal data is easily available in this manner as it is a clear threat to everyone's privacy. The focus of this presentation is on the commercialisation of various register data exemplified by some cases of mass distribution of personal data in Sweden.

The paper raises the question how to remedy these cases. It is proposed that the EU Directive's 'right of access' to personal data by the data subject should be replaced by an exclusive 'right to mediate' granted to the e-citizen.

2. Objectives

This paper aims to discuss how citizens (in particular, Internet users) can be empowered to control personal data about themselves. The discussion is based on an account of how sensitive economical data has been made available for free or for small fees by web sites. The incentives for the data providers have been to sell advertisement space. In the concluding section, a proposal based on the individual data subject as a mediator is suggested as a solution to the problem of mass distribution of personal data in electronic form.

3.   Personal Data Mediated by Commercial Web Services

3.1   Some Swedish Cases

A couple of years ago, certain credit-rating agencies in Sweden began exploiting the act of the freedom of press to make sensitive information available on websites. Credit-ranking information is normally electronically accessible only by employers and credit institutes, but now websites were registered with named persons as publisher – this is enough to be covered by the laws on freedom of the press and freedom of speech (the latter law covers registered radio stations, etc., nowadays including Internet-based publishers). Such web sites can publish anything and this fact was used to publish information usually used for credit ranking on individual citizens. Such requests should normally be followed by information to the one concerned (i.e., the 'data subject' in legal texts).

In spring 2006 there was a debate in Sweden about this as the web services took only a small fee from their customers, which made many people signing up for such services. Newspapers published articles on this fact, and although many citizens were shocked, the debate made more people aware of these services and possibly spurred the use of these services. Also the national data protection authority and foreign news media commented on the matter (see, e.g., [1] and [2]). The Orwellian 'Big Brother Is Watching You' had turned into a threat from Little Brother – your friends, foes, neighbours, colleagues, employees, old partners and prospective ones could make a check of your economic status. During the following year there were three important developments:

- In November 2006, there was a service (ratsit.se) providing the data for free attracting lots of people and selling advertisement slots on its web pages.
- In March 2007, the National Tax Board declared its intention to deliver information only in printed form and not electronically to credit information agencies which passed information on to websites. (There were further issues: ratsit.se did not register as a publisher until March so the legality of its data dissemination activities between November and March was in doubt. This aspect will not be discussed here.)
- From June 11, 2007, there is an agreement within the credit-rating branch. When individuals order information, a copy will be sent to the one concerned including data about who made the request, while a company may inquire without any copy being sent.

The June-11 agreement contains a further restriction that for a request from an individual "a legitimate need must exist". Companies could be thought of having a legitimate reason, such as checking job applicants or customers placing large orders or landlords checking prospective tenants. At least in older 'paper-based' times it would be expensive for company managers to misuse the possibility to check individuals, and for many years only larger companies had electronic access to credit-ranking data.

One might think that this agreement should stifle data supervision by 'little brothers'. Who could have a legitimate reason to get credit-ranking data for his/her neighbour or boss? Furthermore, the demand that a copy is sent to the data subject also brings with it costs, so it is difficult to have gratis services any longer. One euro per data request must be charged to cover postage and the paper-based process of sending a copy (the copy has to be in print as there are not legally valid e-mail addresses for people in general; only physical addresses can be used). One may moreover note that if customers of these web services have to pay, they will be identified by their physical address (invoice) or credit card numbers. Thus, the information about who requested the data will be certified in an implicit manner (at least in most cases).

In principle, this should be the end of unwarrantable supervision by hundreds of thousand little brothers (by the time of the agreement, ratsit.se claimed to have more than 600.000 registered customers and that more than 14 million inquires had been done;

Sweden has 9 million citizens). But this is only 'in principle' as shown by the following two points concerning the site upplysning.se:

- Testing upplysning.se there were no requests for information about the need for the data requested, but later the paper copy to the person being investigated contained a sentence "If you have questions about why John Sören Pettersson has taken this information about you, you can turn directly to him at the address [Pettersson's address]."
- For the limitation that only a company may inquire without copies being sent out, the only check is that the company is registered at the address given. Many persons have their own registered companies and the limitation of anonymity to only companies does not seem to be an important restriction.

As a commentary to the second bullet, it can be noted that, upplysning.se seems really keen to point out that for registered companies nothing has really changed and one will still be totally anonymous. In an e-mail message sent out about a week before the agreement would be effective, they noted this, ending with: "no copy will be sent out and one will be fully anonymous!" (Sic, the clause ends with an exclamation mark!) This e-mail message was sent to all registered customers, not only company customers. Also ratsit.se makes it very clear that companies can inquire without any copy being sent.

The ease with which companies nowadays are registered makes the differentiation between companies and persons questionable when the issue is who gets information. To round off the discussion, we can note that ratsit.se tried to keep to their gratis branding by still offering information about companies free of charge because still no copy needs to be sent if it is a company that is the object of an inquiry. This kind of differentiation between companies and physical persons should be uncontroversial because a company is an economical entity first and foremost.

3.2 Incentives to serve Little Brother

In [3] we speak about 'webification' of data processing. A particular feature of the webification is not only the easy access people have, but also the ease with which new distribution spots, i.e. web servers, are set up, registered, etc. It is also easy to set up the economical infrastructure needed to motivate the web site owner to at all bother for publishing data about individuals. Solutions for credit card payment, or other electronic payments nowadays available (e.g., paynova), are easily installed. Also the other major economic source, advertisement, has found easily implementable forms, both technically speaking and economically. For the business perspective, it is noteworthy that organisations interested in advertising have an efficient means of doing cost-benefit analysis: they do not have to pay for the advertisement itself but for each view of it or click on it. This makes it safe to invest in advertisements – the organisation only pays if the web ad has some effect. There are marketing companies such as Google selling advertisement slots on a huge variety of web sites – the organisation only has to tell what types of site should host its advertisement and then the ads are put at the relevant web sites more or less automatically.

As pointed out in [3], the webification concerns more than databases with personal data. The webification of payment and advertisement infrastructures makes these means for income available to everyone – it is easy to set up a 'professional' hobby site. Google's way of handling adverts has been accused for stimulating the setting up of empty web sites with domain names that look like popular web sites' addresses to fish for users who misspell addresses [4]. Advertisements on these sites will inevitably be clicked resulting in a small revenue for the site owner. We will not deal with this issue here. Rather, we wish to highlight the kind of advertisement-driven sites that try to attract visitors by providing a real but improper content. A single person could set up a site for the dissemination of personal data and hope the adverts will generate a positive return on the (minimal) investment without charging the users anything, at least if personal data is easily accessible electronically. An example of this was a recent site, tubo.se, which tried to fill the vacuum left when the credit-ranking information sites no longer can provide information totally free of charge. Tubo made available all salaries in public organisations, because this information is publicly available as are all other official records of public organisations in Sweden. The web site claimed a serious goal, namely to analyse salary differentials revealing, e.g., gender discrimination. However, what stroke the eye when entering the site was, besides the adverts, the Search box where the user immediately and conveniently can type in a name of a person and in a drop-down list select the organisation the person works for and the salary would promptly appear together with some other data. Now, this limited service was perhaps not too successful as in spring 2008 it was shutting down after six months.

3.3   And Finally: the Privacy of Users of the Web Services

To the problems for the data subjects that low-fee, public available databases entail, there is another privacy problem looming in the shadow, namely the customer registers of the web services selling personal data. Who would admit that he has done a hundred searches covering friends, neighbours, colleagues, ex-girlfriends, etc.? Considering the way credit card numbers and other things are available on the black markets of Internet, it would not be surprising to find web servers offering searches in stolen customer registers. That the inclusion in such registers really is sensitive has been proven in the Swedish case – there have been disputes between some customers and services on the fee charged, but such victims do not want to be identified in news media with their names [3].

4. Put More Technology to Work!

The problems for individuals' privacy have been demonstrated in the preceding section. The present section takes a positive stance to the development of data processing in our digitally connected society, but argues for even more technology, namely data processing based on electronic certificates to enhance transparency and privacy. The arguments come from development work conducted within a large EU project (see e.g. [5, 6]) but in particular from a visionary pilot study conducted 2007 ([7, 3]).[i]

4.1   Checking Information About Oneself

It is easy to be critical to the existence of web sites providing personal data. In the same time it should be acknowledged that there are positive sides of the free flow of information allowed in the Swedish example: any data subject can very quickly check what information about him is available to employers, landlords, and prospective partners. In [3] we noted also for the American site Intelius.com selling information on court cases and address history on individuals[ii], that in addition to the questionable state of affairs, that the person being searched does not know he is investigated, people might even get the wrong information about him by mistaking one John Smith for another one; in Sweden such mistakes are less probable as all personal data handling is based on the unique 'personal number' given to every citizen and person in the census register. But just as in the Swedish cases, any American data subject can very quickly check what information about him (and his namesakes) is available to employers, landlords, and others, by paying the 8 to 50 dollars that Intelius wants to have for information about individuals.

What would happen if this possibility is not available? One can compare with the citizens' questions put to the German data protection authority ULD (see [8] with data from the Datenschutz Schleswig-Holstein). A question such as the following could presumably be answered very quickly by the individual himself had he lived in Sweden: "The telco provider told me that they won't offer me a mobile phone contract. What may be the reason for that?" It is likely that the German telephone company screened applicants based on credit-rating data and then found that this individual had a bad ranking. If this person could have checked what economic data about him is available, he would most probably have found the answer to his question. What is more, he might even be able to explain his present situation better to the telephone company than what these data do lagging a year or so behind as they often do.

4.2   Legal Support Not Enough

So, when taking the data subject's interest in getting to know what information about him or her is available to companies, these web services seem to provide a really useful service. One may object, though, that such checking on oneself should be available anyhow without allowing neighbours and other people to look on one's data. In Europe, the EU Directive 95/46/EC and its implementation in national laws grant this 'right of access' to information on data concerning oneself. The possibility to identify oneself by electronic identity cards now exists and should give swift web access to relevant data.[iii] However, there are two reasons for why this legal support is not enough.

First, as noted in [13], the formulation found in the EU Directive is not appropriate in our digitally connected era: there is room for each member state to set restriction as to how often such inquircs can be forced upon the data controllers. Traditionally, there is an cconomic burden connected to the processing of such requests as they have to be answered in the paper medium. In Sweden, e.g., a data controller can limit the free access to data to once per annum, which may leave the citizen with too old information if he has already accessed his information less than a year ago. In a world with e-IDs such restrictions should not exist (in Germany, this restriction was removed before electronic ID cards [13]).

Second, to really evaluate the contribution from sites such as Intelius.com and upplysning.se one important aspect has to be added: The essence of what these sites do (or the companies delivering data to them) is to collect data from different sources which makes it much casier for the inquirer to get a relevant picture of a certain individual or firm. Thus, a really useful function for checking data about oneself cannot solely be based on e-IDs. There is a need for assistance functions aiding the user to the right compilation of requests, in the same way as Hansen et al. [5] describe assistance functions for ordinary Internet users for exercising their legal rights to access and correct personal data (cf. [7]).

A 'right of access' is a good thing, but there must be guidance how to access relevant data. That is, there must be organisations well informed of what credit-ranking institutes deliver to their customers and these organisations must make this information public (and prefcrably machine-readable in order to let users' computer systems process it automatically) so that the user will make the right combination of requests. The same would hold for other strands of life, such as what prospective employers look for.

4.3   Extension of the 'Right of Access' to an Exclusive 'Right to Mediate'

It has just becn noted that the possibility to identify oneself by electronic identity cards now exists and could potentially give swift web access to relevant data. One can add that it should also ensure uniquc access by the one concerned, blocking other citizens from watching his or her data. We will round off the discussion of composition of data requests by elaborating the idea of unique access by the data subject.

It should not be controversial to force 'normal' users of credit data (organisations of all kinds) to ask the data subject before data is released. The release could in fact be done by the subject him/herself because there are means to let the data be supplemented by proofs of the authentic origin in banks, tax registers, court records, etc., of the data.[iv] If the individual does not release data, he will not get the loan, employment, apartment he wants. (A non-user, i.e. a citizen without digital equipment, would then have to ask to get the information in paper or give consent already at the time of application, which often is the case when one subscribe to certain services.) Such an order of things would allow customers of credit-ranking agencies to go directly to the individual which would potentially restructure the whole business of credit-ranking. There would not be any need for agencies amassing data about people outside the sources for such information. And the many Little Brothers of our modern society would not be so easily served; by law, it could even be mandatory to request each individual's consent for electronic release of data as there would be little need for any such processing that is not actively supported by the individual in question.

Naturally, there still has to be some open records for such things as the property register. But for other things, such as court and tax registers, it is time to demand a return to solely paper-based routines for all inquires that are not made by the one concerned.

This prospect for very transparent data transfers would need further refinement regarding the citizen's ability to consent to data requests. A person who is really keen on an apartment or for an object that is subject to instalment purchase, or a person in need of a loan, may be prone to agree to excessive data requests from the other party. The assistance functions "aiding the user to the right compilation of requests" mentioned in 4.2, should warn the user against data requests that are excessive in relation to the purpose of the request. Many people would probably allow excessive data requests in certain situations, so some sort of cautious guidance to data collection and mediation is surely needed.

Noteworthy, the assistive system on people's computers could in fact also inform the data protection authorities and consumer organisations about breeches against good standards for credit ranking of individuals. This could be done in anonymous formats if the individual thinks his case is sensitive. This use of the assistance functions will in general make it easier to develop useful market standards and to follow up liability issues.

5.   Conclusions and Recommendations

Above, we have presented an account of the debate in Sweden spring 2006 – summer 2007 about the existence of web services selling or giving away personal data that credit-ranking agencies normally would sell only to credit-giving institutions or to certain other legal entities, such as employers. The public availability of economic data and the possibility to register web sites so that they are protected in the same way as mass media institutions are protected by the act of the freedom of press, has made it possible to present personal data to every individual who wants to take part of other people's circumstances.

We noted the inappropriateness of providing access to register data about ordinary citizens on the web but admitted that this accessibility also makes it possible for every registered person to very swiftly and cheaply get the same information about himself that various banks and companies have. Then we took the discussion further by discussing why the intermediates are needed at all. It should not be extremely controversial to force also the 'normal' users of register data to ask the data subject before data are released from the source. There are means to embed data in certificates warranting the authentic origin in banks, tax registers, court records, etc., of the data and we concluded that there would not be any need for agencies amassing data about people outside the sources for such information. The many Little Brothers of our modern society would not be served. Such an order of things would allow secondary users of register data to go to the individual concerned which would increase the transparency and also make it possible to enter corrections or additional facts by the individual himself.

Further research is needed on the question whether users will be able to act as mediators for data about themselves which would stifle data collection (and dissemination) by web sites. This is both a technical issue and a usability question. It also raises questions concerning how and by whom assistance is given because the more automatic the assistance is, the more liability issues are influenced. Naturally, it is also a question of changing business behaviour. We are confident that with the availability of new technology business processes change under the pressure of legislation and the public opinion. As for the latter, which can drive both legislation and business change, we refer to the latest *Flash Eurobarometer* on "Data Protection in the European Union – Citizens' perceptions" where it is stated that 64% of the respondents reported a concern about whether their personal information was protected, and half of these were "very concerned" [15].

References

[1] Datainspektionen (web, 2006-05-15) Lillebror vet allt om dina skulder. ("Little brother knows all about your debts".) Press release in Swedish available at: http://www.datainspektionen.se

[2] *Süddeutsche Zeitung* (web, 2007-07-06) Datenschutz in Schweden: Einblick beim Nachbarn. By Elmar Jung. http://www.sueddeutsche.de/computer/artikel/403/122239/

[3] J.S. Pettersson. Little Brother Is Watching You – commercialisation of personal data through 'webification'. Presented at "Security of the digitized man" (Réflexions prospectives et internationales: *«La sécurité de l'individu numérisé»*) the concluding colloquium of project Asphalès, Paris November 22-23, 2007. Will appear in proceedings published 2008 by CNRS with a summary in French.

[4] *Computer Sweden* (2007-11-26) Danny Aerts: "Google gräver sin egen grav". (In Swedish "Danny Aerts (i.e. the CEO of .se): 'Goggle is digging its own grave' .")

[5] M. Hansen, S. Fischer-Hübner, J.S. Pettersson, & M. Bergmann. Transparency Tools for User-Controlled Identity Management. Presented at *eChallenges e-2007*, 24-26 October 2007, The Hague. Published in: *Expanding the Knowledge Economy: Issues, Applications, Case Studies*, ed. by Cunningham & Cunningham. IOS Press, Amsterdam 2007; pp. 1360-1367.

[6] J.S Pettersson, S. Fischer-Hübner, & M. Bergmann. Outlining "Data Track": Privacy-friendly Data Maintenance for End-users. Presented at *The 15th International Conference on Information Systems Development (ISD 2006)*, Budapest, 31st August - 2nd September 2006. Published in *Advances in Information Systems Development, Volume 2*, ed. by G. Magyar, G. Knapp, W. Wojtkowski, G. Wojtkowski & J. Zupancic; Springer, 2007; pp. 215-226.

[7] J.S. Pettersson. Reports from the pilot study on privacy technology in the framework of consumer support infrastructure. Working Reports R1, R2, R3. December 2006-November 2007. Dept. of Information Systems and Centre for HumanIT, Karlstad University.
    http://www.humanit.org/projects.php?projekt_id=48&lang=en

[8] ULD (2006) Erhöhung des Datenschutzniveaus zugunsten der Verbraucher Unabhängiges Landeszentrum für Datenschutz, Kiel, 201+27 pages. https://www.datenschutzzentrum.de/verbraucherdatenschutz/. [7], page R2-20, contains English sample translations by Marit Hansen, ULD.

[9] *Computer Sweden* (2007-11-30) Dödläge för e-id. (In Swedish "Deadlock for e-ID".) http://computersweden.idg.se/2.2683/1.133781

[10] *Computer Sweden* (2008-03-26) Hårt tryck på Verva att ta fram nytt e-id. (In Swedish about e-ID) http://computersweden.idg.se/2.2683/1.152277

[11] Verva (2007a) Säkert informationsutbyte och säker hantering av elektroniska handlingar. Verket för förvaltningsutveckling, 2007:13.

[12] Verva (2007b) eID 2007. Elektronisk identifieng och underskrift. Verket för förvaltningsutveckling, 2007:16.

[13] J.S. Pettersson & S. Fischer-Hübner (forthcoming) Transparency as the Key to User-controlled Processing of Personal Data. To be published in *Human IT: Technology in Social Context*, ed. by Ch. Christensen. Cambridge Scholars Press.

[14] E. Bangerter, J Camenisch & A. Lysyanskaya. A Cryptographic Framework for the Controlled Release of Certified Data. Published in: *Security Protocols. 12th International Workshop, Cambridge, UK, April 26-28*, 2004, ed. by B. Christianson, B. Crispo, J.A. Malcolm & M. Roe. *Lecture Notes in Computer Science , Vol. 3957*, Springer Verlag 2006.

[15] *Eurobarometer 2008*, Data Protection in the European Union, Citiznes' perceptions, Analytical Report. Flash Euroarometer 225: http://ec.europa.eu/public_opinion/flash/fl_225_en.pdf

---

[i] The EU 6th Framework project PRIME, *Privacy and Identity Management for Europe*, ran March 2004 to February 2008; project web site at www.prime-project.eu . Fundamental in the architecture elaborated in the PRIME project is the use of *network pseudonyms* to allow users to be anonymous and *digital credentials* to allow users to prove their identity or parts thereof, such as being a Swedish citizen. Other features involve aid to the users to gauge the privacy policies of service providers (that is, data handling polices) and to negotiate about policies.

The pilot study "Privacy technology in the framework of consumer support infrastructure" [7] was in part financed by the Swedish agency for innovation systems, VINNOVA, by grant no. 29644-1.

[ii] The Intelius wait page (when searching) says: "Intelius is searching billions of current utility records, court records, county records, change of address records, property records, business records, and other public and publicly available information to find what you're looking for."

[iii] Presently there is a debate in Sweden about the cumbersomeness of these solutions. The present business model underlying the agreements that public bodies are supposed to make has received sharp criticism. See articles in *Computer Sweden* [9] and [10]. Swedish agency Verva released a pilot study October 2007 [12], cf. [11]. On the other hand, in Norway, the MinSide ("MyPage", a service at http://www.norge.no/minside/) allows Norwegian citizens online access to their data stored at authorities (similar service developing in Denmark at www.borger.dk; see www.modernisering.dk/da/vision_strategi/strategi_for_digital_forvaltning/).

[iv] Some certificate-based mechanism must be used if the source of the data is not directly involved in the data release transactions. However, using traditional certificates (X.509 style) based on signature schemes such as RSA or DSA, it is not possible to select a subset of data from a certified record. For alternatives, see [14] (the present author's gratitude to Dieter Sommer, IBM Zürich, for this reference). Sending only a subset might be desired by the data subject in many mediation scenarios unless it is easy and costless to acquire a new certified record each time which in its content is limited to exactly the desired subset.

Collaboration and the Knowledge Economy: Issues, Applications, Case Studies
P. Cunningham and M. Cunningham (Eds.)
IOS Press, 2008

Multimodal Biometric Authentication in Secure Environments

Savvas ARGYROPOULOS, Yannis DAMOUSIS, Dimitrios TZOVARAS

Informatics and Telematics Institute, 1ˢᵗ km Thermi-Panorama Rd.,
P.O. Box 60361 Thermi-Thessaloniki, GR-57001, Greece
Tel: +30 2310 464160, Fax: + 30 2310 464164, Email: {Savvas.Argyropoulos, Damousis,
Dimitrios.Tzovaras}@iti.gr

Abstract: This paper presents the multimodal biometric authentication framework of the EU Specific Target Research Project (STREP) called HUMABIO (Human Monitoring and Authentication using Biodynamic Indicators and Behavioural Analysis). The project aims to develop a modular, robust, multimodal biometrics security authentication system, which improves state-of-the-art methods in biometrics, such as face, speech, and gait and increases unobtrusiveness. For each modality, the data acquisition, feature extraction and matching procedures are briefly discussed. Subsequently, a comparative evaluation of multimodal score-level fusion methods ranging from simple classification schemes to more sophisticated machine learning algorithms, such as support vector machines and fuzzy expert systems is presented and their advantages over unimodal classification are highlighted. Experimental evaluation on data recorded in adverse environmental conditions shows that despite the increased unobtrusiveness the multimodal authentication system can achieve very satisfactory performance.

1. Introduction

Human identification has always been a field of primary concern in applications such as access control in secure infrastructures. In contrast to passwords or tokens which can be easily lost, stolen, forgotten, or shared, biometrics offer a reliable solution to the problem of identity management. Especially, the development of systems that integrate two or more biometric traits has received increased interest during the last years as the advantages of multimodal biometric systems become more evident. Most of the limitations imposed by unimodal biometric systems, e.g., low accuracy, high failure-to-enrol rate, sensitivity to noise etc., can be overcome in multimodal biometric systems [1].

A major shortcoming of current biometric systems is the obtrusive process for obtaining the biometric feature. The subject has to stop, go through a specific measurement procedure, which depends on the biometric that can be very obtrusive, wait for a period of time, and get clearance after authentication is positive. Emerging biometrics such as gait and technologies such as automated person/face detection can potentially allow the non-stop (on-the-move) authentication or even identification which is unobtrusive and transparent to the subject and become part of an ambient intelligence environment.

This article describes the multimodal biometric authentication system which was implemented during the course of the Human Monitoring and Authentication using Biodynamic Indicators and Behavioural Analysis (HUMABIO) FP6 EU project [2]. In particular, the application scenario for non-stop and unobtrusive authentication of employees in a controlled area is examined. Authentication is based on gait, voice, and face modalities in order to limit the cooperation of the user as much as possible, increase unobtrusiveness and user convenience and maximize user acceptance.

2.   Objectives

HUMABIO is a Specific Targeted Research Project (STREP) that focuses its research on emerging and novel biometrics, aiming to enhance unobtrusiveness of biometrics-based access control systems. HUMABIO's application scenarios aim at increased unobtrusiveness for the subject, by taking into account varying factors and allow flexibility in the system operation. Such examples are the inclusion of noise models during the development of the voice recognition module for robust operation in noisy environments and the operation of the face module even with various facial expressions. However, increased unobtrusiveness has its toll on authentication accuracy. Even the more conventional HUMABIO biometrics present lower accuracy than the corresponding algorithms in the literature which refer to strictly controlled conditions. Multiple biometrics are combined within HUMABIO with the objective to increase the authentication accuracy of the multimodal system with respect to the biometrics it comprises. Based on criteria such as unobtrusiveness level, maturity of the technology, and biometric capacity, face, voice, and gait recognition biometrics were selected to be included in the airport application scenario of the HUMABIO system. It should be also noted that the authentication instead of identification scenario was targeted due to increased time constraints and requirements.

Unobtrusive authentication involves automatic authentication of authorized personnel that can move freely in restricted areas. The operational setup of the system, which is installed in a controlled area in Euroairport in Basel, Switzerland, is depicted in Figure 1 (a). The subject walks along a narrow corridor. When the subject enters the corridor the (claimed) identity is transmitted wirelessly to the system via radio frequency identification (RFID) tag. The aim of HUMABIO is to authenticate the claimed identity by the time the subject reaches the end of the corridor. As the subject walks through the corridor, the gait sequence is captured and the subject's height is estimated. Height information is used to calibrate the position of the camera and the microphone, as shown in Figure 1 (b). Face and voice recognition take place at the end of the corridor. By the time the subject reaches the camera and the microphone, their position is already calibrated allowing the unobtrusive face and voice recognition without the need of specific procedures for the collection of the biometric data as it is usually the case with current biometric solutions.

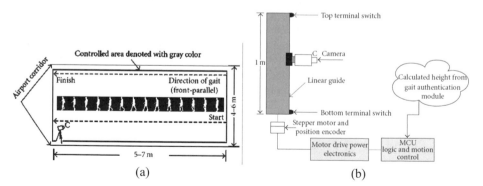

Figure 1: (a) HUMABIO Airport Pilot and (b) Calibration of Camera and Microphone.

3.   Description of Biometric Modalities

a.   Face Classifier

Face feature extraction is carried out in three steps: face detection, face normalization and subspace projection. The first step for facial feature extraction is the accurate localization of face in an input image using a component based approach using detectors similar to those proposed in [3]. Subsequently, the detected face is normalized by applying a similarity transform (rotation, translation and scaling) to the image region containing the face [4]. In the final stage, the input is regarded as a N-dimensional pixel vector containing the concatenated rows of the normalized face image. The feature space for representing faces is then computed by Bayesian subspace analysis, presented in [5]. The dimensionalities for the subspaces were determined beforehand on a large training database containing faces of different individuals exhibiting various facial variations. Thus, the face classifier is robust to facial expressions, poses, illumination conditions and occlusions (e.g. glasses).

b.   Speech Classifier

The speech signal is considered as a sequence of short-term frames (about 10 ms) that are processed by a Mel cepstral analysis method [6]; The cepstral transformation decorrelates the subband energies producing a low dimensional feature vector. Since the silence does not contain any speaker discriminant information, silence is withdrawn using an energy based voice activity detector. During the enrolment procedure, the subject is asked to pronounce a set of utterances covering at best the range of phonemes and speaking styles that could be used while being authenticated.

Typically, the amount of speech recorded during the enrolment process could be from 30 seconds to several minutes. Those utterances are then used in order to create the voice profile of the subject. The voice profile is created using statistical modelling of the sequence of feature parameters which aims at estimating a probability that the sentence has been pronounced by a given speaker. Particularly, due to their simplicity, Gaussian Mixture Models (GMM) were used to approximate the true probability density functions. A GMM-based speaker profile is fully depicted by the mean and standard deviation vectors of each Gaussian (on the order of 128) and the Gaussian weights. The focus of the module development has been put on practical side issues such as the robustness to environment noise, the rejection of unreliable speech samples, the limited amount of enrolment data, and so forth. Several noise models were added to examine the robustness of the system in conditions that simulate real application environments.

c.   Gait Classifier

The first step in the gait recognition module is the extraction of the walking subject's silhouette from the input image sequence. Subsequently, a set of transforms is applied to the silhouette to represent meaningful shape characteristics. In particular, the Radial Integration Transform (RIT) and Circular Integration (CIT) transform are applied due their capability to represent significant shape characteristics and their robustness to noise (e.g., illumination, different clothing, etc.). Additionally, the use of a new set of orthogonal moments is used based on the discrete classical weighted Krawtchouk polynomials due to their highly discriminative power. Thus, the gait recognition module output three matching scores, one for each descriptor: RIT, CIT, and Krawtchouk. Since the description the gait recognition module lies out of the scope of this paper, the interested reader are referred to [7] for further details.

4.   Multimodal Biometric Fusion

Fusion at matching score level is the most common approach in multimodal biometric systems due to the easy accessibility and availability of the matching scores in most biometric modules [1]. In our approach, the output scores of the individual matching algorithms constitute the components of a multidimensional vector from face, gait, and voice classifiers, as illustrated in Figure 2. In the following, we briefly review two advanced machine learning techniques, support vector machines (SVM) and fuzzy expert systems (FES), which are widely used due to their reliability, performance, and effectiveness.

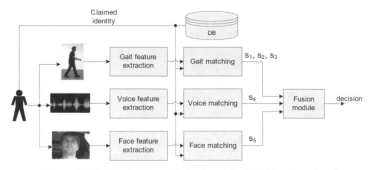

Figure 2: Multimodal Biometric Fusion at the Matching Score Level

a.   Support Vector Machines

SVM map a given set of binary labeled training data to a high-dimensional feature space and separate the two classes of data with a maximum margin hyperplane [8], [9]. Thus, an initial fusion function $f(\overline{x}) = \langle w, \varphi(\overline{x}) \rangle + w_0$ is trained by solving the quadratic problem:

$$\min_{w, w_0, \xi_1, ..., \xi_N} \left(\frac{1}{2} \|w\|^2 + \sum_{i=1}^{N} C_i \cdot \xi_i \right)$$

subject to: $y_i \left(\langle w, \varphi(\overline{x}) \rangle + w_0 \right) \geq 1 - \xi_i, \ i = 1, ..., N$

$$\xi_i \geq 0, \ i = 1, ..., N$$

where $\overline{x} = [s_1, s_2, s_3, s_4, s_5]$ and the function $\varphi : \Re^5 \to F$ maps the data into a feature space F. Thus, the training vectors are mapped into a higher dimensional space by the function φ. Then, the SVM algorithm finds a linear separating hyperplane with the maximal margin in this kernel dimensional space. Also, ξ_i denote the slack variables which are misclassified, C_i is the cost weight (or penalty parameter) associated with training data $\overline{x}_i$, and y_i represents the label of $\overline{x}_i$. It is easy to prove that the margin is maximized when [8]:

$$w = \sum_i a_i y_i \varphi(\overline{x}_i) \tag{1}$$

where α_i are positive real numbers that maximize:

$$\sum_i a_i - \sum_{ij} a_i a_j y_i y_j \langle \varphi(\overline{x}_i), \varphi(\overline{x}_j) \rangle \tag{2}$$

subject to:

$$\sum_i a_i y_i = 0, \ a_i > 0 \tag{3}$$

The decision function can equivalently be expressed as:

$$f(\overline{x}) = \sum_i a_i y_i \langle \varphi(\overline{x}_i), \varphi(\overline{x}) \rangle - w_0 \tag{4}$$

It is important to note that neither the learning algorithm nor the decision function need to represent explicitly the image of points in the feature space F, since both use only the dot products $\langle \varphi(\overline{x}_i), \varphi(\overline{x}_j) \rangle$. Hence, given the kernel function $K(\mathbf{X}, \mathbf{Y}) = \langle \varphi(\mathbf{X}), \varphi(\mathbf{Y}) \rangle$ one could learn and use the maximum margin hyperplane in the feature space without explicitly performing the mapping. In our case, the radial basis function (RBF) kernel was employed, which is given by $K(\mathbf{X}, \mathbf{Y}) = e^{-\gamma \|\mathbf{X} - \mathbf{Y}\|^2}$, $\gamma \geq 0$.

b.   Fuzzy Expert Systems

Fuzzy expert systems (FES) use soft linguistic variables and a continuous range of truth-values in the interval [0, 1] [10]. In order to construct the fuzzy model structure, a number of premise inputs $\overline{X}_p = [x_{p,1}, ..., x_{p,NPI}]$ should be properly selected. These are the decision variables that constitute the premise space and allow the formulation of rules. Each premise variable is then partitioned by a certain number of fuzzy sets that cover adequately its universe of discourse. These fuzzy sets allow the linguistic description of a variable. The linguistic description (fuzzy sets) of the inputs is attained using membership functions of appropriate form.

In our model, each premise input $x_{p,i}$, $i=1,2,3$ is partitioned by three Trapezoid type membership functions. The linguistic description (partitioning) of the premise inputs results to the formation of several fuzzy regions $\mathbf{A}^{(j)}$, formed by the combinations of the memberships along each input. This leads to a number of $NR = 3 \times 3 \times 3 = 27$ rules, as depicted in *Figure 3*.

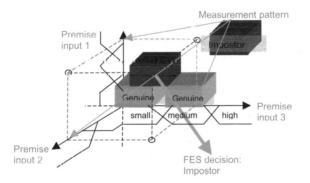

Figure 3: Three membership functions with linguistic expressions "small", "medium", "high" are used for the partitioning of three premise inputs, leading to the formation of 27 fuzzy rules.

Each rule $R^{(j)}$, $j=1,..., NR$ corresponds to a particular category or case, having an IF-THEN description:

$$R^{(j)} : \quad IF \ \overline{X}_p \ is \ A^{(j)} \ THEN \ y_j = F_j(\overline{X}_c) \tag{5}$$

where $y_j = F(\overline{X}_c)$ represents the j-th rule output which is a crisp function of the input vector $\overline{X}_c = [s_1, s_2, s_3, s_4, s_5]$ consisting of the face, voice and gait matching scores:

$$y_j = F(\overline{X}_c) = \lambda_0^j + \sum_{i=1}^{NCI} \lambda_i^j x_{c,i} \tag{6}$$

where λ_i^j are weight coefficients and λ_0^j is a bias term. The lambda coefficients are determined from the training set using genetic algorithms.

5.   Results

The multimodal biometric database for the training and evaluation of the authentication algorithms was formed by aggregating unimodal databases forming "virtual subjects" [11]. The face database consists of 29 subjects captures in two different sessions: one with neutral expression and one with facial expression (smiling or talking). The voice database contains 40 subjects from the YOHO database and consists of "combination lock" phrases (e.g. 36-24-36). Finally, the gait database consists of 75 people recorded at two different conditions: one with a slight difference in appearance (e.g., wearing a hat) and one with a different type of shoe. The N-th multimodal virtual user was created using the N-th user trait from each database. Thus, the multimodal database consists of 29 subjects and two recordings. The evaluation was performed using the first 15 subjects for training and the remaining 14 for testing. The sets slide for each run by one subject. Thus, the total number of genuine and impostor transactions in the training set is 15 x 2 x 29 = 870 and 15 x 14 x 2 x 29 = 12180, respectively. The test set contains 14 x 2 x 29 = 812 genuine and 14 x 13 x 2 x 29 = 10556 impostor transactions.

The performance of the biometric system is evaluated in terms of the False Acceptance Rate (FAR) and the False Rejection Rate (FRR). Additionally, the performance of the unimodal classifiers is shown in Table 1 which illustrates their Equal Error Rate (EER). It must be stressed that the relatively high error rates compared to corresponding results in the literature are attributed to the flexible conditions during the measurements to increase unobtrusiveness. Furthermore, Table 2 summarizes the results of the investigated machine learning algorithms for multimodal fusion. More specifically, classification was performed using the SVM, FES, Gaussian Mixture Modelling (GMM) [12], and Neural Network (NN) fusion schemes. The first conclusion we can reach from the results illustrated in the table is that all the fusion schemes perform better that the best performing unimodal expert (voice classifier) and the gain is approximately 1.4%. This corroborates the statement that the effective combination of information from different experts can improve significantly the performance of a biometric system. Moreover, this table also confirms the superiority of the SVM fusion scheme. More specifically, the FAR and FRR error rates using the SVM fusion classifier are approximately 0.40% and 0.37%, respectively.

Table 1: EER of the Unimodal Biometric Classifiers

Biometric trait	Face	Voice	Gait	EER (%)
EER	12.8	1.76	18.88	12.8

Table 2: Evaluation Results for Initial Authentication in the Airport Pilot Using Different Fusion Methods

Fusion method	Training		Testing	
	FAR (%)	FRR (%)	FAR (%)	FRR (%)
SVM	0.16	0.11	0.40	0.37
FES	0.28	0.22	0.76	0.72
NN	0.65	0.71	0.92	0.98
GMM	0.95	1.03	1.05	1.11

6.   Conclusions

In this paper, the multimodal biometric authentication framework of the HUMABIO project was presented. Specifically, the application scenario for non-stop and unobtrusive authentication of employees in a controlled area based on face, voice, and gait modalities was examined. The main challenge was to address the use of biometrics in specific pilot plans which allow flexible conditions and user unobtrusiveness while at the same time imposing stringent performance requirements. The critical point in such applications is the effective exploitation of the various unimodal experts and their integration in order to provide a global assessment about the person's identity authenticity and physiological state.

The HUMABIO taskforce identified a set of assessment types for the detailed evaluation of the system. These assessment types include the technical and performance assessment (i.e., whether the system can operate as designed), the impact assessment (i.e., to what extent the workplace and societal safety, the operational cost and efficiency, and the user comfort and Quality of Life (QoL) will be affected by the systems' introduction into the market), and the user acceptance assessment (i.e., whether the user groups involved may benefit from the system).

Moreover, a large number of participants were used to evaluate the HUMABIO system under various evaluation scenarios. The performance of both the users and the system were tracked through objective measurements (data from physiological, behavioural, and other biometrics, as well as from data from the systems' performance) and subjective measurement tools (i.e., questionnaires from both the users and the industrial clients). All the users participating in this project had to complete a series of evaluation scenarios, in order to evaluate the effectiveness and efficiency of HUMABIO operation modes. Subsequently, the users' objective and subjective performance was analysed to allow us to draw some conclusions regarding the success and efficacy of the project and its future potential.

The most considerable impact of HUMABIO relates to the innovations that were developed in technology and biometrics. That is, in order for HUMABIO to be able to create a unique physiological signature for each individual, it had to explore the use of novel physiological indicators combined with state of the art behavioural measurements. Such a laborious task has never been attempted before, while, to-date, no systematic study using extensive physiological measurement databases has been presented. Additionally, the development of the HUMABIO system will lead towards a new way of authentication (one that resembles DNA authentication) that will "intimidate" intruders and will be unobtrusive to its users.

The next most important impact of the HUMABIO system can be identified in the realm of security and public safety. HUMABIO attempts to accomplish the combination of physiological and behavioural indicators that will allow de facto aliveness checks to the security/authentication system. Furthermore, this system will provide industry the ability to reduce (if not to eliminate) possible identity fraud and industrial espionage. The creation of such an innovative system will set new safety standards for a variety of application environments (e.g., laboratory, airport, etc.) and at the same time reduce the violation of the user's privacy (by using obstructive security checks). Consequently, the most probable candidates for the system's installation in this case would be environments with high security requirements (such as government agencies, R&D facilities, defence industry, etc.).

Additionally, HUMABIO's impact is not limited to industry, but can also extent to education and research. That is, this system can also offer significant advancements in fields related to human biology and psychology, health, technology, and biometrics. The HUMABIO system will offer researchers working in different modalities, the possibility to work on a modality fusion setting, which will allow an increased reliability in authentication algorithms. The creation of multimodal biometric databases and standardised evaluation methodologies will promote the quality of research conducted by scientists and will allow them to accelerate their research findings and quality.

Regarding exploitation and marketing, it should be noted that multimodal biometrics take only a 2.7% of the global market share in 2007 leaving a lot of room for expansion. In addition the unimodal biometrics developed within HUMABIO can be marketed as commercial products on their own. Several biometric modules are based on emerging biometrics such as EEG and ECG, while others such as anthropometric biometrics based on sensing seats are completely new but can be applied in a variety of systems such as vehicle security. For HUMABIO separate modules and as a whole a detailed bussiness plan has been produced and there is already interest from industries such as Volvo and Siemens for integration to existing security systems that they develop. The main actors identified as potential users of the HUMABIO system are final users (high security environments, supervisors/employees in government agencies, etc.), industrial users (application facilities, such as airports, laboratories, etc.), authentication systems and modules developers, authorities (e.g., police, security officers, etc.) and society (e.g., individuals, medical community, etc.).

References

[1]   K. Jain and A. Ross, "Multibiometric systems," *Communication of the ACM*, vol. 47, no. 1, pp. 34-40, Jan. 2004.
[2]   I. G. Damousis, D. Tzovaras, and E. Bekiaris, "Unobtrusive Multimodal Biometric Authentication: The HUMABIO Project Concept," *EURASIP Journal on Advances in Signal Processing*, vol. 2008, Article ID 265767, 11 pages, 2008.
[3]   P. Viola and M. Jones, "Rapid object detection using a boosted cascade of simple features," in *Proc. IEEE Conf. on Computer Vision and Pattern Recognition*, 2001.
[4]   S. Z. Li, "Face detection," in Handbook of Face Recognition, J. A. K. Li, Stan Z., Ed. Berlin, Germany: Springer-Verlag, 2004.
[5]   B. Moghaddam, T. Jebara, and A. Pentland, "Bayesian face recognition," *Pattern Recognition*, vol. 33, no. 11, pp. 1771–1782, 2000.
[6]   F. Bimbot, et al., "A tutorial on text-independent speaker verification," *EURASIP Journal on Applied Signal Processing*, vol. 2004, no. 4, pp. 430–451, 2004.
[7]   D. Ioannidis, D. Tzovaras, I. G. Damousis, S. Argyropoulos, and K. Moustakas, "Gait recognition using compact feature extraction transforms and depth information," *IEEE Trans. on Information Forensics and Security*, vol. 2, no. 3, pp. 623–630, Sep. 2007.
[8]   N. Christianini, and J. Shawe-Taylor, "An Introduction to Support Vector Machines and Other Kernel-based Learning Methods," Cambridge University Press, 2000.
[9]   S. Hearst et al., "Trends and controversies - support vector machines," *IEEE Intelligent Systems*, vol. 13, no. 4, pp. 18-28, Apr. 1998.
[10] H. J. Zimmermann, "Fuzzy Set Theory and its Applications," Kluwer, Boston, USA, 1996.
[11] N. Poh and S. Bengio, "Using Chimeric Users to Construct Fusion Classifiers in Biometric Authentication Tasks: An Investigation," ICASSP, pp. 1077-1080, Toulouse, France, 2006.
[12] Y. Stylianou et al., "GMM-Based Multimodal Biometric Verification," eINTERFACE'05 Summer Workshop on Multimodal Interfaces, 2005.

Author Index